Interest, Principal, Rate, and Time Formulas	Interest $\quad I = PRT$ $\qquad$ Time $\quad$ Time in years

Principal $\quad P = \dfrac{I}{RT}$ $\qquad$ Time in days $= \dfrac{I}{PR} \times 360$

Rate $\qquad R = \dfrac{I}{PT}$

Maturity Value

The *maturity value*, M, of a principal of P dollars at a rate of interest R for T years is either

$$M = P + I$$

or, since $I = PRT$,

$$M = P(1 + RT)$$

Present Value at Simple Interest

The *present value at simple interest*, P, of a future value M at a rate of interest R for a time T is

$$P = \frac{M}{1 + RT}$$

Simple Interest and Simple Discount

Variables Used for Simple Interest	Variables Used for Simple Discount
I = Interest	B = Discount
P = Principal (Face value)	P = Proceeds
R = Rate of interest	D = Discount rate
T = Time in years, or $\quad$ Fraction of a year	T = Time in years, or $\quad$ Fraction of a year
M = Maturity value	M = Maturity value

	Simple Interest	Simple Discount
Face value	Stated on note, or $P = \dfrac{M}{1 + RT}$	Same as maturity value, or $M = \dfrac{P}{1 - DT}$
Interest charge	$I = PRT$	$B = M \cdot D \cdot T$
Maturity value	$M = P + I$ or $M = P(1 + RT)$	Same as face value, or $M = \dfrac{P}{1 - DT}$
Amount received by borrower	Face value or principal	Proceeds: $P = M - B$ or $P = M(1 - DT)$
Identifying phrases	Interest at a certain rate Maturity value greater than face value	Discounted at a certain rate Proceeds Maturity value equal to face value
Annual interest rate	Same as stated rate, R	Greater than stated rate, D

Mathematics for Business

NINTH EDITION

Stanley A. Salzman
American River College

Gary Clendenen
Siena College

Charles D. Miller

Prentice Hall

Boston   Columbus   Indianapolis   New York   San Francisco   Upper Saddle River   Amsterdam
Cape Town   Dubai   London   Madrid   Milan   Munich   Paris   Montreal   Toronto   Delhi
Mexico City   Sao Paulo   Sydney   Hong Kong   Seoul   Singapore   Taipei   Tokyo

Editor in Chief: Vernon Anthony
Acquisitions Editor: Gary Bauer
Development Editor: Linda Cupp
Editorial Assistant: Megan Heintz
Director of Marketing: David Gesell
Marketing Manager: Leigh Ann Sims
Senior Marketing Coordinator: Alicia Wozniak
Marketing Assistant: Les Roberts
Senior Managing Editor: JoEllen Gohr
Project Manager: Rex Davidson
Senior Operations Supervisor: Pat Tonneman
Operations Specialist: Laura Weaver
Art Director: Diane Ernsberger
Cover Designer: Ali Mohrman
Manager, Rights and Permissions: Zina Arabia
Manager, Visual Research: Beth Brenzel
Manager, Cover Visual Research and Permissions: Karen Sanatar
Image Permission Coordinator: Silvana Attanasio
Cover Art: Getty Images/Digital Vision
Media Director: Allyson Graesser
Lead Media Project Manager: Karen Bretz
Full-Service Project Management: Tracy Duff/Pre-Press PMG
Composition: PrePress PMG
Printer/Binder: Edwards Brothers
Cover Printer: Lehigh-Phoenix
Text Font: Times Roman

Credits and acknowledgments for materials borrowed from other sources and reproduced, with permission, in this textbook appear on the appropriate page within text.

Library of Congress Cataloging-in-Publication Data

Salzman, Stanley A.
  Mathematics for business / Stanley A. Salzman, Gary Clendenen, Charles D. Miller.—9th ed.
    p. cm.
  Includes index.
  ISBN 978-0-13-506394-1 (student edition)
  ISBN 978-0-13-506562-4 (instructor edition)
  1. Business mathematics.   I. Clendenen, Gary.   II. Miller, Charles David   III. Title.
  HF5691.S26 2011
  650.01'513—dc22   2009039794

10 9 8 7 6 5 4 3 2

Prentice Hall
is an imprint of

www.pearsonhighered.com   ISBN 13: 978-0-13-506394-1
                             ISBN 10: 0-13-506394-9

Contents

PART 1   **Basic Mathematics**

PART 3   **Mathematics of Retailing**

PART 4   **Mathematics of Finance**

Preface

The ninth edition of *Mathematics for Business* continues to provide solid, practical, and up-to-date coverage of those topics students must master to attain success in business today. The aim of this edition has been to put more focus on graphs, data, and analysis throughout the book. To accomplish this, the chapter on business statistics has been moved towards the front of the book and is now Chapter 4. This chapter shows students numerous graphs/tables and asks them to read/interpret that data. These skills are then reinforced throughout the rest of the chapters with numerous charts, graphs, and tables of relevant data.

The combination of increased use of graphs and tables throughout the book with the new Stop and Think feature has made the text more focused and integrated. This will give the students a better concept of how business math relates to the economic and business world around them as well as their personal finances.

Unique to this text is coverage on topics such as payroll records and quarterly returns, inflation and the time value of money, distribution of profits in a corporation, range and standard deviation, and index numbers. It also covers retirement plans including regular and Roth IRAs.

A new feature called Stop and Think includes data and related open-ended thought questions about issues relevant to students' financial lives and world. The globalization of our society is emphasized through examples and exercises that highlight foreign countries and international topics. The text also includes two Business Application Cases at the end of each chapter.

The new edition reflects the extensive business and teaching experience of the authors, as well as the suggestions of many reviewers nationwide. Providing solid, practical, and up-to-date coverage of business mathematics topics, the text begins with a brief review of basic mathematics and introduces the basic concepts in statistics. It then goes on to introduce key business topics, such as bank services, payroll, taxes, insurance, business discounts and markups, stocks and bonds, consumer loans, depreciation, and financial statements. The text is accompanied by a greatly enhanced supplements package that provides many avenues—both print and media—for students to practice and further explore the concepts discussed in the chapters. (Please see pages x to xii of this preface for full descriptions of the student and instructor supplements available.)

New to This Edition

- Chapter 1, "Problem Solving and Operations with Fractions," begins with a review of problem solving. Chapters 1 and 2 then review the basics of fractions and algebra and contain numerous drill problems.
- Chapter 3, "Percents," contains over 360 exercises, most of which are application problems. The wide selection of application problems offers the instructor the chance to work on the reading and comprehension skills of students while reviewing the concepts of percent.
- Many of the problems in Chapter 4, "Business Statistics," have been changed, and a number of graphs showing data from the business world have been added to increase the chapter's sense of realism.
- The material in Chapter 5, "Banking Services," has been updated in keeping with the latest banking trends and practices. Banking charges, online banking, the recent federal law known as Check 21, and credit-card deposit slips reflect the latest available materials. The reconciliation form has been simplified to reflect current industry changes.
- In Chapter 6, "Payroll," all wages and salaries have been updated along with FICA, Medicare, and tax-withholding rates. State withholding tax has been modified to more accurately represent state income taxes throughout the nation.
- In Chapter 7, "Taxes," the latest available tax forms and tables have been included in Section 7.3, on the personal income tax. In Chapter 8, "Risk Management," the insurance rates for motor vehicles and life insurance have been updated to more accurately reflect today's insurance costs.

■ Chapter 12, "Simple Interest," has been updated to reflect current interest rates, and substantial new material on inflation and the consumer price index has been added. New examples show that a raise may not be of much help to an employee, depending on the increase in the cost of living that the employee experiences.

■ Chapter 14, "Compound Interest," has been updated, and several application problems have been changed.

■ Chapter 15, "Annuities and Sinking Funds," includes information and examples on IRAs and Roth IRAs.

■ Chapter 16, "Business and Consumer Loans," has been updated to reflect current interest rates, and the last section of the chapter, related to mortgages and loans, has been updated. It includes some discussion of the financial crisis that began in the U.S. in 2007.

■ Data from recent Wal-Mart Stores, Inc. financial statements are included in Chapter 18, "Financial Statements and Ratios," so that students learn about financial statements using actual data from a company they know.

■ The sections on stocks and bonds in Chapter 19, "Securities and Distribution of Profit and Overhead," have been updated to reflect more current price information. Emphasis is placed on using mutual funds to save for retirement and other long-term purposes, including the education of children.

■ Appendix A.1, "Scientific Calculators," contains greatly expanded coverage of scientific calculators for professors who allow students to use calculators. Appendix A.2, "Financial Calculators," reviews the basic functions of financial calculators. Appendix B, "The Metric System," gives students the information needed to understand and use the metric system.

Features

Stop and Think   Each chapter opens with a graphic or table with data that relates to business followed by a thought-provoking question. Applications have been chosen that will increase both student and faculty interest. For example, Chapter 4 ("Business Statistics") opens with a graph showing forecasts of world population and world oil production. It demonstrates a belief held by many experts that world oil production will reach a peak and then begin to fall a few decades before world population is forecast to peak. The Stop and Think questions that follow ask students to describe possible major issues if world oil production is falling as world population continues to grow.

Enhanced Treatment of Real-World Applications   The ninth edition places a greater emphasis on real-world applications. The application problems have been updated throughout the text to be as relevant as possible to today's students. Financial statements from the giant retailer Wal-Mart are used throughout Chapter 18.

Art Program   The art program of the ninth edition includes graphs and charts that utilize actual data from a variety of recognized sources. Rendered to draw student attention while emphasizing the data itself, the graphs and charts help students see that the mathematics of business is inherent to the world around them. See pages 1, 69, and 91.

Business Application Cases   Two business application cases are found at the end of each chapter. These are slightly more involved, realistic scenarios that integrate concepts from that chapter. For example, one of the business cases at the end of Chapter 14 ("Compound Interest") illustrates how a global bank makes profit based on the spread or difference in interest rates between funds borrowed and funds loaned to businesses.

Cumulative Reviews   Five Cumulative Reviews, found after Chapters 4, 8, 11, 16, and 19, help students review groups of related chapter topics and reinforce their understanding of the material. See pages 155, 315, 407, 592, and 715.

Metric System   The metric system of measurement, found in Appendix B, gives students the information needed to understand and use the metric system. See page 736.

Financial Calculator Solutions   Several financial calculator solution boxes demonstrate to the student how this tool can be used to solve problems. Financial calculators are also illustrated in Appendix A.2, which includes exercises that students may solve using the financial calculator of their choice. See 484, 520, and 729.

Quick Review with Chapter Terms   The end-of-chapter Quick Review feature begins with a list of key terms from the chapter and the pages on which they first appear. The Quick Review uses a two-column format (Concepts and Examples) to help students review all the main points presented in the chapter. See pages 30, 64, and 104.

Additional Features

Numerous Exercises   Mastering business mathematics requires working many exercises, so we have included more than 3,850 in the ninth edition. They range from simple drill problems to real-life application exercises that require several steps to solve. All problems have been independently checked to ensure accuracy. See pages 132, 200, and 306.

Graded Application Exercises   The application exercises in each section of this text increase in difficulty level. Each even-numbered application exercise is the same type of problem as the preceding odd-numbered exercise. This allows the student to solve an odd-numbered exercise, check the answer in the answer section of the text, and then solve the following even-numbered exercise with confidence. See pages 119, 200, and 324.

Scientific Calculator Solutions   Scientific calculators are covered in depth in Appendix A.1, and scientific calculator solution boxes are shown throughout the text. See pages 14, 203, and 551.

Supplementary Exercises   Three sets of supplementary exercises, in Chapter 3 and in Chapter 10, are designed to help students review and synthesize difficult concepts. Answers to the odd-numbered supplementary exercises are located in the back of the text. See pages 87, 94, and 374.

Writing Exercises   Designed to help students better understand and relate to the concepts within a section, these exercises, marked with ✎ , require a short written answer. They often include references to specific learning objectives to help students formulate their answer. See pages 50, 118, and 306.

Pretest   A pretest for business mathematics is included in the text's introduction. This tool helps students and instructors identify individual and class strengths and weaknesses. See pages xxii–xxiv.

Notes   These notes provide helpful suggestions to the students and are located throughout the text. See pages 2, 40, and 80.

Glossary   A glossary of key words, located at the back of the book, provides a quick reference for the main ideas of the course.

Summary of Formulas   The inside covers of *Mathematics for Business* provide a handy summary of commonly used information and business formulas from the book.

Student Supplements

Business Math Review Card   A six-page foldout that covers basic math topics, the card also covers specific business math topics such as gross earnings, markup and markdown, and finding gross profit and gross income, insurance, taxes, simple and compound interest, present value, annuities, sinking funds, stocks and bonds, depreciation, financial statements, and business statistics and can be packaged with the textbook.

MyMathLab® Online Course (access code required) MyMathLab® is a text-specific, easily customizable online course that integrates interactive multimedia instruction with textbook content. MyMathLab gives instructors the tools they need to deliver all or a portion of the course online, whether students are in a lab setting or working from home.

■ **Interactive homework exercises**, correlated to your textbook at the objective level, are algorithmically generated for unlimited practice and mastery. Most exercises are free-response and provide guided solutions, sample problems, and learning aids for extra help.
■ **Personalized Study Plan**, generated when students complete a test or quiz, indicates which topics have been mastered and links to tutorial exercises for topics students have not mastered. Instructors can customize the available topics in the study plan to match their course concepts.
■ **Multimedia learning aids**, such as video lectures, animations, and a complete multimedia textbook, help students independently improve their understanding and performance.
■ **Assessment Manager** lets you assign media resources (such as a video segment or a textbook passage), homework, quizzes, and tests. If you prefer, you can create your own online homework, quizzes, and tests that are automatically graded. Select just the right mix of questions from the MyMathLab exercise bank, instructor-created custom exercises, and/or TestGen® test items.
■ **Gradebook**, designed specifically for mathematics and statistics, automatically tracks students' results, lets you stay on top of student performance, and gives you control over how to calculate final grades. You can also add off-line (paper-and-pencil) grades to the gradebook.
■ **MathXL® Exercise Builder** allows you to create static and algorithmic exercises for your online assignments. You can use the library of sample exercises as an easy starting point, or you can edit any course-related exercise.
■ **Pearson Tutor Center** (www.pearsontutorservices.com) access is automatically included with MyMathLab. The Tutor Center is staffed by qualified math instructors who provide textbook-specific tutoring for students via toll-free phone, fax, email, and interactive Web sessions.

The new, Flash®-based MathXL Player is compatible with almost any browser (Firefox®, Safari™, or Internet Explorer®) on almost any platform (Macintosh® or Windows®). MyMathLab is powered by CourseCompass™, Pearson Education's online teaching and learning environment, and by MathXL®, our online homework, tutorial, and assessment system. MyMathLab is available to qualified adopters. For more information, visit www.mymathlab.com or contact your Pearson representative.

MathXL® Online Course (access code required) MathXL® is a powerful online homework, tutorial, and assessment system that accompanies Pearson Education's textbooks in mathematics or statistics. With MathXL, instructors can:

Create, edit, and assign online homework and tests using algorithmically generated exercises correlated at the objective level to the textbook.
Create and assign their own online exercises and import TestGen tests for added flexibility.
Maintain records of all student work tracked in MathXL's online gradebook.
With MathXL, students can:

■ Take chapter tests in MathXL and receive personalized study plans based on their test results.
■ Use the study plan to link directly to tutorial exercises for the objectives they need to study and retest.
■ Access supplemental animations and video clips directly from selected exercises.

MathXL is available to qualified adopters. For more information, visit our website at www.mathxl.com, or contact your Pearson representative.

MathXL® Tutorials on CD This interactive tutorial CD-ROM provides algorithmically generated practice exercises that are correlated at the objective level to the exercises in the textbook.

Every practice exercise is accompanied by an example and a guided solution designed to involve students in the solution process. Selected exercises may also include a video clip to help students visualize concepts. The software provides helpful feedback for incorrect answers and can generate printed summaries of students' progress.

Instructor Supplements

Supplements Available in Print

Annotated Instructor's Edition (AIE) A printed AIE consists of the student edition with answers for all exercises printed directly on the pages. ISBN: 0-13-506562-3

Supplements Available for Download

Instructor's Solutions Manual (ISM)   The ISM contains worked solutions to all exercises in the student edition.

Test Generator (TestGen)   TestGen enables instructors to build, edit, print, and administer tests from a bank of questions developed to cover all test objectives. The test questions are algorithmically generated, making it easy to generate multiple versions of the same test with different numbers in the questions.

To access supplementary materials online, instructors need to request an instructor access code. Go to **www.pearsonhighered.com/irc**, where you can register for a code. Within 48 hours of registering, you will receive a confirming e-mail including an instructor access code. Once you have received your code, locate your text in the online catalog and click on the Instructor Resources button on the left side of the catalog product page. Select a supplement and a log-in page will appear. Once you have logged in, you can access instructor material for all Pearson textbooks.

Acknowledgments

We would like to thank the many users of the eighth edition for their insightful observations and suggestions for improving this book. We also wish to express our appreciation and thanks to the following reviewers for their contributions:

> Daniel W. Biddlecom, Erie Community College, North Campus
> Bruce Broberg, Central Community College
> Jacqueline Dlatt, College of Du Page
> Acie B. Earl, Black Hawk College
> Merilyn Linney, Guilford Technical Community College
> Justine Moore, New England Institute of Technology
> Ellen Sawyer, College of Du Page
> Shelia Walker, Catawba Valley Community College
> Edna May Wierenga, Central Community College

Our appreciation also goes to Deana Richmond for her careful accuracy checking of all the exercises and examples in the book and for the preparation of the Instructor's Solution Manual. We also would like to express our gratitude to our colleagues at American River College and Siena College who have helped us immeasurably with their support and encouragement.

The following individuals at Prentice Hall had a large impact on this edition, and we are grateful for their work and professionalism: Gary Bauer, Linda Cupp, Megan Heint, and Rex Davidson. Thanks are due as well to Tracy Duff at Pre-PressPMG for adeptly managing the production of this edition.

Stanley A. Salzman
Gary Clendenen

Index of Applications

Photograph Credits

Introduction for Students

Success in Business Mathematics

With our growing need for record keeping, establishing budgets, and understanding finance, taxation, and investment opportunities, mathematics has become a greater part of our daily lives. This text applies mathematics to daily business experience. Your success in future business courses and pursuits will be enhanced by the knowledge and skills you will learn in this course.

Studying business mathematics is different from studying subjects such as English or history. The key to success is regular practice. This should not be surprising. After all, can you learn to ski or to play a musical instrument without a lot of regular practice? The same is true for learning mathematics. Working problems nearly every day is the key to becoming successful. Here are some suggestions to help you succeed in business mathematics:

1. **Attend class regularly. Pay attention to what your instructor says, and take careful notes.** Note the problems the instructor works on the board and copy the complete solutions. Keep these notes separate from your homework to avoid confusion.

2. **Don't hesitate to ask questions in class.** Asking questions is not a sign of weakness, but of strength. There are always other students with the same question who are too shy to ask.

3. **Read your text carefully.** Many students read only enough to get by, usually only the examples. Reading the complete section will help you to be successful with the homework problems. As you read the text, work the example problems and check the answers. This will test your understanding of what you have read. Pay special attention to highlighted statements and those labeled "Note."

4. **Before you start on your homework assignment, rework the problems the instructor worked in class.** This will reinforce what you have learned. Many students say, "I understand it perfectly when you do it, but I get stuck when I try to work the problem myself."

5. **Do your homework assignment only after reading the text and reviewing your notes from class.** Estimate the answer before you begin working the problem in the text. Check your work before looking at the answers in the back of the book. If you get a problem wrong and are unable to see why, mark that problem and ask your instructor.

6. **Work as neatly as you can using a *pencil,* and organize your work carefully.** Write your symbols clearly, and make sure the problems are clearly separated from each other.

7. **After you have completed a homework assignment, look over the text again.** Try to decide what the main ideas are in the lesson. Often they are clearly highlighted or boxed in the text.

8. **Determine whether tutoring is available and know how to get help when needed.** Use the instructor's office hours to contact the instructor for suggestions and direction and call the Addison-Wesley Math Tutor Center (see page xiii for details).

9. **Keep any quizzes and tests that are returned to you for studying for future tests and the final exam.** These quizzes and tests indicate what your instructor considers most important. Be sure to correct any test problems that you missed. Write all quiz and test scores on the front page of your notebook.

10. **Don't worry if you do not understand a new topic right away.** As you read more about it and work through the problems, you will gain understanding. No one understands each topic completely right from the start.

Pretest in Business Mathematics

This pretest measures your business mathematics skills at the beginning of the course. The solutions to each of these problems are found as examples throughout the book. The answers are on page xxiii.

(page 9)   **1.**   Convert to an improper fraction: $25\frac{3}{4}$

(page 10)   **2.**   Convert to a mixed number: $\frac{23}{3}$

(page 12)   **3.**   Find the least common denominator of the fractions $\frac{5}{12}$, $\frac{7}{18}$, and $\frac{11}{20}$.

(page 14)   **4.**   Mixed numbers—add: $34\frac{1}{2} + 23\frac{3}{4} + 34\frac{1}{2} + 23\frac{3}{4}$

(page 15)   **5.**   Common fractions—subtract: $\frac{17}{18} - \frac{20}{27}$

(page 15)   **6.**   Mixed numbers—subtract: $\begin{array}{r} 36\frac{2}{9} \\ -27\frac{5}{6} \end{array}$

(page 21)   **7.**   Mixed numbers—multiply: $5\frac{5}{8} \times 4\frac{1}{6}$

(page 22)   **8.**   Common fractions—divide: $\frac{25}{36} \div \frac{15}{18}$

(page 24)   **9.**   Convert the decimal 0.028 to a fraction.

(page 38)   **10.**   Solve $y + 12.3 = 20.5$ for y.

(page 42)   **11.**   Solve $5r - 2 = 2(r + 5)$ for r.

(page 52)   **12.**   Solve for T in the formula $M = P(1 + RT)$

(page 58)   **13.**   Find x in the proportion: $\frac{4}{9} = \frac{36}{x}$

(page 71)   **14.**   Express as a percent: 0.7

(page 72)   **15.**   Express as a decimal: 142%

(page 77)   **16.**   Solve for part: 1.2% of 180 is _____.

(page 83)   **17.**   Solve for base: 135 is 15% of _____.

(page 84)   **18.**   The 5% sales tax collected by Famous Footwear was $780. What was the amount of total sales?

(page 96)   **19.**   The price of a home sold by real estate agent Tricia Marinaro this year is $187,000, which is 10% more than last year's value. Find the value of the home last year.

(page 100)   **20.**   After Fleetfeet deducted 10% from the price of a pair of running shoes, Craig Bleyer paid $135. What was the original price of the shoes?

(page 131)   **21.**   The diameter of a part coming out of a machining process is measured regularly. The diameters vary some, as shown in the frequency table. Find the (a) mean, (b) median, and (c) mode.

Diameter (inches)	Frequency
0.720–0.729	3
0.730–0.739	12
0.740–0.749	8
0.750–0.759	9
0.760–0.769	2

(page 232)   **22.**   Suppose that during a certain quarter Leslie's Pool Supplies has collected $2765.42 from its employees for FICA tax, $638.17 for Medicare tax, and $3572.86 in federal withholding tax. Compute the total amount due to the Internal Revenue Service from Leslie's Pool Supplies.

(page 253)   **23.**   Find the taxes on each of the following pieces of property. Assessed valuations and tax rates are given.

(a) $58,975; 8.4%   (b) $875,400; $7.82 per $100

(c) $129,600; $64.21 per $1000   (d) $221,750; 94 mills (page 263) 24. Chris Kelly is single and has no dependents. He had an adjusted gross income of $26,735 last year, with deductions of $1352 for other taxes, $4118 for mortgage interest, and $317 for charity. Find his taxable income and his income tax.

(page 281) 25. Jo O'Neill owns an industrial building valued at $760,000. Her fire insurance policy (with an 80% coinsurance clause) has a face value of $570,000. The building suffers a fire loss of $144,000. Find the amount of the loss that the insurance company will pay and the amount that O'Neill must pay.

(page 321) 26. Oaks Hardware is offered a series discount of 20/10 on a Porter-Cable cordless drill with a list price of $150. Find the net cost after the series discount.

(page 334) 27. An invoice received by Bass Bait Shop for $840 is dated July 1 and offers terms of 2/10, n/30. If the invoice is paid on July 8 and the shipping and insurance charges, which were "FOB shipping point," are $18.70, find the total amount due.

(page 356) 28. The owner of Rose Fine Wines buys several cases of a popular wine bottled in Spain at a wholesale cost of $15 per bottle. In order to bring new customers into the store, the manager widely advertises a special promotion on this particular wine for $18.75 per bottle, or for considerably less than it can be purchased at competing stores. Find the percent of markup based on cost.

(page 371) 29. An athletic shoe manufacturer makes a walking shoe at a cost of $33.60 per pair. Based on past experience, 10% of the shoes will be defective and must be sold as irregulars for $48 per pair. If the manufacturer produces 1000 pairs of the shoes and desires a markup of 100% on cost, find the selling price per pair.

(page 394) 30. Olympic Sports and Leisure made the following purchases of the Explorer External Frame backpack during the year.

Beginning inventory	20 backpacks at $70
January	50 backpacks at $80
March	100 backpacks at $90
July	60 backpacks at $85
October	40 backpacks at $75

At the end of the year there are 75 backpacks in inventory. Use the weighted average method to find the inventory value.

(page 413) 31. After a large down payment, Jessica Warren borrowed $9000 from her credit union to purchase a previously owned Toyota Camry. Find the interest rate given that the loan was for 9 months and the interest was $540.

(page 468) 32. On February 27, Andrews Lincoln-Mercury receives a 150-day simple interest note with a face value of $3500 at 8% interest per year. On March 27, the firm discounts the note at the bank. Find the proceeds if the discount rate is 12%. (Use ordinary or banker's interest.)

(page 483) 33. Jonathan Simons invests $2500 in an account paying 4% compounded semiannually for 5 years. (a) Estimate the future value using simple interest. Then find (b) the compound amount, (c) the compound interest, and (d) the amount by which simple interest calculations underestimate the compound interest that is earned.

(page 536) 34. Arctic Drilling, Inc. borrowed money by selling bonds with a maturity value in 15 years totaling $10,000,000. Find the amount of each payment into a sinking fund needed to build the required amount in 15 years to pay off the bonds. Assume 9% compounded annually.

(page 581) 35. Bob Jones used a $75,000 loan for 25 years at 8% to purchase a summer cabin. Annual insurance and taxes on the property are $654 and $1329, respectively. Find the monthly payment.

(page 610) 36. City Saturn purchased an electronic smog analyzer for $9000. Using the sum-of-the-years'-digits method of depreciation, find the first and second years' depreciation if the analyzer has an estimated life of 4 years and no salvage value.

(page 618) 37. A boat dock with a life of 10 years is installed on April 12 at a cost of $72,000. If the double-declining-balance method is used, find the depreciation for the first partial year and the next full year.

(page 643) 38. Write each of the following items as a percent of net sales.

Gross sales	$209,000	Salaries and wages	$11,000
Returns	$9000	Rent	$6000
Cost of goods sold	$145,000	Advertising	$11,000

(page 675) 39. Due to excessive debt, Alamo Energy paid no dividend last year. The company has done much better this year and the board of directors has set aside $175,000 for the payment of dividends. The company has outstanding 12,500 shares of cumulative preferred stock having par value of $50, with an 8% dividend. The company also has 40,000 shares of common stock. What dividend will be paid to the owners of each type of stock?

(page 697) 40. Laura Cameron, Jay Davis, and Donna Friedman opened a tool rental business. Cameron contributed $250,000 to the opening of the business, which will be operated by Davis and Friedman. The partners agree that Cameron will first receive a 10% return on her investment before any further division of profits. Additional profits will be divided in the ratio 1:2:2. Find the amount that each partner would receive from a profit of $75,000.

Answers: 1. $\frac{103}{4}$ **2.** $7\frac{2}{3}$ **3.** 180 **4.** $116\frac{1}{2}$ **5.** $\frac{11}{54}$ **6.** $8\frac{7}{18}$ **7.** $23\frac{7}{16}$ **8.** $\frac{5}{6}$ **9.** $\frac{7}{250}$ **10.** 8.2 **11.** 4 **12.** $T = \frac{M-P}{PR}$ **13.** 81 **14.** 70% **15.** 1.42 **16.** 2.160 **17.** 900 **18.** $15,600 **19.** $170,000 **20.** $150 **21. (a)** 0.743 **(b)** 0.7445 **(c)** 0.7345 **22.** $10,380.04 **23. (a)** $4953.90 **(b)** $68,456.28 **(c)** $8321.62 **(d)** $20,844.50 **24.** $17,898; $2334.70 **25.** $135,000; $9000 **26.** $108 **27.** $841.90 **28.** 25% **29.** $69.33 **30.** $6249.75 **31.** 8% **32.** $3469.59 **33. (a)** $3000 **(b)** $3047.49 **(c)** $547.49 **(d)** $47.49 **34.** $340,588.80 **35.** $744.25 **36.** $3600; $2700 **37.** $10,800; $12,240 **38.** 104.5%; 4.5%; 72.5%; 5.5%; 3%; 5.5% **39.** $8; $1.88 **40.** $35,000; $20,000; $20,000

CHAPTER

1

Problem Solving and Operations with Fractions

Mathematics is very much a part of our lives. We use mathematics when we calculate the amount of money we earn, the interest and finance charges on our loans, the interest earned on our investments, and the cost of those things most important to our future. For example, Figure 1.1 shows the average annual earnings for workers between the ages of 25 and 64, depending on the level of education that they achieved.

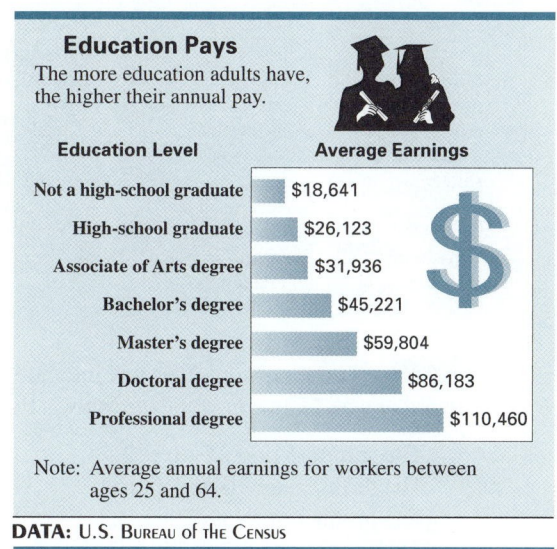

Education Pays
The more education adults have, the higher their annual pay.

Education Level	Average Earnings
Not a high-school graduate	$18,641
High-school graduate	$26,123
Associate of Arts degree	$31,936
Bachelor's degree	$45,221
Master's degree	$59,804
Doctoral degree	$86,183
Professional degree	$110,460

Note: Average annual earnings for workers between ages 25 and 64.

DATA: U.S. Bureau of the Census

Figure 1.1 Average annual earnings of adults based on education.

STOP *and think*

Estimate the lifetime benefit from earning an Associate of Arts degree versus stopping with a high-school diploma. Then estimate the lifetime benefit from earning a Bachelor's degree versus stopping with an Associate of Arts degree. List the nonmonetary pros and cons of earning a Bachelor's degree.

Businesses use mathematics every day to prepare payrolls, find the interest on loans, determine the markups and markdowns on items to be sold, maintain the firm's financial records, or calculate the amount of taxes owed.

It is important for you to understand the fundamentals of mathematics so that you can solve more advanced problems in business mathematics. The first chapter reviews problem solving and fractions, **Chapter 2** looks briefly at basic equations and formulas, **Chapter 3** discusses the very important topic of percents, and **Chapter 4** introduces basic concepts of statistics. The remaining chapters apply these math skills to various problems in business.

1.1 Problem Solving

OBJECTIVES

1 *Identify indicator words in application problems.*

2 *List the four steps for solving application problems.*

3 *Learn to estimate answers.*

It is important to carefully read and fully understand a problem or situation before doing any math. The suggestions given in this section will help you work the many word problems you will encounter both in this course and when working for an employer.

Objective

1 *Identify Indicator Words in Application Problems.* Look for **indicators** in the application problem—words that indicate the necessary operations—addition, subtraction, multiplication, or division. Some of these words appear below.

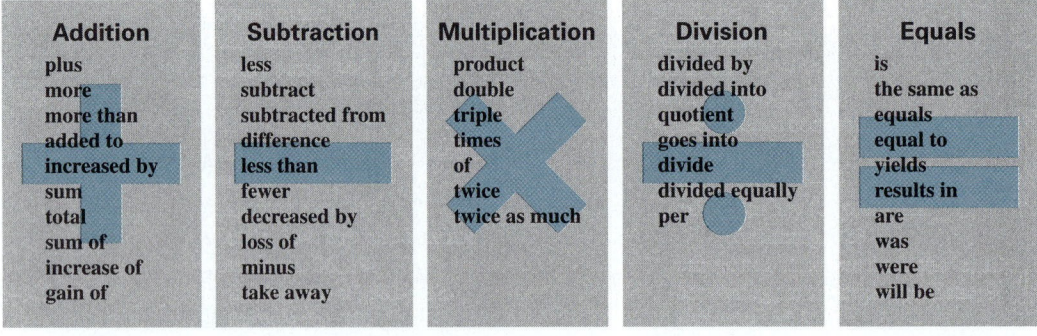

Addition	Subtraction	Multiplication	Division	Equals
plus	less	product	divided by	is
more	subtract	double	divided into	the same as
more than	subtracted from	triple	quotient	equals
added to	difference	times	goes into	equal to
increased by	less than	of	divide	yields
sum	fewer	twice	divided equally	results in
total	decreased by	twice as much	per	are
sum of	loss of			was
increase of	minus			were
gain of	take away			will be

NOTE The word *and* does not indicate addition and does not appear as an indicator word above. Notice how the *and* shows the *location* of an operation sign.

The sum of 6 *and* 2 is 6 + 2.
The difference of 6 *and* 2 is 6 − 2.
The product of 6 *and* 2 is 6 × 2.
The quotient of 6 *and* 2 is 6 ÷ 2.

Objective

2 *List the Four Steps for Solving Application Problems.* Students sometimes make the mistake of trying to solve a problem before understanding it. Believe it or not, this actually wastes your time and often results in more mistakes. The first step in solving a problem is to try to ***fully understand***. Look carefully at the following steps and try to use them on every problem you do.

Solving Application Problems

Step 1 Read the problem carefully. You may need to read it more than once to fully understand. Know what the problem is asking before you try to solve it. Clearly identify the unknown and keep it in mind.

Step 2 Develop a plan to work the problem. Indicator words may help.

Step 3 Estimate a reasonable answer using rounding.

Step 4 Solve the problem.

Step 5 Check to see if the answer is reasonable.

Each of these steps is very important. We suggest you do not take shortcuts—go through all of the steps every time. Getting in the habit of going through all of the steps will be a benefit to you later in life since employers will pay you more if you can solve more complex problems.

Objective

3   *Learn to Estimate Answers.*   It is particularly important to estimate a reasonable answer and then check to see if the final answer is, in fact, reasonable. Doing so will allow you to catch your own mistakes before going on to something else.

What is a *reasonable answer*? Read the problem and try to determine the approximate size of the answer. Should the answer be part of a dollar, a few dollars, hundreds, thousands, or even millions of dollars? For example, if a problem asks for the cost of a man's shirt, would an answer of $20 be reasonable? $1000? $0.65? $65?

EXAMPLE 1   **Applying Division**

At a group yard sale the total sales were $3584.20. The money was divided equally among the boys soccer club, the girls soccer club, the boys softball team, and the girls softball team. How much did each group receive?

Solution

STEP 1 Total sales of $3584.20 are to be divided equally among four different groups. The unknown is the amount that goes to each of the four groups.

STEP 2 Plan: Divide $3584.20 by 4.

STEP 3 Estimate by rounding $3584.20 to $3600. Dividing $3600 by 4 suggests that each group will receive about $900.

STEP 4 Find the answer by dividing.

$$
\begin{array}{r}
896.05 \\
4\overline{)3584.20} \\
\underline{32} \\
38 \\
\underline{36} \\
24 \\
\underline{24} \\
2 \\
\underline{0} \\
20 \\
\underline{20} \\
0
\end{array}
$$

STEP 5 The answer of $896.05 is close to $900, so our answer seems reasonable. Check it as follows.

$$
\begin{array}{r}
\$896.05 \\
\times 4 \\
\hline
\$3584.20
\end{array}
$$
   Amount received
   Number of groups
   Answer checks

EXAMPLE 2 **Applying Addition**

Mandy Crandall works part-time at Starbucks, where her hours vary by day. Her daily earnings for the 5 days of one week were $62.35, $75.40, $88.50, $48.30, and $55.80. Find total earnings.

Solution

STEP 1 The problem gives daily earnings for five days and asks for total earnings for the week.

STEP 2 Plan: Add the five daily earnings.

STEP 3 Glancing at the daily earnings shows an average daily earnings of about $70 per day. Multiply $70 per day $\times$ 5 days to get an estimate of $350 for the week.

STEP 4 Solve by adding exact numbers.

$$
\begin{array}{r}
\$\ 62.35 \\
75.40 \\
88.50 \\
48.30 \\
55.80 \\
\hline
\$330.35
\end{array}
$$ Total earnings for the week

STEP 5 The answer of $330.35 is relatively close to the estimate of $350. It is also a reasonable answer. An answer of, say, $1303.50 for the week would not be reasonable for one week's earnings by a part-time worker at a Starbucks.

EXAMPLE 3 **Applying Subtraction**

The number of students enrolled in Chabot College this year is 1012 fewer than the number enrolled last year. Enrollment last year was 21,382. Find the enrollment this year.

Solution

STEP 1 Last year's enrollment of 21,382 decreased by 1012 this year. The unknown is this year's enrollment.

STEP 2 Plan: The indicator work *fewer* suggests that subtraction should be used to find the number of students enrollment this year. Subtract the decrease in enrollment from last year's enrollment.

STEP 3 Estimate as follows.

$$
\begin{array}{r}
21,000 \\
-\ \ 1,000 \\
\hline
20,000
\end{array}
$$
Estimate of last year's enrollment
Estimate of decrease in enrollment
Estimate of number enrolled this year

STEP 4 Find exact answer.

$$
\begin{array}{r}
21,382 \\
-\ \ 1,012 \\
\hline
20,370
\end{array}
$$ Current enrollment

STEP 5 The exact number of 20,370 students is close to the estimate of 20,000. Check by adding.

$$
\begin{array}{r}
20,370 \\
1,012 \\
\hline
21,382
\end{array}
$$
Current enrollment
Decrease in enrollment compared to last year
Enrollment last year

EXAMPLE **4** **Solving a Problem with Two Steps**

The owner of a small apartment house rents the seven apartments for $975 each. After paying $5920 in expenses, including a mortgage payment, in one month, find the amount that remains.

Solution

STEP 1 The unknown is the amount remaining after expenses for the month.

STEP 2 Plan: First find total rents for the month. Then subtract the expenses.

STEP 3 Estimate by assuming that each renter pays $1000 per month and that total expenses for the month are $6000.

$$7 \text{ apartments} \times \$1000 = \$7000 \text{ total rent}$$

$$\$7000 \text{ total rent} - \$6000 \text{ in expenses} = \$1000 \text{ remaining}$$

STEP 4 Solve for exact answer.

$975	$6825 Total rent
× 7	− 5920 Expenses
$6825 Total rent	$ 905 Remaining after paying expenses

STEP 5 The exact answer of $905 is close to the estimate of $1000. An answer, for example, of $4200 would not have been reasonable since total rents are only $6825.

We suggest that you try to use all five problem-solving steps every time you work a problem. It will make you a much better problem solver in the long run. Firms want individuals who are able to think and solve problems.

NOTE   Recall the Order of Operations. Operations must be done in the following order.

1. Contents of parentheses
2. Exponents and square roots
3. Multiplication and division from left to right
4. Addition and subtraction from left to right

1.1 | **Exercises**

Solve the following application problems.

1. **COMPETITIVE CYCLIST TRAINING**   During a week of training, Beth Andrews rode her bike 80 miles on Monday, 75 miles on Tuesday, 135 miles on Wednesday, 40 miles on Thursday, and 52 miles on Friday. What is the total number of miles she rode in the five-day period?

2. **COFFEE SALES**   During a recent week, Starbucks Coffee sold 325 pounds of Estate Java coffee, 75 pounds of Encanta Blend coffee, 137 pounds of Ethiopia Sidamo coffee, 495 pounds of Starbucks House-Blend Decaf coffee and 105 pounds of New Guinea Peaberry coffee. Find the total number of pounds of these coffees sold.

3. **CRUISE SHIP TRAVEL**   A cruise ship has 1815 passengers. When in port at Grand Cayman, 1348 passengers go ashore for the day while the others remain on the ship. How many passengers remain on the ship?

4. **ATM CASH**   The amount of cash in an ATM ranges from $15,000 in small machines to $250,000 in large bank machines. How much more money is there in the large machines than in the small machines?

5. **GREENHOUSE GASES** Estimates indicate that about 2.5 billion tons of the greenhouse gas carbon dioxide are emitted each year in the United States by utility companies that generate electricity. If scientists estimate that no more than 0.8 billion tons can be emitted in the United States annually to keep global warming at bay, find the required reduction in carbon dioxide emissions.

6. **WORLD POPULATION GROWTH** The world population grows by 8900 people each hour. Find the increase in world population in one year of 365 days.

7. **AUTOMOBILE WEIGHT** A car weighs 2425 pounds. If its 582-pound engine is removed and replaced with a 634-pound engine, how much will the car weigh after the engine change?

8. **PRESCHOOL MANAGER** Tiffany Connolly has $2324 in her preschool operating account. After spending $734 from this account, the class parents raise $568 in a rummage sale. Find the balance in the account after depositing the money from the rummage sale.

9. **BUSINESS ENTERPRISES** There are 24 million business enterprises in the United States. Only 7000 of these businesses are large businesses having 500 or more employees, while the rest are small and midsize businesses. Find the number of small and midsize businesses.

10. **WEIGHING FREIGHT** A truck weighs 9250 pounds when empty. After being loaded with firewood, the truck weighs 21,375 pounds. What is the weight of the firewood?

11. **WORLD WAR II VETERANS** World War II veterans, part of what is now called "the greatest generation," are dying at the rate of 900 each day. How many World War II veterans are projected to die in the next year of 365 days?

12. **FINANCIAL CRISIS** To avoid bankruptcy during a recent financial crisis, a global bank offered a $30,000 bonus to 12,600 employees if they would take an early retirement. If all of the employees retire early, find the total cost to the bank.

13. **HOTEL ROOM COSTS** In a recent study of hotel/casinos, the cost per night at Harrah's Reno was $89, while the cost at Harrah's Lake Tahoe was $239 per night. Find the amount saved on a 5-night stay at Harrah's Reno instead of staying at Harrah's Lake Tahoe.

14. **LUXURY HOTELS** The most expensive hotel room in a recent study was the Ritz-Carlton at $625 per night, while the least expensive was Motel 6 at $75 per night. Find the amount saved on a 4-night stay at Motel 6 over the cost of staying at the Ritz-Carlton.

15. **PHYSICALLY IMPAIRED** The Enabling Supply House purchases 6 wheelchairs at $1256 each and 15 speech compression recorder-players at $895 each. Find the total cost of the equipment.

16. **OFFICE EQUIPMENT** Find the total cost if Krispy Kreme Doughnuts buys 27 computers at $986 each and 12 printers at $179 each.

17. **THEATER RENOVATION** A theater owner is remodeling and wants to provide enough seating for 1250 people. The main floor has 30 rows of 25 seats in each row. If the balcony has 25 rows, how many seats must be in each row of the balcony to satisfy the owner's seating requirements?

18. **PACKING AND SHIPPING** Nancy Hart makes 24 grapevine wreaths per week to sell to gift shops. She works 30 weeks a year and packages 6 wreaths per box. If she ships equal quantities to each of five shops, find the number of boxes each shop will receive.

19. **MALL-SHOPPING FACTS** A recent study showed that the average trip to the mall lasts 4.4 hours, which is longer than a football game. How many hours would be needed for eight of these trips to the mall?

20. **VENDING MACHINE** The Selective End Cold-Drink vending machine is priced at $2679.99 at Costco. Find the cost of 14 of these machines.

21. **STOCKHOLDER LOSSES** Bagoda Imports announced a $38 million loss, or $0.58 a share. Find the number of shares of stock in the company. Round to the nearest tenth of a million.

22. **SHARES OF STOCK** Money Store officials said that they expect to post a loss of $42 million, or $0.65 a share. Find the number of shares of stock in the company. Round to the nearest million.

23. **OLYMPIC GOLD COINS** If a 5-dollar Olympic gold coin weighs 8.359 grams, find the number of coins that can be produced from 221 grams of gold. Round down to the nearest whole number.

24. **MEDICINE DOSAGE** Each dosage of a medication contains 1.62 units of a certain ingredient. Find the number of dosages that can be made from 57.13 units of the ingredient. Round down to the nearest whole number.

25. **U.S. PAPER MONEY** The thickness of one piece of paper money is 0.0043 inch.
    (a) If you had a pile of 100 bills, how high would it be?
    (b) How high would a pile of 1000 bills be?

26. Use the information from Exercise 25.
    (a) Find the number of bills in a pile that is 43 inches high.
    (b) How much money would you have if the pile was all $20 bills?

27. **MANAGERIAL EARNINGS** A parts department manager earns $3250 each month working a 42-hour week. Assume one month is 4.3 weeks and find
    (a) the number of hours worked each month, and
    (b) the manager's hourly earnings. Round to the nearest cent.

28. **MANAGER AT TARGET** An assistant manager at Target earns $3539.76 after taxes each month for working a 48-hour week. Assume 1 month is 4.3 weeks and find
    (a) the number of hours worked each month, and
    (b) the manager's hourly after-tax earnings.

29. **REAL ESTATE FEES** Robert Gonzalez recently sold his home for $246,500. He paid a sales fee of 0.06 times the price of the house. What was the amount of the fee?

30. **BASEBOARD TRIM** Kathy West bought 6.5 yards of baseboard trim to complete her kitchen remodeling. If she paid $8.70 per yard for the trim, what was her total cost?

1.2 Addition and Subtraction of Fractions

OBJECTIVES

1 *Recognize types of fractions.*
2 *Convert mixed numbers to improper fractions.*
3 *Write fractions in lowest terms.*
4 *Use the rules for divisibility.*
5 *Add or subtract like fractions.*
6 *Find the least common denominator.*
7 *Add unlike fractions.*
8 *Add mixed numbers.*
9 *Subtract unlike fractions.*
10 *Subtract mixed numbers.*

This section looks at **fractions**—numbers, like decimals, that can be used to represent parts of a whole. Fractions and decimals are two ways of representing the same quantity. Fractions are used in business and in our personal lives. For example, one restaurant uses the following recipe to make a cake that is a favorite of many of its customers. Notice that the recipe contains several fractions.

Chocolate Decadence Cake

2 cups unsalted butter, room temperature
$1\frac{1}{4}$ pounds bittersweet chocolate, chopped
10 eggs, separated and room temperature
2 tablespoons pure vanilla extract
$1\frac{3}{4}$ cups granulated sugar
$\frac{1}{4}$ teaspoon salt
$\frac{1}{4}$ cup cocoa powder

A **fraction** represents parts of a whole. Fractions are written as one number over another, with a line between the two numbers, as in the following.

$$\frac{5}{8} \quad \frac{1}{4} \quad \frac{9}{7} \quad \frac{13}{10} \begin{array}{l} \longrightarrow \text{Numerator} \\ \longrightarrow \text{Denominator} \end{array}$$

The number above the line is called the **numerator**, and the number below the line is called the **denominator**. In the fraction $\frac{2}{3}$, for example, the numerator is 2 and the denominator is 3. The denominator tells the number of equal parts into which the whole is divided, and the numerator tells how many of these parts we are talking about. For example, $\frac{2}{3}$ of an apple is "2 parts out of an apple cut into 3 equal parts," as shown in Figure 1.2.

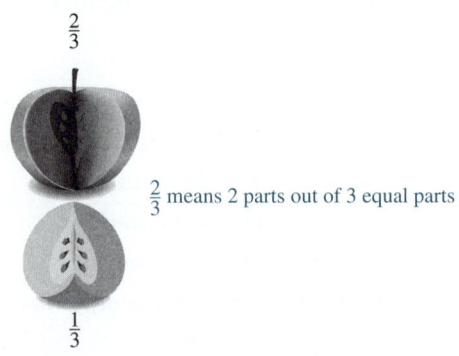

$\frac{2}{3}$ means 2 parts out of 3 equal parts

Figure 1.2

Objective

1 *Recognize Types of Fractions.* A **proper fraction**, or common fraction, is one in which the numerator is *smaller than* the denominator. An **improper fraction** is one in which the numerator is *greater than or equal to* the denonimator.

	Examples					
Proper fractions	$\frac{1}{4}$	$\frac{3}{5}$	$\frac{5}{8}$	$\frac{1}{15}$	$\frac{19}{20}$	$\frac{71}{100}$
Improper fractions	$\frac{5}{2}$	$\frac{7}{3}$	$\frac{5}{5}$	$\frac{9}{5}$	$\frac{53}{45}$	$\frac{80}{62}$

A proper fraction has a value that is less than 1. An improper fraction has a value that is greater than or equal to 1. To write a whole number as a fraction, place the whole number over 1, as in the following examples.

$$7 = \frac{7}{1} \qquad 12 = \frac{12}{1} \qquad 55 = \frac{55}{1}$$

Objective

2 *Convert Mixed Numbers to Improper Fractions.* The sum of a whole number and a fraction is called a **mixed number**. Example of mixed numbers include $2\frac{1}{4}$, $5\frac{3}{4}$, and $12\frac{3}{8}$. The mixed number $2\frac{1}{4}$ is a shortcut way of writing $2 + \frac{1}{4}$. Similarly, $5\frac{3}{4}$ is the same as $5 + \frac{3}{4}$, etc.

To Convert a Mixed Number to an Improper Fraction

Step 1 To find the numerator of the improper fraction, multiply the whole number by the denominator of the fraction and add to the numerator.

Step 2 Keep the same denominator.

$$\text{For example: } 4\frac{5}{8} = \frac{(4 \times 8) + 5}{8} = \frac{37}{8}$$

EXAMPLE 1 **Converting Mixed Numbers to Improper Fractions**

An opening in the kitchen cabinet is for a microwave oven that is $25\frac{3}{4}$ inches wide and $16\frac{1}{2}$ inches high. Convert both mixed numbers to improper fractions.

(a) $25\frac{3}{4}$ **(b)** $16\frac{1}{2}$

Solution

(a) First multiply the whole number (25) by the denominator (4), and then add the numerator (3). This gives $(25 \times 4) + 3 = 100 + 3 = 103$. The parentheses are used to show that 25 and 4 are multiplied first.

$$25\frac{3}{4} = \frac{(25 \times 4) + 3}{4} = \frac{103}{4}$$

(b) $16\frac{1}{2} = \frac{(16 \times 2) + 1}{2} = \frac{33}{2}$

Convert an improper fraction to a mixed number by dividing the numerator of the improper fraction by the denominator. The quotient is the whole number part of the mixed number, and the remainder is used as the numerator of the fraction part. The denominator stays the same.

EXAMPLE **2**   **Converting Improper Fractions to Mixed Numbers**

Convert $\frac{23}{3}$ to a mixed number.

Solution   Divide 23 by 3.

$$3\overline{)23} \\ \underline{21} \\ 2 \quad ^{7}$$

The whole-number part is the quotient 7. The remainder 2 is used as the numerator of the fraction part. Keep 3 as the denominator.

$$\frac{23}{3} = 7\frac{2}{3}$$

NOTE   A proper fraction has a value that is smaller than 1. An improper fraction has a value that is 1 or greater.

Objective

3   *Write Fractions in Lowest Terms.*   A fraction is said to be in **lowest terms** if no number other than 1 divides evenly (with no remainder) into both the numerator and denominator. Effectively, a fraction in lowest terms has been written in the simplest form possible for a fraction. For example, the fractions $\frac{1}{4}, \frac{1}{2},$ and $\frac{5}{6}$ are in lowest terms. However, the fraction $\frac{15}{25}$ is not in lowest terms since both 15 and 25 can be divided by 5. Write $\frac{15}{25}$ in lowest terms by dividing both the numerator and denominator by 5.

$$\frac{15}{25} = \frac{15 \div 5}{25 \div 5} = \frac{3}{5}$$

⬆— Divide by 5.

EXAMPLE **3**   **Writing Fractions in Lowest Terms**

Write the following fractions in lowest terms.

(a) $\frac{15}{40}$ **(b)** $\frac{33}{39}$

Solution   Look for the largest number that divides both numerator and denominator without remainder.

(a) Both 15 and 40 can be divided by 5.

$$\frac{15}{40} = \frac{15 \div 5}{40 \div 5} = \frac{3}{8}$$

(b) Divide both numerator and denominator by 3.

$$\frac{33}{39} = \frac{33 \div 3}{39 \div 3} = \frac{11}{13}$$

Objective

4   *Use the Rules for Divisibility.*   Deciding which numbers will divide into another number without remainder is sometimes difficult. The following **rules for divisibility** can help.

Rules for Divisibility

A number can be divided evenly by:

2	if the last digit is 0, 2, 4, 6, or 8
3	if the sum of the digits is divisible by 3
4	if the last two digits form a number divisible by 4
5	if the last digit is 0 or 5
6	if the number is even and the sum of the digits is divisible by 3
8	if the last three digits form a number divisible by 8
9	if the sum of the digits is divisible by 9
10	if the last digit is 0

EXAMPLE 4 Using the Divisibility Rules

Determine whether the following statements are true.

(a) 3,746,892 is divisible by 4.   (b) 15,974,802 is divisible by 9.

Solution

(a) The number 3,746,892 is divisible by 4, since the last two digits form a number divisible by 4.

$$3, 746, 892$$
⌐ **92** is divisible by 4.

(b) See if 15,974,802 is divisible by 9 by adding the digits of the number.

$$1 + 5 + 9 + 7 + 4 + 8 + 0 + 2 = 36$$
⌐ **36** is divisible by 9.

Since 36 is divisible by 9, the given number is divisible by 9.

NOTE The rules for divisibility only help to identify which single-digit numbers divide evenly into a larger number. The division must actually be done in order to find the number of times one number divides into another.

Objective

5 *Add or Subtract Like Fractions.* Fractions with the same denominator are called **like fractions**. Such fractions have a **common denominator**. For example, $\frac{3}{4}$ and $\frac{1}{4}$ are like fractions and 4 is the common denominator, but $\frac{4}{7}$ and $\frac{4}{9}$ are not like fractions. Add or subtract like fractions by adding or subtracting the numerators and then placing the result over the common denominator. The answer can then be written in lowest terms, if necessary.

EXAMPLE 5 Adding and Subtracting Like Fractions

Add or subtract the following fractions.

(a) $\frac{3}{4} + \frac{1}{4} + \frac{5}{4}$ (b) $\frac{13}{25} - \frac{7}{25}$

Solution The fractions in both parts of this example are like fractions. Add or subtract the numerators and place the result over the common denominator. Write as a mixed number in lowest terms, as necessary.

(a) $\frac{3}{4} + \frac{1}{4} + \frac{5}{4} = \frac{3 + 1 + 5}{4} = \frac{9}{4} = 2\frac{1}{4}$

Add numerators. Write the answer as a mixed number. Use the common denominator.

(b) $\frac{13}{25} - \frac{7}{25} = \frac{13 - 7}{25} = \frac{6}{25}$

Objective

6 *Find the Least Common Denominator.* Fractions with different denominators are called **unlike fractions**. Add or subtract unlike fractions by first converting them to like fractions with a common denominator.

The **least common denominator (LCD)** for two or more fractions is the smallest whole number that can be divided, without remainder, by all the denominators of the fractions. For example, the least common denominator of the fractions $\frac{3}{4}$, $\frac{5}{6}$, and $\frac{1}{2}$ is 12, since 12 is the smallest number that can be divided without remainder by 4, 6, and 2.

In the cabinet specifications from American Landmark Cabinetry (shown below), the fractions in the Shelf-End Base drawing are **like fractions**, $23\frac{3}{16}$, $10\frac{9}{16}$, and $11\frac{3}{16}$, since 16 is the denominator of each fraction. However, in the drawing of the Shelf-End Peninsula Base, the fractions are **unlike fractions**, $22\frac{7}{16}$, $11\frac{3}{32}$, and $11\frac{5}{8}$, since the denominators differ.

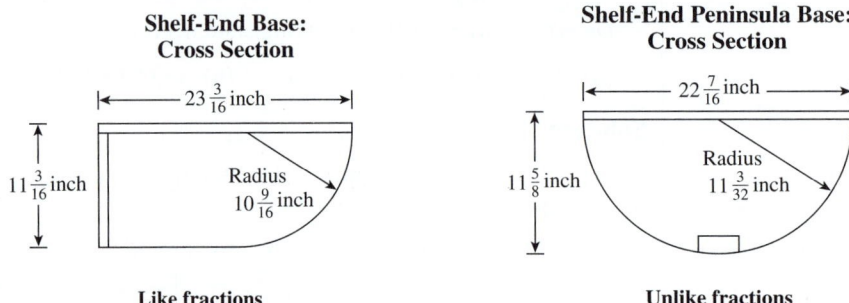

There are two methods of finding the least common denominator: the *inspection method* and the *method of prime numbers*.

Inspection. Check to see if the least common denominator can be found by inspection. For example, the least common denominator of $\frac{1}{3}$ and $\frac{1}{4}$ is 12, since 12 is the smallest number into which 3 and 4 both divide with remainder zero. This method works best when the denominators involved are small.

Method of prime numbers. If you cannot find the least common denominator by inspection, use the method of prime numbers, as shown in the next example.

A **prime number** is a number that can be divided without remainder only by itself and by 1. Prime numbers are 2, 3, 5, 7, 11, 13, 17, and so on.

NOTE All prime numbers other than 2 are odd numbers. However, not all odd numbers are prime numbers. For example, 27 is the product of 3 and 9, and it is not a prime number.

EXAMPLE 6 **Finding the Least Common Denominator**

Use the method of prime numbers to find the least common denominator of the fractions $\frac{5}{12}$, $\frac{7}{18}$, and $\frac{11}{20}$.

Solution First write down the three denominators.

$$12 \qquad 18 \qquad 20$$

Begin by trying to divide the three denominators by the smallest prime number, 2. Write each quotient directly above the given denominator. (This way of writing the division process is just a handy way of writing the separate problems $2\overline{)12}$, $2\overline{)18}$, and $2\overline{)20}$.)

$$\begin{array}{r} 6 \quad\; 9 \quad 10 \\ \hline 2\overline{)12 \quad 18 \quad 20} \end{array}$$

Two of the new quotients, 6 and 10, can still be divided by 2, so perform the division again. Since 9 cannot be divided by 2, just bring up the 9.

$$
\begin{array}{r}
\quad\ 3 \quad 9 \quad 5 \quad \text{Just bring 9 up.} \\
2\overline{)\ 6 \quad 9 \quad 10} \\
2\overline{)12 \quad 18 \quad 20}
\end{array}
$$

None of the new quotients in the top row can be divided by 2, so try the next prime number, 3. The number 9 can be divided twice by 3, as shown below on the left.

$$
\begin{array}{r}
\quad\quad\quad\quad\quad\quad\quad 1 \quad 1 \quad 1 \\
\quad\quad\quad 1 \quad 1 \quad 5 \quad\quad 5\overline{)\ 1 \quad 1 \quad 5} \\
3\overline{)\ 1 \quad 3 \quad 5} \quad\quad 3\overline{)\ 1 \quad 3 \quad 5} \\
3\overline{)\ 3 \quad 9 \quad 5} \quad\quad 3\overline{)\ 3 \quad 9 \quad 5} \\
2\overline{)\ 6 \quad 9 \quad 10} \quad\quad 2\overline{)\ 6 \quad 9 \quad 10} \\
2\overline{)12 \quad 18 \quad 20} \quad\quad 2\overline{)12 \quad 18 \quad 20}
\end{array}
$$

Since none of the new quotients in the top row can be divided by 3, try the next prime number, 5. The number 5 can be used only once. Now that the top row contains only 1s, find the least common denominator by multiplying the prime numbers in the left column.

$$2 \times 2 \times 3 \times 3 \times 5 = 180$$

The least common denominator for $\frac{5}{12}$, $\frac{7}{18}$, and $\frac{11}{20}$ is 180.

NOTE It is **not necessary** to start dividing by the smallest prime number as shown in Example 6. In fact, no matter which prime number you start with, you still get the same least common denominator.

Objective

7 *Add Unlike Fractions.* Add unlike fractions by rewriting the fractions with a common denominator. Since Example 6 shows that 180 is the least common denominator for $\frac{5}{12}$, $\frac{7}{18}$, and $\frac{11}{20}$, these three fractions can be added if each fraction is first written with a denominator of 180.

STEP 1 $\quad \dfrac{5}{12} = \dfrac{\quad}{180} \qquad \dfrac{7}{18} = \dfrac{\quad}{180} \qquad \dfrac{11}{20} = \dfrac{\quad}{180}$

Rewrite these fractions with a common denominator by first dividing the common denominator by the denominator of the original fractions.

$$180 \div 12 = 15 \qquad 180 \div 18 = 10 \qquad 180 \div 20 = 9$$

STEP 2 Next, multiply each quotient by the original numerator.

$$15 \times 5 = 75 \qquad 10 \times 7 = 70 \qquad 9 \times 11 = 99$$

STEP 3 Now, rewrite the fractions.

$$\frac{5}{12} = \frac{75}{180} \qquad \frac{7}{18} = \frac{70}{180} \qquad \frac{11}{20} = \frac{99}{180}$$

STEP 4 Add the fractions.

$$\frac{5}{12} + \frac{7}{18} + \frac{11}{20} = \frac{75}{180} + \frac{70}{180} + \frac{99}{180} = \frac{75 + 70 + 99}{180}$$

$$= \frac{244}{180} = 1\frac{64}{180} = 1\frac{16}{45} \quad \begin{array}{l}\text{Write the answer as a mixed number}\\\text{with the fraction in lowest terms.}\end{array}$$

EXAMPLE 7 **Adding Unlike Fractions**

Add the following fractions.

(a) $\dfrac{3}{4} + \dfrac{1}{2} + \dfrac{5}{8}$ (b) $\dfrac{9}{10} + \dfrac{4}{5} + \dfrac{3}{8}$

Solution

(a) Inspection shows that the least common denominator is 8. Rewrite the fractions so they each have a denominator of 8. Then add.

$$\frac{3}{4} + \frac{1}{2} + \frac{5}{8} = \frac{6}{8} + \frac{4}{8} + \frac{5}{8} = \frac{6 + 4 + 5}{8} = \frac{15}{8} = 1\frac{7}{8}$$

(b) The method of prime numbers shows that the least common denominator is 40. Rewrite the fractions so they each have a denominator of 40. Then add.

$$\frac{9}{10} + \frac{4}{5} + \frac{3}{8} = \frac{36}{40} + \frac{32}{40} + \frac{15}{40} = \frac{36 + 32 + 15}{40} = \frac{83}{40} = 2\frac{3}{40}$$

Scientific Calculator Approach

All calculator solutions are shown using a scientific calculator. The calculator solution to Example 7(b) uses the fraction key on the scientific calculator.

$$9 \boxed{a^{b}\!/_{\!c}} \ 10 \ \boxed{+} \ 4 \ \boxed{a^{b}\!/_{\!c}} \ 5 \ \boxed{+} \ 3 \ \boxed{a^{b}\!/_{\!c}} \ 8 \ \boxed{=} \ 2\frac{3}{40}$$

Objective

8 *Add Mixed Numbers.* Add two mixed numbers by first adding the fraction parts. Then add the whole number parts and combine the two sums.

EXAMPLE 8 **Adding Mixed Numbers**

A rubber gasket must extend around all four edges (perimeter) of the dishwasher panel shown below before it is installed. Find the length of gasket material needed.

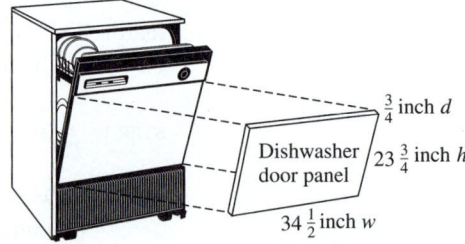

$\frac{3}{4}$ inch d

Dishwasher door panel $23\frac{3}{4}$ inch h

$34\frac{1}{2}$ inch w

Add $34\frac{1}{2}$ inches and $23\frac{3}{4}$ inches and $34\frac{1}{2}$ inches and $23\frac{3}{4}$ inches.

Solution

$$34\frac{1}{2} = 34\frac{2}{4}$$

$$23\frac{3}{4} = 23\frac{3}{4}$$

$$34\frac{1}{2} = 34\frac{2}{4}$$

$$+ 23\frac{3}{4} = 23\frac{3}{4}$$

$$\frac{10}{4} = 2\frac{2}{4}$$

$$114\frac{10}{4} = 114 + 2\frac{2}{4} = 116\frac{2}{4} = 116\frac{1}{2} \text{ inches}$$

> **NOTE** When adding mixed numbers, first add the fraction parts, then add the whole number parts. Then combine the two answers.

Objective

9 *Subtract Unlike Fractions.* If the fractions to be subtracted have different denominators, first find the least common denominator. For example, to subtract $\frac{1}{3}$ from $\frac{5}{8}$, first find the least common denominator, 24. Now write each fraction with a denominator of 24 and subtract.

$$\frac{5}{8} - \frac{1}{3} = \frac{15}{24} - \frac{8}{24} = \frac{15 - 8}{24} = \frac{7}{24}$$

EXAMPLE 9 **Subtracting Fractions**

Subtract the following fractions.

(a) $\frac{3}{4} - \frac{5}{9}$ (b) $\frac{17}{18} - \frac{20}{27}$

Solution Find the common denominator and then subtract.

(a) $\frac{3}{4} - \frac{5}{9} = \frac{27}{36} - \frac{20}{36} = \frac{7}{36}$ (b) $\frac{17}{18} - \frac{20}{27} = \frac{51}{54} - \frac{40}{54} = \frac{11}{54}$

Objective

10 *Subtract Mixed Numbers.* To subtract two mixed numbers, first, change the mixed numbers, if necessary, so that the fraction parts have a common denominator. Then subtract the fraction parts and the whole number parts separately. For example, subtract $3\frac{1}{12}$ from $8\frac{5}{8}$ by first finding that the least common denominator of the two fractions is 24. Then rewrite the problem as shown.

$$8\frac{5}{8} - 3\frac{1}{12}$$

Use 24 as a common denominator.

$$8\frac{15}{24} - 3\frac{2}{24}$$

Now subtract the fraction parts, and subtract the whole number parts.

$$\begin{array}{r} 8\frac{15}{24} \\ -\ 3\frac{2}{24} \\ \hline 5\frac{13}{24} \end{array}$$

— Subtract fractions.
— Subtract whole numbers.

The following example shows how to subtract when **borrowing** is needed.

EXAMPLE 10 **Subtracting with Borrowing**

Subtract $27\frac{5}{6}$ from $36\frac{2}{9}$.

Solution Start by rewriting the problem with a common denominator.

$$\begin{array}{r} 36\frac{2}{9} = 36\frac{4}{18} \\ -\ 27\frac{5}{6} = 27\frac{15}{18} \\ \hline \end{array}$$

The fraction $\frac{15}{18}$ cannot be subtracted from $\frac{4}{18}$, since it is larger than $\frac{4}{18}$. First, borrow 1 from 36.

$$36\frac{4}{18} = 35 + 1 + \frac{4}{18}$$

$$= 35 + \frac{18}{18} + \frac{4}{18} \qquad 1 = \frac{18}{18}$$

$$= 35\frac{22}{18}$$

$$35\frac{22}{18} = \left(36\frac{4}{18}\right)$$
$$-\,27\frac{15}{18}$$
$$\overline{8\frac{7}{18}}$$

Check by adding $8\frac{7}{18}$ and $27\frac{5}{6}$. The answer is $36\frac{2}{9}$, so no mistakes were made.

Scientific Calculator Approach

The calculator solution to Example 10 uses the fraction key.

$$36 \boxed{a^{b}/_{c}} 2 \boxed{a^{b}/_{c}} 9 \boxed{-} 27 \boxed{a^{b}/_{c}} 5 \boxed{a^{b}/_{c}} 6 \boxed{=} 8\frac{7}{18}$$

1.2 | Exercises

Convert the following mixed numbers to improper fractions:

1. $1\frac{3}{8}$ 2. $2\frac{4}{5}$ 3. $4\frac{1}{4}$ 4. $2\frac{8}{11}$

5. $22\frac{7}{8}$ 6. $15\frac{2}{3}$ 7. $12\frac{5}{8}$ 8. $17\frac{5}{8}$

Write the following fractions in lowest terms. Use the divisibility rules as needed.

9. $\frac{8}{16}$ 10. $\frac{15}{20}$ 11. $\frac{40}{75}$ 12. $\frac{36}{42}$

13. $\frac{25}{40}$ 14. $\frac{27}{45}$ 15. $\frac{120}{150}$ 16. $\frac{24}{64}$

17. $\frac{132}{144}$ 18. $\frac{40}{96}$ 19. $\frac{96}{180}$ 20. $\frac{32}{128}$

Convert the following improper fractions to mixed numbers and write them in lowest terms.

21. $\frac{7}{2}$ 22. $\frac{9}{5}$ 23. $\frac{76}{20}$ 24. $\frac{42}{15}$

25. $\frac{14}{11}$ 26. $\frac{55}{8}$ 27. $\frac{21}{15}$ 28. $\frac{85}{52}$

29. $\frac{124}{64}$ 30. $\frac{190}{35}$ 31. $\frac{81}{32}$ 32. $\frac{360}{64}$

 33. Your classmate asks you how to change a mixed number to an improper fraction. Write a couple of sentences explaining how this is done. (See Objective 2.)

 34. Explain in a sentence or two how to change an improper fraction to a mixed number. (See Objective 2.)

Add each of the following and reduce to lowest terms.

35. $\dfrac{2}{5} + \dfrac{1}{5}$

36. $\dfrac{2}{9} + \dfrac{4}{9}$

37. $\dfrac{7}{10} + \dfrac{3}{20}$

38. $\dfrac{3}{8} + \dfrac{1}{4}$

39. $\dfrac{7}{12} + \dfrac{8}{15}$

40. $\dfrac{5}{8} + \dfrac{7}{12}$

41. $\dfrac{9}{11} + \dfrac{1}{22}$

42. $\dfrac{5}{6} + \dfrac{7}{9}$

43. $\dfrac{3}{4} + \dfrac{5}{9} + \dfrac{1}{3}$

44. $\dfrac{1}{4} + \dfrac{1}{8} + \dfrac{1}{12}$

45. $\dfrac{5}{6} + \dfrac{3}{4} + \dfrac{5}{8}$

46. $\dfrac{7}{10} + \dfrac{8}{15} + \dfrac{5}{6}$

47. $\begin{aligned} 82\tfrac{3}{5} \\ + 15\tfrac{1}{5} \\ \hline \end{aligned}$

48. $\begin{aligned} 25\tfrac{2}{7} \\ + 14\tfrac{3}{7} \\ \hline \end{aligned}$

49. $\begin{aligned} 51\tfrac{1}{4} \\ + 29\tfrac{1}{2} \\ \hline \end{aligned}$

50. $\begin{aligned} 38\tfrac{5}{6} \\ 29\tfrac{1}{3} \\ + 47\tfrac{1}{2} \\ \hline \end{aligned}$

51. $\begin{aligned} 32\tfrac{3}{4} \\ 6\tfrac{1}{3} \\ + 14\tfrac{5}{8} \\ \hline \end{aligned}$

52. $\begin{aligned} 16\tfrac{7}{10} \\ 26\tfrac{1}{5} \\ + 8\tfrac{3}{8} \\ \hline \end{aligned}$

53. $\begin{aligned} 89\tfrac{5}{9} \\ 10\tfrac{1}{3} \\ + 87\tfrac{1}{9} \\ \hline \end{aligned}$

54. $\begin{aligned} 74\tfrac{1}{5} \\ 58\tfrac{3}{7} \\ + 21\tfrac{3}{10} \\ \hline \end{aligned}$

Subtract each of the following and reduce to lowest terms.

55. $\dfrac{7}{8} - \dfrac{3}{8}$

56. $\dfrac{11}{12} - \dfrac{5}{12}$

57. $\dfrac{2}{3} - \dfrac{1}{6}$

58. $\dfrac{7}{8} - \dfrac{1}{2}$

59. $\dfrac{5}{12} - \dfrac{1}{16}$

60. $\dfrac{5}{6} - \dfrac{7}{9}$

61. $\dfrac{3}{4} - \dfrac{5}{12}$

62. $\dfrac{5}{7} - \dfrac{1}{3}$

63. $\begin{aligned} 16\tfrac{3}{4} \\ - 12\tfrac{3}{8} \\ \hline \end{aligned}$

64. $\begin{aligned} 25\tfrac{13}{24} \\ - 18\tfrac{5}{12} \\ \hline \end{aligned}$

65. $\begin{aligned} 9\tfrac{7}{8} \\ - 6\tfrac{5}{12} \\ \hline \end{aligned}$

66. $\begin{aligned} 24\tfrac{5}{6} \\ - 18\tfrac{5}{9} \\ \hline \end{aligned}$

67. $\begin{aligned} 71\tfrac{3}{8} \\ - 62\tfrac{1}{3} \\ \hline \end{aligned}$

68. $\begin{aligned} 19\tfrac{5}{6} \\ - 12\tfrac{3}{4} \\ \hline \end{aligned}$

69. $\begin{aligned} 19 \\ - 12\tfrac{3}{4} \\ \hline \end{aligned}$

70. $\begin{aligned} 374 \\ - 211\tfrac{5}{6} \\ \hline \end{aligned}$

 71. Prime numbers are used to find the least common denominator. Give the definition of a prime number in your own words. (See Objective 6.)

72. Can you add or subtract fractions without using the least common denominator? Describe how you would do this.

73. Where are fractions used in everyday life? Think in terms of business applications, hobbies, and vacations. Give three examples.

74. When subtracting mixed numbers, explain when you need to borrow. Use an example to explain how to borrow.

Solve the following application problems.

75. **CABINET INSTALLATION** When installing cabinets, Kate Morgan must be certain that the proper type and size of mounting screw is used. Find the total length of the screw.

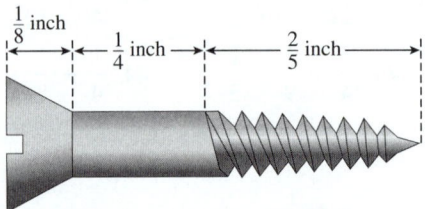

76. **COMPUTER ASSEMBLY** When installing a printer cable to a computer, Ann Kuick must be certain that the proper type and size of mounting hardware is used. Find the total length of the bolt shown.

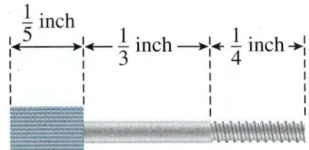

77. **WETLANDS RESERVE** A wetlands reserve has four sides, which measure $1\frac{7}{8}$ miles, $\frac{1}{2}$ mile, $1\frac{2}{3}$ miles, and $\frac{1}{3}$ mile. What is the total distance around the wetlands reserve?

78. **MEASURING BRASS TRIM** To complete a custom accessory order for a customer, Ruth Berry of Home Depot must find the number of inches of brass trim needed to go around the four sides of the lamp base plate shown below. Find the length of brass trim needed.

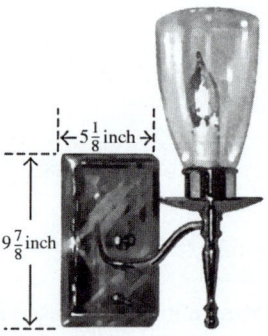

79. **CABINET INSTALLATION** Find the diameter of the hole in the mounting bracket pictured below.

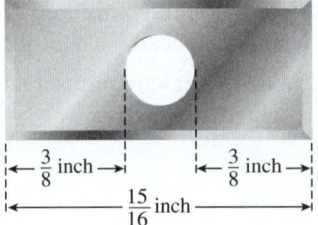

80. **HYDRAULIC FLUID** A hydraulic jack contains $\frac{7}{8}$ liter of hydraulic fluid. A cracked seal resulted in a loss of $\frac{1}{6}$ liter of fluid in the morning and another $\frac{1}{3}$ liter in the afternoon. Find the amount of fluid remaining.

81. **HIGHWAY DRIVING** On a recent vacation to Canada, Hernando Ramirez drove for $5\frac{1}{2}$ hours on the first day, $6\frac{1}{4}$ hours on the second day, $3\frac{3}{4}$ hours on the third day, and 7 hours on the fourth day. How many hours did he drive altogether?

82. **WHOLESALE PRODUCE SALES** Last month, Lim's Wholesale Vegetable Market sold $3\frac{1}{4}$ tons of broccoli, $2\frac{3}{8}$ tons of spinach, $7\frac{1}{2}$ tons of corn, and $1\frac{5}{16}$ tons of turnips. Find the total number of tons of these vegetables sold by the firm last month.

83. **DELIVERING CONCRETE** Chuck Stone has $8\frac{7}{8}$ cubic yards of concrete in a truck. If he unloads $2\frac{1}{2}$ cubic yards at the first stop, 3 cubic yards at the second stop, and $1\frac{3}{4}$ cubic yards at the third stop, how much concrete remains in the truck?

84. **TAILORED CLOTHING** Marv Levenson bought 15 yards of Italian silk fabric. He made two tops with $3\frac{3}{4}$ yards of the material, a suit for his wife with $4\frac{1}{8}$ yards, and a jacket with $3\frac{7}{8}$ yards. Find the number of yards of material remaining.

85. **ORANGES** One week, sales of oranges at four different Price Chopper grocery stores were $4\frac{1}{2}$ cases, $5\frac{1}{4}$ cases, $3\frac{3}{4}$ cases, and $6\frac{1}{3}$ cases. Find the total number of cases sold.

86. **PART-TIME WORK** Andrea Abriani, a college student, works part-time at the Cyber Coffeehouse. She worked $3\frac{3}{8}$ hours on Monday, $5\frac{1}{2}$ hours on Tuesday, $4\frac{3}{4}$ hours on Wednesday, $3\frac{1}{4}$ hours on Thursday, and 6 hours on Friday. How many hours did she work altogether?

87. **WORK WEEK** Julie Davis worked 40 hours during one week. She worked $8\frac{1}{4}$ hours on Monday, $6\frac{1}{6}$ hours on Tuesday, $7\frac{2}{3}$ hours on Wednesday, and $8\frac{3}{4}$ hours on Thursday. How many hours did she work on Friday?

88. **LEADED GLASS FRAMING** A craftsperson must attach a lead strip around all four sides of a leaded glass window before it is installed. The window measures $34\frac{1}{2}$ by $23\frac{3}{4}$ inches. Find the length of lead stripping needed.

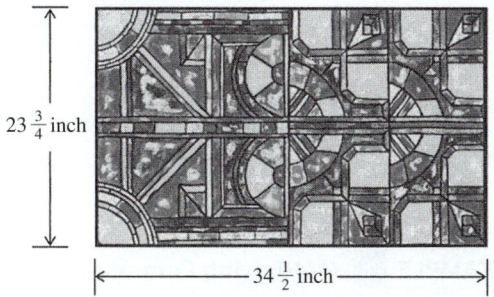

89. **PARKING LOT FENCING** Three sides of a parking lot are $108\frac{1}{4}$ feet, $162\frac{3}{8}$ feet, and $143\frac{1}{2}$ feet. If the distance around the lot is $518\frac{3}{4}$ feet, find the length of the fourth side.

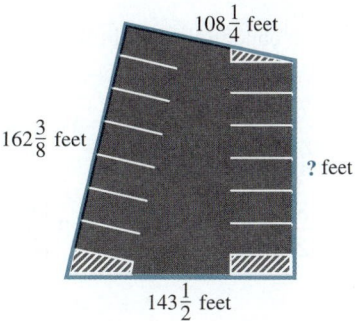

90. **SECURITY FENCING** The exercise yard at the correction center has four sides and is enclosed with $527\frac{1}{24}$ feet of security fencing around it. If three sides of the yard measure $107\frac{2}{3}$ feet, $150\frac{3}{4}$ feet, and $138\frac{5}{8}$ feet, find the length of the fourth side.

| 1.3 | **Multiplication and Division of Fractions** |

OBJECTIVES

1 *Multiply fractions.*

2 *Divide fractions.*

3 *Convert decimals to fractions.*

4 *Round decimals.*

5 *Convert fractions to decimals.*

6 *Know common decimal equivalents.*

Objective

1 *Multiply Fractions.* Multiply two fractions by first multiplying the numerators to form a new numerator and then multiplying the denominators to form a new denominator. Write the answer in lowest terms. For example, multiply $\frac{2}{3}$ and $\frac{5}{8}$.

Multiply numerators.

$$\frac{2}{3} \times \frac{5}{8} = \frac{2 \times 5}{3 \times 8} = \frac{10}{24} = \frac{5}{12} \quad \text{(in lowest terms)}$$

Multiply denominators.

This problem can be simplified by **cancellation**, a modification of the method of writing fractions in lowest terms. If a number divides evenly into a numerator and a denominator without remainder, then divide (cancel).

$$\frac{\overset{1}{\cancel{2}}}{3} \times \frac{5}{\underset{4}{\cancel{8}}} = \frac{1 \times 5}{3 \times 4} = \frac{5}{12} \quad \text{Divide 2 into both 2 and 8.}$$

> **NOTE** It is not necessary to use a common denominator when multiplying or dividing fractions.

EXAMPLE **1** **Multiplying Common Fractions**

Multiply the following fractions.

(a) $\dfrac{6}{11} \times \dfrac{7}{8}$ **(b)** $\dfrac{35}{12} \times \dfrac{32}{25}$

Solution Use cancellation in both of these problems.

(a) $\dfrac{\overset{3}{\cancel{6}}}{11} \times \dfrac{7}{\underset{4}{\cancel{8}}} = \dfrac{3 \times 7}{11 \times 4} = \dfrac{21}{44}$ 2 was divided into both 6 and 8.

(b) $\dfrac{\overset{7}{\cancel{35}}}{\underset{3}{\cancel{12}}} \times \dfrac{\overset{8}{\cancel{32}}}{\underset{5}{\cancel{25}}} = \dfrac{7 \times 8}{3 \times 5} = \dfrac{56}{15} = 3\dfrac{11}{15}$ 4 was divided into both 12 and 32, while 5 was divided into both 35 and 25.

> **NOTE** In order to cancel, the numerator and denominator must both be evenly divisible without remainder by the same number.

To multiply mixed numbers, first change the mixed numbers to improper fractions, then multiply. For example, multiply $6\frac{1}{4}$ and $2\frac{2}{3}$.

First change to improper fractions.

$$6\frac{1}{4} \times 2\frac{2}{3} = \frac{25}{4} \times \frac{8}{3} = \frac{25}{\overset{}{\underset{1}{4}}} \times \frac{\overset{2}{8}}{3} = \frac{25 \times 2}{1 \times 3} = \frac{50}{3} = 16\frac{2}{3}$$

Cancel.   Multiply.

EXAMPLE **2** **Multiplying Mixed Numbers**

Multiply the following.

(a) $5\frac{5}{8} \times 4\frac{1}{6}$ (b) $1\frac{3}{5} \times 3\frac{1}{3} \times 1\frac{3}{4}$

Solution

(a) $\dfrac{\overset{15}{\cancel{45}}}{8} \times \dfrac{25}{\underset{2}{\cancel{6}}} = \dfrac{15 \times 25}{8 \times 2} = \dfrac{375}{16} = 23\frac{7}{16}$

(b) $\dfrac{\overset{2}{\cancel{8}}}{\underset{1}{\cancel{5}}} \times \dfrac{\overset{2}{\cancel{10}}}{3} \times \dfrac{7}{\underset{1}{\cancel{4}}} = \dfrac{2 \times 2 \times 7}{1 \times 3 \times 1} = \dfrac{28}{3} = 9\frac{1}{3}$

Scientific Calculator Approach

The calculator solution to Example 2(b) uses the fraction key.

$$1 \boxed{a^b/_c} 3 \boxed{a^b/_c} 5 \boxed{\times} 3 \boxed{a^b/_c} 1 \boxed{a^b/_c} 3 \boxed{\times} 1 \boxed{a^b/_c} 3 \boxed{a^b/_c} 4 \boxed{=} 9\tfrac{1}{3}$$

Multiply by a whole number by first writing the whole number as a fraction with 1 in the denominator.

$$3\frac{3}{4} \times 16 = 3\frac{3}{4} \times \frac{16}{1} \quad \text{Whole number over 1}$$

$$= \frac{15}{4} \times \frac{16}{1}$$

$$= \frac{15}{\underset{1}{\cancel{4}}} \times \frac{\overset{4}{\cancel{16}}}{1} = 15 \times 4 = 60$$

NOTE   Mixed numbers must always be changed to *improper fractions* before multiplying. When multiplying by mixed numbers, do not multiply whole numbers by whole numbers and fractions by fractions.

Objective

2   *Divide Fractions.*   Divide two fractions by inverting the divisor and then multiplying. A fraction is inverted by exchanging the numerator and denominator.

NOTE   It is not necessary to use a common denominator when dividing fractions.

EXAMPLE 3 **Dividing Common Fractions**

Divide.

(a) $\dfrac{25}{36} \div \dfrac{15}{18}$ (b) $\dfrac{21}{8} \div \dfrac{14}{16}$

Solution Invert the second fraction, then multiply.

(a) $\dfrac{25}{36} \div \dfrac{15}{18} = \dfrac{\overset{5}{\cancel{25}}}{\underset{2}{\cancel{36}}} \times \dfrac{\overset{1}{\cancel{18}}}{\underset{3}{\cancel{15}}} = \dfrac{5 \times 1}{2 \times 3} = \dfrac{5}{6}$ (b) $\dfrac{21}{8} \div \dfrac{14}{16} = \dfrac{\overset{3}{\cancel{21}}}{\underset{1}{\cancel{8}}} \times \dfrac{\overset{\overset{1}{\cancel{2}}}{\cancel{16}}}{\underset{\underset{1}{\cancel{2}}}{\cancel{14}}} = \dfrac{3 \times 1}{1 \times 1} = 3$

NOTE When dividing by a fraction, the second fraction (divisor) is inverted. Cancellation is done *only after inverting*.

Divide mixed numbers by first changing all mixed numbers to improper fractions, as follows.

$$3\dfrac{5}{9} \div 2\dfrac{2}{5} = \dfrac{32}{9} \div \dfrac{12}{5} = \dfrac{\overset{8}{\cancel{32}}}{9} \times \dfrac{5}{\underset{3}{\cancel{12}}} = \dfrac{8 \times 5}{9 \times 3} = \dfrac{40}{27} = 1\dfrac{13}{27}$$

To divide a mixed number by a whole number, first write the whole number as a fraction over a denominator of 1. Then proceed as if dividing fractions.

$$2\dfrac{2}{5} \div 3 = \dfrac{12}{5} \div \dfrac{3}{1} = \dfrac{\overset{4}{\cancel{12}}}{5} \times \dfrac{1}{\underset{1}{\cancel{3}}} = \dfrac{4 \times 1}{5 \times 1} = \dfrac{4}{5}$$

After opening her bakery, Jacquelene Dlat taste tested various cookie recipes with her customers. The following recipe was a customer favorite and is easy to follow using the proper measuring cups and spoons. Sometimes she needs to double or triple the recipe or perhaps, baking a small order, she needs to cut the recipe in half. To double the recipe, multiply each ingredient by 2. To triple the recipe, multiply by 3. To halve the recipe, divide by 2.

Chocolate/Oat-Chip Cookies

1 cup (2 sticks) margarine or butter, softened
$1\dfrac{1}{4}$ cups firmly packed brown sugar
$\dfrac{1}{2}$ cup granulated sugar
2 eggs
2 tablespoons milk
2 teaspoons vanilla

$1\dfrac{3}{4}$ cups all-purpose flour
1 teaspoon baking soda
$\dfrac{1}{2}$ teaspoon salt (optional)
$2\dfrac{1}{2}$ cups uncooked oats
One 12-ounce package (2 cups) semisweet chocolate morsels
1 cup coarsely chopped nuts (optional)

Heat oven to 375°F. **Beat** margarine and sugars until creamy.

Add eggs, milk, and vanilla; beat well.

Add combined flour, baking soda, and salt, mix well. **Stir** in oats, chocolate morsels, and nuts; mix well.

Drop by rounded measuring tablespoonfuls onto ungreased cookie sheet.

Bake 9 to 10 minutes for a chewy cookie or 12 to 13 minutes for a crisp cookie.

Cool 1 minute on cookie sheet; remove to wire rack. Cool completely.

MAKES ABOUT 5 DOZEN

| EXAMPLE | 4 | Multiplying a Whole Number by a Mixed Number |

(a) Find the amount of uncooked oats needed if the preceding recipe for chocolate/oat-chip cookies is doubled (multiplied by 2).

(b) How many cups of all-purpose flour are needed when 12 times the recipe is needed?

Solution Change mixed numbers to improper fractions, use cancellation, and then multiply.

(a) $2\frac{1}{2} \times 2 = \frac{5}{\cancel{2}} \times \frac{\cancel{2}^{1}}{1} = \frac{5 \times 1}{1 \times 1} = \frac{5}{1} = 5$ cups

(b) $1\frac{3}{4} \times 12 = \frac{7}{\cancel{4}} \times \frac{\cancel{12}^{3}}{1} = \frac{7 \times 3}{1 \times 1} = 21$ cups

Objective

3 *Convert Decimals to Fractions.* A **decimal number** is really a fraction with a denominator that is a power of 10, such as 10, 100, or 1000. The digits written to the right of the decimal point have place values as shown in Figure 1.3.

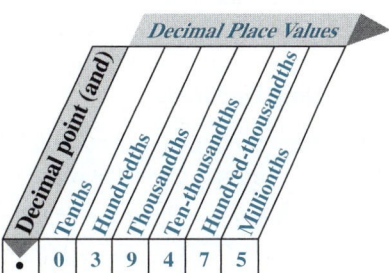

Figure 1.3

Convert a decimal to a fraction by thinking of the decimal as being written in words. For example, think of 0.47 as "forty-seven hundredths." Then write this in fraction form.

$$0.47 = \frac{47}{100}$$

In the same way, 0.3, read as "three tenths," is written in fraction form as follows.

$$0.3 = \frac{3}{10}$$

Also, 0.963, read as "nine hundred sixty-three thousandths," is written

$$\frac{963}{1000}$$

> **NOTE** To read a number, use the word *and* for the decimal point. For example, the number 2.71 is read as "two and seventy-one hundredths." The mixed number form, $2\frac{71}{100}$ is read exactly the same.

EXAMPLE 5 **Converting Decimals to Fractions**

Convert the following decimals to fractions.

(a) 0.75   **(b)** 0.028

Solution

(a) 0.75 is read as "seventy-five hundredths."

$$0.75 = \frac{75}{100} = \frac{3}{4}$$

Here, $\frac{75}{100}$ is written in lowest terms as $\frac{3}{4}$.

(b) 0.028 is read as "twenty-eight thousandths," and the resulting fraction is written in lowest terms.

$$0.028 = \frac{28}{1000} = \frac{7}{250}$$

Objective

4 *Round Decimals.* It is important to be able to round decimals. For example, the 7-Eleven store sells two small candy bars for $0.79, but you want to buy only one candy bar. The price of one bar is $0.79 ÷ 2, which is $0.395. Since you cannot pay part of a cent, the store rounds the price to $0.40 for one bar.

Use the following steps for rounding decimals.

Rounding Decimals

Step 1 Find the place to which the rounding is being done. Draw a vertical line immediately after that place to show that you are deleting the digits to the right.

Step 2A Look only at the first digit to the right of your cutoff line. If the first digit is **5 or more**, increase by 1 the digit in the place to which you are rounding.

Step 2B If the first digit to the right of the line is **4 or less**, do not change the digit in the place to which you are rounding.

Step 3 **Drop** all digits to the right of the place to which you have rounded.

NOTE Do not move the decimal point when rounding.

EXAMPLE 6 **Rounding to the Nearest Tenth**

Round 98.5892 to the nearest tenth.

Solution

STEP 1 Locate the tenths digit and draw a line immediately to the right.

$$98.5\,|\,892$$

Tenths digit

The tenths digit is 5.

STEP 2 Locate the digit just to the right of the line.

$$98.5\,|\,892$$

First digit to the right of the line

The digit just to the right of the line is 8.

STEP 3 If the digit found in Step 2 is 4 or less, leave the digit of Step 1 alone. If the digit found in Step 2 is 5 or more, increase the digit of Step 1 by 1. The digit found in Step 2 is 8, so 98.5892 rounded to the nearest tenth is 98.6.

EXAMPLE 7 **Rounding to the Nearest Thousandth**

Round 0.008572 to the nearest thousandth.

Solution   Locate the thousandths digit and draw a line.

$$0.008 \,|\, 572$$

↑——— Thousandths digit

Since the digit to the right of the line is 5, increase the thousandths digit by 1. Therefore, 0.008572 rounded to the nearest thousandth is 0.009.

EXAMPLE 8 **Rounding Decimals**

When doing business with a foreign country, you must convert the foreign currency using the U.S. exchange rate. Round the following currencies to the indicated place value.

(a) Euro (dollar): 0.8086 to the nearest thousandth
(b) Canada (dollar): 1.0750 to the nearest tenth
(c) Britain (pound): 0.5459 to the nearest hundredth
(d) Mexico (peso): 10.62351 to the nearest ten-thousandth

Solution   Use the method described.

(a) 0.8086 to the nearest thousandth is 0.809.
(b) 1.0750 to the nearest tenth is 1.1.
(c) 0.5459 to the nearest hundredth is 0.55.
(d) 10.62351 to the nearest ten-thousandth is 10.6235.

Objective

5   *Convert Fractions to Decimals.*   To convert a fraction to a decimal, divide the numerator of the fraction by the denominator. Place a decimal point after the numerator and attach additional zeros, one at a time, to the right of the decimal point as the division is performed. Keep going until the division ends or until the desired degree of precision is reached. As a general rule, divide until the quotient has one more digit than the desired degree of precision, then round from the last digit. The result is the decimal equivalent to the fraction.

For example, to convert $\frac{1}{8}$ to a decimal, divide 1 by 8.

$$8\overline{)1}$$

Since 8 will not divide into 1, place a 0 to the right of the decimal point. Now 8 divides into 10 once, with a remainder of 2.

$$
\begin{array}{r}
0.1 \\
8\overline{)1.0} \\
\underline{8} \\
2
\end{array}
$$

Be sure to move the decimal point up.

Continue placing 0s to the right of the decimal point and continue dividing. The division now gives a remainder of 0.

$$
\begin{array}{r}
0.125 \\
8\overline{)1.000} \quad \text{Keep attaching zeros.} \\
\underline{8} \\
20 \\
\underline{16} \\
40 \\
\underline{40} \\
0 \quad \text{Remainder of 0.}
\end{array}
$$

Therefore, $\frac{1}{8} = 0.125$.

> **NOTE** The decimal answer of 0.125 was not rounded. Instead, the division was continued until there was no remainder. In most problems, the answer must be rounded to the required accuracy.

EXAMPLE 9 **Rounding of a Repeating Decimal**

Convert $\frac{2}{3}$ to a decimal. Round to the nearest ten-thousandth.

Solution Divide 2 by 3.

$$
\begin{array}{r}
0.66666 \\
3\overline{)2.00000} \quad \text{Keep attaching zeros.} \\
\underline{1\,8} \\
20 \\
\underline{18} \\
20 \\
\underline{18} \\
20 \\
\underline{18} \\
20 \\
\underline{18} \\
2
\end{array}
$$

This division results in a **repeating decimal**, which is often indicated by placing a bar over the digit or digits that repeat. The answer could be written as follows.

$$0.\overline{6} \qquad \text{or} \qquad 0.6\overline{6} \qquad 0.6666\overline{6}$$

However, rounded to the nearest ten-thousandth:

$$\frac{2}{3} = 0.6667$$

 **Scientific Calculator Approach**

The calculator solution to Example 9 follows.

$$2 \boxed{\div} 3 \boxed{=} \; 0.666666667$$

Objective

6 *Know Common Decimal Equivalents.* Some of the more common **decimal equivalents** of fractions are listed on the following page. These decimals appear from least to greatest value and are rounded to the nearest ten-thousandth. Sometimes decimals must be carried out further to give greater accuracy. At other times they are not carried out as far and are rounded sooner.

Decimal Equivalents

$\frac{1}{16} = 0.0625$	$\frac{5}{16} = 0.3125$	$\frac{11}{16} = 0.6875$
$\frac{1}{10} = 0.1$	$\frac{1}{3} = 0.3333$ (rounded)	$\frac{7}{10} = 0.7$
$\frac{1}{9} = 0.1111$ (rounded)	$\frac{3}{8} = 0.375$	$\frac{3}{4} = 0.75$
$\frac{1}{8} = 0.125$	$\frac{2}{5} = 0.4$	$\frac{4}{5} = 0.8$
$\frac{1}{7} = 0.1429$ (rounded)	$\frac{7}{16} = 0.4375$	$\frac{13}{16} = 0.8125$
$\frac{1}{6} = 0.1667$ (rounded)	$\frac{1}{2} = 0.5$	$\frac{5}{6} = 0.8333$ (rounded)
$\frac{3}{16} = 0.1875$	$\frac{9}{16} = 0.5625$	$\frac{7}{8} = 0.875$
$\frac{1}{5} = 0.2$	$\frac{3}{5} = 0.6$	$\frac{9}{10} = 0.9$
$\frac{1}{4} = 0.25$	$\frac{5}{8} = 0.625$	$\frac{15}{16} = 0.9375$
$\frac{3}{10} = 0.3$	$\frac{2}{3} = 0.6667$ (rounded)	

1.3 | Exercises

Multiply each of the following and write in lowest terms.

1. $\frac{5}{8} \times \frac{2}{3}$

2. $\frac{3}{8} \times \frac{1}{6}$

3. $\frac{9}{10} \times \frac{11}{16}$

4. $1\frac{1}{4} \times 3\frac{1}{2}$

5. $1\frac{2}{3} \times 2\frac{7}{10}$

6. $6 \times 4\frac{2}{3}$

7. $4\frac{3}{5} \times 15$

8. $\frac{3}{4} \times \frac{8}{9} \times 2\frac{1}{2}$

9. $\frac{5}{9} \times 2\frac{1}{4} \times 3\frac{2}{3}$

10. $\frac{2}{3} \times \frac{9}{8} \times 3\frac{1}{4}$

11. $12 \times 2\frac{1}{2} \times 3$

12. $18 \times 1\frac{2}{3} \times 2$

Divide each of the following and write in lowest terms.

13. $\frac{1}{6} \div \frac{1}{3}$

14. $\frac{5}{8} \div \frac{3}{16}$

15. $\frac{13}{20} \div \frac{26}{30}$

16. $\frac{7}{8} \div \frac{3}{4}$

17. $\frac{15}{16} \div \frac{5}{8}$

18. $\frac{12}{11} \div \frac{3}{22}$

19. $2\frac{1}{2} \div 3\frac{3}{4}$

20. $6\frac{1}{2} \div \frac{1}{2}$

21. $3\frac{1}{8} \div \frac{15}{16}$

22. $5\frac{1}{2} \div 4$

23. $6 \div 1\frac{1}{4}$

24. $3 \div 1\frac{1}{4}$

 25. Write in your own words the rule for multiplying fractions. Make up an example problem of your own showing how this works. (See Objective 1.)

26. Use cancellation before multiplying fractions as a useful shortcut. Describe how to do this and give an example. (See Objective 1.)

Find the time-and-a-half pay rates for the following regular hourly pay rates.

27. $8

28. $14

29. $17

30. $9

31. $10.50

32. $18.50

Convert the following decimals to fractions and reduce to lowest terms.

33. 0.8   **34.** 0.6   **35.** 0.24   **36.** 0.64

37. 0.73   **38.** 0.625   **39.** 0.875   **40.** 0.805

41. 0.0375   **42.** 0.8125   **43.** 0.1875   **44.** 0.3125

Round the following decimals to the nearest tenth and to the nearest hundredth.

45. 3.5218   **46.** 4.8361   **47.** 0.0837
48. 2.548   **49.** 8.643   **50.** 86.472
51. 58.956   **52.** 8.065   **53.** 23.047
54. 65.464   **55.** 39.496   **56.** 92.337

Convert the following fractions to decimals. Round the answer to the nearest thousandth if necessary.

57. $\dfrac{3}{4}$ **58.** $\dfrac{7}{8}$ **59.** $\dfrac{3}{8}$ **60.** $\dfrac{5}{6}$

61. $\dfrac{1}{6}$ **62.** $\dfrac{2}{3}$ **63.** $\dfrac{13}{16}$ **64.** $\dfrac{19}{50}$

65. $\dfrac{8}{25}$ **66.** $\dfrac{1}{3}$ **67.** $\dfrac{1}{99}$ **68.** $\dfrac{73}{93}$

69. $\dfrac{5}{8}$ **70.** $\dfrac{5}{9}$ **71.** $\dfrac{5}{6}$ **72.** $\dfrac{7}{16}$

 73. A classmate of yours is confused about how to convert a decimal to a fraction. Write an explanation of this for your classmate, including changing the fraction to lowest terms. (See Objective 3.)

 74. Explain how to convert a fraction to a decimal. Be sure to mention rounding in your explanation. (See Objective 5.)

 75. Explain in your own words the difference between hundreds and hundredths. (See Objective 3.)

 76. Write the directions for rounding an answer involving money to the nearest cent. Why must this be done? (See Objective 4.)

Solve the following application problems.

77. PRODUCING CRAFTS   Angela Gragg wants to make 16 holiday wreaths to sell at the craft fair. Each wreath needs $2\frac{1}{4}$ yards of ribbon. How many yards does she need?

78. FILL DIRT   A contractor needs to add 345 cubic yards of fill dirt before compacting the soil and building a parking lot at a community college. His truck carries an average of $11\frac{1}{2}$ cubic yards of dirt each trip. Find the number of trips required by the truck.

79. DISPENSING EYEDROPS   How many $\frac{1}{8}$-ounce eyedrop dispensers can be filled with 11 ounces of eyedrops?

80. CONCRETE FOOTINGS   Each building footing requires $\frac{5}{16}$ cubic yard of concrete. How many building footings can be constructed from 10 cubic yards of concrete?

81. FINISH CARPENTRY   Each home of a certain design needs $109\frac{1}{2}$ yards of prefinished baseboard. How many homes can be fitted with baseboards if there are 1314 yards of baseboard available?

82. COMMERCIAL FERTILIZER   For 1 acre of crop, $7\frac{1}{2}$ gallons of fertilizer must be applied. How many acres can be fertilized with 1200 gallons of fertilizer?

83. **INSECT CONTROL** An insect spray manufactured by Dutch Chemicals Inc. is mixed with $1\frac{3}{4}$ ounces of chemical per gallon of water. How many ounces of chemical are needed for $12\frac{1}{2}$ gallons of water?

84. **RESIDENTIAL ROOFING** Each home in a new development requires $37\frac{3}{4}$ pounds of roofing nails. How many pounds of roofing nails are needed for 36 homes?

85. **FUEL CONSUMPTION** A fishing boat uses $12\frac{3}{4}$ gallons of fuel on a full-day fishing trip and $7\frac{1}{8}$ gallons of fuel on a half-day trip. Find the total number of gallons of fuel used in 28 full-day trips and 16 half-day trips.

86. **HANDCRAFTED JEWELRY** One necklace can be completed in $6\frac{1}{2}$ minutes, and a bracelet takes $3\frac{1}{8}$ minutes. Find the total time that it takes to complete 36 necklaces and 22 bracelets.

87. **FIREWOOD SALES** Linda Reynolds had a small pickup truck that would carry $\frac{2}{3}$ cord of firewood. Find the number of trips needed to deliver 40 cords of wood.

88. **AUTOMOBILE DEALERSHIP** An automobile dealer has 220 cars on the lot. If $\frac{1}{5}$ of them are sold in a month, find the number of cars remaining on the lot.

89. **MATERIALS MANAGEMENT** A manufacturer of floor jacks is ordering steel tubing to make the handles for this jack. How much steel tubing is needed to make 135 of these jacks? (The symbol for inch is ".)

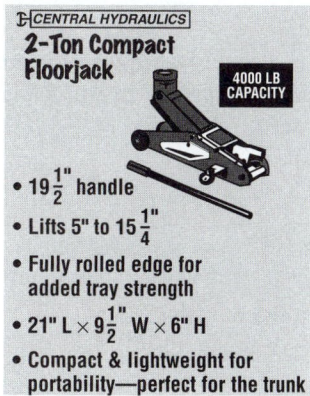

90. **MATERIALS MANAGEMENT** A wheelbarrow manufacturer uses handles made of hardwood. Find the amount of wood that is necessary to make 182 handles. The longest dimension shown is the handle length.

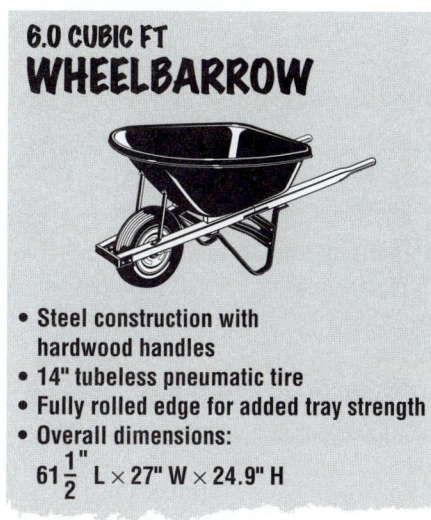

Quick Review

CHAPTER TERMS

Review the following terms to test your understanding of the chapter. For each term you do not know, refer to the page number found next to that term.

borrowing [p. 15]
cancellation [p. 20]
common denominator [p. 11]
common fraction [p. 9]
decimal equivalent [p. 26]

decimal number [p. 23]
denominator [p. 8]
divisibility rules [p. 11]
fraction [p. 8]
improper fraction [p. 9]
indicators [p. 2]
inspection [p. 12]

least common denominator (LCD) [p. 12]
like fractions [p. 11]
lowest terms [p. 10]
method of prime numbers [p. 12]
mixed number [p. 9]

numerator [p. 8]
prime number [p. 12]
proper fraction [p. 9]
repeating decimal [p. 26]
rounding decimals [p. 24]
rules for divisibility [p. 10]
unlike fractions [p. 12]

CONCEPTS

EXAMPLES

1.1 Solving application problems

Step 1 Read the problem carefully and identify the unknown.
Step 2 Develop a plan to work the problem.
Step 3 Estimate a reasonable answer using rounding.
Step 4 Solve the problem.
Step 5 Check to see if the answer is reasonable.

Mr. Rice earns $118 on Sunday, $87 on Monday, and $83 on Tuesday. Find his total earnings.

Using an average of $100 in earnings per day, the total earnings are about $300. Add to find the exact amount and check to see if the answer is reasonable.

$$
\begin{array}{ll}
\$118 & \text{Sunday's earnings} \\
87 & \text{Monday's earnings} \\
\underline{83} & \text{Tuesday's earnings} \\
\$288 & \text{Total earnings (which is close to \$300)}
\end{array}
$$

1.2 Types of fractions

Proper (common): Numerator smaller than denominator.

Improper: Numerator equal to or greater than denominator.

Mixed: Whole number and proper fraction.

Proper $\dfrac{2}{3}, \dfrac{3}{4}, \dfrac{15}{16}, \dfrac{1}{8}$

Improper $\dfrac{17}{8}, \dfrac{19}{12}, \dfrac{11}{2}, \dfrac{5}{3}, \dfrac{7}{7}$

Mixed $2\dfrac{2}{3}, 3\dfrac{5}{8}, 9\dfrac{5}{6}$

1.2 Converting fractions

Mixed to improper: Multiply whole number by denominator and add numerator. The denominator is unchanged.

Improper to mixed: Divide numerator by denominator and place remainder over denominator.

$$7\frac{2}{3} = \frac{(7 \times 3) + 2}{3} = \frac{23}{3}$$

$$\frac{17}{5} = 3\frac{2}{5} \qquad 5\overline{)17} \\ \underline{15} \\ 2$$

1.2 Writing fractions in lowest terms

Divide the numerator and denominator by the same number.

$$\frac{30}{42} = \frac{30 \div 6}{42 \div 6} = \frac{5}{7}$$

1.2 Adding like fractions

Add numerators and reduce to lowest terms. The denominator is unchanged.

$$\frac{3}{4} + \frac{1}{4} + \frac{5}{4} = \frac{3+1+5}{4} = \frac{9}{4} = 2\frac{1}{4}$$

1.2 Finding a least common denominator

Inspection method: Look to see if the least common denominator can be found.

Method of prime numbers: Use prime numbers to find the least common denominator.

$$\frac{1}{3} + \frac{1}{4} + \frac{1}{10}$$

$$
\begin{array}{r|ccc}
 & 1 & 1 & 1 \\
5) & 1 & 1 & 5 \\
3) & 3 & 1 & 5 \\
2) & 3 & 2 & 5 \\
2) & 3 & 4 & 10 \\
\end{array}
$$

Multiply the prime numbers.

$$2 \times 2 \times 3 \times 5 = 60 \text{ LCD}$$

1.2 Adding unlike fractions

1. Find the least common denominator.
2. Rewrite fractions with the least common denominator.
3. Add numerators, placing answers over LCD, and reduce to lowest terms.

$$\frac{1}{3} + \frac{1}{4} + \frac{1}{10} \quad \text{LCD} = 60$$

$$\frac{1}{3} = \frac{20}{60}, \frac{1}{4} = \frac{15}{60}, \frac{1}{10} = \frac{6}{60}$$

$$\frac{20 + 15 + 6}{60} = \frac{41}{60}$$

1.2 Adding mixed numbers

1. Add fractions.
2. Add whole numbers.
3. Combine the sums of whole numbers and fractions. Write answer in simplest terms.

$$
\begin{aligned}
9\frac{2}{3} &= 9\frac{8}{12} \\
+ 6\frac{3}{4} &= 6\frac{9}{12} \\
\hline
15\frac{17}{12} &= 16\frac{5}{12}
\end{aligned}
$$

1.2 Subtracting fractions

1. Find the least common denominator.
2. Subtract numerators, borrowing if necessary.
3. Write the difference over the LCD and reduce to lowest terms.

$$\frac{5}{8} - \frac{1}{3} = \frac{15}{24} - \frac{8}{24} = \frac{7}{24}$$

1.2 Subtracting mixed numbers

1. Subtract fractions, borrowing if necessary.
2. Subtract whole numbers.
3. Combine the differences of whole numbers and fractions.

$$
\begin{aligned}
8\frac{5}{8} &= 8\frac{15}{24} \\
- 3\frac{1}{12} &= 3\frac{2}{24} \\
\hline
5\frac{13}{24}
\end{aligned}
$$

1.3 Multiplying proper fractions

1. Cancel if possible, then multiply numerators and denominators.
2. Reduce answer to lowest terms if canceling was not done.

$$\frac{6}{11} \times \frac{7}{8} = \frac{6}{11} \times \frac{\overset{3}{\cancel{6}}}{\underset{4}{\cancel{8}}} \times \frac{7}{} = \frac{21}{44}$$

1.3 Multiplying mixed numbers

1. Change mixed numbers to improper fractions.
2. Cancel if possible.
3. Multiply as you do with proper fractions. Always reduce to lowest terms.

$$1\frac{3}{5} \times 3\frac{1}{3} = \frac{8}{\underset{1}{\cancel{5}}} \times \frac{\overset{2}{\cancel{10}}}{3} = \frac{8}{1} \times \frac{2}{3}$$

$$= \frac{16}{3} = 5\frac{1}{3}$$

1.3 Dividing proper fractions

Invert the divisor, cancel, then multiply as fractions.

$$\frac{25}{36} \div \frac{15}{18} = \frac{\overset{5}{\cancel{25}}}{\underset{2}{\cancel{36}}} \times \frac{\overset{1}{\cancel{18}}}{\underset{3}{\cancel{15}}} = \frac{5}{2} \times \frac{1}{3} = \frac{5}{6}$$

1.3 Dividing mixed numbers

Change mixed numbers to improper fractions. Then invert the divisor, cancel if possible, and multiply as proper fractions.

$$3\frac{5}{9} \div 2\frac{2}{5} = \frac{32}{9} \div \frac{12}{5} = \frac{\overset{8}{\cancel{32}}}{9} \times \frac{5}{\underset{3}{\cancel{12}}}$$

$$= \frac{40}{27} = 1\frac{13}{27}$$

1.3 Converting decimals to fractions

Think of the decimal as being written in words, then write in fraction form. Reduce to lowest terms.

Convert 0.47 to a fraction. Think of 0.47 as "forty-seven hundredths," then write as $\frac{47}{100}$.

1.3 Rounding decimals

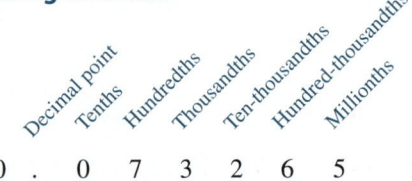

$$0.\ \ 0\ \ 7\ \ 3\ \ 2\ \ 6\ \ 5$$

Round 0.073265 to the nearest ten-thousandth.

$$0.0732|65$$
↑
Ten-thousandths position

Since the digit to the right of the line is 6, increase the ten-thousandths digit by 1. Thus, 0.073265 rounds to 0.0733.

1.3 Converting fractions to decimals

Divide the numerator by the denominator. Round if necessary.

Convert $\frac{1}{8}$ to a decimal.

$$
\begin{array}{r}
0.125 \\
8\overline{)1.000} \\
\underline{8} \\
20 \\
\underline{16} \\
40 \\
\underline{40} \\
0
\end{array}
$$

So, $\frac{1}{8} = 0.125$

The answer section includes answers to all Review Exercises.

Write the following fractions in lowest terms. [1.2]

1. $\dfrac{24}{40}$

2. $\dfrac{32}{64}$

3. $\dfrac{27}{81}$

4. $\dfrac{147}{294}$

5. $\dfrac{63}{70}$

6. $\dfrac{84}{132}$

7. $\dfrac{24}{1200}$

8. $\dfrac{375}{1000}$

Convert the following improper fractions to mixed numbers and write in lowest terms. [1.2]

9. $\dfrac{65}{8}$

10. $\dfrac{56}{12}$

11. $\dfrac{38}{24}$

12. $\dfrac{55}{7}$

13. $\dfrac{120}{45}$

14. $\dfrac{196}{24}$

15. $\dfrac{258}{32}$

16. $\dfrac{194}{64}$

Solve the following problems and write in lowest terms. [1.2]

17. $\dfrac{5}{8} + \dfrac{7}{12}$

18. $\dfrac{1}{5} + \dfrac{3}{10} + \dfrac{3}{8}$

19. $\dfrac{5}{7} - \dfrac{1}{3}$

20. $\dfrac{3}{4} - \dfrac{2}{3}$

21. $\quad 25\dfrac{1}{6}$
$\quad + 46\dfrac{2}{3}$
$\quad \overline{}$

22. $\quad 18\dfrac{3}{5}$
$\quad 47\dfrac{7}{10}$
$\quad + 25\dfrac{8}{15}$
$\quad \overline{}$

23. $\quad 6\dfrac{7}{12}$
$\quad - 2\dfrac{1}{3}$
$\quad \overline{}$

24. $\quad 92\dfrac{5}{16}$
$\quad - 11\dfrac{1}{4}$
$\quad \overline{}$

Solve the following application problems. [1.1 and 1.2]

25. A quality oak floor costs $3.80 per square foot. Additionally, a capable installer charges $2.75 per square foot for labor. Find the total cost, not including any taxes, to lay the flooring in a 580-square-foot living room.

26. A federal law requires that all residential toilets sold in the United States use no more than 1.6 gallons of water per flush. Prior to this legislation, conventional toilets used 3.4 gallons of water per flush. Find the amount of water saved in one year by a family flushing the toilet 22 times each day.

27. Desiree Ramirez worked $5\dfrac{1}{2}$ hours on Wednesday, $6\dfrac{1}{4}$ hours on Thursday, $3\dfrac{3}{4}$ hours on Friday, and 7 hours on Saturday. How many hours did she work altogether?

28. A painting contractor arrived at a 60-unit apartment complex with $147\dfrac{1}{2}$ gallons of exterior paint. His crew sprayed $68\dfrac{1}{2}$ gallons on the wood siding, rolled $37\dfrac{3}{8}$ gallons on the masonry exterior, and brushed $5\dfrac{3}{4}$ gallons on the trim. Find the number of gallons of paint remaining.

29. Three sides of Sheri Minkner's kiwi ranch are $202\dfrac{1}{8}$ feet, $370\dfrac{3}{4}$ feet, and $274\dfrac{1}{2}$ feet. If the distance around the ranch is $1166\dfrac{7}{8}$ feet, what is the length of the fourth side?

30. The Catering Crew served $12\dfrac{2}{3}$ pounds of American cheese, $16\dfrac{1}{8}$ pounds of jack cheese, $15\dfrac{1}{2}$ pounds of sharp cheddar cheese, and $10\dfrac{1}{6}$ pounds of muenster cheese at a catered event. Find the total weight of the cheese served.

Solve each problem and reduce to lowest terms. [1.2]

31. $\dfrac{5}{8} \times \dfrac{2}{3}$

32. $\dfrac{1}{3} \times \dfrac{7}{8} \times \dfrac{3}{5}$

33. $\dfrac{1}{6} \div \dfrac{1}{3}$

34. $10 \div \dfrac{5}{8}$

35. $2\dfrac{1}{2} \div 3\dfrac{3}{4}$

36. $3\dfrac{3}{4} \div \dfrac{27}{16}$

37. $12\dfrac{1}{2} \times 1\dfrac{2}{3}$

38. $12\dfrac{1}{3} \div 2$

Solve the following application problems. [1.1 and 1.3]

39. Barry bought 16.5 meters of rope at $0.48 per meter and 3 meters of wire at $1.05 per meter. How much change did he get from three $5 bills? [1.4 and 1.5]

40. The earnings of Sierra West Bancorp last year were $1.4 million, or $0.39 per share of stock. Find the number of shares of stock in the company. Round to the nearest tenth of a million.

41. The area of a piece of land is $63\frac{3}{4}$ acres. One-third of the land is sold. What is the area of the land that is left?

42. A fishing boat anchor requires $10\frac{3}{8}$ pounds of steel. Find the number of anchors that can be manufactured with 25,730 pounds of steel.

43. Find the number of window-blind pull cords that can be made from $157\frac{1}{2}$ yards of cord if $4\frac{3}{8}$ yards of cord are needed for each blind.

44. Waterford Plumbing is a partnership formed by three people. After-tax profits one year amounted to $562,200. The partners decided to retain $\frac{1}{4}$ of the profit in the firm for remodeling costs and disburse the remaining profit equally to the partners. Find the amount going to each partner.

Convert the following decimals to a fraction and reduce to lowest terms. [1.3]

45. 0.25	**46.** 0.625	**47.** 0.93	**48.** 0.005

Round the following decimals to the nearest tenth and to the nearest hundredth. [1.3]

49. 68.433	**50.** 975.536
51. 0.3549	**52.** 8.025
53. 6.965	**54.** 0.428
55. 0.955	**56.** 71.249

Convert the following fractions to a decimal. Round to the nearest thousandth when necessary. [1.3]

57. $\dfrac{5}{8}$	**58.** $\dfrac{3}{4}$	**59.** $\dfrac{5}{6}$	**60.** $\dfrac{7}{16}$

CHAPTER 1 **Business Application Case #1**
Operating Expenses

It is often said that a picture is worth a thousand words. Visual presentation of data is often used in business in the form of graphs. A commonly used graph that shows the relationships of various data is the circle graph, also called a pie chart. The circle is divided into slices or fractional parts. The size of each slice helps to show the relationship of the various slices to each other and to the whole.

The annual operating expenses for Woodline Moldings and Trim are shown below. Use this information to answer the questions that follow.

WOODLINE MOLDINGS AND TRIM (OPERATING EXPENSES)

Expense Item	Monthly Amount	Annual Amount	Fraction of Total
Salaries	$15,000	_____	___
Rent	$ 9,000	_____	___
Utilities	$ 3,000	_____	___
Advertising	$ 2,250	_____	___
Insurance	$ 2,250	_____	___
Miscellaneous	$ 4,500	_____	___
Total Expenses		_____	

(a) Find the total annual operating expenses for Woodline Moldings and Trim.

(b) What fraction should be used to represent each expense item as part of the total expenses?

(c) Draw a circle (pie) graph using the fractions you found in (b) to represent each expense item. Approximate the fractional part of the circle needed for each expense item. Label each segment of the circle graph with the fraction and the expense item.

| CHAPTER 1 | # Business Application Case #2
Home Repair |

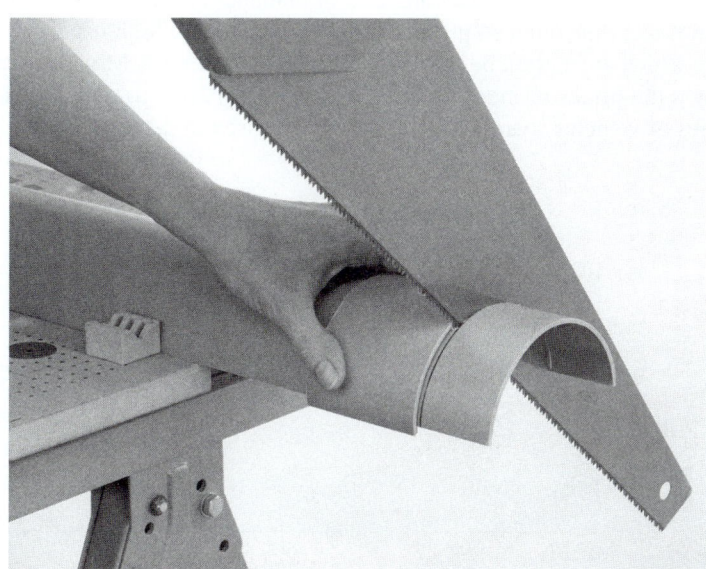

Pete and Barbara Johnson buy an old house. They plan to make the necessary repairs before moving in with their two children, one dog, and two cats. The Johnsons buy all of the needed supplies at a local Home Depot store (see www.homedepot.com) and work on the house during evenings and weekends as they have time and money. Pete believes it will take about 6 months before they can move into the house.

(a) A gutter downspout is 10 feet long. If a piece of gutter downspout 8 feet $8\frac{3}{8}$ inches is needed for a job, find the length of the remaining piece. (*Hint:* 1 foot equals 12 inches.)

(b) Home Depot stock is selling for $25.80 per share. Find the number of shares that can be purchased for $10,000.

(c) Give three specific situations in which fractions and mixed numbers would be used in a home-improvement store.

(d) From your own experiences and those of family members and classmates, list three specific activities where the ability to work with fractions would be needed.

Equations and Formulas

General Motors (GM) has been producing automobiles in the United States since 1908. The company manufactures Chevrolets, Buicks, Oldsmobiles, Cadillacs, GMCs, Pontiacs, Saturns, Isuzus, Opels, and Saabs. In 2007, GM sold nearly 9.3 million automobiles worldwide. Sales were okay during the first nine months of 2008, but collapsed in the last quarter of the year as the world entered a financial crisis and people delayed vehicle purchases. The precipitous drop in sales from 2007 to 2008 is easily seen in Figure 2.1. The figure helps explain why GM was in very serious financial trouble as 2009 began.

Managers use sophisticated algebra-based models to forecast demand. It is to their advantage to have very accurate forecasts of demand. A forecast that is too low may result in lost sales and thus reduced profit. A forecast that is too high usually results in excessive inventory which must often be marked down before selling. GM was forced to significantly mark down the prices of many of its new vehicles in 2009 as demand slowed rapidly and inventories of vehicles soared. Markdown is discussed in detail in Chapter 11.

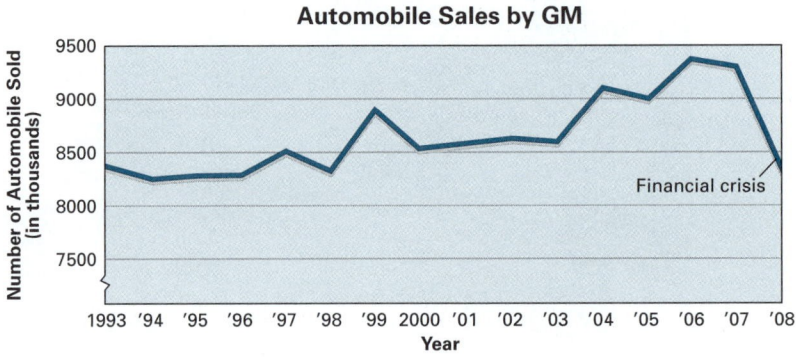

Figure 2.1

STOP —and think

Discuss the effects of a sharp decrease in company sales on the managers, employees, and stockholders of a company. In times of financial stress, companies often lay off some of their employees. Is this fair? What is the alternative?

Equations and formulas are often used in business. For example, formulas are used to find markup, interest, depreciation, annuities, and several other values as well. In this chapter, we show how to work with and solve basic equations and formulas.

2.1	**Solving Equations**

OBJECTIVES

1 *Learn the basic terminology of equations.*

2 *Use basic rules to solve equations.*

3 *Combine like terms in equations.*

4 *Use the distributive property to simplify equations.*

An **equation** is a statement that says two expressions are equal. For example, the equation

$$x + 5 = 9$$

says that the expression $x + 5$ and 9 are equal.

Objective

1 *Learn the Basic Terminology of Equations.* A **variable** is a letter, such as x or s, that is used to represent an unknown number. The variable x, in the equation above, as well as the numbers 5 and 9, are called terms. A **term** is a single letter, a single number, or the product (or quotient) of a number and one or more letters. Examples of terms include $80z$, $30y$, $19.5z$, and $3\frac{1}{2}t$. The number in front of the variable in a term is called the **coefficient**. So the coefficient in the term $3\frac{1}{2}t$ is $3\frac{1}{2}$ and the variable is t. Terms in expressions are separated from one another by addition $(+)$ or subtraction $(-)$ signs, as in the following **expression** that has two terms: $75z - 15y$.

In a way, an equation in math is similar to a sentence in written language. An equation shows a complete relationship, just as each sentence must give a complete thought. Each equation has a left side and a right side. For example, Albert Einstein made the equation $E = mc^2$ famous. The **left side** of this equation is E (Energy) and the **right side** of the equation is mc^2 (mass times the speed of light squared). Einstein's theoretical work showed that energy and mass were two different forms of the same thing—essentially mass can be converted into energy (think of a nuclear bomb) and energy can be converted into mass (humans are still trying to do this).

The **solution** to an equation is the number that makes the equation true. In fact, we solve equations to find the value of the variable that makes the equation true. The solution to the equation $x + 5 = 9$ is 4, since replacing the variable x with the number 4 makes the equation true.

$$x + 5 = 9$$
$$4 + 5 \overset{?}{=} 9 \quad \text{Let } x = 4.$$
$$9 = 9 \quad \text{True.}$$

The preceding check is an example of **substitution:** the variable x was replaced with 4.

Objective

2 *Use Basic Rules to Solve Equations.* We solve an equation to find the number that the variable must equal to make the equation true. The equation is true if the left side equals the right side. This is done by modifying the equation so that all terms containing a variable are on one side of the equation and all numbers are on the other side. The two sides of an equation remain equal if the same change is made to both sides.

The rules for solving equations follow.

> **Addition Rule:** The same number may be added to or subtracted from both sides of an equation.
>
> **Multiplication Rule:** Both sides of an equation may be multiplied or divided by the same nonzero number.

NOTE Remember, whatever arithmetic operation you do to one side of an equation must also be done to the other side.

EXAMPLE 1 **Solving Equations Using Addition**

Solve $x - 17 = 34$.

Solution To solve this equation, x must be alone on one side of the equal sign, and all numbers collected on the other side. To change the $x - 17$ to x, perform the opposite operation to "undo" what was done. The *opposite* of subtraction is addition, so add 17 to both sides.

$$x - 17 = 34$$
$$x - 17 + 17 = 34 + 17 \quad \text{Add 17 to both sides.}$$
$$x + 0 = 51 \quad \text{The sum of } -17 + 17 \text{ is 0.}$$
$$x = 51$$

To check this answer, substitute 51 for x in the original equation.

$$x - 17 = 34 \quad \text{Original equation.}$$
$$51 - 17 \overset{?}{=} 34 \quad \text{Replace } x \text{ with 51.}$$
$$34 = 34 \quad \text{True.}$$

The answer checks, so $x = 51$.

EXAMPLE 2 **Solving Equations Using Subtraction**

Solve $y + 12.3 = 20.5$.

Solution To isolate y on the left side, do the opposite of adding 12.3, which is *subtracting* 12.3 from both sides.

$$y + 12.3 = 20.5$$
$$y + 12.3 - 12.3 = 20.5 - 12.3 \quad \text{Subtract 12.3 from both sides.}$$
$$y + 0 = 8.2$$
$$y = 8.2$$

Check the answer by substituting 8.2 for y in the original equation.

$$y + 12.3 = 20.5$$
$$51 - 17 \overset{?}{=} 34$$
$$20.5 = 20.5$$

The answer checks.

EXAMPLE 3 **Solving Equations Using Division**

Solve $5p = 60$.

Solution The term $5p$ indicates the product of 5 and p. Since the opposite of multiplication is division, solve the equation by *dividing* both sides by 5.

$$5p = 60$$
$$\frac{\cancel{5}p}{\cancel{5}} = \frac{60}{5} \quad \text{Divide both sides by 5.}$$
$$p = 12$$

Check by substituting 12 for p in the original equation.

EXAMPLE 4 **Solving Equations Using Multiplication**

Solve $\dfrac{r}{8} = 13$.

Solution The bar in the fraction $\dfrac{r}{8}$ means to divide ($r \div 8$). Since the opposite operation of division is multiplication, multiply both sides of the equation by 8. Note in the following that a heavy dot is used to indicate multiplication.

$$\frac{r}{8} = 13$$

$$\frac{r}{8} \cdot 8 = 13 \cdot 8 \qquad \text{Multiply both sides by 8.}$$

$$\frac{r}{\cancel{8}} \cdot \cancel{8} = 104 \qquad \text{Cancel } \tfrac{8}{8}, \text{ which is 1.}$$

$$r = 104$$

Example 5 shows how to solve an equation using a reciprocal. The product of a number and its **reciprocal** is 1. To get the reciprocal of a nonzero fraction, exchange the numerator and the denominator. For example, the reciprocal of $\frac{7}{9}$ is $\frac{9}{7}$.

$$\frac{\cancel{7}^{1}}{\cancel{9}_{1}} \cdot \frac{\cancel{9}^{1}}{\cancel{7}_{1}} = 1$$

EXAMPLE 5 **Solving Equations Using Reciprocals**

Solve $\frac{4}{5}n = 20$.

Solution Solve this equation by multiplying both sides by $\frac{5}{4}$, which is the reciprocal of $\frac{4}{5}$. This process will give just $1n$, or n, on the left.

$$\frac{4}{5}n = 20$$

$$\frac{\cancel{5}^{1}}{\cancel{4}_{1}} \cdot \frac{\cancel{4}^{1}}{\cancel{5}_{1}}n = \frac{5}{4} \cdot 20 \qquad \text{Multiply both sides by } \tfrac{5}{4}.$$

$$n = \frac{100}{4}$$

$$n = 25$$

The equation in Example 6 requires two steps to solve.

EXAMPLE 6 **Solving Equations Involving Several Steps**

Solve $2m + 5 = 17$.

Solution To solve equations that require more than one step, first isolate the terms involving the unknown (variable) on one side of the equation and constants (numbers) on the other side by using addition and subtraction.

$$2m + 5 = 17$$

$$2m + 5 - 5 = 17 - 5 \qquad \text{Subtract 5 from both sides.}$$

$$2m = 12$$

$$\frac{2m}{2} = \frac{12}{2}$$ Divide both sides by 2.

$$m = 6$$

Check by substituting 6 for m in the original equation.

$$2m + 5 = 17$$
$$2(6) + 5 \stackrel{?}{=} 17$$
$$17 = 17$$

Thus, $m = 6$ is the solution.

◼

> **NOTE**   The unknown can be on either side of the equal sign. The equation $6 = m$ is the same as $m = 6$. The number is the solution whether the equation has the variable by itself on either the left *or* the right side.

Objective

3   *Combine Like Terms in Equations.*   Some equations have more than one term with the same variable. Terms with the same variables are called **like terms**, or **similar terms**. Like terms can be *combined* by adding or subtracting the coefficients, as shown. Intuitively, you can think of $(8x + 2x)$ below as (8 apples + 2 apples). Since 8 apples + 2 apples is 10 apples, then $8x + 2x$ is equal to $10x$. Terms such as $3x$ and $5y$ are *not* like terms, so they cannot be combined into one term, just as 3 apples + 5 oranges cannot be combined.

$$8x + 2x = 10x$$
$$11y - 3y = 8y$$
$$12p - 5p + 2p = 9p$$
$$2z + z = 2z + 1z = 3z$$

Terms such as $3x$ and $2y$ are *not* like terms, so $2x + 3y$ cannot be combined into one term.

> **NOTE**   Since multiplying by 1 does not change the value of a quantity, $1 \cdot z$ is the same as z.

EXAMPLE 7   Solving Equations with Like Terms

Solve the equation $9z - 3z + 2z = 50$ for the unknown.

Solution   The unknown in this equation is the variable z. The three terms on the left-hand side of the equation are like terms since they all contain the same variable z. So, the first step is to combine the three terms on the left-hand side of the equation.

$$9z - 3z + 2z = 50$$

$$8z = 50$$ Combine the coefficients, that is, $9 - 3 + 2 = 8$.

$$\frac{8z}{8} = \frac{50}{8}$$ Divide both sides by 8.

$$z = 6\frac{1}{4} \text{ or } 6.25$$

Substitute 6.25 for the variable z in the original equation to verify that it is the solution.

◼

Objective

4   *Use the Distributive Property to Simplify Equations.*   One very useful property from mathematics is called the **distributive property**. Actually, we already used the distributive property to add the coefficients of like terms in the previous example. However, this property also allows us to multiply a number on the outside of the parentheses by each term inside the parentheses, as shown here.

$$a(b + c) = ab + ac$$

The following diagram may help in remembering the distributive property.

$$a(b + c) = ab + ac$$

The term on the outside, *a*, is *distributed* over all terms in the parentheses.

$$2(m + 7) = 2m + 2 \cdot 7 = 2m + 14$$
$$8(k - 5) = 8k - 8 \cdot 5 = 8k - 40$$

EXAMPLE **8**   **Solving Equations Using the Distributive Property**

Solve $6(p - 2) = 30$.

Solution   First use the distributive property on the left to remove the parentheses.

$$6(p - 2) = 30$$
$$6p - 12 = 30$$
$$6p - 12 + 12 = 30 + 12 \quad \text{Add 12 to both sides.}$$
$$6p = 42$$
$$\frac{6p}{6} = \frac{42}{6} \quad \text{Divide by 6.}$$
$$p = 7$$

NOTE   Recall that the product of a positive and a negative number is negative. For example, $6(-2) = -12$, so $6(p - 2) = 6p - 12$.

NOTE   Also recall that a negative number times a negative number is a positive number, so $(-10)(-5) = +50$. A negative number divided by a negative number is also a positive number, so $(-10) \div (-5) = +2$.

The distributive property can be used to help understand the adding or subtracting of like terms, as follows.

$$6y + 14y = (6 + 14)y = 20y$$

$$2t + 7t - 3.5t = (2 + 7 - 3.5)t = 5.5t$$

Use the following steps to solve an equation.

Solving Linear Equations

> **Step 1** Remove all parentheses on both sides of the equation using the distributive property.
>
> **Step 2** Combine all similar terms on both sides of the equation.
>
> **Step 3** Add to or subtract from both sides whatever is needed to produce a term with the variable on one side and a number on the other side.
>
> **Step 4** Multiply or divide the variable term by whatever is needed to produce a term with a coefficient of 1. Multiply or divide the number term on the other side by the same quantity.

EXAMPLE 9 **Solving Equations Involving Several Steps**

Solve $5r - 2 = 2(r + 5)$.

Solution

$$5r - 2 = 2(r + 5)$$

$$5r - 2 = 2r + 10 \qquad \text{Use distributive property on the right.}$$

$$5r - 2 + 2 = 2r + 10 + 2 \qquad \text{Add 2 to both sides to get all numbers on the right-hand side.}$$

$$5r = 2r + 12$$

$$5r - 2r = 2r + 12 - 2r \qquad \text{Subtract } 2r \text{ from both sides to get all variables on the left-hand side.}$$

$$5r - 2r = 12$$

$$3r = 12 \qquad \text{Combine like terms on the right.}$$

$$\frac{3r}{3} = \frac{12}{3} \qquad \text{Divide both sides by 3 to get 1 as a coefficient.}$$

$$r = 4$$

NOTE Be sure to check the answer in the *original* equation and not in any other step.

2.1	**Exercises**

Solve each equation. Check each answer.

1. $z + 8 = 50$ **2.** $r + 13 = 83$ **3.** $z + 95 = 400$

4. $v - 29 = 17$ **5.** $25 = x + 12$ **6.** $312 = m - 40$

7. $10k = 42$ **8.** $7s = 84$ **9.** $12q = 144$

10. $8z = 136$ **11.** $60 = 30m$ **12.** $94 = 2z$

13. $5.9y = 17.7$ **14.** $16.5x = 39.6$ **15.** $1.54 = 0.7y$

16. $3.9a = 15.6$ **17.** $3.92w = 3.136$ **18.** $2.773m = 3.3276$

19. $0.0002x = 0.08$ **20.** $0.0324 = 0.0135y$ **21.** $\dfrac{s}{7} = 42$

22. $\dfrac{m}{5} = 6$ **23.** $\dfrac{r}{7} = 1$ **24.** $\dfrac{c}{7} = 2$

25. $\frac{2}{3}b = 8$

26. $22 = \frac{5}{4}s$

27. $35 = \frac{7}{5}t$

28. $\frac{7}{3}s = 21$

29. $2x = \frac{5}{3}$

30. $4y = \frac{1}{3}$

31. $3p = \frac{5}{12}$

32. $\frac{3}{4} = 9a$

33. $7b + 9 = 37$

34. $4x + 12 = 75$

35. $7y - 23 = 58$

36. $12r - 60 = 100$

37. $6p + 41.5 = 69.4$

38. $12.2s + 13.8 = 47.96$

39. $6c + \frac{3}{4} = 8$

40. $5z + \frac{2}{3} = 2$

41. $7q - \frac{2}{3} = 4$

42. $7a - \frac{5}{4} = \frac{9}{4}$

43. $5.2z - 4 = 1.2$

44. $3.6m + 2 = 6.32$

45. $27.85 = 3 + 7.1p$

46. $0.9 = 4t - 3.5$

47. $7m + 4m - 5m = 78$

48. $13r - 7r + 3r = 81$

49. $2s + s + 3s = 12$

50. $3.5k + k + k = 11.55$

51. $5y + 2 = 3(y + 4)$

52. $4z + 2 = 2(z + 2)$

53. $3(m - 4) = m + 2$

54. $s + 8 = 3(s - 6)$

55. $4(y + 8) = 3(y + 14)$

56. $7(z - 5) = 4(z + 8)$

57. $\frac{3}{4}s + \frac{1}{5}s = \frac{4}{5}$

58. $\frac{3}{4}q - \frac{1}{9} = \frac{1}{3} + \frac{1}{4}q$

59. $\frac{3}{8}y + \frac{1}{4} = \frac{9}{8}y - \frac{1}{4}$

60. $3(2p - 1) = 4(2.2 - p)$

61. $2(y + 1) = 4(4 - 2.5y)$

62. $9.1765y + 0.3284y = 6.65343$

63. $0.7452(3k - 1) = 3.94956$

64. $0.3255(1 + 7.5s) = 6.67275$

65. $1.2(2 + 3r) = 0.8(2r + 5)$

 66. Explain why all terms with a variable should be placed on one side of the equation and all terms without a variable should be placed on the opposite side when solving an equation.

 67. A student obtains the equation $6x = 5x$ after applying several steps correctly. The student then divides both sides by x and obtains the result $6 = 5$ and gives "no solution" as the answer. Is this correct? If not, state why not and give the correct solution. (See Objective 3.)

 68. Explain the distributive property and give an example. (See Objective 4.)

2.2   Applications of Equations

OBJECTIVES

1 *Translate phrases into mathematical expressions.*

2 *Write equations from given information.*

3 *Solve application problems.*

Most problems in business are expressed in words. Before these problems can be solved, they must be converted into mathematical language.

Objective

1   *Translate Phrases into Mathematical Expressions.*   Applied problems tend to have certain phrases that occur again and again. The key to solving such problems is to correctly translate these phrases into mathematical expressions. The next few examples illustrate this process.

EXAMPLE **1**   **Translating Phrases Involving Addition**

Write the following verbal expressions as mathematical expressions. Use p to represent the unknown number.

Verbal Expression	Mathematical Expression	Comments
(a) q plus a number	$q + p$	p represents the number and "plus" means addition
(b) Add 17 to a number	$p + 17$	p represents the number to which 17 is added
(c) The sum of a number and 12.7	$p + 12.7$	"sum" indicates addition
(d) 18 more than a number	$p + 18$	"more than" indicates addition

EXAMPLE **2**   **Translating Phrases Involving Subtraction**

Write each of the following verbal expressions as a mathematical expression. Use y as a variable.

Verbal Expression	Mathematical Expression	Comments
(a) 5.5 less than a number	$y - 5.5$	"less than" indicates subtraction
(b) A number decreased by $12\frac{1}{4}$	$y - 12\frac{1}{4}$	"decreased" indicates subtraction
(c) Eight fewer than a number	$y - 8$	"fewer than" indicates subtraction
(d) Eighteen minus a number	$18 - y$	"minus" indicates subtraction

EXAMPLE **3**   **Translating Phrases Involving Multiplication and Division**

Write the following verbal expressions as mathematical expressions. Use z as the variable.

Verbal Expression	Mathematical Expression	Comments
(a) The product of a number and 7.5	$7.5z$	"product" indicates multiplication
(b) Ten times a number	$10z$	"times" indicates multiplication
(c) One-fourth of a number	$\frac{1}{4}z$	"of" indicates multiplication
(d) The quotient of a number and 9	$\frac{z}{9}$	"quotient" indicates division
(e) The quotient of 8 and a number	$\frac{8}{z}$	"quotient" indicates division
(f) The sum of 6 and a number, multiplied by 8.3	$8.3(6 + z)$	multiplying a sum requires parentheses

NOTE   If you are adding or multiplying, the order of the variable and the number does not matter. For example,

$$3 + x = x + 3 \quad \text{and} \quad 5 \cdot y = y \cdot 5$$

However, the order *does make a difference* in both division and subtraction, as you can see.

is not equal to

$$8 - 3 \neq 3 - 8$$
$$12 \div 5 \neq 5 \div 12$$

Translating statements into mathematical expressions and equations helps us solve many real-world application problems. Use the following steps *every time* you solve a problem to become a better problem solver.

Solving Application Problems

> **Step 1 First, read the problem very carefully**. Then reread the problem to make sure that its meaning is clear. Sometimes a sketch helps.
>
> **Step 2 Identify the unknown** and give it a variable name such as x. If possible, write other unknowns as mathematical expressions in terms of the same variable.
>
> **Step 3 Write an equation** describing the relationship given in the problem.
>
> **Step 4 Solve the equation**.
>
> **Step 5 Answer the question(s)** asked in the problem.
>
> **Step 6 Check the solution** using the *original* words of the problem.
>
> **Step 7 Be sure your answer is reasonable**.

NOTE   The third step is often the hardest. To write an equation from the information given in the problem, convert the facts stated in words into mathematical expressions and then into equations.

Objective

2   *Write Equations from Given Information.*   Any words that mean *equals* or *same* translate into an equal sign $(=)$, producing an equation that can be solved for the unknown.

EXAMPLE 4   Solving Number Problems

Translate the following statement into an equation: The product of 5, and a number decreased by 8, is 100. Use y as the variable. Solve the equation.

Solution   The phrase "and a number decreased by 8" is set off by commas from the other parts of the sentence. So, it should have parentheses around it to keep that logic intact.

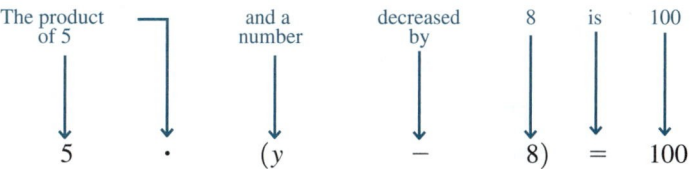

Simplify and complete the solution of the equation.

$$5 \cdot (y - 8) = 100$$
$$5y - 40 = 100 \qquad \text{Apply the distributive property.}$$
$$5y = 140 \qquad \text{Add 40 to both sides.}$$
$$y = 28 \qquad \text{Divide by 5.}$$

Check the answer to make sure it is correct.

NOTE   If Example 4 had been written as "The product of 5 and a number, decreased by 8, is 100," then the corresponding equation would be $5y - 8 = 100$ rather than $5(y - 8) = 100$.

Objective

3   *Solve Application Problems.*

EXAMPLE 5   **Solving an Application Problem**

A mattress for a single bed is on sale for $200, which is $\frac{4}{5}$ of its original price. Find the original price.

Solution

STEP 1 The mattress is on sale for $200, so it must have been priced at more than $200 originally. Let p represent the original price; $200 is the sale price, and the sale price is $\frac{4}{5}$ of the original price. Use all this information to write the equation.

STEP 2 Identify the unknown.   Sale price is $\frac{4}{5}$ of original price.

$$\downarrow \qquad \downarrow \qquad \qquad \downarrow$$

STEP 3 Write the equation. $\$200 = \frac{4}{5} \cdot p$

STEP 4 Solve the equation.

$$200 = \frac{4}{5} \cdot p$$

$$\frac{5}{4} \cdot 200 = \frac{5}{4} \cdot \frac{4}{5} \cdot p \qquad \text{Multiply by reciprocal.}$$

$$\frac{1000}{4} = 1 \cdot p$$

$$250 = p$$

STEP 5 The original price was $250.

STEP 6 Check the solution.

$$\$200 = \frac{4}{5} \cdot p$$

$$\$200 \stackrel{?}{=} \frac{4}{5} \cdot \$250 \qquad \text{Substitute \$250 for } p.$$

$$\$200 = \$200$$

The answer checks.

STEP 7 Is $250 a reasonable price for a mattress before it was on sale? Yes.

EXAMPLE 6   **Solving an Inventory Problem**

The Eastside Nursery ordered 27 saplings. Some of the saplings were elms, costing $17 each, while the rest were maples at $11 each. The total cost of the saplings was $375. Find the number of elms and the number of maples.

Solution

STEP 1 Let x represent the number of elm saplings, then $(27 - x)$ is the number of maple saplings. The total cost of the elm saplings is $17x$ and the total cost of the maple saplings is $11(27 - x)$. A table can be very helpful in identifying the knowns and unknowns.

STEP 2

	Number of Saplings	Cost per Sapling	Total Cost
Elms	x	$17	$17x$
Maples	$(27 - x)$	$11	$11(27 - x)$
Totals	27		375

STEP 3 The information in the table is used to produce the following equation.

$$\text{Cost of elms} + \text{cost of maples} = \text{total cost}$$
$$17x + 11(27 - x) = 375$$

STEP 4 Now solve this equation. First use the distributive property.

$$17x + 297 - 11x = 375$$
$$6x + 297 = 375 \quad \text{Combine terms.}$$
$$6x = 78 \quad \text{Subtract 297 from each side.}$$
$$x = 13 \quad \text{Divide each side by 6.}$$

STEPS 5–6 We have only part of the answer; 13 elm saplings. Now we need to find the number of maple saplings, which is $27 - x$, or $27 - 13 = 14$ maple saplings. Check that the total number of saplings is 27 and the total cost of the saplings is $(13 \times \$17) + (14 \times \$11) = \$375$.

STEP 7 Are the values reasonable? Yes.

EXAMPLE 7 Solving Investment Application Problems

Laurie Zimmerman has $15,000 to invest. She places a portion of the funds in a savings account and $3000 more than twice this amount in a retirement account. How much is put into the savings account? How much is placed in the retirement account?

Solution Let z be the amount invested in the savings account. To find the amount invested in the retirement account, translate as follows.

3000	more than	2 times the amount
↓	↓	↓
3000	+	$2z$

Since the sum of the two investments must be $15,000, an equation can be formed as follows.

Amount invested in savings	+	amount invested in retirement account	=	total amount invested
z	+	$(3000 + 2z)$	=	$15,000

Now solve the equation.

$$z + (3000 + 2z) = 15{,}000$$
$$z + 3000 + 2z = 15{,}000 \quad \text{Remove parentheses.}$$
$$3z + 3000 = 15{,}000 \quad \text{Combine like terms.}$$
$$3z = 12{,}000 \quad \text{Subtract 3000 from both sides.}$$
$$z = 4000 \quad \text{Divide by 3.}$$

The amount invested in the savings account is $4000. The amount invested in the retirement account is $3000 + 2z$, or $3000 + 2(4000) = \$11,000$.

Check the solution as follows:

$$\$4000 + (\$3000 + 2 \cdot \$4000) = \$15{,}000$$

The answer checks.

■

> **NOTE**   In the parentheses above, remember to multiply $2 \cdot \$4000$ before adding $\$3000$.

| 2.2 | **Exercises** |

Write the following as mathematical expressions. Use x as the variable.

1. 27 plus a number
2. the sum of a number and $16\frac{1}{2}$
3. a number added to 22
4. 6.8 added to a number
5. 4 less than a number
6. 12 fewer than a number
7. subtract $3\frac{1}{2}$ from a number
8. subtract a number from 5.4
9. triple a number
10. the product of a number and 9
11. three-fifths of a number
12. four-thirds of a number
13. the quotient of 9 and a number
14. the quotient of a number and 11
15. 16 divided by a number
16. a number divided by 4
17. the product of 2.1 and the sum of 4 and a number
18. the quantity of a number plus 4, divided by 9
19. 7 times the difference of a number and 3
20. the difference of a number and 2, multiplied by 7

Write mathematical expressions for each of the following.

21. **PURCHASING CDs**   Find the cost of 12 CDs at y dollars each.
22. **TUITION FEES**   Find the cost of x students paying tuition of $2800 each.
23. **LIVESTOCK FEED**   The demand forecast for next month is 472 tons of livestock feed. Find the amount that should be ordered if inventory is x tons.
24. **COMPUTER USERS**   Eighty-three of the x employees have computers. How many do not have computers?
25. **UNION MEMBERSHIP**   A company has 73 employees of whom x are members of a union. How many employees are not union members?
26. **CARD SALES**   The inventory of a small card shop is valued at $73,000. The value of the greeting cards is x. Find the value of the rest of the inventory.
27. **TEXTBOOK PURCHASES**   A college bookstore paid $20,210 to purchase x textbooks for a biology class. Find the cost of one textbook.
28. **ADMISSION FEES**   A lodge paid $1853 for tickets for its x members to visit the state capitol. Find the cost of one ticket.
29. **CHARITABLE DONATIONS**   Robin has 21 books on computers. She donates x of them to the school library. How many does she have left?
30. **VIDEO STORE**   A video rental store is x years old. How old will it be in 8 years?

Solve the following application problems. Steps 1–7 are repeated here for your convenience—use them.

Solving Applied Problems

Step 1 Read the problem carefully. Sometimes a sketch helps.

Step 2 Identify the unknown and choose a variable to represent it. If possible, write any other unknowns in terms of the same variable.

Step 3 Translate the problem into an equation.

Step 4 Solve the equation.

Step 5 Answer the question(s) asked in the problem.

Step 6 Check your solution using the original words of the problem.

Step 7 Be sure your answer is reasonable.

31. Four times a number, plus 6, equals 58. Find the number.

32. Seventeen times a number, plus 5, equals 107. Find the number.

33. Six times the quantity of 4 minus a number is 15. Find the number.

34. Twelve times the quantity of a number less 1 is 72. Find the number.

35. When 6 is added to a number, the result is 7 times the number. Find the number.

36. If 6 is subtracted from three times a number, the result is 4 more than the number. Find the number.

37. When 5 times a number is added to twice the number, the result is 10. Find the number.

38. If 7 times a number is subtracted from 11 times the number, the result is 9. Find the number.

39. CAR STEREO   Last month, Ben Jamison sold 17 more car stereos than did the other salesperson at the store. If the two salespeople sold a total of 101 stereos, find the number sold by Jamison.

40. SODA SALES   A grocery store sold 19 more cases of Coke than Sprite. Given that 43 cases were sold, find the number of cases of Coke sold.

41. SHIPBUILDING   One hundred eighty-five more people work in building the ships than are in management, accounting, finance, and marketing. Given a total of 229 employees, find the number working in building the ships.

42. EXCHANGE PROGRAM TO MEXICO   Twenty-one students went on a student exchange program to Guadalajara, Mexico. There were 11 more women than men. Find the number of women.

43. AUTOMOBILE   A one-year-old automobile is marked "on sale" for $18,450, which is $\frac{9}{10}$ of its original price. Find the original price.

44. INTERNATIONAL SHIPMENTS   Because of handling and freight charges, Western Oil Equipment charges $\frac{5}{4}$ of the list price for an item shipped to Indonesia. Find the list price of an item that was charged at $725.

45. HOME CONSTRUCTION   A contractor built 105 homes last year, some economy models and some deluxe models. The number of economy models was $\frac{3}{2}$ the number of deluxe models. Find the number of each type of home that was built.

46. CULINARY SCHOOL   Last quarter, the Regency Culinary School spent $18,000 on advertising using radio and newspaper. The amount spent on newspaper advertising was $\frac{5}{4}$ that spent on radio advertising. Find the amount spent on each type of advertising.

47. RADIO STATION SALARIES   Radio station KLRS spent $21,000 on salaries one month. The amount spent on announcers was $\frac{3}{5}$ the amount spent on all other employees. Find the amount spent on announcers and on all other employees.

48. BUSY INTERSECTION   An engineer is studying a busy intersection. In 1 hour, the number of cars going north-south was $\frac{3}{4}$ of those going east-west, and the total number of cars was 1400. Find the number of cars going north-south and east-west.

49. COMMERCIAL BUILDING   Jane Anderson purchased a run-down, empty commercial building and plans to fix it up. The building can be used for both retail stores and office space. She thinks she can get a total annual rent of $135,000 with $3\frac{1}{2}$ times as much rent coming from retail stores as from office space. Find the rent she expects from office space and also the rent she expects from retail stores.

50. MATERIAL   Karen Cherie has a piece of fabric that is 106 inches long. She wishes to cut it into two pieces so that one piece is 12 inches longer than the other. What should be the length of each piece?

51. HARLEY DAVIDSON   Excluding managers, there are 22 full-time employees working at a large Harley Davidson shop. New employees receive $9.50 per hour, while more experienced workers average $12.90 per hour. The company spends $273.60 per hour in wages, not counting benefits. Find the number of each type of nonmanagement worker.

52. VEGETABLE SALES   Jumbo Market makes $0.10 on a head of lettuce and $0.08 on a bunch of carrots. Last week, a total of 12,900 heads of lettuce and bunches of carrots were sold, with a total profit of $1174. How many heads of lettuce and how many bunches of carrots were sold?

53. NISSAN SALES   Profits on Nissan Altimas and Sentras average $1200 and $850, respectively, at one dealership. The total profit in a month in which they sold 120 of these models was $130,350. Find the number of each sold.

54. AUTO REPAIR   One month, revenue from the 95 repairs at an auto repair shop totaled $20,040. The average charges for repairs on personal and commercial vehicles were $250 and $180, respectively. Find the number of each type of vehicle repaired.

 55. Are the problems in this section difficult for you? Explain why or why not. Explain two things you would recommend to a classmate who is having difficulty.

 56. Write out the steps necessary to solve an applied problem. (See Objective 3.)

2.3   Formulas

OBJECTIVES

1 *Evaluate formulas for given values of the variables.*

2 *Solve formulas for a specific variable.*

3 *Use standard business formulas to solve word problems.*

4 *Evaluate formulas containing exponents.*

Many of the most useful rules and procedures in business are given as **formulas**, or equations, showing the relationships among different variables. For example, the formula for simple interest is

$$\text{Interest} = \text{principal} \times \text{rate} \times \text{time}$$

or, using the first letter for each word,

$$I = P \times R \times T$$

Objective

1   *Evaluate Formulas for Given Values of the Variables.*   Once any three values are substituted into the formula $I = PRT$, we can then find the value of the remaining variable.

> **NOTE**   The variable T is always expressed as a fraction of a year in $I = PRT$. P and I are always in dollars and R is a percent.

EXAMPLE 1   **Finding Interest**

Use the formula $I = PRT$ and find I if $P = \$12{,}500$, R is 8%, or 0.08, and $T = 1$ year.

Solution   Substitute \$12,500 for P, 0.08 for R, and 1 for T in the formula $I = PRT$.

$$I = PRT$$
$$I = \$12{,}500 \times 0.08 \times 1 \quad \text{Substitute values.}$$
$$I = 1000 \quad\quad\quad\quad \text{\$1000 interest.}$$

EXAMPLE 2   **Finding Time**

Use the formula $I = PRT$ and find T if $P = \$4000$, $I = \$720$, and R is 9%, or 0.09.

Solution   Substitute the given numbers for the letters of the formula.

$$I = PRT$$
$$\$720 = \$4000(0.09)T$$
$$\$720 = 360T$$
$$\frac{\$720}{360} = \frac{360T}{360} \quad \text{Divide by 360.}$$
$$2 = T$$

Since T is in years, the answer is 2 years. Check by substituting values for P, R, and T.

$$I = PRT$$
$$= \$4000 \cdot 0.09 \cdot 2$$
$$= \$720$$

The interest checks.

Objective

2   *Solve Formulas for a Specific Variable.*   In Example 2 we found the value of T when given the values of P, I, and R. If several problems of this type must be solved, it may be better to rewrite the formula $I = PRT$ so that T is alone on one side of the equation. Do this using the rules to solve equations given earlier. Since T is multiplied by PR, get T alone by dividing both sides of the equation by PR.

$$I = PRT$$
$$\frac{I}{PR} = \frac{PRT}{PR} \quad \text{Divide by } PR.$$
$$\frac{I}{PR} = \frac{\cancel{P}\,\cancel{R}\,T}{\cancel{P}\,\cancel{R}} \quad \text{Cancel.}$$
$$\frac{I}{PR} = T \quad or \quad T = \frac{I}{PR}$$

This process of rearranging a formula is sometimes called *solving a formula for a specific variable*.

> **NOTE** The formula $M = P(1 + RT)$ in Example 3 is explained in **Chapter 11**. For now, just substitute in the known values and solve for the unknown value.

EXAMPLE 3 **Solving for a Specific Variable**

Solve for T in the formula $M = P(1 + RT)$.

Solution This formula expresses the maturity value (M) of an initial amount of money (P) invested at a specified rate (R) for a certain period of time (T).

Start by using the distributive property on the right side.

$$M = P(1 + RT)$$
$$M = P + PRT$$

Now subtract P from both sides.

$$M - P = P + PRT - P$$
$$M - P = PRT$$

Divide each side by PR.

$$\frac{M - P}{PR} = \frac{\cancel{P}R T}{\cancel{P}\cancel{R}} \quad \text{Cancel.}$$

$$\frac{M - P}{PR} = T \quad \text{or} \quad T = \frac{M - P}{PR}$$

The original formula is now solved for *T*.

EXAMPLE 4 **Solving for a Specific Variable**

An employee earns \$7.89 per hour plus \$0.45 for each circuit board she assembles. **(a)** Write an equation for her total income (T) in terms of hours (H) and number of circuit boards assembled (C). **(b)** Solve for the variable C. **(c)** Use this to find the number of circuit boards she must assemble in a 40-hour week in order to earn \$450.

Solution

(a) Her total earnings are the sum of her hourly wage times the number of hours plus the amount for each circuit board times the number of circuit boards assembled.

$$T = 7.89H + 0.45C$$

(b)
$$T - 7.89H = 7.89H + 0.45C - 7.89H \quad \text{Subtract } 7.89H \text{ from both sides.}$$
$$T - 7.89H = 0.45C$$
$$\frac{T - 7.89H}{0.45} = \frac{0.45C}{0.45} \quad \text{Divide by 0.45.}$$
$$C = \frac{T - 7.89H}{0.45}$$

(c) Substitute $450 in place of T and 40 in place of H.

$$C = \frac{450 - 7.89(40)}{0.45}$$

$$C = \frac{450 - 315.6}{0.45} \qquad \text{Multiply first.}$$

$$C = \frac{134.4}{0.45}$$

$$C = 298.666\ldots \qquad \text{Round to 299.}$$

She must assemble 299 circuit boards.

Scientific Calculator Approach

The calculator solution to Example 4 uses chain calculation and the order of operations.

$$(\;\; 450 \;\; - \;\; 7.89 \;\; \times \;\; 40 \;\;) \;\; \div \;\; .45 = 298.6666\ldots$$

Objective

3 *Use Standard Business Formulas to Solve Word Problems.* In the following two examples, application problems that use some common business formulas are solved. These formulas are discussed in more detail later in the book.

EXAMPLE 5 **Finding Gross Sales**

Use $G = NP$ to find the gross sales from selling 339 CDs at $14.95 each.

Solution In this formula, N is the number of items sold and P is the price per item.

$$G = NP$$
$$G = 339 \cdot \$14.95$$
$$G = \$5068.05$$

The gross sales are $5068.05.

EXAMPLE 6 **Finding Selling Price**

Use $S = C + M$ to find the selling price of a battle-simulator computer game if the cost is $19.08 and the markup is $10.87.

Solution The variable C is the cost of the item, and M is the markup, which is added to cover expenses and profit.

$$S = C + M$$
$$S = \$19.08 + \$10.87$$
$$= \$29.95$$

The selling price of each game is $29.95.

Objective

4   *Evaluate Formulas Containing Exponents.*   Exponents are used to show repeated multiplication of some quantity. For example,

Exponent: number of times quantity is multiplied by itself

$$x \cdot x = x^2$$

Base: quantity being multiplied

Similarly, $z \cdot z \cdot z = z^3$ and $5 \cdot 5 \cdot 5 \cdot 5 = 5^4$, which is 625. Exponents are also referred to as "powers." For example, x^5 is "x to the fifth power."

EXAMPLE **7** **Finding Monthly Sales**

Trinity Home Furnishings has found that total monthly sales for its small chain of stores can be estimated as follows.

$$\text{Sales} = \$148{,}500 + 0.48 \cdot A^2$$

where A = amount spent on advertising. Estimate sales for a month when $500 is spent for advertising.

Solution   Substitute $500 in place of A in the equation.

$$
\begin{aligned}
\text{Sales} &= \$148{,}500 + 0.48 \cdot A^2 \\
&= \$148{,}500 + 0.48 \cdot \$500^2 &&\text{Substitute \$500 in place of } A. \\
&= \$148{,}500 + 0.48 \cdot \$250{,}000 &&\text{First find the exponent.} \\
&= \$268{,}500 &&\text{Then multiply, and finally add.}
\end{aligned}
$$

Total monthly sales are projected to be $268,500 for the month.

| 2.3 | **Exercises** |

In the following exercises a formula is given, along with the values of all but one of the variables in the formula. Find the value of the variable that is not given. Round to the nearest hundredth, if applicable.

1. $I = PRT$; $P = \$4600$, $R = 0.085$, $T = 1\frac{1}{2}$

2. $F = ma$; $m = 820$, $a = 12$

3. $P = B \times R$; $B = \$168{,}000$, $R = 0.06$

4. $B = \dfrac{P}{R}$; $P = \$1200$, $R = 0.08$

5. $s = c + m$; $c = \$14$, $m = \$2.50$

6. $m = s - c$; $s = \$24{,}200$, $c = \$2800$

7. $P = 2L + 2W$; $P = 40$, $W = 6$

8. $P = 2L + 2W$; $P = 340$; $L = 70$

9. $P = \dfrac{1}{RT}$; $T = 3$, $I = 540$, $R = 0.08$

10. $M = P(1 + RT)$; $R = 0.15$, $T = 2$, $M = 481$

11. $y = mx^2 + c$; $m = 3$, $x = 7$, $c = 4.2$

12. $C = \$5 + \$0.10N$; $N = 38$

13. $M = P(1 + i)^n$; $P = \$640$, $i = 0.02$, $n = 8$
14. $M = P(1 + i)^n$; $M = \$2400$, $i = 0.05$, $n = 4$

15. $E = mc^2$; $m = 7.5$, $c = 1$

16. $x = \dfrac{1}{2}at^2$; $t = 5$, $x = 150$

17. $A = \dfrac{1}{2}(b + B)h$; $A = 105$, $b = 19$, $B = 11$

18. $A = \dfrac{1}{2}(b + B)h$; $A = 70$, $b = 15$, $B = 20$

19. $P = \dfrac{S}{1 + RT}$; $S = 24{,}600$, $R = 0.06$, $T = \dfrac{5}{12}$

20. $P = \dfrac{S}{1 + RT}$; $S = 23{,}815$, $R = 0.09$, $T = \dfrac{11}{12}$

Solve each formula for the indicated variable.

21. $A = LW$; for L 22. $d = rt$; for t

23. $PV = nRT$; for V 24. $I = PRT$; for R

25. $M = P(1 + i)^n$; for P 26. $R(1 - DT) = D$; for R

27. $P = \dfrac{A}{1 + i}$; for i 28. $M = P(1 + RT)$; for R

29. $P = M(1 - DT)$; for D 30. $P = \dfrac{M}{1 + RT}$; for R

31. $A = \dfrac{1}{2}(b + B)h$; for h 32. $P = 2L + 2W$; for L

Solve the following application problems.

33. **CARNIVAL**   A carnival purchases 1800 stuffed animals to give to people who win at carnival games. Given a total cost of $4320, find the cost per stuffed animal.

34. **WEB PAGES**   A retailer paid $1305 to a college student who built and added 15 pages to the firm's Web site. Find the cost per Web page.

35. **MUSICAL INSTRUMENTS**   The Guitar Shoppe bought 6 sets of bongo drums and 7 Alvarez guitars for $2445.80. The guitars cost $269 apiece. Find the cost for a set of bongo drums.

36. **REFRIGERATORS**   An appliance store bought 8 large refrigerators and 10 washer/dryer combination sets. The store's cost for a washer/dryer was $462 and the total paid for all of the appliances was $10,860. Find the cost of a refrigerator.

37. **CLOTHING STORE**   The weekly salary for each salesperson at a clothing store is found using the formula $S = \$280 + 0.05x$, where x = employee's total sales for the week. Find the salary of two employees with the following weekly sales: **(a)** $2940 and **(b)** $4450.

38. **LENGTH OF AN INVESTMENT**   A principal (P) of $3500 invested over an unknown amount of time (T) at 9.5% $(R = 0.095)$ yields $748.13 in interest (I). Use $I = PRT$ to find the time rounded to the nearest hundredth of a year.

39. **COMPUTER CHIPS**   A computer chip manufacturer had net sales of $230 million with returns equal to $\dfrac{1}{40}$ of gross sales. Find gross sales rounded to the nearest million given that net sales equals gross sales less returns.

40. BRIDAL SHOP One month, the Bridal Shop had net sales of $33,000 and return(s) of $\frac{1}{12}$ of gross sales. If net sales equal gross sales minus returns, find gross sales.

41. MOVIES The manager of one theatre marks up the cost of chocolate-covered raisins by $\frac{3}{4}$ of the cost of the raisins. Find the cost to the nearest cent if the theatre sells the raisins for $4.00. (*Hint:* Selling price is cost plus markup.)

42. TEXTBOOK COSTS A college bookstore marks textbooks up by $\frac{1}{4}$ the cost of the book. Find the cost to the bookstore of a book it sells for $160, where selling price is cost plus markup.

43. PIZZA Last year, the expenses at Mack's Pizzeria were $\frac{5}{6}$ of the total revenue and the remainder was profit. The profit, or the total revenue less expenses, was $107,400. Find the total revenue.

44. COMPUTER SALES Computerworld has expenses that run $\frac{15}{16}$ of revenue. One month's profit (the difference between revenue and expenses) was $18,000. Find the revenue.

In Exercises 45–49, use the formula $I = PRT$ where $I = interest$ in dollars, $P = principal$ or loan amount, $R = interest\ rate$ written as a decimal, and $T = time$ in years.

45. FINDING INTEREST Find the interest if principal of $5200 is invested at $7\frac{1}{2}$% (or 0.075) for 1 year. ($I = PRT$)

46. LOAN TO AN UNCLE Ben Cross loaned $8000 to his uncle for 4 years and received $1920 in interest. Find the interest rate. ($I = PRT$)

47. AUTO PARTS STARTUP Terry Twitty made a $22,000 loan so that Melissa Graves could start an auto parts business. The loan was for 2 years, and interest was $5720. Find the rate of interest. ($I = PRT$)

48. FINDING TIME Fred Tausz loaned $39,000 to his sister. The loan was at 7% (or 0.07), with interest of $13,650. Find the time for the loan. ($I = PRT$)

49. STUDENT LOAN Joan Summers borrowed $5850 ($P$) from her brother to help pay for her last year in college. They agreed to an interest rate (R) of 3% and a final interest amount (I) of $702. Use $I = PRT$ to find the time of the loan.

In Exercises 50–54, $M = maturity\ value$ at the end of the loan, $P = principal$ or loan amount, $I = interest\ rate$ written as a decimal, $n = number\ of\ years,$ and $R = annual\ interest\ rate$ written as a decimal.

50. MATURITY VALUE Mary Scott invests $1000 at 8% (or 0.08) for 5 years. What maturity value M did Mary have in her account at the end of 5 years? $[M = P(1 + RT)]$

51. SAVING John Wood had $4560 in his retirement account after 2 years. If the account earned 7% (or 0.07), how much did John initially deposit in his account. $[M = P(1 + RT)]$

52. ANTIQUES Jan Reus borrowed $12,500 from her uncle to help start an antique shop. She repaid $14,750 exactly 2 years later. Find the interest rate. $[M = P(1 + RT)]$

53. LOAN AMOUNT Bill Abel paid a maturity value of $5989.50 on a 3-year note with annual interest of 10% (or 0.10). Use $M = P(1 + i)^n$, where n is the number of years in this problem, to solve for the amount borrowed.

54. INHERITANCE Maybelle Jackson inherited $8500 when her grandfather died. She placed the money in a bank certificate of deposit that paid 3.5% per year and planned to leave it there for 20 years until she retires. Use $M = P(1 + i)^n$ to solve for the maturity value.

 55. Write a step-by-step explanation of the procedure you would use to solve the equation $A = P + PRT$ for R. (See Objective 2.)

56. Formulas are used in business, physics, biology, chemistry, engineering, and many other fields. Why are formulas so commonly used? (See Objective 1.)

2.4	**Ratios and Proportions**

OBJECTIVES

1 *Define a ratio.*

2 *Set up a proportion.*

3 *Solve a proportion for any unknown value.*

4 *Use proportions to solve problems.*

Objective

1 *Define a Ratio.*   A **ratio** is a quotient of two quantities that is used to compare the quantities. The ratio of the number a to the number b is written in any of the following ways.

$$a \text{ to } b \qquad a : b \qquad \frac{a}{b}$$

This last way of writing a ratio is most common in algebra, and $a : b$ is perhaps most common in business. Read $a : b$ as "a is to b." Both quantities in a ratio should be in *the same units if possible*—that is, cents to cents or dollars to dollars, not dollars to cents. However, many ratios will not have the same units in the numerator and denominator, such as one involving a worker's pay of $9 per hour or a rate such as 45 miles per hour.

EXAMPLE **1** **Writing Ratios from Words**

Write a ratio in the form $\frac{a}{b}$ for each phrase. (Notice in each phrase that the number mentioned first always becomes the numerator.)

Solution

(a) The ratio of 3 women to 5 children is $\frac{3}{5}$.

(b) To find the ratio of $12 to 20 cents, first convert $12 to cents ($12 = 1200 cents), then write the ratio.

$$\frac{1200}{20} = \frac{60}{1} \qquad or \qquad 60 : 1$$

The exact same ratio results if you first convert 20 cents to $0.20 (dollars) and then work in dollars, as shown here.

$$\frac{12}{0.20} = \frac{60}{1} \qquad or \qquad 60 : 1$$

(c) General Motors car and truck sales fell from 1,900,000 units in 1929 to 525,000 units during 1932, the worst year of the Depression. Write unit sales as a ratio.

$$\frac{1,900,\cancel{000}}{525,\cancel{000}} = \frac{1900}{525} = \frac{76}{21}$$

$\hookrightarrow$ Cancel matching final zeros.

(d) A dairy farmer received $650 for 5000 pounds of milk. Write this as a ratio.

$$\frac{650}{5000} = \frac{13}{100} \qquad or \qquad \$13 \text{ per 100 pounds}$$

NOTE   As done in Example 1(b), always change the numbers to the same units before writing as a ratio.

Objective

2 *Set Up a Proportion.* A ratio is used to compare two numbers or amounts. A **proportion** says that two ratios are equal, as in the following example.

$$\frac{3}{4} = \frac{15}{20}$$

The ratios $\frac{a}{b}$ and $\frac{c}{d}$ are said to form a proportion if $\frac{a}{b} = \frac{c}{d}$. This can be determined by multiplying both sides of the equation by the product of the two denominators.

$$\frac{a}{b} = \frac{c}{d}$$

$$bd \cdot \frac{a}{b} = bd \cdot \frac{c}{d} \quad \text{Multiply both sides by } bd.$$

$$ad = bc$$

Therefore, $\frac{a}{b} = \frac{c}{d}$ if, and only if, $ad = bc$. This is referred to as the **method of cross products.**

$$\frac{a}{b} \bowtie \frac{c}{d}$$

is equivalent to $ad = bc$.

NOTE The numbers in a proportion need not be whole numbers.

EXAMPLE 2 **Determining True Proportions**

Decide if the following proportions are true.

(a) $\dfrac{3}{4} = \dfrac{25}{30}$ (b) $\dfrac{6.5}{\frac{3}{4}} = \dfrac{130}{15}$

Solution

(a) Find each cross product.

$$\frac{3}{4} \bowtie \frac{25}{30}$$

$$3 \cdot 30 = 4 \cdot 25$$

$$90 \neq 100 \quad \text{The symbol } \neq \text{ means "not equal."}$$

Since the cross products are not equal, the proportion is false.

(b) Find each cross product.

$$\frac{6.5}{\frac{3}{4}} \bowtie \frac{130}{15}$$

$$6.5 \cdot 15 = \frac{3}{4} \cdot 130$$

$$97.5 = 0.75 \cdot 130$$

$$97.5 = 97.5$$

The proportion is true.

Objective
_____

3 *Solve a Proportion for Any Unknown Value.* Four numbers are used in a proportion. If *any* three of these numbers are known, *the fourth can be found.*

EXAMPLE 3 **Finding Unknown Values in a Proportion**

Find the unknown that makes each proportion true.

(a) $\dfrac{4}{9} = \dfrac{36}{x}$ **(b)** $\dfrac{3.4}{12} = \dfrac{z}{96}$

Solution

(a) Set the cross products equal to one another, then solve the resulting equation.

$$4 \cdot x = 9 \cdot 36$$
$$4x = 324$$
$$\frac{4x}{4} = \frac{324}{4} \qquad \text{Divide by 4.}$$
$$x = 81$$

Check by confirming that $\dfrac{4}{9}$ does equal $\dfrac{36}{81}$.

(b) Set the cross products equal to one another.

$$3.4 \cdot 96 = 12 \cdot z$$
$$326.4 = 12z$$
$$\frac{326.4}{12} = \frac{12z}{12} \qquad \text{Divide by 12.}$$
$$27.2 = z$$

Objective
_____

4 *Use Proportions to Solve Problems.* Proportions are used in many practical applications, including the following.

EXAMPLE 4 **Foreign Currency Exchange**

While in Mexico on an exchange trip, Laura Axtell needed to exchange $75 U.S. for Mexican pesos. If $1 U.S. is equivalent to 11 Mexican pesos, how many pesos will she receive?

Solution Set the problem up as a proportion and solve for the unknown.

$$\frac{\text{U.S. \$1}}{11 \text{ Mexican pesos}} = \frac{\text{U.S.\$75}}{x \text{ Mexican pesos}}$$
$$1 \cdot x = 11 \times 75$$
$$x = 825$$

Axtell will receive 825 Mexican pesos.

EXAMPLE 5 **Solving Applications**

A hospital charges a patient $117 for 12 capsules. How much will it charge for 18 capsules?

Solution Let x be the cost of 18 capsules. Set up a proportion: one ratio in the proportion can involve the number of capsules, while the other ratio can use the costs. Make sure that corresponding numbers appear in the numerator and the denominator. Use this pattern.

$$\frac{\text{Capsules}}{\text{Capsules}} = \frac{\text{cost}}{\text{cost}}$$

Now substitute the given information.

$$\frac{12}{18} = \frac{\$117}{x}$$

Use cross products to solve the proportion.

$$12x = 18(\$117)$$
$$12x = \$2106$$
$$x = \$175.50$$

The 18 capsules will cost $175.50.

NOTE In Example 5, you can also arrange the proportion as follows.

$$\frac{\text{cost}}{\text{capsule}} = \frac{\text{cost}}{\text{capsule}} \quad \text{or as} \quad \frac{\$117}{12 \text{ capsules}} = \frac{x}{18 \text{ capsules}}$$

EXAMPLE 6 **Solving Applications**

A firm in Hong Kong and one in Thailand agree to jointly develop a controller chip to be sold to North American auto manufacturers. They agree to split the development costs in a ratio of $8:3$ (Hong Kong firm to Thailand firm), resulting in a cost of $9,400,000 to the Hong Kong firm. Find the cost to the Thailand firm.

Solution Let x represent the cost to the Thailand firm, then

$$\frac{8}{3} = \frac{9,400,000}{x}$$
$$8x = 3 \cdot 9,400,000 \quad \text{Cross multiply.}$$
$$8x = 28,200,000$$
$$x = 3,525,000 \quad \text{Divide by 8.}$$

The Thailand firm's share of the costs is $3,525,000.

EXAMPLE 7 **Solving Applications**

Bill Thomas wishes to estimate the amount of timber on some forested land that he owns. One value he needs to estimate is the average height of the trees. One morning, Thomas notices that his own 6-foot body casts an 8-foot shadow at the same time that a tree casts a 34-foot shadow. Find the height of the tree.

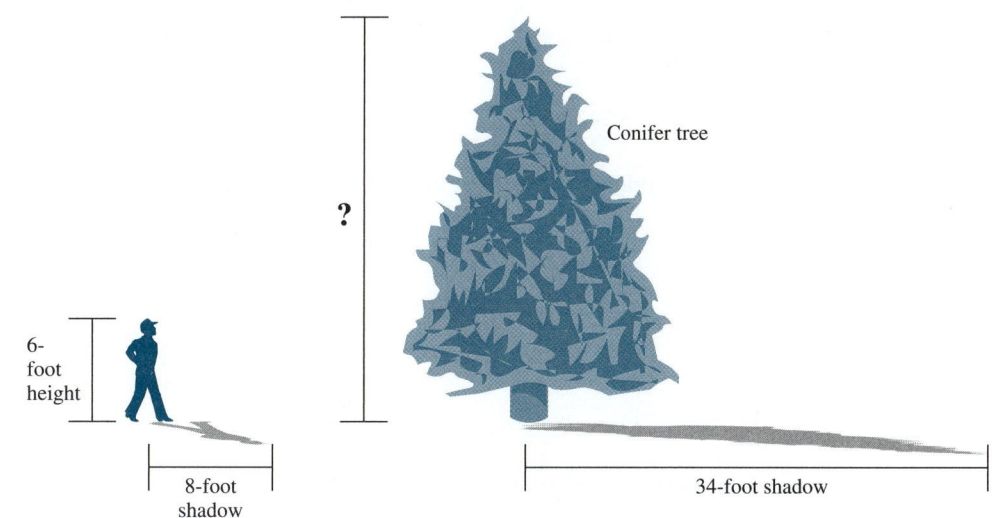

Conifer tree

?

6-foot height

8-foot shadow

34-foot shadow

Solution   Set up a proportion in which the height of the tree is given the variable name x. Set up the ratios as height to length of shadow. All numbers are in feet.

$$\frac{6}{8} = \frac{x}{34}$$

$$6 \cdot 34 = 8 \cdot x \qquad \text{Cross multiply.}$$

$$\frac{204}{8} = \frac{8 \cdot x}{8} \qquad \text{Divide by 8.}$$

$$x = 25.5 \text{ feet}$$

Bill Thomas estimates that the tree is 25.5 feet tall.

2.4	**Exercises**

Write the following ratios. Write each ratio in lowest terms.

1. 18 kilometers to 64 kilometers

2. 18 defects out of 580 items

3. 216 students to 8 faculty

4. $80 in returns to $8360 in sales

5. 8 men to 6 women

6. 12 feet to 1 inch

7. 30 kilometers (30,000 meters) to 8 meters

8. 30 inches to 5 yards

9. 90 dollars to 40 cents

10. 148 minutes to 4 hours

11. 4 dollars to 10 quarters

12. 35 dimes to 6 dollars

13. 20 hours to 5 days

14. 6 days to 9 hours

15. $0.80 to $3

16. $1.20 to $0.75

17. $3.24 to $0.72

18. $3.57 to $0.42

Decide whether the following proportions are true or false.

19. $\dfrac{3}{5} = \dfrac{21}{35}$

20. $\dfrac{6}{13} = \dfrac{30}{65}$

21. $\dfrac{9}{7} = \dfrac{720}{480}$

22. $\dfrac{54}{14} = \dfrac{270}{70}$

23. $\dfrac{69}{320} = \dfrac{7}{102}$

24. $\dfrac{17}{19} = \dfrac{72}{84}$

25. $\dfrac{19}{32} = \dfrac{33}{77}$

26. $\dfrac{19}{30} = \dfrac{57}{90}$

27. $\dfrac{110}{18} = \dfrac{160}{27}$

28. $\dfrac{46}{17} = \dfrac{212}{95}$

29. $\dfrac{32}{75} = \dfrac{61}{108}$

30. $\dfrac{28}{75} = \dfrac{224}{600}$

31. $\dfrac{7.6}{10} = \dfrac{76}{100}$

32. $\dfrac{95}{64} = \dfrac{320}{217}$

33. $\dfrac{2\frac{1}{4}}{5} = \dfrac{9}{20}$

34. $\dfrac{\frac{3}{4}}{80} = \dfrac{\frac{9}{8}}{120}$

35. $\dfrac{4\frac{1}{5}}{6\frac{1}{8}} = \dfrac{27}{41}$

36. $\dfrac{1\frac{1}{2}}{12} = \dfrac{5\frac{1}{4}}{42}$

37. $\dfrac{8.15}{2.03} = \dfrac{61.125}{15.225}$

38. $\dfrac{423.88}{17.119} = \dfrac{330.6264}{13.35282}$

Solve the following proportions.

39. $\dfrac{x}{15} = \dfrac{49}{105}$

40. $\dfrac{y}{35} = \dfrac{27}{315}$

41. $\dfrac{6}{9} = \dfrac{r}{108}$

42. $\dfrac{16}{41} = \dfrac{112}{t}$

43. $\dfrac{63}{s} = \dfrac{3}{5}$

44. $\dfrac{260}{390} = \dfrac{x}{3}$

45. $\dfrac{1}{2} = \dfrac{r}{7}$

46. $\dfrac{2}{3} = \dfrac{5}{s}$

47. $\dfrac{\frac{3}{4}}{6} = \dfrac{3}{x}$

48. $\dfrac{3}{x} = \dfrac{11}{9}$

49. $\dfrac{12}{p} = \dfrac{23.571}{15.714}$

50. $\dfrac{86.112}{57.408} = \dfrac{k}{15}$

51. Explain the difference between ratio and proportion. (See Objective 2.)

52. Explain cross products using the rules of algebra. (See Objective 2.)

Solve the following application problems.

53. **TICKET SALES**   One Ticketmaster outlet sold 350 rock-concert tickets in 2 days. At that rate, find the number of tickets it can expect to sell in 9 days.

54. **BLOOD CELLS**   A 170-pound person has about 30 trillion blood cells. Estimate the number of blood cells in a 140-pound person to the nearest tenth of a trillion.

55. **REAL ESTATE DEVELOPMENT**   Mike George paid $215,000 for a very nice 5-unit apartment house. Find the cost for a 12-unit apartment house.

56. **TIGER FOOD**   A 450-pound circus tiger eats 15 pounds of meat per day. How many pounds of meat would you expect a 360-pound tiger to eat per day?

57. **SEWING**   If 22 children's dresses cost $660, what is the cost of 12 dresses?

58. **BISCUITS**   A biscuit recipe that feeds 7 requires 2 cups of flour. How much flour is needed for enough biscuits to feed a church group of 125? Round to the nearest whole number.

59. GLOBAL WARMING The concentration of carbon dioxide in the atmosphere has increased from 315 parts per million to 380 parts per million in the past 48 years. During the same period of time, the global average temperature increased by 1° Fahrenheit. Estimate the amount of further increase in global average temperature to the nearest tenth of a degree if the concentration of carbon dioxide in the atmosphere increases from 380 parts per million up to 550 parts per million.

60. FERTILIZER COVERAGE Suppose that 7 sacks of fertilizer cover 3325 square feet at a rose farm. Find the number of sacks needed for 7125 square feet.

61. MAP READING The distance between two cities on a road map is 2 inches. Actually, the cities are 120 miles apart. The distance between two other cities is 17 inches. How far apart are these cities?

62. WOMEN'S CLOTHING SHOP Martha Vinn opened a women's clothing shop and had sales of $3720 during the first 3 weeks. At that rate, estimate sales for the first 4 weeks.

63. SALES OF HEALTH FOOD Natural Harvest had sales of $274,312 for the first 20 weeks of the year. Estimate sales for the entire 52-week year.

64. PARTNERSHIP PROFITS Chester and Gaines have a partnership agreement that calls for profits to be paid in the ratio of 2 : 5, respectively. Find the amount that goes to Chester if Gaines receives $45,000.

65. OIL PROFITS The two partners in Alamo Energy agreed to split profits in a ratio of 3 : 8. If the first partner received $48,000 in profits one year, find the profit earned by the second partner.

66. PRODUCTION EMPLOYEES The owner of a factory has always kept the ratio of salespeople to production employees at 2 : 7. If she currently has 24 salespeople, how many production employees are there?

67. SONGBIRD MIGRATION Small songbirds in one area migrate at about 20 miles per hour, whereas eider ducks migrate at 35 miles per hour. How far would the eider ducks migrate in the same amount of time it would take songbirds to migrate 200 miles?

68. ISLAND AREA Indonesia has an area of 741,101 square miles and is made up of 13,677 islands. Assume the United States, with an area of 3,618,770 square miles, were similarly broken up into islands. How many islands would there be (to the nearest whole number)?

69. ICEBERG VOLUME Seven-eighths of an iceberg is below the water since icebergs are made up of freshwater, which is not as dense as seawater. Find the amount of an iceberg that is under water if the amount above water has a volume of 500,000 cubic meters. (*Hint:* $1 - \frac{7}{8} = \frac{1}{8}$ above water.)

70. AUTO PRODUCTION An auto plant produces 3 red sports models for every 7 blue family models. Find the number of red sports models produced if the plant produces 868 blue family models.

71. JAPANESE YEN Benjamin Lopez was in Japan for 2 months on a business trip. Find the number of U.S. dollars he will receive for 20,355 Japanese yen if $1 U.S. can be exchanged for 95 yen. Round to the nearest cent.

72. WORKING IN CHINA Gina Harden was offered a job as a teacher at an elite private high school in Beijing at an annual salary of 471,200 yuan. Find the salary in U.S. dollars if 7.25 yuan can be exchanged for $1 U.S.

CHAPTER TERMS

Review the following terms to test your understanding of the chapter. For each term you do not know, refer to the page number found next to that term.

addition rule [p. 37]
coefficient [p. 37]
distributive property [p. 41]
equation [p. 37]
expression [p. 37]

formulas [p. 50]
left side [p. 37]
like terms [p. 40]
method of cross products [p. 58]
multiplication rule [p. 37]

proportion [p. 57]
ratio [p. 57]
reciprocal [p. 39]
right side [p. 37]
similar terms [p. 40]

solution [p. 37]
substitution [p. 37]
term [p. 37]
variable [p. 37]

CONCEPTS	EXAMPLES

2.1 Solving equations

1. Remove all parentheses on each side of the equation using the distributive property.
2. Combine all like terms on each side of the equation.
3. **Addition Rule** Add to or subtract from both sides whatever is needed to produce a term with the variable on one side and a number on the other side.
4. **Multiplication Rule** Multiply or divide the variable term by whatever is needed to produce a term with a coefficient of 1. Multiply or divide the number term on the other side by the same quantity.

$$12(y + 2) = 84$$
$$12y + 24 = 84 \qquad \text{Use distributive rule.}$$
$$12y + 24 - 24 = 84 - 24 \quad \text{Subtract 24 from both sides.}$$
$$12y = 60 \qquad \text{Simplify.}$$
$$y = 5 \qquad \text{Divide both sides by 12.}$$

2.2 Translating phrases

Use mathematical symbols to represent verbal expressions.

6 times a number plus 3: $6x + 3$

14 minus $2\frac{1}{2}$ times a number: $14 - 2\frac{1}{2}y$

2.2 Solving applied problems

1. **First, read the problem very carefully**. Reread the problem to make sure that its meaning is clear. Sometimes a sketch helps.
2. **Identify the unknown** and give it a variable name such as x. If possible, write other unknowns as mathematical expressions in terms of the same variable.
3. **Write an equation** describing the relationship given in the problem.
4. **Solve the equation.**
5. **Answer the question(s)** asked in the problem.
6. **Check the solution** using the *original* words of the problem.
7. **Be sure your answer is reasonable.**

A committee had 7 fewer men than women. The total number of people on the committee was 19. Find the number of women.
Let x represent the number of women.

$$x + (x - 7) = 19$$
$$2x - 7 = 19$$
$$2x = 26$$
$$x = 13 \text{ women}$$

Check the answer.

$$13 + (13 - 7) \overset{?}{=} 19$$
$$19 = 19$$

The answer checks.

2.3	**Evaluating formulas for given values of the variable**	Use $I = PRT$ with $P = \$10{,}500$, $R = 9\%$, or 0.09, and $T = \frac{3}{4}$ year to find interest (I).

Substitute numerical values for variables and evaluate.

$$I = PRT$$

$$I = 10{,}500 \cdot 0.09 \cdot \frac{3}{4}$$

$$= \$708.75$$

2.3	**Solving formulas for a specific variable**	Solve $M = P + PRT$ for T.

Use the rules for solving equations.

$$M = P + PRT$$

$$M - P = PRT \qquad \text{Subtract } P \text{ from both sides.}$$

$$\frac{M - P}{PR} = T \qquad \text{Divide both sides by } PR.$$

2.3	**Working with exponents**	Find 6^4.

The exponent tells how many times a number is to be multiplied by itself.

$$6^4 = 6 \cdot 6 \cdot 6 \cdot 6$$

$$= 1296$$

2.4	**Solving a proportion for a missing part**	Find x in the proportion.

Use the principle of cross products and solve the resulting equation.

$$\frac{a}{b} = \frac{c}{d} \text{ if } a \cdot d = b \cdot c$$

$$\frac{5}{x} \diagup\!\!\!\!\diagdown \frac{35}{63}$$

$$5 \cdot 63 = 35x \qquad \text{Cross products.}$$

$$315 = 35x$$

$$9 = x$$

2.4	**Using proportions to solve problems**	A retail store charges \$20 to rent 5 movies. How much does it charge for 8 movies?

Set up the proportion, use the principle of cross products, and solve the resulting equation.

$$\frac{20}{5} = \frac{x}{8}$$

$$20 \cdot 8 = 5 \cdot x$$

$$160 = 5x$$

$$32 = x$$

It charges \$32 for 8 movies.

The answer section includes answers to all Review Exercises.

Solve each equation. [2.1]

1. $x + 45 = 96$

2. $r - 36 = 14.7$

3. $8t + 45 = 175.4$

4. $4t - 6 = 15$

5. $\dfrac{s}{6} = 42$

6. $\dfrac{5z}{8} = 85$

7. $\dfrac{m}{4} - 5 = 9$

8. $5(x - 3) = 3(x + 4)$

9. $6y = 2y + 28$

10. $3r - 7 = 2(4 - 3r)$

11. $0.15(2x - 3) = 5.85$

12. $0.6(y - 3) = 0.1y$

Write a mathematical expression. Use x as the variable. [2.2]

13. Ninety-four times a number

14. One half times a number

15. Six times a number is added to the number

16. Five times a number is decreased by 11

17. The sum of 3 times a number and 7

Solve the following application problems. [2.2]

18. Molly Videtto wishes to purchase 3 CDs at $14.95 each and a Liz Claiborne sweater for $95. Given that she has $47.50, find the additional amount she needs. (Ignore taxes.)

19. The owner of 3 bicycle stores has found that profits *(P)* are related to advertising *(A)* according to $P = 18.5A + 4.5$, where all figures are in thousands of dollars. How much must she spend on advertising in order to obtain a quarterly profit of $60,000?

20. Phone and water bills together cost a company $540 for March. If the phone bill costs 4 times as much as the water bill, find each.

21. Five more than $\frac{1}{4}$ of the employees of a company have 25 years or more of service. If 24 employees have 25 or more years of service, how many employees does the company have?

22. The local movie theater sold 100 tickets for $780. If children's tickets cost $6 and adult tickets $12, how many of each were sold?

Use the formula to find the value of the variable that is not given. [2.3]

23. $I = PRT;\ I = \$960,\ R = 0.12,\ T = 2$

24. $M = P(1 + RT);\ M = \$3770,\ R = 0.04,\ T = 4$

25. $M = P(1 + i)^n;\ M = \$14{,}526.80,\ i = 0.1,\ n = 6$

Solve the equation for the variable indicated. [2.3]

26. $I = PRT$; for R

27. $M = P(1 + RT)$; for T

28. $B = PR$; for P

Write the following ratios and simplify. [2.4]

29. $17 to 50 cents

30. 9 days to 12 hours

31. $5000 to $250

32. 3 years to 15 months

33. $2 to 75 cents

Solve the following proportions. [2.4]

34. $\dfrac{v}{14} = \dfrac{27}{126}$

35. $\dfrac{5}{y} = \dfrac{20}{27}$

36. $\dfrac{3}{8} = \dfrac{z}{12}$

37. $\dfrac{6}{11} = \dfrac{90}{t}$

38. $\dfrac{20}{r} = \dfrac{60}{72}$

Solve the following application problems. [2.4]

39. Bass in a lake are sampled for a particular parasite; 14 of 60 bass have the parasite. Given that there are an estimated 18,400 bass in the lake, find the number with parasites. Round to the nearest whole number.

40. A college student majoring in petroleum engineering worked on an oil-drilling site. She noticed a down-hole pressure of 3220 pounds per square inch at 6700 feet below the surface. Estimate the pressure at the 9850-foot total depth of the well to the nearest pound per square inch. Assume that the ratio of pressure to depth does not change with different depths.

41. Last year, a shelter purchased 5760 pounds of beef to feed its 120 inhabitants. Find the total amount of beef needed next year if the manager anticipates 138 inhabitants.

42. John proofreads 7 pages in 12 minutes. How many pages does he proofread in 3 hours?

43. A company makes pension contributions of $89,391 per quarter for its 83 employees. It anticipates a merger that will bring in another 21 employees, and managers plan to give them the same average pension. Find the new quarterly pension contribution required.

44. If 8 shirts cost $223.20, how much would 5 shirts cost?

45. DVDs in a discount store average $12.78 each, including sales tax. Maria Timons received $36.10 in change from a $100 bill. Find the number of DVDs she bought.

CHAPTER 2	**Business Application Case #1**
	Breakeven in Retail

The average selling price of a book at Discount Books is $24.80. Typically, just $\frac{7}{10}$ of this amount goes to pay for the cost of the book, including shipping and handling. Monthly expenses at Discount Books are:

Salaries with benefits	$8500 includes owner's salary
Rent and utilities	$2100
Janitorial	$350
Other	$1620

These definitions may help you:

> *Gross revenue* is the total of all revenue from all sales.
> *Breakeven* is the point at which total revenues equals cost of goods sold plus total expenses.
> *Profit, or net profit,* is the amount left over after all expenses have been paid.
> *Percents* are parts out of 100, so $\frac{7}{10}$ is 70 parts out of 100 equal parts, or 70%.

(a) Find the total monthly expenses.

(b) If $\frac{7}{10}$ of the revenues is used to pay for books, what fraction of the revenue remains?

(c) Write an equation for monthly net profit. Net profit is gross revenue from the sale of books less monthly expenses. Use N for the number of books sold in a month.

(d) How many books must the store sell to break even? Round to the nearest whole number.

(e) What happens if the store does not sell enough books to break even one month?

(f) How many books must the store sell to reach a profit of $6000 over and above all expenses in a month? Round to the nearest whole number.

CHAPTER 2	# Business Application Case #2
	### *Expanding the Number of Stores*

McDonald's (see www.mcdonalds.com) is a successful company that has stores (restaurants) in more than 100 countries. In fact, managers predict that at some point in the future as much as 80% of company profits will be from countries other than the United States. In 2010, the chain had about 26,000 stores, and managers expect total revenue of over $25 billion. Now that is a lot of hamburgers, or actually veggie burgers in India! Most people in India are vegetarians, so when McDonald's goes to India the menus are radically changed.

(a) Estimate the average sales per store to the nearest dollar.

(b) Use the average sales per store found in part (a) and write an algebraic expression for total revenue if managers add N stores next year. Assume that average sales for all of the stores remain the same and that none of the stores are closed.

(c) Estimate revenue for McDonald's if the revenue is increased by $\frac{1}{5}$ in 2 years.

(d) List the pros and cons of working at a fast-food restaurant such as McDonald's. Why might upper management not want to hire someone to manage a store unless he or she has worked in one?

Percent

The word **percent** means "parts out of one hundred." Percents are often used to compare different amounts. They are used daily in newspapers, on the Internet, and in business. One example of the use of percents is shown in Figure 3.1, which shows the monthly and annual growth rate in sales at retail stores in the United States. The vertical shaded bars in Figure 3.1 show the percent change in total retail sales for a month compared to the previous month. The percent is shown by the scale on the left side of the figure. The monthly data are difficult to understand because a month with an increase in retail sales is often followed by a month with a decrease in retail sales. In other words, there is a lot of **variability** in the monthly data.

As a result, Figure 3.1 also shows the percent increase or decrease in annual retail sales, as shown by the blue line graph at the top of the figure. Read the change in the growth of annual retail sales using the scale on the right-hand side of the chart. Notice that the line graph is much easier to interpret than the monthly vertical bars, since there is less variability in the data. The line graph shows that annual retail sales were growing rapidly, at 8% in 2000. But the growth in annual sales slowed to about 5% per year during 2001–2003 following the destruction of the World Trade Center in New York. The annual growth in retail sales went back up to over 5% per year during 2004–2006, but fell sharply at the end of 2008. In fact, annual retail sales actually shrank in 2009 compared to a year earlier as consumers became very worried about the effects of the financial crisis that began in 2007.

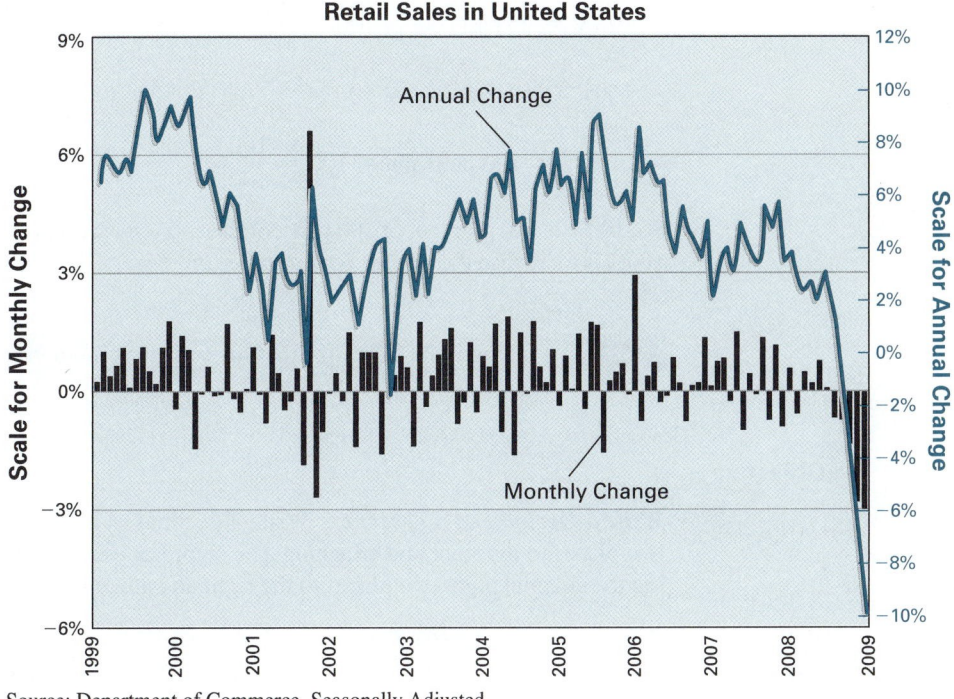

Source: Department of Commerce, Seasonally Adjusted

Figure 3.1

STOP
and think

Imagine that you are a manager at your favorite retail store. Explain the meaning of the data in Figure 3.1 in terms of possible effects on your business, especially retail sales in 2009. Think in terms of salaries, company profits, inventory, and whether the company will be hiring or laying off employees.

Many of the topics in the following chapters of this book use percents. As a result, it is very important for you to understand the material in this chapter fully and to work many of the exercises. Taking the time to learn this material well and working exercises will help you throughout the remainder of this course and in your future career. Think of working the exercises as similar to *working out at a gym* to prepare your body for your favorite sport. However, you are preparing your mind by working exercises.

3.1	Writing Decimals and Fractions as Percents

OBJECTIVES

1 *Write a decimal as a percent.*

2 *Write a fraction or mixed number as a percent.*

3 *Write a percent as a decimal.*

4 *Write a percent as a fraction.*

5 *Write a fractional percent as a decimal.*

Percents represent parts of a whole, just as fractions or decimals do. **Percents** are **hundredths**, or parts of a hundred. "One percent" means 1 of 100 parts. Percents are written with a percent sign, %. For example:

$$25\% = 25 \text{ parts out of } 100 = \frac{25}{100}$$

$$50\% = 50 \text{ parts out of } 100 = \frac{50}{100}$$

$$100\% = 100 \text{ parts out of } 100 = \frac{100}{100}$$

So, 100% is 100 parts out of 100 parts, or the entire (or whole) amount. Any percent greater than 100% is more than the whole. For example, 250% is 250 parts out of 100, or 2.5 times the whole.

NOTE It is important to realize that the % sign is *not* a variable.

Objective

1 *Write a Decimal as a Percent.* Write a decimal as a percent by moving the decimal point two places to the right and attaching a % sign. For example, write 0.75 as a percent by moving the decimal point two places to the right and attaching a % sign, giving 75% as the result.

Decimal	*Percent*
0.75 (0.75.)	75% ← Attach a percent sign.

↑ 2 places to the right

EXAMPLE 1 **Changing Decimals to Percents**

When completing some market research you must express your findings as percents. Write the following decimals as percents.

(a) 0.25   **(b)** 0.38   **(c)** 0.65

Solution   Move the decimal point two places to the right and attach a percent sign.

(a) 25%   **(b)** 38%   **(c)** 65%

If there is nothing in the hundredths position, place zeros to the right of the number to hold the hundredths position. For example, the decimal 0.5 is expressed as 50%, and the number 1.2 is 120%.

$$0.5 = 0.50. = 50\% \qquad 1.2 = 1.20. = 120\%$$

⬆ — Attach a zero.   ⬆ — Attach a zero.

NOTE   Another method of changing a decimal to a percent is to multiply the decimal by 100%. For example,

$$0.25 \times 100\% = 25\% \qquad 0.5 \times 100\% = 50\% \qquad 1.2 \times 100\% = 120\%$$

EXAMPLE 2 **Writing Decimals as Percents**

Write the following decimals as percents.

(a) 0.7   **(b)** 1.3   **(c)** 0.1   **(d)** 3

Solution   Attach zeros to the right side of each number before moving the decimal point two places to the right and adding a % sign.

(a) 70%   **(b)** 130%   **(c)** 10%   **(d)** 300%

If the decimal extends farther than the hundredths position, the resulting percent includes decimal parts of whole percents.

EXAMPLE 3 **Writing Decimals as Percents**

When reading a newsletter, an auto parts manager sees the following decimals. Write these decimals as percents.

(a) 0.857   **(b)** 0.0057   **(c)** 0.0025

Solution

(a) 85.7%   **(b)** 0.57%   **(c)** 0.25%

NOTE   In Example 3 both (b) and (c) are less than 1%; they are decimal parts of 1%.

Objective

2   *Write a Fraction or Mixed Number as a Percent.*   There are two ways to write a fraction as a percent. One way is to first convert the fraction to a decimal, as explained in **Section 1.3**. For example, to express the fraction $\frac{2}{5}$ as a percent, write $\frac{2}{5}$ as a decimal by dividing 2 by 5. Then write the decimal as a percent.

Fraction	*Decimal*	*Percent*
$\frac{2}{5}$	0.4	40%

EXAMPLE 4   **Writing Fractions and Mixed Numbers as Percents**

An advertising account representative is given the following data in fraction form and must change the data to percent.

(a) $\frac{1}{4}$ **(b)** $\frac{3}{5}$ **(c)** $\frac{7}{8}$ **(d)** $1\frac{3}{4}$ **(e)** $1\frac{2}{3}$

Solution   First write each as a decimal. Then write the decimal as a percent.

(a) $\frac{1}{4} = 0.25 = 25\%$ **(b)** $\frac{3}{5} = 0.6 = 60\%$ **(c)** $\frac{7}{8} = 0.875 = 87.5\%$

(d) $1\frac{3}{4} = 1.75 = 175\%$ **(e)** $1\frac{2}{3} = 1.667$ (rounded) $= 166.7\%$

A second way to write a fraction as a percent is to multiply the fraction by 100%. For example, write the fraction $\frac{2}{5}$ as a percent by multiplying $\frac{2}{5}$ by 100%.

$$\frac{2}{5} = \frac{2}{5} \times 100\% = \frac{200\%}{5} = 40\%$$

EXAMPLE 5   **Writing Fractions and Mixed Numbers as Percents**

Write the following fractions as percents.

(a) $\frac{3}{4}$ **(b)** $\frac{1}{3}$ **(c)** $\frac{5}{8}$ **(d)** $1\frac{1}{2}$ **(e)** $2\frac{1}{3}$

Solution   Write as percents by multiplying each by 100%.

(a) $\frac{3}{4} \times 100\% = 75\%$ **(b)** $\frac{1}{3} \times 100\% = 33.3\%$ (rounded)   **(c)** $\frac{5}{8} \times 100\% = 62.5\%$

(d) $1\frac{1}{2} \times 100\% = 150\%$ **(e)** $2\frac{1}{3} \times 100\% = 233.3\%$ (rounded)

Objective

3   *Write a Percent as a Decimal.*   Write a percent as a decimal by moving the decimal point two places to the left and dropping the percent sign. For example, 50% becomes 0.50 or 0.5, 100% becomes 1, and 352% becomes 3.52.

EXAMPLE 6   **Writing Percents as Decimals**

To calculate some insurance claims an insurance agent must change the following percents to decimals.

(a) 25%   **(b)** 142%   **(c)** $37\frac{1}{2}\%$ (*Hint:* $37\frac{1}{2}\% = 37.5\%$)

Solution   Move the decimal point two places to the left and drop the percent sign.

(a) 0.25   **(b)** 1.42   **(c)** 0.375

> **NOTE** Another method of changing a percent to a decimal number is to divide by 100%. For example,
>
> $$25\% \div 100\% = 0.25 \qquad 142\% \div 100\% = 1.42 \qquad 37.5\% \div 100\% = 0.375.$$

Objective

4 *Write a Percent as a Fraction.* Write a percent as a fraction by first changing the percent to a decimal. Then write the decimal as a fraction in lowest terms.

EXAMPLE 7 Writing Percents as Fractions

The table below has data from the American Red Cross, an organization that helps people in times of need, such as after hurricanes, floods, and tornadoes. Convert each percent to a fraction and reduce the fraction to its lowest term.

Are People Ready for Disasters?

People along the Gulf Coast
who have:

(a) Disaster supply kits	28%
(b) Evacuation plans	36%
(c) First aid or CPR training	40%

Source: Data from American Red Cross.

Solution First write each as a decimal. Then convert to a fraction and reduce if possible.

(a) $28\% = 0.28 = \dfrac{28}{100} = \dfrac{7}{25}$ **(b)** $36\% = 0.36 = \dfrac{36}{100} = \dfrac{9}{25}$

(c) $40\% = 0.40 = \dfrac{40}{100} = \dfrac{2}{5}$

Objective

5 *Write a Fractional Percent as a Decimal.* A fractional percent such as $\frac{1}{2}\%$ has a value less than 1%. In fact, $\frac{1}{2}\%$ is equal to $\frac{1}{2}$ of 1%. Write a fractional percent as a decimal by first changing the fraction to a decimal, leaving the percent sign. For example, first write $\frac{1}{2}\%$ as 0.5%. Then write 0.5% as a decimal by moving the decimal point two places to the left and dropping the percent sign.

$$\frac{1}{2}\% = 0.5\% = 0.005$$
$$\quad\quad\quad \uparrow\!\!\text{—— Written as decimal}$$

EXAMPLE 8 Writing Fractional Percents as Decimals

Write each fractional percent as a decimal.

(a) $\frac{1}{5}\%$ **(b)** $\frac{3}{4}\%$ **(c)** $1\frac{1}{8}\%$

Solution Begin by writing the fraction as a decimal.

(a) $\frac{1}{5}\% = 0.2\% = 0.002$

(b) $\frac{3}{4}\% = 0.75\% = 0.0075$

(c) $1\frac{1}{8}\% = 1.125\% = 0.01125$

> **NOTE** When writing a fractional percent as a decimal, first, change the fraction to a decimal, leaving the percent sign. Then move the decimal point two places to the left and drop the percent sign.

The following chart shows many fractions, as well as their decimal and percent equivalents. **It is helpful to memorize the more commonly used ones.**

FRACTION, DECIMAL, AND PERCENT EQUIVALENTS

$\frac{1}{100} = 0.01 = 1\%$	$\frac{9}{16} = 0.5625 = 56.25\%$ or $56\frac{1}{4}\%$
$\frac{1}{50} = 0.02 = 2\%$	$\frac{3}{5} = 0.6 = 60\%$
$\frac{1}{25} = 0.04 = 4\%$	$\frac{5}{8} = 0.625 = 62.5\%$ or $62\frac{1}{2}\%$
$\frac{1}{20} = 0.05 = 5\%$	$\frac{2}{3} = 0.666\overline{6} = 66\frac{2}{3}\%$
$\frac{1}{16} = 0.0625 = 6.25\%$ or $6\frac{1}{4}\%$	$\frac{11}{16} = 0.6875 = 68.75\%$ or $68\frac{3}{4}\%$
$\frac{1}{12} = 0.083\overline{3} = 8\frac{1}{3}\%$	$\frac{7}{10} = 0.7 = 70\%$
$\frac{1}{10} = 0.1 = 10\%$	$\frac{3}{4} = 0.75 = 75\%$
$\frac{1}{9} = 0.111\overline{1} = 11\frac{1}{9}\%$	$\frac{4}{5} = 0.8 = 80\%$
$\frac{1}{8} = 0.125 = 12.5\%$ or $12\frac{1}{2}\%$	$\frac{13}{16} = 0.8125 = 81.25\%$ or $81\frac{1}{4}\%$
$\frac{1}{7} = 0.1428 = 14\frac{2}{7}\%$	$\frac{5}{6} = 0.833\overline{3} = 83\frac{1}{3}\%$
$\frac{1}{6} = 0.166\overline{6} = 16\frac{2}{3}\%$	$\frac{7}{8} = 0.875 = 87\frac{1}{2}\%$
$\frac{3}{16} = 0.1875 = 18.75\%$ or $18\frac{3}{4}\%$	$\frac{9}{10} = 0.9 = 90\%$
$\frac{1}{5} = 0.2 = 20\%$	$\frac{15}{16} = 0.9375 = 93.75\%$ or $93\frac{3}{4}\%$
$\frac{1}{4} = 0.25 = 25\%$	$1 = 1.00 = 100\%$
$\frac{3}{10} = 0.3 = 30\%$	$1\frac{1}{10} = 1.1 = 110\%$
$\frac{5}{16} = 0.3125 = 31.25\%$ or $31\frac{1}{4}\%$	$1\frac{1}{4} = 1.25 = 125\%$
$\frac{1}{3} = 0.333\overline{3} = 33\frac{1}{3}\%$	$1\frac{1}{3} = 1.333\overline{3} = 133\frac{1}{3}\%$
$\frac{3}{8} = 0.375 = 37.5\%$ or $37\frac{1}{2}\%$	$1\frac{1}{2} = 1.5 = 150\%$
$\frac{2}{5} = 0.4 = 40\%$	$1\frac{2}{3} = 1.666\overline{6} = 166\frac{2}{3}\%$
$\frac{7}{16} = 0.4375 = 43.75\%$ or $43\frac{3}{4}\%$	$1\frac{3}{4} = 1.75 = 175\%$
$\frac{1}{2} = 0.5 = 50\%$	$2 = 2.00 = 200\%$

3.1 Exercises

Write the following decimals as percents.

1. 0.2	**2.** 0.5	**3.** 0.72	**4.** 0.86
5. 1.4	**6.** 3.017	**7.** 0.375	**8.** 0.875
9. 4.625	**10.** 7.8	**11.** 0.0025	**12.** 0.0008
13. 0.0015	**14.** 0.221	**15.** 3.45	**16.** 5.5

Write the following fractions as percents.

17. $\dfrac{1}{4}$ **18.** $\dfrac{5}{8}$ **19.** $\dfrac{1}{10}$ **20.** $\dfrac{1}{20}$

21. $\dfrac{1}{50}$ **22.** $\dfrac{1}{125}$ **23.** $\dfrac{3}{8}$ **24.** $\dfrac{4}{5}$

25. $\dfrac{1}{8}$ **26.** $\dfrac{13}{20}$ **27.** $\dfrac{1}{200}$ **28.** $\dfrac{1}{400}$

29. $\dfrac{7}{8}$ **30.** $\dfrac{1}{100}$ **31.** $\dfrac{3}{50}$ **32.** $\dfrac{4}{25}$

Write the following percents as decimals.

33. 65%   **34.** 32%   **35.** 75%   **36.** 58%

37. 0.6%   **38.** 0.5%   **39.** 0.25%   **40.** 0.125%

41. 315%   **42.** 150%   **43.** 200.6%   **44.** 475.6%

45. 540.6%   **46.** 135.6%   **47.** 0.07%   **48.** 0.05%

 49. Fractions, decimals, and percents are all used to describe a part of something. The use of percent is much more common than fractions and decimals. Why do you suppose this is true?

 50. List five uses of percent that are or will be part of your life. Consider the activities of working, shopping, saving, borrowing, and planning for the future.

 51. To change a fraction to a percent you must first change the fraction to a decimal. Why is this? (See Objective 2.)

 52. The fractional percent $\frac{1}{2}\%$ is equal to 0.005. Explain each step as you change $\frac{1}{2}\%$ to its decimal equivalent. (See Objective 5.)

Determine the fraction, decimal, or percent equivalents for each of the following, as necessary. Write fractions in lowest terms.

	Fraction	Decimal	Percent
53.	$\frac{1}{2}$	_____	_____
54.	$\frac{3}{25}$	_____	_____
55.	_____	_____	15%
56.	_____	_____	87.5%
57.	_____	0.25	_____
58.	_____	0.35	_____
59.	$6\frac{1}{8}$	_____	_____
60.	$3\frac{1}{2}$	_____	_____
61.	_____	7.25	_____
62.	$1\frac{3}{4}$	_____	_____
63.	_____	0.0025	_____
64.	_____	0.00125	_____

	Fraction	Decimal	Percent
65.	$\frac{1}{3}$	_____	_____
66.	_____	_____	$4\frac{1}{4}\%$
67.	_____	_____	$\frac{3}{4}\%$
68.	$\frac{9}{200}$	_____	_____
69.	_____	_____	12.5%
70.	_____	0.025	_____
71.	_____	2.5	_____
72.	_____	_____	375%
73.	_____	_____	1038.35%
74.	_____	23.82	_____
75.	$4\frac{3}{8}$	_____	_____
76.	_____	_____	$37\frac{1}{2}\%$
77.	_____	_____	$6\frac{3}{4}\%$
78.	$\frac{35}{200}$	_____	_____
79.	_____	8.8	_____
80.	$6\frac{3}{8}$	_____	_____
81.	_____	_____	$\frac{1}{4}\%$
82.	_____	_____	$\frac{4}{5}\%$

3.2   Applications: Finding the Part

OBJECTIVES

1 *Identify the three elements of a percent problem.*
2 *Use the percent formula.*
3 *Apply the percent formula to a business problem.*
4 *Recognize the terms associated with base, rate, and part.*
5 *Use the basic percent equation.*

Objective

1   ***Identify the Three Elements of a Percent Problem.***   Problems involving percent have three main quantities. Usually two of these quantities are given and the third must be found. The three key quantities in a percent problem are as follows.

Base. The whole or total, the starting point, or that to which something is being compared.

Rate. A number followed by "%" or "percent."

Part. The result of multiplying the base and the rate. It is a part of the base.

Here are some examples you may recognize.

Part (*P*)	= Base (*B*)	× Rate (*R*)
Sales tax	= Total cost	× Sales tax rate
Commission	= Sale price of home	× Commission rate
Markdown	= Original price	× Discount rate
Increase	= Original amount	× Percent of increase
Interest	= Investment	× Interest rate

Objective

2 *Use the Percent Formula.*   The above three quantities are related by the basic **percent formula.**

$$\textbf{Part} = \textbf{Base} \times \textbf{Rate} \quad or \quad P = B \times R \quad or \quad P = BR$$

A couple selling their home for $220,000 discovered that they must pay a 6% real estate commission. Use the **basic percent equation** to find the commission.

$$\textbf{Part } (P) = \textbf{Base } (B) \times \textbf{Rate } (R)$$

$$\text{Commission} = \$220{,}000 \times 0.06 \qquad \text{Write 6\% as 0.06.}$$

$$\text{Commission} = \$13{,}200$$

The couple must pay $13,200 in commission. The commission is often split among four parties: the real estate broker of the agent that listed the house, the listing agent at that brokerage, the real estate broker of the selling agent, and the agent that actually sold the house. The commission is not necessarily split evenly among the four parties and varies from one location to another.

EXAMPLE 1 Solving for Part

Solve for part (*P*) using $P = B \times R$.

(a) 4% of 50   **(b)** 1.2% of 180

(c) 140% of 225   **(d)** $\frac{1}{4}$% of 560 (*Hint:* $\frac{1}{4}$% = 0.25%)

Solution

(a) $\begin{aligned} B \times R &= P \\ 50 \times 0.04 &= 2 \end{aligned}$ **(b)** $\begin{aligned} B \times R &= P \\ 180 \times 0.012 &= 2.16 \end{aligned}$

(c) $\begin{aligned} B \times R &= P \\ 225 \times 1.4 &= 315 \end{aligned}$ **(d)** $\begin{aligned} B \times R &= P \\ 560 \times 0.0025 &= 1.4 \end{aligned}$

Objective

3 *Apply the Percent Formula to a Business Problem.* Calculating **sales tax** is an excellent example of finding part. States, counties, and cities often collect taxes on sales to the consumer. The sales tax is a percent or portion of the sale. This percent varies from as low as 3% in some states to 8% or more in other states. The percent formula is used for finding sales tax.

$$P \quad = B \times \quad R$$

Sales tax = sales × sales tax rate

EXAMPLE 2 **Calculating Sales Tax**

Racy Feed and Pet Supply sold $284.50 worth of merchandise. If the sales tax rate was 5%, what was the sales tax and the total sale, including the tax?

Solution The amount of sales, $284.50, is the starting point or base, and 5% is the rate. Since the tax is a *part* of total sales, use the formula $P = BR$ to find the part.

$$P = \$284.50 \times 5\%$$
$$P = \$284.50 \times 0.05$$
$$P = 14.225 = \$14.23 \quad \text{Rounded}$$

The tax, or part, was $14.23.

$$
\begin{aligned}
\text{Total} &= \text{Amount of Sale} + \text{Tax} \\
&= \$284.50 \quad\quad\quad + \$14.23 \\
&= \$298.73
\end{aligned}
$$

NOTE An alternative approach to finding the combined sales and tax is to multiply $284.50 by 105% (100% sales + 5% sales tax).

$$\$284.50 \times 105\% = 284.5 \times 1.05 = \$298.73$$

EXAMPLE 3 **Finding Part**

Bob and Rhonda Ray live in Florida and have a combined income of $68,300. They are debating moving to Wisconsin to be near Rhonda's ailing mother and they wonder what the increase in taxes might be if they make the same income there. Use information from the figure to estimate any increase in taxes.

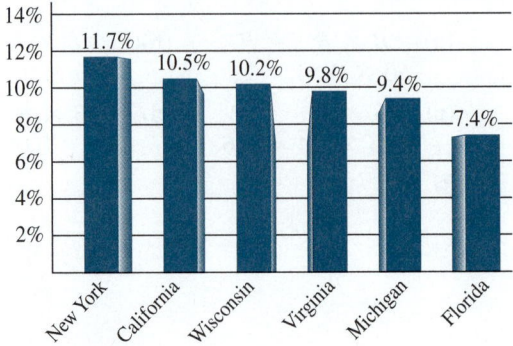

Combined State and Local Tax as a Percentage of Average Household Income (2008)

New York 11.7%, California 10.5%, Wisconsin 10.2%, Virginia 9.8%, Michigan 9.4%, Florida 7.4%

Source: Tax Foundation.

Solution   First estimate the tax (the part) on the combined income (the base) of $68,300 for each state.

$$P = B \times R$$

Tax in Florida $= \$68,300 \times 0.074 = \$5054.20$

Tax in Wisconsin $= \$68,300 \times 0.102 = \$6966.60$

Next subtract the two taxes to find the increase.

Difference $= \$6966.60 - \$5054.20 = \$1912.40$

Each year, the couple would pay about $2000 more in taxes if they move to Wisconsin and have the same income there.

 Scientific Calculator Approach

The calculator solution to Example 3 follows.

68300 $\boxed{\times}$ 7.4 $\boxed{\%}$ $\boxed{=}$ 5054.20

68300 $\boxed{\times}$ 10.2 $\boxed{\%}$ $\boxed{=}$ 6966.60 $\boxed{\text{STO}}$

$\boxed{\text{RCL}}$ $\boxed{-}$ 5054.20 $\boxed{=}$ 1912.40

Objective

4   *Recognize the Terms Associated with Base, Rate, and Part.*   Percent problems have certain similarities. For example, some phrases are associated with the base in the problem. Other phrases lead to the part, while "%" or "percent" following a number identifies the rate. Table 3.1 helps distinguish between the base and the part.

Table 3.1   **WORDS AND PHRASES ASSOCIATED WITH BASE AND PART**

Usually Indicates the Base (B)	Usually Indicates the Part (P)
Sales $\longrightarrow$	Sales tax
Investment $\longrightarrow$	Return
Savings $\longrightarrow$	Interest
Value of bonds $\longrightarrow$	Dividends
Retail price $\longrightarrow$	Discount
Last year's anything $\longrightarrow$	Increase or decrease
Value of real estate $\longrightarrow$	Rents
Old salary $\longrightarrow$	Raise
Total sales $\longrightarrow$	Commission
Value of stocks $\longrightarrow$	Dividends
Earnings $\longrightarrow$	Expenditures
Original $\longrightarrow$	Change

Objective

5   *Use the Basic Percent Equation.*   Most percent problems can be written in the form of the basic percent equation.

$$R \quad \times \quad B \quad = \quad P$$

Rate $\times$ Base $=$ Part
$\downarrow$ $\qquad$ $\downarrow$ $\quad$ $\downarrow$ $\quad$ $\downarrow$ $\quad$ $\downarrow$

____% $\quad$ of $\quad$ ____ $\quad$ is $\quad$ ____

Examples: $\qquad$ 5% of the automobiles are red.

4.2% of the workers are unemployed.

28% of the income is income tax.

75% of the students are full-time.

> **NOTE**   Rate is identified by "%" (the percent sign); the word "of" means "×" (multiplication); the *multiplicand,* or number being multiplied, is the base; the word "is" means "=" (equals); and the product, or answer, is a part of the base.

EXAMPLE 4   Identifying the Elements in Percent Problems

Identify the values given in the following percent problems and determine which value must be found.

(a) During a recent sale, Stockdale Marine offered a 15% discount on all new recreational equipment. Find the discount on a jet ski originally priced at $4895.

Solution   Identify the values in the percent equation: Rate = 15%; Base = Price = $4895; and Part = discount, which is the unknown.

$$R \quad \times \quad B \quad = \quad P$$

____% $\quad$ of $\quad$ ____ $\quad$ is discount.

15% $\quad$ of $\quad$ $4895 $\quad$ = discount

0.15 $\quad$ × $\quad$ $4895 $\quad$ = P

$P = \$734.25$ discount

(b) Round Table Pizza spends an amount equal to 5.8% of its sales on advertising. If sales for the month were $28,500, find the amount spent on advertising.

Solution   Identify the values in the percent equation: Rate = 5.8%; Base = Sales = $28,500; and Part = amount spent on advertising, which is the unknown.

$$R \quad \times \quad B \quad = \quad P$$

____% $\quad$ of $\quad$ ____ $\quad$ is $\quad$ amount spent on advertising.

5.8% $\quad$ of $\quad$ $28,500 $\quad$ = $\quad$ amount spent on advertising

0.058 $\quad$ × $\quad$ $28,500 $\quad$ = $\quad$ P

$P = \$1653$ spent on advertising

3.2	**Exercises**

Solve for part in each of the following.

1. 20% of 80 bicycles

2. 25% of 3500 Web sites

3. 22.5% of $1086

4. 20.5% of $1500

5. 4% of 120 feet

6. 125% of 2000 products

7. 175% of 5820 miles

8. 15% of 75 cases

9. 17.5% of 1040 homes

10. 52.5% of 1560 trucks

11. 118% of 125.8 yards

12. 500% of 142 units

13. $90\frac{1}{2}$% of $5930

14. $7\frac{1}{2}$% of $150

15. 0.5% of $1300

16. 0.75% of 180,000 calls

17. Name the three components in a percent problem and tell how you can identify each of these components. (See Objective 1.)

18. There are words and phrases that are usually associated with base and part. Give three examples of words that usually identify base and the accompanying word for the part. (See Objective 4.)

Solve for part in the following application problems. Round to the nearest cent unless otherwise indicated.

19. WEDDING PREFERENCES In a recent survey of 480 adults, 55% said that they would prefer to have their wedding at a religious site. How many said they would prefer the religious site?

20. NEWS ON INTERNET One poll of 822 people showed that 47.2% get their news from the Internet. Find the number of people who said they get their news from the Internet.

21. SALES TAX A real estate broker wants to purchase a Blackberry priced at $256. If the sales tax rate is 7.75%, find the total price including the sales tax.

22. MORTGAGE BROKER Thomas Dugally of Century 21 Realty works with a mortgage company that charges borrowers a fee of $350 plus 2% of the loan amount. What is the total charge for a home loan of $128,000?

23. SUPERMARKET SHOPPING The Point of Purchase Advertising Institute says that 55% of all supermarket shoppers have a written list of their needs. If there are 3680 shoppers per day entering the supermarket that you manage, what number of shoppers would you expect to have a written shopping list?

24. BAR SOAP A bar of Ivory Soap is $99\frac{44}{100}$% pure. If the bar of soap weighs 9 ounces, how many ounces are pure? Round to the nearest hundredth.

25. GLOBAL WARMING Of 240 climate scientists polled, 85.8% strongly believe that humans contribute significantly to global warming. Find the number of scientists that strongly believe.

26. DRIVING DISTRACTIONS It is estimated that 29.5% of automobile crashes are caused by driver distractions, such as text messaging. If there are 16,450 automobile crashes in a study, what number would be caused by driver distractions? Round to the nearest whole number.

27. GERMAN LABOR FORCE The size of the workforce in Germany is 44 million. If 62.5% of the labor force is male, find (a) the percent of the labor force that is female and (b) the number of workers who are female.

28. U.S. LABOR FORCE In the United States, there are 158 million people in the labor force. If 68% of the labor force is male, find (a) the percent of the workforce that is female and (b) the number of workers who are female to the nearest tenth of a million.

29. WORKPLACE REQUIREMENTS A study of office workers found that 27% would like more storage space. If there are 14 million office workers, how many would want more storage space?

30. **FEMALE LAWYERS** There are 1,143,050 active lawyers living in the United States. If 53.1% of these lawyers are male, find (a) the percent of the lawyers who are female and (b) the number of lawyers who are female. Round to the nearest whole number.

31. **NEW PRODUCT FAILURE** Marketing Intelligence Service says that there were 15,401 new products introduced last year. If 86% of the products introduced last year failed to reach their business objectives, find the number of products that did reach their objectives. Round to the nearest whole number.

32. **FAMILY BUDGET** A family of four with an after-tax monthly income of $4400 spends 90% and saves the balance. Find (a) the monthly savings and (b) the annual savings.

33. **ORANGE JUICE IN CHINA** This year the sales of Tropicana orange juice in China are $100 million. Seagram's Tropicana Beverage Group estimates that sales will increase by 35% next year. Find the amount of orange juice sales estimated for next year.

34. **SUPER BOWL ADVERTISING** The average cost of a 30-second ad during the Super Bowl four years ago was $2.4 million. If the increase in cost is 5.7% per year, find the average cost this year. Round to the nearest tenth of a million.

35. **SALES TAX COMPUTATION** As the owner of a copy and print shop, you must collect $6\frac{1}{2}$% of the amount of each sale for sales tax. If sales for the month are $48,680, what is the combined amount of sales and tax?

36. **DIGITAL TV** A digital TV is priced at $524. If sales tax of $7\frac{3}{4}$% is charged, find the total cost paid by the customer.

37. **REAL ESTATE COMMISSIONS** Thomas Dugally of Century 21 Realty sold a home for $174,900. The commission was 6% of the sale price. However, Dugally receives only 20% of the total commission. Find the amount of commission received by Dugally.

38. **BUSINESS OWNERSHIP** Rick Wilson has an 82% ownership in a company called Puppets and Clowns. The company has a value of $49,200 and Wilson receives an income of 30% of the value of his ownership. Find the amount of his income.

CONSUMER INTERNET SALES Country Store has a unique selection of merchandise that it sells by mail and over the Internet. Use the shipping and insurance delivery chart below and a sales tax rate of 5% to solve Exercises 39–42. There is no sales tax on shipping and insurance.

Shipping and Insurance Delivery Chart

Up to $25.00	add $3.95
$25.01 to $50.00	add $6.95
$50.01 to $99.99	add $8.95
$100.00 or more	add $10.95

39. Find the total cost of 6 electric skillets at a price of $29.99 each.

40. A customer ordered 5 sets of flour-sack towels at a price of $12.99 each. What is the total cost?

41. Find the total cost of 3 pop-up hampers at a price of $18.99 each and 4 nonstick mini-donut pans at $10.99 each.

42. Find the total cost of a small night lamp at a price of $49.99 and 2 sweaters at a price of $38.50 each.

| 3.3 | **Applications: Finding the Base** |

OBJECTIVES

1 *Use the basic percent equation to solve for base.*

2 *Find the amount of sales when taxes and rate of tax are known.*

3 *Find the amount of investment when expense and rate of expense are known.*

4 *Find the base when rate and part are for different quantities.*

Objective

1 *Use the Basic Percent Equation to Solve for Base.* In some problems, the rate and part are given and the base must be found. For example, suppose that a couple, interested in purchasing a home, can make a monthly payment of $1155, which is 28% of their monthly income. To find their monthly income, use the rate (28%) and part ($1155) to find the base by using the basic percent equation, rate × base = part. The word "of" in "28% of their monthly income" is the key word that indicates monthly income is the base.

$$R \times B = P$$

$$28\% \text{ of } \underline{\hspace{1cm}} = \$1155$$

$$0.28 \times B = \$1155$$

$$\frac{0.28B}{0.28} = \frac{\$1155}{0.28} \quad \text{Divide both sides by 0.28.}$$

$$B = \frac{\$1155}{0.28}$$

$$B = \$4125 \quad \text{Monthly income.}$$

EXAMPLE 1 Solving for Base

Solve for base using the basic percent equation.

(a) 8 is 4% of _____   **(b)** 135 is 15% of _____   **(c)** 1.25 is 25% of _____

Solution

(a)
$$P = R \times B$$
$$8 = 4\% \text{ of } \underline{\hspace{1cm}}$$
$$8 = 4\% \times B$$
$$8 = 0.04B$$
$$\frac{8}{0.04} = \frac{0.04B}{0.04}$$
$$B = \frac{8}{0.04} = 200$$

(b)
$$P = R \times B$$
$$135 = 15\% \text{ of } \underline{\hspace{1cm}}$$
$$135 = 15\% \times B$$
$$135 = 0.15B$$
$$\frac{135}{0.15} = \frac{0.15B}{0.15}$$
$$B = \frac{135}{0.15} = 900$$

(c)
$$P = R \times B$$
$$1.25 = 25\% \text{ of } \underline{\hspace{1cm}}$$
$$1.25 = 25\% \times B$$
$$1.25 = 0.25B$$
$$\frac{1.25}{0.25} = \frac{0.25B}{0.25}$$
$$B = \frac{1.25}{0.25} = 5$$

Objective

2   ***Find the Amount of Sales When Taxes and Rate of Tax Are Known.***   A common business application of percent involves sales tax and the sales tax rate.

EXAMPLE 2   **Finding Sales When Sales Tax Is Given**

The 5% sales tax collected one week by Famous Footwear was $780. What was the amount of total sales?

Solution   Here the rate of tax collection is 5% and taxes collected are a part of total sales. The rate is 5% and the part is $780. Use the percent equation.

$$R \times B = P$$

$$5\% \text{ of } \underline{\hspace{1.5cm}} = \$780$$

$$0.05B = \$780$$

$$\frac{0.05B}{0.05} = \frac{\$780}{0.05}$$

$$B = \frac{\$780}{0.05} = \$15,600$$

The total sales of the company were $15,600.

Scientific
Calculator
Approach

In the calculator solution to Example 2, the percent key may be used when dividing.

780 $\div$ 5 % = 15600

NOTE   It is important to the consider whether an answer is reasonable. A common error in a base problem is to confuse the base and part. In Example 2, if the taxes, $780, had been mistakenly used as the base, the resulting answer would have been $39 ($780 × 5%). Obviously, $39 is not a reasonable amount for total sales, given $780 as sales tax.

Objective

3   ***Find the Amount of Investment When Expense and Rate of Expense Are Known.***   The amount of an investment is the base. When the amount of expenses and the rate of expenses are known, the percent equation may be used to find the amount of the investment.

EXAMPLE 3   **Finding the Amount of an Investment**

The yearly lawn and pool maintenance cost of an apartment complex is $3\frac{1}{2}\%$ of its value. If the maintenance cost amounts to $73,500 per year, find the value of the complex.

Solution   To find the total value of the complex, which is the base, use the percent equation.

$$R \times B = P$$

$$3\frac{1}{2}\% \text{ of } \underline{\hspace{1.5cm}} = \$73,500$$

$$0.035B = \$73,500$$

$$\frac{0.035B}{0.035} = \frac{\$73,500}{0.035}$$

$$B = \frac{\$73,500}{0.035} = \$2,100,000$$

The total value of the complex is $2,100,000.

> **NOTE** When working with a fraction of a percent, it is best to change the fraction to a decimal. In Example 3, $3\frac{1}{2}\%$ was changed to 3.5%, which equals 0.035.

Objective

4 *Find the Base When Rate and Part Are for Different Quantities.* The rate used and the part given in a problem do not always refer to the same quantity. *Always pay careful attention when reading to understand a problem.*

Sometimes you need to subtract a percent from 100% to solve a problem. For example, assume 8% of the bananas in a shipment have been damaged. The percent of the bananas with good quality is found as follows.

$$
\begin{array}{ll}
100\% & \text{All bananas in the shipment} \\
-8\% & \text{Damaged bananas} \\
\hline
92\% & \text{Good quality bananas}
\end{array}
$$

The value 92% is said to be the **complement** with respect to 100% of 8%, or it is simply called the complement of 8%.

EXAMPLE 4 **Finding Base When Rate and Part Are for Different Quantities**

United Hospital finds that 25% of its employees are men and 720 are women. Find the total number of employees.

Solution First find the percent of women employees.

$$
\begin{array}{ll}
100\% & \text{All employees} \\
-25\% & \text{Men} \\
\hline
75\% & \text{Women}
\end{array}
$$

Then use the percent equation knowing that the 720 women employees (part) correspond to 75% of the total number of employees.

$$R \times B = P$$
$$75\% \text{ of } \underline{\hspace{1cm}} = 720$$
$$0.75B = 720$$
$$\frac{0.75B}{0.75} = \frac{720}{0.75}$$
$$B = \frac{720}{0.75} = 960$$

The total number of employees is 960.

3.3	**Exercises**

Solve for base in each of the following. Round to the nearest hundredth.

1. 265 bowlers is 25% of _____ bowlers.
2. 240 letters is 80% of _____ letters.
3. 75 miles is 40% of _____ miles.
4. 32 shipments is 8% of _____ shipments.
5. 55 packages is 5.5% of _____ packages.

6. $850 is $4\frac{1}{4}\%$ of _____.

7. 36 employees is 0.75% of _____ employees.

8. 23 workers is 0.5% of _____ workers.

9. 33 rolls is 0.15% of _____ rolls.

10. 54,600 boxes is 60% of _____ boxes.

11. 50 doors is 0.25% of _____ doors.

12. 39 bottles is 0.78% of _____ bottles.

13. $33,870 is $37\frac{1}{2}\%$ of _____.

14. $8,500 is $27\frac{1}{2}\%$ of _____.

15. 20% of _____ sacks is 350 sacks.

16. 16% of _____ is $45.

17. 375 crates is 0.12% of _____ crates.

18. 3.5 quarts is 0.07% of _____ quarts.

19. 0.5% of _____ homes is 327 homes.

20. 6.5 barrels is 0.05% of _____ barrels.

21. 12 audits is 0.03% of _____ audits.

22. 8 banks is 0.04% of _____ banks.

 23. The basic percent formula is $P = B \times R$. Show how to find the formula to solve for B (base). (See Objective 1.)

 24. A problem includes amount of sales, sales tax, and a sales tax rate. Explain how you could identify the base, rate, and part in this problem. (See Objective 2.)

Solve for base in the following application problems.

25. **STUDENT DEBT** A survey at one large university showed that 1843 juniors and seniors had more than $10,000 in student loans. This amounted to 36.7% of the entire group of juniors and seniors. Find the number of juniors and seniors at the college.

26. **EMPLOYEE POPULATION BASE** In a large metropolitan area 81% of the employed population is enrolled in a health maintenance organization (HMO). If 700,650 employees are enrolled, find the total number of people in the employed population.

27. **COLLEGE ENROLLMENT** This semester there are 1785 married students on campus. If this figure represents 23% of the total enrollment, what is the total enrollment? Round to the nearest whole number.

28. **WOMEN MOTORCYCLISTS** The Motorcycle Industry Council estimated that there were 635,000 women motorcycle riders in the United States. Since this is 9.6% of all motorcycle riders in the United States, what is the total number of motorcycle riders? Round to the nearest thousand.

29. **LOAN QUALIFICATION** Lauren Morse found a home for Sharon and Howard Martin that will require a monthly loan payment of $1140. If the lender insists that the buyer's monthly payment not exceed 30% of the buyer's monthly income, find the minimum monthly income required by the lender.

30. **PERSONAL BUDGETING** Byron Hopkins spends 30% of his income on rent, 24% on food, 8% on clothing, 15% on transportation, 11% on education, and 7% on recreation and saves the balance. If his savings amount to $150 per month, what are his monthly earnings?

31. **DIABETES SURVEY** In a telephone survey, 749 people said that diabetes is a serious problem in the United States. If this was 71% of the survey group, find the total number of people in the telephone survey. Round to the nearest whole number.

32. **DRIVING TESTS** In analyzing the success of driver's license applicants, the state finds that 58.3% of those examined received a passing mark. If the records show that 8370 new driver's licenses were issued, what was the number of applicants? Round to the nearest whole number.

33. **WAL-MART PROFITS** After paying income taxes, Wal-Mart Stores, Inc. earned $3.5 billion in profit one year. Estimate total revenue to the nearest tenth of a billion if profit was 3.36% of total revenue.

34. **COMMUNICATIONS INDUSTRY LAYOFFS** Telecommunications equipment maker Nortel Networks says it will lay off 4000 workers globally. If this amounts to 4% of its total workforce, how many workers will remain after the layoffs?

35. **GAMBLING PAYBACK** An Atlantic City casino advertises that it gives a 97.4% payback on slot machines, and the balance is retained by the casino. If the amount retained by the casino is $4823, find the total amount played on the slot machines.

36. **SMOKERS AND CANCER** The National Cancer Institute estimates that 87% of all deaths due to lung cancers are caused by smoking. Assume that 1.1 million people who developed lung cancer from smoking died from the cancer. Find the number who died of lung cancer from all causes. Round to the nearest tenth of a million.

Supplementary Exercises: Base and Part

Solve for base or part as indicated in the following application problems.

1. **SHAMPOO INGREDIENTS** Most shampoos contain 75% to 90% water. If there are 12.5 ounces of water in a bottle of shampoo that contains 78% water, what is the size of the bottle of shampoo? Round to the nearest whole number.

2. **HOUSEHOLD LUBRICANT** The lubricant WD-40 is used in 82.3 million U.S. homes, which is 79% of all homes. Find the total number of homes in the United States. Round to the nearest tenth of a million.

3. **PROPERTY INSURANCE** A dental office is valued at $423,750 and is insured for 68% of its value. Find the amount of insurance coverage.

4. **FLU SHOTS** In a survey of 3860 people who were 18–49 years of age, 16.3% had received an influenza vaccination (flu shot). How many of those surveyed received the vaccination? Round to the nearest whole number.

5. **CAMAROS AND MUSTANGS** The Chevy Camaro was introduced in 1967. Sales that year were 220,917, which was 46.2% of the number of Ford Mustangs sold in the same year. Find the number of Mustangs sold in 1967. Round to the nearest whole number.

6. **AUTO-LOAN INDUSTRY** The Money Store Inc. announced that it has auto loans valued at $776 million. If this is 5.1% of the company's total loan portfolio, what is the total amount of loans? Round to the nearest tenth of a million.

7. **FROZEN YOGURT SALES** The total sales of frozen yogurt were $594 million in the past 12 months. If 15.8% of the sales were private-label brands, what is the amount of sales that were private-label brands? Round to the nearest tenth of a million.

8. **CALORIES FROM FAT** Häagen-Dazs vanilla ice cream has 270 calories per serving. If 60% of these calories come from fat, find the number of calories coming from fat.

9. **RETIREMENT ACCOUNTS** Jo O'Neill has 9.5% of her earnings deposited into a retirement account. This amounts to $308.75 per month. Find her annual earnings.

10. **SOCIAL SECURITY** After graduating from college, James O'Neill was surprised that $52.08 was taken out of his first weekly paycheck for something he had never heard of called FICA. He learned that FICA is also called Social Security tax, and that the tax rate was 6.2%. Find his income for the week.

11. **DRIVER SAFETY SURVEY** A survey at an intersection found that of 2200 drivers, 38% were wearing seat belts. How many drivers in the survey were wearing seat belts?

12. **BLOOD CHOLESTEROL LEVELS** At a recent health fair 32% of the people tested were found to have high blood cholesterol levels. If 350 people were tested, find the number having high blood cholesterol.

13. **CAT FOOD SALES** Sales of Whiskas canned cat food dropped 3%, or $1.9 million, in the past year. Find the sales of Whiskas cat food after the decrease. Round to the nearest tenth of a million.

14. **CANNED CAT FOOD** In the past year there has been a 14% increase in the sales of Tender Morsels canned cat food. If this increase amounts to $1.41 million, find the sales of Tender Morsels canned cat food after the increase. Round to the nearest tenth of a million.

3.4   Applications: Finding the Rate

OBJECTIVES

1 *Use the percent equation to solve for rate.*

2 *Find the rate of return when the amount of the return and the investment are known.*

3 *Solve for the percent remaining when the total amount and amount used are given.*

4 *Find the percent of change.*

In the third type of percent problem, the part and base are given and the rate must be found. The rate is identified by the "%" sign, or "percent." For example, what percent of 32 is 8? Use the percent equation as shown next.

Objective

1   *Use the Percent Equation to Solve for Rate.*

$$R \times B = P$$
$$\underline{\qquad}\% \text{ of } 32 = 8$$
$$R \times 32 = 8$$
$$32R = 8$$

Now divide both sides by 32.

$$\frac{\cancel{32}R}{\cancel{32}} = \frac{8}{32}$$

$$R = \frac{8}{32} = 0.25 = 25\%$$

Finally, 8 is 25% of 32, or 25% of 32 is 8.

NOTE   When solving for rate, you *must* change the resulting decimal answer to a percent.

EXAMPLE 1 **Solving for Rate**

Solve for rate.

(a) 63 is what percent of 180?
(b) What percent of 500 is 100?
(c) 54 is what percent of 12?

Solution

(a) 63 is _____ % of 180

$$R \times B = P$$
$$\underline{\qquad}\% \text{ of } 180 = 63$$
$$180R = 63$$
$$\frac{\cancel{180}R}{\cancel{180}} = \frac{63}{180} \qquad \text{Divide both sides by 180.}$$
$$R = \frac{63}{180} = 0.35 = 35\%$$

(b) 100 is _____ % of 500

$$R \times B = P$$
$$\underline{\qquad}\% \text{ of } 500 = 100$$
$$500R = 100$$
$$\frac{\cancel{500}R}{\cancel{500}} = \frac{100}{500} \qquad \text{Divide both sides by 500.}$$
$$R = \frac{100}{500} = 0.2 = 20\%$$

(c) 54 is _____ % of 12

$$R \times B = P$$
$$\underline{\qquad}\% \text{ of } 12 = 54$$
$$12R = 54$$
$$\frac{\cancel{12}R}{\cancel{12}} = \frac{54}{12} \qquad \text{Divide both sides by 12.}$$
$$R = \frac{54}{12} = 4.5 = 450\%$$

■

Objective

2 *Find the Rate of Return When the Amount of the Return and the Investment Are Known.*
It is often necessary to find the rate of return when the amount of the return and investment are known.

EXAMPLE 2 **Finding the Rate of Return**

Joan Baker invested $3000 in a CD and received interest of $123.60 one year later. Find the rate of return (the interest rate) to the nearest tenth of a percent.

Solution   The original investment of $3000 is the base and the interest of $123.60 is the part.

$$R \times B = P$$
$$\underline{\hspace{1.5cm}}\% \times \$3000 = \$123.60$$
$$R \times \$3000 = \$123.60$$
$$\$3000R = \$123.60$$
$$\frac{\$3000R}{\$3000} = \frac{\$123.60}{\$3000} \qquad \text{Divide both sides by \$3000.}$$
$$R = 4.12\%$$

The annual interest rate was 4.12%, which rounds to 4.1%.

Objective

3   *Solve for the Percent Remaining When the Total Amount and Amount Used Are Given.* When the total amount of something and the amount used are known, it is common to solve for the percent remaining.

EXAMPLE 3   Solving for the Percent Remaining

A roof is expected to last 12 years before it needs replacement. If the roof is 10 years old, what percent of the roof's life remains? Round to the nearest tenth of a percent.

Solution   The total life of the roof is 12 years, which is the whole or base. The number of years of life remaining is $12 - 10 = 2$ years, which is the part.

$$R \times B = P$$
$$\underline{\hspace{1.5cm}}\% \text{ of } 12 \text{ is } 2$$
$$R \times 12 = 2$$
$$12R = 2$$
$$\frac{12R}{12} = \frac{2}{12} \qquad \text{Divide both sides by 12.}$$
$$R = \frac{2}{12} = \frac{1}{6} = 0.166\ldots = 16.7\% \quad \text{Rounded}$$

This problem can also be solved by first finding the percent of the life that has been used (10 years/12 years), which is 83.3% rounded to the nearest tenth of a percent. The percent of total life remaining is found as follows.

$$\begin{array}{ll} 100.0\% & \text{Total life of the roof} \\ -83.3\% & \text{Amount of life that has been used} \\ \hline 16.7\% & \text{Remaining life} \end{array}$$

This results in the same answer found above.

NOTE   Remember that the base is always 100%.

Objective

4   *Find the Percent of Change.*   A common business problem is to find the percent of change in amounts involved in operating a business, such as sales and returns, and to determine the percent of gain or loss of an investment.

| EXAMPLE | 4 | Finding the Percent of Increase |

Slow sales at Consumer Electronics, Inc., early in the fall prompted the managers to mark down prices by 15% and to advertise the sale widely on radio and in the newspaper. Sales climbed from $36,600 in the month before the advertising campaign to $113,460 the next month. Find the percent increase.

Solution   The base is the sales last month, or $36,600. Find the part, the increase in sales, as follows.

$$\text{Increase in sales} = \$113{,}460 - \$36{,}600 = \$76{,}860$$

Use the basic percent equation as follows.

$$R \times B = P$$

$$\underline{\qquad}\% \text{ of } \$36{,}600 = \$76{,}860$$

$$R \times \$36{,}600 = \$76{,}860$$

$$\$36{,}600R = \$76{,}860$$

$$\frac{\$36{,}600R}{\$36{,}600} = \frac{\$76{,}860}{\$36{,}600} \qquad \text{Divide both sides by \$36,600.}$$

$$R = \frac{76{,}860}{36{,}600} = 2.1 = 210\%$$

Sales increased by 210%. Since this percent is over 200%, the *increase in sales* was more than twice the original sales amount of $36,600. Clearly, customers responded strongly to the advertising campaign. This is a *huge increase* for only one month!

 Scientific Calculator Approach

The calculator solution to this example is to subtract to find the difference and then divide.

| (| 113460 | − | 36600 |) | ÷ | 36600 | = | 2.1 |

NOTE   Remember, to find the percent of increase, the first step is to determine the amount of increase. The base is *always* the original amount, such as last year's or last month's amount, and the amount of increase is the part.

Percents are commonly used to show the amount of change. The figure below shows the recent annual change in the price of some basic foods. For example, from 2007 to 2008, the price of fresh fruit increased by 9.2%. This change is high for one year and can be expected to greatly affect lower-income families. To find out why the price of fresh fruit has changed so much in the year, it would be necessary to dig further into the data at the United States Department of Agriculture.

Annual Increase in Food Prices (2008)

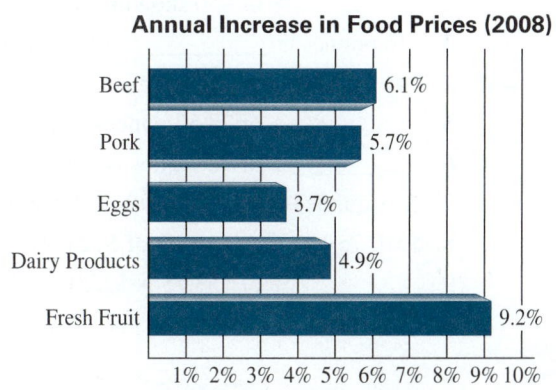

Source: United States Department of Agriculture.

EXAMPLE 5 | **Finding the Percent of Decrease**

As a result of lower mortgage interest rates, Scott and Andrea Abriani will be able to decrease their monthly mortgage payment from $1155 to $1050. Find the percent of decrease.

Solution   The base is the old monthly payment of $1155. First find the part, which is the
decrease in the payment.

$$\text{Decrease in payment} = \text{old payment} - \text{new payment}$$
$$= \$1155 - \$1050 = \$105$$

Use the basic percent equation.

$$R \times B = P$$
$$\underline{\qquad}\% \text{ of } \$1155 = \$105$$
$$R \times \$1155 = \$105$$
$$\$1155R = \$105$$
$$\frac{\$1155R}{\$1155} = \frac{\$105}{\$1155} \qquad \text{Divide both sides by \$1155.}$$
$$R = \frac{105}{1155} = 0.0909 = 9.1\% \quad \text{Rounded to the nearest tenth of a percent}$$

The monthly mortgage payment went down by 9.1%.

 **Scientific Calculator Approach**

The calculator solution to this example is to subtract to find the difference and then divide.

$$1155 \; \boxed{-} \; 1050 \; \boxed{=} \; 105 \; \boxed{\div} \; 1155 \; \boxed{=} \; 0.0909 = .091 \text{(rounded)}$$

NOTE   To find the percent of decrease, the first step is to determine the *amount of
decrease*. The amount of decrease is the part in the problem and the base is the original
amount or last year's, last month's, or last week's amount.

| **3.4** | **Exercises** |

Solve for rate in each of the following. Round to the nearest tenth of a percent.

1. _____ % of 2760 listings is 276 listings.

2. _____ % of 850 showings is 340 showings.

3. 310 phones is _____ % of 248 phones.

4. 144 desks is _____ % of 300 desks.

5. _____ % of 78.57 ounces is 22.2 ounces.

6. _____ % of 728 miles is 509.6 miles.

7. 73.1 quarts is _____ % of 786.8 quarts.

8. $310.75 is _____ % of $124.30.

9. _____ % of $53.75 is $2.20.

10. _____ % of 850 liters is 3.4 liters.

11. 46 shirts is _____ % of 780 shirts.

12. 5.2 vats is _____ % of 28.4 vats.

13. _____ % of 2 acres is 2.05 acres.

14. _____ % of $8 is $0.06.

15. 13,830 books is _____ % of 78,400 books.

16. _____ % of 73 cases is 350.4 cases.

17. _____ % of $330 is $91.74.

18. _____ % of 752 employees is 470 employees.

19. The basic percent formula is $P = B \times R$. Show how to use the formula to solve for R (rate). (See Objective 1.)

20. A problem includes last year's sales and this year's sales and asks for the percent of increase. Explain how you would identify the base, rate, and part in this problem. (See Objective 4.)

Solve for rate in the following application problems. Round to the nearest tenth of a percent.

21. ADVERTISING EXPENSES   Fernanda Lai of Wired Education Systems reports that sales were $132,900 while advertising expenses were $7442.40. What percent of last month's sales was spent on advertising?

22. MUSIC STORES   Music Land Group, Inc. will close 150 of its 1119 Sam Goody and Suncoast Motion Picture Company Stores. What percent of the stores will close?

23. WOMEN IN THE MILITARY   A recent study by Rand's National Defense Research Institute examined 48,000 military jobs, such as Army attack-helicopter pilot or Navy gunner's mate. It was found that only 960 of these jobs were filled by women. What percent of these jobs were filled by women?

24. VOCABULARY KNOWLEDGE   There are 55,000 words in Webster's Dictionary, but most educated people can identify only 20,000 of these words. What percent of the words in the dictionary can these people identify?

25. ADVERTISING MEDIA   Advertising expenditures for Bailey's Roofers are as follows.

Newspaper	$2250	Television	$1425
Radio	$954	Yellow Pages	$1605
Outdoor	$1950	Miscellaneous	$2775

What percent of the total advertising expenditures is spent on radio advertising?

26. MAIL DELIVERY   The manager of a small country post office estimates that of the roughly 3850 mailings handled each day, about 2400 fall in the category that some homeowners called junk mail advertising. Find the percent of the mailings that are advertising.

27. HARLEY-DAVIDSON MOTORCYCLES   Harley-Davidson, the only major U.S.-based motorcycle maker, says that it expects to build 317,000 motorcycles this year, up from 290,600 last year. Find the percent of increase in production.

28. AVERAGE HOME PRICE   The average selling price of a home in the United States last year was $202,250 while the average selling price this year was $207,300. What is the percent of increase? Round to the nearest tenth of a percent.

29. FALLING PHONE BILLS   Sarah Walker's long-distance phone bills plummeted to an average of $24.40 a month from last year's monthly average of $30.50. What was the percent of decrease?

30. SOLAR POWER   In the past 5 years, the cost of generating electricity from the sun has been brought down from 24 cents per kilowatt hour to 7 cents per kilowatt hour. Find the percent of decrease.

Supplementary Exercises: Rate, Base, and Part

Solve for rate, base, or part as indicated in the following. Round rates to the nearest tenth of a percent.

1. **OVERWEIGHT PATIENTS**   A telephone survey of doctors found that 63% of the doctors reported an increase in the number of patients who are overweight. If the number of doctors reporting this was 189, find the number of doctors in the survey.

2. **EMPLOYEE HEALTH PLANS**   When larger firms (over 1000 employees) were surveyed, it was found that 27% of the firms offered only one health plan to employees. If 1800 firms were surveyed, find the number offering only one health plan.

3. **MOTORCYCLE SAFETY**   Only 20 of the 50 states require motorcycle riders to wear helmets. What percent of the states require motorcycle riders to wear helmets?

4. **DANGER OF EXTINCTION**   Scientists tell us that there are 9688 species of birds and that 1211 of these species are in danger of extinction. What percent of the bird species are in danger of extinction?

5. **ECONOMY LODGING**   According to industry figures, there are 44,500 hotels and motels in America. Economy hotels and motels account for 38% of this total. Find the number of economy hotels and motels.

6. **AMERICAN CHIROPRACTIC ASSOCIATION**   There are 60,000 licensed chiropractors in the nation. If 25% of these chiropractors belong to the American Chiropractic Association (ACA), find the number of chiropractors in the ACA.

7. **DRUNK-DRIVING ACCIDENTS**   In the United States, 275,000 people were injured in alcohol-related driving accidents last year. This was 9.48% of all traffic injuries. Find the number of traffic injuries last year. Round to the nearest whole number.

8. **LAPTOP COMPUTER SALES**   Last year, Get Wired Computer Company sold 7038 laptop computers. If this was 56% of its total computer sales, find the total number of computers sold. Round to the nearest whole number.

9. **COST AFTER MARKDOWN**   A fax machine priced at $398 is marked down 7% to promote the new model. If the sales tax is also 7%, what is the cost of the fax machine including sales tax?

10. **TEAM SWEATERS**   After a losing basketball season, a college bookstore offers sweaters emblazoned with a large, colorful team mascot at a 10% discount. If the original price was $58 and sales tax is 7.5%, find the total cost with sales tax. (*Hint:* First find the discount, then add the tax.)

11. **BLOOD-ALCOHOL LEVELS**   In the United States, 15 of the 50 states limit blood-alcohol levels for drivers to 0.08%. The remaining states limit these levels to 0.10%.

    (a) What percent of the states have a blood alcohol limit of 0.08%?

    (b) What percent have a limit of 0.10%?

12. **ENDANGERED FROGS**   About 2700 of the 6000 known species of frogs are threatened with extinction. Find the percent threatened with extinction.

13. **WOMEN'S COATS**   A "60%-off sale" begins today. What is the sale price of women's wool coats normally priced at $335?

14. **APPLIANCES**   What is the sale price of a $769 Sears Kenmore washer/dryer set with a discount of 25%?

15. **SOCIAL SECURITY BENEFITS**   The Social Security Administration announced that the average monthly benefit to single retirees will be increased from $1108 to $1141. Find the percent of increase. Round to the nearest hundredth of a percent.

16. **BENEFIT INCREASE**   The average monthly Social Security benefit to couples will be increased to $1523. If the current monthly benefit is $1492, what is the percent of increase?

CELL PHONE SALES   The cell phone sales by one company in four regions of the country are shown in the table. Use this data to answer Exercises 17–20.

CELL PHONE SALES		
Region	Last Year	This Year
Northeast	32,000	36,000
Midwest	65,000	66,300
South	82,000	77,500
West	54,000	49,600

17. Find the percent of increase in sales in the northeastern region.

18. Find the percent of increase in sales in the midwestern region.

19. What is the percent of decrease in sales in the southern region?

20. What is the percent of decrease in sales in the western region?

21. **VENDING MACHINE SALES**   Of the total candy bars contained in a vending machine, 240 bars have been sold. If 25% of the bars have been sold, find the total number of candy bars that were in the machine.

22. **TOTAL SALES**   If the sales tax rate is 6% and the sales tax collected is $478.20, what are the sales?

23. **FAMILY BUDGETING**   Toni and Jay Shellan set up a budget allowing 30% for rent and household expenses, 25% for food, 8% for clothing, 10% for car payments and insurance, and 20% for medical and recreation. The balance is put into savings. Jay takes home $2950 per month after taxes and Toni brings home $28,500 per year after taxes. Assuming no emergencies that use up funds, find the amount the couple will save in a year.

24. **CHICKEN NOODLE SOUP**   In one year there were 350 million cans of chicken noodle soup sold (all brands). If 60% of this soup is sold in the cold-and-flu season (October through March), how many cans were sold in the cold-and-flu season?

25. **FLOOD INSURANCE**   According to the Federal Emergency Management Agency (FEMA), there are 11 million buildings at risk of flooding. The agency finds that only 2.6 million of these are currently insured for flooding. Find the percent that are insured.

26. **REFRIGERATION CAPACITY**   A Hotpoint refrigerator has a capacity of 11.5 cubic feet in the refrigerator and 5.5 cubic feet in the freezer. What percent of the total capacity is the capacity of the freezer?

27. **INTERNET USERS**   Worldwide, about 1.1 billion people use the Internet. At 35.5% of the total, Asians are the largest group of users. Find the number of Asian Internet users to the nearest million.

28. **YOUNG DRIVERS**   Of the 5136 teenagers killed in car accidents last year, 66.3% were males. Find the number of teenaged males killed in car accidents.

29. **U.S. PATENT RECIPIENTS**   Among the 50 companies receiving the greatest number of U.S. patents last year, 18 were Japanese companies. What percent of the top 50 companies were Japanese companies?

30. **LAYOFF ALTERNATIVE**   Instead of laying off workers, a company cut all employee hours from 40 hours a week to 30 hours a week. What was the percent cut in employee hours?

| 3.5 | **Increase and Decrease Problems** |

OBJECTIVES

1 *Learn to identify an increase or a decrease problem.*

2 *Apply the basic diagram for increase problems.*

3 *Use an equation to solve for base in increase problems.*

4 *Apply the basic diagram for decrease problems.*

5 *Use an equation to solve for base in decrease problems.*

Businesses commonly look at how amounts change, either up or down. For example, a manager might need to know the percent by which sales have increased, or the percent by which costs have decreased, while a consumer might need to know the percent by which the price of an item has changed. Identify these **increase and decrease problems** as follows.

Objective

1   *Learn to Identify an Increase or a Decrease Problem.*

Increase Problem

The base (100%) plus some portion of the base, gives a new value, which is part. Phrases such as *after an increase of, more than,* or *greater than* often indicate an increase problem. The basic formula for an increase problem is

$$\text{Original} + \text{Increase} = \text{New value}$$
$$\qquad\uparrow \qquad\qquad\qquad\qquad \uparrow$$
$$\qquad\text{Base} \qquad\qquad\qquad\qquad \text{Part}$$

Decrease Problem

The part equals the base (100%) minus some portion of the base, resulting in a new value. Phrases such as *after a decrease of, less than,* or *after a reduction of* often indicate a decrease problem. The basic formula for a decrease problem is

$$\text{Original} - \text{Decrease} = \text{New value}$$
$$\qquad\uparrow \qquad\qquad\qquad\qquad \uparrow$$
$$\qquad\text{Base} \qquad\qquad\qquad\qquad \text{Part}$$

NOTE   Base is always the original amount and we can solve for base in both increase and decrease problems. Base is always 100%.

EXAMPLE 1   Using a Diagram to Understand an Increase Problem

The price of a home sold by real estate agent Tricia Marinaro this year is $187,000, which is 10% more than last year's value. Find the value of the home last year.

Solution   Use a diagram, such as Figure 3.2 below, to help solve this problem. Since base is the starting point, or that to which something is compared, the base here is last year's sales. Call the base 100% and remember that

$$\text{Original} + \text{Increase} = \text{New value}$$

Objective

2   *Apply the Basic Diagram for Increase Problems.*

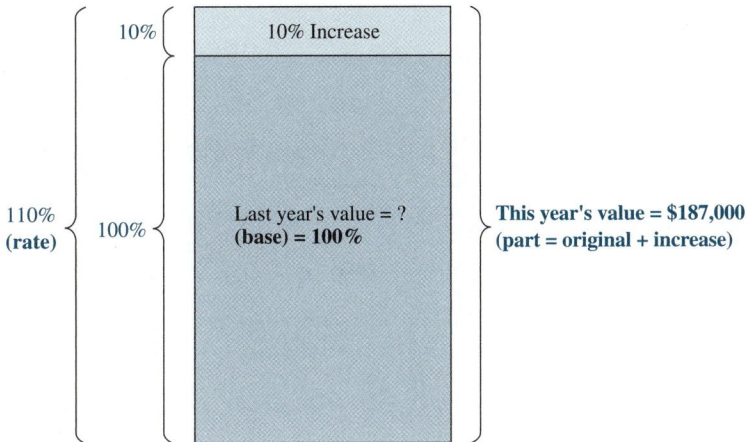

Figure 3.2

Objective

3   *Use an Equation to Solve for Base in Increase Problems.*   As shown in Figure 3.2, the 10% increase is based on last year's value (which is unknown) and not on this year's value of $187,000. This year's value is the *result* of adding 10% of last year's value to the amount of last year's value. Therefore, this year's value is all of last year's value (100%) plus 10% of last year's value (100% + 10% = 110%). Solve with the increase formula, using B to represent base.

$$\text{Original} + \quad\quad\quad \text{Increase} = \text{New value}$$
$$\text{Last year's value} + 10\% \text{ of last year's value} = \text{This year's value}$$
$$100\% \times B + 10\% \times B = \$187{,}000$$
$$110\% \times B = \$187{,}000$$
$$1.1B = \$187{,}000$$
$$\frac{\cancel{1.1}B}{\cancel{1.1}} = \frac{\$187{,}000}{1.1} \quad\quad \text{Divide both sides by 1.1.}$$
$$B = \frac{\$187{,}000}{1.1}$$
$$B = \$170{,}000 \quad\quad \text{Last year's value}$$

Check the answer by finding 10% of last year's value and adding it to last year's value.

$$
\begin{array}{r}
\$170{,}000 \quad \text{Last year's value} \\
+ \quad 17{,}000 \quad \text{(10\% of \$170,000)} \\
\hline
\$187{,}000 \quad \text{This year's value}
\end{array}
$$

> **NOTE**   The common error in solving for the base in an increase problem is thinking that the base is given and that the solution can be found by solving for part. Remember that the number given in Example 1, $187,000, is the result of having added 10% of the base to the base (100% + 10% = 110%). In fact, the $187,000 is the part, and base must be found.

The following figure shows world population over time with forecasts to 2050. Although world population growth has slowed since early in the last century, experts at the United Nations predict that it will still grow rapidly for decades since there are so many young people of childbearing age in the world. To capture some of the uncertainty in the rate of population growth over the next few decades, three different forecasts of population in 2050 are shown in the figure.

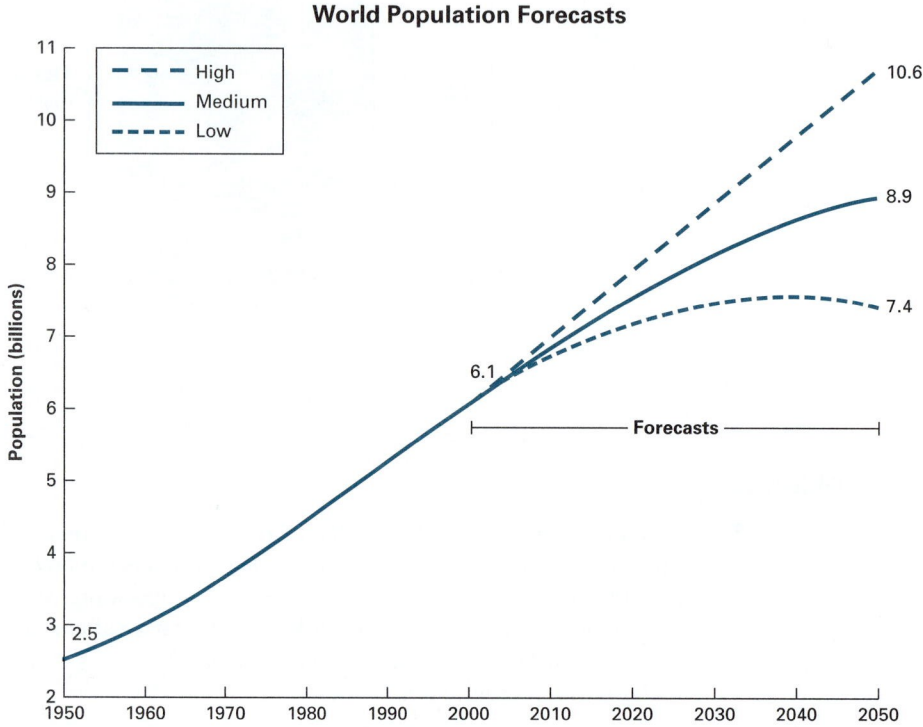

World Population Forecasts

Source: Data from United Nations Department of Economic and Social Affairs – World Population to 2300.

The low rate of population growth results in a peak in population of about 7.5 billion in 2038. World population in 2050 will be 8.9 billion under the medium growth rate and 10.6 billion under the high growth rate. Clearly, this information is very relevant to industry and world leaders trying to make plans to ensure sufficient food, water, energy, etc. for the growing population on planet Earth.

Example 2 shows how to solve a problem with two increases.

EXAMPLE 2   Finding Base after Two Increases

Sales of Icon's newest Web-enabling device have grown by 20% per year for each of the past 2 years. If 93,600 are sold this year, find sales 2 years ago.

Solution   The two 20% increases cannot be added together because these increases are from two different years, with two separate bases. The problem must be solved in two steps. First, use a diagram to find last year's production.

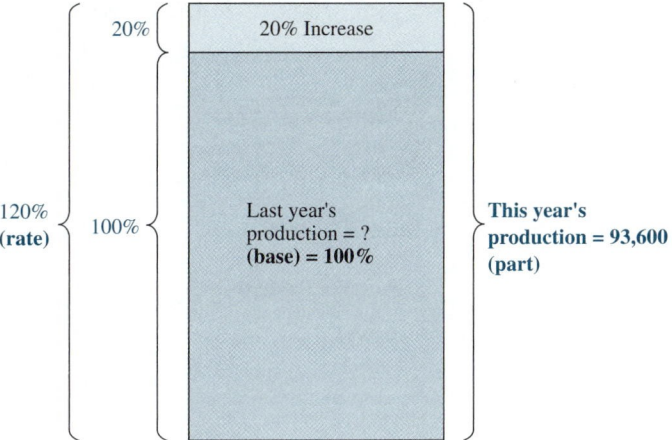

Figure 3.3

From Figure 3.3, last year's production plus 20% of last year's production equals this year's production. Use the following formula:

$$100\% \times B + 20\% \times B = 93{,}600$$
$$120\% \times B = 93{,}600$$
$$1.2B = 93{,}600$$
$$\frac{\cancel{1.2}B}{\cancel{1.2}} = \frac{93{,}600}{1.2}$$
$$B = \frac{93{,}600}{1.2}$$
$$B = 78{,}000 \quad \text{Last year's production}$$

Production last year was 78,000 units. Production for the preceding year (2 years ago) must now be found. Use another diagram (Figure 3.4).

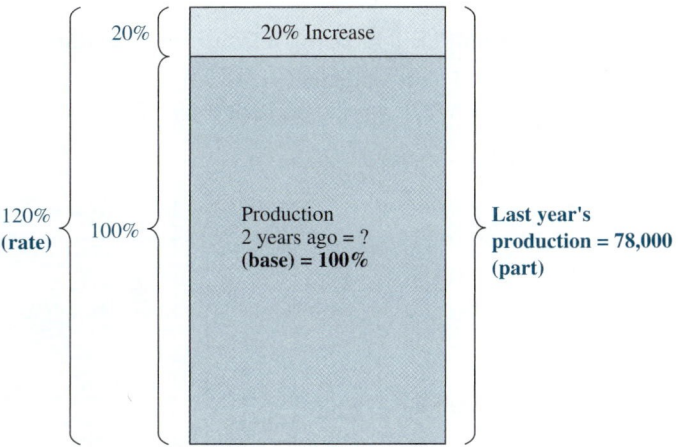

Figure 3.4

Thus, production 2 years ago + 20% of production 2 years ago = last year's production. In the following solution, b is used for the unknown since B was used above.

$$100\% \times b + 20\% \times b = 78{,}000$$

$$120\% \times b = 78{,}000$$

$$1.2b = 78{,}000$$

$$\frac{\cancel{1.2}b}{\cancel{1.2}} = \frac{78{,}000}{1.2}$$

$$b = \frac{78{,}000}{1.2}$$

$$b = 65{,}000 \qquad \text{Production 2 years ago}$$

Check the answer.

65,000	Production 2 years ago
+ 13,000	20% increase
78,000	Production last year
+ 15,600	20% increase
93,600	Production this year

 **Scientific Calculator Approach**

The calculator solution to this example divides in a series.

93,600 $\div$ 1.2 $\div$ 1.2 $=$ 65,000

NOTE It is important to realize that the two 20% increases cannot be added together to equal one increase of 40%. Each 20% increase is calculated on a *different base*.

Objective

4 *Apply the Basic Diagram for Decrease Problems.*

EXAMPLE 3 **Using a Diagram to Understand a Decrease Problem**

After Fleetfeet deducted 10% from the price of a pair of running shoes, Craig Bleyer paid $135. What was the original price of the shoes?

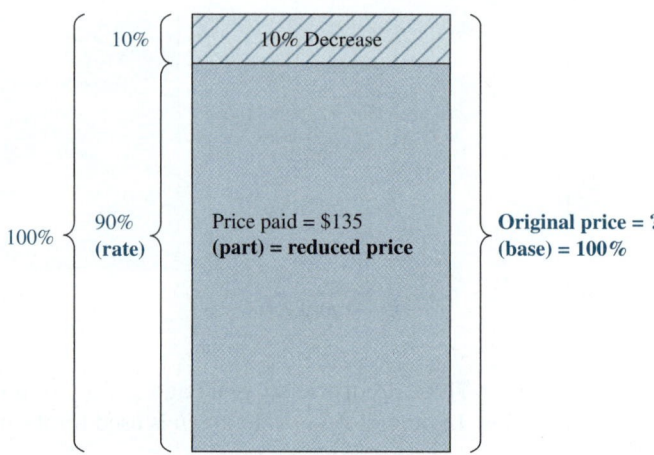

Figure 3.5

Solution Use a diagram (Figure 3.5) again and remember that the base is the starting point—in this case, the original price. As always, the base is 100%. Use the decrease formula because the price went down.

Objective

5 *Use an Equation to Solve for Base in Decrease Problems.* As Figure 3.5 shows, 10% was deducted from the original price. The result equals the price paid, which is 90% of the original price.

Be careful in finding the rate: 10% cannot be used because the original price on which 10% was calculated is not given. The rate 90% (the difference, $100\% - 10\% = 90\%$) must be used since 90% of the original price is the *resulting* $135 price paid. Now find the original price.

$$\text{Original} - \text{Decrease} = \text{New value}$$
$$\text{Original price} - 10\% \text{ of the original price} = \text{Price paid}$$
$$100\% \times B - 10\% \times B = \$135$$
$$90\% \times B = \$135$$
$$0.9B = \$135$$
$$\frac{0.9B}{0.9} = \frac{\$135}{0.9}$$
$$B = \frac{\$135}{0.9}$$
$$B = \$150 \qquad \text{Original price}$$

Check the answer.

$$
\begin{array}{r l}
\$150 & \text{Original price} \\
-\quad 15 & \text{10\% discount} \\
\hline
\$135 & \text{Price paid}
\end{array}
$$

NOTE The common mistake made in Example 3 is thinking that the reduced price, $135, is the base. The original price is the base, while the reduced price, $135, is a *result* of subtracting 10% of the base from the base. The reduced price is the part or 90% *of the base* ($100\% - 10\% = 90\%$).

3.5	**Exercises**

Solve for base in each of the following. Round to the nearest cent.

	Part (After Increase)	Rate of Increase
1.	$450	20%
2.	$800	25%
3.	$30.70	10%
4.	$10.09	5%

Solve for base in each of the following. Round to the nearest cent.

	Part (After Decrease)	Rate of Decrease
5.	$20	20%
6.	$1530	15%
7.	$598.15	30%
8.	$98.38	15%

9. Certain words or word phrases help to identify an increase problem. Discuss how you will identify an increase problem. (See Objective 1.)

10. Certain words or word phrases help to identify a decrease problem. Discuss how you will identify a decrease problem. (See Objective 1.)

Solve the following application problems. Read each carefully to determine which are increase or decrease problems and work accordingly. Round to the nearest cent, when necessary.

11. HOME VALUE APPRECIATION　Zoe Werner of Century 21 Realty just listed a home for $178,740. If this is 3% more than what the home sold for last year, what was last year's selling price to the nearest dollar?

12. DEALER'S COST　John Chavez Auto Stereos sold a high-quality auto stereo for $337.92, a loss of 12% of the dealer's original cost. Find the original cost.

13. FAMILY RESTAURANT　Santiago Rowland owns a small restaurant and charges 8% sales tax on all orders. At the end of the day, he has a total of $2052, including the sales and sales tax in his cash register. (a) What were his sales not including sales tax? (b) Find the amount that is sales tax.

14. SALES TAX　A hotel manager purchased a notebook computer for $958.50, including $6\frac{1}{2}\%$ sales tax. Find (a) the price of the personal computer, and (b) the amount of sales tax.

15. STARBUCKS　Revenue at Starbucks increased to $2.5 billion this quarter, or 8.7% higher than the same quarter last year. Find the total revenue for the same quarter last year to the nearest tenth of a billion.

16. ANTILOCK BRAKES　In a recent test of an automobile antilock braking system (ABS) on wet pavement, the stopping distance was 114 feet. If this was 28.75% less than the distance needed to stop the same automobile without the ABS, find the distance needed to stop without the antilock braking system.

17. WEDDING COSTS　The average cost of a wedding today is $19,104, which is 26% more than the average cost 5 years ago. Find the average cost of a wedding 5 years ago. Round to the nearest cent.

18. POPULATION OF CHINA　The population of China is about 1.35 billion. It has grown at a rate of 1.1% per year for each of the past 2 years. Find the population 2 years ago and round to the nearest hundredth of a billion.

19. WALLPAPER SALES　Erika Guitierrez, owner of Wallpaper Plus, says that her sales have increased exactly 20% per year for the last 2 years. Her sales this year are $170,035.20. Find her sales 2 years ago.

20. VOLVO SALES　In 5 years, Volvo plans to boost worldwide sales 25%, to 500,000 units a year. Find the Volvo sales this year.

21. **NURSING HOME COSTS**   Next year, the average annual cost of nursing home care is expected to increase to $83,585. Find the cost this year to the nearest dollar if costs increase by 6%.

22. **INTERNET SALES**   Netflix rents DVDs on the Internet. The firm recently announced that it has 8.4 million subscribers, or 25% more than last year. Find the number of subscribers last year rounded to the nearest tenth of a million.

23. **SURPLUS-EQUIPMENT SALES**   In a 3-day public sale of Jackson County surplus equipment, the first day brought $5750 in sales and the second day brought $4186 in sales, with 28% of the original equipment left to be sold on the third day. Find the value of equipment left to sell.

24. **COLLEGE EXPENSES**   After spending $4800 for tuition and $4350 for dormitory fees, Donald Cole finds that 15% of his original savings remains. Find the amount of his savings that remains.

25. **TIRE MANUFACTURING**   International Tires reported a 16% drop in third quarter earnings. If earnings dropped to $122 million, find the earnings before the drop. Round to the nearest hundredth of a million.

26. **NATIONAL HOME SALES**   Sales of existing homes decreased 7.4% to an annual number of 6.2 million units. Find the annual number of homes sold before the decrease. Round to the nearest hundredth of a million.

27. **WINTER-WHEAT PLANTING**   Even though wheat prices are rising during the planting season, farmers have planted only 50.2 million acres of winter-wheat varieties. If this is 2% fewer acres than last year, find the number of acres planted last year. Round to the nearest tenth of a million.

28. **LEATHER-CLOTHING SALES**   Department stores and specialty chains sold 4.1 million leather jackets and coats this year. If this is a 38% drop in sales from last year, find last year's sales. Round to the nearest tenth of a million.

29. **COMMUNITY COLLEGE**   For the past 2 years, the enrollment at American River College has grown by 3.2% per year. If there are currently 37,000 students enrolled, estimate the number of students enrolled 2 years ago.

30. **TUITION**   The tuition and fees at one public university have increased by an average of 8.2% for each of the past 2 years. If tuition and fees are currently $4600 per semester, find the cost 2 years ago.

31. **CONE ZONE DEATHS**   This year there were 1181 deaths related to road construction zones in the United States. If this is an increase of 70% in the last 5 years, what was the number of deaths 5 years ago? Round to the nearest whole number.

32. **MINORITY LOANS**   A mortgage lender made 8% more loans to minorities this year than last year. If the number of loans to minorities this year is 2660, find the number of loans made to minorities last year.

33. **CELL PHONE SALES**   Sales of one model of cell phone fell 18% in one year, to 296,398 units. Find the number of these phones sold last year rounded to the nearest whole number.

34. **JOB LOSSES**   Jameson Foundry announced that it expects to reduce its union workforce to 59,000 workers, a decrease of 20%. Find the size of the workforce before the decrease.

CHAPTER TERMS

Review the following terms to test your understanding of the chapter. For each term you do not know, refer to the page number found next to that term.

base [p. 77]
basic percent equation
 [p. 77]
complement [p. 85]
decrease problem [p. 96]

equation for rate [p. 88]
hundredths [p. 70]
increase problem [p. 96]
part [p. 77]
percent [p. 69]

percent formula [p. 77]
percent of decrease [p. 92]
percent of increase
 [p. 91]
percents [p. 70]

rate [p. 77]
sales tax [p. 78]
variability [p. 69]

CONCEPTS

EXAMPLES

3.1 Writing a decimal as a percent

Move the decimal point two places to the right and attach a % sign.

$$0.75 \ (0.75.) = 75\%$$

3.1 Writing a fraction as a percent

First change the fraction to a decimal, then write the decimal as a percent.

$$\frac{2}{5} = 0.4$$
$$0.4 \ (0.40.) = 40\%$$

3.1 Writing a percent as a decimal

Move the decimal point two places to the left and drop the % sign.

$$50\% \ (0.50.\%) = 0.5$$

3.1 Writing a percent as a fraction

First change the percent to a decimal. Then write the decimal as a fraction in lowest terms.

$$15\% \ (0.15.\%) = 0.15 = \frac{15}{100} = \frac{3}{20}$$

3.1 Writing a fractional percent as a decimal

First change the fraction to a decimal leaving the % sign, then move the decimal point two places to the left and drop the % sign.

$$\frac{1}{2}\% = 0.5\%$$
$$0.5\% = 0.00.5$$
$$\frac{1}{2}\% = 0.005$$

3.2 Solving for part using the percent formula

$$\text{Part} = \text{Base} \times \text{Rate}$$
$$P = B \times R$$
$$P = BR$$
$$\_\_\_\_\_ \% \text{ of } \_\_\_\_\_ \text{ is } \_\_\_\_\_$$

A company offered a 15% discount on all sales. Find the discount on sales of $1850.

$$\_\_\_\_\_\% \text{ of } sales \text{ is discount}$$
$$15\% \text{ of } \$1850 = \text{discount}$$
$$R \times B = P$$
$$0.15 \times \$1850 = P$$
$$0.15 \times \$1850 = \$277.50 \text{ discount}$$

3.3 Using the basic percent equation to solve for base

Remember that base is the starting point, reference point, all of something, or 100%.

$$\text{Rate} \quad \times \quad \text{Base} \quad = \quad \text{Part}$$
$$\underline{}\% \times \underline{} \quad \text{is} \quad \underline{}$$

If the sales tax rate is 4%, find the sales if the sales tax is $18.

$$R \times B = P$$
$$4\% \times \underline{} = \$18$$
$$0.04B = \$18$$
$$\frac{0.04B}{0.04} = \frac{\$18}{0.04}$$
$$B = \frac{\$18}{0.04}$$
$$= \$450 \text{ sales}$$

3.4 Using the basic percent equation to solve for rate

Remember that rate is a percent and is followed by a % sign.

$$\text{Rate} \quad \times \quad \text{Base} \quad = \quad \text{Part}$$
$$\underline{}\% \times \underline{} \quad \text{is} \quad \underline{}$$

The return is $307.80 on an investment of $3420. Find the rate of return.

$$R \times B = P$$
$$\underline{}\% \text{ of } \$3420 \text{ is } \$307.80$$
$$R \times \$3420 = \$307.80$$
$$\$3420R = \$307.80$$
$$\frac{\$3420R}{\$3420} = \frac{\$307.80}{\$3420}$$
$$R = 0.09$$
$$R = 9\%$$

3.4 Finding the percent of change

Calculate the change (increase or decrease), which is the part. Base is the amount before the change.

$$\text{Use } R = \frac{P}{B}$$

Air conditioner production rose from 3820 units to 5157 units. Find the percent of increase.

$$5157 - 3820 = 1337 \text{ increase}$$
$$R = \frac{1337}{3820} = 0.35 = 35\%$$

3.5 Drawing a diagram and using an equation to solve an increase problem

Solve for base given rate (110%) and part (after increase).

This year sales of $121,000 are 10% more than last year's sales. Find last year's sales.

$$\text{Original} + \text{Increase} = \text{New value}$$
$$100\% \times B + 10\% \times B = \$121,000$$
$$1B + 0.1B = \$121,000$$
$$1.1B = \$121,000$$
$$B = \frac{\$121,000}{1.1}$$
$$B = \$110,000 \text{ last year's sales}$$

3.5 **Drawing a diagram and using an equation to solve a decrease problem**

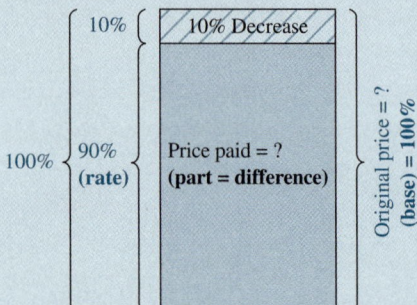

Solve for base given rate (90%) and part (after decrease).

After a deduction of 10% from the price, a customer paid $135. Find the original price.

$$\text{Original} - \text{Decrease} = \text{New value}$$
$$100\% \times B - 10\% \times B = \$135$$
$$1B - 0.1B = \$135$$
$$0.9B = \$135$$
$$B = \frac{\$135}{0.9}$$
$$B = \$150 \text{ original price}$$

CHAPTER 3	Review Exercises

The answer section includes answers to all Review Exercises.

Solve each of the following. [3.1–3.4]

1. 18 members is 12% of what number of members?

2. What is 5% of 480 vans?

3. 33 shippers is 3% of what number of shippers?

4. 36 accounts is what percent of 1440 accounts?

5. What is $\frac{1}{4}$% of $1500?

6. Find the fractional equivalent of 24%.

7. 24 loads is $2\frac{1}{2}$% of how many loads?

8. Change 87.5% to its fractional equivalent.

9. $70.55 is what percent of $830?

10. What is the fractional equivalent of $\frac{1}{2}$%?

Solve the following application problems, reading each carefully to determine whether base, part, or rate is being asked for. Also, check to see which are increase or decrease problems, and work accordingly. Round to the nearest cent or tenth of a percent, as necessary.

11. Due to low demand related to high gas prices, a Ford Explorer is offered at 17% off the manufacturer's suggested retail price. Find the discount and the sale price of this Explorer, originally priced at $30,500. **[3.2]**

12. A supervisor at Barrett Manufacturing finds that rejects amount to 1120 units per month. If this amounts to 0.5% of total monthly production, find the total monthly production. **[3.3]**

13. During a recent economic downturn in the United States, automobile sales were expected to fall 1.2% from the previous year's sales of 6.30 million. Find the expected sales for this year, rounded to the nearest hundredth of a million. **[3.2]**

14. It is estimated that 3 million people in the United States who are between the ages 55 and 64 have no health insurance. If this is 14% of the people in this age bracket, find the number of Americans in this age bracket. Round to the nearest hundredth of a million. **[3.3]**

15. A regional manager for Blockbuster has a monthly advertising budget of $6800. She budgets 25% for television, 40% for radio, and the remainder for newspapers. (a) Find the percent of the total budget to be spent on newspapers. (b) Find the total amount to be spent on newspaper advertising for an entire year. **[3.2]**

16. The government is offering a $25,000 bonus to federal employees for retiring early. After taxes and other deductions, the employee will receive only $17,000. What percent of the bonus will each employee actually receive? **[3.4]**

17. A digital camera is marked "reduced 25%, now only $262.50." Find the original price of the digital camera. **[3.5]**

18. Last year's backpack sales were 10% more than they were the year before. This year's sales are 1452 units, which is 10% more than last year. Find the number of backpacks sold 2 years ago. **[3.5]**

19. One day on the London Stock Exchange, Unilever's stock shares increased 12.3 pence to 449.5 pence. Find the percent of increase. **[3.4]**

20. Automobile sales in Asia were 23.4 million this year, a 9.4% increase over last year. Find the number of auto sales in Asia last year, rounded to the nearest tenth of a million. **[3.5]**

21. Americans lose about 300 million golf balls each year, and about 225 million of these are recovered and resold in what has become a $200 million annual business. What percent of the lost golf balls are recovered and resold? **[3.4]**

22. Most window cleaners contain 75% to 90% water. If a 16-ounce bottle of window cleaner contains 78% water, find the number of ounces of water in the 16-ounce bottle. Round to the nearest tenth of an ounce. **[3.2]**

23. Bookstore sales of the *Physicians Desk Reference,* which contains prescription drug information, rose 13.7% this year. If sales this year were 111,150 copies, find last year's sales. Round to the nearest whole number. **[3.5]**

24. After deducting 11.8% of total sales as her commission, George-Ann Hornor, a salesperson for Marx Toy Company, deposited $35,138.88 to the company account. Find the total amount of her sales. **[3.5]**

25. The U.S. Patent Office received 230,000 patent applications last year and issued 112,091 patents. What percent of the patent applications resulted in patents? Round to the nearest tenth of a percent. **[3.4]**

26. Doctors in Argentina reported that 240,000 Argentines will have plastic surgery this year. If the population of the entire country is 33 million, what percent of the Argentines will have plastic surgery this year? **[3.4]**

27. World population is about 6,925,000,000. If 4.54% of the world's population lives in the United States, estimate the number of people living in the United States. **[3.2]**

28. Tupperware, which was built on parties in people's homes where sellers demonstrated the use of plastic containers, is part of Premark International, Incorporated. Last year, Tupperware products accounted for 39% of Premark's $3.5 billion in sales. Find the amount of the Tupperware sales. **[3.2]**

29. The whooping crane, which is the tallest bird (5 feet) in North America, now has a population of 266 after dropping to near extinction in 1941, when there were only 15 birds. Find the percent of increase, to the nearest percent, in the number of whooping cranes since 1941. **[3.4]**

30. The Small Business Administration (SBA) guaranteed 42,500 loans this year, compared with 40,100 loans last year. Find the percent of increase in the number of loans guaranteed. **[3.4]**

31. The number of business failures this year was 64,031, compared with 64,743 business failures last year. Find the percent of decrease. **[3.4]**

32. The number of Canadian tourists traveling to Florida this year has decreased 25% since 1990, when a record 2.4 million visited the "Sunshine State." Find the number of Canadian tourists visiting Florida this year. **[3.2]**

33. Sales at Baker Electronics increased 1.7% this quarter to $143.2 million. Find sales last quarter to the nearest tenth of a million. **[3.4]**

34. Online sales of an item were up 2% from last year. If sales this year were 151,477 units, find the number of units sold last year. Round to the nearest whole number. **[3.5]**

35. Average hourly wages at a distribution center have risen 4.2% to $12.40 over the last year. Find the average hourly wages last year. **[3.5]**

36. Navistar International Corporation will cut daily production of class 8 trucks—those that can haul more than 33,000 pounds—by 26%, reducing daily production to 72 units. Find the daily production before the cutback. Round to the nearest whole number. **[3.5]**

CHAPTER 3	Business Application Case #1 *Stocks*

Understanding the stock market can be an important part of financial planning. Looking toward retirement, you may invest a portion of your savings by buying stock in various companies. Every day the changes in stock prices are shown in most major newspapers. Listed below are some well-known companies along with stock price information for this year and last year. Find the stock price last year, the percent of change from last year, or the stock price this year, as necessary. Round dollar amounts to the nearest cent and percents to the nearest tenth.

THE UPS AND DOWNS OF LAST YEAR

Company Name	Stock Symbol	Stock Price Last Year	Stock Price This Year	% Change from Last Year
Amazon.com	AMZN	18.89	51.51	_____
DaimlerChrysler	DCX	30.65	_____	28.7%
Dell Computer	DELL	_____	40.40	1186.6%
Krispy Kreme	KKD	33.77	40.02	_____
McDonald's	MCD	16.08	24.46	_____
Merck	MRK	_____	43.63	−21.1%
Pepsi Bottling	PBG	25.71	_____	−9.5%
R. J. Reynolds	RJR	_____	56.38	33.9%
Wal-Mart	WMT	50.51	_____	4.3%
Yahoo	YHOO	16.35	42.50	_____

CHAPTER 3	Business Application Case #2
	Real Estate Sales

Century 21 Real Estate Corporation (www.century21.com) is the world's largest franchiser of real estate offices and operates in more than 60 countries. The firm provides comprehensive training, management, administrative, and market support for more than 6000 independently owned and operated offices. It is considered the number-one consumer brand in the real estate industry.

Sometimes homeowners complain when they see the 6% sales commission that they must pay when listing their homes for sale with Century 21. However, realize that the commission is usually split among the following four parties: listing agent, selling agent, and the two offices for which each of these real estate agents work.

(a) The value of homes in one area went up by an average of 2.3% in the past year. Estimate the value today of a home that was valued at $265,000 last year.

(b) This year, the annual sales through one Century 21 office with 12 sales agents were $42 million. Estimate the revenue for the office if it received an average of 20% of the 6% commission on sales.

(c) From the revenue in part (b) above, the office manager must pay all costs of operating the sales office, including advertising, utilities, phones, insurance, and salaries for all noncommission employees. For the current year, these costs amount to $468,000. Find the profit as a percent of total revenue to the real estate office and round to the nearest tenth of a percent.

(d) Describe at least four examples in which percent is used in the real estate industry.

(e) Visit any local real estate office. Ask the manager and/or agents about advantages and disadvantages of a career as a real estate agent. Would a career as a real estate agent interest you? Why or why not?

Business Statistics

Sometimes the word **statistics** refers to data from business, economics, or other areas. At other times, *statistics* refers to techniques used to study data, such as looking for trends or making forecasts. For example, Figure 4.1 shows two different sets of data on the same line graph. One set is world population with a forecast to 2100 made by the United Nations. World population is read in billions of people using the scale on the left side of the graph. Notice that world population is predicted to peak at about 2080, followed by a slow decline.

The other set of data in the figure is total world oil production from a projection made by Cambridge Energy Research Associates (CERA), a well-respected group of experts on oil. Actually, CERA assumes higher levels of oil production for a longer period of time than many other groups of scientists studying the same issue. So, some suggest the world oil production line in Figure 4.1 is optimistic. The idea that there will be a peak in world oil production followed by a decline is known as **peak oil**. World oil production in millions of barrels per day is read using the scale on the right-hand side of the graph. Notice that world oil production is predicted to peak about 2040, or about 40 years before world population peaks in 2080. It is important to remember that everything beyond 2008 in the graph is a forecast and therefore subject to significant error.

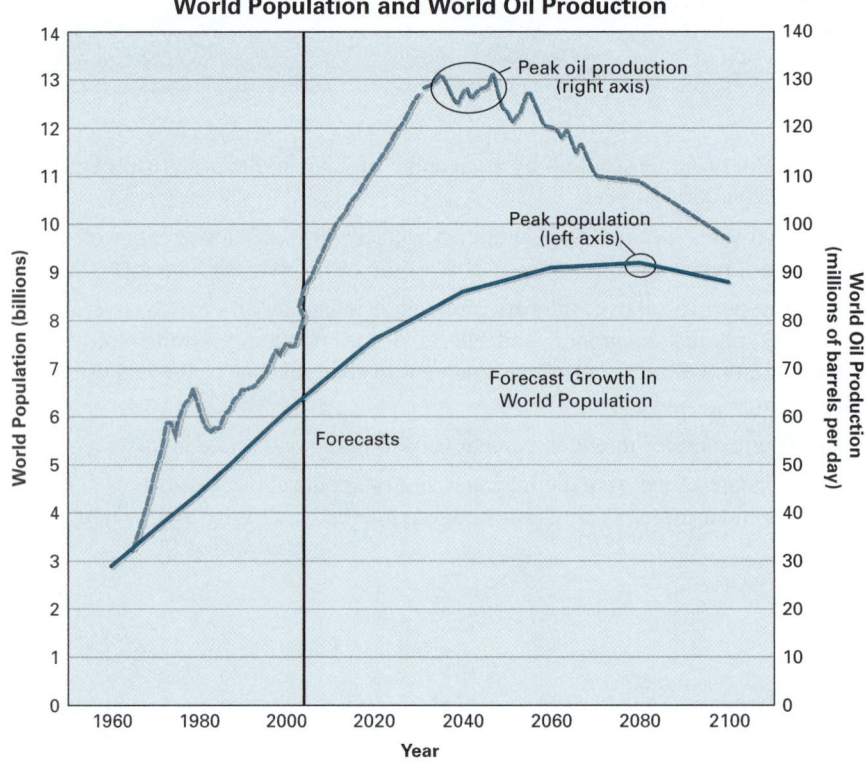

Figure 4.1

STOP —and think

> The forecasts in Figure 4.1 predict that world oil production will peak about 40 years before the peak in world population. First, list as many things as you can think of for which we humans use oil—it may help to use the Internet. Then, describe possible major issues if oil production peaks and falls off as population continues to grow. Finally, describe how business and government may be affected.

Managers use statistics daily. Sometimes the data are given in tables, but frequency distributions and graphs are often used as well. This chapter introduces basic concepts in statistics. To learn more on this important subject, we encourage you to take a class in statistics at your college.

4.1 Frequency Distributions and Graphs

OBJECTIVES

1 *Construct a frequency distribution.*

2 *Make a bar graph.*

3 *Make a line graph.*

4 *Make a circle graph.*

Objective

1 *Construct a Frequency Distribution.* It can be difficult to interpret or find patterns in a large group of numbers called **raw data**. One way of analyzing the numbers is to organize them into a table that shows the frequency of occurrence of the various numbers. This type of table is called a **frequency distribution**.

EXAMPLE 1 Constructing a Frequency Distribution

Stephanie Simpson is analyzing sales over the past 24 weeks at her new outdoor restaurant, Garden Plaza Coffee. The weekly sales data have been rounded to the nearest thousand dollars. Read down the columns, beginning with the left column, for successive weeks of the year.

Construct a table that shows each value of sales. Then go through the data and place a tally mark (|) next to each corresponding value. By counting the number of occurrences of each sales number, you are creating a frequency distribution table.

Solution Table 4.1 shows that the most common weekly sales amount was $4800, although there were 3 weeks with sales of $5300.

Table 4.1   FREQUENCY DISTRIBUTION TABLE

Sales (thousands)	Tally	Frequency	Sales (thousands)	Tally	Frequency	Sales (thousands)	Tally	Frequency
$3.2	|	1	$4.2	|	1	$5.1	|	1
$3.3	|	1	$4.3	|	1	$5.2	|	1
$3.5	|	1	$4.6	|	1	$5.3	|||	3
$3.9	||	2	$4.8	||||	4	$5.6	|	1
$4.0	|	1	$4.9	|	1			
$4.1	||	2	$5.0	||	2			

The frequency distribution given in the previous example contains a great deal of information, perhaps more than is needed. It can be simplified by combining weekly sales into groups, forming the grouped data shown in Table 4.2.

NOTE   The number of groups in the left column of Table 4.2 is arbitrary and usually varies between 5 and 15.

Table 4.2   GROUPED DATA

Sales (thousands)	Frequency (number of weeks)
$3.1–$3.5	3
$3.6–$4.0	3
$4.1–$4.5	4
$4.6–$5.0	8
$5.1–$5.5	5
$5.6–$6.0	1

Simpson must pay all expenses, including cost of foods and beverages, equipment repairs, employee salaries, rent, taxes, utilities, and insurance before anything is left for her to take out of the company as profit.

EXAMPLE 2   Analyzing Data

Based on the grouped data in Table 4.2, answer the following questions.

(a) If sales are $4000 or less per week, Simpson can take no salary and she must actually put money into the company to pay the bills. Find the number of weeks during which this occurred. Show this as a percent of the total number of weeks.

(b) If weekly sales are greater than $4000 but not more than $5000, Simpson does not have to put money into the company, but she still cannot take anything out of the company for herself in profit. Find the number of weeks during which this occurred. Show this as a percent of the total number of weeks.

(c) Simpson can take out at least a small profit for herself if sales exceed $5000 per week. Find the number of weeks during which this occurred and show this as a percent of the total number of weeks.

Solution   First, add the numbers in the right column in Table 4.2 to find that there are 24 weeks of data. Then answer the questions.

Sales	Number of Occurrences	Percent
(a) Less than $4000 per week	6 weeks	25%
(b) From $4000 to $5000 per week	12 weeks	50%
(c) Over $5000 per week	6 weeks	25%

Simpson had to put money into her business during 25% of the weeks. She was only able to take a salary out of the company during 25% of the weeks—the weeks with the highest sales. Example 3 gives a better sense of which weeks she was able to take a salary.

Objective

2 *Make a Bar Graph.* The next step in analyzing this information is to use it to make a **graph**. In statistics, a graph is a visual presentation of numerical data. One of the most common graphs is a **bar graph**, where the height of a bar represents the frequency of a particular value. A bar graph for the sales data is shown in Figure 4.2.

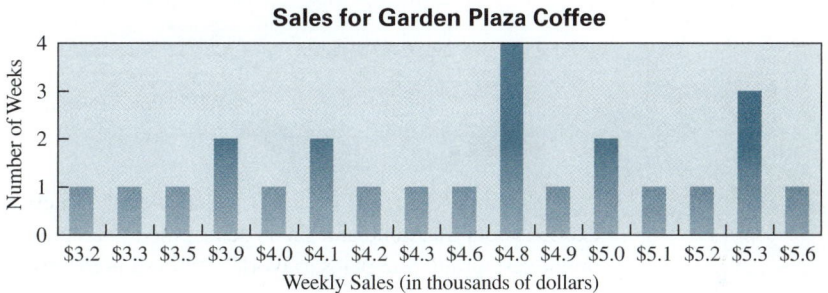

Figure 4.2

The information from the grouped data is shown in Figure 4.3. This graph shows that weekly sales of between $4600 and $5000 were the most common. Notice that this graph *does not* show any trend that may be occurring over time.

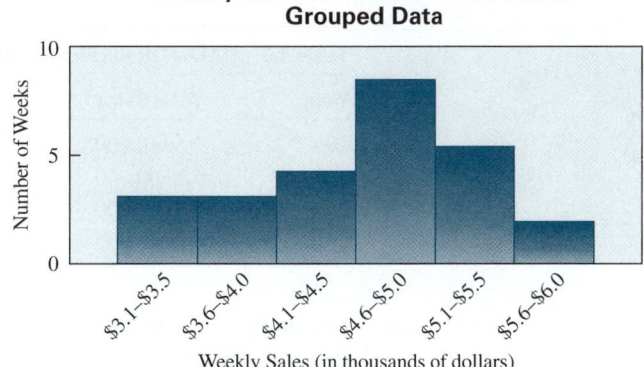

Figure 4.3

Objective

3 *Make a Line Graph.* Bar graphs show which numbers occurred and how many times but do not necessarily show the order in which the numbers occurred. To discover any trends that may have developed, draw a **line graph** of the data over time.

EXAMPLE 3 Draw a Line Graph

Show the progression of weekly sales at Garden Plaza Coffee through the year using a line graph. Do this by totaling the first 4 weeks (the first column) of data in Example 1 for the first data point. Similarly, total the second 4 weeks (second column) of data for the next data point, and so on.

Solution First find total sales for each 4-week period of time. We will just show the calculations for the first two 4-week time periods to show how it is done.

First 4 weeks' sales = $3.9 + $3.2 + $3.3 + $3.5 = $13.9 *or* $13,900

Next 4 weeks' sales = $4.0 + $4.2 + $4.1 + $3.9 = $16.2 *or* $16,200

Continuing in this manner, the six data points for the graph are $13.9, $16.2, $18, $19.7, $20.2, and $21 in thousands of dollars.

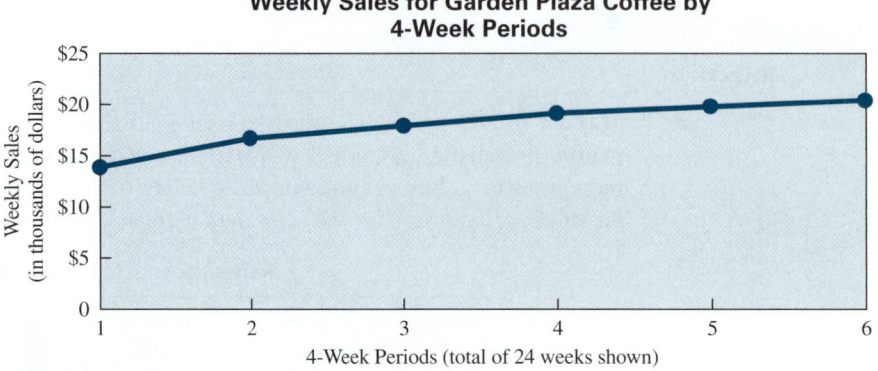

Figure 4.4

It is apparent from Figure 4.4 that weekly sales are increasing. Stephanie Simpson is excited about this trend and she is determined to continue the trend since her livelihood depends on the restaurant. She plans to work very hard in the restaurant over the next few months.

One advantage of line graphs is that two or more sets of data can be shown on the same graph. For example, suppose the managers of a company called River City Auto Parts want to compare total sales, profits, and overhead. Assume that they have extracted the following data from their records.

Table 4.3   DATA FOR RIVER CITY AUTO PARTS

Year	Total Sales	Overhead	Profit
2007	$740,000	$205,000	$83,000
2008	$860,000	$251,000	$102,000
2009	$810,000	$247,000	$21,000
2010	$1,040,000	$302,000	$146,000

Separate lines can be made on a line graph for each category so that necessary comparisons can be made. A graph such as this is called a **comparative line graph** (see Figure 4.5).

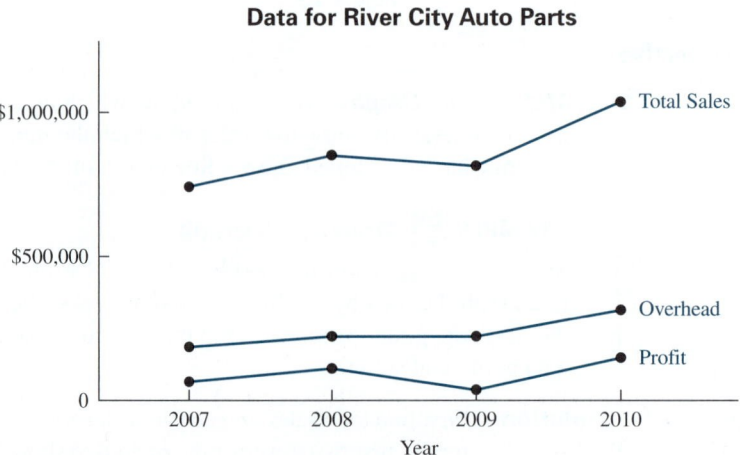

Figure 4.5

> **NOTE** Including zero on one or both scales of a line graph *often helps* the viewer understand and relate to the data.

4 *Make a Circle Graph.* Suppose a sales manager for Novel Recording makes a record of the expenses involved in keeping a salesforce on the road. After finding the total expenses, she converts each expense into a percent of the total, as shown in Table 4.4.

Table 4.4 NOVEL RECORDING EXPENSES

Item	Percent of Total
Car and plane	30%
Lodging	25%
Food	15%
Entertainment	10%
Sales meetings	10%
Other	10%
Total:	100%

> **NOTE** The percents should total 100%, although the total sometimes differs slightly due to rounding.

The sales manager can show these percents using a **circle graph**, which is sometimes called a **pie chart**. Every circle has 360 degrees, which is written as 360°. The degrees used here have nothing to do with temperature degrees such as 75° Fahrenheit or 15° Celsius. A degree as used in a circle graph simply represents $\frac{1}{360}$ of the circle in the shape of a piece of pie. To find the portion of the circle graph for each expense, multiply the percents in Table 4.4 by 360°.

Item	Percent × 360°	Fraction of Circle
Car and plane	$30\% \times 360° = 108°$	$\frac{108°}{360°} = \frac{3}{10}$
Lodging	$25\% \times 360° = 90°$	$\frac{90°}{360°} = \frac{1}{4}$
Food	$15\% \times 360° = 54°$	$\frac{54°}{360°} = \frac{3}{20}$
Entertainment	$10\% \times 360° = 36°$	$\frac{36°}{360°} = \frac{1}{10}$
Sales meetings	$10\% \times 360° = 36°$	$\frac{36°}{360°} = \frac{1}{10}$
Other	$10\% \times 360° = 36°$	$\frac{36°}{360°} = \frac{1}{10}$

These figures are used to build the pie chart in Figure 4.6.

**Novel Recording
Breakdown of Expenses**

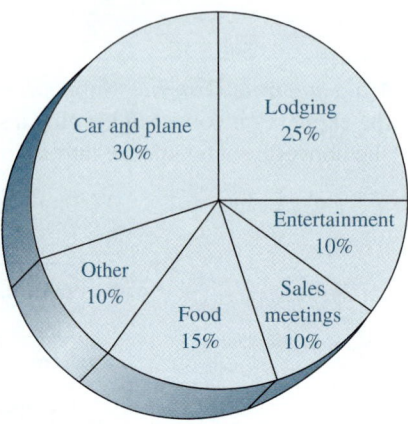

Figure 4.6

Circle graphs are used to show comparisons when one item represents a small portion compared to another. In the circle graph shown here, an item representing 1% of the total could be drawn as a small but noticeable slice; such a small item would hardly show up in a line graph.

EXAMPLE 4 Interpreting a Circle Graph

Based on the circle graph of expenses, answer the following questions.

(a) What percent of expenses was spent on travel and entertainment?
(b) What percent of expenses was spent on food and lodging?

Solution

(a) Travel is   30%   Car and plane
    Entertainment is + 10%
    Total spent   40%

(b) Food is   15%
    Lodging is   + 25%
    Total spent   40%

One of the most rapidly growing health problems worldwide is diabetes, a disease that causes sugar to build up in the blood. This disease may contribute to serious health problems, including heart disease, blindness, and kidney failure. It may result in the need to amputate leg(s) or other extremities. Figure 4.7 shows that diabetes is more common in some groups than in others.

Information on the American Diabetes Association Web site (www.diabetes.org) indicates that individuals can decrease their chances of being affected by this life-altering disease by getting 30 minutes a day of moderate physical activity, changing eating habits, and reducing body fat. The association recommends a diet with a lot of vegetables and fruits and a reduction in fats, sugary soft drinks, and candy.

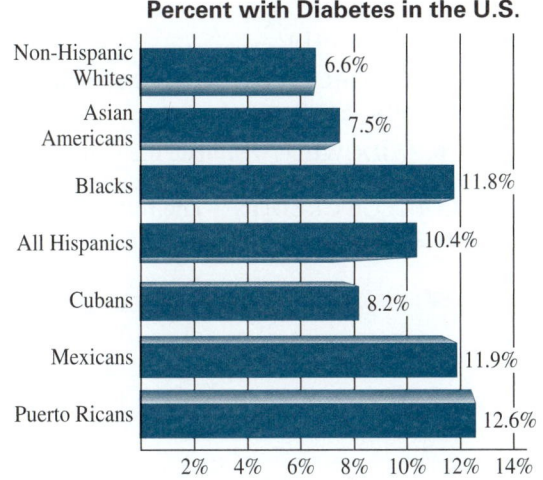

Percent with Diabetes in the U.S.

Source: Centers for Disease Control.

Figure 4.7

4.1	**Exercises**

Solve the following application problems using the information provided.

Answer Exercises 1–3 from the bar chart on the left and answer Exercises 4–6 from the line graph on the right.

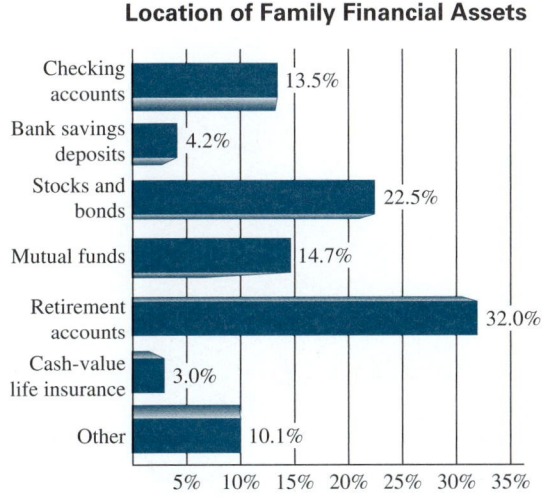

Location of Family Financial Assets

Source: Federal Board Survey of Consumer Finances.

Getting Together

The percentage of people who live together is rising while the marriage rate is in decline.

Source: U.S. Bureau of the Census.

1. **BANK DEPOSITS** Find the total percent on deposit at banks, including checking accounts and savings deposits.

2. **INVESTMENT DEPOSITS** Find the total percent in investments, including stocks and bonds, mutual funds, and retirement accounts.

3. **RATIO COMPARISON** Compare the percent in investment deposits to the percent in bank deposits using the answers in Exercises 1 and 2 above.

4. **MARRIED** Approximately what percent of the U.S. population was married in 1950 and in 2010?

5. **DIVORCED** What has happened to the percent of people divorced during the past 50+ years?

6. **WIDOWED** Estimate the percent of widowed people in 2010.

COLLEGE CREDITS **The following list shows the number of college credits completed by 30 employees of Franklin Bank.**

74	133	4	127	20	30
103	27	139	118	138	121
149	132	64	141	130	76
42	50	95	56	65	104
4	140	12	88	119	64

Use these numbers to complete the following table.

Number of Credits Completed	Frequency
7. 0–24	_____
8. 25–49	_____
9. 50–74	_____
10. 75–99	_____
11. 100–124	_____
12. 125–149	_____

13. Make a line graph using the frequencies that you found.

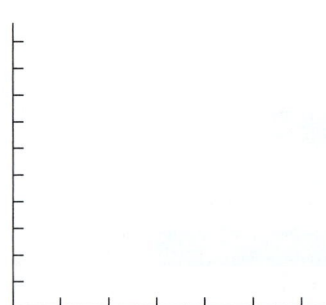

14. How many employees completed fewer than 25 credits?

15. How many employees completed 50 or more credits?

16. How many employees completed from 50 to 124 credits?

17. How many employees completed from 0 to 49 credits?

18. What percent of the employees have completed at least 100 credits? Round to the nearest tenth of a percent.

19. Compare bar graphs, line graphs, and circle graphs. (See Objectives 2–4.)

20. Explain the purpose of a comparative line graph. (See Objective 3.)

21. **FARM TRACTOR**   The following graph is used to estimate the acreage covered by a farm implement per hour, when its width and speed of travel are known. For example, a $7\frac{1}{2}$-foot (90-inch) mower blade moving 4 miles per hour would cover about $3\frac{5}{8}$ acres per hour. This is found by going across the graph from the working width (90 inches) to the diagonal line for speed (4 mph), then down to the bottom to find acreage per hour.

    (a) What is the acreage per hour for a 36-inch implement moving $2\frac{1}{2}$ miles per hour?

    (b) What is the acreage per hour for an 8-foot-wide combine moving 4 miles per hour?

    (c) How fast must a tractor pull a 48-inch plow in order to plow 1 acre per hour?

    (d) How wide a spray pattern is needed in order to spray $4\frac{1}{2}$ acres per hour at a speed of $4\frac{1}{2}$ miles per hour?

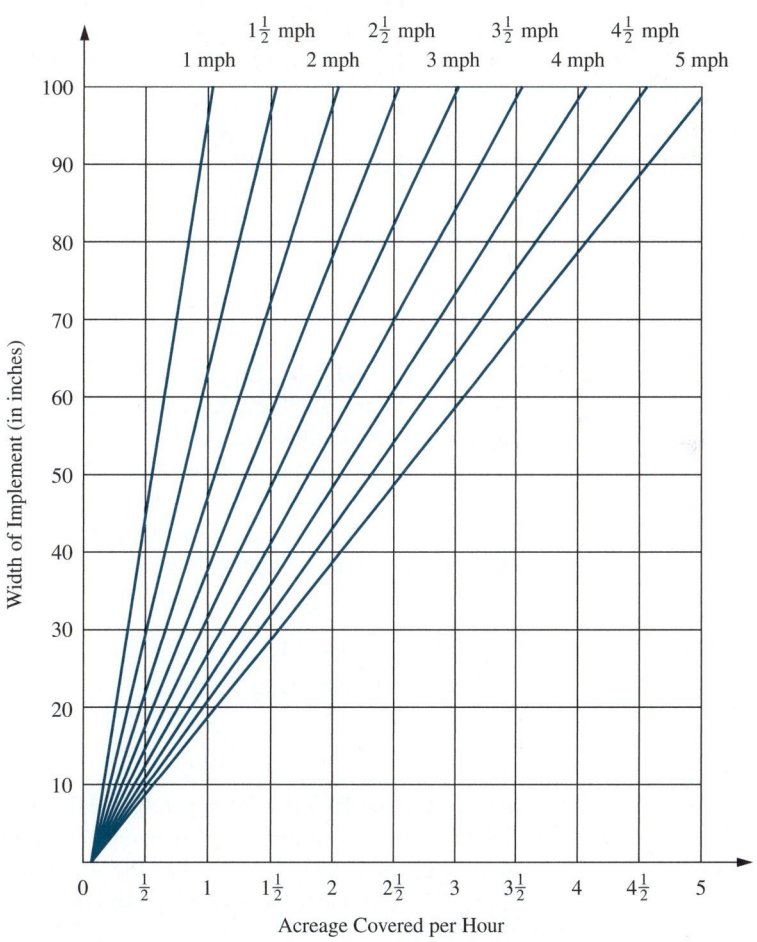

Acreage Covered by Farm Tractor

22. **AVERAGE WEIGHT AND HEIGHT**   The comparative line graph shows the change in average weight (in pounds) for a recent 20-year period for various categories of American adults. Find the change in weight for each of the following groups of people.

    (a) Men aged 20–24 who are 5 feet 10 inches tall (*Hint:* First find 5′ 10″ on the horizontal line in the center of the graph.)

    (b) Women aged 40–49 whose height is 5 feet 8 inches

    (c) 5-foot-tall women aged 20–24

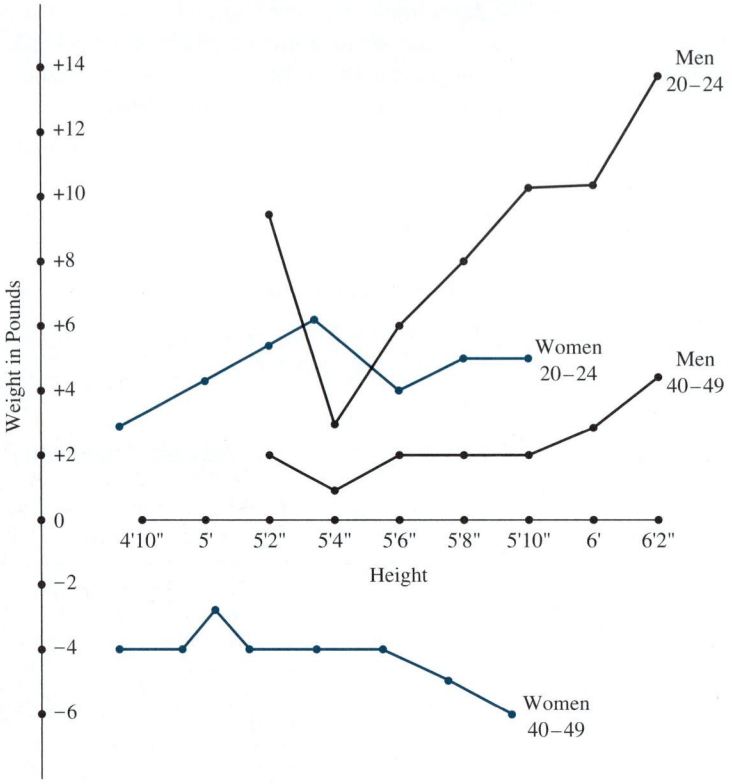

Average Weight and Height

20-Year Change in Average Weight of Americans

23. **COMPUTER SKILLS**   In today's business environment it is important for administrative and office-support professionals to possess computer skills. A recent survey asked this question of employers: "What does your company use as the primary method for evaluating a job candidate's software proficiency?" Draw a circle graph using the data.

The interview only	47%
Reference checking	26%
A test on a computer	8%
Other	19%
	100%

24. **SOURCES OF RETIREMENT INCOME**   The Social Security Administration recently found that the average retired couple has the following sources of retirement income. Show the data in a circle graph.

Social Security	40%
Personal assets	21%
Earnings	17%
Pensions	19%
Other	3%
	100%

25. INTEREST RATES Interest rates in the United States have changed considerably during the past 100 years, creating an environment that either nourishes business growth and associated stock market rallies or stunts their growth. Use the data in the line chart to answer the questions that follow.

Interest Rates in U.S.

*1900–1919, average long-term corporate bonds;
1920–2005, average 10-year Treasury bonds.

Source: Moody's Investor Service. Reprinted by permission.

(a) Estimate the average annual yield at the end of the Great Depression.

(b) Over what range did yields fluctuate between 1980 and 1990?

(c) Over what range did yields fluctuate between 2000 and 2010?

(d) Identify the long-term trend of rates during 1940–1982 and during 1982–2010.

26. MARKET SHARE Sales data for several fast-food companies were taken from recent financial statements. Show the data in a pie chart.

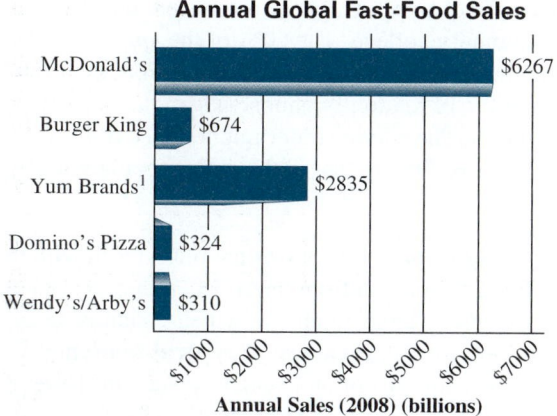

Annual Global Fast-Food Sales

McDonald's $6267
Burger King $674
Yum Brands[1] $2835
Domino's Pizza $324
Wendy's/Arby's $310

Annual Sales (2008) (billions)

[1]Yum Brands owns Pizza Hut, Kentucky Fried Chicken, and Taco Bell.

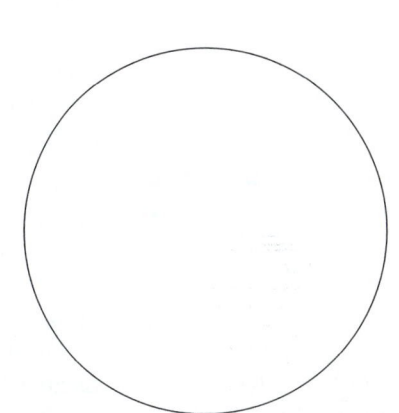

27. COLLEGE COSTS   Tuition and fees for a public 4-year college or university continue to rise. Show the data in a bar chart using horizontal bars.

Rising Tuition and Fees at Colleges (adjusted for inflation)

2003–2004	$11,859
2004–2005	$12,481
2005–2006	$12,824
2006–2007	$13,089
2007–2008	$13,589
2008–2009	$14,160 (estimate)

Source: College Board.

4.2   The Mean

OBJECTIVES

1 *Understand the difference between population and sample.*

2 *Find the mean of a set of data.*

3 *Find a weighted mean.*

4 *Find the mean for grouped data.*

Objective

1   *Understand the Difference between Population and Sample.*   In statistics, it is important to distinguish between the concepts of population and sample. **Population** is the entire group being studied, whereas **sample** is a portion of the entire group. Samples should be chosen randomly, meaning that no one individual in the population is more likely to be chosen than is another. The idea is for the sample to represent the population.

An administrator, for example, might be interested in the grade point average (GPA) of all freshmen at a community college. The GPA of the *entire population* of freshmen can be obtained, but this might be time-consuming to compile. Or, if an estimate of the GPA is adequate, the administrator can randomly choose a sample of perhaps 50 freshmen and find their grade point averages. The administrator might then *assume* that the grade point average of *this sample of students* is close to that of the entire population of all freshmen.

Objective

2   *Find the Mean of a Set of Data.*   Businesses are often faced with the problem of analyzing a mass of raw data. Reports come in from many different branches of a company. For example, salespeople may send in a large number of expense claims. In analyzing all the data, one of the first things to look for is a **measure of central tendency**—a single number that is designed to represent the entire list of numbers. One such measure of central tendency is the **mean**, which is just the common **average** used in everyday life.

For example, suppose the sales of carnations at Tom's Flower Shop for each of the days last week were $86, $103, $118, $117, $126, $158, and $149. To find a single number that is representative of this list, use the following formula.

$$\text{Mean} = \frac{\text{sum of all values}}{\text{number of values}}$$

For Tom's Flower Shop, the mean is

$$\text{Mean} = \frac{\$86 + \$103 + \$118 + \$117 + \$126 + \$158 + \$149}{7}$$

$$= \frac{\$857}{7}$$

$$= \$122.43 \quad \text{Rounded to the nearest cent}$$

EXAMPLE **1** **Finding the Mean**

Stephanie Simpson has promised 7 of her employees at Garden Plaza Coffee that they will all work about the same number of hours. One employee complained that she worked considerably more hours than the other employees last month. The number of hours worked by each of the 7 employees during the past month are given. Find the mean to the nearest hour.

Hours worked: 75, 63, 76, 82, 70, 81, 149

Solution The mean can be *estimated* by first rounding each number to the tens position. Therefore, 75 rounds to 80, 63 to 60, and so on, providing the following.

80, 60, 80, 80, 70, 80, 150

Add these numbers and divide by 7 to find an estimate of the mean.

$600 \div 7 = 86$ Rounded to the nearest whole number

Now find the exact value by adding the original numbers and dividing by 7. Check that the sum of numbers is 596.

$$\text{Mean} = \frac{596}{7} = 85 \quad \text{Rounded}$$

The mean of 85 seems a bit large since 1 employee did work a lot more than the other 6 employees. The mean without this value of 149 is the sum of the remaining hours worked divided by 6.

$$\text{Mean} = \frac{447}{6} = 75 \quad \text{Rounded}$$

This value seems more in line with the average number of hours worked. Perhaps there was an unusual reason why the one employee worked 149 hours (someone else was sick, etc.).

Notice that our estimate of 86 is close to the exact mean of 85. Estimating an answer before calculating the exact value helps minimize errors.

Averages are commonly used. Figure 4.8 shows the average credit-card debt owed by students at one private college. To find the averages in Figure 4.8, someone went through the following steps for just the freshman class:

1. Identify all freshmen students at the college (the population);
2. Take a random sample from the population of all freshmen; and
3. Estimate the average credit-card debt of freshmen in the random sample.

If the sample was taken randomly, then results from the sample can be used as an estimate of the average credit-card debt for the population of all freshman students at the college. All three steps must be done separately for sophomores, again for juniors, and again for seniors to get the data in the table. As you can see, a lot of work was needed to get the data, including taking four different samples from four different populations of students at the one college.

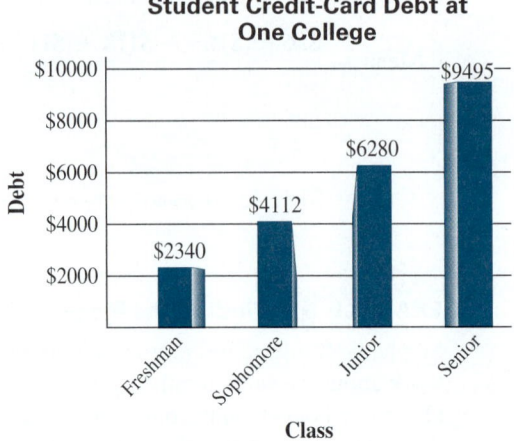

Student Credit-Card Debt at One College

Figure 4.8

Objective

3 *Find a Weighted Mean.*   Table 4.5 shows a frequency distribution of annual salaries received by employees of a medium-sized corporation. The table shows that 27 employees were paid $32,000 each, 16 were paid $40,000 each, and so on. The average salary paid to these employees cannot be found by just adding the salaries, since different salaries are earned by different numbers of employees.

To find the mean of the salaries, it is necessary to first multiply each annual salary by the number of employees receiving that salary. This process produces a **weighted mean**, where each number (a salary here) is "weighted" by multiplying it by the number of times it occurs.

Table 4.5   SALARIES OF EMPLOYEES

Salary	Number of Employees	Salary × Number of Employees
$32,000	27	$864,000
40,000	16	640,000
50,000	11	550,000
72,000	6	432,000
90,000	4	360,000
96,000	4	384,000
110,000	3	330,000
160,000	2	320,000
$296,000	1	296,000
	Total: 74	**Total: $4,176,000**

Use the totals of both columns of data in the table to find the mean by dividing total salaries by total number of employees.

$$\text{Mean salary} = \frac{\$4,176,000}{74} = \$56,432 \quad \text{Rounded}$$

Importantly, look at the large size of the total salary: $4,176,000. The company must pay this amount in salaries *each year* for the 74 employees. This may not be a problem for a company making money, but imagine the difficulty paying this amount in salaries if the company is facing a severe financial problem. In fact, managers at companies in financial trouble often lay off employees to save funds. One long-standing argument in society relates to the fairness of laying workers off even as top managers continue to earn high salaries and bonuses.

As you can see in the next example, weighted means are also used to find grade point averages.

EXAMPLE 2 Finding Grade Point Average

Find the grade point average for the following student. Assume $A = 4$, $B = 3$, $C = 2$, and $D = 1$, and $F = 0$.

Solution

Course	Units	Grade	Grade × Units
Business mathematics	3	$A\ (= 4)$	$4 \times 3 = 12$
Retailing	4	$C\ (= 2)$	$2 \times 4 = 8$
English	3	$B\ (= 3)$	$3 \times 3 = 9$
Computer science	2	$A\ (= 4)$	$4 \times 2 = 8$
Lab for computer science	2	$A\ (= 4)$	$1 \times 2 = 2$
	Total: 14		**Total:** 39

The grade point average for this student is

$$\frac{39}{14} = 2.79 \ or \ a \ B-$$

NOTE Grade point averages are frequently rounded to the nearest hundredth.

Objective

4 *Find the Mean for Grouped Data.* The mean can also be found for data that have been grouped into a frequency distribution. To do so, find the midpoint of each interval or class. This midpoint is found by averaging the highest and lowest numbers that can go into a class. For example, the midpoint, or **class mark**, of the interval 100–109 is the mean of 100 and 109.

$$\text{Class midpoint} = \frac{100 + 109}{2} = \frac{209}{2} = 104.5$$

EXAMPLE 3 Finding the Mean for Grouped Data

A researcher surveyed a number of farmers on their use of a particular brand of fertilizer. Although the recommended usage is 135 pounds per acre, she found that the usage varied from that. Find the mean for the frequency distribution shown.

	Intervals	Frequency	
	100–109	9	
	110–119	12	
Pounds per acre	120–129	17	Number of farmers
	130–139	28	
	140–149	21	
	150–159	16	
	160–169	4	

Solution Begin by finding the class mark for each class of fertilizer use. As explained, the class mark or midpoint of the first class is 104.5, and the midpoint of the second class is

$$\frac{110 + 119}{2} = \frac{229}{9} = 114.5$$

Find the other midpoints in a similar way. Then multiply the frequencies by the class marks, completing the column at the right labeled Frequency × Class Mark. Next, find the totals in the Frequency column and the Frequency × Class Mark column.

Intervals	Frequency	Class Mark	Frequency × Class Mark
100–109	9	104.5	9 × 104.5 = 940.5
110–119	12	114.5	12 × 114.5 = 1,374.0
120–129	17	124.5	17 × 124.5 = 2,116.5
130–139	28	134.5	28 × 134.5 = 3,766.0
140–149	21	144.5	21 × 144.5 = 3,034.5
150–159	16	154.5	16 × 154.5 = 2,472.0
160–169	4	164.5	4 × 164.5 = 658.0
	Total: 107		**Total:** 14,361.5

NOTE The intervals in a frequency table should not overlap with one another.

Finally, the mean is the quotient of these totals, or

$$\text{Mean} = \frac{14,361.5}{107} = 134.2 \quad \text{To the nearest tenth}$$

The mean usage rate of 134.2 pounds per acre is close to the recommended usage rate of 135 pounds per acre. The researcher was concerned with fertilizer use. Farmers using too much fertilizer could damage their crops, and those using too little fertilizer could have reduced yields. Either way, farmers would produce less for the markets and make less profit.

NOTE When a set of data is divided up into classes, it is no longer possible to tell where a particular item falls in a class. For this reason, *a mean found from grouped data is only approximate.*

4.2 Exercises

Find the mean for the following sets of data. Round to the nearest tenth.

1. 128, 240, 164, 380

2. 60, 65, 67, 62, 59, 58, 70

3. 3800, 3625, 3904, 3296, 3400, 3650, 3822, 4020

4. 10.3, 11.7, 12.4, 8.6, 9.9, 12.1, 13.2, 10.8, 9.6, 8.8

Round to the nearest whole number or as indicated.

5. **DOG WEIGHTS** A kennel owner likes Labs and owns four adult Labs with the following weights: 65 pounds, 58 pounds, 90 pounds, and 79 pounds. Find the mean weight.

6. **AUTO PRODUCTS** Weekly sales of products from the automotive department at a large discount store to the nearest dollar were: $7327, $6849, $8104, and $6598. Find the mean.

7. **COST OF DINING ROOM SET** A young couple is shopping for a dining room set. The prices of the ones they have looked at so far are $1280, $2650, $870, $940, and $760. Find the mean.

8. **LIFE INSURANCE SALES** Life insurance sold last quarter by the 6 new agents of National Insurance Agency totaled $294,000, $580,000, $722,000, $463,000, $814,000, and $1,785,000. Find the mean total of life insurance sold.

9. **RAINFALL** Annual rainfall in a small city in the desert of southern Arizona is given for the past few years: 12 inches, 9.8 inches, 12.2 inches, 9.3 inches, 10.2 inches, and 8 inches. Find the mean amount of rainfall to the nearest tenth.

10. **TELEPHONE SALES** TeleSales employs 9 people to make telephone calls to sell magazines. Last year, these people produced total sales of $492,811, $763,455, $901,852, $179,806, $244,193, $382,574, $591,873, $1,003,058, and $473,902. Find the mean sales per employee.

Find the weighted mean for the following. Round to the nearest tenth.

11. Value	Frequency
30	5
40	3
45	2
48	4

12. Value	Frequency
10	8
12	5
15	1
18	1

13. Value	Frequency
125	6
130	4
150	5
190	3
220	2
230	5

14. Value	Frequency
25	1
26	2
29	5
30	4
32	3
33	5

15. Explain the difference between population and sample. (See Objective 1.)

16. Think of an example in which the mean really does not give a good understanding of the situation involving the data. (See Objective 2.)

In the following problems, find the weighted mean salary for the employees. Round to the nearest thousand dollars.

17. Salary	Number of Employees
$18,000	8
$21,000	10
$28,000	8
$29,000	6
$38,000	4
$41,000	3
$53,000	2
$162,000	1

18. Salary	Number of Employees
$15,000	8
$20,000	15
$22,000	13
$25,000	9
$30,000	4
$42,000	3
$57,000	2
$260,000	1

Find the grade point average for the following students. Assume A = 4, B = 3, C = 2, D = 1, and F = 0. Round to the nearest hundredth.

19. Credits	Grade
4	D
2	A
3	C
1	F
3	D

20. Credits	Grade
4	B
3	B
3	C
3	C
3	D

Find the mean for the following grouped data. Rounded to the nearest tenth.

21. Interval	Frequency
50–59	15
60–69	20
70–79	21
80–89	27
90–99	18
100–109	2

22. Interval	Frequency
320–339	7
340–359	9
360–379	12
380–399	11
400–419	6
420–439	5

23. Interval	Frequency
25–49	18
50–74	15
75–99	30
100–124	18
125–149	32
150–174	14
175–199	7

24. Interval	Frequency
150–154	4
155–159	7
160–164	9
165–169	12
170–174	16
175–179	8
180–184	3

Solve the following application problems.

25. **MINIMUM GRADE TO PASS** The final grade in a history class is the average of three tests taken during the semester. Wanda Kroll made 74% and 68% on the first two tests. Find the minimum score she can make on the third test and still have a 70% average.

26. **CATTLE TRAILER** A trailer can hold 4200 pounds. The front of the trailer is loaded with scrap steel weighing 1300 pounds and an engine block weighing 840 pounds. Find the number of cows with a mean weight of 660 pounds that can be safely added to the trailer.

27. **STUDENT HEIGHT** A teacher wanted to demonstrate the mean of the grouped data to her class and she asked everyone to write down his or her height to the nearest inch. Find the mean to the nearest inch.

Interval	Frequency
46–50 inches	4
51–55 inches	12
56–60 inches	9
61–65 inches	3

28. **WEIGHT LIFTING** At the end of a one-semester class in weight lifting, a high school football coach tabulated data showing the amount of weight each student could dead lift. Find the mean to the nearest pound.

Interval	Frequency
101–150 pounds	1
151–200 pounds	9
201–250 pounds	16
251–300 pounds	5

4.3	The Median and the Mode

OBJECTIVES

1 *Find the median of a set of data.*

2 *Find the mode of a set of data.*

3 *Find the median and the mode of data in a frequency table.*

In everyday life, the word "average" usually refers to the mean. However, there are two other "averages" in common use, the **median** and the **mode**. Median and mode are discussed in this section.

Suppose the owner of a small company pays 5 employees annual salaries of $17,500, $18,000, $18,200, $19,000, and $20,000. The average, or mean, salary paid to the employees is

$$\text{Mean} = \frac{\$17,500 + \$18,000 + \$18,200 + \$19,000 + \$20,000}{5}$$

$$= \frac{\$92,700}{5} = \$18,540$$

Now suppose that the employees go on strike and demand a raise. To get public support, they appear on television to talk about their low salaries, which average only $18,540 per year.

The television station sends a reporter to interview the owner of the company. Before the interviewer arrives, the owner decides to find the average salary of *all employees*, including the 5 on strike, plus his own. To do this, he adds the 5 salaries given to the employees, plus his salary of $127,000. This gives an average of

$$\text{Mean} = \frac{\$17,500 + \$18,000 + \$18,200 + \$19,000 + \$20,000 + \$127,000}{6}$$

$$= \frac{\$219,700}{6} = \$36,617 \quad \text{Rounded}$$

When the television reporter arrives, the owner says that there is no reason for the employees to be on strike, since "the average salary of all company employees is $36,617."

There are two points to this story. First, both averages are correct, depending on what is being measured. *This shows how easily statistics can be manipulated.* Second, *the mean is often a poor indicator of the "middle"* of a list of numbers. In fact, when the mean was computed by the owner, it was greater than 5 of the 6 employees' salaries. The mean may be greatly affected by extreme values, such as the owner's salary of $127,000.

Objective

1 *Find the Median of a Set of Data.* To avoid such a misleading result, use a different measure of the "middle" of a list of numbers, the **median**. The median divides a list of numbers in half: one-half of the numbers lie at or above the median and one-half lie at or below the median.

Since the median divides an ordered list of numbers in half, the first step in finding a median is to rewrite the list of numbers as an **ordered array**, or list, with the numbers going from *smallest to largest*. For example, the list of numbers 9, 6, 11, 17, 14, 12, 8 would be written in order as the following ordered array.

$$6, 8, 9, 11, 12, 14, 17$$

The median is found from the ordered array as explained in the following box. Notice that the procedure for finding the median depends on whether the number of numbers in the list is even or odd.

Finding the Median

1. If the ordered array has an *odd* number of values, divide the number of values by 2. The next higher whole number gives the *location* of the median.

2. If the ordered array has an *even* number of values, there is no single middle number. Find the median by first dividing the number of values by 2. The median is the average (mean) of the number in this position and the number in the next higher position.

Example 1 shows a list of numbers having an *odd* number of values. Example 2 shows an *even* number of values.

EXAMPLE **1**   **Finding the Median (Odd Number of Numbers)**

Find the median for the annual salaries of the 5 employees introduced earlier in this section ($18,000, $20,000, $17,500, $19,000, and $18,200).

Solution   First, list the numbers from smallest to largest.

$$\$17,500, \$18,000, \$18,200, \$19,000, \$20,000$$

There are 5 numbers in the list. Divide 5 by 2 to get $\frac{5}{2} = 2.5$. The *next higher number* is 3 so that the median is the third number, or $18,200. Two numbers are larger than $18,200 and two are smaller.

EXAMPLE **2**   **Finding the Median (Even Number of Numbers)**

Find the median of the salaries of the employer and the 5 employees introduced earlier in this section ($127,000, $17,500, $18,000, $18,200, $19,000, and $20,000).

Solution   First arrange the numbers from smallest to largest.

$$\$17,500, \$18,000, \$18,200, \$19,000, \$20,000, \$127,000$$

There are 6 numbers (an even number of numbers) in the list. Divide 6 by 2 to get 3. The median is the *mean of the numbers in the third and fourth positions.*

$$\text{Median} = \frac{\$18,200 + \$19,000}{2} = \$18,600$$

The median of this set of numbers is $18,600 and the mean is $36,617. The median is probably a better measure of central tendency for this set of numbers than is the mean, which is distorted by one large number, i.e., $127,000.

Objective

2   ***Find the Mode of a Set of Data.***   The last important statistical measure of central tendency is called the **mode**. The mode is the number that occurs *most often*. For example, 10 students earned the following scores on a business law examination.

$$74, 81, 39, 74, 82, 80, 100, 92, 74, 85$$

The mode is 74, since more students obtained this score than any other.

NOTE   A bar graph can be used to find the mode.

EXAMPLE 3 Finding the Mode

Professor Miller gave the same test to both his day and evening sections of business math at American College. Find the mode of the tests given in each class. Which class had the lower mode?

(a) Day class: 85, 92, 81, 73, 78, 80, 83, 80, 74, 69, 80, 65, 71, 65, 80, 93, 54, 78, 80, 45, 70, 76, 73, 80, 71, 68

(b) Evening class: 68, 73, 59, 76, 79, 73, 85, 90, 73, 69, 73, 75, 93, 73, 76, 70, 73, 68, 82, 84, 77

Solution

(a) The number 80 is the mode for the day class because it occurs more often than any other number.

(b) The number 73 is the mode for the evening class because it occurs more often than any other number.

The evening class has the lower mode.

NOTE   It is not necessary to place the numbers in numerical order when looking for the mode, but it helps with a large array of numbers.

A set of data is called **bimodal** if it has two different modes, i.e., two numbers that occur the same number of times with each occurring more than any other number in the data set. A data set in which every number occurs the same number of times is said to have *no mode*.

NOTE   The mean, median, and mode are different ways of estimating the middle or center of a list of numbers. Each of these three ways is a measure of central tendency.

Objective

3   *Find the Median and the Mode of Data in a Frequency Table.*   The same basic ideas of median and mode are applied to data in a frequency table, as shown in the next example.

EXAMPLE 4 Finding the Mean, Median, and Mode

The diameter of a part coming out of a machining process is measured regularly. The diameters vary some, as shown in the frequency table. Find (a) the mean, (b) the median, and (c) the mode.

Diameter (inches)	Frequency
0.720–0.729	3
0.730–0.739	12
0.740–0.749	8
0.750–0.759	9
0.760–0.769	2

Solution

(a) The mean of the grouped data is found using the technique shown in the previous section. The class mark for the first class is

$$\frac{0.720 + 0.729}{2} = 0.7245$$

and so on for the other classes.

Class Mark	Frequency × Class Mark
0.7245	3 × 0.7245 = 2.1735
0.7345	12 × 0.7345 = 8.814
0.7445	8 × 0.7445 = 5.956
0.7545	9 × 0.7545 = 6.7905
0.7645	2 × 0.7645 = 1.529
Total: 34	= 25.263

The group average is

$$\frac{25.263}{34} = 0.743 \quad \text{Rounded}$$

(b) There are 34, or an even number, of values. Divide 34 by 2 to get 17. Thus, the 17th and 18th numbers from the smallest are averaged to find the median. The numbers have already been arranged from smallest to largest in the table. Three numbers fall in the first class (0.720–0.729) and 15 numbers fall in the first and second classes combined (0.720–0.729 and 0.730–0.739). The 17th and 18th numbers fall in the third class (0.740–0.749). The median is the class mark of the class containing the 17th and 18th values, or 0.7445.

(c) The mode is the class mark of the class with the highest frequency of occurrences, or 0.7345.

Thus, we have the following.

$$\text{Mean} = 0.743 \qquad \text{Median} = 0.7445 \qquad \text{Mode} = 0.7345$$

4.3	**Exercises**

Find the median for the following sets of data.

  1. 37, 14, 65, 12, 32

  2. 46, 27, 91, 34, 68, 53, 39

  3. 95, 98, 75, 81

  4. 6.8, 9.7, 5.2, 6.0, 6.8, 6.3

  5. 0.81, 0.82, 0.86, 0.84

  6. 900, 860, 840, 880, 920, 940

Find the mode or modes for the following sets of data.

  7. 60, 50, 60, 40, 70, 60, 40

  8. 12, 13, 10, 13, 14, 13

  9. 65, 60, 68, 72, 56, 70, 85

  10. 180, 195, 162, 173, 184, 195, 186, 170

  11. 6, 4, 8, 4, 6, 9, 3, 2

  12. 5.8, 5.6, 5.8, 5.5, 5.3, 5.4, 5.6, 5.2

  13. Compare mean, median, and mode. (See Objectives 1–3.)

  14. Give an example in which values for the mean, median, and mode of a set of data still do not provide a good understanding of the situation involving the data. (See Objectives 1–3.)

Solve the following application problems.

15. **SCUBA DIVING**   A scuba diver used his log book to review the depths of his last 5 dives in the waters of the Caribbean.

68 feet, 90 feet, 56 feet, 82 feet, 110 feet

Find the mean and median.

16. **SKYDIVING**   The altitudes of a skydiver's recent jumps are given in feet.

4300, 5000, 3800, 4800, 3400, 3600

Find the mean and median.

17. If you want to avoid a single extreme value having a large effect on the average, would you use the mean or the median? Explain.

18. **SHOE INVENTORY**   A manager trainee at a shoe store is trying to figure out how many pairs of each size shoe of a particular style to order. Should she use the mean, median, or mode of the number of each size sold? Or, are none of these values adequate? Explain. (See Sections 4.2 and 4.3.)

Find the mean, median, and mode for the following grouped data sets. Round to the nearest tenth.

19.
Interval	Frequency
100–109	10
110–119	12
120–129	8
130–139	2

20.
Interval	Frequency
10–14	2
15–19	1
20–24	5
25–29	7

Solve the following application problems.

21. **HEATING OIL**   A manufacturing company made 4 purchases of 3000 gallons each of heating oil to heat its facility during the winter. The prices it paid for the heating oil follow: $1.70 per gallon, $1.72 per gallon, $1.71 per gallon, and $1.78 per gallon. Find the mean and median.

22. **WHALE WATCH**   Blue Ray Tours takes people off the coast of Newfoundland twice daily and records the number of whales spotted. The number of whales varies by season of the year. Late one spring, the following weekly counts were observed during four successive weeks: 14, 21, 48, and 37. Find the mean, median, and mode.

23. **CHEMICAL PRODUCTION**   A biochemical company tries to place exactly 3 pounds of a particular enzyme in each bag that it produces. However, a tolerance of ±0.1 pound is considered acceptable. A recent sample of 56 bags of enzyme showed the following.

Pounds of Enzyme	Frequency
2.76–2.85	0
2.86–2.95	3
2.96–3.05	48
3.06–3.15	5
3.16–3.25	0

Find the mean of the grouped data. Based on the data available, does the company appear to have a successful bagging operation rounded to the nearest one-hundredth of a pound?

24. ROBOT-DRILLED HOLES A robot designed to drill a hole to a depth of 1.5 centimeters in a block of steel is being tested, with the following results.

Depth of Hole (centimeters)	Frequency
1.16–1.25	0
1.26–1.35	1
1.36–1.45	18
1.46–1.55	20
1.56–1.65	0

Find the mean of the grouped data. Does the robot appear to be working as desired?

4.4	**Range and Standard Deviation**

OBJECTIVES

1 *Find the range for a set of data.*

2 *Find the standard deviation.*

3 *Use the normal curve to estimate data.*

The mean and median can be used to indicate the middle, or central tendency, of a set of data, but *more is needed* to gain a good understanding of the data. It is also very important to get some sense about how widely the data are scattered.

To see why, look at the data in Table 4.6. Both sets of numbers have the same mean and median. The number of admittances in emergency room A go from a low of 5 to a high of 9 and the number of admittances in data set B go from a low of 1 to a high of 13. Even though the means and medians are the same, the manager of emergency room B needs to plan for a higher number of people since that emergency room sometimes has significantly more admittances per hour. The term used to describe the scatter of the data is **dispersion**.

Table 4.6 HOURLY ADMITTANCES TO EMERGENCY ROOMS

	A	B
	5	1
	6	2
	7	7
	8	12
	9	13
Mean	7	7
Median	7	7

Objective

1 *Find the Range for a Set of Data.* Two of the most common measures of dispersion, the range and the standard deviation, are discussed here.

The **range** for a set of data is defined as the *difference between the largest value and the smallest value in the set*. The range is *never* a negative number. In column A in Table 4.6, the largest value is 9 and the smallest is 5. The range is

$$\text{Highest} - \text{lowest} = \text{range}$$
$$9 - 5 = 4$$

In column B, the range is $13 - 1 = 12$, or much lower than the range in column A.

The range can be misleading if it is interpreted unwisely. For example, suppose three executives rate two employees, Mark and Myrna, on five different jobs, as shown in the following table.

Job	Mark	Myrna
1	28	27
2	22	27
3	21	28
4	26	6
5	18	27
Mean	23	23
Median	22	27
Range	10	22

By looking at the range for each person, we might be tempted to conclude that Mark is a more consistent worker than Myrna. However, by checking more closely, we might decide that Myrna is actually more consistent with the exception of one very poor score, which may be due to some special circumstance. Myrna's median score is not affected much by the single low score and is more typical of her performance as a whole than is her mean score.

One of the most useful measures of dispersion, the standard deviation, is based on the *deviation (or spread) from the mean* of the data. To find how much each value deviates from the mean, first find the mean, and then subtract the mean from each data value.

EXAMPLE 1   Finding Deviations from the Mean

Find the deviations from the mean for the data values 32, 41, 47, 53, 57.

Solution   Add these numbers and divide by 5. *The mean is 46.* To find the deviations from the mean, subtract 46 from each data value. (Subtracting 46 from a smaller number produces a negative result.)

Data value	32	41	47	53	57
Deviation	-14	-5	1	7	11

NOTE   To check the work in Example 1, add the deviations. The sum of the deviations for a set of data is always 0, as long as the mean was not rounded.

NOTE   The deviation between a number and the mean is 0 if the two numbers are identical.

Objective

2   *Find the Standard Deviation.*   To find the measure of dispersion or scatter in the data, it might be tempting to find the mean of the deviations. However, this number always turns out to be 0 no matter how much the dispersion in the data is, because the positive deviations simply cancel out the negative ones.

Get around this problem of adding positive and negative numbers by first *squaring* each deviation. (The square of a negative number is positive.) Take Example 1 one step further.

Data value	32	41	47	53	57
Deviation from mean	−14	−5	1	7	11
Square of deviation	196	25	1	49	121

Before defining standard deviation, we need to define square root. The **square root** of a number n is written $\sqrt{n}$. It is the number that when multiplied by itself equals n. Thus, $\sqrt{144} = 12$ since $12 \times 12 = 144$, $\sqrt{1} = 1$ since $1 \times 1 = 1$, and so on.

Here is the formula to find the **standard deviation**.

$$\text{Standard deviation} = \sqrt{\frac{\Sigma(\text{deviation}^2)}{\text{number of observations}}}$$

where (deviation^2) is the deviation from the mean for each value squared, so that $\Sigma(\text{deviation}^2)$ is the sum of the squared deviations.

Finding the Standard Deviation

1. For each number, find the deviation from the mean.
2. Square each deviation.
3. Add the squared deviations together.
4. Divide the sum of the squared deviations by the number of observations.
5. Find the square root of the result found in Step 4.

Find the standard deviation using the data in the previous table, which is the same raw data as found in Example 1.

$$s = \sqrt{\frac{196 + 25 + 1 + 49 + 121}{5}}$$

$$= \sqrt{\frac{392}{5}}$$

$$= \sqrt{78.4}$$

$$= 8.9 \qquad \text{Rounded to the nearest tenth}$$

Scientific Calculator Approach

The calculator solution to this problem is as follows.

$$(\;\; 196 \;\; + \;\; 25 \;\; + \;\; 1 \;\; + \;\; 49 \;\; + \;\; 121 \;\;) \;\; \div \;\; 5 \;\; = \;\; \sqrt{x} \;\; 8.854377448$$

The algebraic expression for the standard deviation is

$$s = \sqrt{\frac{\Sigma d^2}{n}}$$

where $d = $ a deviation from the mean, n is the *number of data points in the group of numbers*, and the Greek letter Σ (sigma) represents a "sum of."

NOTE   Some calculators have statistical function keys that can be used to calculate means and standard deviations. Check your calculator manual to see if your calculator has these keys.

EXAMPLE 2   Finding Standard Deviation

The number of attendees at recent children's soccer games is 7, 9, 18, 22, 27, 29, 32, 40. Find the standard deviation.

Solution

STEP 1 Find the mean of the values.

$$\frac{7 + 9 + 18 + 22 + 27 + 29 + 32 + 40}{8} = 23$$

STEP 2 Find the deviations from the mean.

Data values	7	9	18	22	27	29	32	40
Deviations	-16	-14	-5	-1	4	6	9	17

STEP 3 Square each deviation.

Squares of deviations: 256   196   25   1   16   36   81   289

These numbers are the d^2 values in the formula.

STEP 4 Find the sum of the d^2 values.

$$\Sigma d^2 = 256 + 196 + 25 + 1 + 16 + 36 + 81 + 289 = 900$$

Now divide Σd^2 by n, which is 8 in this example.

$$\frac{\Sigma d^2}{n} = \frac{900}{8} = 112.5$$

STEP 5 Take the square root of the answer in Step 4. The standard deviation of the given list of numbers is

$$s = \sqrt{112.5} = 10.6$$

   The standard deviation is an important measure of the scatter in data. For example, suppose two different soccer teams score the following number of goals in subsequent games.

Team	Number of Goals Scored
Rockets	2, 1, 2, 2, 1
Bulls	0, 4, 5, 1, 7

The data for the Bulls is more widely scattered and will have a much larger standard deviation than that for the Rockets. It is important to know both measures of central tendency, such as the mean, median, or mode, and measures of dispersion (or scatter), such as range and standard deviation. Information on both is needed to better understand the data.

NOTE   The **variance**, which is used in some textbooks, is the square of the standard deviation.

$$\text{Variance} = (\text{standard deviation})^2$$

Similarly, the standard deviation is the square root of the variance.

$$\text{Standard deviation} = \sqrt{\text{variance}}$$

Objective

3   *Use the Normal Curve to Estimate Data.*   Soft-drink bottlers such as the Coca-Cola Company wish to deliver a quality product to their customers. Of course, a primary measure of quality is taste. The level of liquid placed in each container during the bottling process affects the level of carbonation, which, in turn, influences taste. Thus, these bottlers try to put a very specific amount of the liquid drink into each container. Some even X-ray each bottle as it rapidly moves down the production line in order to make sure that the amount of liquid is "close enough" to the desired level.

If the bottling process is working well, the amount of liquid in successive containers will be centered around the desired amount. However, there will always be **variation** since not every bottle will be filled with exactly the same amount of fluid. Even though the difference in the amount of fluid in each bottle may be small, it is an important measure of quality that producers are very concerned about. The differences in the fluid levels between bottles can usually be described by the **normal curve**. The normal curve is also called the **normal probability distribution** or the **bell-shaped curve**. The normal curve is shown in Figure 4.9.

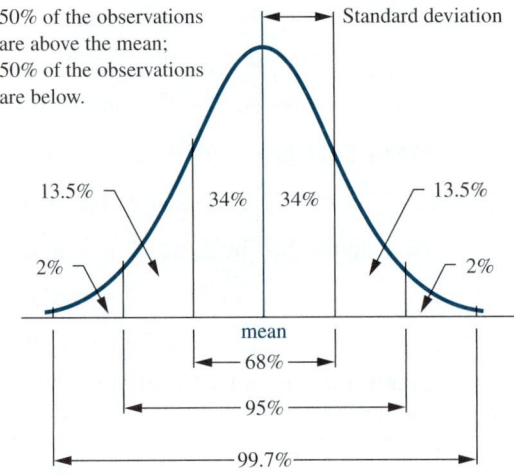

Figure 4.9 Normal Distribution

To illustrate how the normal curve shown in Figure 4.9 is used, assume that the amount of fluid in bottles being produced at a bottling company is normally distributed with a mean of 16 ounces and a standard deviation of 0.1 ounce. Then the following is true.

50% of the bottles contain 16 ounces or less.
50% of the bottles contain 16 ounces or more.

The following is also true.

68% of the bottles are filled to within 1 standard deviation of the mean of 16 ounces.
95% of the bottles are filled to within 2 standard deviations of the mean of 16 ounces.
99.7% of the bottles are filled to within 3 standard deviations of the mean of 16 ounces.

Although the amount of fluid in the next bottle is never known exactly, the output of the process can be approximated by the normal curve using this information.

In this example, the amount of fluid is measured in ounces. However, the next example discusses fluid levels in bottles using the height of fluid in a bottle. The same percentages that are shown above apply to this example as well. In fact, the same percentages *apply to every application* of the normal probability distribution!

EXAMPLE 3 **Using the Normal Distribution**

Measurements are used by a worker to determine the fluid-level fill of bottles. The worker has found that the fluid-level fill can be described by the normal curve with a mean of 6 inches and a standard deviation of 0.04 inch.

(a) Find the mean minus 3 standard deviations and the mean plus 3 standard deviations.

(b) Use Figure 4.9 to find the number of bottles out of 1000 that should fall between the two limits found in part (a). This represents the number of appropriately filled bottles.

(c) Find the number of bottles out of 1000 expected to have a fluid-level fill of less than 5.96 inches.

Solution

(a) Mean $-$ 3 standard deviations = $6 - (3 \cdot 0.04) = 5.88$ inches
Mean $+$ 3 standard deviations = $6 + (3 \cdot 0.04) = 6.12$ inches

(b) Simply add the percents within 3 standard deviations of the mean in Figure 4.9 to find the total percent of the bottles that should fall within the limits found in (a) above.

$$2\% + 13.5\% + 34\% + 34\% + 13.5\% + 2\% = 99\%$$

Now multiply this percent by the 1000 bottles to find the number of bottles that should fall within the limits found in (a).

$$99\% \text{ of } 1000 = 0.99 \times 1000 = 990 \text{ containers}$$

If a random sample of 100 results in more than 1 bottle outside the acceptable range of 5.88 inches to 6.12 inches, then the production line is stopped and the equipment is checked for quality problems. This is done to prevent poor-quality products from coming off the production line. No company wants to produce poor-quality products.

(c) The mean minus 1 standard deviation is 5.96 inches. So, we are looking for the area under the normal curve that is to the left of the mean minus 1 standard deviation. The area from the mean all the way to the left is 50%. The area between the mean and 1 standard deviation to the left of the mean is 34%. The area to the left of the mean minus 1 standard deviation is $50\% - 34\% = 16\%$. Now multiply 0.16 by the 1000 bottles sampled to find the number.

$$0.16 \times 1000 = 160 \text{ bottles}$$

NOTE   Workers from all over the world have been trained in statistics so that they can monitor the quality of their own work.

4.4	**Exercises**

Find the mean and standard deviation for each set of data. Round answers to the nearest tenth.

1. 15, 18, 20, 19

2. 6.8, 5.4, 3.7, 7.2, 6.4

3. 20, 22, 23, 18, 21, 22

4. 120, 118, 109, 115, 112, 110

5. 55, 58, 54, 52, 51, 59, 58, 60

6. 7.5, 7.3, 7.2, 7.5, 7.8, 7.1, 7.4, 8.0, 7.2, 7.6

Find the range for each set of data.

7. 18, 24, 60, 42, 51, 61

8. 10, 15, 12, 17, 21, 13

9. 500, 274, 361, 295, 112

10. 10.3, 7.4, 8.1, 6.5, 9.7

11. When can the range of a set of numbers be misleading? (See Objective 1.)

12. Explain the meaning of range and standard deviation. (See Objectives 1 and 2.)

STUDENT WEIGHT The weights of two hundred 11-year-old students were measured. The results can be approximated by a normal curve with a mean weight of 80 pounds and a standard deviation of 0.5 pound. Use the following graph to find the number of students weighing as indicated in Exercises 13–20.

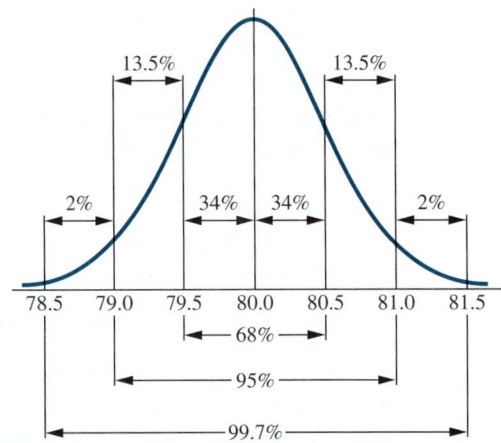

13. More than 80 pounds

14. More than 79.5 pounds

15. Between 79.5 and 80.5 pounds

16. Between 79 and 81 pounds

17. Between 80.5 and 81 pounds

18. Between 79.5 and 81 pounds

19. Within 1 pound of the mean

20. More than $1\frac{1}{2}$ pounds away from the mean

JOCKEY WEIGHT The weight of each jockey who rides horses at the race track is carefully measured before any race. The jockeys at one race had a mean weight of 107.8 pounds with a standard deviation of 2.6 pounds. Use the concepts of the normal curve to estimate the likelihood that one jockey chosen at random falls in the following weight classes.

21. Less than 107.8 pounds

22. More than 110.4 pounds

23. Between 102.6 and 113 pounds

24. Between 100 and 115.6 pounds

IQ = TEST RESULTS On standard IQ tests, the mean is 100 and the standard deviation is 15. The results are very close to fitting a normal curve. Suppose an IQ test is given to a very large group of people. Find the percent of people whose IQ score is the following.

25. More than 100

26. Less than 100

27. Greater than 115

28. Between 85 and 115

29. Between 70 and 130

30. Between 55 and 145

31. Less than 55

32. More than 145

TIRE WEAR After a 30,000-mile road test, the average wear on a particular brand of tire averaged 0.2 inch, with a standard deviation of 0.015 inch. The tire wear fits a normal curve closely. What percent of the tire wear would be the following?

33. 0.185 inch or more?

34. Less than 0.185 inch?

35. 0.23 inch or less?

36. More than 0.23 inch?

RACE TIMES The average amount of time taken by runners to complete a 10-kilometer race was 47.6 minutes, with a standard deviation of 2.7 minutes. Given that the times are approximately normally distributed, what percent of the runners required the following?

37. At least 44.9 minutes?

38. No more than 44.9 minutes?

39. No more than 53 minutes?

40. At least 53 minutes?

41. Between 44.9 minutes and 50.3 minutes?

42. Between 42.2 minutes and 53 minutes?

43. **SWIMMING** A graduate student is doing research using students on a high school swim team. She found that the average time to swim the 100-yard freestyle was 54.6 seconds, with a standard deviation of 1.2 seconds. Out of 20 swimmers, use the normal distribution to estimate the number that would be expected to swim 100 yards freestyle in less than 53.4 seconds.

44. **TEST GRADES** The exact same final exam in world history was given to 263 students. The results can be approximated by the normal probability distribution, with a mean of 72% and a standard deviation of 9%. Find the number of students scoring less than 63% on the test.

4.5 Index Numbers

OBJECTIVES

1 *Find the price relative.*

2 *Use the Consumer Price Index to compare costs.*

Objective

1 *Find the Price Relative.* A house that cost $85,000 ten years ago now sells for $182,500. Tuition at one community college has increased from $380 per semester 15 years ago to $2600 per semester today. The price of both the house and college tuition increased over time. In fact, the cost of most items, including houses, cars, food, and beverages, tends to go up from year to year. Salaries also often increase from year to year.

Rather than thinking that prices continually increase, you can also think of it as the value of each dollar continuing to fall as time passes. Over the years, each dollar buys less and less, so the value of the dollar goes down. This is true for most currencies in the world, most of the time.

Price relatives are used to study the increase in prices over time. They can be used to compare two different items to see which price has increased more during a certain period of time. The **price relative** is the current price divided by the price in a specific past year, which is called the **base year**. The formula for price relative follows.

$$\text{Price relative} = \frac{\text{price this year}}{\text{price in base year}} \times 100$$

EXAMPLE 1 **Finding the Price Relative**

Using the prices just given, find the price relative for the house.

$$\text{Price relative} = \frac{\$182,500}{\$85,000} \times 100 = 214.7 \quad \text{Rounded}$$

Today, the house sells for 214.7% of the price it did 10 years ago. Notice that a price relative is really just a percent. It gives the percent that this year's price is compared to the base year.

Find the price relative for the community college tuition as follows.

$$\text{Price relative} = \frac{\$2600}{\$380} \times 100 = 684.2 \quad \textcolor{blue}{\text{Rounded}}$$

Since the price relative of 684.2 for the increase in college tuition is much larger than the price relative of 214.7 for the house, it is clear that the price of the college tuition has increased far more rapidly than the price of the house.

EXAMPLE 2   Finding the Price Relative

The price of a particular Intel computer chip dropped from $500 two years ago to $200 today. The price relative is found as follows.

$$\frac{\$200}{\$500} \times 100 = 40$$

The computer chip sells for 40% of its original price. This example shows that a price relative is below 100 when the price of the item falls. Although the price of most items increases with time, the price of a few items goes down with time. Most price relatives are over 100 during periods of high inflation when prices are generally increasing.

NOTE   The price relative gives a way of comparing the two prices and showing a percent increase.

Objective

2   *Use the Consumer Price Index to Compare Costs.*   The **Consumer Price Index (CPI)**, published by the Bureau of Labor Statistics, can be given in terms of price relatives. The bureau keeps track of the costs of a great many items in different cities throughout the country and publishes its findings monthly. A recent portion of the report for one month is included in Table 4.5.

Table 4.5   URBAN PRICES INDEX*

Item	Chicago	Houston	Los Angeles	New York
All items	213.4	191.1	226.2	238.4
Food and beverages	219.2	202.3	237.8	229.6
Transportation	186.3	168.5	189.7	200.3
Medical	371.9	340.4	354.3	367.6
Recreation	112.4	108.3	117.1	115.5

*All figures are expressed as a percent of the 1982–1984 base of 100.

Source: U.S Bureau of Labor Statistics.

The numbers in Table 4.5 show the price relatives using a base year of 1982–1984. For example, medical costs in New York are now 367.6% of those in 1982–1984. The price relatives in Table 4.5 can be used to compare price increases for the different cities shown. For example, since 1982–1984 the cost of recreation has gone up by 108.3% in Houston versus 117.1% in Los Angeles. The data in the table cannot be used to estimate the actual cost of recreation in, say, Houston without first knowing what recreation costs were in the base year.

NOTE It is easy to see that the largest price relatives in Table 4.5 are those for medical costs. Thus, medical costs have increased far more rapidly than any of the other costs shown in the table.

Medical Costs Increase

The results of a recent survey of area firms indicate that increasing medical costs have become a big concern for managers. The survey showed an average annual increase in the cost of medical insurance of 12.7%. Managers are debating how to keep medical costs under control and wondering how they can pass part of the costs along to consumers and to employees. . . .

EXAMPLE 3 Using the CPI

One kidney transplant in Chicago cost $11,050 in 1984. Use the price relative to estimate the cost of the same surgery today.

Solution The price relative for medical costs in Chicago is 317.9, or 371.9%.

$$\text{Today's cost} = \$11,050 \times 371.9\% = \$41,094.95$$

This high cost shows why people need help with the expenses from any catastrophic illness.

4.5 Exercises

Find the price relatives for the following items. Round to the nearest tenth.

Item	Price Then	Price Now
1. Rent	$225 per month	$550 per month
2. Ski boat	$2600	$4800
3. Computer	$2000	$1200
4. Jeans	$25 per pair	$40 per pair
5. Natural gas	$1.25 per thousand cubic feet	$7.00 per thousand cubic feet
6. House	$60,000	$95,000

Use the Urban Prices Index in Table 4.5 to complete the following chart.

Urban Area	Item	$100 Worth in 1982 Will Cost Today
7. Chicago	All items	_____
8. New York	Food and beverage	_____
9. Houston	Transportation	_____
10. Los Angeles	Food and beverage	_____
11. Chicago	Medical	_____
12. Los Angeles	Recreation	_____

Solve the following application problem using Table 4.5.

13. **HEART BYPASS** Assume the total cost of a heart bypass in New York in 1982 was $34,500. Estimate the cost today to the nearest $1000.

14. **FAMILY BUDGET** Find today's equivalent of $22,000 family budget in 1982 in Houston to the nearest $1000. This would include all items.

15. **FOOD AND BEVERAGE** Assume a 1983 food and beverage budget for a family of 4 in Chicago of $310 per month. Find today's equivalent amount.

16. **RECREATION** Assume a 1982 family budget of $3000 for recreation in Los Angeles and find today's equivalent amount.

17. **INCREASING PRICES** Of the items listed in Table 4.5, which has increased the most?

18. **INCREASING PRICES** Use Table 4.5 to find the city in which all item costs increased the least.

19. Explain price relative and inflation. Are they identical to one another? Explain. (See Objectives 1 and 2.)

20. Go to the library or use the Internet and find the government's estimate of the CPI for the past 3 years. Compare the average inflation of these 3 years to inflation during the early 1930s, when inflation was actually negative. Also compare to inflation in the late 1970s, when inflation was very high. (See Objective 2.)

CHAPTER TERMS

Review the following terms to test your understanding of the chapter. For any terms you do not know, refer to the page number found next to that term.

average [p. 122]
bar graph [p. 113]
base year [p. 141]
bell-shaped curve [p. 138]
bimodal [p. 131]
circle graph [p. 115]
class mark [p. 125]
comparative line graph [p. 114]
Consumer Price Index (CPI) [p. 142]

dispersion [p. 134]
frequency distribution [p. 111]
graph [p. 113]
line graph [p. 113]
mean [p. 122]
measure of central tendency [p. 122]
median [p. 129]
mode [p. 130]
normal curve [p. 138]

normal probability distribution [p. 138]
ordered array [p. 129]
peak oil [p. 110]
pie chart [p. 115]
population [p. 122]
price relative [p. 141]
range [p. 134]
raw data [p. 111]
sample [p. 122]
square root [p. 136]

standard deviation [p. 136]
statistics [p. 110]
variance [p. 137]
variation [p. 138]
weighted mean [p. 124]

CONCEPTS

EXAMPLES

4.1 Constructing a frequency distribution from raw data

1. Construct a table listing each value and the number of times this value occurs.
2. For a distribution with grouped data, combine the data into classes.

For the following data, construct a frequency distribution.
12, 15, 15, 14, 13, 20, 10,
12, 11, 9, 10, 12, 17, 20, 16,
17, 14, 18, 19, 13

Data	Tally	Frequency
9	|	1
10	||	2
11	|	1
12	|||	3
13	||	2
14	||	2
15	||	2
16	|	1
17	||	2
18	|	1
19	|	1
20	||	2

Classes	Frequency
9–11	4
12–14	7
15–17	5
18–20	4

4.1 Constructing a bar graph from a frequency distribution

Draw a bar for each class using the frequency of the class as the height of the bar.

Construct a bar graph from the frequency distribution of the previous example.

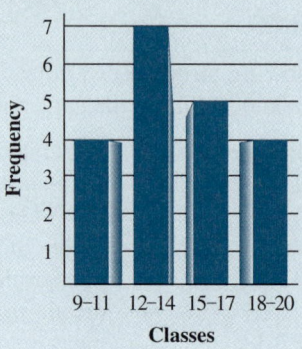

4.1 Constructing a line graph

1. Plot each year on the horizontal axis.
2. For each year, find the value for that year and plot a point for each value.
3. Connect all points with straight lines.

Construct a line graph for the following data.

Year	Value
2007	$850,000
2008	920,000
2009	875,000
2010	975,000

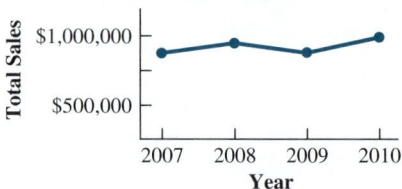

4.1 Constructing a circle graph

1. Determine the percent of the total for each item.
2. Find the number of degrees represented by each percent.
3. Draw the circle.

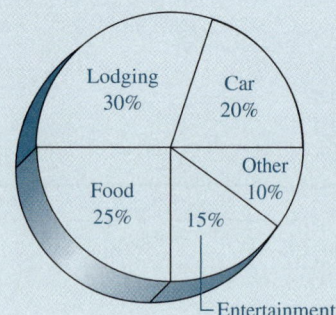

Construct a circle graph for the following expenses.

Item	Amount	Percent
Car	$200	20%
Lodging	300	30%
Food	250	25%
Entertainment	150	15%
Other	100	10%

Multiply each percent by 360° to find the angle for each sector.

Car: $360° \times 0.2 = 72°$
Lodging: $360° \times 0.3 = 108°$
Food: $360° \times 0.25 = 90°$
Entertainment: $360° \times 0.15 = 54°$
Other: $360° \times 0.1 = 36°$

4.2 Finding the mean of a set of data

Divide the sum of the data by the number of data points.

The test scores for Pat Phelan in her business math course were 85, 76, 93, 91, 78, 82, 87, and 85. Find Phelan's test average.

$$\text{Mean} = \frac{85 + 76 + 93 + 91 + 78 + 82 + 87 + 85}{8}$$

$$= \frac{677}{8} = 84.63$$

4.2 Finding the weighted mean

1. Multiply frequency by value.
2. Add all products obtained in Step 1.
3. Divide the sum in Step 2 by the total number of data points.

No. of School-Age Children	Frequency
0	12
1	6
2	7
3	3
4	2
	Total families: 30

Find the mean number of school-age children per family.

No.	Frequency	No. × Frequency
0	12	0
1	6	6
2	7	14
3	3	9
4	2	8
		37

$$\text{Mean} = \frac{37}{30} = 1.23$$

4.2 Finding the mean of a grouped frequency distribution

1. Determine the class mark (the midpoint) for each class.
2. Multiply the class mark by the frequency of each class.
3. Add all the products obtained in Step 2.
4. Divide by the number of observations.

Find the mean.

Intervals	Frequency
3–5	2
6–8	10
9–11	12
12–14	9
15–17	7

Intervals	Freq.	Class Mark	Frequency × Class Mark
3–5	2	4	8
6–8	10	7	70
9–11	12	10	120
12–14	9	13	117
15–17	7	16	112
Total: 40			**Total:** 427

$$\text{Mean} = \frac{427}{40} = 10.68$$

| 4.3 | **Finding the median of a set of data** | Find the median for Pat Phelan's grades from an earlier |

4.3 Finding the median of a set of data

1. Arrange the data from lowest to highest.
2. If there is an *odd* number of numbers, the median is the number in the middle.
3. If there is an *even* number of numbers, the median is the average of the two in the middle.

Find the median for Pat Phelan's grades from an earlier example. The data arranged from lowest to highest are 76, 78, 82, 85, 85, 87, 91, and 93.

The average of the middle two values is $\dfrac{85 + 85}{2} = 85$.

4.3 Determining the mode of a set of data

The mode is the most frequently occurring value.

Find the mode for Phelan's grades in the previous example.
The mode is 85, which occurs most frequently (twice).

4.3 Finding the median of a grouped frequency distribution

The median is the class mark associated with the middle number or with the average of the middle numbers.

Intervals	Frequency
10–19	5
20–29	8
30–39	2

There are 15 observations. Divide 15 by 2 to find 7.5. Thus, the class mark associated with the eighth value from the smallest, or 24.5, is the median.

4.3 Finding the mode of a grouped frequency distribution

The mode is the class mark of the class with the highest frequency.

Intervals	Frequency
10–19	5
20–29	8
30–39	2

The second class has the highest frequency. The mode is the associated class mark of 24.5.

4.4 Finding the range of a set of data

$$\text{Range} = \text{Highest} - \text{Lowest}$$

Find the range of the values 7, 6, 10, 7, 9, 5, 2, 8, and 9.

$$\text{Range} = \text{Highest} - \text{Lowest}$$
$$= 10 - 2 = 8$$

4.4 Finding the standard deviation

1. Determine the mean of the data.
2. Subtract the mean from each value to obtain individual deviations, d.
3. Square each deviation.
4. Sum all the squared deviations.
5. Divide the sum by the number of observations.
6. Take the square root of the number obtained in Step 5.

$$s = \sqrt{\frac{\Sigma d^2}{n}}$$

Find the standard deviation of the values, 7, 6, 10, 7, 9, 5, 2, 8, and 9.

Data Value	Deviation d	Deviation Squared, d^2
7	0	0
6	−1	1
10	3	9
7	0	0
9	2	4
5	−2	4
2	−5	25
8	1	1
9	2	4
Total: 63		**Total:** 48

$$\text{Mean} = 63 \div 9 = 7$$

$$\text{Variance} = \frac{\Sigma d^2}{n} = \frac{48}{9} = 5.33$$

$$\text{Std. deviation} = \sqrt{5.33} = 2.31$$

4.5 Finding the price relative

Divide the price this year by the price in a base year and multiply by 100.

A car cost $16,000 10 years ago. It now costs $22,500. Find the price relative for the car.

$$\text{Price relative} = \frac{\text{Price this year}}{\text{Price in base year}} \times 100$$

$$= \frac{\$22,500}{\$16,000} \times 100 = 140.6$$

4.5 Finding cost today using the Consumer Price Index (CPI)

Multiply CPI by cost in the base year to estimate current cost.

A family budget in Los Angeles in 1982 was $23,500. Estimate the same budget today using Table 4.5.

$$\text{Cost today} = \$23,500 \times 226.2\%$$

$$= \$23,500 \times 2.262$$

$$= \$53,157$$

CHAPTER 4   Review Exercises

The answer section includes answers to all Review Exercises.

Work the following application problems. The following numbers are the number of gallons of gasoline sold at a convenience store by week for the past 20 weeks. [4.1]

12,450	11,300	12,800	10,850	14,100
14,900	12,300	11,600	12,400	12,900
13,300	12,500	13,390	12,800	12,500
15,100	13,700	12,200	11,800	12,600

1. Use these numbers to complete the following table.

Gallons of Gasoline	Number of Weeks
10,000–10,999	_____
11,000–11,999	_____
12,000–12,999	_____
13,000–13,999	_____
14,000–14,999	_____
15,000–15,999	_____

2. How many weeks had sales of 13,000 gallons or more?

3. Use the numbers in Exercise 1 to draw a bar graph. Be sure to put a heading and labels on the graph.

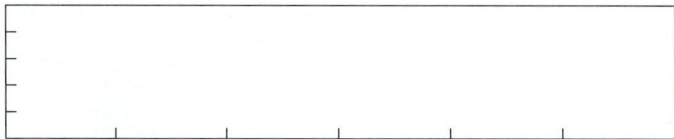

4. During a 1-year period, the campus newspaper at Comfort Community College had the following expenses. Find all numbers missing from the table.

Item	Dollar Amount	Percent of Total	Degrees of a Circle
Newsprint	$12,000	20%	_____
Ink	$6,000	_____	36°
Wire service	$18,000	30%	_____
Salaries	$18,000	30%	_____
Other	$6,000	10%	_____

5. Draw a circle graph using the information in Exercise 4.

6. What percent of the expenses were for newsprint, ink, and wire service?

Calculate the mean, median, and mode for the following sets of data. Round answers to the nearest tenth. **[4.2–4.3]**

7. 25, 20, 18, 35, 19

8. 85, 80, 82, 82, 88, 90, 92

9. 21, 20, 20, 18, 21, 19, 21, 22

10. 42, 44, 41, 44, 45, 44

11. 8, 7, 6, 6, 7, 7, 5, 9

12. 2.5, 2.4, 2.4, 2.3, 2.4, 2.6, 2.0, 2.2

Calculate the mean for the frequency distribution given in Exercises 13 and 14. Round answers to the nearest tenth. **[4.2]**

13.

Intervals	Frequency
10–14	6
15–19	3
20–24	5
25–29	7
30–34	5
35–39	9

14.

Intervals	Frequency
10–19	6
20–29	5
30–39	9
40–49	4
50–59	7

Calculate the median and the mode for the frequency distributions given in Exercises 15 and 16. **[4.3]**

15.

Intervals	Frequency
1–5	20
6–10	12
11–15	14
16–20	10
21–25	5

16.

Intervals	Frequency
50–59	3
60–69	5
70–79	18
80–89	12
90–99	4

Find the range and standard deviation for Exercises 17–20. Round answers to the nearest hundredth. **[4.4]**

17. 62, 24, 38, 91, 56

18. 5, 7, 12, 10, 7, 12, 18

19. 82, 86, 78, 74, 65

20. 150, 145, 130, 120, 162, 158

Find the price relative for Exercises 21–24. Round to the nearest tenth. **[4.5]**

Item	Price in Base Year	Price in Current Year
21. Automobile	$22,500	$32,300
22. Television	$250	$410
23. Personal computer	$1800	$950
24. Lawn mower	$185	$300

Solve the following application problems.

25. A Brazilian brought his critically ill 18-year-old daughter to Houston, Texas, to receive the same medical procedure he had received there in 1984 as a young man. The cost of the procedure in 1984 was $12,170. Use the price relatives in Table 4.5 to estimate the cost of the medical procedure to the nearest dollar. **[4.5]**

26. The thickness of an alloy coating on a military weapon can be approximated by a normal curve with mean 7.2 millimeters and standard deviation 0.08 millimeter. Find the percent of items expected to have a coating thicker than 7.12 millimeters. **[4.4]**

27. Okba Asad, the owner of Current's Restaurant, has monitored weekly sales for the past 6 weeks. Plot these data in a line graph. Do sales appear to be increasing or can you tell from the data given? **[4.1]**

Week	Sales	Week	Sales
1	$4227	4	$5009
2	$4806	5	$4198
3	$4559	6	$5126

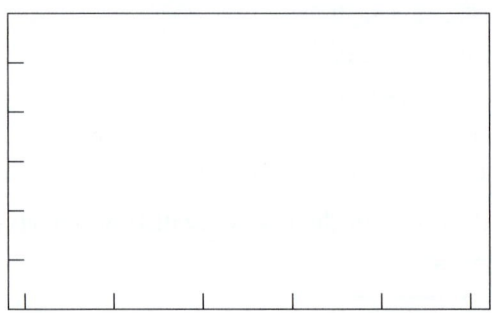

28. Marie Dee wishes to calculate her grade point average for the semester. Round your answers to the nearest hundredth. (A = 4.0, B = 3.0, C = 2.0, D = 1.0, F = 0.0)

    Also, find her grade point average if she had been unable to pull her Spanish grade up from the F she had in the course prior to the final exam. **[4.2]**

Course	Semester Hours	Grade
Business Math	3	A
English	3	C
Biology	4	B
Spanish	3	D

29. The average price of a nursing home in Philadelphia went from $1950 per month in 1990 to $4630 per month today. Find the price relative. **[4.5]**

30. Ted Smith sells stocks and bonds at Merrill Lynch. His wife developed a serious illness at the beginning of 2010 and her condition slowly improved through the balance of the year. Do you think his personal problems may have influenced his work performance? **[4.1]**

Year	Quarterly Commissions			
2008	$14,250	$12,375	$15,750	$13,682
2009	$13,435	$14,230	$11,540	$15,782
2010	$8,207	$7,350	$10,366	$11,470

Support your view by drawing a line graph. Be sure to label the quarter in which Mrs. Smith became ill.

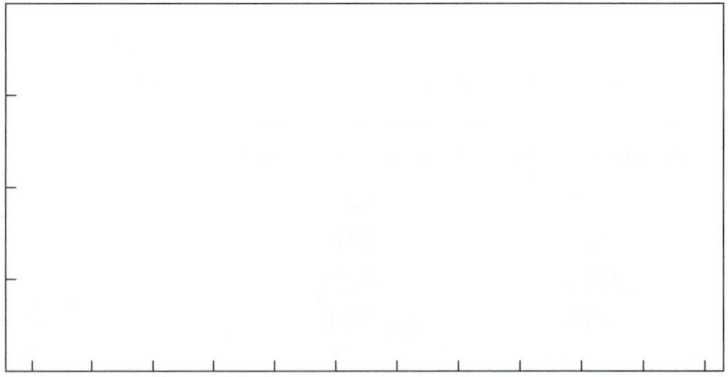

CHAPTER 4	Business Application Case #1
	Growth of a New Business

For years, Pat Farmer managed an oil and gas services company in Midland, Texas, that provided well services for oil and gas operators. Finally, she decided to start her own company in Midland, where she knew a lot of people. Six months later, she opened a second office in Lockhart, Texas, to service oil and gas operators in that area even though she did not know nearly as many people in that area. Here are the sales in thousands of dollars for the two shops.

	Mar.	Apr.	May	June	July	Aug.	Sep.	Oct.	Nov.	Dec.
Midland	8.9	12.2	15.4	18.4	18.9	16.1	18.5	20.2	28.3	31.4
Lockhart							4.8	8.6	10.2	10.2

(a) Find the mean, median, and mode for both stores to the nearest tenth of a thousand.

Midland:

Lockhart:

(b) Plot sales for both stores on the same line graph. Put month on the horizontal axis and sales on the vertical axis.

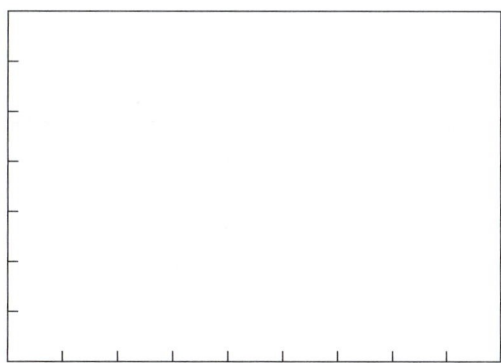

(c) Identify any trends in the line graph.

(d) In which city have sales grown more rapidly? Explain why this may be the case.

CHAPTER 4	Business Application Case #2
	Sales at the Retailing Giant: Wal-Mart Stores, Inc.

Sam Walton opened the first Wal-Mart store in Arkansas in 1962. The first giant supercenters were built 26 years later in 1988. Wal-Mart now serves more than 49 million customers each week, employs more than 620,000 people, and has over 3100 international stores in 13 different countries, including Mexico, Canada, China, the United Kingdom, and Japan. Amazingly, more than 1,000,000 different products are for sale on the Wal-Mart Web site, www.walmart.com. The following financial data were taken from Wal-Mart's financial statements, which are public.

Wal-Mart Stores, Inc. (all numbers in billions)			
Year	Net Sales	Income Taxes Paid	After-tax Profit
2004	$252.8	$4.4	$9.1
2005	$281.5	$5.6	$10.3
2006	$308.9	$6.0	$11.2
2007	$345.0	$6.7	$11.3
2008	$374.5	$6.3	$12.7

(a) First, find the mean and median income taxes paid. Then find the mean and median profit.

(b) Add mean income taxes paid during the past 5 years to the mean after-tax profit during the past 5 years using the data found in part (a). You have found the average before-tax profit. Then, find mean income taxes paid as a percent of before-tax profit to determine the percent of profit Wal-Mart has paid in income taxes.

(c) Graph net sales versus year using a line graph. Identify any particular trend.

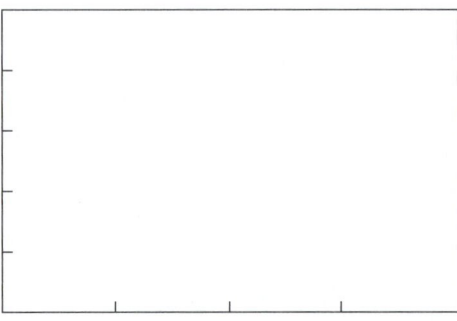

| PART 1 | Cumulative Review: Chapters 1–4 |

To help you review, the numbers in brackets show the section in which the topic was introduced.

Solve the following application problem. [1.1]

1. One of the first things Alyssa Datoli did after getting a divorce was to set up a budget for herself and her young son. She spends $875 for rent and utilities, $400 for food, $320 for child care, and $182 for transportation and plans to limit herself to $600 for all other expenses. She puts any remaining money in a saving account at a local bank. Find the amount going into savings each month if her take-home pay is $2437 per month including child-care payments.

2. The Enabling Supply House purchases 6 wheelchairs at $1256 each and 15 speech compression recorder-players at $895 each. Find the total cost.

3. Software Supply had a bank balance of $29,742.18 at the beginning of April. During the month, the firm made deposits of $14,096.18 and $6529.42. A total of $18,709.51 in checks was paid by the bank during the month. Find the firm's checking account balance at the end of April.

4. Jessica Waters purchases a hot tub on contract and must pay $185 per month until she has paid a total of $4440. Find the number of payments she must make.

Solve the following problems. [1.2–1.3]

5. Write $\dfrac{48}{54}$ in lowest terms.

6. Write $8\dfrac{1}{8}$ as an improper fraction.

7. Write $\dfrac{107}{15}$ as a mixed number.

8. $1\dfrac{2}{3} + 2\dfrac{3}{4} =$

9. $5\dfrac{7}{8} + 7\dfrac{2}{3} =$

10. $6\dfrac{1}{3} - 4\dfrac{7}{12} =$

11. $8\dfrac{1}{2} \times \dfrac{9}{17} \times \dfrac{2}{3} =$

12. $3\dfrac{3}{4} \div \dfrac{27}{16} =$

Solve the following application problems. [1.2–1.3]

13. The area of a piece of land is $63\dfrac{3}{4}$ acres. One-third of the land is sold. What is the area of the land that is left?

14. To prepare for the state real estate exam, Pam Prentiss studied $5\dfrac{1}{2}$ hours on the first day, $6\dfrac{1}{4}$ hours on the second day, $3\dfrac{3}{4}$ hours on the third day, and 7 hours on the fourth day. How many hours did she study altogether?

15. The storage yard at American River Raft Rental has four sides and is enclosed with $527\dfrac{1}{24}$ feet of security fencing around it. If three sides of the yard measure $107\dfrac{2}{3}$ feet, $150\dfrac{3}{4}$ feet, and $138\dfrac{5}{8}$ feet, what is the length of the fourth side?

16. Play-It-Now Sports Center has decided to divide $\dfrac{2}{3}$ of the company's profit-sharing funds evenly among the 8 store managers. What fraction of the total amount will each receive?

Solve the following problems. [1.3]

17. Change 0.35 to a fraction.

18. Change $\dfrac{2}{3}$ to a decimal. Round to the nearest thousandth.

Round each of the following numbers as indicated. [1.3]

19. 78.572 to the nearest hundredth

20. 4732.489 to the nearest hundredth

21. 62.65 to the nearest tenth

22. 215.6749 to the nearest thousandth

Solve each equation. [2.1]

23. $x + 17 = 43$

24. $y - 33 = 52.4$

25. $\dfrac{z}{4} - 10 = 18$

26. $4(r - 2) = 2(r + 8)$

Write a mathematical expression. Use *x* as the variable. [2.2]

27. $\frac{3}{4}$ times a number

28. 5 times a number is added to the number

29. 8 times a number is decreased by 8

30. The sum of 6 times a number and 5

For each problem, use the formula to find the value of the variable that is not given. [2.3]

31. $I = PRT$; $I = \$2880$, $R = 0.08$, $P = \$12,000$

32. $M = P(1 + RT)$; $M = \$2035$, $R = 0.05$, $T = 2$

Write the following ratios. [2.4]

33. $2000 to $400

34. 21 feet to 5 yards

Solve the following proportions. [2.4]

35. $\frac{3}{x} = \frac{14}{42}$

36. $\frac{5}{8} = \frac{22}{y}$

Solve the following application problems. [2.4]

37. Thirty-five out of a random sample of 200 students at a 4-year liberal arts college play some type of sport. Based on results of this sample, estimate the number playing sports out of a student body of 3000 students.

38. A company spends 4 times as much on product development as it does on advertising. If $38,500 is spent on advertising, how much is spent on product development?

Solve the following problems. [3.1–3.4]

39. Change $\frac{5}{8}$ to a percent.

40. Change 0.25% to a decimal.

41. Find 18% of 2500 prospects.

42. Find 134% of $80.

43. 275 sales is what percent of 1100 sales?

44. 375 patients is what percent of 250 patients?

Solve the application problems.

45. During the real estate crisis of 2007–2010, a mayor in California estimated that 13,000 of the 140,000 homes in his community went through foreclosure. Foreclosure occurs when the homeowner cannot make the payments and the mortgage company takes over ownership of the home. Find the percent of foreclosures to the nearest tenth of a percent. **[3.4]**

46. The population of Elk Grove is 76,800 people. If 28.5% of the population is under the age of 18, find the number of people under the age of 18. **[3.2]**

47. The number of students enrolled in the Los Rios Community College District rose 9.5% this year. If the number of students enrolled this year is 64,040, find last year's enrollment. Round to the nearest whole number. **[3.5]**

48. As an antique dealer, Clarence Hanks charges a 25% selling fee. After deducting this fee, Hanks recently paid out $12,570 to his sellers. Find the total amount of his sales. **[3.5]**

49. Early investors in Dell Computer stock saw the value of the stock go up 900 times their original cost. What percent increase did they experience? Show your work explaining how you arrived at your answer. **[3.1]**

50. The value of a stock used to be 6 times what it is worth today. The value today is what percent of the past value? Round to the nearest tenth of a percent. Show your work explaining how you arrived at your answer. **[3.1]**

51. The graph shows the actual minimum wage and the minimum wage in constant 2009 dollars, which has been adjusted for inflation. Use the graph to (a) estimate the actual minimum wage in 1990 and in 2009 and find the percent increase to the nearest percent. Then find (b) the minimum wage in constant 2009 dollars in 1990 and in 2009 and find the percent increase or decrease to the nearest percent. (c) What has been the general trend since 1980 in the minimum wage in constant 2009 dollars? **[4.1]**

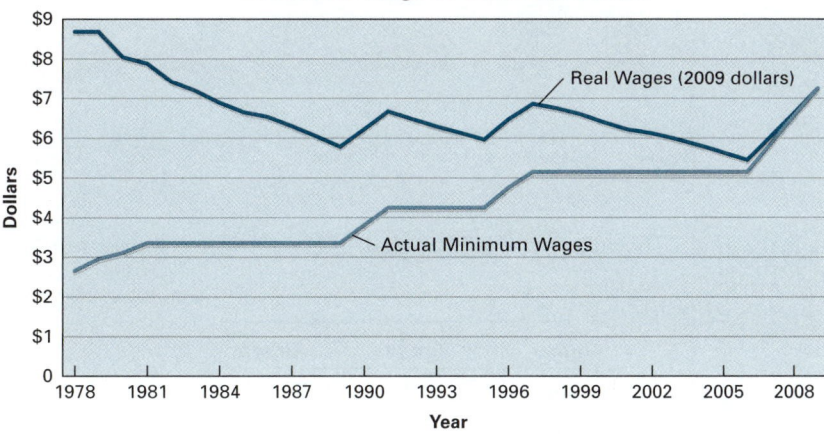

U.S. Actual Minimum Wage and Minimum Wage in Constant Dollars

Source: Bureau of Labor Statistics.

52. Use the data in the table to construct a bar chart. **[4.1]**

PRICE OF A GALLON OF REGULAR GASOLINE

Year	Price	Year	Price
1995	$1.14	2002	$1.35
1996	$1.23	2003	$1.55
1997	$1.23	2004	$1.85
1998	$1.06	2005	$2.28
1999	$1.16	2006	$2.58
2000	$1.50	2007	$2.82
2001	$1.42	2008	$3.41

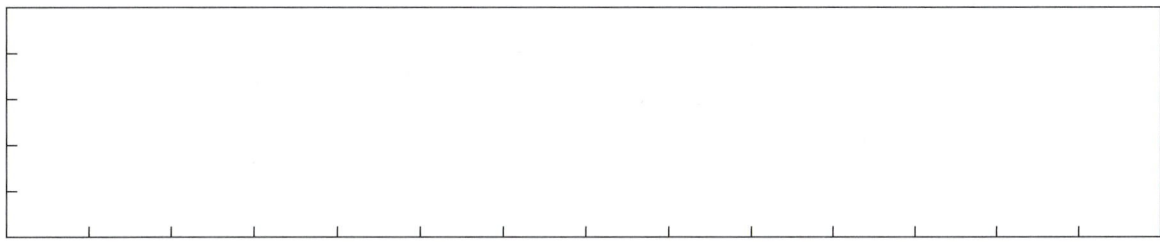

53. Benson's Medical Supplies had quarterly sales of $85,200, $102,000, $92,000, and $124,000 last year. Show this data using both a bar chart and a pie chart. **[4.1]**

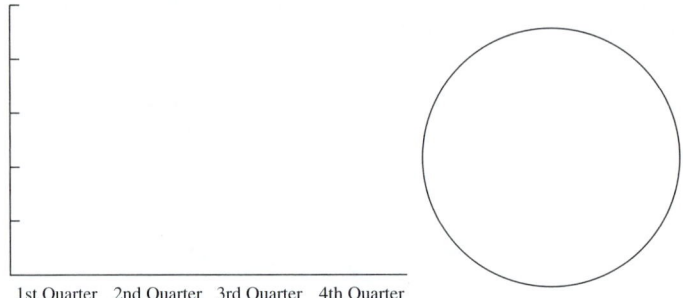

1st Quarter   2nd Quarter   3rd Quarter   4th Quarter

54. Glenda Hickey made the grades shown below. Find her grade point average to the nearest hundredth. (Note: A = 4, B = 3, C = 2, D = 1, and F = 0.) **[4.2]**

Course	Credits	Grade
Math	3	B (= 3)
English	4	C (= 2)
Sociology	3	C (= 2)
Music	3	A (= 4)
Total: 13		

55. Find the mean, range, and standard deviation for the following data: 78, 82, 71, 69. Round to the nearest tenth where applicable. **[4.2 and 4.3]**

56. The diameter of a metal transmission shaft fits a normal curve, with a mean of 0.625 inch and a standard deviation of 0.045 inch. Find the percent of the shafts with a diameter of between 0.625 inch and 0.715 inch, assuming a normal curve. **[4.4]**

57. The price of a network card for a computer network dropped from $1200 one year ago to $680 today. Find the price relative, rounded to the nearest whole number. **[4.5]**

58. A family of 4 in Los Angeles averaged $270 per month for food and beverages in 1984. Use Table 4.5 on page 142 to estimate the monthly cost of food and beverages for a family of 4 in Los Angeles today. Round to the nearest dollar. **[4.5]**

Banking Services

Banks and savings institutions are far more than simply places to deposit funds and take out loans. They also offer many services, including automated teller machines (ATMs), credit cards, debit cards, safe deposit boxes, online banking, investment services, automatic withdrawals and payments, and even payroll services for businesses. This chapter explores checking accounts and registers, business checking account services, credit-card transactions, and bank reconciliation, which is also referred to as balancing a checking account.

The use of **electronic banking** on the Internet does not come without risk. For example, Figure 5.1 shows the increasing losses from Internet theft. The level of theft grew from only about $18 million in 2001 to nearly $250 million in 2007. Experts predict rapid continuing growth. This type of crime has become a major issue in the world of commerce for both individuals and businesses. It affects everyone.

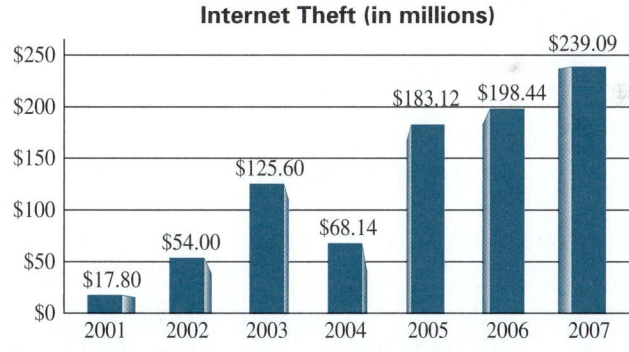

Internet Theft (in millions)

Source: Bureau of Justice; FBI.

Figure 5.1

STOP
—and think

Do you think that Internet theft will continue to be a problem in the future? List several ways in which people may be able to steal from you, or access your personal records, using the Internet. How can law enforcement control this growing threat? Can you think of job opportunities related to this growing threat? What training would be needed?

5.1	**Checking Accounts and Check Registers**

OBJECTIVES

1 *Identify the parts of a check.*

2 *Know the types of checking accounts.*

3 *Find the monthly service charges.*

4 *Identify the parts of a deposit slip.*

5 *Identify the parts of a check stub.*

6 *Complete the parts of a check register (transaction register).*

Electronic commerce or e-commerce refers to the buying and selling of products and services over computer networks or the Internet. Most large firms use e-commerce extensively and even tie their supply chains together with information through the Internet. Many smaller firms also use electronic banking extensively. However, a number of smaller firms and many individuals, particularly in the United States, still use checks. Europeans tend to write few checks, preferring electronic banking instead. However, the continued heavy reliance on checks in the United States makes it important to understand how to use checks and checking accounts. Figure 5.2 shows the parts of a check.

Checking Facts for the United States

- Three of every four families have a checking account.
- The average adult writes over 100 checks each year.
- Checks became common after World War II.
- Today, 135 billion checks are processed each year.

Objective

1   *Identify the Parts of a Check.*

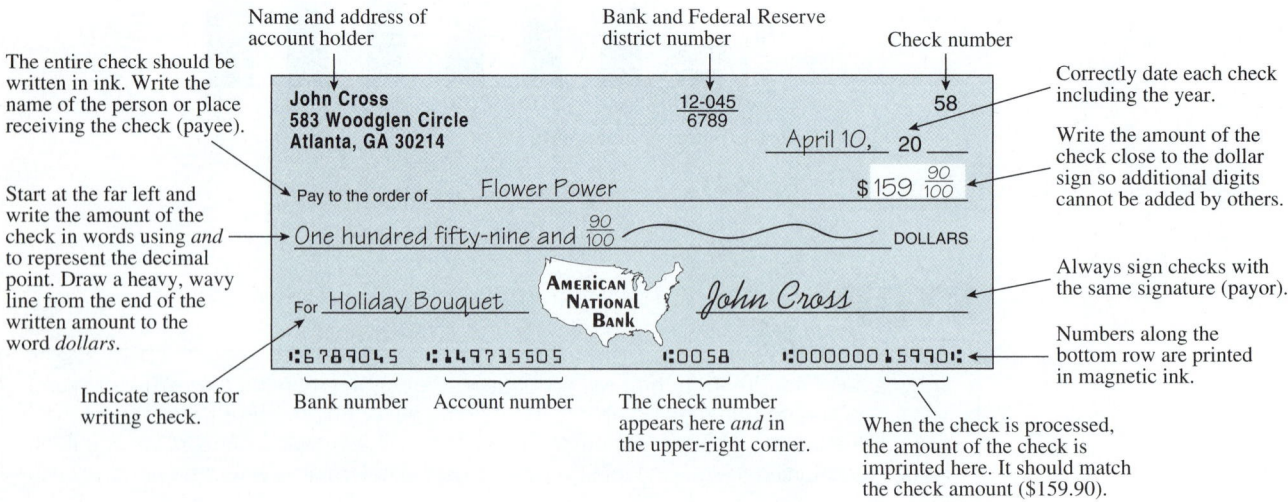

Figure 5.2

Objective

2 *Know the Types of Checking Accounts.* Two main types of checking accounts are available.
Personal checking accounts are used by individuals. The bank supplies printed checks (normally charging a check-printing fee) for the customer to use. Some banks offer the checking account at no charge to the customer, but most require that a minimum monthly balance remain in the checking account. If the minimum balance is not maintained during any month, a service charge is applied to the account. Today, the **flat-fee checking account** is common. For a fixed charge per month, the bank supplies the checking account, check printing, a bank credit card, an ATM card, a debit card, and a host of other services. **Interest paid on checking account balances** is common with personal checking accounts. **Money market** accounts are offered by savings and loan associations, credit unions, and banks and are available to individuals as well as business customers. These accounts often require much higher minimum balances than regular accounts, but pay higher interest.

Business checking accounts often receive more services than do personal accounts. For example, banks often arrange to receive payments on debts payable to business firms. The bank automatically credits the amount to the business account.

A popular service available to personal and business customers is the **automated teller machine (ATM)**. Offered by many banks, savings and loans, and credit unions, an ATM allows the customer to perform a great number of transactions. The ATM card and **electronic banking** allow cash withdrawals and deposits, transfer of funds from one account to another including the paying of credit-card accounts or other loans, and account-balance inquiries at *any* time. The bar graph shows other services people would like to have available at ATMs.

Not Just Cash

A recent survey indicated that people would like ATMs to also offer the following additional services.

Stamps	50%
Check cashing	48%
Event tickets	36%
Phone cards	20%

Source: eFunds, a Harris Poll interactive survey.

NOTE Those on vacation in Europe, Canada, Mexico, and many other countries can often obtain cash in the local currency using ATM machines.

An **ATM card** is a card issued by a bank or other financial institution that is used for deposits, withdrawals, or other types of transactions. A **debit card** is an ATM card with a Visa or MasterCard logo on it. The use of an ATM or debit card at a **point-of-sale terminal** results in the immediate subtraction of funds from your bank account and credit to the seller's bank account. All of the large retailers use a point-of-sale system that results in immediate transfers of money even on weekends or at night. You can confirm an immediate subtraction to your account balance by looking at your account on the Internet immediately after a purchase.

The use of a credit card such as Visa or MasterCard usually requires that you sign a receipt. The use of a debit card generally requires that you enter your **personal identification number** (**PIN**). Your PIN number is a special code that only you know, which authorizes the transaction. Your liability for losses on a stolen credit card is limited to $50 by law as long as you notify your credit-card company of the loss of the card promptly. However, stolen debit cards can potentially result in a *much higher loss*. So be sure to protect your PIN from prying eyes and do not give it out to friends!

> **NOTE** When using an ATM or debit card, keep receipts so that you can subtract the amount of the transaction from your checking account balance.

Transaction Costs

The cost of different payment transactions.

Bank branch	$1.07
U.S. mail	$0.73
Telephone	$0.54
Debit card	$0.29
ATM	$0.27
Internet	$0.01

Source: Jupiter Communication Home Banking Report.

Most banks and credit unions offer **online banking**, which allows **electronic funds transfer (EFT)**. Online banking is also referred to as **home banking**, **Internet banking**, and **electronic banking**. Banks that offer these services are sometimes called **brick-to-click banks**, indicating the trend of moving away from going to a bank building and instead banking by clicking the mouse on a personal computer. Actually, there are **virtual banks** that do not have any physical branches or tellers.

Some people set up automatic payments, such as the payment on a home mortgage, for the same day each month so that they do not have to go to the trouble of writing a check or making an electronic payment each month. The Internet has changed banking for banks and also for individuals. To see why banks prefer electronic banking, look at the table at the side: **Transaction Costs**. Clearly, transactions done on the Internet are far cheaper than the other types of transactions. Competition requires firms to continually find ways to cut costs. Banks use the Internet and ATMs to decrease costs, improve profit, and be competitive. Combine lower costs of transactions on the Internet with a higher level of convenience for consumers and it is easy to see why business on the Internet has grown so rapidly since the World Wide Web first became available in 1993.

Objective

3   *Find the Monthly Service Charges.*   Service charges for business checking accounts are based on the average balance for the period covered by the statement. This average balance determines the **maintenance charge per month**, to which a **per debit charge** (per check charge) is added. The charges generally apply regardless of the amount of account activity. Some typical bank charges for a business checking account appear in Table 5.1.

Table 5.1   TYPICAL BANK CHARGES FOR A BUSINESS CHECKING ACCOUNT

Average Balance	Maintenance Charge per Month	Per Check Charge
Less than $500	$12.00	$0.20
$500–$1999	$ 7.50	$0.20
$2000–$4999	$ 5.00	$0.10
$5000 or more	$ 0	$0

> **EXAMPLE 1** **Finding the Checking Account Service Charge**
>
> Find the monthly service charge for the following business accounts using Table 5.1.
>
> **(a)** Pittsburgh Glass, 38 checks written, average balance $833

Solution

> **(a)** An account with an average balance between $500 and $1999 has a maintenance charge of $7.50 per month plus a debit (check) charge of $0.20 each.
>
> Monthly charge = Maintenance Charge + Number of checks × per Check Charge
>
> $= \qquad \$7.50 \qquad + \qquad 38 \qquad × \qquad \$0.20$
>
> $= \$15.10$
>
> **(b)** Fargo Western Auto, 87 checks written, average balance $2367

Solution

> **(b)** An account with an average balance between $2000 and $4999 has a maintenance charge of $5.00 and a per check charge of $0.10.
>
> Monthly charge = Maintenance Charge + Number of checks × per Check Charge
>
> $= \qquad \$5.00 \qquad + \qquad 87 \qquad × \qquad \$0.10$
>
> $= \$13.70$

 Scientific Calculator Approach

The calculator solutions to Example 1 use chain calculations, with the calculator observing the order of operations.

(a) 7.5 $\boxed{+}$ 38 $\boxed{×}$ .2 $\boxed{=}$ 15.1

(b) 5 $\boxed{+}$ 87 $\boxed{×}$ .1 $\boxed{=}$ 13.7

Objective

4   *Identify the Parts of a Deposit Slip.*   Money, either cash or checks, is placed into a checking account with a **deposit slip** or **deposit ticket**, such as the one in Figure 5.3. The account number is written at the bottom of the slip in magnetic ink. The slip contains blanks in which are entered any cash (either currency or coins), as well as checks that are to be deposited.

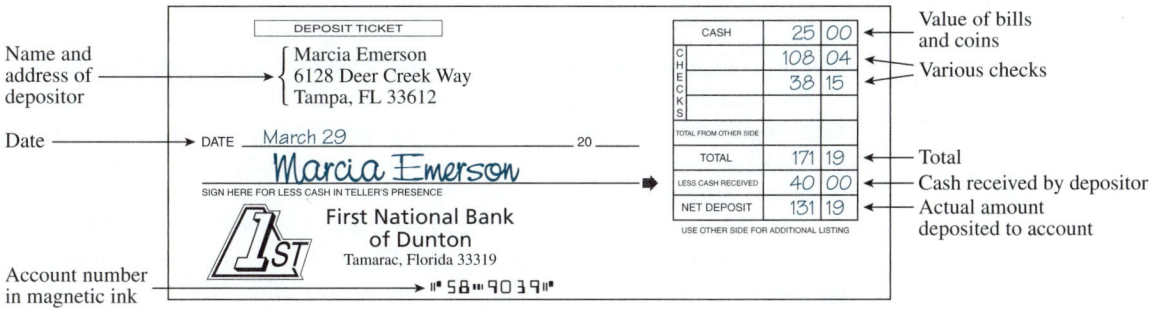

Figure 5.3

     When a check is deposited, it should have "for deposit only" and either the depositor's signature or the company stamp placed on the back within 1.5 inches of the vertical top edge. In this way, if a check is lost or stolen on the way to the bank, it will be worthless to anyone finding it. Such an endorsement, which limits the ability to cash a check, is called a **restricted endorsement**. An example of a restricted endorsement is shown in Figure 5.4, along with two other types of endorsements. The most common endorsement by individuals is the **blank endorsement**, where only the name of the person being paid is signed. This endorsement should be used only at the moment of cashing a check. The **special endorsement**, used to pass on the check to someone else, might be used to pay a bill on another account.

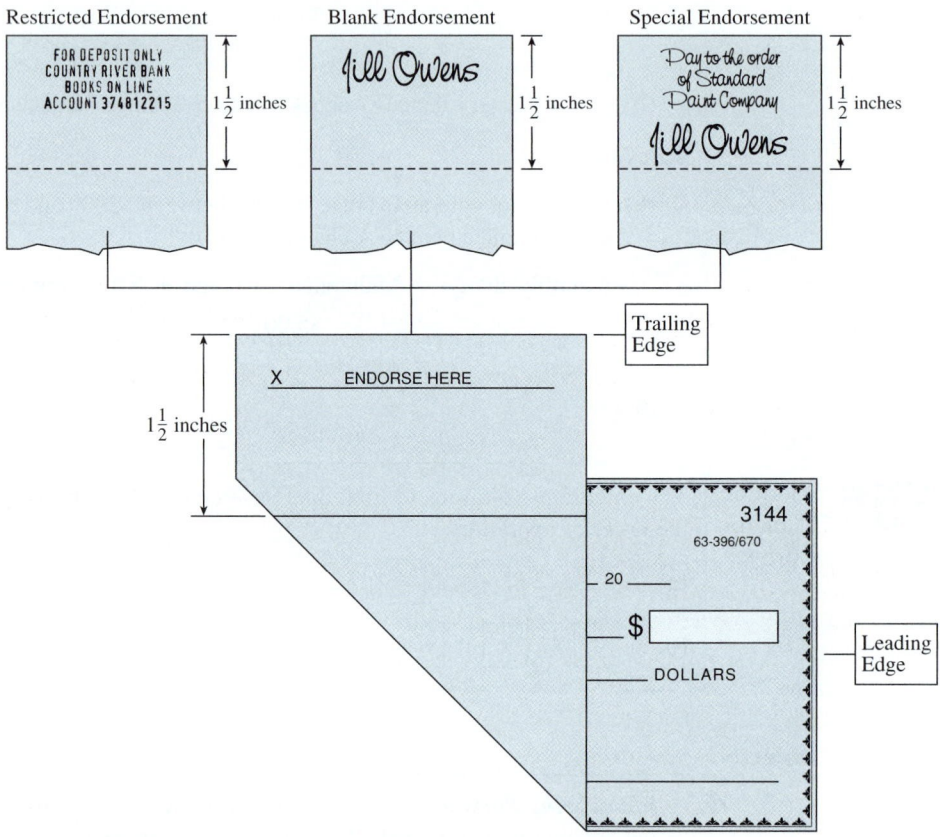

Figure 5.4

After the check is endorsed, it is normally cashed or deposited at a bank. The payee either is given cash or receives a credit in the account for the amount of the check. The check is then routed to a Federal Reserve bank, which forwards the check to the payer's bank. After going through this procedure, known as **processing**, the check is then **canceled** and returned to the payer. The check will now have additional processing information on its back, as shown in Figure 5.5.

A federal law known as **Check 21** took effect in October of 2004. Check 21, short for the 21st Century Act, resulted in several changes to the handling of checking account transactions. These changes in the federal banking laws allow banks to take electronic photos of all canceled checks and to exchange checks electronically. The bank retains the photos and the canceled checks are destroyed instead of being returned to the payer. The 1-to-5-day window between the time you write a check and the time your money is withdrawn from your account (known as "**float**") has been reduced greatly.

The date that the bank debited (deducted funds from) the payer's account.

The date and bank where the check was deposited are important proof against claims that a check was late or was never received.

Restricted endorsement for deposit only

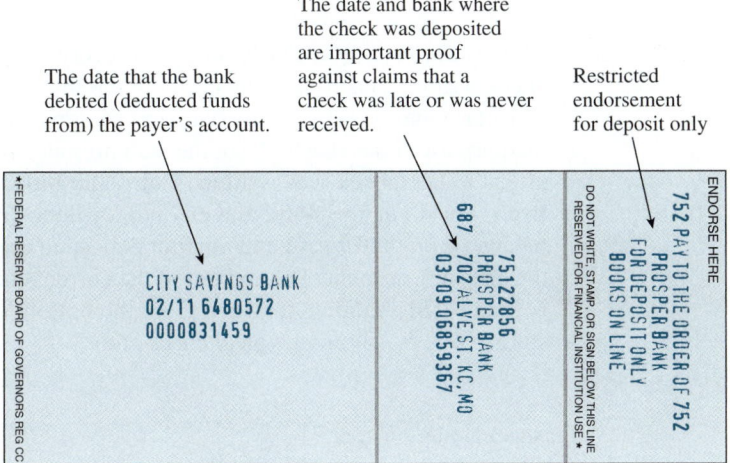

Figure 5.5

A two-sided commercial deposit slip is shown in Figure 5.6. Notice that more space is given for an itemized list of customers' checks that are being deposited to the business account. Some financial institutions require that the bank and Federal Reserve district numbers be shown in the description column of the deposit slip. These numbers appear in the upper center portion of the check and are identified in the sample check on page 160.

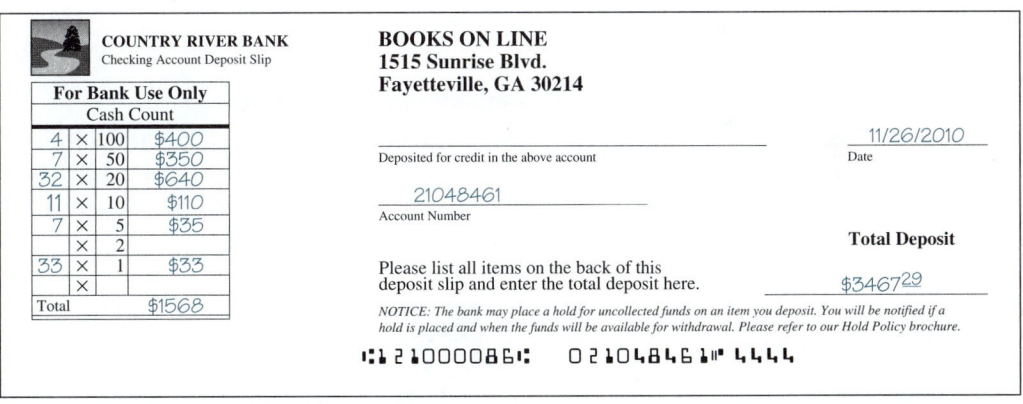

Figure 5.6

Objective

5 *Identify the Parts of a Check Stub.* A record must be kept of every deposit made and every check written. Business firms normally do this with one **check stub** for each check. These stubs provide room to list the date, the person or firm to whom the check will be paid, and the purpose of the check. Also, the stub provides space to record the balance in the account after the last check was written (called the **balance brought forward**, abbreviated Bal. Bro't. For'd., on the stub), and any money deposited since the last check was written. The balance brought forward and amount deposited are added to provide the current balance in the checking account. The amount of the current check is then subtracted, and a new balance is found. This **balance forward** from the bottom of the stub should be written on the next stub. Figure 5.7 shows a typical check stub.

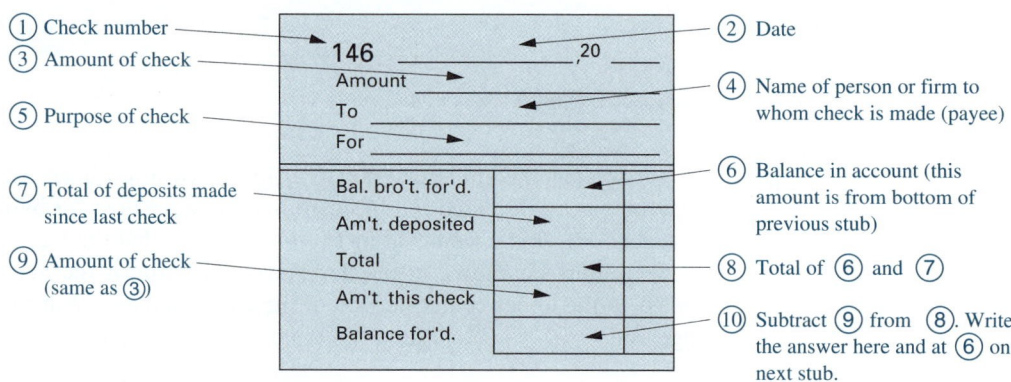

Figure 5.7

EXAMPLE 2 Completing a Check Stub

Check number 2724 is made out on June 8 to Lillburn Utilities as payment for water and power. Assume that the check is for $182.15, that the balance brought forward is $4245.36, and that deposits of $337.71 and $193.17 have been made since the last check was written. Complete the check stub as shown in Figure 5.8.

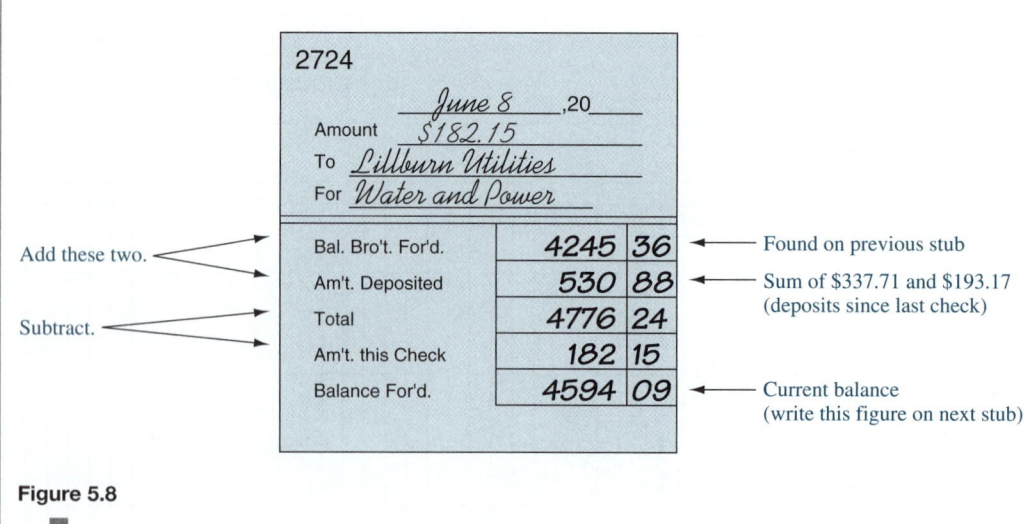

Figure 5.8

Banks offer many styles of checkbooks. Notice that the two styles shown in Figure 5.9 offer two stubs and may be used for payrolls. The stub next to the check can be used as the employee's record of earnings and deductions. The second style provides space on the check itself for listing a group of invoices or bills that are being paid with that same check.

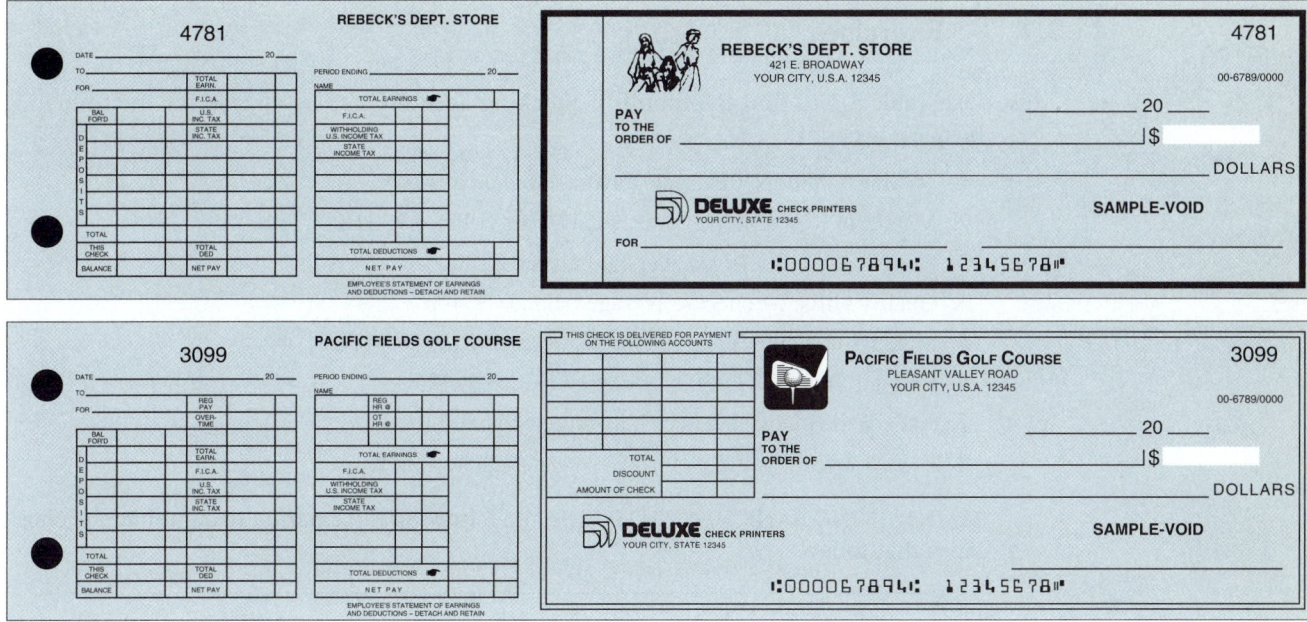

Figure 5.9

Objective

6 *Complete the Parts of a Check Register (Transaction Register).* Some depositors prefer a check register to the check stubs, while others use both. The **check register**, also called a **transaction register**, shows at a glance the checks written and deposits made, as seen in Figure 5.10. The column headed ✓ is used to check off each check or check image after it is received back from the bank.

CHECK NO.	DATE	CHECK ISSUED TO	AMOUNT OF CHECK		✓	DATE OF DEP.	AMOUNT OF DEPOSIT		BALANCE	
							BALANCE BROUGHT FORWARD →		3518	72
1435	5/8	Swan Brothers	378	93					3139	79
1436	5/8	Class Acts	25	14					3114	65
1437	5/9	Mirror Lighting	519	65					2595	00
		Deposit				5/10	3821	17	6416	17
1438	5/10	Woodlake Auditorium	750	00					5666	17
		Deposit				5/12	500	00	6166	17
1439	5/12	Rick's Clowns	170	80					5995	37
1440	5/14	Y.M.C.A.	219	17					5776	20
	5/14	ATM	120	00					5656	20
		Deposit				5/15	326	15	5982	35
1441	5/16	Stage Door Playhouse	825	00					5157	35
1442	5/17	Gilbert Eckern	1785	00					3372	35
		Deposit				5/19	1580	25	4952	60

Figure 5.10

NOTE ATM transactions for cash withdrawals and purchases must be entered on check stubs or in the check register. The transaction amount and the charge for each transaction must then be subtracted to maintain an accurate balance.

5.1	Exercises

Use Table 5.1 to find the monthly checking account service charge for the following business accounts.

1. Maxine Vitamins, 92 checks, average balance $4618
2. Mandarin Restaurant, 76 checks, average balance $3318
3. Auto Parts, 112 checks, average balance $7832
4. Quality Gifts, 64 checks, average balance $3490
5. Mak's Smog and Tune, 48 checks, average balance $1763
6. Cellular One, 315 checks, average balance $6424
7. Jim's Bail Bonds, 28 checks, average balance $1965
8. Ben's Lawn Repair, 74 checks, average balance $875

MAINTAINING BANK RECORDS Use the following information to complete the check stubs that follow.

	Date	To	For	Amount	Bal. Bro't. For'd.	Deposits
9.	Mar. 8	Patty Demko	Tutoring	$380.71	$3971.28	$79.26
10.	Oct. 15	Elizabeth Linton	Rent	$850.00	$2973.09	$1853.24
11.	Dec. 4	Paul's Pools	Chemicals	$37.52	$1126.73	—

9.

```
857
                    _____ 20 ____
Amount    _____
To        _____
For       _____

Bal. Bro't. For'd.    |      |   |
Am't. Deposited       |      |   |
Total                 |      |   |
Am't. this Check      |      |   |
Balance For'd.        |      |   |
```

10.

```
1248
                    _____ 20 ____
Amount    _____
To        _____
For       _____

Bal. Bro't. For'd.    |      |   |
Am't. Deposited       |      |   |
Total                 |      |   |
Am't. this Check      |      |   |
Balance For'd.        |      |   |
```

11.

```
735
                    _____ 20 ____
Amount    _____
To        _____
For       _____

Bal. Bro't. For'd.    |      |   |
Am't. Deposited       |      |   |
Total                 |      |   |
Am't. this Check      |      |   |
Balance For'd.        |      |   |
```

12. List and explain at least six parts of a check. Draw a sketch showing where these parts appear on a check. (See Objective 1.)

  13. Explain to a friend at least two advantages and two possible disadvantages of using an ATM card. Do this in writing. (See Objective 2.)

  14. Write an explanation for a friend of two types of check endorsements. Describe where these endorsements must be placed. (See Objective 4.)

  15. Explain in your own words the factors that determine the service charges on a business checking account. (See Objective 3.)

COMPLETING CHECK STUBS Using the information below, complete the following check stubs for Books On Line. The balance brought forward for check stub 5311 is $7223.69.

CHECKS WRITTEN					DEPOSITS MADE	
Number	**Date**	**To**	**For**	**Amount**	**Date**	**Amount**
5311	Oct. 7	Anessa Davis	Books	$1250.80	Oct. 8	$752.18
5312	Oct. 10	County Clerk	License	$39.12	Oct. 9	$23.32
5313	Oct. 15	United Parcel	Shipping	$356.28	Oct. 13	$1025.45

16.

```
5311

_____ 20 _____
Amount   _____
To       _____
For      _____

Bal. Bro't. For'd.  |        |    |
Am't. Deposited     |        |    |
Total               |        |    |
Am't. this Check    |        |    |
Balance For'd.      |        |    |
```

17.

```
5312

_____ 20 _____
Amount   _____
To       _____
For      _____

Bal. Bro't. For'd.  |        |    |
Am't. Deposited     |        |    |
Total               |        |    |
Am't. this Check    |        |    |
Balance For'd.      |        |    |
```

18.

```
5313

_____ 20 _____
Amount   _____
To       _____
For      _____

Bal. Bro't. For'd.  |        |    |
Am't. Deposited     |        |    |
Total               |        |    |
Am't. this Check    |        |    |
Balance For'd.      |        |    |
```

BANK BALANCES   For Exercises 19–22, complete the balance column in the following check registers after each check or deposit transaction.

19.

CHECK NO.	DATE	CHECK ISSUED TO	AMOUNT OF CHECK		✓	DATE OF DEP.	AMOUNT OF DEPOSIT	BALANCE	
		BALANCE BROUGHT FORWARD →						1629	86
861	7/3	Ahwahnee Hotel	250	45					
862	7/5	Willow Creek	149	00					
863	7/5	Void							
		Deposit				7/7	117	73	
864	7/9	Del Campo High School	69	80					
		Deposit				7/10	329	86	
		Deposit				7/12	418	30	
865	7/14	Big 5 Sporting Goods	109	76					
866	7/14	Dr. Yates	614	12					
867	7/16	Greyhound	32	18					
		Deposit				7/16	520	95	

20.

CHECK NO.	DATE	CHECK ISSUED TO	AMOUNT OF CHECK		✓	DATE OF DEP.	AMOUNT OF DEPOSIT	BALANCE	
		BALANCE BROUGHT FORWARD →						832	15
1121	3/17	AirTouch Cellular	257	29					
1122	3/18	Curry Village	190	50					
		Deposit				3/19	78	29	
		Deposit				3/21	157	42	
1123	3/22	San Juan District	38	76					
1124	3/23	Macy's Gourmet	175	88					
		Deposit				3/23	379	28	
1125	3/24	Class Video	197	20					
1126	3/24	Water World	25	10					
1127	3/25	Bel Air Market	75	00					
		Deposit				3/28	722	35	

21.

CHECK NO.	DATE	CHECK ISSUED TO	AMOUNT OF CHECK		✓	DATE OF DEP.	AMOUNT OF DEPOSIT	BALANCE	
		BALANCE BROUGHT FORWARD →						3852	48
2308	12/6	Web Masters	143	16					
2309	12/7	Water and Power	118	40					
		Deposit				12/8	286	32	
	12/10	ATM (cash)	80	00					
2310	12/11	Ann Kuick	986	22					
2311	12/11	Account Temps	375	50					
		Deposit				12/14	1201	82	
2312	12/14	Central Chevrolet	735	68					
2313	12/15	Miller Mining	223	94					
		Deposit				12/17	498	01	
2314	12/18	Federal Parcel	78	24					

22.

CHECK NO.	DATE	CHECK ISSUED TO	AMOUNT OF CHECK	✓	DATE OF DEP.	AMOUNT OF DEPOSIT	BALANCE
		BALANCE BROUGHT FORWARD ⟶					8284 18
1917	6/4	Valley Electric	188 18				
1918	6/5	Harrold Ford	433 56				
1919	6/5	Paul Altier (photography)	138 17				
		Deposit			6/6	453 28	
		Deposit			6/8	1475 69	
1920	6/9	U.S. Rentals	335 82				
1921	6/11	Quick Turn Merchandise	573 27				
	6/11	ATM (wine)	16 35				
1922	6/14	Broadly Plumbing	195 15				
		Deposit			6/16	635 85	
1923	6/16	National Dues F.F.A.	317 20				

5.2 Checking Services and Depositing Credit-Card Transactions

OBJECTIVES

1 *Identify bank services available to customers.*

2 *Deposit credit-card transactions.*

3 *Calculate the discount fee on credit-card deposits.*

Objective

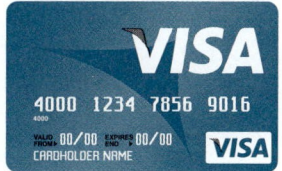

1 *Identify Bank Services Available to Customers.* Banks must make a profit in order to survive and prosper. Furthermore, banking has become so fiercely competitive that bank managers must continually look for ways to increase revenue and cut costs. They have cut costs by moving to online banking and increased revenue by charging for many services. Listed below are some of the services that banks offer along with possible associated charges. Of course, charges vary greatly and also depend on the amount the customer has on deposit at the bank. Fees are usually waived for individuals with a lot of money on deposit. Still, U.S. banks pull in over $50 billion a year in charges!

ATM services—Banks often let their own customers use the bank's ATM machine for free but charge $1.00 or more to a noncustomer. The ATM charges can be even higher for any out-of-country users.

Bank teller—Some banks now charge if you talk to a teller.

Cashier's check (bank check)—This is a check guaranteed by the bank. The charge for a cashier's check depends on the amount of the check, but it is commonly $5 or more.

Credit card—Banks often offer credit cards such as Visa or MasterCard to their customers. They charge interest on cash advances or on any balances carried over from one month to the next. The interest rates are often quite high, up to 20%, so avoid *credit-card debt* if possible.

Debit card—Most banks do not charge for a customer's use of a debit card. Banks tend to like debit cards for two reasons. First, the card reduces their transaction costs. Second, it allows banks to have less cash on hand. Working with cash is expensive since it must be protected from theft. Debit cards also result in higher insufficient funds charges to the bank from individuals who do not track account balances and do not have enough in their account to cover the charge.

Money order—A money order is proof that funds have been prepaid in cash. In addition to banks, retail stores such as Wal-Mart and even U.S. post offices sell money orders. Depending on the amount of money involved, money orders can cost up to $4.

Notary—Some documents require a signature by a person called a notary. Once this service was free, but bank customers now often have to pay for it.

Online banking—Online banking allows individuals to check account balances, make payments, and transfer funds between accounts from any personal computer anywhere in the world. This service is often free but some banks charge a small fee.

Overdraft or insufficient funds (NSF)—You will get an insufficient funds charge of $20 to $45 if you write a check for more than you have on deposit in your account. The same charge may be applied if a check is returned because it was not completed correctly.

Overdraft protection—The bank will honor the check even though there are currently insufficient funds in the account to cover it. Charges for overdraft protection vary, but some banks give overdraft protection to those with sufficient funds on deposit, for example, in a certificate of deposit.

Returned deposit—A fee of $10 to $40 is charged on any item deposited that is then returned to the bank due to insufficient funds.

Stop payment—Banks charge as much as $35 to stop payment on a check you have written.

The following table shows that students rely widely on credit cards. In fact, reliance on debt was so great the 2000 Census reported that more than 25% of all 18- to 34-year-olds in the United States had moved back to live with their parents partly due to debt.

Students and Credit Cards

75% have credit cards.

25% have paid a late fee.

Average balance is $2200 for undergraduates, $5800 for graduates.

Devote 22% of their income to servicing debt.

Some students see a penalty of 30% after one late payment.

Source: Nellie Mae.

Objective

2 *Deposit Credit-Card Transactions.* Most retailers and chain stores complete credit-card transactions electronically. After your credit card is swiped, the system either authorizes or does not authorize the purchase, depending on your credit. The verification of your ability to buy and the actual purchase both happen at the same time. To be effective, this process requires a high-speed network link to the merchant's bank. The magnetic "strip" on the back of the credit card contains information that uniquely identifies you, the number of the credit card, and the bank that issued the card. The use of electronic verification systems allows merchants to eliminate paper transactions and reduce costs.

However, some small retailers continue to process their credit-card sales mechanically. These credit-card sales are deposited into a business checking account with a **merchant batch header ticket**, such as the one shown in Example 1. This form is used with Visa or

MasterCard credit-card deposits. Notice that the form lists both sales slips and credit slips (refunds). Credit slips are used when merchandise purchased with a credit card is returned to the store. Entries in each of these categories are totaled, and the total credits are subtracted from the total sales to give the gross amount of deposit.

EXAMPLE 1 **Determining Deposits with Credit-Card Transactions**

Books On Line had the following credit-card sales and refunds. Complete a merchant batch header ticket.

Sales		Refunds (Credit)
$82.31	$146.50	$13.83
$38.18	$78.80	$25.19
$65.29	$63.14	$78.56
$178.22	$208.67	

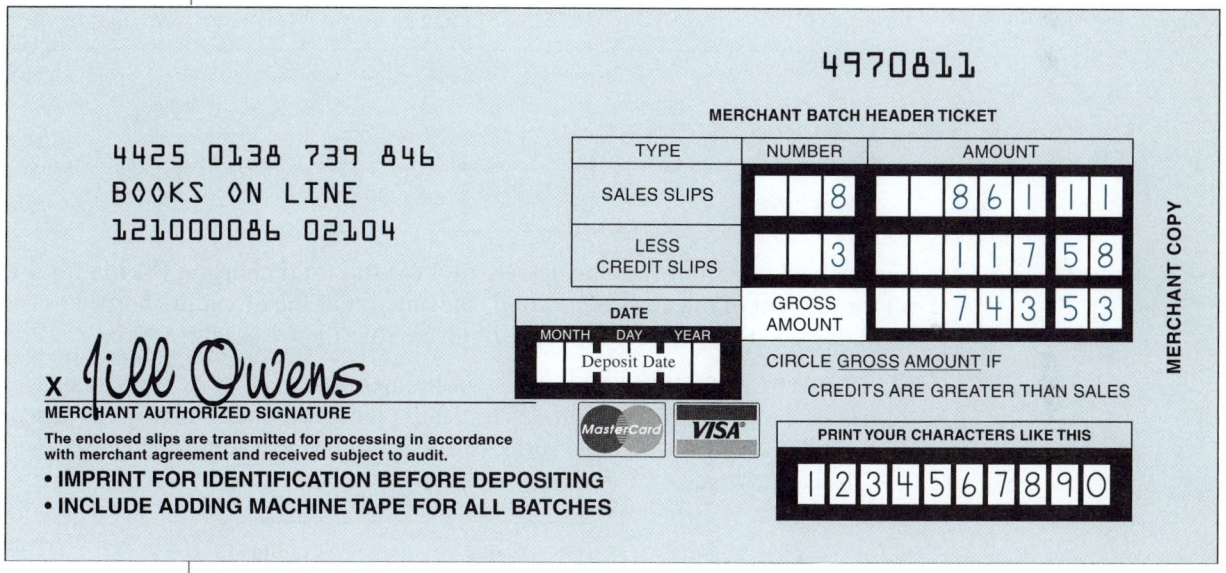

Solution All credit slips and sales slips must be totaled. The number of each of these and the totals are written at the right on the form. The total sales slips are $861.11 and the credit slips total $117.58. The difference is the gross amount. Here, $743.53 is the gross deposit.

Objective

3 *Calculate the Discount Fee on Credit-Card Deposits.* The bank collects a **discount fee** (a percent of sales) from the merchant and also an interest charge from the card user on all accounts not paid in full at the first billing. Although credit-card transactions are deposited frequently by a business, the bank calculates the discount fee on the gross amount of the credit-card deposits since the last bank statement date. The fee paid by the merchant is usually about 2%, but sometimes more, of the sales slip amount. It is determined by the type of processing used (electronic or manual), the dollar volume of credit-card usage by the merchant, and the average amount of the sale at the merchant's store. All credit-card deposits for the month are added, and the fee is subtracted from the total at the statement date.

EXAMPLE **2** **Finding the Discount and the Credit Given on a Credit-Card Deposit**

The deposit in Example 1 represents total credit-card deposits for the month. Find the fee charged and the credit given to the merchant at the statement date if Books On Line pays a 2% fee.

Solution   Since the total credit-card deposit for Books On Line is $743.53 and the fee is 2%, the discount charged is found as follows.

$$\$743.53 \times 0.02(2\%) = \$14.87 \text{ discount charge (rounded)}$$

Out of a deposit of $743.53, the merchant will receive a credit of $743.53 − $14.87 = $728.66.

Scientific
Calculator
Approach

The calculator solution to Example 2 is

$743.53 $\boxed{-}$ 2 $\boxed{\%}$ $\boxed{=}$ 728.6594

5.2	**Exercises**

For each of the following businesses, find (a) the total charges, (b) the total credits, (c) the amount of the gross deposit, (d) the amount of the discount charged at the statement date, and (e) the amount of credit given after the fee is subtracted.

1. **CREDIT-CARD DEPOSITS**   Fry's Electronics does most of its business on a cash basis or through its own credit department, although it does honor major bank charge cards. In a recent period, the business had the following credit-card charges and credits. The bank charges a 3% discount.

Sales		Credits
$78.56	$38.15	$29.76
$875.29	$18.46	$102.15
$330.82	$22.13	$71.95
$55.24	$707.37	
$47.83	$245.91	

2. **CREDIT-CARD DEPOSITS**   Baker Auto accepts credit cards from customers for work ranging from oil changes to small repairs on automobiles. The following credit-card transactions occurred during a recent period. The bank charges a 2% discount.

Sales		Credits
$66.68	$18.95	$62.16
$119.63	$496.28	$106.62
$53.86	$21.85	$38.91
$178.62	$242.78	
$219.78	$176.93	

3. CREDIT-CARD DEPOSITS Bayside Jeepers does most of its business on a cash basis or through its own credit department, although it does honor major bank charge cards. In a recent period, the business had the following credit-card charges and credits. The bank charges a 4% discount.

Sales			Credits
$25.18	$77.51	$14.73	$38.15
$15.73	$357.18	$106.78	$106.86
$138.97	$72.73	$88.34	$44.38
$58.73	$29.68	$72.21	
$255.18	$15.76	$262.73	

4. CREDIT-CARD DEPOSITS Jamison Hardware had the following credit-card transactions during a recent period. The bank charges a 2% discount.

Sales		Credits
$42.60	$29.50	$22.10
$38.25	$72.85	$14.67
$16.60	$19.30	$30.30
$52.40	$6.75	
$14.38	$88.98	

5. CREDIT-CARD DEPOSITS Maureen Tomlin Studios had the following credit-card transactions during a recent period. The bank charges a 3% discount.

Sales		Credits
$7.84	$98.56	$13.86
$33.18	$318.72	$58.97
$50.76	$116.35	
$12.72	$23.78	
$9.36	$38.95	
$118.68	$235.82	

6. CREDIT-CARD DEPOSITS Jena's Small Gifts is located near a college campus. The following credit-card charges and credits took place during a recent period. The bank charges a 2% discount.

Sales		Credits
$16.40	$184.16	$23.17
$18.98	$137.61	$7.26
$6.76	$24.69	$14.53
$11.75	$86.17	
$29.63		

7. List and describe in your own words four services offered to business checking account customers. (See Objective 1.)

8. The merchant accepting a credit card from a customer must pay a fee of 2% to 5% of the transaction amount. Why is the merchant willing to do this? Who really pays this fee?

| 5.3 | **Reconciliation** |

1 *Reconcile a bank statement with the checkbook.*

2 *List outstanding checks.*

3 *Find the adjusted bank balance or current balance.*

4 *Use the T-account form of reconciliation.*

The activity in a checking account is compiled by the bank each month in a **bank statement**. The statement can be mailed to customers and/or made available online. The bank statement shows all account activity during the month, including checks paid, debits, ATM transactions, online transactions, deposits, and, of course, any charges by the bank. Occasionally, a deposit includes a check that was deposited and must be returned due to **insufficient funds**, also called **nonsufficient funds** (**NSF**). This is also sometimes referred to as **bouncing a check**. A check that has been returned because of nonsufficient funds is a **returned check**. The amount of a returned check must be subtracted from the checkbook balance along with any other charges in order to balance the account for the month.

Bouncing a check is illegal in most states. Here are a few things that can happen if you bounce a check:

1. Your bank may charge a fee of $25 or more.
2. The merchant may choose not to accept a check from you in the future.
3. The merchant may report you to a database and other merchants may refuse to accept your checks.
4. It may affect your credit rating.
5. It may result in problems with local authorities.

The authorities are more concerned about someone who bounces checks often than someone who accidently bounces one check, but it can be stressful to bounce a check. The way to avoid this problem is to always know how much you have in your account. In truth, this has become more difficult for all of us since the advent of debit cards, electronic bill payments, and automatic deductions. It takes a little effort to avoid bouncing a check, but it is worth your time!

Objective

1 *Reconcile a Bank Statement with the Checkbook.*   Many businesses have automatic deposits from customers and other sources made to their accounts. These amounts must be added to the checkbook balance. When the bank statement is received, it is very important to verify its accuracy. In addition, it is a good time to check the accuracy of the check register, making certain that all checks written have been listed and subtracted and that all deposits have been added to the checking account balance. This process of checking the bank statement and the check register is called **reconciliation**.

Reconciliation is best done using the forms usually printed on the back of the bank statement. A sample bank statement is shown in Figure 5.11, and an example of the reconciliation process follows. Note the codes used by the bank, and their meaning, listed at the bottom of the statement. The codes on this bank statement indicate the following: RC means Returned Check, SC means Service Charge, IC means Interest Credit, ATM means Automated Teller Machine.

> **NOTE**   Reconciling the bank statement is an important step in maintaining accurate checking account records and in helping to avoid writing checks for which there are nonsufficient funds. In addition to nonsufficient funds charges, which can be costly, many businesspeople view a person or business who writes "bad checks" as irresponsible.

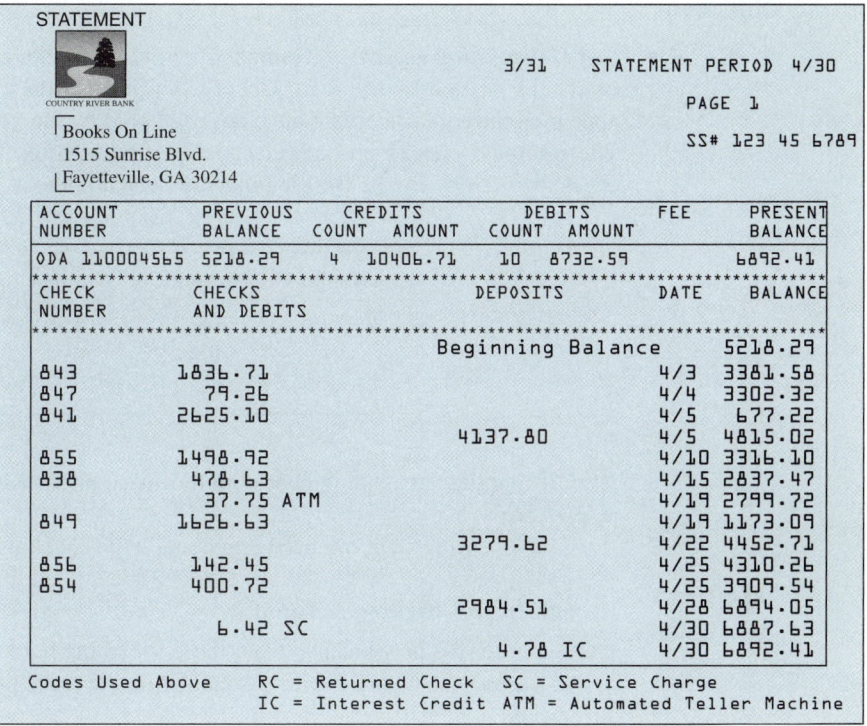

```
STATEMENT

                                         3/31    STATEMENT PERIOD 4/30

COUNTRY RIVER BANK                                        PAGE 1

  Books On Line                                  SS# 123 45 6789
  1515 Sunrise Blvd.
  Fayetteville, GA 30214

 ACCOUNT       PREVIOUS     CREDITS          DEBITS         FEE     PRESENT
 NUMBER        BALANCE   COUNT  AMOUNT    COUNT  AMOUNT             BALANCE
ODA 110004565  5218.29     4   10406.71    10   8732.59            6892.41
*****************************************************************************
 CHECK         CHECKS                     DEPOSITS         DATE    BALANCE
 NUMBER        AND DEBITS
*****************************************************************************
                                  Beginning Balance              5218.29
   843          1836.71                                    4/3    3381.58
   847            79.26                                    4/4    3302.32
   841          2625.10                                    4/5     677.22
                                    4137.80                4/5    4815.02
   855          1498.92                                    4/10   3316.10
   838           478.63                                    4/15   2837.47
                  37.75 ATM                                4/19   2799.72
   849          1626.63                                    4/19   1173.09
                                    3279.62                4/22   4452.71
   856           142.45                                    4/25   4310.26
   854           400.72                                    4/25   3909.54
                                    2984.51                4/28   6894.05
                   6.42 SC                                 4/30   6887.63
                                       4.78 IC             4/30   6892.41

 Codes Used Above    RC = Returned Check   SC = Service Charge
                     IC = Interest Credit  ATM = Automated Teller Machine
```

Figure 5.11

EXAMPLE **1** **Reconciling a Checking Account**

Books On Line received its bank statement. The statement shows a balance of $6892.41, after a bank service charge of $6.42 and an interest credit of $4.78. The Books On Line checkbook now shows a balance of $7576.38. Reconcile the account using the following steps (illustrated in Figure 5.12).

Solution

Checks Outstanding		
Number	Amount	
846	$ 42	73
852	598	71
853	68	12
857	79	80
858	160	30
Total	$ 949	66

Compare the list of checks paid by the bank with your records. List and total the checks not yet paid.

(1) Enter new balance from bank statement: $ 6892.41

(2) List any deposits made by you and not yet recorded by the bank:
+ 892.41
+ 739.58
+
+

(3) Add all numbers from lines above.
Total: 8524.40

(4) Write total of checks outstanding: − 949.66

(5) Subtract (4) from (3).
This is adjusted bank balance: $ 7574.74

To reconcile your records:

(6) List your checkbook balance: $ 7576.38

(7) Write the total of any fees or charges deducted by the bank and not yet subtracted by you from your checkbook: − 6.42

(8) Subtract line (7) from line (6). 7569.96

(9) Enter interest credit: (Add to your checkbook) + 4.78

(10) Add line (9) to line (8).
Adjusted checkbook balance: $ 7574.74

New balance of your account; this number should be same as (5).

Figure 5.12

Objective

2 *List Outstanding Checks.* Compare the list of checks on the bank statement with the list of checks written by the firm. Checks that have been written by the firm but do not yet appear on the bank statement have not been paid by the bank as of the date of the statement. These unpaid checks are called **checks outstanding**. The following table shows those checks written by Books On Line that are outstanding.

Number	Amount	Number	Amount
846	$42.73	857	$79.80
852	$598.71	858	$160.30
853	$68.12		

After listing the outstanding checks in the space provided on the form, total them. The total is $949.66.

The following steps are used to reconcile the checking account.

Reconciling a Checking Account

STEP 1 Enter the new balance from the front of the bank statement. As given, the new balance is $6892.41. Write this number in the space provided on the reconcilement form.

STEP 2 List any deposits made that have not yet been recorded by the bank. These are deposits in transit (DIT). Suppose that Books On Line has deposits of $892.41 and $739.58 that are not yet recorded. These numbers are written at Step 2 on the form.

STEP 3 All the numbers from Steps 1 and 2 are added. Here the total is $8524.40.

STEP 4 Write down the total of outstanding checks. The total is $949.66.

STEP 5 Subtract the total in Step 4 from the number in Step 3. The result here is $7574.74, called the **adjusted bank balance** or the **current balance**. This number should represent the current checking account balance.

Objective

3 *Find the Adjusted Bank Balance or Current Balance.* Now look at the firm's own records.

STEP 6 List the firm's checkbook balance. As mentioned before, the checkbook balance for Books On Line is $7576.38. This number is entered on line 6.

STEP 7 Enter any charges not yet deducted. The service charge here is $6.42. Since there are no other fees or charges, enter $6.42 on line 7.

STEP 8 Subtract the charges on line 7 from the checkbook balance on line 6 to get $7569.96.

STEP 9 Enter the interest credit on line 9. The interest credit here is $4.78. This amount is interest paid on the money in the account.

STEP 10 Add the interest on line 9 to get $7574.74, the same result as in Step 5.

Since the result from Step 10 is the same as the result from Step 5, the account is balanced (reconciled). The correct current balance in the account is $7574.74.

There are several typical reasons why checking accounts do not balance.

Why Checking Accounts Do Not Balance

- Forgetting to enter a check in the check register.
- Forgetting to enter an ATM transaction in the check register.
- Forgetting to enter a deposit in the check register.
- Transposing numbers (writing $961.20 as $916.20, for example).
- Addition or subtraction errors.
- Forgetting to subtract one of the bank service fees, such as those charged for using your debit card or for ATM use.
- Forgetting to enter interest or other credits.
- The bank may have charged the customer an amount different from the check amount.
- A check may be altered or forged.

Objective

4   *Use the T-Account Form of Reconciliation.*   Many businesspeople and accountants prefer a **T-account form** for bank reconciliation. With this method, the bank statement balance is written on the left and the checkbook balance is written on the right. Adjustments are made to either the bank balance or the checkbook balance, depending on which side was unaware of the transaction or charge. T-account reconciliation uses the format in Figure 5.13. The adjusted balances must agree, with the result showing the actual amount remaining in the account.

Bank Reconciliation

Bank statement balance	$ _____		Checkbook balance	$ _____
Add:			**Add:**	
1. Add all deposits not yet recorded.	$ _____		1. Add all miscellaneous credits, collections, and interest.	$ _____
Less:			**Less:**	
2. Subtract all outstanding checks.	$ _____		2. Subtract previously deposited overdrafts and bank charges.	$ _____
Adjusted balance	$ =======		**Adjusted balance**	$ =======

Figure 5.13

EXAMPLE 2   **Using the T-Account Form**

The bank statement of Hazel Nut Gifts shows a balance of $4385.88. Checks outstanding are $292.70, $75.16, and $636.55. Deposits not yet recorded are $483.11 and $89.95. Also appearing are a service charge of $7.90, a check-printing charge of $9.20, a returned check (NSF) for $94.25, and an interest credit of $10.06. The checkbook now shows a balance of $4055.82. Use the T-method to reconcile the checking account.

Solution   The reconciliation is shown using a T-account in Figure 5.14.

Bank Reconciliation

Bank statement balance	$4385.88		Checkbook balance		$4055.82

Add:

Deposits not recorded
$483.11
+ 89.95　　*add these to get* →　　+ 573.06

　　　　4958.94

Add:

Interest credit　　　　+ 10.06

　　　　　　　　　4065.88

Less:

Outstanding checks

$292.70
75.16
+636.55　　*add these to get* →　　−1004.41

Less:

Service charge　　$7.90
Check printing charge　　9.20　　*add these to get* →
Returned check　　+94.25　　　− 111.35

Adjusted balance	→	$3954.53	**Adjusted balance**	$3954.53 ←

found by adding $4385.88 and $573.06, and subtracting $1004.41

found by adding $4055.82 and $10.06, and subtracting $111.35

Figure 5.14

EXAMPLE 3　Reconciling a Checking Account

A checking account register is shown in Figure 5.15. A ✓ on the register indicates that the check appeared on the previous month's bank statement. Reconcile the account with a bank statement shown in Figure 5.16. (Codes on the statement have the following meaning: RC, Returned Check; SC, Service Charge; IC, Interest Credit; ATM, Automated Teller Machine.)

CHECK NO.	DATE	CHECK ISSUED TO	AMOUNT OF CHECK	✓	DATE OF DEP.	AMOUNT OF DEPOSIT	BALANCE
		BALANCE BROUGHT FORWARD →					2782 95
721	7/11	Miller's Outpost	138 50	✓			2644 45
722	7/12	Barber Advertising	73 08				2571 37
723	7/18	Wayside Lumber	318 62	✓			2252 75
		Deposit			7/20	1060 37	3313 12
724	7/25	I.R.S.	836 15				2476 97
725	7/26	John Lessor	450 00				2026 97
726	7/28	Sacramento Bee	67 80				1959 17
727	8/2	T.V.A.	59 25				1899 92
728	8/3	Carmichael Office	97 37				1802 55
		Deposit			8/6	795 45	2598 00
ATM	8/5	ATM Cash	80 00				2518 00

Figure 5.15

```
Bank Statement
*************************************************************
CHECK    CHECKS                    DEPOSITS     DATE    BALANCE
NUMBER   AND DEBITS
*************************************************************
                                              7/20    2325.83
722      73.08                                7/22    2252.75
                             1060.37          7/24    3313.12
724      836.15                               7/28    2476.97
725      450.00    49.07 RC                   7/30    1977.90
727      59.25                    3.22 IC     8/4     1921.87
                   80.00 ATM                  8/5     1841.87
                    7.60 SC                   8/5     1834.27
```

Figure 5.16

Bank Reconciliation

Bank statement balance	$1834.27		Checkbook balance		$2518.00
Add:			**Add:**		
Deposits not recorded	+ 795.45		Interest credit (IC)		+3.22
	2629.72				2521.22
Less:			**Less:**		
Outstanding checks			*Bank charges* Returned check (RC)	$49.07	
$67.80 +97.37	−165.17		Service charge (SC)	+7.60	−56.67
Adjusted balance	$2464.55		**Adjusted balance**		$2464.55

Figure 5.17

Solution Follow the instructions on the form in Figure 5.13. The completed reconciliation is shown in T-form in Figure 5.17.

NOTE It is important to guard against identity theft and other criminal activities. Destroy all documents that include savings, checking, and credit-card account numbers, Social Security numbers, and all bank records. Check washing is a crime in which the thief removes the amount written on the check and changes it to a higher amount.

5.3	Exercises

Find the current balance for each of the following accounts.

	Balance from Bank Statement	Checks Outstanding		Deposits Not Yet Recorded
1.	$4572.15	$97.68 $418.25	$348.17	$816.14 $571.28
2.	$6274.76	$381.40 $875.14	$681.10 $83.15	$346.65 $198.96
3.	$7911.42	$52.38 $95.42	$528.02 $76.50	$492.80 $38.72
4.	$9343.65	$840.71 $78.68	$665.73 $87.00	$971.64 $3382.71
5.	$19,523.20	$6853.60 $795.77	$340.00 $22.85	$6724.93 $78.81
6.	$32,489.50	$3589.70 $263.15	$18,702.15 $7269.78	$7110.65 $2218.63

RECONCILING CHECKING ACCOUNTS Use the steps given in Example 1 and Figure 5.12 to reconcile the following accounts.

		7.		8.
Balance from bank statement		$6875.09		$14,928.42
Checks outstanding (check number is given first)	421	$371.52	112	$84.76
	424	$429.07	115	$109.38
	427	$883.69	117	$42.03
	429	$35.62	119	$1429.12
Deposits not yet recorded		$701.56		$54.21
		$421.78		$394.76
		$689.35		$1002.04
Bank charge		$8.75		$7.00
Interest credit		$10.71		$22.86
Checkbook balance		$6965.92		$14,698.28

RECONCILING CHECKING ACCOUNTS Use the T-account form, Figure 5.13, to reconcile the following accounts.

9. The checkbook of Toys for Tots, Inc. shows a balance of $7779. When the bank statement was received, it showed a balance of $6237.44, a returned check amounting to $246.70, a service charge of $15.60, and a check-printing charge of $18.50. There were unrecorded deposits of $1442.44 and $479.50 and checks outstanding of $146.36, $91.52, $43.78, and $379.52.

10. Carole Venezio received a bank statement showing a balance of $1248.63, a returned check amounting to $35.17, a service charge of $7.70, and an interest credit of $2.51. Checks outstanding were $380, $36.66, $15.29, and $143.18; deposits not yet recorded were $478.18 and $359.12. The checkbook showed a balance of $1551.16.

11. The bank statement of William Poole Enterprises showed a bank balance of $4074.65, a returned check amounting to $168.40, a service charge of $7.08, and an interest credit

of $10.18. There were unrecorded deposits of $907.82 and $1784.15 and checks outstanding of $642.55, $1082.98, $73.25, and $471.83. The checkbook showed a balance of $4661.31.

12. The bank statement of Allysa Paige Decorating showed a balance of $1270.08. The checkbook balance showed $1626.63. There were unrecorded deposits of $370.64 and $219.38 and outstanding checks of $38.18, $185.10, $14.75, and $90.14. Check-printing charges were $8.50; the service charge was $3.80; there was a returned check of $83.85 and an interest credit of $1.45.

13. Explain in your own words the significance of writing a bad check. What might the cost be in dollars? What are the other consequences? (See Objective 1.)

14. What happens when you as a businessperson receive a bad check? What are the financial costs to the business? What are you likely to do regarding this customer? (See Objective 1.)

15. Briefly describe the importance of reconciling a checking account. What are the benefits derived from keeping good checking records? (See Objective 1.)

16. Suppose your checking account will not balance. Name four types of errors that you will look for in trying to correct this problem.

Reconcile the following checking accounts. Compare the items appearing on the bank statement to the check register. A ✓ indicates that the check appeared on the previous month's statement. (Codes indicate the following: RC means Returned Check, SC means Service Charge, CP means Check-Printing Charge, IC means Interest Credit, ATM means Automated Teller Machine.)

17.

CHECK NO.	DATE	CHECK ISSUED TO	AMOUNT OF CHECK		✓	DATE OF DEP.	AMOUNT OF DEPOSIT		BALANCE	
		BALANCE BROUGHT FORWARD →							7682	07
662	3/3	Action Packing Supplies	451	16					7230	91
663	3/3	Crown Paper	954	29	✓				6276	62
664	3/5	ATM Cash	80	00	✓				6196	62
		Deposit				3/7	913	28	7109	90
665	3/10	Fairless Water District	72	37					7037	53
666	3/12	Audia Temporary	340	88					6696	65
667	3/13	Car Repair	618	65					6078	00
668	3/14	Fairless Hills Power	100	50					5977	50
		Deposit				3/16	450	18	6427	68
		Deposit				3/18	163	55	6591	23
669	3/20	Plumber	238	50					6352	73
670	3/22	Standard Brands	315	62					6037	11
671	3/23	Penny-Saver Products	67	29					5969	82
		Deposit				3/24	830	75	6800	57

Bank Statement

```
*****************************************************************************
CHECK            CHECKS                    DEPOSITS        DATE      BALANCE
NUMBER           AND DEBITS
*****************************************************************************
                                                           3/5       6647.78
                                           913.28          3/7       7561.06
662              451.16                                     3/11      7109.90
666              340.88      82.15 RC      450.18           3/16      7137.05
665              72.37                      22.48 IC        3/20      7087.16
667              618.65                    163.55           3/22      6632.06
669              238.50      12.70 SC                       3/26      6380.86
```

18.

CHECK NO.	DATE	CHECK ISSUED TO	AMOUNT OF CHECK		✓	DATE OF DEP.	AMOUNT OF DEPOSIT		BALANCE	
						BALANCE BROUGHT FORWARD →			6669	34
760	2/8	Rugs to Go	248	96					6420	38
762	2/9	Healthways Dist.	125	63					6294	75
		Deposit				2/11	618	34	6913	09
763	2/12	Franchise Tax	770	41	✓				6142	68
764	2/14	Phone Bill	22	86	✓				6119	82
765	2/15	Yellow Pages	91	24					6028	58
		Deposit				2/17	826	03	6854	61
766	2/17	Morning Herald	71	59					6783	02
767	2/18	San Juan Electric	63	24					6719	78
ATM	2/22	ATM Gas	15	26					6704	52
769	2/23	West Construction	405	07					6299	45
770	2/24	Electrician	525	00					5774	45
		Deposit				2/26	220	16	5994	61
771	2/28	Capital Alarm	135	76					5858	85

Bank Statement

```
****************************************************************************
CHECK          CHECKS                     DEPOSITS        DATE     BALANCE
NUMBER         AND DEBITS
****************************************************************************
                                                          2/14     5876.07
765            91.24                       618.34         2/16     6403.17
760            248.96                       826.03        2/17     6980.24
766            71.59                                      2/19     6908.65
762            125.63                                     2/21     6783.02
                          198.17 RC                       2/22     6584.85
                          15.26 ATM         8.12 IC       2/24     6577.71
769            405.07      4.85 CP                        2/26     6167.79
                          6.28 SC                         2/27     6161.51
770            525.00                                     2/28     5636.51
```

CHAPTER TERMS

Review the following terms to test your understanding of the chapter. For each term you do not know, refer to the page number found next to that term.

adjusted bank balance [p. 178]

ATM card [p. 162]

automated teller machine (ATM) [p. 161]

balance brought forward [p. 166]

balance forward [p. 166]

bank check [p. 171]

bank statement [p. 176]

bank teller [p. 171]

blank endorsement [p. 164]

bouncing a check [p. 176]

brick-to-click banks [p. 162]

business checking account [p. 161]

canceled (check) [p. 164]

cashier's check [p. 171]

Check 21 [p. 164]

check register [p.167]

checks outstanding [p. 178]

check stub [p. 166]

credit card [p. 171]

current balance [p. 178]

debit card [p. 162]

deposit slip [p. 163]

deposit ticket [p. 163]

discount fee [p. 173]

e-commerce [p. 160]

electronic banking [p. 159]

electronic funds transfer (EFT) [p. 162]

flat-fee checking account [p. 161]

float [p. 164]

insufficient funds [p. 176]

interest-paying checking accounts [p. 161]

Internet banking [p. 162]

maintenance charge per month [p. 162]

merchant batch header ticket [p. 172]

money market [p. 161]

money order [p. 172]

nonsufficient funds (NSF) [p. 176]

notary service [p. 172]

online banking [p. 162]

overdraft [p. 172]

overdraft protection [p. 172]

per debit charge [p. 162]

personal checking account [p. 161]

personal identification number (PIN) [p. 162]

point-of-sale terminal [p. 162]

processing (check) [p. 164]

reconciliation [p. 176]

restricted endorsement [p. 164]

returned check [p. 176]

returned-deposit item [p. 172]

special endorsement [p. 164]

stop-payment order [p. 172]

T-account form [p. 179]

transaction costs [p. 162]

transaction register [p. 167]

virtual bank [p. 162]

CONCEPTS

5.1 Checking account service charges

There is usually a checking account maintenance charge and often a per check charge.

EXAMPLES

Find the monthly checking account service charge for a business with 36 checks and transactions, given a monthly maintenance charge of $7.50 and a $0.20 per check charge.

$$\$7.50 + 36(\$0.20) = \$7.50 + \$7.20$$
$$= \$14.70 \text{ monthly service charge}$$

5.2 Banking services offered

The checking account customer must be aware of various banking services that are offered.

Overdraft protection: offered to protect the customer from bouncing a check (NSF)

ATM card: used at automated teller machine to get cash or used as a debit card to make purchases

Stop-payment order: stops payment on a check written in error or a lost check

Cashier's check: a check written by the financial institution itself

Money order: an instrument used in place of cash

Notary service: an official certification of a signature or document

Online banking: allows the customer to perform banking functions using the Internet

Safe deposit box: box in a bank vault in which important and valuable items can be stored

5.2 Depositing credit-card transactions

Subtract credit-card refunds from total credit-card sales to find the gross deposit. Then subtract the discount charge from this total.

The following are credit-card charges and credits.

Sales		Credits
$28.15	$78.59	$21.86
$36.92	$63.82	$19.62

(a) Find total sales.

$$\$28.15 + \$36.92 + \$78.59 + \$63.82 = \$207.48$$

(b) Find total credits.

$$\$21.86 + \$19.62 = \$41.48$$

(c) Find gross amount.

$$\$207.48 - \$41.48 = \$166$$

(d) Given a 2% fee, find the amount of the charge.

$$\$166 \times 0.02 = \$3.32$$

(e) Find the amount of credit given to the business.

$$\$166 - \$3.32 = \$162.68$$

5.3 Reconciliation of a checking account

A checking account customer must periodically verify checking account records with those of the bank or financial institution. The bank statement is used for this.

The accuracy of all checks written, deposits made, service charges incurred, and interest paid is checked and verified. The customer's checkbook balance and bank balance must be the same for the account to reconcile, or balance.

CHAPTER 5 | Review Exercises

The answer section includes answers to all Review Exercises.

Use Table 5.1 on page 162 to find the monthly checking account service charge for the following accounts. [5.1]

1. The Sub Shop, 42 checks, average balance $1478

2. Sangi Market, 35 checks, average balance $485

3. Old English Chimney Sweep, 52 checks, average balance $3017

Complete the following three check stubs for Cypert Propane. The balance brought forward for stub 1561 is $16,409.82. Find the balance forward at the bottom of each stub. [5.1]

CHECKS WRITTEN

Number	Date	To	For	Amount
1561	Aug. 6	Fuel Depot	Fuel	$6892.12
1562	Aug. 8	First Bank	Payment	$1258.36
1563	Aug. 14	Security Service	Guard dogs	$416.14

Deposits made: $1572 on Aug. 7, $10,000 on Aug. 10.

4.

1561		
_____20____		
Amount _____		
To _____		
For _____		
Bal. Bro't. For'd.		
Am't. Deposited		
Total		
Am't. this Check		
Balance For'd.		

5.

1562		
_____20____		
Amount _____		
To _____		
For _____		
Bal. Bro't. For'd.		
Am't. Deposited		
Total		
Am't. this Check		
Balance For'd.		

6.

1563		
_____20____		
Amount _____		
To _____		
For _____		
Bal. Bro't. For'd.		
Am't. Deposited		
Total		
Am't. this Check		
Balance For'd.		

Jim Havey owns The Toy Train Shop. The shop sells new and collectible toy trains and does repairs as well. The following credit-card transactions occurred during a recent period. [5.2]

Sales		Credits
$118.68	$235.82	$15.36
$7.84	$98.56	$57.47
$33.18	$318.72	
$50.76	$116.35	
$12.72	$23.78	
$9.36	$38.95	

7. Find the total charges for the store.

8. What is the total amount of the credits?

9. Find the amount of the gross deposit when these credit-card transactions are deposited.

10. If the bank charges the retailer a 2% discount charge, what is the amount of the discount charge at the statement date?

11. Find the amount of credit given to The Toy Train Shop after the fee is subtracted.

Solve the following application problems.

12. Clancy Strock Collectibles received a bank statement showing a balance of $4964.52, a returned check amounting to $140.68, a service charge of $30.84, and an interest credit of $10.04. Checks outstanding are $1520, $146.64, $31.16, and $572.76; deposits not yet recorded are $1912.72 and $1436.48. The checkbook shows a balance of $6204.64. Use Figure 5.12 to reconcile the checking account. **[5.3]**

13. The bank statement of Jerry's Pizza showed a bank balance of $8149.30, a returned check amounting to $336.80, a service charge of $14.16, and an interest credit of $20.36. There were unrecorded deposits of $1815.64 and $3568.30, and checks outstanding of $1285.10, $2165.96, $146.50, and $943.66. The checkbook shows a balance of $9322.62. Use Figure 5.13 to reconcile the checking account. **[5.3]**

14. Use Figure 5.13 and the following check register and bank statement to reconcile the checking account. Compare the items appearing on the bank statement to the check register. A ✓ indicates that the check appeared on the previous month's statement. (Codes indicate the following: RC means Returned Check, SC means Service Charge, CP means Check-Printing Charge, IC means Interest Credit, ATM means Automated Teller Machine.) **[5.3]**

CHECK NO.	DATE	CHECK ISSUED TO	AMOUNT OF CHECK	✓	DATE OF DEP.	AMOUNT OF DEPOSIT	BALANCE
		BALANCE BROUGHT FORWARD →					1876 93
318	$9/6$	MUIR TRAVEL	76 18	✓			1800 75
319	$9/6$	NORTH COAST TOURS	322 40				1478 35
320	$9/8$	AMES PHOTO	41 12	✓			1437 23
		DEPOSIT			$9/10$	851 62	2288 85
321	$9/14$	AMERICAN FLYERS	970 40				1318 45
322	$9/15$	REVERE INTER.	386 92				931 53
		DEPOSIT			$9/18$	995 20	1926 73
324	$9/20$	IDAHO EDISON	68 17				1858 56
325	$9/20$	WESSON SUPPLY	195 76				1662 80
326	$9/22$	PARKER PACKERS	348 33				1314 47
327	$9/23$	FREEZE DRY SUPPLY	215 84				1098 63
328	$9/24$	COUNTY WATER	169 56				929 07
		DEPOSIT			$9/28$	418 35	1347 42

BANK STATEMENT

Check Number	Checks and Debits		Deposits	Date	Balance
				9/9	1759.63
			851.62	9/10	2611.25
321	970.40			9/15	1640.85
319	322.40			9/18	1318.45
322	386.92	78.93 RC	995.20	9/20	1847.80
325	195.76		6.52 IC	9/23	1658.56
326	348.33	7.80 SC		9/25	1302.43

CHAPTER 5   Business Application Case #1
Retailer Banking

Keiah Fulgham owns a retail store specializing in track-and-field equipment and accessories. She sells athletic shoes, clothing, and equipment to individuals, athletic clubs, and schools. Many of her customers use credit cards for their purchases and her credit-card sales in a recent week amounted to $8752.40. During the same period she had $573.94 in credit slips; Ms. Fulgham pays a credit-card fee of $2\frac{1}{2}\%$.

When she received her bank statement, the balance was $4228.34. The checks outstanding were $758.14, $38.37, $1671.88, $120.13, $2264.75, $78.11, $3662.73, $816.25, and $400. Both her credit-card deposit and bank deposits of $458.23, $771.18, $235.71, $1278.55, $663.52, and $1475.39 were not recorded.

(a) Find the gross deposit when the credit-card sales and credits are deposited.

(b) Find the amount of the credit given to Ms. Fulgham after the fee is subtracted.

(c) What is the total of the checks outstanding?

(d) Find the total of the deposits that were not recorded.

(e) Find the current balance in Ms. Fulgham's checking account.

<table>
<tr><td>CHAPTER 5</td><td><h1>Business Application Case #2</h1>Internet Startup</td></tr>
</table>

After having a baby, Melissa Hilton started her own business on Ebay (www.ebay.com). She buys items on sale at various stores in the mall or at garage sales. She then sells them to the highest bidder on Ebay and also on a Web site she has created where people can make purchases using a credit card.

   Melissa likes working at home since it allows her to take care of her new baby and supplement the family income at the same time. She also likes the fact that being active with a new business keeps her mentally stimulated. At the recommendation of an accountant, she uses a separate checking account for all of her business transactions. Although many of her payments are made online, she still writes checks to some individuals.

(a) If Hilton pays a monthly checking account fee of $5 plus $0.05 per check, find the total charge for a month in which 48 checks were written.

(b) The total credit-card sales during one month were $2682 with only a single credit-card return of $112. Find (i) the gross amount of the credit-card deposit and (ii) the amount of credit after a fee of $1\frac{1}{2}\%$ is subtracted.

(c) List items you or your friends have purchased on the Internet. Would you buy again on the Internet? What was the service like? Did you have any problems or issues? Do you trust the Internet as a place to shop and buy?

(d) List pros and cons from your perspective of having a home-based business on the Internet. Have you ever tried to sell something on Ebay? If not, we suggest you try it. It is easier than you may think.

Payroll

Business owners, managers, and employees alike take a strong interest in payroll. The amount of pay earned by an employee is most often determined by the number of hours worked or by specific tasks accomplished. Workers' pay varies around the world. Figure 6.1 shows average hourly manufacturing wages in different countries. Clearly, the highest hourly wages are paid in Germany, the United States, Japan, the United Kingdom, and Canada. China, Mexico, and Taiwan have the lowest wages.

The primary reason companies **offshore**, or move jobs abroad, is to take advantage of the lower wage rates. Factory workers in China may not speak English and may not have the training of U.S. or German workers, but they will work for about $1 per hour. Other problems that arise when firms offshore jobs include differences in time zones, high shipping costs to transport goods, language problems, quality problems, unreliable electricity and water, and cultural differences. Figure 6.2 shows that more and more women are working in the U.S.

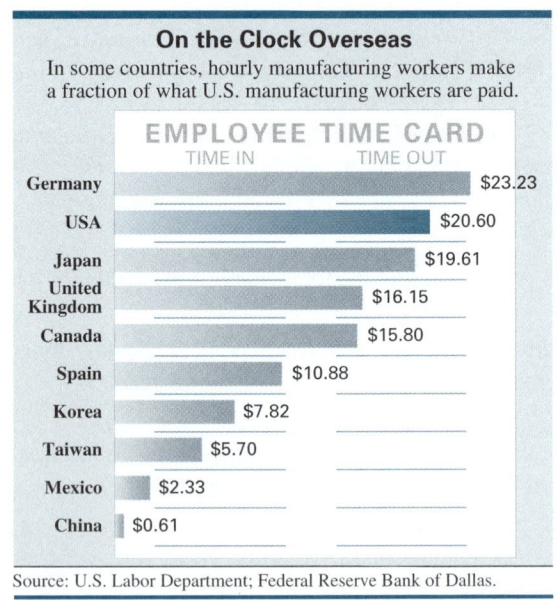

On the Clock Overseas

In some countries, hourly manufacturing workers make a fraction of what U.S. manufacturing workers are paid.

EMPLOYEE TIME CARD

	TIME IN	TIME OUT
Germany		$23.23
USA		$20.60
Japan		$19.61
United Kingdom		$16.15
Canada		$15.80
Spain		$10.88
Korea		$7.82
Taiwan		$5.70
Mexico		$2.33
China		$0.61

Source: U.S. Labor Department; Federal Reserve Bank of Dallas.

Figure 6.1

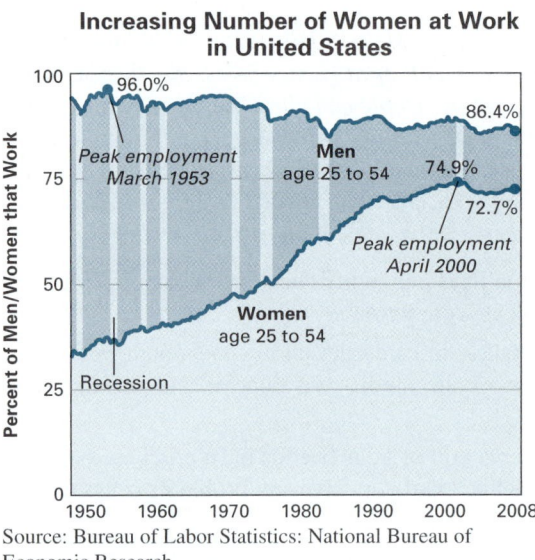

Increasing Number of Women at Work in United States

96.0%
86.4%
Peak employment March 1953
Men age 25 to 54
74.9%
72.7%
Peak employment April 2000
Women age 25 to 54
Recession

Source: Bureau of Labor Statistics: National Bureau of Economic Research.

Figure 6.2

STOP and think

First use Figure 6.2 to find the percent of women in the workforce outside the home in 1950 and in 2008. Since women also tend to spend more time than men working in the home and raising kids, women in general have become very busy. Identify ways in which this trend has affected families, society, and business.

Preparing the payroll is one of the most important jobs in any office. Payroll records must be accurate, and the payroll must be prepared on time so that the necessary checks can be written. The first step in preparing the payroll is to determine the **gross earnings** (the total amount earned) for each employee. There are many methods used to find gross earnings and several of these are discussed in this chapter. A number of **deductions** may be subtracted from gross earnings to find **net pay**, the amount actually received by the employee. These deductions and employer payroll records will also be discussed in this chapter.

| 6.1 | Gross Earnings (Wages and Salaries) |

OBJECTIVES

1 *Use hourly rate to calculate gross earnings.*

2 *Find overtime earnings for over 40 hours of work per week.*

3 *Use overtime premium method of calculating gross earnings.*

4 *Find overtime earnings for over 8 hours of work per day.*

5 *Understand double time, shift differential, and split-shift premiums.*

6 *Find equivalent earnings for different pay periods.*

7 *Find gross earnings when overtime is paid to salaried employees.*

Several methods are used to determine an employee's pay. Two of these methods, salaries and wages, are discussed in this section. Commissions and piecework are discussed in the next two sections.

In many businesses, the first step in preparing the payroll is to look at the **time card** maintained for each employee. An example of a time card is shown in Figure 6.3. The card includes the dates of the pay period and the employee's name and other personal information. It also shows the days, times, and hours worked, the total number of hours worked, and requires a signature verification by the employee as to the accuracy of the card. Although the card in Figure 6.3 is filled in by hand, many companies use a time clock that automatically stamps the days, dates, and times on the card. The information on these cards is then transferred to a **payroll ledger** (a chart showing all payroll information), as shown in Example 1.

Objective

1 *Use Hourly Rate to Calculate Gross Earnings.* Eboni Perkins, whose time card is shown in Figure 6.3, is paid an **hourly wage** of $14.80 (see the time card). Her gross earnings would be calculated with the following formula.

$$\text{Gross earnings} = \text{Number of hours worked} \times \text{Rate per hour}$$

For example, if Perkins works 8 hours at $14.80 per hour, her gross earnings would be

$$\text{Gross earnings} = 8 \times \$14.80 = \$118.40$$

| **EXAMPLE** 1 | **Completing a Payroll Ledger** |

Meg Holden is doing the payroll for two employees, S. Abruzzo and N. Williams. The first thing she must do is complete a payroll ledger.

Employee	Hours Worked							Total Hours	Rate	Gross Earnings
	S	M	T	W	Th	F	S			
Abruzzo, S.	—	2	4	8	6	3	—		$8.40	
Williams, N.	—	3.5	3	7	6.75	7	—		$10.40	

PAYROLL CARD
NO TIME CLOCK REQUIRED

EMPL. NO. 1375   CARD NO. _____

FULL NAME   Eboni Perkins   AGE (IF UNDER 18) _____

ADDRESS 412 Fawndale Drive   SOCIAL SECURITY NO. 123–45–6789

DATE EMPLOYED   POSITION Shift MGR   RATE $14.80

PAY PERIOD STARTING   7/23   ENDING 7/27

DATE	REGULAR TIME					OVER TIME		
	IN	OUT	IN	OUT	DAILY TOTALS	IN	OUT	DAILY TOTALS
7/23	8:00	11:50	12:20	4:30	8	4:30	6:30	2
7/24	7:58	12:00	12:30	4:30	8	5:00	7:30	2.5
7/25	8:00	12:00	12:30	4:32	8			
7/26	7:58	12:05	12:35	4:30	8	4:30	5:00	0.5
7/27	8:01	12:00	1:00	5:00	8			

APPROVED BY   MJH

TOTAL REGULAR TIME   40   5

REGULAR DAYS WORKED   5 @   8 HRS.   @   EARNINGS 14.80 $ 592.00

ADDITIONAL COMPENSATION: VALUE OF MEALS, LODGING, GIFTS, ETC.   AMOUNT $ _____

COMMISSIONS, FEES, BONUSES, GOODS, ETC.   OT 5 @ 22.20   AMOUNT $ 111.00

OTHER REMUNERATIONS (KIND) $ _____

DEDUCTIONS: TOTAL EARNINGS $ 703.00

I CERTIFY THE FOREGOING TO BE A CORRECT ACCOUNT OF THE TIME WORKED AND WAGES RECEIVED:

SIGNATURE   DATE PAID

Figure 6.3

Solution   The first step is to find the total number of hours worked by each person.

$$\text{Abruzzo:}\qquad 2 + 4 + 8 + 6 + 3 = 23 \text{ hours}$$

$$\text{Williams: } 3.5 + 3 + 7 + 6.75 + 7 = 27.25 \text{ hours}$$

To find the gross earnings, multiply the number of hours worked and the rate per hour.

$$\text{Abruzzo:}\qquad 23 \times \$8.40 = \$193.20$$

$$\text{Williams: } 27.25 \times \$10.40 = \$283.40$$

The payroll ledger can now be completed.

Employee	Hours Worked							Total Hours	Rate	Gross Earnings
	S	M	T	W	Th	F	S			
Abruzzo, S.	—	2	4	8	6	3	—	23	$8.40	$193.20
Williams, N.	—	3.5	3	7	6.75	7	—	27.25	$10.40	$283.40

Objective

2 *Find Overtime Earnings for Over 40 Hours of Work Per Week.* The **Fair Labor Standards Act (FLSA)** is a federal law that establishes a workweek of 40 hours per week and requires **overtime** pay for hours worked beyond 40 per week. It also sets the federal **minimum wage**, which is $7.25 per hour as of July 24, 2009. Some states, such as California, set their minimum wage at levels higher than the federal minimum wage. FLSA does not control vacation or sick pay, holidays off, vacations, or fringe benefits such as medical insurance. Many employees are not covered by FLSA, including executives, professionals, managers, administrative workers, teachers, outside sales employees, waiters and waitresses, salespeople, farm workers, and casual babysitters. So, for example, FLSA does not require that mangers or teachers who work more than 40 hours per week be paid overtime.

Many companies not covered by the FLSA follow the practice of paying **time-and-a-half**, or 1.5 times the normal wage rate, for any work over 40 hours per week. Calculate overtime earnings as follows. Add regular earnings to overtime earnings to find gross earnings.

$$\text{Overtime earnings} = \textbf{Hourly wage} \times \textbf{1.5}$$

$$\text{Gross earnings} = \text{Earnings at regular rate} + \text{Overtime earnings}$$

EXAMPLE 2 **Completing a Payroll Ledger with Overtime**

Complete the following payroll ledger.

Employee	\multicolumn{7}{c}{Hours Worked}	\multicolumn{2}{c}{Total Hours}		\multicolumn{3}{c}{Gross Earnings}
	S	M	T	W	Th	F	S	Reg.	O.T.	Reg. Rate	Reg.	O.T.	Total
Chung, E.	6	9	8.25	8	9	4.5	—			$8.30			
Jenders, P.	—	10	6.75	9	6.25	10	4.25			$9.48			

Solution First find the total number of hours worked.

Chung: $6 + 9 + 8.25 + 8 + 9 + 4.5 = 44.75$ hours

Jenders: $10 + 6.75 + 9 + 6.25 + 10 + 4.25 = 46.25$ hours

Both employees worked more than 40 hours. Gross earnings at the regular rate can now be found as discussed previously. Chung earned $40 \times \$8.30 = \$332$ at the regular rate, and Jenders earned $40 \times \$9.48 = \$379.20$ at the regular rate. To find overtime earnings, first find the number of overtime hours worked by each employee.

┌── regular hours

Chung: $44.75 - 40 = 4.75$ overtime hours

Jenders: $46.25 - 40 = 6.25$ overtime hours

The regular rate given for each employee can be used to find the time-and-a-half rate.

$$\text{Chung:} = 1\frac{1}{2} \times \$8.30 = \$12.45 \quad \text{Per hour of overtime}$$

$$\text{Jenders:} = 1\frac{1}{2} \times \$9.48 = \$14.22 \quad \text{Per hour of overtime}$$

Now find the overtime earnings.

Chung: 4.75 hours $\times \$12.45$ per hour $= \$59.14$ Rounded to the nearest cent

Jenders: 6.25 hours $\times \$14.22$ per hour $= \$88.88$ Rounded

The ledger can now be completed.

Employee	Hours Worked							Total Hours		Reg. Rate	Gross Earnings		
	S	M	T	W	Th	F	S	Reg.	O.T.		Reg.	O.T.	Total
Chung, E.	6	9	8.25	8	9	4.5	—	40	4.75	$8.30	$332	$59.14	$391.14
Jenders, P.	—	10	6.75	9	6.25	10	4.25	40	6.25	$9.48	$379.20	$88.88	$468.08

Objective

3   *Use Overtime Premium Method of Calculating Gross Earnings.*   Gross earnings with overtime is sometimes calculated with the **overtime premium method** (sometimes called the **overtime excess method**). This method produces the exact same result as the method just described. The total hours at the regular rate are added to the overtime hours at one-half of the regular rate to arrive at gross earnings.

The formula for the overtime premium method is

$$\text{Total hours} \times \text{Regular rate} = \text{Straight-time earnings}$$

$$\underline{+ \text{Overtime hours} \times \frac{1}{2}\text{Regular rate} = \text{Overtime premium}}$$

$$= \text{Gross earnings}$$

EXAMPLE 3   Using the Overtime Premium Method

This week, Marcy Pleu worked 40 regular hours and 12 overtime hours. Her regular rate of pay is $17.40 per hour. Find her total gross pay using the overtime premium method.

Solution   The total number of hours worked by Pleu is 52 (40 + 12) and her overtime premium rate is $8.70 ($\frac{1}{2} \times$ $17.40).

52 hours × $17.40 =	$904.80	Regular-rate earnings
12 overtime hours × $8.70 =	$104.40	Overtime
	$1009.20	Gross earnings

 Scientific Calculator Approach

Using chain calculations and the order of operations to solve Example 3, the regular earnings are calculated. Next the overtime earnings are calculated. Finally, they are added together.

52 × 17.4 + 12 × 17.4 × .5 = 1009.2

NOTE   Some companies prefer the overtime premium method since it readily identifies the extra cost of overtime labor and can be seen easily. Quite often, excessive use of overtime indicates inefficiencies in management.

Objective

4   *Find Overtime Earnings for Over 8 Hours of Work Per Day.*   Some companies pay the time-and-a-half rate for all time worked over 8 hours in any one day, no matter how many hours are worked in a week. This **daily overtime** is shown in the next example.

EXAMPLE 4 Finding Overtime Each Day

Peter Harris worked 10 hours on Monday, 5 on Tuesday, 7 on Wednesday, and 12 on Thursday. His regular rate of pay is $10.10. Find his gross earnings for the week if everything over 8 hours in one day is overtime.

	S	M	T	W	Th	F	S	Total Hours
Reg.	—	8	5	7	8	—	—	28
O.T.	—	2	—	—	4	—	—	6

Solution Harris worked more than 8 hours on both Monday and Thursday. On Monday, he had $10 - 8 = 2$ hours of overtime, with $12 - 8 = 4$ hours of overtime on Thursday. For the week, he earned $2 + 4 = 6$ hours of overtime. His regular hours are 8 on Monday, 5 on Tuesday, 7 on Wednesday, and 8 on Thursday, or

$$8 + 5 + 7 + 8 = 28 \text{ hours at the regular rate.}$$

His hourly earnings are $10.10, giving

$$28 \times \$10.10 = \$282.80 \text{ at the regular rate.}$$

If the regular rate is $10.10, the time-and-a-half rate is

$$\$10.10 \times 1\frac{1}{2} = \$15.15$$

He earned time-and-a-half for 6 hours.

$$6 \times \$15.15 = \$90.90$$

His gross earnings are found by adding regular earnings and overtime earnings.

$$\underbrace{\$282.80}_{\substack{\text{Total} \\ \text{regular pay}}} + \underbrace{\$90.90}_{\substack{\text{Total} \\ \text{overtime}}} = \underbrace{\$373.70}_{\substack{\text{Gross} \\ \text{earnings}}}$$

NOTE There are many careers that require unusual schedules and do not pay overtime for over 40 hours worked in one week or over 8 hours worked in one day. One example is a firefighter, who may work 24 hours and then get 48 hours off.

Objective

5 *Understand Double Time, Shift Differential, and Split-Shift Premiums.* In addition to premiums paid for overtime, other **premium payment plans** include **double time** for holidays and, in some industries, Saturdays and Sundays. A **shift differential** is often given to compensate employees for working less desirable hours. For example, an additional amount per hour or per shift might be paid to swing shift (4:00 P.M. to midnight) and graveyard shift (midnight to 8:00 A.M.) employees. These shifts are worked by nurses, emergency personnel, telephone operators, and workers at power plants.

Restaurant employees and telephone operators often receive a **split-shift premium**. The employees' hours are staggered so that the employees are on the job only during the busiest times. For example, an employee may work 4 hours, be off 4 hours, then work 4 hours. The employee is paid a premium because of this less desirable schedule.

Some employers offer **compensatory time**, or **comp time**, for overtime hours worked. Instead of receiving additional money, an employee is given time off from the regular work schedule as compensation for overtime hours already worked. Quite often, the compensatory time is given at $1\frac{1}{2}$ times the overtime hours worked. For example, 12 hours might be given as compensation for 8 hours of previously worked overtime. Occasionally an employee is given a choice of overtime pay or comp time. Many companies reserve the use of compensatory time for their supervisors or managerial employees. Also, compensatory time is very common in government agencies.

Objective

6 *Find Equivalent Earnings for Different Pay Periods.* The second common method of finding gross earnings uses a **salary**, a fixed amount given as so much per **pay period** (time between paychecks). Common pay periods are weekly, biweekly, semimonthly, and monthly (Table 6.1).

TABLE 6.1   COMMON PAY PERIODS

Monthly	12 paychecks each year
Semimonthly	Twice each month or 24 paychecks each year
Biweekly	Every two weeks or 26 paychecks each year
Weekly	52 paychecks each year

In Chapter 1, Figure 1.1 shows the average earnings for workers, depending on the level of education that they had achieved. Figure 6.4 shows that, although many careers require a 4-year college degree, there are still careers that do not. Notice, however, that many of these careers do require special training or an associate's degree.

Jobs That Do Not Require an Undergraduate Degree

Profession	Median Annual Earnings		
Air traffic controller	$107,780	Registered nurse	$62,480
Real estate broker	$79,800	Funeral director	$57,660
Commercial pilot	$71,270	Police officer	$50,670
Nuclear power		Aircraft mechanic	$49,670
reactor operator	$71,220	Court reporter	$48,330
Elevator installer/		Electrician	$48,100
repairer	$66,330	Flight attendant	$33,470
Dental hygienist	$64,910	Pest control worker	$30,280
Locomotive		Restaurant cook	$21,960
engineer	$63,180	Bartender	$19,740

Source: U.S. Department of Labor.

Figure 6.4

EXAMPLE 5 Determining Equivalent Salaries

You are a career counselor and want to compare the earnings of four clients for whom you have helped find jobs. John Cross receives a weekly salary of $546, Melanie Goulet a biweekly salary of $1686, Carla Lampsa a semimonthly salary of $736, and Tom Shaffer a monthly salary of $1818. For each worker, find the following: (a) earnings per year, (b) earnings per month, and (c) earnings per week.

Solution **John Cross**

(a) $546 × 52 = $28,392 per year
(b) $28,392 ÷ 12 = $2366 per month
(c) $546 per week

Melanie Goulet

(a) $1686 × 26 = $43,836 per year (biweekly = 26 per year)
(b) $43,836 ÷ 12 = $3653 per month
(c) $1686 ÷ 2 = $843 per week

Carla Lampsa

(a) $736 × 24 = $17,664 per year
(b) $736 × 2 = $1472 per month
(c) $17,664 ÷ 52 = $339.69 per week

Tom Shaffer

(a) $1818 × 12 = $21,816 per year
(b) $1818 per month
(c) $21,816 ÷ 52 = $419.54 per week

Objective

7 ***Find Gross Earnings When Overtime Is Paid to Salaried Employees.*** A salary is paid for the performance of a certain job, without keeping track of the number of hours worked. However, the Fair Labor Standards Act requires that certain salaried positions receive additional compensation for overtime. Just as with wage earners, the salaried employee is often paid time-and-a-half for all hours worked over the normal number of hours per week.

EXAMPLE 6 **Finding Overtime for Salaried Employees**

Caralee Woods is paid $872 a week as an executive assistant. If her normal workweek is 40 hours, and she is paid time-and-a-half for all overtime, find her gross earnings for a week in which she works 45 hours.

Solution The executive assistant's salary has an hourly equivalent of

$$\frac{\$872}{40 \text{ hours}} = \$21.80 \text{ per hour}$$

Since she must be paid overtime at the rate of $1\frac{1}{2}$ times her regular pay, she will get $32.70 per hour ($1\frac{1}{2}$ × $21.80) for overtime. Her gross earnings for the week are calculated as follows:

Salary for 40 hours =	$ 872.00	Regular-rate earnings
Overtime for 5 hours (5 × $32.70) =	163.50	Overtime
	$1035.50	Gross earnings

Scientific Calculator Approach

The calculator solution to Example 6 is as follows:

872 + 872 ÷ 40 × 1.5 × 5 = 1035.5

EXAMPLE 7   **Finding Gross Earnings with Overtime**

A technician working in a crime lab is paid a salary of $648 per week. If his regular work-week is 36 hours, find his gross earnings for a week in which he works 46 hours. All overtime hours are paid at time-and-a-half.

Solution   The technician's salary has an hourly equivalent of

$$\frac{\$648}{36 \text{ hours}} = \$18 \text{ per hour}$$

Since he is paid $1\frac{1}{2}$ times the regular rate per hour, he will receive $27 per hour ($1\frac{1}{2} \times$ $18) for overtime. His gross earnings for the week are as follows.

Salary for 36 hours	=	$648	Regular-rate earnings
Overtime for 10 hours (10 × $27)	=	270	Overtime
		$918	Gross earnings

Figure 6.5 lists the 10 best firms to work for as rated by *Fortune* magazine. Besides salaries, the editors making the choice also look at factors such as benefits and working environment when trying to identify the best companies.

Best Companies to Work For

- Google
- Quicken Loans
- Wegmans Food Markets
- Edward Jones
- Genentech
- Cisco Systems
- Starbucks
- Qualcomm
- Goldman Sachs
- Methodist Hospital System

Figure 6.5   Source: *Fortune* Magazine.

6.1	**Exercises**

THE PAYROLL LEDGER   **Find the number of regular hours and overtime hours (any hours over 40) for each of the following employees. Then calculate the overtime rate (time-and-a-half) for each employee.**

	Employee	S	M	T	W	Th	F	S	Reg. Hrs.	O.T. Hrs.	Reg. Rate	O.T. Rate
1.	Allen, K.	—	7	4	7	10	8	4			$8.10	
2.	Doran, C.	—	6.5	9	7.5	8	9.5	7			$8.24	
3.	Jaworski, B.	3	6	8.25	8	8.5	5	—			$7.80	
4.	Sheehan, A.	8.5	9	7.5	8	10	8.25	—			$9.50	
5.	Ulman, L.	—	9.5	7	9	9.25	10.5	—			$11.48	
6.	Fuqua, B.	—	8	8	9	7.25	6	7			$9.80	

GROSS EARNINGS Find the earnings at the regular rate, the earnings at the overtime rate, and the gross earnings for each of the employees in Exercises 1–6.

7. Allen, K.

8. Doran, C.

9. Jaworski, B.

10. Sheehan, A.

11. Ulman, L.

12. Fuqua, B.

Find the overtime rate at time-and-a-half, the amount of earnings at regular pay, the amount at overtime pay, and the total gross wages for each employee.

	Employee	Total Hours Reg.	O.T.	Reg. Rate	O.T. Rate	Gross Earnings Reg.	O.T.	Total
13.	Fenton, C.	39.5	—	$8.80				
14.	Klein, A.	36.25	—	$10.20				
15.	Schultz, J.	40	4.5	$14.40				
16.	Light, P.	40	6.75	$9.80				
17.	Weisher, W.	40	4.25	$9.18				
18.	Dong, L.	40	5	$8.25				

OVERTIME PREMIUM Some companies use the overtime premium method to determine gross earnings. Use this method to complete the following partial payroll register. Overtime is paid at time-and-a-half rate for all hours over 40.

	Employee	S	M	T	W	Th	F	S	Total Hours	Reg. Rate	O.T. Hours	O.T. Premium Rate	Gross Earnings Reg.	O.T.	Total
19.	Aragona, B.	10	9	8	5	12	7	—		$7.40					
20.	Biron, C.	7.75	10	5	9.75	8	10	—		$9.50					
21.	Cheever, P.	—	12	11	8	8.25	11	—		$8.60					
22.	Abeya, C.	—	8.5	5.5	10	12	10.5	7		$7.50					
23.	Sherlock, F.	—	10	9.25	9.5	11.5	10	—		$10.20					
24.	Firavich, S.	8.5	7	9.75	—	10.5	12	—		$12.50					

DAILY OVERTIME PAYMENT Some companies pay overtime for all time worked over 8 hours in a given day. Use this method to complete the following payroll register. Overtime is paid at time-and-a-half rate.

		Hours Worked							Total Hours		Reg.	O.T.	Gross Earnings		
	Employee	S	M	T	W	Th	F	S	Reg.	O.T.	Rate	Rate	Reg.	O.T.	Total
25.	Belinder, M.	—	10	9	11	6	5	—			$9.50				
26.	Cechvala, C.	—	9	8.75	7	8.5	10	—			$7.60				
27.	Deininger, M.	—	7.5	8	9	10.75	8	—			$11.40				
28.	Gingrich, D.	—	9	10	8	6	9.75	—			$8.60				
29.	Kaplan, L.	—	9.5	8.5	7.75	8	9.5	—			$10.20				
30.	Lerner, M.	6	8	6.5	8.75	—	10.25	—			$14.40				

31. Explain in your own words what premium payment plans are. Select a premium payment plan and describe it. (See Objective 5.)

32. If you were given a choice of overtime pay or compensatory time, which would you choose? Why? (See Objective 5.)

EQUIVALENT EARNINGS Find the equivalent earnings for each of the following salaries as indicated.

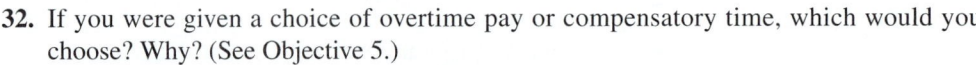

	Weekly Earnings	Biweekly Earnings	Semimonthly Earnings	Monthly Earnings	Annual Earnings
33.	$248	_____	_____	_____	_____
34.	_____	_____	$480	_____	_____
35.	_____	$852	_____	_____	_____
36.	_____	_____	_____	$2300	_____
37.	_____	_____	$1087.50	_____	_____
38.	$436	_____	_____	_____	_____
39.	_____	_____	_____	$2680	_____
40.	_____	$768	_____	_____	_____
41.	_____	_____	_____	_____	$43,160
42.	_____	_____	_____	_____	$52,200

SALARY WITH OVERTIME Find the weekly gross earnings for the following people who are on salary and are paid time-and-a-half for overtime. (*Hint:* Round hourly equivalents and overtime amounts to the nearest cent.)

	Employee	Regular Hours per Week	Weekly Salary	Hours Worked	Weekly Gross Earnings
43.	Atkins, G.	40	$520	56	_____
44.	Berry, M.	40	$360	42	_____
45.	Bridges, C.	45	$418	50	_____
46.	Kelley, R.	38	$340	40	_____
47.	Magot, D.	32	$450	44	_____
48.	Sypniewski, D.	30	$484	45	_____

Solve the following application problems. Round hourly equivalents, regular rates, and overtime rates to the nearest cent.

49. RETAIL EMPLOYMENT Last week, Lori Merrill worked 48 hours at Starbucks. Find her gross earnings for the week if she is paid $8.40 per hour and earns time-and-a-half for all hours over 40.

50. ACCOUNTS PAYABLE CLERK Angela Gragg is a receptionist in a doctor's office and is paid $13.60 per hour for straight time and time-and-a-half for all hours over 40 worked in a week. Find her gross earnings for a week in which she worked 52 hours.

51. WELDER James Simpson is paid $14.60 per hour to work as a welder. He is paid time-and-a-half for all hours over 8 hours worked on a given day. Find his gross earnings for a week during which he worked the following hours: Monday, 9.5 hours; Tuesday, 7 hours; Wednesday, 8 hours; Thursday, 10 hours; and Friday, 9.5 hours.

52. OFFICE ASSISTANT Jenny Fang is a dental assistant and worked 10 hours on Monday, 9.75 hours on Tuesday, 5.5 hours on Wednesday, 12 hours on Thursday, and 7.25 hours on Friday. Her regular rate of pay is $11.50 an hour, with time-and-a-half paid for all hours over 8 worked in a given day. Find her gross earnings for the week.

53. ESCROW OFFICER Anne Felsted is paid $920 a week as an escrow officer at a bank. Her normal workweek is 40 hours. She is paid time-and-a-half for overtime. Find her gross earnings for a week in which she worked 46 hours.

54. FEEDSTORE SALES An employee at Valley Feed Stores is paid $298 for a normal workweek of 35 hours. If she is paid time-and-a-half for overtime, find her gross earnings for a week in which she worked 48 hours.

55. SALARY WITH OVERTIME Charles Dawkins, manager of the Cellular Phone Center, is paid a salary of $638 per week, has a normal workweek of 40 hours, and is paid time-and-a-half for overtime. Find his gross earnings in a week in which he worked 52 hours.

56. HOME MORTGAGE BUSINESS Lesly Jaramillo, assistant manager of Countrywide Mortgage, worked 54 hours this week. If she is paid a weekly salary of $800 and has a normal workweek of 45 hours, find her gross earnings for the week. She is paid time-and-a-half for all overtime.

57. EQUIVALENT EARNINGS An employee earns $630 weekly. Find the equivalent earnings if paid (a) biweekly, (b) semimonthly, (c) monthly, and (d) annually.

58. ANNUAL SALARY Angelica Canales is a plant supervisor and is paid $42,900 annually. Find the equivalent earnings if this amount is paid (a) weekly, (b) biweekly, (c) semimonthly, and (d) monthly.

59. Semimonthly pay periods result in 24 paychecks per year. Biweekly pay periods result in 26 paychecks per year. Which of these pay periods gives three checks in two months of the year? Will it always be the same two months? Explain.

60. Which would you prefer: a monthly pay period or a weekly pay period? What special budgetary considerations might you consider regarding the pay period that you choose?

6.2	**Gross Earnings (Commission)**

OBJECTIVES

1 *Find gross earnings using commission rate × sales (P = R × B).*

2 *Determine commission using a variable commission rate.*

3 *Use salary and commission rate to find gross earnings.*

4 *Use a drawing account and quota to find gross earnings.*

5 *Determine override as part of gross earnings.*

Many people in sales and marketing are paid on **commission**, usually a fixed percent of sales. This is an incentive system of compensation and the commissions are designed to produce maximum employee output, since pay is directly dependent on sales. This section discusses several common types of sales commissions.

Objective

1 *Find Gross Earnings Using Commission Rate × Sales (P = R × B).* With a **straight commission**, the salesperson is paid a fixed percent of sales. Gross earnings are found by the following formula.

$$P \quad = \quad R \quad \times \quad B$$

Gross earnings = commission rate × amount of sales

EXAMPLE 1   **Determining Earnings Using Commission**

The real estate commission to sell a house is 6% of the sale price. Find the commission on a small three-bedroom, two-bath home that sold for $188,500.

Solution

$$\text{Commission} = 6\% \text{ of } \$188,500$$
$$= 0.06 \times \$188,500 = \$11,310$$

Any returned items must be subtracted from gross sales before calculating a commission. Gross sales less **returns** is called **net sales**.

EXAMPLE 2   **Subtracting Returns When Using Commissions**

Jessie Winkler sells food supplements and vitamins and is paid commission of 4.5% of net sales. His territory includes several states in the northeastern part of the United States and also Quebec, Canada. Find his commission for a month with $98,450 in sales and $2650 in returns.

Solution

$$\text{Net sales} = \$98,450 - \$2650 = \$95,800$$
$$\text{Commission} = 4.5\% \text{ of } \$95,800$$
$$= 0.045 \times \$95,800 = \$4311$$

Objective

2 *Determine Commission Using a Variable Commission Rate.* The **sliding-scale** or **variable commission** plan is a method of pay designed to retain top-producing salespeople. With these plans, a higher rate of commission is paid as sales get larger and larger.

EXAMPLE 3 Finding Earnings Using Variable Commission

Bob Kilpatrick sells food and bakery products to businesses and is paid as follows:

Sales	Rate
Up to $10,000	6%
$10,001–$20,000	8%
$20,001 and up	9%

Find Kilpatrick's earnings on sales of $32,768.

Solution Use the three commission rates as follows:

(Total sales)	$32,768	
(First $10,000)	− 10,000 at 6% =	$600.00
	$22,768	
(Next $10,000)	− 10,000 at 8% =	$800.00
(Over $20,000)	$12,768 at 9% =	$1149.12
Total commissions	=	$2549.12

Kilpatrick had gross earnings of $2549.12.

Scientific Calculator Approach

The first thing to do is find the commission earned at the highest rate and *place* it in memory.

(32768 − 20000) × 9 % = STO

Next, find the commission at the second-highest rate and *add* this to memory.

(20000 − 10000) × 8 % = + RCL = STO

Finally, find the commission at the lowest rate and *add* it to memory. The result is the total commission.

10000 × 6 % = + RCL = 2549.12

Objective

3 *Use Salary and Commission Rate to Find Gross Earnings.* With a **salary plus commission**, the salesperson is paid a fixed sum per pay period, plus a commission on all sales. This method of payment is commonly used by large retail stores. Gross earnings with salary plus commission are found by the following formula.

Gross earnings = Fixed amount per pay period + Amount earned on commission

Many salespeople favor this method of determining gross earnings. It is especially attractive to the beginning salesperson who lacks selling experience and personal self-confidence. While providing an incentive, it offers the security of a guaranteed income to cover basic living costs.

EXAMPLE 4 Adding Commission to a Salary

Pat Quinlin is paid $225 per week by the Potters Exchange, plus 3% on all sales. Find her gross earnings for a week in which her sales were $7250.

Solution

$$\text{Gross earnings} = \text{Fixed earnings} + \text{Commission}$$
$$= \$225 + (0.03 \times \$7250)$$
$$= \$225 + \$217.50$$
$$= \$442.50$$

NOTE   Workers paid by commission may include salespeople in clothing stores and even waiters and waitresses in high-end restaurants who are paid a commission on sales of wine or other items.

Objective

4   *Use a Drawing Account and Quota to Find Gross Earnings.*   The fixed amount of earnings is often a **draw**, or loan, against future commissions. A **drawing account** is set up with the amounts drawn repaid with future commissions. This is a loan against future commissions but offers the salesperson the assurance of a fixed sum per pay period. The salesperson must repay the drawing account as commissions are earned.

EXAMPLE 5 Subtracting a Draw from Commission

Elizabeth Owens, a computer sales representative, has sales of $77,120 for the month and is paid a 7% commission rate. She had draws of $750 for the month. Find her gross earnings after repaying the drawing account.

Solution

$$\text{Gross earnings} = \text{Commissions} - \text{Draw}$$
$$= (0.07 \times 77{,}120) - \$750$$
$$= \$5398.40 - \$750$$
$$= \$4648.40$$

NOTE   It can be risky to work only for commissions since sales can be low some months, resulting in low earnings for the month. As a result, many companies offer a plan that includes a low base salary plus a commission used to motivate people to greater achievements.

Figure 6.6 shows the occupations with the highest number of projected jobs.

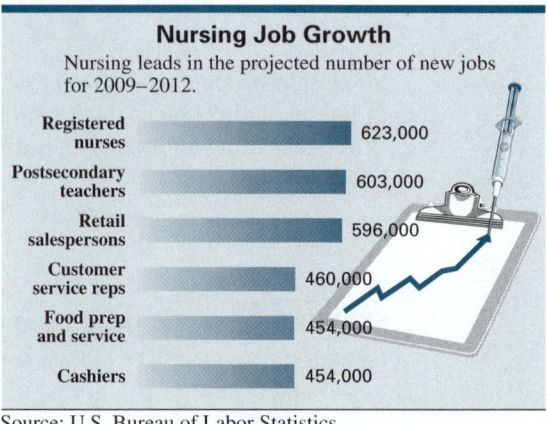

Nursing Job Growth

Nursing leads in the projected number of new jobs for 2009–2012.

Registered nurses	623,000
Postsecondary teachers	603,000
Retail salespersons	596,000
Customer service reps	460,000
Food prep and service	454,000
Cashiers	454,000

Source: U.S. Bureau of Labor Statistics.

Figure 6.6

A sales quota is often established for salespeople. The **quota** is the minimum amount of sales expected from the employee. If the salesperson continually falls short of the sales quota, the person may be terminated. Normally, however, the salesperson is rewarded with a bonus or commission for passing the sales quota. This plan is called a **quota bonus system**.

EXAMPLE 6   Using the Quota Bonus System

David Shea is a sales representative for a mountain bike manufacturer. During a recent week, he had sales of $18,780 and was paid a commission of 8% after meeting the sales quota of $5000. Find his gross earnings.

Solution

$$\text{Gross earnings} = \text{Commission rate} \times (\text{Sales} - \text{Quota})$$
$$= 0.08 \times (\$18,780 - \$5000) \qquad \text{No commission on}$$
$$= 0.08 \times \$13,780 \qquad \qquad \text{the first } \$5000$$
$$= \$1102.40$$

Objective

5   *Determine Override as Part of Gross Earnings.*   Sales supervisors and department heads are often paid from two sources. First, they receive a commission on their own personal sales. Second, they also receive a commission called an **override** on the total sales of their department. The override is used to reward the manager for training and motivating sales staff. It is difficult to do a great job managing people, and managers are usually rewarded by making more than nonmanagers, although some salespeople earn high incomes.

EXAMPLE 7   Finding Gross Earnings with Commission and Override

Taylor's Men's Shoppe pays the manager a salary plus commission and override on department sales. Find the earnings for a manager given the following information for one week.

	Manager	Department
Sales	$5850	$23,650
Returns	$187	$768
Base Salary	$400	—
Quota	$2000	—
Commission Rate	5%	
Override Rate	1%	

Solution   First, find the commission on personal sales.

$$\text{Personal Sales} - \text{Returns} - \text{Quota} = \$5850 - \$187 - \$2000$$
$$= \$3663$$
$$\text{Commission on Personal Sales} = 5\% \times \$3663 = \$183.15$$

Then, find the override commission on department sales.

$$\text{Department Sales} - \text{Returns} = \$23,650 - \$768 = \$22,882$$
$$\text{Override on Department Sales} = \$22,882 \times 0.01 = \$228.82$$

Finally, find the manager's gross earnings.

$$\text{Gross earnings} = \text{Salary} + \text{Commission} + \text{Override}$$
$$= \$400 + \$183.15 + \$228.82$$
$$= \$811.97$$

Scientific
Calculator
Approach

In solving Example 7, the approach here is to first find the manager's commission on personal sales and *place* it in memory.

$$(\boxed{5850} \boxed{-} \boxed{187} \boxed{-} \boxed{2000} \boxed{)} \boxed{\times} \boxed{5} \boxed{\%} \boxed{=} \boxed{STO}$$

Next, find the override on department sales and *add* it to memory.

$$(\boxed{23650} \boxed{-} \boxed{768} \boxed{)} \boxed{\times} \boxed{1} \boxed{\%} \boxed{=} \boxed{+} \boxed{RCL} \boxed{=} \boxed{STO}$$

Finally, *add* the salary to the commission and override in memory. The result is the gross earnings.

$$\boxed{400} \boxed{+} \boxed{RCL} \boxed{=} 811.97$$

6.2 | Exercises

COMMISSION WITH RETURNS   Find the gross earnings for each of the following salespeople.

	Employee	Total Sales	Returns and Allowances	Rate of Commission
1.	McKee, J.	$2810	$208	8%
2.	Brown, D.	$5734	$415	5%
3.	Pasnick, J.	$2875	$64	15%
4.	Beckenstein, J.	$2603	$76	18%
5.	Brown, K.	$25,658	$4083	9%
6.	Dramatinos, M.	$18,765	$386	8%
7.	Dobbins, G.	$45,618	$2281	1%
8.	Phares, H.	$34,183	$1169	2%

VARIABLE COMMISSION   In addition to a small monthly base salary, Jetta Pools and Spas pays its salespeople a monthly commission, determined as follows:

    6% on first $7500 in sales
    8% on next $7500 in sales
    10% on any sales over $15,000

Find the commission for each of the following employees.

	Employee	Total Sales			Employee	Total Sales
9.	Dean, D.	$18,550		**10.**	Davis, C.	$17,640
11.	Brueck, G.	$10,480		**12.**	Koch, R.	$16,250
13.	Sanchez, J.	$11,225		**14.**	Fisher, L.	$22,650
15.	Butter, M.	$25,860		**16.**	Manly, C.	$23,340

17. When you are paid a commission, there is always the possibility of higher earnings and also the uncertainty about a paycheck. Explain in your own words the special budgetary planning you would have to do if you were paid on commission.

18. A variable commission plan is often referred to as an incentive within an incentive. Explain why this might be an accurate description of a variable commission plan. (See Objective 2.)

COMMISSION PAYROLL LEDGER Complete the following commission payroll to find gross earnings.

	Employee	Gross Sales	Sales Returns	Net Quota	Commission Sales	Commission Rate	Gross Commission	Salary	Gross Earnings
19.	Potter, D.	$5250	$220	—		4%		$290	
20.	Schwartz, A.	$9370	$840	$3000		10%		—	
21.	Reska, L.	$6380	$295	$2000		6%		$500	
22.	Wetherbee, S.	$3270	$420	—		7%		$280	
23.	Chen, C.	$22,420	$390	$2500		3%		—	
24.	Ng, B.	$10,680	$490	$1500		6%		—	
25.	Jidobu, B.	$4215	$318	$1000		5%		$210	
26.	Kroeger, T.	$3850	$310	$1400		6%		$350	

Solve the following application problems.

27. **ART SUPPLIES** Laura Akahori is a sales representative for wholesale art. She is paid an 11% commission rate and has had a draw of $450 this week. If her sales are $12,420 this week, find her gross earnings after repaying the drawing account.

28. **COMMISSION DRAW** Kim Craft has sales of $78,560 for the month and is paid a 6% commission rate. She has had draws totaling $1500 for the month. Find her gross earnings after repaying the drawing account.

29. **SALARY PLUS COMMISSION** Stacy Dwyer, a salesperson for Zapp Music, has sales of $194,800 this month and is paid a 2% commission by her company. She also receives a salary of $1750 each month. Find her gross earnings for the month.

30. **EDUCATIONAL SALES** Nancy White, an account representative for Kreative Kids, is paid a 4% commission rate and a salary of $200 each week. If her sales are $25,510 this week, find her gross earnings for the week.

31. **OFFICE SYSTEMS** Arthur Zinshyang is a commissioned salesperson for Office Systems, Inc., which allows him to draw $800 per month. His commission is 6% of the first $6000 in sales, 8% of the next $16,000, and 15% of all sales over $22,000. If his sales for the month were $27,700, find (a) his total commission and (b) the earnings due at the end of the month after repaying the drawing account balance of $800.

32. **GREETING CARD SALES** Irma Easterly is a sales representative for Hi Side Greeting Card Company. She is paid a monthly draw of $650. Her commission is 10% of the first $2000 in sales, 12% of the next $4000, and 20% of all sales over $6000. If her sales for the month were $13,750, find (a) her total commission and (b) the gross earnings due at the end of the month after repaying the drawing account.

33. **COMMISSION PLUS OVERRIDE** A manager at Medco Health is paid a weekly salary plus commission and an override. Find his gross earnings given the following.

Personal sales	$5650	Personal returns	$168
Department sales	$17,312	Department returns	$634
Salary	$400	Personal quota	$1000
Commission rate	5%	Override	$1\frac{1}{2}\%$

34. APPLIANCE SALES MANAGER The sales manager for A&A Appliance is paid a salary plus commission and an override. Find her gross earnings given the following.

Personal sales	$5856	Personal returns	$185
Store sales	$19,622	Store returns	$358
Salary	$250	Personal quota	$3000
Commission rate	3%	Override	2%

6.3 Gross Earnings (Piecework)

OBJECTIVES

1 *Find the gross earnings for piecework.*

2 *Find the gross earnings for differential piecework.*

3 *Determine chargebacks or dockings.*

4 *Find overtime earnings for piecework.*

The salaries and wages discussed in **Section 6.1** are called **time rates**, since they depend only on the amount of time an employee was actually on the job. Commission earnings in **Section 6.2** and the piecework methods discussed in this section are called **incentive rates**. These gross earnings are based on production and pay an employee for actual performance on the job. The 10 help-wanted ads from the classified section of the newspaper are for jobs offering incentive rates of pay. The ad for lathers and stucco construction workers offers piecework and hourly compensation; the ad for truck drivers lists piece rates of $0.45 per mile (cpm). The ads for bill collectors and commercial roofing, health insurance, Better Business Bureau membership, automobile, swimming pool, and home security system sales positions pay on a commission plan.

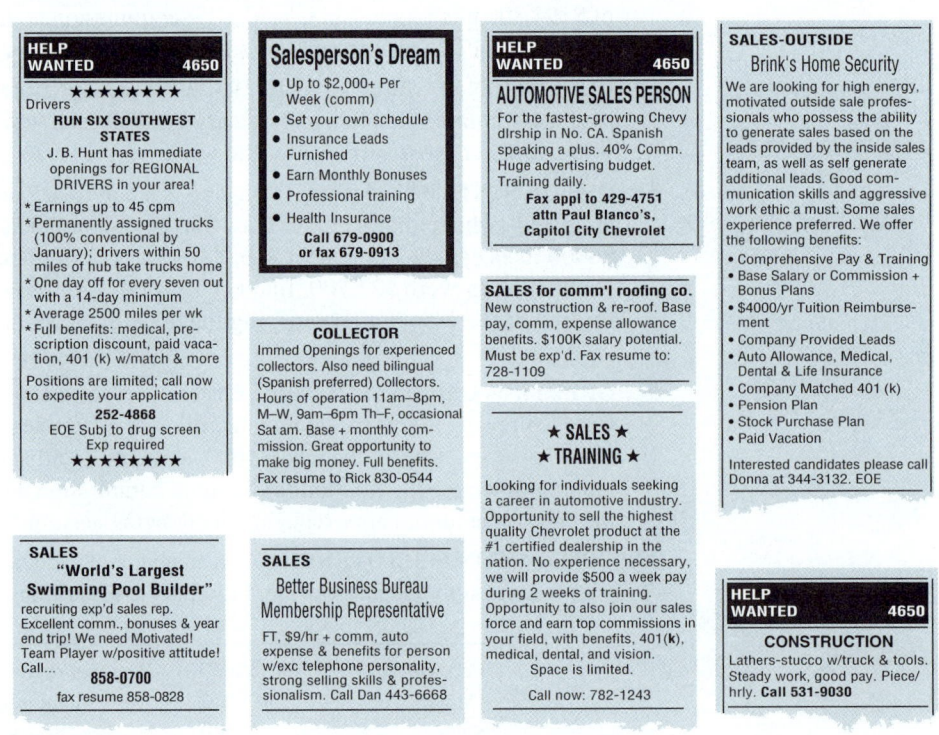

Objective

1 *Find the Gross Earnings for Piecework.* A **piecework rate** pays an employee so much per item produced. Gross earnings are found using the following formula.

$$\text{Gross earnings} = \text{Pay per item} \times \text{Number of items}$$

For example, a truck driver who drives 2000 miles in a week and is paid a piecework rate of $0.45 per mile earns

$$\text{Gross earnings} = 2000 \times \$0.45 = \$900$$

for the week.

EXAMPLE 1   **Finding Gross Earnings for Piecework**

Dona Kenly was paid $0.85 for sewing a jacket collar, $0.98 for a sleeve with a cuff, and $1.10 for a lapel. One week she sewed 318 jacket collars, 112 sleeves with cuffs, and 37 lapels. Find her gross earnings.

Solution   Multiply the rate per item by the number of that type of item.

Item	Rate × Number = Total
Jacket collars	$0.85 × 318 = $270.30
Sleeves with cuffs	$0.98 × 112 = $109.76
Lapels	$1.10 × 37 = $40.70
	Gross Earnings = $420.76

Objective

2   *Find the Gross Earnings for Differential Piecework.*   A **straight-piecework plan**, such as in Example 1, is perhaps the oldest of all incentive payment plans. It is used in many manufacturing and production jobs such as fine jewelry finishing, agricultural and farm work, garment manufacturing, as well as in the building trades for structural framing, roofing, and floor laying. While many workers prefer working under a piecework plan, there are just as many who dislike it. Labor unions and other employee organizations, senior employees, and others claim that piecework plans result in unsafe work habits and poor workmanship.

Companies still using piecework have often made various modifications and changes to the straight-piecework plan. Many of these modified plans incorporate initial quotas and then offer an additional **premium rate** for each item produced beyond the quota. These plans offer an added incentive within an incentive. For example, in the **differential-piecework plan** the rate paid per item depends on the number of items produced.

EXAMPLE 2   **Using Differential Piecework**

Metro Electric pays assemblers as follows.

1–100 units	$2.10 each
101–150 units	$2.25 each
151 or more units	$2.40 each

Find the gross earnings of an employee producing 214 items.

Solution   The gross earnings of a worker producing 214 items would be found as follows.

(Total units)	214	
(First 100 units)	−100 at $2.10 each =	$210.00
	114	
(Next 50 units)	− 50 at $2.25 each =	$112.50
(Number over 150)	64 at $2.40 each =	+$153.60
	=	$476.10

The gross earnings are $476.10.

> **NOTE** With differential piecework, the highest amount paid applies only to the last units produced. In Example 2, $2.10 is paid for units 1–100, $2.25 is paid for units 101–150, and $2.40 is paid only on those units beyond unit 150, which in this case is 64 units.

Objective

3 *Determine Chargebacks or Dockings.* While companies are often pleased to reward employees with premium rates for surpassing quotas, management is very concerned with unacceptable quality and unusable production. Ruined items may produce a total loss of material and labor or correctable flaws that require additional handling, resulting in added costs and decreased profits. To discourage carelessness and mistakes, many companies require the employee to share in the cost of the spoiled item. These penalties, called **chargebacks** or **dockings,** are normally at a lower rate than the employee receives for producing that piece. This lower rate is used because a small amount of production error is expected.

EXAMPLE 3 **Understanding and Using Chargebacks**

In Example 2, suppose the company had a chargeback of $2.50 per spoiled item and the employee had spoiled 14 items. Find the gross earnings after the chargeback.

Solution Gross earnings are found by subtracting the chargeback from piece rate earnings.

$$\text{Gross earnings} = \text{Piecework earnings} - (\text{Spoiled items} \times \text{Chargeback rate})$$
$$= \$476.10 - (14 \text{ items} \times \$2.50)$$
$$= \$476.10 - \$35$$
$$= \$441.10$$

Piecework and differential-piecework rates are frequently modified to include some guaranteed hourly rate of pay. Often this is necessary to meet minimum wage laws. To satisfy the law, the employer may either pay minimum wage or piecework earnings, *whichever is higher.*

EXAMPLE 4 **Finding Earnings with a Guaranteed Hourly Wage**

A tire installer at the Tire Center is paid $8.40 per hour for an 8-hour day, or $0.95 per tire installed—whichever is higher. Find the weekly earnings for an employee having the following rate of production.

Monday	86 installations
Tuesday	70 installations
Wednesday	88 installations
Thursday	68 installations
Friday	82 installations

Solution The hourly earnings for an 8-hour day are $67.20 (8 × $8.40). If the piecework earnings for the day are less than this amount, the hourly earnings will be paid.

Monday	86 × $0.95 =	$81.70	Piece rate
Tuesday	~~70 × $0.95~~ =	$67.20	Hourly (piece rate is $66.50)
Wednesday	88 × $0.95 =	$83.60	Piece rate
Thursday	~~68 × $0.95~~ =	$67.20	Hourly (piece rate is $64.60)
Friday	82 × $0.95 =	$77.90	Piece rate
		$377.60	Weekly earnings

> **NOTE** The worker *cannot* earn less than $8.40 per hour or $67.20 ($8.40 × 8) for the day. Since the piecework earnings on Tuesday and Thursday in Example 3 fall below the hourly minimum, the hourly rate, or $67.20 for the day, is paid on those days.

Objective

4 ***Find Overtime Earnings for Piecework.*** Piecework employees, just as other workers, are paid time-and-a-half for overtime. The overtime rate may be computed as $1\frac{1}{2}$ times the hourly rate, but most often the overtime rate is $1\frac{1}{2}$ times the regular rate per piece.

EXAMPLE 5 Determining Earnings with Overtime Piecework

Ryan Andrews is paid $0.98 per child's tricycle assembled. During one week, he assembles 480 tricycles on regular time and 104 tricycles during overtime hours. Find his gross earnings for the week if time-and-a-half per assembly is paid for overtime.

Solution

$$\text{Gross earnings} = \text{Earnings at regular piece rate} + \text{Earnings at overtime piece rate}$$
$$= 480 \times \$0.98 + (104 \times 1\tfrac{1}{2} \times \$0.98)$$
$$= \$470.40 + \$152.88$$
$$= \$623.28$$

 Scientific Calculator Approach

The calculator solution to Example 5 uses parentheses to first calculate the overtime piece rate.

480 ⨉ .98 + (104 ⨉ 1.5 ⨉ .98) = 623.28

6.3	**Exercises**

PET DIETARY PRODUCTS Complete the following payroll ledger for Pet Salt Products. Employees are paid a straight piece rate. Rates per unit vary depending on worker skills involved.

	Employee	Units Produced					Total Pieces	Rate per Unit	Gross Earnings
		M	T	W	Th	F	Total Pieces	Rate per Unit	Gross Earnings
1.	Mora, E.	150	124	172	110	96		$0.58	
2.	Motton, T.	120	108	89	130	95		$0.87	
3.	Young, C.	98	86	79	108	80		$0.75	
4.	McIntosh, R.	67	54	72	83	59		$0.93	
5.	Todd, R.	118	124	143	132	148		$0.68	
6.	Eckern, G.	157	148	169	145	178		$0.59	
7.	King, M.	125	118	115	132	98		$0.46	
8.	Demaree, D.	152	136	170	144	192		$0.43	
9.	Parker, R.	149	135	118	125	143		$0.78	
10.	Pearson, D.	96	84	115	102	96		$0.72	

FRUIT INSPECTION Production workers at Classic Fruit Distributors are paid as follows to inspect and package crates of fruit.

1–200 crates	$1.00 each
201–400 crates	$1.08 each
Over 400 crates	$1.15 each

Find the weekly gross earnings for each.

	Employee	Number of Crates		Employee	Number of Crates
11.	Dalton, S.	190	12.	Peterson, K.	180
13.	Zhao, F.	228	14.	Nguyen, A.	310
15.	Simms, B.	405	16.	Getz, J.	420

HOURLY/PIECEWORK RATES Find the gross earnings for each of the following agricultural employees. Each has an 8-hour workday and is paid $0.75 for each unit of production or the hourly rate, whichever is greater. Note that agricultural workers are not covered by the Fair Labor Standards Act, so they are often paid less than the minimum wage.

	Employee	Units Produced M	T	W	Th	F	Hourly Rate	Gross Earnings
17.	Knab, C.	66	75	58	72	68	$6.18	
18.	DeCicco, A.	62	78	79	80	81	$7.20	
19.	Wilson, M.	80	60	75	78	74	$6.80	
20.	Viale, D.	72	70	62	88	82	$6.50	
21.	Zurcher, S.	75	84	72	93	67	$6.75	
22.	Frase, E.	63	57	67	75	70	$5.70	
23.	Pantera, A.	73	62	78	64	81	$6.30	
24.	Enos, C.	90	77	89	102	99	$8.10	

PIECEWORK WITH OVERTIME Find the gross earnings for each of the following employees. Overtime is $1\frac{1}{2}$ times the normal per piece rate. Rejected units are charged at the chargeback rate.

	Employee	Units Produced Reg.	O.T.	Rejected Units	Rate per Unit	Chargeback per Unit	Gross Earnings
25.	Miller, J.	510	74	20	$0.72	$0.38	
26.	Kavanagh, M.	380	26	6	$0.69	$0.56	
27.	Boghoussian, A.	493	74	34	$0.86	$0.46	
28.	Carlson, K.	508	38	16	$0.59	$0.42	
29.	Balbi, G.	286	38	4	$0.95	$0.82	
30.	Fukano, H.	315	64	35	$0.74	$0.65	
31.	Hughes, G.	403	72	15	$0.68	$0.45	
32.	Dos Reis, A.	452	12	6	$0.59	$0.50	

33. Wages and salaries are known as time rates, while commissions are called incentive rates of pay. Explain in your own words the difference between these payment methods.

 34. Describe what a chargeback or docking is for rejected units. Why do you think that the chargeback per unit is usually less than the rate paid per unit? (See Objective 3.)

Solve the following application problems.

35. KEYBOARD ASSEMBLY Greg Jackson is paid $4.75 for each keyboard assembled, charged $2.25 for each rejection, and paid time-and-a-half for overtime production. Find his gross earnings for the week when he assembles 142 keyboards at the regular rate, 26 keyboards at the overtime rate, and has 7 chargebacks.

36. CAKE DECORATING John Davis decorates cakes at the French Meadow Bakery, for which he is paid $2.42 each. He is charged $1.40 per rejection and paid time-and-a-half for all overtime production. Find his gross earnings when production for the week is 128 cakes at the regular rate and 19 cakes at the overtime rate. He has a total of 5 chargebacks.

37. FAUCET ASSEMBLY Mike Kinney is paid $2.35 per faucet assembled, charged $1.05 for each rejection, and paid time-and-a-half for overtime production. Find his gross earnings for the week when he assembles 228 faucets at the regular rate, 74 faucets at the overtime rate, and has 18 chargebacks.

38. COSTUME PRODUCTION Kristen Clement sews lace on dance costumes, for which she is paid $1.18 each. She is charged $0.90 per rejection and is paid time-and-a-half for all overtime production. Find her gross earnings when production during a 3-day workweek is 138 costumes at the regular rate and 28 costumes at the overtime rate. She has a total of 9 chargebacks.

39. TOY TRAIN PACKAGING Anna Kauffman packages toy train sets. She is paid $1.15 per unit and is charged $0.45 for each rejection. Find her gross earnings for the week given the following production.

	M	T	W	Th	F	Totals
Production	142	106	118	98	110	574
Chargebacks	6	3	5	8	4	26

40. PACKING AND SHIPPING Steve Zagorin checks and ships customer orders for Feathers and Stream Fishing Lures. He receives $0.48 per package and is charged $0.40 for each rejection. Find his gross earnings for the week given the following production.

	M	T	W	Th	F	Totals
Production	178	165	186	171	174	874
Chargebacks	5	3	2	7	4	21

6.4 Social Security, Medicare, and Other Taxes

OBJECTIVES

1 *Understand FICA.*

2 *Find the maximum FICA tax paid by an employee in one year.*

3 *Understand Medicare tax.*

4 *Find FICA tax and Medicare tax.*

5 *Determine the FICA tax and the Medicare tax paid by a self-employed person.*

6 *Find state disability insurance deductions.*

Finding gross earnings is only the first step in preparing a payroll. The employer must then subtract all required deductions from gross earnings. For most employees, these deductions include Social Security tax, Medicare tax, federal income tax withholding, and state income tax withholding. Other deductions may include state disability insurance, union dues, retirement contributions, credit union savings or loan payments, purchase of bonds, uniform expenses, group insurance plans, and charitable contributions. Subtracting these deductions from gross earnings results in net pay, the amount the employee receives.

Objective

1 *Understand FICA.* The **Federal Insurance Contributions Act (FICA)** was passed into law in the 1930s during the middle of the Great Depression. This plan, now called **Social Security,** was originally designed to give monthly benefits to retired workers and their survivors. Also included today are death benefits and **Medicare** payments. As the number of people receiving benefits has increased along with the individual benefit amounts, people paying into Social Security have had to pay a larger amount of earnings into this fund each year. From 1937 through 1950 an employee paid 1% of income into Social Security, up to a maximum of $30 per year. This amount has increased over the years until an employee in 2009 paid 6.2% of income to FICA and 1.45% to Medicare, which together can total $8170 or more per year.

For many years, both the Social Security tax rate and the Medicare tax rate were combined. However, since 1991 these tax rates have been expressed individually. Table 6.2 shows the tax rates and the maximum earnings on which Social Security and Medicare taxes are paid by the employee. The employer pays the same rate as the employee, matching all employee contributions dollar for dollar. Self-employed people pay double the rate paid by those who are employees, since they are effectively both the employee and the employer.

Table 6.2 MAXIMUM EARNINGS ON WHICH SOCIAL SECURITY AND MEDICARE TAXES ARE PAID

	Social Security Tax		Medicare Tax	
Year	Social Security Tax Rate	Employee Earnings Subject to the Tax	Medicare Tax Rate	Employee Earnings Subject to the Tax
2000	6.2%	$76,200	1.45%	all
2001	6.2%	$80,400	1.45%	all
2002	6.2%	$84,900	1.45%	all
2003	6.2%	$87,000	1.45%	all
2004	6.2%	$87,900	1.45%	all
2005	6.2%	$90,000	1.45%	all
2006	6.2%	$94,200	1.45%	all
2007	6.2%	$97,500	1.45%	all
2008	6.2%	$102,000	1.45%	all
2009	6.2%	$106,800	1.45%	all

Notice in Table 6.2 that the Social Security and Medicare tax rates have remained constant since 2000. However, the maximum amount of earnings subject to the FICA and Medicare taxes increased each year. At first glance, one might think that these data suggest that more of the cost of these programs is being shifted to people with higher earnings. But, the increase in maximum earnings subject to tax is really just an adjustment for inflation. In other words, earnings of $76,200 in 2000 provided about the same purchasing power as earnings of $106,800 in 2009. (Inflation is a very important topic and we cover it in more detail in Chapter 12.) So the cost of these programs is not being shifted to higher earners.

NOTE Since both the maximum amount of earnings subject to tax and the tax rates change annually, we will use 6.2% of the first $110,000 for Social Security taxes and 1.45% of all earnings for Medicare taxes. Use the Social Security Administration's Web page at www.ssa.gov to find the current rates and maximum earnings subject to taxes.

Each employee in the United States must have a Social Security number. You can apply for one at a local post office. Future benefits depend on the amount of money contributed to the fund during an individual's working years. Each year, the Social Security Administration sends out a statement to workers 25 and older showing how much they will be paid in the event of retirement, disability, or death. You can submit a **Request for Earnings and Benefit Estimate Statement**, as shown in Figure 6.7, to get an estimate of your future benefits. Check it carefully for errors! Errors can only be corrected within the first three years. Not catching an error may be like throwing money into the trash!

Request for *Social Security Statement*

☐ Please check this box if you want to get your *Statement* in Spanish instead of English.

Please print or type your answers. When you have completed the form, fold it and mail it to us. If you prefer to send your request using the Internet, go to *www.socialsecurity.gov.*

1. Name shown on your Social Security card:

   First Name _____ Middle Initial _____

   Last Name Only _____

2. Your Social Security number as shown on your card:

   ☐☐☐-☐☐-☐☐☐☐

3. Your date of birth (Mo.-Day-Yr.)

   ☐☐-☐☐-☐☐☐☐

4. Other Social Security numbers you have used:

   ☐☐☐-☐☐-☐☐☐☐
   ☐☐☐-☐☐-☐☐☐☐

5. Your Sex: ☐ Male ☐ Female

For items 6 and 8, show only earnings covered by Social Security. Do NOT include wages from state, local or federal government employment that are NOT covered by Social Security or that are covered ONLY by Medicare.

6. Show your actual earnings (wages and/or net self-employment income) for last year and your estimated earnings for this year.

   A. Last year's actual earnings: *(Dollars Only)*

   $ ☐☐☐,☐☐☐.☐☐

   B. This year's estimated earnings: *(Dollars Only)*

   $ ☐☐☐,☐☐☐.☐☐

7. Show the age at which you plan to stop working:

   ☐☐ *(Show only one age)*

8. Below, show the average yearly amount (not your total future lifetime earnings) that you think you will earn between now and when you plan to stop working. Include performance or scheduled pay increases or bonuses, but not cost-of-living increases.

   If you expect to earn significantly more or less in the future due to promotions, job changes, part-time work or an absence from the work force, enter the amount that most closely reflects your future average yearly earnings.

   If you don't expect any significant changes, show the same amount you are earning now (the amount in 6B).

   Future average yearly earnings: *(Dollars Only)*

   $ ☐☐☐,☐☐☐.☐☐

9. Do you want us to send the *Statement*:
   • To you? Enter your name and mailing address.
   • To someone else (your accountant, pension plan, etc.)? Enter your name with "c/o" and the name and address of that person or organization.

"C/O" or Street Address (Include Apt. No., P.O. Box, Rural Route)

Street Address

Street Address (If Foreign Address, enter City, Province, Postal Code)

U.S. City, State, ZIP code (If Foreign Address, enter Name of Country only)

NOTICE:
I am asking for information about my own Social Security record or the record of a person I am authorized to represent. I declare under penalty of perjury that I have examined all the information on this form, and on any accompanying statements or forms, and it is true and correct to the best of my knowledge. I authorize you to use a contractor to send the *Social Security Statement* to the person and address in item 9.

▶

Please sign your name (Do Not Print)

Date _____ (Area Code) Daytime Telephone No.

Form **SSA-7004-SM** (06-2008) EF (06-2008)
10-2006 edition may be used

♻ Printed on recycled paper

Figure 6.7

Objective

2 *Find the Maximum FICA Tax Paid by an Employee in One Year.* Since Social Security rates and maximum earnings change annually, we assume throughout the book that the taxes are paid only on gross earnings up to $110,000 per year.

Social Security tax = 6.2% of gross earnings up to $110,000 per year

No Social Security taxes are paid on any gross earnings above $110,000 in one year.

NOTE Only about 7% of all income earners reach the cutoff point of $110,000 for Social Security taxes.

Objective

3   ***Understand Medicare Tax.***   Medicare tax is paid on **all** earnings. Multiply the earnings by 1.45% to find the tax.

Objective

4   ***Find FICA Tax and Medicare Tax.***   When finding the amounts to be withheld for Social Security tax and Medicare tax, the employer must use the current rates and the maximum earnings amount.

EXAMPLE 1   **Finding FICA Tax and Medicare Tax**

Find the Social Security tax and the Medicare tax for the following gross earnings.

(a) D. Horwitz; $478.15   **(b)** C. Christensen; $522.83

Solution

(a) Social Security tax $= 6.2\% \times \$478.15$

$$= 0.062 \times \$478.15 = \$29.65 \quad \text{Rounded}$$

Medicare tax $= 1.45\% \times \$478.15$

$$= 0.0145 \times \$478.15 = \$6.93 \quad \text{Rounded}$$

(b) Social Security tax $= 6.2\% \times \$522.83$

$$= 0.062 \times \$522.83 = \$32.42 \quad \text{Rounded}$$

Medicare tax $= 1.45\% \times \$522.83$

$$= 0.0145 \times \$522.83 = \$7.58 \quad \text{Rounded}$$

EXAMPLE 2   **Finding FICA Tax**

Shannon Woolums has earned $107,634.05 so far this year. Her gross earnings for the current pay period are $5224.03. Find her Social Security tax.

Solution   Social Security tax is paid on only the first $110,000 earned in a year. Woolums has already earned $107,634.05. Subtract $107,634.05 from $110,000, to find that she has to pay Social Security tax on only $2365.95 of her earnings for the current pay period.

$110,000.00	Maximum earnings subject to Social Security tax
− $107,634.05	Earnings to date
$2,365.95	Earnings on which tax is due

The Social Security tax on $2365.95 is $146.69 ($2365.95 × 6.2%) (rounded). Therefore, Woolums pays $146.69 for the current pay period and no additional Social Security tax for the rest of the year.

Table 6.3 compares the contributions to social programs (Social Security and Medicare) in selected countries around the world. How do U.S. workers' (employee) contributions compare to those in other countries?

Table 6.3 **SOCIAL INSURANCE CONTRIBUTIONS AS A PERCENT OF TOTAL GROSS EARNINGS**

Country	Employee	Employer
Italy	10.26	48.00
France	20.66	42.57
Sweden	33.00	7.00
Belgium	14.24	32.73
Mexico	22.00	3.00
Germany	21.12	21.12
Netherlands	7.04	13.05
Japan	11.00	12.00
Ireland	5.52	10.54
U.K.	7.08	10.00
Switzerland	6.55	8.37
Canada	5.00	8.00
U.S.A.	7.65	7.65

Sources: Benefits Report Europe, USA, and Canada; Watson Wyatt Worldwide, and Knight Ridder Tribune.

Have you ever wondered why we haven't run out of Social Security numbers? Marilyn Vos Savant answers this question for a reader in her weekly column in *Parade* magazine. The reader's question and her answer are shown at the left.

Objective

5 *Determine the FICA Tax and the Medicare Tax Paid by a Self-Employed Person.* People who are self-employed pay higher Social Security tax and higher Medicare tax than people who work for others. There is no employer to match the employee contribution so the self-employed person pays a rate that is double that of the employee. The gross earnings of the self-employed person are first multiplied by 92.35% (0.9235) to find the adjusted earnings. These adjusted earnings are then multiplied by the current rates. In our examples the self-employed person pays 12.4% (6.2% $\times$ 2) of adjusted earnings for Social Security tax and 2.9% (1.45% $\times$ 2) of adjusted earnings for Medicare tax.

EXAMPLE 3 **Finding FICA and Medicare Tax for the Self-Employed**

Find the Social Security tax and the Medicare tax paid by Sashaya Davis, a self-employed Web-page designer who had adjusted earnings of $53,820 this year.

Solution

$$\text{Social Security tax} = \$53,820 \times 12.4\% = \$53,820 \times 0.124 = \$6673.68$$
$$\text{Medicare tax} = \$53,820 \times 2.9\% = \$53,820 \times 0.029 = \$1560.78$$

NOTE Social Security taxes apply only to the first $110,000 in self-employment income, whereas Medicare taxes apply to total gross earnings with no upper limit.

> **NOTE** Always use the current tax rates for both Social Security and Medicare. These can always be found in Circular E, *Employer's Tax Guide*, which is available from the Internal Revenue Service.

Objective

6 *Find State Disability Insurance Deductions.* Many states have a state disability insurance program that is paid for by employees. If disabled, the employee would receive weekly benefits. A typical state program defines "disability" as "any illness or injury incurred on or off the job, either physical or mental, including pregnancy, childbirth, or related condition, that prevents you from doing your regular work." The employee processes the claim after obtaining certification from a doctor or other qualified examiner. Weekly disability benefits are determined by the highest quarter's earnings within the last year of employment.

A typical state program also requires the qualifying employee to pay a **state disability insurance (SDI)** deduction of 1% of the first $31,800 earned each year. There are no payments on earnings above this amount. Some states have similar programs, but their insurance is placed with private insurance companies rather than with the state.

EXAMPLE 4 Finding State Disability Insurance Deductions

Find the state disability deduction for an employee at Comet Auto Parts with gross earnings of $418 this pay period. The SDI rate is 1%, and the employee has not earned $31,800 this year.

Solution

$$\text{State disability deduction} = 1\% \text{ of } \$418$$
$$= 0.01 \times \$418 = \$4.18$$

EXAMPLE 5 Finding State Disability Insurance Deductions

Milo Lacy has earned $30,620 so far this year. Find the SDI deduction if gross earnings this pay period are $3096. Use an SDI rate of 1% on the first $31,800.

Solution The SDI deduction will be taken on $1180 of the current gross earnings.

$31,800	Maximum earnings subject to SDI
− $30,620	Earnings this year
$1,180	Earnings this year subject to SDI

The SDI deduction is $11.80 ($1180 × 1%).

> **NOTE** Those involved in payroll work must always be up-to-date on the current rates and the maximum annual earning amounts against which FICA, Medicare, and SDI payroll deductions may be taken.

6.4	**Exercises**

SOCIAL SECURITY AND MEDICARE TAX Find the Social Security tax and the Medicare tax for each of the following amounts of gross earnings. Assume a 6.2% FICA rate and a 1.45% Medicare tax rate.

1. $324.72   **2.** $207.25

3. $463.24   **4.** $606.35

5. $854.71   **6.** $683.65

7. $1086.25   **8.** $1243.18

MAXIMUM SOCIAL SECURITY TAX   Find the Social Security tax for each of the following managers for the current pay period. Assume a 6.2% FICA rate up to a maximum of $110,000.

Manager	Gross Earnings This Year (So Far)	Earnings Current Pay Period
9. Dandridge, T.	$98,460.10	$4218.48
10. Hale, R.	$107,950.10	$3200
11. Hall, T.	$109,360.40	$5260
12. Maurin, J.	$112,040.18	$2487.52
13. Saraniti, S.	$109,540.96	$1053.73
14. De Bouchel, V.	$108,820.12	$4160.86

PAYROLL DEDUCTIONS   Find the regular earnings, overtime earnings, gross earnings, Social Security tax (6.2%), Medicare tax (1.45%), and state disability insurance deduction (1%) for each of the following employees. Assume that no employee will have earned more than the FICA or SDI maximum at the end of the current pay period. Assume time-and-a-half is paid for any overtime in a 40-hour week.

Employee	Hours Worked	Regular Rate
15. Thunstrom, P.	45.5	$9.22
16. Fernandez, P.	47.75	$7.52
17. Odom, R.	44	$10.30
18. Ruppart, A.	45	$12.40
19. Leonard, B.	45	$8.18
20. Taggart, G.	47	$11.68
21. Zhao, T.	46.75	$17.50
22. Shotwell, E.	48.25	$7.40

Solve the following application problems. Assume that the FICA rate is 6.2%, the Medicare rate is 1.45%, the SDI rate is 1%, and that earnings will not exceed $31,800.

23. SOCIAL SECURITY AND MEDICARE   Kwei Riang worked 43.5 hours last week at McDonald's. He is paid $8.58 per hour, plus time-and-a-half for overtime (over 40 hours per week). Find his (a) Social Security tax and (b) Medicare tax for the week.

24. SOCIAL SECURITY AND MEDICARE   Beth Kaufman receives 7% commission on all sales. Her sales on Monday of last week were $1412.20, with $1928.42 on Tuesday, $598.14 on Wednesday, $1051.12 on Thursday, and $958.72 on Friday. Find her (a) Social Security tax and (b) Medicare tax for the week.

25. STATE DISABILITY DEDUCTION   Lynn Peterson is paid an 8% commission on sales. During a recent pay period, she had sales of $19,482 and returns and allowances of $193. Find the amount of (a) her Social Security tax, (b) her Medicare tax, and (c) her state disability for this pay period.

26. STATE DISABILITY DEDUCTIONS   Peter Phelps is a representative for Delta International Machinery and is paid $675 per week plus a commission of 2% on sales. His sales last week were $17,240. Find the amount of (a) his Social Security tax, (b) his Medicare tax, and (c) his state disability for the pay period.

SELF-EMPLOYMENT DEDUCTIONS　The following problems refer to self-employed individuals. These people pay Social Security tax of 12.4% and Medicare tax of 2.9%. Find the taxes on each of the following annual adjusted earnings. (See Example 3.)

27. Tony Romano, owner of The Cutlery, earned $58,238.74.

28. Rachel Leach, an interior decorator, earned $28,286.20.

29. Krystal McClellan, accountant, earned $34,817.16.

30. Ron Morris, a Chick-fil-A franchise owner, earned $48,007.14.

31. Lauren Midgley, shop owner, earned $26,843.60.

32. Eric Lemmon, commission salesperson, earned $52,748.32.

 33. A young person who has just received her first paycheck is puzzled by the amounts that have been deducted from gross earnings. Briefly explain both the FICA and Medicare deductions to this person. (See Objectives 1–4.)

 34. Describe the difference between the FICA paid by an employee and that paid by a self-employed person. (See Objective 5.)

6.5　Income Tax Withholding

OBJECTIVES

1　*Understand the Employee's Withholding Allowance Certificate (Form W-4).*

2　*Find the federal withholding tax using the wage bracket method.*

3　*Find the federal tax using the percentage method.*

4　*Find the state withholding tax using the state income tax rate.*

5　*Find net pay when given gross wages, taxes, and other deductions.*

The **personal income tax** is the largest single source of money for the federal government. The law requires that the bulk of this tax owed by an individual be paid periodically, as the income is earned. For this reason, employers must deduct money from the gross earnings of almost every employee. These deductions, called **income tax withholdings**, are sent periodically to the Internal Revenue Service. The Internal Revenue Service has introduced an **electronic funds transfer payment system** (**EFTPS**) that allows employers to transfer these funds electronically. The amount of money withheld depends on the employee's earnings. Generally, the withholding tax for a married person is less than the withholding tax for a single person making the same income.

Objective

1　*Understand the Employee's Withholding Allowance Certificate (Form W-4).*　Each employee must file with the employer a W-4 form, as shown in Figure 6.8. On this form the employee states the number of **withholding allowances** being claimed along with additional information so that the employer can withhold the proper amount for income tax.

A W-4 form is usually completed at the time of employment. A married person with three children will normally claim five allowances (one each for the employee and spouse, plus one for each child). However, when both spouses are employed, each may claim himself or herself. The number of allowances may be raised if an employee has been receiving a refund of withholding taxes, or the number may be lowered if the employee has had a balance due in previous tax years. The W-4 form has instructions to help determine the proper number of allowances. Some people enjoy receiving a tax refund when filing their income tax return, so they claim fewer allowances, having more withheld from each check. Other individuals would rather receive more of their income each pay period, so they claim the maximum number of allowances to which they are entitled. The exact number of allowances *must* be claimed when the income tax return is filed.

Form **W-4**	**Employee's Withholding Allowance Certificate**	OMB No. 1545-0074
Department of the Treasury Internal Revenue Service	▶ Whether you are entitled to claim a certain number of allowances or exemption from withholding is subject to review by the IRS. Your employer may be required to send a copy of this form to the IRS.	20**09**

1 Type or print your first name and middle initial. Last name **2** Your social security number

Home address (number and street or rural route) **3** ☐ Single ☐ Married ☐ Married, but withhold at higher Single rate.
Note. If married, but legally separated, or spouse is a nonresident alien, check the "Single" box.

City or town, state, and ZIP code **4** If your last name differs from that shown on your social security card, check here. You must call 1-800-772-1213 for a replacement card. ▶ ☐

5 Total number of allowances you are claiming (from line **H** above **or** from the applicable worksheet on page 2) **5**

6 Additional amount, if any, you want withheld from each paycheck . . . . **6** $

7 I claim exemption from withholding for 2009, and I certify that I meet **both** of the following conditions for exemption.
• Last year I had a right to a refund of **all** federal income tax withheld because I had **no** tax liability **and**
• This year I expect a refund of **all** federal income tax withheld because I expect to have **no** tax liability.
If you meet both conditions, write "Exempt" here . . . . ▶ **7**

Under penalties of perjury, I declare that I have examined this certificate and to the best of my knowledge and belief, it is true, correct, and complete.

Employee's signature
(Form is not valid unless you sign it.) ▶ Date ▶

8 Employer's name and address (Employer: Complete lines 8 and 10 only if sending to the IRS.) **9** Office code (optional) **10** Employer identification number (EIN)

For Privacy Act and Paperwork Reduction Act Notice, see page 2. Cat. No. 10220Q Form **W-4** (2009)

Figure 6.8

Objective

2 *Find the Federal Withholding Tax Using the Wage Bracket Method.* The withholding tax is found using the gross earnings per pay period. Income tax withholding is applied to all earnings, unlike Social Security tax. Generally, the higher a person's gross earnings, the more withholding tax is paid.

There are two methods that employers use to determine the amount of federal withholding tax to deduct from paychecks: the **wage bracket method** and the **percentage method**.

The Internal Revenue Service supplies withholding tax tables to be used with the wage bracket method. These tables are extensive and cover weekly, biweekly, monthly, and daily pay periods. Figures 6.9 and 6.10 show samples of the withholding tables. Figure 6.9 is for both single and married people who are paid weekly and Figure 6.10 is for both single and married people who are paid monthly.

EXAMPLE 1 **Finding Federal Withholding Using the Wage Bracket Method**

Lisa Revies is single and claims no withholding allowances so that she will receive a refund from the government or avoid owing taxes at the end of the year. The proper number will be used when filing her income tax return. Use the wage bracket method to find her withholding tax if her weekly gross earnings are $334.88.

Solution Use the table in Figure 6.9 for Single Persons—Weekly Payroll Period. The given earnings are found in the row "at least $330 but less than $340." Go across this row to the column headed "0" (for no withholding allowances). From the table, the withholding is $35 per week.

EXAMPLE 2 **Using the Wage Bracket Method for Federal Withholding**

Larry Sifford is married, claims three withholding allowances, and has monthly gross earnings of $3016.47. Find his withholding tax using the wage bracket method.

Solution Use the table in Figure 6.10 for Married Persons—Monthly Payroll Period. Look down the two left columns and find the range that includes Sifford's gross earnings: "at least $3000 but less than $3040." Read across the table to the column headed "3" for the three withholding allowances. The withholding tax is $157 per month.

SINGLE Persons—WEEKLY Payroll Period

(For Wages Paid in 2008)

If the wages are—		And the number of withholding allowances claimed is—										
At least	But less than	0	1	2	3	4	5	6	7	8	9	10
		The amount of income tax to be withheld is—										
250	260	23	14	7	0	0	0	0	0	0	0	0
260	270	25	15	8	1	0	0	0	0	0	0	0
270	280	26	16	9	2	0	0	0	0	0	0	0
280	290	28	18	10	3	0	0	0	0	0	0	0
290	300	29	19	11	4	0	0	0	0	0	0	0
300	310	31	21	12	5	0	0	0	0	0	0	0
310	320	32	22	13	6	0	0	0	0	0	0	0
320	330	34	24	14	7	0	0	0	0	0	0	0
330	340	35	25	15	8	1	0	0	0	0	0	0
340	350	37	27	17	9	2	0	0	0	0	0	0
350	360	38	28	18	10	3	0	0	0	0	0	0
360	370	40	30	20	11	4	0	0	0	0	0	0
370	380	41	31	21	12	5	0	0	0	0	0	0
380	390	43	33	23	13	6	0	0	0	0	0	0
390	400	44	34	24	14	7	1	0	0	0	0	0
400	410	46	36	26	15	8	2	0	0	0	0	0
410	420	47	37	27	17	9	3	0	0	0	0	0
420	430	49	39	29	18	10	4	0	0	0	0	0
430	440	50	40	30	20	11	5	0	0	0	0	0
440	450	52	42	32	21	12	6	0	0	0	0	0
450	460	53	43	33	23	13	7	0	0	0	0	0
460	470	55	45	35	24	14	8	1	0	0	0	0
470	480	56	46	36	26	16	9	2	0	0	0	0
480	490	58	48	38	27	17	10	3	0	0	0	0
490	500	59	49	39	29	19	11	4	0	0	0	0
500	510	61	51	41	30	20	12	5	0	0	0	0
510	520	62	52	42	32	22	13	6	0	0	0	0
520	530	64	54	44	33	23	14	7	0	0	0	0
530	540	65	55	45	35	25	15	8	1	0	0	0
540	550	67	57	47	36	26	16	9	2	0	0	0

MARRIED Persons—WEEKLY Payroll Period

(For Wages Paid in 2008)

If the wages are—		And the number of withholding allowances claimed is—										
At least	But less than	0	1	2	3	4	5	6	7	8	9	10
		The amount of income tax to be withheld is—										
440	450	29	22	16	9	2	0	0	0	0	0	0
450	460	30	23	17	10	3	0	0	0	0	0	0
460	470	32	24	18	11	4	0	0	0	0	0	0
470	480	33	25	19	12	5	0	0	0	0	0	0
480	490	35	26	20	13	6	0	0	0	0	0	0
490	500	36	27	21	14	7	0	0	0	0	0	0
500	510	38	28	22	15	8	1	0	0	0	0	0
510	520	39	29	23	16	9	2	0	0	0	0	0
520	530	41	31	24	17	10	3	0	0	0	0	0
530	540	42	32	25	18	11	4	0	0	0	0	0
540	550	44	34	26	19	12	5	0	0	0	0	0
550	560	45	35	27	20	13	6	0	0	0	0	0
560	570	47	37	28	21	14	7	1	0	0	0	0
570	580	48	38	29	22	15	8	2	0	0	0	0
580	590	50	40	30	23	16	9	3	0	0	0	0
590	600	51	41	31	24	17	10	4	0	0	0	0
600	610	53	43	33	25	18	11	5	0	0	0	0
610	620	54	44	34	26	19	12	6	0	0	0	0
620	630	56	46	36	27	20	13	7	0	0	0	0
630	640	57	47	37	28	21	14	8	1	0	0	0
640	650	59	49	39	29	22	15	9	2	0	0	0
650	660	60	50	40	30	23	16	10	3	0	0	0
660	670	62	52	42	31	24	17	11	4	0	0	0
670	680	63	53	43	33	25	18	12	5	0	0	0
680	690	65	55	45	34	26	19	13	6	0	0	0
690	700	66	56	46	36	27	20	14	7	0	0	0
700	710	68	58	48	37	28	21	15	8	1	0	0
710	720	69	59	49	39	29	22	16	9	2	0	0
720	730	71	61	51	40	30	23	17	10	3	0	0
730	740	72	62	52	42	32	24	18	11	4	0	0

Figure 6.9

SINGLE Persons—MONTHLY Payroll Period

(For Wages Paid in 2008)

If the wages are—		And the number of withholding allowances claimed is—										
At least	But less than	0	1	2	3	4	5	6	7	8	9	10
		The amount of income tax to be withheld is—										
840	880	64	35	6	0	0	0	0	0	0	0	0
880	920	70	39	10	0	0	0	0	0	0	0	0
920	960	76	43	14	0	0	0	0	0	0	0	0
960	1,000	82	47	18	0	0	0	0	0	0	0	0
1,000	1,040	88	51	22	0	0	0	0	0	0	0	0
1,040	1,080	94	55	26	0	0	0	0	0	0	0	0
1,080	1,120	100	59	30	0	0	0	0	0	0	0	0
1,120	1,160	106	63	34	4	0	0	0	0	0	0	0
1,160	1,200	112	68	38	8	0	0	0	0	0	0	0
1,200	1,240	118	74	42	12	0	0	0	0	0	0	0
1,240	1,280	124	80	46	16	0	0	0	0	0	0	0
1,280	1,320	130	86	50	20	0	0	0	0	0	0	0
1,320	1,360	136	92	54	24	0	0	0	0	0	0	0
1,360	1,400	142	98	58	28	0	0	0	0	0	0	0
1,400	1,440	148	104	62	32	3	0	0	0	0	0	0
1,440	1,480	154	110	67	36	7	0	0	0	0	0	0
1,480	1,520	160	116	73	40	11	0	0	0	0	0	0
1,520	1,560	166	122	79	44	15	0	0	0	0	0	0
1,560	1,600	172	128	85	48	19	0	0	0	0	0	0
1,600	1,640	178	134	91	52	23	0	0	0	0	0	0
1,640	1,680	184	140	97	56	27	0	0	0	0	0	0
1,680	1,720	190	146	103	60	31	2	0	0	0	0	0
1,720	1,760	196	152	109	65	35	6	0	0	0	0	0
1,760	1,800	202	158	115	71	39	10	0	0	0	0	0
1,800	1,840	208	164	121	77	43	14	0	0	0	0	0
1,840	1,880	214	170	127	83	47	18	0	0	0	0	0
1,880	1,920	220	176	133	89	51	22	0	0	0	0	0
1,920	1,960	226	182	139	95	55	26	0	0	0	0	0
1,960	2,000	232	188	145	101	59	30	1	0	0	0	0
2,000	2,040	238	194	151	107	63	34	5	0	0	0	0

MARRIED Persons—MONTHLY Payroll Period

(For Wages Paid in 2008)

If the wages are—		And the number of withholding allowances claimed is—										
At least	But less than	0	1	2	3	4	5	6	7	8	9	10
		The amount of income tax to be withheld is—										
2,040	2,080	144	110	81	52	23	0	0	0	0	0	0
2,080	2,120	150	114	85	56	27	0	0	0	0	0	0
2,120	2,160	156	118	89	60	31	2	0	0	0	0	0
2,160	2,200	162	122	93	64	35	6	0	0	0	0	0
2,200	2,240	168	126	97	68	39	10	0	0	0	0	0
2,240	2,280	174	130	101	72	43	14	0	0	0	0	0
2,280	2,320	180	136	105	76	47	18	0	0	0	0	0
2,320	2,360	186	142	109	80	51	22	0	0	0	0	0
2,360	2,400	192	148	113	84	55	26	0	0	0	0	0
2,400	2,440	198	154	117	88	59	30	0	0	0	0	0
2,440	2,480	204	160	121	92	63	34	4	0	0	0	0
2,480	2,520	210	166	125	96	67	38	8	0	0	0	0
2,520	2,560	216	172	129	100	71	42	12	0	0	0	0
2,560	2,600	222	178	135	104	75	46	16	0	0	0	0
2,600	2,640	228	184	141	108	79	50	20	0	0	0	0
2,640	2,680	234	190	147	112	83	54	24	0	0	0	0
2,680	2,720	240	196	153	116	87	58	28	0	0	0	0
2,720	2,760	246	202	159	120	91	62	32	3	0	0	0
2,760	2,800	252	208	165	124	95	66	36	7	0	0	0
2,800	2,840	258	214	171	128	99	70	40	11	0	0	0
2,840	2,880	264	220	177	133	103	74	44	15	0	0	0
2,880	2,920	270	226	183	139	107	78	48	19	0	0	0
2,920	2,960	276	232	189	145	111	82	52	23	0	0	0
2,960	3,000	282	238	195	151	115	86	56	27	0	0	0
3,000	3,040	288	244	201	157	119	90	60	31	2	0	0
3,040	3,080	294	250	207	163	123	94	64	35	6	0	0
3,080	3,120	300	256	213	169	127	98	68	39	10	0	0
3,120	3,160	306	262	219	175	131	102	72	43	14	0	0
3,160	3,200	312	268	225	181	137	106	76	47	18	0	0
3,200	3,240	318	274	231	187	143	110	80	51	22	0	0

Figure 6.10

Objective

3 *Find the Federal Tax Using the Percentage Method.* Many companies today prefer to use the **percentage method** to determine federal withholding tax. The percentage method does not require the many pages of tables needed with the wage bracket method and is more easily adapted to computer applications in the processing of payrolls. Instead, the table shown in Figure 6.11 is used.

EXAMPLE **3** **Finding Federal Withholding Using the Percentage Method**

Joseph Fillipi is married, claims four withholding allowances, and has weekly gross earnings of $1575. Use the percentage method to find his withholding tax.

Solution

STEP 1 Find the withholding allowance for *one* on the weekly payroll period in Figure 6.11. The amount is $67.31. Since Fillipi claims four allowances, multiply the one withholding allowance ($67.31) by the number of withholding allowances (4).

$$\$67.31 \times 4 = \$269.24$$

Amount for one withholding allowance ⬆   ⬆ Amount for four withholding allowances

STEP 2 Subtract the amount in Step 1 from gross earnings.

$$\$1575 - \$269.24 = \$1305.76$$

Gross earnings ⬆   ⬆ Amount used in Table 1(b)

STEP 3 Find the "married person weekly" section of the percentage method withholding in Figure 6.11. Since $1305.76 is over $453 but below $1388, the amount that should be withheld for tax is $29.90 plus 15% of the excess over $453.

$$
\begin{aligned}
\text{Amount to withhold} &= \$29.90 + 15\% \text{ of excess over } \$453 \\
&= \$29.90 + 0.15 \times (\$1305.76 - \$453) \\
&= \$29.90 + \$127.91 = \$157.81
\end{aligned}
$$

The amount that should be withheld each week for income taxes is $157.81.

NOTE In Step 1, for an employee who is paid monthly, the number of withholding allowances would be multiplied by $291.67, the amount from the table for one monthly withholding allowance.

 Scientific Calculator Approach

The calculator solution to Example 3 follows.

1575 $-$ 67.31 $\times$ 4 $-$ 453 $=$ $\times$ .15 $+$ 29.9 $=$ 157.814

This number rounds to $157.81.

**Percentage Method—2008 Amount
for One Withholding Allowance**

Payroll Period	One Withholding Allowance
Weekly	$ 67.31
Biweekly	134.62
Semimonthly.......................................	145.83
Monthly...	291.67
Quarterly	875.00
Semiannually	1,750.00
Annually	3,500.00
Daily or miscellaneous (each day of the payroll period)	13.46

Tables for Percentage Method of Withholding

(For Wages Paid in 2008)

TABLE 1—WEEKLY Payroll Period

(a) SINGLE person (including head of household)—

If the amount of wages (after subtracting withholding allowances) is: The amount of income tax to withhold is:

Not over $51 . . . . $0

Over—	But not over—		of excess over—
$51	—$198	. . . 10%	—$51
$198	—$653	. . $14.70 plus 15%	—$198
$653	—$1,533	—$82.95 plus 25%	—$653
$1,533	—$3,202	. . $302.95 plus 28%	—$1,533
$3,202	—$6,916	. . $770.27 plus 33%	—$3,202
$6,916	. . . .	. . $1,995.89 plus 35%	—$6,916

(b) MARRIED person—

If the amount of wages (after subtracting withholding allowances) is: The amount of income tax to withhold is:

Not over $154 . . . . $0

Over—	But not over—		of excess over—
$154	—$453	. . . 10%	—$154
$453	—$1,388	. . $29.90 plus 15%	—$453
$1,388	—$2,651	. . $170.15 plus 25%	—$1,388
$2,651	—$3,994	. . $485.90 plus 28%	—$2,651
$3,994	—$7,021	. . $861.94 plus 33%	—$3,994
$7,021	. . . .	. . $1,860.85 plus 35%	—$7,021

TABLE 2—BIWEEKLY Payroll Period

(a) SINGLE person (including head of household)—

If the amount of wages (after subtracting withholding allowances) is: The amount of income tax to withhold is:

Not over $102 . . . . $0

Over—	But not over—		of excess over—
$102	—$396	. . . 10%	—$102
$396	—$1,306	. . $29.40 plus 15%	—$396
$1,306	—$3,066	. . $165.90 plus 25%	—$1,306
$3,066	—$6,404	. . $605.90 plus 28%	—$3,066
$6,404	—$13,833	. . $1,540.54 plus 33%	—$6,404
$13,833	. . . .	. . $3,992.11 plus 35%	—$13,833

(b) MARRIED person—

If the amount of wages (after subtracting withholding allowances) is: The amount of income tax to withhold is:

Not over $308 . . . . $0

Over—	But not over—		of excess over—
$308	—$906	. . . 10%	—$308
$906	—$2,775	. . $59.80 plus 15%	—$906
$2,775	—$5,302	. . $340.15 plus 25%	—$2,775
$5,302	—$7,988	. . $971.90 plus 28%	—$5,302
$7,988	—$14,042	. . $1,723.98 plus 33%	—$7,988
$14,042	. . . .	. . $3,721.80 plus 35%	—$14,042

TABLE 3—SEMIMONTHLY Payroll Period

(a) SINGLE person (including head of household)—

If the amount of wages (after subtracting withholding allowances) is: The amount of income tax to withhold is:

Not over $110 . . . . $0

Over—	But not over—		of excess over—
$110	—$429	. . . 10%	—$110
$429	—$1,415	. . $31.90 plus 15%	—$429
$1,415	—$3,322	. . $179.80 plus 25%	—$1,415
$3,322	—$6,938	. . $656.55 plus 28%	—$3,322
$6,938	—$14,985	. . $1,669.03 plus 33%	—$6,938
$14,985	. . . .	. . $4,324.54 plus 35%	—$14,985

(b) MARRIED person—

If the amount of wages (after subtracting withholding allowances) is: The amount of income tax to withhold is:

Not over $333 . . . . $0

Over—	But not over—		of excess over—
$333	—$981	. . . 10%	—$333
$981	—$3,006	. . $64.80 plus 15%	—$981
$3,006	—$5,744	. . $368.55 plus 25%	—$3,006
$5,744	—$8,654	. . $1,053.05 plus 28%	—$5,744
$8,654	—$15,213	. . $1,867.85 plus 33%	—$8,654
$15,213	. . . .	. . $4,032.32 plus 35%	—$15,213

TABLE 4—MONTHLY Payroll Period

(a) SINGLE person (including head of household)—

If the amount of wages (after subtracting withholding allowances) is: The amount of income tax to withhold is:

Not over $221 . . . . $0

Over—	But not over—		of excess over—
$221	—$858	. . . 10%	—$221
$858	—$2,830	. . $63.70 plus 15%	—$858
$2,830	—$6,644	. . $359.50 plus 25%	—$2,830
$6,644	—$13,875	. . $1,313.00 plus 28%	—$6,644
$13,875	—$29,971	. . $3,337.68 plus 33%	—$13,875
$29,971	. . . .	. . $8,649.36 plus 35%	—$29,971

(b) MARRIED person—

If the amount of wages (after subtracting withholding allowances) is: The amount of income tax to withhold is:

Not over $667 . . . . $0

Over—	But not over—		of excess over—
$667	—$1,963	. . . 10%	—$667
$1,963	—$6,013	. . $129.60 plus 15%	—$1,963
$6,013	—$11,488	. . $737.10 plus 25%	—$6,013
$11,488	—$17,308	. . $2,105.85 plus 28%	—$11,488
$17,308	—$30,425	. . $3,735.45 plus 33%	—$17,308
$30,425	. . . .	. . $8,064.06 plus 35%	—$30,425

Figure 6.11

EXAMPLE 4   Finding Federal Withholding Using the Percentage Method

Sharon MacDonald is married, claims three withholding allowances, and has monthly gross earnings of $6820. Use the percentage method to find her withholding tax.

Solution

STEP 1 Find the withholding allowance for *one* on the monthly payroll period in the percentage method income tax withholding table. The amount is $291.67. Since MacDonald claims three withholding allowances, multiply the one withholding allowance ($291.67) by her number of withholding allowances (3).

$$\$291.67 \times 3 = \$875.01$$

Amount for one withholding allowance —↑   ↑— Amount for three withholding allowances

STEP 2 Subtract the amount in Step 1 from gross earnings.

$$\$6820 - \$875.01 = \$5944.99$$

Gross earnings —↑   ↑— Amount used in Table 4(b)

STEP 3 Find the "married person monthly" section of the percentage method withholding table. Since $5944.99 is more than $1963 but less than $6013, the monthly withholding amount is found by adding $129.60 to 15% of the excess over $1963.

$$\text{Excess over } \$1963: \$5944.99 - \$1963 = \$3981.99$$

$$\begin{aligned}
\text{Monthly withholding tax} &= \$129.60 + 15\% \text{ of } \$3981.99 \\
&= \$129.60 + \$597.30 \\
&= \$726.90
\end{aligned}$$

EXAMPLE 5   Finding Federal Withholding Using the Percentage Method

Jessica Peters is divorced (single) and claims a withholding allowance for herself and her baby. Use the percentage method to find her withholding tax for a week with gross earnings of $1980.

Solution   Jessica Peters claims two withholding allowances. So, first multiply the $67.31 withholding allowance for one person times two allowances to find the weekly withholding allowance.

STEP 1 Weekly withholding allowance: $67.31 × 2 allowances = $134.62

STEP 2 Gross Earnings − Weekly withholding allowance = $1980 − $134.62

$$= \$1845.38$$

STEP 3 $1845.38 falls between $1533 and $3202 in the table for single, weekly payroll period.

$$\begin{aligned}
\text{Withholding tax} &= \$302.95 + 28\% \text{ of excess over } \$1533 \\
&= \$302.95 + 0.28\,(\$1845.38 - \$1533) \\
&= \$302.95 + 0.28 \times \$312.38 \\
&= \$390.42
\end{aligned}$$

The amount that will be withheld is $390.42.

NOTE   The amount of withholding tax found using the wage bracket method can vary slightly from the amount of withholding tax found using the percentage method. Any differences would be eliminated when the income tax return is filed.

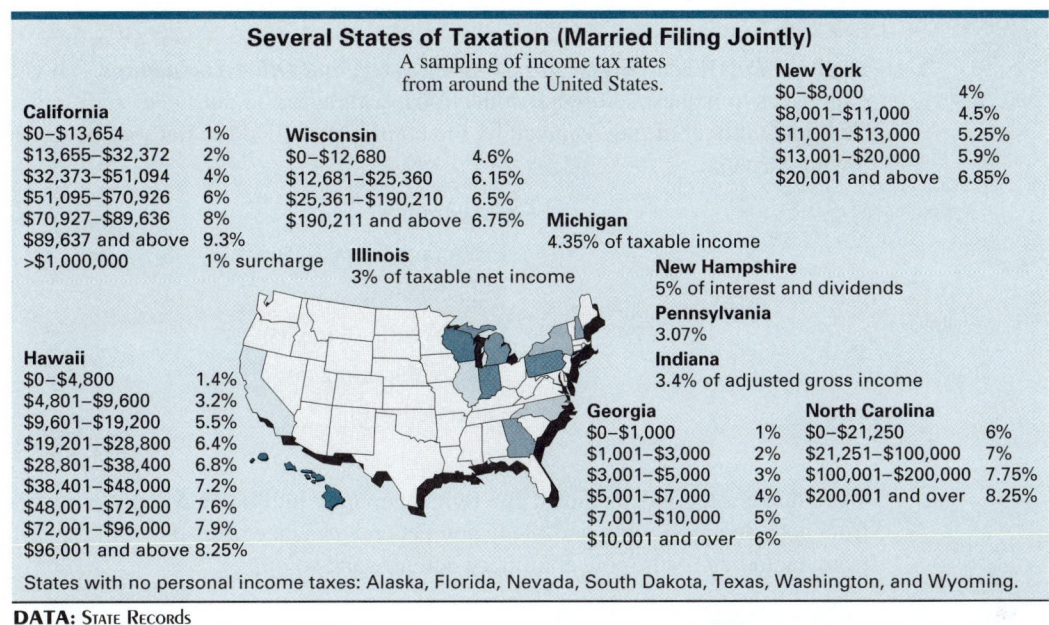

Several States of Taxation (Married Filing Jointly)
A sampling of income tax rates
from around the United States.

New York
$0–$8,000	4%
$8,001–$11,000	4.5%
$11,001–$13,000	5.25%
$13,001–$20,000	5.9%
$20,001 and above	6.85%

California
$0–$13,654	1%
$13,655–$32,372	2%
$32,373–$51,094	4%
$51,095–$70,926	6%
$70,927–$89,636	8%
$89,637 and above	9.3%
>$1,000,000	1% surcharge

Wisconsin
$0–$12,680	4.6%
$12,681–$25,360	6.15%
$25,361–$190,210	6.5%
$190,211 and above	6.75%

Michigan
4.35% of taxable income

Illinois
3% of taxable net income

New Hampshire
5% of interest and dividends

Pennsylvania
3.07%

Hawaii
$0–$4,800	1.4%
$4,801–$9,600	3.2%
$9,601–$19,200	5.5%
$19,201–$28,800	6.4%
$28,801–$38,400	6.8%
$38,401–$48,000	7.2%
$48,001–$72,000	7.6%
$72,001–$96,000	7.9%
$96,001 and above	8.25%

Indiana
3.4% of adjusted gross income

Georgia
$0–$1,000	1%
$1,001–$3,000	2%
$3,001–$5,000	3%
$5,001–$7,000	4%
$7,001–$10,000	5%
$10,001 and over	6%

North Carolina
$0–$21,250	6%
$21,251–$100,000	7%
$100,001–$200,000	7.75%
$200,001 and over	8.25%

States with no personal income taxes: Alaska, Florida, Nevada, South Dakota, Texas, Washington, and Wyoming.

DATA: STATE RECORDS

Figure 6.12

Objective

4 *Find the State Withholding Tax Using the State Income Tax Rate.* Many states and cities also have an income tax collected by withholding. Income taxes vary from state to state, with no state income tax in the states of Alaska, Florida, Nevada, South Dakota, Texas, Washington, and Wyoming. New Hampshire and Tennessee tax only dividend and interest income. A few states have a flat tax rate (percent of income) as a **state income tax**, while the majority of the states issue tax tables with taxes going as high as 9% and 10%. A few of the states' income tax rates are shown in Figure 6.12.

EXAMPLE 6 **Finding State Withholding Tax**

After receiving his Bachelor's degree in computer science, Imtiaz Ahmed moved to Michigan and began a new job. The gross amount of his first paycheck is $4240. Use Figure 6.12 to **(a)** find the applicable state tax rate and then **(b)** find the tax.

Solution

(a) The tax rate for Michigan is 4.35% of taxable income.

(b) State tax = Gross earnings × Tax rate

$= \$4240 \times 0.0435$

$= \$184.44$

NOTE Several software programs are available to find state income tax. For example, Quickbooks, Turbo Tax, and Peachtree Accounting are often used.

Objective

5 *Find Net Pay When Given Gross Wages, Taxes, and Other Deductions.* It is common for employees to request additional deductions, such as union dues and credit union payments. The final amount of pay received by the employee, called the **net pay**, is given by the following formula.

$$
\begin{array}{l}
\text{Gross earnings} \\
-\ \text{FICA tax (Social Security)} \\
-\ \text{Medicare tax} \\
-\ \text{Federal withholding tax} \\
-\ \text{State withholding tax} \\
\underline{-\ \text{Other deductions}} \\
\text{Net pay}
\end{array}
$$

Wow, that is a lot of deductions! But remember, later in life you will probably benefit greatly from both Social Security and Medicare. Federal and state taxes pay for things we all benefit from, including roads, police, military defense, and so on.

EXAMPLE 7 **Determining Net Pay after Deductions**

Brittany White is married and claims three withholding allowances. Her weekly gross earnings are $643.35. Her state withholding is 2.5% and her union dues are $25. Find her net pay using the percentage method of withholding.

Solution First, we will find the federal withholding tax since it requires several steps.

From Figure 6.11, one withholding allowance is $67.31.

Total withholding allowance = $67.31 $\times$ 3 allowances = $201.93

Gross earnings – Total withholding allowance = $643.35 − $201.93 = $441.42

From Figure 6.11, married, weekly, the federal tax is 10% of ($441.42 − $154) = $28.74

Next, find the other deductions and add them to find the total of weekly deductions.

$$
\begin{array}{lr}
\text{FICA: } \$643.35 \times 0.062 & = \$39.89 \\
\text{Medicare: } \$643.35 \times 0.0145 & = \$\ 9.33 \\
\text{Federal: (from above)} & = \$28.74 \\
\text{State: } \$643.35 \times 0.025 & = \$16.08 \\
\text{Union dues:} & = \$25.00 \\
\text{Total deductions} & \underline{\$119.04}
\end{array}
$$

Finally, find the net pay by subtracting total deductions from gross earnings.

$$
\begin{array}{ll}
\$643.35 & \text{Gross earnings} \\
\underline{-\ 119.04} & \text{Total deductions} \\
\$524.31 & \text{Net pay}
\end{array}
$$

White will receive a paycheck for $524.31, or for only 81.5% of her total gross earnings of $643.35. The remaining 18.5% (100% − 81.5%) of her gross earnings is used to pay the various taxes and union dues.

6.5	Exercises

FEDERAL WITHHOLDING TAX   Find the federal withholding tax for each of the following employees. Use the wage bracket method.

	Employee	Gross Earnings	Married?	Withholding Allowances
1.	Stanegna, J.	$3128.51 monthly	yes	3
2.	De Simone, D.	$325.76 weekly	no	2
3.	Koehler, J.	$507.52 weekly	yes	0
4.	Jones, C.	$2416.88 monthly	yes	1
5.	Jenders, P.	$1268.29 monthly	no	2
6.	Hollabaugh, A.	$1953.35 monthly	no	1
7.	Esposito, C.	$2817.32 monthly	yes	6
8.	Miller, M.	$341.18 weekly	no	1
9.	Mehta, S.	$1622.41 monthly	no	4
10.	Sommerfield, K.	$465.92 weekly	yes	0
11.	Weisner, W.	$1834.57 monthly	no	3
12.	NgauTibbits, C.	$618.43 weekly	yes	2

STATE WITHHOLDING TAX   Use the state income tax rate given to find the state withholding tax for each of the following employees. Round to the nearest cent.

	Employee	Gross Weekly Earnings	State Income Tax Rate	
13.	Owens, E.	$188.60	4.4%	_____
14.	Childs, M.	$235.68	5.0%	_____
15.	Christensen, C.	$317.43	2.8%	_____
16.	deJamaer, K.	$547.54	3.4%	_____
17.	Galvin, M.	$1476.32	6.0%	_____
18.	Hampson, N.	$2720.85	5.95%	_____

EMPLOYEE NET PAY   Use the percentage method of withholding to find federal withholding tax, a 6.2% FICA rate to find FICA tax, and 1.45% to find Medicare tax for each of the following employees. Then find the net pay for each employee. The number of withholding allowances and the marital status are listed after each employee's name. Assume that no employee has earned over $110,000 so far this year. (See Examples 3 and 5.)

	Employee	Gross Earnings	FICA	Medicare Tax	Federal Withholding Tax	Net Pay
19.	Hamel; 4, M	$576.28 weekly	_____	_____	_____	_____
20.	Guardino; 3, S	$2878.12 monthly	_____	_____	_____	_____
21.	Foster; 1, S	$2512.53 monthly	_____	_____	_____	_____
22.	Erb; 2, M	$625 weekly	_____	_____	_____	_____
23.	Terry; 3, M	$2276.83 semimonthly	_____	_____	_____	_____
24.	Galluccio; 1, S	$420.17 weekly	_____	_____	_____	_____
25.	Derma; 6, M	$1971.06 semimonthly	_____	_____	_____	_____

Employee	Gross Earnings	FICA	Medicare Tax	Federal Withholding Tax	Net Pay
26. Eddy; 2, M	$1020 weekly	_____	_____	_____	_____
27. Tang; 3, S	$2710 biweekly	_____	_____	_____	_____
28. Zamost; 2, S	$6625.24 monthly	_____	_____	_____	_____
29. Reilly; 1, S	$1786.44 weekly	_____	_____	_____	_____
30. Gertz; 4, M	$2618.50 biweekly	_____	_____	_____	_____
31. Bryn; 3, M	$1852.20 semimonthly	_____	_____	_____	_____
32. Hahn; 2, S	$1240 weekly	_____	_____	_____	_____

 33. Write an explanation of how to determine the federal withholding tax using the wage bracket (tax tables) method. (See Objective 2.)

 34. Write an explanation of how to find the federal withholding tax using the percentage method. (See Objective 3.)

Use the percentage method of withholding, a FICA rate of 6.2%, a Medicare rate of 1.45%, an SDI rate of 1%, and a state withholding tax of 3.4% in the following problems.

35. MARKETING REPRESENTATIVE Doug Gilbert, marketing representative, has weekly earnings of $975. He is married and claims four withholding allowances. His deductions include FICA, Medicare, federal withholding, state disability insurance, state withholding, union dues of $15.50, and credit union savings of $25. Find his net pay for a week in February.

36. TEACHER PAY Sheila Jones received her 4-year degree and is in her first year of teaching mathematics at a high school in the Midwest. Her semimonthly income is $1835 before deductions for FICA, Medicare, federal withholding, state disability insurance, state withholding, a United Way contribution of $20, and a savings deduction of $30. If she is single and claims four withholding allowances, find her net pay.

37. EDUCATIONAL SALES A new salesperson for Pearson Education is paid a salary of $410 per week plus 7% of all sales over $5000. She is single and claims two withholding allowances. Her deductions include FICA, Medicare, federal withholding, state disability insurance, state withholding, credit union savings of $50, and a Salvation Army contribution of $10. Find her net pay for a week in April during which she has sales of $11,284 with returns and allowances of $425.

38. TRAVEL AGENCY SALES Mindy Carter, an account executive for a travel agency specializing in executive travel to Asia, is paid on a variable commission, is married, and claims four withholding allowances. She receives 3% of the first $20,000 in sales, 4% of the next $10,000 in sales, and 6% of all sales over $30,000. This week she has sales of $45,550 and the following deductions: FICA, Medicare, federal withholding, state disability insurance, state withholding, a retirement contribution of $45, a savings bond of $50, and charitable contributions of $20. Find her net pay after subtracting all of her deductions.

39. HEATING COMPANY REPRESENTATIVE Sheri Minkner, a commission sales representative for Alternative Heating Company, is paid a monthly salary of $4200 plus a bonus of 1.5% on monthly sales. She is married and claims three withholding allowances. Her deductions include FICA, Medicare, federal withholding, state disability insurance, credit union savings of $150, charitable contributions of $25, and a savings bond of $50. Find her net pay for a month in which her sales were $42,618. The state in which Minkner works has no state income tax.

40. RIVER RAFTING MANAGER River Raft Adventures pays its manager Susan Estey a monthly salary of $2880 plus a commission of 0.8% based on total monthly sales volume. In the month of May, River Raft Adventures has total sales of $86,280. Estey is married and claims five withholding allowances. Her deductions include FICA, Medicare, federal withholding, state disability insurance, state withholding of $159.30, credit union payment of $300, March of Dimes contributions of $20, and savings bonds of $250. Find her net pay for May.

| 6.6 | **Payroll Records and Quarterly Returns** |

OBJECTIVES

1 *Understand payroll records kept by employers.*

2 *Calculate employer's matching Social Security and Medicare contributions.*

3 *Find the quarterly amount due the Internal Revenue Service.*

4 *Find the amount of federal unemployment tax due.*

Employers keep payroll records for many reasons. Individual payroll records for each employee are used to keep track of Social Security tax, Medicare tax, federal and state withholding, and many other items. The amounts withheld from employee earnings are sent periodically to the proper agency; most are paid entirely by the employee and others are matched by the employer. Usually these records are filed quarterly. These quarters and the filing dates are shown in Table 6.4.

Objective

1 *Understand Payroll Records Kept by Employers.* The payroll ledger, discussed in **Section 6.1**, was a record of the number of hours worked by all of the employees during a certain time period. The Employee's Earnings Record shown in Figure 6.13 details quarterly totals for an individual employee. This record shows the gross earnings, deduction amounts, and net pay for each pay period during the quarter.

Objective

2 *Calculate Employer's Matching Social Security and Medicare Contributions.* The employer must check the earnings of each employee to make sure that the FICA and the federal unemployment tax cutoff points are not passed. Since the employer must also give an end-of-year wage and tax statement (Form W-2) to each employee, the records are also used as the source of this information. In addition, accurate payroll records are important because the employer is required by law to match the employee's Social Security and Medicare contributions.

Objective

3 *Find the Quarterly Amount Due the Internal Revenue Service.* An employee's contribution to Social Security and Medicare must be matched by the employer.

Table 6.4 COMPANY FILING SCHEDULES FOR EMPLOYEE WITHHOLDING

Quarter	Ending	Due Date
January, February, March	March 31	April 30
April, May, June	June 30	July 31
July, August, September	September 30	October 31
October, November, December	December 31	January 31

NAME Lisa Kamins		CLOCK NUMBER 114	DEPT Production	MARITAL STATUS M	NO. OF EXEMPT 3	RECORD OF PAY CHANGES 1/1/20__ 7.20
STREET 407 Glen Oak Dr.		SOC.SEC. NUMBER 123-45-6789		☐ M. ☒ F.		
CITY Fort Worth, Texas		PHONE NO. 482-6319	DATE STARTED DATE LEFT			

TIME WORKED	DATE PAY PERIOD ENDING	YEAR 200__ TIME WORKED						ENCIRCLE QUARTERS ① 2 3 4	GROSS PAYROLL	F.W.T.	SOC. SEC.	MEDI	S.W.T.	U.D.	D. INS.	CHECK NO.	DEDUCTION AMOUNTS / NET PAY	
		SUN	M	TU	W	TH	F	SAT				DEDUCTIONS						
	BROUGHT FORWARD →																	
	1/7		8	8	7	8	10		298^{80}	18^{00}	19^{42}	4^{48}	13^{80}	5^{00}	18^{00}	1186	220^{10}	1
	1/14		8	8	8	8	8		288^{00}	16^{00}	18^{72}	4^{32}	13^{40}	5^{00}	18^{00}	1295	212^{56}	2
	1/21		8	10	8	9	8	4	363^{60}	28^{00}	23^{63}	5^{45}	15^{06}	5^{00}	18^{00}	1378	268^{46}	3
	1/28		8	8	8	8	8		288^{00}	16^{00}	18^{72}	4^{32}	13^{40}	5^{00}	18^{00}	1498	212^{56}	4
	2/4		8	8	6	8	8	2	288^{00}	16^{00}	18^{72}	4^{32}	13^{40}	5^{00}	18^{00}	1601	212^{56}	5
	2/11		8	8	8	8	8		288^{00}	16^{00}	18^{72}	4^{32}	13^{40}	5^{00}	18^{00}	1738	212^{56}	6
	2/18		8	8	8	8	8		288^{00}	16^{00}	18^{72}	4^{32}	13^{40}	5^{00}	18^{00}	1856	212^{56}	7
	2/25		10	8	10	6	6	5	342^{00}	25^{00}	22^{23}	5^{13}	14^{70}	5^{00}	18^{00}	2023	251^{94}	8
	3/3		8	8	8	8	8		288^{00}	16^{00}	18^{72}	4^{32}	13^{40}	5^{00}	18^{00}	2186	212^{56}	9
	3/10		8	7	8	9	10		309^{60}	19^{00}	20^{12}	4^{64}	13^{90}	5^{00}	18^{00}	2316	228^{94}	10
	3/17		8	8	8	8	8		288^{00}	16^{00}	18^{72}	4^{32}	13^{40}	5^{00}	18^{00}	2479	212^{56}	11
	3/24		10	8	10	8	8		391^{00}	33^{00}	25^{42}	5^{87}	16^{60}	5^{00}	18^{00}	2632	287^{11}	12
	3/31		8	8	8	9	8	4	403^{75}	34^{00}	26^{24}	6^{06}	17^{06}	5^{00}	18^{00}	2801	297^{39}	13
																		14
																		15
																		16
	QTR. TO DATE								4124^{75}	269^{00}	268^{10}	61^{87}	184^{92}	65^{00}	234^{80}		3041^{88}	

Figure 6.13

EXAMPLE 1 Finding the Amount of FICA and Medicare Tax Due

If the employees at Fair Oaks Automotive Repair pay a total of $789.10 in Social Security tax and $182.10 in Medicare tax, how much must the employer send to the Internal Revenue Service?

Solution The employer must match this and send a total of $971.20 ($789.10 + $182.10 from employees) + $971.20 (from employer) = $1942.40 to the government.

NOTE In addition to the employee's Social Security tax and a matching amount paid by the employer, the employer must also send the amount withheld for income tax to the Internal Revenue Service on a quarterly basis.

EXAMPLE 2 Finding the Employer's Amount Due the IRS

Suppose that during a certain quarter Leslie's Pool Supplies has collected $2765.42 from its employees for FICA tax, $638.17 for Medicare tax, and $3572.86 in federal withholding tax. Compute the total amount due to the Internal Revenue Service from Leslie's Pool Supplies.

Solution

$2,765.42	Collected from employees for FICA tax
$2,765.42	Equal amount paid by employer
$638.17	Collected from employees for Medicare tax
$638.17	Equal amount paid by employer
$3,572.86	Federal withholding tax
$10,380.04	Total due to Internal Revenue Service

The firm must send $10,380.04 to the Internal Revenue Service.

■ ■ ■ Scientific
■ ■ Calculator
■ Approach

| The calculator solution for Example 2 is as follows:

2765.42 $\boxed{\times}$ 2 $\boxed{+}$ 638.17 $\boxed{\times}$ 2 $\boxed{+}$ 3572.86 $\boxed{=}$ 10380.04

Objective

4 *Find the Amount of Federal Unemployment Tax Due.* The **Federal Unemployment Tax Act (FUTA)** requires employers to pay an additional tax. This **unemployment insurance tax** is paid entirely by employers. These funds are used to pay unemployment benefits to individuals who have lost their jobs and cannot find work. Unemployment benefits are often very benefical to families in times of economic recession when many people are unemployed. One difference between the **developed world** and poorer **third-world countries** is that most countries in the developed world offer benefits to help people when they are sick, lose their jobs, or retire. The poorest countries in the world usually have no benefits to pay to individuals who are ill, elderly, or without sufficient food.

In general, all employers who paid wages of $1500 or more in a calendar quarter or had one or more employees for some part of a day in any 20 different weeks in a calendar year must file an employer's annual *Federal Unemployment Tax Return.* This federal return must be filed each January for the preceding year. The FUTA tax that must be paid by the employer is 6.2% of the first $7000 in earnings for that year for each employee.

States also require employers to pay unemployment taxes. Any **state unemployment tax (SUTA)** paid by an employer becomes a credit on the federal unemployment tax return. Many states decrease the unemployment tax rate for any company with low labor turnover. Since the tax rates and maximum amount subject to tax vary widely by state, we will not include them in our calculations here. However, you can be sure that your employer is paying both SUTA and FUTA taxes on your behalf.

EXAMPLE **3** **Finding the Amount of Unemployment Tax Due**

Betty Clifton earns $4800 each quarter. Find (**a**) the amount of her earnings that are subject to the FUTA tax in the second quarter and (**b**) the amount of the tax in that quarter.

Solution

(**a**) The FUTA tax applies only to the first $7000 in earnings each year. So the earnings in the second quarter subject to the FUTA tax are: $7000 − $4800 = $2200.

(**b**) FUTA tax = $2200 × 0.062 = $136.40

NOTE Employers pay several expenses on behalf of each employee that the employee does not see. These include the employer's one-half of FICA and Medicare taxes, unemployment taxes, and usually worker's compensation insurance which insures employees in the event they are injured on the job. Many employers also pay portions of the employee's health insurance and make contributions to a retirement plan for the employee. So the salary is only part of an employer's cost to hire someone.

6.6	Exercises

EMPLOYER PAYROLL RECORDS   Find the total combined amount of Social Security and Medicare tax (employee's contribution plus employer's contribution) for each of the following firms. Use a FICA rate of 6.2% and a Medicare tax rate of 1.45%, and assume no employee has earned over $110,000 so far this year.

Firm	Total Employee Earnings
1. Atlasta Ranch	$15,634.18
2. Norm's Cell Phones	$10,046.53
3. Adin Feed and Fuel	$17,462.10
4. Leisure Outdoor Furniture	$15,324.15
5. Computers Plus	$14,131.59
6. Owl Drugstore	$21,281.60
7. Plescia Produce	$62,475.80
8. Brownstone Music	$122,819.50

TOTAL EMPLOYER PAYMENT   Calculate the total amount due from each of the following firms. Use a FICA rate of 6.2% and a Medicare tax rate of 1.45%.

Firm	Total Employee Earnings	Total Withholding for Income Tax
9. Web Design	$6150.82	$629.18
10. McIntosh Meats	$8714.55	$2008.76
11. Childlike Publishers	$32,121.85	$8215.08
12. Mart & Bottle	$20,255.60	$4436.80
13. Todd Consultants	$37,271.39	$7128.64
14. UPS Store	$10,158.24	$2768.62
15. Tony Balony's	$34,547.86	$12,628.19
16. Oaks Hardware	$21,394.77	$5671.30

17. Without changes, Social Security is projected to be bankrupt by 2038. What changes do you think should be made to the system to keep it solvent?

18. Describe in your own words four differences between Social Security and FUTA. Consider the purpose, amount paid, and who pays.

Solve the following application problems. Assume no employee has earned over $110,000 so far this year. Use a FICA rate of 6.2% and a Medicare tax rate of 1.45%.

19. HAIR SALON OWNER   Total employee earnings at City Hair Care are $21,928.10. Find the combined total amount of FICA and Medicare taxes sent to the IRS by the employer.

20. PAVING CONTRACTOR   Biondi Paving has a weekly payroll of $13,650.30. How much FICA and Medicare taxes should be sent to the IRS?

21. AM-PM OWNER   The AM-PM Mart has an employee payroll of $7622.84. During the same time period, $1625.68 was withheld as income tax. Find the total amount due to the IRS.

22. FLORIST SHOP OWNER   The payroll at the Oak Mill Florist is $22,607.72. During the same pay period, $3898.14 was withheld as income tax. Find the total amount that must be sent to the IRS.

FEDERAL UNEMPLOYMENT TAX   **Assume a FUTA rate of 6.2% of the first $7000 in earnings in each of the following.**

23. An employee earns $3280 in the first quarter of the year, $2600 in the second quarter, and $3156 in the third quarter. Find (a) the amount of earnings subject to unemployment tax in the third quarter and (b) the amount of unemployment tax due on third-quarter earnings.

24. As a part-time employee at an apartment complex, James Berry earns an average of $850 per month. Find (a) the amount of income subject to unemployment tax in the third quarter and (b) the amount of tax due on third-quarter earnings.

25. Emma Price is paid $1800 per month. Find (a) the amount of earnings subject to unemployment tax in the second quarter and (b) the amount of unemployment tax due on second-quarter earnings.

26. Michael Booth received $4820 in earnings in the first quarter of the year. His earnings in the second quarter are $3815. Find (a) the amount of his earnings subject to FUTA in the second quarter and (b) the amount of tax due in the second quarter.

CHAPTER TERMS

Review the following terms to test your understanding of the chapter. For each term you do not know, refer to the page number found next to that term.

chargebacks [p. 210]
commission rate [p. 202]
compensatory (comp) time [p. 195]
daily overtime [p. 194]
deductions [p. 190]
developed world [p. 233]
differential-piecework plan [p. 209]
dockings [p. 210]
double time [p. 195]
drawing account [p. 204]
Electronic Funds Transfer Payment System (EFTPS) [p. 220]
Fair Labor Standards Act (FLSA) [p. 193]
Federal Insurance Contributions Act (FICA) [p. 214]
Federal Unemployment Tax Act (FUTA) [p.233]

gross earnings [p. 190]
hourly wage [p. 191]
incentive rates [p. 208]
income tax withholdings [p. 220]
Medicare [p. 214]
minimum wage [p. 193]
net pay [p. 28]
net sales [p. 202]
offshoring [p. 190]
override [p. 205]
overtime [p. 193]
overtime premium (excess) method [p. 194]
pay period [p. 196]
payroll ledger [p. 191]
percentage method [p. 221]
personal income tax [p. 220]
piecework rate [p. 208]
premium payment plan [p. 195]

premium rate [p. 209]
quota bonus system [p. 205]
quotas [p. 205]
Request for Earnings and Benefit Estimate Statement [p. 215]
returns [p. 202]
salary [p. 196]
salary plus commission [p. 203]
shift differential [p. 195]
sliding-scale commission [p. 202]
Social Security [p. 214]
split-shift premium [p. 195]
state disability insurance (SDI) [p. 218]
state income tax [p. 227]
state unemployment insurance tax (SUTA) [p. 233]

straight commission [p. 202]
straight-piecework plan [p. 209]
third-world country [p. 233]
time card [p. 191]
time rates [p. 208]
time-and-a-half rate [p. 193]
unemployment insurance tax [p. 233]
variable commission [p. 202]
wage bracket method [p. 221]
withholding allowances [p. 220]

CONCEPTS

EXAMPLES

6.1 Gross earnings

Gross earnings = Hours worked × Rate per hour

40 hours at $8.40 per hour

Gross earnings = 40 × $8.40 = $336

6.1 Gross earnings with overtime

First, find regular earnings. Then, determine overtime pay at overtime rate. Finally, add regular and overtime earnings.

40 hours at $8.40 per hour; 10 hours at time-and-a-half.

$$\text{Gross earnings} = (40 \times \$8.40) + \left(10 \times \$8.40 \times 1\tfrac{1}{2}\right)$$
$$= \$336 + \$126$$
$$= \$462$$

6.1 Common pay periods

Pay Period	Paychecks per Year
Monthly	12
Semimonthly	24
Biweekly	26
Weekly	52

Find the earnings equivalent to $2000 per month for other pay periods.

$$\text{Semimonthly} = \frac{\$2000}{2} = \$1000$$

$$\text{Biweekly} = \frac{\$2000 \times 12}{26} = \$923.08$$

$$\text{Weekly} = \frac{\$2000 \times 12}{52} = \$461.54$$

6.1	**Overtime for salaried employees**	Salary is $648 per week for 36 hours. Find earnings for 46 hours.

First, find the equivalent hourly rate. Next, multiply the rate by the overtime hours by $1\frac{1}{2}$. Finally, add overtime earnings to salary.

$$\$648 \div 36 = \$18.00 \text{ per hour}$$
$$\$18.00 \times 10 \times 1\frac{1}{2} = \$270 \text{ overtime}$$
$$\$648 + \$270 = \$918$$

6.2   Straight commission

Gross earnings = Commission rate × Amount of sales

Sales of $25,800; commission rate is 5%.

$$0.05 \times \$25,800 = \$1290$$

6.2   Variable commission

Commission rate varies at different sales levels.

Up to $10,000, 6%; $10,001–$20,000, 8%; $20,001 and up, 9%. Find the commission on sales of $32,768.

$0.06 \times \$10,000 =$	$\$600.00$	(First $10,000)
$0.08 \times \$10,000 =$	$\$800.00$	(Next $10,000)
$0.09 \times \underline{\$12,768} =$	$\underline{\$1149.12}$	(Over $20,000)
Totals $32,768	$2549.12	

6.2   Salary and commission

Gross earnings = Fixed earnings + Commission

Salary, $250 per week; commission rate, 3%. Find gross earnings on sales of $6848.

$$\text{Gross earnings} = \$250 + (0.03 \times \$6848)$$
$$= \$250 + \$205.44$$
$$= \$455.44$$

6.2   Commissions with a drawing account

Gross earnings = Commission − Draw

Sales for month, $54,640; commission rate, 7%; draw, $750 for month. Find the gross earnings.

$$\text{Gross earnings} = (0.07 \times \$54,640) - \$750$$
$$= \$3824.80 - \$750$$
$$= \$3074.80$$

6.2   Commissions with a quota bonus

Gross earnings = Commission rate × (Sales − Quota)

Sales for week, $14,370; commission rate, 10% after meeting the sales quota of $4000. Find gross earnings.

$$\text{Gross earnings} = 0.1 \times (\$14,370 - \$4000)$$
$$= 0.1 \times \$10,370$$
$$= \$1037$$

6.3   Gross earnings for piecework

Gross earnings = Payment per item × Number of items

Items produced, 275; payment per item, $1.28. Find the gross earnings.

$$\$1.28 \times 275 = \$352$$

6.3   Gross earnings for differential piecework

The rate paid per item produced varies with level of production.

1–100 items, $1.20 each; 101–200 items, $1.30 each; over 200 items, $1.45 each. Find the gross earnings if 292 items are produced.

$100 \times \$1.20 =$	$\$120.00$	First 100 items
$100 \times \$1.30 =$	$\$130.00$	Second 100 items
$\underline{92} \times \$1.45 =$	$\underline{\$133.40}$	Above 200 items
292	$383.40	

6.3	**Gross earnings with piece rate and chargebacks**	Items produced, 318; piece rate, $1.35; spoiled items, 26; chargeback, $1.60. Find the gross earnings.

6.3 Gross earnings with piece rate and chargebacks

Find piece rate earnings; then calculate chargebacks and subtract them from piece rate earnings to find gross earnings.

Items produced, 318; piece rate, $1.35; spoiled items, 26; chargeback, $1.60. Find the gross earnings.

Total: $318 \times \$1.35 = \$429.30$

Chargeback: $26 \times \$1.60 = \$41.60$

Gross earnings: $\$429.30 - \$41.60 = \$387.70$

6.3 Overtime earnings on piecework

Gross earnings = Earnings at regular rate + Earnings at overtime rate

Items produced on regular time, 530; items produced on overtime, 110; piece rate, $0.60. Find the gross earnings.

$$\text{Gross earnings} = 530 \times \$0.60 + 110 \left(1\frac{1}{2} \times \$0.60 \right)$$

$$= \$318 + \$99$$

$$= \$417$$

6.4 FICA; Social Security tax

The gross earnings are multiplied by the rate. When the maximum earnings are reached, no additional FICA is withheld that year.

Gross earnings, $458; Social Security tax rate, 6.2%. Find Social Security tax.

$$\$458 \times 0.062 = \$28.40$$

6.4 Medicare tax

The gross earnings are multiplied by the tax rate. There is no maximum earnings limit on Medicare.

Gross earnings, $458; Medicare tax rate, 1.45%. Find Medicare tax.

$$\$458 \times 0.0145 = \$6.64$$

6.4 State disability insurance deductions

Multiply the gross earnings by the SDI tax rate. When maximum earnings are reached, no additional taxes are paid in that year.

Gross earnings, $3210; SDI tax rate 1%. Find SDI tax.

$$\$3210 \times 0.01 = \$32.10$$

6.5 Withholding Federal Tax—Wage Bracket

Find the amount to be withheld using the tables for Wage Bracket Method of Withholding.

Single, 3 withholding allowances, weekly wage of $535. Go to the table for single and weekly. Look at the row "at least $530 but less than $540" and column with 3 allowances.

Withholding amount = $35

6.5 Withholding Federal Tax—Percentage Method

Find

1. Amount for one withholding allowance
2. Multiply amount times number of allowances
3. Wages − amount found in Step 2 above
4. Appropriate table for Percentage Method Withholding Allowance
5. Appropriate row in table
6. Amount to withhold by following directions

Married, 4 withholding allowances, monthly wage of $3400.

1. one monthly withholding allowance = $291.67
2. $291.67 \times 4 = \$1166.68$
3. $\$3400 - \$1166.68 = \$2233.32$
4. table for married, monthly
5. "over 1,963 but not over $6,013"
6. $\$129.60 + 15\% \times (\$2233.32 - \$1963)$
   $= \$129.60 + \$40.55$
   $= \$170.15$

6.5 State withholding tax

Tax is paid on total earnings. No maximum as with FICA.

Married employee with weekly earnings of $392. Find the state withholding tax given a state withholding tax rate of 4.5%.

$$4.5\% \times \$392 = 0.045 \times \$392 = \$17.64$$

6.6 Quarterly report

Filed each quarter; FICA and federal withholding are sent to the IRS.

(FICA + Medicare) × 2 (employer) + federal withholding tax

Quarterly FICA withheld from employees is $5269, Medicare tax is $1581, and federal withholding tax is $14,780. Find the total due the IRS.

($5269 + $1581) × 2 + $14,780 = $28,480

6.6 Federal Unemployment Tax (FUTA)

FUTA is paid by the employer on the first $7000 of earnings each year for each employee.

An employee earned $3850 in the first quarter of a year. Find the amount of unemployment tax using a 6.2% tax rate.

$3850 × 6.2% = $238.70

CHAPTER 6	Review Exercises

The answer section includes answers to all Review Exercises.

Complete the following partial payroll ledger. Find the total gross earnings for each employee. Time-and-a-half is paid on all hours over 40 in one week. [6.1]

	Employee	Hours Worked	Reg. Hours	O.T. Hours	Reg. Rate	Gross Earnings
1.	Darasz, B.	48.5			$9.14	
2.	Davidson, D.	48			$8.50	
3.	Mandler, S.	38.25			$10.85	
4.	Rosenthal, L.	57.25			$12.20	

Find the equivalent earnings for each of the following salaries as indicated. [6.1]

	Weekly	Biweekly	Semimonthly	Monthly	Annually
5.	$410.80	_____	_____	_____	_____
6.	_____	$1060	_____	_____	_____
7.	_____	_____	_____	_____	$18,000
8.	_____	_____	$875	_____	_____

Find the weekly gross earnings for the following people who are on salary and are paid time-and-a-half for overtime. [6.1]

	Employee	Regular Hours per Week	Weekly Salary	Hours Worked	Weekly Gross Earnings
9.	Uldall, E.	40	$640	45	_____
10.	Donovan-Dickerson, K.	36	$342	42	_____

Find the gross earnings for each of the following salespeople. [6.2]

	Employee	Total Sales	Returns	Rate of Commission
11.	Gonsalves, R.	$48,620	$3106	8%
12.	Kaufman, B.	$38,740	$1245	9%

Solve the following application problems. [6.3]

13. Twenty Minute Lube and Oil pays its employees $2.50 for an oil change, $2.60 for each car lubed, and $3.75 if a car gets both an oil change and a lube. This week, Andre Herrebout changed the oil in 63 cars, lubed 46 cars, and gave an oil change and lube to 68 cars. Find his gross pay for the week.

14. At Jalisco Electronics in Mexicali, Mexico, assemblers are paid as follows: 1–20 units in a week, $4.50 each; 21–30 units, $5.50 each; and more than 30 units, $7 each. Adrian Ortega assembled 28 units in one week. Find his gross pay.

15. Samantha Walker receives a commission of 6% for selling a $235,000 house. Half the commission goes to the broker and half of the remainder to another salesperson. Walker gets the rest. Find the amount she receives.

Employees at Appliance Giant are paid a commission on the following schedule: first $2000 in sales, 6%; next $2000 in sales, 8%; sales over $4000, 10%. Use this information for Exercises 16 and 17. [6.2]

16. Find the gross earnings for an employee with total sales of $5850.

17. Find the gross earnings for an employee with total sales of $7200.

18. Pat Rowell ties bows on Christmas wreaths and is paid $0.12 for each bow tied. She is charged $0.09 for each rejection and is paid time-and-a-half for overtime production. Find her gross earnings for a week when she produces 1850 at the regular rate, 285 at the overtime rate, and has 92 rejections.

An employee is paid a salary of $9300 per month. If the FICA rate is 6.2% on the first $110,000 of earnings and the Medicare tax rate is 1.45% on all earnings, how much will the employee pay in (a) FICA tax and (b) Medicare tax during the following months? [6.4]

19. March   20. December

Find the federal withholding tax using the wage bracket method for each of the following employees. [6.5]

21. Flahive: 2 withholding allowances, single, $515 weekly earnings

22. Hoffa: 2 withholding allowances, married, $705.91 weekly earnings

23. Howard: 3 withholding allowances, married, $3210.55 monthly earnings

24. Kluesner: 4 withholding allowances, single, $1859.62 monthly earnings

25. Lawrence: 6 withholding allowances, married, $2864.57 monthly earnings

26. Tewell: 2 withholding allowances, single, $318.36 weekly earnings

Find the net pay for each of the following employees after FICA, Medicare, federal withholding tax, state disability, and other deductions have been made. Assume that no one has earned over $110,000 so far this year. Assume a FICA rate of 6.2%, Medicare rate of 1.45%, and a state disability rate of 1%. Use the percentage method of withholding. [6.5]

27. Precilo: $1852.75 monthly earnings, 1 withholding allowance, single, $37.80 in other deductions

28. Martinez: $684.20 weekly earnings, 4 withholding allowances, married, state withholding of $15.34, credit union savings of $20

29. Watson: $1040 weekly earnings, 6 withholding allowances, married, state withholding of $34.80, union dues of $38, charitable contribution of $15

Solve the following application problems. Assume no employee has earned over $110,000 so far this year. Use a FICA rate of 6.2% and a rate of 1.45% for Medicare. [6.6]

30. Total employee earnings for Round Table Pizza are $12,720.15. Find the combined total of FICA and Medicare taxes sent to the IRS by the employer.

31. San Juan Electric has an employee payroll of $29,185.17. During the same period $4921 was withheld as income tax. Find the total amount due the IRS.

Solve the following application problems.

32. A salesperson is paid $452 per week plus a commission of 2% on all sales. The salesperson sold $712 worth of goods on Monday, $523 on Tuesday, $1002 on Wednesday, $391 on Thursday, and $609 on Friday. Returns and allowances for the week were $114. Find the employee's (a) Social Security tax (6.2%), (b) Medicare tax (1.45%), and (c) state disability insurance (1%) for the week.

33. Kerry Conley has earned $108,210 this year and his income for the current week is $2650. Find his (a) FICA tax and (b) Medicare tax for the current week.

34. The employees of Miracle Floor Covering paid a total of $1496.11 in Social Security tax last month, $345.30 in Medicare tax, and $1768.43 in federal withholding tax. Find the total amount that the employer must send to the Internal Revenue Service.

For Exercises 35 and 36, find (a) the Social Security tax and (b) the Medicare tax for each of the following self-employed people. Use a FICA tax rate of 12.4% and a Medicare tax rate of 2.9%. [6.4]

35. Kula, S.: $38,795.22

36. Biondi, E.: $27,618.53

Assume a FUTA rate of 6.2% on the first $7000 in earnings in each of the following. [6.6]

37. An employee earns $2875 in the first quarter of the year, $3212 in the second quarter, and $2942 in the third quarter. Find (a) the amount of earnings subject to unemployment tax in the third quarter and (b) the amount of unemployment tax due on third quarter earnings.

38. Amy Berk earns $810 per month. Find (a) the amount of earnings subject to unemployment tax in the third quarter and (b) the amount of unemployment tax due on third-quarter earnings.

CHAPTER 6 | Business Application Case #1
Diesel Mechanic

Jim Waters is a diesel mechanic working on truck engines for Hunter Trucking. His annual salary based on a 40-hour workweek is $38,480, but he is paid time-and-a-half for all overtime. He is single and claims two withholding allowances. Deductions include FICA, federal withholding using the percentage method, state disability insurance at 1%, state withholding at 3.5%, credit union payments of $125, retirement deductions of $55, association dues of $15, and a contribution to the Diabetes Association of $25. Find each of the following for a 52-hour workweek.

(a) Regular wages

(b) Overtime wages

(c) Total gross earnings

(d) FICA

(e) Medicare

(f) Federal withholding

(g) State disability insurance

(h) State withholding

(i) Other deductions

(j) Net pay

CHAPTER 6	Business Application Case #2
	Social Security (www.ssa.gov)

The Great Depression of the 1930s was a very difficult time across much of the world. In the United States, unemployment rose to 25% and widespread bank failures wiped out the savings of many families. Poverty among the elderly and disabled grew dramatically, and by 1934 more than 50% of the elderly did not have enough income to support themselves.

Due to the great problems of that era, Congress and the president acted and passed the Social Security Act of 1935. It required employees and employers to contribute to a fund that would then be used to make monthly payments to retired workers. Social Security includes benefits to retired workers and dependents, child survivors of a deceased worker, and disabled workers and dependents. The graph shows the number of beneficiaries of benefits over time. It is important to notice that Social Security payments amount to more than one-half of the income of many retired people in the United States. Presumably, you or your dependents will receive Social Security benefits at some point.

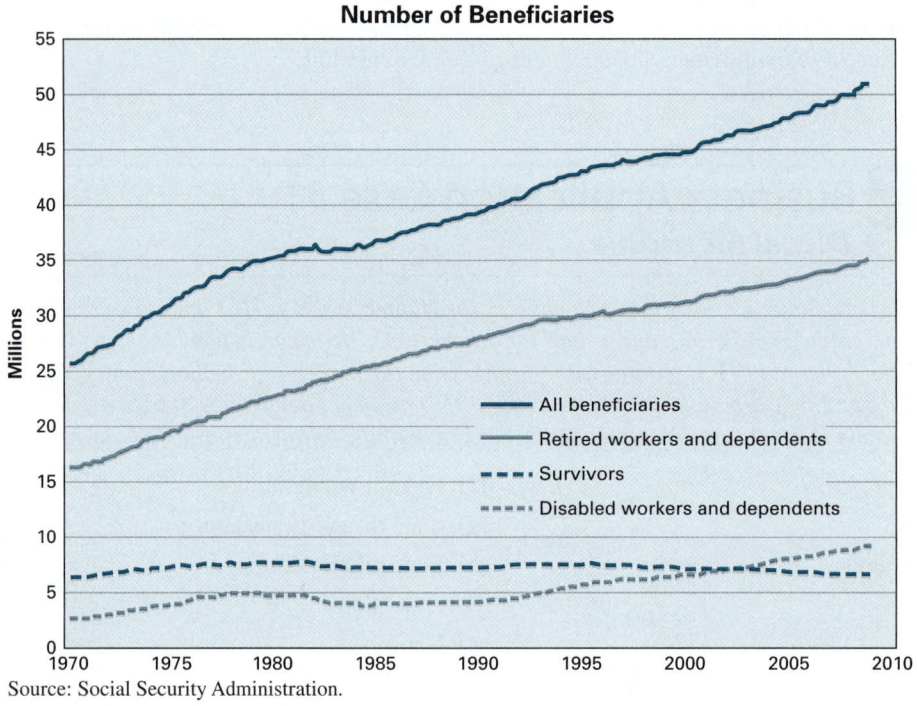

Source: Social Security Administration.

(a) Estimate the total number of beneficiaries of Social Security payments in 1970 and also in 2008. Then find the percent increase from 1970 to 2008.

(b) A high school senior by the name of Dong Yi has started up her own business that designs and builds Web pages for area businesses. Yi hires another high school student to assist her. Find the total FICA taxes and Medicare taxes that must be sent to the government for a quarter in which Dong made $5700 and the assistant was paid $2600.

Taxes

Tax dollars pay for education, health services, national defense, streets and highways, parks and recreation facilities, police and fire protection, public assistance for the poor, libraries, and even street lights. As government provides more services, taxes go up. Figure 7.1 shows the number of days that the "average American" must work to pay the taxes for the year. Note that the number of days fell sharply during 2001–2003 as tax rates were reduced. But taxes have since gone back up.

> Taxes are the price we pay to live in a civilized society.
>
> —Oliver Wendell Holmes, Jr.

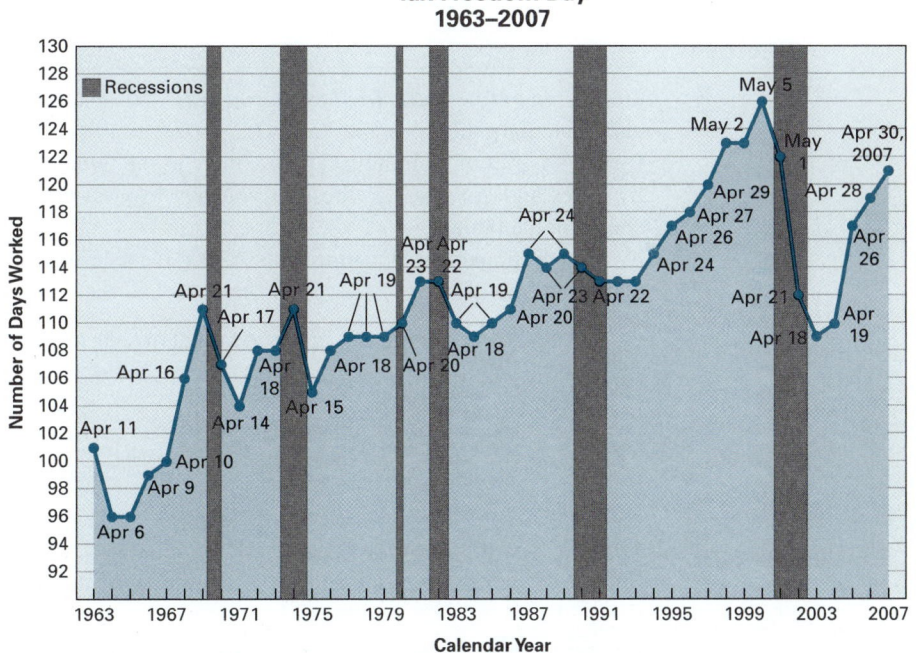

Source: Data from www.taxfoundation.org.

Figure 7.1

List all the different kinds of taxes that you pay. Do you believe that the wealthy pay significant taxes? Do you believe they pay their fair share of the total tax burden? Search the Internet for information to support your views.

Most taxes are levied on sales, property, and income. This chapter examines the basics of taxation and discusses the calculations necessary to work with each type of tax.

7.1	Sales Tax

OBJECTIVES

1 *Understand how sales tax is determined.*

2 *Find the amount of sales tax and the total sale.*

3 *Find the selling price when the sales tax is known.*

4 *Find the amount of the sale when the total price including tax is known.*

5 *Define excise tax.*

6 *Find the total cost including sales tax and excise tax.*

Most states and many cities and counties levy a **sales tax** on sales at retail stores. The tax rate varies from one location to another, but it is always given as a percent of the retail price. Although most states tax restaurant sales, many do not tax food items purchased in grocery stores.

Objective

1 *Understand How Sales Tax Is Determined.*   Most stores have cash registers that automatically calculate the sales tax. Table 7.1 shows 2008 sales tax rates for all 50 states and also for the District of Columbia. The tax rates in the table do not include any sales taxes levied by cities and counties, so the rate you pay in your state is probably higher than the one shown in the table.

The basic percent equation is used to solve sales tax problems. The amount of *sales tax* is the part, the *amount of the sale* is the base, and the *sales tax rate* is the rate.

$$\text{Sales tax} = \text{Amount of sale} \times \text{Sales tax rate}$$

$$P \quad = \quad B \quad \times \quad R$$

$$\text{Part} \quad = \quad \text{Base} \quad \times \quad \text{Rate}$$

Objective

2 *Find the Amount of Sales Tax and the Total Sale.*   A common calculation in business is to find the amount of sales tax and the total amount of the sale, including tax.

EXAMPLE 1   Finding Sales Tax and the Total Sale

A customer at Round Table Pizza purchases several large pizzas for $49.95. Sales tax in the state is 5%. Find (a) the amount of sales tax and (b) the total amount collected from the customer.

Solution

(a) The amount of sales tax (part) is found by multiplying the sales tax rate (rate) by the amount of the sale (base). Use the percent equation to find the sales tax.

$$P = BR$$
$$= \$49.95 \times 5\%$$
$$= \$49.95 \times 0.05 = \$2.50 \quad \text{Rounded}$$

The sales tax is $2.50.

(b) Add to find the total amount collected from the customer.

$49.95   Amount of sale
+ 2.50   Sales tax
$52.45   Total sale including tax

Table 7.1   2008 SALES TAX RATES (EXCLUDES CITY, COUNTY, AND OTHER LOCAL SALES TAXES)

Alabama	4%	Montana	0%
Alaska	0%	Nebraska	5.5%
Arizona	5.6%	Nevada	6.5%
Arkansas	6%	New Hampshire	0%
California	7.25%	New Jersey	7%
Colorado	2.9%	New Mexico	5%
Connecticut	6%	New York	4%
Delaware	0%	North Carolina	4.25%
District of Columbia	5.75%	North Dakota	5%
Florida	6%	Ohio	5.5%
Georgia	4%	Oklahoma	4.5%
Hawaii	4%	Oregon	0%
Idaho	6%	Pennsylvania	6%
Illinois	6.25%	Rhode Island	7%
Indiana	6%	South Carolina	6%
Iowa	5%	South Dakota	4%
Kansas	5.3%	Tennessee	7%
Kentucky	6%	Texas	6.25%
Louisiana	4%	Utah	4.65%
Maine	5%	Vermont	6%
Maryland	6%	Virginia	5%
Massachusetts	6.25%	Washington	6.5%
Michigan	6%	West Virginia	6%
Minnesota	6.5%	Wisconsin	5%
Mississippi	7%	Wyoming	4%
Missouri	4.225%		

Note: Alaska, Delaware, Montana, New Hampshire, and Oregon do not have a state sales tax.

NOTE   The sales tax on any one sale may be small, but the sales taxes on all transactions in a state add up to a *lot of money*. States depend on revenue from sales taxes to pay expenses such as the salaries of state employees, to maintain and improve roads, to operate museums, to staff police departments, etc.

Objective

3   *Find the Selling Price When the Sales Tax Is Known.*   If the amount of sales tax and the sales tax rate are known, it is possible to determine the selling price.

EXAMPLE 2   Finding Price When Sales Tax Is Known

The sales tax on a new sound system is $16.14. Find the price of the sound system if the sales tax rate is 6%.

Solution   Since sales tax (part) is found by multiplying the sales tax rate (rate) by the amount of the sale (base), the amount of sale is found using the percent equation and solving for base.

$$P = B \times R$$

$$\$16.14 = B \times 6\% \quad \text{Write 6\% as 0.06.}$$

$$\$16.14 = 0.06B$$

$$\frac{\$16.14}{0.06} = \frac{0.06B}{0.06}$$

$$\$269 = B$$

The sound system sells for $269.

Objective

4   *Find the Amount of the Sale When the Total Price Including Tax Is Known.*   When the total price, including sales tax and the **sales tax rate** are known, the sale amount can be found as shown in the next example.

EXAMPLE 3   **Determining the Sale Price When the Total Cost Is Known**

Coleman Headstart Preschool purchased some playground equipment at a total cost of $3663.36, including sales tax of 6%. Find the price of the equipment before the sales tax.

Solution   The sales tax rate of 6% applies to the cost of the equipment (base) and not to the total of $3663.36, which includes the sales tax. Let B be the cost of the equipment. Then the cost of the equipment plus the sales tax equals $3663.36.

$$\text{Cost of equipment} + \text{Sales tax} = \text{Total price}$$

$$B + (6\%)B = \$3663.36$$

$$1B + 0.06B = \$3663.36$$

$$1.06B = \$3663.36$$

$$B = \frac{\$3663.36}{1.06} \quad \text{Divide by 1.06.}$$

$$B = \$3456$$

The cost of the equipment is $3456.

Check the answer by finding the sales tax (part) and adding it to the original price.

$$\text{Sales tax} = \$3456 \times 0.06 = \$207.36$$

$$\text{Total cost} = \$3456 + \$207.36 = \$3663.36$$

The answer checks, so the cost before sales tax is $3456.

Objective

5   *Define Excise Tax.*   Besides state sales taxes, an **excise tax**, sometimes called a **luxury tax**, is charged on certain items by the federal, state, and local governments. Similar to sales taxes, excise taxes are paid by, or passed on to, the consumer of goods and services. Excise taxes are charged on gasoline, tires, luxury cars, and services such as telephone, entertainment, air transportation, and business licenses.

Excise taxes may be either a percent of the sale price of an item, a fixed amount for each unit sold, or a combination of the two. Table 7.2 shows the current federal excise taxes charged on several items.

Table 7.2   FEDERAL EXCISE TAXES*

Product or Service	Rate	Product or Service	Rate
Local telephone service	3%	Bows	11%
Cigarettes	39¢ per pack	Gasoline	18.4¢/gal.
Tires	$0.0945 for each 10 pounds	Diesel fuel	24.4¢/gal.
	of the maximum rated load	Aviation fuel	21.9¢/gal.
	capacity over 3500 pounds	Truck and trailer, chassis	12%
Air transportation	7.5%	and bodies	
International air travel	$15.40 per person	Inland waterways fuel	20¢/gal.
Air freight	6.25%	Ship passenger tax	$3/passenger
Fishing rods	10%	Vaccines	$0.75 per dose

Source: Publication 510, I.R.S., Excise Taxes for 2008.

*In addition to the federal excise taxes shown here, there are a number of additional excise taxes that apply to alcoholic beverages, tobacco products, and firearms. Special ATF forms are used by businesses when selling these products.

Objective

6   *Find the Total Cost Including Sales Tax and Excise Tax.*   Excise taxes are added to the price of an item in addition to sales tax. The excise tax is calculated on the base price of the item before sales tax is added. The amount of the excise tax is not subject to sales tax.

EXAMPLE 4   Finding the Total Cost with Sales and Excise Taxes

The purchasing manager of a large sporting goods chain orders 1230 fishing rods. The marketing manager expects to sell the fishing rods at an average price of $26.40, not including excise or sales taxes. The excise tax is 10% of the average price and sales taxes average 7.75% in that part of the country. Find the total revenue expected from the sale of all of the fishing rods, including all taxes.

Solution   First, find the total revenue per fishing rod.

$$\text{Excise tax per rod} = \$26.40 \times 10\% = \$2.64$$
$$\text{Sales tax per rod} = \$26.40 \times 7.75\% = \$2.05$$
$$\text{Total revenue per rod} = \$26.40 + \$2.64 + \$2.05 = \$31.09$$

Then, find the total revenue expected from the sale of all 1230 fishing rods.

$$\text{Total revenue} = 1230 \times \$31.09 = \$38,240.70$$

Excise and sales taxes are applied separately to the price of the item. So, another way to work this problem is to first add the two tax rates together ($10\% + 7.75\% = 17.75\%$) and then apply this rate to the price of the item.

$$\text{Excise tax} + \text{Sales tax} = 17.75\% \text{ of } \$26.40$$
$$= \$4.69$$

This method results in the exact total revenue.

7.1	Exercises

SALES AND EXCISE TAX   Find (a) the amount of sales tax, (b) the amount of excise tax, and (c) the total sale price including taxes in each of the following problems.

	Sale Price	Sales Tax Rate	Excise Tax Rate
1.	$76.20	3%	11%
2.	$59.80	6%	10%
3.	$47.70	4.5%	3%
4.	$21.15	8.25%	12%
5.	$148.50	5%	18.4¢/gal.; 165 gal.

	Sale Price	Sales Tax Rate	Excise Tax Rate
6.	$216.75	3%	14¢ gal.; 190 gal.
7.	$822.18	7%	12%
8.	$648.52	4%	10%
9.	$29,400	6.25%	$3/person; 168 people
10.	$57,552	4.5%	$3/person; 218 people

SALES TAX COMPUTATIONS   Find the sale price and total cost when given the amount of sales tax and the sales tax rate. Round to the nearest cent.

	Amount of Sales Tax	Sales Tax Rate
11.	$9.60	6%
12.	$4.58	5%
13.	$6.30	4%
14.	$21.84	8%
15.	$21.45	6.5%
16.	$58.00	7.25%
17.	$63.84	5%
18.	$22.32	4%

SALES TAX APPLICATIONS   Find the amount of the sale before sales tax was added and the amount of sales tax in each of the following. Round to the nearest cent.

	Total Sale	Sales Tax Rate
19.	$107.31	5%
20.	$273.92	7%
21.	$551.52	6%
22.	$312.66	5.5%
23.	$20.60	4.25%
24.	$85.28	4%
25.	$333.90	6%
26.	$1352.01	3%
27.	$2945.76	7%
28.	$4469.64	5%

29. What is the sales tax where you live? Is there a different tax rate in a county or city near you? Explain why this difference exists.

30. List three items that you, your family, or your employer purchased within the last year on which an excise tax was paid. (See Objective 5.)

Solve the following application problems.

31. **ARCHERY EQUIPMENT** Open Range Archery sells an archery set for $119.80. If sales tax is 6% and the excise tax is 11%, find (a) the amount of the sales tax, (b) the amount of the excise tax, and (c) the total sale including sales tax and excise tax.

32. **TRUCK PURCHASE** Cross Town Trucking pays $43,135.20 for a truck. If sales tax is 7% and excise tax is 12%, find (a) the amount of the sales tax, (b) the amount of the excise tax, and (c) the total price including sales tax and excise tax.

33. **MOUNTAIN BICYCLE PURCHASE** The sales tax on a mountain bike is $19.39. If the sales tax rate is $7\frac{1}{2}$%, find the sales price of the mountain bike.

34. **HARLEY-DAVIDSON** Sales tax on a motorcycle was $1584. If the tax rate was 8.25%, find the sales price of the motorcycle.

35. **LAPTOP COMPUTER PURCHASE** The price of a Dell laptop computer is $1350, including an 8% sales tax. Find the sales price before tax.

36. **FLIGHT TO AFRICA** Jeb Britney visits his son in the Peace Corps in Cameroon, Africa. The cost of the flight is $1645 before taxes. Sales taxes are 8% and the excise tax rate is given in Table 7.2 for air transportation. Find the total cost including the international air travel fee also in Table 7.2.

37. **CHARTER PLANE** A group of retired people charter an airplane for a round-trip from Houston, Texas, to Paris, France. The cost of each ticket is $462 not including a 6.5% sales tax and an excise tax as given in Table 7.2 for air transportation. Find the total cost for everyone given that 108 people sign up for the trip. (*Hint:* Don't forget the international air travel fee also in Table 7.2.)

38. **TROPICAL FISH SALES** The Tropical Fish Place has total receipts for the day of $875.43. This includes 6.5% sales tax on all sales. Find the amount that is sales tax.

39. **EMPLOYEE MATH ERROR** At the close of business one day, Mike Roche, a new employee, totaled the amount in the cash register and found $1908.01. He multiplied this sum by the sales tax rate of $8\frac{1}{2}$% to find the amount of sales tax. This procedure is incorrect. Find (a) the correct amount of sales tax and (b) the amount of error made by Roche.

40. **TAX OVERPAYMENT** Santiago Rowland has total daily receipts of $1856. His lounge manager multiplies this total by 5.5%, the tax rate in the area. This procedure is incorrect. Find (a) the correct amount of sales tax and (b) the amount of error made by the manager.

41. **CIGARETTE SALES** Ryman Market purchased 800 packs of cigarettes last week for $2.35 per pack. Note that the store does not have to pay sales taxes when purchasing the cigarettes since sales taxes are paid by the final buyer. Find the total cost of buying the 800 packs including excise tax.

42. **JET FUEL** Bombay Aviation purchased 850,000 gallons of aviation fuel at a cost of $3.48 per gallon. Find the total cost including excise tax assuming no sales tax is paid.

43. **VACCINES** The manager of a very active free clinic in Los Angeles anticipates giving 22,000 vaccines in the coming year. Find the total excise tax.

44. **GASOLINE TAX** An accountant at a corporation wants to know the amount of excise taxes the firm pays on behalf of their outside salespeople. The accountant estimates the firm purchased 4909 gallons of gasoline last year. Find the excise tax.

7.2	Property Tax

OBJECTIVES

1　*Understand fair market value and find assessed valuation.*

2　*Use the tax rate formula.*

3　*Use the formula for property tax.*

4　*Express tax rates in percent, dollars per $100, dollars per $1000, and mills.*

5　*Find taxes given the assessed valuation and the tax rate.*

6　*Find the assessed valuation given the tax rate and the tax.*

7　*Find the tax rate given the assessed valuation and the tax.*

Virtually everywhere in the nation, the owners of **real property** such as homes or land pay a property tax every year based on the value of their property. In many areas **personal property** (such as mobile homes, furnishings, appliances, motor homes, trailers, boats, and other non–real estate items) is also taxed. Some areas handle these two taxes separately, while others combine them. The money raised by this property tax is used to provide services in the local community, such as police and fire protection, roads, schools, and parks.

　　Table 7.3 shows property tax rates on homes as a percent of the value of the home for a few states. Note that states often choose to get their funding from different sources. For example, California has low property taxes but high state income tax rates. On the other hand, Texas has high property taxes but no state income tax. Due to revenues from abundant oil and gas production, Alaska has no state income tax, low property taxes, and no sales taxes. Alaska even gives rebates to its citizens. However, some cities in Alaska levy and collect sales taxes on sales within the city.

Table 7.3　PROPERTY TAX RATES ON HOMES (2009)

State	Annual Tax as a Percent of Home Value
Arizona	0.52%
California	0.50%
Florida	0.80%
Georgia	0.75%
Illinois	1.53%
Michigan	1.38%
Nebraska	1.74%
Pennsylvania	1.39%
Texas	1.84%
Wisconsin	1.74%

Source: Data from www.taxfoundation.org.

NOTE　Although churches and nonprofit charitable organizations are exempt from both property taxes and income taxes, the individuals who work for these organizations are required to pay these taxes.

Objective

1　*Understand Fair Market Value and Find Assessed Valuation.*　The first step in calculating the property tax on real estate is to get the property assessed. In this process, a local official, called the assessor, makes an estimate of the **fair market value** of the property, the price for which the property could reasonably be expected to be sold. The **assessed valuation** of the property is then found by multiplying the fair market value by a certain percent called the **assessment rate**. The percent that is used varies from location to location.

In some areas assessed valuation is 25% of fair market value, while in other areas, the assessed valuation is 40% to 60% or even 100% of fair market value. Occasionally, different rates will be used for homes and for businesses. In theory, this step is unnecessary in calculating property tax. However, using an assessed valuation that is a percent of fair market value has become an accepted practice over the years.

NOTE   The assessed value of a property is often far below the fair market value. Assessed value only has meaning when calculating the property taxes. It is not used for any other purpose.

EXAMPLE 1   Finding the Assessed Value of Property

Find the assessed valuation for the following pieces of property owned by Lynn Colgin.

(a) Fair market value, $112,000; assessment rate (percent), 25%

(b) Fair market value, $1,382,500; assessment rate (percent), 60%

Solution   Multiply the fair market value by the assessment rate.

(a) $112,000 \times 0.25 = $28,000$ assessed valuation

(b) $1,382,500 \times 0.60 = $829,500$ assessed valuation

■

NOTE   Property is often reassessed every few years, especially in areas with rapidly increasing or decreasing property values.

Objective

2   *Use the Tax Rate Formula.*   After calculating the assessed valuation of all the taxable property in an area and determining the amount of money needed to provide the necessary services (the budget), the agency responsible for levying the tax announces the annual **property tax rate**. This tax rate is determined by the following formula.

$$R = \frac{P}{B}$$

$$\text{Tax rate} = \frac{\text{Total tax amount needed}}{\text{Total assessed value}}$$

EXAMPLE 2   Finding the Tax Rate on Property

Find the tax rate on property that is needed to generate the total tax amounts shown.

	Total Tax Amount Needed	Total Assessed Value
(a)	$1,105,200	$36,840,000
(b)	$1,900,800	$86,400,000

Solution   In each situation, divide the total tax amount needed by the total assessed value.

(a) $1,105,200 \div $36,840,000 = 3.0\%$ (b) $1,900,800 \div $86,400,000 = 2.2\%$

■

NOTE   Some states reduce property taxes on homes to make home ownership more affordable. Some further reduce property taxes on homes owned by individuals who are elderly or disabled.

Senior Fights High Property Taxes

Tom and Becky Smith purchased their home in 1989. Tom retired from his engineering job in 2009 after being diagnosed with lung cancer. He died this year. His 66-year-old widow Becky is trying to figure out how to pay the bills, including the medical bills and the property taxes. The property taxes on their home have increased from $407 per year to $6870 per year in the 20+ years they have owned the home. So, Becky has decided to protest . . .

Objective

3 *Use the Formula for Property Tax.* Property tax rates are expressed in different ways in different parts of the country. However, property tax is always found with the formula

$$P = R \times B$$

Tax = Tax rate × Assessed valuation

Objective

4 *Express Tax Rates in Percent, Dollars per $100, Dollars per $1000, and Mills.*

Percent. Some areas express tax rates as a percent of assessed valuation. The tax on some acreage with an assessed valuation of $86,500 at a tax rate of 4.87% is found as follows.

$$\text{Tax} = 0.0487 \times \$86,500 = \$4212.55$$

Dollars per $100. In other areas, the rate is expressed as a number of dollars per $100 of assessed valuation. For example, the rate might be expressed as $11.42 per $100 of assessed valuation. Assuming a tax rate of $11.42 per $100, find the tax on a piece of land having an assessed valuation of $42,000 as follows. First divide the assessed valuation by 100 by moving the decimal point two places to the left to find the number of hundreds in $42,000.

$$\$42,000 = 420 \text{ hundreds} \quad \text{Move the decimal two places to the left.}$$

Then, find the tax.

$$\text{Tax} = \text{Tax rate} \times \text{Number of hundreds of valuation}$$
$$= \$11.42 \times 420 = \$4796.40$$

Dollars per $1000. In other areas, the tax rate is expressed as a number of dollars per $1000 of assessed valuation. If the tax rate is $98.12 per $1000, a piece of property having an assessed valuation of $197,000 would be taxed as follows.

$$\$197,000 = 197 \text{ thousands} \quad \text{Move the decimal three places to the left.}$$
$$\text{Tax} = \$98.12 \times 197 = \$19,329.64$$

Mills. Finally, some areas express tax rates in mills, where a **mill** is one-tenth of a cent, or one-thousandth of a dollar. For example, a tax rate might be expressed as 46 mills per dollar, or $0.046 per dollar of assessed evaluation. The tax on a property having an assessed valuation of $81,000, at a tax rate of 46 mills follows.

$$\text{Tax} = 0.046 \times \$81,000 \quad 46 \text{ mills} = \$0.046$$
$$= \$3726$$

Table 7.4 shows the same tax rates written in the four different systems. Although expressed differently, they are equivalent tax rates.

Table 7.4	WRITING TAX RATES IN FOUR SYSTEMS		
Percent	**Per $100**	**Per $1000**	**In Mills**
12.52%	$12.52	$125.20	125.2
3.2%	$3.20	$32.00	32
9.87%	$9.87	$98.70	98.7

Objective

5 *Find Taxes Given the Assessed Valuation and the Tax Rate.* Property taxes are found by multiplying the tax rate by the assessed valuation, as shown in the following example. Regardless of assessment rate or tax rate, property owners are concerned with the actual tax.

EXAMPLE 3 **Finding the Property Tax**

Find the taxes on each of the following pieces of property. Assessed valuations and tax rates are given.

(a) $58,975; 8.4%   (b) $875,400; $7.82 per $100

(c) $129,600; $64.21 per $1000   (d) $221,750; 94 mills

Solution Multiply tax rate by the assessed valuation.

(a) 8.4% = 0.084

$$\text{Tax} = \text{Tax rate} \times \text{Assessed valuation}$$
$$\text{Tax} = 0.084 \times \$58,975 = \$4953.90$$

(b) $875,400 = 8754 hundreds

$$\text{Tax} = \$7.82 \times 8754 = \$68,456.28$$

(c) $129,600 = 129.6 thousands

$$\text{Tax} = \$64.21 \times 129.6 = \$8321.62$$

(d) 94 mills = 0.094

$$\text{Tax} = 0.094 \times \$221,750 = \$20,844.50$$

Objective

6 *Find the Assessed Valuation Given the Tax Rate and the Tax.* The tax formula can also be used to find the assessed valuation when given the amount of tax and the tax rate.

EXAMPLE 4 **Finding the Assessed Valuation**

The county property tax on a car wash in Boden County is $1024. If the tax rate is $1.65 per $100, find the assessed valuation.

Solution Use the formula for finding tax.

$$\text{Tax} = \text{Tax rate} \times \text{Assessed valuation}$$
$$\$1024 = \$1.65 \times \text{Assessed valuation}$$
$$\frac{\$1024}{\$1.65} = \text{Assessed valuation} \qquad \text{Divide by \$1.65.}$$
$$620.61 \text{ hundreds} = \text{Assessed valuation}$$

The assessed valuation is $62,061 ($620.61 × 100).

■■▨ Scientific
▨▨ Calculator
▨ Approach

The calculator solution to Example 4 is as follows.

1024 ÷ 1.65 × 100 = 62061   Rounded to the nearest dollar.

NOTE The total property tax is usually the sum of taxes from several different taxing entities, including state, school district, county, city, and perhaps even from local community college districts.

Objective

7 *Find the Tax Rate Given the Assessed Valuation and the Tax.* The tax rate may be found by using the tax formula when the assessed valuation and the amount of tax are given.

EXAMPLE 5 **Finding the Tax Rate Given Assessed Valuation and Tax**

A commercial property in Hampton County has an assessed valuation of $480,000 and an annual property tax of $14,500. Find the tax rate per $1000.

Solution Use the formula for finding tax.

$$\text{Tax} = \text{Tax rate} \times \text{Assessed valuation}$$

The assessed valuation is 480 thousands ($480,000 ÷ 1000).

$$\$14,500 = \text{Tax rate} \times 480$$

$$\frac{\$14,500}{480} = \text{Tax rate} \qquad \text{Divide by 480.}$$

$$\$30.21 = \text{Tax rate per } \$1000$$

The tax rate per $1000 is $30.21.

■

7.2 | **Exercises**

ASSESSED VALUATION Find the assessed valuation for each of the following pieces of property.

Fair Market Value	Rate of Assessment
1. $341,200	40%
2. $136,500	50%
3. $173,800	35%
4. $587,300	42%
5. $1,300,500	25%
6. $2,450,000	80%

PROPERTY TAX RATES   Find the tax rate for the following. Write the tax rate as a percent rounded to the nearest tenth.

Total Tax Amount Needed	Total Assessed Value
7. $12,342,000	$220,440,000
8. $8,650,000	$346,000,000
9. $12,480,000	$337,297,297
10. $2,751,375	$108,750,000
11. $1,224,000	$40,800,000
12. $2,941,500	$81,700,000

TAX RATE COMPARISON   Complete the following list comparing tax rates.

	Percent	Per $100	Per $1000	In Mills
13.	(a) _____ %	(b) _____	(c) _____	28
14.	(a) _____ %	$6.75	(b) _____	(c) _____
15.	2.41%	(a) _____	(b) _____	(c) _____
16.	7.42%	(a) _____	(b) _____	(c) _____
17.	(a) _____ %	$7.08	(b) _____	(c) _____
18.	(a) _____ %	(b) _____	$35	(c) _____

19. What is the difference between fair market value and assessed value? How is the assessment rate used when finding the assessed value? (See Objective 1.)

20. Select any tax rate and express it as a percent. Write this tax rate in three additional equivalent forms and explain what each form means. (See Objective 4.)

FINDING PROPERTY TAX   Find the tax for each of the following.

Assessed Valuation	Tax Rate
21. $86,200	$6.80 per $100
22. $41,300	$46.40 per $1000
23. $685,400	6.93%
24. $128,200	42 mills
25. $248,000	$1.80 per $100
26. $38,250	$89.70 per $1000

ASSESSED VALUE, TAX RATE, AND TAX   Find the missing quantity.

	Assessed Valuation	Tax Rate	Tax
27.	$49,250	_____ %	$2856.50
28.	_____	$7.18 per $100	$15,652.40
29.	$73,800	85 mills	_____
30.	_____	$48.18 per $1000	$1903.11
31.	$152,680	_____ per $100	$8015.70
32.	$435,500	37.6 mills	_____
33.	_____	4.3%	$10,182.40
34.	$96,200	_____ per $1000	$3367

Solve the following application problems. Round percents to the nearest tenth of a percent.

35. **RETAIL CENTER** Wilma James owns a retail center with many different shops that has a fair market value of $2,870,000. Property in the area is assessed at 60% of market value and the property tax is $58,400. Find the tax rate as a percent of assessed value.

36. **MEDICAL CLINIC** Dr. Robertson owns a clinic that is occupied by physicians and their medical equipment. The building has a fair market value of $1,880,000 and property is assessed at 50% of market value. Given a property tax of $52,400, find the tax rate as a percent of assessed value.

37. **FM RADIO BROADCASTING** A new FM radio station broadcasts from a building having a fair market value of $734,000. The building is in an area where property is assessed at 25% of market value and the tax rate is $75.30 per $1000 of assessed value. Find the property tax.

38. **ICE SKATING RINK** The building containing a small ice skating rink has a fair market value of $628,000, not including the value of the equipment inside the building. Property is assessed at 35% and the tax rate is $42 per $1000 of assessed value. Find the property tax.

39. **COMMERCIAL PROPERTY** Plaza Office Park has a fair market value of $5,700,000. Property is assessed in the area at 25% of market value. The tax rate is $14.10 per $100 of assessed valuation. Find the property tax.

40. **HARLEY-DAVIDSON SHOP** Harley-Davidson of Lincoln has property with a fair market value of $1,037,200. The property is located in an area that is assessed at 15% of market value. The tax rate for the local school district is $7.35 per $100. Find the school district property tax.

41. **COUNTY PROPERTY TAX** In one county, property is assessed at 40% of market value, with a tax rate of 32.1 mills. In a second county, property is assessed at 24% of market value with a tax rate of 50.2 mills. Custom Cabinets is trying to decide where to place a building with a fair market value of $380,000. (a) Which county would charge the lower property tax? (b) Find the amount saved each year.

42. **PROPERTY TAX COMPARISON** Property taxes vary from one county to the next. In one county, property is assessed at 30% of market value, with a tax rate of 45.6 mills. In a second county, property is assessed at 48% of market value, with a tax rate of 29.3 mills. Misty Arce is trying to decide where to build a home that she expects to have a market value of $210,000. (a) Which county would charge the lower property tax? (b) Find the annual amount saved.

43. **MANSION** Last year the property tax on a mansion was $28,600 at a tax rate of $12.50 per $1000. After a reassessment this year, the assessed value was increased by $140,000 and the property tax due is $31,100. Find the percent increase in the tax rate.

44. **INDUSTRIAL PROPERTY TAX** Last year the property tax on a small warehouse was $3042, and the tax rate was $3.60 per $100. After a reassessment this year, the assessed value was increased by $10,500 and the property tax due is $3705. Find the percent of increase in the tax rate. Round to the nearest tenth of a percent.

45. **UNDEVELOPED LAND TAX** A commercial corner lot was assessed at $45,000, and the tax was $1327.50. The following year the property tax increased to $1353.75 while the tax rate decreased by $0.10 per $100. Find the amount of increase in the assessed value of the commercial lot.

46. **INVESTMENT PROPERTY TAX** An investment property was assessed at $240,000, and the tax was $5400. The following year the property tax increased to $5805, while the tax rate decreased by $1.00 per $1000. Find the amount of increase in the assessed value of the property.

7.3 Personal Income Tax

OBJECTIVES

1 *Know the four steps that determine tax liability.*

2 *Identify information needed to find adjusted gross income.*

3 *Calculate adjusted gross income.*

4 *Know the standard deduction amounts.*

5 *Know the tax rates.*

6 *List possible itemized deductions to find taxable income.*

7 *Calculate income tax.*

8 *Determine a balance due or a refund from the Internal Revenue Service.*

9 *Prepare a 1040A and a Schedule 1 federal tax form.*

Income taxes are calculated based on income. They are a source of revenue for the federal government, most states, and many local governments. The pie charts in Figure 7.2 show the major categories of income and outlays for the United States government. Notice that personal income taxes and corporate income taxes combine to generate 50% of the government's income. Social Security, Medicare, unemployment, and other retirement taxes are an additional 35% of the government's income. The government's largest outlay is Social Security, Medicare, and other retirement, which amounts to 38% of the total outlay.

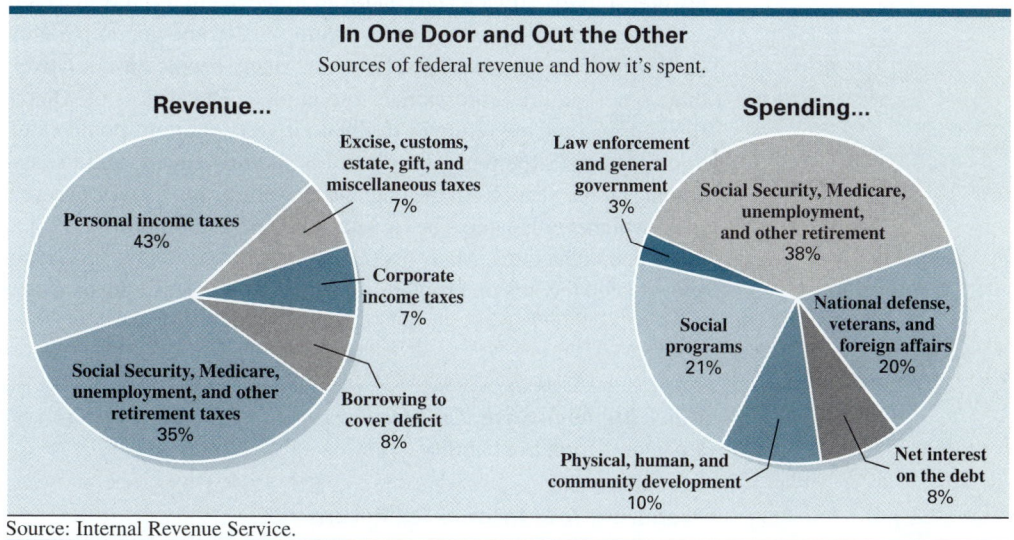

Source: Internal Revenue Service.

Source: www.irs.gov.

Figure 7.2 Major Categories of Federal Income and Outlays

Some people believe that individuals with high incomes pay little or no income taxes. Figure 7.3 shows that the top 1% of all earners pay an average of 31.2% of their income in federal taxes, or about $1 out of every $3 earned. Of course, this does not include the state, property, sales, or gasoline taxes paid by these same individuals. In fact, the top 1% of all earners pay more in federal income tax than the lowest 90% of all earners combined!

The **Internal Revenue Service (IRS)** is the organization in the U.S. government that is responsible for collecting income taxes from individuals and businesses. Most working adults are required to file income tax returns with the IRS each year. Married couples usually submit one joint tax return showing income and deductions for both spouses, but spouses can file separately. The most recent forms and tax rates can be found on the IRS Web site at www.irs.gov. Last year, more than 80 million families, or about 80% of the number filing in the United States,

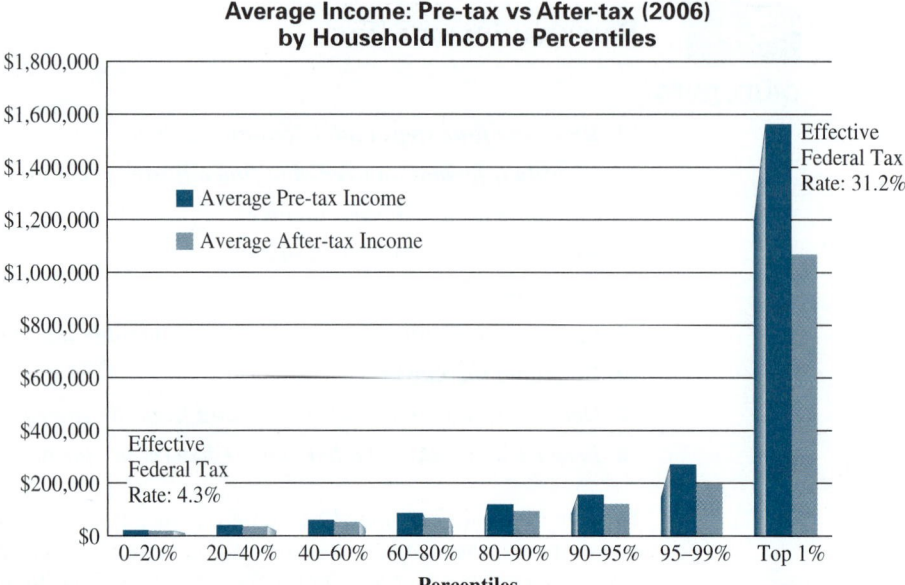

Average Income: Pre-tax vs After-tax (2006) by Household Income Percentiles

Source: Congressional Budget Office.

Figure 7.3

filed electronically. Filing electronically allows most filers access to free, commercial, online tax preparation software and can result in receiving refunds in as few as 10 days.

There are thousands of rules relating to income tax preparation and many different forms, each with its own instructions. However, many people have relatively simple income tax returns that do not require professionals to complete. Regardless of whether you use a professional to file your income tax return or if you do it yourself, you should carefully save all records related to income and expenses. These records should be kept until the statute of limitations runs out, which is three years from the date the tax return was filed or two years from the date the tax was paid, whichever is later. The IRS can audit you during this period and they require proof of income and deductions. Many accountants recommend you keep records for seven years, but you should keep records on property such as your home as long as they are needed.

Objective

1   *Know the Four Steps That Determine Tax Liability.*   There are four basic steps in finding a person's total tax liability.

Preparing Your Income Tax Return

Step 1 Find the adjusted gross income (AGI) for the year.

Step 2 Find the taxable income.

Step 3 Find the tax.

Step 4 Check to see if a refund is due or if more money is owed to the government.

Objective

2   *Identify Information Needed to Find Adjusted Gross Income.*   The first step in finding personal income tax is to find **adjusted gross income**. Adjusted gross income is the total of all income, less certain adjustments. Employers are required to send employees **W-2 forms** showing wages paid, federal income taxes withheld, Social Security tax withheld, and Medicare tax withheld. Other types of income such as interest, dividends, and self-employment income are shown on **1099 forms**, which are also mailed to each individual. Sample W-2 and 1099-INT forms are shown.

22222	Void ☐	**a** Employee's social security number	For Official Use Only ▶ OMB No. 1545-0008	

b Employer identification number (EIN) 94-1287319		**1** Wages, tips, other compensation $24,738.41	**2** Federal income tax withheld $3275.60

c Employer's name, address, and ZIP code

The Doll House
1568 Liberty Heights Ave.
Baltimore, MD 21230

3 Social security wages $24,738.41	**4** Social security tax withheld $1533.78
5 Medicare wages and tips $24,738.41	**6** Medicare tax withheld $358.71
7 Social security tips	**8** Allocated tips

d Control number 123-45-6789

| **9** Advance EIC payment | **10** Dependent care benefits |

e Employee's first name and initial Jennifer | Last name Crum | Suff.

11 Nonqualified plans	**12a** See instructions for box 12
13 Statutory employee ☐ Retirement plan ☐ Third-party sick pay ☐	**12b**
14 Other	**12c**
	12d

2136 Old Road
Towson, MD 21285

f Employee's address and ZIP code

15 State MD	Employer's state ID number 600-5076	**16** State wages, tips, etc.	**17** State income tax	**18** Local wages, tips, etc.	**19** Local income tax	**20** Locality name

Form **W-2** **Wage and Tax Statement**   **20**

Copy A For Social Security Administration — Send this entire page with Form W-3 to the Social Security Administration; photocopies are **not** acceptable.

Department of the Treasury—Internal Revenue Service
For Privacy Act and Paperwork Reduction Act Notice, see back of Copy D.
Cat. No. 10134D

9292   ☐ VOID   ☐ CORRECTED

PAYER'S name, street address, city, state, ZIP code, and telephone no. Employees Credit Union 2572 Brookhaven Drive Dundalk, MD 21222 301-125-3661	Payer's RTN (optional)	OMB No. 1545-0112	**Interest Income**

| **1** Interest income $ 1624.01 | **20** |
| **2** Early withdrawal penalty $ | Form **1099-INT** |

PAYER'S federal identification number 94-1287319	RECIPIENT'S identification number 123-45-6789	**3** Interest on U.S. Savings Bonds and Treas. obligations $	**Copy A** **For Internal Revenue Service Center** File with Form 1096.

RECIPIENT'S name Jennifer Crum

| **4** Federal income tax withheld $ | **5** Investment expenses $ |

Street address (including apt. no.) 2136 Old Road

| **6** Foreign tax paid $ | **7** Foreign country or U.S. possession |

For Privacy Act and Paperwork Reduction Act Notice, see the **2008 General Instructions for Forms 1099, 1098, 5498, and W-2G.**

City, state, and ZIP code Towson, MD 21285

| **8** Tax-exempt interest $ | **9** Specified private activity bond interest $ |

Account number (see instructions) | 2nd TIN not. ☐

Form **1099-INT**   Cat. No. 14410K   Department of the Treasury - Internal Revenue Service

260 Chapter 7 *Taxes*

Objective

3 *Calculate Adjusted Gross Income.*

Finding Adjusted Gross Income

1. **Add** amounts from all W-2 and 1099 forms along with dividends, capital gains, unemployment compensation, and tips or other employee compensation.
2. From this sum, subtract adjustments such as contributions to a *regular* **individual retirement account (IRA)** or alimony payments.

EXAMPLE **1** **Finding Adjusted Gross Income (AGI)**

As an assistant manager at The Doll House, Jennifer Crum earned $24,738.41 last year and $1624.01 in interest from her credit union (see her W-2 and 1099 forms). She had $1500 in IRA contributions. Find her adjusted gross income.

Solution

$$\text{Adjusted gross income} = \text{wages} + \text{interest} - \text{IRA contribution}$$
$$= \$24{,}738.41 + \$1624.01 - \$1500$$
$$= \$24{,}862.42$$

NOTE A copy of all W-2 forms must be sent to the Internal Revenue Service along with the completed tax forms. However, the IRS does not require the taxpayer to send in copies of 1099 forms.

Objective

4 *Know the Standard Deduction Amounts.* Most people are almost finished at this point. A taxpayer next subtracts *the larger of* either the itemized deductions or the standard deduction from adjusted gross income. Itemized deductions are described in Objective 5 in this section and are associated with several limitations based on adjusted gross income. The **standard deduction** amounts change each year, so be sure to use the most recent numbers when preparing your income taxes. Here are the most recent standard deductions.

$5,350—Single taxpayers

$10,700—Married couples filing jointly or qualifying widower

$5,350—Married taxpayers filing separately

$7,850—Head of household

NOTE Additional standard deductions are given for taxpayers and dependents who are blind or 65 years of age or older.

Head of household refers to an unmarried person who provides a home for other people such as a dependent child or a dependent parent of the taxpayer.

The next step is to find the number of **personal exemptions**. One exemption is allowed for yourself, another for your spouse if filing a joint return, and yet another exemption for each child or other dependent. The number of exemptions does not depend on whether the filing status is single or married. The deduction for personal exemptions is $3400 times the number of exemptions. Here are some examples.

	Number of Exemptions	Personal Exemption(s)
Single individual	1	$1 \times \$3400 = \$3400$
Married couple filing jointly, with 3 children	5	$5 \times \$3400 = \$17,000$
Single woman, head of household with 2 dependent children	3	$3 \times \$3400 = \$10,200$

Taxable income is found by subtracting the sum of the standard (or itemized) deduction amount and personal exemptions from adjusted gross income. Taxes are then calculated based on taxable income, as shown next.

NOTE Both the standard deduction amounts and the personal exemption amounts change each year. It is always important to use current information.

Objective

5 *Know the Tax Rates.* As shown in Table 7.4, income tax rates for individuals range from 10% to 35% depending on taxable income and filing status. Assume a single filer has a taxable income of $37,300. According to the tax rate schedule for a single filer, $37,300 falls in the over $31,850, but not over $77,100 row. Therefore, find the tax as follows.

$$\text{Federal income tax} = \$4386.25 + 25\% \text{ of the amount over } \$31,850$$
$$= \$4386.25 + 0.25 \times (\$37,300 - \$31,850)$$
$$= \$5748.75$$

The 25% tax rate applies only to the amount above $31,850 and not to the entire taxable income.

EXAMPLE 2 Finding Taxable Income and the Income Tax Amount

Find the taxable income and tax for each.

(a) Peter Chin, single, 1 exemption; adjusted gross income $32,480
(b) The Richfields, married, filing jointly, 4 exemptions; adjusted gross income $68,250

Solution

(a)

	Adjusted	Standard	Personal
Taxable income =	Gross Income −	Deduction −	Exemption(s)
Taxable income =	$32,480 −	$5350 −	$1 \times \$3400$
	= $23,730		

$$\text{Tax} = \$782.50 + 0.15 \times (\$23,730 - \$7825)$$
$$= \$3168.25$$

(b)

	Adjusted	Standard	Personal
Taxable income =	Gross Income −	Deduction −	Exemption(s)
Taxable income =	$68,250 −	$10,700 −	$4 \times \$3400$
	= $43,950		

$$\text{Tax} = \$1565 + 0.15 \times (\$43,950 - \$15,650)$$
$$= \$5810$$

Table 7.4   2008 TAX RATE SCHEDULES

Schedule X—Single

If taxable income is over–	But not over–	The tax is:
$0	$7,825	10% of the amount of $0
$7,825	$31,850	$782.50 plus 15% of the amount over $7,825
$31,850	$77,100	$4,386.25 plus 25% of the amount over $31,850
$77,100	$160,850	$15,698.75 plus 28% of the amount over $77,100
$160,850	$349,700	$39,148.75 plus 33% of the amount over $160,850
$349,700	no limit	$101,469.25 plus 35% of the amount over $349,700

Schedule Y-1—Married Filing Jointly or Qualifying Widow(er)

If taxable income is over–	But not over–	The tax is:
$0	$15,650	10% of the amount over $0
$15,650	$63,700	$1,565.00 plus 15% of the amount over $15,650
$63,700	$128,500	$8,772.50 plus 25% of the amount over $63,700
$128,500	$195,850	$24,972.50 plus 28% of the amount over $128,500
$195,850	$349,700	$43,830.50 plus 33% of the amount over $195,850
$349,700	no limit	$94,601.00 plus 35% of the amount over $349,700

Schedule Y-2—Married Filing Separately

If taxable income is over–	But not over–	The tax is:
$0	$7,825	10% of the amount over $0
$7,825	$31,850	$782.50 plus 15% of the amount over $7,825
$31,850	$64,250	$4,386.25 plus 25% of the amount over $31,850
$64,250	$97,925	$12,486.25 plus 28% of the amount over $64,250
$97,925	$174,850	$21,915.25 plus 33% of the amount over $97,925
$174,850	no limit	$47,300.50 plus 35% of the amount over $174,850

Schedule Z—Head of Household

If taxable income is over–	But not over–	The tax is:
$0	$11,200	10% of the amount over $0
$11,200	$42,650	$1,120.00 plus 15% of the amount over $11,200
$42,650	$110,100	$5,837.50 plus 25% of the amount over $42,650
$110,100	$178,350	$22,700.00 plus 28% of the amount over $110,100
$178,350	$349,700	$41,810.00 plus 33% of the amount over $178,350
$349,700	no limit	$98,355.50 plus 35% of the amount over $349,700

NOTE   When taxable income goes beyond the 15% tax rate amount, do not make the mistake of using the 25% tax rate on the entire amount of taxable income. Just apply the 25% rate to the amount over and above the amount listed in the table.

Objective

6   *List Possible Itemized Deductions to Find Taxable Income.*   Actually, taxpayers may deduct *the larger of* **itemized deductions** *or* the standard deduction from their adjusted gross income *before* finding taxable income. This is particularly applicable to individuals who own their own homes and pay mortgage interest and property taxes. The most common **tax deductions** for individuals are listed here. Business deductions differ from those for individuals.

Medical and dental expenses. Only medical and dental expenses exceeding 7.5% of adjusted gross income may be deducted. This deduction is effectively limited to catastrophic illnesses for most taxpayers. Expenses reimbursed by an insurance company are not deductible.

Taxes. Taxes that can be deducted include state and local income taxes, real estate taxes, and personal property taxes. Taxes that individuals cannot deduct include federal income taxes, excise taxes, and taxes on gasoline.

Interest. Home mortgage interest on the taxpayer's principal residence and a qualified second home is deductible. Other interest charges (such as credit-card interest) may *not* be deducted.

Contributions. Contributions to qualifying charities may be deducted.

Miscellaneous deductions. These expenses are deductible only to the extent that the total exceeds 2% of the taxpayer's adjusted gross income. They include the following: unreimbursed employee expenses, tax preparation fees, appraisal fees for tax purposes, and legal fees for tax planning or tax litigation.

> **NOTE**   The taxpayer may take the larger of the standard deduction or the itemized deductions. You must have documentation to show itemized expenses if you itemize.

Objective

7   *Calculate Income Tax.*   After the taxable income is determined, the amount of income tax must be found (see Objective 5).

EXAMPLE 3   Using Itemized Deductions to Find Taxable Income and Income Tax

Chris Kelly is single and has no dependents. He had an adjusted gross income of $26,735 last year. He had deductions of $1352 for other taxes, $4118 for mortgage interest, and $317 for charity. Find his taxable income and his income tax.

Solution

$$\text{Itemized deductions} = \$1352 + \$4118 + \$317 = \$5787$$

Kelly's itemized deductions of $5787 are larger than the $5350 standard deduction for a single person. Therefore, taxable income is adjusted gross income minus the itemized deductions minus the one personal exemption for being single with no dependents.

$$
\begin{aligned}
\text{Taxable income} &= \$26,735 - \underset{\substack{\text{Itemized} \\ \text{deductions}}}{\$5787} - 1 \times \underset{\substack{\text{Personal} \\ \text{exemption}}}{\$3400} = \$17,548 \\
\text{Income tax} &= \$782.50 + 15\% \text{ of amount over } \$7825 \\
&= \$782.50 + 0.15 \times (\$17,548 - \$7825) \\
&= \$2240.95
\end{aligned}
$$

Chris Kelly must pay $2240.95 in income taxes for the year.

> **NOTE**   The federal government demands that individuals pay taxes due. Not paying a tax can result in legal troubles, fines, and potentially the loss of an asset such as your home. Lying on a tax return is a criminal issue and may result in a prison sentence.

Objective

8   *Determine a Balance Due or a Refund from the Internal Revenue Service.*   A taxpayer may have paid more to the IRS than is due. Add up the total amount of income tax paid using the W-2 forms (usually no taxes are withheld on 1099 forms). If the amount withheld is greater than the tax owed, the taxpayer is entitled to a refund. If the amount withheld is less than the tax owed, then the taxpayer must send the difference along with the tax return to the IRS.

EXAMPLE 4 **Determining Tax Due or Refund**

Tim Owen works as an attorney and his wife stays at home with their young daughter. Last year Tim had an adjusted gross income of $94,800 and $820 was withheld from his paycheck each month for federal income taxes. The Owens file a joint return and use the standard deduction and 3 exemptions. Find either the amount of income taxes they must pay or the amount they overpaid.

Solution

Adjusted gross income	$94,800	
Standard deduction	− 10,700	Married filing jointly
Personal exemptions	− 10,200	3 exemptions × $3400
Taxable income	$73,900	

$$\text{Income tax} = \$8772.50 + 25\% \text{ of amount over } \$63,700$$
$$= \$8772.50 + 0.25 \times (\$73,900 - \$63,700)$$
$$= \$11,322.50$$

Total amount withheld last year = $820 × 12 = $9840
Amount owed to IRS = $11,322.50 − $9840 = $1482.50

The Owens must send a payment of $1482.50 with their tax return.

It is best to use the simplest form needed when filing with the IRS. The **1040EZ** is the simplest form and is used by many students, but many people are not allowed to use it. Here are the IRS guidelines to help you determine the appropriate form.

Form 1040EZ—You must

1. file single or married filing jointly;
2. claim no dependents;
3. have no adjustments to income;
4. claim no tax credit other than the Earned Income Credit;
5. be under age 65 and not blind at end of tax year;
6. have taxable income less than $100,000;
7. have income only from wages, salaries, tips, taxable scholarship, and unemployment compensation and taxable interest that does not exceed $1500;
8. claim no advanced Earned Income Credit payments;
9. not owe any taxes to a household employee; and
10. not owe any alternative minimum tax.

Form 1040A—You must

1. have income only from wages, salaries, tips, ordinary dividends, interest, capital gains, unemployment, pension plans, and certain other sources;
2. claim no adjustments other than educator expenses, IRA deduction, student loan interest, and tuition and fees;
3. not itemize deductions;
4. have a taxable income of less than $100,000; and
5. use only the following tax credits: child, education, earned income, and certain other credits.

Form 1040—Use this form if

1. taxable income is $100,000 or more;
2. income includes any of the following: unreported tips, self-employment earnings, income received as a partner or a shareholder in a Subchapter S corporation;
3. deductions are itemized; or
4. household employment taxes are owed.

Objective

9   *Prepare a 1040A and a Schedule 1 Federal Tax Form.*   Figure 7.4 shows that income taxes vary considerably by country and that married couples in many countries pay a far higher percent of their income in taxes than they do in the United States. Actually, income taxes in the United States are relatively low compared to many countries in the figure. However, many of the countries with higher taxes have more safety nets for employees, including higher unemployment benefits and coverage of medical expenses compared to the United States. So, generally countries with higher income tax rates offer more benefits and countries with lower levels of income taxes have fewer benefits.

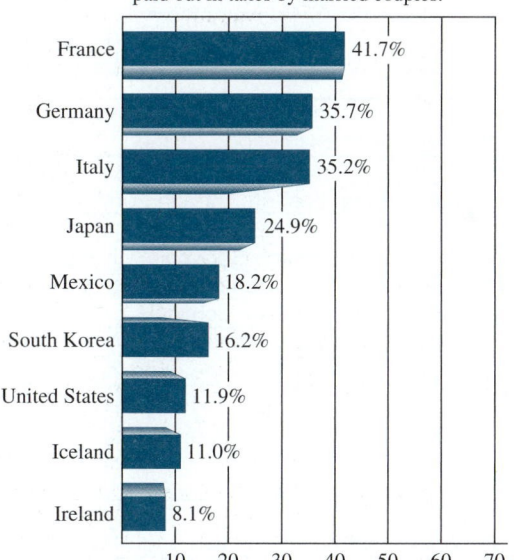

Comparing Income Taxes by Country (2006)
The average percent of gross income paid out in taxes by married couples.

Country	Percent
France	41.7%
Germany	35.7%
Italy	35.2%
Japan	24.9%
Mexico	18.2%
South Korea	16.2%
United States	11.9%
Iceland	11.0%
Ireland	8.1%

Source: Organization for Economic Cooperation and Development.

Figure 7.4

The next example shows how to complete an income tax return using **Form 1040A** and a **Schedule 1 (Form 1040A)**. When completing income tax forms and calculations, notice that all amounts may be rounded to the nearest dollar.

EXAMPLE 5   **Preparing a 1040A and a Schedule 1**

Jennifer Crum is single and claims one exemption. Her income appears on the W-2 and 1099 forms on page 259. Crum contributes $1500 to an IRA. Crum satisfies the requirements to use Form 1040A but must also fill out Schedule 1 (Form 1040A) since she has more than $1500 in interest.

Form	Department of the Treasury—Internal Revenue Service		
1040A	**U.S. Individual Income Tax Return**	**20**	IRS Use Only—Do not write or staple in this space.

Label
(See page 15.)

Use the IRS label.
Otherwise, please print or type.

L A B E L   H E R E

Your first name and initial	Last name		OMB No. 1545-0074
Jennifer	Crum		**Your social security number** 123 :45: 6789
If a joint return, spouse's first name and initial	Last name		**Spouse's social security number**
Home address (number and street). If you have a P.O. box, see page 15.		Apt. no.	▲ You **must** enter ▲ your SSN(s) above.
2136 Old Road			
City, town or post office, state, and ZIP code. If you have a foreign address, see page 15.			Checking a box below will not change your tax or refund.
Towson, MD 21285			

Presidential Election Campaign ▶ Check here if you, or your spouse if filing jointly, want $3 to go to this fund (see page 15) ▶ ☑ **You** ☐ **Spouse**

Filing status
Check only one box.

1 ☑ Single
2 ☐ Married filing jointly (even if only one had income)
3 ☐ Married filing separately. Enter spouse's SSN above and full name here. ▶
4 ☐ Head of household (with qualifying person). (See page 16.) If the qualifying person is a child but not your dependent, enter this child's name here. ▶ _____
5 ☐ Qualifying widow(er) with dependent child (see page 17)

Exemptions

If more than six dependents, see page 18.

6a ☑ **Yourself.** If someone can claim you as a dependent, **do not** check box 6a.
b ☐ **Spouse**
c **Dependents:**

(1) First name Last name	(2) Dependent's social security number	(3) Dependent's relationship to you	(4) ✓ if qualifying child for child tax credit (see page 18)
			☐
			☐
			☐
			☐
			☐
			☐

Boxes checked on 6a and 6b ___1___

No. of children on 6c who:
• lived with you _____
• did not live with you due to divorce or separation (see page 19) _____

Dependents on 6c not entered above _____

Add numbers on lines above ▶ [1]

d Total number of exemptions claimed.

Income

Attach Form(s) W-2 here. Also attach Form(s) 1099-R if tax was withheld.

If you did not get a W-2, see page 21.

Enclose, but do not attach, any payment.

7	Wages, salaries, tips, etc. Attach Form(s) W-2.	7	$24,738
8a	**Taxable** interest. Attach Schedule 1 if required.	8a	$1,624
b	**Tax-exempt** interest. **Do not** include on line 8a. 8b		
9a	Ordinary dividends. Attach Schedule 1 if required.	9a	
b	Qualified dividends (see page 22). 9b		
10	Capital gain distributions (see page 22).	10	
11a	IRA distributions. 11a	11b Taxable amount (see page 22). 11b	
12a	Pensions and annuities. 12a	12b Taxable amount (see page 23). 12b	
13	Unemployment compensation and Alaska Permanent Fund dividends.	13	
14a	Social security benefits. 14a	14b Taxable amount (see page 25). 14b	
15	Add lines 7 through 14b (far right column). This is your **total income.** ▶	15	$26,362

Adjusted gross income

16	Educator expenses (see page 25).	16		
17	IRA deduction (see page 27).	17	$1,500	
18	Student loan interest deduction (see page 29).	18		
19	Tuition and fees deduction. Attach Form 8917.	19		
20	Add lines 16 through 19. These are your **total adjustments.**	20		$1,500
21	Subtract line 20 from line 15. This is your **adjusted gross income.** ▶	21		$24,862

For Disclosure, Privacy Act, and Paperwork Reduction Act Notice, see page 74.   Cat. No. 11327A   Form **1040A** (2007)

Form 1040A (2007)   Page **2**

Tax, credits, and payments	**22**	Enter the amount from line 21 (adjusted gross income).	22	$24,862

23a Check if: ☐ **You** were born before January 2, 1943, ☐ Blind ☐ **Spouse** was born before January 2, 1943, ☐ Blind } **Total boxes checked ▶** 23a ☐

b If you are married filing separately and your spouse itemizes deductions, see page 30 and check here ▶ 23b ☐

Standard Deduction for—

• People who checked any box on line 23a or 23b **or** who can be claimed as a dependent, see page 30.

• All others:

Single or Married filing separately, $5,350

Married filing jointly or Qualifying widow(er), $10,700

Head of household, $7,850

24 Enter your **standard deduction** (see left margin).	24	$5,350
25 Subtract line 24 from line 22. If line 24 is more than line 22, enter -0-.	25	$19,512
26 If line 22 is $117,300 or less, multiply $3,400 by the total number of exemptions claimed on line 6d. If line 22 is over $117,300, see the worksheet on page 32.	26	$3,400
27 Subtract line 26 from line 25. If line 26 is more than line 25, enter -0-. This is your **taxable income.** ▶	27	$16,112
28 **Tax,** including any alternative minimum tax (see page 30).	28	$2,026

29 Credit for child and dependent care expenses. Attach Schedule 2.	29	
30 Credit for the elderly or the disabled. Attach Schedule 3.	30	
31 Education credits. Attach Form 8863.	31	
32 Child tax credit (see page 35). Attach Form 8901 if required.	32	
33 Retirement savings contributions credit. Attach Form 8880.	33	

34 Add lines 29 through 33. These are your **total credits.**	34	$0
35 Subtract line 34 from line 28. If line 34 is more than line 28, enter -0-.	35	$2,026
36 Advance earned income credit payments from Form(s) W-2, box 9.	36	
37 Add lines 35 and 36. This is your **total tax.** ▶	37	$2,026
38 Federal income tax withheld from Forms W-2 and 1099. 38 $3,276		

If you have a qualifying child, attach Schedule EIC.

39 2007 estimated tax payments and amount applied from 2006 return. 39		
40a **Earned income credit (EIC).** 40a $0		
b Nontaxable combat pay election. 40b		
41 Additional child tax credit. Attach Form 8812. 41		
42 Add lines 38, 39, 40a, and 41. These are your **total payments.** ▶	42	$3,276

Refund

Direct deposit? See page 52 and fill in 44b, 44c, and 44d or Form 8888.

43 If line 42 is more than line 37, subtract line 37 from line 42. This is the amount you **overpaid.**	43	$1,250
44a Amount of line 43 you want **refunded to you.** If Form 8888 is attached, check here ▶ ☐	44a	$1,250

▶ **b** Routing number `1 2 3 4 5 6 7 0 9` ▶ **c** Type: ☑ Checking ☐ Savings

▶ **d** Account number `5 5 4 1 1 0 0 0 1 1 0 0 5 9 0 0 1`

45 Amount of line 43 you want **applied to your 2008 estimated tax.** 45		$0

Amount you owe

46 **Amount you owe.** Subtract line 42 from line 37. For details on how to pay, see page 53. ▶	46	$0
47 Estimated tax penalty (see page 53). 47 $0		

Third party designee

Do you want to allow another person to discuss this return with the IRS (see page 54)? ☐ **Yes.** Complete the following. ☑ **No**

Designee's name ▶	Phone no. ▶ ( )	Personal identification number (PIN) ▶

Sign here

Joint return? See page 15. Keep a copy for your records.

Under penalties of perjury, I declare that I have examined this return and accompanying schedules and statements, and to the best of my knowledge and belief, they are true, correct, and accurately list all amounts and sources of income I received during the tax year. Declaration of preparer (other than the taxpayer) is based on all information of which the preparer has any knowledge.

Your signature	Date	Your occupation	Daytime phone number
Jennifer Crum	4/14/	Assistant manager	(410) 286-2594
Spouse's signature. If a joint return, **both** must sign.	Date	Spouse's occupation	

Paid preparer's use only

Preparer's signature ▶	Date	Check if self-employed ☐	Preparer's SSN or PTIN
Firm's name (or yours if self-employed), address, and ZIP code ▶		EIN	
		Phone no. ( )	

Form **1040A** (2007)

Schedule 1
(Form 1040A)

Department of the Treasury—Internal Revenue Service

Interest and Ordinary Dividends for Form 1040A Filers

20

OMB No. 1545-0074

Name(s) shown on Form 1040A

Jennifer Crum

Your social security number

123 ¦45¦ 6789

Part I

Interest

(See back of schedule and the instructions for Form 1040A, line 8a.)

Note. If you received a Form 1099-INT, Form 1099-OID, or substitute statement from a brokerage firm, enter the firm's name and the total interest shown on that form.

			Amount	
1	List name of payer. If any interest is from a seller-financed mortgage and the buyer used the property as a personal residence, see back of schedule and list this interest first. Also, show that buyer's social security number and address.			
	Employees Credit Union	1	$1,624	
2	Add the amounts on line 1.	2	$1,624	
3	Excludable interest on series EE and I U.S. savings bonds issued after 1989. Attach Form 8815.	3		
4	Subtract line 3 from line 2. Enter the result here and on Form 1040A, line 8a.	4	$1,624	

Part II

Ordinary dividends

(See back of schedule and the instructions for Form 1040A, line 9a.)

Note. If you received a Form 1099-DIV or substitute statement from a brokerage firm, enter the firm's name and the ordinary dividends shown on that form.

			Amount	
5	List name of payer.	5		
6	Add the amounts on line 5. Enter the total here and on Form 1040A, line 9a.	6		

For Paperwork Reduction Act Notice, see Form 1040A instructions.   Cat. No. 12075R   **Schedule 1 (Form 1040A) 2007**

7.3	**Exercises**

ADJUSTED GROSS INCOME Find the adjusted gross income for each of the following.

Name	Income from Jobs	Interest	Misc. Income	Dividend Income	Adjustments to Income	Adjusted Gross Income
1. R. Jacob	$22,840	$234	$1209	$48	$1200	
2. K. Chandler	$38,156	$285	$73	$542	$317	
3. The Hanks	$21,380	$625	$139	$184	$618	
4. The Jazwinskis	$33,650	$722	$375	$218	$473	
5. The Brashers	$38,643	$95	$188	$105	$0	
6. The Ameens	$41,379	$1174	$536	$186	$2258	

TAXABLE INCOME AND TAX Find the amount of taxable income and the tax for each of the following. Use the tax rate schedule (Table 7.4). The letter following the name indicates marital status. Assume that all married people are filing jointly. Round figures to nearest dollar.

Name	Number of Exemptions	Adjusted Gross Income	Total Itemized Deductions	Taxable Income	Tax Owed
7. R. Rodriguez, S	1	$32,400	$2398		
8. Lesly Pacas, S	1	$22,770	$898		
9. The Cooks, M	3	$38,751	$5968		
10. The Loveridges, M	7	$52,532	$6972		
11. The Jordans, M	5	$71,800	$12,200		
12. G. Clarke, S	1	$48,600	$6080		
13. D. Collins, S	2	$35,350	$6240		
14. K. Tang, Head of Household	2	$93,240	$11,800		
15. B. Kammerer, S	1	$43,500	$5107		
16. G. Nation, M	3	$153,420	$11,700		
17. B. Albert, Head of Household	2	$62,613	$8490		
18. B. Nelson, Head of Household	4	$58,630	$6290		

TAX REFUND OR TAX DUE Find the amount of any refund or tax due for the following people. The letter following the name indicates marital status. Assume a 52-week year and that married people are filing jointly.

Name	Taxable Income	Federal Income Tax Withheld from Checks	Tax Refund or Tax Due
19. Karecki, S	$13,378	$243.10 monthly	
20. Turner, K., S	$32,060	$347.80 monthly	
21. Hunziker, S	$23,552	$72.18 weekly	
22. The Fungs, M	$38,238	$119.27 weekly	
23. The Todds, M	$68,420	$510 monthly	
24. The Bensons, M	$46,850	$165.30 weekly	

25. List four sources of income for which an individual might receive W-2 and 1099 forms. Which form would commonly be received for each? (See Objective 3.)

26. List four possible tax deductions, and explain the effect that a tax deduction will have on taxable income and on income tax due. (See Objective 6.) Round to the nearest dollar.

Find the taxable income and income tax in the following application problems. Round to the nearest dollar.

27. **MARRIED—INCOME TAX**   Paul and Joanna Kidman had an adjusted gross income of $121,420 last year. Deductions included $3184 for state income tax, $1208 for city income tax, $8145 for property tax on their home, $13,512 for mortgage interest, and $1425 in charitable contributions. They file a joint return and claim 4 exemptions.

28. **SINGLE—INCOME TAX**   Ronda Biondi works at Fashion Shoppe and had an adjusted gross income of $34,975 last year. She had deductions of $971 for state income tax, $2564 for property tax, $3820 in mortgage interest, and $235 in contributions. Biondi claims 1 exemption and files as a single person.

29. **SINGLE—INCOME TAX**   Martha Crutchfield has an adjusted gross income of $79,300 and files as a single person with only 1 exemption. Her itemized deductions amounted to $4630.

30. **MARRIED—INCOME TAX**   The Simpsons had an adjusted gross income of $48,260 last year. They had deductions of $1078 for state income tax, $253 for city income tax, $4850 for property tax, $5218 in mortgage interest, and $386 in contributions. They claim 3 exemptions and file a joint return.

31. **HEAD OF HOUSEHOLD**   Martha Spencer, owner of The Doll House, had wages of $98,645, dividends of $385, interest of $672, and adjustments to income of $1058 last year. She had deductions of $877 for state income tax, $342 for city income tax, $3840 for property tax, $8250 in mortgage interest, and $855 in contributions. She claims 4 exemptions and files as head of household.

32. **HEAD OF HOUSEHOLD**   John Walker had wages of $30,364, other income of $2892, dividends of $240, interest of $315, and a regular IRA contribution of $750 last year. He had deductions of $1163 for state income tax, $3220 for property tax, $3680 in mortgage interest, and $540 in contributions. Walker claims 2 exemptions and files as head of household.

33. **MARRIED TAXPAYER**   Bruce and Sally Feldstein work full-time as registered nurses and had combined wages of $128,450, other income of $3200, dividend income of $530, and interest income of $1848. They do not own a home but are thinking of buying one. They contributed $10,300 to a tax-deductible retirement plan at work. Deductions include $6400 in state income tax and $1230 in charitable donations. They file a joint return and claim 3 exemptions.

34. **SINGLE TAXPAYER**   Sheila Spinney works as a freelance editor and earned $78,450 last year along with interest of $2450 and dividends of $432. She contributed $1500 to an IRA and donated $3600 to her church and an additional $200 for hurricane relief. She does not own a home and lives in a state that has no state income tax. She files as a head of household with 3 exemptions.

CHAPTER TERMS

Review the following terms to test your understanding of the chapter. For each term you do not know, refer to the page number found next to that term.

1099 forms [p. 259]
adjusted gross income [p. 258]
assessed valuation [p. 250]
assessment rate [p. 250]
contributions [p. 263]
dollars per $100 [p. 252]
dollars per $1000 [p. 252]
excise (luxury) tax [p. 246]
fair market value [p. 250]
Form 1040A [p. 265]

Form 1040EZ [p. 264]
head of household [p.260]
income taxes [p. 257]
individual retirement account (IRA) [p. 260]
interest [p. 263]
Internal Revenue Service (IRS) [p. 257]
itemized tax deduction [p. 262]
luxury tax [p. 246]

medical and dental expenses [p. 263]
mills [p. 252]
miscellaneous deductions [p. 263]
percent [p. 252]
personal exemptions [p. 260]
personal property [p. 250]
property tax rate [p. 251]
real property [p. 250]

sales tax [p. 244]
sales tax rate [p. 246]
Schedule 1 (Form 1040A) [p. 265]
standard deduction [p. 260]
tax deduction [p. 262]
taxable income [p. 261]
W-2 forms [p. 259]

CONCEPTS

EXAMPLES

7.1 Finding sales tax

Collected by most states, and some counties and cities. Use $P = BR$, where P is the sales tax, B is the amount of the sale, and R is the sales tax rate.

Sales tax of $7\frac{1}{2}\%$ is charged on a sale of $45.75. Find the amount of sales tax and the total including tax.

$$P = 0.075 \times \$45.75 = \$3.43 \quad \text{Rounded}$$

$\$45.75$ sale $+ \$3.43$ tax $= \$49.18$ Total

7.1 Finding selling price when the sales tax is known

Use the basic percent equation.

$$P = B \times R$$

Sales tax = Selling price × Tax rate

Sales tax is $4.59 and the sales tax rate is 6%. Find the amount of the sale.

$$\$4.59 = B \times 0.06$$

$$\frac{\$4.59}{0.06} = B$$

$$\$76.50 = B \qquad \text{Selling price}$$

7.1 Finding the amount of the sale when the total price is known

Use the percent equation and remember

Amount of sale + Sales tax = Total

Total price including tax, $128.96; sales tax, 7%. Find the amount of the sale.

$$B + (0.07)B = \$128.96$$

$$1.07B = \$128.96$$

$$B = \frac{\$128.96}{1.07} = \$120.52$$

7.1 Excise tax (luxury tax)

A tax charged on certain items by the federal, state, or local government. It may be either a percent of the sale price or a certain amount per item.

A firm buys a truck costing $48,700. Sales taxes are 8% and excise taxes are as shown in Table 7.2. Find the total cost.

$48,700	Truck
$3,896	Sales tax: 0.08 × $48,700
$5,844	Excise tax: 0.12 × $48,700
$58,440	Total cost

7.2	**Fair market value and assessed valuation**	The assessment rate is 30%; fair market value is $115,000. Find the assessed valuation.

Fair market value and assessed valuation

Multiply the market value of the property by the assessment rate (a local assessed percent) to arrive at the assessed valuation.

The assessment rate is 30%; fair market value is $115,000. Find the assessed valuation.

$$0.3 \times \$115,000 = \$34,500$$

7.2 Tax rate

The tax rate formula follows.

$$\text{Tax rate} = \frac{\text{Total tax amount needed}}{\text{Total assessed value}}$$

Tax amount needed, $2,456,000; total assessed value, $144,470,000. Find the tax rate to nearest tenth of a percent.

$$\frac{\$2,456,000}{\$144,470,000} = 1.7\% \quad \text{Rounded}$$

7.2 Expressing tax rates in different forms and finding tax

1. Percent: multiply assessed valuation by rate.

   Assessed value, $90,000; tax rate, 2.5%.

   $$\$90,000 \times 0.025 = \$2250$$

2. Dollars per $100: move decimal 2 places to left in assessed valuation and multiply.

   Tax rate, $2.50 per $100

   $$900 \times \$2.50 = \$2250$$

3. Dollars per $1000: move decimal 3 places to left in assessed valuation and multiply.

   Tax rate, $25 per $1000

   $$90 \times \$25 = \$2250$$

4. Mills: move decimal 3 places to the left in rate and multiply by assessed valuation.

   Tax rate, 25 mills

   $$\$90,000 \times 0.025 = \$2250$$

7.3 Adjusted gross income

Adjusted gross income includes wages, salaries, tips, dividends, and interest. Regular IRA contributions or alimony payments are subtracted.

Salary, $32,540; interest income, $875; dividends, $315. Find adjusted gross income.

$$\$32,540 + \$875 + \$315 = \$33,730$$

7.3 Standard deduction amounts

The majority of taxpayers use the standard deduction allowed by the IRS.

$5350 for single people; $10,700 for married couples filing jointly; $5350 for married taxpayers filing separately; $7850 for head of household

7.3 Taxable income

The larger of either the total of itemized deductions or the standard deduction is subtracted from adjusted gross income along with $3400 for each personal exemption.

Adjusted gross income, $18,200; single taxpayer; 1 exemption; itemized deductions total $2850; find taxable income. Standard deduction is $5350; larger than $2850 itemized deduction.

$$\text{Taxable income} = \$18,200 - \$5350 - \$3400$$
$$= \$9450$$

7.3 Tax Rates

The tax rate shown applies to earnings over the amount shown in the appropriate column.

Tax Rates	Single Amount over	Married Filing Jointly Amount over	Married Filing Separately Amount over	Head of Household Amount over
10%	$0	$0	$0	$0
15%	$7,825	$15,650	$7,825	$11,200
25%	$31,850	$63,700	$31,850	$42,650
28%	$77,100	$128,500	$64,250	$110,100
33%	$160,850	$195,850	$97,925	$178,350
35%	$349,700	$349,700	$174,850	$349,700

7.3 Income tax

The amount of income tax is found by using the correct tax table and the proper tax rates.

Taxable income, $72,508; married filing jointly; find income tax.

$$\$8772.50 + 0.25 \times (\$72,508 - \$63,700) = \$10,974.50$$

7.3 Tax due or refund

If the total amount withheld by employers is greater than the tax owed, a refund results. If the tax owed is the greater amount, a balance is due.

Tax owed, $2506; tax withheld, $226 per month for 12 months. Find balance due or refund.

$$\$226 \times 12 = \$2712 \text{ withheld}$$
$$\$2712 \text{ withheld} - \$2506 \text{ owed} = \$206 \text{ refund}$$

CHAPTER 7   Review Exercises

The answer section includes answers to all Review Exercises.

Find the amount of the sales tax, the excise tax, and the total cost including taxes in each of the following problems. **[7.1]**

	Sale Price	Sales Tax Rate	Excise Tax Rate
1.	$852.15	6%	10%
2.	$86.15	8%	11%
3.	$16,500	5%	$12.20/person; 110 people
4.	$345.96	7%	18.3¢/gal.; 285 gal.

Find the item cost when given the amount of tax and the sales tax rate. **[7.1]**

	Amount of Sales Tax	Sales Tax Rate
5.	$68.04	6%
6.	$14.20	5%
7.	$19.60	7%
8.	$26.99	$8\frac{1}{4}\%$

Find the amount of the sale before sales tax was added in each of the following. [7.1]

Total Sale	Sales Tax Rate
9. $447.32	6%
10. $133.75	7%
11. $292.95	5%
12. $172.06	$7\frac{3}{4}\%$

Complete the following list comparing tax rates. Do not round. [7.2]

	Percent	Per $100	Per $1000	In Mills
13.		$4.06		
14.				27
15.	1.27%			
16.			$19.50	

Find the missing quantity. [7.2]

	Assessed Valuation	Tax Rate	Tax
17.	$426,000	32 mills	
18.	$98,200	_____ per $1000	$1816.70
19.	_____	3.5%	$1627.50
20.	$140,500	____ %	$3934
21.	_____	$3.80 per $100	$3655.60
22.	$103,600	27 mills	

Find the taxable income and the tax rounded to the nearest dollar for the following. The letter following the name indicates the marital status. All married people are filing jointly. [7.3]

Name	Number of Exemptions	Adjusted Gross Income	Total Itemized Deductions
23. G. Eckern, S	1	$38,415	$4516
24. The Bridges, M	5	$88,628	$9834
25. R. McIntosh, M	3	$68,490	$11,420
26. B. Thomas, S (head of household)	2	$122,380	$14,320

Solve the following application problems. [7.1–7.2]

27. The Oak Glen Park District budgets on the basis that it will collect $1,978,000. If the total assessed value of the property in the district is $90,550,000, find the tax rate as a percent rounded to the nearest tenth.

28. Total receipts for the day at the Toy Circus are $3442.88. If this includes 6% sales tax, find the amount of the sales tax.

29. A shopping center has a fair market value of $2,608,300. Property in the area is assessed at 40% of fair market value, with a tax rate of $37.50 per $1000. Find the annual property tax.

Find the taxable income and income tax owed in each of the following application problems. [7.3]

30. The Bakers, married and filing a joint return, have a combined adjusted gross income of $94,320, 3 exemptions, and itemized deductions of $9450.

31. Permelia Pervine had an adjusted gross income of $37,450 last year. She had deductions of $960 for state income tax, $3840 for property tax, $5280 in mortgage interest, and $830 to her church. She claims 2 exemptions and files as head of household.

32. Jennifer and Tony Romano had total wages and salaries of $69,750, other income of $852, and interest income of $2880. They are allowed an adjustment to income of $2450. Their itemized deductions are $7218 in mortgage interest, $1680 in state income taxes, and $1040 in charitable contributions. The Romanos are filing a joint return and claim 4 exemptions.

Find the amount of any refund or tax due for the following people. The letter following the name indicates marital status. Assume a 52-week year and that married people are filing jointly. [7.3]

Name	Taxable Income	Federal Income Tax Withheld from Checks
33. The Smiths, M	$60,850	$188.40 weekly
34. Maria Jales, S	$32,507	$387.30 monthly
35. The Flores, M	$52,970	$105.07 weekly
36. Jake Kraft, HH	$48,300	$685.20 monthly

CHAPTER 7	Business Application Case #1

Business Application Case #1
Locating a Truck Stop

Jack Armstrong, owner of All American Truck Stop, is considering two separate locations along the interstate, Anderson and Bentonville. The two locations are about 200 miles apart, and while the sites offer similar business potential, there are differences in land acquisition costs, building costs, and, importantly, property taxes. Armstrong feels that he needs 5.5 acres of land and buildings and improvements that will total 90,000 square feet. The land and building costs and property tax information are as follows.

	Anderson	Bentonville
Land cost (per square foot)	$0.80	$0.70
Building and improvement cost (per square foot)	$32.80	$36.90
Assessment rate	25%	20%
Tax rate	32 mills	$7.50 per $100

Knowing that there are 43,560 square feet in an acre and that the total cost of land improvements will be used as fair market value in both locations, Armstrong needs to answer the following questions to help him in his decision.

(a) What is the cost of the land and improvements in each location?

(b) Find the assessed valuation of the land and improvements in each location.

(c) Find the annual property tax in each location.

(d) What is the total cost including land, building, and property taxes over a 10-year period in each location? Assume taxes remain constant.

(e) On the basis of cost over a 10-year period, which location should Armstrong select?

CHAPTER 7	Business Application Case #2
	Taxes Paid by a Family

To help understand why it is so difficult to pay the bills every month, Todd and Samantha Baker decided to estimate the various annual taxes they pay. Since they inherited their home from Samantha's mother, the interest on the monthly payments is too small to be a deduction on their income tax return. As a result, they plan to file using form 1040A. They also bought an inexpensive, used car this year for their 17-year-old daughter, which increased the amount spent subject to sales tax. Use the following information to answer the questions.

Estimated amount spent subject to sales tax: $23,700; sales tax rate: 7.25%

Market value of home: $173,000; assessment rate: 40%; property tax rate: $54.30 per $1000

Combined wages: $52,500; taxable interest: $3840; IRA contribution: $2000; married filing jointly with 3 deductions

Miles driven by family in year: 32,890; average miles per gallon of gasoline: 18.5; average state and federal tax on a gallon of gasoline: $0.45

(a) Sales tax   =

(b) Property tax   =

(c) FICA and Medicare tax   =

(d) Taxable income   =

(e) Income tax (use Table 7.4)   =

(f) Tax on gasoline   =

(g) Total of taxes   =

(h) Taxes as a percent of combined wages and interest =

At first, the Bakers were surprised that their total taxes amount to over $14,500, or over 25% of their combined wages and interest income. But after talking it over, they recognized that there was no charge for the high school education for their daughter, the roads in their neighborhoods were nicely paved, the area they lived in was relatively free of crime, and they knew that the police would come quickly when called. They also knew that Social Security would pay them an income for many years after they retire and that Medicare would pay most of their medical expenses then, too. All in all, the Bakers felt they were getting a lot out of the taxes they were paying each year.

Risk Management

We buy insurance to protect us against catastrophic loss such as damage to our home by a fire or the theft of our automobile. Without insurance, one large, catastrophic loss could financially destroy a family or business. **Insurance** protects against risk. **Peril insurance** provides protection against financial loss, whereas life insurance provides protection against a death, and medical insurance provides protection against illness.

An insured such as a person, family, or business pays a small **premium** to the insurance company, called the **insurer** or **carrier**. The insurance company pools the many small payments together into large sums of money. Of course, the insurance company must pay its expenses, including commissions to insurance agents, employee salaries, mortgage payments on real estate, property taxes, and utilities. The company then uses its financial resources to pay claims made by any insured that has an accident or suffers damages for which it is insured. For example, insurance companies collect premiums for wind and flood damages from many different property owners in hurricane-prone areas along the Gulf of Mexico. However, Figure 8.1 shows that insurance companies have paid out *billions of dollars* in damages from huge hurricanes.

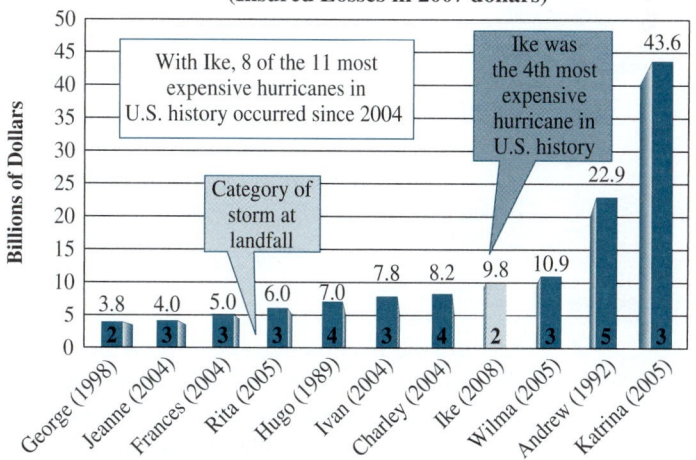

Top 11 Most Costly Hurricanes in U.S. History
(Insured Losses in 2007 dollars)

Sources: ISO/PCS; AIR Worldwide, RMS, Eqecat; Insurance Information Institute inflation adjustments.

Figure 8.1

List all insurance premiums that you (or your parents) pay and add up the combined annual cost. Why buy insurance? How do you choose the policy limits? Why do businesses buy insurance? Why do states require automobile owners to carry insurance?

Individuals buy insurance to protect against losses due to fire, theft, illness or health problems, disability, car wrecks, lawsuits, and even death. Companies buy insurance to protect against losses due to fire, automobile accidents, employee illnesses, lawsuits, and worker accidents on the job. This chapter looks first at business insurance, including fire and liability coverage. Next, motor vehicle insurance is discussed. Then, the many types of life insurance policies are examined.

8.1	**Business Insurance**

OBJECTIVES

1 *Define the terms: policy, face value, and premium.*

2 *Identify the factors that determine the premium.*

3 *Find the annual premium for fire insurance given rating and property values.*

4 *Calculate short-term rates and cancellations.*

5 *Calculate prorated insurance premium cancellations.*

6 *Use the coinsurance formula to solve problems.*

7 *Find the insurance liability when there are multiple carriers.*

8 *Find liability of multiple carriers when coinsurance requirement is not met.*

9 *List additional risks against which a business may be insured.*

There is only a slight chance that any particular building will suffer fire damage during a given year. However, if such fire damage were to occur, the financial loss to the owner could be very large. To protect against this small chance of a large loss, people pay an amount equal to a small percent of the value of their property to a fire insurance company. Each year the company collects money from a large number of property owners, then pays for expenses due to fire damage for those few buildings that are damaged that year.

Objective

1 *Define the Terms: Policy, Face Value, and Premium.* The contract between the owner of a building and a fire insurance company is called a **policy**. The amount of insurance provided by the company is called the **face value** of the policy. The charge for the policy is called the **premium**.

Objective

2 *Identify the Factors That Determine the Premium.* The amount of premium charged by the insurance company depends on several factors, such as the type of construction of the building, the contents and use of the building, the location of the building, and the type of fire protection that is available. Wood-frame buildings are generally more likely to be damaged by fire and thus require a larger premium than masonry buildings. Building types are assigned to categories by insurance company employees called **underwriters**. These categories are usually named by letters, such as A, B, C, and so on. Underwriters also assign ratings, called **territorial ratings**, to each area served, which describe the quality of fire protection in the area. Although fire insurance rates vary from state to state, the rates in Table 8.1 are typical.

Objective

3 *Find the Annual Premium for Fire Insurance Given Rating and Property Values.* The annual premium rate for fire insurance is expressed as a certain amount for each $100. The basic percent equation is used to find the annual insurance premium. The replacement cost

Table 8.1 ANNUAL RATES FOR EACH $100 OF FIRE INSURANCE

Territorial Rating	Building Rating: A		Building Rating: B		Building Rating: C	
	Building	Contents	Building	Contents	Building	Contents
1	$0.28	$0.40	$0.36	$0.49	$0.45	$0.60
2	$0.30	$0.44	$0.45	$0.55	$0.54	$0.75
3	$0.37	$0.46	$0.54	$0.60	$0.63	$0.80
4	$0.50	$0.52	$0.75	$0.77	$0.84	$0.90
5	$0.62	$0.58	$0.92	$0.99	$1.05	$1.14

of the building in hundreds of dollars is the base, the insurance premium per $100 of fire insurance is the rate, and the annual insurance premium is the part.

$$\text{Annual premium} = \text{Building replacement cost} \times \text{Insurance premium}$$
$$\text{(in \$100s)} \qquad \text{(per \$100)}$$
$$P \qquad = \qquad B \qquad \times \qquad R$$

EXAMPLE 1 Finding the Annual Fire Insurance Premium

Flowers For You is in a building with a class B rating. The territory is rated 3. Find the annual premium to insure the building, which has a replacement cost of $378,000 and has contents with a replacement cost of $92,000.

Solution From Table 8.1, the rates per $100 for a class B building in area 3 are $0.54 for the building and $0.60 for the contents. The premium for the building is found by solving the following formula.

$$\text{Replacement cost of building} = \$378,000 \div 100 = 3780 \text{ hundreds}$$
$$\text{Rate for building} = \textbf{\$0.54 (from table)}$$
$$\text{Premium for building} = \text{Value (in hundreds)} \times \text{Rate}$$
$$= 3780 \times \textbf{\$0.54} = \$2041.20$$

The premium for the contents can be found in the same way.

$$\text{Replacement cost of contents} = \$92,000 \div 100 = 920 \text{ hundreds}$$
$$\text{Rate for contents} = \textbf{\$0.60 (from table)}$$
$$\text{Premium for contents} = \text{Value (in hundreds)} \times \text{Rate}$$
$$= 920 \times \textbf{\$0.60} = \$552$$

$$\text{Total premium} = \$2041.20 \text{ (building)} + \$552 \text{ (contents)}$$
$$= \$2593.20 \text{ (building and contents)}$$
$$= \$2593 \text{ (rounded)}$$

NOTE Fire insurance preminums are rounded to the nearest dollar.

Objective

4 *Calculate Short-Term Rates and Cancellations.* Insurance is sometimes purchased for part of a year, perhaps even for just a few months. Perhaps only a short period of time remains on a lease. Also, if a business is sold or the owner wishes to change insurance carriers during the period of a policy, the existing policy must be canceled. In each of these cases, the insurance company will charge a **short-term** or **cancellation rate**. When the short-term rate is used, a penalty results.

As shown in Table 8.2, one month's insurance costs 18% of an annual premium while one month is only $8\frac{1}{3}\%$ of a year ($1 \div 12 = 0.083333$). The premium for a 6-month policy or a policy canceled after 6 months costs 70% of the annual premium.

Table 8.2　SHORT-TERM RATE SCHEDULE

Time in Months	Percent of Annual Premium	Time in Months	Percent of Annual Premium
1	18%	7	75%
2	35%	8	80%
3	45%	9	85%
4	55%	10	90%
5	65%	11	95%
6	70%	12	100%

EXAMPLE 2　Determining Short-Term Rates

Bob Garrett sold his Irving, Texas, grocery store. Because of the sale, he canceled his fire insurance after 4 months. The annual premium was $4680. Use the short-term rate schedule in Table 8.2 to find the amount of refund to the insured.

Solution　The short-term rate for 4 months is 55% of the annual premium.

$$\$4680 \text{ (annual premium)} \times 0.55 = \$2574 \text{ (premium for 4 months)}$$

The refund is found by subtracting the 4-month premium from the annual premium.

$$\$4680 \text{ (annual premium)} - \$2574 \text{ (4-month premium)}$$
$$= \$2106 \text{ (refund)}$$

Objective

5　*Calculate Prorated Insurance Premium Cancellations.*　Occasionally, an insurance company may cancel an insurance policy. This is normally the result of fraud on the part of the insured or any violation of the insurance agreement with the insurance company.

When the insurance company initiates a policy cancellation, the insured is not penalized as with the short-term or cancellation rate. Instead, the insured is charged only for the exact amount of time that the insurance was in force. It is normal for this proration to be to the exact day. Here, we will prorate on a monthly basis, which results in the insured paying only for the number of months that the insurance was provided.

EXAMPLE 3　Calculating Prorated Insurance Cancellations

Your Creations Art Supplies had a fire insurance policy with an annual premium of $2832. Because the insured was in violation of fire codes, the insurance company canceled the policy after 7 months and prorated the premium. Find (a) the amount of the premium retained by the insurance company and (b) the amount of refund to the insured.

Solution　Since the cancellation is after 7 months, the insured is charged for $\frac{7}{12}$ of the year.

(a) The amount of the premium retained by the company is found by multiplying the annual premium by $\frac{7}{12}$.

$$\$2832 \text{ (annual premium)} \times \tfrac{7}{12} = \$1652 \text{ (premium for seven months)}$$

(b) The refund is found by subtracting the premium for 7 months from the annual premium.

$$\$2832 \text{ (annual premium)} - \$1652 \text{ (7-month premium)} = \$1180 \text{ (refund)}$$

The refund is equal to $\frac{5}{12}$ of the annual premium.

Objective

6 *Use the Coinsurance Formula to Solve Problems.* Most fires damage only a portion of a building and its contents. Since complete destruction of a building is rare, many owners try to save money by buying insurance for only a portion of the value of the building and contents. Realizing this, insurance companies place a **coinsurance clause** in fire insurance policies. With coinsurance, part of the risk of fire, under certain conditions, is assumed by the business firm taking out the insurance. For example, an 80% coinsurance clause provides that for full protection, the amount of insurance taken out must be at least 80% of the replacement cost of the building and contents insured.

If the amount of insurance is less than 80% of the replacement cost, the insurance company pays only a portion of any loss. For example, if a business firm took out insurance with a face value of only 40% of the replacement cost of the building insured and then had a loss, the insurance company would pay only half the loss, since 40% is half of 80%.

Use the following coinsurance formula to find the portion of a loss that will be paid by the insurance company.

Amount insurance companies will pay (assuming 80% coinsurance)

$$= \text{Amount of loss} \times \frac{\text{Amount of policy}}{80\% \text{ of replacement cost}}$$

NOTE The insurance company will never pay more than the face value of the policy, nor will the insurance company pay more than the amount of the loss.

EXAMPLE 4 Using the Coinsurance Formula

Jo O'Neill owns an industrial building valued at $760,000. Her fire insurance policy has an 80% coinsurance clause and a face value of $570,000. The building suffers a fire loss of $144,000. Find the amount of the loss that the insurance company will pay and the amount that O'Neill must pay.

Solution For full coverage, the policy should be for at least 80% of the value of the building, or

$$0.80 \times \$760,000 = \$608,000$$

Since the face value of the policy is less than 80% of the replacement cost of the building, the company will pay only a portion of the loss. Use the coinsurance formula.

$$\text{Amount insurance company pays} = \$144,000 \times \frac{\$570,000}{\$608,000} = \$135,000$$

The company will pay $135,000 towards the loss, and O'Neill must pay the additional $9000 ($144,000 − $135,000).

Scientific Calculator Approach

The calculator solution to Example 4 uses chain calculations and parentheses to set off the denominator. The result is then subtracted from the fire loss.

144000 $\times$ 570000 $\div$ (80 % $\times$ 760000) = 135000

144000 − 135000 = 9000

EXAMPLE 5 Finding the Amount of Loss Paid by the Insurance Company

A Swedish investment group owns a warehouse with a replacement cost of $3,450,000. The company has a fire insurance policy with a face value of $2,950,000. The policy has an 80% coinsurance feature. If the firm has a fire loss of $233,500, find the part of the loss paid by the insurance company.

Solution The value of the warehouse is $3,450,000. Take 80% of this value.

$$0.80 \times \$3,450,000 = \$2,760,000$$

The business has a fire insurance policy with a face value of more than 80% of the value of the warehouse. Therefore, the insurance company will pay the entire $233,500 loss.

Objective

7 *Find the Insurance Liability When There Are Multiple Carriers.* A business may have fire insurance policies with several companies at the same time. Perhaps additional insurance coverage was purchased over a period of time, as new additions were made to a factory or building complex. Or perhaps the value of the building is so high that no one insurance company wants to take the entire risk by itself, so several companies each agree to take a portion of the insurance coverage and thereby share the risk. In either event, the insurance coverage is divided among **multiple carriers**. When an insurance claim is made against multiple carriers, each insurance company pays its fractional portion of the total claim on the property equal to its prorated share of the total coverage.

EXAMPLE 6 Understanding Multiple Carrier Insurance

World Recycling Conglomerate (WRC) has an insured loss of $1,800,000 while having insurance coverage greater than its coinsurance requirement. The insurance is divided among Company A with $5,900,000 coverage, Company B with $4,425,000 coverage, and Company C with $1,475,000 coverage. Find the amount of the loss paid by each of the insurance companies.

Solution Start by finding the total face value of all three policies.

$$\$5,900,000 + \$4,425,000 + \$1,475,000 = \$11,800,000 \text{ total face value}$$

$$\$5,900,000 \quad \text{Company A pays } \frac{\$5,900,000}{\$11,800,000} = \frac{1}{2} \text{ of the loss}$$

$$\$4,425,000 \quad \text{Company B pays } \frac{\$4,425,000}{\$11,800,000} = \frac{3}{8} \text{ of the loss}$$

$$+ \ \$1,475,000 \quad \text{Company C pays } \frac{\$1,475,000}{\$11,800,000} = \frac{1}{8} \text{ of the loss}$$

$$\$11,800,000 \text{ total face value}$$

Since the insured loss is $1,800,000, the amount paid by each of the multiple carriers follows.

$$\text{Company A} \quad \frac{1}{2} \times \$1,800,000 = \$900,000$$

$$\text{Company B} \quad \frac{3}{8} \times \$1,800,000 = \$675,000$$

$$\text{Company C} \quad \frac{1}{8} \times \$1,800,000 = \underline{\$225,000}$$

$$\text{Total loss} = \$1,800,000$$

Objective

8 *Find Liability of Multiple Carriers When Coinsurance Requirement Is Not Met.* If the coinsurance requirement is not met, the total amount of the loss paid by the insurance coverage is found, and then the amount that each of the carriers pays is found by the method shown in Example 7.

EXAMPLE 7 Finding Liability of Multiple Carriers When Coinsurance Requirements Are Not Met

The Carpet Solution warehouse has a replacement cost of $2,000,000 and is insured under an 80% coinsurance clause for $1,200,000. The insurance consists of an $800,000 policy with Company A and a $400,000 policy with Company B. If the warehouse suffers a loss of $200,000, find (a) the part of any loss that is covered, (b) the amount of the loss the insurance companies will pay, (c) each insurance company's portion of the $200,000 loss, and (d) the amount paid by the insured.

Solution

(a) First, find the amount of insurance needed to satisfy the 80% coinsurance clause.

$$0.80 \times \$2,000,000 = \$1,600,000$$

Since the face value of the policy ($1,200,000) is less than 80% ($1,600,000), the insurance companies will pay only pay only a portion of the loss.

$$\text{Part insurance companies pay} = \frac{\$1,200,000}{\$1,600,000}$$

(b) Use the coinsurance formula to find the amount of the loss that the insurance companies will pay.

$$\text{Amount insurance companies pay} = \$200,000 \times \frac{\$1,200,000}{\$1,600,000} = \$150,000$$

(c) The total face value of the insurance is $1,200,000. Since the amount of the loss that the insurance companies will pay is $150,000, the amount paid by each of the multiple carriers is as follows.

$$\frac{\$800,000}{\$1,200,000} \times \$150,000 = \$100,000 \quad \text{Company A}$$

$$\frac{\$400,000}{\$1,200,000} \times \$150,000 = \underline{\$50,000} \quad \text{Company B}$$

$$\$150,000 \quad \text{Amount of loss paid}$$

(d) The Carpet Solution must pay $50,000, the difference between the loss and the amount paid by the insurance companies.

Fire Damage, Water Damage

Betty Davis experienced a fire in an apartment house she owned. Thanks to the quick action of a neighbor, a fire truck was there in minutes and the firemen quickly went to work. In the process, they kicked in the doors to two apartments that backed up to the utility room and sprayed foam throughout both apartments. They did this to keep the fire from coming into the apartments and spreading, but it made a mess. As a result, repairs had to be made to the two apartments in addition to the laundry room, and someone had to pay for the clothes that tenants lost in the washers and dryers. Betty was thankful that she had insurance.

Objective

9 *List Additional Risks Against Which a Business May Be Insured.* There are many types of insurance coverage that a business might want. One of the most common is liability coverage, which protects against monetary awards from personal-injury lawsuits caused by the business. Another common coverage protects property against damage caused by windstorm, hail, or fire. Homeowners usually buy a **homeowner's policy**, which protects against these losses and many others, including all credit cards and automated teller cards, business property brought home, and medical costs for guests who are injured. Other policies are designed for condominium owners, rental property owners, and apartment dwellers. Many types of additional coverage, such as flooding and earthquake protection, are available to give complete and comprehensive insurance coverage.

A business owner's package policy, known in the insurance industry as a **special multiperils policy**, or **SMP**, typically includes coverage of the following:

- Replacement cost for the building and contents
- Contents coverage that provides for a 25% peak-season increase
- Business property that is in transit or temporarily away from the premises
- Money, securities, accounts receivable, and other valuable papers up to $1000
- Loss of income, including coverage for rents and interruption of business for up to 12 months
- Liability and medical coverage resulting from personal injury, advertising injury, and medical malpractice

In addition to coverage of these standard risks, a list of optional coverages is also available. The businessperson may select those that he or she feels are necessary. A few of these are:

- Replacement cost coverage on exterior signs
- Replacement cost coverage for glass
- Computer coverage
- Coverage for loss of refrigeration
- Professional liability coverage for barbers, beauticians, pharmacists, hearing aid sellers, morticians, optometrists, and veterinarians
- Coverage for nonowned and hired automobiles
- Liquor liability coverage

In addition to the many coverages for business property and personal liability, the employer may be required to provide **worker's compensation insurance** for employees. This coverage provides payments to an employee who is unable to work because of a job-related injury or illness.

An employer may pay the entire premium or part of the premium for employee health insurance, **disability insurance**, dental insurance, and group life insurance. Most often these **group insurance plans** offer slightly reduced premiums to those participating in the plan. Participation in group insurance plans is sometimes an incentive for remaining with an employer, since changing jobs may eliminate participation in the group insurance plan.

8.1	Exercises

Find the total annual premium for fire insurance for each of the following. Round to the nearest dollar. Use Table 8.1.

	Territorial Rating	Building Classification	Building Replacement Cost	Contents Value
1.	4	C	$480,000	$75,000
2.	1	C	$285,000	$152,000
3.	3	A	$596,400	$206,700
4.	3	C	$220,500	$105,000
5.	5	B	$782,600	$212,000
6.	2	B	$345,700	$174,500
7.	5	C	$583,200	$221,400
8.	4	A	$850,500	$425,800

Find the amount of refund to the insured using the Short-Term Rate Schedule in Table 8.2.

	Annual Premium	Months in Force
9.	$2162	8
10.	$1382	2
11.	$4860	1
12.	$964	2
13.	$1507	3
14.	$1866	10
15.	$4860	11
16.	$13,420	6

Find (a) the amount of premium retained by the company and (b) the amount of refund to the insured using proration.

	Annual Premium	Months in Force
17.	$2680	9
18.	$1936	8
19.	$4375	7
20.	$876	11
21.	$5308	6
22.	$3192	3

Find the amount of each of the following losses that will be paid by the insurance company. Assume that each policy includes an 80% coinsurance clause.

	Replacement Cost of Building	Face Value of Policy	Amount of Loss
23.	$277,000	$223,500	$19,850
24.	$780,000	$585,500	$10,400
25.	$868,000	$650,000	$98,500
26.	$750,000	$500,000	$56,000
27.	$218,500	$195,000	$36,500
28.	$124,800	$80,000	$25,000
29.	$147,850	$100,000	$14,850
30.	$285,000	$150,000	$18,500

Find the amount paid by each insurance company in the following problems involving multiple carriers. Assume that the coinsurance requirement is met. Round all answers to the nearest dollar.

	Insurance Loss	Companies and Coverage	
31.	$80,000	Company A	$750,000
		Company B	$250,000
32.	$360,000	Company 1	$1,200,000
		Company 2	$800,000
33.	$650,000	Company 1	$1,350,000
		Company 2	$1,200,000
		Company 3	$450,000
34.	$1,600,000	Company A	$4,800,000
		Company B	$800,000
		Company C	$2,400,000

Find (a) the amount of the loss paid by the insurance companies, (b) each insurance company's payment, and (c) the amount paid by the insured in each of the following problems involving coinsurance and multiple carriers. Assume an 80% coinsurance clause and round all answers to the nearest dollar.

	Property Value	Insurance Loss	Companies and Coverage	
35.	$900,000	$360,000	Company A	$350,000
			Company B	$250,000
36.	$160,000	$70,000	Company A	$90,000
			Company B	$30,000
37.	$250,000	$20,000	Company 1	$75,000
			Company 2	$50,000
38.	$480,000	$100,000	Company 1	$180,000
			Company 2	$60,000

Use Table 8.1 to find the annual fire insurance premium for each of the following application problems. Round to the nearest dollar.

39. **FURNITURE STORE FIRE INSURANCE** Billings Furniture owns a building with a replacement cost of $1,400,000 and with contents of $360,000. The building is class C with a territorial rating of 5.

40. **INDUSTRIAL FIRE INSURANCE** Valley Crop Dusting owns a class B building with a replacement cost of $107,500. Contents are worth $39,800. The territorial rating is 2.

41. **RESTAURANT FIRE INSURANCE** The Rocklin Grill owns a building with a replacement cost of $235,000. The contents are worth $48,500. The building is class B, with a territorial rating of 1.

42. **INDUSTRIAL BUILDING INSURANCE** London's Dredging Equipment is in a C-rated building with a territorial rating of 4. The building has a replacement cost of $305,000 and the contents are worth $682,000.

Find the amount of refund to the insured using the Short-Term Rate Schedule in Table 8.2 for each of the following.

43. **REAL ESTATE OFFICE** RE/MAX Realty pays an annual fire insurance premium of $2350. It transfers insurance companies after 4 months.

44. **JOB PRINTING** Postal Printers pays an annual fire insurance premium of $1960. The business is sold and insurance canceled after 6 months.

45. **HARDWARE SUPPLY** Ace Hardware cancels its fire insurance after 8 months. The annual premium was $4650.

46. **HORSE STABLES** Martinez Horse Stables pays an annual fire insurance premium of $3960. It changes insurance companies after 2 months.

Find (a) the amount of premium retained by the company and (b) the amount of refund to the insured using proration.

47. **CONSTRUCTION BUSINESS** West Construction pays an annual fire insurance premium of $2670. The insurance company cancels the policy after 5 months.

48. **SPORTING GOODS** The Sports Center had its fire insurance canceled after 10 months. The annual premium is $3380.

49. **DRUG STORE** As the result of a recent claim, Buy-Rite Drug Store had its fire insurance policy canceled after 7 months. The annual premium is $1944.

50. **COFFEE SHOP** Java City Coffee pays an annual fire insurance premium of $4270. The insurance company cancels the policy after 3 months.

 51. Describe three factors that determine the premium charged for fire insurance. (See Objective 2.)

52. Explain the coinsurance clause and describe how coinsurance works. (See Objective 6.)

In each of the following application problems, find the amount of the loss paid by (a) the insurance company and (b) the insured. Assume an 80% coinsurance requirement.

53. **GIFT SHOP FIRE LOSS** Indonesian Wonder Gift Shop has a building with a replacement cost of of $395,000. The shop is insured for $280,000. Fire loss is $22,500.

54. **WELDING FIRE LOSS** Flashpoint Welding Supplies owns a building with a replacement cost of $540,000 and is insured for $308,000. Fire loss is $34,000.

55. **SALVATION ARMY LOSS** The main office of the Salvation Army suffers a loss from fire of $45,000. The building has a replacement cost of $550,000 and is insured for $300,000.

56. **CAR PARTS** Acme Motors owns a plant that builds electric engines for General Electric. The plant has a replacement cost of $2,850,000 and it is insured for $2,200,000. The fire loss is $185,000.

57. Explain in your own words multiple carrier insurance. Give two reasons for dividing insurance among multiple carriers. (See Objective 7.)

58. Several types of insurance coverage beyond basic fire coverage are included in a homeowner's policy. List and explain three losses that would be covered. (See Objective 9.)

In each of the following, find the amount paid by each of the multiple carriers. Assume that the coinsurance requirement has been met and round to the nearest dollar.

59. **COINSURED FIRE LOSS** Camp Curry Stable had an insured fire loss of $548,000. It had insurance coverage as follows: Company A, $600,000; Company B, $400,000; and Company C, $200,000.

60. **FIRE LOSS** The Harley Shoppe had an insured fire loss of $382,000. It has insurance as follows: Company 1, $300,000; Company 2, $180,000; and Company 3, $120,000.

In each of the following application problems, find (a) the amount that the insured would receive and (b) the amount that each of the insurance companies would pay. Round to the nearest dollar.

61. **AUTO DEALERSHIP** Sullivan Chevrolet owns a showroom with a replacement cost of $4,000,000. The fire insurance policies contain an 80% coinsurance clause. The fire policies include $1,800,000 with Company A and $600,000 with Company B. The dealership suffers a $500,000 fire loss.

62. **MANUFACTURING COMPANY** The fire insurance policies on the Global Manufacturing Company contain an 80% coinsurance clause and the warehouse has a replacement cost of $2,400,000. Fire policies on the warehouse are $900,000 with Company A and $300,000 with Company B. Global Manufacturing has a fire loss of $800,000.

63. **RESTAURANT FIRE LOSS** Jack Pritchard's Steakhouse has a replacement cost of $360,000. The fire policies are $100,000 with Company 1, $50,000 with Company 2, and $30,000 with Company 3, while each contains an 80% coinsurance clause. There is a fire at the steakhouse causing a $120,000 loss.

64. **HIGH-RISE CONDOMINIUMS** The Peace Lake Condo tower has a replacement cost of $5,500,000. Fire insurance policies are $1,500,000 with Company 1, $1,000,000 with Company 2, and $800,000 with Company 3. The policies contain an 80% coinsurance clause and the tower suffers a $1,200,000 fire loss.

8.2 Motor Vehicle Insurance

OBJECTIVES

1 *Describe the factors that affect the cost of motor vehicle insurance.*

2 *Define liability insurance and determine the premium.*

3 *Define property damage insurance and determine the premium.*

4 *Describe comprehensive and collision insurance and determine the premium.*

5 *Define no-fault and uninsured motorist insurance.*

6 *Apply youthful-operator factors.*

7 *Calculate a motor vehicle insurance premium.*

8 *Find the amounts paid by the insurance company and the insured.*

Objective

1 *Describe the Factors That Affect the Cost of Motor Vehicle Insurance.* Automobile accidents increase in number each year, and the average cost of repairing a motor vehicle after an accident continues to rise dramatically. Businesses and individuals buy motor vehicle insurance to protect against the possible large cost of an accident. The cost of this insurance, the **premium**, is determined by people called **actuaries**, who classify accidents according to location, age and sex of the drivers, and other factors. Insurance companies use these results to determine the premiums. For example, there is a higher percentage of accidents in heavily populated cities than in rural areas. Certain makes and models of automobiles are stolen more often than others. Young male drivers (16–25 years of age) are involved in many more accidents than they should be, considering their proportion of the population. The more expensive a vehicle and the newer a vehicle, the more it costs to repair. These are several of the factors that determine the cost of motor vehicle insurance.

Figure 8.2 shows where insurance companies spent their revenues. Of every $100 in premium and return on investment, $63 went to pay claims, $24 was used to pay for insurance company expenses such as employees and maintenance on buildings, $5 was spent on taxes, and $8 was company profit. The figure of 8% is called the **profit margin**. The data show that in 2006, insurance companies averaged a profit of 8% of premiums and return on investments. Of course, some insurance companies did better and others did worse.

**Where the Revenue Dollar Went, 2009
(Premiums and Investments)**

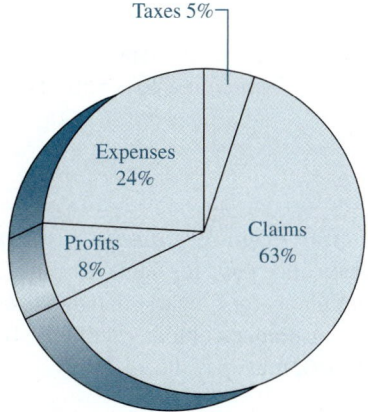

Source: Insurance Information Institute.

Figure 8.2

Objective

2 *Define Liability Insurance and Determine the Premium.* **Liability** or **bodily injury insurance** protects the insured in case he or she injures someone with a car. Many states have minimum amounts of liability insurance coverage set by law. The amount of liability insurance is expressed as two numbers with a slash between them, such as 15/30. The numbers 15/30 mean that the insurance company will pay up to $15,000 for injury to one person, and a maximum of $30,000 for all persons injured in the same accident. Table 8.3 shows typical premium rates for various amounts of liability coverage.

> **NOTE** Each year more than 5000 teenagers between the ages of 16 and 20 die due to fatal injuries caused in car accidents. An additional 400,000 drivers age 16 to 20 are seriously injured in car accidents each year.

Table 8.3   LIABILITY (BODILY INJURY) AND MEDICAL INSURANCE (PER YEAR)

Territory	Liability and Medical Expense Limits				
	15/30 $1000	25/50 $2000	50/100 $3000	100/300 $5000	250/500 $10,000
1	$268	$273	$294	$321	$368
2	269	302	341	378	392
3	310	314	375	398	459
4	216	218	253	284	310

Medical insurance is included in the cost of the liability insurance provided to the driver and passengers of a vehicle in case of injury. For example, the column of the table headed "15/30" shows that the insured can also receive reimbursement for up to $1000 of his or her own medical expenses in an accident.

For purposes of setting premiums, insurance companies divide the nation into territories—as many as thirty or more. These territories are established on the basis of population, the number of motor vehicles, and the number of accidents and other claims within the territory. Four territories are shown in Table 8.3. All tables in this section show annual premiums.

EXAMPLE 1   Finding the Liability and Medical Premium

Zallia Todd, owner of Flowers For You, is in territory 2 and wants 100/300 liability coverage. Find the amount of the premium for this coverage and the amount of medical coverage included.

Solution   Look up territory 2 in Table 8.3 and 100/300 coverage to find a premium of $378, which includes $5000 of medical coverage.

Objective

3   *Define Property Damage Insurance and Determine the Premium.*   **Property damage insurance** pays for damages caused to another vehicle or other property. Table 8.4 shows the premiums for property damage insurance. The coverage amount is the maximum amount that the insurance company will pay. If a claim for damages exceeds this maximum amount, the insured must pay the excess.

EXAMPLE 2   Finding the Premium for Property Damage

Zallia Todd, in territory 2, wants property damage coverage of $50,000. Find the premium.

Solution   Property damage coverage of $50,000 in territory 2 requires a premium of $223, as Table 8.4 shows.

Table 8.4   PROPERTY DAMAGE INSURANCE (PER YEAR)

Territory	Property Damage Limits			
	$10,000	$25,000	$50,000	$100,000
1	$119	$128	$141	$162
2	168	192	223	251
3	129	134	145	158
4	86	101	112	124

Many insurance companies give discounts on insurance premiums based on good driving records, completing courses in driving safety, and insuring more than one car. Some even reduce car insurance premiums for students who make good grades. Be sure and ask for discounts—they can save you money. The graphic shows the number of states requiring discounts on automobile insurance.

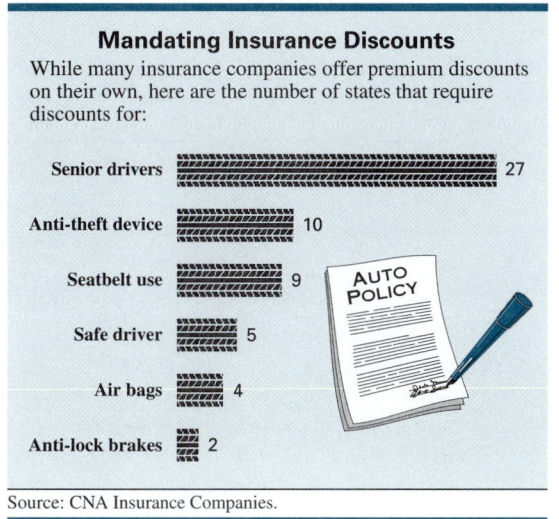

Mandating Insurance Discounts

While many insurance companies offer premium discounts on their own, here are the number of states that require discounts for:

Senior drivers	27
Anti-theft device	10
Seatbelt use	9
Safe driver	5
Air bags	4
Anti-lock brakes	2

Source: CNA Insurance Companies.

Objective

4   *Describe Comprehensive and Collision Insurance and Determine the Premium.* **Comprehensive insurance** pays for damage to the insured's vehicle caused by fire, theft, vandalism, falling trees, and other such events. **Collision insurance** pays for repairs to the insured's vehicle in case of an accident. Collision insurance often includes a **deductible**. The deductible is paid by the insured in the event of a claim, with the insurance company paying all amounts above the deductible. Common deductible amounts are $100, $250, $500, and $1000. For example, if the cost of repairing damage caused by an accident is $2045 and the deductible amount is $500, the insured pays $500, and the insurance company pays $1545 ($2045 − $500 = $1545).

> **NOTE**   The higher the deductible amount, the lower the cost of the collision coverage. The insured shares a greater portion of the risk as the deductible amount increases.

Table 8.5 shows some typical rates for comprehensive and collision insurance. Rates are determined not only by territories but also by age group and cost category of the vehicle. Age group 1 refers to a vehicle that is 1 year old or less; age group 6 is a vehicle 6 years old or older.

> **NOTE**   Different models fall into different catagories. For example, the cost category for a Ford Escape might be a category 6 and a Lincoln Navigator might be a category 8. The collision coverage in Table 8.5 is for $500 deductible coverage.

EXAMPLE 3   Finding the Comprehensive and Collision Premium

Zallia Todd, owner of Flowers For You, is in territory 2 and has a 2-year-old minivan that has a category of 8. Use Table 8.5 to find the annual premium for (a) comprehensive coverage and (b) collision coverage.

Solution

(a) The annual premium for comprehensive coverage is $74.
(b) The annual premium for collision coverage is $215.

Table 8.5 COMPREHENSIVE AND COLLISION INSURANCE

Territory	Age Group	Comprehensive			Collision ($500 Deductible)		
		6	**7**	**8**	**6**	**7**	**8**
1	1	$58	$64	$90	$153	$165	$184
	2–3	50	56	82	135	147	171
	4–5	44	52	76	116	128	147
	6	34	44	64	92	110	128
2	1	44	62	81	196	219	241
	2–3	42	59	74	178	194	215
	4–5	38	51	63	169	189	201
	6	33	44	58	148	154	183
3	1	70	78	108	145	157	174
	2–3	60	66	90	128	139	162
	4–5	52	64	92	111	122	139
	6	44	58	66	149	163	196
4	1	50	58	77	192	223	245
	2–3	42	46	71	187	209	233
	4–5	40	45	68	179	192	218
	6	38	42	65	165	177	201

Automobile theft is a major problem in the United States since over 1.2 million cars are stolen each year. Figure 8.3 shows the most frequently reported stolen automobiles in 2007.

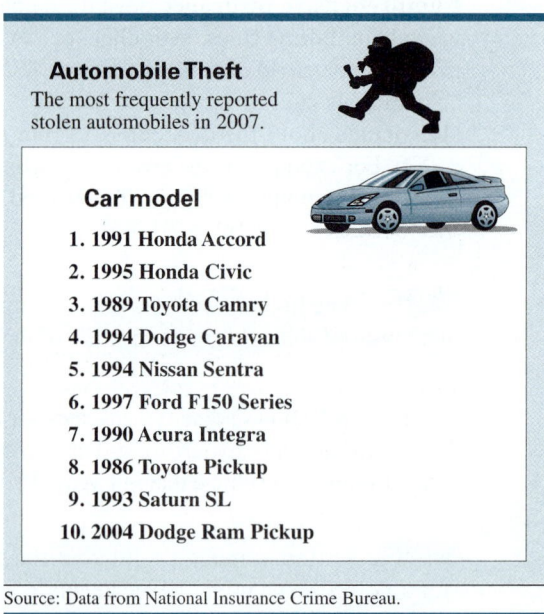

Automobile Theft
The most frequently reported stolen automobiles in 2007.

Car model

1. 1991 Honda Accord
2. 1995 Honda Civic
3. 1989 Toyota Camry
4. 1994 Dodge Caravan
5. 1994 Nissan Sentra
6. 1997 Ford F150 Series
7. 1990 Acura Integra
8. 1986 Toyota Pickup
9. 1993 Saturn SL
10. 2004 Dodge Ram Pickup

Source: Data from National Insurance Crime Bureau.

Figure 8.3

Objective

5 *Define No-Fault and Uninsured Motorist Insurance.*   **No-fault insurance** refers to a state insurance program that allows an injured insured to recover financial losses from his or her own insurance company, no matter who caused the accident. An original goal of no-fault insurance was to limit lawsuits for accidents with less serious injuries. Under no fault, damages for pain and suffering are eliminated except in cases of permanent injury or death. Insurance compaines argue that no-fault insurance removes lawyers and courts from the process and results in lower overall costs. Trial lawyers and some consumer groups argue that no-fault insurance leaves accident victims unable to recover all of their damages.

The New York State Insurance Department has stated that a "no-fraud industry" has emerged in which criminal rings recruit people, often immigrants, to pile into automobiles and deliberately stage accidents. As a result of this criminal activity and other issues, only about a dozen states still have no-fault insurance although many states have experimented with it.

In the states that do not have no-fault insurance a driver must be concerned about an accident with an uninsured driver. Drivers in these states need **uninsured motorist insurance**, which protects the vehicle owner in a collision with a vehicle that is not insured. Some insurance companies offer **underinsured motorist insurance**, which provides protection in the event that there is a collision with a vehicle that is underinsured. Typical costs for uninsured motorist insurance are shown in Table 8.6.

Table 8.6 UNINSURED MOTORIST INSURANCE (PER YEAR)

Territory	Basic Limit
1	$66
2	44
3	76
4	70

EXAMPLE 4 **Determining the Premium for Uninsured Motorist Coverage**

Zallia Todd, living in territory 2, wants uninsured motorist coverage. Find the premium in Table 8.6.

Solution The annual premium for uninsured motorist coverage in territory 2 is $44.

Objective

6 *Apply Youthful-Operator Factors.* Youthful drivers are involved in more accidents than adult drivers. The graph below helps to explain why most insurance companies distinguish between **youthful** and **adult operators**. Although the age at which a driver becomes an adult varies from company to company, drivers of age 24 or less are usually considered youthful drivers and drivers 25 or older are considered adults. Owing to the higher proportion of accidents in the 24-and-under bracket, insurance companies add an additional amount to the insurance premium. In Table 8.7, there are two categories of youthful drivers, age 20 or less

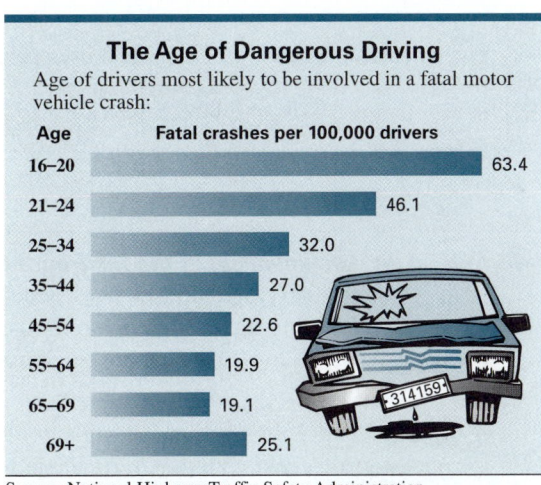

The Age of Dangerous Driving

Age of drivers most likely to be involved in a fatal motor vehicle crash:

Age	Fatal crashes per 100,000 drivers
16–20	63.4
21–24	46.1
25–34	32.0
35–44	27.0
45–54	22.6
55–64	19.9
65–69	19.1
69+	25.1

Source: National Highway Traffic Safety Administration.

and age 21–24. Consideration is also given to the youthful operator who has had driver's training. Some companies give discounts to youthful drivers who are "good students" (a B average or better). To use the youthful-operator table, first determine the premium for all coverage desired and then multiply this premium by the appropriate youthful-operator factor to find the total premium.

Table 8.7   YOUTHFUL-OPERATOR FACTOR

Age	With Driver's Training	Without Driver's Training
20 or less	1.55	1.75
21–24	1.25	1.40

Objective

7   *Calculate a Motor Vehicle Insurance Premium.*   The total annual insurance premium is found by adding the costs of each type of insurance coverage.

> **EXAMPLE 5**   **Using the Youthful–Operator Factor**
>
> James Ito lives in territory 4, is 22 years old, has had driver's training, and drives a 5-year-old car in category 7. He wants a 25/50 liability policy, $10,000 property damage coverage, a comprehensive and collision policy, and uninsured motorist coverage. Find his annual insurance premium.
>
> **Solution**
>
> | Table | Coverage | Premium |
> |---|---|---|
> | 8.3 | 25/50 liability | $218 |
> | 8.4 | $10,000 property damage | 86 |
> | 8.5 | Comprehensive | 45 |
> | 8.5 | Collision | 192 |
> | 8.6 | Uninsured motorist | 70 |
> | | Sum | $611 |
>
> Multiply this sum by the youthful–operator factor of 1.25, found in Table 8.7.
>
> $$\text{Total premium} = \$611 \times 1.25 = \$763.75$$

Scientific Calculator Approach

The calculator solution to Example 5 uses parentheses and chain calculations.

$$(\boxed{218} + \boxed{86} + \boxed{45} + \boxed{192} + \boxed{70}) \times \boxed{1.25} = 763.75$$

Objective

8   *Find the Amounts Paid by the Insurance Company and the Insured.*   The cost of increasing insurance coverage limits is usually quite small. For example, in Table 8.3 the additional cost of increasing liability coverage in territory 1 from 50/100 to 100/300 is only $27 per year ($321 − $294). Medical coverage would also be increased.

> **NOTE**   Since the insurance company pays only up to the maximum amount of insurance coverage and with the driver liable for all additional amounts, many people pay an additional premium for increased coverage.

> **EXAMPLE** 6 **Finding the Amounts Paid by the Insurance Company and the Insured**
>
> Eric Liwanag has 25/50 liability limits, $25,000 property damage limits, and $250 deductible collision insurance. While on vacation he was at fault in an accident that caused $5800 damage to his car and $3380 in damage to another car and resulted in severe injuries to the other driver and her passenger. A subsequent lawsuit for injuries resulted in a judgment of $45,000 and $35,000, respectively, to the other parties. Find the amounts that the insurance company will pay for (a) repairing Liwanag's car, (b) repairing the other car, and (c) paying the court judgment resulting from the lawsuit. (d) How much will Liwanag have to pay to the injured parties?
>
> **Solution**
>
> (a) The insurance company will pay $5550 ($5800 − $250 deductible) to repair Liwanag's car.
>
> (b) Repairs on the other car will be paid to the property damage limits; here, the total repairs of $3380 are paid.
>
> (c) Since more than one person was injured, the insurance company pays the limit of $50,000 ($25,000 to each of the two injured parties).
>
> (d) Liwanag is liable for $30,000 ($80,000 − $50,000), the amount awarded over the insurance limits.

Additional factors may affect the annual premium for motor vehicle insurance, such as whether the vehicle is used for pleasure, as transportation to and from work, or for business purposes, how far the vehicle is driven each year, whether the youthful driver is male or female, the marital status of the male youthful driver, the past driving record of the driver, and whether the driver has more than one car insured with the insurance company. Quite often, discounts are given to nonsmokers and good students. There are also discounts for automobiles equipped with air bags and antilock braking systems. Many insurance companies charge an annual policy fee, which covers the cost of processing the policy each year.

> **NOTE** Car insurance premiums often go up sharply for those who receive moving violations (tickets) from police and for those who cause accidents. Drive safely or pay the price in more ways than one!

8.2 Exercises

Find the annual premium for each of the following people.

Name	Territory	Age	Driver's Training	Liability	Property Damage	Comprehensive Collision Age Group	Category	Uninsured Motorist
1. Maxey	4	35	—	100/300	$50,000	2	8	yes
2. Morrissey	1	20	yes	25/50	$25,000	4	7	no
3. Shraim	3	52	—	250/500	$50,000	2	8	yes
4. Waldron	2	67	—	50/100	$100,000	1	6	yes
5. Carter	1	35	—	100/300	$25,000	5	6	no
6. Tao	2	24	yes	100/300	$50,000	5	7	yes
7. Baeta	4	52	—	250/500	$50,000	1	8	yes
8. Gualco	1	31	—	250/500	$50,000	none	none	no

Name	Territory	Age	Driver's Training	Liability	Property Damage	Comprehensive Collision Age Group	Category	Uninsured Motorist
9. Harrison	3	44	—	50/100	$25,000	5	6	yes
10. Ballinger	2	17	yes	15/30	$10,000	4	8	yes
11. Green	2	43	—	100/300	$100,000	6	6	no
12. Rodriquez	3	60	—	50/100	$100,000	5	7	yes

 13. Describe four factors that determine the premium on an automobile insurance policy. (See Objective 1.)

 14. Explain the difference between comprehensive insurance and collision insurance. (See Objective 4.)

Solve each of the following application problems.

15. YOUTHFUL OPERATOR—NO DRIVER'S TRAINING Karen Roberts's father gave her a new Honda Accord to use at college under the condition she pay her own insurance. She is 17, has not had driver's training, lives in territory 1, and her vehicle has a category of 6. She wants 50/100 liability limits, $25,000 property damage limits, comprehensive and collision insurance, and uninsured motorist coverage. Find her annual insurance premium.

16. ADULT AUTO INSURANCE Bill Poole is 47 years old, lives in territory 4, and drives a 2-year-old car with a category of 7. He wants 250/500 liability limits, $100,000 property damage limits, comprehensive and collision insurance, and uninsured motorist coverage. Find his annual insurance premium.

17. STUDENT AUTO INSURANCE Martha Vickers is 22, has taken driver's training, and has a 5-year-old car. She lives in territory 3 and wants the following coverage: liability 25/50, property damage $25,000, no comprehensive, no collision, and uninsured motorist.

18. YOUTHFUL OPERATOR—NO DRIVER'S TRAINING Michelle Massa is 17 years old, has not had driver's training, lives in territory 2, and purchased a new Jeep Cherokee with a category of 6. She wants 50/100 liability limits, $25,000 property damage limits, comprehensive and collision insurance, and uninsured motorist coverage. Find her annual insurance premium.

19. BODILY INJURY INSURANCE Suppose your bodily injury policy has limits of 25/50, and you injure a person on a bicycle. The judge awards damages of $36,500 to the cyclist. (a) How much will the company pay? (b) How much will you pay?

20. BODILY INJURY INSURANCE Your best friend causes injury to three people and they receive damages of $50,000 each. She has a policy with bodily injury limits of 100/300. (a) How much will the company pay to each person? (b) How much must your friend pay?

21. INSURANCE CLAIMS PAYMENT A reckless driver caused Leslie Silva to collide with a car in another lane. Silva had 50/100 liability limits, $25,000 property damage limits, and collision coverage with a $250 deductible. Silva's car had damage of $1878, and the other car suffered $6936 in damage. The resulting lawsuit gave injury awards of $60,000 and $55,000, respectively, to the two people in the other car. Find the amount that the insurance company will pay for (a) repairing Silva's car, (b) repairing the other car, and (c) personal injury damages. (d) How much must Silva pay beyond her insurance coverage, including the collision deductible?

22. **INSURANCE CLAIMS PAYMENT**   Driving a vehicle at excessive speed caused Bob Armstrong to crash into another car. Armstrong had 15/30 liability limits, $10,000 property damage limits, and collision coverage with a $250 deductible. Damage to Armstrong's car was $2980; the other car, with a value of $22,800, was totaled. The results of a lawsuit awarded $75,000 and $45,000, respectively, in damages for personal injury to the two people in the other car. Find the amount that the insurance company will pay for (a) repairing Armstrong's car, (b) repairing the other car, and (c) personal injury damages. (d) How much must Armstrong pay beyond his insurance coverage?

23. **COMPANY/INSURED LIABILITY**   An employee for Safeco Security was driving to a job when a ladder fell from the truck into the path of an oncoming car. Damage to the car was $10,250. Both the driver and the passenger suffered injuries and were given court awards of $30,000 and $40,000, respectively. The security company had 25/50 liability insurance limits and $10,000 property damage limits. (a) Find the total amount paid by the insurance company for both property damage and liability and (b) find the total amount beyond the insurance limits for which the business owner was liable.

24. **COMPANY/INSURED LIABILITY**   A trailer-mounted concrete mixer being towed by a contractor broke loose on the beltway and caused a serious accident involving a car and three occupants. Damage to the car was $10,807. The driver and two passengers were given court awards for personal injury of $25,000, $35,000, and $38,000, respectively. The contractor had 25/50 liability insurance limits and $10,000 property damage limits. Find (a) the total amount paid by the insurance company for both property damage and liability and (b) the total amount beyond the insurance limits for which the contractor was liable.

25. Explain why insurance companies charge a higher premium on auto insurance sold to a youthful operator. Do you think that this higher premium is a good idea or not? (See Objective 6.)

26. Property damage insurance pays for damage caused by the insured to the property of others. Since the average cost of a new car today is over $20,000, what amount of property damage coverage would you recommend to a friend who owns her own business? Why is this your recommendation? (See Objective 3.)

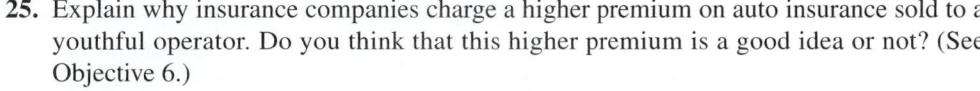

8.3   Life Insurance

OBJECTIVES

1   *List reasons for purchasing life insurance.*

2   *Define term, decreasing term, and whole-life policies.*

3   *Understand universal life, variable life, limited payment, and endowment policies.*

4   *Find the annual premium for life insurance.*

5   *Use premium factors with different modes of premium payment.*

6   *Describe discounts, conditions, and additional coverage.*

7   *Understand nonforfeiture options.*

8   *Calculate income under various settlement options.*

Objective

1   *List Reasons for Purchasing Life Insurance.*   Individuals buy life insurance for a variety of reasons. Most often, the insured wants to provide for the needs of others in the event of early death or disability. Parents may want to guarantee that their children will have enough money for college even if the parents die. Also, some types of life insurance provide paybacks upon retirement, paybacks that allow a retired person to live better than he or she might otherwise live. Insurance money can also be used to pay off mortgages. According to the American Council of Life Insurers, the average amount of a life insurance policy sold in the United States today exceeds $100,000.

Life insurance is also important for businesses, particularly for an owner or partner in a small business. A business often takes a number of years to grow and may be the owner's main asset. The unexpected death of the owner might leave the business without proper guidance and control, and the business may suffer drastically before it can be sold. Life insurance on the partners in a business supplies the surviving partner with the necessary money to buy out a deceased partner's interest in the partnership.

The following table lists the six leading causes of death in the United States and things that individuals can do to reduce the risk of each. Notice that several themes occur repeatedly: quit smoking, increase physical activity, and eat more vegetables/fish/fruit. In fact, scientists believe that smoking is one of the highest health risks, but diet, exercise, and excessive weight are also very important factors.

Biggest Causes of Death	To Reduce Risk:
1. Heart disease	Quit smoking, lose weight, eat more fish and less red meat, increase physical activity
2. Cancer	Eat more vegetables, fruit, and fish
3. Accidents	Do not drink and drive
4. Stroke	Quit smoking, reduce salt in diet, increase physical activity
5. Lung disease	Quit smoking, increase physical activity
6. Diabetes	Eat more vegetables, lose weight, increase physical activity, avoid simple sugars such as candy

Source: National Institute of Health Statistics, 2007.

Objective

2 *Define Term, Decreasing Term, and Whole-Life Policies.*   There are several types of life insurance policies available. The most common types are term, decreasing term, and whole-life insurance.

Term insurance is the least expensive type of life insurance. It provides the most insurance per dollar spent but it does not build up any cash values for retirement. This type of insurance coverage is usually renewable until some age such as 70, when the insured is no longer allowed to renew it. As a result, most people discontinue term insurance before they die. However, term insurance is an excellent way to protect against an early death.

The premium on **renewable term** policies increases each year as the insured ages. Premiums on this type of policy become expensive by the time a person is 50 years of age or so. As a result, many people prefer **level premium term** policies. Initially, these policies require a higher premium than policies with annually increasing premiums. However, the premium on a level premium policy is constant for a period of time, such as 10 years or 20 years. Thereafter, the premiums would increase significantly.

Decreasing term insurance is a modification of term insurance where the insured pays a fixed premium until age 60 or 65, with the amount of life insurance decreasing periodically. This policy is designed to fit the ages and stages of life as life insurance needs change. For the person just starting out, it gives more protection for less money. A typical policy, costing $11 per month, is shown in Table 8.8. Decreasing term insurance is commonly available to employees of large companies as a fringe benefit, paid for by either the employee, the employer, or both. Most mortgage insurance policies are this type. The amount of life insurance coverage decreases as the amount of the mortgage is reduced.

Table 8.8	A TYPICAL DECREASING TERM INSURANCE POLICY
Age of insured	**Coverage**
Under 29	$40,000
30–34	35,000
35–39	30,000
40–44	25,000
45–49	18,000
50–54	11,000
55–59	7000
60–66	4000
67 and over	0

Whole-life insurance (also called **straight life, ordinary life insurance**, or **permanent**) combines life insurance protection with savings. The insured pays a constant premium until death or until retirement, whichever occurs sooner. Upon retirement, monthly payments may be made by the company to the insured until his or her death.

Whole-life insurance builds up **cash value**, or money used to pay retirement benefits to the insured. Also, these cash values can be borrowed by the insured at favorable interest rates. Cash value accumulation is guaranteed by the company. The rate of interest used to calculate cash values by the company is very conservative. For this reason many consumer finance experts recommend the purchase of term insurance, with the difference in premiums between term insurance and whole-life insurance invested in a good no-load mutual fund or money market fund. See **Section 19.2** for a discussion of mutual funds.

> **NOTE** Many people plan to save the additional money they would have paid for whole-life insurance, but they neglect to do so. One advantage of whole-life insurance is that regular payments are required. Remember that term insurance has no cash value, whereas whole-life does.

In general, people in the United States are living longer, as shown in the graph. But many doctors are worried about an epidemic of diabetes this century due partly to poor diet and increased weight of adults across much of the world. Such an epidemic threatens to shorten the average life span.

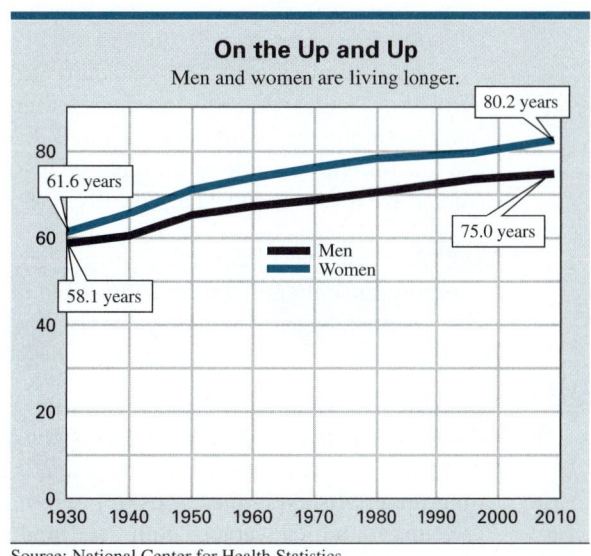

On the Up and Up
Men and women are living longer.

Source: National Center for Health Statistics.

Objective

3   *Understand Universal Life, Variable Life, Limited Payment, and Endowment Policies.*
Universal and variable life policies provide the life insurance coverage of term insurance (high coverage per premium dollar), plus a tax-deferred way to accumulate assets and earn interest at money market rates. Unlike traditional whole-life insurance policies, **universal life insurance** allows the insured to vary the amount of premium depending on the changing needs of the insured. A younger insured person with limited funds may want maximum insurance protection for the family. At a later date, the insured may want to begin actively building assets and may increase the premium to build cash value for retirement benefits. Universal life insurance is sensitive to interest rate changes. The portion of the premium going into retirement benefits receives money market interest rates and is usually guaranteed a minimum rate of return, regardless of what happens to market rates. The insured person profits from higher interest rates but is also protected if interest rates drop below the guaranteed rate. The idea is that returns will be greater than those given to ordinary life policyholders.

Variable life is the latest attempt to encourage sales of the insurance industry's main product, whole-life insurance. It allows you to allocate your premiums among one or more separate investments that offer varying degrees of risk and reward—stocks, bonds, combinations of both, or accounts that provide for guarantees of interest and principal. Typical policies available today allow the policyholder to switch investments from one fund to another twice each year. These features coupled with some tax benefits have resulted in the variable life policy accounting for 25% and 35% of the new policies sold in recent years by two of the largest life insurance companies.

Limited-payment life insurance is similar to ordinary life, except that premiums are paid for only a certain fixed number of years, such as 20 years. For this reason, this insurance is often called "20-pay life," representing payments of 20 years. The premium for limited-payment life is higher than for ordinary life policies. Limited-payment life is commonly used by athletes, actors, and others whose income is likely to be high for several years and then decline.

An **endowment policy** is the most expensive type of policy. These policies guarantee payment of a fixed amount of money to a given individual, whether or not the insured lives. Endowment policies might be taken out by parents to guarantee a sum of money for their children's college education. Because of the high premiums, this is one of the least popular types of policies today.

It is not always easy to decide on the best type of policy. While term insurance gives the greatest amount of insurance for each premium dollar, it pays only when the insured dies. Since term insurance costs increase rapidly with age, most people buying term insurance drop it before they die. Ordinary life insurance provides less coverage for each premium dollar in the event of death; however, it does provide a return to the insured at retirement. The only certain method for determining which policy will give the best return is for the insured to know when he or she will die, and this is not possible.

The Commissioners 2001 Standard Ordinary Table of Mortality (Table 8.9) shows the number of deaths per 1000 and the remaining life expectancy in years for both males and females among the people in the United States having life insurance. Insurance companies use this **mortality table** to evaluate their life insurance reserves, from which benefits are paid. This table is updated periodically. The most recent one is shown in Table 8.9.

NOTE   Life expectancy for women is greater than for men, so a woman pays a lower life insurance premium than does a man of the same age. Find the insurance premium for a woman by subtracting 5 years from her age before using the table of premiums.

Objective

4   *Find the Annual Premium for Life Insurance.*   Calculation of life insurance rates and premiums uses complex mathematics and is done by actuaries. The results of such calculations are published in the tables of premiums. A typical table is shown in Table 8.10. The premium for a life insurance policy is found with the following formula.

$$\text{Annual premium} = \text{Number of thousands} \times \text{Rate per \$1000}$$

Table 8.9 COMMISSIONERS 2001 STANDARD ORDINARY TABLE OF MORTALITY SHOWING THE LIFE EXPECTANCY OF MEN AND WOMEN AT VARIOUS AGES

	Males		Females			Males		Females	
Age	Deaths per 1000	Expectation of Life (years)	Deaths per 1000	Expectation of Life (years)	Age	Deaths per 1000	Expectation of Life (years)	Deaths per 1000	Expectation of Life (years)
Newborn	1.0	76.6	0.5	80.8	65	16.9	16.8	11.9	20.1
5	0.2	71.8	0.2	76.0	70	25.8	13.3	17.8	16.4
10	0.2	66.9	0.2	71.0	75	41.9	10.2	27.9	13.0
15	0.6	62.0	0.4	66.1	80	70.1	7.5	43.9	9.9
20	1.0	57.2	0.5	61.3	85	116.6	5.4	74.5	7.3
25	1.1	52.5	0.5	56.4	90	187.7	3.8	121.9	5.3
30	1.1	47.8	0.7	51.6	95	269.2	2.8	193.7	3.6
35	1.2	43.1	1.0	46.8	100	363.2	2.1	275.7	2.6
40	1.7	38.3	1.3	42.0	105	459.2	1.6	410.6	1.7
45	2.7	33.7	1.9	37.3	110	589.6	1.1	581.8	1.2
50	3.8	29.2	3.1	32.7	115	765.7	0.8	763.4	0.8
55	6.2	24.8	5.1	28.3	120	1000.0	0.5	1000.0	0.5
60	9.9	20.6	8.0	24.1					

Source: American Council of Life Insurance, *Life Insurance Fact Book* (Washington, D.C, 2006).

Table 8.10 ANNUAL PREMIUM RATE* PER $1000 OF LIFE INSURANCE

Age	Renewable Term	Whole Life	Universal Life	20-Pay Life
20	2.28	4.07	3.48	12.30
21	2.33	4.26	3.85	12.95
22	2.39	4.37	4.10	13.72
23	2.43	4.45	4.56	14.28
24	2.52	4.68	4.80	15.95
25	2.58	5.06	5.11	16.60
30	2.97	5.66	6.08	18.78
35	3.41	7.68	7.45	21.60
40	4.15	12.67	10.62	24.26
45	4.92	19.86	15.24	28.16
50		26.23	21.46	32.59
55		31.75	28.38	38.63
60		38.42	36.72	45.74

*For women, subtract 5 years from the actual age. For example, to find the rates for a 30-year-old woman, use the rates for age 25.

EXAMPLE **1** **Finding the Life Insurance Premium**

Judith Allen, owner of Canadian Book Sales, is 40 years old and wants to buy a life insurance policy with a face value of $50,000. Use Table 8.10 to find her annual premium for (a) a renewable term policy, (b) a whole-life policy, (c) a universal life policy, and (d) a 20-pay life plan.

Solution Since the table gives rates per $1000 of face value, first find the number of thousands in $50,000.

$$50,000 = 50 \text{ thousands}$$

	Rate/$1000 (from Table 8.10)		Amount of Insurance (in thousands)		Annual Premium
(a) Renewable term	$3.41	×	50	=	$170.50
(b) Whole life	$7.68	×	50	=	$384.00
(c) Universal life	$7.45	×	50	=	$372.50
(d) 20-pay life	$21.60	×	50	=	$1080.00

NOTE   Remember to subtract 5 years from the age of a female before using the table of premiums.

Objective

5   *Use Premium Factors with Different Modes of Premium Payment.*   The annual life insurance premium is not always paid in one single payment. Many companies give the insured the option of paying the premium semiannually, quarterly, or monthly. For this convenience, the policyholder pays an additional amount, determined by a **premium factor**. Table 8.11 shows typical premium factors.

Table 8.11   PREMIUM FACTORS

Mode of Payment	Premium Factor
Semiannually	0.51
Quarterly	0.26
Monthly	0.0908

EXAMPLE 2   Using a Premium Factor

The annual insurance premium on a $50,000 whole-life policy for Michelle Lee is $384. Use Table 8.11 to find the amount of the premium and the total annual cost if she pays at the following periods: (a) semiannually, (b) quarterly, (c) monthly.

Solution

	Annual Premium		Premium Factor		Premium Payment
(a) Semiannual	$384	×	0.51	=	$195.84 each 6 months
(b) Quarterly	$384	×	0.26	=	$99.84 each quarter
(c) Monthly	$384	×	0.0908	=	$34.87 each month

The annual costs are found as follows.

	Premium		Number of Payments/Year		Total Annual Cost
Annual Payment	$384	×	1	=	$384
Semiannual	$195.84	×	2	=	$391.68
Quarterly	$99.84	×	4	=	$399.36
Monthly	$34.87	×	12	=	$418.44

Paying for the policy monthly results in a nearly 9% increase in the annual cost of the policy. Try to pay your premiums annually to save on cost.

Objective

6 *Describe Discounts, Conditions, and Additional Coverage.* Many companies today offer a **nonsmokers discount** because they feel that nonsmokers are better insurance risks. Normally, not having smoked for 12 months qualifies one as a nonsmoker. Most policies also contain a **suicide clause**. This clause states that suicide is not covered, usually for the first 2 years of the policy.

Additional coverage is often available for small increases in the premium. The **accidental death benefit** coverage will pay an additional death benefit if the insured dies as the result of an accident. An optional benefit known as **waiver of premium** allows the life insurance policy to remain in force without payment of premium when the insured becomes disabled. A **guaranteed conversion privilege** lets the insured convert term insurance to any type of whole-life or universal life insurance without physical examination. **Companion** or **spouse insurance** allows an insured to add a companion or spouse to a policy and results in both being insured on one policy.

Objective

7 *Understand Nonforfeiture Options.* Fire insurance, automobile insurance, property insurance, and term life insurance protect against specific hazards in the years during which the policy is in force. These policies rarely have any benefits remaining after premiums are no longer paid. However, whole-life, universal-life, and 20-pay life policies build up funds called **cash values** that can be withdrawn. The benefits available upon cancellation of this type of policy are called **nonforfeiture options**. The cash values that have built up in these policies can be used in any of the following ways.

1. Cancel the policy and withdraw the cash in one lump sum.
2. Leave the policy in force and borrow some of the cash value.
3. Cancel the policy and receive fixed payments during a period of time, such as 10 years.
4. Use the cash value to buy paid-up insurance that lasts for life.
5. Use the cash value to buy term insurance for a period of time after which policy is canceled.

The owner of the policy no longer has to make premium payments under the last two nonforfeiture options. Typical nonforfeiture options for a policy issued at age 25 appear in Table 8.12.

Table 8.12 NONFORFEITURE OPTIONS PER $1000/POLICY ISSUED AT AGE 25

Years in Force	Whole Life				20-Pay Life				Universal Life
	Cash Value	Paid-up Ins.	Ext. Term		Cash Value	Paid-up Ins.	Ext. Term		Cash Value
			Years	Days			Years	Days	
3*	$5	$16	1	192	$29	$93	11	18	$40
5	28	84	10	190	70	228	20	96	96
10	96	258	18	112	187	554	29	115	310
15	169	415	20	312	339	789	33	215	680
20	283	579	23	315	491	1000	Life	Life	1125
25	394	637	25	130	506	1000			1495
30	491	698	26	210	523	1000			1968

*Normally, there is no cash value accrued in the first 2 years. The cash value of universal life is an estimate, not a guarantee, of the value and will vary depending on the performance of the portfolio of investments chosen by the insured.

EXAMPLE **3** **Determining Nonforfeiture Options**

Lois Stevens purchased an $80,000 whole-life insurance policy when she was 25 years old and has paid on the policy for 20 years. Determine the following values for her policy: (a) cash value, (b) the amount of paid-up insurance that she could receive, and (c) the time period for which she could have extended-term insurance.

Solution

(a) The cash value found in Table 8.12 under whole life for 20 years is $283 per $1000 of insurance. The cash value of her policy is as follows.

$$\$283 \times 80 \text{ (number of \$1000s)} = \$22,640$$

(b) Again, from Table 8.12, the amount of paid-up insurance that she could receive is $579 per $1000, or

$$\$579 \times 80 = \$46,320 \text{ paid-up insurance.}$$

This coverage would remain in force until her death without paying any additional premium.

(c) The time period for which she could have extended-term insurance of the same amount, $80,000, is 23 years and 315 days.

So, Lois Stevens has the option of canceling the policy and (a) taking out $22,640 in cash, (b) using the cash value to buy $46,320 in life insurance without ever having to make another payment, or (c) having $80,000 in term life insurance for 23 years and 315 days without having to make another payment. The last option would result in no insurance after the 23 years and 315 days.

There are two types of insurance companies—**mutual companies** and **stock companies**. The policyholders are the owners in a mutual company, with the policies called **participating policies**. The owners (policyholders) share in any profits of the company; the profits are paid in the form of dividends. If the company prospers, the policyholders receive a dividend or refund of premium. In a stock company, the stockholders are the owners of the company, with the policies called **nonparticipating policies**. If the company prospers, the stockholders, not the policyholders, receive a dividend. The distinction is important in determining the **net cost of insurance policies**.

Objective

8 *Calculate Income under Various Settlement Options.* At the death of a life insurance policyholder, the **beneficiary**, the individual chosen by the insured to receive benefits upon death, has several **settlement options** when choosing how the death benefits are to be received. In many cases the beneficiary elects to receive a single lump-sum payment of the face value of the policy. In other cases, the beneficiary allows the life insurance company to invest the face value and to pay the beneficiary the proceeds and interest over a period of time in the form of an **annuity**. These are the more common options available.

1. A fixed-amount annuity may be paid each month. The monthly payments continue, including interest, until all the proceeds are used up.
2. The beneficiary may prefer the payments of a fixed-period annuity. The insurance company determines the amount that may be paid monthly, for example, for 10 years. The payment continues for exactly that period of time, even if the beneficiary dies.
3. Payments for life is another option. Based upon the age and sex of the beneficiary, the insurance company calculates an amount to be paid to the beneficiary for as long as he or she lives.
4. A last option is payments for life with a guaranteed number of years. Here, if the beneficiary dies before receiving the benefits for the guaranteed time period, the payments continue to the beneficiaries' heirs until the guarantee is satisfied. The guarantees usually range from 5 to 25 years.

Table 8.13 shows the monthly income per $1000 of insurance coverage under various settlement options.

Table 8.13   MONTHLY PAYMENTS PER $1000 OF FACE VALUE

Options 1 and 2: Fixed Amount or Fixed Number of Year		Options 3 and 4: Income for Life				
		Age When Payments Begin			Life with 10 Years	Life with 15 Years
Years	Amount	Male	Female	Life Annuity	Certain	Certain
10	$9.78	50	55	$4.63	$4.49	$4.38
12	8.46	55	60	5.36	5.16	4.78
14	7.63	60	65	5.94	5.73	4.91
16	6.91	65	70	6.93	6.51	5.34
18	6.07	70	75	7.86	6.93	6.28
20	5.78					

EXAMPLE 4   Finding Settlement Options

Chris Bowler is the beneficiary of a $40,000 life insurance policy. Find (a) the monthly payment if he decides to receive payments for 18 years and (b) the number of years payments will continue if he selects a monthly payment of $300.

Solution

(a) The monthly payment from Table 8.13 for 18 years is $6.07 per $1000 of face value. The monthly payment he receives is

$$\$6.07 \times 40 \text{ (thousands)} = \$242.80$$

(b) A monthly payment of $300 is equivalent to

$$\frac{\$300}{40(\text{thousands})} = \$7.50 \text{ per } \$1000 \text{ face value}$$

Reading the amount column under Options 1 and 2, find $7.63 (closest to $7.50). The $300 payment will continue for a little over 14 years.

EXAMPLE 5   Finding Settlement Options

Ron Hill, 60 years of age, is the beneficiary of a $20,000 life insurance policy. Find (a) his monthly payment from a life annuity and (b) his monthly payment from a life annuity with 15 years certain.

Solution

(a) Under Options 3 and 4 in Table 8.13, look up male, age 60. Look across to the life annuity column, to find $5.94. His monthly payment for life is

$$\$5.94 \times 20 \text{ (thousands)} = \$118.80$$

(b) The monthly payment from a life annuity with 15 years certain is

$$\$4.91 \times 20 \text{ (thousands)} = \$98.20$$

8.3	Exercises

Find the annual premium, the semiannual premium, the quarterly premium, and the monthly premium for each of the following. (Note: Subtract 5 years for females.) Use Tables 8.10 and 8.11.

	Face Value of Policy	Age of Insured	Sex of Insured	Type of Policy
1.	$30,000	60	F	Whole life
2.	$60,000	30	M	Whole life
3.	$35,000	40	M	20-pay life
4.	$80,000	40	F	Universal life
5.	$85,000	30	M	Universal life

	Face Value of Policy	Age of Insured	Sex of Insured	Type of Policy
6.	$150,000	45	F	Renewable term
7.	$100,000	35	F	Renewable term
8.	$10,000	22	M	20-pay life
9.	$50,000	45	F	Universal life
10.	$40,000	29	F	20-pay life
11.	$70,000	50	M	Whole life
12.	$60,000	35	M	Renewable term
13.	$100,000	60	F	Whole life
14.	$100,000	27	F	Universal life

 15. Explain in your own words the advantages and disadvantages of buying renewable term life insurance. Would you buy renewable term life insurance for yourself? Why or why not? (See Objective 2.)

 16. If you were the beneficiary of a $40,000 life insurance policy, what settlement option would you choose? Why? (See Objective 8.)

Find the nonforfeiture values of the following policies. The policies were issued at age 25. Use Table 8.12.

	Years in Force	Type of Policy	Face Value	Nonforfeiture Option
17.	10	Universal life	$50,000	Cash value
18.	15	Universal life	$75,000	Cash value
19.	30	20-pay life	$30,000	Paid-up insurance
20.	15	Whole life	$35,000	Extended term
21.	30	Universal life	$100,000	Cash value
22.	15	20-pay life	$25,000	Paid-up insurance
23.	20	Whole life	$100,000	Extended term
24.	10	Whole life	$40,000	Extended term

Find the monthly payment or period of payment under the following policy settlement options. Use Table 8.13.

	Beneficiary		Face		Monthly Payment	
	Age	Sex	Value	Settlement Option	Years	Amount
25.	55	M	$50,000	Fixed amount per month	20	_____
26.	65	F	$75,000	Life, 10 years certain	10	_____
27.	65	M	$10,000	Fixed number of years	_____	$60.70
28.	60	M	$40,000	Fixed number of years	_____	$338.40
29.	70	F	$30,000	Life, 15 years certain	15	
30.	60	F	$100,000	Fixed amount per month	10	

Solve the following application problems.

31. WHOLE-LIFE POLICY   Linda Davis buys a $50,000 whole-life policy at age 40. Her son Matthew is the beneficiary and will collect the face value of the policy. (a) Find the annual premium. (b) How much will Matthew get if his mother dies after paying premiums for 9 years?

32. 20-PAY LIFE POLICY   Luan Lee buys a $100,000, 20-pay life policy at age 45. Her son Bryan is the beneficiary and will collect the face value of the policy. (a) Find the annual premium. (b) How much will Bryan get if his mother dies after making payments for 12 years?

33. EMPLOYEE LIFE INSURANCE   Ozark Steel Foundry feels that it would suffer considerable hardship if the firm's head moldmaker died suddenly. Therefore, the firm takes out a $280,000 policy on the moldmaker's life. The moldmaker is a 45-year-old woman, and the company buys a renewable term policy. Find the semiannual premium.

34. KEY EMPLOYEE INSURANCE   Ellen Sawyer owns the Doll Shop and has a 40-year-old male key employee who she wants to insure for $100,000. Find the quarterly premium for a renewable term policy.

35. UNIVERSAL LIFE   Leticia Adams is a 35-year-old single mom who has a daughter with severe Down syndrome. To protect her daughter, she purchases a $200,000 universal life insurance policy on herself. Find the monthly premium.

36. WHOLE LIFE   At 25, Aaron Clinton is the primary wage earner for his family, which includes three young children. To protect his family in the event of his death and also save some funds for eventual retirement, he decides to buy $150,000 in whole-life insurance. Find the quarterly premium.

37. PREMIUM FACTORS   The annual premium for a whole-life policy is $872. Using premium factors, find (a) the semiannual premium, (b) the quarterly premium, (c) the monthly premium, and (d) the total annual cost of each of the plans.

38. UNIVERSAL LIFE   A universal life policy has an annual premium of $1806. Use premium factors to find (a) the semiannual premium, (b) the quarterly premium, (c) the monthly premium, and (d) the total annual cost for each of the plans.

39. NONFORFEITURE OPTIONS   Catherine Konradt purchased a $20,000 whole-life policy 20 years ago when she was 25 years old. Use the table of nonforfeiture options (Table 8.12) to determine (a) the cash value, (b) the amount of paid-up insurance which she could receive, and (c) the time period for which she could have paid-up insurance.

40. **NONFORFEITURE OPTIONS** Lee Hardesty purchased a 20-pay life policy 15 years ago when he was 25 years old. The face value of the policy is $80,000. Find the following values using the nonforfeiture options table (Table 8.12): (a) cash value, (b) the amount of paid-up insurance that he could have, and (c) the time period for which he could have paid-up term insurance.

41. **POLICY CASH VALUE** The face value of a universal life policy purchased by Patty Gillette is $100,000. She purchased the policy 25 years ago when she was 25 years of age. Use the nonforfeiture options table (Table 8.12) to find the cash value of the policy today.

42. **NONFORFEITURE OPTIONS** When he was 25 years old, Chuck Manly purchased a $40,000 whole-life policy. Now that 30 years have passed, Manly wants to know the options available when canceling his policy. Use the nonforfeiture options table (Table 8.12) to find (a) the cash value, (b) the amount of paid-up insurance he could have, and (c) the time period for which he could have paid-up term insurance.

43. **SETTLEMENT OPTIONS** Ryan Polstra is the beneficiary of a $25,000 life insurance policy. Polstra is 50 years of age and is considering the various settlement options available. Use Table 8.13 to find (a) the monthly payment if he selects payments for 12 years, (b) the number of years he will receive payments of $145 per month, (c) the monthly payment from a life annuity, and (d) the amount he would receive monthly if he chooses a life annuity with 15 years certain.

44. **SETTLEMENT OPTIONS** Krista Bauer is the beneficiary of a $30,000 life insurance policy. Bauer is 65 years of age and is considering the various settlement options available. Use Table 8.13 to find (a) the monthly payment she would receive if she selects a fixed amount for 10 years, (b) the number of years she can receive $225 per month, (c) the amount she can receive per month as a life annuity, and (d) the monthly amount she could receive as a life annuity with 10 years certain.

45. **SETTLEMENT OPTIONS** James Marcotte is the beneficiary of a $50,000 life insurance policy. Marcotte is 60 years of age and is considering the various settlement options available. Use Table 8.13 to find (a) the monthly payment he would receive if he selects a fixed amount for 16 years, (b) the number of years he can receive $305 per month, (c) the amount he can receive per month as a life annuity, and (d) the monthly amount he could receive as a life annuity with 10 years certain.

46. **SETTLEMENT OPTIONS** Kristen Clement is the beneficiary of a $70,000 life insurance policy. Clement is 60 years of age and is considering the various settlement options available. Use Table 8.13 to find (a) the monthly payment she would receive if she selects a fixed amount for 18 years, (b) the number of years she can receive $405 per month, (c) the amount she can receive as a life annuity, and (d) the monthly amount she could receive as a life annuity with 10 years certain.

47. The greatest advantage of a renewable term policy is that you get the most coverage for your premium dollar. However, renewable term provides no cash value for retirement. Explain how you would provide for retirement to offset this disadvantage of a renewable term life policy. (See Objective 2.)

48. The additional charge for paying an insurance premium semiannually, quarterly, or monthly is determined by a premium factor. Would you select something other than the single premium payment? Why or why not? How could you justify the additional charge (premium factor)? (See Objective 5.)

CHAPTER TERMS

Review the following terms to test your understanding of the chapter. For each term you do not know, refer to the page number found next to that term.

accidental death benefit [p. 303]

actuaries [p. 289]

adult operator [p. 293]

annuity [p. 304]

beneficiary [p. 304]

bodily injury insurance [p. 289]

cash value [p. 299]

coinsurance clause [p. 281]

collision insurance [p. 291]

companion or spouse insurance [p. 303]

comprehensive insurance [p. 291]

decreasing term insurance [p. 298]

deductible [p. 291]

disability insurance [p. 284]

endowment policy [p. 300]

extended-term insurance [p. 303]

face value [p. 278]

group insurance plans [p. 284]

guaranteed conversion privilege [p. 303]

homeowner's policy [p. 284]

insurance [p. 277]

insured policyholder [p. 300]

insurer or carrier [p. 277]

level premium term [p. 298]

liability insurance [p. 289]

limited-payment life insurance [p. 300]

medical insurance [p. 290]

mortality table [p. 300]

multiple carriers [p. 282]

mutual companies [p. 304]

net cost of insurance policies [p. 304]

no-fault insurance [p. 292]

nonforfeiture options [p. 303]

nonparticipating policies [p. 304]

nonsmokers discount [p. 303]

ordinary life insurance [p. 299]

paid-up insurance [p. 303]

participating policies [p. 304]

peril insurance [p. 277]

permanent life insurance [p. 299]

policy [p. 278]

premium [p. 277]

premium factor [p. 302]

profit margin [p. 289]

property damage insurance [p. 290]

renewable term [p. 298]

settlement option [p. 304]

short-term or cancellation rate [p. 279]

special multiperils policy (SMP) [p. 284]

stock companies [p. 304]

straight life insurance [p. 299]

suicide clause [p. 303]

term insurance [p. 298]

territorial ratings [p. 278]

underinsured motorist insurance [p. 293]

underwriter [p. 278]

uninsured motorist insurance [p. 293]

universal life policy [p. 300]

variable life policy [p. 300]

waiver of premium [p. 303]

whole-life insurance [p. 299]

worker's compensation insurance [p. 284]

youthful operator [p. 293]

CONCEPTS

EXAMPLES

8.1 Annual premium for fire insurance

Use the building and territorial rating in Table 8.1 to find the premiums per $100 for the building and for the contents. Add the two premiums.

Building replacement cost, $160,000; contents, $35,000; territorial rating, 4; building rating, B. Find the annual premium.

Building: $1600 \times \$0.75 = \$1200$

Contents: $350 \times \$0.77 = \$269.50$

Total premium: $\$1200 + \$269.50 = \$1469.50$

8.1 Short-term rates and cancellations

Annual premium is multiplied by the short-term rate. Use Table 8.2.

Annual premium is $2320. Short-term rate for 9 months is 85%. Premium for 9 months is

$\$2320 \times 0.85 = \$1972$ Premium

$\$2320 - \$1972 = \$348$ Refund

8.1 Calculate prorated insurance premium cancellations

Multiply annual premium by a fraction with months of insurance in force as the numerator and 12 as the denominator.

Annual premium, $1620; policy canceled after 4 months. Find refund. Premium for 4 months is

$$\$1620 \times \frac{4}{12} = \$540$$

$\$1620 - \$540 = \$1080$ refund

8.1 Coinsurance formula

Part of the risk is taken by the insured. An 80% coinsurance clause is common.

Loss paid by insurance company =

$$\text{Amount of loss} \times \frac{\text{Policy amount}}{80\% \text{ of replacement cost}}$$

Building replacement cost, $125,000; policy amount, $75,000; loss, $40,000; 80% coinsurance clause. Find the amount of loss paid by insurance company.

$$\$40,000 \times \frac{\$75,000}{\$100,000} = \$30,000$$

Insurance company pays $30,000.

8.1 Multiple carriers

Several companies insure the same property to limit their risk; each company pays its fractional portion of any claim.

Insured loss, $500,000; insurance is Company A with $1,000,000; Company B with $750,000; Company C with $250,000. Find the amount of loss paid by each company.

Total insurance is

$$
\begin{array}{r}
\$1,000,000 \\
750,000 \\
+\quad 250,000 \\
\hline
\$2,000,000
\end{array}
$$

Company A pays

$$\frac{\$1,000,000}{\$2,000,000} \times \$500,000 = \$250,000$$

Company B pays

$$\frac{\$750,000}{\$2,000,000} \times \$500,000 = \$187,500$$

Company C pays

$$\frac{\$250,000}{\$2,000,000} \times \$500,000 = \$62,500$$

8.2 Annual auto insurance premium

Most drivers are legally required to purchase automobile insurance. The premium is determined by the types of coverage selected, the type of car, geographic territory, past driving record, and other factors. See Tables 8.3 to 8.6.

Determine the premium: territory, 2; liability, 50/100; property damage, $50,000; comprehensive and collision, 3-year-old car with a category of 8; uninsured motorist coverage; driver, age 23 with driver's training.

$$
\begin{array}{rl}
\$341 & \text{Liability} \\
223 & \text{Property damage} \\
74 & \text{Comprehensive} \\
215 & \text{Collision} \\
+\quad 44 & \text{Uninsured motorist} \\
\hline
\$897 & \times 1.25 \text{ youthful-operator factor} \\
& = \$1121.25
\end{array}
$$

8.2 Amount paid by insurance company and by insured

The company pays up to the maximum amount of insurance coverage; insured pays the balance.

Policy terms: liability, 15/30; property damage, $10,000; collision, $250 deductible. Accident caused $2850 damage to insured's car; $3850 to other car; injury liability of $20,000 and $25,000, respectively.

Company pays $2600 ($2850 − $250) to repair insured's car.

Company pays $3850 to repair other car ($10,000 limit).

Company pays $30,000 for two injured people ($15,000 each).

Insured pays $15,000 ($45,000 − $30,000), amount over limit.

| 8.3 | **Annual life insurance premium** | Find the premiums on a $50,000 policy for a 30-year-old male. |

8.3 **Annual life insurance premium**

There are several types of life policies. Use Table 8.10 and multiply by the number of $1000s of coverage. Subtract 5 years from the age for females.

Premium =
number of thousands × rate per $1000

Find the premiums on a $50,000 policy for a 30-year-old male.

Renewable term: 50 × $2.97 = $148.50

Whole life: 50 × $5.66 = $283

Universal life: 50 × $6.08 = $304

20-Pay life: 50 × $18.78 = $939

8.3 **Premium factors**

If not paid annually, life insurance premiums may be paid semiannually, quarterly, or monthly. The annual premium is multiplied by the premium factor to determine the premium amount. Use Table 8.11.

The annual life insurance premium is $740. Find the semiannual, quarterly, and monthly premium.

Semiannual: $740 × 0.51 = $377.40

Quarterly: $740 × 0.26 = $192.40

Monthly: $740 × 0.0908 = $67.19

8.3 **Nonforfeiture options**

Upon cancellation of a policy, the insured may receive a cash settlement, paid-up insurance, or extended-term insurance as a nonforfeiture option. Use Table 8.12.

Insurance is a $40,000, 20-pay life policy; in force for 10 years; issued at age 25.

Cash value: $187 × 40 = $7480

Paid-up insurance: $554 × 40 = $22,160

Extended-term insurance period is 29 years, 115 days.

8.3 **Settlement options**

Upon the death of the insured, the beneficiary often has choices as to how the money may be received. These range from all cash to various types of payment arrangements. Use Table 8.13.

Insurance is a $30,000 policy; female beneficiary, age 60. Find monthly payments for:

16 years: 30 × $6.91 = $207.30

Life annuity: 30 × $5.36 = $160.80

Life with 15 years certain: 30 × $4.78 = $143.40

For how many years would $200 a month be paid?

$$\frac{\$200}{30} = \$6.67 \text{ per } \$1000$$

A little more than 16 years: $6.67 is closest to $6.91.

The answer section includes answers to all Review Exercises.

Find the total annual premium for fire insurance for each of the following. Use Table 8.1. **[8.1]**

	Territorial Rating	Building Classification	Replacement Cost of Building	Contents Value
1.	4	A	$640,000	$275,000
2.	2	C	$375,000	$198,000
3.	3	A	$80,000	$30,000
4.	1	B	$193,000	$68,000

Find the amount of refund to the insured using the Short-Term Rate Schedule (Table 8.2). **[8.1]**

	Annual Premium	Months in Force
5.	$1773	2
6.	$1078	6
7.	$1486	9
8.	$2878	5

Find (a) the amount of premium retained by the company and (b) the amount of refund to the insured using proration. **[8.1]**

	Annual Premium	Months in Force
9.	$3150	5
10.	$1975	9
11.	$1476	10
12.	$2784	2

Find the amount of each of the following losses that will be paid by the insurance company. Assume that each policy includes an 80% coinsurance clause. **[8.1]**

	Replacement Cost of Building	Face Value of Policy	Amount of Loss
13.	$456,000	$320,000	$45,000
14.	$277,500	$165,000	$97,800
15.	$186,700	$120,000	$3400
16.	$325,000	$220,000	$42,200

Find the annual motor vehicle insurance premium for the following people. **[8.2]**

	Name	Territory	Age	Driver's Training	Liability	Property Damage	Comprehensive Collision Age Group	Category	Uninsured Motorist
17.	Larik	1	42	—	50/100	$100,000	1	8	yes
18.	Ramos	3	18	yes	15/30	$10,000	5	7	yes
19.	Verano	2	24	no	25/50	$25,000	2	8	yes
20.	Wilson	4	29	—	250/500	$100,000	1	6	yes

Find the annual premium for each of the following life insurance policies. [8.3]

21. Carolyn Phelps: 20-pay life; $70,000 face value; age 55

22. Ralph Todd: renewable term; $50,000 face value; age 45

23. Gilbert Eckern: whole life: $30,000 face value; age 23

24. Irene Chang: universal life; $40,000 face value; age 29

Solve the following application problems.

25. Dave's Body and Paint has an insurable loss of $72,000, while having insurance coverage beyond the coinsurance requirement. The insurance is divided between Company A with $250,000 coverage, Company B with $150,000 coverage, and Company C with $100,000 coverage. Find the amount of loss paid by each of the insurance companies. **[8.1]**

26. The headquarters building of Western States Life is valued at $820,000, and the fire insurance policies contain an 80% coinsurance clause. The policies include $350,000 with Company 1 and $200,000 with Company 2. The Western building suffered a $150,000 fire loss. Find (a) the amount that Western would receive after the loss and (b) the amount of loss paid by each insurance company. Round to the nearest dollar. **[8.1]**

27. Tim Martinez was late for work and driving too fast. He was unable to avoid a bicycle rider and injured her badly. He had policy liability limits of 25/50, but the judge awarded damages of $38,400 to the injured bicycle rider. Find (a) the amount that the insurance company will pay and (b) the amount that Martinez must pay. **[8.2]**

28. Three people are injured in an automobile accident and receive $15,000 each in damages. The driver has bodily injury insurance of 50/100. (a) How much will the company pay to each person and (b) how much must the driver pay? **[8.2]**

29. Some scaffolding falls off a truck and into the path of a car, resulting in serious damage and injury. The car had damage of $16,800, and the driver and passenger of the car were given court awards of $25,000 and $35,000, respectively. The driver of the truck had 15/30 liability insurance limits and $10,000 property damage limits. Find (a) the total amount paid by the insurance company for both property damage and liability and (b) the total amount beyond the insurance limits for which the driver was liable. **[8.2]**

30. The annual premium for a whole-life policy is $970. Use premium factors to find (a) the semiannual premium, (b) the quarterly premium, (c) the monthly premium, and (d) the total annual cost for each of the plans. **[8.3]**

31. Lori Johnson purchased a universal life policy 20 years ago when she was 25 years old. The face value of the policy is $60,000. Find the cash value of the policy using the nonforfeiture options table (Table 8.12). **[8.3]**

32. Glenn Lewis purchased a $40,000 whole-life policy 20 years ago when he was 25 years old. Use Table 8.12 to determine (a) the cash value, (b) the amount of paid-up insurance he could receive, and (c) the time period for which he could have paid-up term insurance. **[8.3]**

33. Pete White is the beneficiary of an $80,000 life insurance policy. White is 60 years old and is considering the various settlement options available. Use Table 8.13 to find (a) the monthly payment he would receive if he selects a fixed payment for 16 years, (b) the number of years he can receive $675 per month, (c) the amount he can receive as a life annuity, and (d) the monthly amount he could receive as a life annuity with 15 years certain. **[8.3]**

34. Ann-Marie Sargent is the beneficiary of a $40,000 life insurance policy. Sargent is 55 years old and is considering the various settlement options available. Use Table 8.13 to find (a) the monthly payment she would receive if she selects a fixed payment for 20 years, (b) the number of years she can receive $245 per month, (c) the amount she can receive as a life annuity, and (d) the monthly amount she could receive as a life annuity with 10 years certain. **[8.3]**

CHAPTER 8	Business Application Case #1
	Financial Planning for Insurance

Childcare Playground Toys imports parts from Thailand and Malaysia and assembles quality playground equipment and riding toys. Planning ahead, the company set aside $41,700 to pay fire insurance premiums on the company property and a semiannual life insurance premium for the president. Both were due in the same month. Find each of the following.

(a) The building occupied by the company is a class B building with a replacement cost of $1,730,000. The contents are worth $3,502,000 and the territorial rating is 4. Find the annual insurance premium.

(b) The president of Childcare Playground Toys is a 45-year-old woman and the company is buying a $175,000, renewable term life insurance policy on the president's life. Find the semiannual premium.

(c) Find the total amount needed to pay the fire insurance premium and the semiannual life insurance premium.

(d) How much more than the amount needed had the company set aside to pay these expenses?

CHAPTER 8	Business Application Case #2
	Employee Benefits and Fire Insurance

After working for a large manufacturer for 19 years, Sherrie Bennett is establishing her own company to market low-cost wind turbines to Europe. She plans to purchase a small commercial building and hire the following people with salaries as shown. Answer the questions that follow.

Employee	Age, Sex	Duty	Annual Salary
P. Russo	30, F	Secretary	$23,500
E. Martin	45, M	Sales	$44,800
T. Hicks	50, F	Office Manager	$58,000

(a) Find the fire insurance premium for a building: replacement cost, $235,000; contents, $28,900; building rating, C; territory 5.

(b) Bennett decides to purchase life insurance for each employee in the amount shown. Find the annual life insurance premium for renewable term coverage. Then, find the amount of the FICA and Medicare taxes for each employee for which Bennett is responsible as the employer (FICA: 6.2%; Medicare; 1.45%). Finally, find the total expenditure for each employee.

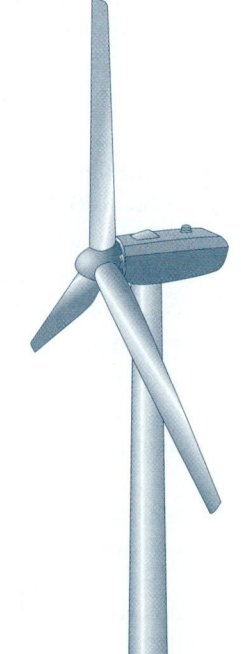

Employee	Amount of Life Insurance	Cost of Life Insurance	FICA	Medicare	Total
P. Russo	$50,000	_____	_____	_____	_____
E. Martin	$100,000	_____	_____	_____	_____
T. Hicks	$200,000	_____	_____	_____	_____

(c) Find the total annual cost of employee salaries, fire insurance, and employee benefits including life insurance, FICA, and Medicare.

Note that these are not all of the expenses that Bennett must pay in her first year of business. Presumably, she will pay at least part of the medical insurance, worker's compensation insurance, and unemployment insurance on her employees. She will also have to buy supplies and pay for telephone service, Internet access, travel to and from Europe, and shipping services in addition to many other costs.

PART 2	Cumulative Review: Chapters 5–8

The following credit card transactions were made at Gifts and Such. Answer Questions 1 to 5 using this information. **[5.2]**

	Sales		Credits
$93.50	$315.26	$22.51	$99.84
$117.75	$38.00	$162.15	$72.68
$173.05	$92.18		$35.63

1. Find the total amount of the sales slips.

2. What is the total amount of the credit slips?

3. Find the total amount of the deposit.

4. Assuming that the bank charges the retailer a $2\frac{1}{4}\%$ discount charge, find the amount of the discount charge at the statement date.

5. Find the amount of the credit given to the retailer after the fee is subtracted.

Solve the following application problems

6. The bank statement of Adam Hamel Productions shows a balance of $16,298.60, a returned check amounting to $673.60, a service charge of $28.32, and an interest credit of $40.72. There were unrecorded deposits of $3631.28 and $7136.60, and checks outstanding are $2570.20, $4331.92, $293, and $1887.32. The checkbook shows a balance of $18,645.24. Use the T-account form, Figure 5.13, to find the adjusted balance of this checking account. **[5.3]**

7. Angela Perez worked 7 hours on Monday, 10 hours on Tuesday, 8 hours on Wednesday, 9 hours on Thursday, and 10 hours on Friday. Her regular hourly pay is $12.80. Find her gross earnings for the week if Perez is paid overtime (time-and-a-half) for all hours over 8 worked in a day. **[6.1]**

8. Laura Rogers is a commission salesperson for Education Specialties, which allows her a draw of $1200 per month. Her commision is 5% of the first $5000 in sales, 8% of the next $15,000, and 15% of all sales over $20,000. Her sales for the month were $28,400. Find (a) her total commission and (b) the earnings due at the end of the month after repaying the drawing account balance of $1200. **[6.2]**

9. Eric Means is paid $2.18 for each computer keyboard assembled, is charged $1.05 for each rejection, and is paid time-and-a-half for overtime production. Find his gross earnings for the week when he assembles 268 keyboards at the regular rate and 32 keyboards at the overtime rate and has 9 chargebacks. **[6.3]**

10. Greg Baker is a salesperson for Petco Wholesalers and is paid $650 per week plus a commission of 3% of all sales. His sales last week were $33,482. Find the amount of (a) his Social Security tax (6.2%), (b) his Medicare tax (1.45%), and (c) his state disability (1%) for the pay period. **[6.4]**

11. As a nurse, Connie Zhao earned $1240 one week including overtime. She is single and has two children, so she claims 3 exemptions. Her deductions include FICA (6.2%), Medicare (1.45%), federal withholding, state disability insurance (1%), state withholding of 3.2%, and a savings bond of $50. Use the percentage method of withholding to find her net pay for the week. **[6.5]**

12. The employees of Highland Farms paid a total of $968.50 in Social Security tax last month, $223.50 in Medicare tax, and $1975.38 in federal withholding tax. Find the total amount that the employer must send to the Internal Revenue Service. **[6.6]**

13. The Custom Fireside Shop charges $286.96, including 5.5% sales tax, for a custom fireplace screen. Find the price of the fireplace screen without the tax. **[7.1]**

Complete the following list comparing tax rates. **[7.2]**

Percent	Per $100	Per $1000	In Mills
14. (a) _____	$2.68	(b) _____	(c) _____
15. 4.62%	(a) _____	(b) _____	(c) _____

16. Phyllis Beaton earned $38,514.75 last year from Bel Air Supermarket as assistant manager and $675.18 in interest from her credit union. She had $1800 in IRA contributions. Find her adjusted gross income. **[7.3]**

17. Feather's Custom Cabinets owns a class A building with a replacement cost of $179,480. The replacement cost of the contents is $83,300 and the territorial rating is 4. Find the annual fire insurance premium. **[8.1]**

18. One Outback Restaurant has a replacement cost of $720,000. The fire policies are $200,000 with Company A, $100,000 with Company B, and $60,000 with Company C, and each contains an 80% coinsurance clause. There is a fire at the restaurant causing a $240,000 loss. Find (a) the amount that the insured would receive and (b) the amount that each of the insurance companies would pay. Round to the nearest dollar. **[8.1]**

19. James Follain is 57, lives in territory 2, and wants the following automobile coverage: liability, 50/100; property damage, $50,000; comprehensive and collision (age group 3 and category 7); and uninsured motorist. Find his annual premium. **[8.2]**

20. Del Nelson was distracted by his cell phone as he drove along the interstate. He didn't notice that cars were braking and he crashed into the car in front of him. Nelson had 25/50 liability limits, $25,000 property damage limits, and collision coverage with a $250 deductible. Damage to Nelson's car was $6340, while the car in front of him, with a value of $34,800, was totaled. The results of a lawsuit awarded $100,000 and $65,000 in damages for personal injury to the two people in the other car. Find the amount that the insurance company will pay for (a) repairing Nelson's car, (b) repairing the other car, and (c) personal injury damages. (d) How much must Nelson pay beyond his insurance coverage? **[8.2]**

21. Jim Havey purchased a 20-pay life policy with a face value of $100,000. He is 50 years old. Use the premium factors to find (a) the semiannual premium, (b) the quarterly premium, (c) the monthly premium, and (d) the total annual cost of each of the plans. **[8.3]**

CHAPTER

9

Mathematics of Buying

Retail is a huge business that provides millions of jobs around the world. Think of the many retail stores you have been in, from the giant stores of Wal-Mart, Target, or Home Depot to tiny cell phone outlets at your local mall. Retailers make a profit by purchasing items at one price and then selling them for a higher price. We study the mathematics of buying products in this chapter and discuss markup and markdown in the next chapter.

A **supply chain** consists of **raw materials suppliers**, which supply **manufacturers**, which ship finished products to **wholesalers** (or **distributors**), which ship products to retailers. **Retailers** sell directly to the ultimate user: the **consumer**.

Suppliers ▷ Manufacturer ▷ Wholesaler ▷ Retailer ▷ Consumer

Inventory refers to all items that a company owns that are for sale, or that are being readied for sale. It is very costly for a firm to have too much inventory since products become outdated or spoil, among other reasons. Too little inventory is also very costly since it often results in lost sales. So, managers try to hold just the right amount of inventory everywhere in the supply chain. Figure 9.1 shows the ratio of average inventories held by businesses to annual sales. Notice that the ratio has generally fallen since 1999. In other words, since 1999 managers have continued to cut costs by decreasing the average amount of inventory held for each dollar in sales. Doing so not only benefits the firm in terms of costs and profits, it usually also results in lower prices to consumers!

Ratio of Average Inventory to Annual Sales
(Data adjusted for seasonal, holiday and trading-day differences but not for price changes)

Source: Census.gov.

Figure 9.1

STOP
—and think

> Notice that the ratio of average inventory to sales in Figure 9.1 increased sharply in late 2008 as consumer demand dropped sharply during the real estate and credit crisis of 2008–2010. Use the idea of supply chains to explain why. What are the possible effects on business of a rapid increase in inventory?

9.1	Invoices and Trade Discounts

OBJECTIVES

1. *Complete an invoice.*
2. *Understand common shipping terms.*
3. *Identify invoice abbreviations.*
4. *Calculate net cost and trade discounts.*
5. *Differentiate between single and series discounts.*
6. *Calculate each series discount separately.*
7. *Use complements to calculate series discounts.*
8. *Use a table to find the net cost equivalent of series discounts.*

An **invoice** is a document issued by a seller to a buyer as a record of a transaction. For a seller, the invoice is a **sales invoice** that records a sale. For a buyer, an invoice is a **purchase invoice** that records a purchase. An invoice shows the seller, buyer, items purchased, quantity, price, and any discounts. It shows the **extension total**, which is the number of items purchased times the price per unit. It also shows any discounts applied, the shipping and insurance charges, and the **invoice total**, which is the sum of the extension totals.

Originally, invoices were printed on paper. Today, most invoices are sent electronically over the Internet, although they are often printed out on paper for record-keeping purposes. **Electronic commerce** refers to the very widespread buying and selling of products over the Internet. Electronic commerce allows financial transactions to occur much more rapidly and with a much lower cost than before. Electronic commerce is used for much of global trade.

Objective

1 *Complete an Invoice.* The invoice in Figure 9.2 serves as a sales invoice for J. B. Sherr Company and as a purchase invoice for Kitchens Galore. The number of items shipped column multiplied by the **unit price** gives the amount or total for each item. The **total invoice amount** is the sum of the amount totals.

Trade and cash discounts, discussed later in this section, **are never applied to shipping and insurance charges**. For this reason shipping and insurance charges are often not included in the invoice total, so the purchaser must add them to the invoice total to find the total amount due. In the J. B. Sherr Company invoice, the freight (shipping) charges ($39.95) are included in the INVOICE TOTAL space.

Objective

2 *Understand Common Shipping Terms.* A common shipping term appearing on invoices is **free on board (FOB)**, followed by the words **shipping point** or **destination**. The term "FOB shipping point" means that the *buyer* pays for shipping and that ownership of the merchandise passes to the purchaser when the merchandise is given to the shipper. The term

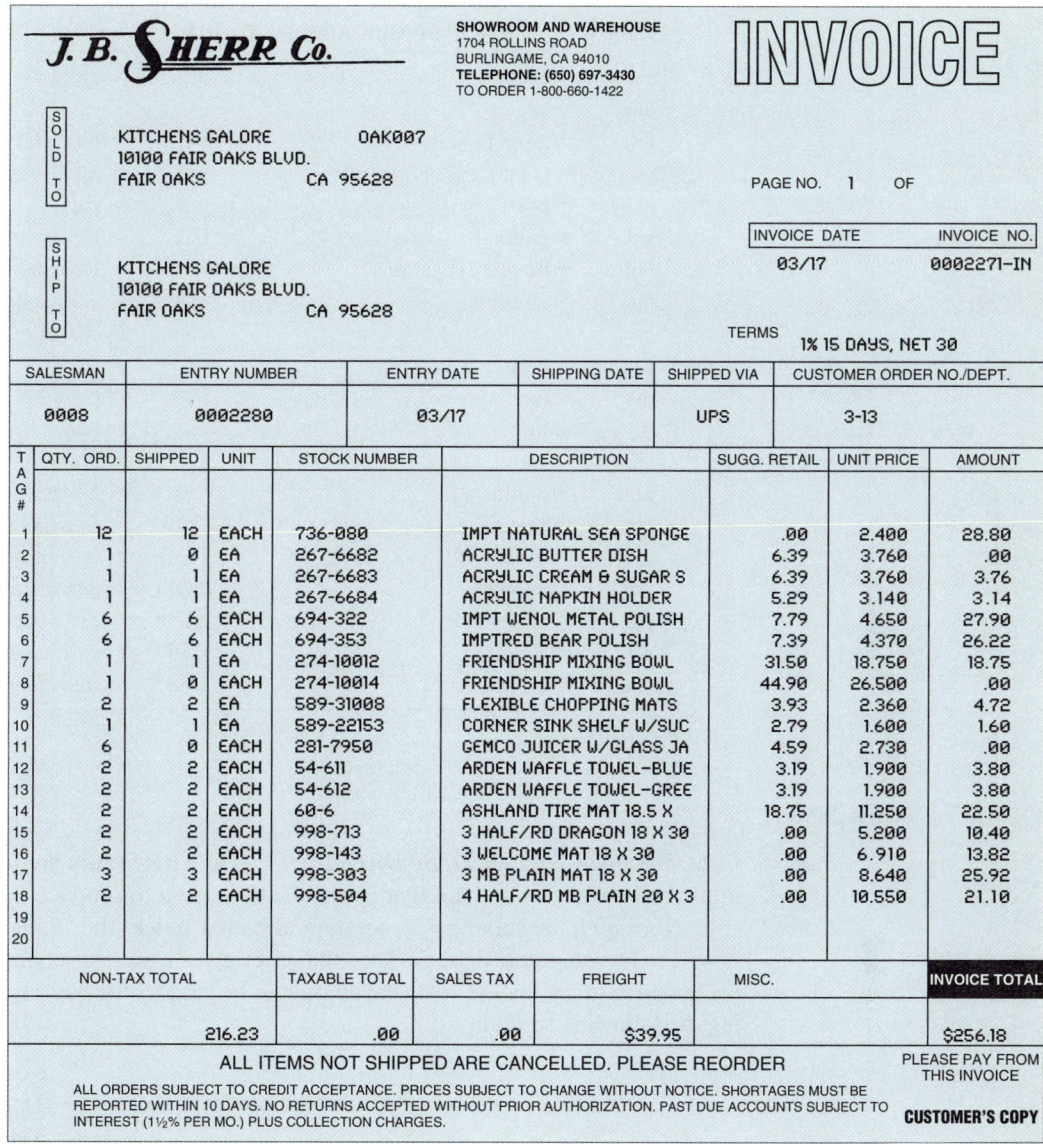

Figure 9.2

"FOB destination" means that the *seller* pays the shipping charges and retains ownership until the goods reach the destination. This distinction is important in the event that the merchandise is lost or damaged during shipment.

The shipping term **COD** means **cash on delivery**. Here, the shipper makes delivery to the purchaser on the receipt of enough cash to pay for the goods. A shipping term used when goods are moved by ship is **FAS**, which means **free alongside ship**. Here, the goods are delivered to the receiving dock with all freight charges to that point paid by the seller.

Objective

3 *Identify Invoice Abbreviations.*   A number of abbreviations are used on invoices to identify measurements, quantities of merchandise, shipping terms, and additional discounts. Those most commonly used are shown in Table 9.1. (Some of these measurements are from the metric system. These measurements often appear on invoices for imported goods.)

Table 9.1   COMMON INVOICE ABBREVIATIONS

ea.	= each	drm.	= drum
doz.	= dozen	cs.	= case
gro.	= gross (144 items)	bx.	= box
gr. gro.	= great gross (12 gross)	sk.	= sack
qt.	= quart	pr.	= pair
gal.	= gallon (4 quarts)	C	= Roman numeral for 100
bbl.	= barrel $\left(31\frac{1}{2} \text{ gallons}\right)$	M	= Roman numeral for 1000
ml	= milliliter	cwt.	= per hundred weight
cl	= centiliter	cpm.	= cost per thousand
L	= liter	@	= at
in.	= inch	lb.	= pound
ft.	= foot	oz.	= ounce
yd.	= yard	g	= gram
mm	= millimeter	kg	= kilogram
cm	= centimeter	FOB	= free on board
m	= meter	ROG	= receipt-of-goods
km	= kilometer	EOM	= end-of-month
ct.	= crate	ex. or x	= extra dating
cart.	= carton	COD	= cash on delivery
ctn.	= carton	FAS	= free alongside ship

Objective

4   *Calculate Net Cost and Trade Discounts.*   **Trade discounts** are offered to businesses or individuals who buy an item that is to be sold or used to produce an item that will then be sold. Normally, the seller prices an item at its **list price** (the suggested price at which the item is to be sold to the public). Then the seller gives a trade discount that is subtracted from the list price to get the **net cost** (the amount to be paid by the buyer). Find the net cost by using the following formula.

$$\text{Net cost} = \text{List price} - \text{Trade discount} \qquad \text{or} \qquad \begin{array}{r} \textbf{List price} \\ - \textbf{ Trade discount} \\ \hline \textbf{Net cost} \end{array}$$

NOTE   The terms *net cost* and *net price* both refer to the amount paid by the buyer. However, net cost is the preferred term since this is the cost of an item to the business.

EXAMPLE 1   Calculating a Single Trade Discount

The list price of a Shredmaster home paper shredder is $99.80, and the trade discount is 25%. Find the net cost.

Solution   First find the amount of the trade discount by taking 25% of $99.80.

$$R \times B = P$$
$$25\% \times \$99.80 = 0.25 \times \$99.80 = \$24.95$$

Find the net cost by subtracting $24.95 from the list price of $99.80.

$$\$99.80 \,(\text{list price}) - \$24.95 \,(\text{trade discount}) = \$74.85 \,(\text{net cost})$$

The net cost of the shredder is $74.85.

Objective

5   *Differentiate between Single and Series Discounts.*   In Example 1 a **single discount** of 25% was offered. Another type of discount combines two or more discounts into a **series** or **chain discount**. A series discount written as 20/10 means that a 20% discount is subtracted from the list price, and *from this difference* another 10% discount is subtracted.

Another discount of 15% could be attached to the series discount of 20/10, giving a new series discount of 20/10/15.

Why Trade Discounts May Change

1. *Price changes* may cause trade discounts to be raised or lowered.
2. As the *quantity purchased* increases, the discount may increase.
3. The buyer's position in *marketing channels* may determine the amount of discount offered (a wholesaler would receive a larger discount than the succeeding retailer).
4. *Geographic location* may influence the trade discount. An additional discount may be offered to increase sales in one particular area.
5. *Seasonal fluctuations* in sales may influence the trade discounts offered.
6. *Competition* from other companies may cause trade discounts to be raised or lowered.

Objective

6   *Calculate Each Series Discount Separately.*   Three methods can be used to calculate a series discount and the net cost. The first of these is to *calculate each series discount separately and subtract it before finding the next discount.*

EXAMPLE 2   **Calculating Series Trade Discounts**

Oaks Hardware is offered a series discount of 20/10 on a Porter-Cable cordless drill with a list price of $150. Find the net cost after the series discount.

Solution   First, find the 20% discount and subtract it from $150.

$$20\% \text{ discount} = 20\% \text{ of } \$150 = \$30$$
$$\text{Amount after } 20\% \text{ discount} = \$150 - \$30 = \$120$$

Then, find the 10% discount and subtract it from the $120 amount. Notice that the 10% discount applies to the amount *after* the first discount, or to $120.

$$10\% \text{ discount} = 10\% \text{ of } \$120 = \$12$$
$$\text{Amount after both discounts} = \$120 - \$12 = \$108$$

NOTE   When finding series discounts separately, remember to apply each discount after the previous discount has been subtracted from the price.

It is important to realize that discounts in a series are never added together. For example, a series discount of 30/15 is not the same thing as a single discount of 45% (the sum of 30% and 15%). A discount of 35/15 indicates that a 35% discount is applied first. Then, a discount of 15% is applied to the amount remaining after the first discount has been subtracted.

Objective

7   *Use Complements to Calculate Series Discounts.*   The second method is to *use complements.* First, find the **complement** (with respect to 1, or 100%) of each single discount. The complement with respect to 1 is found by subtracting the discount from 100%. Several examples are shown in Table 9.2. Note that you must first convert any fraction in a discount to a decimal number before subtracting from 100%. For example, $16\frac{2}{3}\%$ is first converted to 16.667 (rounded) in the table before being subtracted from 100%.

Table 9.2   TYPICAL COMPLEMENTS WITH RESPECT TO 1

Discount	Calculation	Complement	Decimal Equivalent of Complement
20%	100% − 20%	= 80%	0.80
15%	100% − 15%	= 85%	0.85
35%	100% − 35%	= 65%	0.65
$12\frac{1}{2}\%$	100% − 12.5%	= 87.5%	0.875
$16\frac{2}{3}\%$	100% − 16.667%	= 83.334%	0.833 (rounded)
$33\frac{1}{3}\%$	100% − 33.333%	= 66.667%	0.667 (rounded)

The complement of the discount is the portion actually paid. For example,

- 10% discount means 90% paid.
- 25% discount means 75% paid.
- $33\frac{1}{3}\%$ discount means $66\frac{2}{3}\%$ $\left(\frac{2}{3}\right)$ paid.
- 50% discount means 50% paid.

The **net cost equivalent** or **percent paid** is the product of the complements. Usually, there are only two or perhaps three complements, but there can be more.

$$\text{Net cost equivalent} = \text{First complement} \times \text{Second complement} \times \dots$$

Multiply the list price by the net cost equivalent to find the net cost.

$$\text{Net cost} = \text{List price} \times \text{Net cost equivalent}$$

EXAMPLE 3   Using Complements to Solve Series Discounts

Kitchens Galore is offered a series discount of 20/10 on a George Foreman Grilling Machine with list price of $150. Find the net cost after the series discount.

Solution   The discounts are 20% and 10%. First, find the complement of each discount.

Discount	Complement	Decimal Form of Complement
20%	100% − 20% = 80%	0.8
10%	100% − 10% = 90%	0.9

Then, multiply the decimal form of the two complements to find the net cost equivalent and net cost.

$$\text{Net cost equivalent} = 0.8 \times 0.9 = 0.72$$

$$\text{Net cost} = \text{List price} \times \text{Net cost equivalent}$$
$$= \$150 \quad \times \quad 0.72$$
$$= \$108$$

The discount is the difference between the list price and the net cost, or $150 − $108 = $42 in this example.

Scientific
Calculator
Approach

On many calculators you can subtract the discount percents from the list price in a series calculation. For Example 3, this would be calculated as follows:

$$150 \boxed{-} 20 \boxed{\%} \boxed{-} 10 \boxed{\%} \boxed{=} 108$$

EXAMPLE 4 **Using Complements to Solve Series Discounts**

The list price of a Heartland 30-inch combination gas and electric stove is $3095. Find the net cost if a series discount of 20/10/10 is offered.

Solution   Start by finding the complements with respect to 1 of each discount. Then multiply the complements to find the net cost equivalent.

20/10/10   Series discount

$0.8 \times 0.9 \times 0.9 = \mathbf{0.648}$ **Net cost equivalent (percent paid)**

Complements with respect to 1

Net cost = List price × Net cost equivalent

= $3095   ×   **0.648**

= $2005.56

Amount of discount = List price − Net cost

= $3095   − $2005.56

= $1089.44

> **NOTE**   *Never round the net cost equivalent.* If a repeating decimal results, use the fraction equivalent. In Example 4, if the net cost equivalent had been rounded to 0.65, the resulting net cost would have been $2011.75 (0.65 × $3095). This error of $6.19 demonstrates the importance of not rounding the net cost equivalent.

Objective

8   *Use a Table to Find the Net Cost Equivalent of Series Discounts.*   The third method is to *use a table of net cost equivalents.* For example, to use Table 9.3 for a series discount of 20/10/10, find the number located to the right of 10/10 and below 20%. The number is 0.648, the net cost equivalent for a discount of 20/10/10. Multiply this number by the list price to get the net cost.

The order of the discounts in the series makes no difference. A 10/20 series is the same as a 20/10 series, and a 15/10/20 series is identical to a 20/15/10 series. This is true because changing the order in which complements are multiplied does not change the net cost equivalent.

> **NOTE**   The net cost equivalent (percent paid) found using Table 9.3 and the list price are multiplied to find the net cost.

EXAMPLE 5 **Using a Table of Net Cost Equivalents**

Use Table 9.3 to find the net cost equivalent for the following series discounts.

(a) 10/20   **(b)** 10/10/40   **(c)** 25/25/5   **(d)** 35/20/15

Solution

(a) 0.72   **(b)** 0.486   **(c)** 0.534375   **(d)** 0.442

Table 9.3 NET COST EQUIVALENTS OF SERIES DISCOUNTS

	5%	10%	15%	20%	25%	30%	35%	40%
5	0.9025	0.855	0.8075	0.76	0.7125	0.665	0.6175	0.57
10	0.855	0.81	0.765	0.72	0.675	0.63	0.585	0.54
10/5	0.81225	0.7695	0.72675	0.684	0.64125	0.5985	0.55575	0.513
10/10	0.7695	0.729	0.6885	0.648	0.6075	0.567	0.5265	0.486
15	0.8075	0.765	0.7225	0.68	0.6375	0.595	0.5525	0.51
15/10	0.72675	0.6885	0.65025	0.612	0.57375	0.5355	0.49725	0.459
20	0.76	0.72	0.68	0.64	0.6	0.56	0.52	0.48
20/15	0.646	0.612	0.578	0.544	0.51	0.476	0.442	0.408
25	0.7125	0.675	0.6375	0.6	0.5625	0.525	0.4875	0.45
25/20	0.57	0.54	0.51	0.48	0.45	0.42	0.39	0.36
25/25	0.534375	0.50625	0.478125	0.45	0.421875	0.39375	0.365625	0.3375
30	0.665	0.63	0.595	0.56	0.525	0.49	0.455	0.42
40	0.57	0.54	0.51	0.48	0.45	0.42	0.39	0.36

NOTE *Do not round any of the net cost equivalents.* Doing so will cause an error in the net cost.

9.1 Exercises

ABBREVIATIONS ON INVOICES What do each of the following abbreviations represent?

1. ft.   **2.** mm

3. sk.   **4.** qt.

5. gr. gro.   **6.** kg

7. cs.   **8.** gro.

9. drm.   **10.** yd.

11. cpm.   **12.** bbl.

13. gal.   **14.** cwt.

15. COD   **16.** FOB

17. USING INVOICES Compute each of the following extension totals, find the invoice total, and the total amount due.

HOME ACCESSORIES WHOLESALERS

Sold to: Kitchens Galore
10100 Fair Oaks Blvd.
Fair Oaks, CA 95628

Date: June 10
Order. No.: 796152
Shipped by: UPS
Terms: Net

Quantity	Order No./Description	Unit Price	Extension Total
6 doz.	pastry brush, wide	$37.80 doz.	
3 gro.	napkins, cotton	$12.60 gro.	
9 doz.	cherry pitters	$14.04 doz.	
8	food processors (3 qt.)	$106.12 ea.	
53 pr.	stainless tongs	$68.12 pr.	
		Invoice Total	
		Shipping and Insurance	$37.45
		Total Amount Due	

18. USING INVOICES Compute each of the following extension totals, find the invoice total, and the total amount due.

J & K'S MUSTANG PARTS New and Used				
Sold to: Dave's Auto Body & Paint 4443-B Auburn Blvd. Sacramento, CA 95841			**Date:** July 17 **Order. No.:** 100603 **Shipped by:** Emery **Terms:** Net	
Quantity	**Order No./Description**	**Unit Price**	**Extension Total**	
24	filler tube gaskets	$2.25 ea.		
12 pr.	taillight lens gaskets	$4.75 pr.		
6 pr.	taillight bezels to body	$10.80 pr.		
2 gr.	door panel fasteners	$14.20 gr.		
18	bumper bolt kits	$16.50 ea.		
		Invoice Total		
		Shipping and Insurance	$23.75	
		Total Amount Due		

 19. Explain the difference between "FOB shipping point" and "FOB destination." In each case, who pays for shipping? When does ownership of the merchandise transfer? (See Objective 2.)

 20. Name six items that appear on an invoice. Try to do this without looking at an invoice. (See Objective 1.)

Using complements (with respect to 1) of the single discounts, find the net cost equivalent for each of the following discounts. Use Table 9.3 for the first four problems.

21. 10/20   **22.** 10/10   **23.** 20/20/20

24. 10/15/20   **25.** 10/20/25   **26.** 40/20/10

27. $30/42\frac{1}{2}$ **28.** $10/16\frac{2}{3}$ **29.** 20/30/5

30. 20/20/10   **31.** 50/10/20/5   **32.** 25/10/20/10

Find the net cost for each of the following. Round to the nearest cent.

33. $418 less 20/20   **34.** $148 less 25/10

35. $8.20 less 5/10   **36.** $860 less 20/40

37. $9.80 less 10/10/10   **38.** $8.80 less 40/10/20

39. $8220 less 30/5/10   **40.** $15.70 less 5/10/20

41. $25 less $30/32\frac{1}{2}$ **42.** $590 less $10/12\frac{1}{2}/10$

43. $1250 less 20/20/20   **44.** $1410 less 10/20/5

 45. Explain the difference between a single trade discount and a series or chain trade discount. (See Objectives 4 and 5.)

46. Identify and explain four reasons that might cause series trade discounts to change. (See Objective 5.)

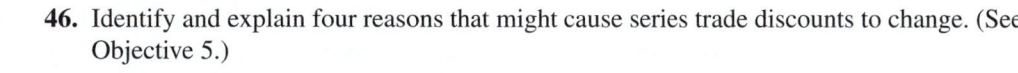 **47.** Explain what a complement (with respect to 1 or 100%) is. Give an example. (See Objective 7.)

 48. Using complements, explain how to find the net cost equivalent of a 25/20 series discount. Explain why a 25/10/10 series discount is not the same as a 25/20 series discount. (See Objective 7.)

Solve the following application problems in trade discount. Round to the nearest cent.

49. **PURCHASING A DIGITAL CAMERA** The list price of a new digital camera is $399.99. If the series discount offered is 10/10/25, what is the net cost after trade discounts?

50. **ADJUSTABLE WALKERS** Roger Wheatley, a restorative nurse assistant (RNA), finds that the list price of one dozen adjustable walkers is $1680. Find the cost per walker if a series discount of 40/25 is offered.

51. **KITCHEN CABINETS** Modern Cabinets purchases a tile-topped wooden kitchen island list-priced at $480. It is available at either a 10/15/10 discount or a 20/15 discount. (a) Which discount gives the lower price? (b) Find the difference in net cost.

52. **TANNING SALON** Electric Beach buys a tanning gel with a list price per bottle of $17.21. Since he buys in volume for their chain of tanning salons, the purchasing manager prices the gel at two different wholesalers. One offers a 15/10/5 discount and the second offers a 15/20 discount. (a) Which discount gives the lower cost? (b) Find the difference per bottle.

53. **BULK CHEMICALS** Brazilian Chemical Supply offers a series discount of 20/20/10 on all bulk purchases. A tank (bulk) of industrial solvent is list-priced at $28,500. What is the net cost after trade discounts?

54. **KITCHEN SUPPLIES** Kitchens Galore receives a 10/5/20 series trade discount from a supplier. If it purchases 3 dozen 32-ounce smoothie makers list-priced at $468 per dozen, find the net cost.

55. **MUSIC PLAYER** This is Jennifer Rainwater's first week working as a purchaser for an electronics store. She searches for a particular portable music player and finds one priced at $107 with discounts of 20/10 at the quantity needed. She mistakenly understands 20/10 to mean a 30% discount. Find the difference in price due to this error.

56. **BILLING ERROR** The Office Depot offers a series trade discount of 30/20 to its regular customers. Chris Hutchinson, a new man in the billing department, understood the 30/20 terms to mean 50% and computed this trade discount on a list price of $5440. How much difference did this error make in the amount of the invoice?

57. **STICKER PURCHASES** The AAA Foto and Copy Shop purchases stickers at a list price of $135 per 1000. If it receives a trade discount of $40/33\frac{1}{3}$, find the net cost of 3500 stickers.

58. **STATIONERY SALES** One brand of file folders is list-priced at $6.60 per dozen. A wholesale stationer offers a trade discount of 10/5/15 on the folders. Find the net cost of $5\frac{1}{2}$ dozen folders.

59. **BRASS DEADBOLTS** The list price of brass deadbolts is $9.95. A retailer has a choice of two suppliers, one offering a discount of 10/25/15 and the other offering a discount of 20/15/10. If the retailer purchases 4 dozen deadbolts, find (a) the total cost of the less expensive supplier and (b) the amount saved by selecting the lower price.

60. **FIBER OPTICS** Cindy Herring has a choice of two suppliers of fiber optics for her business. Tyler Supplies offers a 20/10/25 discount on a list price of $5.70 per unit. Irving Optics offers a 30/20 series discount on a list price of $5.40 per unit. (a) Which supplier gives her the lower price? (b) How much does she save if she buys 12,500 units from the lower-priced supplier? (*Hint:* Do not round.)

9.2	**Single Discount Equivalents**

OBJECTIVES

1 *Express a series discount as an equivalent single discount.*

2 *Find the net cost by multiplying list price by the complements of single discounts.*

3 *Find the list price if given the series discount and the net cost.*

4 *Determine a single trade discount rate.*

5 *Find the trade discount that must be added to match a competitor's price.*

Objective

1   *Express a Series Discount as an Equivalent Single Discount.*   Series or chain discounts must often be expressed as a single discount rate. Find a **single discount equivalent** to a series discount by multiplying the complements (with respect to 1 or 100%) of the individual discounts. As in the previous section, the result is the net cost equivalent. Then, subtract the net cost equivalent from 1. The result is the single discount that is equivalent to the series discount. *The single discount is expressed as a percent.*

$$\text{Single discount equivalent} = 1 - \text{Net cost equivalent}$$

EXAMPLE 1   **Finding a Single Discount Equivalent**

If Air Clean Manufacturing offered a 20/10 discount to wholesale accounts on all heater filters, what would be the single discount equivalent?

Solution   Find the net cost equivalent (percent paid).

$$20/10$$

$$0.8 \times 0.9 = 0.72 \quad \text{Net cost equivalent}$$

Subtract the net cost equivalent from 1.

$$1.00 \,\text{base} \,(100\%) - 0.72 \,\text{remains} = 0.28$$

The single discount equivalent of a 20/10 series discount is 28%.

This method may also be used with the table of net cost equivalents of series discounts. For example, Table 9.3 shows 0.72 as the net cost equivalent for the series discount 20/10. The single discount is therefore 28% $(1.00 - 0.72 = 0.28 = 28\%)$.

Objective

2   *Find the Net Cost by Multiplying List Price by the Complements of Single Discounts.*   The net cost can also be found by multiplying the list price by the complements of each of the single discounts in a series, as shown in Example 2.

EXAMPLE 2   **Finding the Net Cost Using Complements**

The list price of an oak entertainment center is $970. Find the net price if trade discounts of $20/15/27\frac{1}{2}$ are offered.

Solution

$$\text{Net cost} = \text{List price} \times \text{Complements of individual discounts}$$

$$\text{Net cost} = \$970 \times 0.8 \times 0.85 \times 0.725$$

$$20/15/27\tfrac{1}{2}$$

$$= \$478.21$$

 Scientific Calculator Approach

For the calculator solution to Example 2, enter the list price and multiply by the complements to find the net price.

$$970 \;\boxed{\times}\; .8 \;\boxed{\times}\; .85 \;\boxed{\times}\; .725 \;\boxed{=}\; 478.21$$

Objective

3   *Find the List Price If Given the Series Discount and the Net Cost.*   Sometimes the net cost after trade discounts is known along with the series discount, and the list price must be found.

EXAMPLE 3   **Solving for List Price**

Find the list price of a Kohler kitchen sink that has a net cost of $243.20 after trade discounts of 20/20.

Solution   Use a net cost equivalent, along with knowledge of percent. Start by finding the percent paid, using complements.

$$20/20 \qquad \text{Series discount}$$

$$0.8 \times 0.8 = 0.64 \qquad \text{Net cost equivalent}$$
$$\text{(percent paid)}$$

Complements with respect to 1

As the work shows, 0.64, or 64% of the list price, or $243.20, was paid. Use the basic percent equation to find the list price.

$$R \times B = P$$
$$0.64 \times \text{List price} = \$243.20$$
$$0.64 \times B = \$243.20$$
$$0.64B = \$243.20$$
$$\frac{0.64B}{0.64} = \frac{\$243.20}{0.64} = \$380 \quad \text{List price}$$

Check the answer.

$$
\begin{array}{ll}
\$380 & \text{List price} \\
-\ 76 & (0.2 \times \$380) \\
\hline
\$304 & \\
-\ 60.80 & (0.2 \times \$304) \\
\hline
\$243.20 & \text{Net cost}
\end{array}
$$

The list price of the sink is $380.

EXAMPLE 4   Solving for List Price

Find the list price of a 6-foot fiberglass stepladder having a series discount of 10/30/20 and a net cost of $45.36.

Solution   Find the percent paid.

10/30/20   Series discount

$$0.9 \times 0.7 \times 0.8 = 0.504$$ Net cost equivalent (percent paid)

Complements with respect to 1

Therefore, 0.504 of the list price is $45.36. Now use the basic percent equation.

$$R \times B = P$$
$$0.504 \times \text{List price} = \$45.36$$
$$0.504 \times B = \$45.36$$
$$0.504B = \$45.36$$
$$\frac{0.504B}{0.504} = \frac{\$45.36}{0.504} = \$90 \quad \text{List price}$$

The list price of the stepladder is $90. Check this answer as in the previous example.

NOTE   Notice that Examples 3 and 4 are decrease problems similar to those shown in **Chapter 3, Section 5**. They are still base problems but may look different because the discount is now shown as a series of two or more discounts rather than a single percent decrease as in **Chapter 3**. If you need help, refer to **Section 3.5**.

Objective

4   *Determine a Single Trade Discount Rate.*

EXAMPLE 5   Finding the Single Trade Discount Rate

The list price of a gas-powered pressure washer is $550. If the wholesaler offers the system at a net cost of $341, find the single trade discount rate being offered.

Solution   Use the following formula.

$$\text{Percent paid} \times \text{List price} = \text{Net cost}$$
$$P \times L = N$$
$$P \times \$550 = \$341$$
$$\$550P = \$341$$
$$\frac{550P}{550} = \frac{341}{550} = 0.62 \text{ or } 62\% \quad \text{Percent paid}$$

Since 62% is paid, the discount offered is 38% (100% − 62% = 38%).

For an alternative approach, first find the amount of discount, or $550 - $341 = $209. Next, find the rate of discount by using the basic percent equation.

$$R \times B = P$$

_____ % of List price is Discount

_____ % of $550 = $209

$$R \times \$550 = \$209$$

$$\$550R = \$209$$

$$\frac{\cancel{550}R}{\cancel{550}} = \frac{\$209}{550}$$

$$R = \frac{209}{550} = 0.38 = 38\%$$

By either method, the discount is 38%.

Objective

5   *Find the Trade Discount That Must Be Added to Match a Competitor's Price.*

EXAMPLE **6**   **Adding a Discount to Match a Competitor's Price**

S and B Distributors offers a 20% trade discount on a digital camera list-priced at $450. What additional trade discount must be offered to match a competitor's price of $342?

Solution   First use the formula

$$P \times L = N$$

to find the single discount needed. The percent paid is found by multiplying together the complement of the 20% discount already given and the new, unknown discount.

$$0.8 \times \text{Complement of additional discount} \times L = N$$

$$0.8 \times d \times \$450 = \$342$$

$$\$360d = \$342$$

$$\frac{\cancel{360}d}{\cancel{360}} = \frac{\$342}{360}$$

$$d = 0.95 \text{ or } 95\%$$

Therefore, 95% is the complement of the trade discount that must be added. The additional discount needed is 5% (100% − 95%). To match the competition, S and B Distributors must give a 20/5 series discount.

9.2   Exercises

Find the net cost equivalent and the percent form of the single discount equivalent for each of the following series discounts.

1. 10/20	**2.** 10/10
3. 15/35	**4.** 10/50
5. 20/20	**6.** 20/20/20
7. 20/20/10	**8.** 15/5/10

9. 25/10   10. $30/37\frac{1}{2}$

11. $16\frac{2}{3}/10$ 12. 30/25

13. 10/10/20   14. 20/20/10

15. 55/40/10   16. 10/30/10

17. 40/25   18. 5/5/5

19. $20/12\frac{1}{2}$ 20. $10/33\frac{1}{3}$

21. 20/10/20/10   22. 10/20/25/10

23. 5/20/30/5   24. 10/5/30/20

25. Using complements, show that the single discount equivalent of a 20/25/10 series discount is 46%. (See Objective 1.)

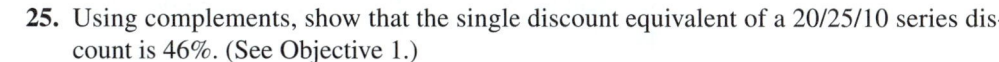

26. Suppose that you own a business and are offered a choice of a 10/20 trade discount or a 20/10 trade discount. Which do you prefer? Why? (See Objective 1.)

Find the list price given the net cost and the series discount.

27. Net cost, $518.40; trade discount, 20/10

28. Net cost, $343.35; trade discount, 10/30

29. Net cost, $279.30; trade discount, 40/5/30

30. Net cost, $5250; trade discount, $25/33\frac{1}{3}$

31. Net cost, $1313.28; trade discount, 5/10/20

32. Net cost, $2697.30; trade discount, 10/10/10

Solve the following application problems in trade discount.

33. **COMPARING DISCOUNTS** A S'mores Maker kit has a list price of $39.95 and is offered to wholesalers with a series discount of 20/10/10. The same appliance is offered to retailers with a series discount of 20/10. (a) Find the wholesaler's price. (b) Find the retailer's price. (c) Find the difference between the two prices.

34. **COMPARING DISCOUNTS** Kathy Miller is offered oak stair railing by The Turning Point for $1370 less 30/10. Sierra Stair Company offers the same railing for $1220 less 10/10. (a) Which offer is better? (b) How much does Miller save by taking the better offer?

35. **PRICING POTTED PLANTS** Irene's Plant Place paid a net price of $414.40 for a shipment of potted plants after a trade discount of 30/20 from the list price. Find the list price.

36. **VITAMINS, MINERALS, AND SUPPLEMENTS** SJ's Nutrition Center received a shipment of vitamins, minerals, and diet supplements at a net cost of $1125. This cost was the result of a trade discount of 25/20 from list price. Find the list price of this shipment.

37. **REFRIGERATOR** The manufacturer's list price on an energy-saver refrigerator is $840. The manufacturer offers it to wholesalers at a series discount of 10/20/10, and directly to retailers at a series discount of 10/20. Find (a) the price to wholesalers, (b) the price to retailers, and (c) the difference between the two.

38. **VIDEOCONFERENCING DEVICE** A videoconferencing device is list-priced at $395. The manufacturer offers a series discount of 25/20/10 to wholesalers and a 25/20 series discount to retailers. (a) What is the wholesaler's price? (b) What is the retailer's price? (c) What is the difference between the prices?

39. **PORTABLE GENERATORS** A portable generator with a list price of $295.95 is sold by a wholesaler at a net cost of $221.95. Find the single trade discount rate being offered. Round to the nearest tenth of a percent.

40. TRUCK-BED LINERS Truck Stuff offers a fiberglass truck-bed liner at a net cost of $180. If the list price of the bed liner is $281.25, find the single trade discount rate.

41. SECURITY ALARM SYSTEMS Capitol Alarm purchased a security alarm system at a net cost of $2733.75 and a series discount of $10/10/12\frac{1}{2}$. Find the list price.

42. FLAT-SCREEN TV A 42-inch flat-screen, digital television is on sale for $447.12. Find the original list price if the series discount is 10/20/10.

43. MOTOR OIL PRICING An auto wholesaler offers a 10% trade discount on a case of oil priced at $27.60. A competitor offers the same oil at $23.60. What additional trade discount must be given to meet the competitor's price? Round to the nearest tenth of a percent.

44. PERSONAL COMPUTERS A personal computer distributor has offered a computer system at a $1450 list price less a 30% trade discount. Find the additional trade discount needed to meet a competitor's net price of $933.80.

9.3	**Cash Discounts: Ordinary Dating Method**

OBJECTIVES

1 *Calculate net cost after discounts.*

2 *Use the ordinary dating method.*

3 *Determine whether cash discounts are earned.*

4 *Use postdating when calculating cash discounts.*

5 *Determine the amount due when goods are returned.*

Objective

1 *Calculate Net Cost after Discounts.* **Cash discounts** are offered by sellers to encourage prompt payment by customers. In effect, the seller is saying, "Pay me quickly, and receive a discount." Businesses often borrow money for their day-to-day operation. Immediate cash payments from customers *decrease* the need for the seller to borrow money. However, immediate cash payments may *increase* the need for the buyer to borrow money. Still, many buyers pay in time to receive the cash discount, to lower their cost. Most businesses can *only* be successful if they control costs.

To find the net cost when a cash discount is offered, begin with the list price and subtract any trade discounts. From this amount subtract the cash discount. Use the following formula to find the net cost.

$$\text{Net cost} = (\text{List price} - \text{Trade discount}) - \text{Cash discount}$$

> **NOTE** If an invoice amount includes shipping and insurance charges, subtract these charges first, before a cash discount is taken. Then add them back to find net cost after the cash discount is subtracted.

The type of cash discount appears on the invoice under "Terms," which can be found in the bottom right-hand corner of the Hershey Chocolate U.S.A. invoice in Figure 9.3. Many companies using automated billing systems state the exact amount of the cash discount at the bottom of the invoice. This eliminates all calculations on the part of the buyer. The Hershey invoice is an example of an invoice stating the exact amount of the cash discount, which is found at the bottom of the invoice. However, not all businesses do this, so it is important to know how to determine cash discounts.

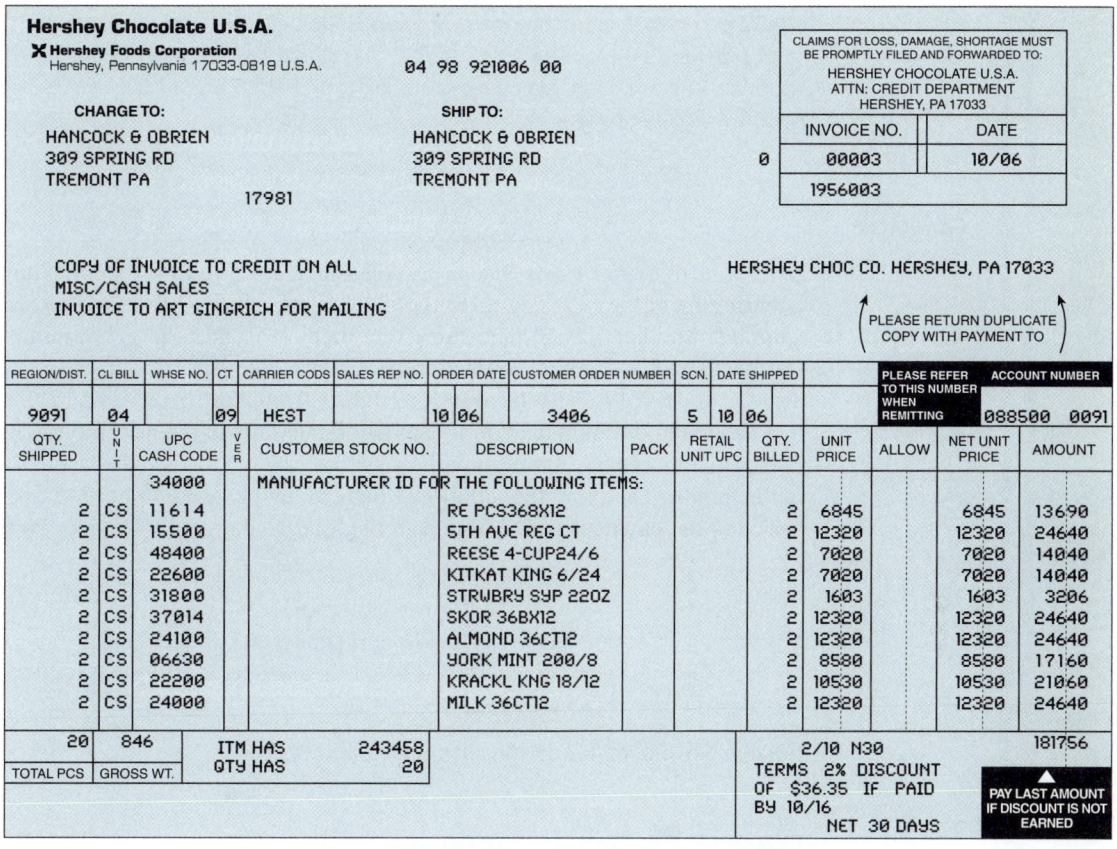

Figure 9.3

There are many methods for determining cash discounts, but nearly all of these are based on the "ordinary dating method." The methods discussed in this section and the methods discussed in the next section are the ones most commonly used today.

Objective

2   *Use the Ordinary Dating Method.*   The **ordinary dating method** of cash discount, for example, is expressed on an invoice as

$$\text{2/10, n/30 or sometimes 2/10, net/30}$$

and is read "two ten, net thirty." The first digit is the rate of discount (2%), the second digit is the number of days allowed to take the discount (10 days), and n/30 or net/30 is the total number of days given to pay the invoice in full, if the buyer does not use the cash discount. The 2% discount may be subtracted from the amount owed if the invoice is paid within 10 days from the date of the invoice. If payment is made between the 11th and 30th days from the invoice date, the entire amount of the invoice is due. After 30 days from the date of the invoice, the invoice is considered overdue and may be subject to a late charge.

To find the due date of an invoice, use the number of days in each month given in Table 9.4.

Table 9.4   THE NUMBER OF DAYS IN EACH MONTH

30-Day Months	31-Day Months		Exception
April	January	August	February
June	March	October	(28 days normally; 29 days in leap years)
September	May	December	
November	July		

> **NOTE** Leap years occur every 4 years. They are the same as Summer Olympic years and presidential election years in the United States. If a year is evenly divisible by the number 4, it is a leap year. The years 2012 and 2016 are all leap years because they are evenly divisible by 4.

Objective

3 *Determine Whether Cash Discounts Are Earned.* Find the date that an invoice is due by counting from the next day after the date of the invoice. *The date of the invoice is never counted.* Another way to determine due dates is to add the given number of days to the starting date. For example, to determine 10 days from April 7, add the number of days to the date $(7 + 10 = 17)$. The due date, or 10 days from April 7, is April 17.

When the discount date or net payment date falls in the next month, find the number of days remaining in the current month by subtracting the invoice date from the number of days in the month. Then find the number of days in the next month needed to equal the discount period or net payment period. For example, find 15 days from October 20 as follows.

$$
\begin{array}{rl}
31 & \text{Days in October} \\
-\ 20 & \text{The beginning date, October 20} \\
\hline
11 & \text{Days remaining in October} \\
+\ \ 4 & \text{Additional days needed in November to equal 15 days} \\
\hline
15 & \text{Days}
\end{array}
$$

Finally, November 4 is 15 days from October 20.

EXAMPLE 1 Finding Cash Discount Dates

A Hershey Chocolate invoice is dated January 2 and offers terms of 2/10, net 30. Find (a) the last date on which the 2% discount may be taken and (b) the net payment date.

Solution

(a) Beginning with the invoice date, January 2, the last date for taking the discount is January 12 $(2 + 10)$.

(b) The net payment date is February 1 (29 days remaining in January plus 1 day in February).

EXAMPLE 2 Finding the Amount Due on an Invoice

An invoice received by Bass Bait Shop for $840 is dated July 1 and offers terms of 2/10, n/30. If the invoice is paid on July 8 and the FOB shipping and insurance charges are $18.70, find the total amount due.

Solution The 2/10 means that the discount of 2% applies only if the invoice is paid within 10 days of the invoice date. The discount of 2% does apply, since the invoice date is July 1 and the invoice was paid on July 8, or only 7 days after the invoice date.

$$
\begin{aligned}
\textbf{Amount due} &= \textbf{Invoice amount} - \textbf{Cash discount of 2\%} \\
&= \$840 \qquad\qquad - \$840 \times 0.02 \\
&= \$823.20
\end{aligned}
$$

However, shipping and insurance charges must be added to find the total amount due.

Total amount due = $823.20 + $18.70 = $841.90 (Shipping and insurance)

Complements can also be used to work Example 2. A discount of 2% means that the complement of 2%, or 98% (100% − 2%) of the invoice amount must be paid. Find the total amount due as follows.

Invoice amount		Complement of 2%		Shipping charge		Total due
$840	×	0.98	+	$18.70	=	$841.90

> **NOTE** A cash discount is never taken on shipping and insurance charges. Be certain that shipping and insurance charges are excluded from the invoice amount before calculating the cash discount. Shipping and insurance charges must then be added back to find the total amount due.

Objective

4 *Use Postdating When Calculating Cash Discounts.* In the ordinary dating method, the cash discount date and net payment date are both counted from the date of the invoice. Occasionally, the seller places a date later than the actual invoice date, sometimes labeling it **"as of."** This is called **postdating**. Notice that the Levi Strauss invoice in Figure 9.4 is dated "07/25 as of 08/01." The cash discount period and the net payment date are counted from 08/01 (August 1). This results in giving additional time for the purchaser to pay the invoice and receive the discount. The date due (9/10) is the due date on the invoice. The phrase "terms: 8%/10 EOM" is explained in **Section 9.4**.

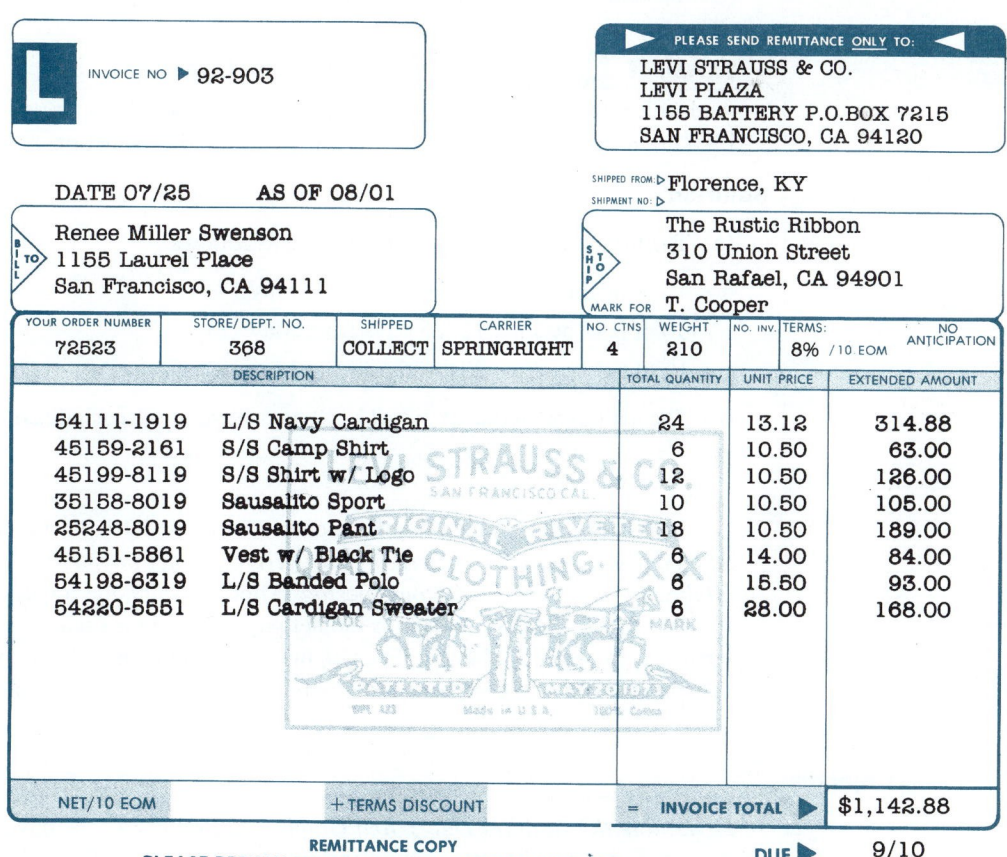

Figure 9.4

> **EXAMPLE 3** **Using Postdating "as of" with Invoices**
>
> An invoice for some Henckles Cutlery from Germany is dated October 21 AS OF November 1 with terms of 3/15, n/30. Find (a) the last date on which the cash discount may be taken and (b) the net payment date.

Solution

(a) Beginning with the postdate (AS OF) of November 1, the last date for taking the discount is November 16 (1 + 15).

(b) The net payment date is December 1 (29 days remaining in November and 1 day in December).

Sometimes a sliding scale of cash discounts is offered. For example, consider terms of 3/10, 2/20, 1/30, n/60. The buyer will receive only one of these discounts and then only if paid by the time required. Here is how to interpret terms of 3/10, 2/20, 1/30, n/60.

Term	Discount	If Payment Received
3/10	3%	In the first 10 days from date of invoice
2/20	2%	Between 11 days and 20 days from date of invoice
1/30	1%	Between 21 days and 30 days from date of invoice
n/60	0%	Between 31 days and 60 days from date of invoice

The full amount must be paid no later than 60 days from the date of the invoice or it will be overdue and may be subject to a penalty.

> **EXAMPLE 4** **Determining Cash Discount Due Dates**
>
> An invoice from Cellular Products is dated May 18 and offers terms of 4/10, 3/25, 1/40, n/60. Find (a) the three final dates for cash discounts and (b) the net payment date.

Solution

(a) The three final cash discount dates are as follows.

   4% if paid by May 28 (10 days from May 18)

   3% if paid by June 12 (25 days from May 18)

   1% if paid by June 27 (40 days from May 18)

(b) The net payment date is July 17 (20 days beyond the cash discount period).

Never take more than one of the cash discounts. *With all methods of giving cash discounts, if the net payment period is not given, the net payment due date is assumed to be 20 days beyond the cash discount period.* After that date, the invoice is considered overdue. If either the final discount date or the net payment date is on a Sunday or holiday, the next business day is used. Many companies insist that payment is made when it is received. It is general practice, however, to consider payment made when it is mailed.

Objective

5 *Determine the Amount Due When Goods Are Returned.* A buyer receiving incorrect or damaged merchandise may return the goods to the seller. The value of the returned goods must be subtracted from the amount of the invoice before calculating the cash discount.

| EXAMPLE 5 | **Finding the Amount Due When Goods Are Returned** |

An invoice from Homeproducts.com amounts to $380, is dated March 9, and offers terms of 4/10, net 30. If $75 of goods are returned and the invoice is paid on March 17, what amount is due?

Solution The invoice was paid 8 days after its date ($17 - 9 = 8$), so the 4% cash discount is taken. The discount is taken on $305.

$$\$380 \,(\text{invoice amount}) - \$75 \,(\text{goods returned}) = \$305 \,(\text{goods retained})$$

The cash discount is subtracted from the $305. Since $\$305 \times 0.04 = \$12.20$, the amount due is

$$\$305 \,(\text{goods retained}) - \$12.20 \,(\text{cash discount}) = \$292.80 \,(\text{amount due})$$

| **9.3** | **Exercises** |

Find the final discount date and the net payment date for each of the following problems.

	Invoice Date	As of	Terms
1.	Oct. 8		3/10, n/30
2.	April 12		2/10, n/30
3.	Feb. 25	Mar. 10	3/15, n/20
4.	Nov. 7	Nov. 18	3/10, n/30
5.	Sept. 11		4/10, n/60
6.	Mar. 23		2/10, n/30
7.	Jan. 14		2/10, n/60
8.	Oct. 3		3/10, n/15
9.	Dec. 7	Jan. 5	5/15, n/60
10.	July 31	Aug. 15	3/10, n/30

Solve for the amount of discount and the amount due on each of the following invoices.

	Invoice Amount	Invoice Date	Terms	Shipping and Insurance	Goods Returned	Date Invoice Paid
11.	$151.35	June 6	2/10 net 30	$12.58		June 15
12.	$66.10	Mar. 8	6/10, n/30	$4.39		Mar. 14
13.	$96.06	Nov. 30	net 30	$5.22		Dec. 20
14.	$148	July 19	3/15, 1/25, n/60	$7.45		Aug. 16
15.	$724	Jan. 20	5/10, 2/20, n/30	$38.14		Feb. 5
16.	$1282	July 1	4/15, n/40	$21.40		July 7
17.	$780.70	May 5	net 30	$3.80	$125	June 1
18.	$162	Jan. 15	2/15, net 30	$8.18	$12	Jan. 23
19.	$635	Oct. 10	5/10, n/30	$53.18	$52	Oct. 18
20.	$1623.08	Nov. 12	2/10, n/30	$122.14	$187	Nov. 25

21. Describe the difference between a trade discount and a cash discount. Why are cash discounts offered? (See Objective 1.)

22. Using 2/10, n/30 as an example, explain what an ordinary cash discount means. (See Objective 2.)

Solve the following application problems.

23. HOME BAKING Grainworks Supply offers cash discounts of 2/10, 1/15, net 30 to all customers. An invoice dated May 18 amounting to $2010.70 is paid on June 1. Find the amount needed to pay the invoice.

24. RUSSIAN ELECTRICAL SUPPLIES A shipment of electrical supplies is received from the Lyskovo Electrotechnical Works. The invoice is dated March 8, amounts to $6824.58, and has terms of 2/15, 1/20 as of March 20. Find the amount needed to pay the invoice on April 2.

25. AGRICULTURAL PRODUCTS Agricultural Wholesale Products offers customers a trade discount of 10/20/5 on all products, with terms of net 30. Find the customer's price for products with a total list price of $986 if the invoice was paid within 30 days.

26. FISHING EQUIPMENT Joe Nejad received an invoice for $586.12 for fishing tackle. The invoice was dated February 21, as of March 4, with terms of 4/10, 3/30, n/60. Find the total amount necessary to pay the invoice in full on March 22.

27. COMPUTERS A high-speed work station with dual processing chips and 10 gigabytes of memory has a list price of $2140, but sells to distributors with trade discounts of 15/10 and terms of 4/15, n/30. If the retailer receives all discounts, find the net cost to the retailer.

28. HOME FURNACE A manufacturer of home furnaces lists an ultra-high-efficiency model for $3900 with trade discounts to a wholesaler of 10/5 and terms of 3/20, n/60. The invoice is dated July 30 and the wholesaler pays the invoice on August 10. Find the net cost.

29. RECREATION EQUIPMENT The list price of a popular brand of snowmobile is $5190. If a dealer can obtain trade discounts of 10/20/30 and cash terms of 4/10, n/30, find the lowest possible net cost.

30. PETROCHEMICAL PRODUCTS Century Petrochemical Products offers customers a trade discount of 10/20/5 on all products, with terms of net 30. Find the customer's price for products with a total list price of $2630 if the invoice was paid within 30 days.

31. NUTRITIONAL PRODUCTS Village Nutrition offers retailers a trade discount of 10/20/10 on all purchases, with terms of 3/10, n/30. If the total list price of an order is $3215.80, find the retailers' net cost if both discounts are earned.

32. GEORGE FOREMAN GRILL A George Foreman Jumbo Grill plus a free Toastmaster Ultravection oven is list-priced at $140 with a trade discount of 20/5/10 and terms of 4/10, n/30. Find the cost assuming that both discounts are earned.

33. RECREATION PRODUCTS An invoice from Tower Recreation is dated April 14 and offers terms of 6/10, 4/20, 1/30, n/50. Find (a) the three final discount dates and (b) the net payment date.

34. INVOICE TERMS An invoice with terms of 4/15, 3/20, 1/30, n/60 is dated September 4. Find (a) the three final discount dates and (b) the net payment date.

35. INVOICE TERMS Truck Stuff receives an invoice dated March 28 AS OF April 5 with terms of 4/20, n/30. Find (a) the final discount date and (b) the net payment date.

36. AS OF DATING An invoice is dated May 20 AS OF June 5 with terms of 2/10, n/30. Find (a) the final discount date and (b) the net payment date.

37. **NURSERY SUPPLIES** Valley Nursery received an invoice for supplies amounting to $3724.40. The invoice is dated October 19 AS OF November 10 and offers terms of 2/20, n/40. Find the amount necessary to pay in full on November 28 if $104.50 worth of supplies are returned.

38. **INTERIOR DESIGN** Sarah Bryn Interiors received an invoice for drapery hardware amounting to $218.80. The invoice is dated July 12 AS OF July 20 and offers terms of 3/20, n/60. Find the amount necessary to pay in full on August 3 if $24.30 worth of goods are returned.

39. **APPLIANCE REPAIRS** An invoice received by Capital Appliance for repair parts amounts to $3322.80. The invoice is dated August 22 AS OF September 10 and offers terms of 4/10, 2/20, n/30. Find the amount necessary to pay in full on September 26 if $152.80 worth of goods are returned.

40. **CHILDREN'S RETAILER** An invoice received by Sydney's Baby Barn amounts to $380.50. The invoice is dated October 25 AS OF November 2 and offers terms of 3/15, n/30. Find the amount necessary to pay in full on November 18 if $56.50 worth of goods are returned.

 41. How do you remember the number of days in each month of the year? List the months and the number of days in each.

 42. Explain how "AS OF" dating (postdating) works. Why is it used? (See Objective 4.)

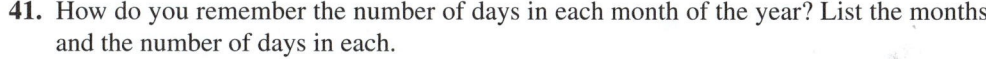

9.4 | Cash Discounts: Other Dating Methods

OBJECTIVES

1 *Solve cash discount problems with end-of-month dating.*

2 *Use receipt-of-goods dating to solve cash discount problems.*

3 *Use extra dating to solve cash discount problems.*

4 *Determine credit given for partial payment of an invoice.*

In addition to the ordinary dating method of cash discounts, there are several other cash discount methods that are in common use.

Objective

1 *Solve Cash Discount Problems with End-of-Month Dating.* **End-of-month dating** and **proximo dating**, abbreviated **EOM** and **prox.**, are both treated the same way. For example, both "3/10 EOM" and "3/10 prox." mean that a 3% cash discount may be taken if payment is made within 10 days. *However*, the 10 days are counted from the end of the month in which the invoice is dated. For example, an invoice dated July 14 with terms of 3/10 EOM would have a discount date 10 days from the end of the month, or August 10.

Since this is a method of increasing the length of time during which a discount may be taken, it has become common business practice with EOM and prox. dating to **add a month** *when the date of an invoice is the 26th of the month or later.* For example, if an invoice is dated March 25 and the discount offered is 3/10 prox., the last date on which the discount may be taken is April 10. ***However, if the invoice is dated March 26 (or any later day in March) and the cash discount offered is 3/10 prox., then the last date on which the discount may be taken is May 10.***

> **NOTE**   The practice of adding an extra month when the invoice is dated the 26th of a month or after is used *only* with the end-of-month (proximo) dating cash discount. It does *not* apply to any of the other cash discount methods.

EXAMPLE 1   Using End-of-Month Dating

An invoice from Harley-Davidson is dated June 10, with terms of 3/20 EOM. Find (a) the final date on which the cash discount may be taken and (b) the net payment date.

Solution

(a) Terms of 3/20 EOM mean that a 3% discount applies if payment is made within 20 days of the end of the month of the invoice date. So, the last date on which the discount applies is July 20.

(b) When no net payment due date is given, allow 20 days after the last discount date. Therefore, the net payment date is August 9, or 20 days after the last discount date of July 20.

> **NOTE**   With all methods of cash discounts, if the net payment period is not given, the net payment due date is assumed to be 20 days beyond the cash discount date.

EXAMPLE 2   Understanding Proximo Dating

Find the amount due on an invoice of $782 for some threaded fasteners that is dated August 3 if terms are 1/10 prox., and the invoice is paid on September 4.

Solution   The last date on which the discount may be taken is September 10 (10 days after the end of August). The discount of 1% applies since September 4 is within the discount period.

$$\text{Amount due} = \text{Invoice amount} - \text{Cash discount of 1\%}$$
$$= \$782 \qquad - 1\% \text{ of } \$782$$
$$= \$782 \qquad - 0.01 \times \$782$$
$$= \$774.18$$

Objective

2   *Use Receipt-of-Goods Dating to Solve Cash Discount Problems.*   **Receipt-of-goods dating**, abbreviated **ROG**, offers discounts determined from the date the goods are actually received. This method is often used when shipping time is long. The invoice might arrive overnight by mail, but the goods may take several weeks. Under the ROG method of cash discount, the buyer is given time to receive and inspect the merchandise and then benefit from a cash discount. For example, the discount "3/15 ROG" allows a 3% cash discount if paid within 15 days from receipt of goods. If the invoice was dated March 5 and goods were received on April 7, the last date to take the 3% cash discount is April 22 (April 7 plus 15 days). The net payment date, since it is not stated, is 20 days after the last discount date, or May 12 (April 22 plus 20 days).

EXAMPLE **3**   **Using Receipt-of-Goods Dating**

Java City received an invoice dated December 12, with terms of 2/10 ROG. The goods were received on January 2. Find (a) the final date on which the cash discount may be taken and (b) the net payment date.

Solution

(a) The discount date is January 12 (10 days after receipt of goods, January 2 + 10 days).

(b) The net payment date is February 1 (20 days after the last discount date).

EXAMPLE **4**   **Working with ROG Dating**

Stabel Printing receives an invoice for $485 for printing supplies. The terms are 3/10 ROG, the invoice is dated June 8, and goods are received June 18. The invoice is paid on June 30. Find the amount due.

Solution   The last date to take the 3% cash discount is June 28, 10 days after June 18. Since the invoice is paid on June 30, 2 days after the last discount date, no cash discount may be taken. The entire amount of the invoice must be paid.

$$
\begin{aligned}
\text{Amount due} &= \text{Invoice amount} - \$0\,\text{discount} \\
&= \$485 \qquad\quad - \qquad \$0 \\
&= \$485
\end{aligned}
$$

Objective

3   *Use Extra Dating to Solve Cash Discount Problems.*   **Extra dating**, abbreviated **extra, ex.,** or **x**, gives the buyer additional time to take a cash discount. For example, the discount "2/10-50 extra" or "2/10-50 ex." or "2/10-50 x" allows a 2% cash discount if paid within (10 + 50) or 60 days from the date of the invoice. The discount is expressed as 2/10-50 ex. (rather than 2/60) to show that the 50 days are *extra*, or in addition to the normal 10 days offered.

There are several reasons for using extra dating. A supplier might extend the discount period during a slack season to generate more sales or perhaps to gain a competitive advantage. For example, the seller might offer Christmas merchandise with extra dating to allow the buyer to take the cash discount after the holiday selling period.

EXAMPLE **5**   **Using Extra Dating**

An invoice for paint accessories is dated November 23 with terms 2/10–50 ex. Find (a) the final date on which the cash discount may be taken and (b) the net payment date.

Solution

(a) The discount date is January 22 (7 days remaining in November + 31 days in December = 38; thus, 22 more days are needed in January to total 60).

(b) The net payment date is February 11 (20 days after the last discount date).

> **EXAMPLE 6   Understanding Extra Dating**
>
> An invoice from KitchenAid is dated August 5, amounts to $2250, offers terms of 3/10–30 x, and is paid on September 12. Find the net payment.
>
> **Solution**   The last day to take the 3% cash discount is September 14 (August 5 + 40 days = September 14). Since the invoice is paid on September 12, the 3% discount may be taken. The 3% cash discount is computed on $2250, the amount of the invoice.
>
> $$3\% \times \$2250 = 0.03 \times \$2250 = \$67.50$$
>
> The discount to be taken is $67.50. The cash discount is subtracted from the invoice amount to determine the amount of payment.
>
> $$\$2250 \text{ (invoice amount)} - \$67.50 \text{ (cash discount)} = \$2182.50 \text{ (amount of payment)}$$

When customers pay invoices quickly, there is less need for a business to borrow money. In certain industries it is common to deduct interest that would have to be paid on borrowed money from the invoice amount. To do this, the company uses the current rate of interest and calculates the amount of interest over the remaining days on which the cash discount is allowable. This deduction, known as **anticipation**, is taken in addition to the cash discount earned. Anticipation involves the use of simple interest, which is discussed in **Chapter 12**.

Objective

4   *Determine Credit Given for Partial Payment of an Invoice.*   Occasionally, a customer may pay only a portion of the total amount due on an invoice. If this **partial payment** is made within a discount period, the customer is entitled to a discount on the portion of the invoice that is paid.

If the terms of an invoice are 3%, 10 days, then only 97% (100% − 3%) of the invoice amount must be paid during the first 10 days. So, for each $0.97 paid, the customer is entitled to $1.00 of credit. When a partial payment is made, the credit given for the partial payment is found by dividing the partial payment by the complement of the cash discount percent. Then, to find the balance due, subtract the credit given from the invoice amount. The cash discount is found by subtracting the partial payment from the credit given.

> **EXAMPLE 7   Finding Credit for Partial Payment**
>
> Dave's Body and Paint receives an invoice for $1140, dated March 8, that offers terms of 2/10 proximo. A partial payment of $450 is made on April 5. Find (a) the amount credited for the partial payment, (b) the balance due on the invoice, and (c) the cash discount earned.
>
> **Solution**
>
> **(a)** The cash discount is earned on the $450 partial payment made on April 5 (April 10 was the last discount date).
>
> $$100\% - 2\% = 98\% = 0.98$$
> $$\text{Amount paid} = 0.98 \times \text{Credit given}$$
> $$\$450 = 0.98 \times C$$
> $$\$450 = 0.98C$$
> $$\frac{\$450}{0.98} = \frac{0.98C}{0.98}$$
> $$\frac{\$450}{0.98} = C$$
> $$= \$459.18 \quad \text{Credit given (rounded)}$$

(b) Balance due = Invoice amount − Credit given

$$= \$1140 - \$459.18$$

$$= \$680.82$$

(c) Cash discount = Credit given − Partial payment

$$= \$459.18 - \$450$$

$$= \$9.18$$

Scientific Calculator Approach

A calculator solution to Example 7 will include these three steps.

(a) First, find the amount of credit given.

$$450 \boxed{\div} 0.98 \boxed{=} 459.18 \text{ (rounded)}$$

(b) Next, store the amount of credit and subtract this amount from the invoice amount to find the balance due.

$$\boxed{STO} \, 1140 \boxed{-} \boxed{RCL} \boxed{=} 680.82 \text{ (rounded)}$$

(c) Finally, subtract the partial payment from the amount of credit given to find the cash discount.

$$\boxed{RCL} \boxed{-} 450 \boxed{=} 9.18 \text{ (rounded)}$$

NOTE Cash discounts are important, and a business should make the effort to pay invoices early to earn the cash discounts. In many cases the money saved through cash discounts has a great effect on the profitability of a business. Often companies will borrow money to enable them to take advantage of cash discounts. The mathematics of this type of loan is discussed in **Section 12.1**, "Basics of Simple Interest."

The cash discounts discussed here are normally not used when selling to foreign customers or purchasing from foreign suppliers. Instead, other types of discounts may be offered to reduce the price of goods sold to foreign buyers. These discounts may be given as allowances for tariffs paid (import duties) by the customer, reimbursement for shipping, and insurance paid by the customer or in the form of an advertising allowance.

9.4	**Exercises**

Find the discount date and net payment date for each of the following (the net payment date is 20 days after the final discount date).

	Invoice Date	Terms	Date Goods Received
1.	Feb. 8	3/10 EOM	
2.	July 14	2/15 ROG	Sept. 3
3.	Nov. 22	1/10–20 x	
4.	May 17	6/30 EOM	
5.	April 12	3/15–50 x	
6.	Oct. 30	1/10 ROG	Dec. 12

	Invoice Date	Terms	Date Goods Received
7.	June 26	2/10 EOM	
8.	Sept. 27	3/15 prox.	
9.	July 6	2/20 ROG	Aug. 4
10.	Jan. 15	3/15 ROG	Feb. 5

Solve for the amount of discount and the amount due on each of the following.

	Invoice Amount	Invoice Date	Terms	Date Goods Received	Date Invoice Paid
11.	$682.28	June 4	3/20 ROG	July 25	Aug. 10
12.	$356.20	May 17	3/15 prox.		June 12
13.	$194.04	Aug. 22	5/10–60 ex.		Nov. 5
14.	$9240.40	Jan. 8	1/20 ROG	Mar. 10	Mar. 23
15.	$2960	Oct. 31	2/10 EOM		Dec. 5
16.	$127.50	Feb. 17	3/20 ROG	Mar. 19	Apr. 10
17.	$4220	Oct. 4	4/15 prox.		Nov. 10
18.	$256.50	July 17	3/10–40 extra		Sept. 2
19.	$12.38	Mar. 29	2/15 ROG	April 15	April 30
20.	$11,480	April 6	2/15 prox.		April 30
21.	$3250.60	Oct. 17	3/15–20 x		Oct. 20
22.	$8318	June 9	3/20 EOM		July 18
23.	$1708.18	Nov. 13	4/10 prox.		Dec. 10
24.	$13,728.34	April 6	2/10 ROG	April 28	May 6

 25. Quite often there is no mention of a net payment date on an invoice. Explain the common business practice when no net payment date is given. (See Objective 1.)

 26. Describe why receipt-of-goods dating (ROG) is offered to customers. Use an example in your description. (See Objective 2.)

Find the credit given and the balance due on the invoice after making the following partial payments.

	Invoice Amount	Invoice Date	Terms	Date Invoice Paid	Partial Payment
27.	$3150	Jan. 9	2/10 EOM	Feb. 8	$1862
28.	$484	June 6	5/10–30 x	July 10	$209
29.	$1750	Aug. 12	5/10–30 x	Sept. 15	$684
30.	$920	Jan. 11	3/10, 2/15, n/30	Jan. 23	$450.80
31.	$160	Dec. 8	3/10, n/30	Dec. 15	$97
32.	$8120	Oct. 4	4/20 prox.	Nov. 15	$2016

 33. Write a short explanation of partial payment. Why would a company accept a partial payment? Why would a customer make a partial payment? (See Objective 4.)

 34. Of all the different types of cash discounts presented in this section, which type seemed most interesting to you? Explain your reasons.

Solve the following application problems in cash and trade discounts.

35. **BATHROOM DECOR** An invoice received by Bath and Home is dated August 18 with terms of 2/15 EOM. Find (a) the final date on which the discount may be taken and (b) the net payment date.

36. **RADIATOR SUPPLIES** An invoice from Steamer's Radiator Supply is dated February 23 with terms of 3/20 ROG and the goods are received on March 2. Find (a) the final date on which the cash discount may be taken and (b) the net payment date.

37. **GLASS REPAIR SUPPLIES** An invoice from Carmichael Glass is dated November 11 with terms of 3/20 ROG and the goods are received on December 3. Find (a) the final date on which the cash discount may be taken and (b) the net payment date.

38. **STAINED GLASS SUPPLIES** An invoice received from the Stained Glass Exchange is dated June 16 with terms of 2/10 prox. Find (a) the final date on which the cash discount may be taken and (b) the net payment date.

39. **TOYOTA** Find the amount due on an invoice of $283,480 for several Toyotas with terms of 1/20 ROG. The invoice is dated October 20, goods are received on December 1, and the invoice is paid on December 20.

40. **CANADIAN FOOD PRODUCTS** Abigail Shellist, a wholesaler of Canadian food products, offers terms of 4/15–40 ex. to encourage the sales of her products. In a recent order, a retailer purchased $9864.18 worth of Canadian foods and was offered the above terms. If the invoice was dated March 10, find (a) the final date on which the cash discount may be taken and (b) the amount paid if the discount was earned.

41. **CERAMIC DINNERWARE** Fiesta, a dinnerware manufacturer, offers terms of 2/10–30 x to stimulate slow sales in the winter months. Kitchens Galore purchased $2382.58 worth of dinnerware and was offered the above terms. If the invoice was dated November 3, find (a) the final date on which the cash discount may be taken and (b) the amount paid if the discount was earned.

42. **RACING BIKE** An ultra-light-weight racing bicycle has a list price of $3850. The invoice is dated September 28 and has terms of 3/10–50 x. The invoice is paid on November 25. Find the amount due.

43. **ELECTRIC SCOOTER** A recent invoice for a Scoot-'N-Go electric scooter with a list price of $758 was dated February 20 and offered terms of 2/20 ROG. If the scooter was received on March 20 and the invoice was paid on April 8, find the amount due.

44. **CUSTOM WHEELS** Scott Ryder purchased several 19-inch and 21-inch custom wheels for his performance auto parts store and was offered a cash discount of 2/10 EOM. The invoice amounted to $7218.80 and was dated June 2. The wheels were received 7 days later, and the invoice was paid on July 7. Find the amount necessary to pay the invoice in full.

45. **INVOICE PARTIAL PAYMENT** An invoice amounting to $1920 is dated July 23 by Lexington Foot Locker and offers cash terms of 6/30–120 x. If a partial payment of $940 is made on November 28, find (a) the credit given for the partial payment and (b) the balance due on the invoice.

46. **LIGHTING SALES** Lamps For Less receives an invoice amounting to $5832 with cash terms of 3/10 prox. and dated August 9. If a partial payment of $3350 is made on August 15, find (a) the credit given for the partial payment and (b) the balance due on the invoice.

47. **ENGLISH SOCCER EQUIPMENT**   An invoice dated December 8 is received with a shipment of soccer equipment from England on April 18 of the following year. The list price of the equipment is $2538, with allowed series discounts of 25/10/10. If cash terms of sale are 3/15 ROG, find the amount necessary to pay in full on April 21.

48. **WATERFORD CRYSTAL**   William Glen receives an invoice for some Waterford Crystal from Ireland amounting to $3628.10 and dated May 17. The terms of the invoice are 5/20–90 x and the invoice is paid on September 2. Find the amount necessary to pay the invoice in full.

49. **BEAUTY SUPPLIES**   Michael Anderson Beauty Supplies offers series discounts of 15/10 with terms of 5/15–30 x. On an invoice dated June 4 for items list-priced at $128, find the amount necessary to pay the invoice in full on July 15.

50. **COPY SUPPLIES**   The Copy Corner receives an invoice amounting to $388.20 with terms of 8/10, net/30 and dated August 20 AS OF September 1. If a partial payment of $225 is made on September 8, find (a) the credit given for the partial payment and (b) the balance due on the invoice.

51. **FROZEN DESSERT SHOP**   The Frozen Dessert Shop receives an invoice amounting to $526.80 with terms of 2/20 prox. and dated October 5. If a partial payment of $300 is made on November 12, find (a) the credit given for the partial payment and (b) the balance due on the invoice.

52. **CONSTRUCTION COMPANY**   An invoice of $7819.20 with terms of 4/10 prox. is received by Penny Carter Construction and is dated May 2. If a partial payment of $6000 is made on May 8, find (a) the credit given for the partial payment and (b) the balance due on the invoice.

53. **PARTIAL INVOICE PAYMENT**   An invoice received for some precision hand tools from Germany has terms of 3/15–30 x and is dated May 20. The amount of the invoice is $1120.15, and a partial payment of $580 is made on July 1. Find (a) the credit given for the partial payment and (b) the balance due on the invoice.

54. **JEEP SUPPLIES**   Jeepers Supply makes a partial payment of $660 on an invoice of $1491.54. If the invoice is dated April 14 with terms of 4/20 prox. and the partial payment is made on May 13, find (a) the credit given for the partial payment and (b) the balance due on the invoice.

55. **PARTIAL INVOICE PAYMENT**   The UPS Store receives an invoice amounting to $672.30 with terms of 8/10, net 30 and dated August 20 AS OF September 1. If a partial payment of $450 is made on September 8, find (a) the credit given for the partial payment and (b) the balance due on the invoice.

56. **FROZEN YOGURT**   Yogurt for You receives an invoice amounting to $263.40 with terms of 2/20 EOM and dated September 6. If a partial payment of $150 is made on October 15, find (a) the credit given for the partial payment and (b) the balance due on the invoice.

CHAPTER TERMS

Review the following terms to test your understanding of the chapter. For each term you do not know, refer to the page number found next to that term:

anticipation [p. 342]
amount of
  invoice [p. 318]
cash discount [p. 332]
cash on delivery (COD)
  [p. 319]
chain discount [p. 321]
complement [p. 321]
consumer [p. 317]
distributor [p. 317]
electronic commerce (EC)
  [p. 318]
EOM (end of month)
  [p. 339]

extension total [p. 318]
extra dating (extra, ex., x)
  [p. 341]
free alongside ship (FAS)
  [p. 319]
free on board (FOB)
  [p. 318]
inventory [p. 317]
invoice [p. 318]
invoice total [p. 318]
list price [p. 320]
manufacturer [p. 317]
net cost [p. 320]
net cost equivalent [p. 322]

net price [p. 320]
ordinary dating method
  [p. 333]
partial payment [p. 342]
percent paid [p. 322]
postdated "as of" [p. 335]
proximo (prox.) dating
  [p. 339]
purchase invoice [p. 318]
raw materials supplier
  [p. 317]
receipt-of-goods dating
  (ROG) [p. 340]
retailer [p. 317]

sales invoice [p. 318]
series discount [p. 321]
single discount [p. 321]
single discount
  equivalent [p. 327]
supply chain [p. 317]
total invoice amount
  [p. 318]
trade discounts [p. 320]
unit price [p. 318]
wholesaler [p. 317]

CONCEPTS

EXAMPLES

9.1 Trade discount and net cost

First find the amount of the trade discount. Then use the formula:

Net cost = List price − Trade discount

List price, $28; trade discount, 25%. Find the net cost.

$$\text{Trade discount} = \$28 \times 0.25 = \$7$$
$$\text{Net cost} = \$28 - \$7 = \$21$$

9.1 Complements with respect to 1

The complement is the number that must be added to a given discount to get 1 or 100%.

Find the complement with respect to 1 for each of the following.

(a) $10\% + x = 100\%$
    $x = 100\% - 10\%$
    $x = 90\%$

(b) $12\frac{1}{2}\%$; complement = 87.5%

(c) 50%; complement = 50%

9.1 Complement and series discounts

The complement of a discount is the percent paid. Multiply the complements of the discounts in the series to get the net cost equivalent.

Series discount, 10/20/10. Find the net cost equivalent.

10 / 20 / 10
↓   ↓   ↓
$0.9 \times 0.8 \times 0.9 = 0.648$

9.1 Net cost equivalent (percent paid) and the net cost

Multiply the net cost equivalent (percent paid) by the list price to get the net cost.

Percent paid × List price = Net cost

List price, $280; series discount 10/30/20. Find the net cost.

10 / 30 / 20
↓   ↓   ↓
$0.9 \times 0.7 \times 0.8 = 0.504$ percent paid
$0.504 \times \$280 = \$141.12$

9.2	**Single discount equivalent to a series discount**	What single discount is equivalent to a 10/20/20 series discount?

Often needed to compare one series discount to another, the single discount equivalent is found by subtracting the net cost equivalent from 1.

$$10 \ / \ 20 \ / \ 20$$
$$\downarrow \quad \downarrow \quad \downarrow$$
$$0.9 \times 0.8 \times 0.8 = 0.576$$

$$1 - \text{Net cost equivalent} = \text{Single discount equivalent}$$

$$1 - 0.576 = 0.424 = 42.4\%$$

9.2	**Finding net cost using complements of individual discounts**	List price, $510; series discount, 30/10/5. Find the net cost.

To find the net cost, multiply the list price by the product of the complements of the individual discounts.

$$30 \ / \ 10 \ / \ 5$$
$$\downarrow \quad \downarrow \quad \downarrow$$
$$\$510 \times 0.7 \times 0.9 \times 0.95 = \$305.24 \quad \text{(Rounded)}$$

9.2	**Finding list price if given the series discount and the net cost**	Net cost, $224; series discount, 20/20. Find list price.

First, find the net cost equivalent (percent paid), then use the formula to find the list price.

$$P \times L = N$$

Percent paid $\times$ List price $=$ Net cost

$$20 \ / \ 20$$
$$\downarrow \quad \downarrow$$
$$0.8 \times 0.8 = 0.64$$
$$0.64 \times \text{List price} = \$224$$
$$0.64L = \$224$$
$$L = \$350 \quad \text{List price}$$

9.2	**Determining the trade discount that must be added to meet a competitor's price**	List price $640; trade discount 25%. Find the trade discount that must be added to match the competitor's price of $432.

First use the formula $P \times L = N$ to find the single discount needed. The answer is the complement of the discount that must be added; subtract it from 100% to get the discount.

$$P \times L = N$$
$$0.75 \times \text{Complement of discount} \times L = N$$
$$0.75 \times d \times \$640 = \$432$$
$$\$480d = \$432$$
$$d = 0.9 = 90\%$$
$$100\% - 90\% = 10\% \text{ additional discount}$$

9.3	**Determining number of days and dates**	Date, July 24. Find 10 days from date.

30-day months	31-day months
April	All the rest except
June	February with 28 days
September	(29 days in leap year)
November	

July $31 - 24 = 7$ remaining in July

10	Total number of days
$-\ \ 7$	Days remaining in July
3	August—future date

9.3 Ordinary dating and cash discounts

With ordinary dating, count days from the date of the invoice. Remember:

$$
\begin{array}{cccc}
2 & / & 10, & n & / & 30 \\
\downarrow & & \downarrow & \downarrow & & \downarrow \\
\% & & \text{days} & \text{net} & & \text{days}
\end{array}
$$

Invoice amount $182; terms 2/10, n/30. Find cash discount and amount due.

Cash discount: $182 × 0.02 = $3.64

Amount due: $182 − $3.64 = $178.36

9.3 Returned goods

Subtract returned goods amount from invoice before calculating the cash discount.

Invoice amount, $95; returned goods, $15; terms, 3/15, n/30. Find amount due if discount is earned.

Cash discount: ($95 − $15) × 0.03 = $2.40

Amount due: $95 − $15 − $2.40 = $77.60

9.4 Cash discounts with end-of-month dating (EOM or proximo)

Count the final discount date and the net date from the end of the month. If the invoice is dated the 26th or after, add the entire following month when determining the dates. If not stated, the net date is 20 days beyond the discount date.

Terms, 2/10 EOM; invoice date, Oct. 18. Find the final discount date and the net payment date.

Final discount date: November 10, which is 10 days from the end of October

Net payment date: November 30, which is 20 days beyond the discount date

9.4 Receipt-of-goods dating and cash discounts (ROG)

Time is counted from the date goods are received to determine the final cash discount date and the net payment date. If not stated, the net date is 20 days beyond the discount date.

Terms, 3/10 ROG; invoice date, March 8; goods received, May 10. Find the final discount date and the net payment date.

Final discount date: May 20 (May 10 + 10 days)

Net payment date: June 9 (May 20 + 20 days)

9.4 Extra dating and cash discounts

Extra dating adds extra days to the usual cash discount period, so 3/10–20 x is the same as 3/30. If not stated, the net date is 20 days beyond the discount date.

Terms, 3/10–20 x; invoice date, January 8. Find the final discount date and the net payment date.

Final discount date: February 7 (23 days in January + 7 days in February = 30)

Net payment date: February 27 (February 7 + 20 days)

9.4 Partial payment credit

When only a portion of an invoice amount is paid within the cash discount period, credit is given for the partial payment. Use the formula

Amount paid = (1 − Discount rate) × Credit given

Invoice, $400; terms, 2/10, n/30; invoice date, Oct. 10; partial payment of $200 on Oct. 15. Find credit given for partial payment and the balance due on the invoice.

$200 = (1 − 0.02) × Credit given

$200 = 0.98C

$C = \dfrac{200}{0.98} = 204.08 (rounded)   Credit

$= $400 − $204.08 = 195.92 Balance due

The answer section includes answers to all Review Exercises.

Find the net cost (invoice amount) for the following. Round to the nearest cent. [9.1]

1. List price: $480 less 20/10
2. List price: $276 less $10/12\frac{1}{2}/10$
3. List price: $2830 less 5/15/20
4. List price: $1620 less 20/25/15

Find (a) the net cost equivalent and (b) the percent form of the single discount equivalent for the following series discounts. [9.2]

5. 25/15
6. 20/10/20
7. $20/32\frac{1}{2}$
8. 10/20/10/30

Find the list price, given the net cost and the series discount. [9.2]

9. Net cost, $361.50; trade discount, 10/20
10. Net cost, $1050.74; trade discount, 15/20
11. Net cost, $328.70; trade discount, 10/20/15
12. Net cost, $1289.40; trade discount, 5/20/25

Find the final discount date and net payment date for the following. (The net payment date is 20 days after the final discount date.) [9.3 and 9.4]

	Invoice Date	Terms	Date Goods Received
13.	Feb. 10	4/15 EOM	Feb. 16
14.	May 8	2/10 ROG	May 20
15.	Dec. 4	3/10 prox	Dec. 8
16.	Oct. 20	2/20–40 extra	Oct. 31

Solve for the amount of discount and the amount due on the following. [9.4]

	Invoice Amount	Invoice Date	Terms	Shipping and Insurance	Date Goods Received	Date Invoice Paid
17.	$1280.40	March 16	3/15 ROG	$76.18	April 7	April 20
18.	$945.60	May 9	3/15 proximo		May 20	June 12
19.	$875.50	Feb. 20	4/15 EOM	$67.18	Mar. 1	Mar. 12
20.	$2210.60	Aug. 5	2/10–60 x		Sept. 10	Oct. 13

Find the credit given and the balance due on the invoice after making the following partial payments. Round to the nearest cent. [9.4]

	Invoice Amount	Invoice Date	Terms	Date Invoice Paid	Partial Payment
21.	$660	February 2	2/10, n/30	February 10	$300
22.	$5310	April 22	3/15 EOM	May 14	$2520
23.	$860	July 23	1/10 prox.	August 5	$500
24.	$3850	September 17	3/10–40 x	November 2	$2050

Solve the following application problems in cash and trade discounts.

25. The following invoice was paid on November 15. Find (a) the invoice total, (b) the amount that should be paid after the cash discount, and (c) the total amount due, including shipping and insurance. **[9.1 and 9.3]**

GOURMET KITCHEN WHOLESALERS			
Terms: 2/10, 1/15, n/60			November 6

Quantity	Description	Unit Price	Extension Total
16	tablecloths, linen	@ 17.50 ea.	
8	rings, napkin	@ 3.25 ea.	
4	cups, ceramic	@ 12.65 ea.	
12	bowls, 1 qt. stainless	@ 3.15 ea.	
		(a) Invoice Total	
		Cash Discount	
		(b) Due after Cash Discount	
		Shipping and Insurance	$11.55
		(c) Total Amount Due	

26. Fireside Shop offers chimney caps for $120 less 25/10. The same chimney cap is offered by Builders Supply for $111 less 25/5. Find (a) the firm that offers the lower price and (b) the difference in price. **[9.1]**

27. Bergen Snow Tractors purchased several snowmobiles for $41,424.75 after a series discount of 10/5. Find the list price. **[9.2]**

28. Restaurant Distributing offers a commercial pasta maker for $980 with a trade discount of 25%. Find the trade discount that must be added to match a competitor's price of $661.50. **[9.2]**

29. An invoice amounting to $2018 is dated September 18 and offers terms of 3/20 EOM. If $183 of goods are returned and the invoice is paid on October 18, what amount is due? **[9.4]**

30. Subway Sandwich Shop purchased paper products list-priced at $348 less series discounts of 10/20/10 with terms of 3/10–50 extra. If the retailer paid the invoice within 60 days, find the amount paid. **[9.4]**

31. An invoice of $838 from Kara-Dolls has cash terms of 2/15 EOM and is dated March 8. Find (a) the final date on which the cash discount may be taken and (b) the amount necessary to pay the invoice in full if the cash discount is earned. **[9.4]**

32. An invoice from Round Table Pizza Products amounts to $5280, was dated November 1, and offers terms of 4/15 proximo. A partial payment of $1800 is made on December 12. Find (a) the amount credited for the partial payment, (b) the balance due on the invoice, and (c) the cash discount earned. **[9.4]**

CHAPTER 9	Business Application Case #1
	Retailer Discounts

Andrew Ryan of Specialty Kitchens buys much of his merchandise from Gourmet Kitchen Wholesalers. In early September, he ordered kitchen flatware, dinnerware, and cutlery having a total list price of $9748, and appliances and cookware having a list price of $17,645. Gourmet Kitchen Wholesalers offers trade discounts of 20/10/10 on these items and charges for shipping. The invoice for this order arrived a few days later, is dated September 4, has terms of 3/15 EOM, and shows a shipping charge of $748.38. Specialty Kitchens will need to know all of the following. Round to the nearest cent.

(a) The total amount of the invoice excluding shipping.

(b) The final discount date.

(c) The net payment date.

(d) The amount necessary to pay the invoice in full on October 11 including the shipping.

(e) Suppose that on October 11 the invoice is not paid in full, but a partial payment of $10,000 is made instead. Find the credit given for the partial payment and the balance due on the invoice including shipping.

CHAPTER 9	Business Application Case #2
	Purchasing Decisions at a Retailer

Thomas Rugby works as a purchasing manager for a large retailer. He needs to buy 1200 vacuum cleaners with a specific power and efficiency rating. After considerable discussion with potential suppliers, he has narrowed the decision of which to use to one of the two following firms.

Company	Cost of Each Vacuum Cleaner	Trade Discount	Shipping Charge
Trident, Inc.	$117.20	5/10 net 30	$1585
Shanghai Industries	$124	2/20 ROG	$2200

(a) Assume all discounts are taken and find the total cost to purchase 1200 vacuum cleaners from each company including the shipping charges.

(b) Based on cost alone, which company should Thomas buy from and what would be the savings to his firm?

(c) However, Mr. Rugby has heard a rumor of possible quality problems with Trident, Inc. products. He has been unable to verify the rumor, but he is worried about quality problems since his firm would have to handle any poor-quality vacuum cleaners returned to a store. At the same time, his boss is constantly pushing him to save costs. In this situation, which company would you choose if you had Mr. Rugby's job? Justify your choice.

Markup

The success of a business depends on many things. It greatly depends on managers' skills and knowledge about their customers. It also depends on keeping costs low, including the costs of borrowed money. Importantly, a firm must be able to charge a high enough price to pay operating expenses, including wages, and have some left over for profit. This chapter is about markup, which is the difference between the selling price and the purchase price.

Managers continually monitor expenses. Table 10.1 shows some of Wal-Mart Stores' expenses for a recent quarter. Notice that Wal-Mart paid 75.1% of its gross quarterly revenue of $98.6 billion for Cost of Sales, which includes payments to thousands of suppliers. Most of Wal-Mart's revenue is simply passed on to its thousands of suppliers. The company also paid out 19.5% of its gross revenue for selling and administrative expenses that included wages for more than 2 million employess. Only 3.1% of their total revenue was profit. In other words, the firm saw an average profit of just over 3 cents on every $1 in sales. Clearly, Wal-Mart Stores must mark up the price of goods the company buys by enough to cover its many costs in order to make any profit.

Table 10.1   WAL-MART STORES (3RD QUARTER, 2008)

	(in billions)	Percent of Gross Revenue
Gross Revenue	$98.6	—
Cost of Sales	$74.1	75.1%
Selling, General, & Administrative	$19.2	19.5%
Interest	$0.4	0.4%
After-tax Profit	$3.1	3.1%

Source: Wal-Mart financial statements.

STOP —and think

The percent of gross revenue that goes to profit is less than 5% at many large discount retailers and grocery stores. Estimate the amount you spend at the grocery store each week. Assume profit at the store averages 3% of gross sales and estimate the amount of profit the firm makes from you *each year.* If a grocery store experiences a theft of $850 in products during one week, how much extra must it sell to have the same profit at the end of the quarter?

10.1	**Markup on Cost**

OBJECTIVES

1 *Recognize the terms used in selling.*

2 *Use the basic markup formula.*

3 *Calculate markup based on cost.*

4 *Apply percent to markup problems.*

Objective

1 *Recognize the Terms Used in Selling.*　The following terms are used in markup.

Cost is the price paid to the manufacturer or supplier after trade and cash discounts have been taken. Shipping and insurance charges are included in the cost. This is often called the **wholesale price**.

Selling price, or **retail price**, is the price at which merchandise is offered for sale to the public.

Markup, also called **margin** or **gross profit**, is the difference between the cost and the selling price. These three terms are often used interchangeably.

Operating expenses, or **overhead**, include the many expenses of business operation, such as wages and salaries of employees, rent for buildings and equipment, utilities, insurance, and advertising. Even an expense item such as postage can add up. Mailing costs average from 6.2% of operating expense to as high as 9.2% for some companies.

Net profit (net earnings) is the amount, if any, remaining for the business after the cost of goods and operating expenses have been paid. (Income tax for the business is computed on net profit.)

We usually think of markup in terms of products. But a similar concept applies to a service industry, such as the delivery of mail by the U.S. Postal Service. Since the U.S. Postal Service is not supposed to lose money on behalf of taxpayers, managers must fully understand and carefully control costs. They must mark the price of postage up to the point where the Postal Service does not lose money. Figure 10.1 shows historical postal rates. Using techniques from later chapters, we can see that the cost to mail a letter has increased at the rate of 4.6% per year since 1971. Inflation is a major reason that prices have increased so much over the years. For example, wages and fuel have increased since 1971, requiring higher postage costs. Inflation is discussed in Chapter 12.

Figure 10.1

Most manufacturers, many wholesalers, and some retailers calculate markup as a percent of cost, called **markup on cost**. Manufacturers, who usually evaluate their inventories on the basis of cost, find this method to be most consistent with their business operations. Retailers, on the other hand, usually compute **markup on selling price** since retailers compare most areas of their business operations to sales revenue. Such items as sales commissions, sales taxes, advertising, and other items of expense are expressed as a percent of sales. It is reasonable, then, for the retailer to express markup as percent of sales. Wholesalers, however, use either cost or selling price, so be sure to find out which a wholesaler is using.

Objective

2 *Use the Basic Markup Formula.* Whether markup is based on cost or on selling price, the same basic **markup formula** is always used. This formula is as follows.

$$\textbf{Cost + Markup = Selling price}$$
$$C \quad + \quad M \quad = \quad S$$

The markup formula is illustrated in Figure 10.2. Most problems in markup give two of the items in the formula and ask for the third.

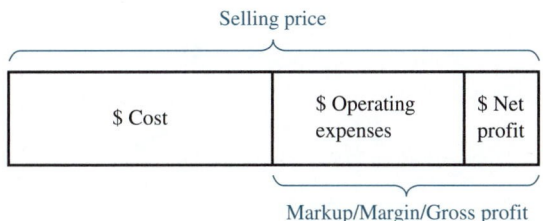

Figure 10.2

EXAMPLE 1 **Using the Basic Markup Formula**

Disney Books and Music received some new children's music CDs. Use the markup formula to determine the selling price, markup, and cost of the CDs in the following problems.

(a)   Cost = $10   **(b)**   Cost = $10

      Markup = $5   Selling price = $15

      Selling price = _____   Markup = _____

(c)   Markup = $5

    Selling price = $15

        Cost = _____

Solution

(a) $C + M = S$ **(b)** $C + M = S$

    $\$10 + \$5 = S$ $\$10 + M = \$15$

         $\$15 = S$ $M = \$15 - \$10$

                   $M = \$5$

(c) $C + M = S$

   $C + \$5 = \$15$

       $C = \$15 - \$5$

       $C = \$10$

Objective

3 *Calculate Markup Based on Cost.* **Markup based on cost** is expressed as a percent of cost. As shown in the work with percent, the base (that to which a number is being compared) is 100%, so cost will have a value of 100%. Markup and selling price will also have percent values found by comparing their dollar values to the dollar value of cost. Solve markup problems with the basic markup formula $C + M = S$.

Objective

4   *Apply Percent to Markup Problems.*

> **EXAMPLE** **2**   **Calculating Markup on Cost**
>
> The owner of Rose Fine Wines buys several cases of a popular wine bottled in Spain at a wholesale cost of $15 per bottle. In order to bring new customers into the store, the manager widely advertises a special promotion on this particular wine for $18.75 per bottle, or for considerably less than it can be purchased at competing stores. Find the percent of markup based on cost.
>
> **Solution**   Use the markup formula
>
> $$C + M = S$$
>
> with C = $15 and S = $18.75.
>
> $$\$15 + M = \$18.75$$
> $$M = \$18.75 - \$15$$
> $$M = \$3.75$$
>
> The markup is $3.75. Now, find the percent of markup based on cost with the basic percent equation, $R \times B = P$. The base is the cost, or $15, and the markup is the part, or $3.75. Substitute these values into $R \times B = P$.
>
> $$R \times B = P$$
> $$R \times \$15 = \$3.75 \qquad \text{Base is 15.}$$
> $$\$15R = \$3.75$$
> $$\frac{\cancel{15}R}{\cancel{15}} = \frac{3.75}{15} \qquad \text{Divide both sides by 15.}$$
> $$R = 0.25 = 25\%$$
>
> The $3.75 markup on the wine corresponds to 25% markup on cost. For your information, quality wines are often marked up by more than 50% and sometimes by 100%. So, the manager is using advertising and a lower-than-normal markup on this popular wine to bring new customers into the store. He probably anticipates that the nice selection of wines combined with the friendly and knowledgeable service will result in customers returning to the store.

 **Scientific Calculator Approach**

The calculator solution for Example 2 uses the parentheses to find the markup and then divides by the cost.

$$(\boxed{18.75} \boxed{-} \boxed{15}) \boxed{\div} \boxed{15} \boxed{=} \; 0.25$$

NOTE   The markup formula and the basic percent equation can be used for solving various types of problems involving markup, as shown in the next examples.

EXAMPLE 3 **Finding Cost When Cost Is Base**

Olympic Sports and Leisure has a markup on a Spalding basketball of $14, which is 50% based on cost. Find the cost and the selling price.

Solution   The markup is 50% of the cost.

$$P = R \times B$$
$$M = 50\% \times C \quad \text{Markup is part, cost is base.}$$
$$M = 0.50C$$

Since the markup is $14, substitute 14 for M.

$$\$14 = 0.50C$$
$$\frac{14}{0.50} = \frac{0.50C}{0.50}$$
$$28 = C$$

The cost of the basketball is $28. Now use the basic markup formula to find the selling price.

$$C + M = S$$
$$\$28 + \$14 = S$$
$$\$42 = S$$

The selling price of the basketball is $42.

EXAMPLE 4 **Finding the Markup and the Selling Price**

Find the markup and selling price for a Casio solar-powered watch if the cost is $23.60 and the markup is 25% of cost.

Solution   Since the markup is 25% of cost, or $M = 0.25C$,

$$M = 0.25(\$23.60)$$
$$M = \$5.90$$

The markup is $5.90. Now use the markup formula, with $C = \$23.60$ and $M = \$5.90$.

$$C + M = S$$
$$\$23.60 + \$5.90 = S$$
$$\$29.50 = S$$

The selling price of the watch is $29.50.

Scientific Calculator Approach

The calculator solution for Example 4 uses the percent add-on feature found on many calculators.

$$23.6 \boxed{+} \ 25 \boxed{\%} \ \boxed{=} \ 29.5$$

EXAMPLE 5 **Finding Cost When Cost Is Base**

Olympic Sports and Leisure is selling a Wilson baseball glove for $42, which is 140% of the cost. How much did Olympic Sports and Leisure pay for the baseball glove?

Solution   If the selling price is 140% of cost, then the markup must be 40% of cost. (The cost is always 100% when markup is based on cost.)

$$M = 0.4C$$

Now use the basic formula.

$$C + M = S$$
$$C + 0.4C = \$42$$
$$1C + 0.4C = \$42$$
$$1.4C = \$42$$
$$\frac{1.4C}{1.4} = \frac{\$42}{1.4}$$
$$C = \$30$$

The cost of the glove is $30. Check: $0.40(\$30) = \$12$ markup, and $\$30 + \$12 = \$42$.

EXAMPLE 6 **Finding the Cost and the Markup**

The retail selling price of a Kenmore Elite 21.6-cubic-foot refrigerator is $978.75. If the markup is 35% of cost, find the cost and the markup.

Solution   Use the formula, with $M = 0.35C$.

$$C + M = S$$
$$C + 0.35C = \$978.75$$
$$1C + 0.35C = \$978.75$$
$$1.35C = \$978.75$$
$$\frac{1.35C}{1.35} = \frac{\$978.75}{1.35}$$
$$C = \$725$$

The cost of the refrigerator is $725. Now find the markup.

$$C + M = S$$
$$\$725 + M = \$978.75$$
$$M = \$978.75 - \$725$$
$$M = \$253.75$$

The markup is $253.75.

NOTE   Remember, when calculating markup on cost, cost is *always* the base, 100%.

10.1	**Exercises**

Find the missing quantities. Round rates to the nearest tenth of a percent and money to the nearest cent.

	Cost	Markup	% Markup on Cost	Selling Price
1.	$12.40	_____	40%	_____
2.	_____	$7.20	_____	$43.20
3.	$23.50	$11.75	_____	_____
4.	_____	_____	100%	$68.98
5.	$158.70	_____	_____	$198.50
6.	_____	$14.40	60%	_____
7.	_____	$13.50	_____	$81
8.	$33.80	_____	25%	_____
9.	$210	_____	_____	$328
10.	_____	$25.25	_____	$73.80
11.	$495	_____	27%	_____
12.	_____	_____	16%	$90.83

13. Markup may be calculated on cost or on selling price. Explain why most manufacturers prefer to use cost as base when calculating markup. (See Objective 1.)

14. Write the basic markup formula. Define each term. (See Objective 2.)

Solve the following application problems using cost as base. Round rates to the nearest tenth of a percent and money to the nearest cent.

15. HARD-TO-FIND TOOLS   The Brookstone Company sells a precision tool kit for $138. If the markup is 35% of cost, find the cost.

16. DENTAL TOOLS   The cost of a dentist's handpiece is $560 and the markup is 25% of cost. Find the markup.

17. GARDEN TOOLS   Orchard Supply sells garden sprayers at a price of $18.95. If markup is 38% of cost, find the cost.

18. LAWN FERTILIZER   Orchard Supply sells lawn fertilizer at a price of $12.50 per bag. If the markup is 25% of cost, find the cost.

19. ELECTRIC WHEELCHAIR   A retailer purchases an electric wheelchair for $2820. The firm uses a markup of 28% on cost. Find the selling price.

20. RECREATION EQUIPMENT   Water Sports purchases jet skis at a cost of $2880 each. If its operating expenses are 25% of its cost, and it wishes to make a net profit of 15% of its cost, find the selling price.

21. HEARING AIDS   Benson Hearing pays $1540 for specialized hearing aids, which it then sells for $1999. Find the percent of markup on cost.

22. MARKUP ON ASPIRIN   The Tower Market sells aspirin (50-tablet bottle) for $3.38 per bottle. If it pays $2.60 per bottle, find the markup percent on cost.

23. OUTDOOR LIGHTING   Patios Plus sold an outdoor lighting set for $119.95. The markup on the set was $23.99. Find (a) the cost, (b) the markup percent on cost, and (c) the selling price as a percent of cost.

24. ATHLETIC SHOES   Fleet Feet had a markup of $11.66 on some shoes that it sold for $55.66. Find (a) the cost, (b) the markup percent on cost, and (c) the selling price as a percent of cost.

25. **FARM EQUIPMENT** Fairfield Tractor put a markup of 32% on cost on a part for which it paid $73.50. Find (a) the selling price as a percent of cost, (b) the selling price, and (c) the markup.

26. **BRASS LAMPS** A lighting manufacturer offers brass lamps at a selling price that is 175% of the cost. The markup is $61.50. Find (a) the markup percent on cost, (b) the cost, and (c) the selling price.

27. **HIKING BOOTS** Nature Trails, a manufacturer of hiking equipment, prices light-weight hiking boots at $89.04, which is 127.2% of their cost. Find (a) the cost, (b) the markup as a percent of cost, and (c) the markup.

28. **COIN COLLECTING** North Area Coins priced an 1800s uncirculated silver dollar at $868, which was 112% of cost. Find (a) the cost, (b) the markup as a percent of cost, and (c) the markup.

29. **WELDING SUPPLIES** Welder's Supply purchases arc welding units for $3860 each. The company has operating expenses of 22% of cost and a net profit of 12% of cost. Find the selling price of each arc welding unit.

30. **MOTOR SCOOTER** Kragen Auto Supply purchases 4-stroke gas scooters at a cost of $280 each. The company's operating expenses are 16% of cost, and a net profit of 7% of cost is desired. Find the selling price of one scooter.

31. **RETAIL HARDWARE** Bell Hardware has operating expenses of 18% of cost and desires a 17% net profit on cost. The selling price of a tube of 20-year silicone caulk is $8.95. Find the cost.

32. **SLIDING PATIO DOORS** American Glass Company sells 8-foot sliding patio doors for $299.90. Its operating expenses are 15% of cost and its net profit is 15% of cost. Find the cost.

10.2	**Markup on Selling Price**

OBJECTIVES

1 *Calculate markup based on selling price.*

2 *Solve markup problems when selling price is base.*

3 *Use the markup formula to solve variations of markup problems.*

4 *Determine percent markup on cost and the equivalent percent markup on selling price.*

5 *Convert markup percent on cost to markup percent on selling price.*

6 *Convert markup percent on selling price to markup percent on cost.*

As mentioned, wholesalers sometimes calculate markup based on cost and other times calculate **markup based on selling price**. Retailers use sales figures in almost all aspects of their business. Almost all expense and income amounts are calculated as a percent of sales. Therefore, it is common for retailers to calculate markup based on selling price. In each case, markup will be given as "on cost" or "on selling price." Remember that if markup is based on selling price, then selling price *is* the base. Since the base is 100%, selling price will have a value of 100%. This section discusses markup on selling price.

Objective

1 *Calculate Markup Based on Selling Price.* The same basic markup formula is used with markup on selling price.

$$\text{Cost} + \text{Markup} = \text{Selling price}$$
$$C + M = S$$

Objective

2 *Solve Markup Problems When Selling Price Is Base.*

EXAMPLE **1** **Solving for Markup on Selling Price**

To compete against other discount stores, Target sells a calculator for $15 that it buys for $10. Find the markup and the percent of markup on selling price.

Solution   First, solve for markup.

$$C + M = S$$
$$\$10 + M = \$15$$
$$M = \$15 - \$10$$
$$M = \$5$$

   Now solve for percent of markup on selling price. Use the basic percent equation, $R \times B = P$. In this example, P is the markup, or $5, and the base B is the selling price, or $15. Substitute these values into $R \times B = P$, and solve the equation.

$$R \times B = P$$
$$R \times \$15 = \$5$$
$$R = \frac{\$5}{\$15}$$
$$R = \frac{1}{3} = 0.333\ldots$$
$$= 33\frac{1}{3}\%$$

The percent of markup on selling price is $33\frac{1}{3}\%$.

Objective

3 *Use the Markup Formula to Solve Variations of Markup Problems.*   As with problems where markup is based on cost, the basic formula $C + M = S$ may be used for all variations of markup problems when selling price is the base.

EXAMPLE **2** **Finding Markup When Selling Price Is Given**

Find the markup on a movie in high-definition Blu-ray Disc format that sells for $22.79, if the markup is 30% of the selling price. Then find the cost paid by the retailer.

Solution

$$\text{Markup} = 30\% \text{ of Selling price}$$
$$= 0.3 \times \$22.79$$
$$= \$6.84 \qquad \text{Rounded}$$

$$\textbf{Cost to retailer} = \textbf{Selling price} - \textbf{Markup}$$
$$= \$22.79 \quad - \$6.84$$
$$= \$15.95$$

EXAMPLE 3   Finding Cost When Selling Price Is Base

A bookstore employee knows that the three-hole binders have a markup of $2.38, which is 40% based on selling price. Find the cost of the binders.

Solution   Start by finding selling price and then subtract markup to find cost. Here $R = 40\%$ (the rate of markup), $P = \$2.38$ (the markup), and B is the unknown (selling price). Use $R \times B = P$ as follows.

$$R \times B = P$$
$$40\% \times S = \$2.38$$
$$0.4S = \$2.38$$
$$S = \frac{\$2.38}{0.4}$$
$$S = \$5.95$$

The selling price is $5.95. Now solve for cost.

$$C + M = S$$
$$C + \$2.38 = \$5.95$$
$$C + \$2.38 - \$2.38 = \$5.95 - \$2.38$$
$$C = \$5.95 - \$2.38$$
$$C = \$3.57$$

The cost is $3.57.

EXAMPLE 4   Finding the Selling Price and the Markup When Cost Is Given

An employee at The Home Depot is told to calculate the selling price and markup on a 6-pack container of tomato plants if the cost is $3.16 and the markup is 20% of selling price.

Solution   Use the formula $C + M = S$. Since the markup is 20% of the selling price, $M = 0.2S$.

$$C + M = S$$
$$\$3.16 + 0.2S = S$$
$$\$3.16 + 0.2S - 0.2S = 1S - 0.2S$$
$$\$3.16 = 1S - 0.2S$$
$$\$3.16 = 0.8S$$
$$\frac{3.16}{0.8} = \frac{0.8S}{0.8}$$
$$\$3.95 = S$$

The selling price is $3.95.
   Now find the markup using the markup formula.

$$C + M = S$$
$$\$3.16 + M = \$3.95$$
$$M = \$3.95 - \$3.16$$
$$M = \$0.79$$

The markup is $0.79.

Markups vary widely from industry to industry and from business to business. This variation is a result of different costs of merchandise, operating costs, level of profit margin, and local competition. Table 10.2 shows average markups for different types of retail stores.

Table 10.2   AVERAGE MARKUPS FOR RETAIL STORES (MARKUP ON SELLING PRICE)

Type of Store	Markup	Type of Store	Markup
General merchandise	29.97%	Furniture and home furnishings	35.75%
Grocery	22.05%	Drinking places	52.49%
Other food	27.31%	Eating places	56.35%
Motor vehicle dealers (new)	12.83%	Drug and proprietary	30.81%
Gasoline service stations	14.47%	Liquor	20.19%
Other automotive dealers	29.57%	Sporting goods and bicycle	29.72%
Apparel and accessories	37.64%	Gift, novelty, and souvenir	41.86%

Source: Sole Proprietorship Income Tax Returns, U.S. Treasury Dept., Internal Revenue Service, Statistics Division.

Do not make the mistake of thinking of the markup percents in Table 10.2 as profit. Included in markup are the following costs: wages, employee benefits, transportation, taxes, maintenance, rent, utilities, insurance, etc. Profit is what remains after everything has been paid. Sometimes a firm makes a profit, but many firms also lose money in rough economic times such as a recession.

Objective

4 *Determine Percent Markup on Cost and the Equivalent Percent Markup on Selling Price.*   Sometimes, a markup based on cost must be compared to a markup based on selling price. Such a conversion might be necessary for a manufacturer who thinks in terms of cost and wants to understand a wholesaler or retail customer. Or, perhaps, a retailer or wholesaler might convert markup on selling price to markup on cost to better understand the manufacturer. Make these comparisons by first computing the markup on cost, then computing the markup on selling price.

EXAMPLE 5   Determining Equivalent Markups

Claire Magersky sells fishing lures to both fishing-equipment wholesalers and sporting-goods stores. If the lure costs her $4.20 and she sells it for $5.25, what is the percent of markup on cost? What is the percent of markup on selling price?

Solution   To solve for markup, use the formula $C + M = S$, with $C = \$4.20$ and $S = \$5.25$.

$$C + M = S$$
$$\$4.20 + M = \$5.25$$
$$M = \$5.25 - \$4.20$$
$$M = \$1.05 \qquad \text{Markup}$$

Next, to solve for the percent of markup on cost, use the percent equation, $R \times B = P$, with $B = \$4.20$ (the cost, since markup is on cost) and $P = \$1.05$ (the markup).

$$R \times B = P$$
$$R \times \$4.20 = \$1.05$$
$$\$4.20R = \$1.05$$
$$R = \frac{1.05}{4.2}$$
$$R = 0.25 = 25\% \quad \text{Markup on cost}$$

To find the percent of markup on selling price, use the percent equation again. While P is still \$1.05, B changes to \$5.25 since the markup on selling price must be found. Substitute into the equation as follows.

$$R \times B = P$$
$$R \times \$5.25 = \$1.05$$
$$\$5.25R = \$1.05$$
$$R = \frac{1.05}{5.25}$$
$$R = 0.2 = 20\% \quad \text{Markup on selling price}$$

Example 5 shows that a 25% markup on cost is the exact same thing as a 20% markup on selling price. The process to convert from markup on cost to markup on selling price and vice versa is shown in the next two objectives in this section.

Objective

5   *Convert Markup Percent on Cost to Markup Percent on Selling Price.*   Another method for making markup comparisons is to use **conversion formulas**. *No dollar amounts are needed to use these formulas.* Only the percent of markup is needed. If you have markup percent on cost, you can convert the markup percent on cost to markup percent on selling price with the following formula.

$$\% \text{ Markup on selling price} = \frac{\% \text{ Markup on cost}}{100\% + \% \text{ Markup on cost}}$$

Or, if M_c represents markup on cost and M_s represents markup on selling price.

$$M_s = \frac{M_c}{100\% + M_c}$$

EXAMPLE 6   Converting Markup on Cost to Markup on Selling Price

Convert a markup of 25% on cost to its **equivalent percent markup** on selling price.

Solution   Use the markup on cost (M_c) of 25% in the formula to solve for markup on selling price.

$$M_s = \frac{M_c}{100\% + M_c}$$
$$= \frac{25\%}{100\% + 25\%}$$
$$= \frac{25\%}{125\%} = 20\%$$

So a 25% markup on cost is the same as a 20% markup on selling price.

Scientific Calculator Approach

The markup on cost (25%) is divided by 100% plus the markup on cost. The parentheses keys are used here.

25 % ÷ (100 % + 25 %) = 0.2

Objective

6 *Convert Markup Percent on Selling Price to Markup Percent on Cost.* Convert markup percent on selling price to markup percent on cost with the following formula.

$$\% \text{ Markup on cost} = \frac{\% \text{ Markup on selling price}}{100\% - \% \text{ Markup on selling price}}$$

Or, if M_c represents markup on cost and M_s represents markup on selling price.

$$M_c = \frac{M_s}{100\% - M_s}$$

EXAMPLE 7 **Converting Markup on Selling Price to Markup on Cost**

Convert a markup of 30% on selling price to its **equivalent percent markup** on cost.

Solution Use the markup on selling price (M_s) of 30% in the formula to solve for markup on cost.

$$M_c = \frac{M_s}{100\% - M_s}$$

$$= \frac{30\%}{100\% - 30\%}$$

$$= \frac{30\%}{70\%} = 42.9\%$$

Therefore, a 30% markup on selling price is the same as a 42.9% markup on cost.

 Scientific Calculator Approach

For Example 7, the markup on selling price (30%) is divided by 100% minus the markup on selling price. The parentheses keys are used here.

30 % ÷ (100 % − 30 %) = 0.429 *Rounded*

NOTE Retailers and wholesalers commonly use both markup on cost and markup on selling price. One is not better than the other; the two simply represent different ways to talk about markup.

Table 10.3 shows common markup equivalents expressed as percents on cost and also on selling price. A table like this would be helpful to anyone using markup equivalents on a regular basis.

Table 10.3 COMMON MARKUP EQUIVALENTS

Markup on Cost	Markup on Selling Price
20%	$16\frac{2}{3}\%$
25%	20%
$33\frac{1}{3}\%$	25%
50%	$33\frac{1}{3}\%$
$66\frac{2}{3}\%$	40%
75%	$42\frac{6}{7}\%$
100%	50%

10.2	**Exercises**

Find the missing quantities. Round rates to the nearest tenth of a percent and money to the nearest cent.

	Cost Price	Markup	% Markup on Selling Price	Selling Price
1.	$21	_____	25%	_____
2.	$145	_____		$250
3.	_____	$112	46%	_____
4.	_____	$72	_____	$189.50
5.	$18.60	_____	$66\frac{2}{3}\%$	_____
6.	$17.28	_____	_____	$29.95
7.	_____	_____	35%	$71.32
8.	$178	_____	$33\frac{1}{3}\%$	_____
9.	_____	$42.18	_____	$120
10.	$193.15	_____	42.5%	_____

Find the missing quantities by first computing the markup on one base and then computing the markup on the other. Round rates to the nearest tenth of a percent and money to the nearest cent.

	Cost	Markup	Selling Price	% Markup on Cost	% Markup on Selling Price
11.	_____	$57.50	_____	25%	20%
12.	_____	$0.23	$0.73	_____	_____
13.	$13.80	_____	_____	_____	38%
14.	$33.75	_____	$67.50	_____	_____
15.	_____	$300	_____	40%	_____
16.	$5.15	_____	$15.45	_____	_____
17.	_____	$78.48	$436	_____	18%
18.	_____	$480	_____	25%	_____

Find the equivalent markups on either cost or selling price using the appropriate formula. Round to the nearest tenth of a percent.

	Markup on Cost	Markup on Selling Price
19.	_____	20%
20.	_____	50%
21.	_____	26%
22.	_____	15.3%
23.	50%	_____
24.	$33\frac{1}{3}\%$	_____
25.	_____	40%
26.	_____	$16\frac{2}{3}\%$

27. Why do you suppose that grocery stores have an average markup of 22.05%, while eating places have an average markup of 56.35%?

28. To have a markup of 100% or greater, the markup must be calculated on cost. Show why this is always true. (See Objectives 5 and 6.)

Solve the following application problems. Round rates to the nearest tenth of a percent and money to the nearest cent.

29. LEATHER HANDBAG Jelica's Handbags pays $32.33 for a leather handbag and uses a markup of 34% on selling price. Find the selling price.

30. AUTO PARTS DEALER An auto parts dealer pays $14.28 per dozen gallons of windshield washer fluid and the markup is 50% on selling price. Find the selling price per gallon.

31. HOME ENTERTAINMENT SYSTEM Fry's Electronics sells a home theater speaker package for $595 and maintains a markup of 35% on selling price. Find the cost.

32. HOT TUB SYSTEM Lowe's sells a hot tub system for $3522 and maintains a markup of 35% on selling price. Find the cost.

33. CEILING FANS The cost of a ceiling fan is $92.82 and the markup is 22% on selling price. Find the selling price.

34. FLY FISHING Field and Stream Sports pays $20.80 for a fly rod and sells it for $32. Find the percent of markup on selling price.

35. BELGIAN FLOOR TILE Handmade floor tile from Belgium has a markup of 36% on the selling price. The tile has a markup of $1.62 per tile. Find (a) the selling price, (b) the cost, and (c) the cost as a percent of the selling price per tile.

36. DVD RECORDER Direct Electronics pays $196.78 for a Philips DVD recorder. The markup is 18% on selling price. Find (a) the cost as a percent of selling price, (b) the selling price, and (c) the markup.

37. CLOCK RADIOS Best Products buys clock radios for $258 per dozen and has a gross profit of $7.74 per clock radio. Find the percent of gross profit based on selling price.

38. HOME-WORKOUT EQUIPMENT Olympics Sports has a markup of $280 on a Schwinn Bowflex. If this is a 35% markup on selling price, find (a) the selling price, (b) the cost, and (c) the cost as a percent of selling price.

39. SWIMMING POOL PUMP Leslie's Pool Supply pays $187.19 for a Hydramax II pump. If the markup is 28% on the selling price, find (a) the cost as a percent of selling price, (b) the selling price, and (c) the markup.

40. LEVI'S DOCKER SHIRTS Mervyn's Department Store priced some Levi's Docker shirts at $29.95. The cost of the shirts was 58% of the selling price. Find (a) the cost, (b) the markup, and (c) the markup as a percent of selling price.

41. RECYCLING ALUMINUM Recyclable aluminum can be sold for $2880 per ton (1 ton = 2000 pounds). If Alcan Recycling wants a 50% markup on selling price, (a) how much per pound can it pay local residents for their recycled aluminum? (b) What is the equivalent markup percent on cost?

42. RETAIL SILK FLOWERS A retailer purchases silk flowers for $31.56 per dozen and sells them for $4.78 each. (a) Find his percent of markup on selling price. (b) What is the equivalent markup on cost?

43. RIVER RAFT SALES White Water Supply purchased a job lot of 380 river rafts for $7600. If it sold 158 of the rafts at $45 each, 74 at $35 each, 56 at $30 each, and the remainder at $25 each, what is (a) the total amount received for the rafts, (b) the total markup, (c) the markup percent on selling price, and (d) the equivalent markup percent on cost?

44. ITALIAN SILK TIES Dress for Success purchased 240 Italian silk ties for $2280. It sold 162 ties at $25 each, 45 ties at $15 each, 20 ties at $10 each, and the remainder at $5 each. Find (a) the total amount received for the ties, (b) the total markup, (c) the markup percent on selling price, and (d) the equivalent markup percent on cost.

45. GOLD JEWELRY Zarrima Jewels sells a diamond necklace for $1180, which includes a markup of 60% on selling price. Find (a) the cost and (b) the percent of markup on cost.

46. SMOKING SUPPLIES The Tinder Box Smoke Shop buys a special blend of pipe tobacco in 10-pound tins at a cost of $24 per tin. The shop sells the tobacco for $1.20 per ounce. Find (a) the markup percent on selling price and (b) the equivalent markup percent on cost. (*Hint:* 1 pound = 16 ounces).

47. RESTAURANT SUPPLIES A restaurant supplier sells coffee filters for $6.90 per box. If the cost of the filters is $4.80, find (a) the percent of markup on cost and (b) the equivalent percent of markup on selling price.

48. ALL-PURPOSE FERTILIZER Home Base sells a 40-pound bag of Pax All-Purpose Fertilizer for $10.98. The cost of the fertilizer is $7.32 per bag. Find (a) the percent of markup on cost and (b) the equivalent percent of markup on selling price.

49. CORDLESS PHONES A discount store purchased 5.8-GHz cordless phones at a cost of $576 per dozen. If it needs 20% of cost to cover operating expenses and 15% of cost for net profit, what is (a) the selling price per phone and (b) the percent of markup on selling price?

50. BOWLING EQUIPMENT The Bowler's ProShop determines that operating expenses are 23% of selling price and desires a net profit of 12% of selling price. If the cost of a team shirt is $29.25, what is (a) the selling price and (b) the percent of markup on cost?

51. MOUNTAIN BIKE SALES Cycle City advertises mountain bikes for $199.90. If its cost is $2100 per dozen, what is (a) the markup per bicycle, (b) the percent of markup on selling price, and (c) the percent of markup on cost?

52. HAND TOOL SALES The Tool Shed advertises standard/metric socket sets (manufactured in the U.S.A.) for $39. Its cost is $351 per dozen sets. Find (a) the markup per set, (b) the percent of markup on selling price, and (c) the percent of markup on cost.

10.3 Markup with Spoilage

OBJECTIVES

1 *Solve markup problems when items are unfit for sale.*
2 *Solve markup problems when a certain percent of items are unsaleable.*
3 *Calculate markup when a percent of the merchandise must be sold at a reduced price.*

Shrinkage refers to the loss of products between the point of creation (manufacturer, farmer, etc.) and the point of sale to a final customer. It includes spoilage, which we discuss in this section, but it also includes losses related to theft and breakage. Figure 10.3 shows that 79% of all shrinkage comes from either employee theft or shoplifting. Managers are well aware of this fact and work hard to establish systems designed to reduce theft. The retailing industry has worked with legislators across the country to make shoplifting a crime. Even helping a shoplifter is a crime. Shoplifters are sometimes surprised at how much trouble they are in once caught.

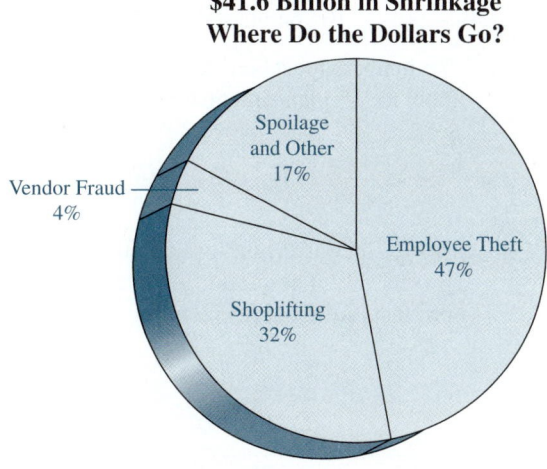

**$41.6 Billion in Shrinkage
Where Do the Dollars Go?**

Source: 2007 National Retail Security Survey,
University of Florida.

Figure 10.3

Objective

1 ***Solve Markup Problems When Items Are Unfit for Sale.***   **Spoilage** refers to products that have been damaged or blemished. Spoilage is a common problem for firms that work with fresh food such as fruit or dairy, but it also affects businesses that sell clothing, for example. Clothing items with small defects or blemishes are known as **irregulars**. A firm usually has to mark the price down to sell any product with blemishes or small defects. Any items that cannot be sold are a total loss. In either case, the markup on the good-quality items must make up for any losses on the spoiled or blemished items. The process of marking regular items at a higher price to make up for losses on damaged products is called **markup with spoilage**.

| **EXAMPLE** 1 | **Finding Selling Price with Spoilage** |

Village Nursery purchases 105 5-gallon-size juniper shrubs for $351. If a markup of 40% on selling price is necessary and 15 of the plants are unfit for sale, what is the selling price per plant?

Solution   First, find the total revenue from the sale of all the plants using a 40% markup on selling price and a cost of $351.

$$C + M = S$$
$$C + 40\%S = S$$
$$\$351 + 0.4S = S$$
$$\$351 = 1.00S - 0.4S$$
$$\$351 = 0.6S$$
$$\frac{\$351}{0.6} = S$$
$$\$585 = S$$

The total revenue from all the plants is $585. Now, divide the total selling price by the number of saleable plants to find the selling price per plant.

$$\frac{\$585}{105 \text{ purchased } - \text{ 15 unsaleable}} = \frac{\$585}{90} = \$6.50 \quad \text{Selling price per plant}$$

The junipers must be priced at $6.50 each to realize a markup of 40% on selling price and to allow for 15 plants that cannot be sold.

◼

NOTE Controlling loss due to spoilage is critical in business. As spoilage increases, profits fall. These additional costs due to spoilage may be added to the price of the products sold, but the resulting higher price may be too high and no longer competitive.

Objective

2 *Solve Markup Problems When a Certain Percent of Items Are Unsaleable.*

EXAMPLE 2 **Finding Selling Price When a Percent of Items Are Unsaleable**

The Bagel Boys bakes 60 dozen bagels at a cost of $3.24 per dozen. If a markup of 50% on selling price is needed and 5% of the bagels will not be sold and must be donated or thrown away, what is the selling price per dozen bagels?

Solution To begin, find the total cost of the bagels.

$$\text{Cost} = 60 \text{ dozen} \times \$3.24 = \$194.40$$

Now find the selling price, using a markup of 50% of selling price.

$$C + M = S$$
$$C + 50\% = S$$
$$\$194.40 + 0.5S = S$$
$$\$194.40 = 1.00S - 0.5S$$
$$\$194.40 = 0.5S$$
$$\frac{\$194.40}{0.5} = S$$
$$\$388.80 = S$$

The total revenue from sales is $388.80.

Next, find the number of dozen bagels that will be sold. Since 5% will not be sold, 95% (100% − 5%) will be sold.

$$95\% \times 60 \text{ dozen} = 57 \quad \text{Number of dozens sold}$$

The total revenue from sales of $388.80 must be received from 57 dozen bagels.

Find the selling price per dozen bagels by dividing the total selling price by the number of dozens to be sold.

$$\frac{\text{Total revenue from sales}}{\text{Number saleable}} = \frac{\$388.80}{57} = \$6.82 \quad \text{Selling price per dozen (rounded)}$$

A selling price of $6.82 per dozen gives the desired markup of 50% on selling price while allowing for 5% of the bagels to be unsold.

◼

Objective

3 *Calculate Markup When a Percent of the Merchandise Must Be Sold at a Reduced Price.*

EXAMPLE **3** **Finding Selling Price When Some Items Are Sold at a Reduced Price**

An athletic shoe manufacturer makes a walking shoe at a cost of $33.60 per pair. Based on past experience, 10% of the shoes will be defective and must be sold as irregulars for $48 per pair. If the manufacturer produces 1000 pairs of shoes and desires a markup of 100% on cost, what is the selling price per pair?

Solution First, find the cost of the total production.

$$1000 \text{ pairs} \times \$33.60 = \$33,600 \quad \text{Total production cost}$$

The total revenue from sales is

$$C + M = S$$
$$C + 100\%C = S$$
$$2C = S$$

The total cost (C) is $33,600, so $S = 2C = \$67,200$, where S is the total revenue that must be earned from the sale of all shoes, irregular and regular. First, find the revenue from the sale of irregular pairs.

$$
\begin{aligned}
\text{Revenue from sale of irregulars} &= \text{Number of irregulars} \times \text{Price per pair of irregulars} \\
&= \quad 10\% \text{ of } 1000 \quad \times \quad \$48 \\
&= \quad\quad 100 \quad\quad \times \quad \$48 \\
&= \quad\quad \$4800
\end{aligned}
$$

Next find the revenue that must be received from regular pairs of shoes.

$$
\begin{aligned}
\text{Revenue needed from regulars} &= \text{Total amount needed} - \text{Sales of irregulars} \\
&= \quad \$67,200 \quad\quad - \quad \$4800 \\
&= \quad \$62,400
\end{aligned}
$$

Finally, find the price at which regular pairs must be sold.

$$
\begin{aligned}
\text{Price per regular pair} &= \text{Revenue needed from regulars} \div \text{Number of regulars} \\
&= \quad \$62,400 \quad\quad \div \quad 900 \\
&= \quad \$69.33 \quad \text{Rounded}
\end{aligned}
$$

An average selling price of $69.33 per regular pair gives the manufacturer approximately 100% markup on cost when allowing the 10% that are irregulars to sell at $48 per pair.

 **Scientific Calculator Approach**

The calculator solution to Example 3 requires several steps.

1. Find the total revenue, and store in memory.

$$1000 \;\boxed{\times}\; 33.6 \;\boxed{\times}\; 2 \;\boxed{=}\; \boxed{\text{STO}}$$

2. Find the total revenue received from the sale of irregular pairs.

$$0.1 \;\boxed{\times}\; 1000 \;\boxed{\times}\; 48 \;\boxed{=}$$

3. Subtract the revenue from sales of irregulars from the total sales revenue.

$$\boxed{+/-} \;\boxed{+}\; \boxed{\text{RCL}} \;\boxed{=}$$

4. Divide by the number of regular pairs sold.

$$\boxed{\div}\; 900 \;\boxed{=}\; 69.33 \quad \text{Rounded}$$

The following bar graph shows the annual sales of the top ten retailers in the United States. Which of these sell perishables? The answer is Wal-Mart, Kroger, Costco, and SuperValu. Which of these face issues related to spoilage? The answer is every company on the list, since each receives items that may be defective.

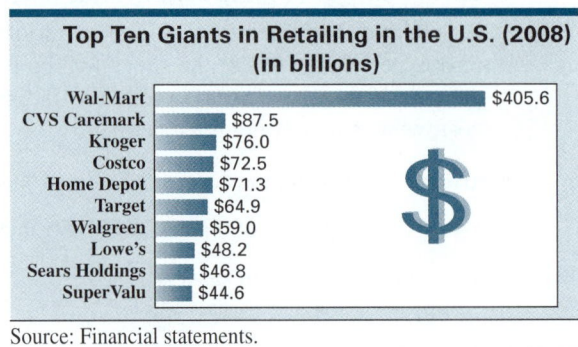

Top Ten Giants in Retailing in the U.S. (2008)
(in billions)

Wal-Mart	$405.6
CVS Caremark	$87.5
Kroger	$76.0
Costco	$72.5
Home Depot	$71.3
Target	$64.9
Walgreen	$59.0
Lowe's	$48.2
Sears Holdings	$46.8
SuperValu	$44.6

Source: Financial statements.

10.3 | Exercises

Find the selling price per item.

	Total Cost	Quantity Purchased	Number Unsaleable	% Markup on Selling Price	Selling Price per Item
1.	$81	90	9	10%	_____
2.	$540	36	6	25%	_____
3.	$340	1 gr.	8	20%	_____
4.	$189	4 doz.	6	40%	_____
5.	$120	25	5	$33\frac{1}{3}\%$	_____
6.	$2750	120	10	50%	_____
7.	$126	8 doz.	6	15%	_____
8.	$2025	250	25	25%	_____

Find the missing quantities.

	Total Cost	Quantity Purchased	Percent Unsaleable	% Markup on Selling Price	Number to Sell	Selling Price per Item
9.	$161	25	4%	25%	_____	_____
10.	$342	120	5%	20%	_____	_____
11.	$198	2 doz.	25%	50%	_____	_____
12.	$162	20 cs.	10%	30%	_____	_____
13.	$190	80 pr.	5%	$33\frac{1}{3}\%$	_____	_____
14.	$8750	100	30%	15%	_____	_____
15.	$25,200	2000 gal.	5%	20%	_____	_____
16.	$7200	100 bbl.	10%	80%	_____	_____

Find the missing quantities. Markup is based on total cost.

	Total Cost	Quantity Purchased	Percent Sold at Reduced Price	% Markup on Total Cost	Number at Regular Price	Number at Regular Price	Reduced Price	Regular Selling Price
17.	$500	200	20%	25%	_____	_____	$2.00	_____
18.	$360	120	10%	20%	_____	_____	$2.00	_____
19.	$2200	40	15%	35%	_____	_____	$50.00	_____
20.	$270	90	20%	40%	_____	_____	$4.00	_____
21.	$432	1 gr.	25%	25%	_____	_____	$2.50	_____
22.	$3000	600	10%	$33\frac{1}{3}$%	_____	_____	$5.00	_____
23.	$2800	1000 pr.	30%	50%	_____	_____	$3.00	_____
24.	$7500	1000	50%	25%	_____	_____	$5.00	_____

25. When merchandise is unsaleable it is as if the items were not received. Explain how the price of the saleable items must be adjusted to offset this loss. (See Objective 1.)

26. Explain how we all pay for the spoiled fruit and vegetables in the produce department of the grocery store. (See Objective 1.)

Solve the following application problems.

27. POTTERY SHOP SALES The Aztec Pottery Shop finds that 15% of its production cannot be sold. It produces 100 items at a cost of $2.15 each and desires a markup of 40% on selling price. Find the selling price per item.

28. PRODUCE SALES Country Produce knows that 20% of the strawberries purchased will spoil and must be thrown out. If it buys 200 baskets of strawberries for $1.20 per basket and wants a markup of 50% on selling price, find the selling price per basket of strawberries.

29. FALL FASHIONS Jasmon Boutique purchased 25 mohair sweaters designed by a well-known designer for a total cost of $1200. The manager estimates that she will have to sell 5 sweaters at a discount at the end of the fall season, receiving only $225 for all. If she wants a markup of $33\frac{1}{3}$% on selling price, find the price for each sweater.

30. IMPORTED CANDLES Cost Plus Imports purchased 30 crates of candles from Mexico for a total cost of $237.60. Each crate contains 3 dozen candles. If 4 crates of the candles are sold at the reduced price of $0.25 per candle and Cost Plus Imports wants a markup of 100% on cost, find the regular price per candle.

31. LONG-STEMMED ROSES Farmers Flowers purchased 12 gross of long-stemmed roses at a cost of $1890. If 25% of the roses must be sold at $15.00 per dozen and a markup of 100% on cost is needed, find the regular selling price per dozen roses.

32. CUSTOM BASEBALL CAPS Custom Caps buys 2000 baseball hats at $7.50 per hat. If a markup of 50% on selling price is needed and 5% of the hats are unsaleable, what is the selling price of each hat?

33. STOVE SHELL CASTINGS Bethel Metals finds that 20% of its stove shell castings are unsaleable. If the cost of manufacturing 55 stoves is $10,450 and Bethel Metals needs a markup of 30% on cost, what is the selling price per stove?

34. HALLOWEEN PUMPKINS River Market purchased 120 small but perfect pumpkins before Halloween for $320. The manager expects 15 pumpkins to spoil. If she needs a markup of 100% on cost, find the average selling price needed.

35. **RECAPPED TRUCK TIRES**   Wheelco Tire recaps truck tires at a cost of $80.50 per tire. Past experience shows that 12% of the recaps must be sold as blemishes for $105. If it recaps 500 tires and a markup of 110% on cost is desired, what is the regular selling price per tire?

36. **ROOFING TILE**   Solano Tile manufactures roof tile at a cost of $42 per square. Past experience shows that 8% of a production run are irregulars and must be sold for $45 per square. If a production run of 10,000 squares is completed and Solano Tile desires a markup of 80% on cost, what is the selling price per square?

37. **BOOK PUBLISHING**   U.S. Publishing Company prints a book on sports memorabilia at a production cost of $10.80 per copy. It knows that 20% of the production will be sold for $11.50 per copy. It prints 50,000 books and it wants a markup of 50% on selling price. Find the selling price per book. Round to the nearest cent.

38. **IMPORTED WALLPAPER**   Wallpaper Specialty Imports purchased 7000 rolls of wallpaper manufactured in France at a cost of $18.90 per roll. Past experience shows that 25% of the wallpaper will have to be sold for $20.25 per roll. Find the selling price per roll if the store wants a markup of 50% on selling price.

Supplementary Exercises: Markup

Solve the following application problems. Round rates to the nearest tenth of a percent and dollar amounts to the nearest cent.

1. **TELESCOPES**   Olympic Sports pays $74.50 for a Bushnell telescope and the markup is 30% of cost. Find the markup.

2. **BED IN A BAG**   A comforter and sheet set has a cost of $132 to the retailer and is marked up 45% on cost. Find the markup.

3. **SNOWBOARD PACKAGES**   What percent of markup on cost must be used if an Atlantis Snowboard package costing $335 is sold for $399?

4. **LAWNMOWER**   Benson Hardware sells a self-propelled, mulching lawnmower for $399. If it pays $308 for the mower, find the markup on cost.

5. **AUTOMOTIVE SUPPLIES**   An auto parts dealer pays $41.88 per dozen cans of fuel-injection cleaner and the markup is 50% on selling price. Find the selling price per can.

6. **GIFT SHOP SALES**   Goodies Gifts pays $26.91 for a half dozen stoneware milk jug banks. If the markup is 35% of the selling price, what is the selling price per bank?

7. **KITCHEN REMODELING**   A new kitchen range hood has a cost of $100.40 to The Home Depot. If its markup is 25% on cost, find the selling price.

8. **ART AND FRAMING**   Yen's Art and Framing pays $41.60 for a 27″ × 30″ frame and sells it for $64. Find the markup percent on cost.

9. **PING-PONG TABLE**   Olympic Sports pays $136.79 for a Ping-Pong table. The markup is 24% on selling price. Find (a) the cost as a percent of selling price, (b) the selling price, and (c) the markup.

10. **DOUBLE-PANE WINDOWS**   Eastern Building Supply pays $3808 for the double-pane windows needed for a 3-bedroom, 2-bath home. If the markup on the windows is 15% on selling price, what is (a) the cost as a percent of selling price, (b) the selling price, and (c) the markup?

11. **SELLING BANANAS**   The produce manager at Tom Thumb Market knows that 10% of the bananas purchased will become unsaleable and will have to be thrown out. If she buys 500 pounds of bananas for $0.32 per pound and wants a markup of 45% on the selling price, find the selling price per pound of bananas.

12. **BAKERY CAKES**   Folsom Bakery finds that 12% of the cakes that it bakes do not sell, so they will be donated to the Twin Lakes Food Bank. If it bakes 150 cakes at a cost of $2.37 each and desires a markup of 70% on selling price, find the selling price per cake.

CHAPTER TERMS

Review the following terms to test your understanding of the chapter. For each term you do not know, refer to the page number found next to that term.

conversion formulas [p. 364]

cost [p. 354]

equivalent percent markup [p. 364]

gross profit [p. 354]

irregulars [p. 369]

margin [p. 354]

markup [p. 354]

markup based on cost [p. 355]

markup based on selling price [p. 360]

markup formula [p. 355]

markup on cost [p. 354]

markup on selling price [p. 354]

markup with spoilage [p. 369]

net earnings [p. 354]

net profit [p. 354]

operating expenses [p. 354]

overhead [p. 354]

retail price [p. 354]

selling price [p. 354]

shrinkage [p. 368]

spoilage [p. 369]

wholesale price [p. 354]

CONCEPTS

EXAMPLES

10.1 Markup on cost

Use Rate × Base = Part $(R \times B = P)$, with cost as base (100%), markup % as rate, and markup as part.

Cost, $160; markup, 25% on cost. Find the markup.

$$R \times B = P$$
$$0.25 \times \$160 = \$40 \quad \text{Markup}$$

10.1 Calculating the percent of markup

Use Cost + Markup = Selling price $(C + M = S)$ and the basic percent equation, $R \times B = P$.

Cost, $420; selling price, $546. Find the percent of markup based on cost.

$$C + M = S$$
$$\$420 + M = \$546$$
$$M = \$126$$
$$R \times B = P$$
$$R \times \$420 = \$126$$
$$R = \frac{126}{420} = 0.3 = 30\% \quad \text{Markup percent on cost}$$

10.1 Finding the cost and selling price

Use $P = R \times B$ to solve for cost; then use $C + M = S$ to find selling price.

Markup, $56; markup on cost, 50%. Find cost and selling price.

$$P = R \times B$$
$$\$56 = 0.5C$$
$$C = \frac{56}{0.5} = \$112 \quad \text{Cost}$$
$$C + M = S$$
$$\$112 + \$56 = \$168 \quad \text{Selling price}$$

10.2 Markup on selling price

Use Rate × Base = Part $(R \times B = P)$, with selling price as base (100%), markup % as rate, and markup as part.

Selling price, $6; markup, 25% on selling price. Find the markup.

$$P = R \times B$$
$$\text{Markup} = 25\% \times \text{Selling price}$$
$$M = 0.25(\$6) = \$1.50 \quad \text{Markup}$$

10.2 Finding the cost

Use the formulas $R \times B = P$ and $C + M = S$.

Markup, \$87.50; markup on selling price, 35%. Find the cost.

First, use $R \times B = P$ to find selling price.

$$35\% \times \text{Selling price} = \$87.50$$
$$0.35S = \$87.50$$
$$S = \$250$$

Now find cost.

$$C + M = S$$
$$C + \$87.50 = \$250 \qquad \text{Selling price}$$
$$C = \$250 - \$87.50 = \$162.50 \qquad \text{Cost}$$

10.2 Calculating the selling price and the markup

Use the formula $C + M = S$.

Cost, \$150; markup, 25% of selling price. Find the selling price and the markup.

$$C + M = S$$
$$\$150 + 0.25S = S$$
$$\$150 = 0.75S$$
$$\frac{\$150}{0.75} = \frac{\cancel{0.75}S}{\cancel{0.75}}$$
$$\$200 = S \qquad \text{Selling price}$$
$$C + M = S$$
$$\$150 + M = \$200 \qquad \text{Selling price}$$
$$M = \$200 - \$150$$
$$= \$50 \qquad \text{Markup}$$

10.2 Converting markup on cost to markup on selling price

Use the following formula.

$$M_s = \frac{M_c}{100\% + M_c}$$

Markup on cost, 25%. Convert to markup on selling price.

$$M_s = \frac{25\%}{100\% + 25\%}$$
$$= \frac{0.25}{1.25} = 0.2 = 20\%$$

10.2 Converting markup on selling price to markup on cost

Use the following formula.

$$M_c = \frac{M_s}{100\% - M_s}$$

Markup on selling price, 20%. Convert to markup on cost.

$$M_c = \frac{20\%}{100\% - 20\%}$$
$$= \frac{0.2}{0.8} = 0.25 = 25\%$$

10.3 Solving markup with spoilage or unsaleable items

1. Find total cost and selling price.
2. Subtract total sales at reduced prices from total sales.
3. Divide the remaining sales amount by the number of saleable units to get selling price per unit.

60 doughnuts cost \$0.15 each; 10 are not sold; 60% markup on selling price. Find selling price per doughnut.

$$\text{Cost} = 60 \times \$0.15 = \$9$$
$$C + M = S$$
$$\$9 + 0.6S = S$$
$$\$9 = 0.4S$$
$$\$22.50 = S$$
$$\$22.50 \div 50 = \$0.45 \qquad \text{Sale price per doughnut}$$

The answer section includes answers to all Review Exercises.

Find the missing quantities. Round rates to the nearest tenth of a percent and money to the nearest cent. [10.1]

	Cost Price	Markup	% Markup on Cost	Selling Price
1.	$32	_____	20%	_____
2.	_____	$6.15	25%	_____
3.	_____	$73.50	_____	$220.50
4.	$108	_____	_____	$153.90

Find the missing quantities. Round rates to the nearest tenth of a percent and money to the nearest cent. [10.2]

	Cost Price	Markup	% Markup on Selling Price	Selling Price
5.	$72.32	_____	20%	_____
6.	_____	$35	_____	$140
7.	_____	$17.35	$33\frac{1}{3}$%	_____
8.	$283.02	$177.18	_____	_____

Find the missing quantities by first computing the markup on one base and then computing the markup on the other. Round rates to the nearest tenth of a percent and money to the nearest cent. [10.2]

	Cost	Markup	Selling Price	% Markup on on Cost	% Markup on Selling Price
9.	_____	$480	_____	_____	20%
10.	$64.50	_____	$129	_____	_____
11.	_____	$3.68	$11.68	_____	_____
12.	_____	$474.28	_____	100%	_____
13.	$44.16	_____	$66.24	_____	_____
14.	$375.40	_____	_____	40%	_____

Find the equivalent markups on either cost or selling price using the appropriate formula. Round to the nearest tenth of a percent. [10.2]

	% Markup on Cost	% Markup on Selling Price
15.	_____	20%
16.	100%	_____
17.	_____	15.3%
18.	20%	_____

Find the selling price per item. [10.3]

	Total Cost	Quantity Purchased	Number Unsaleable	% Markup on Selling Price	Selling Price per Item
19.	$324	360	36	20%	_____
20.	$780	52	12	40%	_____
21.	$970	9 doz.	6	30%	_____
22.	$12,650	1500 pr.	150 pr.	45%	_____

Find the missing quantities. Markup is based on total cost. **[10.3]**

	Total Cost	Quantity Purchased	Percent Sold at Reduced Price	% Markup on Total Cost	Number at Regular Price	Number at Reduced Price	Reduced Price	Regular Selling Price Each
23.	$750	150	10%	25%	____	____	$2.50	____
24.	$135	90 pr.	20%	40%	____	____	$1.00	____
25.	$1728	2 gr.	25%	20%	____	____	$4.00	____
26.	$2800	1000 pr.	30%	50%	____	____	$3.00	____

Solve the following application problems on markup.

27. Premont Pools purchases chlorine tables in 10-pound containers for $22.30 per container. Find the selling price if the markup is 35% on selling price. **[10.2]**

28. Best Buy sells a washer and dryer set for $790 while using a markup of 25% on cost. Find the cost. **[10.1]**

29. The Computer Service Center sells a DeskJet print cartridge for $37.50. The print cartridge costs the store $22.50. Find the markup as a percent of selling price. **[10.2]**

30. Wild Rivers offers an inflatable boat for $199.95. If the boats cost $1943.52 per dozen, what is (a) the markup, (b) the percent of markup on selling price, and (c) the percent of markup on cost? Round to the nearest tenth of a percent. **[10.1 and 10.2]**

31. Raley's Superstore bought 1820 swimming pool blow-up toys for a total cost of $10,010. The toys were sold as follows: 580 at $13.95 each, 635 at $9.95 each, 318 at $8.95 each, 122 at $7.95 each, and the balance at $5.00 each. Find (a) the total selling price of all the toys and (b) the markup as a percent of selling price (to the nearest whole percent). **[10.2]**

32. Fan Fever purchased 200 posters at a cost of $540. If 20% of the posters must be sold at $3 each and a markup of 100% on cost is needed, find the regular selling price of each poster. **[10.3]**

33. Office Depot pays $3.96 for a package of 20-pound paper and sells it for $4.95. Find (a) the percent of markup on selling price and (b) the percent of markup on cost. **[10.2]**

34. Fosters' Doughnuts bakes lemon squares at a cost of $5.79 per dozen. Markup on cost is 100% and 15% of the lemon squares will have to be sold at $7.20 per dozen. If Fosters bakes 180 dozen lemon squares, what is the regular selling price per dozen? Round to the nearest cent. **[10.3]**

CHAPTER 10	Business Application Case #1
	Discounts and Markups in Retailing

The Hallmark Shop buys 3400 boxes of holiday greeting cards directly from the manufacturer. The list price of the cards is $9.90 per box, there is a trade discount of 30/10/20, and a cash discount of 5/10–40x. The Hallmark Shop earns and receives both discounts.

The cards were sold as follows: 1080 boxes at $7.90, 1250 boxes at $5.90, 660 boxes at $5.00, 230 boxes at $4.00, and the remaining boxes were unsaleable. To better manage greeting card sales next year, determine each of the following.

(a) The net cost of the greeting cards after trade and cash discounts. (First find total cost, then apply discounts.)

(b) The total sales amount received from all the holiday greeting cards.

(c) The amount of net profit from the sales of the cards.

(d) The markup as a percent of selling price to the nearest whole percent.

(e) The equivalent percent of markup on cost to the nearest whole percent.

CHAPTER 10	Business Application Case #2
	Estimating Needed Markup

After a careful analysis, the manager of a retail store has estimated the following costs as a percent of the sales price, based on total annual sales. Use these figures to answer the questions that follow.

Item	Percent of Selling Price
Cost of Goods Sold Including Transportation Costs	61.2%
Wages and Benefits	19.8%
Rent, Taxes, Utilities, Maintenance, Insurance	8.3%
Theft	1.9%
Spoilage and Other	3.6%

(a) Find the percent of sales that remains as profit.

(b) If annual sales at the store this year are $7,180,300, estimate the profit for the year.

(c) Estimate the average markup on cost needed to pay all costs and leave a profit as indicated in (a) above. (*Hint:* Assume a sale of exactly $100 not including taxes. Then 61.2% of that or $61.20, is the cost of goods sold. From that you can find the markup on cost.)

(d) Use the appropriate formula in **Section 10.2** to find the markup on selling price.

Markdown and Inventory Control

Markdowns and sales are the cornerstone of many businesses today. The word "free" in advertising gets the greatest response from consumers, and the word "sale" is not far behind. While there can be many reasons for offering markdowns, the resulting increase in sales volume helps move out existing inventory to make room for new merchandise.

The financial crisis that began in 2008 resulted in some very difficult issues for managers around the world. At the time, many consumers struggled with falling equities in their homes, sharp reductions in retirement accounts as stock prices fell, and difficulty obtaining loans. Unemployment was also rising and some worried about their jobs even as few firms gave raises or bonuses. As a result, consumers across the world became cautious and "tightened their belts" by buying less. The slowdown in sales at the end of 2008 is apparent in Figure 11.1, which shows the growth (or decline) in sales compared to the same month of the previous year. As sales fell sharply, inventories built up in stores and along the supply chains. Managers were forced to mark down prices significantly in order to move inventory out of the stores.

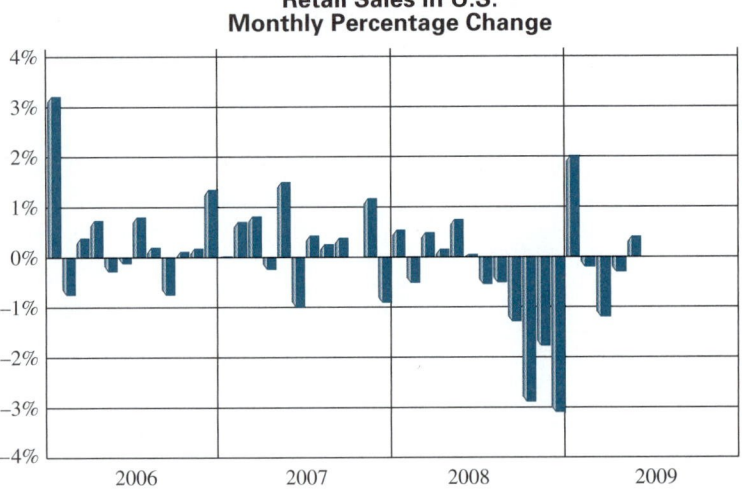

Retail Sales in U.S. Monthly Percentage Change

Source: Commerce Department.

Figure 11.1

> Suppose that you are the manager of a large retail store and that demand falls sharply. What would be the first sign(s) of a sharp falloff in sales? If sales stayed low, what would happen to your inventory? What could you do as a manager to respond? How bad would things need to be before you would consider laying people off, or should layoffs ever happen?

Managers spend a great deal of time controlling inventory. Inventories that are too high simply sit on shelves and require sales or markdowns to be sold. Inventories that are too low result in lost sales as customers go elsewhere. This chapter discusses some of the main ideas of inventory control.

11.1   **Markdown**

OBJECTIVES

1 *Calculate markdown and reduced price.*

2 *Calculate the percent of markdown.*

3 *Find the original selling price.*

4 *Identify the terms associated with loss.*

5 *Determine the break-even point and operating loss.*

6 *Determine the amount of absolute loss and the percent of absolute loss.*

7 *Find the maximum percent of markdown to be given.*

Merchandise often does not sell at its marked price, for any of several reasons. The retailer may have ordered too much, or the merchandise may have become soiled or damaged, or perhaps only odd sizes and colors remain. Also, merchandise may not sell because of lower prices at other stores, seasonal changes, economic fluctuations, or changes in fashion.

Objective

1   *Calculate Markdown and Reduced Price.*   When merchandise does not sell at its marked price, its price is often reduced. The difference between the original selling price and the reduced selling price is called the **markdown**. The selling price after the markdown is called the **reduced price, sale price**, or **actual selling price**. The basic **formula for markdown** is as follows.

$$\text{Reduced price} = \text{Original price} - \text{Markdown}$$

EXAMPLE 1   **Finding the Reduced Price**

A La-Z-Boy store has marked down a leather recliner. What is the reduced price if the original price was $960 and the markdown is 25%?

Solution

$$
\begin{aligned}
\text{Reduced price} &= \text{Original price} - \text{Markdown} \\
&= \quad \$960 \quad - 25\% \text{ of } \$960 \\
&= \quad \$960 \quad - 0.25 \times \$960 \\
&= \quad \$720
\end{aligned}
$$

 Scientific Calculator Approach

The calculator solution to Example 1 uses the complement, with respect to 1, of the 25% discount.

960 ☒ (1 − 0.25) = 720

Objective

2   *Calculate the Percent of Markdown.*   The next example shows how to find a **percent, or rate, of markdown**.

NOTE   The original selling price is always the base or 100% and the percent of markdown is always calculated on the original selling price.

EXAMPLE 2 **Calculating the Percent of Markdown**

A necklace and earring set with small rubies has a retail value of $785. Find the percent markdown on the original price if it has been marked down to $530.

Solution First find the markdown.

$$\text{Markdown} = \text{Original price} - \text{Reduced price}$$
$$= \quad \$785 \quad - \quad \$530 = \$255$$

To solve for percent of markdown on original price, use the percent equation: Rate × Base = Part. The base is the original price of $785, the rate is unknown, and the part is the amount of markdown, or $255.

$$R \times B = P$$
$$\underline{\quad\quad}\% \times \$785 = \$255$$
$$R \times \$785 = \$255$$
$$\$785R = \$255$$
$$R = \frac{255}{785}$$
$$R = 0.3248 = 32\% \quad \text{Rounded to the nearest percent}$$

The jewelry was sold at a markdown of 32%.

Scientific Calculator Approach

In the calculator solution to Example 2, the reduced price is subtracted from the original price using parentheses. This results in the markdown, which is then divided by the original price.

$$(\boxed{785} \boxed{-} \boxed{530}) \boxed{\div} \boxed{785} \boxed{=} 0.3248$$

Objective

3 *Find the Original Selling Price.*

EXAMPLE 3 **Finding the Original Price**

Bouza's Baby News offers a child's car seat at a reduced price of $63 after a 25% markdown from the original price. Find the original price.

Solution After the 25% markdown, the reduced price of $63 represents 75% of the original price. Find the original price, which is the base.

$$R \times B = P$$
$$75\% \times B = \$63$$
$$0.75B = \$63$$
$$B = \frac{63}{0.75}$$
$$B = \$84$$

The original price of the car seat was $84.

NOTE In Example 3, notice that 75%, not 25%, is used in the formula. The reduced price, $63, is represented by 75%.

Objective

4   *Identify the Terms Associated with Loss.*   The amount of markdown must be large enough to sell the merchandise while providing as much profit as possible. Merchandise that is marked down will result in either a reduced net profit, a break-even point, an operating loss, or an absolute loss. Figure 11.2 illustrates the meanings of these terms.

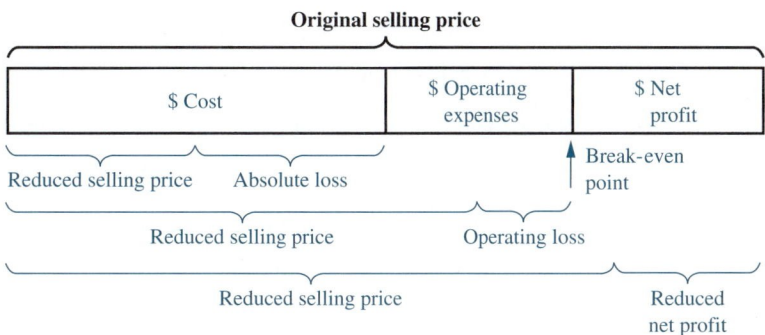

Figure 11.2

    Reduced net profit results when the reduced price is still within the net profit range, that is, when it is greater than the total cost plus overhead (operating expenses).

    The **break-even point** is the point at which the reduced price just covers cost plus overhead (operating expenses). At this point the business neither makes money nor loses money.

    An **operating loss** occurs when the reduced price is less than the break-even point. The operating loss is the difference between the break-even point and the reduced selling price.

    An **absolute loss** is the result of a reduced price that not only covers none of the operating expenses but is also below the cost of the merchandise. The absolute loss is the difference between the cost and reduced selling price.

    The following formulas are helpful when working with markdowns.

$$\text{Break-even point} = \text{Cost} + \text{Operating expenses}$$

$$\text{Operating loss} = \text{Break-even point} - \text{Reduced selling price}$$

$$\text{Absolute loss} = \text{Cost} - \text{Reduced selling price}$$

Objective

5   *Determine the Break-Even Point and Operating Loss.*

EXAMPLE **4**   **Determining a Profit or a Loss**

Cordova Appliance paid $40 for a blender. If operating expenses are 30% of cost and the blender is sold for $50, find the break-even point and the amount of loss.

Solution   Use the following formula to find the break-even point.

$$\text{Cost} + \text{Operating expenses} = \text{Break-even point}$$

$$\$40 + (0.3 \times \$40) = \$40 + \$12 = \$52 \quad \text{Break-even point}$$

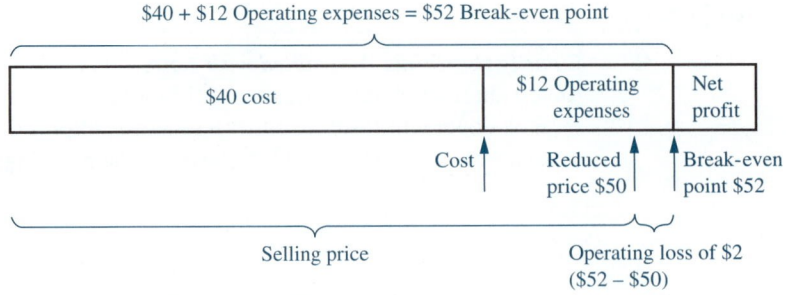

Figure 11.3

Since the break-even point is $52 and the selling price is $50, there is a loss of

$$\$52 - \$50 = \$2$$

This $2 loss is an operating loss since the selling price is less than the break-even point but greater than the cost. See Figure 11.3.

Scientific Calculator Approach

The calculator solution to Example 4 is as follows.

$$40 \boxed{+} \boxed{(} 0.3 \boxed{\times} 40 \boxed{)} \boxed{-} 50 \boxed{=} 2$$

Objective

6   *Determine the Amount of Absolute Loss and the Percent of Absolute Loss.*

EXAMPLE 5   **Determining the Operating Loss and the Absolute Loss**

A new, voice-activated GPS sells for $360. However, one retailer marks it down by 30% due to slow sales before Christmas. The unit costs the retailer $260 and the operating expenses are 20% of the cost. Find (a) the operating loss, (b) the absolute loss, and (c) the percent of absolute loss based on cost (round to the nearest percent).

Solution

(a) The break-even point (cost + operating expenses) is $312 ($260 + 0.2 × $260 = $260 + $52).

$$\text{Reduced price} = \$360 - (0.3 \times \$360) = \$360 - \$108 = \$252$$
$$\text{Operating loss} = \$312 \text{ break-even point} - \$252 \text{ reduced price} = \$60$$

(b) The absolute or gross loss is the difference between the cost and the reduced price.

$$\$260 \text{ cost} - \$252 \text{ reduced price} = \$8 \text{ absolute loss}$$

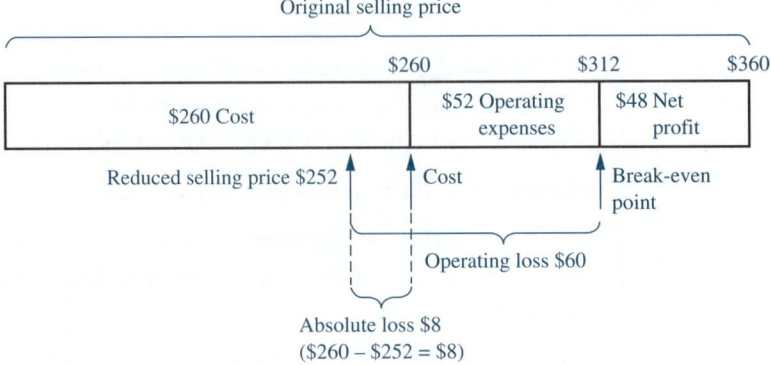

Figure 11.4

(c) The percent of absolute loss is always expressed as a percent of cost, so find the percent of cost that is the absolute loss using the percent equation.

$$R \times B = P$$
$$\underline{\quad\quad}\% \times \$260 = \$8$$
$$\$260R = \$8$$
$$R = \frac{8}{260}$$
$$R = 0.0308 = 3\% \quad \text{Rounded}$$

The rate of absolute loss is approximately 3%. See Figure 11.4.

Objective

7   *Find the Maximum Percent of Markdown to Be Given.*

> **EXAMPLE** 6   **Finding the Original Price and Maximum Percent of Markdown to Be Given**

A wood-burning pellet stove cost a retailer $1890. If the store's operating expenses are 25% of cost, and net profit is 15% of cost, what is (a) the original selling price of the stove and (b) the maximum percent of markdown that may be given without taking an operating loss (round to the nearest tenth of a percent)?

Solution

(a) The markup is 40% (25% + 15%) on cost. The selling price is found from the basic markup formula.

$$C + M = S$$
$$\$1890 + (0.4 \times \$1890) = S$$
$$\$1890 + \$756 = S$$
$$\$2646 = S$$

The original selling price is $2646.

(b) Break-even point = Cost   + Operating expenses
$$= \$1890 \;+\; 0.25 \times \$1890$$
$$= \$2362.50$$

The maximum amount of markdown that may be taken without an operating loss is as follows.

Markdown = Original price − Reduced price
$$= \quad \$2646 \quad - \quad \$2362.50$$
$$= \quad \$283.50$$

Since the maximum markdown is $283.50, the maximum percent of markdown can be found by asking: What percent of original selling price is markdown?

$$R \times B = P$$
$$\underline{\quad\quad}\% \times \$2646 = \$283.50$$
$$\$2646R = \$283.50$$
$$R = \frac{283.50}{2646}$$
$$R = 0.1071 = 10.7\% \quad \text{Rounded}$$

A maximum of 10.7% may be given as markdown without an operating loss.

Figure 11.5 shows the percent of adults who get an emotional high as a result of making certain purchases. Customers love buying things—they especially love buying things when they are on sale. In fact, many marketing professionals view their work as helping customers satisfy basic psychological needs versus just "selling a product."

In the Sweet Buy and Buy

Percent of adults that say they feel euphoric after shopping for the following items:

Item	Percent
Car	28%
Gift for someone	17%
House	11%
Clothes	8%
Home electronics	5%
Jewelry	4%
Vacations	4%
Furniture	4%

Source: Yankelovich Partners.

Figure 11.5

11.1 | Exercises

Find the missing quantities. Round rates to the nearest whole percent and money to the nearest cent.

	Original Price	% Markdown	$ Markdown	Reduced Price
1.	$860	_____	$215	_____
2.	$240	_____	$96	_____
3.	$30.80	_____	_____	$16.94
4.	$1450	_____	_____	$725
5.	_____	20%	_____	$5.20
6.	_____	$66\frac{2}{3}$%	_____	$3.10
7.	_____	40%	$1.08	_____
8.	_____	20%	$0.77	_____
9.	$43.50	50%	_____	_____
10.	$2327.50	44%	_____	_____
11.	_____	_____	$175	$682
12.	_____	_____	$276.93	$1261.57

Complete the following. If there is no operating loss or absolute loss, write "none." Use Figure 11.2 as a guide.

	Cost	Operating Expense	Break-even Point	Reduced Price	Operating Loss	Absolute Loss
13.	$48	$12	_____	$50	_____	_____
14.	$25	$8	_____	$22	_____	_____
15.	$50	_____	$66	$44	_____	_____
16.	$12.50	_____	$16.50	$11	_____	_____
17.	$310	$75	_____	_____	$135	_____
18.	$78	$22	_____	_____	$30	_____
19.	_____	_____	_____	$25	$14	$4
20.	_____	_____	_____	$100	$56	$16

21. Describe five reasons why a store will reduce (mark down) the price of merchandise to get it sold.

22. As a result of a markdown, there are four possible results: reduced net profit, breaking even, operating loss, and absolute loss. As a business owner, which would concern you the most? Explain. (See Objective 4.)

Solve the following application problems. Round rates to the nearest whole percent and money to the nearest cent.

23. **GAS BARBECUE MARKDOWN** A Sunbeam Grill Master gas barbecue is marked down $76.48, a reduction of 32%. Find the original price.

24. **RACING BICYCLE** An ultra-light racing bicycle is marked down 15% to $3939.75. Find the original price.

25. **OAK DESK** An oak desk originally priced at $837.50 is reduced to $686.75. Find the percent of markdown on the original price.

26. **AUTOMOBILE SOUND SYSTEMS** Fry's Electronics prices its entire inventory of 200-watt AM/FM MP3/CD players with removable face at $133,509. If the original price of the inventory was $226,284, find the percent of markdown on the original price.

27. **IMPORTED RUGS** The Persian and Oriental Rug Gallery paid $2211 for an imported rug from Iran. Its operating expenses are $33\frac{1}{3}\%$ of cost. If it sells the rug at a clearance price of $2650, find the amount of profit or loss.

28. **EXERCISE BICYCLES** Ship Shape Shop has an end-of-season sale during which it sells a Proform Upright Bike for $265. If the cost was $198 and the operating expenses were 25% of cost, find the amount of profit or loss.

29. **ANTIQUES** American Antique paid $153.49 for a fern stand. Its original selling price was $208.78, but this was marked down 46% in order to make room for incoming merchandise. Operating expenses are 14.9% of cost. Find (a) the operating loss, (b) the absolute loss, and (c) the percent of absolute loss based on cost.

30. **TRUCK BED LINERS** Pep Boys Automotive paid $208.50 for a pickup truck bed liner. The original selling price was $291.90, but this was marked down 35%. Operating expenses are 28% of cost. Find (a) the operating loss, (b) the absolute loss, and (c) the percent of absolute loss based on cost.

31. PHOTOGRAPHIC ENLARGERS Photo Supply, a retailer, pays $190 for an enlarger. The store's operating expenses are 20% of cost, and net profit is 15% of cost. Find (a) the selling price of the enlarger and (b) the maximum percent of markdown that may be given without taking an operating loss. Round to the nearest whole percent.

32. AIR CONDITIONERS A room air conditioner cost a retailer $278. The store's operating expenses are 30% of cost, and net profit is 10% of cost. Find (a) the selling price of the air conditioner and (b) the maximum percent of markdown that may be given without taking an operating loss.

11.2   Average Inventory and Inventory Turnover

OBJECTIVES

1 *Determine average inventory.*

2 *Calculate stock turnover.*

3 *Identify considerations in stock turnover.*

Many firms have a lot of inventory on hand. For example, Table 11.1 shows inventory levels at the largest retailer in the world: Wal-Mart Stores. The company holds billions of dollars in inventory even though managers know it is very expensive to keep inventory on hand since inventory is sometimes stolen, items go out of style requiring markdowns in order to sell them, and holding inventory ties up much-needed cash, which is often borrowed from a bank. Yet, retailers *must hold inventory* in order to have it available for customers to examine and purchase.

Table 11.1 WAL-MART STORES (IN BILLIONS)			
Year	Total Revenue	Inventory at End of Year	Inventory as a Percent of Total Revenue
2006	$315.7	$32.19	10.2%
2007	$348.7	$33.69	9.7%
2008	$378.8	$35.18	9.3%

Source: Wal-Mart financial statements.

Since it is so expensive to carry inventory, managers have spent a lot of time trying to create systems to make sure the stores have product the customers want on hand but that do not result in too much inventory. To better manage inventories, management has improved point-of-sale and database systems that track sales as they are made. Today, management has much more information about what customers buy than ever before. This information allows them to adjust quickly the product mix they are buying from suppliers as demand patterns change. In turn, this results in reduced inventory levels, less waste, and, importantly, it reduces costs.

One very important measure of the efficiency of a firm is **inventory turnover**, also called **stock turnover** or just **turns**. Inventory turnover is a measure of the number of times a firm's average inventory is turned over (or sold) each year. A company with inventory turns of 52 is selling its average inventory every week, whereas a company with turns of 12 is selling its average inventory only once every month.

A higher turnover means that the firm is selling goods at a faster rate. A slower turnover may mean that the company is having difficulty selling items, or perhaps that it is poorly managed. To survive, businesses selling perishables such as fruit, dairy products, and flowers must have a high turnover since products remaining on the shelves quickly spoil. On the other hand, other businesses, such as furniture stores or hardware stores, will normally have much lower inventory turns.

Objective

1 *Determine Average Inventory.* Find stock turnover by first calculating the **average inventory**. The average inventory for a certain time period is found by adding the inventories taken during the time period and then dividing the total by the number of times that the inventory was taken.

EXAMPLE 1 **Determining Average Inventory**

The inventory value at Medco Health Supplies was $285,672 on April 1 and $198,560 on April 30. What was the average inventory?

Solution First, add the inventory values.

$$
\begin{array}{ll}
\$285,672 & \text{April 1} \\
+ \ \$198,560 & \text{April 30} \\
\hline
\$484,232 &
\end{array}
$$

Then divide by the number of times inventory was taken.

$$\frac{\$484,232}{2} = \$242,116$$

The average inventory was $242,116.

EXAMPLE 2 **Finding Average Inventory for the Quarter**

The retail value of inventory at a small gift shop was $22,615 on January 1, $18,321 on February 1, $26,718 on March 1, and $16,228 on March 31. Find the average inventory for the first quarter of the year.

Solution First add the inventories and then divide by the number of inventories taken.

$$\frac{\$22,615 + \$18,321 + \$26,718 + \$16,228}{4} = \$20,970.50$$

The average inventory for the first quarter of the year is $20,970.50.

In Example 2, inventory was taken 4 times to find the average inventory for the first quarter of the year. To find the average inventory for a period of time, an inventory must be taken at the beginning of the period and one final time at the end of the period. To find average inventory for a full year, it is common to find inventory on the first day of each month and on the last day of the last month. Average inventory is found by adding all these inventory amounts (13 of them) and then dividing by 13, the number of inventories taken. Methods of taking inventory and inventory valuation are discussed in the next section.

Keeping a close watch on inventory is an ongoing concern of management. Year-end sales promotions are designed to quickly reduce inventory.

Objective

2 *Calculate Stock Turnover.* Most inventories are taken at retail because products or shelf locations are marked with the retail price and not the cost. Also, statistical averages are usually shown as average turnover at retail. Many businesses, however, value inventory at cost. For this reason, stock turnover is found by either of these formulas.

$$\text{Turnover at retail} = \frac{\text{Retail sales}}{\text{Average inventory at retail}}$$

$$\text{Turnover at cost} = \frac{\text{Cost of goods sold}}{\text{Average inventory at cost}}$$

As long as there is no theft, markdowns, or unsaleable merchandise, the two turnover ratios will be equal. However, since there is usually some shrinkage, the **turnover at cost** is usually slightly higher than the **turnover at retail**. For this reason, many managers prefer to use the more conservative turnover at retail.

EXAMPLE 3   Finding Stock Turnover at Retail

During May, The Book Barn has sales of $32,032 and an average retail inventory of $9856. Find the stock turnover at retail.

Solution

$$\text{Turnover at retail} = \frac{\text{Retail sales}}{\text{Average inventory at retail}} = \frac{\$32{,}032}{\$9856} = 3.25 \text{ at retail}$$

On average, the store turned over its entire inventory 3.25 times during the month.

EXAMPLE 4   Finding Stock Turnover at Cost

If The Book Barn in Example 3 used a markup of 40% on selling price and if the cost of goods sold was $19,396, what is the stock turnover on cost?

Solution   Inventory at retail in the store was $9856. Since markup is 40% on selling price, the cost is 60% of the inventory.

$$C = 0.6 \times \$9856$$
$$= \$5913.60$$

Inventory value at cost is $5913.60.

$$\text{Turnover at cost} = \frac{\text{Cost of goods sold}}{\text{Average inventory at cost}}$$

$$= \frac{\$19{,}396}{\$5913.60} = 3.28 \text{ at cost} \qquad \text{Rounded}$$

The turnover on cost is 3.28.

NOTE   In Example 4, the average inventory at cost needed to be calculated. To do this, the rate of markup was used along with the average inventory at retail. Since the markup was 40% on selling price, the average inventory at cost was 60% of the average inventory at retail.

Objective

3 *Identify Considerations in Stock Turnover.* Stock turnover is useful only for comparison purposes. Many trade organizations publish such operating statistics to permit businesses to compare their operation with the industry as a whole. In addition to this, management uses these rates to compare turnover from period to period and from department to department.

A rapid stock turnover is usually given high priority by management. Here are some of the benefits.

1. Capital invested in inventory is kept at a minimum. This allows additional funds to be used for special purchases and discounts.
2. Items in inventory are up-to-date, fresher, and are therefore less likely to be sold at a reduced price or loss.
3. Costly storage space and the other expenses of handling inventory can be minimized.

On the other hand, a high inventory turnover may cause problems that result in reduced profits.

1. Orders for smaller quantities of goods from wholesalers may result in losses of quantity discounts and thus incur additional processing, handling, and bookkeeping expenses.
2. Items can be sold out and customers may be dissatisfied.

Both inventory selection and inventory turnover are very important management decisions, and much attention is typically given to this part of the business.

11.2	**Exercises**

Find the average inventory in the following.

	Date	Inventory Amount at Retail		Date	Inventory Amount at Retail
1.	April 1	$10,603	**2.**	January 1	$42,312
	April 30	$12,757		July 1	$38,514
3.	July 1	$18,300		December 31	$30,219
	October 1	$26,580	**4.**	January 31	$69,480
	December 31	$23,139		April 30	$55,860
5.	January 1	$16,250		July 31	$80,715
	March 1	$20,780		October 31	$88,050
	May 1	$28,720		January 31	$63,975
	July 1	$24,630	**6.**	January 1	$65,430
	September 1	$23,550		April 1	$58,710
	November 1	$34,800		July 1	$53,410
	December 31	$22,770		October 1	$78,950
				December 31	$46,340

Find the stock turnover at retail and turnover at cost for the following. Round to the nearest hundredth.

	Average Inventory at Cost	Average Inventory at Retail	Cost of Goods Sold	Retail Sales
7.	$26,745	$53,085	$75,591	$149,175
8.	$15,140	$24,080	$67,408	$106,193
9.	$22,390	$32,730	$178,687	$259,876
10.	$30,280	$48,160	$134,816	$212,386
11.	$26,400	$42,660	$270,600	$437,260
12.	$72,120	$138,460	$259,123	$487,379
13.	$180,600	$256,700	$846,336	$1,196,222
14.	$411,580	$780,600	$1,905,668	$3,559,536

15. Identify three types of businesses that you think would have a high turnover. Identify three types of businesses that you think would have a low turnover.

16. Which departments in a grocery store do you think have the highest turnover? Which ones have the lowest turnover?

Solve the following application problems. Round stock turnover to the nearest hundredth.

17. **CERAMIC TILE**   Bedrosian's Tile took inventory at the first of each month for the full year. The sum of these inventories was $596,428. On December 31, inventory was again taken and amounted to $49,895. Find the average inventory for the year.

18. **PHARMACY INVENTORY**   Inventory at retail at Sid's Pharmacy was $38,864 on April 1, $47,536 on May 1, and $26,128 on June 1. Find the average inventory.

19. **GLASS SHOP**   The Glass Works has an average inventory at cost of $15,730 and cost of goods sold for the same period is $85,412. Find the stock turnover at cost.

20. **CELL PHONES**   A cell phone booth in a local mall had an average inventory of $6320 at retail. Cell phone sales for the year were $249,400. Find the stock turnover at retail.

21. **METAL PLATING**   Capital Plating had an average inventory of $27,250 at retail. The cost of goods sold for the year was $103,400 and a markup of 40% on selling price was used. What was the turnover at cost?

22. **UNDERWATER DIVING**   Associated Divers uses a markup of 30% on selling price. If its average inventory is $15,650 at retail and the cost of goods sold is $53,023, what is the stock turnover at cost?

23. **ELECTRICAL SUPPLIES**   The cost of goods sold at Capitol Electric was $2,108,410. The following inventories were taken at cost: $208,180, $247,660, and $114,438. Find the stock turnover at cost.

24. **HOBBY SALES**   Inventory at Harbortown Hobby was taken at retail value four times and found to be at $53,820, $49,510, $60,820, and $56,380. Sales during the same period were $252,077. Find the stock turnover at retail.

25. **POSTERS AND CARDS**   Posters and Cards had the following inventories at retail: $33,820, $46,240, $39,830, $52,040, and $48,700. This business uses a 35% markup on cost, and the cost of goods sold during this period was $136,450. Find the turnover at cost.

26. **APPLIANCE DEALER**   Inventory at Standard Appliance was taken at retail four different times and found to be $98,500, $135,820, $107,420, and $124,300. The company uses a markup of 25% on cost, and the cost of goods sold for this period was $305,920. Find the inventory turnover at cost.

11.3	**Valuation of Inventory**

OBJECTIVES

    1 *Define perpetual inventory.*

    2 *Understand universal product codes (UPC).*

    3 *Use the specific-identification method to value inventory.*

    4 *Use the weighted-average method to value inventory.*

    5 *Use the FIFO method to value inventory.*

    6 *Use the LIFO method to value inventory.*

    7 *Use the gross-profit method to estimate inventory.*

    8 *Use the retail method to estimate inventory.*

Objective

1   *Define Perpetual Inventory.*   Placing a value on the merchandise that a firm has in stock is called **inventory valuation**. It is not always easy to place this value on each of the items in inventory. Many large companies keep a **perpetual inventory** by using a computer. As new items are received, the quantity, size, and cost of each are placed in the computer. Clerks enter product codes into the cash register by scanning the code attached to the item. Since inventory records are constantly updated, managers can find out the quantity on hand of any item.

Objective

2   *Understand Universal Product Codes (UPC).*   **Universal product codes (UPC)** are the stripes known as bar codes that appear on many items sold in stores. Each product and product size is assigned its own code number. These UPCs are a great help in keeping track of inventory.

0-87720-071 – 8

    A Cracker Jack box has a UPC number (also called the *bar code*) of 0-87720-071-8. The checkout clerk or customer in a retail store passes the coded lines over an optical scanner. The numbers are picked up by a computer, which recognizes the product by its code. The computer then forwards the price of the item to the cash register. At the same time the price is being recorded, the computer is subtracting the item automatically from inventory. After all the items being purchased have passed over the scanner, the customer receives a detailed cash register receipt that gives a description of each item, the price of each item, and a total purchase price.

    Most firms have programmed their systems to automatically place an order with the warehouse or supplier when the number of items on hand becomes low. This technique has allowed firms to have better control over their inventory with lower cost, compared to manually monitoring inventory and placing orders. However, computer database records are sometimes not accurate due to mistakes, theft, etc. As a result, most businesses take a **physical inventory** at regular intervals, such as at the end of every month. This type of inventory is called **periodic inventory** since it is done periodically or at regular time intervals. This helps detect theft and corrects mistakes that have collected in the database.

    There are four major methods used for inventory valuation. They are the specific-identification method, the weighted-average method, the first-in, first-out method, and the last-in, first-out method.

Objective

3   *Use the Specific-Identification Method to Value Inventory.*   The **specific-identification method** of inventory valuation is useful where items are easily identified and costs do not fluctuate. If the number of items is large and the exact cost of each unit is not known, then it may be difficult or impossible to use this method of inventory. With specific identification, each item is cost coded, either with numerals or a letter code. The cost may be included in a group of numbers written on the item or in a 10-letter code (where each letter is different).

For example, if a store uses the code SMALPROFIT, or

1	2	3	4	5	6	7	8	9	0
S	M	A	L	P	R	O	F	I	T

then an item bearing the cost code ARF would have a cost of

A	R	F
↓	↓	↓
3	6	8

or $3.68. An item coded PMITT would have a cost of $529.

EXAMPLE 1 **Finding the Value of Inventory**

Hoig's Marine has four small fishing boats in stock. Cost codes indicate the following costs to the store.

Model A	$2718
Model B	$2571
Model C	$3498
Model D	$3974

Find the value of the fishing boat inventory using the specific-identification method.

Solution   The value of the inventory is found by adding the costs of the four fishing boats.

Model A	$ 2,718	
Model B	2,571	
Model C	3,498	
Model D	+ 3,974	
	$12,761	Total value of inventory

Objective

4 *Use the Weighted-Average Method to Value Inventory.*   Since the cost of many items changes over time, there may be several of the same items that were purchased at different costs. Because of this variation, there are several common methods used to value an inventory. One method, the **weighted-average (average-cost) method**, values the items in an inventory at the average cost of buying them.

EXAMPLE 2 **Using Weighted-Average (Average-Cost) Inventory Valuation**

Olympic Sports and Leisure made the following purchases of the Explorer External Frame backpack during the year.

Beginning inventory	20 backpacks at $70
January	50 backpacks at $80
March	100 backpacks at $90
July	60 backpacks at $85
October	40 backpacks at $75

At the end of the year there are 75 backpacks in inventory. Use the weighted-average method to find the inventory value.

Solution Find the total cost of all the backpacks.

Beginning inventory	$20 \times \$70 =$	$\$1,400$
January	$50 \times \$80 =$	$\$4,000$
March	$100 \times \$90 =$	$\$9,000$
July	$60 \times \$85 =$	$\$5,100$
October	$40 \times \$75 =$	$\$3,000$
Total	270	$\$22,500$

Find the average cost per backpack by dividing this total cost by the number purchased. The average cost per backpack is

$$\frac{\$22,500}{270} = \$83.33 \quad \text{Rounded}$$

Since the average cost is $83.33 and 75 backpacks remain in inventory, the weighted-average method gives the inventory value of the remaining backpacks as $83.33 \times 75 = $6249.75.

Scientific
Calculator
Approach

The calculator solution to Example 2 has several steps.
    First, find the total number of backpacks purchased and place the total in memory.

$$20 \boxed{+} 50 \boxed{+} 100 \boxed{+} 60 \boxed{+} 40 \boxed{=} 270 \boxed{\text{STO}}$$

Next, find the total cost of all the backpacks purchased and divide by the number stored in memory. This gives the average cost per backpack.

$$20 \boxed{\times} 70 \boxed{+} 50 \boxed{\times} 80 \boxed{+} 100 \boxed{\times} 90 \boxed{+} 60 \boxed{\times} 85$$

$$\boxed{+} 40 \boxed{\times} 75 \boxed{=} \boxed{\div} \boxed{\text{RCL}} \boxed{=} 83.3333$$

Finally, round the average cost to the nearest cent and multiply by the number of backpacks in inventory to get the weighted-average inventory value.

$$83.33 \boxed{\times} 75 \boxed{=} 6249.75$$

Objective

5 *Use the FIFO Method to Value Inventory.* The **first-in, first-out (FIFO) method** of inventory valuation assumes a natural flow of goods through the inventory: the first goods to arrive are the first goods to be sold, so, the most recent items purchased by the company are the items remaining in inventory.

EXAMPLE 3 Using FIFO Inventory Valuation

Use the FIFO method to find the inventory value of the 75 backpacks from Olympic Sports and Leisure in Example 2.

Solution With the FIFO method, the 75 remaining backpacks are assumed to consist of the last 75 backpacks purchased, or 40 backpacks bought in October and 35 $(75 - 40 = 35)$ backpacks from the previous purchase in July.

The value of the inventory is as follows.

October	40 backpacks at $75 = $3000	Value of last 40
July	35 backpacks at $85 = $2975	Value of previous 35
	75 valued at = $5975	Inventory value

The value of the backpack inventory is $5975 using the FIFO method.

Objective

6   *Use the LIFO Method to Value Inventory.*   The **last-in, first-out (LIFO) method** of inventory valuation assumes a flow of goods through the inventory that is just the opposite of the FIFO method. With LIFO, the goods remaining in inventory are the first goods purchased.

EXAMPLE 4   **Using LIFO Inventory Valuation**

Use the LIFO method to value the 75 backpacks in inventory at Olympic Sports and Leisure (see Example 2).

Solution   The calculation starts with the beginning inventory and moves through the year's purchases, resulting in 75 backpacks. The beginning inventory and January purchases come to 70 backpacks, so the cost of 5 more $(75 - 70 = 5)$ backpacks from the March purchase is needed.

Beginning inventory	20 backpacks at $70 = $1400	Value of first 20
January	50 backpacks at $80 = $4000	Value of next 50
March	5 backpacks at $90 = $450	Value of last 5
Total	75 valued $5850	Inventory value

The value of the backpack inventory is $5850 using the LIFO method.

Depending on the method of valuing inventories that is used, Olympic Sports and Leisure may show the inventory value of the 75 backpacks as follows.

Average-cost method	$6249.75
FIFO	$5975.00
LIFO	$5850.00

The preferred inventory valuation method would be determined by Olympic Sports and Leisure, perhaps on the advice of an accountant. The comparison of inventory evaluation methods below would help them in selecting the method.

Comparing Inventory Valuation Methods

- When the market is stable, prices do not fluctuate. Since prices are not changing, all methods give the *same* inventory value.
- In a market where prices are rising and falling, each method gives a *different* inventory value.
- Weighted-average costs tend to *smooth out* inventory values that might result from price fluctuations.
- The FIFO method results in an inventory value that most closely reflects the *current* replacement cost of inventory.
- The LIFO method results in the last cost of inventory being assigned to the cost of merchandise sold. This results in a *closer matching* of current costs with sales revenues.

NOTE   Accepted accounting practice insists that the method used to evaluate inventory be stated on the company financial statements.

The large quantities and varied types of items that are often in inventory make it time-consuming and expensive to take an actual physical inventory. Where this is the case, a physical inventory may be taken only once or twice a year. However, the need to monitor the performance of the business throughout the year is extremely important. To do this, methods of approximating inventory value have been developed. Two common methods for doing this are the gross-profit method and the retail method.

Objective

7 *Use the Gross-Profit Method to Estimate Inventory.* An estimate of inventory using the **gross-profit method** is found as follows.

> Beginning inventory (at cost)
> + Purchase (at cost)
> ─────────────────────
> Merchandise available for sale (at cost)
> − Cost of goods sold
> ─────────────────────
> Ending inventory (at cost)

The beginning inventory and amount of purchases are taken from company records, and the cost of goods sold is normally determined by applying the rate of markup to the amount of net sales.

EXAMPLE 5 **Estimating Inventory Value Using the Gross-Profit Method**

Inventory on June 30 was $242,000. During the next 3 months, the company had purchases of $425,000 and net sales of $528,000. Use the gross-profit method to estimate the value of the inventory on September 30 if the company uses a markup of 25% on selling price.

Solution First, find the cost of goods sold. Since markup is 25% of selling price, find cost.

$$C + M = S$$
$$C + 0.25S = S$$
$$C + 0.25S - 0.25S = S - 0.25S$$
$$C = S - 0.25S$$
$$C = 0.75S$$
$$C = 0.75 \times \$528,000$$
$$C = \$396,000$$

The cost of goods sold is $396,000. Now use the gross-profit method.

$242,000	Beginning inventory (June 30)
+ 425,000	Purchases
$667,000	Merchandise available for sale
− 396,000	Cost of goods sold
$271,000	Ending inventory (September 30)

The estimated value of the inventory on September 30 is $271,000.

Objective

8 *Use the Retail Method to Estimate Inventory.* The **retail method** of estimating inventory requires that a business keep records of all purchases at both cost and retail prices. The format for estimating inventory value at retail is the same as that used in estimating inventory using the gross-profit method. The difference, however, is that all amounts used are at retail. Inventory at retail is estimated as follows.

> Beginning inventory (at retail)
> + Purchases (at retail)
> ─────────────────────
> Merchandise available for sale (at retail)
> − Net sales
> ─────────────────────
> Ending inventory (at retail)

Notice that net sales are used in this method instead of cost of goods sold. Also, ending inventory value at retail must now be changed to an estimated value at cost. This is done by multiplying the ending inventory value at retail by a ratio determined by comparing the merchandise available for sale at cost to the merchandise available for sale at retail.

EXAMPLE 6   **Estimating Inventory Value Using the Retail Method**

At one booth in the mall, inventory on March 31 was valued at $9000 at cost and $15,000 at retail. During the next 3 months, the company made purchases of $36,000 at cost, or $60,000 at retail, and had total sales of $54,000. Use the retail method to estimate the value of inventory at cost on June 30.

Solution

At Cost	At Retail	
$9,000	$15,000	Beginning inventory
+ 36,000	+ 60,000	Purchases
$45,000	$75,000	Merchandise available for sale
	− 54,000	Net sales
	$21,000	June 30 inventory (at retail)

Now find the ratio of merchandise available for sale at cost to merchandise available for sale at retail.

$$\frac{\$45,000}{\$75,000}$$

$45,000 — Merchandise available for sale at cost

$75,000 — Merchandise available for sale at retail

Finally, the estimated inventory value at cost on June 30 is found by multiplying inventory at retail on June 30 by this ratio.

$$\$21,000 \times \frac{45,000}{75,000} = \$12,600 \quad \text{June 30 inventory (at cost)}$$

The retail method of estimating inventory value assumes that the ratio of the merchandise available for sale at cost to the merchandise available for sale at retail is the same as the ratio of the ending inventory at cost to ending inventory at retail. Both the gross-profit method and the retail method of estimating inventories must be updated from time to time with physical inventory counts to assure accurate record keeping.

Companies selling on the Internet are often able to have products shipped directly from a manufacturer or wholesaler to their customers. This will usually result in decreased inventory requirements in the supply chain since the Internet retailer doesn't need to carry inventory.

11.3 | **Exercises**

Find the inventory value for the following using the specific-identification method.

Description	Cost
1. Fair	$208
Good	$274
Excellent	$345
3. Good	$79
Excellent	$186
Mint	$295

Description	Cost
2. Economy	$1215
Standard	$1509
Luxury	$1873
Deluxe	$2116
4. Incomplete	$835
Cheap	$972
Improved	$1170
Tolerable	$1360

Find the inventory values using (a) the weighted-average method, (b) the FIFO method, and (c) the LIFO method for each of the following. Round to the nearest dollar.

Purchases		Now in Inventory
5. Beginning inventory:	10 units at $8	
June:	25 units at $9	
August:	15 units at $10	20 units
6. Beginning inventory:	80 units at $14.50	
July:	50 units at $15.80	
October:	70 units at $13.90	90 units
7. Beginning inventory:	50 units at $30.50	
March:	70 units at $31.50	
June:	30 units at $33.25	
August:	40 units at $30.75	75 units
8. Beginning inventory:	700 units at $1.25	
May:	400 units at $1.75	
August:	500 units at $2.25	
October:	600 units at $3.00	720 units

Solve the following application problems. Round to the nearest dollar.

9. **SPECIFIC-IDENTIFICATION INVENTORY VALUE** Towne Furniture had the following coffee tables in stock.

Model Number	Cost
P6251	$182
C3852	$210
PC623	$132
RW778	$921
WO335	$325

Find the inventory value using the specific-identification method.

10. **HEATING AND AIR-CONDITIONING** Foothill Heat and Cool had the following refrigeration compressors in stock. Use the specific-identification method to find the inventory value.

Model Number	Cost
AC129	$428
AC428	$715
AC2207	$526
AC78C	$1718
AC3107	$635

11. **BANDAGE INVENTORY** A Rite-Aid drug store made the following purchases of elastic bandages made in Brazil.

Beginning inventory:	24 units at $1.50
June:	40 units at $1.35
August:	48 units at $1.25
November:	18 units at $1.60

    Inventory at the end of the year shows that 35 units remain. Find the inventory value using (a) the weighted-average method, (b) the FIFO method, and (c) the LIFO method.

12. **CANDLES** The Hobby House purchased of a variety of scented candles during the year as follows.

Beginning inventory:	200 candles at $1.10
March:	400 candles at $1.20
May:	700 candles at $1.00
August:	500 candles at $1.15
November:	300 candles at $1.30

    At the end of the year, it had 450 candles in stock. Find the inventory value using (a) the weighted-average method, (b) the FIFO method, and (c) the LIFO method.

13. **GREETING CARDS** The warehouse manager for DV Pharmacy made the following purchases of boxes of greeting cards.

Beginning inventory:	200 boxes at $3.10
July:	250 boxes at $3.50
August:	300 boxes at $4.25
October:	280 boxes at $4.50

    Inventory at the end of October shows that 320 boxes remain. Find the inventory value using (a) the weighted-average method, (b) the FIFO method, and (c) the LIFO method.

14. **GAME BOY** Online Electronics made the following purchases of Game Boy consoles throughout the year.

Beginning inventory:	300 consoles at $21.60
March:	400 consoles at $24.00
August:	450 consoles at $24.30
November:	350 consoles at $22.50

    An inventory at the end of December shows that 530 consoles remain. Find the inventory value using (a) the weighted-average method, (b) the FIFO method, and (c) the LIFO method.

15. **PARTY SUPPLIES**   Party Tyme Wholesalers made the following purchases of 11-inch paper plates.

Beginning inventory:	350 cases at $8.25
October:	300 cases at $9.50
November:	360 cases at $11.45
December:	240 cases at $10.10

The January inventory found that there were 625 cases remaining. Find the inventory value using (a) the weighted-average method, (b) the FIFO method, and (c) the LIFO method.

16. **LINEN SUPPLY**   Industrial Linen Supply made the following purchases of shop towels.

Beginning inventory:	650 towels at $3.80
June:	500 towels at $4.20
September:	450 towels at $3.95
December:	600 towels at $4.05

In January an inventory found that there were 775 towels remaining. Find the inventory value using (a) the weighted-average method, (b) the FIFO method, and (c) the LIFO method.

17. **SECURITY DOORS**   The inventory on December 31 at Safe Security Doors was $136,000 at cost. During the next 3 months, the company made purchases of $148,000 (cost) and had net sales of $236,000. Use the gross-profit method to estimate the value of the inventory at cost on March 31 if the company uses a markup of 35% on selling price.

18. **TOY STORE INVENTORY**   Happy Toys has an inventory of $52,000 at cost on June 30. Purchases during the next 3 months were $68,000 (cost), and net sales were $126,000. If the company uses a 40% markup on selling price, use the gross-profit method to estimate the value of the inventory at cost on September 30.

19. **PIANO REPAIR**   The September 30 inventory at Liverpool Piano Repair was $43,750 at cost and $62,500 at retail. Purchases during the next 3 months were $51,600 at cost and $73,800 at retail, and net sales were $92,500. Use the retail method to estimate the value of inventory at cost on December 31.

20. **EVALUATING INVENTORY**   Uptown Sound had an inventory of $27,000 at cost and $45,000 at retail on March 31. During the next 3 months, it made purchases of $108,000 at cost and $180,000 at retail and had net sales of $162,000. Use the retail method to estimate the value of inventory at cost on June 30.

21. In your opinion, what are the benefits to a merchant who is using universal product codes (UPC)? (See Objective 2.)

22. List the four inventory valuation methods discussed in this section. Explain how one of these methods is used to determine inventory value.

Quick Review

CHAPTER TERMS

Review the following terms to test your understanding of the chapter. For each term you do not know, refer to the page number found next to that term.

absolute loss [p. 383]
actual selling price
  [p. 381]
average inventory
  [p. 389]
break-even point [p. 383]
first-in, first-out (FIFO)
  method [p. 395]
formula for markdown
  [p. 381]
gross-profit method
  [p. 397]

inventory turnover
  [p. 388]
inventory valuation
  [p. 393]
last-in, first-out (LIFO)
  method [p. 396]
markdown [p. 381]
operating loss [p. 383]
percent of markdown
  [p. 381]
periodic inventory
  [p. 393]

perpetual inventory
  [p. 393]
physical inventory
  [p. 393]
rate of markdown [p. 381]
reduced net profit [p. 383]
reduced price [p. 381]
retail method [p. 397]
sale price [p. 381]
specific-identification
  method [p. 393]
stock turnover [p. 388]

turnover at cost [p. 390]
turnover at retail [p. 390]
turns [p. 388]
universal product code
  (UPC) [p. 393]
weighted-average
  (average-cost) method
  [p. 394]

CONCEPTS

EXAMPLES

11.1 Percent of markdown

Markdown is always a percent of the original price. Use the following formula.

$$\text{Markdown percent} = \frac{\text{Markdown amount}}{\text{Original price}}$$

Original price, $76; markdown, $19. Find the percent of markdown.

$$\text{Markdown percent} = \frac{19}{76}$$
$$= 0.25 = 25\%$$

11.1 Break-even point

Add cost to operating expenses to find the break-even point.

Cost, $54; operating expenses, $16. Find the break-even point.

$$\$54 + \$16 = \$70 \quad \text{Break-even point}$$

11.1 Operating loss

When the reduced price is below the break-even point, subtract the reduced price from the break-even point to find the operating loss.

Break-even point, $70; reduced price, $58. Find the operating loss.

$$\$70 - \$58 = \$12 \quad \text{Operating loss}$$

11.1 Absolute loss

When the reduced price is below cost, subtract the reduced price from the cost to find the absolute loss.

Cost, $54; reduced price, $48. Find the absolute loss.

$$\$54 - \$48 = \$6 \quad \text{Absolute loss}$$

11.2 Average inventory

Take inventory 2 or more times; add the totals and divide by the number of inventories to get the average.

Inventories: $22,635, $24,692, and $18,796. Find the average inventory.

$$\frac{\$22,635 + \$24,692 + \$18,796}{3} = \frac{\$66,123}{3}$$
$$= \$22,041 \quad \text{Average inventory}$$

11.2 Turnover at retail

Use the following formula.

$$\text{Turnover} = \frac{\text{Retail sales}}{\text{Average inventory at retail}}$$

Sales, $78,496; average inventory at retail, $18,076. Find turnover at retail.

$$\frac{\$78,496}{\$18,076} = 4.34 \text{ at retail} \quad \text{Rounded}$$

11.2 Turnover at cost

Use the following formula.

$$\text{Turnover} = \frac{\text{Cost of goods sold}}{\text{Average inventory at cost}}$$

Cost of goods sold, $132,710; average inventory at cost, $32,960. Find the turnover at cost.

$$\frac{\$132,710}{\$32,960} = 4.03 \text{ at cost} \quad \text{Rounded}$$

11.3 Specific-identification to value inventory

Each item is cost coded and the cost of each of the items is added to find total inventory.

Costs: item 1, $593; item 2, $614; item 3, $498. Find total value of inventory.

$593 + $614 + $498 = $1705 \quad Total value of inventory

11.3 Weighted-average method of inventory valuation

This method values items in an inventory at the average cost of buying them.

Beginning inventory of 20 at $75; purchases of 15 at $80; 25 at $65; 18 at $70; 22 remain in inventory. Find the inventory value.

$$
\begin{array}{rl}
20 \times \$75 = & \$1500 \\
15 \times \$80 = & \$1200 \\
25 \times \$65 = & \$1625 \\
18 \times \$70 = & \$1260 \\
\hline
\text{Totals } 78 & \$5585
\end{array}
$$

$$\frac{\$5585}{78} = \$71.60 \text{ Rounded} \times 22 = \$1575.20 \quad \text{Value of inventory}$$

11.3 First-in, first-out (FIFO) method of inventory valuation

First items in are first sold. Inventory is based on cost of most recent items purchased.

Beginning inventory of 25 items at $40; purchase on Aug. 7, 30 items at $35; 35 remain in inventory. Find the inventory value.

$$
\begin{array}{rll}
30 \times \$35 = & \$1050 & \text{Value of last 30} \\
5 \times \$40 = & \$200 & \text{Value of previous 5} \\
\hline
\text{Totals } 35 & \$1250 & \text{Value of inventory}
\end{array}
$$

11.3 Last-in, first-out (LIFO) method of inventory valuation

The goods remaining in inventory are the first goods purchased.

Beginning inventory of 48 items at $20 each; purchase on May 9, 40 items at $25 each; 55 remain in inventory. Find the inventory value.

$$
\begin{array}{rll}
48 \times \$20 = & \$960 & \text{Value of first 48} \\
7 \times \$25 = & \$175 & \text{Value of last 7} \\
\hline
\text{Totals } 55 & \$1135 & \text{Value of inventory}
\end{array}
$$

11.3 Estimating inventory value using the gross-profit method

Beginning inventory (at cost)
+ Purchases (at cost)
Merchandise available for sale (at cost)
− Cost of goods sold
Ending inventory (at cost)

Find cost using $C + M = S$; $C = \$198,000$

$$
\begin{array}{rl}
\$121,000 & \text{Beginning inventory} \\
+ 212,500 & \text{Purchases} \\
\hline
\$333,500 & \text{Merchandise available for sale} \\
- 198,000 & \text{Cost of goods sold} \\
\hline
\$135,500 & \text{Ending inventory (at cost)}
\end{array}
$$

11.3	**Estimating inventory value using the retail method**			At Cost	At Retail

11.3 Estimating inventory value using the retail method

$$\frac{\text{Goods available for sale at cost}}{\text{Goods available for sale at retail}} = \%(\text{cost ratio})$$

$$\begin{array}{c}\text{Ending inventory} \\ \text{at retail}\end{array} \times \%(\text{cost ratio}) = \begin{array}{c}\text{Inventory} \\ \text{at cost}\end{array}$$

	At Cost	At Retail
Beginning inventory	$7,000	$10,000
Purchases	+ 21,000	+ 30,000
Goods available for sale	$28,000	$40,000
Net sales		− 25,000
Ending inventory		$15,000

$$\frac{\$28,000 \quad \text{Goods available for sale at cost}}{\$40,000 \quad \text{Goods available for sale at retail}}$$

$$= 0.7 = 70\%$$

$$\$15,000 \times 0.7 = \$10,500 \quad \text{Inventory value at cost}$$

CHAPTER 11	Review Exercises

The answer section includes answers to all Review Exercises.

Find the missing quantities. Round rates to the nearest whole percent and money to the nearest cent. [11.1]

	Original Price	% Markdown	$ Markdown	Reduced Price
1.	$96	30%	_____	_____
2.	_____	$33\frac{1}{3}\%$	_____	$10
3.	_____	50%	$2.70	_____
4.	$2340	_____	_____	$1755

Complete the following. If there is no operating loss or absolute loss, write "none." Use Figure 11.2 as a guide. [11.1]

	Cost	Operating Expense	Break-even Point	Reduced Price	Operating Loss	Absolute Loss
5.	$150	_____	$198	$132	_____	$18
6.	$80	$20	_____	$93	_____	_____
7.	$78	$22	_____	_____	$30	_____
8.	$5	$1.25	_____	$5.50	_____	_____

Find the average inventory in each of the following. [11.2]

	Date	Inventory Amount at Retail
9.	Beginning inventory	$44,398
	March 31	$37,704
11.	Beginning inventory	$77,159
	April 1	$67,305
	July 1	$80,664
	October 1	$95,229
	December 31	$61,702

	Date	Inventory Amount at Retail
10.	Beginning inventory	$316,481
	July 1	$432,185
	December 31	$296,738
12.	Beginning inventory	$36,502
	April 1	$27,331
	July 1	$28,709
	October 1	$32,153
	December 31	$39,604

Find the stock turnover at retail and at cost in each of the following. Round to the nearest hundredth. [11.2]

	Average Inventory at Cost	Average Inventory at Retail	Cost of Goods Sold	Retail Sales
13.	$14,120	$25,572	$81,312	$146,528
14.	$11,195	$16,365	$89,343	$129,938
15.	$90,300	$128,350	$423,168	$598,111
16.	$102,895	$195,150	$476,417	$889,884

Find the inventory value in each of the following using the specific-identification method. [11.2]

Description	Cost		Description	Cost
17. Small	$122	18.	Poor	$314
Medium	$199		Fair	$422
Large	$235		Good	$506
19. Economy	$795	20.	Good	$1283
Standard	$850		Better	$1398
Luxury	$915		Best	$1564
Deluxe	$1080		Designer	$1772

Solving the following application problems.

21. A one-year-old Harley-Davidson motorcycle originally priced at $13,875 is marked down to $9990. Find the percent of markdown on the original price. [11.1]

22. A cordless telephone costs a retailer $56. The store's operating expenses are 30% of cost, and net profit is 10% of cost. Find (a) the selling price of the cordless telephone and (b) the maximum percent of markdown that may be given without taking an operating loss. Round to the nearest whole percent. [11.1]

23. Party Supplies had an inventory of $29,332 on January 1, $36,908 on July 1, and $31,464 on December 31. Find the average inventory. [11.2]

24. The Natural Grocer has an average inventory of $25,380 at cost. If the cost of goods sold for the year was $273,375, find the stock turnover at cost. Round to the nearest hundredth. [11.2]

25. Western Boots manufactures cowboy boots. Inventory at retail value at the end of each quarter of the past year was $78,230, $46,590, $63,980, and $104,125. Sales during the same period were $925,370. Find the stock turnover at retail rounded to the nearest hundredth. [11.3]

26. Thunder Manufacturing made the following purchases of rivet drums during the year: 25 at $135 each, 40 at $165 each, 15 at $108.50 each, and 30 at $142 each. An inventory shows that 45 rivet drums remain. Find the inventory value using (a) the weighted-average method, (b) the FIFO method, and (c) the LIFO method. [11.3]

27. The inventory on December 31 at Modern Clothiers was $118,000 at cost. During the next 3 months, the company made purchases of $186,000 (cost) and had net sales of $378,000. Use the gross-profit method to estimate the value of the inventory at cost on March 31 if the company uses a markup of 50% on selling price. [11.3]

28. Tap Plastics had an inventory of $54,000 at cost and $90,000 at retail on June 30. During the next 3 months, it made purchases of $216,000 at cost and $360,000 at retail and had net sales of $324,000. Use the retail method to estimate the value of the inventory at cost on September 30. [11.3]

CHAPTER 11	Business Application Case #1
	Reducing Prices to Move Merchandise

Surf and Skate purchased two dozen pairs of Roces 5th Element adults' inline skates at a cost of $2925. Markup on this type of product is 35% of selling price, while operating expenses for the store are 25% of cost. Only 6 pairs of the skates sell at the original price and the manager decides to mark down the remaining skates. The price is reduced 25% and 6 more pairs sell. The remaining 12 pairs of skates are marked down 50% of the original selling price and are finally sold.

(a) Find the original selling price of each pair of skates.

(b) Find the total sales of all the skates.

(c) Find the operating loss.

(d) Find the absolute loss.

CHAPTER 11	Business Application Case #2
	Going Out of Business

Jetson Boats is going out of business. The company has a long history of selling and servicing boats, but debts piled up during Mr. Jetson's long illness and inventories fell as he stopped purchasing from manufacturers. Since no one wants to buy the business, Mr. Jetson's son has temporarily taken over, and he must mark down the following in order to close the business.

Item	Total Cost	Original Selling Price
Small boats	$92,350	$117,500
Mid-sized boats	$127,900	$172,400
Parts	$32,900	$52,640
Miscellaneous	$18,740	$28,280

(a) Find the average markup on cost Mr. Jetson used for each. Round to the nearest tenth of a percent.

(b) Sum the Total Cost and Original Selling Prices columns in the table above and then find the average markup on total cost to the nearest tenth.

(c) Assume the son marks down the total of the original selling prices found in (b) above by 15% and sells one-half of the inventory. Further assume he marks the remaining inventory down an additional 20% from that already reduced price, and then sells it. Find the total revenue received.

(d) Find the total revenue received from (c) as a percent of total cost from (b) to determine the final markup actually received. Round to the nearest tenth of a percent.

PART 3	Cumulative Review: Chapters 9–11

Find the net cost (invoice amount) for each of the following. **[9.1]**

1. List price $280, less 10/20
2. List price $375, less 25/10/5

Find the net cost equivalent and the percent form of the single discount equivalent for the following series discounts. **[9.2]**

3. 10/20   4. 20/20   5. 20/30/5   6. 50/40/10

Solve for the amount of discount and the amount due on each of the following. **[9.4]**

	Invoice Amount	Invoice Date	Terms	Shipping and Insurance	Date Goods Received	Date Invoice Paid
7.	$740.58	Mar. 20	2/10/ROG	$36.80	April 6	Apr. 14
8.	$874.22	Feb. 12	4/15 proximo		Feb. 22	Mar. 12
9.	$3788.20	Jul. 19	3/15 EOM	$71.18	Aug. 7	Aug. 9
10.	$4692.50	Nov. 5	2/15-50x		Nov. 10	Jan. 6

Find the missing quantities by first computing the markup on one base and then computing the markup on the other. Round rates to the nearest tenth of a percent and money to the nearest cent. **[10.2]**

	Cost	Markup	Selling Price	% Markup on Cost	% Markup on Selling Price
11.	_____	$288.14	$576.28	_____	_____
12.	_____	$38.22	_____	$33\frac{1}{3}\%$	_____

Find the missing quantities. Markup is based on total cost. **[10.3]**

	Total Cost	Quantity Purchased	Percent Sold at Reduced Price	% Markup on Total Cost	Number at Regular Price	Number at Reduced Price	Reduced Price	Regular Selling Price Each
13.	$1400	1000 pr.	30%	50%	_____	_____	$1.50	_____
14.	$2250	150	10%	25%	_____	_____	$7.50	_____

Complete the following. If there is no operating loss or absolute loss, write "none." Use Figure 11.2 as a guide. **[11.1]**

	Cost	Operating Expense	Break-even Point	Reduced Price	Operating Loss	Absolute Loss
15.	$150	_____	$198	$132	_____	_____
16.	$39	$11	_____	_____	$15	_____

Find the average inventory in each of the following. **[11.2]**

	Date	Inventory Amount at Retail
17.	Beginning inventory	$74,422
	July 1	$58,320
	December 31	$61,889

Date	Inventory Amount at Retail
18. Beginning inventory	$218,143
April 1	$186,326
July 1	$275,637
October 1	$207,448
December 31	$172,351

Find the stock turnover at retail and at cost in each of the following. Round to the nearest hundredth. [11.2]

	Average Inventory at Cost	Average Inventory at Retail	Cost of Goods Sold	Retail Sales
19.	$14,120	$25,572	$81,312	$146,528
20.	$45,150	$64,175	$211,584	$299,056

Solve the following application problems.

21. A home-security system is list-priced at $2995. The manufacturer offers a series discount of 20/20/20 to wholesalers and a 20/20 series discount to retailers. (a) What is the wholesaler's price? (b) What is the retailer's price? (c) What is the difference between the prices? **[9.2]**

22. Pet Supply Wholesalers receives an invoice dated June 22 for $3578 with terms of 2/10 EOM. The invoice is paid on July 8. Find the amount necessary to pay the invoice in full. **[9.4]**

23. An appliance store sells a dishwasher for $949 while using a 30% markup on cost. Find the cost. **[10.1]**

24. Office Max sells a Texas Instruments financial calculator for $19.95. The calculator costs the store $15.96. Find the markup as a percent of selling price. **[10.2]**

25. Area Rugs Galore offers an 8-by-10-foot Persian rug for $499.95. If the rugs cost $4499.55 per dozen, find (a) the markup, (b) the percent of markup on selling price, and (c) the percent of markup on cost. Round to the nearest tenth of a percent. **[10.1 and 10.2]**

26. A commercial riding lawn mower, originally priced at $9250, is marked down to $6660. Find the percent of markdown on the original price. **[11.1]**

27. John Cross Pool Supply, a retailer, pays $285 for a diving board. The original selling price was $399 but was marked down 40%. If operating expenses are 30% of cost, find (a) the operating loss and (b) the absolute loss. **[11.1]**

28. Boise Medical Supplies had an inventory of $58,664 on January 1, $73,815 on July 1, and $62,938 on December 31. Find the average inventory. **[11.2]**

Round to the nearest dollar amount.

29. Craighead Products made the following purchases of fuel tanks during the year: 25 at $270 each, 40 at $330 each, 15 at $217 each, and 30 at $284 each. An inventory shows that 45 fuel tanks remain. Find the inventory value, using the weighted-average method. **[11.3]**

30. Find the inventory value listed in Exercise 29 using (a) the FIFO method and (b) the LIFO method. **[11.3]**

CHAPTER
12

Simple Interest

Some of the oldest documents in existence—clay tablets dating back almost 5000 years—show the calculation of interest charges. Interest, a fee for borrowing money, is about as old as civilization itself. Interestingly, the Koran forbids Muslims from charging interest. Instead, Islamic banks take an ownership interest in firms to which they "lend" money and are repaid through profits.

The largest and most secure companies, such as Microsoft, borrow at a very favorable interest rate called the **prime rate**. Many interest rates, including interest rates on many loans and on savings deposits, move up and down more or less with the prime rate. In other words, when the prime rate moves up, the interest rates on automobile and home loans also tend to increase, and vice versa. Figure 12.1 shows prime rate and housing start data for the United States. Notice that the prime rate fell from a high of nearly 20% in 1980 to below 5% in 2009. Since high interest rates make it expensive to borrow, the high prime rate and other interest rates in 1980 caused housing starts to fall to a low level, as you can see in the figure. But why were housing starts low in 2008 when interest rates were low?

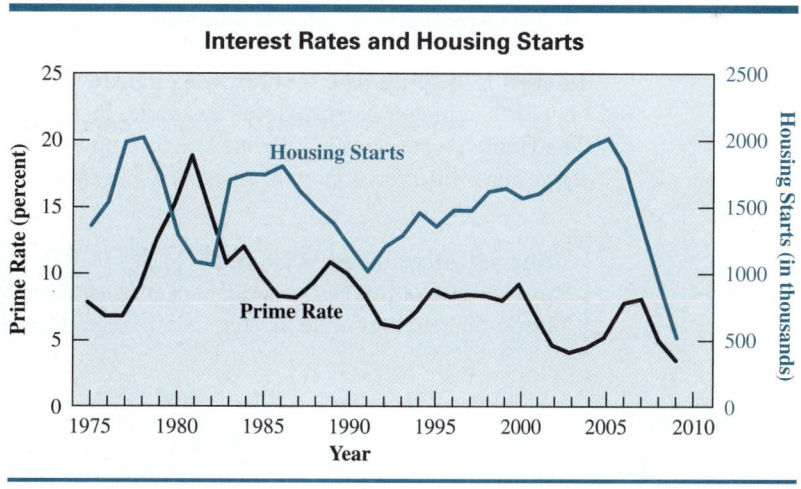

Source: U.S. Bureau of Census.
Figure 12.1

In contrast to what you might expect, housing starts collapsed to a very low level in 2008–2009 even though the prime rate was very low. Why? Low interest rates mean low monthly payments so more new houses should be started. The answer lies in the severe financial crisis that began in 2008. The financial crisis began as home prices fell rapidly, then some companies went bankrupt and it was difficult for businesses and individuals to find loans. The stock market also fell sharply, reducing the value of retirement plans. Unemployment soared and people worried about their jobs. Spending for high-cost items such as automobiles, houses, jewelry, and even clothes slowed sharply as consumers retrenched. Government regulators worked feverishly to bring interest rates down, keep the banking system going, and support some large firms such as the automobile makers. The belief is that lower interest rates will, in time, result in buyers coming back into the market to buy homes and firm up prices.

The financial crisis that began in 2008 was originally centered around subprime home loans made in the United States to individuals or families without good credit. Why did it spread so quickly around the world? What does "global economy" really mean? How can rapidly falling home values in a few states in the United States result in the near bankruptcy of the small city of Norvik, Norway, as happened in 2008?

Two basic types of interest are in common use today: **simple interest** and **compound interest**. Simple interest is interest paid on only the principal. Compound interest is interest paid on *both principal and past interest*. This chapter discusses simple interest, and **Chapter 14** covers compound interest.

12.1   Basics of Simple Interest

OBJECTIVES

1   *Find simple interest.*
2   *Find interest for less than a year.*
3   *Find principal if given rate and time.*
4   *Find rate if given principal and time.*
5   *Find time if given principal and rate.*

Interest is the price paid for borrowing money. Interest rates are usually expressed as a percent of the amount borrowed. For example, in some states, retail companies such as Sears, The Home Depot, and J.C. Penney charge up to 21% interest per year on money owed to them. Here are three important terms *you must learn*.

> **Principal**—the amount borrowed.
> **Rate** (or **rate of interest**)—percent of interest charged by lender.
> **Time**—the length of time in years before repayment is due.

Objective

1   *Find Simple Interest.*   **Simple interest** is interest charged on the entire principal for the entire length of the loan and is usually used for short-term loans that last less than a year. It is found using a modification of the basic percent formula.

$$\text{Simple interest} = \text{Principal} \times \text{Rate} \times \text{Time}$$
$$I = \quad P \quad \times \quad R \quad \times \quad T \quad \text{or}$$
$$I = PRT$$

The rate, *R,* is expressed as a decimal or fraction, and time, *T,* is expressed as the number of years, or the fraction of a year.

> **NOTE**   It is important to remember that time is in years. This means that a time period given in months or days *must* be converted to a fraction of a year before being substituted into the formula for *T*.

EXAMPLE 1 **Finding Simple Interest**

In addition to using some of their own money, Gilbert Construction Company must borrow $60,000 to build an 1800-square-foot home. The owner, Susan Gilbert, is considering whether she should borrow the funds at (a) 8% per year for 1 year or (b) $8\frac{1}{2}$% per year for $1\frac{1}{2}$ years. Find the simple interest on both loans and (c) the difference between the two.

Solution

(a) Use the formula $I = PRT$. Substitute $60,000 for P, 0.08 (the decimal form of 8%) for R, and 1 for T.

$$I = PRT$$
$$= \$60,000 \times 0.08 \times 1$$
$$= \$4800 \qquad \text{Simple interest}$$

Check the answer by dividing $4800 by $60,000 to find 0.08, or 8% interest.

(b) Again use the simple interest formula. However, now use $R = 0.085\ (8\frac{1}{2}\%)$ and $T = 1.5$ $(1\frac{1}{2}$ years$)$.

$$I = PRT$$
$$= \$60,000 \times 0.085 \times 1.5$$
$$= \$7650 \qquad \text{Simple interest}$$

(c) Difference $= \$7650 - \$4800 = \$2850$

The second loan has a higher interest rate and a longer time. It adds $2850 to the cost of building the house and therefore reduces any profit on the house by that amount. Gilbert chooses the 1-year loan since she already has a contract with the individual who will buy the home and she can build and deliver the home within 1 year. Gilbert constantly fights to keep costs, including interest charges, as low as possible to make profit.

Objective

2 *Find Interest for Less Than a Year.* Notice in part (a) of the next example how 9 months is written as $\frac{9}{12}$ of a year and in part (b) that 13 months (obviously more than 1 year) is written as $\frac{13}{12}$ or $1\frac{1}{12}$ of a year. Also notice that sometimes it is necessary to round interest to the nearest cent, as shown next in part (b) of Example 2.

EXAMPLE 2 **Finding Simple Interest Using Months**

Jodie Luk needs to borrow $2800 to finish her last semester in college. Her uncle offers to lend her the money either at (a) 8% simple interest for 9 months or (b) $8\frac{1}{2}$% simple interest for 13 months. Find the interest on both options and (c) the difference between the two.

Solution

(a) Since there are 12 months in a year, 9 months is $\frac{9}{12}$, or 0.75, of a year. Find the interest as follows.

$$I = PRT$$
$$= \$2800 \times 0.08 \times \frac{9}{12}$$
$$= \$168$$

(b) Use $\frac{13}{12}$ to represent 13 months in terms of number of years.

$$I = PRT$$

$$= \$2800 \times 0.085 \times \frac{13}{12}$$

$$= \$257.83 \qquad \text{Rounded}$$

(c) Difference $= \$257.83 - \$168 = \$89.83$

The difference in interest is small since the loan amount (principal) is small.

Scientific Calculator Approach

The calculator solution to Example 2 follows.

2800 $\boxed{\times}$ 0.08 $\boxed{\times}$ 9 $\boxed{\div}$ 12 $\boxed{=}$ 168 $\boxed{\text{STO}}$

2800 $\boxed{\times}$ 0.085 $\boxed{\times}$ 13 $\boxed{\div}$ 12 $\boxed{=}$ 257.83 (rounded)

257.83 $\boxed{-}$ $\boxed{\text{RCL}}$ $\boxed{=}$ \$89.83 difference

---

Objective

3 ***Find Principal If Given Rate and Time.*** Sometimes the amount of interest is known, but the principal, rate, or time must be found. Do this with the following modifications of the formula for simple interest.

$$I = PRT$$

$$\frac{I}{RT} = \frac{P\cancel{R}\cancel{T}}{\cancel{R}\cancel{T}} \qquad \text{Divide both sides by } RT$$

$$\frac{I}{RT} = P \quad \text{or} \quad P = \frac{I}{RT}$$

Similarly, dividing both sides of $I = PRT$ by PT gives the formula for *R*.

$$R = \frac{I}{PT}$$

And dividing both sides of $I = PRT$ by PR gives the formula for *T*.

$$T = \frac{I}{PR}$$

> **NOTE** You do not have to remember all of the formulas above. Just remember $I = PRT$ and use algebra to solve for the unknown **(Section 2.3)**. Do not forget that the *rate must be a decimal or fraction* and *time must be in years*.

EXAMPLE 3 **Finding the Principal**

Ajax Coal borrows funds at 10.5% for 10 months to buy a tractor that will be used to keep the roads in the firm's coal mine in good condition. Find the principal that results in interest of \$13,125.

Solution Find the principal by dividing both sides of $I = PRT$ by RT.

$$P = \frac{I}{RT}$$

$$= \frac{\$13,125}{0.105 \times \frac{10}{12}} \qquad \text{Substitute values for variables.}$$

$$= \$150,000$$

The principal or loan amount is \$150,000.

Scientific Calculator Approach

> For the calculator solution to Example 3, divide using the chain calculation.
>
> $\boxed{13125}$ $\boxed{\div}$ $\boxed{(}$ $\boxed{0.105}$ $\boxed{\times}$ $\boxed{10}$ $\boxed{\div}$ $\boxed{12}$ $\boxed{)}$ $\boxed{=}$ $\boxed{150000}$

Objective

4 *Find Rate If Given Principal and Time.* The next example shows how to find the interest rate if the principal and time are given.

EXAMPLE **4** **Finding the Rate**

After a large down payment, Jessica Warren borrowed \$9000 from her credit union to purchase a previously owned Toyota Camry. Find the interest rate if the loan was for 9 months and the interest was \$540.

Solution Divide both sides of $I = PRT$ by PT to get the following.

$$R = \frac{I}{PT}$$

$$= \frac{\$540}{\$9000 \times \frac{9}{12}} \qquad \text{Substitute values for variables.}$$

$$= 0.08$$

The rate was 8%.

> **NOTE** In order to avoid rounding errors, it is important not to round off any calculations until the very end when solving these types of problems.

Objective

5 *Find Time If Given Principal and Rate.* The simple interest formula can also be used to find the time of a loan.

EXAMPLE **5** **Finding the Time**

Jennifer Wells, a loan officer at Midwest Bank, made a loan of \$9600 at 10%. How many months will it take to produce \$560 in interest?

Solution Use $I = PRT$ and divide both sides by PR to get

$$T \text{ (in years)} = \frac{I}{PR}$$

We included "(in years)" to emphasize this important point—time of the loan is measured in years. Now substitute $560 for I, $9600 for P, and 0.10 for R.

$$T \text{ (in years)} = \frac{\$560}{\$9600 \times 0.10} \qquad \text{Substitute values for variables.}$$

$$= \frac{\$560}{\$960}$$

Reduced to lowest terms

$$T \text{ (in years)} = \frac{\$560}{\$960} = \frac{7}{12} \text{ year} = 7 \text{ months}$$

NOTE In all the examples of this section, time has been expressed in years or months. **Section 12.2** will deal with interest problems in which the time is expressed in days.

12.1 | Exercises

Find the simple interest for each of the following. Round to the nearest cent.

1. $6800 at 10% for $1\frac{1}{4}$ years
2. $9500 at 12% for $1\frac{1}{2}$ years
3. $12,400 at $9\frac{1}{2}$% for 8 months
4. $4800 at 8% for 8 months
5. $8250 at 13% for 15 months
6. $2830 at 15% for 6 months
7. $9874 at $7\frac{1}{8}$% for 11 months
8. $10,745 at $4\frac{5}{8}$% for 9 months
9. $74,986.15 at 12.23% for 5 months
10. $39,072.76 at 11.23% for 7 months

Complete this chart. Round money to the nearest cent, rate to the nearest tenth of a percent, and time to the nearest month.

	Principal	Interest	Rate	Time in Months
11.	$10,000	_____	10%	6
12.	$15,000	_____	$12\frac{1}{2}$%	10
13.	_____	$162.50	8%	6
14.	_____	$84	10%	7
15.	$3800	$199.50	_____	9
16.	$2600	$144.08	_____	7
17.	$5350	$749	12%	_____
18.	$24,800	$3534	$9\frac{1}{2}$%	_____

Solve the following application problems. Round money to the nearest cent, rate to the nearest tenth of a percent, and time to the nearest month.

19. Find the time, in years, necessary for an $8200 loan to produce $1353 in interest at 11%.

20. A $10,400 loan resulted in interest charges of $1248 at 12% interest. Find the time in years.

21. Find the principal if $245 in interest is due after 10 months at 7%.

22. What amount of principal produces $55 in interest after 1 month at 11%?

23. What time (in months) is necessary for a principal of $8400 to produce $770 in interest at 10%?

24. How many months are necessary for $4800 to produce $44 in interest at 11%?

25. Find the rate if a principal of $1890 produces $138.60 in interest after 11 months.

26. A loan of $8500 produces interest of $595 in 7 months. Find the rate.

27. **LATE-PAYMENT PENALTY**   Casey Watkins is 3 months late on a car payment to a finance company. She has agreed to a penalty rate of 10% per year on the loan balance of $5850. Find the penalty.

28. **CONSTRUCTION**   Denver Construction, Inc. is 2 months late on a payment. The penalty is based on a loan amount of $682,500 and a rate of 14%. Find the penalty.

29. **LOAN TO BUY TIMBER**   Georgia Plantations borrows funds to buy land and agrees to pay interest of $114,375 in 9 months at 10% interest. Find the principal.

30. **AUTOMOBILE LOAN**   Michael George borrows money to replace his Chevrolet. He agrees to pay $1170 in interest at 9% in 10 months. Find the principal (loan amount).

31. **LAWN MOWERS**   The Green Care Company needs to borrow $7000 to buy new lawn mowers. The firm wants to pay no more than $560 in interest. If the interest rate is 12%, what is the longest time for which the money may be borrowed?

32. **NEW STORE**   Max Perry wants to borrow $50,000 to move his vitamin store to a better location. However, his credit history is not excellent. His bank will lend him only $30,000 and then only at a high interest rate of 14%. If Perry cannot pay more than $3500 in interest, find the longest period of time the money may be borrowed.

33. **SAVINGS**   June Peters deposits $6400 in a savings account at her bank. When she withdraws the money 8 months later, she receives a check for $6506.67. Assume simple interest and find the rate of interest paid by the bank.

34. **SAVINGS**   Latoya Johnson deposited $5000 in a certificate of deposit for 6 months and will receive interest of $95. Find the simple interest rate.

35. A $2000 loan was made for 3 months at 7% simple interest. A student calculates the interest due on the loan as follows.

$$I = \$2000 \times 0.07 \times 3 = \$420$$

Is this correct? If not, explain why not and state the correct answer. (See Objective 1.)

36. Are you willing to invest your own funds in an account paying 1% per year for several years? Why or why not? What interest rate should a bank charge you when you borrow? Why?

37. **DENTAL WORK**   Lupe Garcia needs to borrow $3200 for 8 months for dental work that she needs this month. She can choose between a credit union charging 10% or a loan company charging 18%. How much will she save by using the credit union?

38. **CAR REPAIR**   Tomas Rodriguez needs to borrow $3900 so he can repair damages to his car. He plans to pay the loan back in full in 5 months using his income tax refund. He can go to a finance company that will charge him 18% or to his uncle, who has agreed to charge him 9%. Find the difference in the interest charges.

39. **SPORTING GOODS**   A sporting goods store needs to borrow $30,000 to purchase several bikes made of a new, lightweight alloy after a recent Tour de France bike race stimulated interest for the bike. The manager wants to pay back no more than $32,500 in 9 months. What is the highest interest rate the manager can accept?

40. **STUDENT LOAN** A student needs to borrow $3500 for living expenses for a study abroad program in Hong Kong. She feels that she will be able to pay back only $3750 in 7 months after she works in the summer. What is the highest interest rate she is able to pay?

41. **DRESS SHOP** Gladys's Dress Shop received an invoice for $2543, with terms of 2/15, n/60 (see Section 9.3). The store can borrow money at the bank at 12%. How much would be saved by borrowing money for 60 − 15 = 45 days to take advantage of the cash discount? (*Hint:* If discount is earned, firm does not need to borrow full amount of invoice.)

42. **PET SUPPLIES** Westside Pet Supplies received an invoice of $1796, with terms 1/10, n/30 (see Section 9.3). Due to a poor credit history, the store must pay 14.5% interest. How much would the store save by borrowing money for 30 − 10 = 20 days to take advantage of the cash discount? (*Hint:* If discount is earned, firm does not need to borrow full amount of invoice.)

43. **HOME ADDITION** Ricky and Gina Hardin borrow $49,800 to add a den to their home. They finance the loan at 10% simple interest for 4 months. They hope to pay the loan off then, using proceeds from the sale of a rental house. Find the interest.

12.2	Simple Interest for a Given Number of Days

OBJECTIVES

1 *Find the number of days from one date to another using a table.*

2 *Find the number of days from one date to another using the actual number of days.*

3 *Find exact and ordinary interest.*

The previous section showed how to find simple interest for loans of a given number of months or years. In this section, *loans for a given number of days* are discussed. In business, it is common for loans to be for a given number of days, such as "due in 90 days," or else to be due at some fixed date in the future, such as "due on April 17." You will find this topic useful if you own your own business or if you are involved in the finances of a business.

Objective

1 *Find the Number of Days from One Date to Another Using a Table.* There are two ways to find the number of days from one date to another. One way is by the use of Table 12.1. This table assigns a different number to each day of the year. For example, the number for June 11 is found by locating 11 at the left, and June across the top. You will find that June 11 is day 162. Also, December 29 is day 363. The number of days from June 11 to December 29 is found by subtracting.

$$
\begin{array}{lr}
\text{December 29 is day} & 363 \\
\text{June 11 is day} & \underline{-\ 162} \quad \text{Subtract.} \\
& 201
\end{array}
$$

There are 201 days from June 11 to December 29. (Throughout this book, ignore leap years unless otherwise stated.)

NOTE When counting the number of days of a loan, do not count the day the loan is made, but do count its due date.

Table 12.1 THE NUMBER OF EACH OF THE DAYS OF THE YEAR (ADD 1 TO EACH DATE AFTER FEBRUARY 29 FOR A LEAP YEAR)

Day of Month	Jan.	Feb.	March	April	May	June	July	Aug.	Sept.	Oct.	Nov.	Dec.	Day of Month
1	1	32	60	91	121	152	182	213	244	274	305	335	1
2	2	33	61	92	122	153	183	214	245	275	306	336	2
3	3	34	62	93	123	154	184	215	246	276	307	337	3
4	4	35	63	94	124	155	185	216	247	277	308	338	4
5	5	36	64	95	125	156	186	217	248	278	309	339	5
6	6	37	65	96	126	157	187	218	249	279	310	340	6
7	7	38	66	97	127	158	188	219	250	280	311	341	7
8	8	39	67	98	128	159	189	220	251	281	312	342	8
9	9	40	68	99	129	160	190	221	252	282	313	343	9
10	10	41	69	100	130	161	191	222	253	283	314	344	10
11	11	42	70	101	131	162	192	223	254	284	315	345	11
12	12	43	71	102	132	163	193	224	255	285	316	346	12
13	13	44	72	103	133	164	194	225	256	286	317	347	13
14	14	45	73	104	134	165	195	226	257	287	318	348	14
15	15	46	74	105	135	166	196	227	258	288	319	349	15
16	16	47	75	106	136	167	197	228	259	289	320	350	16
17	17	48	76	107	137	168	198	229	260	290	321	351	17
18	18	49	77	108	138	169	199	230	261	291	322	352	18
19	19	50	78	109	139	170	200	231	262	292	323	353	19
20	20	51	79	110	140	171	201	232	263	293	324	354	20
21	21	52	80	111	141	172	202	233	264	294	325	355	21
22	22	53	81	112	142	173	203	234	265	295	326	356	22
23	23	54	82	113	143	174	204	235	266	296	327	357	23
24	24	55	83	114	144	175	205	236	267	297	328	358	24
25	25	56	84	115	145	176	206	237	268	298	329	359	25
26	26	57	85	116	146	177	207	238	269	299	330	360	26
27	27	58	86	117	147	178	208	239	270	300	331	361	27
28	28	59	87	118	148	179	209	240	271	301	332	362	28
29	29		88	119	149	180	210	241	272	302	333	363	29
30	30		89	120	150	181	211	242	273	303	334	364	30
31	31		90		151		212	243		304		365	31

EXAMPLE 1 Finding the Number of Days

Find the number of days from (a) March 24 to July 22 and (b) November 8 to February 17 of the next year.

Solution

(a) The number of days can be estimated. There are about 4 months from March 24 to July 22. Assume 30 days per month and multiply to find about 120 days. Now to find the exact number of days, note that March 24 is day 83 and July 22 is day 203.

$$\begin{array}{r} \text{July 22 is day} \quad 203 \\ \text{March 24 is day} \quad -\ 83 \\ \hline 120 \end{array}$$

There are 120 days from March 24 to July 22. It turns out that our estimate was the exact number of days. Estimates rarely provide the exact answer, but they can help minimize errors by providing approximate values.

(b) Since November 8 is in one year and February 17 is in the next year, first find the number of days from November 8 to the end of the year.

$$
\begin{array}{lr}
\text{Last day of the year is number} & 365 \\
\text{November 8 is day} & -\ 312 \\
\hline
& 53
\end{array}
$$

There are 53 days from November 8 to the end of the year.

Then find the number of days from the beginning of the next year to February 17. According to the chart, February 17 is the 48th day of the year. The total number of days is found as follows.

$$
\begin{array}{lr}
\text{November 8 to end of year} & 53 \\
\text{January 1 to February 17} & +\ 48 \\
\hline
& 101
\end{array}
$$

There are 101 days from November 8 to February 17 of the next year.

Objective

2 *Find the Number of Days from One Date to Another Using the Actual Number of Days.* The number of days from one date to another can also be found using the number of days in each month of the year, as shown in Table 12.2.

Table 12.2   THE NUMBER OF DAYS IN EACH MONTH

31 Days		30 Days	28 Days
January	August	April	February
March	October	June	(29 days in leap year)
May	December	September	
July		November	

EXAMPLE 2 **Finding the Number of Days from One Date to Another Using Actual Days**

Find the number of days from (a) March 12 to June 7 and (b) November 4 to February 21.

Solution

(a) Since March has 31 days, there are $31 - 12 = 19$ days left in March, then 30 days in April, 31 in May, and an additional 7 days in June, for a total as follows.

$$
\begin{array}{rl}
19 & \text{Remaining in March} \\
30 & \text{April} \\
31 & \text{May} \\
+\ 7 & \text{June} \\
\hline
87 & \text{Days from March 12 to June 7}
\end{array}
$$

(b) Add the days in each of the months.

$$
\begin{array}{rl}
26 & \text{Remaining in November} \\
31 & \text{December} \\
31 & \text{January} \\
+\ 21 & \text{February} \\
\hline
109 &
\end{array}
$$

There are 109 days from November 4 to February 21.

Two other ways of remembering the number of days in each month are the rhyme method and the knuckle method, as seen below.

Rhyme Method:

30 days hath September

April, June, and November.

All the rest have 31, except February,

which has 28 and in a leap year 29.

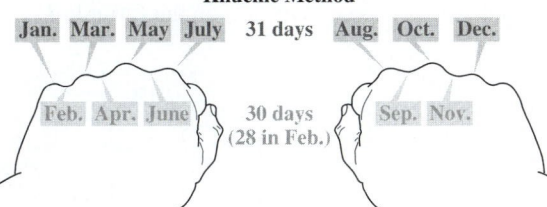

Knuckle Method

Jan. Mar. May July 31 days Aug. Oct. Dec.

Feb. Apr. June   30 days   Sep. Nov.
                    (28 in Feb.)

EXAMPLE 3 Finding Specific Dates

Find the date that is 90 days from (a) March 25 and (b) November 7.

Solution

(a) From Table 12.1, March 25 is day 84. Add 90.

$$\begin{array}{r} \text{March 25 is day} \quad 84 \\ +\ \ 90 \ \text{days} \\ \hline 174 \end{array}$$

As shown in Table 12.1, day 174 is June 23, so 90 days from March 25 is June 23. Alternatively, work as follows.

$$\begin{array}{lr} \text{March 25 to end of month} & 6 \\ \text{April} & 30 \\ \text{May} & +\ 31 \\ \hline & 67 \end{array}$$

Since $90 - 67 = 23$, an additional 23 days in June are needed, giving June 23.

(b) November 7 is day 311. Add 90 days to get the following.

$$\begin{array}{r} 311 \\ +\ \ 90 \\ \hline 401 \end{array}$$

Since there are only 365 days in a year, subtract 365.

$$\begin{array}{r} 401 \\ -\ 365 \\ \hline 36 \quad \text{Day of the following year} \end{array}$$

Day 36 of the following year is February 5, so that 90 days from November 7 is February 5 of the following year.

Objective

3   *Find Exact and Ordinary Interest.*   In the formula for simple interest, time is always measured in years or parts of years. In the examples of the previous section, time was in months, with *T* in the formula $I = PRT$ written as follows.

$$T = \frac{\text{Given number of months}}{12}$$

Things are not so simple when the loan is given in days. There are two common methods for calculating simple interest for a given number of days: **exact interest** and **ordinary** (or **banker's interest**).

In the formula $I = PRT$, the fraction for time is found as follows.

Exact interest	$T = \dfrac{\text{Exact number of days in the loan}}{365}$
Ordinary or banker's interest	$T = \dfrac{\text{Exact number of days in the loan}}{360}$

Government agencies and the Federal Reserve Bank use exact interest, as do many credit unions and banks. However, there are still many banks that use ordinary interest for loans. Exact interest is used for savings accounts. Ordinary interest may have been used originally because it was easier to calculate than exact interest. With the modern use of calculators and computers, however, ordinary interest is probably used today out of tradition and because it produces a *greater dollar amount* of interest than does exact interest, as shown in the next example.

EXAMPLE 4 Finding Exact and Ordinary Interest

Alameda Printing borrowed $35,300 on May 12. The loan, at an interest rate of 12%, is due on August 27. Find the interest on the loan using (a) exact interest and (b) ordinary interest.

Solution Use Table 12.1 or calculate the number of days in each month to find that there are 107 days from May 12 to August 27. In both situations, $P = \$35,300$, $R = 0.12$, and the loan is for 107 days. The only difference between the two situations is the number of days in the denominator of the fraction for time. *Exact interest* uses 365 days, and *ordinary interest* uses 360 days.

(a) Exact Interest

$$I = PRT$$

$$I = \$35,300 \times 0.12 \times \frac{107}{365}$$

$$I = \$1241.79 \qquad \text{Rounded}$$

(b) Ordinary Interest

$$I = PRT$$

$$I = \$35,300 \times 0.12 \times \frac{107}{\mathbf{360}}$$

$$I = \$1259.03 \qquad \textbf{Rounded}$$

The difference between the two is $1259.03 - \$1241.79$ or $17.24. Ordinary interest results in an additional $17.24 in interest.

NOTE If P and R are the same, more interest is generated using ordinary interest than using exact interest.

The formula from **Sections 12.1** and **12.2** are repeated here for your convenience.

Interest $I = PRT$

Principal $P = \dfrac{I}{RT}$ *T* is in years.

Rate $R = \dfrac{I}{PT}$

Time *T* (in years) $T = \dfrac{I}{PR}$

Time *T* (in months) $T = \dfrac{I}{PR} \times 12$ T is a fraction of a year.

Time *T* (in days) $T = \dfrac{I}{PR} \times 360$ Use 360 days for banker's (ordinary) interest.

Time *T* (in days) $T = \dfrac{I}{PR} \times 365$ Use 365 days for exact interest.

NOTE   Throughout the balance of this book, assume ordinary (or banker's) interest unless stated otherwise.

12.2	**Exercises**

Find the exact number of days from the first date to the second. (In Exercises 5–6, assume that the second month given is in the following year.)

1. May 7 to December 2   **2.** April 24 to July 7

3. October 27 to December 2   **4.** July 12 to October 29

5. September 2 to March 17   **6.** July 24 to March 30

Find the date that is the indicated number of days from the given date.

7. 120 days from June 14   **8.** 45 days from July 28

9. 30 days from February 8   **10.** 90 days from November 18

11. 120 days from December 12   **12.** 150 days from November 1

Find the amount of ordinary interest you would pay for each of the following. Round to the nearest cent.

13. $18,000 at 10% for 90 days   **14.** $11,400 at $8\frac{1}{4}$% for 200 days

15. $3250 at 12% for 150 days   **16.** $8620 at 11.25% for 120 days

17. A loan of $8500 at 9.5% made on June 3 and due October 31

18. A loan of $6800 at 12% made on June 20 and due December 26

19. A loan of $1520 at 10% made on February 27 and due August 5

20. A loan of $3600 at 11% made on December 2 and due February 20

Find the exact interest for each of the following. Round to the nearest cent.

21. $3800 at 10% for 100 days   **22.** $6900 at 8% for 200 days

23. $7400 at 9.5% for 60 days   **24.** $5000 at 8% for 90 days

25. A loan of $6500 at 7% made on July 12 and due on October 12

26. A loan of $8120 at 9% made on January 30 and due May 20

27. A loan of $2050 at 12% made on June 24 and due February 12 of the next year

28. A loan of $14,000 at 8% made on August 12 and due March 19 of the next year

29. Explain the difference between exact and ordinary interest. (See Objective 3.)

30. As a borrower, would you prefer exact or ordinary interest? Why? (See Objective 3.)

Solve the following application problems using exact interest. Round to the nearest cent.

31. **IRS PENALTY**   Fred Thomas accidentally paid $1800 in employee taxes 40 days late. Unbelievably, the Internal Revenue Service charged a penalty at a rate of 60% per year. Find the penalty.

32. **MISSED TAX PAYMENT**   Bella Steinem missed an income tax payment. The payment was due June 15 and was paid September 7. The penalty was 14% simple interest on the unpaid tax of $4600. Find the penalty.

33. **PLAYGROUND EQUIPMENT**   The manager of a franchised kindergarten borrowed $46,800 on October 30 at 12% simple interest. Find the interest due on March 15.

34. **GRAPHIC ARTS**   Ben Peterson borrowed $38,500 on November 7 for a digital printer and some other equipment. He agreed to repay the 10.5% rate loan on March 30 of the following year. Find the interest.

Solve the following application problems using ordinary interest. Round to the nearest cent.

35. **PHOTOGRAPHY STUDIO**   Nolan Brinkman borrowed $48,000 on June 10 to open a photography studio. Given a rate of $12\frac{1}{4}\%$, find the interest due on Christmas (December 25).

36. **WESTERN WEAR**   On May 18, the Wilson Dude Ranch bought a supply of assorted Western wear and saddles for $11,270. The ranch agreed to pay for it on August 30, with $10\frac{1}{2}\%$ interest. Find the interest owed.

37. **PLUMBING**   Suarez Plumbing can borrow $1,250,000 for 300 days at $10\frac{1}{2}\%$ interest. A few years ago when interest rates were low, the same loan would have had an interest rate of $8\frac{3}{4}\%$. Find the difference in the interest charges.

38. **CONSTRUCTION IN MEXICO**   A construction company in Mexico City borrows 300,000 pesos for 90 days at an interest rate of 18%. The same loan would have been at a rate of 35% several years ago. Find the difference in the interest charges based on the two rates.

In Exercises 39–42 find the (a) exact interest and (b) ordinary interest for the following, rounded to the nearest cent. Then (c) find the amount by which the ordinary interest is larger.

39. $18,000 at 9% for 120 days

40. $75,000 at 11% for 120 days

41. $145,000 at $9\frac{1}{2}\%$ for 240 days

42. $250,000 at $12\frac{1}{8}\%$ for 180 days

Solve the following application problems. Round to the nearest cent.

43. **FIRE TRUCK**   Bergen County borrows $385,000 to purchase a new pumper. The loan will be repaid once property taxes are paid for the year, or in 200 days, at a rate of 8.5%. How much more interest would it be required to pay using ordinary interest compared to exact interest?

44. **SKI EQUIPMENT**   Ski Mountain Ltd. borrows $120,000 for extra inventory for the coming ski season. The owners expect to repay the loan after the ski season is over, in 140 days, at a rate of $10\frac{1}{2}\%$. How much more would the firm pay using ordinary interest compared to exact interest?

45. **NEW TRUCKS**   Blaine Trucking wishes to borrow $880,000 for new trucks on September 20 and plans to pay off the loan on May 1 of the following year. State Bank will lend it the funds at 9% based on exact interest calculations. First Bank will lend it the funds at $8\frac{7}{8}\%$ interest based on ordinary interest calculations. Which bank is asking for less interest? How much less?

46. **INTERNATIONAL CONSTRUCTION**   A Canadian construction firm needs to borrow an additional $3,500,000 for 150 days to build a bridge linking Mexico to the United States. National Bank will lend it the funds at $10\frac{1}{2}\%$ simple interest based on exact interest calculations, and Laredo Bank will lend it the funds at $10\frac{5}{8}\%$ simple interest based on ordinary interest calculations. Which bank is asking for less interest? How much less?

12.3   Maturity Value

OBJECTIVES

1 *Find maturity value.*
2 *Find principal if given maturity value, time, and rate.*
3 *Find rate if given principal, maturity value, and time.*
4 *Find time if given maturity value, principal, and rate.*

Suppose you borrow $15,000 at $9\frac{1}{2}\%$ and must pay the loan off in 9 months.

$$\text{Interest} = \text{PRT}$$
$$= \$15,000 \times 0.095 \times \frac{9}{12} = \$1068.75$$

However, the amount you must repay includes the loan amount (principal) plus interest. The sum of these two values is called the **maturity value**. This is the amount that must be paid on the **maturity date** of the loan.

Objective

1 *Find Maturity Value.*   The maturity value is also sometimes called the **future value**, since it is the value of the loan including interest at a specific future date. The principal amount received by the borrower when the loan is made is called the **present value**. Find the maturity value of the loan above that had interest of $1068.75.

$$\text{M} = \text{P} + \text{I}$$
$$\text{Maturity value} = \text{Principal} + \text{Interest}$$
$$= \$15,000 + \$1068.75$$
$$= \$16,068.75$$

The borrower must pay a maturity value of $16,068.75 on the maturity date of the loan. Not doing so will result in a penalty to the borrower.

NOTE   The maturity value of a loan always exceeds the principal (the original loan amount) since maturity value is principal *plus* interest.

EXAMPLE **1** **Finding Interest and Maturity Value**

Jim Wilcox would like to remodel his gift kiosk at the mall. To remodel the kiosk, he borrows $7200 for 21 months at 9.25% interest. Find the interest due on the loan and the maturity value.

Solution Interest due is found using $I = PRT$, where T is in years $\left(21 \text{ months} = \frac{21}{12} \text{ years}\right)$.

$$I = PRT$$

$$= \$7200 \times 0.0925 \times \frac{21}{12} = \$1165.50$$

Find the maturity value using $M = P + I$, where $P = \$7200$ and $I = \$1165.50$.

$$M = P + I$$

$$= \$7200 + \$1165.50 = \$8365.50$$

The formula for maturity value, $M = P + I$, can be written in a different way if I is replaced with PRT (since $I = PRT$).

$$M = P + I$$

$$= P + PRT \qquad \text{Substitute } PRT \text{ for } I.$$

$$= P(1 + RT) \qquad \text{Use the distributive property.}$$

Therefore, the maturity value M, of a principal of P dollars, at a rate of interest R, for T years can be written in either of the following forms.

$$M = P + I \qquad \text{or} \qquad M = P(1 + RT)$$

NOTE Do not round off values too soon when using a formula to do interest rate problems. Round *after* finding the final value.

EXAMPLE **2** **Finding Maturity Value**

Use the formula $M = P(1 + RT)$ to find the maturity value for a loan of $6000 for 120 days at 9% interest.

Solution Substitute $6000 for P, 9% or 0.09 for R, and $\frac{120}{360}$ for T $\left(\text{since 120 days is } \frac{120}{360} \text{ of a year}\right)$. The maturity value is as follows.

$$M = P(1 + RT)$$

$$= \$6000 \times \left[1 + \left(0.09 \times \frac{120}{360}\right)\right]$$

NOTE Parentheses were placed around $0.09 \times \frac{120}{360}$ to emphasize that these numbers are multiplied as a first step.

$$M = \$6000 \times (1 + 0.03)$$

$$= \$6000 \times 1.03$$

$$= \$6180$$

The interest can be found by subtracting the principal from the maturity value.

$$I = \$6180 - \$6000 = \$180$$

The calculator solution to this example uses parentheses on the calculator in place of the brackets.

$$6000 \boxed{\times} \boxed{(} 1 \boxed{+} 0.09 \boxed{\times} 120 \boxed{\div} 360 \boxed{)} \boxed{=} 6180$$

Subtract the principal from \$6180 to obtain the interest.

$$6180 \boxed{-} 6000 \boxed{=} 180$$

Objective

2 *Find Principal If Given Maturity Value, Time, and Rate.* Sometimes the maturity value is given, and either the principal, rate, or time must be found. For example, given the maturity value, rate, and time, find principal as follows.

$$M = P(1 + RT)$$

$$\frac{M}{(1 + RT)} = \frac{P(1 + RT)}{(1 + RT)} \qquad \text{Divide both sides by } (1 + RT).$$

$$\frac{M}{(1 + RT)} = \frac{P\cancel{(1 + RT)}}{\cancel{(1 + RT)}} \qquad \text{Divide out common factors.}$$

$$\boxed{\frac{M}{1 + RT} = P \qquad \text{or} \qquad P = \frac{M}{1 + RT}}$$

Principal is also called the *present value* of the loan.

EXAMPLE **3** **Finding Principal Given Time, Rate, and Maturity Value**

Find the principal that would produce a maturity value of \$15,300 in 4 months at 6% interest.

Solution Use the formula above and substitute \$15,300 for M, 0.06 for R, and $\frac{4}{12}$ for T.

$$P = \frac{M}{1 + RT}$$

$$= \frac{\$15,300}{1 + \left(0.06 \times \frac{4}{12}\right)}$$

As shown by the parentheses, first multiply 0.06 and $\frac{4}{12}$, and then add 1.

$$P = \frac{\$15,300}{1 + 0.02}$$

$$= \frac{\$15,300}{1.02}$$

$$= \$15,000$$

The principal is \$15,000 and the interest is \$15,300 − \$15,000 = \$300.

The calculator solution to Example 3 uses parentheses for the entire denominator.

$$15300 \boxed{\div} \boxed{(} 1 \boxed{+} 0.06 \boxed{\times} 4 \boxed{\div} 12 \boxed{)} \boxed{=} 15000$$

Objective

3   *Find Rate If Given Principal, Maturity Value, and Time.*   If principal, maturity value, and time are given, rate can be found as follows.

$$M = P(1 + RT)$$

$$M = P + PRT \qquad \text{Use the distributive property.}$$

$$M - P = PRT \qquad \text{Subtract } P \text{ from both sides.}$$

$$\frac{M - P}{PT} = \frac{\cancel{P}R\cancel{T}}{\cancel{P}\cancel{T}} \qquad \text{Divide both sides by } PT.$$

$$\boxed{\frac{M - P}{PT} = R \qquad \text{or} \qquad R = \frac{M - P}{PT}}$$

EXAMPLE **4**   **Finding Rate Given Principal, Maturity Value, and Time**

Lin Pao invests a principal of $14,400 and receives a maturity value of $15,080 in 200 days. Find the interest rate.

Solution   Use the formula above and substitute values.

$$R = \frac{M - P}{PT}$$

$$= \frac{\$15{,}080 - \$14{,}400}{\$14{,}400 \times \frac{200}{360}}$$

$$= 0.085 \qquad \text{or} \qquad 8.5\%$$

Scientific Calculator Approach

The calculator solution to Example 4 uses parentheses for the numerator ($15,080 − $14,400) and for the denominator $\left(\$14{,}400 \times \frac{200}{360}\right)$.

| (| 15080 | − | 14400 |) | ÷ | (| 14400 | × | 200 | ÷ | 360 |) | = | 0.085 |

Notice that maturity value minus principal $(M - P)$ is interest I. Therefore,

$$R = \frac{M - P}{PT} = \frac{I}{PT}$$

and Example 4 can be solved using this formula.

$$\text{Interest} = \$15{,}080 - \$14{,}400 = \$680$$

$$R = \frac{I}{PT}$$

$$= \frac{\$680}{\$14{,}400 \times \frac{200}{360}}$$

$$= 0.085 \qquad \text{or} \qquad 8.5\%$$

Objective

4 *Find Time If Given Maturity Value, Principal, and Rate.* Given maturity value, principal, and rate, time can be found as follows.

$$M = P(1 + RT)$$

$$M = P + PRT \qquad \text{Use the distributive property.}$$

$$M - P = PRT \qquad \text{Subtract } P \text{ from both sides.}$$

$$\frac{M - P}{PR} = \frac{\cancel{P}\cancel{R}T}{\cancel{P}\cancel{R}} \qquad \text{Divide both sides by } PR.$$

$$\frac{M - P}{PR} = T \text{ (in years)} \qquad \text{or} \qquad T = \frac{M - P}{PR}$$

This gives a value for time T in *years*. To convert to *days* multiply by 360. For example, $\frac{1}{2}$ of a year is $\frac{1}{2} \times 360 = 180$ days.

$$T \text{ (in days)} = \frac{M - P}{PR} \times 360$$

Since $I = M - P$, this is the same as

$$T \text{ (in days)} = \frac{I}{PR} \times 360$$

EXAMPLE 5 **Finding the Time in Days**

Mustang Signs borrowed $18,250 at $10\frac{1}{8}\%$ interest for the construction of two new signs and agreed to repay $19,687.19. Find the time in days and round to the nearest day if necessary.

Solution Use the formula above and substitute values.

$$T = \frac{M - P}{PR} \times 360$$

$$= \frac{\$19,687.19 - \$18,250}{\$18,250 \times 0.10125} \times 360$$

$$= \frac{1437.19}{1847.81} \times 360$$

$$= 280 \text{ days} \qquad\qquad \text{Rounded}$$

Scientific
Calculator
Approach

The calculator solution to Example 5 uses parentheses to set off both the numerator and the denominator.

| (| 19687.19 | − | 18250 |) | ÷ | (| 18250 | × | 0.10125 |) | × | 360 | = | 280 |

The formulas from Section 12.3 are repeated here for your convenience.

Interest	$I = PRT$
Maturity Value	$M = P(1 + RT)$
Principal	$P = \dfrac{I}{RT} = \dfrac{M - P}{RT} = \dfrac{M}{1 + RT}$
Rate	$R = \dfrac{I}{PT} = \dfrac{M - P}{PT}$
Time (in years)	$T = \dfrac{I}{PR} = \dfrac{M - P}{PR}$
Time (in days)	$T = \dfrac{I}{PR} \times 360 = \dfrac{M - P}{PR} \times 360$

12.3	**Exercises**

Find the interest and the maturity value for the following loans. Round to the nearest cent.

1. $8500 at 10% for 9 months
2. $12,200 at $9\frac{1}{2}$% for 10 months
3. $5800 at 8.5% for 140 days
4. $10,800 at $7\frac{3}{4}$% for 220 days
5. $8640 at 10% for $1\frac{1}{4}$ years
6. $34,600 at 13% for $1\frac{1}{2}$ years

Complete this chart. Round money to the nearest cent, rate to the nearest tenth of a percent, and time to the nearest day.

	Principal	Interest	Rate	Time in Days	Maturity Value
7.	$4800	_____	10%	100	_____
8.	$7500	_____	12%	120	_____
9.	$8600	$133.78	8%	_____	_____
10.	$7400	$292.92	$9\frac{1}{2}$%	_____	_____
11.	$14,000	$490	_____	120	_____
12.	$12,800	$544	_____	180	_____
13.	_____	_____	$7\frac{7}{8}$%	200	$17,117.50
14.	_____	_____	$10\frac{1}{2}$%	240	$30,602
15.	_____	$666	9%	_____	$15,466
16.	_____	$8086.05	9.1%	_____	$89,086.05
17.	$1800	_____	14%	_____	$1926
18.	$11,250	_____	12.8%	_____	$11,710
19.	_____	$3272.92	_____	185	$45,732.36
20.	_____	$1963.33	_____	76	$76,963.33

Solve the following application problems. Round to the nearest cent.

21. **HOT-TUB ENCLOSURE** José Garcia borrowed $12,000 for 140 days at $10\frac{1}{2}\%$ to add a hot tub and enclosure to his home. Find the interest and the maturity value.

22. **FUNERAL EXPENSES** Jessica Singleton's grandfather had been ill for several years, so everything he owned was used for medical expenses. At his death, Singleton had to borrow $12,000 for 120 days at 11% to pay for the balance of her grandfather's funeral and for related attorney expenses and court costs. Find the interest and maturity value on the loan.

23. **WEDDING COSTS** Joey Patrick and Lori Hooten borrowed $12,400 at $10\frac{5}{8}\%$ interest for wedding expenses and a honeymoon to Hawaii. Given that they must repay $12,912.36, find the time in days and the amount of interest. Round to the nearest day.

24. **BOAT DEALERSHIP** James Wilson borrows $845,000 at 9% interest to expand his inventory of fishing and pleasure boats. He agrees to repay $904,150 on the maturity date of the loan. Find the amount of interest paid and time in days.

25. **PERSONAL TRAINER** James Wicker borrowed $12,000 for equipment so that he could do some of his personal training work in his garage. He agreed to repay $13,200 after 300 days. Find the amount of interest and the interest rate.

26. **BURGLAR ALARMS** Belinda Tate received a contract to install burglar alarms in 7 houses and needed to borrow $28,000 for related equipment and supplies. Since she used a certificate of deposit for collateral for the loan, she was required to repay only $29,166.67 in 250 days. Find the amount of interest and the interest rate rounded to the nearest tenth of a percent.

27. **AUTO MECHANIC** Mona Melton likes to work on cars. She signs a simple interest note with a maturity value of $65,000 at 11.5% for 300 days to open a small auto repair shop. Find the principal and the interest.

28. **SETTLING A LAWSUIT** Jill Phan borrowed some money to settle a lawsuit against her restaurant—a customer slipped on a puddle of water from the icemaker and fell. The 180-day loan was at 9% interest and Phan must repay $44,412.50. Find the principal and the interest.

 29. List the two basic equations from which all of the other equations in this section can be derived. Use the two equations to derive the equation for time given maturity value, principal, and rate. (See Objectives 1 and 3.)

 30. Using $I = PRT$ and $M = P + I$, explain the steps to derive the equation for principal given maturity value, rate, and time. (See Objective 2.)

| 12.4 | **Inflation and the Time Value of Money** |

OBJECTIVES

1 *Define inflation and the consumer price index.*

2 *Understand the time value of money.*

3 *Define present value and future value.*

4 *Calculate present and future values using simple interest.*

5 *Find present value for a given maturity value.*

6 *Find present value after a loan is made.*

Believe it or not, in 1960 a family of four would have done well with an income of only $500 per month. Today, it costs $500 or more a month just to rent a low-end apartment or house. Five hundred dollars will not buy nearly as much today as it did in 1960. Why? The answer is inflation.

Think about the last raise you or someone you know received. Was it enough to cover the increased costs associated with inflation? It doesn't mean much if your raise is 2% in a year when prices of the things you buy go up by, say, 4.3%. Even though inflation usually increases prices slightly in any one year, in the long run it has a very large effect on purchasing power.

Objective

1 *Define Inflation and the Consumer Price Index.* **Inflation** is the rise in the overall price of goods and services. As shown in the following bar graph, food costs sometimes go up sharply—a sign of inflation.

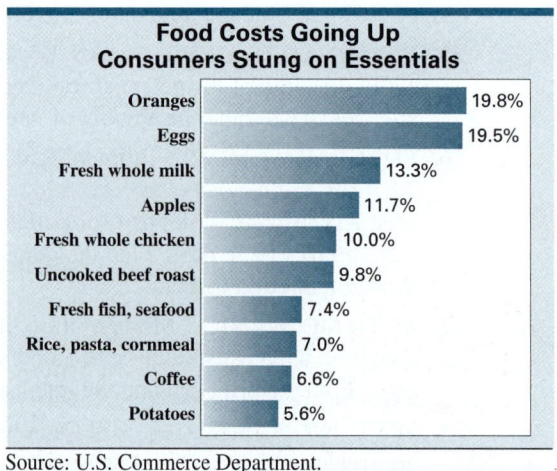

Food Costs Going Up
Consumers Stung on Essentials

Oranges	19.8%
Eggs	19.5%
Fresh whole milk	13.3%
Apples	11.7%
Fresh whole chicken	10.0%
Uncooked beef roast	9.8%
Fresh fish, seafood	7.4%
Rice, pasta, cornmeal	7.0%
Coffee	6.6%
Potatoes	5.6%

Source: U.S. Commerce Department.

The **consumer price index (CPI)** is calculated by the government annually in the United States and is often referred to as the "cost-of-living index." Other countries have similar indexes. The CPI can be used to track inflation. It measures the average change in prices from one year to the next for a common bundle of goods and services bought by the average consumer on a regular basis. Figure 12.2 shows yearly inflation for the past 28 years. Note that inflation was very high in 1980—prices were increasing very rapidly. However, inflation has continued to decrease and is at a record low during the financial crisis that began in 2008.

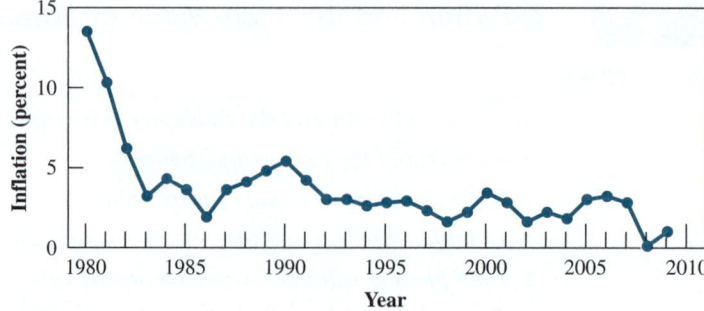

Annual Inflation Rate
Based on Consumer Price Index

Figure 12.2
Source: U.S. Bureau of Census.

> **EXAMPLE** **1** **Estimating the Effect of Inflation**
>
> Inflation from one year to the next was 4.8% as measured by the CPI. (a) Find the effect of the increase on a family with an annual income and budget of $239,600 (after taxes). (b) What is the overall effect if the family receives only a 2% after-tax increase in pay for the year?
>
> **Solution**
>
> **(a)** First, estimate the increase in the costs of the goods and services that the family buys. Then find the total cost of buying those items next year.
>
> $$\text{Increase in costs} = 0.048 \times \$39{,}600 = \$1900.80$$
> $$\text{Cost of goods and services next year} = \$39{,}600 + \$1900.80 = \$41{,}500.80$$
>
> **(b)** Find the increase in income, then find the new income.
>
> $$\text{After-tax increase in income} = 0.02 \times \$39{,}600 = \$792$$
> $$\text{Family's new after-tax income} = \$39{,}600 + \$792 = \$40{,}392$$
>
> So the amount the family has to spend increases from $39,600 to $40,392, but an estimate of the cost of the goods and services the family buys increases from $39,600 to $41,500.80. The loss in purchasing power is the difference between the two numbers.
>
> $$\text{Loss of purchasing power} = \$41{,}500.80 - \$40{,}392 = \$1108.80$$
>
> The family will have to buy less or go into debt in order to buy the same goods and services.
>
> ■

Inflation can erode people's purchasing power *even as their annual salaries are increasing*. Retired people are particularly concerned with inflation since they must live off Social Security and the assets they have accumulated during their lifetime. Some retired people do not have ways of increasing their income to keep pace with inflation and therefore must lower their standards of living substantially during their retirement. Other retired people have investments such as stocks that help them stay ahead of inflation. Newspaper headlines such as those below cause concern to elderly people on fixed incomes.

High Cost of Inflation

The figures assume a 3.5% average annual rate of inflation.

	A new car	A new house	Heart surgery	A vacation
Today	$26,500	$183,200	$97,200	$1900/person
20 years from now	$52,729	$364,529	$193,407	$3780/person

The federal government works to keep inflation at moderate levels since high inflation can be so harmful. When the economy becomes overheated and inflationary pressures increase, the Federal Reserve nudges interest rates upward. This reduces borrowing slightly, slows the economy, and reduces inflationary pressures. Conversely, if inflation is low and the economy is growing very slowly or not at all, the Federal Reserve nudges interest rates downward, thereby stimulating the economy and creating more jobs. The Federal Reserve has the very difficult task of maintaining a growing and healthy economy with low levels of inflation.

> **NOTE** Inflation rates in the United States have generally been low since 1990. However, some experts believe that the expenditures related to the big bailout plans by many governments in 2008–2009 will cause inflation to increase sharply during 2010–2012. Watch for inflation—it affects you.

Objective

2 *Understand the Time Value of Money.* Would you leave $1000 on deposit with your bank for 2 years (in a savings account) and expect only $1000 back when the money is returned? Probably not! You would expect interest in addition to the return of your principal. The **time value of money** is the idea that the loaning of money to someone or to a firm has value, and that value is typically repaid by returning interest in addition to principal.

The time value of money is an important concept in modern society. Regular investments of relatively small sums of money can result in large sums at later dates. For example, how would you like to turn $54,000 into over $150,000? Simply invest $150 per month for 30 years, say from age 30 to age 60, at 6% interest compounded monthly. This topic is discussed in **Chapters 14** and **15**.

Application of the time value of money will help you send your children to college, purchase a home, and prepare for your own retirement. The time value of money is equally important to firms that invest to build factories, develop new technologies, or need capital for many other reasons.

Objective

3 *Define Present Value and Future Value.* The principal amount that must be invested today to produce a given future amount is called the **present value**. The amount that this sum grows to at some future date is called the **future value**. We have been calculating the future value in the earlier sections of this chapter when we were calculating the maturity amount.

$$\text{Future value} = M = P(1 + RT)$$

We have also been calculating the present value in the earlier sections of this chapter when we were calculating the principal with the following form of the above equation.

$$\text{Present value} = P = \frac{M}{(1 + RT)}$$

Objective

4 *Calculate Present and Future Values Using Simple Interest.*

EXAMPLE 2 **Finding Future Value**

Joan Waters loans part of her inheritance of $28,500 to her aunt at $6\frac{1}{2}\%$ simple interest on May 30. Find the future value of this amount on February 4 of the following year. Round to the nearest cent.

Solution First find the number of days from May 30 to February 4 by finding the number of days from May 30 to the end of the year. Then find the number of days from the beginning of the year to February 4.

The end of the year is day	365
May 30 is day	− 150
May 30 to end of year	215

February 4 is day 35 of the next year. The total number of days is $215 + 35 = 250$ days. Now use the formula for the maturity value (future value) using simple interest.

$$M = P(1 + RT)$$
$$= \$28,500 \left(1 + 0.065 \times \frac{250}{360}\right)$$
$$= \$29,786.46 \qquad \text{Rounded}$$

The future value on February 4 is $29,786.46.

EXAMPLE 3   Finding Present Value

KLTV Television plans to spend $280,000 for a new satellite dish and associated electronic equipment in 18 months. What present value must be invested today at 6% simple interest so that the firm will have the needed future value?

Solution   Use the following form of the simple interest formula.

$$P = \frac{M}{(1 + RT)}$$
$$= \frac{\$280,000}{\left(1 + 0.06 \times \frac{18}{12}\right)}$$
$$= \frac{\$280,000}{(1 + 0.09)}$$
$$= \frac{\$280,000}{1.09}$$
$$= \$256,880.73$$

KLTV Television must invest a present value of $256,880.73 today at 6% simple interest in order to have a future value of $280,000 in 18 months.

 **Scientific Calculator Approach**

For the calculator solution to Example 3, the denominator $\left(1 + 0.06 \times \frac{18}{12}\right)$ should be considered a single number. Set it apart using parentheses.

$$280000 \;\boxed{\div}\; \boxed{(} \; 1 \; \boxed{+} \; .06 \; \boxed{\times} \; 18 \; \boxed{\div} \; 12 \; \boxed{)} \; \boxed{=} \; 256880.73$$

Objective

5   *Find Present Value for a Given Maturity Value.*   Example 3 showed how to find the present value of an amount needed at a specific future date. Sometimes a company needs cash, so it sells a loan it has made rather than continuing to receive payments. Notes are sold for their present value on the date sold. The amount they are sold for depends on the interest rate on the date sold. The market interest rate often differs from the interest rate on the original note.

Finding the Present Value of a Loan

Step 1 Find the future value (maturity value) of the loan using the original terms of the loan.

Step 2 Find the present value of this amount using the market interest rate and the time remaining until maturity.

EXAMPLE 4 **Finding Present Value of a Loan**

Joplin Laugherty borrowed $365,000 for 10 months from Bank USA at 9% simple interest to remodel the lobby of his seafood restaurant, Laugherty's. Economic data released later the same day indicate that the economy in the area is slowing. Bank management decides the bank needs cash and immediately sells the loan to an investment company. Managers at the investment company also see that the economy is slowing and require a higher interest rate on the loan of 12%, since the risk of repayment has increased. Find (**a**) the present value received by the bank and (**b**) the loss the bank took on the loan.

Solution   First, find the maturity value of the loan to Laugherty's using the terms of the loan.

$$M = P(1 + RT)$$
$$= \$365,000\left(1 + 0.09 \times \frac{10}{12}\right)$$
$$= \$392,375$$

The investment company is buying the right to receive $392,375 from Laugherty's in 10 months. Find the present value using the market rate of 12%.

$$P = \frac{M}{1 + RT}$$
$$= \frac{\$392,375}{1 + 0.12 \times \frac{10}{12}}$$
$$= \frac{\$392,375}{1 + 0.1}$$
$$= \frac{\$392,375}{1.1}$$
$$= \$356,704.55 \qquad \text{Rounded}$$

Here are the numbers:

$$\text{Amount loaned by bank} = \$365,000$$
$$\text{Maturity value that must be paid} = \$392,375$$
$$\text{Amount bank receives for loan} = \$356,704.55$$

The loss the bank took is found as follows.

$$\text{Loss to bank} = \$365,000 - \$356,704.55 = \$8295.45$$

Normally, a bank would not make a loan and then sell it immediately at a loss. However, in this case the bank needed the cash and was forced to sell the loan at a loss.

NOTE   In Example 4, the money was lent to the restaurant owner at 9% simple interest. However, since the slowing economy increased the risk of a default on the loan, the market interest rate went up to 12%. If the interest rate had remained at 9%, the bank would not have lost any money when selling the loan.

 Scientific Calculator Approach

The calculator solution to Example 4 follows.

365000 $\times$ (1 + 0.09 $\times$ 10 $\div$ 12) = 392375

392375 $\div$ (1 + 0.12 $\times$ 10 $\div$ 12) = 356704.55

Objective

6 *Find Present Value after a Loan Is Made.* Sometimes the present value of a loan is needed when the amount currently owed is not known. In that event, you must still find the maturity value of the loan and then find the present value of this amount on the date the loan is to be sold using the market interest rate at that time.

EXAMPLE **5** **Finding Present Value on a Date after Loan Is Made**

An Argentinean made a loan of $6500 to a business partner on May 13 for 90 days. The interest rate on the loan is 8%. After the loan is made, the general level of interest rates in Argentina rises quickly to 12%. Find the present value of the loan on June 26.

Solution First find the maturity value of the loan. The principal is $6500, the rate is 8%, and the time is 90 days, or $\frac{90}{360}$ year.

$$M = P(1 + RT)$$

$$= \$6500\left[1 + \left(0.08 \times \frac{90}{360}\right)\right]$$

$$= \$6500(1 + 0.02)$$

$$= \$6630$$

The loan was made on May 13, for 90 days. The loan is due on August 11. As shown in Figure 12.3, the number of days from June 26 (the day for which the present value is desired) to August 11 is as follows.

4	Days in June
31	Days in July
+ 11	Days in August
46	Total days

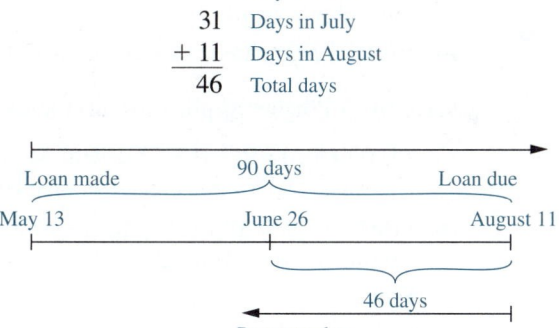

Figure 12.3

The total number of days could also be found by using Table 12.1.

To find the present value 46 days before the loan is paid off, use the formula for present value, with $M = \$6630$, $R = 12\%$, and $T = \frac{46}{360}$ year.

$$P = \frac{M}{1 + RT}$$

$$= \frac{\$6630}{1 + \left(0.12 \times \frac{46}{360}\right)}$$

$$= \$6529.88 \qquad \text{Rounded}$$

The businessman should be willing to accept $6529.88 on June 26 in full payment of the loan, both principal and interest. This amount would grow to $6630 at 12% by August 11.

NOTE Since $\frac{46}{360}$ in the example above does not produce a terminating decimal, it is important that it not be rounded at an intermediate step. Wait and round the final answer.

| **12.4** | **Exercises** |

In the following problems, find the present value or future value, as indicated, to the nearest cent.

	Present Value	Interest Rate	Time	Future Value
1.	$4800	9%	110 days	_____
2.	$8000	$8\frac{1}{2}\%$	140 days	_____
3.	$10,500	11%	10 months	_____
4.	$6800	$12\frac{1}{2}\%$	9 months	_____
5.	$4100	$8\frac{3}{8}\%$	$1\frac{1}{4}$ years	_____
6.	$7400	$10\frac{1}{4}\%$	$1\frac{1}{2}$ years	_____
7.	_____	6%	100 days	$2440.00
8.	_____	9%	180 days	$1985.50
9.	_____	$11\frac{1}{8}\%$	6 months	$8867.25
10.	_____	12%	11 months	$10,323.00
11.	_____	$5\frac{7}{8}\%$	$1\frac{1}{8}$ years	$9275.02
12.	_____	$7\frac{1}{4}\%$	$1\frac{1}{2}$ years	$7096.00

13. Explain the difference between the interest rate on a loan and the time value of money. (See Objective 4.)

14. Explain the meaning of inflation and the CPI. (See Objective 1.)

Solve the following application problems. Round to the nearest cent.

15. **AUTO DEALERSHIPS** General Motors loaned one of its auto dealers $6,500,000 on August 4 at $9\frac{1}{2}\%$ simple interest. Find the future value as of December 31.

16. **LOAN TO A SUPPLIER** Karl's Kameras loaned a supplier $28,300 on July 14 at 8% simple interest. Find the future value of the loan on March 15 of the following year.

17. **BANK OPERATIONS** Chase Bank loaned a large Canadian firm $8.5 million (U.S.) at $9\frac{1}{2}\%$ simple interest for 90 days and simultaneously paid $6\frac{3}{4}\%$ interest for the same funds to its depositors. Find the difference between the interest earned by Chase Bank and the interest paid to the depositors.

18. **FINANCE COMPANY** A finance company borrows $250,000 at $9\frac{1}{2}\%$ interest per year. It lends the money to many different small borrowers with poor credit history at $16\frac{1}{2}\%$ per year. Find the difference in interest earned and interest paid out assuming all loans are for 1 year.

19. **CREDIT RISK** Ben Aflack made a loan of $80,000 at 8% for 200 days. Due to severe injuries received in a car accident on the same day the loan was made, Aflack immediately had to sell the loan to an investor. The investor believes the credit risk of the borrower is high and requires 12% simple interest. Find the present value of the loan.

20. **PRESENT VALUE** Find the present value, on the date it was made, of a loan of $14,700 at 12% for 210 days if money is worth 10%.

21. **PRESENT VALUE** A loan of $6980 was made on May 24, for 214 days, at 11%. Find the present value of the loan on July 9, if the time value of money is 10%.

22. **PRESENT VALUE** On February 24, an 89-day loan of $980 at 12% is made. Find the present value of the loan on March 10, if the time value of money is 10%.

23. **COLLEGE EXPENSES** Worried about college expenses, Lupe Martinez sold a diamond ring she had inherited for $3200 and invested the funds at $4\frac{3}{4}\%$ simple interest for 14 months. Find the future value.

24. **LAWSUIT AWARD** A marketing company misrepresented a product, was sued by a plaintiff, and the judge awarded the plaintiff $280,000. The plaintiff received this amount on July 17 and deposited it in an account earning 3.5% simple interest on the same day. Find the future value on November 30.

25. **INFLATION AND PURCHASING POWER** A family with a spending budget of $26,500 receives an increase in wages of 3% in a year in which inflation was 4.5%. Find the net gain or loss in its purchasing power, ignoring taxes.

26. **GAIN IN PURCHASING POWER** Ben Thomas spends $34,300 and receives a 6% raise in a year in which inflation was 2.5%. Ignoring taxes, find the net gain in his purchasing power.

Three different bids are given in each of the following two exercises. For each, find the lowest bid using the concept of present value. Assume that the time value of money is 10%.

27. $16,800 today, $17,400 in 150 days, $18,000 in 210 days

28. $41,250 today, $41,102 in 210 days, $45,000 in 300 days

29. Describe some possible effects of inflation on people earning minimum wage.

30. What effects can you foresee of a rapid increase in inflation from 6% to 10%?

CHAPTER TERMS

Review the following terms to test your understanding of the chapter. For each term you do not know, refer to the page number found next to that term.

banker's interest [p. 420]	future value [p. 423]	ordinary interest [p. 420]	simple interest [p. 410]
compound interest [p. 410]	inflation [p. 430]	present value [p. 423]	time [p. 410]
consumer price index (CPI) [p. 430]	interest [p. 410]	prime rate [p. 409]	time value of money [p. 432]
exact interest [p. 420]	maturity date [p. 423]	principal [p. 410]	
	maturity value [p. 423]	rate of interest [p. 410]	

CONCEPTS

EXAMPLES

12.1 Finding simple interest given time expressed in years

Use the formula $I = PRT$ with R in decimal form and time in years.

Find the simple interest on $65,000 for 2 years at 8% per year.

$$I = PRT$$
$$= \$65,000 \times 0.08 \times 2$$
$$= \$10,400$$

12.1 Finding simple interest given time expressed in months

Use $I = PRT$. Express time in years by dividing time in months by 12.

Find the simple interest on $8600 for 14 months at $6\frac{1}{2}\%$ per year.

$$I = PRT$$
$$= \$8600 \times 0.065 \times \frac{14}{12}$$
$$= \$652.17 \qquad \text{Rounded}$$

12.1 Determining principal given interest, rate, and time

Use the formula

$$P = \frac{I}{RT}$$

with R in decimal form and time in years.

Find the principal that would produce an interest of $150 in 8 months at 6%.

$$P = \frac{I}{RT}$$
$$= \frac{\$150}{0.06 \times \frac{8}{12}}$$
$$= \$3750$$

12.1 Finding rate given interest, principal, and time

Use the formula

$$R = \frac{I}{PT}$$

with T in years.

Find the rate on a $15,000 loan for 60 months if the interest was $6750.

$$R = \frac{I}{PT}$$
$$= \frac{\$6750}{\$15,000 \times \frac{60}{12}}$$
$$= 0.09, \text{ or } 9\%$$

12.1 Determining time given interest, principal, and rate Use the formula $$T = \frac{I}{PR}$$ with R in decimal form.	Find the time for a loan of \$12,000 at 10% to produce \$2400 in interest. $$T = \frac{I}{PR}$$ $$= \frac{\$2400}{\$12,000 \times 0.10}$$ $$= 2 \text{ years}$$
12.2 Finding the number of days from one date to another using a table Find the day corresponding to each date and subtract.	Find the number of days from February 15 to July 28. July 28 is day 209 Feb. 15 is day – 46 163 days
12.2 Determining the number of days from one date to another using the actual number of days in a month Add the actual number of days in each month or partial month from one date to the next.	Find the number of days from January 17 to April 15. 14 Remaining in January 28 February 31 March + 15 April 88 days
12.2 Finding exact interest Use the formula $I = PRT$ with $$T = \frac{\text{Time in days}}{365}$$	Find the exact interest on \$7300 at 7% for 100 days. $$I = PRT$$ $$= \$7300 \times 0.07 \times \frac{100}{365}$$ $$= \$140$$
12.2 Finding ordinary interest (bankers' interest) Use the formula $I = PRT$ with $$T = \frac{\text{Time in days}}{360}$$	Find the **ordinary interest** on \$11,000 at 7% for 90 days. $$I = PRT$$ $$= \$11,000 \times 0.07 \times \frac{90}{360}$$ $$= \$192.50$$
12.3 Determining the maturity value of a loan when principal, rate, and time are known Use the formula $$M = P(1 + RT)$$ with R in decimal form and T in years.	Find the maturity value of a \$25,000 loan that is made for 2 years at 6%. $$M = P(1 + RT)$$ $$= \$25,000[1 + (0.06 \times 2)]$$ $$= \$28,000$$
12.3 Finding the principal when maturity value, rate, and time are known Use the formula $$P = \frac{M}{1 + RT}$$ with R in decimal form and T in years.	Find the principal that would produce a maturity value of \$15,000 in 9 months at 7%. $$P = \frac{M}{1 + RT}$$ $$= \frac{\$15,000}{1 + \left(0.07 \times \frac{9}{12}\right)}$$ $$= \$14,251.78 \quad \text{Rounded}$$

12.3 Determining the time in days when maturity value, rate, and principal are known

Use the formula

$$T = \frac{M - P}{PR} \times 360$$

to find time in days.

A principal of \$12,000 produces a maturity value of \$12,540 at a 6% rate. Find the time of the loan in days.

$$T = \frac{M - P}{PR} \times 360$$

$$= \frac{\$12,540 - \$12,000}{\$12,000 \times 0.06} \times 360$$

$$= 0.75 \times 360$$

$$= 270 \text{ days}$$

12.3 Finding rate given principal, maturity value, and time

Use the formula

$$R = \frac{M - P}{PT}$$

with time expressed in years.

A principal of \$8400 produces a maturity value of \$8718.50 in 210 days. Find the rate of interest.

$$R = \frac{M - P}{PT}$$

$$= \frac{\$8718.50 - \$8400}{\$8400 \times \frac{210}{360}}$$

$$= 0.065, \text{ or } 6.5\%$$

12.3 Finding time in days when principal, rate, and interest are known

Use the formula

$$T = \frac{I}{PR} \times 360$$

with R in decimal form.

\$8500 was invested at 8% and \$141.67 interest was earned. Find the time in days.

$$T = \frac{I}{PR} \times 360$$

$$= \frac{\$141.67}{\$8500 \times 0.08} \times 360$$

$$= 75 \text{ days}$$

12.4 Finding the effect of inflation on the cost of living

Use the percent formula.

Find the increase in the cost of living for a family with a budget of \$24,600 after taxes in a year with $3\frac{1}{2}\%$ inflation.

$$0.035 \times \$24,600 = \$861$$

They experience an \$861 increase in the cost of living.

12.4 Determining present value given maturity or future value, rate, and time

Use the formula

$$P = \frac{M}{1 + RT}$$

with R in decimal form and T in years.

A debt of \$8000 must be paid in 9 months. Find the amount that could be deposited today at 5% interest so that enough money will be available.

$$P = \frac{M}{1 + RT}$$

$$= \frac{\$8000}{1 + \left(0.05 \times \frac{9}{12}\right)}$$

$$= \$7710.84 \qquad \text{Rounded}$$

12.4 Finding present value of a loan

Use the formula

$$M = P(1 + RT)$$

with R in decimal form and time in years. Then use the formula

$$P = \frac{M}{1 + RT}$$

with R = time value of money and T in years.

A loan of $7500 at 12% is due in 15 months. Find the present value of the loan if the time value of money is 9%.

$$M = P(1 + RT)$$
$$= \$7500 \times \left[1 + \left(0.12 \times \frac{15}{12}\right)\right]$$
$$= \$8625$$

$$P = \frac{M}{1 + RT}$$
$$= \frac{\$8625}{1 + \left(0.09 \times \frac{15}{12}\right)}$$
$$= \$7752.81$$

12.4 Finding present value of a loan after it is made

Use the formula $M = P(1 + RT)$ with R in decimal form and T in years. Next, use the formula

$$P = \frac{M}{1 + RT}$$

with R = time value of money, and T = fraction of a year using days from present value date to due date.

An $8000 loan is made on June 5 for 90 days at 9%. The time value of money is 11%. Find the present value of the loan on August 10. First find maturity value of the loan.

$$M = P(1 + RT)$$
$$= \$8000 \times \left[1 + \left(0.09 \times \frac{90}{360}\right)\right]$$
$$= \$8180$$

Now, find time in days from Aug. 10 to maturity date.

$$P = \frac{M}{1 + RT}$$
$$= \frac{\$8180}{1 + \left(0.11 \times \frac{24}{360}\right)}$$
$$= \$8120.45$$

CHAPTER 12   Review Exercises

The answer section includes answers to all Review Exercises.

Complete this table. Round money to the nearest cent, rate to the nearest tenth of a percent, and time to the nearest month. [12.1]

	Interest	Principal	Rate	Time
1.	_____	$8400	5%	2 years
2.	_____	$9600	$10\frac{1}{2}\%$	10 months
3.	$696.80	_____	12%	8 months
4.	$144	_____	8%	9 months

Interest	Principal	Rate	Time
5. $810	$12,000	_____	9 months
6. $750	$8000	_____	15 months
7. $540	$12,000	6%	_____
8. $1600	$8000	8%	_____

Find the number of days from the first date to the second. [12.2]

9. April 15 to August 7

10. July 12 to November 4

Find the exact interest for the following. Round to the nearest cent. [12.2]

Interest	Principal	Rate	Time
11. _____	$10,500	$7\frac{1}{2}\%$	120 days
12. _____	$8400	$9\frac{3}{4}\%$	150 days
13. _____	$7200	8%	From July 12 to November 30
14. _____	$16,500	10%	From February 4 to August 15

Find ordinary interest for the following. Round to the nearest cent. [12.2]

Interest	Principal	Rate	Time
15. _____	$7400	7%	30 days
16. _____	$52,000	10.2%	220 days

Complete the following table. Round money to the nearest cent, rate to the nearest tenth of a percent, and time to the nearest day. Use ordinary interest. [12.3]

Principal	Rate	Time	Interest
17. _____	$7\frac{1}{2}\%$	80 days	$203.33
18. _____	11%	180 days	$340
19. $6000	_____	60 days	$70
20. $8400	_____	120 days	$231
21. $7800	9%	_____	$78
22. $4900	$10\frac{1}{8}\%$	_____	$124.03

Complete the following table. Round money to the nearest cent and rate to the nearest tenth of a percent. [12.3]

Maturity Value	Principal	Rate	Time
23. _____	$5500	8%	$1\frac{3}{4}$ years
24. _____	$6900	7.2%	9 months
25. $12,180.00	_____	9%	60 days
26. $6752.78	_____	10%	140 days
27. $8120.00	$8000	_____	60 days
28. $17,537.50	$15,250	_____	15 months

Find the present value of each of the following. Round to the nearest cent. [12.4]

Present Value	Maturity Value	Rate	Time
29. _____	$6600	$8\frac{1}{2}\%$	120 days
30. _____	$12,000	12%	100 days

Find the present value of the following loans on the day they are made. Round to the nearest cent. **[12.4]**

Present Value	Principal Amount	Interest Rate of Loan	Length of Loan	Time Value of Money
31. _____	$8000	$9\frac{1}{2}\%$	10 months	8%
32. _____	$20,000	7%	15 months	9%

Find the present value for the following loans on the indicated dates. Assume that the time value of money is 9%. Round to the nearest cent. **[12.4]**

Present Value	Amount	Interest Rate of Loan	Length of Loan	Loan Made	Find Present Value On
33. _____	$800	10%	60 days	Feb. 1	March 15
34. _____	$15,000	8%	300 days	Apr. 1	October 15

Solve the following application problems. Round money to the nearest cent, rate to the nearest tenth of a percent, and time to the nearest day.

35. Christina Barrett borrowed $4500 at $7\frac{1}{2}\%$ for 90 days to go on an exchange trip to Seoul, Korea. Find the simple interest. **[12.1]**

36. CenterStage Music borrowed $18,600 at 9% simple interest for 150 days to obtain a trade discount on guitars purchased from Martin. Find the maturity value. **[12.3]**

37. A loan to an auto shop of $34,200 at $7\frac{1}{2}\%$ has a maturity value of $35,981.25. Find the time in days. **[12.3]**

38. An 8-month, 9% loan had a maturity value of $3816. Find the amount originally borrowed. **[12.3]**

39. Collins Dairy just bought new milking machines. The machines must be paid for with a single payment of $12,000 in 270 days. The firm has $11,200 that it can invest today. What rate of interest must it earn on this deposit to have the necessary $12,000? **[12.2]**

40. Quik Print is ordering a new $27,500 printing press. The seller of the press wants payment in 120 days. The print shop has $26,000 available for investment today. What rate of interest must it earn on this deposit to have the needed $27,500? Is it reasonable to earn this rate? **[12.2]**

41. Angela Rueben needs $14,000 but has only $13,400. How many days will it take to get the needed amount if she can earn 5% per year? **[12.3]**

42. Find the present value of a loan on the day it was made if the loan is for $9100 at 11% for 85 days. Assume that money has a time value of 9.7% **[12.4]**

43. A loan of $19,250 is made on October 15, at 12%. The loan is for 75 days. Find the present value of the loan on November 27 if money has a time value of 11.7%. **[12.4]**

44. Suppose a loan of $11,800 is made on July 12, for 153 days, at 9%. Find the present value of the loan on September 20, if money has a time value of 11%. **[12.4]**

45. Sherri Woods makes and spends $28,400 per year. She receives an increase in her annual salary of 6% during a year in which inflation is 3%. Ignoring taxes, find her net gain or loss in purchasing power. **[12.4]**

46. Bob and Jane Shaw have been spending their entire after-tax income of $46,850. Assume they receive no increase in their after-tax salary for a particular year during which inflation was 6%. Find the net gain or loss in their purchasing power. **[12.4]**

 47. Explain the possible effects of inflation on individuals who are retired. **[12.4]**

48. Use intuition to decide which of the following you would prefer: (a) a salary of $35,000 per year with no raises for 10 years or (b) a salary of $32,000 per year with annual raises of 3% per year for each of the next 10 years. Explain the reason for your choice. **[12.4]**

CHAPTER 12	Business Application Case #1
	Financing a Startup

Wes Whitmeyer started an appraisal company to estimate the value of homes and commercial real estate. During the first few months of operation of his new business, he received the following simple-interest loans.

Loan Number	Date Loan Made	Principal	Length of Loan	Interest Rate	Purpose of Loan
1	March 3	$12,000	6 months	10%	Used truck
2	April 17	$6200	90 days	12%	Computer equipment
3	July 9	$18,400	200 days	$9\frac{1}{2}\%$	Remodel the office

Complete the following table. Round to the nearest cent if needed.

Loan Number	Maturity Date	Simple Interest	Maturity Value
1	_____	_____	_____
2	_____	_____	_____
3	_____	_____	_____
Totals:		_____	_____

CHAPTER 12	Business Application Case #2
	Financing a Tanker to Ship Chemicals

Navistar Shipping needs another tanker (ship) to be used to carry chemicals from the Middle East to North America. The firm needs to borrow $12,800,000 to purchase the ship, and managers are debating the following three simple-interest loans.

Lender	Interest Rate	Length
Shanghai Bank	8.72%	6 months
Bacon Funds	9.6%	12 months
Jidlaka Investments	9.47%	7 months

(a) Find the interest and maturity value of each loan. (b) Then decide on the best loan if the firm believes it will take some time to make enough money to pay off the loan.

Notes and Bank Discount

The ability to borrow money is at the foundation of modern society. Without the ability to borrow, most individuals and families would not be able to buy a house or a car, for example. Figure 13.1 shows the median debt that students have accrued when in college, so students also clearly need to borrow. Businesses borrow extensively to finance operating costs or to build something such as a dam or a new factory.

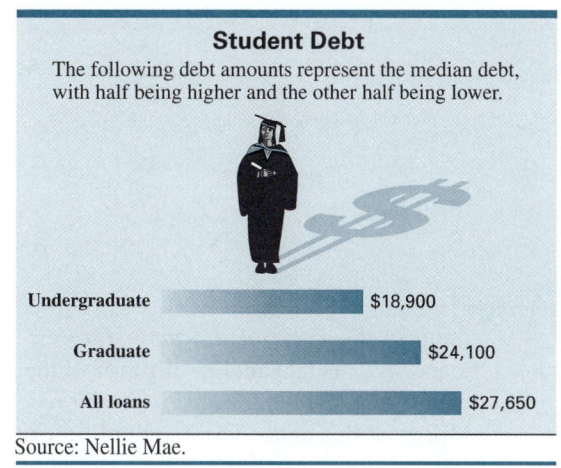

Student Debt

The following debt amounts represent the median debt, with half being higher and the other half being lower.

Undergraduate	$18,900
Graduate	$24,100
All loans	$27,650

Source: Nellie Mae.

Figure 13.1

STOP
and think

Think about your own situation or that of a student friend. First, estimate your total debt today including student loans, automobile loans, charge card balances, and any other loans you may have. Then, try to estimate how much you will need to borrow each semester for the remainder of your degree program. Approximately how much will you owe when you graduate? What salary do you expect when you graduate? How long do you think it will it take you to pay off that debt?

When an individual or business borrows money, written proof of the loan often takes the form of a **promissory note**, which documents a loan. A promissory note is a legal and, frequently, a transferable document in which one person or firm agrees to pay a stated amount of money, at a stated date and interest rate, to another. Banks typically require business owners to sign promissory notes when lending them money. Sometimes, simple interest notes are used, while at other times, simple discount notes are used. Both types of notes are discussed in this chapter.

NOTE   A year is assumed to have 360 days for all calculations in this chapter.

<table>
<tr><td>

13.1
</td><td>

Simple Interest Notes
</td></tr>
</table>

OBJECTIVES

1 *Identify the parts of a simple interest promissory note.*

2 *Find the due date of a note.*

3 *Find the face value, time, and rate of a note.*

An example of a promissory note is shown in Figure 13.2.

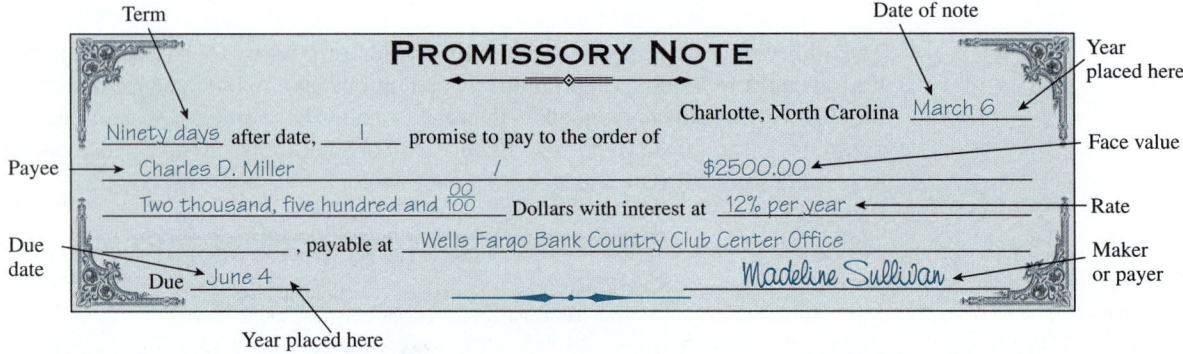

Figure 13.2

Objective

1 *Identify the Parts of a Simple Interest Promissory Note.* The person borrowing the money is called the **maker** or **payer** of the note (Madeline Sullivan for this note). The person who loaned the money, and who will receive the payment, is called the **payee** (Charles D. Miller for this note). The length of time until the note is due is called the **term of the note** (90 days for this note). The **face value**, or principal, of the note ($2500 for this note) is the amount written on the line in front of *dollars*. The interest rate on the note is 12% per year.

The **maturity value** of the loan is the face value plus any interest that is due. Since the interest for this note is found by using formulas for simple interest, this note is a **simple interest note**. When using the formulas for simple interest, the face value of the note is used as the value for the principal, *P.* Find the interest on the note shown in Figure 13.2 as follows.

$$\text{Interest} = \text{Face value} \times \text{Rate} \times \text{Time}$$

$$= \$2500 \times 0.12 \times \frac{90}{360} = \$75$$

The maturity value of the loan is

$$\text{Maturity value} = \text{Face value} + \text{Interest}$$

$$= \$2500 + \$75 = \$2575$$

Madeline Sullivan must pay $2575 to Charles D. Miller at the note's maturity, or June 4, which is 90 days after March 6.

The promissory note shown in Figure 13.2 contains all the information needed to calculate interest owed and maturity value. However, banks and other financial institutions use a more comprehensive note containing very detailed listings of necessary payment dates and amounts, as well as paragraphs describing the bank's rights in case of nonpayment of the note. A typical promissory note from a large bank is shown in Figure 13.3.

FIXED RATE CONSUMER NOTE, DISCLOSURE AND SECURITY AGREEMENT

BORROWER
Joan WaTers

ADDRESS

2705 4Th ST., Kansas CiTy, MO

TELEPHONE NO.   IDENTIFICATION NO.

HA69724

OFFICER INITIALS	INTEREST RATE	PRINCIPAL AMOUNT	FUNDING DATE	MATURITY DATE	CUSTOMER NUMBER	LOAN NUMBER
GWS	12%	$10,000	4/1	8/1	3627014	HA69724

** ANNUAL PERCENTAGE RATE **	** FINANCE CHARGE **	AMOUNT FINANCED	TOTAL OF PAYMENTS
THE COST OF THE CREDIT AS A YEARLY RATE.	THE DOLLAR AMOUNT THE CREDIT WILL COST.	THE AMOUNT OF CREDIT PROVIDED TO THE BORROWER OR ON BORROWER'S BEHALF.	THE AMOUNT BORROWER WILL HAVE PAID AFTER PAYMENTS HAVE BEEN MADE AS SCHEDULED.
12%	$1957.04	$10,000	$11,957.04

NUMBER OF PAYMENTS	AMOUNT OF PAYMENTS	WHEN PAYMENTS ARE DUE
36	$332.14 monThly	beginning April 11

DEMAND FEATURE: ☐ This Note has a demand feature.

REQUIRED DEPOSIT ACCOUNT: ☐ If checked, the Lender requires that Borrower maintain a deposit balance with Lender. The Annual Percentage Rate does not take into account required deposits.

SECURITY: A security interest has been granted in: ☐ Collateral securing other loans with Lender may also secure this loan; ☐ Any deposit accounts of Borrower with Lender; ☒ The goods or property being purchased; ☐ Other (describe): LOT 167, BILL MORRIS SURVEY

FILING FEES: $ ___NONE___ in fees are being paid to public officials in order to research, perfect or release a security interest in the Collateral.

PREPAYMENT: If Borrower pays off early, Borrower ☐ may ☐ will not have to pay a penalty; ☐ may ☐ will not be charged a minimum finance charge; ☐ may ☐ will not be entitled to a refund of part of the finance charge.

ITEMIZATION: Borrower has the right to receive at this time an itemization of the Amount Financed. Borrower ☐ does ☐ does not want an itemization.

LATE CHARGES: If an installment is received more than ___10___ days late, Borrower will be charged a late payment charge of: ☐ _____ % of the unpaid late installment; ☒ ___5___ % of the unpaid late installment or $ ___15.00___ , whichever is ☒ greater ☐ less; as permitted by law.

ASSUMPTION: ☐ This loan may not be assumed on its original terms. ☐ This loan may be assumed on its original terms, subject to certain conditions.

See your contract documents for additional information about nonpayment, default, prepayment penalties and refunds and acceleration.   • means an estimate

Figure 13.3

Almost all notes written by banks are secured by **collateral**. That is, the person borrowing the money *must pledge assets* such as cars, stock, or real estate that are of equal value or greater value than the amount of the loan. The collateral for the note in Figure 13.3 is Lot 167 located in the Bill Morris Survey. In the event of nonpayment, the bank will take the collateral and sell or liquidate it. The bank then uses the proceeds to pay off the note. Any excess is returned to the maker of the note.

Objective

2 *Find the Due Date of a Note.*   When a promissory note is given in months, the loan is due on the same day of the month, after the given number of months has passed. For example, a 4-month note made on May 25 would be due 4 months in the future on September 25. Other examples follow.

A loan made on January 31 for 3 months would normally be due on April 31. However, there are only 30 days in April, so the loan is due on April 30. Whenever a due date does not exist, such as February 30 or November 31, use the last day of the month (February 28 or November 30 in these examples). February 29 must be used if it is a leap year.

Date Made	Length of Loan	Date Due
March 12	5 months	August 12
April 24	7 months	November 24
October 7	9 months	July 7
January 31	3 months	April 30

| **EXAMPLE** | **1** | **Finding Due Date, Interest, and Maturity Value** |

Fred Romero needs to borrow money to purchase equipment needed to start his own graphic arts company. He signs a note with a face value of $15,000, a term of 10 months, and a rate of $11\frac{1}{2}\%$ on April 30. Find the due date, interest, and maturity value.

Solution   Ten months from April 30 is February 30 of the following year, which does not exist. So the due date is the last day of February, or February 28. It would be due February 29 if it is a leap year.

$$\text{Interest} = \$15{,}000 \times 0.115 \times \frac{10}{12} = \$1437.50$$

$$\text{Maturity value} = \$15{,}000 + \$1437.50 = \$16{,}437.50$$

NOTE   When the length of the loan is given in months, do *not* convert the time to days in order to find the date due.

The term of a promissory note is often given as a number of days. For example, a loan might be signed on March 12, and be due in 90 days. To find the date due, use the exact number of days in a month. This can be done in either of two ways, as shown in **Chapter 12**.

One way is to look back at Table 12.1, which shows the number of each day. From the table, March 12 is the 71st day of the year. The loan is due 90 days after March 12. The number of the day on which the loan is due is found as follows.

71	Number of the day loan is made.
+ 90	Number of days until due.
161	Number of the day loan is due is 161.

From Table 12.1, day 161 is June 10. A 90-day loan made on March 12 is due on June 10.

As an alternate method, use the actual number of days in each month. The loan is made on March 12. Since March has 31 days, there are 19 more days in March.

$$\begin{array}{r} 31 \\ -\ 12 \\ \hline 19 \end{array}$$

There are 30 days in April, and 31 in May. Find the total as follows.

19	Rest of days in March
30	Days in April
+ 31	Days in May
80	

The loan is for 90 days, which is 10 more than 80, making the loan due on June 10.

The following table shows several more examples.

Date Made	Length of Loan	Due Date
January 9	60 days	March 10
May 28	120 days	September 25
November 21	100 days	March 1
October 9	180 days	April 7

Objective

3 *Find the Face Value, Time, and Rate of a Note.* The next examples show how to find the face value, time, or rate for a note. Each of these examples uses formulas from **Chapter 12**.

> **NOTE** Face value for simple interest notes is the same as the principal, *P*, as used in **Chapter 12**.

EXAMPLE 2 Finding Face Value and Interest

Sheila Walker signed a 120-day note at 9% for funds she used for a vacation to Europe. A single payment of $7725 paid off the note when it was due. Find the face value and interest for the note.

Solution The payment of $7725 is the maturity value of the note. The maturity value is found with the following formula from **Chapter 12**.

$$M = P(1 + RT)$$

Since *P* is not known in this example, solve for *P* by dividing both sides by $1 + RT$.

$$P = \frac{M}{1 + RT}$$

Now substitute $7725 for *M*, 0.09 for *R*, and $\frac{120}{360}$ for *T*.

$$P = \frac{\$7725}{1 + \left(0.09 \times \frac{120}{360}\right)}$$

$$= \frac{\$7725}{1 + 0.03}$$

$$= \frac{\$7725}{1.03}$$

$$= \$7500$$

The face value of the note was $7500. The interest charge was $7725 − $7500 = $225.

EXAMPLE 3 Finding the Time of a Note

The owner of Jay's Country Music in Nashville signed a note with a face value of $45,000 to buy digital recording equipment. The interest rate is 10% and the maturity value is $47,250. Find the time of the note, in days.

Solution Recall the formula for time in days using banker's interest from **Chapter 12**.

$$T \text{ (in days)} = \frac{M - P}{PR} \times 360$$

Find the time by substituting $47,250 for *M*, $45,000 for *P*, and 10%, or 0.10, for *R*.

$$T \text{ (in days)} = \frac{\$47,250 - \$45,000}{\$45,000 \times 0.10} \times 360$$

$$= \frac{\$2250}{\$4500} \times 360$$

$$= 0.125 \times 360$$

$$= 180 \text{ days}$$

The loan was for 180 days. Since $M - P = I$, the same time in days can also be found using the equation from **Chapter 12**.

$$T(\text{in days}) = \frac{I}{PR} \times 360$$

NOTE A common error when solving for time T (in days) is forgetting to multiply by 360.

EXAMPLE 4 **Finding the Rate of a Note**

Leslie Graham, owner of Graham's Fine Wines, signed a note with a face value of $12,500 on April 12. She needed the funds to pay additional income taxes. On August 30, a maturity value of $12,961.81 is to be repaid. Find the rate on the note.

Solution Find the rate by starting with the formula for simple interest, $I = PRT$, and dividing both sides by PT.

$$R = \frac{I}{PT}$$

Interest $(I) = \$12,961.81 - \$12,500 = \$461.81$

Principal $(P) = \$12,500$

Time $(T) = \frac{140}{360}$ since there are 140 days from April 12 to August 30.

$$R = \frac{\$461.81}{\$12,500 \times \frac{140}{360}}$$

$$= 9.5\% \qquad \text{Rounded}$$

The rate is 9.5%. The same rate can be found using the alternative form of the equation $R = \dfrac{M - P}{PT}$ found in **Chapter 12**.

NOTE Do not round before the final answer in problems such as Example 4.

13.1 | **Exercises**

Identify each of the following from the promissory note that follows.

1. maker
2. payer
3. payee
4. face value
5. term of loan
6. day loan made
7. day loan due
8. maturity value

PROMISSORY NOTE

Jackson, Mississippi <u>October 27</u>

<u>Ninety days</u> after date, ____|____ promise to pay to the order of

<u>Leta Clendenen</u> / <u>$7500.00</u>

<u>Seven thousand five hundred and</u> ⁰⁰/₁₀₀ Dollars with interest at <u>12% per year</u>

_____, payable at <u>Crocker–Citizens Bank, Oak Park Branch</u>

Due <u>January 25</u>   <u>Helen Spence</u>

Find the due date of each of the following.

	Date Made	Term of Loan
9.	April 20	5 months
10.	July 12	3 months
11.	December 31	6 months
12.	May 31	4 months
13.	January 6	70 days
14.	September 14	125 days
15.	November 24	150 days
16.	December 8	160 days

Find the date due and the maturity value for each of the following. Use Table 12.1 on page 417 in your textbook. Round money to the nearest cent.

	Date Made	Face Value	Term of Loan	Rate
17.	June 12	$6000	150 days	9%
18.	March 18	$9500	200 days	10%
19.	August 14	$5000	300 days	$8\frac{1}{2}\%$
20.	October 20	$4500	180 days	12%

Complete the following table. Round money to the nearest cent, time to the nearest day, and rate to the nearest tenth of a percent.

	Principal	Rate	Time	Maturity Value
21.	_____	10%	180 days	$8820
22.	_____	9%	240 days	$7632
23.	$3600	8%	_____	$3696
24.	$8500	7.5%	_____	$8942.71
25.	$8400	_____	140 days	$8759.33
26.	$6800	_____	180 days	$7225
27.	$12,240	$10\frac{1}{2}\%$	200 days	_____
28.	$15,000	9%	150 days	_____

29. State and explain the different parts of a simple interest promissory note. (See Objective 1.)

30. Name at least five reasons why a small firm such as a bicycle or boat shop might need to borrow money. List three reasons you might need to borrow money.

Solve the following application problems. Round to the nearest cent.

31. **WEDDING SUPPLIES** On October 7, Janet Nastor signed a 200-day note with a face value of $18,400 for an inventory of wedding dresses and other supplies for her store. If the rate on the note was $9\frac{3}{4}\%$, find (a) the due date and (b) the maturity value.

32. **SKI PURCHASE** Jill Sample's Ski House bought $15,900 worth of skis from Rossignol on September 19. The firm signed a 200-day, $11\frac{1}{2}\%$ note for the skis. Find (a) the due date and (b) the maturity value of the note.

33. **FITNESS GYM** On April 15, Bobby and Jill Watson signed a 7-month note with a face value of $85,000 for equipment to start a fitness gym. If the rate on the note was $10\frac{1}{2}\%$, find (a) the due date and (b) the maturity value.

34. **HOBBY STORE** Ted Jenson borrowed $24,500 for 9 months at 8.5% to purchase numerous remote-control race cars and helicopters and also a few high-tech robots made in Japan. If he signed the note with the bank on July 5, find (a) the due date and (b) the maturity value.

35. **COFFEE SHOP** In order to buy a large quantity of Columbian coffee beans at a very special price, Gourmet Coffee signs a 320-day note at 9% with a maturity value of $13,500. Find the face value.

36. **STARTUP COMPANY** A 15-year-old computer whiz needs two computers and some software to start a home business. His parents help him by signing a note with a maturity value of $5400, rate of 12%, and time of 240 days. Find the face value.

37. **FLOWER SHOP** Marie's Flowers uses the proceeds from an 11%, 7-month note with a maturity value of $30,222.33 to build a garden area with a fountain in front of her store. If the note is due on November 7, find (a) the date the loan was made and (b) the face value.

38. **PHYSICAL THERAPIST** A physical therapist signed an 11-month, $9\frac{1}{2}\%$ note with a maturity value of $92,836.92 due on March 30. Find (a) the date the loan was made and (b) the face value.

39. **STATIONERY SHOP** West Stationery is getting ready to pay a note that is due. The interest rate is 12%, the face value is $4000, and the interest is $120. Find the time (in days) of the note.

40. **SCUBA SHOP** Ocean Scuba just paid the $7536 maturity value on a note with a face value of $7200. The interest rate was 8%. Find the time (in days) of the note.

41. **SECURITY SYSTEM PURCHASE** The manager of the local electronics plant bought a security system for $12,000, paying for it with a 120-day note with a maturity value of $12,320. Find the interest rate she paid on the note.

42. **COFFEE SHIPMENT** Dunn Brothers Coffee Company signed a $17,000, 90-day note for a shipment of coffee. The maturity value of the note was $17,382.50. Find the interest rate paid.

43. **ALASKA CRUISE** Bob and Sheryl Robinson sign a $6800 note at 12% simple interest for 90 days and use the funds to help pay for a 2-week cruise to Alaska. If Sheryl receives an after-tax year-end bonus of $5000 in 90 days, how much additional money will they need to pay off the note?

44. **INCOME TAX REFUND** The owner of Ben's Package Goods expects a $7400 refund on his taxes from the government in 100 days. He signs a 100-day note for $8600 at 9% to purchase extra inventory in order to get large-quantity discounts. How much additional money beyond his tax refund will he need at maturity?

13.2	**Simple Discount Notes**

OBJECTIVES

1 *Define simple discount notes.*

2 *Find bank discount and proceeds.*

3 *Calculate proceeds if given face value, discount rate, and time.*

4 *Distinguish between discount rates and simple interest rates.*

5 *Find effective interest rates.*

6 *Understand T-bills.*

7 *Find the face value that produces the desired proceeds.*

8 *Find discount rate, face value, or time.*

Objective

1 *Define Simple Discount Notes.*   The dollar amount written on the front of a simple interest note is called the face value (or principal). The face value of a simple interest note is the amount actually loaned to the borrower. In this section we discuss simple discount notes. It is important that you know that face value is defined *differently* for simple discount notes than for simple interest notes.

A **simple discount note** has the interest deducted *in advance* from the face value written on the note. In this type of note, the borrower *never receives* the face value—rather, the borrower receives the face value *less interest*. These notes are sometimes called **interest-in-advance notes** since the interest is subtracted *before* any money is given to the borrower.

> **NOTE**   A simple discount note is simply another way to write a note. It is not necessarily better or worse for a borrower or for a lender than a simple interest note.

The face value and the maturity value of a simple discount note are the same. The amount of interest charged is called the **bank discount**, or just the **discount**. Discount here is *not* the same as a discount received at a store when an item is on sale. Rather, the borrower receives a sum of money called the **proceeds**, which equals the face value of the note *less the discount*.

Type of Note	Amount Received by Borrower		Interest		Repayment Amount
Simple interest	Face value (Principal)	+	Interest	=	Maturity value
Simple discount	Proceeds	+	Discount (Interest)	=	Face value (Maturity value)

As an example of a simple discount note, suppose a borrower signs a note with a face value of $2000 and a discount of $150 as follows. Then,

$2000	Face value or maturity value of the note
− $150	Discount or interest that must be paid at maturity
$1850	Proceeds that the borrower actually receives at the time loan is made

> Simple *interest* is calculated on the *principal,* while simple *discount* is calculated on the *maturity value.*

Objective

2 *Find Bank Discount and Proceeds.* The formula for finding the bank discount is similar to the formula for calculating simple interest. Different letters are used to emphasize that the loan is a *discount loan* and that interest charges are computed based on maturity value rather than on the amount received by the borrower.

Calculating Bank Discount

$$B \qquad\qquad M \quad \times \quad D \quad \times \quad T$$

Bank discount = Face value $\times$ Discount rate $\times$ Time

where B = bank discount
M = face value (maturity value)
D = discount rate
T = time (in years)

Then, if P is the proceeds:

Proceeds amount received (loan amount) = Face value $-$ Bank discount

or $P = M - B$

The maturity value, or face value, M, is the sum of the discount and the proceeds.

$$M = P + B$$

EXAMPLE **1** **Finding Discount and Proceeds**

Marie Gostowski borrowed $12,000 for 10 months from Bank of America so that she could buy a new, larger commercial oven for her bakery. The banker discounted the note at 9%. Find the amount of the discount and the proceeds.

Solution Find the discount with the formula $B = MDT$, with $M = \$12,000$, $D = 9\%$, and $T = \frac{10}{12}$, or $\frac{5}{6}$.

$$B = MDT$$

$$= \$12,000 \times 0.09 \times \frac{5}{6} = \$900$$

The discount of $900 is the interest charge on the loan. The value of the proceeds that Gostowski actually received when making the loan is found using $P = M - B$.

$$P = M - B$$

$$= \$12,000 - \$900 = \$11,100$$

After signing the note for $12,000, Gostowski will be given $11,100. Then, 10 months later, she must make a single payment of $12,000 to the bank.

NOTE In Example 1, the value of the proceeds of $11,100 is the present value, and the maturity value of $12,000 is the future value.

Objective

3   *Calculate Proceeds If Given Face Value, Discount Rate, and Time.*   The value of the proceeds of a simple discount note is the face value (maturity value) *minus* the discount $(M - B)$. The discount equals maturity value $\times$ discount rate $\times$ the time in years. Look at the following.

$$P = M - B$$
$$= M - MDT \qquad \text{Substitute } MDT \text{ for } B.$$
$$= M(1 - DT) \qquad \text{Use the distributive property.}$$

> **NOTE**   Time must be in years or a fraction of a year for simple discount notes, just as it was for simple interest notes.

EXAMPLE 2   **Finding Proceeds**

Josh Crandall borrows $25,000 (in U.S. currency) from a bank in Cameroon to purchase a used Land Rover for use by his African safari company. Find the proceeds if the loan is for 90 days and has a discount rate of $10\frac{1}{2}\%$.

Solution   There are two ways to find the proceeds. One way would be to use the formula $B = MDT$ to find the discount and then subtract the discount from the face value to find the proceeds.

$$B = MDT$$
$$= \$25{,}000 \times 0.105 \times \frac{90}{360} = \$656.25$$

The proceeds are then

$$P = M - D$$
$$= \$25{,}000 - \$656.25 = \$24{,}343.75$$

As a second method and a check for finding the proceeds, use the formula $P = M(1 - DT)$. Here, $M = \$25{,}000$, $D = 10\frac{1}{2}\%$, and $T = \frac{90}{360}$.

$$P = M(1 - DT)$$
$$= \$25{,}000\left[1 - \left(0.105 \times \frac{90}{360}\right)\right]$$

Inside the brackets, be sure to first multiply $0.105 \times \frac{90}{360}$, and then subtract.

$$P = \$25{,}000(1 - 0.02625)$$
$$= \$25{,}000(0.97375)$$
$$= \$24{,}343.75$$

The proceeds of a simple discount note can be found using either method.

> **NOTE**   Do not round when making calculations within any one formula. Round only after all calculations in the formula have been made.

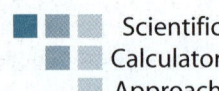
Scientific
Calculator
Approach

For the calculator solution to Example 2, think of the problem as

$$\$25,000\left(1 - 0.105 \times \frac{90}{360}\right)$$

and enter the parentheses accordingly.

25000 $\boxed{\times}$ $\boxed{(}$ 1 $\boxed{-}$ 0.105 $\boxed{\times}$ 90 $\boxed{\div}$ 360 $\boxed{)}$ $\boxed{=}$ 24343.75

Objective

4   *Distinguish Between Discount Rates and Simple Interest Rates.*   A discount rate of 12% is not the same as a simple interest rate of 12%. The next example shows why.

EXAMPLE 3   **Comparing Discount Rates and Simple Interest Rates**

Two different notes each have a face value of $7500 and a time of 90 days. One has a simple interest rate of 12%, and the other has a discount rate of 12%.

(a) Find the interest owed on each.

Solution

For the Simple Interest Note	For the Simple Discount Note
$I = PRT$	$B = MDT$
$= \$7500 \times 0.12 \times \dfrac{90}{360}$	$= \$7500 \times 0.12 \times \dfrac{90}{360}$
$= \$225$	$= \$225$

In each case, the interest is $225.

(b) Find the amount *actually received* by the borrower in each case.

Solution

For the Simple Interest Note	For the Simple Discount Note
Principal = Face value	Proceeds = $M - B$
= $7500	= $7500 − $225
	= $7275

With the simple interest note, the borrower has the use of $7500, but only $7275 is available with the simple discount note. In each case, the interest charge is the same, $225, but *more money is available to the borrower with the simple interest note.*

(c) Find the maturity value of each note.

Solution

For the Simple Interest Note	For the Simple Discount Note
$M = P + I$	Maturity value = Face value
= $7500 + $225	= $7500
= $7725	

The differences between these two notes can be summarized as follows.

	Simple Interest	Simple Discount
Face value	$7500	$7500
Interest	$225	$225
Amount available to borrower	$7500	$7275
Maturity value	$7725	$7500

The borrower in the 12% simple interest note uses $7500 for 90 days and pays $225 in interest. The borrower in the 12% simple discount note is able to use only $7275 for 90 days and must pay the same interest. Therefore, in this particular case, the 12% simple interest note is better than the 12% discount note.

Objective

5 *Find Effective Interest Rates.*

Example 3 shows that interest rates can be stated in different ways, which can be confusing. The **nominal interest rate**, also called the **stated rate**, is the rate that is written or stated on a note. The **effective interest rate**, also called the **true interest rate**, or the **annual percentage rate**, is the actual interest rate on the amount received by the borrower. The nominal rate for a loan may differ from the effective interest rate.

The **Federal Truth in Lending Act** was passed in 1969 because of the confusion resulting from the different ways of calculating interest charges. This act requires that all interest rates be given in a standard way, so that they can quickly and easily be compared to one another. The next example shows how to find the effective interest rate corresponding to the discount rate given in Example 3. Effective interest rates are more fully discussed in **Chapter 14**.

EXAMPLE 4 Finding Rate of Interest for Discount Notes

Find the rate of simple interest for the simple discount note in Example 3.

Solution The discount rate of 12% in the simple discount note in Example 3 is the nominal rate for that note and not the effective rate. This is because the 12% applies to the maturity value of $7500 and *not* to the proceeds of $7275 actually received by the borrower. Find the effective interest rate using the formula for simple interest, $I = PRT$, with $I = \$225$, $P = \$7275$, and $T = \frac{90}{360}$.

Start with $I = PRT$, and divide both sides by PT.

$$R = \frac{I}{PT}$$

Then substitute the given numbers.

$$R = \frac{\$225}{\$7275 \times \frac{90}{360}}$$

$$= \frac{\$225}{\$1818.75}$$

$$= 0.1237, \quad \text{or} \quad 12.37\% \quad \text{Rounded}$$

The effective rate of interest is 12.37%, and not 12%, which is the nominal rate written on the note. Federal regulations require that a borrower be told the effective rate of interest.

However, the regulations allow the rate to be rounded to the nearest quarter of a percent, so 12.37% could be reported as 12.25% in this case. In Example 3, we were comparing a simple interest loan with an effective rate of 12.00%, so it becomes obvious which is better from the borrower's perspective.

■

Objective

6 *Understand T-Bills.* **U.S. Treasury bills (T-bills)** are a common use of discount notes. The U.S. government uses T-bills to borrow money from investors. These financial instruments are available with 13-week, 26-week, or 52-week maturities. Rather than paying the face value for a T-bill, investors pay the face value minus the discount, which is based on the current interest rate and length to maturity of the bill. The investor receives the face amount of the T-bill when it matures. T-bills are considered to be very safe investments since they are loans to the U.S. government. A T-bill may be bought and sold many times during its lifetime.

NOTE Effective April 7, 2008, the minimum purchase amount of treasury bills is $100. Banks and financial institutions are usually the largest purchasers, but individuals can buy Treasury bills directly or through mutual funds or exchange-traded funds that buy Treasury bills.

EXAMPLE 5 Finding Facts about T-Bills

Managers at a bank in Brazil are worried about devaluation of the Brazilian currency. They purchase $1 million in 26-week U.S. T-bills with a stated rate of 4%, so that this money is in a safe place for a short period of time. Find (a) the total purchase price, (b) the total maturity value, (c) the interest earned, and (d) the effective rate of interest.

Solution

$$M = \$1,000,000; D = 0.04; T = \tfrac{26}{52} \quad \text{(The denominator is 52 when time is in weeks.)}$$

(a) Bank discount = Face value × Discount rate × Time

$$= \$1,000,000 \times 0.04 \times \tfrac{26}{52} = \$20,000$$

Purchase price = Face value − Bank discount

$$= \$1,000,000 - \$20,000 = \$980,000$$

Maturity value
$1,000,000

Bank discount

(b) Maturity value = Face value

$$= \$1,000,000$$

(c) Interest = Bank discount

$$= \$20,000$$

Purchase price
$980,000

(d) Effective rate $= \dfrac{\text{Interest earned}}{\text{Purchase price (proceeds)} \times \text{Time}}$

$$= \dfrac{\$20,000}{\$980,000 \times \tfrac{26}{52}} = 0.04081 = 4.08\% \quad \text{Rounded}$$

The T-bills have a stated rate of 4% but have an effective rate of 4.08%.

■

Objective

7 *Find the Face Value That Produces the Desired Proceeds.* Normally, a borrower has in mind a certain amount of money needed. The next example shows how to use the amount needed by a borrower to find the face value of the discount note.

EXAMPLE 6 **Find the Face Value That Produces the Desired Proceeds**

Mike Collins needs $4000 to repair his roof. Find the value of a note that will provide the $4000 in proceeds if he plans to repay the note in 180 days and the bank charges a 10% discount rate.

Solution Start with the formula $P = M(1 - DT)$. Since M is not known, find a formula for M by dividing both sides by $1 - DT$.

$$M = \frac{P}{1 - DT}$$

Replace P with $4000, D with 10%, or 0.1, and T with $\frac{180}{360}$.

$$M = \frac{\$4000}{\left(1 - 0.1 \times \frac{180}{360}\right)}$$

$$= \frac{\$4000}{1 - 0.05} = \$4210.53 \quad \text{Rounded}$$

Collins must sign a note with a face value of $4210.53 to get the $4000 that he needs.

Scientific
Calculator
Approach

The calculator solution to Example 6 follows.

4000 ÷ (1 − 0.1 × 180 ÷ 360) = 4210.53

Objective

8 ***Find Discount Rate, Face Value, or Time.*** The formula for simple interest, $I = PRT$, can be solved for P, R, or T. Similarly, the formula for simple discount, $B = MDT$, can be solved for M, D, or T. Do this as shown in the next example.

EXAMPLE 7 **Finding Discount**

Sheila Watts borrowed proceeds of $4480 on a discount note to help with college expenses. Her 240-day note had a maturity value of $4800. Find the discount rate.

Solution To find the discount rate, start with the formula $B = MDT$ and divide both sides by MT.

$$D = \frac{B}{MT}$$

The discount is

$$B = \$4800 - \$4480 = \$320$$

also, $M = \$4800$ and $T = \frac{240}{360}$. Now find D.

$$D = \frac{\$320}{\$4800 \times \frac{240}{360}} = 0.10$$

The discount rate is 10%.

13.2 | Exercises

Find the discount and the proceeds. Round money to the nearest cent.

	Maturity Value	Discount Rate	Time in Days
1.	$4600	9%	90
2.	$6800	10%	180
3.	$8500	11%	300
4.	$15,500	12%	200
5.	$8400	$9\frac{1}{2}\%$	30
6.	$9800	$8\frac{3}{4}\%$	50

Find the due date and the proceeds for the following. Round to the nearest cent.

	Maturity Value	Discount Rate	Date Made	Time in Days
7.	$8400	11%	January 3	100
8.	$5400	12%	March 25	90
9.	$12,000	$9\frac{1}{2}\%$	August 21	180
10.	$9750	$10\frac{3}{4}\%$	December 9	200

Complete this table.

	Maturity Value	Discount Rate	Date Made	Due Date	Time in Days	Discount	Proceeds
11.	$24,000	$9\frac{1}{2}\%$	2/4	____	180	_____	_____
12.	$8275	7%	____	9/10	120	_____	_____
13.	$14,400	____	8/7	1/4	150	$660	_____
14.	$8200	____	2/9	5/10	___	$205	_____
15.	_____	____	11/12	____	90	$108	$7092
16.	_____	____	12/2	8/11	___	$1372	$18,228

Solve the following application problems. Round rates to the nearest tenth of a percent and money to the nearest cent.

17. **BOAT PURCHASE**   A Chevron employee bought a boat with funds borrowed from First National Bank. He intends to repay the note with a Christmas bonus of $6000 to be paid to him in 120 days. Given an 11% discount, find the discount and the proceeds.

18. **INCOME TAX PAYMENT**   LaTonya Barker must make a quarterly tax payment to the Internal Revenue Service. She decides to borrow money from her company (Bicycles Unlimited) and repay the loan in 100 days using an $8500 bonus she will receive at that time. Given an 8.5% discount rate, find the discount and the proceeds.

19. **BUSINESS TRIP TO ALASKA**   Walter Bates needed money to go on a business trip to Alaska and he signed a note for $6000. At a $10\frac{1}{2}\%$ discount rate, the discount on the note was $210. Find the length of the loan in days.

20. **DIVORCE SETTLEMENT** Will and Juliet Ramapo divorced. As part of the divorce settlement, the judge required Will to sign a $12,500 note at 8.5% simple discount in favor of his wife, who will keep their two children. Find the length of the loan in days if the discount is $737.85.

21. **COLLATERAL** Ben Ficklin signed a 300-day note for $85,000 using the cash in his life insurance policy as collateral. Find the discount rate if the discount is $4604.17.

22. **TRADE WITH MEXICO** Juan Ramirez borrows $380,000 in U.S. dollars to construct a warehouse in Juarez, Mexico near the border with Texas. He signed the 250-day note with proceeds of $354,930.56 for a warehouse to store U.S.-made medical equipment before distributing it throughout Mexico. Find the discount rate.

23. **LAPTOP COMPUTER** Jane Peters frequently travels to Hong Kong and needs to purchase a special laptop computer costing $3200. If the discount rate is 10% and the term is 140 days, find the maturity value of the loan.

24. **LAST YEAR AT COLLEGE** Mary Gibb estimates that she needs $10,000 to finish her last year at college. She borrows the funds from her uncle for 12 months at a favorable 4% discount rate. Find the face value of the loan.

25. **HOME REMODELING** Faith Daigle signs an 8.5% discount note with a maturity value of $7800 and a term of 8 months so that she can remodel her kitchen and bathroom. Find the proceeds and the effective interest rate.

26. **PERSONAL DISCOUNT NOTE** Ed Foust goes to the bank and signs a note for $8400. The bank charges a 7% discount rate. Find the proceeds and the effective rate charged by the bank if the note is for 8 months.

27. **JAPANESE FISHING** A Japanese contractor needed proceeds of $410,000 to finish construction of a ship specially designed to catch, harvest, and freeze fish on long voyages such as to the coast of South America. A Japanese bank loaned the contractor the funds at a 4.25% discount rate for 120 days. Find the face value of the note and the effective interest rate.

28. **INTERNATIONAL FINANCE** A Canadian electric company requires proceeds of $720,000 (local currency) and borrows from a bank in Thailand at a 12% discount for 45 days. Find the face value of the note and the effective interest rate.

The following exercises apply to U.S. Treasury bills. (Assume 52 weeks per year for each exercise, and round to the nearest hundredth of a percent.)

29. **PURCHASE OF T-BILLS** A large German investment firm purchases $25,000,000 in U.S. T-bills at a 6% discount for 13 weeks. Find (a) the purchase price of the T-bills, (b) the maturity value of the T-bills, (c) the interest earned, and (d) the effective rate.

30. **T-BILLS** Nina Horn buys a $50,000 T-bill at a 5.8% discount for 26 weeks. Find (a) the purchase price of the T-bill, (b) the maturity value, (c) the interest earned, and (d) the effective rate of interest.

31. Explain the difference between simple interest notes and simple discount notes.

32. Compare the formulas for simple interest rate and simple discount rate. Define all variables for both, and explain the difference between simple interest rate and simple discount rate. (See Objective 4.)

33. As a borrower, would you prefer a simple interest note with a rate of 11% or a simple discount note with a rate of 11%? Explain using an example. (See Objective 4.)

34. Explain why individuals or companies from other parts of the world invest in U.S. T-bills from time to time.

13.3	**Comparing Simple Interest and Simple Discount**

OBJECTIVES

1 *Compare the differences between simple interest and simple discount notes.*

2 *Convert between simple interest and simple discount rates.*

People in business use both simple interest notes (**Section 13.1**) and simple discount notes (**Section 13.2**). In this section, the two types of notes are compared. First, here are the similarities between the two types of notes.

1. The borrower receives a lump sum of money at the beginning of each type of note.
2. Both types of notes are repaid with a single payment at the end of a stated period of time.
3. This length of time is generally one year or less.

Objective

1 *Compare the Differences between Simple Interest and Simple Discount Notes.* Table 13.1 compares these two types of notes.

TABLE 13.1   A COMPARISON OF SIMPLE INTEREST AND SIMPLE DISCOUNT NOTES

Variables Used for Simple Interest	Variables Used for Simple Discount
I = Interest	B = Discount
P = Principal (face value)	P = Proceeds (amount received)
R = Rate of interest	D = Discount rate
T = Time in years, or fraction of a year	T = Time in years, or fraction of a year
M = Maturity value	M = Maturity value (face value)

	Formulas	
Elements	**Simple Interest**	**Simple Discount**
Face value	Stated on note, or $$P = \frac{M}{1 + RT}$$	Same as maturity value, or $$M = \frac{P}{1 - DT}$$
Interest charge	$I = PRT$	$B = MDT$
Maturity value	$M = P + I$ or $M = P(1 + RT)$	Same as face value, or $$M = \frac{P}{1 - DT}$$
Amount received by borrower	Face value or principal	Proceeds $P = M - B$ or $P = M(1 - DT)$
Identifying phrases	Interest at a certain rate Maturity value greater than face value Simple interest	Discounted at a certain rate Proceeds (less than face) Maturity value equal to face value Simple discount rate
True annual interest rate	Same as stated rate, R	Greater than stated rate, D

Objective

2   *Convert between Simple Interest and Simple Discount Rates.*   As shown earlier, a 12% simple interest rate is *not* the same as a 12% simple discount rate. This section shows formulas to convert between simple interest rates and simple discount rates. To find these formulas, start with the basic formulas for simple interest and simple discount.

Simple Interest		Simple Discount
$M = P(1 + RT)$	and	$P = M(1 - DT)$
↳ Principal		↳ Proceeds

Solve both the simple interest formula and the simple discount formula for P, the principal or proceeds received by the borrower.

Simple Interest	Simple Discount
$P = \dfrac{M}{1 + RT}$	$P = M(1 - DT)$

Since the right-hand side of each equation is P, then the two right-hand sides must equal one another.

$$\frac{M}{1 + RT} = M(1 - DT)$$

Divide both sides by M to get

$$\frac{1}{1 + RT} = 1 - DT$$

By going through several more algebraic steps, this equation can be solved for either R or D, giving the results in the box.

The simple interest rate R and the simple discount rate D are calculated by the formulas

$$R = \frac{D}{1 - DT} \quad \text{and} \quad D = \frac{R}{1 + RT}$$

where T is time in years.

NOTE   These two formulas show that neither proceeds nor maturity value is needed to convert between the two types of rates, only rate and time are needed.

EXAMPLE 1   **Converting Interest and Discount Rates**

John Patterson's lawn care business has two outstanding notes. (a) The first note is a 180-day simple discount note with a face value of $16,800 and a discount rate of 10%. Convert this rate to a simple interest (effective interest) rate. (b) The second note is a 140-day simple interest note with a face value of $24,600 and an interest rate of 11%. Find the corresponding simple discount rate.

Solution

(a) Find R with the following formula.

$$R = \frac{D}{1 - DT}$$

Again, notice that no dollar amounts, not even face value, are needed. Here $D = 0.10$ and $T = \frac{180}{360}$.

$$R = \frac{0.10}{1 - \left(0.10 \times \frac{180}{360}\right)} = \frac{0.1}{1 - 0.05} = \frac{0.1}{0.95} = 0.105263$$

Rounding to the nearest hundredth of a percent, the corresponding simple interest rate is 10.53%.

The answer can be checked by first finding the interest on the simple discount loan.

$$B = MDT$$

$$= \$16{,}800 \times 0.10 \times \frac{180}{360}$$

$$= \$840$$

Then find the loan proceeds.

$$P = M - B$$

$$= \$16{,}800 - \$840$$

$$= \$15{,}960$$

Finally, use the formula for a simple interest calculation to find the simple interest rate:

$$R = \frac{I}{PT}$$

$$= \frac{\$840}{\$15{,}960 \times \frac{180}{360}}$$

$$= 10.53\% \qquad \text{Rounded}$$

(b) Find the simple discount rate that corresponds to a simple interest rate of 11% for 140 days. Use the following formula.

$$D = \frac{R}{1 + RT}$$

Replace R with 0.11 and T with $\frac{140}{360}$. Then,

$$D = \frac{0.11}{1 + \left(0.11 \times \frac{140}{360}\right)}$$

$$= \frac{0.11}{1 + 0.042777778}$$

$$= 0.1055 \qquad \text{Rounded}$$

or 10.55%, rounded to the nearest hundredth of a percent.

NOTE In Example 1, the simple interest rate is larger than the equivalent simple discount rate. This is always the case. The simple interest rate is always larger than the equivalent simple discount rate.

■■□ Scientific
■■□ Calculator
□ Approach

The calculator approach to Example 1 uses parentheses to group each denominator.

(a) 0.10 ÷ (1 − 0.10 × 180 ÷ 360) = 0.1053 Rounded

(b) 0.11 ÷ (1 + 0.11 × 140 ÷ 360) = 0.1055 Rounded

13.3	**Exercises**

Find the simple interest rate that corresponds to the given discount rate for the given time. Round to the nearest hundredth of a percent.

1. 9%, 120 days

2. 12%, 180 days

3. 10.5%, 200 days

4. 7%, 100 days

5. 8%, 120 days

6. 9.5%, 300 days

Find the simple discount rate that corresponds to the given simple interest rate for the given time. Round to the nearest hundredth of a percent.

7. 8.5%, 120 days

8. 10.5%, 200 days

9. 12%, 220 days

10. 8%, 240 days

11. 10%, 100 days

12. 9%, 180 days

 13. Is the rate associated with simple discount notes the true annual interest rate? If not, explain why not and show how to calculate the true rate.

14. Use an example to show that a simple interest note at 10% results in less than a simple discount note at 10%.

Solve the following application problems.

15. SURGERY   Sherri Johnson needs to borrow money for an operation. She can borrow at a 13% simple interest rate or at a 12.8% simple discount rate. If she needs the money for 90 days, which loan should she take?

16. WEDDING   Reann Kiang needs to borrow $8600 to pay for her only daughter's wedding. One bank charges 12% simple interest and a second bank charges 11% simple discount. If she needs the money for 120 days, which loan should she take?

17. USED MOTORCYCLE   Sean McTuff wants to borrow $6000 for 180 days to purchase a used Harley-Davidson motorcycle with a "lotta chrome" on it. How much less interest is paid with a 12% simple interest note compared to a 12% simple discount note?

18. VET CLINIC   Dr. Jensen needs a 9-month construction loan with proceeds of $280,000 to construct a clinic including a parking lot. How much less interest is paid with a 9.5% simple interest note compared to a 9.5% simple discount note?

19. REGISTERED BREEDER   Samantha Spade needs $12,000 to purchase several registered poodles and set up cages so she can start a business breeding dogs. She approaches two banks for a 1-year loan. Regions Financial offers her 10% simple discount and First Financial offers her 9.5% simple interest. Identify the better loan and find the difference in interest.

20. eBAY SALES   Nesta Yumong needs to borrow $8500 for 90 days to start a business on eBay buying and selling silver coins and other memorabilia. She has a choice of a 9% simple discount note or a 9.25% simple interest note. Identify the loan with the lower interest amount and find the difference in interest.

 21. Show the algebraic steps needed to solve the following equation for *D*.

$$\frac{1}{1 + RT} = 1 - DT$$

 22. Assume a simple discount rate of 12% and explore the effect of time on the simple interest rate. Do this by substituting three different times, each less than 1 year, into the appropriate formula. (See Objective 2.)

13.4   Discounting a Note

OBJECTIVES

1 *Find the discount and the proceeds of a note.*

2 *Find the proceeds of a rediscounted note.*

Businesses often accept either simple interest or simple discount notes in place of immediate payment for goods or services. For example, a company that manufactures skis, a retailer that sells the skis, and a bank may do business as follows.

1. Ski manufacturer sells skis to a retailer and accepts a promissory note instead of cash.
2. Ski manufacturer needs cash and sells the note to a bank before it matures.
3. Retailer pays the maturity value of the note to the bank when due.

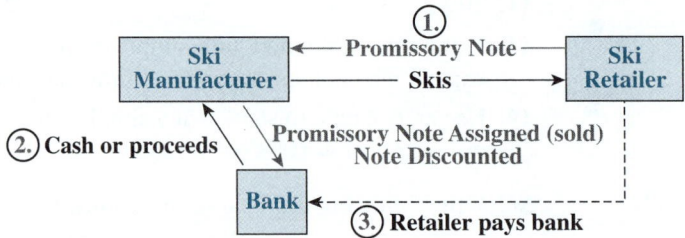

Selling the note to a bank allows the manufacturing company to get cash earlier, but of course the firm gives up the interest, which the bank will earn instead. The maturity value of the note less a fee charged by the bank is called the **bank discount** or **discount**. The process of receiving cash for a note or selling a note is called **discounting a note**.

The amount of cash actually received by the manufacturer from the bank is called the **proceeds**. The bank then collects the maturity value from the maker of each note when it becomes due. Normally, such notes are sold with **recourse**. This means that if the maker of the note does not pay for some reason, the bank collects from the seller of the note. This protects the bank against loss. You may have noticed that banks do not like to lose money!

Objective

1   *Find the Discount and the Proceeds of a Note.*   Use the following procedure to discount a note.

> **Step 1** Find the maturity value of the original note (if necessary). Use $M = P(1 + RT)$.
>
> **Step 2** Find the discount period.
>
> **Step 3** Find the discount using the formula $B = MDT$.
>
> **Step 4** The proceeds are found by $P = M - B$.
>
> This method is shown in the next examples.

EXAMPLE 1   **Finding Proceeds**

Destination Mad is a rock-and-roll band that wants to record an album and produce 1500 CDs both to promote the band and to sell to fans. They sign a 200-day simple interest note with Blues Recording Studio dated March 24. It has a face value of $9600 and simple interest of 12%. On August 15, Blues Recording Studio sells the note at a discount rate of 12.5%. Find the proceeds to the recording studio.

Solution Go through the four steps of discounting a note.

STEP 1 First find the maturity value of the simple interest note.

$$M = P(1 + RT)$$

$$= \$9600\left(1 + 0.12 \times \frac{200}{360}\right) = \$10{,}240$$

STEP 2 Find the **discount period**, or the number of days from August 15 until the note is due. As shown in Figure 13.4, the note is due 200 days after March 24, or October 10. The number of days from August 15 to October 10 is found as follows.

16	Days left in August
30	Days in September
+ 10	Days until note is due in October
56	Days of discount period

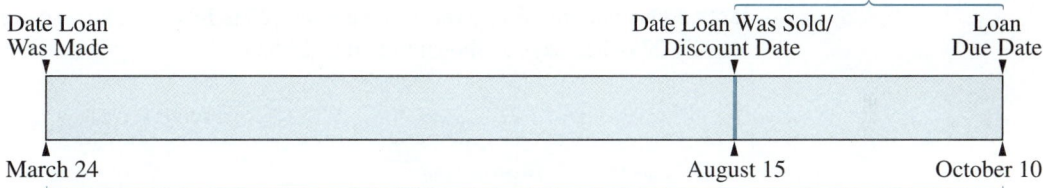

Discount Period = 56 Days

Date Loan Was Made   Date Loan Was Sold/ Discount Date   Loan Due Date

March 24   August 15   October 10

Length of Original Loan: 200 Days

Figure 13.4

STEP 3 Find the *bank discount* using $B = MDT$ with $M = \$10{,}240$ and $T = \frac{56}{360}$.

$$B = \$10{,}240 \times 0.125 \times \frac{56}{360} = \$199.11 \quad \text{Rounded}$$

STEP 4 Find the *proceeds* using the formula $P = M - B$.

$$P = \$10{,}240 - \$199.11 = \$10{,}040.89$$

The bank purchases the note on August 15 for $10,040.89 in cash paid to Blues Recording Studio. Then, on the maturity date of October 10, the bank will collect $10,240 from Destination Mad, shown as follows.

Date	Transaction
March 24	The band signs 200-day simple interest note for $9600.
August 15	Blues Recording Studio sells note to bank for $10,040.89.
October 10	The bank receives $10,240 from the payer (band).

In $141\,(200 - 56)$ days, the recording studio in Example 1 earned the following interest.

$$\text{Interest earned} = \$10{,}040.89 - \$9600 = \$440.89$$

The effective rate of interest is found as follows.

$$R = \frac{I}{PT}$$

$$= \frac{\$440.89}{\$9600 \times \frac{144}{360}}$$

$$= 11.48\% \quad \text{Rounded}$$

Their effective interest rate was a little less than the 12% rate stated on the note.

> **NOTE** In discounting a note, the business receives less money than if it held the note to maturity, but it will receive the money sooner.

EXAMPLE 2 **Finding Proceeds and Discount**

On February 27, Andrews Lincoln-Mercury receives a 150-day simple interest note with a face value of $3500 at 8% interest per year. On March 27, the firm discounts the note at the bank. Find the proceeds if the discount rate is 12%.

Solution Again, go through the four steps to discount a note.

STEP 1 First find the maturity value of the simple interest note.

$$M = P(1 + RT)$$
$$= \$3500\left(1 + 0.08 \times \frac{150}{360}\right) = \$3616.67 \quad \text{Rounded}$$

STEP 2 One hundred fifty days from February 27 is July 27. The discount period from March 27 to July 27 is 122 days as shown in Figure 13.5.

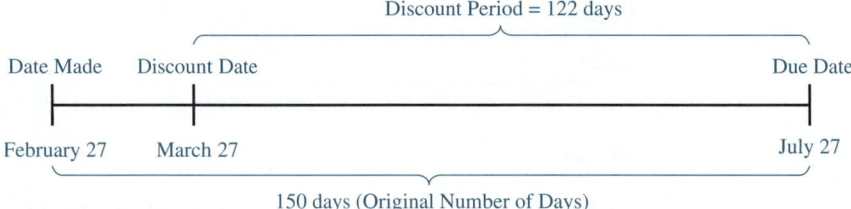

Figure 13.5

> **NOTE** Remember, the discount period is calculated *from the date of sale* to the *due date* of the loan, not from the date the loan was made.

STEP 3 Use $B = MDT$ with the discount rate of 12% to find the discount.

$$B = \$3616.67 \times 0.12 \times \frac{122}{360} = \$147.08 \quad \text{Rounded}$$

STEP 4 Use $P = M - B$ to find the proceeds.

$$P = \$3616.67 - \$147.08 = \$3469.59$$

Andrews receives $3469.59 from the bank on March 27.

Objective

2 ***Find the Proceeds of a Rediscounted Note.*** In the next example, a company borrows money from a bank by signing a *simple discount note.* The bank making the loan then sells the note to a finance company. In this case, with the same note being discounted twice, the note is said to have been **rediscounted**. Notice in the example that the rate charged by the finance company to the bank is lower than the rate charged to the public. This is very common in transactions between large financial institutions, with the lower rate a sort of "wholesale" rate.

Even though the note in Example 3 is rediscounted, the steps used are basically the same as those used in earlier examples. The only difference is that since the original note was a simple discount note instead of a simple interest note, it is not necessary to solve for maturity value. The face value *is* the maturity value.

EXAMPLE **3** **Finding Proceeds of a Rediscounted Note**

The chief financial officer of Communication Networks signed a 180-day note with a discount rate of 12% and a face value of $140,000 with a bank. Fifty-four days after the note was signed, the bank rediscounted the note to Century Finance at 10% for cash. Find the proceeds Century Finance must pay the bank.

Solution   Go through the steps given for discounting a note.

STEP 1 The maturity value of the note is $140,000.

> **NOTE**   The fact that the bank charged a 12% discount rate plays no part in the problem since only the maturity value of the note is needed.

STEP 2 The discount period is $180 - 54 = 126$ days.

STEP 3 The discount (to Century Finance) is

$$\text{Discount} = \$140,000 \times 0.10 \times \frac{126}{360} = \$4900$$

STEP 4 The proceeds are

$$\$140,000 - \$4900 = \$135,100$$

This example can be summarized as follows.

1. Communication Networks signs a note with a maturity value of $140,000. The original proceeds to Communication Networks is found as follows.

$$P = M - MDT$$

$$= \$140,000 - \$140,000 \times 0.12 \times \frac{180}{360}$$

$$= \$131,600$$

   Then, 54 days after the note is signed, the bank rediscounts the note to Century Finance, receiving proceeds of $135,100. Finally, 180 days after signing the note (and 126 days after the note was discounted), Communication Networks pays $140,000 to Century Finance.

2. The bank lends $131,600 for 54 days and makes $135,100 - \$131,600 = \$3500$ in interest. The effective interest rate earned by the bank is found as follows.

$$R = \frac{I}{PT}$$

$$= \frac{\$3500}{\$131,600 \times \frac{54}{360}}$$

$$= 17.73\% \qquad \text{Rounded}$$

Not only notes are discounted. It is very common for a business to sell part of its accounts receivable (money owed to the business—see **Section 18.3**) to a financial institution. This process is called **factoring**, and the people who buy the accounts receivable are called **factors**. The calculations involved with factoring are the same as those discussed in this section.

13.4	Exercises

Find the discount period for each of the following.

	Loan Made	Length of Loan	Date of Discount
1.	June 28	120 days	August 4
2.	March 13	180 days	June 1
3.	August 4	220 days	January 12
4.	November 5	60 days	December 18

Find the proceeds when each of the following simple discount notes are discounted. Round to the nearest cent.

	Maturity Value	Discount Period	Discount Rate
5.	$8200	120 days	8%
6.	$8000	200 days	9%
7.	$15,000	180 days	12%
8.	$18,200	240 days	11%

Each of the following simple interest notes was discounted at 12%. Find the discount period, the discount, and the proceeds for each. Round money to the nearest cent.

	Loan Made	Face Value	Length of Loan	Simple Interest Rate	Discounted
9.	January 9	$3500	120 days	9%	March 9
10.	April 23	$4000	150 days	7%	June 11
11.	May 5	$6800	130 days	$10\frac{1}{2}\%$	July 6
12.	May 29	$4500	80 days	8%	July 8
13.	September 18	$10,000	220 days	10%	February 4
14.	October 11	$17,500	100 days	11%	January 2

Solve the following application problems. Round money to the nearest cent and interest rates to the nearest hundredth of a percent.

15. AIR CONDITIONER   On June 7, Capital Air, Inc. accepted a 150-day simple interest note for $8500 at 10% when it installed an air-conditioning unit on a large commercial building. The note is discounted on August 3 at 12%. Find (a) the discount period, (b) the discount, and (c) the proceeds to Capital Air.

16. ELECTRONIC EQUIPMENT   On October 1, Home Health signed a $90,000 note at $11\frac{1}{2}\%$ simple interest for 180 days for electronic equipment. On February 18, the note was sold to another firm at a discount rate of $12\frac{1}{2}\%$. Find (a) the discount period, (b) the discount, and (c) the proceeds.

17. **FOUNDATION** On April 20, Hendrix Foundations accepts a $18,500 note for work done on the cement foundation for a commercial building. The note is for 180 days at 7.5% simple interest. If Hendrix sells the note at a 9% discount rate 30 days after receipt, find (a) the bank discount and (b) the proceeds.

18. **ELECTRONIC GAMES** Warrior Games accepted a $420,800 note from a large retailer for the sale of electronic games. The note is for 200 days at 7% simple interest. If the firm sells the note at an 8% discount rate 90 days after receipt for funds to make payroll, find (a) the bank discount and (b) the proceeds.

19. **REDISCOUNTING A NOTE** Citizen's First Bank accepted a $24,000 simple discount note from a customer at a discount rate of $10\frac{1}{2}\%$ for 150 days. They rediscounted the note to Northside Bank at 11% exactly 90 days before its maturity date. Find (a) the proceeds to the customer, (b) the proceeds to Citizen's First Bank, and (c) the actual amount of interest earned by Citizen's First Bank on the note.

20. **SIMPLE DISCOUNT NOTE** Farmer's Bank accepted a $17,000 simple discount note from a customer. The note was for 120 days at an 11% discount rate. The bank then rediscounted the note at a second bank, at 8%, 15 days before the maturity date of the note. Find each of the following: (a) the proceeds to the customer of Farmer's Bank, (b) the proceeds to Farmer's Bank when it rediscounted the note, and (c) the actual amount of interest earned by Farmer's Bank on the note.

21. **DISCOUNT NOTE** State Bank accepts a simple discount note at 12% for 280 days on December 3, with a maturity value of $36,500. It rediscounts the note at 10% on May 4 of the following year. Find (a) the proceeds to the maker of the note, (b) the proceeds to State Bank, and (c) the actual interest earned by State Bank.

22. **DISCOUNT NOTE** On March 13, First Bank accepted a note due in 180 days with a face value of $45,000 and a discount rate of 9.8%. The bank discounts the note on July 15 at a rate of 10.5%. Find (a) the proceeds to the customer of the bank, (b) the proceeds to the bank when it rediscounts the note, and (c) the actual amount of interest earned by the bank.

23. **T-BILLS** On behalf of the bank where he works, Jim Jackson purchased $100,000 in 52-week T-bills at a discount rate of 4.8% and sold them 32 weeks later at a discount rate of 5%. Find (a) the total purchase price, (b) the discount at the time of sale, (c) the proceeds to the bank, and (d) the effective interest rate to Jim Jackson. (*Hint:* Treat T-bills as a discount note.)

24. **T-BILLS** On June 1, the finance ministry of Saudi Arabia purchased $10,000,000 in 26-week T-bills at a discount rate of 3.9% and then sold them 15 weeks later at a discount rate of 3.74%. Find (a) the total purchase price, (b) the discount at the time of sale, (c) the proceeds to the Saudi finance ministry, and (d) the effective interest rate. (*Hint:* Treat T-bills as a discount note.)

25. Explain the purpose of discounting a note.

26. Explain why banks or other financial institutions may need to rediscount notes. (See Objective 2.)

CHAPTER TERMS

Review the following terms to test your understanding of the chapter. For any terms you do not know, refer to the page number found next to that term.

annual percentage rate [p. 457]
bank discount [p. 453]
collateral [p. 447]
discount [p. 453 or 466]
discount period [p. 467]
discounting a note [p. 466]
effective interest rate [p. 457]

face value [p. 446]
factors [p. 470]
factoring [p. 470]
Federal Truth in Lending Act [p. 457]
interest-in-advance notes [p. 453]
maker [p. 446]
maturity value [p. 446]

nominal interest rate [p. 457]
payee [p. 446]
payer [p. 446]
proceeds [p. 453]
promissory note [p. 445]
recourse [p. 466]
rediscounted [p. 468]

simple discount note [p. 453]
simple interest note [p. 446]
stated rate [p. 457]
term of the note [p. 446]
true interest rate [p. 457]
U.S. Treasury bills (T-bills) [p. 458]

CONCEPTS

13.1 Maturity value of a loan

Interest $I = PRT$

Maturity value $M = P + I = P(1 + RT)$

13.1 Finding the due date, interest, and maturity value of a note with the term in months

1. Add the number of months to date of note to find due date.
2. Use $I = PRT$ to find interest.
3. Use $M = P + I$ to find maturity value.

13.1 Determining the face value of a note, given rate, time, and maturity value

Use the formula

$$P = \frac{M}{1 + RT}$$

EXAMPLES

A note with a face value of $12,000 is due in 60 days. The rate is 8%. Find the maturity value.

$$I = PRT$$
$$= \$12{,}000 \times 0.08 \times \frac{60}{360} = \$160$$

$$M = P + I$$
$$= \$12{,}000 + \$160 = \$12{,}160$$

Find the due date, interest, and maturity value of a $4800 loan made on May 12 for 9 months at 9%. The due date is 9 months from May 12, which is February 12 of the following year.

$$I = PRT$$
$$= \$4800 \times 0.09 \times \frac{9}{12} = \$324$$

$$M = P + I$$
$$= \$4800 + \$324 = \$5124$$

A 90-day note has an interest rate of 9% and a maturity value of $5726. Find the face value.

$$P = \frac{M}{1 + RT}$$
$$= \frac{\$5726}{1 + \left(0.09 \times \frac{90}{360}\right)} = \$5600$$

13.1	Finding the time of a note in days given maturity value, face value, and interest rate	A note has a face value of $4800, an interest rate of 6%, and a maturity value of $5000. Find the time of the note in days.

Use $T = \dfrac{M - P}{PR} \times 360$ to find time in days.

Alternatively, since $I = M - P$, use

$T = \dfrac{I}{PR} \times 360.$

$$T = \frac{\$5000 - \$4800}{\$4800 \times 0.06} \times 360$$

$$= 250 \text{ days}$$

13.1 Determining the rate of a note given the face value, time, and maturity value

Use $R = \dfrac{M - P}{PT}$ to find the rate. Alternatively,

since $I = M - P$, use $R = \dfrac{I}{PT}.$

A 240-day note has a face value of $9000 and a maturity value of $9300. Find the interest rate.

$$R = \frac{\$9300 - \$9000}{\$9000 \times \frac{240}{360}} = 0.05$$

The rate is 5%.

13.2 Finding the discount and proceeds of a simple discount note

1. Calculate bank discount B using the formula $B = MDT$ with D = discount rate.
2. Calculate proceeds using the formula $P = M - B$.

Tom Jones borrows $5000 for 60 days at a discount rate of 9%. Find the bank discount and proceeds.

$$B = MDT$$

$$= \$5000 \times 0.09 \times \frac{60}{360} = \$75$$

$$P = M - B$$

$$= \$5000 - \$75 = \$4925$$

13.2 Determining the effective rate or true rate of interest given face value, time, and discount rate

First, find the discount (B) using the formula $B = MDT$. Find the proceeds using the formula $P = M - B$. Calculate the true rate of interest from either

$$R = \frac{M - P}{PT} \qquad \text{or} \qquad R = \frac{I}{PT}$$

A note has a face value of $9000, a time of 120 days, and a discount rate of 12%. Find the true rate of interest.

$$B = MDT$$

$$= \$9000 \times 0.12 \times \frac{120}{360} = \$360$$

$$P = M - B$$

$$= \$9000 - \$360 = \$8640$$

$$R = \frac{I}{PT}$$

$$= \frac{\$360}{\$8640 \times \frac{120}{360}} = 0.125$$

The effective rate is 12.5%.

13.2 Finding the face value of a simple discount note

Use the formula $M = \dfrac{P}{1 - DT}$ to find the face value M.

Find the face value of a note that will provide $38,000 in proceeds if the note is repaid in 220 days and the bank charges an 8% discount rate.

$$M = \frac{P}{1 - DT}$$

$$= \frac{\$38,000}{1 - \left(0.08 \times \frac{220}{360}\right)}$$

$$= \$39,953.27 \qquad \text{Rounded}$$

13.2 Determining the discount rate of a note given face value and proceeds

Find the discount B from the formula $B = M - P$.

Find the rate from the formula $D = \dfrac{B}{MT}$.

A 90-day note has a face value of $15,000 and proceeds of $14,568.75. Find the discount rate.

$$B = M - P$$
$$= \$15,000 - \$14,568.75$$
$$= \$431.25$$

$$D = \frac{B}{MT}$$

$$= \frac{\$431.25}{\$15,000 \times \frac{90}{360}} = 0.115$$

The discount rate is 11.5%.

13.3 Finding the simple interest rate that equates to a given discount rate

Find the simple interest rate using the formula

$$R = \frac{D}{1 - DT}$$

A 180-day simple discount note is at 10%. Find the equivalent simple interest rate.

$$R = \frac{D}{1 - DT}$$

$$= \frac{0.10}{1 - 0.10 \times \frac{180}{360}} = 10.53\% \quad \text{Rounded}$$

13.3 Find the simple discount rate that equates to a given simple interest rate

Find the discount rate using the formula

$$D = \frac{R}{1 + RT}$$

A 240-day simple interest note is at $10\frac{3}{4}\%$. Find the equivalent simple discount rate.

$$D = \frac{R}{1 + RT}$$

$$= \frac{0.1075}{1 + 0.1075 \times \frac{240}{360}} = 10.03\% \quad \text{Rounded}$$

13.4 Finding the proceeds, to an individual or firm, after discounting a note

STEP 1 Find the maturity value of the original note (if necessary). Use $M = P(1 + RT)$.

STEP 2 Find the discount period.

STEP 3 Find the discount using the formula $B = MDT$.

STEP 4 The proceeds are found by $P = M - B$.

Moe's Ice Cream converts a 9%, 150-day simple interest note dated March 1 with a face value of $15,000 to cash on June 1. Assume a discount rate of 11%.

1. Find the proceeds.

$$M = P(1 + RT)$$
$$= \$15{,}000 \times \left(1 + 0.09 \times \frac{150}{360}\right)$$
$$= \$15{,}562.50$$

2. Find the discount period.

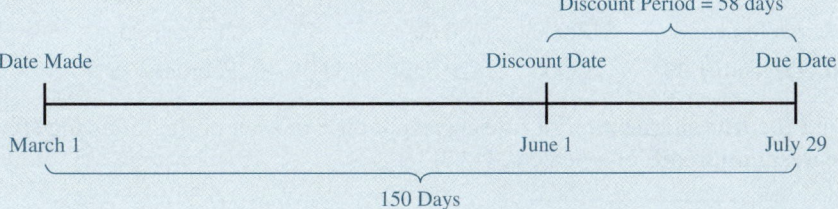

Discount Period = 58 days

Date Made   Discount Date   Due Date

March 1   June 1   July 29

150 Days

3. Find the bank discount.

$$B = \$15{,}562.50 \times 0.11 \times \frac{58}{360}$$
$$= \$275.80 \quad \text{Rounded}$$

4. Find the proceeds.

$$P = \$15{,}562.50 - \$275.80$$
$$= \$15{,}286.70$$

The bank will pay $15,286.70 to Moe on June 1 and collect $15,562.50 on July 29 from the maker of the note.

CHAPTER 13   Review Exercises

The answer section includes answers to all Review Exercises.

Complete the following table for simple interest notes. Round money to the nearest cent. [13.1]

	Face Value	Rate	Time	Interest	Maturity Value
1.	$9800	$8\frac{1}{2}\%$	200 days	_____	_____
2.	$3000		90 days	$78.75	_____
3.	$8000	12%	_____	$640	_____
4.	_____	9.25%	180 days	$670.63	_____

In the following, find the due date and the maturity value. [13.1]

	Date Made	Face Value	Term of Loan	Simple Interest Rate	Date Due	Maturity Value
5.	January 8	$12,000	120 days	9%	_____	_____
6.	June 19	$6000	200 days	$12\frac{1}{2}\%$	_____	_____

Find the discount and the proceeds for the following discounted notes. **[13.2]**

	Face Value	Discount Rate	Time	Discount	Proceeds
7.	$18,000	12%	80 days	_____	_____
8.	$26,000	$10\frac{1}{2}\%$	180 days	_____	_____

Each of the following simple interest notes was discounted 12%. Find the (a) discount period, (b) discount, and (c) proceeds for the following discounted notes. **[13.4]**

	Loan Made	Face Value	Length of Loan	Rate	Date of Discount
9.	September 4	$12,000	150 days	9%	October 25
10.	December 20	$8500	120 days	$11\frac{1}{8}\%$	February 28

Find the true simple interest rate corresponding to each of the following simple discount rates. Round to the nearest hundredth of a percent. **[13.3]**

	Time	Discount Rate
11.	150 days	11%
12.	170 days	9%

Solve the following application problems. Round rates to the nearest hundredth of a percent, time to the nearest day, and money to the nearest cent.

13. What simple discount rate corresponds to a simple interest rate of 12% on a 180-day note? **[13.3]**

14. Ben's Ice Cream borrowed $23,500 for 200 days at $8\frac{3}{4}\%$ simple interest. Find the maturity value. **[13.1]**

15. The note in Exercise 14 was discounted 80 days before maturity at 10%. Find the discount. **[13.2]**

16. Benito Maintenance signed a $45,000 simple interest note for 200 days and was charged $2250 in interest. Find the rate. **[13.1]**

17. Walter Bates borrowed $23,000 at 10% simple interest to start a cabinet-making business. Find the term of the loan if the interest is $1150. **[13.1]**

18. A borrower signed a note with a face value of $50,000 at a $9\frac{1}{2}\%$ discount rate and received $47,361.11. Find the term of the note. **[13.2]**

19. To expand his saw-sharpening business, Chuck Giles signed a note with a face value of $18,500 for 150 days that had proceeds of $17,671.35. Find the discount rate. **[13.2]**

20. A 90-day note has a loan amount of $12,000 and a maturity value of $12,330. Find the simple interest rate and simple discount rate of this note. **[13.3]**

21. Bill Barton needed money for a new automobile and signed a note for $15,000 at a simple discount rate of 12% and a term of 240 days. Find the effective rate of interest. **[13.2]**

22. On December 8, Joan Jones signed a 100-day, 10% discount note at First Bank for $14,000. First Bank sold the note to a finance company on February 12 at a $9\frac{1}{2}\%$ discount. Find the proceeds to First Bank. **[13.4]**

23. West Stables must pay a note given to one of its suppliers. The interest rate on the note is 8%, the face value is $12,300, and the simple interest is $410. Find the time of the note. **[13.1]**

24. Martinez Cleaners borrows $42,000 for 200 days at $9\frac{1}{2}\%$ simple interest. Find the interest. **[13.1]**

25. A company with bad credit signed a $79,000, 120-day note for a shipment of goods. The maturity value of the note is $83,187. Find the rate of interest paid on the note. **[13.1]**

26. Christina Barrett borrowed funds at an 11% discount rate for 180 days. Find the maturity value if the discount was $1012. **[13.2]**

27. Tom Watson Insurance accepted a 270-day, $8000 note on May 25. The simple interest rate on the note is 15%. The note was then discounted at 12% on August 7. Find the proceeds. **[13.4]**

28. An architect sells a note at a 9% discount. The note has a face value of $18,400 and a discount of $782. Find the length in days. **[13.4]**

29. Yami's Kennels signed a 288-day note with a face value of $25,000 and a discount rate of 9.5%. Find the bank discount and proceeds. **[13.2]**

30. The owner of Scarino's Pizza signed a note with a discount of $2880 and proceeds of $33,120. Find the maturity value. **[13.2]**

31. On March 3, National Bank accepted a $25,000, 180-day note at a discount rate of 9%. It rediscounts the note on May 26 at $9\frac{1}{2}\%$. Find the proceeds to National Bank. **[13.4]**

32. Linda Youngman accepted a $16,000, 120-day note from a customer. The note had a discount rate of 9% and was accepted on May 12. The note was then discounted at 11% on July 20. Find the proceeds to Youngman. **[13.4]**

33. Colonial Bank accepted a 200-day note at 10% simple interest with a face value of $83,000. It discounted the note at a 10% simple discount rate 90 days before it matured. Find the proceeds to Colonial Bank. **[13.2]**

34. Marilyn Neault needs to borrow $35,264 for equipment to set up an optometrist office. She signs a 12% simple discount note at the bank for 216 days. Find the face value of the note. **[13.3]**

35. On November 16, the Wedding Shoppe accepted a 9.5% simple interest 200-day note with a face value of $11,200 for a wedding at Clear Lake. Find the proceeds if the note was discounted at 11% on January 13. **[13.4]**

36. Find the simple interest rate that corresponds to an $11\frac{3}{4}\%$ simple discount rate on a 220-day note. Then find the discount rate that corresponds to a 9.5% simple interest rate on a 220-day note. **[13.3]**

37. Would you prefer a $15,000 note at 12% simple interest or one at 12% discount interest? Explain. **[13.3]**

38. Explain the differences between a simple interest note and a simple discount note. Which type of note (if either) is preferred by a borrower? Explain. **[13.3]**

CHAPTER 13	Business Application Case #1
	How Do Global Banks Make Money?

Bank of America borrowed $80,000,000 at 5% simple interest for 180 days from a Chinese investment house. At the same time, the bank made the following loans, each for the exact same 180-day period.

1. A 7% simple interest note for $38,000,000 to a Canadian firm that extracts oil from Canadian tar sands;

2. An 8.2% simple discount note for $27,500,000 to a British contractor building a factory in South Africa; and

3. An 8% simple discount note for $14,500,000 to a Louisiana company building minesweepers in New Orleans for the Mexican government.

(a) Find the difference between interest received and interest paid by the bank on these funds.

(b) The bank did not loan out all $80,000,000. Find the amount it actually loaned out.

CHAPTER 13	Business Application Case #2
	Financing a Refinery

In addition to using cash on hand, Pinston Refining needs to borrow $185,000,000 for 1 year while constructing the first phase of a new refinery. Managers have approached three banks and have been offered the following loans. In each loan, the proceeds to Pinston Refining are $185,000,000.

Lender	Type of Note	Interest or Discount Rate
Bank U.S.	Discount	9.5%
Japan FundCo	Simple	9.8%
Niacin Strong	Discount	10.4%

(a) Find the maturity value for each and determine the best loan.

(b) Find the difference in interest between the worst and best loans.

CHAPTER

14

Compound Interest

Simple interest is paid on the **principal**—not on any past interest. However, bank deposits and many other investments commonly earn **compound interest**. Compound interest is calculated on any interest previously credited (paid) to the account in addition to the original principal.

The great physicist Albert Einstein said, "The most powerful force in the universe is compound interest." This amazing "powerful force" is something that you can use throughout your life if you choose to do so. To show what can be done using compound interest, assume your parent(s) had invested on your behalf $1000 earning 6% per year on the day you were born. As Figure 14.1 shows, the $1000 would grow to over $18,000 by age 50 and nearly $106,000 by age 80. Note that this $106,000 could be used to give you $6360 in interest *each year for the remainder of your life* and that the entire $106,000 would still be in your estate. All of this with only a $1000 initial investment!

NOTE   Nearly every wealthy individual has used compounding.

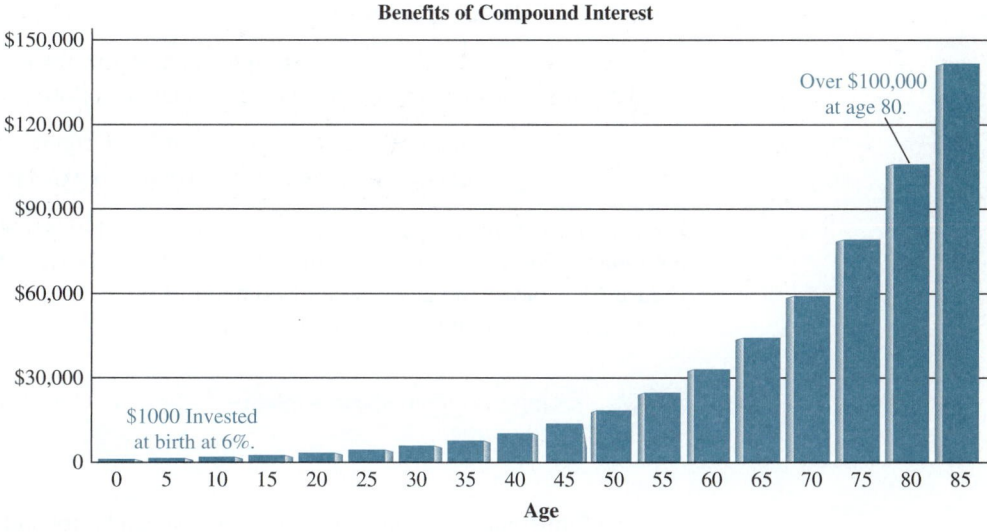

Figure 14.1

STOP
—and think

Why are most wealthy people older? Is it possible to accumulate $1,000,000 in your lifetime? What are some things you would need to do to accomplish that goal?

14.1	**Compound Interest**

OBJECTIVES

1 *Find compound interest and compound amount.*

2 *Determine the number of periods and rate per period.*

3 *Find values in the interest table.*

4 *Use the formula for compound interest to find the compound amount.*

5 *Find the effective rate of interest.*

Objective

1 ***Find Compound Interest and Compound Amount.*** Compound interest includes interest on principal and also interest on interest already paid. Assume that $1000 is deposited into a mutual fund paying 8% per year. Use the formula for simple interest at the end of each year for 3 years to find the compound amount in 3 years.

$$\text{Interest at end of year 1} = \$1000 \times 0.08 \times 1 = \$80$$

Now add the interest to the principal to get the new principal at the beginning of year 2.

$$\text{Principal at end of year 1} = \$1000 + \$80 = \$1080$$

This principal plus interest will earn interest for year 2. Do these same calculations for years 2 and 3.

$$\text{Interest at end of year 2} = \$1080 \times 0.08 \times 1 = \$86.40$$
$$\text{Principal at end of year 2} = \$1080 + \$86.40 = \$1166.40$$

$$\text{Interest at end of year 3} = \$1166.40 \times 0.08 \times 1 = \$93.31$$
$$\text{Principal at end of year 3} = \$1166.40 + \$93.31 = \$1259.71$$

The final amount of $1259.71 is the **compound amount, future amount**, or **future value**. The interest earned during the 3 years is found as follows.

$$\text{Interest} = \text{Compound amount} - \text{Original principal}$$
$$\text{Interest} = \$1259.71 - \$1000 = \$259.71$$

Simple interest on $1000 for 3 years at 8% would be: $1000 × 0.08 × 3 = $240. So, compound interest resulted in an extra $19.71 ($259.71 − $240) interest in 3 years. Figure 14.2 shows the advantage of compound interest over simple interest for a $1000 investment as the number of years increases.

> **NOTE** Compound interest earns interest on principal and it also earns interest on any interest already earned.

The future amount using compound interest can be found by multiplying the principal times the quantity (1 + Rate) once for each period the investment is to be compounded. Rate is the annual interest rate. Therefore, the future amount of $1000 invested at 8% compounded annually for 3 years is shown as follows.

→ Multiply by (1 + 0.08) 3 times

$$\text{Future value} = \$1000 \times (1 + 0.08) \times (1 + 0.08) \times (1 + 0.08)$$
$$= \$1000 \times 1.08 \times 1.08 \times 1.08$$
$$= \$1259.71$$

Compound Interest Versus Simple Interest
$1000 Invested at 10%

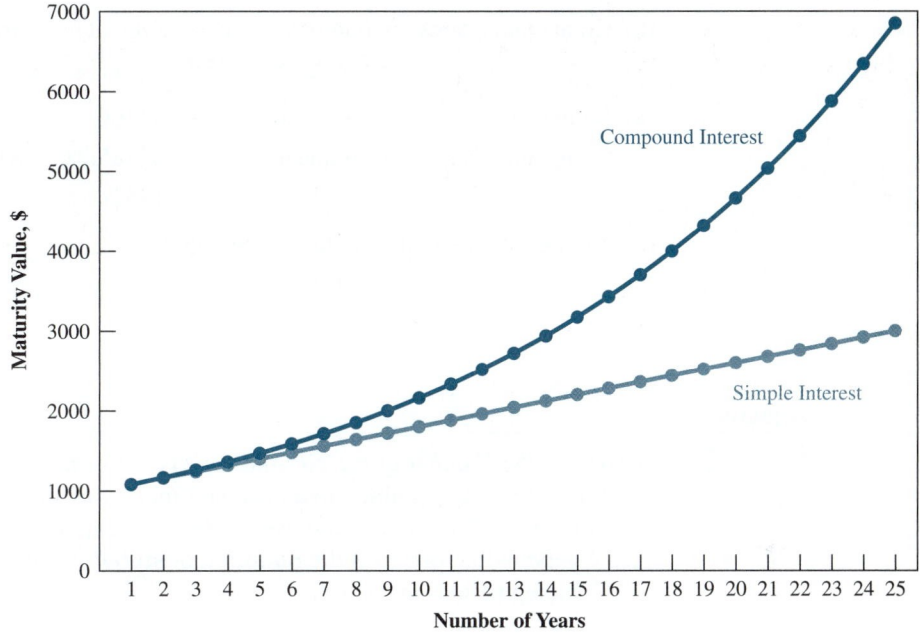

Figure 14.2

Note that $1.08 \times 1.08 \times 1.08$ can be written as $(1.08)^3$, or 1.08^3, using an **exponent** for the number of times 1.08 is multiplied times itself. Thus, the future amount of $1000 invested at 8% compounded annually for 3 years can also be shown as follows.

$$\text{Future value} = \$1000 \times 1.08\overset{\text{Exponent}}{^3} = \$1259.71 \quad \text{(Rounded)}$$

The number 3 is the exponent and is the number of years this investment is compounded. The future value of an investment of $2000 at 8.5% for several different annual periods is shown.

Number of Years	Future Value at 8.5%
5	$2000 \times 1.085^5 = \$3007.31$
10	$2000 \times 1.085^{10} = \$4521.97$
30	$2000 \times 1.085^{30} = \$23{,}116.50$

NOTE The future value of an investment depends on the amount of the initial investment, the interest rate, and the length of time the funds remain invested. The last of these, time, is why many of the wealthy are older. They have had many years to accumulate money and let compound interest work.

EXAMPLE 1 **Finding Compound Interest**

In 4 years, Tony and Lynn Jameson will need $8000 for a down payment on a manufactured home. They have $5500 that they invest in an account earning 5% per year compounded annually. Find (a) the future amount in 4 years, (b) the amount of compound interest earned, (c) the excess of compound interest over simple interest for the 4 years, and (d) the additional amount needed to achieve their goal.

Solution

(a) Future amount $= \$5500 \times 1.05^4 = \$6685.28$ Rounded

(b) Compound interest $=$ Future amount $-$ Original investment

$$= \$6685.28 - \$5500 = \$1185.28$$

(c) Simple interest $= \$5500 \times 0.05 \times 4 = \$1100$

   Compound interest $-$ Simple interest $= \$1185.28 - \$1100$

$$= \$85.28$$

(d) Amount still needed $= \$8000 - \$6685.28$

$$= \$1314.72$$

Objective

2   *Determine the Number of Periods and Rate per Period.*

Interest is often credited to an account more than once a year when calculating compound interest. The interest rate used to find the amount of interest credited at the end of each compounding period is the **nominal**, or **stated**, annual rate divided by the number of compounding periods in one year.

Compounding Period	Interest Credited at the End of Each	Number of Times Interest Is Credited per Year	Number of Times Interest Would Be Credited over 5 Years	Rate per Compounding Period If R Is Rate per Year
Annual	Year	1	$5 \times 1 = 5$	R
Semiannual	6 months	2	$5 \times 2 = 10$	$\frac{R}{2}$
Quarterly	Quarter	4	$5 \times 4 = 20$	$\frac{R}{4}$
Monthly	Month	12	$5 \times 12 = 60$	$\frac{R}{12}$

EXAMPLE 2 **Finding Number of Periods and Rate per Period**

(a) A bank pays interest of 8%, compounded semiannually. This means that semiannually, or twice a year, interest of $8\% \div 2 = 4\%$ is added to all money that has been on deposit for 6 months or more.

(b) An interest rate of 9% per year, compounded quarterly, means that every 3 months (quarterly), interest of $9\% \div 4 = 2.25\%$ is added to all money that has been on deposit for at least a quarter.

NOTE In Example 2(a), the **period of compounding** is semiannual (every 6 months), while it is quarterly (every 3 months) in Example 2(b).

The formula for compound interest is often written using algebraic notation. If P dollars are deposited at a rate of interest i per period for n periods, then the compound amount and interest earned are found as follows.

$$\text{Compound amount} = M = P(1 + i)^n$$
$$\text{Interest earned} = I = M - P$$

NOTE It is important to keep in mind that i is the interest rate *per compounding period*, and not per year, and n is the total number of *compounding periods*, not the number of years.

EXAMPLE **3** **Finding Compound Interest**

Jonathan Simons invests $2500 in an account paying 4% compounded semiannually for 5 years. (a) Estimate the future value using simple interest. Then find (b) the compound amount, (c) the compound interest, and (d) the amount by which simple interest calculations underestimate the compound interest that is earned.

Solution

(a) Simple interest calculations can be used to estimate the compound amount but they will always underestimate the actual amount. Use $4\% \div 2 = 2\%$ per period and $5 \text{ years} \times 2 = 10$ periods for the calculations.

$$\text{Simple interest} = PRT$$
$$= \$2500 \times 0.02 \times 10 = \$500$$
$$\text{Estimate of future amount} = P + I = \$2500 + \$500 = \$3000$$

(b) $\text{Compound amount} = P(1 + i)^n$
$$= \$2500 \times (1 + 0.02)^{10}$$
$$= \$2500 \times 1.02^{10}$$
$$= \$3047.49 \quad \text{Rounded}$$

(c) $\text{Compound interest} = M - P$
$$= \$3047.49 - \$2500 = \$547.49$$

(d) $\text{Underestimation when simple interest is used} = \text{Compound interest} - \text{Simple interest}$
$$= \$547.49 - \$500 = \$47.49$$

Objective

3 ***Find Values in the Interest Table.*** The value of $(1 + i)^n$ can be found by direct calculation using scientific calculators or from tables. One such table is given in the compound interest column (column A) of the interest table in **Appendix D**. The interest rate per compounding period is on the upper left-hand corner of each page.

EXAMPLE **4** **Using the Interest Table**

Find the following values in the compound interest table in **Appendix D**.

Number of compounding periods

(a) $(1 + 5\%)^{12}$ or $(1 + 0.05)^{12} = (1.05)^{12}$

Interest rate per compounding period

Find the 5% page of the interest table. Look in column A, for compound interest, and find 12 (or 12 periods) at the left side. You should find 1.79585633.

Number of compounding periods

(b) $(1 + 8\%)^{27} = (1.08)^{27} = 7.98806147$

Interest rate per compounding period

Find the 8% page. Then look in column A and find 27 at the left.

Scientific Calculator Approach

For the calculator solution to Example 4,

(a) The value of $(1.05)^{12}$ can be found as follows.

$$1.05 \boxed{y^x} 12 \boxed{=} 1.795856326$$

(b) The value of $(1.08)^{27}$ is found as follows.

$$1.08 \boxed{y^x} 27 \boxed{=} 7.988061469$$

NOTE Some calculators have an $\boxed{a^x}$ or $\boxed{x^y}$ key instead of a $\boxed{y^x}$ key. All of these keys are used in the same way.

Objective

4 *Use the Formula for Compound Interest to Find the Compound Amount.* The evaluation of $(1 + i)^n$ using tables or calculators can now be used to find the compound amount and interest.

EXAMPLE 5 **Finding Compound Interest**

John Smith inherits $15,000, which he deposits in a retirement account that pays interest compounded semiannually. How much will he have after 25 years if the funds grow (a) at 6%, (b) at 8%, and (c) at 10%? Round to the nearest cent.

Solution In 25 years, there are $2 \times 25 = 50$ semiannual periods. The semiannual interest rates are (a) $\frac{6\%}{2} = 3\%$, (b) $\frac{8\%}{2} = 4\%$, and (c) $\frac{10\%}{2} = 5\%$. Using factors from the table or using the formula $M = P(1 + i)^n$,

(a) $15,000(1.03)^{50} = 15,000 \times 4.38390602 = 65,758.59$
(b) $15,000(1.04)^{50} = 15,000 \times 7.10668335 = 106,600.25$
(c) $15,000(1.05)^{50} = 15,000 \times 11.46739979 = 172,011.00$

The $15,000 that John Smith inherits is the present value he has today. The future value is the amount he will have in 25 years.

Financial Calculator Approach

Present value, interest per compounding period, and number of compound periods are known. Future value is the unknown. See **Appendix A.2.**

(a) $-15000 \boxed{PV} 3 \boxed{i} 50 \boxed{n} \boxed{FV} 65758.59$

(b) $-15000 \boxed{PV} 4 \boxed{i} 50 \boxed{n} \boxed{FV} 106600.25$

(c) $-15000 \boxed{PV} 5 \boxed{i} 50 \boxed{n} \boxed{FV} 172011$

Answers will vary by a few cents depending on the specific calculator used.

NOTE Simple interest rate calculations are usually indicated by phrases such as *simple interest, simple interest note,* or *discount rate.* Compound interest rate calculations are usually indicated by phrases such as *compounded annually, 6% per quarter,* or *compounded daily.*

The more often interest is compounded, *the more interest is earned.* Use a financial calculator or a compound interest table more complete than the one in this text and use the compound interest formula to get the results shown in Table 14.1. (Leap years were ignored in finding daily interest.)

TABLE 14.1   INTEREST ON $1000 AT 6% PER YEAR FOR 10 YEARS

Frequency of Compounding	Interest per Compounding Period	Number of Compounding Periods	Interest
Not at all (simple interest)	—	—	$600.00
Annually	6%	10	$1790.85
Semiannually	6%/2	20	$1806.11
Quarterly	6%/4	40	$1814.02
Monthly	6%/12	120	$1819.40
Daily	6%/365	3650	$1822.03
Hourly	6%/8760	87,600	$1822.12
Every Minute	6%/525,600	5,256,000	$1822.12

Table 14.1 shows that compounding produces significantly more interest than does simple interest. However, increasing the frequency of compounding makes smaller and smaller differences in the amount of interest earned with an increasing number of compounding periods.

EXAMPLE 6   Finding Compound Amount

Ben Fitzgerald is comparing two different investment options. Find the compound amount on a deposit of $8000 for 3 years at (a) 6% compounded quarterly and (b) 6% compounded monthly.

Solution

(a) Number of compounding periods = 3 years × 4 quarters per year = 12 and interest of 6% ÷ 4 = 1.5% is credited at the end of each quarter.

From the table.

$$\$8000(1.015)^{12} = \$8000 \times \boxed{1.19561817} = \$9564.95 \quad \text{Rounded}$$

(b) Number of compounding periods = 3 years × 12 months per year = 36 and interest of 6% ÷ 12 = 0.5% is credited at the end of each quarter

From the table.

$$\$8000(1.005)^{36} = \$8000 \times \boxed{1.19668052} = \$9573.44 \quad \text{Rounded}$$

 **Scientific Calculator Approach**

Solve Example 6 using a scientific calculator as follows.

(a) 8000 $\times$ 1.015 y^x 12 $=$ 9564.95

(b) 8000 $\times$ 1.005 y^x 36 $=$ 9573.44

Financial
Calculator
Approach

Example 6 can also be solved using a financial calculator, as follows.

(a) -8000 $\boxed{PV}$ 1.5 $\boxed{i}$ 12 $\boxed{n}$ $\boxed{FV}$ 9564.95

(b) -8000 $\boxed{PV}$ 0.5 $\boxed{i}$ 36 $\boxed{n}$ $\boxed{FV}$ 9573.44

Although these values are exactly the same as those found using the Scientific Calculator Approach, values sometimes differ slightly when using different calculators. The difference is usually very small.

Another use of compound interest calculations is to find the effect of **inflation** on real estate values.

EXAMPLE 7 Finding the Effect of Inflation on Real Estate Values

Bill and Joy Lopez purchase a home for $167,200. If the house increases in value by 3% per year, find its value at the end of 4 years.

Solution The value of the house compounds at 3% for 4 years. Use the table to find 1.12550881. You can also use your calculator to work this problem.

$$\text{Future value of home} = \$167,200 \times 1.12550881$$
$$= \$188,185 \qquad \text{Rounded}$$

The home is expected to increase in value by $188,185 - $167,200 = $20,985 during the 4 years.

Objective

5 *Find the Effective Rate of Interest.* The nominal, or stated, interest rate is the annual rate of interest. If interest is compounded more often than once a year, then the actual rate of interest earned *will be greater than* the nominal rate. The rate actually earned is called the **effective rate of interest**. It is necessary to understand effective rate of interest to compare one loan to another, in order to identify which is better.

Consider a deposit of $1000 for 1 year in an investment earning 8% per year compounded quarterly. The maturity value and interest are found as follows.

$$M = \$1000 \times 1.08243216$$
$$= \$1082.43$$
$$\text{Interest} = \$1082.43 - \$1000 = \$82.43$$

The stated interest rate is 8%. However, due to quarterly compounding, the investment earns $82.43 on a $1000 investment. Earning $82.43 on a $1000 investment in a year is an 8.243% return on investment, the effective rate of interest in this case. Notice that the effective rate is greater than the nominal rate. The effective rate of interest takes into consideration how often interest is compounded.

Finding the Effective Rate of Interest

Step 1 Find the entry in column A of the interest table that corresponds to the proper rate per period and the proper number of periods.

Step 2 Subtract 1 from the number.

Step 3 Round to the nearest hundredth of a percent.

NOTE The effective rate can be found on a scientific calculator as $(1 + i)^n - 1$, where i = rate per compounding period and n = number of compounding periods. Round to the nearest hundredth of a percent.

EXAMPLE 8 **Finding the Effective Rate of Interest**

James Suhr is comparing two loans. Loan A has a nominal rate of 10% compounded quarterly and Loan B has a nominal rate of 9% compounded monthly. Find the effective rate of interest for each loan.

Solution Loan A: $10\% \div 4 = 2.5\%$ per quarter for 4 quarters. Look in column A of the interest table for $2\frac{1}{2}\%$ and 4 periods to find the effective interest rate, as follows.

$$\begin{array}{r} 1.10381289 \\ - 1.00000000 \\ \hline 0.10381289, \text{ or } 10.38\% \end{array}$$

Loan B: $9\% \div 12 = 0.75\%$ per month for 12 months. Look in column A of the interest table for $\frac{3}{4}\%$ and 12 periods to find the following.

$$\begin{array}{r} 1.09380690 \\ - 1.00000000 \\ \hline 0.09380690, \text{ or } 9.38\% \end{array}$$

NOTE In Step 2, be sure to subtract 1 from the number in the table to find the interest.

14.1 | **Exercises**

Find the compound amount and the amount of interest earned for the following. Round to the nearest cent. Use your calculator, rather than the tables, in Exercises 1–4.

1. $12,000 at 8% compounded annually for 3 years
2. $8500 at 6% compounded semiannually for $4\frac{1}{2}$ years
3. $6000 at 5% compounded quarterly for 2 years
4. $10,500 at 10% compounded quarterly for 4 years

Find the compound amount when the following deposits are made. Round to the nearest cent.

5. $1000 at 8% compounded annually for 40 years
6. $925 at 5% compounded annually for 12 years
7. $10,000 at 6% compounded semiannually for 9 years
8. $8765.72 at 12% compounded monthly for 4 years

Find the amount of interest earned by the following deposits.

9. $8400 at 7% compounded annually for 8 years
10. $6200 at 11% compounded annually for 5 years
11. $12,600 at 8% compounded quarterly for $4\frac{3}{4}$ years
12. $23,000 at 12% compounded monthly for $2\frac{1}{2}$ years

Find simple interest; then use column A of the interest table and the same interest rate to find the interest compounded annually. Find the amount by which the compound interest is larger. Round to the nearest cent.

	Principal	Rate	Number of Years
13.	$1000	6%	5
14.	$800	7%	6
15.	$7908.42	5%	8
16.	$10,240	10%	11

Find the effective rate corresponding to the following nominal rates. Round to the nearest hundredth of a percent.

17. 8% compounded quarterly

18. 10% compounded quarterly

19. 9% compounded monthly

20. 12% compounded monthly

Solve the following application problems. Round to the nearest cent.

21. FINDING COMPOUND AMOUNT William Gates invested $5000 at 6% for 3 years. Find the compound amount if the compound period is (a) quarterly and (b) monthly.

22. FINDING COMPOUND AMOUNT Bertha James invested $10,000 in a bond mutual fund that pays 8% interest. She plans to leave the money invested for 3 years. Find the compound amount if the compounding period is (a) semiannually and (b) quarterly.

23. COMPOUNDING PERIODS Find the interest earned on $10,000 for 4 years at 6% compounded (a) yearly, (b) semiannually, (c) quarterly, and (d) monthly. (e) Find the simple interest.

24. COMPOUNDING PERIODS Suppose $32,000 is deposited for 2 years at 10% interest. Find the interest earned on the deposit if the interest is compounded (a) yearly, (b) semiannually, (c) quarterly, and (d) monthly. (e) Find the simple interest.

25. LOAN TO A RESTAURANT Benjamin Moore loans $8800 to the owner of a new restaurant. He will be repaid at the end of 4 years, with interest at 8% compounded semiannually. Find how much he will be repaid.

26. BANK CD Brenda Gilliam deposits $8000, earned from testing elementary school students for learning disabilities, in a bank CD paying 5% compounded semiannually. Find the future value in 3 years.

27. COMPARING BANKS There are two banks in Citrus Heights. One pays interest of 4% compounded annually, and the other pays 4% compounded quarterly. If Stan deposits $10,000 in each bank, (a) how much will he have in each bank at the end of 3 years? (b) How much more would he have in the bank that paid more interest?

28. COMPARING YIELDS Barbara Mason is considering two investments. One yields 8% compounded quarterly and a second yields 9% compounded monthly. She deposits $6000 in each for a period of 2 years. (a) Find the amount she will have in each at the end of 2 years. Then (b) find the additional amount in the higher-yielding investment.

29. GUARANTEED PENSION One of the pension funds that Jessica Walters manages must have $3,450,000 in 2 years. The fund currently has $2,600,000 and it earns 5% compounded monthly. Find the expected shortage in the pension in 2 years.

30. **GOVERNMENT CLAIM** The government is requiring Ace Plumbing to have $4.2 million in its pension plan in 18 months. It currently has $3.2 million earning 6% compounded semiannually. Find the expected shortage in the pension in 18 months.

31. **COMPARING INVESTMENTS** Joan Getz is comparing two investment opportunities, the first at 6% compounded semiannually and the second at 5% compounded monthly. Find the effective interest rates for each. Which would produce more income for Getz?

32. **RAISING FUNDS** A church plans to raise funds by selling bonds to individuals and businesses in the community. It is considering two options, the first at 8% compounded annually and the second at 6% compounded monthly. Find the effective interest rate for both. Which would produce the lower cost for the church?

Use either a scientific or financial calculator to solve the following for compound amount.

33. $15,000 at 6.5% compounded annually for 3 years

34. $24,500 at 8.9% compounded semiannually for 2 years

35. $9500 at 10.3% compounded quarterly for $2\frac{1}{2}$ years

36. $18,000 at 6% compounded monthly for $2\frac{1}{4}$ years

37. Explain the basic difference between simple interest and compound interest. (See Objective 1.)

38. Do long-term investments grow more using simple interest or compound interest? Why is this type of interest to your advantage when saving for events several years in the future? (See Objective 1.)

39. **COMPARING YIELDS** Jess Cockrell has $20,000 to invest for 1 year. He can lend it to his brother, who has agreed to pay 7% simple interest, or to a bank paying 4% compounded quarterly. Find the extra interest earned if he lends the funds to his brother.

40. **COMPARING YIELDS** Benson Automotive has $400,000 to invest for 9 months. The firm has the choice of lending it to a local contractor at 8% simple interest or to a bank that will pay 4% compounded monthly. Find the additional interest that would be generated by the simple interest note in this situation.

41. **RETIREMENT INVESTMENT** Peter and Betsy Mueller inherit $12,000 from Peter's aunt. Although they are only in their early thirties, the Muellers decide to set the money aside for their eventual retirement. They invest the funds in a Roth IRA account so that they will not have to pay any taxes on the earnings. Find the amount they will have in 25 years if the funds are invested in a fund that grows at 8% compounded semiannually for 25 years.

14.2 Daily and Continuous Compounding

1 *Define savings account and money market account.*

2 *Calculate interest compounded daily.*

3 *Find compound interest for time deposit accounts.*

4 *Determine the penalty for early withdrawal.*

5 *Find compound amount with continuous compounding.*

One positive result from the financial crisis that began in 2008 was an increase in the level of personal savings. Figure 14.3 shows that household savings in the United States had fallen dramatically and more or less continuously since the early 1990s. In other words, individuals simply saved less and less as the years went by. That has been a worrisome trend. However, savings increased sharply in mid 2008 as the news media talked constantly about the financial problems in the world and many people worried about their debt and began saving.

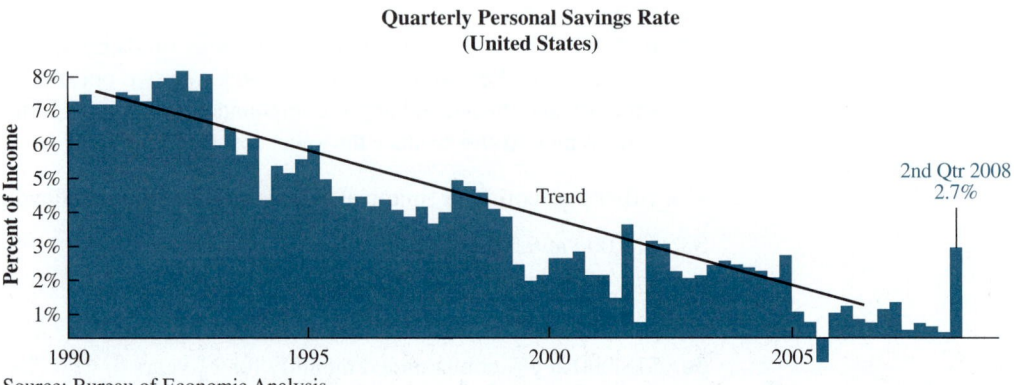

Source: Bureau of Economic Analysis.

Figure 14.3

Objective

1   *Define Savings Account and Money Market Account.*   A **savings account**, or **passbook account**, is an account at a bank or other financial institution that normally requires no minimum balance, no minimum term, and no notice or penalty for withdrawals. Passbook accounts generally show transactions in a small book. They have mostly been replaced by savings accounts that provide monthly statements. Both of these accounts pay interest at a rate stated periodically by the bank.

In contrast, **money market accounts** pay interest rates that change frequently but that are maintained only as long as the balance in the account does not fall below a predetermined minimum, usually between $1000 and $2500. These accounts offer interest rates almost as high as those of time deposits, while permitting funds to be withdrawn at any time. These accounts were set up to compete with the money market funds offered by many stock brokerage and mutual funds firms.

Both savings accounts and money market accounts are used to meet the day-to-day money needs of a person or business. Money can be deposited in, or withdrawn from, savings accounts and money market accounts with no penalty, although most money market funds limit the number of withdrawals per month. Historically, interest rates on both savings accounts and money market accounts have varied widely. Many checking accounts now also pay a small amount of interest, but the banks charge a fee if the balance falls below a specific amount. The Truth in Savings Act of 1991 resulted in **Regulation DD**, which requires that interest on savings accounts be *paid based on the exact number of days*.

Savings accounts and money markets are one of the safest places to place money. These accounts at most, but not all, institutions are insured by either the **Federal Deposit Insurance Corporation (FDIC)** or **Federal Savings and Loan Insurance Corporation (FSLIC)** on deposits up to a specified limit. The limit is currently $250,000, but it is scheduled to be reduced back to $100,000 at the end of 2009. Call your bank to see if your funds are federally insured.

Interest rates on savings accounts have ranged widely from close to 0% currently to as high as 5% in the past. Since most economists expect interest rates to increase from current levels, we arbitrarily choose to use $3\frac{1}{2}\%$ in Table 14.2 and for all of the interest rate calculations in this section.

Table 14.2   VALUES OF $(1 + i)^n$ **FOR** $3\frac{1}{2}\%$ **COMPOUNDED DAILY**

Number of Days n	Value of $(1 + i)^n$	n	Value of $(1 + i)^n$	n	Value of $(1 + i)^n$	n	Value of $(1 + i)^n$	n	Value of $(1 + i)^n$
1	1.000095890	19	1.001823491	37	1.003554076	55	1.005287650	73	1.007024219
2	1.000191790	20	1.001919556	38	1.003650307	56	1.005384048	74	1.007120783
3	1.000287699	21	1.002015631	39	1.003746548	57	1.005480454	75	1.007217357
4	1.000383617	22	1.002111714	40	1.003842797	58	1.005576870	76	1.007313939
5	1.000479544	23	1.002207807	41	1.003939056	59	1.005673296	77	1.007410531
6	1.000575480	24	1.002303909	42	1.004035324	60	1.005769730	78	1.007507132
7	1.000671426	25	1.002400021	43	1.004131602	61	1.005866174	79	1.007603742
8	1.000767381	26	1.002496141	44	1.004227888	62	1.005962627	80	1.007700362
9	1.000863345	27	1.002592271	45	1.004324184	63	1.006059089	81	1.007796990
10	1.000959318	28	1.002688410	46	1.004420489	64	1.006155560	82	1.007893628
11	1.001055300	29	1.002784558	47	1.004516803	65	1.006252041	83	1.007990276
12	1.001151292	30	1.002880716	48	1.004613127	66	1.006348531	84	1.008086932
13	1.001247293	31	1.002976882	49	1.004709460	67	1.006445030	85	1.008183598
14	1.001343303	32	1.003073058	50	1.004805802	68	1.006541538	86	1.008280273
15	1.001439322	33	1.003169243	51	1.004902153	69	1.006638056	87	1.008376958
16	1.001535350	34	1.003265438	52	1.004998513	70	1.006734583	88	1.008473651
17	1.001631388	35	1.003361641	53	1.005094883	71	1.006831119	89	1.008570354
18	1.001727435	36	1.003457854	54	1.005191262	72	1.006927665	90	1.008667067

Note: The value of $(1 + i)^n$ for $3\frac{1}{2}\%$ compounded daily for a quarter with 91 days is 1.008763788 and for a quarter with 92 days is 1.008860519.

Objective

2   *Calculate Interest Compounded Daily.*   Interest on savings accounts is found using compound interest. It is common for banks to pay interest **compounded daily** so that interest is credited for every day that the money is on deposit.

The formula for daily compounding is *exactly* the same as that given in the last section. However, because the annual interest rate must be divided by 365 (for daily compounding), the arithmetic is very tedious. To avoid this, use Table 14.2, which provides the necessary numbers for 1 to 92 days, as well as for one to four 90-day quarters, assuming $3\frac{1}{2}\%$ interest compounded daily. The table goes to only 92 days since interest is normally credited to the depositor's account only quarterly, even with daily compounding. The four quarters in a year begin on January 1, April 1, July 1, and October 1. Although some quarters have 91 or 92 days in them, we assume 90-day quarters for convenience in calculation.

INTEREST BY QUARTER FOR $3\frac{1}{2}\%$ **COMPOUNDED DAILY ASSUMING 90-DAY QUARTERS**

Number of Quarters	Value of $(1 + i)^n$
1	1.008667067
2	1.017409251
3	1.026227205
4	1.035121585

NOTE   See **Appendix A.2** for financial calculators that do not require the use of a table.

EXAMPLE **1**   **Finding Interest Using Daily Compounding**

Mr. Watson wants his 6-year-old son Billy to learn about savings and interest. He took Billy to a bank on September 12 and opened a savings account with $500 to which Billy added $23.50 he had received from doing chores. Find the amount of interest Billy has earned by his birthday, November 20, if he earns $3\frac{1}{2}\%$ compounded daily.

Solution   There are 18 days remaining in September, 31 days in October, and 20 days in November. The money was on deposit for $18 + 31 + 20 = 69$ days. The table value for 69 days is 1.006638056, so the compound amount is

$$\$523.50 \times 1.006638056 = \$526.98 \quad \text{Rounded}$$

and the interest earned is $\$526.98 - \$523.50 = \$3.48$.

Billy is old enough that he isn't impressed with $3.48. Mr. Watson, knowing the power of compound interest over the long term, insists that Billy continue to save part of his earnings.

Scientific Calculator Approach

Using a scientific calculator, Example 1 can be solved as follows.

523.50 $\times$ (1 + 0.035 $\div$ 365) y^x 69 = 526.98

Financial Calculator Approach

Solve for the unknown future value using a financial calculator as follows.

-523.50 PV 0.009589041 i 69 n FV 526.98

$\hookrightarrow$ 3.5 $\div$ 365

Interest rates on savings accounts change often. If the rate is other than $3\frac{1}{2}\%$, use the formula for compound amount from **Section 14.1**, that is,

$$M = P(1 + i)^n$$

where $i = $ *annual rate* and $n = $ number of days.

EXAMPLE 2 **Finding Quarterly Interest**

Tom Blackmore is a private investigator. On January 10, he deposited $2463 in a savings account paying $3\frac{1}{2}\%$ compounded daily. He deposits an additional $1320 on February 18 and $840 on March 3. Find the interest earned through April 10.

Solution Treat each of the three amounts separately. The $2463 was in the account for 21 days in January, 28 days in February, 31 days in March, and 10 days in April for a total of 90 days. The compound amount is found using 1.008667067 from the table.

Compound amount = $2463 $\times$ 1.008667067 = $2484.35   First deposit plus interest

A deposit of $1320 was made on February 18. This amount was on deposit for 10 days in February, 31 days in March and 10 days in April for a total of 51 days.

Compound amount = $1320 $\times$ 1.004902153 = $1326.47   Second deposit plus interest

The final deposit of $840 was on deposit for 28 days in March and 10 days in April for a total of 38 days.

Compound amount = $840 $\times$ 1.003650307 = $843.07   Final deposit plus interest

The total amount in the account is found by adding the three compound amounts together, and the interest earned is the total amount in the account minus deposits.

Total in account = $2484.35 + $1326.47 + $843.07 = $4653.89

Interest earned = $4653.89 − ($2463 + $1320 + $840) = $30.89

The interest earned is $30.89.

NOTE Different financial institutions calculate quarterly interest in slightly different ways. We show one common way to do it in these examples.

EXAMPLE 3 **Finding Quarterly Interest**

Beth Gardner owns Blacktop Paving, Inc. She needs a place to keep extra cash, a place that will earn interest but that will allow her to get funds when needed. She opened a savings account on July 20 with a $24,800 deposit. She then withdrew $3800 on August 29 for an unexpected truck repair and she made another withdrawal for $8200 on September 29 for payroll. Find the interest earned through October 1, if the interest rate is $3\frac{1}{2}\%$ compounded daily.

Solution Of the original $24,800, a total of $24,800 − $3800 − $8200 = $12,800 earned interest from July 20 to October 1, or for $274 − 201 = 73$ days. Find the factor 1.007024219 from the table.

$$\text{Compound amount} = \$12,800 \times 1.007024219 = \$12,889.91$$
$$\text{Interest} = \$12,889.91 − \$12,800 = \$89.91$$

The withdrawn $3800 earned interest from July 20 to August 29, or for $241 − 201 = 40$ days.

$$\text{Compound amount} = \$3800 \times 1.003842797 = \$3814.60$$
$$\text{Interest} = \$3814.60 − \$3800 = \$14.60$$

Finally, the withdrawn $8200 earned interest from July 20 to September 29 or for $272 − 201 = 71$ days.

$$\text{Compound amount} = \$8200 \times 1.006831119 = \$8256.02$$
$$\text{Interest} = \$8256.02 − \$8200 = \$56.02$$

The total interest earned is ($89.91 + $14.60 + $56.02) = $160.53. The total in the account on October 1 is found as follows.

$$\text{Deposits} + \text{Interest} − \text{Withdrawals} = \text{Balance on October 1}$$
$$\$24,800 + \$160.53 − (\$3800 + \$8200) = \$12,960.53$$

Objective

3 *Find Compound Interest for Time Deposit Accounts.* Savings accounts and money market accounts are handy for funds needed on a day-to-day basis but time deposits are better for larger sums that are not needed in the near future. **Time deposits** are deposits that must be left at a bank for a specific period of time such as 6 months, 1 year, or 3 years. Importantly, they pay a higher interest rate than savings accounts. Time deposits often require a minimum investment of $500 or more. There is no law that requires a bank to issue a certificate with a time deposit, but most do issue an accompanying certificate and they refer to it as a **certificate of deposit** or **CD**. A typical CD is shown in Figure 14.4.

It is probably not a good idea to invest all of one's money in a certificate of deposit, since a penalty is charged for early withdrawal. At least some cash should be left in a savings or money market account for daily needs. Additionally, many financial planners recommend that some portion of liquid assets be placed in mutual funds containing stocks or bonds.

The higher interest paid by some certificates of deposit can be found using Table 14.3 on the next page. (This table assumes daily compounding and 365 days per year.)

NEW ENGLAND FEDERAL
— *Savings Bank* —

Certificate of Deposit

1. Account Summary
Accountholder(s)   JOHN DOE

Account Number	123–45670
Date of Issuance	JANUARY 23
Maturity Date	JULY 23

Principal Amount	Term	Nominal Rate / APR	Additional Deposits
$ 6,400.00	30 MONTHS	4.08/4.50%	None

2. General

This is a Certificate of Deposit in the amount set forth above issued to the Accountholder(s) named above, by New England Federal Savings Bank.

3. Account Renewal

Unless the Accountholder(s) has instructed the Bank not to renew this certificate of deposit, it will automatically and repeatedly be renewed at its maturity for an identical term and at the interest rate the Bank is then offering. Notice of maturity will be mailed to the Accountholder(s) at least 15 days prior to each maturity. The Bank reserves the right not to renew this certificate of deposit, but it must mail notice of such intention to the Accountholder(s) at least 15 days prior to maturity.

4. Interest

This certificate of deposit shall earn interest at the rate set forth above. Such interest shall be compounded daily and credited monthly. During renewal terms, this certificate of deposit will earn interest at the rate the Bank is then offering. Interest earned during any term may be withdrawn during that term without penalty. Upon renewal, principal shall include interest earned (but not paid) during the prior term.

5. Interest Checks   N/A

The Accountholder(s) has authorized the Bank to pay interest on the following basis:
☐ Monthly   ☐ Quarterly   ☐ Semi Annually

6. Withdrawal Penalty

In the event of any withdrawal of principal at any time prior to the maturity of this or any renewal term, the Accountholder(s) shall pay a penalty equal to three months' interest, (if the term of this certificate of deposit is equal to or less than one year), or six months' interest, (if the term of this certificate of deposit is greater than one year), on the amount withdrawn, at the rate being paid on this certificate of deposit at the time of withdrawal. If the Accountholder withdraws part or all of the balance of this certificate of deposit during the seven calendar days subsequent to the maturity of this or any renewal term, there will be no withdrawal penalty.

Any withdrawal which reduces the balance of this certificate of deposit below $1,000 will be treated as a withdrawal of the remaining balance.

No penalty will be charged for withdrawal following the death or adjudicated incompetence of the Accountholder.

NEW ENGLAND FEDERAL SAVINGS BANK

By   *Sue Smith*
      Authorized Representative

Figure 14.4

Table 14.3   COMPOUND INTEREST FOR TIME DEPOSIT ACCOUNTS (DAILY COMPOUNDING)

Number of Years	Interest Rate			
	4%	5%	6%	7%
1	1.04080849	1.05126750	1.06183131	1.07250098
2	1.08328232	1.10516335	1.12748573	1.15025836
3	1.12748944	1.16182231	1.19719965	1.23365322
4	1.17350058	1.22138603	1.27122407	1.32309429
5	1.22138937	1.28400343	1.34982552	1.41901993
10	1.49179200	1.64866481	1.82202895	2.01361755

EXAMPLE **4**   **Finding Compound Amount and Interest on Time Deposits**

Vivek Pandey deposits $4000 into each of two separate CDs. The first CD pays 4% compounded daily and matures in 3 years. The second CD pays 5% compounded daily and matures in 4 years. Find the maturity value of each.

Solution   Look in Table 14.3 for 4% and 3 years to find 1.12748944.

$$\text{Maturity value} = \$4000 \times 1.12748944 = \$4509.96$$

Look in Table 14.3 for 5% and 4 years to find 1.22138603.

$$\text{Maturity value} = \$4000 \times 1.22138603 = \$4885.54$$

Alternatively, you can find these values using $M = P(1 + i)^n$ and your calculator. The results might differ a bit from the preceding ones due to rounding.

NOTE   Many time deposits earn interest compounded monthly or quarterly rather than daily. In that event, calculate interest using the techniques of **Section 14.1**.

Objective

4   *Determine the Penalty for Early Withdrawal.*   A penalty is incurred if a depositor withdraws funds from a time deposit, such as a CD, before the maturity date. The procedure for calculating this early withdrawal penalty is not standard. However, many financial institutions use the following rules for calculating the **early withdrawal penalty**.

Calculating the Early Withdrawal Penalty on a Time Deposit

1. If money is withdrawn within 3 months of the deposit, no interest will be paid at all on the money withdrawn.
2. If money is withdrawn after 3 months but before the end of the term, then 3 months interest is deducted from the time the account has been open and regular passbook interest is paid on the account.

EXAMPLE **5**   **Finding Interest When Early Withdrawal Occurs**

Use the rules listed in the box to find the amount of interest earned on each of the following.

(a) On January 5, Raymond Hoyle deposited $5000 in a 1-year certificate of deposit paying 6% compounded daily. He withdrew the money on March 12 of the same year.
(b) Bob Kashir deposited $6000 in a 4-year certificate of deposit paying 5% compounded daily. He withdrew the money 15 months later. The passbook rate at his bank is $3\frac{1}{2}\%$ compounded daily.

Solution

(a) Since March 12 is within 3 months of January 5, no interest at all is earned. The bank will simply return the $5000.
(b) The money is withdrawn early, so 3 months, interest is lost. The money was on deposit for 15 months, but only $15 - 3 = 12$ months, interest will be paid. Also, interest will be paid at the passbook rates, $3\frac{1}{2}\%$ compounded daily, instead of the more generous 5% compounded daily. The compound amount is found using the factor for four 90-day quarters (assume it is not a leap year) at $3\frac{1}{2}\%$. From Table 14.2, this is 1.035121585.

$$\$6000(1.035121585) = \$6210.73$$

The interest is found by subtracting the initial deposit of $6000 from $6210.73.

$$\text{Interest} = \$6210.73 - \$6000 = \$210.73$$

Objective

5 *Find Compound Amount with Continuous Compounding.* In the first section of this chapter, we discussed annual, semiannual, quarterly, and monthly compounding. Then we saw daily compounding at the beginning of this section. There is no reason that interest could not be compounded more frequently, such as every hour or even every minute. Table 14.1 shows the interest earned on $1000 at 6% per year for 10 years, assuming various frequencies of compounding.

Clearly, more frequent compounding results in more interest. However, after a while, increasing the frequency of compounding makes less and less difference. For example, going from compounding daily to compounding every minute produces only 9 cents additional interest on $1000 after 10 years.

It would be possible to extend Table 14.1 to include compounding every second, every half-second, or any desired small time interval. It would even be possible to think of compounding *every instant*. Compounding every instant is called **continuous compounding**. The formula for continuous compounding, given in the next box, uses the number *e*. The number *e* is approximately equal to 2.7182818. Some calculators have an e^x button for working with this number. See **Appendix A** to learn how to use this function on your calculator.

If P dollars are deposited at a rate of interest r per year and *compounded continuously* for t years, the compound interest M is as follows.

$$M = Pe^{rt}$$

Continuous compounding is used by some financial institutions and various government agencies.

EXAMPLE 6 **Finding the Compound Amount for Continuous Compounding**

Find the compound amount for the following deposits.

(a) $1000 at 6% compounded continuously for 10 years
(b) $45,000 at 5% compounded continuously for 3 years

Solution

(a) $1000 at 6% compounded continuously for 10 years

Use the formula in the box with $P = \$1000, r = 0.06$, and $t = 10$. The compound amount is as follows.

$$M = Pe^{rt}$$
$$M = \$1000e^{0.06 \cdot 10}$$
$$= \$1000e^{0.6}$$

The value of $e^{0.6}$ is found in the table in **Appendix C**. Find 0.6 in the column labeled x and read across to the number 1.82211880 in the column labeled e^x.

$$M = \$1000(1.82211880) = \$1822.12$$

Of this amount,

$$\$1822.12 - \$1000 = \$822.12$$

is interest, the same as when interest is compounded every minute as shown in Table 14.1 in this section.

(b) $45,000 at 5% compounded continuously for 3 years (use **Appendix C**).

$$M = \$45,000e^{0.05 \cdot 3}$$
$$= \$45,000e^{0.15}$$
$$= \$45,000 \times 1.16183424 = \$52,282.54$$

Scientific Calculator Approach

Example 6(b) can be solved as follows. Recall that $r \cdot t = 0.05 \times 3 = 0.15$.

$$45000 \boxed{\times} 0.15 \boxed{e^x} \boxed{=} 52282.54$$

NOTE The interest rates paid by banks in some years are quite low compared to the returns from other investments such as stocks. However, in other years, the returns from banks may equal or even exceed returns from stocks.

EXAMPLE 7 Finding the Compound Amount for Continuous Compounding

Find the compound amount for the following deposits in which time is not in an even number of years.

(a) $15,000 at 4.5% compounded continuously for 6 months
(b) $8200 at 4% compounded continuously for 216 days

Solution

(a) Use the formula with $P = \$15,000$, $r = 4.5\% = 0.045$, and $t = \frac{6}{12} = 0.5$.

$$M = Pe^{rt}$$
$$= \$15,000 \cdot e^{0.045 \cdot 0.5}$$
$$= \$15,000 \cdot e^{0.0225}$$
$$= \$15,341.33 \qquad \text{Rounded}$$

(b) Use the formula with $P = \$8200$, $r = 4\% = 0.04$, and $t = \frac{216}{360} = 0.6$.

$$M = Pe^{rt}$$
$$= \$8200 \cdot e^{0.04 \cdot 0.6}$$
$$= \$8200 \cdot e^{0.024}$$
$$= \$8399.18 \qquad \text{Rounded}$$

14.2 Exercises

Find the interest earned by the following. Assume $3\frac{1}{2}\%$ interest compounded daily, and use the exact number of days.

	Amount	Date Deposited	Date Withdrawn
1.	$6200	October 7	December 10
2.	$3850	January 5	February 9
3.	$6500	February 17	April 15
4.	$2830	May 4	June 23

Find the amount on deposit on the first day of the next quarter when the following sums are deposited as indicated. Assume $3\frac{1}{2}\%$ interest compounded daily.

	Amount	Date Deposited
5.	$7235.82	February 14
6.	$3018.25	April 7
7.	$2965.72	July 1
8.	$4031.46	April 1

Find the compound amount for the following certificates of deposit. Assume daily compounding and use Table 14.3.

	Amount Deposited	Interest Rate	Time in Years
9.	$5000	6%	2
10.	$2900	5%	10
11.	$14,000	7%	3
12.	$7500	4%	5

Find the amount of interest earned by the following certificates of deposit. Assume daily compounding and use Table 14.3.

	Amount Deposited	Interest Rate	Time in Years
13.	$20,000	7%	3
14.	$6800	5%	5
15.	$5000	4%	4
16.	$1000	6%	1

17. Explain the difference between passbook accounts, time deposit accounts, certificates of deposit, and insured money market accounts.

18. Use an example to show that continuous compounding is better for a saver than semiannual compounding.

Solve each of the following application problems. Assume $3\frac{1}{2}\%$ interest compounded daily. Round to the nearest cent at each step.

19. SAVINGS ACCOUNT Teresa Tabor had $4300 in her savings account on July 1. She then deposited $1000 on July 30 and $500 on September 5. Find the balance in the account on October 1.

20. SAVINGS ACCOUNT Vicki Phelps had $8600 in her savings account on April 1. She then deposited $800 on May 5 and an additional $350 on June 20. Find the balance in the account on July 1.

21. SAVINGS ACCOUNT FOR EXTRA CASH On April 1, Action Sports opened a savings account with a deposit of $17,500. A withdrawal of $5000 was made 21 days later and another withdrawal of $980 was made 12 days before July 1. Find (a) the interest earned through July 1 and (b) the balance on July 1.

22. EXCESS CASH The owner of Rondo's Magic Shop opened a savings account for the extra cash in the firm. The initial deposit of $7800 was made on July 7. A withdrawal of $1500 was made 46 days later, with an additional withdrawal of $1000 made 30 days before October 1. Find (a) the interest earned through October 1 and (b) the balance on October 1.

For the following application problems on certificates of deposit, use the rules for finding the early withdrawal penalty as given in the text. Assume daily compounding of interest and use Table 14.2.

23. **TIME DEPOSIT**   Alyssa Datolli deposited $8500 in a 4-year time deposit account paying 3.5% interest. She withdrew the funds after 30 days to purchase a car. Find the interest.

24. **TIME DEPOSIT**   Jana Box deposited $6000 in a 3-year account paying 4% interest but needed the money 2 months later and withdrew it. How much interest did she receive?

25. **TIME DEPOSIT**   Emma Gilger placed $20,000 in a 10-year account paying 5% interest. The savings and loan where she placed her money pays a passbook rate of $3\frac{1}{2}\%$ compounded daily. She withdrew $5000 of her money after 15 months. Find the interest that she earned on the $5000.

26. **TIME DEPOSIT**   Trish Hardison deposited $18,680 in a 4-year account paying 6% interest. The bank where she put the money pays a passbook rate of $3\frac{1}{2}\%$ compounded daily. She withdrew $2000 after 15 months. Find the interest that she earned on the $2000.

Use the formulas and the value of *e* (Appendix C) to find the compound amount and the interest for the following deposits. Assume continuous compounding.

	Amount	Interest Rate	Time
27.	$8000	6%	2 years
28.	$4500	4.5%	6 years
29.	$12,000	5%	4 years
30.	$8008.43	6%	6 months

Use the formula $M = Pe^{rt}$ and your calculator to find the compound amount for the following. Assume continuous compounding and use 360 days in a year for Exercise 34.

	Amount	Interest Rate	Time
31.	$4000	4%	2 years
32.	$9000	6%	5 years
33.	$18,000	5.5%	9 months
34.	$25,000	4.5%	324 days

Solve the following application problems. Round to the nearest cent.

35. **PARTIAL COLLATERAL FOR A LOAN**   An Italian engineering firm deposited $800,000 in a 2-year time deposit earning 6% compounded daily as partial collateral for a loan. At maturity, find (a) the compound amount and (b) the interest earned.

36. **WELDING SHOP**   Joni Perez needs to borrow $20,000 to open a welding shop, but the bank will not lend her the money. Joni's uncle agrees to put up collateral for the loan with a $20,000, 4-year certificate of deposit paying 7% compounded daily. This means that the bank will take all or part of his deposit if Joni should fail to repay the loan. Find (a) the compound amount earned by her uncle and (b) the interest earned if the funds remain at the bank for the full 4 years.

37. **RETIREMENT**   Tara Nolan has worked for the same company for 15 years and on retirement has the option of investing her retirement money in either of two funds. One fund pays 6% compounded continuously and the other pays 7% compounded semiannually.

If she has $286,000 to deposit for 2 years, which investment should she choose? Find the extra interest earned by making the better choice. (*Hint:* $e^{0.12} = 1.1275$.)

38. **IRA INVESTMENT** Lee Stringer has just retired and rolls $145,000 from one of his pension plans into an Individual Retirement Account. One investment choice yields 8% compounded quarterly and the other yields 7.5% compounded continuously. Given a term for each investment of 3 years, find the amount of extra interest that will be earned with the better choice. (*Hint:* $e^{0.225} = 1.252322716$.)

39. Is it important to you for your bank to have insurance on your savings account? Why or why not?

40. Go to your bank and find the current interest rates it pays on savings accounts, IMMAs, and CDs.

14.3   Finding Time and Rate

OBJECTIVES

1 *Find time given principal, maturity value, and rate.*
2 *Find rate given time, principal, and maturity value.*
3 *Use more than one table to solve interest problems.*

In **Chapter 12,** we saw how to work with the formula for simple interest, $I = PRT$, to find any one of the variables given the other three. In this section, we do the same thing using the formula for compound interest, $M = P(1 + i)^n$. However, we will wait until the next section when we discuss present value and future value to solve this equation for the principal P.

Objective

1 *Find Time Given Principal, Maturity Value, and Rate.* The next two examples show how to find time.

EXAMPLE 1 Finding Time

James Thompson needs $45,000 to start a small music store but has only $29,000. How long must he wait to start the business if he believes he can earn 10% compounded annually?

Solution   Use the formula $M = P(1 + i)^n$, with $M = $45,000$, $P = $29,000$, and $i = 0.10$. The value of n is unknown.

$$M = P(1 + i)^n$$
$$\$45{,}000 = \$29{,}000(1 + 0.10)^n$$
$$\$45{,}000 = \$29{,}000(1.1)^n$$
$$\frac{\$45{,}000}{\$29{,}000} = (1.1)^n \qquad \text{Divide by \$29,000.}$$
$$1.551724138 = (1.1)^n$$

Solving this equation would require advanced algebra. However, a good approximation can be found by looking down column A of the 10% page of the interest table in **Appendix D**. The number 1.61051000 in row 5 is very close to the number on the left side of the equation above. Since interest is compounded annually, he must wait about 5 years.

EXAMPLE 2   **Finding Time to Double**

Suppose the general level of inflation in the economy averages 4% per year. Find the number of years it would take for the general level of prices to double.

Solution   To find the number of years it will take for $1 worth of goods and services to cost $2, solve for n in the following equation.

$$2 = 1(1 + 4\%)^n$$

or

$$2 = 1(1 + 0.04)^n$$

where $M = 2, P = 1$, and $i = 4\%$. This equation simplifies as follows.

$$2 = (1.04)^n$$

As in the previous examples, look down column A of the 4% page of the interest table to find the number closest to 2. The closest number is 2.02581652. This number corresponds to 18 periods, so to the nearest year, the general level of prices would double in 18 years.

NOTE   Prices would double about every $7\frac{1}{2}$ years if inflation were 10%.

Objective

2   ***Find Rate Given Time, Principal, and Maturity Value.***   The same method we used to find time can be used to find rate, although you must look at several pages in **Appendix D**. This is because only one interest rate is shown on each page. The method is to look on a page for any interest rate and find the value in column A and the row for the number of periods. Go to pages with higher or lower interest rates as needed to get as close to the rate as possible.

EXAMPLE 3   **Finding Rate**

Kaj Songram needs to borrow $8000 for 1 year. He has been offered a loan with interest compounded monthly and a compound amount of $8493.42. Find the rate.

Solution   Use the equation $M = P(1 + i)^n$, with i unknown. Notice that n is the number of compounding periods, which is 12.

$$\$8493.42 = \$8000(1 + i)^{12}$$

Divide both sides by $8000.

$$1.0616775 = (1 + i)^{12}$$

Find the row for 12 periods in column A of the interest tables in **Appendix D**. Check this number in column A under different rates as necessary until you find the number closest to 1.0616775. The closest number is 1.06167781, corresponding to an interest rate of $\frac{1}{2}\%$ per month, or

$$\frac{1}{2} \times 12 = 6\% \text{ per year}$$

Objective

3 *Use More Than One Table to Solve Interest Problems.* Some problems require the use of more than one table, as in the next example.

EXAMPLE 4 **Using More Than One Table**

Jean King deposits $2500 in a fund paying 6% compounded quarterly. After 4 years, the rate drops to 5% compounded semiannually. Find the amount in her account at the end of 7 years.

Solution First find the future value after 4 years. Look in column A of the interest rate table for 4 × 4 = 16 periods and 6% ÷ 4 = 1.5% interest to find 1.26898555.

$$\$2500(1.26898555) = \$3172.46$$

Now find the future value of $3172.46 at the end of another 3 years. Look in column A of the interest rate table for 2 × 3 = 6 periods and 5% ÷ 2 = 2.5% interest to find 1.15969342.

$$\$3172.46(1.15969342) = \$3679.08$$

King will have $3679.08 in her account at the end of 7 years.

■

Scientific Calculator Approach

Example 4 can also be solved in two steps using the equation for maturity value $M = P(1 + i)^n$. First, find the value at the end of year 4 using $n = 16$ periods and $i = 1.5\%$.

Use the $\boxed{y^x}$ key on your scientific calculator and solve the following.

$$M \boxed{=} \$2500 \boxed{(} \boxed{1} \boxed{+} \boxed{0.015} \boxed{)} \boxed{16} \boxed{=} \$3172.46$$

This amount then grows at $i = 2.5\%$ every 6 months for $n = 6$ semiannual periods. Use the $\boxed{y^x}$ key again.

$$M \boxed{=} \$3172.46 \boxed{(} \boxed{1} \boxed{+} \boxed{0.025} \boxed{)} \boxed{6} \boxed{=} \$3679.08$$

Notice the future value is exactly the same as the value obtained using the tables.

14.3 Exercises

Complete this table. Round time to the nearest period, interest to the nearest whole percent per year, and money to the nearest cent. (As a review, some of these problems do not require the methods of this section.)

	Principal	Compound Amount	Interest Rate	Compounded	Time in Years
1.	$6200	$7384.30	6%	annually	___
2.	$12,000	$17,631.94	8%	annually	___
3.	$3600	$4824.34	10%	semiannually	___
4.	$2500	$2760.20	4%	semiannually	___
5.	$12,000	$15,149.72	___	annually	4

	Principal	Compound Amount	Interest Rate	Compounded	Time in Years
6.	$13,200	$22,680.06	____	annually	8
7.	$8500	$13,403.64	____	quarterly	$5\frac{3}{4}$
8.	$3100	$3765.63	____	monthly	$3\frac{1}{4}$

9. During your working career of 40 years, approximately how many times can you double an investment at 6% interest and at 8% interest? (*Hint:* Use column A in **Appendix D**.) What does this mean to you? (See Objective 2.)

10. Explain how to find the interest rate given principal, compound amount, compounding period, and time in years. (See Objective 2.)

Solve the following application problems. Round as in Exercises 1–10.

11. **HOTEL MANAGEMENT**   Management wants to remodel the interior of a hotel and signs a note with proceeds of $344,546.29, a maturity value of $420,000, and a rate of 8% compounded quarterly. Find the length of the loan.

12. **NEW POLICE CARS**   The Otero County Police Department borrows $220,287.35 to purchase several new police cars equipped with sophisticated radar to detect speeders. Find the length of the loan if the maturity value is $252,000 and the rate is 9% compounded monthly.

13. **INVESTING FOR A NEW AUTO**   Gladys Ford will need a new car and invests $12,000 in a mutual fund containing corporate bonds paying about 6% per year compounded quarterly. Find the compound amount in (a) 3 years and (b) 5 years.

14. **TRUST FUND**   Elton Scallion invests the $95,000 he inherited in a trust for his mentally ill son, who cannot work. If the investments yield 5% compounded semiannually, find the compound amount (a) in 10 years and (b) in 25 years.

15. **UNKNOWN INTEREST RATE**   Roy Bledsoe deposits $46,000 in an account that has interest compounded semiannually. In $2\frac{1}{2}$ years the account contains $58,708.95. Find the interest rate paid.

16. **UNKNOWN INTEREST RATE**   Jim Pierce invests $12,500 and expects to receive $13,945.85 in $2\frac{3}{4}$ years. Assume interest is compounded quarterly and find the interest rate.

17. **STUDENT LOAN**   By the time she received her college degree, Samantha Blackstone had borrowed $28,300 in loans. Her father agreed to assume the loans for her and refinanced the loans into one simple interest note. Due to his good credit history, the note has a low interest rate of 7% compounded semiannually and a maturity value of $34,787.93. Find the length of the loan.

18. **HOME CONSTRUCTION LOAN**   A home construction loan of $80,000 at 12% compounded monthly resulted in a maturity value of $92,877.52. Find the term or length of the loan.

Use the ideas of Example 2 in the text to answer the following questions. Find the time, to the nearest year, that it would take for the general level of prices in the economy to double if the average annual inflation rate is as follows.

19. $2\frac{1}{2}\%$

20. 6%

21. $3\frac{1}{2}\%$

22. 4%

23. **GASOLINE DEMAND**   Worldwide, demand for gasoline is increasing at a rate of about 2% per year. If it continues to increase at this rate indefinitely, find the number of years before the oil companies would need to double the supply of gasoline.

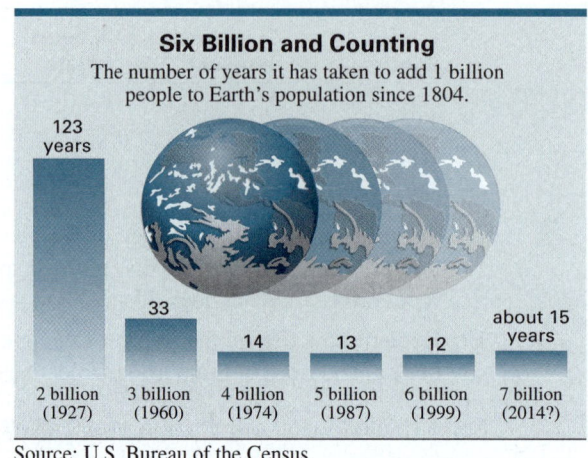

Six Billion and Counting
The number of years it has taken to add 1 billion
people to Earth's population since 1804.

123
years

33

14   13   12

about 15
years

| 2 billion (1927) | 3 billion (1960) | 4 billion (1974) | 5 billion (1987) | 6 billion (1999) | 7 billion (2014?) |

Source: U.S. Bureau of the Census.

Figure 14.5

24. POPULATION GROWTH The rate of growth of world population appears to be further slowing due to (1) the large number of deaths caused by AIDS and (2) women having fewer children. Assume that world population grows at 1.5% per year (Figure 14.5). Use column A in **Appendix D** to estimate the number of years it would require for world population to double.

The remainder of these exercises may require the use of any of the tables presented so far in this chapter.

25. INVESTING Dawn Young deposits $10,000 at 8% compounded quarterly. Two years after she makes the first deposit, she adds another $20,000, also at 8%, compounded quarterly. What total amount will she have 5 years after her first deposit?

26. SAVING FOR COLLEGE Holly Crabtree has decided to help her young grandson pay for college. In 2004, she deposited $5000 in an account paying 6% compounded semiannually. Exactly 2 years later, she deposits another $2000 in a different account paying 5% compounded quarterly. Find the account balance after an additional 5 years (in 2011).

For Exercises 27–30 use Table 14.3 for the certificates of deposit.

27. SAVING FOR COLLEGE Khy Luk wants to save to help a grandchild through college. He deposits $5000 into an account paying 8% per year compounded quarterly. After $3\frac{3}{4}$ years, the compound amount is used to purchase a 4-year CD paying 5% compounded daily. Find the account balance after $7\frac{3}{4}$ years.

28. LONG-TERM SAVINGS Lupe Gonzales puts $4000 in a fund for 5 years that pays 6% compounded annually. After 5 years, she hopes to take the future value and invest it in a mutual fund yielding 8% per year compounded annually for 20 years. Find the final amount that Gonzales will have after 25 years.

29. COMPOUND INTEREST Jean Sides has $11,000 in a mutual fund that pays 10% compounded semiannually. After the money has been on deposit for 4 years, $5000 is invested in a fund that pays 7% compounded daily for 3 years. (The remaining money stays at 10% compounded semiannually.) Find the total amount on deposit in both accounts, both principal and interest, after the 7 years.

30. COMPOUND INTEREST Frank Sabas has $45,000 in an account paying 8% compounded quarterly. After $2\frac{1}{4}$ years, Sabas removes $20,000 and invests for 5 years in a fund paying 6% compounded daily. (The remaining money continues to earn 8% compounded quarterly.) Find the total amount on deposit in both accounts, both principal and interest, after the $7\frac{1}{4}$ years.

14.4	**Present Value at Compound Interest**

OBJECTIVES

 1 *Review the meaning of future value and present value.*
 2 *Find the present value.*

Objective

1   *Review the Meaning of Future Value and Present Value.*   In **Sections 14.1** and **14.2**, the principal, interest rate, and time were given and **future value** was found using $M = P(1 + i)^n$ or using **Appendix D**. In **Section 14.3**, the interest rate and time were found given the other values in the formula. In this section, we look at how to find the **present value**, or the amount that must be deposited today in order to accumulate the needed future value at the needed time. Figure 14.6 shows the idea of present value and future value.

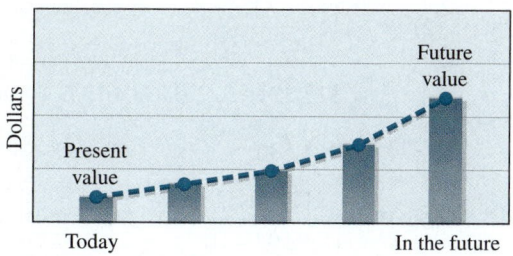

Figure 14.6

Objective

2   *Find the Present Value.*   Earlier, *P* was used for principal or amount borrowed or deposited at the beginning of a term. The phrase *present value* is often used, instead of the word *principal*, if the value is unknown. Thus *P* also represents present value and it can be found as follows.

$$M = P(1 + i)^n$$

$$\frac{M}{(1 + i)^n} = \frac{P(1 + i)^n}{(1 + i)^n} \qquad \text{Divide by } (1 + i)^n.$$

$$P = \frac{M}{(1 + i)^n} \qquad \text{Use this formula for present value.}$$

The present value, *P*, is found by dividing the compound amount, *M*, by $(1 + i)^n$. The values of $(1 + i)^n$ are given in column A of the interest table. Another way to solve this problem is to rewrite the formula as shown below and to then use column B of the interest table, which gives values of $\dfrac{1}{(1 + i)^n}$.

From column B in Appendix D

$$P = \frac{M}{(1 + i)^n} = M \cdot \frac{1}{(1 + i)^n}$$

From column A in Appendix D

EXAMPLE 1   **Finding Present Value**

Eric Long signs a note with an interest maturity value of $17,291.52 to purchase 0.5 acres located on a small creek. The note has an interest rate of 9% compounded semiannually and a period of 2 years. Find the present value, or the amount of proceeds that he receives.

Solution   The interest rate is 9% ÷ 2 or 4.5% per semiannual period, and the number of compounding periods is 2 years × 2 semiannual periods per year or 4. The present value can be found in one of three ways: (1) using column A, **Appendix D**, (2) using column B, **Appendix D**, and (3) using the formula and a calculator.

(1) $P = \dfrac{M}{(1 + i)^n}$

$P = \dfrac{\$17,291.52}{1.1925186}$ Value of $(1 + 0.045)^4$ from column A, Appendix D

$P = \$14,500$

(2) $P = M \cdot \dfrac{1}{(1 + i)^n}$

$P = \$17,291.52 \times 0.83856134$ Value of $\dfrac{1}{(1 + 0.045)^4}$ from column B, Appendix D

$P = \$14,500$

(3) $P = \dfrac{\$17,291.52}{(1 + 0.045)^4}$

$P = \dfrac{\$17,291.52}{1.192518601}$ Use the calculator to find $(1 + 0.045)^4$

$P = \$14,500$

NOTE   In this case, all three methods produce the same answer. In some situations, answers may differ by a few cents due to rounding.

 **Financial Calculator Approach**

Future value, interest rate per compounding period, and number of compounding periods are known in this problem. Present value is the unknown.

17291.52 | FV | 4.5 | i | 4 | n | PV | −14500

The minus sign indicates that Eric Long must pay out $14,500 now to obtain the needed future value.

EXAMPLE 2   **Finding Present Value**

Green Acres Sprinklers, Inc. will receive $185,000 in 3 years as part of a lawsuit settlement. Find the present value if money can be invested at 5% compounded quarterly.

Solution   3 years = 12 quarters and 5% compounded quarterly = $1\frac{1}{4}$% per quarter. Look at the $1\frac{1}{4}$% page in **Appendix D** and column B on the row for 12 periods to find 0.86150860. Multiply to find the present value.

$$\$185,000(0.86150860) = \$159,379.09$$

A deposit of $159,379.09 at 5% compounded quarterly for 3 years will result in $185,000.

Scientific Calculator Approach

Example 2 can also be solved by rewriting $M = P(1 + r)^t$ as $P = \dfrac{M}{(1 + r)^t}$, where $r = \dfrac{5\%}{4}$ and $t = 3 \cdot 4 = 12$.

$$185000 \div \boxed{(} \; 1 \; \boxed{+} \; 0.05 \; \boxed{\div} \; 4 \; \boxed{)} \; \boxed{y^x} \; 12 = 159379.09$$

EXAMPLE 3   Finding the Value of a Business

Tom Fredrickson owns a men's clothing store worth $125,000. The business is doing well, with Fredrickson confident that the value of the business will increase at the rate of 16% per year, compounded semiannually, for the next 4 years. If he sells the business, he will invest the proceeds at 8% compounded quarterly. What sale price should he insist on?

Years

```
       1       2       3       4
|------|-------|-------|-------|
Present value              Future value
```

Solution   This problem requires two steps. First, decide on the future value of the business. This is done with the formula for compound amount, $M = P(1 + i)^n$. Here, $P = \$125,000$, $i = 16\% \div 2 = 8\%$, and $n = 4 \times 2 = 8$ periods.

$$M = \$125,000(1 + 0.08)^8$$
$$= \$125,000(1.85093021) \quad \text{Use column A.}$$
$$= \$231,366.28$$

Now find the present value of this sum, assuming that money can be invested at 8% compounded quarterly. Use the formula

$$P = M \cdot \frac{1}{(1 + i)^n}$$

with $M = \$231,366.28$, $i = 8\% \div 4 = 2\%$, and $n = 4 \times 4 = 16$ periods.

$$P = \$231,366.28 \cdot \frac{1}{(1 + 0.02)^{16}}$$
$$= \$231,366.28(0.72844581) \quad \text{Use column B.}$$
$$= \$168,537.80$$

Fredrickson should not sell the business for less than $168,537.80. An investment of this amount at 8% compounded quarterly for 4 years will produce the same future amount as the growth in the value of the business.

14.4   Exercises

Find the present value and the amount of interest earned for the following deposits. Round to the nearest cent.

	Amount Needed	Time	Interest	Compounded
1.	$4800	3 years	8%	annually
2.	$3300	4 years	11%	annually
3.	$12,200	$2\frac{1}{2}$ years	12%	quarterly

	Amount Needed	Time	Interest	Compounded
4.	$7000	$3\frac{1}{4}$ years	10%	quarterly
5.	$8500	1 year	12%	monthly
6.	$18,000	$1\frac{1}{2}$ years	9%	monthly

7. Explain the difference between present value and future value. (See Objective 1.)

8. List three reasons why a business owner may need to place a value on a business. (See Objective 2.)

Solve the following application problems.

9. **PACK MULES**   David Fontana Backpackers will need to buy some new pack mules in 5 years. These mules will cost a total of $5000. What lump sum should the firm invest today at 7%, compounded annually, in order to be able to buy the mules? How much interest will be earned?

10. **CANDY STORE**   A candy store owner needs $85,000 in 1 year to open a branch in a mall. Find the lump sum that could be invested today at 5% compounded monthly to produce the needed funds. Find the interest earned.

11. **ECOTOUR**   The Datons' accountant told them they will get a refund of $8500 on their income taxes. They are excited and decide to borrow as much as possible now to go on a life-long dream tour of 1 month in the Amazon in South America. They do not want to borrow more than can be repaid with their income tax refund. Find the proceeds if their accountant agrees to lend them the funds at 7% compounded monthly for 2 months.

12. **HOME REMODEL**   Daisy Wadsworth knows she will receive a bonus of $12,000 in 3 months and decides to remodel her home. She does not want to borrow more than she can repay using her bonus. Although the bank usually does not make short, small loans, she has a good relationship with her banker and he lends her the funds at 9% compounded monthly. Find the proceeds.

13. **SMALL GROCERY STORE**   Jose Martinez, an immigrant from Mexico, estimates that he needs $9000 to start a (very) small grocery store in 3 years. How much must he deposit today if his credit union will pay 8% compounded quarterly?

14. **SAVING FOR COLLEGE**   Mrs. Jones wants all of her grandchildren to go to college and decides to help financially. How much must she give to each child at birth if they are to have $10,000 on entering college 18 years later, assuming 6% interest compounded annually?

15. **TIME VALUE OF MONEY**   Assume that money can be invested at 8% compounded quarterly. Which is larger, $2500 now or $3800 in 5 years? (*Hint:* First find the present value of $3800, then compare present values.)

16. **TIME VALUE OF MONEY**   Assume that money can be invested at 10% compounded semiannually. Which is larger, $3000 now or $7500 in 10 years? (*Hint:* First find the present value of $7500, then compare present values.)

17. **FUTURE VALUE**   An investment of $30,000 earns interest of 10% compounded semiannually for $2\frac{1}{2}$ years. Find the future value of the investment. If money can be deposited elsewhere for $2\frac{1}{2}$ years at 8% compounded quarterly, find the present value of this future value.

18. **SELLING AN ESTATE**   Judith McGrath sold her deceased grandfather's home and accepted a note for $65,000 with interest of 9% compounded semiannually for 3 years. Find the future value. Then find the present value of this future value if funds can be invested elsewhere for 3 years at 6% compounded monthly.

19. **CAFE OF MODERN ART** The owner of Cafe of Modern Art signs a note for $16,800 at 10% simple interest for 4 years. Find the maturity value of the note. What should the holder of the note be willing to accept in payment for the note today if funds can be invested for 4 years at 6% per year compounded quarterly?

20. **MATURITY VALUE** In 6 years, Susan Hessney must pay off a note with a face value of $12,000 and simple interest of 9% per year. Find the maturity value of the note. What should the holder of the note be willing to accept in complete payment today, if money can be invested for 6 years at 6% per year compounded quarterly?

21. **VALUING A HAIR SALON** Jessie Jones believes her hair salon is worth $20,000 and estimates that its value will grow at 10% per year compounded annually for the next 3 years. If she sells the business, the funds will be invested at 8% compounded quarterly. (a) Find the future value if she holds onto the business. (b) What price should she insist on now if she sells the business?

22. **BIKE SHOP** Andy Sargent figures his bike shop is worth $88,000 if sold today and that it will grow in value at 8% per year compounded annually for the next 6 years. If he sells the business, the funds will be invested at 5% compounded semiannually. (a) Find the future value of the shop. (b) What price should he insist on at this time if he sells the business?

CHAPTER TERMS

Review the following terms to test your understanding of the chapter. For any
terms you do not know, refer to the page number found next to that term.

certificate of deposit (CD)
[p. 493]
compound amount [p. 480]
compound interest [p. 479]
compounded daily [p. 491]
continuous compounding
[p. 496]
early withdrawal penalty
[p. 495]

effective rate of interest
[p. 486]
exponent [p. 481]
Federal Deposit Insurance
Corporation (FDIC)
[p. 490]
Federal Savings and Loan
Insurance Corporation
(FSLIC) [p. 490]

future amount [p. 480]
future value [p. 480]
inflation [p. 486]
money market account
[p. 490]
nominal rate [p. 482]
passbook account [p. 490]
period of compounding
[p. 482]

present value [p. 505]
principal [p. 479]
Regulation DD [p. 490]
savings account [p. 490]
simple interest [p. 479]
stated rate [p. 482]
time deposit [p. 493]

CONCEPTS

EXAMPLES

14.1 Finding the compound amount and the interest

Determine the interest rate per period and the number of compounding periods. Use the formula $M = P(1 + i)^n$ and the interest table to calculate the compound amount. Then subtract the principal from the compound amount to obtain interest.

Find the compound amount and the interest if $7200 is deposited at 9% compounded monthly for 4 years.

$$i = \frac{0.09}{12} = 0.0075$$

$$n = 4 \times 12 = 48$$

$$M = P(1 + i)^n$$

$$= \$7200(1.0075)^{48}$$

$$= \$7200(1.43140533) = \$10{,}306.12$$

$$I = M - P$$

$$= \$10{,}306.12 - \$7200 = \$3106.12$$

14.1 Determining the effective rate of interest

Determine the value from column A of the interest table in **Appendix D** that corresponds to the rate and number of periods. Subtract 1 from this value and round as required. A calculator can also be used to find $(1 + i)^n - 1$, which should be rounded.

Find the effective rate of interest to the nearest hundredth, if the annual rate is 8% compounded quarterly.

$$i = \frac{0.08}{4} = 0.02; n = 4$$

1.08243216 table value for $i = 2\%, n = 4$

1.08243216 − 1.00000000 = 0.08243216

The effective rate is 8.24%.

14.2 Interest compounded daily

Determine the number of days and then find the value of $(1 + i)^n$ using Table 14.2. Multiply this value by the principal to obtain compound amount. Subtract principal from compound amount to obtain interest. A calculator can also be used to find $(1 + i)^n$.

Janice deposited $1535 on September 5 in an account paying $3\frac{1}{2}\%$ compounded daily and withdrew everything on December 5. How much interest was earned?

There are 25 additional days in September, 31 days in October, 30 days in November, and 5 days in December.

$$25 + 31 + 30 + 5 = 91 \text{ days}$$

$$\text{Compound amount} = \$1535(1.008763788)$$

$$= \$1548.45 \qquad \text{From table}$$

$$\text{Interest} = \$1548.45 - \$1535$$

$$= \$13.45$$

14.2 Finding the interest and balance when withdrawals are made

Find the amount that earns interest for the entire quarter and determine compound amount and interest on this sum using Table 14.2. Then, find compound amount and interest for the amount withdrawn. Find the final balance by adding the total interest to the original balance and subtracting the withdrawal.

Tom had $1500 in his $3\frac{1}{2}\%$ compounded daily savings account on October 1. He withdrew $450 on October 15. How much interest had he earned by January 1 and what was his final balance?

$1500 - $450 = 1050 earns interest for the entire 92-day quarter.

$$\text{Compound amount} = \$1050 \times 1.008860519$$
$$= \$1059.30 \qquad \text{From table}$$
$$\text{Interest} = \$1059.30 - \$1050 = \$9.30$$

The withdrawn $450 earns interest for 14 days.

$$\text{Compound amount} = \$450 \times 1.001343303$$
$$= \$450.60 \qquad \text{From table}$$
$$\text{Interest} = \$450.60 - \$450 = \$0.60$$
$$\text{Total interest} = \$9.30 + \$0.60 = \$9.90$$
$$\text{Final balance} = \$1500 + \$9.90 - \$450$$
$$= \$1059.90$$

14.2 Finding the compound amount and interest earned on time deposits

Use Table 14.3 to find the value corresponding to the rate and number of years. Next, multiply the table value by the initial amount to obtain compound amount. Then subtract initial investment from compound amount to obtain interest.

Mike invests $15,000 in a certificate of deposit paying 5% compounded daily. Find the compound amount and interest after 4 years.

$$\text{Table value} = 1.22138603$$
$$\text{Compound amount} = \$15,000 \times 1.22138603$$
$$= \$18,320.79$$
$$\text{Interest} = \$18,320.79 - \$15,000$$
$$= \$3320.79$$

14.2 Finding the penalty for early withdrawal of funds from a time deposit account

If money is withdrawn within 3 months, no interest is paid. Otherwise, determine the number of months for which interest will be paid. Find value in Table 14.2 for rate and time. Then multiply this by initial deposit to obtain compound amount. Find the interest by subtracting initial deposit from compound amount.

Tom deposited $5000 in a 3-year CD paying 7% compounded daily. He withdrew the money 15 months later. The passbook rate at his bank is $3\frac{1}{2}\%$ compounded daily. Find the amount of interest earned. Tom will get the passbook rate for $15 - 3 = 12$ months, or 4 quarters. Passbook rate of $3\frac{1}{2}\%$ for 4 quarters gives a table value of 1.035121585.

$$\text{Compound amount} = \$5000 \times 1.035121585$$
$$= \$5175.61$$
$$\text{Interest} = \$5175.61 - \$5000 = \$175.61$$

14.2 Determining the interest and compound amount for continuous compounding

Use the formula

$$M = Pe^{rt}$$

Use the table in **Appendix C** or your calculator to find the value of e^{rt}. Find interest from the formula $I = M - P$.

Find the interest and compound amount for $2000 at 6% compounded continuously for 8 years.

$$M = Pe^{rt}$$
$$M = \$2000e^{0.06 \cdot 8}$$
$$= \$2000e^{0.48}$$
$$= \$2000(1.6160744) = \$3232.15$$
$$I = M - P$$
$$I = \$3232.15 - \$2000 = \$1232.15$$

14.3 Finding the time given interest rate, compound amount, and principal

Substitute values for M, P, and i in the formula $M = P(1 + i)^n$; then divide both sides by the value of P. Find the value in column A of the interest table (**Appendix D**), closest to the left-hand side of the equation, for the correct value of i. The corresponding value of n is the number of periods required to obtain the compound amount.

How long would it take for $1800 at 6% compounded semiannually to become $7361.97?

$$i = 6\% \div 2 = 3\%$$
$$M = P(1 + i)^n$$
$$\$7361.97 = \$1800(1.03)^n$$
$$4.0899833 = (1.03)^n$$

In column A of the 3% page, the number 4.13225188 is *close* to 4.0899833, so $n = 48$. It would take 48 6-month periods, or 24 years.

14.3 Finding the rate, given principal, compound amount, and time

Divide the compound amount by the principal. Use the row of the interest table that corresponds to the number of interest periods and find the value of column A in **Appendix D**, closest to the quotient obtained above. You may need to examine several pages. Then find the interest rate per year.

A principal of $7000 is deposited for 18 months with interest compounded monthly. Find the rate if the compound amount is $7657.50.

$$M = P(1 + i)^n$$
$$\$7657.50 = \$7000(1 + i)^{18}$$
$$1.09392857 = (1 + i)^{18}$$

Find the row for 18 periods in the interest table. Check row 18 across the different interest rates (pages) in the table to find the closest entry to 1.09392857. The closest number is 1.09392894 on the 0.5% interest rate page. So the rate is 0.5% × 12, or 6% per year compounded monthly.

14.4 Finding the present value of a future amount

Use the formula

$$P = \frac{M}{(1 + i)^n}$$

where M = future value
i = interest rate per compounding period
n = number of periods.

Substitute values for i, n, and M and find the value of $\frac{1}{(1 + i)^n}$ from column B of the interest table in **Appendix D** or use your calculator.

What amount deposited today at 5% compounded monthly will produce $8000 in 3 years?

$$M = \$8000$$
$$i = \frac{5\%}{12} = 0.4167\% \qquad \text{Rounded}$$
$$n = 3 \times 12 = 36$$
$$P = \frac{M}{(1 + i)^n}$$
$$= M \times \frac{1}{(1 + i)^n}$$
$$P = \$8000 \times \frac{1}{(1 + 0.004167)^{36}}$$
$$= \$8000 \times \frac{1}{(1.004167)^{36}}$$
$$= \$8000(0.86096596)$$
$$= \$6887.73$$

The answer section includes answers to all Review Exercises.

Find the compound amount and the interest earned for the following deposits. Round to the nearest cent. [14.1]

1. \$12,400 at $6\frac{1}{2}\%$ compounded annually for 6 years

2. \$7000 at 6% compounded semiannually for 4 years

3. \$22,500 at 4% compounded quarterly for 5 years

4. \$18,000 at 7% compounded quarterly for 4 years

5. \$9000 at 9% compounded monthly for $2\frac{1}{2}$ years

6. \$12,000 at 6% compounded monthly for $3\frac{1}{4}$ years

Find the effective rate of interest corresponding to the following nominal rates. Round to the nearest hundredth of a percent. [14.1]

7. 7% compounded quarterly

8. 8% compounded quarterly

9. 4% compounded semiannually

10. 9% compounded monthly

Find the interest earned by the following deposits. Assume $3\frac{1}{2}\%$ interest compounded daily. Round to the nearest cent. [14.2]

	Interest	Amount	Date Deposited	Date Withdrawn
11.		\$2900	March 4	May 30
12.		\$6000	May 20	July 1
13.		\$3020.80	July 15	October 1

Find the amount on deposit on the first day of the next quarter when the following sums are deposited as indicated. Assume $3\frac{1}{2}\%$ compounded daily. Round to the nearest cent. [14.2]

	Amount at End of Quarter	Amount	Date Deposited
14.		\$3500	January 22
15.		\$7200.35	April 22
16.		\$9600.40	August 10

Use Table 14.3 to find the compound amount for each of the following certificates of deposit. Assume daily compounding. Round to the nearest cent. [14.2]

	Compound Amount	Amount Deposited	Interest Rate	Time in Years
17.		\$4000	5%	3
18.		\$6500	6%	2
19.		\$10,000	4%	5

Find the compound amount and the interest for the following deposits. Assume continuous compounding. Round to the nearest cent. [14.2]

	Compound Amount	Interest	Amount	Interest Rate	Time
20.			\$12,600	8%	7 years
21.			\$5000	3%	5 years

Complete the following table. Round time to the nearest period, interest to the nearest whole percent per year, and money to the nearest cent. **[14.3]**

	Principal	Amount	Interest Rate	Compounded	Time in Years
22.	$4300	$5754.37	_____	Annually	5
23.	$8600	$11,566.04	_____	Quarterly	3
24.	$7500	$9914.25	_____	Quarterly	$3\frac{1}{2}$
25.	$6000	$6749.18	4%	Annually	_____
26.	$8400	$10,357.20	6%	Monthly	_____

Find the present value for the following future amounts. Round to the nearest cent. Also find the interest earned. **[14.4]**

	Amount Needed	Time	Interest Rate	Compounded	Present Value	Interest Earned
27.	$14,300	3 years	$5\frac{1}{2}\%$	Annually	_____	_____
28.	$4000	3 years	4%	Semiannually	_____	_____
29.	$6000	5 years	10%	Quarterly	_____	_____
30.	$3000	4 years	6%	Monthly	_____	_____

Solve the following application problems.

31. Discount Auto Insurance deposited $1800 in a savings account paying $3\frac{1}{2}\%$ compounded daily on January 1 and deposited an additional $2300 in the account on March 12. Find the balance on April 1. **[14.2]**

32. Susan Chu opens a savings account on June 10 with a deposit of $4000 and makes an additional deposit of $1200 on July 6. Find the balance on September 1 assuming an interest rate of $3\frac{1}{2}\%$ compounded daily. **[14.2]**

33. Kerry Craton deposited $2000 in a 10-year CD earning 4% compounded daily. Find the compound amount and interest at the end of 10 years. **[14.2]**

34. Elizabeth Daigle put $4000 of her divorce settlement in a 5-year CD that paid 6% compounded daily. Find the compound amount and interest at the end of 5 years. **[14.2]**

35. Elegant Interiors needs $65,000 in 3 years for capital improvements at the retail store. What lump sum should be invested today at 9% compounded monthly to generate this amount? **[14.4]**

36. Computers, Inc., accepted a 2-year note for $12,540 in lieu of immediate payment for computer equipment sold to a local firm. Find (a) the maturity value given a rate of 10% compounded annually and (b) the present value of the note at 6% per year compounded semiannually for 2 years. **[14.4]**

37. Jack Taylor invests $15,000 in an account paying 6% per year compounded annually. In how many years will the compound amount become $18,937.15? **[14.3]**

38. The consumption of electricity in one area has increased historically at 6% per year. If it continues to increase at this rate indefinitely, find the number of years before the electric utility would need to double the amount of generating capacity. **[14.3]**

| CHAPTER 14 | # Business Application Case #1
Valuing a Chain of McDonald's Restaurants |

James and Mary Watson own a small chain of McDonald's restaurants that is valued at $2,300,000. They believe that the chain will grow in value at 12% per year compounded annually for the next 5 years. If they sell the chain, the funds will be invested for 5 years at a rate of 6% compounded semiannually. They expect inflation to be 4% per year for the next 5 years. Ignore taxes and answer the following. Round answers to the nearest dollar.

(a) Find the future value of the chain after 5 years. Then find the price they should sell the chain for if they wish to have the same future value at the end of 5 years.

(b) Find the future value of the chain if it only grows at 2% per year for 5 years. Then find the price they should ask for the chain given a 2% growth rate per year.

(c) What future value would the chain be worth if it grew at their expected rate of inflation? Find the price they should ask for the chain if it grows at the rate of inflation.

(d) Complete the following table.

Growth Rate	Future Value	Value Today
2%	_____	_____
4% (inflation)	_____	_____
12%	_____	_____

> **Note**   The value of the chain varies by more than $1 million dollars depending on the rate of growth assumed for the business for the next 5 years.

| CHAPTER 14 | # Business Application Case #2
Replacing a Coal-Fired Power Plant |

PowerCo needs to replace an aging coal-fired power plant in 8 years. Managers hope to replace it with a high-efficiency plant that will sequester carbon emissions rather than allowing carbon to be released into the atmosphere. Managers plan to borrow most of the money needed, but they plan to accumulate at least $50,000,000 of the cost.

(a) If managers invest $32,000,000 now at an estimated 5% compounded semiannually after income taxes, find the amount it will grow to in 8 years.

(b) How much more will they need in 8 years?

(c) Find the present value of the shortage identified in (b) using 5% compounded semiannually. This is the additional amount managers need to set aside today to have the $50,000,000 in 5 years.

Annuities and Sinking Funds

Chapters 12, 13, and 14 involved the deposit of a **lump sum** of cash. However, few can afford to prepare for their children's college education or their own retirement with one large deposit. Rather, most individuals save using regular contributions such as those to a retirement plan. Figure 15.1 shows reasons why employers offer a retirement savings plan.

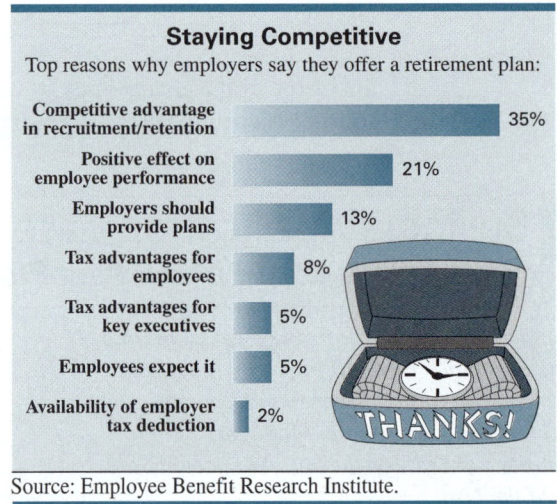

Staying Competitive

Top reasons why employers say they offer a retirement plan:

Competitive advantage in recruitment/retention	35%
Positive effect on employee performance	21%
Employers should provide plans	13%
Tax advantages for employees	8%
Tax advantages for key executives	5%
Employees expect it	5%
Availability of employer tax deduction	2%

Source: Employee Benefit Research Institute.

Figure 15.1

STOP
—and think

Retirement probably seems very far in the future to you. However, everyone who does not die young will retire if financially able to do so. Those without enough income must continue to work even into their seventies. Furthermore, having money in a retirement account makes you feel more secure and in control of your own destiny. First, talk to someone over 60 years old about retirement then answer these questions: Should you think about retirement planning now? How important is it to you that your employer offers a retirement plan?

15.1	**Amount of an Annuity**

OBJECTIVES

1 *Identify the types of annuities.*

2 *Find the amount of an annuity.*

3 *Find the amount of an annuity payment.*

4 *Find the number of payments.*

5 *Find the amount of an annuity due.*

6 *Find the value of an individual retirement account (IRA).*

An **annuity** is a *sequence of equal payments*. It can be used to accumulate money for the future or to pay off a debt. Examples of annuities include car payments, mortgage payments on a home, and a regular contribution to a retirement plan. Another example of an annuity is the regular payments of the life insurance benefits from an insurance company to the spouse of the deceased person. In this chapter, you will see that an annuity is a very effective way to accumulate funds for future needs such as a wedding, a new car, or future college expenses.

The time between the payments of an annuity is the **payment period**, with the time from the beginning of the first payment period to the end of the last called the **term of the annuity**. The **amount of the annuity**, also called the **future value of the annuity**, is the total amount accumulated at the end of the annuity. It is the sum of all payments along with compound interest on each payment to the end of the term.

Objective

1 *Identify the Types of Annuities.* There are many kinds of annuities. A **contingent annuity** has variable beginning or ending dates. For example, an insurance policy that pays a fixed amount per month beginning when a person is age 65 and lasting until that person's death has a variable ending date and is a contingent annuity. A person might prepare a will leaving a fixed annual sum to the surviving spouse for a fixed number of years. This is an example of a contingent annuity with a variable beginning date (because the annual payments do not start until the death of the person making the will). We will not discuss contingent annuities in this book. Instead, we will discuss only annuities certain.

An **annuity certain** has a specified beginning date and a specified ending date. Examples include the 48 monthly payments needed to pay off a car loan or 18 annual payments into a college fund beginning at the birth of a child. Payments in an **ordinary annuity** are made at the *end of each period* whereas payments in an **annuity due** are made at the *beginning of each period*.

A **simple annuity** has payment dates matching the compounding period. For example, an annuity with payments made quarterly and having interest compounded quarterly is a simple annuity. An annuity with payments made quarterly and interest compounded daily is not a simple annuity. There are formulas available for annuities that are not simple, but we discuss only simple annuities in this book.

Consider an annuity with payments of $2500 at the *end of each year* for 6 years into an investment account paying 8% per year compounded annually. The definitions above can be used to identify this annuity as *certain, ordinary,* and *simple.* Find the future value at the end of 6 years by adding the future values of the deposits made at the end of each of the years. The payment of $2500 at the end of the first year will be invested for 5 years. The payment at the end of the 2nd year will be invested for 4 years, etc. The future value of the first payment is found as follows.

$$\$2500(1 + 0.08)^5 = \$2500(1.08)^5$$
$$= \$3673.32$$

The value of $(1.08)^5$ can be found using a calculator or using column A in **Appendix D**.

> **NOTE** We are rounding answers to the nearest cent in this section.

Figure 15.2 shows each payment, the calculation to find the compound amount of that payment, the compound amount of each payment, and the **future value of the annuity of $18,339.82**.

How an Annuity Works

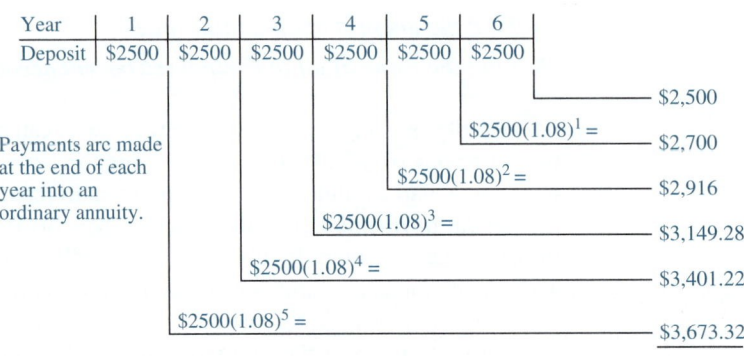

Figure 15.2

 **Scientific Calculator Approach**

The value of $2500 invested for 5 years, or $2500(1.08)^5$, is found as follows.

$$1.08 \boxed{y^x} 5 \boxed{\times} 2500 \boxed{=} 3673.32$$

The other values on the right-hand side of Figure 15.2 can be found in a similar fashion.

Objective

2 *Find the Amount of an Annuity.* This method for finding the amount of the annuity of $2500 at the end of each year for 6 years was tedious, so we use a formula.

Finding the Future Value of an Annuity

A simple annuity is made up of payments of R dollars at the end of each period for n periods, at a rate of interest i per period. The amount or future value of the annuity, S, is given by this equation.

$$S = R\left[\frac{(1 + i)^n - 1}{i}\right]$$

The quantity in brackets is commonly written $s_{\overline{n}|i}$ (read "s-angle-n-at-i") or

$$S = R \cdot s_{\overline{n}|i}$$

where the value of $s_{\overline{n}|i}$ for a specific n and i is found in column C of **Appendix D**.

For our annuity, $R = \$2500$, $n = 6$, and $i = 0.08$. By the formula, the amount of the annuity is as follows.

$$S = R \cdot s_{\overline{n}|i}$$
$$S = \$2500 \cdot s_{\overline{6}|0.08}$$
$$= \$2500\left[\frac{(1 + 0.08)^6 - 1}{0.08}\right] \quad \text{Definition of } s_{\overline{6}|0.08}$$

$$= \$2500\left[\frac{(1.08)^6 - 1}{0.08}\right]$$

$$= \$2500\left(\frac{1.58687432 - 1}{0.08}\right)$$

$$= \$2500(7.33592900)$$

$$= \$18,339.82$$

This is exactly the same result found earlier.

Scientific Calculator Approach

The expression $S = \$2500\left[\dfrac{(1 + 0.08)^6 - 1}{0.08}\right]$ above can be evaluated using a calculator as follows.

$$2500 \boxed{\times} \boxed{(} \boxed{(} \boxed{1} \boxed{+} \boxed{0.08} \boxed{)} \boxed{y^x} \boxed{6} \boxed{-} \boxed{1} \boxed{)} \boxed{\div} \boxed{0.08} \boxed{=} \quad 18339.82$$

Notice that the numerator in the brackets is entered as $((1 + 0.08)^6 - 1)$ in order to maintain the order of operations.

To save time, tables of values of $s_{\overline{n}|i}$ have been calculated using the expression given above for the amount of an annuity for different values of n and i. They appear in column C of the interest table in **Appendix D**. Look in this table for 8% and 6 periods to find the following.

$$s_{\overline{6}|0.08} = 7.33592904$$

NOTE   The number from the table is slightly different than the result found using the formula. This tiny difference is due to rounding.

EXAMPLE 1   **Finding the Amount of an Ordinary Annuity**

The hospital where Tish Baker works as an aide pays $600 at the end of each quarter into her retirement plan. If she chooses an investment that yields 6% per year compounded quarterly, how much will she have in 10 years? How much interest will she have earned?

Solution   Baker's payments form an ordinary annuity, with $R = \$600$, $n = 10 \times 4 = 40$ compounding periods (quarters), and $i = 6\% \div 4 = 1.5\%$ per compounding period (per quarter). The amount, or future value, of the annuity is found as follows.

$$S = \$600(54.26789391) \quad \text{Using column C of table}$$
$$= \$32,560.74$$

The interest earned is the future amount less all payments.

$$I = \$32,560.74 - 40 \times \$600 = \$8560.74$$

The future amount can be checked using the formula for calculating the amount of an annuity.

$$S = R\left[\frac{(1 + i)^n - 1}{i}\right]$$

$$S = \$600\left[\frac{(1 + 0.015)^{40} - 1}{0.015}\right]$$

$$= \$600\left(\frac{1.814018409 - 1}{0.015}\right)$$

$$= \$600(54.26789391)$$

$$= \$32{,}560.74$$

Notice that the factor 54.26789391 found using a scientific calculator is exactly the same as the factor from the table in **Appendix D**.

Scientific Calculator Approach

To solve for S in the preceding problem, first find the fraction.

((1 + 0.015) y^x 40 − 1) ÷ 0.015 STO

Then multiply: 600 × RCL = 32560.74

Financial Calculator Approach

Payment, number of compounding periods, and interest rate per compounding period are known. Future value is the unknown. Be sure to set your calculator to an ordinary annuity with payments at the end of each period, before keying in the following.

−600 PMT 40 n 1.5 i FV 32560.74

EXAMPLE 2 **Finding the Amount of an Ordinary Annuity**

At the birth of her grandson, Junella Smith decides to help pay for his college education. She commits to making deposits of $600 into an account *at the end of each 6 months for 18 years.* Smith has narrowed her choices to an annuity at an insurance company paying 6% compounded semiannually, a CD at a bank paying 5% compounded semiannually, or a savings account at a credit union paying $3\frac{1}{2}\%$ compounded semiannually. (a) Find the amount of the annuity in each case. (b) Which is preferred if all three options are safe?

Solution

(a) There are $2 \times 18 = 36$ semiannual periods in 18 years. The semiannual interest, value from **Appendix D**, and future amount are shown in the table that follows. In each case, the future amount is found using either $S = R\left[\dfrac{(1 + i)^n - 1}{i}\right]$ or $S = R \cdot s_{\overline{n}|i}$ and table values, where $R = \$600$, $n = 36$, and i is the semiannual interest.

	Semiannual Interest	Value from Appendix D	Future Amount
Annuity	$\dfrac{6\%}{2} = 3\%$	63.27594427	$37,965.57
CD	$\dfrac{5\%}{2} = 2.5\%$	57.30141263	$34,380.85
Savings account	$\dfrac{3\frac{1}{2}\%}{2} = 1.75\%$	49.56612949	$29,739.68

The future values of the investments over time are shown in the graph.

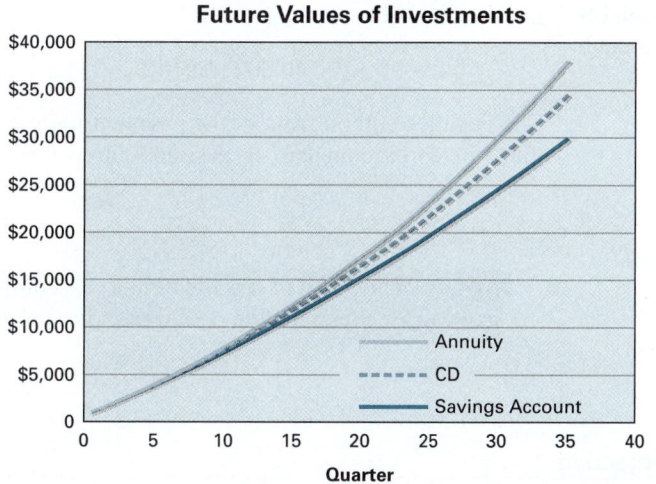

Future Values of Investments

(b) The amount in the account grows more rapidly with the higher interest rate paid by the annuity. So, as long as all of the investment choices have equal risk in terms of losing money, then the annuity is the best investment of the three choices. Junella Smith might make a different choice if the risk associated with the different alternatives were not equal, since she may not want to take any risk of losing money.

> **NOTE** Example 2 in **Appendix A.2** shows how a financial calculator can be used to solve this same type of problem.

Objective

3   *Find the Amount of an Annuity Payment.*   Sometimes the lump sum that will be needed at some time in the future is known, and the amount of each payment into an annuity that will result in the required amount must be found.

EXAMPLE 3   **Finding the Amount of an Annuity Payment**

Fast Copy, Inc. will need several new commercial printers in 3 years and the owner wants to make end-of-quarter payments now toward that goal. She estimates that the equipment will cost $70,000. If funds earn 6% compounded quarterly, find the payment of the annuity needed to accumulate this amount.

Solution   This is an ordinary annuity with $S = \$70{,}000$, $i = 1\frac{1}{2}\%$ ($6\% \div 4$), and $n = 12$ (3 years $\times$ 4 quarters per year). The unknown in the formula for the amount of an annuity is the size of each payment, or R.

$$\$70{,}000 = R \cdot s_{\overline{12}|0.015}$$
$$\$70{,}000 = R \cdot 13.04121143 \qquad \text{From column C, \textbf{Appendix D}}$$
$$R = \$70{,}000 \div 13.04121143$$
$$R = \$5367.60$$

Each end-of-quarter payment must be $5367.60.

Future value, number of compounding periods, and interest rate per compounding period are known. Payment is the unknown.

70,000 $\boxed{FV}$ 12 $\boxed{n}$ 1.5 $\boxed{i}$ $\boxed{PMT}$ −5367.60

The negative sign in front of the payment indicates that the company must make payments into a fund to accumulate the desired future value.

NOTE The value of *n* is the number of compounding periods (*not years*), and *i* is the interest per compounding period (*not interest per year*).

Objective

4 *Find the Number of Payments.* The next example shows how to find the number of periods necessary to accumulate a certain amount of money.

EXAMPLE 4 Finding the Number of Payments

The Dunlaps want to purchase their first home and need $12,000 for a down payment. They can save $825 per quarter. If they deposit this amount in an account paying 3% interest compounded quarterly, how long will it be before they can purchase a home?

Solution Here the amount of the annuity (*S*), the amount of each payment (*R*), and the interest rate per period (*i*) are known. The unknown is *n,* the number of quarters for which deposits must be made. Start with the formula for the amount of an annuity and substitute $12,000 for *S*, $825 for *R*, and $\frac{3}{4}$% (3% ÷ 4) for *i*.

$$S = R \cdot s_{\overline{n}|i}$$
$$\$12,000 = \$825 \cdot s_{\overline{n}|0.0075}$$
$$14.54545455 = s_{\overline{n}|0.0075} \qquad \text{Divide both sides by \$825.}$$

Go to the $\frac{3}{4}$% page in the interest table. Look down column C for the first number *larger* than 14.54545455. The first number that is *larger* is 14.70340370, which corresponds to 14 quarters. The family must save for 14 quarters, or $3\frac{1}{2}$ years. At the end of this period of time they will have a little more than the $12,000 needed.

$$\$825(14.70340370) = \$12,130.31$$

NOTE The table value used is the one *larger* than the calculated value, not closest to it.

Future value, quarterly payment, and interest rate per quarter are known in Example 4. The unknown is *n,* the number of quarters.

−12000 $\boxed{FV}$ 825 $\boxed{PMT}$ 0.75 $\boxed{i}$ $\boxed{n}$ 14

Objective

5 *Find the Amount of an Annuity Due.* As mentioned earlier, with ordinary annuities, payments are made at the *end of each time period*. With **annuities due** the payments are made at the *beginning of the time period*. The difference between an ordinary annuity and an annuity due is subtle, but both are used in the financial services industry. The following charts may help you understand the difference between an ordinary annuity and an annuity due.

In an *ordinary annuity*, payments are made at the *end of each time period*, as shown below. Think of the payments as being made *on the last second of the last day* of each period.

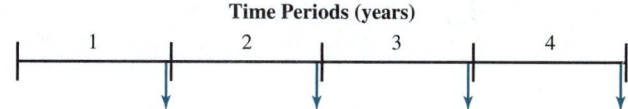

Ordinary annuity payments are at the end of each year.

In an *annuity due*, payments are made at the *beginning of each period*. Think of payments as being made *on the first second of the first day* of each period.

Now look at the following diagrams. The one on top is the annuity due just discussed. Note that the payment is at the first of each period. The one on the bottom is an ordinary

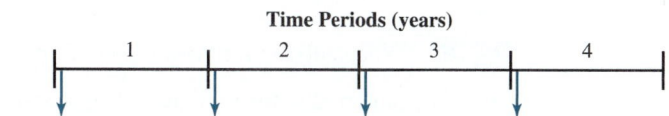

Annuity due payments are at the beginning of each year.

annuity with one additional period added—payments are at the end of each period. Notice the alignment of the arrows representing the payments in both. They are exactly the same, although the ordinary annuity has one extra payment at the end of year 5. We use this similarity to find the amount of an annuity due below.

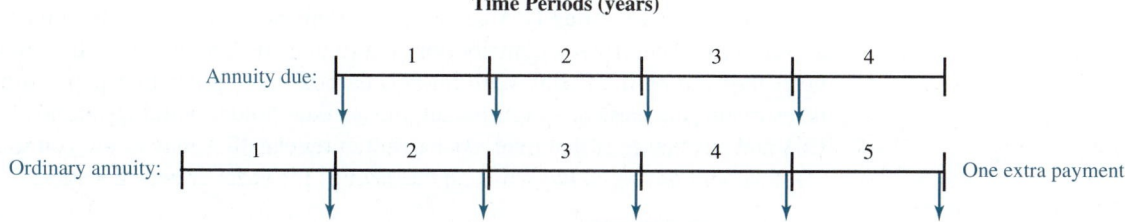

Finding the Amount of an Annuity Due

To find the amount of an annuity due, treat each payment as if it were made at the end of the preceding period. Then follow these steps.

Step 1 Add 1 to the number of periods.

Step 2 Use this number of periods in column C of the interest table to find the amount of the annuity.

Step 3 Subtract one payment from the amount found in Step 2.

EXAMPLE **5** **Finding the Amount of an Annuity Due**

Mr. and Mrs. Thompson set up an investment program using an *annuity due* with payments of $500 *at the beginning of each quarter.* Find the amount of the annuity if they make payments for 7 years in a mutual fund paying 6% compounded quarterly.

Solution   There are $7 \times 4 = 28$ compounding periods.

STEP 1 Add 1 to the number of periods: $28 + 1 = 29$.

STEP 2 Use the $\frac{6\%}{4} = 1.5\%$ interest table with 29 periods in column C of **Appendix D** to find the following number: 35.99870085.

$$\text{Amount} = \$500 \times 35.99870085 = \$17,999.35$$

STEP 3 Subtract one payment.

$$\text{Future value} = \$17,999.35 - \$500 = \$17,499.35$$

Financial Calculator Approach   First change the calculator settings to annuity due (payments at the beginning of each period). Then enter known values for payment, number of periods, and interest rate per period. Finally, press the future value key to find the unknown.

$$-500 \boxed{PMT}\ 28\ \boxed{n}\ 1.5\ \boxed{i}\ \boxed{FV}\ 17499.35$$

NOTE   When solving for the amount of an annuity due, be sure to

1. add one period to the total number of annuity periods, and

2. subtract one payment from the amount found.

Objective

6   *Find the Value of an Individual Retirement Account (IRA).*   A really great investment vehicle that working people can use to save for retirement is an **individual retirement account**, also called an **IRA**. There are two common types of IRA accounts, regular IRAs and Roth IRAs.

Deposits to a **regular IRA** account are often excluded from federal income taxes in the current year. Therefore, a contribution to a regular IRA may reduce the amount of income taxes *that you must pay this year.* Interest earned in a regular IRA is not subject to income taxes in the year earned. At retirement, the account holder withdraws funds from the regular IRA and pays taxes at that time. As a result, a regular IRA may allow you to save for retirement *without having to pay taxes* on the savings for years or even decades!

Roth IRA

WHICH IRA IS BEST FOR YOU?
If you've been contributing to a nondeductible, traditional IRA, the new Roth IRA, where earnings grow tax-free, may be the better option. If you're trying to decide between a deductible IRA and a Roth, here are some facts that may help.

	DEDUCTIBLE IRA	ROTH IRA
Tax deductible?	If you qualify	No
Taxable at withdrawal?	Yes	No
Penalty for early withdrawal?	Yes, prior to age 59.5	Yes*
Mandatory withdrawal age?	70.5	None
Penalty-free withdrawals?	$10,000 for first-time home buyers; unlimited for education	$10,000 for first-time home buyers, after 5 year wait; unlimited for education

*Never any penalty for withdrawing your own contributions, but a penalty applies to withdrawal of any gains within 5 years of opening the account and/or before turning 59.5.

Deposits to a **Roth IRA** are not excluded from federal taxes in the year paid, so they *do not* reduce current income taxes. However, the deposit and interest do grow tax-free. In addition, one huge advantage is that the withdrawals from the Roth IRA at retirement are *not* subject to income taxes. This offers you a great opportunity to save money for retirement without having to pay taxes when you withdraw the funds.

NOTE   Early withdrawal from either a regular IRA or a Roth IRA may result in a penalty.

EXAMPLE 6   Finding the Value of an IRA

At 27, Joann Gretz sets up an IRA with Merrill Lynch where she plans to deposit $2000 at the end of each year until age 60. Find the amount of the annuity if she invests in (a) a Treasury-bill fund, which has historically yielded 6% compounded annually versus (b) a stock fund, which has historically yielded 10% compounded annually. Although past performance is no guarantee of the future, assume that future yields equal historical yields.

Solution   Age 60 is $60 - 27 = 33$ years away.

(a) Treasury-bill fund: Look in column C of **Appendix D** with $n = 33$ and $i = 6\%$ to find 97.34316471.

$$\text{Amount} = \$2000 \times 97.34316471 = \$194,686.33$$

(b) Stock fund: Look in column C of **Appendix D** with $n = 33$ and $i = 10\%$ to find 222.25154420.

$$\text{Amount} = \$2000 \times 222.25154420 = \$444,503.09$$

Gretz can see the projected difference in the results of the Treasury-bill fund and the stock fund using the graph in Figure 15.3. On this basis, she decides to try to maximize return on investment in the future—however, she plans to do so without taking too much risk and decides to use both funds.

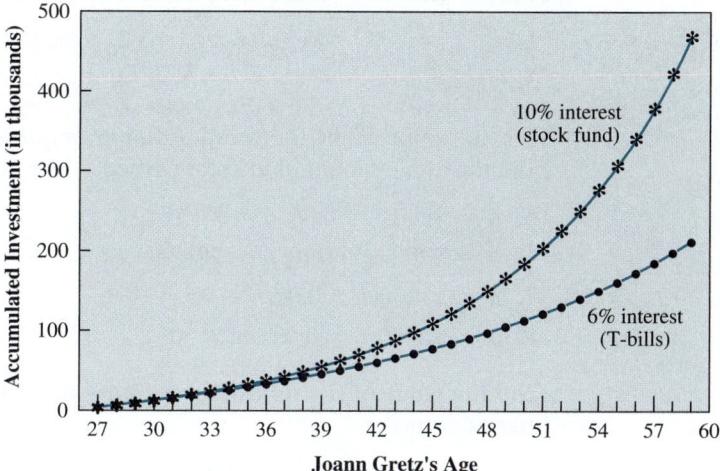

Projected Value of IRA for Joann Gretz

Figure 15.3

EXAMPLE 7   **Saving for Retirement**

At age 20, Tom Jones begins saving for retirement by making end-of-year payments of $400 into an IRA account, until age 65 (a total of 45 years). Becky Smith doesn't begin saving for retirement until age 40, at which time she deposits $1000 at the end of each year until age 65 (a total of 25 years). Assume that each account earns 7% compounded annually and find the amount available at age 65 to each individual.

Solution   Tom Jones saves $400 at the end of each year for 45 years at 7% compounded annually.

$$\text{Future amount} = \$400 \cdot s_{\overline{45}|0.07} = \$400 \times 285.74931084$$
$$= \$114,299.72$$

Becky Smith saves $1000 at the end of each year for 25 years also earning 7% compounded annually.

$$\text{Future amount} = \$1000 \cdot s_{\overline{25}|0.07} = \$1000 \times 63.24903772$$
$$= \$63,249.04$$

Even though Becky Smith deposits much more each year than Tom Jones, Jones ends up with a lot more money at age 65. Why? Tom Jones saved for 45 years giving compound interest a lot of time to work for him. Becky Smith has made it a harder for herself by not starting to save until age 40, but it is still a good idea for her to save. The important idea is to start saving early so that compound interest can also work for you!

NOTE   The last example shows that it is very important to begin saving early in life, but it is never too late to begin saving.

15.1   **Exercises**

Find the following values using column C of the table in Appendix D.

1. $s_{\overline{15}|0.03}$

2. $s_{\overline{30}|0.08}$

3. $s_{\overline{10}|0.09}$

4. $s_{\overline{50}|0.12}$

Find the value of the following ordinary annuities if interest is compounded annually. Find the total amount of interest earned.

5. $R = \$850, i = 0.06, n = 28$

6. $R = \$200, i = 0.10, n = 20$

7. $R = \$1000, i = 0.08, n = 25$

8. $R = \$2000, i = 0.065, n = 50$

Find the value of the following ordinary annuities and then find the total amount of interest earned.

9. $R = \$1400$, 10% per year compounded quarterly for 8 years

10. $R = \$250$, 8% per year compounded quarterly for 10 years

11. $R = \$800$, 9% per year compounded monthly for 4 years

12. $R = \$500$, 6% per year compounded monthly for 3 years

Find the amount of the following annuities due if interest is compounded annually. Find the amount of interest earned.

13. $R = \$1200, i = 0.075, n = 8$

14. $R = \$1400, i = 0.08, n = 10$

15. $R = \$17,544, i = 0.08, n = 6$

16. $R = \$64,715, i = 0.06, n = 12$

Assume that you are able to invest $900 per year in an ordinary annuity where interest is not taxed. Complete the following table by finding the amount of the annuity for each interest rate and time period given.

	Annual Compounding Rate				
	5%	7%	9%	11%	13%
10 years	17. _____	18. _____	19. _____	20. _____	21. _____
20 years	22. _____	23. _____	24. _____	25. _____	26. _____
30 years	27. _____	28. _____	29. _____	30. _____	31. _____

 32. Explain the difference in the methods used to calculate the amount of an ordinary annuity and the amount of an annuity due. (See Objectives 2 and 5.)

 33. Explain the difference between a regular IRA and a Roth IRA. Which is better for a young person? (See Objective 6.)

 34. MILLIONAIRE BY CHOICE   Ben Watson, 22, recently graduated from college and started work at his first professional job. He has set a goal for himself to become a millionaire. Watson's employer invests $2800 at the end of each year into a retirement plan. Is this enough for Watson to be a millionaire in time? If not, what else can he do?

First, find the amount of the following annuities due, then find the amount of interest earned.

35. Payments of $500 made at the beginning of each quarter for 10 years at 4% compounded quarterly

36. $50 deposited at the beginning of each month for 4 years at 6% compounded monthly

37. $100 deposited at the beginning of each quarter for 9 years at 8% compounded quarterly

38. $1500 deposited at the beginning of each semiannual period for 11 years at 9% compounded semiannually

Find the periodic payment that will amount to the following sums under the given conditions.

39. $S = \$20,000$, interest at $7\frac{1}{2}\%$ compounded annually, payments made at the end of each year for 10 years

40. $S = \$30,000$, interest is 5% compounded semiannually, payments made at the end of each 6-month period for 8 years

41. $S = \$50,000$, interest is 12% compounded quarterly, payments made at the end of each quarter for 8 years

42. $S = \$24,000$, interest is 9% compounded monthly, payments are made at the end of each month for $3\frac{1}{4}$ years

Find the minimum number of payments that must be made to accumulate the given amount of money at the stated interest rate. Also, find the amount of the annuity.

43. $15,000 needed, payments of $450 are made at the end of each quarter at 6% compounded quarterly

44. $21,000 needed, payments of $1500 are made at the end of each 6-month period at 10% compounded semiannually

45. $35,000 needed, payments of $825 are made at the end of each month at 9% compounded monthly

46. $37,500 needed, payments of $1250 are made at the end of each month at 12% compounded monthly

Solve the following application problems.

47. INVESTING IN AN IRA   At the end of each quarter, the Thompsons invest $450 in an IRA earning 8% compounded quarterly. Find the amount of their annuity at the end of $3\frac{1}{2}$ years.

48. RETIREMENT ACCOUNT   An employer deposits $1200 at the end of each quarter into Natasha Kimskey's retirement account. Kimskey chooses to put the money into a fund that invests in real estate mortgages that has historically paid 8% compounded quarterly. Find the amount of the annuity in 10 years assuming the yield remains constant.

49. CHILD-SUPPORT PAYMENTS   Becky Smith decides to put the child-support payments from her previous husband into an annuity for the education of her two children. At the end of each month for 4 years, she puts $300 into a mutual fund that has yielded 9% compounded monthly. Find (a) the amount of the annuity and (b) the interest earned.

50. EXCESS CASH   Digital Electronics, Inc. decides to accumulate funds in order to build a building in 4 years. It deposits $20,000 at the end of every month in an account earning 6% compounded monthly. Find the future value.

51. FUTURE VALUE   Pam Parker deposits $2435 at the beginning of each year for 8 years in an account paying 6% compounded annually. She then leaves that money alone, with no further deposits, for an additional 5 years. Find the final amount on deposit after the entire 13-year period. Find the total amount of interest earned.

52. ANNUITY DUE   Tim Bessner invests $500 at the *beginning* of each quarter for 10 years in an account paying 7% compounded quarterly. He then leaves the money alone, with no further deposits, for an additional 6 years. Find the amount on deposit after the 16 years and find total interest earned.

53. RECREATIONAL VEHICLE   Tom and Sandra Kip are trying to save $4000 as the down payment on a new recreational vehicle. If they can deposit $125 at the end of each month in an account paying 4% compounded monthly, how long will it take them to accumulate the necessary amount? How much will they actually accumulate?

54. NEW SHOWROOM   Western Motors needs $120,000 as a down payment on a new showroom. If the company deposits $10,000 at the end of each quarter at 5% compounded quarterly, how long will it take to get the needed money? How much will the company actually have?

55. AFFORDING COLLEGE   In order to help his daughter go to college, Bill Thomas plans to invest $250 per quarter for 10 years in either (a) an ordinary annuity paying 8% compounded quarterly or (b) a CD yielding 6% compounded quarterly. Find the amount of the annuity for both choices.

56. COLLEGE FUND   The Crockers have decided to invest $1500 at the end of each year for 12 years in a college fund for their twin grandsons. They can choose either (a) a mutual fund of domestic stocks expected to yield 10% per year or (b) a savings account expected to yield about 4% per year. Find the amount of the annuity in both cases.

15.2	**Present Value of an Annuity**

OBJECTIVES

1 *Calculate the present value of an annuity.*

2 *Use the formula for the present value of an annuity.*

3 *Find the equivalent cash price.*

The previous section discussed how to find the amount of an annuity after a series of equal, periodic payments. This section considers the present value of such an annuity. There are two ways to think of the **present value of an annuity**.

1. The *present value of an annuity* is a lump sum that can be deposited today that will amount to the same future amount as would the periodic *payments* into an annuity (see Example 1 on page 530).
2. The present value of an annuity is a lump sum that can be deposited today that is needed to generate the payments from an annuity (see Example 2 on page 531).

Objective

1   *Calculate the Present Value of an Annuity.*   As an example of this second way of looking at the present value of an annuity, let us find the amount that *must be deposited today,* at 10% compounded annually, so that $1500 could be removed *at the end of each year for 6 years.*

The amount that must be deposited today is the sum of the present values of each of the separate withdrawals. In other words, today's deposit must include the present value of the withdrawal made at the end of year 1 plus the present value of the withdrawal at the end of year 2 and so forth, all the way to the present value of the withdrawal at the end of year 6.

Use column B of **Appendix D** to find the present value of the payment at the end of the first year with one compounding period and a rate of 10% per year.

$$\text{Present value of 1st payment} = \$1500(0.90909091) = \$1363.64$$

Find the present values for payments at the end of years 2 through 6 in a similar fashion to see the values in Figure 15.4.

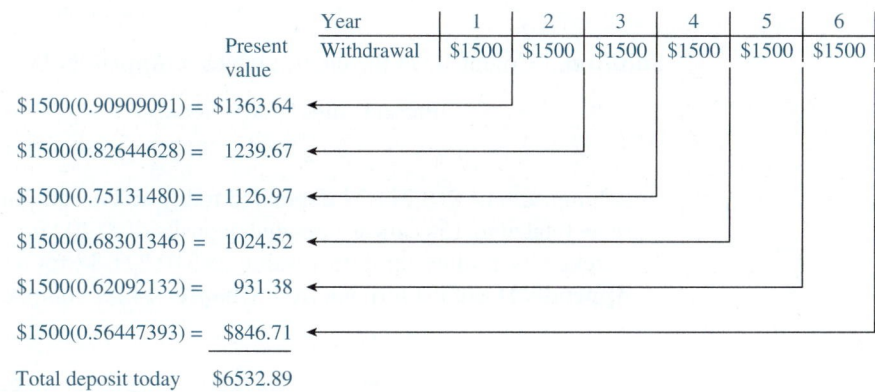

Year	1	2	3	4	5	6
Withdrawal	$1500	$1500	$1500	$1500	$1500	$1500

Present value

$1500(0.90909091) = $1363.64

$1500(0.82644628) = 1239.67

$1500(0.75131480) = 1126.97

$1500(0.68301346) = 1024.52

$1500(0.62092132) = 931.38

$1500(0.56447393) = $846.71

Total deposit today $6532.89

Figure 15.4

A lump sum deposit today of $6532.89 at 10% compounded annually would permit withdrawals of $1500 at the end of each year for 6 years. Also, a lump sum deposit today of $6532.89 left in an account for 6 years would produce *the same final total* as deposits of $1500 at the end of each year for 6 years, with all deposits at 10% compounded annually.

Objective

2   *Use the Formula for the Present Value of an Annuity.*

Finding the Present Value of an Annuity

Here is the formula for the present value A of an annuity with a payment of R dollars at the end of each period. The term is n periods and i is the rate of interest per compounding period. The lump sum deposit must be made at the beginning of year 1.

$$A = R\left[\frac{(1 + i)^n - 1}{i(1 + i)^n}\right]$$

The expression in brackets is abbreviated $a_{\overline{n}|i}$.

$$A = R \cdot a_{\overline{n}|i}$$

$a_{\overline{n}|i}$ is read as "*a*-angle-*n*-at-*i*."

Values of $a_{\overline{n}|i}$ are given in column D of the interest table. We can use the table to check the problem given on the preceding page. Look on the 10% page, for 6 payments at 10%, finding the number 4.35526070. Then multiply, which gives the following.

$$A = \$1500(4.35526070) = \$6532.89$$

This is the same answer found earlier.

EXAMPLE 1   Finding the Present Value of an Annuity

Dion Martinez has decided to make annual payments of $1200 at the end of each year for 15 years into an investment that she thinks will yield 8% compounded annually. What lump sum deposited today at 8% compounded annually will result in the same future value?

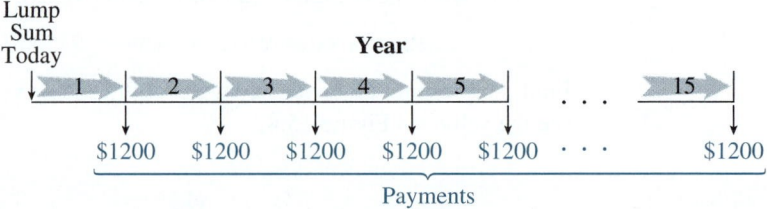

Solution   Column D of the interest tables in **Appendix D** shows that $a_{\overline{15}|0.08} = 8.55947869$.

$$\text{Present value is } A = R \cdot a_{\overline{n}|i}$$
$$A = \$1200 \cdot 8.55947869 = \$10,271.37$$

A lump sum of $10,271.37 deposited today at 8% compounded annually will result in the same total after 15 years as year-end deposits of $1200 for 15 years at 8%. This result can be checked by finding the future value of $10,271.37 for 15 years at 8%. Use column A of **Appendix D** and the formula from **Chapter 14** for compound amount M.

$$M = P(1 + i)^n$$
$$M = \$10,271.37 \cdot 3.17216911 = \$32,582.52$$

On the other hand, using the amount of an annuity that is column C of **Appendix D**, deposits of $1200 at the end of each year for 15 years, at 8% produces the following.

$$S = R \cdot s_{\overline{n}|i}$$
$$S = R \cdot s_{\overline{15}|0.08}$$
$$= \$1200 \cdot 27.15211393 = \$32,582.54$$

The difference of 2 cents is due to rounding.

Financial
Calculator
Approach

Set your calculator to an ordinary annuity (payments at the end of each period). Payment, number of compounding periods, and interest rate per compounding period are known. Present value is the unknown.

$$-1200 \boxed{PMT} \; 15 \; \boxed{n} \; 8 \; \boxed{i} \; \boxed{PV} \; 10271.37$$

NOTE There are two ways to produce $32,582.54 in 15 years at 8% compounded annually: a single deposit of $10,271.37 today or payments of $1200 at the end of each year for 15 years.

EXAMPLE 2 Finding the Present Value

Fred and Sara Zhao recently divorced. As one part of the divorce settlement, Fred must pay Sara $2000 at the end of each year for 10 years. If money can be deposited at 6% compounded annually, find the lump sum he could deposit today to have enough money, with principal and interest, to make the payments.

Solution Look under $n = 10$ and $i = 0.06$ in column D of the interest tables to find $a_{\overline{10}|0.06} = 7.36008705$.

$$A = R \cdot a_{\overline{10}|0.06}$$
$$= \$2000 \cdot 7.36008705$$
$$= \$14{,}720.17$$

A deposit of $14,720.17 today at 6% compounded annually is sufficient to make the 10 year-end payments of $2000 each. The difference between the sum of all payments, $10 \times \$2000 = \$20{,}000$, and the amount deposited today is the interest.

$$\text{Interest} = 10 \times \$2000 - \$14{,}720.17 = \$5279.83$$

NOTE Although the $2000 withdrawals are at the end of each year, the original lump-sum deposit must be made at the beginning of year 1.

EXAMPLE 3 Finding the Present Value

An Australian engineering firm hires a new manager for its North American operations. The contract states that if the new manager works for 5 years, then he will receive a benefit of $15,000 at the end of each semiannual period for 8 years. Find the lump sum the firm could deposit today to satisfy the retirement contract if funds can be invested at 10% compounded semiannually. Ignore taxes.

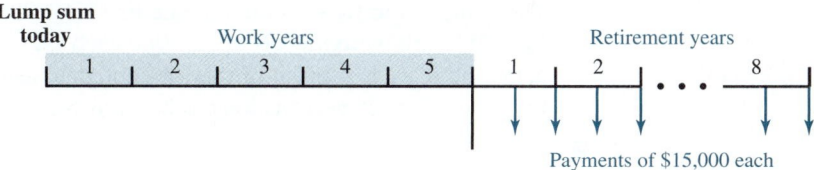

Payments of $15,000 each

Solution First find the present value of an annuity with $2 \times 8 = 16$ periods at 5% per compounding period. Use column D of the interest tables to find $a_{\overline{16}|0.05} = 10.83776956$.

$$A = R \cdot a_{\overline{16}|0.05}$$
$$= \$15,000 \cdot 10.83776956$$
$$= \$162,566.54$$

The firm needs $162,566.54 at the end of the 5-year work period to satisfy the retirement benefits.

It can meet this liability today by depositing the present value of $162,566.54 assuming 10% compounded semiannually over 5 years. Use column B of the interest tables with $n = 5 \times 2 = 10$ and $i = \frac{10\%}{2} = 5\%$ and the formula from **Chapter 14** to find the following.

$$P = \frac{M}{(1 + i)^n} = M\frac{1}{(1 + i)^n}$$
$$P = \$162,566.54 \cdot 0.61391325$$
$$= \$99,801.75$$

A lump sum of $99,801.75 deposited today will grow to $162,566.54 in 5 years which, with interest, is enough to make all 16 retirement payments of $15,000 each.

EXAMPLE 4 Determining Retirement Income

Bill Jones wishes to retire at age 65 and withdraw $25,000 at the end of each year until age 90. (a) If money earns 8% per year compounded annually, how much will he need at age 65? (b) If Jones starts an IRA at age 32 by depositing $2000 per year in an account paying 8% per year compounded annually, will the IRA account contain enough money?

Solution

(a) The amount needed at age 65 is the present value of an annuity of $25,000 per year for $90 - 65 = 25$ years, with interest of 8% compounded annually. Use column D of the interest tables to find $a_{\overline{25}|0.08} = 10.67477619$.

$$A = R \cdot a_{\overline{n}|i}$$
$$A = \$25,000 \cdot 10.67477619$$
$$= \$266,869.40$$

Assuming Jones continues to earn 8% compounded annually, he will need $266,869.40 at age 65 to generate the needed $25,000 at the end of each year until age 90.

(b) Jones makes payments of $2000 at the end of each year for $65 - 32 = 33$ years, at 8% compounded annually. These payments form a regular annuity with $n = 33$ and $i = 0.08$. Use column C of the interest tables to find $s_{\overline{33}|0.08} = 145.95062044$.

$$S = R \cdot s_{\overline{n}|i}$$
$$S = \$2000 \cdot 145.95062044$$
$$= \$291,901.24$$

The value in the IRA account at age 65 ($291,901.24) exceeds the amount needed to fund 25 yearly withdrawals of $25,000 each ($266,869.40). Therefore, $2000 invested at the end of each year for 33 years is enough to generate $25,000 at the end of each year for $90 - 65 = 25$ years as long as he earns 8%.

> **NOTE**   We have ignored the effect of income taxes in our examples. Money in retirement accounts grows free of income tax, but income taxes must be paid on retirement funds in most accounts when withdrawn. An exception is funds from Roth IRA accounts, which are not subject to income tax when withdrawn.

> **NOTE**   Example 7 in **Appendix A.2** shows how a financial calculator can be used to solve a similar problem.

Objective

3   *Find the Equivalent Cash Price.*   One thousand dollars in your hands today is better than $1000 to be paid to you in 8 years. This is true since $1000 in your hands today could earn interest for 8 years, so it would be more than $1000 in 8 years. Thus, the timing of any payment(s) is important when comparing different situations. The next example shows how to convert two different payment situations into present values so that the better of the two becomes clear.

EXAMPLE 5   **Finding Equivalent Cash Price**

Julia Smithers is an attorney trying to settle an estate. The estate owns a piece of property that is desired by two different developers. Delton Properties offers $140,000 in cash, today, for the land. Stoneybrook offers $50,000 now as a down payment, with payments of $8000 at the end of each quarter for 4 years. Money may be invested at 12% compounded quarterly. Stoneybrook offers a bank guarantee that the payment will be made, making each offer equally safe. Which bid should the attorney accept?

Solution   The bids are best compared using the present value of the two offers. The offer from Delton Properties is $140,000 cash today, so $140,000 is the present value for that offer. However, Stoneybrook's offer includes payments and cash. Find the present value of Stoneybrook's offer by adding the present value of the annuity payments to the cash to be paid today. Use column D of the interest table to find the present value of the annuity payments of $8000 at the end of each quarter. Use $n = 4 \times 4 = 16$ periods and $i = 12\% \div 4 = 3\%$ per compounding period.

$$A = R \cdot a_{\overline{n}|i}$$
$$A = \$8000 \cdot a_{\overline{16}|0.03}$$
$$= \$8000(12.56110203)$$
$$= \$100,488.82$$

Present value of Stoneybrook's offer = Cash + Present value of annuity payments
$$= \$50,000 + \$100,488.82$$
$$= \$150,488.82$$

This amount, $150,488.82, is called the **equivalent cash price**. This exceeds the $140,000 in cash offered by Delton Properties, so the attorney should accept Stoneybrook's bid as long as the company has good credit.

15.2	**Exercises**

Find the following values.

1. $a_{\overline{15}|0.075}$

2. $a_{\overline{20}|0.09}$

3. $a_{\overline{15}|0.12}$

4. $a_{\overline{40}|0.06}$

Find the present value of each of the following annuities. Round to the nearest cent.

Amount per Payment	Payment at End of Each	No. of Years	Money Invested at
5. $3000	year	8	10% compounded annually
6. $1500	year	10	$7\frac{1}{2}$% compounded annually
7. $800	6 months	10	6% compounded semiannually
8. $650	6 months	8	7% compounded semiannually
9. $400	quarter	5	8% compounded quarterly
10. $200	month	$3\frac{1}{2}$	5% compounded monthly

 11. Explain the difference between the future value and present value of an annuity. Illustrate the difference with an example.

 12. An individual wins a state lottery that pays $50,000 a year for 20 years. Must the state have $1 million to pay for this prize? If not, how can the state ensure that it has the necessary funds? (See Objective 1.)

Solve the following application problems. Round to the nearest cent.

13. LOTTERY Gina Hardin was elated when she won a state lottery paying $85,480 at the end of each year for 20 years. Find the amount the state must set aside today to satisfy this annuity at 8% compounded annually.

14. DIVORCE SETTLEMENT Tom and Kitty Wysong recently divorced. Ms. Wysong agreed to pay Mr. Wysong $8000 every 6 months for 12 years since he had helped her through medical school. What amount should Ms. Wysong set aside today in an account earning 10% per year compounded semiannually in order to satisfy this obligation?

15. CARE OF DISABLED CHILD Mr. Roberts is retired and wishes to set up a 10-year annuity with quarterly payments of $8000 for the care of his disabled son. Find the amount he should deposit today at 6% interest compounded quarterly.

16. EQUIPMENT REPLACEMENT Physician's Pain Management plans to set aside an annual payment of $18,000 per year for 4 years for replacement of physical therapy equipment. Assuming 8% compounded annually, what lump sum deposited today would result in the same future value?

17. WITHDRAWALS What lump sum deposited today at 8% compounded semiannually would permit withdrawals of $1200 at the end of each 6-month period for 7 years? How much interest is earned?

18. TRUST FUND Henry Worthington sets up a trust fund for his grandson. He wants his grandson to make withdrawals from the trust fund of $3000 at the end of each quarter for 10 years. Find the amount needed in the trust fund, if money will earn 6% compounded quarterly.

19. RETIREMENT INCOME In addition to his income from Social Security and two rental houses that he owns, Chandra Lach needs $18,000 at the end of each year for 25 years at retirement. Find the amount he must accumulate if he earns (a) 5% per year and (b) 7% per year.

20. RETIREMENT INCOME In addition to income from Social Security and a pension, Fernando Martinez needs $12,000 per year for 30 years at retirement. Find the amount he must accumulate if he earns (a) 4% per year and (b) $7\frac{1}{2}$% per year.

21. **PAYING FOR COLLEGE** Tom Potter estimates that his daughter's college needs, beginning in 8 years, will be $3600 at the end of each quarter for 4 years. (a) Find the total amount needed in 8 years assuming 8% compounded quarterly. (b) Will he have enough money available in 8 years if he invests $700 at the end of each quarter for the next 8 years at 8% compounded quarterly?

22. **VAN PURCHASE** In 4 years, Jennifer Videtto will need a delivery van for her office-supply store, that will require a down payment of $10,000 with payments of $1200 per month for 36 months. (a) Find the total amount needed in 4 years assuming 9% compounded monthly. (b) Will she have enough money available if she invests $1000 at the end of each month for the next 4 years at 9% compounded monthly?

23. **SALE OF COMMERCIAL BUILDING** A small commercial building sells for a down payment of $25,000 and payments of $4000 at the end of each semiannual period for 20 years. Find the equivalent cash price of the building, if money may be invested at 10% compounded semiannually.

24. **SALE OF FISHING BOAT** A fishing boat is sold with a down payment of $21,000 and payments of $3500 at the end of each quarter for $7\frac{1}{2}$ years. Find the equivalent cash price of the boat if money may be invested at 12% compounded quarterly.

Based only on present value, which of the following bids should be accepted?

25. $100,000 today, or $51,000 down and $8000 at the end of each year for 12 years; assume money may be invested at 10% compounded annually

26. $140,000 today, or $86,000 down and $2000 at the end of each month for 3 years; assume money may be invested at 12% compounded monthly

27. $335,000 today, or $175,000 down and $9500 at the end of each quarter for $4\frac{1}{2}$ years; assume money may be invested at 7% compounded quarterly

28. $4,000,000 today, or $600,000 down and $300,000 at the end of each 6-month period for 8 years; assume money may be invested at 10% compounded semiannually

Solve the following application problems.

29. **COMMERCIAL FARMING** A manager for a commercial farmer plans to retire in 5 years and is to receive $10,000 at the end of each semiannual period for 15 years. Find the shortage in 5 years if the farmer deposits $12,000 at the end of each semiannual period. Assume his deposits earn 8% compounded semiannually.

30. **SEVERANCE PAY** A large manufacturer plans to move an operation from Texas to India in 2 years, resulting in layoffs in the United States. Management anticipates a severance pay for the laid-off workers of $330,000 per month for 6 months. Find the shortage in 2 years if they deposit $65,000 per month in an account. Assume 6% compounded monthly.

31. **PLANNING AHEAD** George Joyce is terminally ill and expects to live 5 years. He has a daughter who will need $12,000 at the end of each year for 4 years beginning at the time of his death. Assume 8% per year and find the amount that must be deposited today to satisfy his daughter's needs.

32. **LIVE IN EUROPE** Beatrice Rice plans to live in Europe for 3 years beginning in 10 years. Assume an interest rate of 9% per year and assume she needs $35,000 at the end of each year while in Europe. Find the lump sum that must be deposited today to satisfy this need.

15.3	**Sinking Funds**

OBJECTIVES

1 *Find the amount of a sinking fund payment.*

2 *Set up a sinking fund table.*

Section 1 of this chapter showed how to find the amount of an annuity—the sum of money that will be in an account after making a series of equal periodic payments. Businesses often have a need to raise a certain amount of money at some fixed time in the future. In such a case, the problem is turned around. The businessperson knows how much money is needed in the future and must find the amount of each periodic payment.

A **sinking fund** is a fund that is set up to receive these periodic payments. The periodic payments plus the interest produce the necessary lump sum needed in the future.

Sinking funds are set up to provide money to build new factories, buy equipment, and purchase other companies. Also, many corporations and governmental agencies set up sinking funds to cover the face value of **bonds** or other debt that must be paid off at some time in the future.

This section discusses only the mechanics of setting up a sinking fund to pay off a bond when it is due. In **Chapter 19**, the investment aspect of bonds is discussed in detail.

Objective

1 *Find the Amount of a Sinking Fund Payment.* The payments into a sinking fund are just the payments of an annuity. If S is the amount that must be accumulated, R is the amount of each periodic payment, n is the number of periods, and i is the interest rate per period, then

$$S = R \cdot s_{\overline{n}|i}$$

The symbol for future amount needed is S and it is the known quantity in sinking fund problems. The unknown is the amount of each periodic payment, or R. Divide both sides of the formula for S by $s_{\overline{n}|i}$ to solve for R.

$$R = \frac{S}{s_{\overline{n}|i}}$$

Finding the Amount of Each Payment

The amount of each payment R, into a *sinking fund* that must contain S dollars after n payments, with interest of i per period, follows.

$$R = S \cdot \left(\frac{1}{s_{\overline{n}|i}} \right)$$

The right-hand side is read as capital S times 1 divided by *s-angle-n-at-i*.

Values of $1 \div s_{\overline{n}|i}$ are given in column E of the interest table. These values also can be found by dividing the corresponding numbers from column C into 1.

EXAMPLE 1 **Finding Periodic Payments**

Arctic Drilling, Inc. borrowed money by selling bonds with a maturity value in 15 years totaling $10,000,000. Find the amount of each payment into a sinking fund needed to build the required amount in 15 years to pay off the bonds. Assume 9% compounded annually.

Solution Look in column E of the interest table for 9% and 15 years to find 0.03405888. The amount of each payment is calculated as follows:

$$R = S \cdot \left(\frac{1}{s_{\overline{n}|i}} \right)$$

$$R = \$10,000,000 \left(\frac{1}{s_{\overline{15}|0.09}} \right)$$

$$= \$10,000,000(0.03405888)$$

$$= \$340,588.80$$

If the corporation deposits \$340,588.80 at the end of each year for 15 years, it will have the \$10,000,000 needed to pay off the bonds.

NOTE The 9% interest rate in Example 1 is what the corporation *earns* on money it has deposited. The *interest that the corporation pays* to the people who bought the \$10,000,000 in bonds plays no part in this calculation.

Objective

2 *Set Up a Sinking Fund Table.* To keep track of the various payments into a sinking fund, accountants often make up a sinking fund table, as shown in Example 2.

EXAMPLE 2 **Setting Up a Sinking Fund Table**

Arctic Drilling, Inc. in Example 1 deposited \$340,588.80 at the end of each year in a sinking fund earning 9% compounded annually. Set up a sinking fund table for the first 8 years.

Solution The sinking fund contains no money until the end of year 1 when a single deposit of \$340,588.80 is made. This payment earns no interest in the first year since it is made at the end of the year. The balance at the end of the first year is \$340,588.80. This amount earns interest at 9% during the second year and a payment is also made at the end of the second year.

End of second year $=$ (1st payment + interest) + 2nd payment

$$= (\$340,588.80 + \$340,588.80 \times 0.09) + \$340,588.80$$

$$= \$711,830.59$$

Continue in this fashion to find the values in the table. Be sure to round interest to the nearest cent each time before completing each row of the table. This is an excellent application for computer spreadsheet use.

SINKING FUND TABLE

| | Beginning of Period | | End of Period | |
Period	Accumulated Amount	Periodic Deposit	Interest Earned	Accumulated Amount
1	0	\$340,588.80	0	\$340,588.80
2	\$340,588.80	\$340,588.80	\$30,652.99	\$711,830.59
3	\$711,830.59	\$340,588.80	\$64,064.75	\$1,116,484.14
4	\$1,116,484.14	\$340,588.80	\$100,483.57	\$1,557,556.51
5	\$1,557,556.51	\$340,588.80	\$140,180.09	\$2,038,325.40
6	\$2,038,325.40	\$340,588.80	\$183,449.29	\$2,562,363.49
7	\$2,562,363.49	\$340,588.80	\$230,612.71	\$3,133,565.00
8	\$3,133,565.00	\$340,588.80	\$282,020.85	\$3,756,174.65

NOTE Rounding of the payment to the nearest dollar may cause the final result in Example 2 to differ slightly from the future amount needed.

The exact amount of debt at a future date was known in Examples 1 and 2. Example 3 shows how to estimate future debt before setting up the needed sinking fund.

EXAMPLE 3 **Finding Periodic Payments**

Children's Hospital plans to purchase a new MRI machine in 3 years. The machine currently sells for $2,100,000, but the price is expected to increase at 8% per year compounded semiannually. The hospital decides to set up a sinking fund to purchase the machine. Find the amount of each year-end payment into the fund if annual payments are made and the money is expected to earn 6% compounded annually. Round each to the nearest dollar.

Solution First, find the future price of the MRI machine using $\frac{8\%}{2} = 4\%$ interest for $3 \times 2 = 6$ periods using column A in **Appendix D**.

$$\text{Future price} = \$2,100,000 \times 1.26531902 = \$2,657,170 \quad \text{Rounded}$$

This is the total amount that the sinking fund must accumulate. The required payment to a sinking fund is found using column E in **Appendix D** with 3 periods and 6% interest to find 0.31410981.

$$\text{Payment} = \$2,657,170 \times 0.31410981 = \$834,643 \quad \text{Rounded}$$

Payments of $834,643 at the end of each year into a sinking fund paying 6% per year compounded annually will produce enough to pay cash for the MRI machine in 3 years.

Two different interest rates are involved in Example 3. The price is increasing at 8% per year compounded semiannually, but deposits in the sinking fund earn 6% compounded annually. **Interest rate spreads** such as this are common in business. For example, banks use an interest rate spread between what they pay for funds on deposit and what they charge on loans to customers.

15.3	**Exercises**

Find each of the following values.

1. $\dfrac{1}{s_{\overline{12}|0.075}}$

2. $\dfrac{1}{s_{\overline{20}|0.035}}$

3. $\dfrac{1}{s_{\overline{40}|0.09}}$

4. $\dfrac{1}{s_{\overline{30}|0.045}}$

Find the amount of payment to be made into a sinking fund so that the indicated amount will be there when needed. Round to the nearest cent.

5. $8500 in 4 years, money earns $5\frac{1}{2}\%$ compounded annually, 4 annual payments

6. $4850 in $7\frac{1}{2}$ years, money earns 7% compounded semiannually, 15 semiannual payments

7. $14,000 in 5 years, money earns 8% compounded quarterly, 20 quarterly payments

8. $28,000 in 10 years, money earns 10% compounded quarterly, 40 quarterly payments

9. Explain the purpose of a sinking fund. Why is it given a name other than annuity?

10. Define the phrase *interest rate spread.* Why do interest rate spreads exist? (See Objective 2.)

In Exercises 11–14, do the following. Find (a) the present value needed to fund the end-of-period retirement benefit using the interest rate given, and find (b) the end-of-period semiannual payment needed to accumulate the value found in part (a) assuming regular investments for 25 years in an account yielding 8% compounded semiannually.

11. $10,000 per year for 25 years, 8% per year

12. $12,000 every 6 months for 25 years, 7% compounded semiannually

13. $12,000 per quarter for 9 years, 8% compounded quarterly

14. $10,000 per quarter for 12 years, 12% compounded quarterly

Solve the following application problems. Round to the nearest cent.

15. **CATTLE FEED LOT**   The owner of Bainbridge Cattle sets up a sinking fund to accumulate $1,800,000 needed in 3 years to purchase land and construct a cattle feed lot. Find (a) the amount of each end-of-6-month payment assuming 7% compounded semiannually and (b) the total amount of interest earned.

16. **ALLIGATOR HUNTING**   Cajun Jack needs $45,000 in 4 years for a boat used to hunt alligators that are used both for leather and for the meat. (a) Find the amount of each payment if payments are made at the end of each quarter into a fund earning 6% compounded quarterly. (b) Find the total amount of interest earned.

17. **CLEANING MACHINE**   Smith Dry Cleaning must buy a new cleaning machine in 9 years for $110,000. The firm desires to set up a sinking fund for this purpose. Find the payment into the fund at the end of each year if money in the fund earns 6% compounded annually.

18. **TALENT AGENCY**   Catriona Kaplan's Baby Beautiful Talent Agency needs $79,000 in 6 years. To accumulate the necessary funds, the company sets up a sinking fund with payments made into the fund quarterly. Find the payment into this fund if money in the fund earns 5% compounded quarterly.

19. **JAIL**   A city sold $4,000,000 worth of bonds to pay for a new jail. To pay off the bonds when they mature in 8 years, the city sets up a sinking fund. Find the amount of each payment into the fund if the city makes annual payments and the money earns 6% compounded annually. Find the amount of interest earned by the deposits.

20. **CHURCH FUND-RAISING**   A small church-related college sold $1,480,000 in bonds to pay for an addition to the administration building. The bonds must be paid off in 15 years. To accumulate the money to pay off the bonds, the college sets up a sinking fund. If the college makes payments at the end of each 6 months and the money earns 10% compounded semiannually, find the amount of each payment into the fund. Find the amount of interest earned by the deposits.

21. COAL MINING Pennsylvania Coal Co. has contracted to pay $960,211.72 in 4 years to purchase a huge Caterpillar tractor used to scoop up chunks of dirt, rock, and coal. Assume funds on deposit earn 8% interest compounded annually and complete the following sinking fund table.

	Beginning of Period		End of Period	
Period	**Accumulated Amount**	**Periodic Deposit**	**Interest Earned**	**Accumulated Amount**
1	$0	$213,090.95	$0	$213,090.95
2	$213,090.95	$213,090.95	_____	_____
3	_____	_____	_____	_____
4	_____	_____	_____	_____

22. CASINO BOAT PURCHASE Riverside Gambling, Inc. needs $4,000,000 in 8 years to purchase a replacement casino boat to place on a nearby river. Assume annual payments earn 6% compounded annually and complete the sinking fund table.

	Beginning of Period		End of Period	
Period	**Accumulated Amount**	**Periodic Deposit**	**Interest Earned**	**Accumulated Amount**
1	$0	$404,143.76	$0	$404,143.76
2	$404,143.76	$404,143.76	_____	_____
3	_____	$404,143.76	_____	_____
4	_____	$404,143.76	_____	_____
5	_____	$404,143.76	_____	_____
6	_____	$404,143.76	_____	_____
7	_____	$404,143.76	_____	_____
8	_____	_____	_____	_____

23. FOOTBALL STADIUM A school district needs to build a new football stadium at a cost of $8,000,000. It sets up a sinking fund with end-of-quarter payments in an account earning 7% compounded quarterly. Find the amount that needs to be deposited each quarter if it wishes to build the stadium (a) in 3 years and (b) in 4 years.

24. AIRPORT IMPROVEMENTS A city near Chicago sold $9,000,000 in bonds to pay for improvements to an airport. It set up a sinking fund with end-of-quarter payments in an account earning 8% compounded quarterly. Find the amount that should be deposited in this fund each quarter if it wishes to pay off the bonds in (a) 7 years and (b) 12 years.

CHAPTER TERMS

Review the following terms to test your understanding of the chapter. For each term you do not know, refer to the page number found next to the term.

amount of an annuity [p. 517]

annuity [p. 517]

annuity certain [p. 517]

annuity due [p. 517 or 523]

bonds [p. 536]

contingent annuity [p. 517]

equivalent cash price [p. 533]

future value of an annuity [p. 517]

individual retirement account (IRA) [p. 524]

interest rate spread [p. 538]

lump sum [p. 516]

ordinary annuity [p. 517]

payment period [p. 517]

present value of an annuity [p. 529]

regular IRA [p. 524]

Roth IRA [p. 525]

simple annuity [p. 517]

sinking fund [p. 536]

stock fund [p. 525]

term of an annuity [p. 517]

Treasury-bill fund [p. 525]

CONCEPTS

EXAMPLES

15.1 Finding the amount of an annuity

Use n, the number of periods, and i, the interest rate per period, to find $s_{\overline{n}|i}$ in column C of the interest table in **Appendix D**. Find the amount S from the formula $S = R \cdot s_{\overline{n}|i}$ with R the periodic payment into the annuity, or use the formula.

$$S = R\left[\frac{(1+i)^n - 1}{i}\right]$$

Bill Thomas deposits $4500 at the end of each year at 6% compounded annually. How much will Thomas have at the end of 40 years?

$$n = 40; i = 6\%$$

From the table

$$s_{\overline{40}|0.06} = 154.76196562$$

and

$$S = (\$4500)(154.76196562) = \$696,428.85$$

15.1 Finding the amount of each payment into an annuity

Determine the amount needed in the future S, the interest rate per period i, and the number of periods n. Use the interest table in **Appendix D** to find $s_{\overline{n}|i}$, then find R from the formula $S = R \cdot s_{\overline{n}|i}$.

Find the amount of the periodic payment that will produce $18,000 if the interest is 6% compounded monthly and monthly payments are made for 4 years.

$$S = \$18,000$$

$$n = 4 \times 12 = 48$$

$$i = 0.06 \div 12 = 0.005$$

$$s_{\overline{48}|0.005} = 54.09783222$$

$$S = R \cdot s_{\overline{n}|i}$$

$$\$18,000 = R(54.09783222)$$

$$\$332.73 = R$$

15.1 Finding the number of payments

Divide the amount of the annuity S by the amount of the payment R to find $s_{\overline{n}|i}$. Find the page in **Appendix D** corresponding to the interest rate i. Look in column C using the value found for $s_{\overline{n}|i}$ (or the first larger number) to find n.

George Gleine needs $5000. He can put $210 per quarter into an account paying 4% compounded quarterly. How long will it take to accumulate the money?

$$s_{\overline{n}|0.01} = \frac{S}{R} = \frac{\$5000}{\$210}$$

$$s_{\overline{n}|0.01} = 23.80952381$$

Closest table value is 24.47158598, so $n = 22$ quarters; $22 \div 4 = 5\frac{1}{2}$ years.

15.1 Finding the amount of an annuity due

Add 1 to the number of periods and use this as the value of n. Use n and i, the interest rate per period, to find $s_{\overline{n}|i}$ in the interest table. To find the amount, use the formula.

$$S = R \cdot s_{\overline{n}|i} - 1 \text{ payment}$$

Find the amount of an annuity due if payments of $700 are made at the beginning of each month for 3 years into an account paying 5% compounded monthly.

$$n = (12 \times 3) + 1 = 37$$

$$i = 5\% \div 12 = \frac{5}{12}\%$$

$$s_{\overline{37}|0.467} = 39.91480775$$

$$S = \$700(39.91480775) - \$700$$

$$= \$27,240.37$$

15.1 Finding the amount of an IRA

Use n, the number of periods, and i, the interest rate per period, to find $s_{\overline{n}|i}$ in column C of the interest table in **Appendix D**. Find the amount S from the formula $S = R \cdot s_{\overline{n}|i}$ with R the periodic payment into the annuity.

Deposits of $1500 at the end of each year are made into an IRA account paying 10% per year. Find the accumulated amount in 30 years.

$$n = 30; i = 10\%$$

From the table, we have the following.

$$s_{\overline{30}|0.10} = 164.49402269$$

$$S = \$1500 \cdot 164.49402269$$

$$= \$246,741.03$$

15.2 Finding the present value of an annuity

Use the number of periods n, interest rate per period i, and column D of the interest table to find $a_{\overline{n}|i}$. Find the present value of the annuity A, using the formula

$$A = R \cdot a_{\overline{n}|i}$$

with R the payment per period.

What lump sum deposited today at 9% compounded annually will yield the same total as payments of $2500 at the end of each year for 8 years?

$$R = \$2500; n = 8; i = 9\%$$

$$a_{\overline{8}|0.09} = 5.53481911$$

$$A = \$2500(5.53481911)$$

$$= \$13,837.05$$

15.2 Finding equivalent cash price

Use the number of periods n, interest rate per period i, and column D of the interest table to find $a_{\overline{n}|i}$. Find the present value using the formula

$$A = R \cdot a_{\overline{n}|i}$$

Add the value of A to the down payment to obtain the equivalent cash value.

A buyer offers to purchase a business for $75,000 down and quarterly payments of $4000 for 5 years. If money may be invested at 8% compounded quarterly, how much is the buyer actually offering?

$$R = \$4000$$

$$n = 4 \times 5 = 20; i = 8\% \div 4 = 2\%$$

$$a_{\overline{20}|0.02} = 16.3514334$$

$$A = \$4000 \times 16.3514334$$

$$= \$65,405.73$$

Equivalent cash value $= \$75,000 + \$65,405.73$
$= \$140,405.73$

15.3 Determining the payment into a sinking fund

Use the number of payments n, the interest rate per period i, and column E of the interest table to find the value of $1 \div s_{\overline{n}|i}$. Use the formula

$$R = S \cdot \frac{1}{s_{\overline{n}|i}}$$

to calculate the payment.

A company must set up a sinking fund to accumulate $50,000 in 5 years. Find the amount of the payments if they are made at the end of each year and the fund earns 8%.

$$n = 5; i = 0.08$$

$$\frac{1}{s_{\overline{n}|i}} = 0.17045645$$

$$R = \$50,000(0.17045645)$$
$$= \$8522.82$$

15.3 Setting up a sinking fund table

Determine the payment R and the interest at the end of each payment. Then add the previous total, next payment, and interest to find the accumulated amount. Repeat for each period.

A company wants to set up a sinking fund to accumulate $10,000 in 4 years. It wishes to make annual payments into the account, which pays 8% compounded annually. Set up a table.

$$n = 4; i = 0.08$$

$$\frac{1}{s_{\overline{4}|0.08}} = 0.22192080$$

$$R = \$10,000(0.22192080)$$
$$= \$2219.21$$

| | Beginning of Period | | End of Period | |
| | Accumulated | Periodic | Interest | Accumulated |
Period	Amount	Deposit	Earned	Amount
1	$0	$2219.21	$0	$2219.21
2	2219.21	2219.21	177.54	4615.96
3	4615.96	2219.21	369.28	7204.45
4	7204.45	2219.19	576.36	10,000.00

CHAPTER 15 Review Exercises

The answer section includes answers to all Review Exercises.

Find the amount of the following annuities. [15.1]

1. $1500 is deposited at the end of each year for 22 years, money earns $6\frac{1}{2}\%$ compounded annually.

2. $1000 is deposited at the end of each semiannual period for 12 years, money earns 6% compounded semiannually.

3. $3000 is deposited at the end of each quarter for $6\frac{3}{4}$ years, money earns 10% compounded quarterly.

4. $1000 is deposited at the end of each month for $3\frac{1}{2}$ years, money earns 9% compounded monthly.

5. $18,000 is deposited at the beginning of each year for 7 years, money earns $6\frac{1}{2}\%$ compounded annually.

6. $3500 is deposited at the beginning of each quarter for $5\frac{1}{2}$ years, money earns 8% compounded quarterly.

7. Fatima Burke deposits $800 at the end of each quarter for $5\frac{1}{2}$ years in an account she expects to earn 5% compounded quarterly. Find the future value and amount of interest.

8. A firm of attorneys deposits $7500 of profit-sharing money at the end of each semiannual period for $7\frac{1}{2}$ years. Find the final amount in the account if the deposit earns 5% compounded semiannually. Find the amount of interest earned.

Find the present value of the following ordinary annuities. [15.2]

9. Payments of $4200 are made annually at 7% compounded annually for 15 years.

10. Payments of $800 are made semiannually at 8% compounded semiannually for $4\frac{1}{2}$ years.

11. Payments of $450 are made quarterly for $5\frac{1}{4}$ years at 6% compounded quarterly.

12. Payments of $125 are made monthly for $4\frac{1}{6}$ years at 10% compounded monthly.

Find the amount of each payment to be made to a sinking fund so that enough money will be available to pay off the indicated loan. [15.3]

13. $85,000 loan, money earns 9% compounded annually, 6 annual payments

14. $42,000 loan, money earns 6% compounded quarterly, 26 quarterly payments

15. $240,000 loan, money earns 9% compounded semiannually, 9 semiannual payments

16. $35,000 loan, money earns 9% compounded monthly, 47 monthly payments

Solve the following application problems.

17. Jaime Bickers invests $4000 at the end of each semiannual period for 8 years. His financial advisor told him the funds should earn about 6% compounded semiannually. Find the amount of the annuity. **[15.1]**

18. Bill Wild can save $600 at the end of each year in an account earning 10% per year. How many years are required for him to accumulate $100,000? **[15.1]**

19. Jessica Savage purchased her father's home when he went to an assisted-living center. She owes her father $85,000 and plans to pay it off in 3 years. Find the required end-of-quarter payments into a sinking fund if she earns 7% compounded quarterly. **[15.3]**

20. Moira Roberts has promised to give $25,000 to her church in 3 years. If she can earn 6% compounded monthly, find the lump sum she can deposit today to accumulate the necessary funds. **[15.2]**

21. According to the terms of a divorce settlement, one spouse must pay the other $28,000 in 17 months. What lump sum can be invested today, at 6% compounded monthly, so that enough will be available for the payment? **[15.2]**

22. A-1 Plumbing needs $48,000 in 4 years to replace two trucks. Find the amount it must deposit at the end of each quarter in a fund earning 6% compounded quarterly. **[15.3]**

23. A power company needs to replace some large generators at an estimated cost of $680,000 in $5\frac{1}{2}$ years. It expects to receive a payment of $240,000 from another source at that time. Find the payment required at the end of each semiannual period to accumulate the remaining funds needed to purchase the generators. Assume the company can earn 8% compounded semiannually. **[15.3]**

24. Hilda Worth invests $500 at the *beginning* of each semiannual period into an IRA account paying 10% compounded semiannually. Given that she is 30 years old, find the amount she will have accumulated at age 54. **[15.1]**

25. In 3 years, Aqua, Inc. plans to expand operations with the purchase of equipment for a fish farm on the coast of Florida. At that time, the firm expects to begin 5 years of end-of-quarter payments of $54,239.82 assuming 8% compounded quarterly. (a) Find the present value of the payments when they are scheduled to begin in 3 years. (b) Then find the lump sum the firm must deposit today in an account earning $7\frac{1}{2}$% compounded annually to satisfy the debt payments. **[15.2]**

Prepare a sinking fund table for the following. [15.3]

26. A firm sets up a sinking fund to pay off a $100,000 note due in 4 years. The firm makes annual payments into an account earning 9% compounded annually.

| | Beginning of Period | | End of Period | |
Period	Accumulated Amount	Periodic Deposit	Interest Earned	Accumulated Amount
1	$0	$21,866.87	$0	$21,866.87
2				
3				
4				

CHAPTER 15	# Business Application Case #1
	## *Financial Planning*

At age 32, Tish Baker has decided to invest $3600 per year for 33 years until she is 65, in her retirement plan. She has also decided to place one-half of the funds in a stock index fund that roughly tracks the return on the Standard and Poor's index. The other half of the funds will be placed in a mutual fund containing bonds.

(a) Find the amount she will have at 65 assuming the stock fund averages 9% per year compounded annually and the bond fund averages $6\frac{1}{2}$% per year compounded annually.

(b) The amount found in part (a) seems like a lot of money. But Baker knows that inflation will increase her cost of living. She wants to see the effect of 3% annual inflation on her financial goals. Find the income she needs at age 65 to have the same purchasing power as an income of $20,000 today. (*Hint:* Look at the section on inflation in **Section 12.4** and use column A of the tables.)

(c) Baker wishes to fund her retirement for 20 years (to age 85). Find the present value at the time of her retirement of the annual income found in part (b) assuming that the funds earn 8% per year compounded annually.

(d) Will her expected savings from part (a) fund her retirement at a purchasing power of $20,000 per year in today's dollars?

Baker will also receive a monthly check from Social Security during her retirement. The bar chart below shows the importance of Social Security to Americans. If Baker saves as much as she plans and she has correctly estimated her needs at retirement, she will not have to rely on Social Security for more than one-half of her income. This may allow her to travel or do other things she enjoys during retirement.

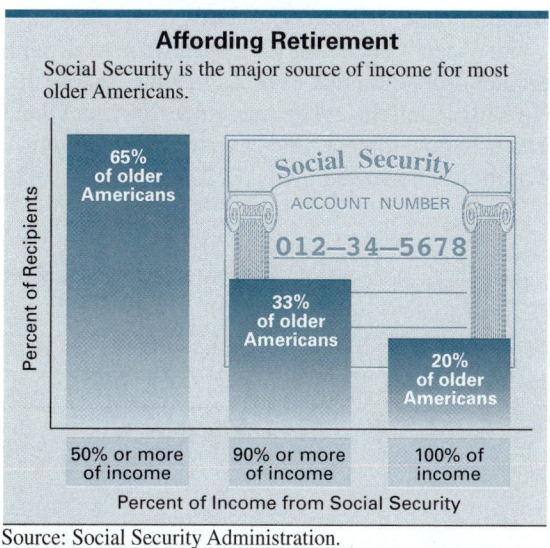

Source: Social Security Administration.

CHAPTER 15	# Business Application Case #2
	## *Financing the Cost of a New Building*

Administrators at Bacon College are debating the construction of a new building to house the School of Business Administration. They have estimated the total amount needed at the time construction starts in 5 years to be $21,300,000. The college already has $4,500,000 earning $6\frac{1}{2}$% per year that can be used to meet that goal.

(a) Find the future value of the $4,500,000.

(b) Find the shortage in 5 years.

(c) Find the amount that must be placed into a sinking fund earning $6\frac{1}{2}$% per year, to accumulate the additional funds needed.

Each year, the president of the college hopes to get donors to contribute the amount just calculated in part (c), but he knows it will be difficult.

Business and Consumer Loans

Paying cash for everything is almost impossible. For example, we use credit to pay for our phone, lights, and running water since we normally pay for these items at the end of a month. Many people buy on credit at the department store, use a credit card at the gas station, or buy cars or furniture on the installment plan. Occasionally it is necessary to borrow to pay taxes, medical expenses, or educational costs. Almost everyone borrows when buying a home.

Most businesses borrow money. Banks borrow money from individuals who deposit money into a savings account or CD at the bank, but banks also borrow from other banks. The person or firm doing the lending is called the **lender** or **creditor**. The person or firm doing the borrowing is the **borrower** or **debtor**.

Even governments borrow. A **budget surplus** refers to income from taxes and other sources that exceeds spending for a specific period, such as a year. A **budget deficit** refers to government spending that exceeds income. Figure 16.1 shows that the United States has had large budget deficits every year since 2002 and that a really huge deficit is expected in 2009. The U.S. government finances deficit spending by borrowing, so there will be a record amount of money borrowed by the U.S. government in 2009 and probably 2010 as well.

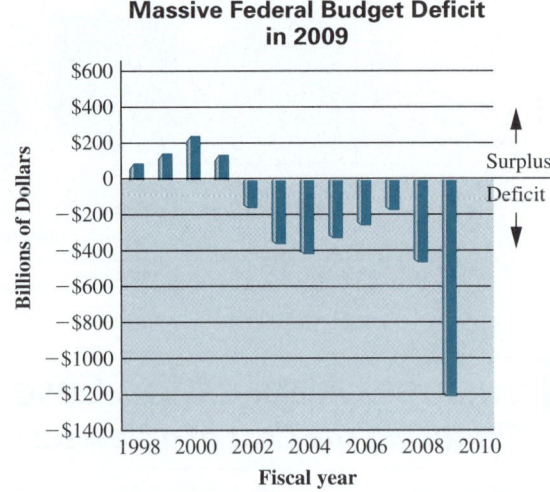

Note: Fiscal year ends Sept. 30

Figure 16.1

STOP
—and think

From whom does the U.S. government borrow money? Do individuals have $1.2 trillion to lend to the government as needed in 2009? If not individuals, then who? Corporations use most of their excess cash for their own business operations. Who has enough money to lend such huge sums to the U.S. government? Who must pay the interest on money borrowed by the government?

Years ago, consumer credit was offered by businesses as an additional service to attract more customers and increase total sales. Today, consumer credit is not merely a service to the customer. For many large retail stores the interest or finance charges on consumer credit represent *a large portion* of company profit. This chapter examines the various methods used in determining interest charges.

In 2005, a new law affecting a borrower's ability to declare both a **Chapter 7** and a **Chapter 13 bankruptcy** was passed. A Chapter 7 bankruptcy results in the liquidation of the borrower's assets with funds going to creditors, even as other remaining debts are canceled, resulting in a "fresh start." In contrast, a Chapter 13 bankruptcy requires borrowers to enter into a repayment plan and make payments until all debt is paid. Under the new law of 2005, fewer people will be allowed to file under Chapter 7 and more will be required to file under Chapter 13. In effect, it has become more difficult to declare bankruptcy, and a borrower is more likely to have to pay off all of the debt in the event of bankruptcy.

There is a fundamental difference between the notes discussed in earlier sections and the loans discussed in this chapter. In the earlier situations, a sum of money was paid back, with interest, with a lump-sum payment at some future date. In this chapter, the principal and interest are paid back in periodic payments.

16.1	Open-End Credit

OBJECTIVES

1 *Define open-end credit.*

2 *Understand revolving charge accounts and credit accounts.*

3 *Use the average daily balance method to calculate finance charges.*

4 *Define loan consolidation.*

Objective

1 *Define Open-End Credit.*   A common way of buying on credit, called **open-end credit**, has no fixed payments. The customer continues making payments until no outstanding balance is owed. With open-end credit, additional credit is often extended before the initial amount is paid off. Examples of open-end credit include most department store credit accounts and credit cards, as well as MasterCard and Visa. Individuals are given a **credit limit** on these accounts based on their income and other factors. They are then allowed to charge up to this amount.

Objective

2 *Understand Revolving Charge Accounts and Credit Accounts.*   Individuals may open **credit accounts** at certain stores. This allows the customer to make frequent purchases from that store during the month without having to pay cash or write a check. Such accounts are often never paid off, although a minimum amount must be paid each month. Since the account may never be paid off, it is called a **revolving charge account**.

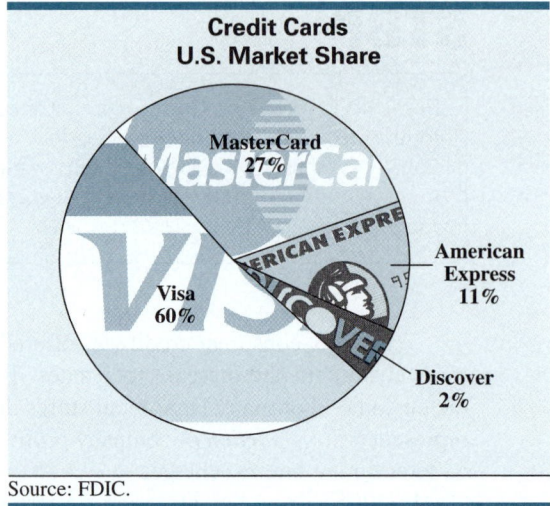

Source: FDIC.

Figure 16.2

Credit cards such as MasterCard and Visa are accepted by most stores and restaurants worldwide. Sometimes there is an annual membership fee or a minimum monthly charge for the use of this service. Credit cards are a convenient way to make purchases and track expenses since they provide a monthly statement. Part of their convenience is due to the fact that they are so widely accepted and can also be used at ATM machines for cash. Figure 16.2 shows the share of the huge U.S. credit-card market by type of card. Figure 16.3 shows a copy of a receipt for a customer using a credit card.

```
                        Hingham
                  Hingham, MA 02043
                   (781) 749-0763

     11-10-07 12:44P   0530/0001/8704/4 1321XXX
     ID# 999-8889-9287-5586-9469-9812-9607



     CARTERS BLANKET 716042011989   *   10.99 T2
     UPDATED SEPARAT 400886657471   C   12.00 T2

                             SUBTOTAL      22.99
     T2=      31.98  @   0.0% TAX           0.00
     T1=       0.00  @   5.0% TAX           0.00
                                TOTAL      22.99


     CREDIT         XXXXXXXXXXXX1234      22.99
     PAYMENT FROM PRIMARY ACCOUNT
     APPROVED
```

```
     NOW HIRING FOR THE HOLIDAY SEASON.
           FLEXIBLE SCHEDULING
     IMMEDIATE ASSOCIATE DISCOUNT. APPLY TODAY
```

Figure 16.3

At the end of a monthly billing period, the customer receives an **itemized billing** similar to that shown in Figure 16.4. Charges over and above the combined cost of the various charges are called **finance charges**. They include interest, credit life insurance, and international transaction fees.

Many lenders charge **late fees** for payments that are received after the due date and **over-the-limit fees** in the event the debt exceeds the amount authorized by the issuer of the card. Both late fees and over-the-limit fees tend to be high, so avoid them if you can. Lenders also typically charge a late fee if the payment made is *less than the minimum payment* requested by the lender. They may even cancel the account or increase the interest rate if two successive payments are less than the minimum requested.

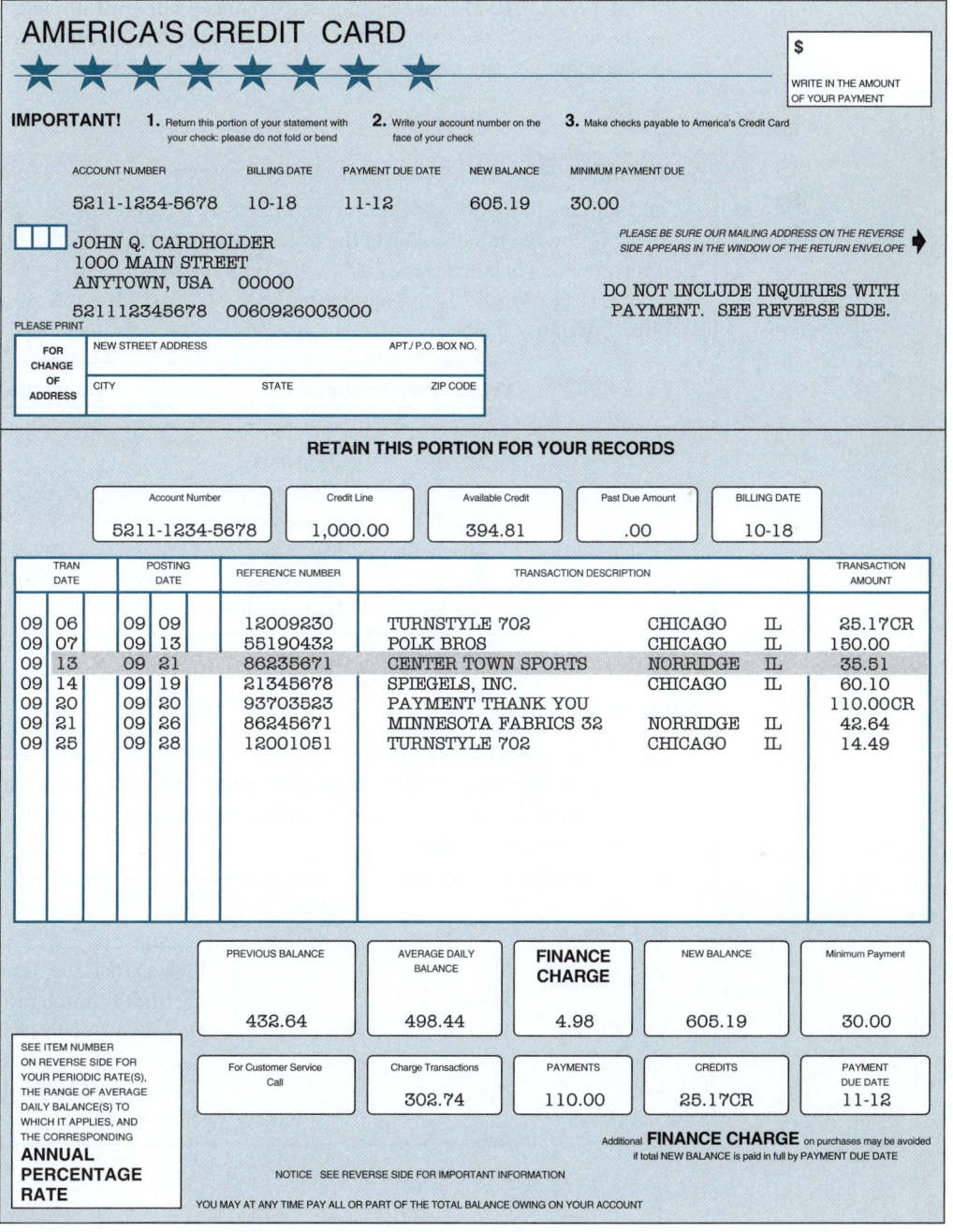

Figure 16.4

> **NOTE**   Lenders may simply deny charges to an account that cause the debt to exceed previously established credit limits.

Objective

3   *Use the Average Daily Balance Method to Calculate Finance Charges.*   Finance charges on many open-ended accounts are zero as long as the borrower *pays the full amount owed each month.* An exception is on cash advances, which result in a finance charge even if the balance is paid in full at the end of the month. Finance charges apply if balances are not paid in full, and they are usually calculated using the **average daily balance** method.

First, the balance owed on the account is found at the end of each day during a month or billing period. All of these ending daily balance amounts are added and the total is divided by the number of days during the billing period. The result is the average daily balance of the account. The finance charge is then calculated on this amount.

EXAMPLE 1   Finding Average Daily Balance

The activity in the MasterCard account of Kay Chamberlin for one billing period is shown in the following table. (a) Find the average daily balance on the next billing date of April 3, if the previous balance was $209.46. (b) Find the finance charge for the month if the monthly charge is $1\frac{1}{2}\%$ of the average daily balance. (c) Find the total amount due at the end of the billing period.

Transaction Description	Transaction Amount
Previous balance, $209.46	
March 3 Billing date	
March 12 Payment	$50.00CR*
March 17 Drug store	$28.46
March 20 Mail order	$31.22
April 1 Auto parts	$59.10
April 3 End of billing cycle	

*CR represents "credit."

Solution

(a) Using the transaction data above, the following table shows the beginning date, end date, and number of days at each specific unpaid balance. Note that March 3 is the first day and April 3 is the last day of the billing month. Each payment or charge results in a separate row in the table.

Beg. Date	End Date	Number of Days		Unpaid Balance
Mar. 3	Mar. 12	9	Previous balance carried forward is	$209.46
Mar. 12	Mar. 17	5	On March 12, subtract $50 to get	$159.46
Mar. 17	Mar. 20	3	On Mar. 17, add $28.46 to get	$187.92
Mar. 20	Apr. 1	12	On Mar. 20, add $31.22 to get	$219.14
Apr. 1	Apr. 3	2	On Apr. 1, add $59.10 to get	$278.24
		31 days in the billing period		

Next find a weighted average of the unpaid balances for the month. Multiply each unpaid balance by the number of days outstanding, total the products, and divide by the 31 days in this billing cycle. Some months will have fewer than 31 days in the cycle.

$$\$209.46 \times 9 = \$1885.14$$
$$\$159.46 \times 5 = 797.30$$
$$\$187.92 \times 3 = 563.76$$
$$\$219.14 \times 12 = 2629.68$$
$$\$278.24 \times 2 = 556.48$$
$$\$6432.36$$

Now divide the total by 31, since there are 31 days in this billing cycle.

Average daily balance = $\$6432.36 \div 31 = \$207.50$ Rounded

Chamberlin will pay a finance charge based on the average daily balance of $207.50.

Scientific Calculator Approach

The calculator solution to part (a) of Example 1 is as follows: Multiply each unpaid balance by the respective number of days until the balance changes. Add these values together and divide by the number of days in the month (31 days).

(209.46 × 9 + 159.46 × 5 + 187.92 × 3 + 219.14 × 12 + 278.24 × 2) ÷ 31 = 207.5

(b) Find the finance charge for the month by multiplying the monthly rate of $1\frac{1}{2}\%$ by the average daily balance.

Finance charge = $0.015 \times \$207.50 = \$3.11$

The finance charge would be different for a month with a different average daily balance.

(c) The amount due at the end of the billing period is the previous balance minus any payments and credits, plus any new charges, including the finance charge.

Previous Balance	− Payment	+ Drug Store	+ Mail Order	+ Auto Parts	+ Finance Charge	
$209.46	− $50	+ $28.46	+ $31.22	+ $59.10	+ $3.11	= $281.35

Ending balance

The amount due on April 3 is $281.35, but the credit-card issuer usually gives card holders a couple of weeks to pay without incurring any penalty charges or additional interest.

NOTE The billing period in Example 1 is 31 days. Some billing periods are 30 days or less. Be sure to use the correct number of days.

NOTE Not all billings for open-end accounts occur on the same day of the month.

If finance charges are expressed on a per month basis, find the **annual percentage rate** by multiplying the monthly rate by 12, the number of months in a year. Table 16.1 shows typical monthly rates and the corresponding annual percentage rates. Notice that the interest rates charged by some credit-card companies are extremely high!

TABLE 16.1   MONTHLY FINANCE CHARGES AND CORRESPONDING ANNUAL PERCENTAGE RATES

Quoted Monthly Finance Charge	Annual Percentage Rate
$\frac{1}{2}$ of 1%	6%
$\frac{2}{3}$ of 1%	8%
$\frac{3}{4}$ of 1%	9%
$\frac{5}{6}$ of 1%	10%
1%	12%
$1\frac{1}{4}\%$	15%
$1\frac{1}{2}\%$	18%
$1\frac{2}{3}\%$	20%
$1\frac{3}{4}\%$	21%
2%	24%

NOTE   The monthly finance charge percent is used only to calculate the finance charge, not the minimum payment.

Objective

4   *Define Loan Consolidation.*   Credit has historically been *so easy to obtain* for individuals in our society *that it has sometimes become problematic*. Figure 16.5 shows students' use of credit cards. Individuals with many high-interest revolving account loans sometimes

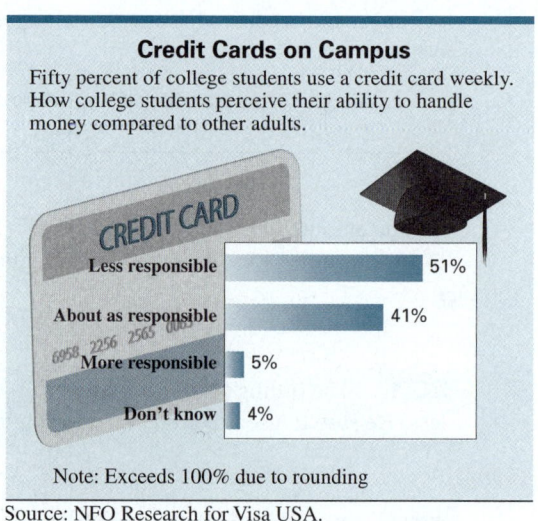

Credit Cards on Campus

Fifty percent of college students use a credit card weekly. How college students perceive their ability to handle money compared to other adults.

Less responsible	51%
About as responsible	41%
More responsible	5%
Don't know	4%

Note: Exceeds 100% due to rounding

Source: NFO Research for Visa USA.

Figure 16.5

consolidate their loans into one lower-interest loan, frequently with a longer term. It may cost to consolidate loans, but it allows people to handle their bills without defaulting on debt and ruining their credit history. Consolidating a loan may help someone afford the payments, but it does not extend the life of the items purchased that created the loans in the first place.

EXAMPLE 2 **Loan Consolidation**

Between auto loans, a home loan, and the revolving account loans shown below, teachers Bill and Cynthia Taylor have more short-term debt than they can handle. They have gone to George Willis at Glaston Credit Union for help.

Revolving Account	Debt	Annual Percentage Rate	Minimum Payment
Sears	$3880.54	18%	$150
Dillards	1620.13	16%	75
MasterCard	3140.65	14%	100
Visa	8940.60	20%	270
Totals	$17,581.92		$595

Solution George Willis (1) put the Taylors on a *strict budget,* (2) consolidated the revolving account debts into one longer-term low-interest loan at the credit union, and (3) decreased the payment on one auto by refinancing it at a lower rate. In all, Willis reduced the Taylors' monthly payments by about $280 per month.

NOTE Families such as the Taylors in Example 2 who consolidate their debts and then take additional loans can develop serious financial problems and may end up with more debt than they can handle. In this event, the only option may be a very stressful experience referred to as bankruptcy.

Unfortunately, families sometimes owe so much on high-interest credit cards and automobile loans that they simply cannot handle the debt even by consolidating loans. In that event the family may have to declare bankruptcy or get second jobs, pushing workloads up to 60 hours per week. This can make life *very* difficult. It is best to avoid high-interest credit-card debt by buying only what you can pay off at the end of the month. Look at the following ideas.

Consider the Following before Buying

1. Do I really need the item *now*, or can I delay the purchase until I have the cash to buy it?
2. Can I get along with a less expensive used one rather than a new one?
3. What is the real cost, including cash price, sales tax, and finance charges, of purchasing this item?
4. Am I getting the best price for the item and best loan terms (such as interest rate and term of loan) possible or should I shop around on the Internet for a better deal?
5. Can I truly afford the payments?
6. If I buy this item, can I still save every month?

16.1	**Exercises**

Find the finance charge for the following revolving credit accounts. Assume interest is calculated on the average daily balance of the account. (See Example 1.)

Average Daily Balance	Monthly Interest Rate
1. $836.15	1.2%
2. $8431.10	1.4%
3. $389.95	$1\frac{1}{4}\%$
4. $2235.46	1.6%

Find the average daily balance for the following credit-card accounts. Assume the billing date is the same day in each month, and use the number of days in each month. Then find the finance charge if interest is 1.5% per month on the average daily balance. (See Example 1.) Finally, find the balance at the end of the billing cycle.

5. Previous balance $139.56

September 12	Billing date	
September 20	Payment	$45
September 21	CDs	$37.25

6. Previous balance $412.48

November 5	Billing date	
November 18	Payment	$150
November 30	Dinner and play	$84.50

7. Previous balance $2737.28

May 4	Billing date	
May 15	Payment	$200
May 19	Airline ticket	$303

8. Previous balance $228.95

January 27	Billing date	
February 9	Cheese	$11.08
February 13	Returns	$26.54
February 20	Payment	$29
February 25	Repairs	$71.19

9. Previous balance $938.34

June 11	Billing date	
June 15	Returns	$319.35
June 20	Jewelry	$347.19
June 24	Car rental	$222.57
July 3	Payment	$345

10. Previous balance $355.72

March 29	Billing date	
March 31	Returns	$209.53
April 2	Cleaning supplies	$28.76
April 10	Gasoline	$14.80
April 12	Returns	$63.54
April 13	Returns	$11.71
April 20	Payment	$72
April 21	Flowers	$29.72

11. Previous balance $714.58

August 17	Billing date	
August 21	Mail order	$26.94
August 23	Returns	$25.41
August 27	Wine	$31.82
August 31	Payment	$128
September 9	Returns	$71.14
September 11	Birthday gift	$110
September 14	Cash advance	$100

12. Previous balance $412.42

March 10	Billing date	
March 13	Returns	$28.18
March 15	School supplies	$16
March 20	Payment	$200
April 3	Gasoline	$28.45
April 5	Clothing	$86.80

Solve the following application problems.

13. **CREDIT-CARD DEBT** Jerry Jasper has an average daily balance of $2800.35 for the month on a credit card that charges 1.5% on the average daily balance. (a) Find the monthly finance charge. (b) Find the finance charge if he can change the loan to a credit card that charges 1% on the average unpaid balance. (c) Find the savings.

14. **REDUCING FINANCE CHARGES** Maria Estefan has an average daily balance of $4509.66 for the month on a credit card that charges 1.8% on the average daily balance. (a) Find the monthly finance charge. (b) Find the finance charge if she can change the loan to a credit card that charges 1% on the average unpaid balance. (c) Find the savings.

15. **DREAM VACATION** After taking his dream vacation to Europe, Benjamin Thompson has an average daily balance of $4850.39 on a credit card that charges 1.5% per month. (a) Find the interest charges. (b) Find the interest charges if he can change the loan to a credit card that charges 0.8% per month. (c) Find the savings.

16. **CREDIT-CARD DEBT** Jerry Johnson has been ill and has an average daily balance of $16,432.51 on a credit card charging 1.6% interest. (a) Find the monthly finance charge. (b) Find the finance charge if he can change the loan to a credit card that charges 0.5% on the average daily balance. (c) Find the savings.

17. Explain how the average daily balance is determined. (See Objective 3.)

18. Explain how consolidating loans may be of some advantage to a credit-card holder. What disadvantages can you think of? (See Objective 4.)

19. Suppose your brother owes $1200, $1500, and $2380 on credit cards charging 15%, 18%, and 24%, respectively. What would you recommend to your brother? Why? (See Objective 4.)

20. Do this for yourself: Make a table listing all of your debts showing the amount owed, monthly payment, and interest rate on each. Compare your debt payments to your monthly income. Try to move any significant credit-card debt to another card with a lower interest rate.

21. Victor Barton crushed his foot in a car accident. His insurance paid only a portion of his medical bills and he was left with $18,400 in related debt that he ended up charging to a credit card that charges 1.5% per month on the average daily balance. Find the amount he can save each month if he can move the debt to a credit card that charges no interest for 1 year on balances transferred.

22. Ben Fuller has a debt of $13,850 from his years as a college student and he currently pays 1.25% per month in interest charges. Find the savings if he can move the debt to a credit card that charges no interest for 1 year on balances transferred.

16.2   Installment Loans

OBJECTIVES

1 *Define installment loan and annual percentage rate.*

2 *Find the total installment cost and finance charge.*

3 *Use a table to find the APR.*

Objective

1   *Define Installment Loan and Annual Percentage Rate.*   A loan is **amortized** if both principal and interest are paid off by a sequence of periodic payments. An example is a payment of $440 per month for 48 months on a car loan. This type of loan is called an **installment loan**. Installment loans are used for cars, boats, home improvements, furniture, and even for consolidating several smaller loans into one affordable payment.

Since the enactment of the **Federal Truth-in-Lending Act (Regulation Z)** in 1969, lenders must report their **finance charge** (the charge for credit) and their **annual percentage rate (APR)** on installment loans. The Truth-in-Lending Act does *not* regulate interest rates or credit charges, but merely requires a standardized and truthful report of what they are to within one-eighth of a percent of the actual APR. In practice, many institutions round to the nearest one-quarter of a percent. Each state sets the allowable interest rates and charges. Lenders normally give borrowers a document such as the one in Figure 16.6, showing all credit charges.

The **nominal**, or **stated**, interest rate can differ from the APR. The APR is the *true effective annual interest rate* for a loan. For example, consider a 1-year loan with $1000 in proceeds and $1120 in maturity value. The interest is $120. Look in the table below at the effect of time on the effective interest rate. Clearly not all loans with $1000 in proceeds and $120 in interest are equivalent.

TIME	CALCULATIONS	EFFECTIVE RATE
1 year	$R = \dfrac{\$120}{(\$1000 \times 1)}$	12%
$\frac{3}{4}$ year	$R = \dfrac{\$120}{\left(\$1000 \times \frac{3}{4}\right)}$	16%
$\frac{1}{2}$ year	$R = \dfrac{\$120}{\left(\$1000 \times \frac{1}{2}\right)}$	24%

Note and Disclosure Statement

BORROWER NAME (Last – First – Middle Initial) AND ADDRESS (Street – City – State – Zip Code)

Smith, John Q.
10123 Fair Oaks Blvd.
Fair Oaks, CA 95628

DATE	MEMBER NUMBER	NOTE NUMBER

CONTRACT NUMBER	REFERENCE NUMBER	MATURITY DATE
012-2719-6	XXXXXXXXX	XXXXXXX

In this agreement "you" and "your" mean each person who signs this agreement. The "credit union" means the credit union whose name appears above and anyone to whom the credit union transfers its rights under this agreement. The terms on the reverse side are part of this agreement. Boxes checked below apply to this agreement.

TRUTH IN LENDING DISCLOSURE

ANNUAL PERCENTAGE RATE The cost of your credit as a yearly rate.	FINANCE CHARGE The dollar amount the credit will cost you.	Amount Financed The amount of credit provided to you or on your behalf.	Total of Payments The amount you will have paid when you have made all payments as scheduled.	Prepayment: If you pay off early you will not have to pay a penalty. e means an estimate
13.99%	$ 1,605.64	$ 6,800.00	$ 8,405.64	

	Number of Payments	Amount of Payments	When Payments Are Due	Property Insurance: You may obtain property insurance from anyone you want that is acceptable to the credit union.
Your Payment Schedule will be:	36	$233.49	monthly beginning May 15	XXXXXXXXXXXXXXXXXXXXXXXXXXXXXX $

Security: Collateral securing other loans with the credit union will also secure this loan. You are giving a security interest in your shares and/or deposits in the credit union; and **X** the goods/property being purchased; ☐ Other (Describe)

Late Charge: N/A	Filing Fees	Non-Filing Insurance
	$ N/A	$ N/A

See your contract documents for any additional information about nonpayment, default, and any required repayment in full before the scheduled date.

ITEMIZATION OF THE AMOUNT FINANCED

ITEMIZATION OF AMOUNT FINANCED OF $	AMOUNT GIVEN TO YOU DIRECTLY $	AMOUNT PAID ON YOUR ACCOUNT $	PREPAID FINANCE CHARGE $
AMOUNT PAID TO OTHERS $	To	$	To
ON YOUR BEHALF $	To	$	To

NOTE AND SECURITY AGREEMENT   CONTINUED ON REVERSE SIDE

Promise to Pay: You promise to pay $ _____ to the credit union plus interest on the unpaid balance at _____ % per year until what you owe has been repaid.

Collection Costs: You promise to pay all costs of collecting the amount you owe under this agreement including court costs and reasonable attorney fees.

Security Offered:	MODEL	YEAR	I.D. NUMBER	TYPE	VALUE
	Chevrolet Caprice		1NA1G1H96XE6811		

Other (Describe):

You Pledge Shares and/or Deposits of $ _____ in account number _____ Key No. _____ This Note is governed by the laws of **Illinois**

SIGNATURE: If you agree to make and be bound by the terms of this Note and Security Agreement sign below. *If you are not a borrower but an owner of the collateral for this loan, sign below and check the box for "Owner of Collateral". By doing so you agree only to the terms of the Security Agreement.*
CAUTION: IT IS IMPORTANT THAT YOU THOROUGHLY READ THIS CONTRACT BEFORE YOU SIGN IT.

Borrower	Date	Borrower ☐ Owner of Collateral (other than a Borrower)	Date
X (SEAL)		X (SEAL)	
Borrower ☐ Owner of Collateral (other than a Borrower)	Date	Witness	Date
X (SEAL)		X (SEAL)	

CREDIT INSURANCE APPLICATION

"You" or "Your" means the member and the joint insured (if applicable).

Credit insurance **is voluntary and not required in order to obtain this loan.** You may select any insurer of your choice. You can get this insurance only if you check the "yes" box below and sign your name and write in the date. The rate you are charged for the insurance is subject to change. You will receive written notice before any increase goes into effect. You have the right to stop this insurance by notifying your credit union in writing. Your signature below means you agree that:

- If you elect insurance, you authorize the credit union to add the charges for insurance to your loan each month.
- You are eligible for disability insurance only if you are working for wages or profit for 25 hours a

week or more on the date of any advance. If you are not, that particular advance will not be insured until you return to work. If you are off work because of temporary layoff, strike or vacation, but soon to resume, you will be considered at work. Are you working for wages or profit for 25 hours a week or more? ☐ Yes ☐ No

- You are eligible for insurance up to the Maximum Age for Insurance. Insurance will stop when you reach that age.

NOTE: THE LIFE AND DISABILITY INSURANCE CONTAINS CERTAIN BENEFIT EXCLUSIONS, INCLUDING A PRE-EXISTING CONDITION EXCLUSION. PLEASE REFER TO YOUR CERTIFICATE FOR DETAILS.

YOU ELECT THE FOLLOWING INSURANCE COVERAGE(S)	YES	NO	PREMIUM SCHEDULE	INSURANCE MAXIMUMS	DISABILITY	LIFE
CREDIT DISABILITY		X	$ e	MONTHLY TOTAL BENEFIT	$ 600	N/A
				INSURABLE BALANCE PER LOAN ACCOUNT	$50,000	N/A
				MAXIMUM AGE FOR INSURANCE	66	N/A

If you are totally disabled for more than **30** days, then the Disability Benefit will begin with the **31st** day of disability. | **SECONDARY BENEFICIARY** (If you desire to name one)

DATE	DATE OF BIRTH	DATE	DATE OF BIRTH
April 3			

SIGNATURE OF BORROWER ELIGIBLE TO BE INSURED (Be sure to check the boxes above.)

X *John Q. Smith*

SIGNATURE OF JOINT INSURED (CO-BORROWER) (Only required if JOINT CREDIT LIFE coverage is selected)

X   N/A

Figure 16.6

Interest charges vary significantly from one loan to another and can be quite high. Look at Figure 16.7, which shows the added interest cost to finance a well-equipped truck. The finance charge for a loan depends on the borrower's past credit record, income, down payment, and other factors. *It pays to shop and make comparisons based on APR figures before borrowing.*

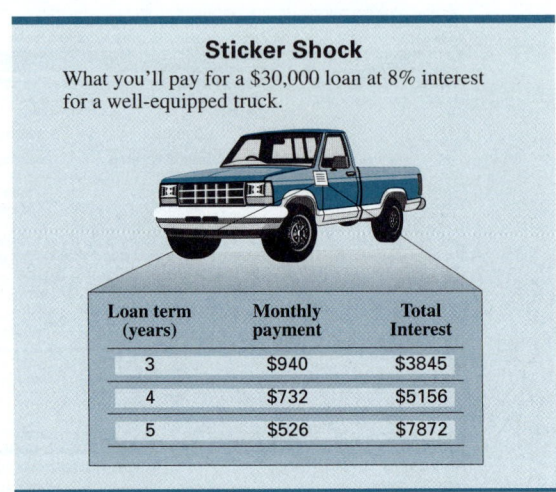

Sticker Shock

What you'll pay for a $30,000 loan at 8% interest for a well-equipped truck.

Loan term (years)	Monthly payment	Total Interest
3	$940	$3845
4	$732	$5156
5	$526	$7872

Figure 16.7

Objective

2 *Find the Total Installment Cost and Finance Charge.* In order to find the annual percentage rate on a loan, it is necessary to first find the **total installment cost (deferred payment price)**, the **finance charge**, and the **amount financed**. We will then show how to find the annual percentage rate for an installment loan in Objective 3.

Finding Amount Financed

Step 1 Find the total installment cost.

Total installment cost = Down payment
+ (Amount of each payment × Number of payments)

Step 2 Find the finance charge.

Finance charge = Total installment cost − Cash price

Step 3 Finally, find the amount financed.

Amount financed = Cash price − Down payment

NOTE Lenders frequently *allow the borrower to choose the day of the month* that installment payments are due. This allows the borrower to pay the bill after a payday for example.

EXAMPLE **1** **Finding Total Installment Cost, Amount Financed, and Finance Charge**

Ed Chamski makes his living by teaching piano both at home and at a nearby community college where he is a professor of music. He purchased a new baby grand piano for $8500 with $1500 down and 48 monthly payments of $184.34 each. Find (a) the total installment cost, (b) the finance charge, and (c) the amount financed.

Solution

(a) Find the total installment cost by adding the down payment to the total amount of all payments.

$$\text{Total installment cost} = \$1500 + 48 \times \$184.34 = \$10{,}348.32$$

(b) The finance charge is the total installment cost less the cash price.

$$\text{Finance charge} = \$10{,}348.32 - \$8500 = \$1848.32$$

(c) The amount financed is $8500 - $1500 = $7000.

NOTE In determining the total installment cost, the down payment is added to the total of the monthly payments.

Students frequently borrow money using a **Stafford loan**, which is a type of installment loan. The government pays the interest on a *subsidized* Stafford loan while the student borrower is in school on at least a half-time basis. On the other hand, the student is responsible for interest on *unsubsidized* Stafford loans. Repayment of a loan begins 6 months after the borrower ceases at least half-time enrollment. You can find information about Stafford loans at the financial aid office of your college or at a bank.

Objective

3 *Use a Table to Find the APR.* Annual percentage rate tables, available from the nearest federal reserve bank or the Board of Governors of the Federal Reserve System, Washington, D.C. 20551, are used for APR rates that *are accurate enough* to satisfy federal law. Table 16.2 is a portion of these tables, which incidentally consist of two volumes.

The APR is found using the annual percentage rate table as follows.

Finding Annual Percentage Rate Using a Table

Step 1 Divide the finance charge by the amount financed, and multiply by $100.

$$\frac{\text{Finance charge}}{\text{Amount financed}} \times \$100$$

The result is the finance charge per $100 of the amount financed.

Step 2 Read down the left column of Table 16.2 to the proper number of payments. Go across to the number closest to the number found in Step 1. Read up the column to find the annual percentage rate.

NOTE Interest rates on installment loans are often higher than home mortgage rates and certainly much higher than the rates paid by banks on deposits.

Table 16.2   ANNUAL PERCENTAGE RATE TABLE FOR MONTHLY PAYMENT PLANS

Annual Percentage Rate (Finance Charge per $100 of Amount Financed)

Number of Payments	10.00%	10.25%	10.50%	10.75%	11.00%	11.25%	11.50%	11.75%	12.00%	12.25%	12.50%	12.75%	13.00%	13.25%	13.50%	13.75%
1	0.83	0.85	0.87	0.90	0.92	0.94	0.96	0.98	1.00	1.02	1.04	1.06	1.08	1.10	1.12	1.15
2	1.25	1.28	1.31	1.35	1.38	1.41	1.44	1.47	1.50	1.53	1.57	1.60	1.63	1.66	1.69	1.72
3	1.67	1.71	1.76	1.80	1.84	1.88	1.92	1.96	2.01	2.05	2.09	2.13	2.17	2.22	2.26	2.30
4	2.09	2.14	2.20	2.25	2.30	2.35	2.41	2.46	2.51	2.57	2.62	2.67	2.72	2.78	2.83	2.88
5	2.51	2.58	2.64	2.70	2.77	2.83	2.89	2.96	3.02	3.08	3.15	3.21	3.27	3.34	3.40	3.46
6	2.94	3.01	3.08	3.16	3.23	3.31	3.38	3.45	3.53	3.60	3.68	3.75	3.83	3.90	3.97	4.05
7	3.36	3.45	3.53	3.62	3.70	3.78	3.87	3.95	4.04	4.12	4.21	4.29	4.38	4.47	4.55	4.64
8	3.79	3.88	3.98	4.07	4.17	4.26	4.36	4.46	4.55	4.65	4.74	4.84	4.94	5.03	5.13	5.22
9	4.21	4.32	4.43	4.53	4.64	4.75	4.85	4.96	5.07	5.17	5.28	5.39	5.49	5.60	5.71	5.82
10	4.64	4.76	4.88	4.99	5.11	5.23	5.35	5.46	5.58	5.70	5.82	5.94	6.05	6.17	6.29	6.41
11	5.07	5.20	5.33	5.45	5.58	5.71	5.84	5.97	6.10	6.23	6.36	6.49	6.62	6.75	6.88	7.01
12	5.50	5.64	5.78	5.92	6.06	6.20	6.34	6.48	6.62	6.76	6.90	7.04	7.18	7.32	7.46	7.60
13	5.93	6.08	6.23	6.38	6.53	6.68	6.84	6.99	7.14	7.29	7.44	7.59	7.75	7.90	8.05	8.20
14	6.36	6.52	6.69	6.85	7.01	7.17	7.34	7.50	7.66	7.82	7.99	8.15	8.31	8.48	8.64	8.81
15	6.80	6.97	7.14	7.32	7.49	7.66	7.84	8.01	8.19	8.36	8.53	8.71	8.88	9.06	9.23	9.41
16	7.23	7.41	7.60	7.78	7.97	8.15	8.34	8.53	8.71	8.90	9.08	9.27	9.46	9.64	9.83	10.02
17	7.67	7.86	8.06	8.25	8.45	8.65	8.84	9.04	9.24	9.44	9.63	9.83	10.03	10.23	10.43	10.63
18	8.10	8.31	8.52	8.73	8.93	9.14	9.35	9.56	9.77	9.98	10.19	10.40	10.61	10.82	11.03	11.24
19	8.54	8.76	8.98	9.20	9.42	9.64	9.86	10.08	10.30	10.52	10.74	10.96	11.18	11.41	11.63	11.85
20	8.98	9.21	9.44	9.67	9.90	10.13	10.37	10.60	10.83	11.06	11.30	11.53	11.76	12.00	12.23	12.46
21	9.42	9.66	9.90	10.15	10.39	10.63	10.88	11.12	11.36	11.61	11.85	12.10	12.34	12.59	12.84	13.08
22	9.86	10.12	10.37	10.62	10.88	11.13	11.39	11.64	11.90	12.16	12.41	12.67	12.93	13.19	13.44	13.70
23	10.30	10.57	10.84	11.10	11.37	11.63	11.90	12.17	12.44	12.71	12.97	13.24	13.51	13.78	14.05	14.32
24	10.75	11.02	11.30	11.58	11.86	12.14	12.42	12.70	12.98	13.26	13.54	13.82	14.10	14.38	14.66	14.95
25	11.19	11.48	11.77	12.06	12.35	12.64	12.93	13.22	13.52	13.81	14.10	14.40	14.69	14.98	15.28	15.57
26	11.64	11.94	12.24	12.54	12.85	13.15	13.45	13.75	14.06	14.36	14.67	14.97	15.28	15.59	15.89	16.20
27	12.09	12.40	12.71	13.03	13.34	13.66	13.97	14.29	14.60	14.92	15.24	15.56	15.87	16.19	16.51	16.83
28	12.53	12.86	13.18	13.51	13.84	14.16	14.49	14.82	15.15	15.48	15.81	16.14	16.47	16.80	17.13	17.46
29	12.98	13.32	13.66	14.00	14.33	14.67	15.01	15.35	15.70	16.04	16.38	16.72	17.07	17.41	17.75	18.10
30	13.43	13.78	14.13	14.48	14.83	15.19	15.54	15.89	16.24	16.60	16.95	17.31	17.66	18.02	18.38	18.74

Table 16.2 (CONTINUED) ANNUAL PERCENTAGE RATE TABLE FOR MONTHLY PAYMENT PLANS

Annual Percentage Rate (Finance Charge per $100 of Amount Financed)

Number of Payments	10.00%	10.25%	10.50%	10.75%	11.00%	11.25%	11.50%	11.75%	12.00%	12.25%	12.50%	12.75%	13.00%	13.25%	13.50%	13.75%
31	13.89	14.25	14.61	14.97	15.33	15.70	16.06	16.43	16.79	17.16	17.53	17.90	18.27	18.63	19.00	19.38
32	14.34	14.71	15.09	15.46	15.84	16.21	16.59	16.97	17.35	17.73	18.11	18.49	18.87	19.25	19.63	20.02
33	14.79	15.18	15.57	15.95	16.34	16.73	17.12	17.51	17.90	18.29	18.69	19.08	19.47	19.87	20.26	20.66
34	15.25	15.65	16.05	16.44	16.85	17.25	17.65	18.05	18.46	18.86	19.27	19.67	20.08	20.49	20.90	21.31
35	15.70	16.11	16.53	16.94	17.35	17.77	18.18	18.60	19.01	19.43	19.85	20.27	20.69	21.11	21.53	21.95
36	16.16	16.58	17.01	17.43	17.86	18.29	18.71	19.14	19.57	20.00	20.43	20.87	21.30	21.73	22.17	22.60
37	16.62	17.06	17.49	17.93	18.37	18.81	19.25	19.69	20.13	20.58	21.02	21.46	21.91	22.36	22.81	23.25
38	17.08	17.53	17.98	18.43	18.88	19.33	19.78	20.24	20.69	21.15	21.61	22.07	22.52	22.99	23.45	23.91
39	17.54	18.00	18.46	18.93	19.39	19.86	20.32	20.79	21.26	21.73	22.20	22.67	23.14	23.61	24.09	24.56
40	18.00	18.48	18.95	19.43	19.90	20.38	20.86	21.34	21.82	22.30	22.79	23.27	23.76	24.25	24.73	25.22
41	18.47	18.95	19.44	19.93	20.42	20.91	21.40	21.89	22.39	22.88	23.38	23.88	24.38	24.88	25.38	25.88
42	18.93	19.43	19.93	20.43	20.93	21.44	21.94	22.45	22.96	23.47	23.98	24.49	25.00	25.51	26.03	26.55
43	19.40	19.91	20.42	20.94	21.45	21.97	22.49	23.01	23.53	24.05	24.57	25.10	25.62	26.15	26.68	27.21
44	19.86	20.39	20.91	21.44	21.97	22.50	23.03	23.57	24.10	24.64	25.17	25.71	26.25	26.79	27.33	27.88
45	20.33	20.87	21.41	21.95	22.49	23.03	23.58	24.12	24.67	25.22	25.77	26.32	26.88	27.43	27.99	28.55
46	20.80	21.35	21.90	22.46	23.01	23.57	24.13	24.69	25.25	25.81	26.37	26.94	27.51	28.08	28.65	29.22
47	21.27	21.83	22.40	22.97	23.53	24.10	24.68	25.25	25.82	26.40	26.98	27.56	28.14	28.72	29.31	29.89
48	21.74	22.32	22.90	23.48	24.06	24.64	25.23	25.81	26.40	26.99	27.58	28.18	28.77	29.37	29.97	30.57
49	22.21	22.80	23.39	23.99	24.58	25.18	25.78	26.38	26.98	27.59	28.19	28.80	29.41	30.02	30.63	31.24
50	22.69	23.29	23.89	24.50	25.11	25.72	26.33	26.95	27.56	28.18	28.80	29.42	30.04	30.67	31.29	31.92
51	23.16	23.78	24.40	25.02	25.64	26.26	26.89	27.52	28.15	28.78	29.41	30.05	30.68	31.32	31.96	32.60
52	23.64	24.27	24.90	25.53	26.17	26.81	27.45	28.09	28.73	29.38	30.02	30.67	31.32	31.98	32.63	33.29
53	24.11	24.76	25.40	26.05	26.70	27.35	28.00	28.66	29.32	29.98	30.64	31.30	31.97	32.63	33.30	33.97
54	24.59	25.25	25.91	26.57	27.23	27.90	28.56	29.23	29.91	30.58	31.25	31.93	32.61	33.29	33.98	34.66
55	25.07	25.74	26.41	27.09	27.77	28.44	29.13	29.81	30.50	31.18	31.87	32.56	33.26	33.95	34.65	35.35
56	25.55	26.23	26.92	27.61	28.30	28.99	29.69	30.39	31.09	31.79	32.49	33.20	33.91	34.62	35.33	36.04
57	26.03	26.73	27.43	28.13	28.84	29.54	30.25	30.97	31.68	32.39	33.11	33.83	34.56	35.28	36.01	36.74
58	26.51	27.23	27.94	28.66	29.37	30.10	30.82	31.55	32.27	33.00	33.74	34.47	35.21	35.95	36.69	37.43
59	27.00	27.72	28.45	29.18	29.91	30.65	31.39	32.13	32.87	33.61	34.36	35.11	35.86	36.62	37.37	38.13
60	27.48	28.22	28.96	29.71	30.45	31.20	31.96	32.71	33.47	34.23	34.99	35.75	36.52	37.29	38.06	38.83

EXAMPLE 2 **Finding Annual Percentage Rate**

Toots McGee placed a $2400 down payment on a new Subaru Outback with a total cost of $25,400. She needed the all-wheel drive (AWD) of the Subaru for the snowy conditions in upstate New York where she lived. She signed a note with payments of $494.40 for 60 months. Find the annual percentage rate.

Solution

$$\text{Total installment cost} = \text{Down payment} + \text{Sum of all payments}$$
$$= \$2400 + 60 \times \$494.40 = \$32{,}064$$
$$\text{Finance charge} = \text{Total installment cost} - \text{Cash price}$$
$$= \$32{,}064 - \$25{,}400 = \$6664$$
$$\text{Amount financed} = \text{Cash price} - \text{Down payment}$$
$$= \$25{,}400 - \$2400 = \$23{,}000$$

Now find the annual percentage rate.

$$\frac{\text{Finance charge}}{\text{Amount financed}} \times \$100 = \frac{\$6664}{\$23{,}000} \times \$100$$
$$= \$28.97 \text{ in finance charges per } \$100 \text{ financed}$$

The nearest value in the table on the 60 payment row is $28.96 which corresponds to an interest rate of 10.50%. The APR is 10.50%.

Financial Calculator Approach

In Example 2, a more precise value of the APR can be found using a financial calculator. Payment, number of compounding periods, and present value (loan amount) are known. The interest rate per compounding period is unknown.

$$-494.40 \boxed{PMT} \ 60 \boxed{n} \ 23000 \boxed{PV} \ \boxed{i} \ 0.87529468$$

Multiply this rate per month by 12 months to get an annual rate of $0.87529468 \times 12 = 10.50\%$ (rounded).

16.2 | **Exercises**

Find the finance charge and the total installment cost for the following. (See Example 1.)

	Amount Financed	Down Payment	Cash Price	Number of Payments	Amount of Payment	Total Installment Cost	Finance Charge
1.	$12,400	$5000	$17,400	60	$264.94	_____	_____
2.	$650	$125	$775	24	$32	_____	_____
3.	$150	None	$150	12	$15	_____	_____
4.	$1200	None	$1200	20	$70	_____	_____
5.	$780	$300	$1080	10	$90	_____	_____
6.	$490	None	$490	12	$43.30	_____	_____

Find the annual percentage rate using Table 16.2. (See Example 2.)

	Amount Financed	Finance Charge	No. of Monthly Payments	APR
7.	$1850	$157.30	15	_____
8.	$345	$24.62	12	_____
9.	$442	$28.68	14	_____
10.	$4690	$1237.22	48	_____
11.	$145	$13.25	18	_____
12.	$650	$73.45	24	_____

 13. Explain the difference between open-end credit and installment loans. (See **Section 16.1** and Objective 1 of this section.)

14. Find the APR on one of your personal loans. (See Objective 3.)

Solve the following application problems. Express annual percentage rate to the nearest one hundredth of a percent.

15. FLAT-SCREEN TV Rudolf Heston bought a flat-screen TV with special sound speakers for $1800 so that he and his friends could watch sports together. He paid $200 down and agreed to payments of $142.16 per month for 12 months. Find the annual percentage rate.

16. REFRIGERATOR PURCHASE Sears offers a refrigerator for $960 with no down payment, $176.44 in interest charges, and 30 equal payments. Find the annual percentage rate.

17. LIVING ROOM SET Judy and Charles Bitters purchased a complete living room set for $2725. They paid $500 down and financed the balance with payments of $258.69 for 9 months. Find the annual percentage rate.

18. SOFA ON SALE A department store has a sofa on sale for $900. A buyer paying 20% down finances the balance by paying $34.30 per month for 2 years. Find the annual percentage rate that the store must include in its advertising.

19. COMPUTER SYSTEM PURCHASE A contractor in Mexico City purchases a computer system for 650,000 pesos. After making a down payment of 100,000 pesos, he agrees to payments of 26,342.18 pesos per month for 24 months. Find (a) the total installment cost and (b) the annual percentage rate.

20. TRUCK PURCHASE An electrical contractor in Hiroshima, Japan, purchases a truck costing 2,700,000 yen. He makes a down payment of 1,000,000 yen and agrees to monthly payments of 54,855 yen for 36 months. Find (a) the total installment cost and (b) the annual percentage rate.

21. STORE EXPANSION Dillon Sporting Goods borrows $180,000 to expand its store to include winter sporting supplies such as skis and snowmobiles. It makes no down payment but agrees to monthly payments of $6974.66 for 30 months. Find (a) the total installment cost and (b) the annual percentage rate.

22. ENGINE REPLACEMENT Jose Yaki purchased a new 505-horsepower engine for his 2006 Corvette for $11,450. He made a down payment of $5000 and agreed to make 24 payments of $305.15. Find the annual percentage rate.

 23. When are people more likely to use installment loans rather than open-end credit? (*Hint:* Search your local newspaper for examples.)

 24. Which type of loan tends to have higher interest rates—installment loans or credit loans? Document this with several examples of each type of loan.

16.3	**Early Payoffs of Loans**

OBJECTIVES

1 *Use the United States Rule when prepaying a loan.*

2 *Find the amount due on the maturity date using the United States Rule.*

3 *Find the balance due after missing a payment.*

4 *Use the Rule of 78 when prepaying a loan.*

Objective

1 *Use the United States Rule When Prepaying a Loan.* It is common for a payment to be made on a loan *before it is due.* This may occur when a person receives extra money or when a debt is refinanced elsewhere. Prepayments of loans are discussed in this section.

The first method for calculating the effect of an early loan payment is the **United States Rule**, which is used by the U.S. government as well as most states and financial institutions. Under the United States Rule, any payment is first applied to any interest owed. The balance of the payment is then used to reduce the principal amount of the loan.

The United States Rule

Step 1 Find the simple interest due from the date the loan was made until the date the partial payment is made. Use the formula $I = PRT$.

Step 2 Subtract this interest from the amount of the payment.

Step 3 Any difference is used to reduce the principal.

Step 4 Treat additional partial payments in the same way, always finding interest on *only* the unpaid balance after the last partial payment.

The remaining unpaid principal plus interest on this unpaid principal is then due on the maturity date of the loan.

Objective

2 *Find the Amount Due on the Maturity Date Using the United States Rule.* If the partial payment is not large enough to pay the interest due, the payment is either held in suspension until enough money is available to pay the interest due or the payment is rejected and returned. Either way, the borrower is contacted. This means that making a partial payment smaller than the interest due *offers no advantage* to the borrower—the lender just holds the partial payment until enough money is available to pay the interest owed.

EXAMPLE 1 Finding the Amount Due

On August 14, Jane Ficker signed a 180-day note for $28,500 for an X-ray machine for her dental office. The note has an interest rate of 10%. On October 25, a payment of $8500 is made. (a) Find the balance owed on the principal. (b) If no additional payments are made, find the amount due at maturity of the loan.

Solution

(a) First, find that there are 72 days from August 14 to October 25. Then find simple interest using $I = PRT$.

$$\text{Interest} = \$28,500 \times 0.10 \times \frac{72}{360} = \$570$$

Subtract the interest from the October 25 payment to find the amount of the payment to be applied to principal. Then reduce the original principal by this amount.

$$\text{Applied to principal} = \$8500 - \$570 = \$7930$$
$$\text{New principal} = \$28,500 - \$7930 = \$20,570$$

(b) The note was originally for 180 days with the partial payment made after 72 days. Thus, interest on the new principal of $20,570 will be charged for $180 - 72 = 108$ days.

$$\text{Interest} = \$20,570 \times 0.10 \times \frac{108}{360} = \$617.10$$

If no additional partial payments are made, the amount due at the maturity date is the remaining principal plus interest on that remaining principal.

$$\text{Amount due at maturity} = \$20,570 + \$617.10 = \$21,187.10$$

In order to find the total interest paid when partial payments are made, the individual interest payments are added.

EXAMPLE 2 Finding Total Interest Paid

A lawn furniture manufacturer signs a 140-day note on February 5. The note, for $45,600, is to a supplier of aluminum tubing for the furniture and carries a simple interest rate of 12%. On March 19, the manufacturer receives an unexpected payment from one of its customers and applies $16,000 toward the note. A further early payment permits a second $13,250 partial payment on April 23. Find the interest paid on the note and the amount paid on the due date of the note.

Solution   The first partial payment was made on March 19, which is 42 days after the loan was made. In 42 days, the interest on the note is found using $I = PRT$.

$$I = \$45,600 \times 0.12 \times \frac{42}{360} = \$638.40$$

A partial payment of $16,000 was made on March 19. Of this amount, $638.40 is applied to interest.

$16,000.00	Amount of payment
− 638.40	Interest owed
$15,361.60	Applied to principal

After the partial payment on March 19, the balance on the loan is found as follows.

$45,600.00	Original amount of loan
− 15,361.60	Applied to principal
$30,238.40	New amount owed

A second partial payment is made on April 23, which is $12 + 23 = 35$ days later. Find interest on $30,238.40 for 35 days.

$$I = \$30,238.40 \times 0.12 \times \frac{35}{360} = \$352.78$$

A payment of $13,250 is made on April 23. Of this, $352.78 applies to interest, leaving

$$\$13,250 - \$352.78 = \$12,897.22$$

to reduce the principal. After the partial payment on April 23, the principal is as follows.

$30,238.40	Previous balance
− 12,897.22	Applied to principal
$17,341.18	New principal

The first partial payment was made 42 days after the note was signed, with the second payment made 35 days after that. The second payment was made $42 + 35 = 77$ days after the note was signed. Since the note was for 140 days, the note is due

$$140 - 77 = 63$$

days after the second partial payment. Interest on the new balance of $17,341.18 for 63 days is

$$I = \$17{,}341.18 \times 0.12 \times \frac{63}{360} = \$364.16$$

On the date the loan matures, a total of

$$\$17{,}341.18 + \$364.16 = \$17{,}705.34$$

must be paid. The total interest paid over the life of the loan is

$$\$638.40 + \$352.78 + \$364.16 = \$1355.34$$

All this work is summarized in the following table.

Date Payment Made	Amount of Payment	Applied to Interest	Applied to Principal	Remaining Balance
March 19	$16,000	$638.40	$15,361.60	$30,238.40
April 23	13,250	352.78	12,897.22	17,341.18
Date of maturity (June 25)	17,705.34	364.16	17,341.18	0
Totals		$1355.34	$45,600.00	

Objective

3 *Find the Balance Due after Missing a Payment.*   The next example shows what happens when a payment is missed.

EXAMPLE 3 Finding Balance Due after a Missed Payment

On March 5, Sally Richter bought 1 acre of land with a 2-year-old mobile home for $49,900 from an elderly couple. She paid $2000 down and signed a promissory note with monthly payments of $887.39 for 6 years at 10% interest. She made the first payment on April 1, but missed the May 1 payment due to expenses related to a car accident. Richter called the elderly couple and discussed her situation. They agreed not to charge her a penalty for the missed payment, but interest charges would continue to apply. Find the loan balance if Richter makes a regular payment on June 1 if interest is based on the number of days since the last payment.

Solution

$$\text{Amount financed} = \$49{,}900 - \$2000 = \$47{,}900$$

1ST PAYMENT MADE ON APRIL 1:

Number of days from March 5 to April 1 is 27.

$$\text{Interest from March 5 to April 1} = \$47{,}900 \times 0.10 \times \frac{27}{360} = \$359.25$$

$$\text{Amount applied to principal} = \$887.39 - \$359.25 = \$528.14$$
$$\text{Balance after 1st payment} = \$47{,}900 - \$528.14 = \$47{,}371.86$$

2ND PAYMENT WAS NOT MADE:

Lender agreed not to charge a penalty.
Interest continues to accrue.

3RD PAYMENT WAS MADE ON JUNE 1:

Number of days from April 1 to June 1 is 61.

Interest from April 1 to June 1 $= \$47{,}371.86 \times 0.10 \times \dfrac{61}{360} = \$802.69$

Payment of $887.39 on June 1 is larger than interest due of $802.69.
Amount applied to principal $= \$887.39 - \$802.69 = \$84.70$
Principal after June 1 payment $= \$47{,}371.86 - \$84.70 = \$47{,}287.16$

Her loan balance will go down as long as she makes the regular payments. Many lenders would have charged Richter a penalty for a missed or late payment. If the elderly couple had charged Richter a penalty, it would have been taken out of the June 1 payment before interest. Thus, a payment is used first to pay a penalty and to then pay interest. Finally, anything remaining is used to reduce the principal.

Objective

4   *Use the Rule of 78 When Prepaying a Loan.*   A variation of the United States Rule, called the **Rule of 78**, is still used by many lenders. The rule of 78 is sometimes called the **sum-of-the-balances method** when the length of the contract is other than 1 year. This rule allows a lender to earn more of the finance charge during the early months of the loan compared to the United States Rule. Lenders typically use this rule to protect against early payoffs on *small loans*. Effectively, the lender will earn a higher rate of interest in the event of an early payoff under the Rule of 78 than under the United States Rule. The Rule of 78 *favors the lender* in the event of an early payoff.

NOTE   Some individuals suggest that the Rule of 78 should be banned, believing that it gives lenders unfair advantage. On the other hand, some lenders support the rule, saying that it compensates them for the costs of setting up loans for borrowers who repay a loan quickly.

The Rule of 78 gets its name from a loan of 12 months—the sum of the months $1 + 2 + 3 + \cdots + 12 = 78$. The finance charge for the first month is $\frac{12}{78}$ of the total finance charge, with $\frac{11}{78}$ in the second month, $\frac{10}{78}$ in the third month, and $\frac{1}{78}$ in the final month. The Rule of 78 can be applied to loans with terms other than 12 months. For example, the sum of the months in a 6-month contract is $1 + 2 + 3 + 4 + 5 + 6 = 21$. The finance charge for the first month would be $\frac{6}{21}, \frac{5}{21}$ for the second month, and so on.

The **unearned interest**, or interest not earned by the lender under the Rule of 78 for a loan of 12 months, depends on the month in which the loan is paid off. The unearned interest is returned to the borrower. If the loan is paid off at the end of 2 months, then the interest earned by the lender is $\frac{12}{78} + \frac{11}{78} = \frac{23}{78}$ of the finance charge. Thus, the interest not earned by the lender is

$$1 - \frac{23}{78} \qquad \text{or, equivalently,} \qquad \frac{1}{78} + \frac{2}{78} + \cdots + \frac{10}{78}$$

which is $\frac{55}{78}$ of the finance charges. The process is similar for loans of lengths other than 12 months.

Finding Unearned Interest

The unearned interest is given by

$$U = F\left(\frac{N}{P}\right)\left(\frac{1+N}{1+P}\right)$$

where $U =$ unearned interest, $F =$ finance charge, $N =$ number of payments remaining, and $P =$ total number of payments.

EXAMPLE 4 Finding Payoff Value

Richard Buck borrowed $1800 that he is paying back in 24 monthly payments of $88.50 each. With 9 payments remaining, he decides to repay the loan in full. Find (a) the amount of unearned finance charge and (b) the amount necessary to repay the loan in full.

Solution

(a) Total installment cost = 24 × $88.50 = $2124

Finance charge = $2124 − $1800 = $324

The amount of unearned interest is found as follows. The finance charge is $324, the scheduled number of payments is 24, and the loan is paid off with 9 payments left. Use the formula.

$$\text{Unearned interest} = \$324 \times \left(\frac{9}{24}\right) \times \frac{(1+9)}{(1+24)}$$

$$= \$324 \times \left(\frac{9 \times 10}{24 \times 25}\right)$$

$$= \$48.60$$

Paying off the loan 9 months early produces a savings of $48.60 in interest.

(b) When Buck decides to pay off the loan, he has 9 payments of $88.50 left. These payments total as follows.

$$9 \times \$88.50 = \$796.50$$

By paying the loan early, Buck saves the unearned interest of $48.60, so

$$\$796.50 - \$48.60 = \$747.90$$

is needed to pay the loan in full.

Scientific Calculator Approach

The calculator solution to Example 4 is as follows.

(a) First think of the problem as $\dfrac{(324 \times 9 \times (1+9))}{(24 \times (1+24))}$ or as $\dfrac{324 \times 9 \times 10}{24 \times 25}$, then solve.

(324 × 9 × (1 + 9)) ÷

(24 × (1 + 24)) = 48.6

(b) 9 × 88.5 − 48.6 = 747.9

16.3 Exercises

Find the balance due on the maturity date of the following notes. Find the total amount of interest paid on the note. Use the United States Rule.

	Principal	Interest	Time in Days	Partial Payments
1.	$6500	8%	100	$1500 on day 56
2.	$5800	10%	120	$2500 on day 60
3.	$8500	12%	150	$5000 on day 45
4.	$6000	$10\frac{1}{2}\%$	130	$3000 on day 100
5.	$10,000	$8\frac{1}{4}\%$	180	$6000 on day 120
6.	$12,600	$11\frac{1}{2}\%$	140	$8000 on day 100

Each of the following loans is paid in full before its date of maturity. Find the amount of unearned interest. Use the Rule of 78.

	Finance Charge	Total Number of Payments	Remaining Number of Payments When Paid in Full
7.	$975	48	30
8.	$325	36	6
9.	$460	20	4
10.	$325	24	22
11.	$3653.82	48	9
12.	$3085.54	60	15

 13. Explain the concept of the United States Rule. When is the United States Rule likely to be applied? (See Objective 1.)

 14. Explain the concept of the Rule of 78. When is the Rule of 78 likely to be applied? (See Objective 4.)

 15. Why is it of no advantage to the borrower to make a partial payment smaller than the amount of interest due? What would the lender do with this payment? (See Objective 2.)

 16. List some advantages of paying loans off faster than required.

Solve the following application problems.

17. **COMPUTER CONSULTANT** The computer system at Genome Therapy crashed several times last year. On January 10, the company borrows $125,000 at 11% for 250 days to pay a consultant for some equipment and work on their Novell network. However, managers decide to pay the loan in full on July 1. Find (a) the interest due and (b) the total amount due using the United States Rule.

18. **LOAN REPAYMENT** Titus Czech signed a 100-day note for $2800 at 15% compounded annually but repaid the loan in full in 80 days instead. Find (a) the interest paid and (b) the amount due in 80 days using the United States Rule.

19. **HOME REMODELING** Freida Batherson signed a note with proceeds of $8400 and a monthly payment of $383.75 for 24 months to remodel her kitchen. Find the amount of unearned interest using the Rule of 78 if she uses her income tax refund to pay off the loan in month 14.

20. **EARLY PAYOFF** George Duda has decided that making the small monthly payment on a 6-month loan is a nuisance. The total finance charge is only $34, and the loan is paid in full with 3 months remaining. Find the unearned interest using the Rule of 78.

21. **EASY PAYMENT PLAN** Anne Kelly purchased a refrigerator on the "easy payment plan" with only $100 down and 18 equal monthly payments of $45.20. The total cash price of the refrigerator was $800. After making 6 monthly payments, she decided to pay the loan in full. Use the Rule of 78 and find (a) the amount of unearned interest and (b) the amount necessary to pay the loan in full.

22. **FINANCING A USED CAR** A used car costs $8850. After a down payment of $2000, the balance is financed with 48 payments of $194.25 each. The loan is paid off with 15 payments left. Use the Rule of 78 to find (a) the amount of unearned interest and (b) the amount necessary to pay the loan in full.

23. **PAPER GOODS INVENTORY** To save on freight charges, Wholesale Paper orders large quantities of basic paper goods every 4 months. For its last order, the firm signed a note on February 18 that matures on May 15. The face value of the note was $104,500, with interest of 11%. The firm made a partial payment of $38,000 on March 20,

with a second partial payment of $27,200 on April 16. Find the amount due on the maturity date of the note and the amount of interest paid on the note using the United States Rule.

24. **TESTING EQUIPMENT** Mid-City Electronics bought new testing equipment, paying for it with a note for $32,000. The note was made on July 26 and is due on November 20. The interest rate is 13%. The firm made a partial payment of $6000 on August 31, with a second partial payment of $11,700 on October 4. Find the amount due on the maturity date of the note and the amount of interest paid on the note using the United States Rule.

25. **MISSED PAYMENT** James Thompson's loan balance after his May 3 payment was $11,832.20. He missed the June 3 payment but made a payment of $463.12 on July 8. No penalty was charged and the loan has an interest rate of 9% simple interest. Find (a) the number of days from May 3 to July 8 and (b) the loan balance on July 8.

26. **MISSED PAYMENT** Pam Cunningham borrowed money to start up a pet store and owed $14,940.87 on November 7. She missed the December payment but she was able to make a larger-than-usual payment of $800 on January 4. No penalty was charged and the loan has an interest rate of 12% simple interest. Find (a) the number of days from November 7 to January 4 and (b) the loan balance on January 4.

16.4	**Personal Property Loans**

OBJECTIVES

1 *Define personal property and real estate.*

2 *Use the formula for amortization to find payment.*

3 *Set up an amortization table.*

4 *Find monthly payments.*

Objective

1 *Define Personal Property and Real Estate.* Items that can be moved from one location to another, such as an automobile, a boat, or a stereo, are called **personal property**. In contrast, buildings, land, and homes cannot be moved and are called **real estate** or **real property**. Personal property loans are discussed in this section and real estate loans are discussed in the next section. Both types are installment loans.

As the following headline suggests, people can end up with more debt than they can afford. In that event, individuals are sometimes forced to return personal property such as an automobile to the lender. When this happens, the property is said to be **repossessed** by the lender.

Students Cautioned about Too Much Debt

Objective

2 *Use the Formula for Amortization to Find Payment.* Paying for something in full up front means that no loan is needed. But usually more expensive items are purchased on credit and require a series of regular payments. A loan is said to be **amortized** if both principal and interest are paid off in a *sequence of equal payments made at regular intervals*.

The amount of each payment can be calculated using the formula, given in **Section 15.2**, for the present value A of an annuity with payment R, interest rate per period i, and n periods. The formula is repeated here for convenience.

$$A = R\left[\frac{(1 + i)^n - 1}{i(1 + i)^n}\right]$$

The unknown in **Section 15.2** was the present value A. Now the present value (loan amount) is known along with the interest rate per compounding period and number of periods—the payment R is the unknown. The equation above can be solved for R and a scientific calculator can be used to calculate payments. Alternatively, you can use the tables in **Appendix D** and solve the equation $A = R \cdot a_{\overline{n}|i}$ for R.

The periodic payment R needed to amortize a loan of A dollars with interest of i per period for n periods follows.

$$R = A\left(\frac{1}{a_{\overline{n}|i}}\right)$$

The notation $a_{\overline{n}|i}$ is read "a-angle–n-at-i." Values of $\frac{1}{a_{\overline{n}|i}}$ for different n's and i's can be found in column F of **Appendix D**. Thus, the periodic payment R is found by multiplying the loan amount A by a number taken from the table in **Appendix D**.

EXAMPLE 1 **Finding Amortization Information**

Pablo Valdez recently accepted a job as a designer of World Wide Web pages. Valdez and his spouse, a teacher and avid water skier, decide to borrow $15,000 to purchase a new ski boat. They borrow the funds for 36 months at 12% per year. Find (a) the monthly payment, (b) the portion of the first payment that is interest, (c) the balance due after one payment, (d) the interest owed for the second month, and (e) the balance after the second payment.

Solution

(a) Use $\dfrac{12\%}{12} = 1\%$ per period for i and 36 periods for n in the amortization table in **Appendix D** to find 0.03321431.

$$\text{Monthly payment} = \$15,000 \times 0.03321431 = \$498.21 \quad \text{Rounded}$$

(b) Interest for the month is found using the simple interest formula $I = PRT$.

$$I = \$15,000 \times 0.12 \times \frac{1}{12} = \$150$$

$$\text{Amount used to reduce principal} = \$498.21 - \$150$$
$$= \$348.21$$

(c) Balance after 1st payment $= \$15,000 - \$348.21$
$$= \$14,651.79$$

(d) Interest for 2nd month $= \$14,651.79 \times 0.12 \times \dfrac{1}{12}$

$$= \$146.52$$

$$\text{Amount used to reduce principal} = \$498.21 - \$146.52$$
$$= \$351.69$$

(e) Balance after 2nd payment $= \$14,651.79 - \$351.69$
$$= \$14,300.10$$

Financial Calculator Approach

The unknown payment in Example 1 can also be found using a financial calculator. Enter the known values for present value, number of compounding periods, and interest rate per compounding period.

15000 $\boxed{PV}$ 36 $\boxed{n}$ 1 $\boxed{i}$ $\boxed{PMT}$ −498.21

↳ 12% ÷ 12 months = 1% per month

Objective

3 *Set up an Amortization Table.* An **amortization table** or **schedule** shows the amount of each payment that goes to interest and to principal. It also shows the debt remaining after each payment. One excellent way to calculate an amortization table is to use spreadsheet software. Sometimes, amortization tables are referred to as **loan repayment tables**.

NOTE Be sure to round interest to the nearest cent each time before proceeding.

EXAMPLE 2 **Finding Payments, Interest, and Loan Balances**

A contractor agrees to pay $15,000 for a new computer system. This amount will be repaid in 3 years with semiannual payments at an interest rate of 8% compounded semiannually. Set up an amortization schedule for this loan.

Solution The interest rate per 6-month compounding period is $\frac{8\%}{2}$ = 4%. Use 4% and 6 periods in column F in **Appendix D** to find 0.1907619.

Payment = $15,000 × 0.1907619 = $2861.43

This is the payment for all periods other than the last one. To complete the amortization table, follow these steps.

1. Calculate interest at 4% of the balance at end of previous period using $I = PRT$ and round to the nearest cent.
2. Portion applied to principal = Amount of payment − Interest for period
3. Balance at end of period = Balance at end of prior period − Portion applied to principal

The payment for the last period sometimes differs slightly since it is whatever is required to pay the loan off in full. It usually differs by only a few cents from the regular payment.

Payment Number	Amount of Payment	Interest for Period	Portion Applied to Principal	Balance at End of Period
0	—	—	—	$15,000.00
1	$2861.43	$600.00	$2261.43	12,738.57
2	2861.43	509.54	2351.89	10,386.68
3	2861.43	415.47	2445.96	7,940.72
4	2861.43	317.63	2543.80	5,396.92
5	2861.43	215.88	2645.55	2,751.37
6	2861.42	110.05	2751.37	0

Objective

4 *Find Monthly Payments.* Table 16.3 can also be used to find the monthly payment. Determine the table value corresponding to the annual percentage rate (APR) and the number of monthly payments. Then find the monthly payment by multiplying the number from the table by the amount to be financed.

Table 16.3   LOAN PAYOFF TABLE

APR \ Months	18	24	30	36	42	48	54	60
8%	0.059138	0.045229	0.036887	0.031336	0.027376	0.024413	0.022113	0.020277
9%	0.0596	0.045683	0.037347	0.0318	0.027845	0.024885	0.022589	0.020758
10%	0.060056	0.046146	0.03781	0.032267	0.028317	0.025363	0.023072	0.021247
11%	0.060516	0.046608	0.038277	0.032739	0.028793	0.025846	0.023561	0.021742
12%	0.060984	0.047075	0.038747	0.033214	0.029276	0.026333	0.024057	0.022245
13%	0.06145	0.047542	0.03922	0.033694	0.029762	0.026827	0.024557	0.022753
14%	0.061917	0.048013	0.0397	0.034178	0.030252	0.027327	0.025065	0.023268
15%	0.062383	0.048488	0.04018	0.034667	0.03075	0.027831	0.025578	0.02379
16%	0.062855	0.048963	0.040663	0.035159	0.03125	0.02834	0.026096	0.024318
17%	0.063328	0.049442	0.04115	0.035653	0.031755	0.028854	0.026620	0.024853
18%	0.063806	0.049925	0.04164	0.036153	0.032264	0.029369	0.027152	0.025393
19%	0.064283	0.050408	0.042133	0.036656	0.032779	0.0299	0.027687	0.02594
20%	0.064761	0.050896	0.04263	0.037164	0.033298	0.030431	0.02823	0.026493
21%	0.065244	0.051388	0.04313	0.037675	0.033821	0.030967	0.028776	0.027053

EXAMPLE 3   Finding Monthly Payments

After a down payment, Linda Dean owes $8700 on a 1-year-old Toyota Prius. She wishes to pay the loan off in 60 monthly payments. Find the amount of each payment and the finance charge, if the APR on her loan is 18%. Her interest rate is high because she has a poor credit history.

Solution   Multiply the amount to be financed of $8700 by the number from Table 16.3 for 60 months and 18%, which is 0.025393.

$$\text{Payment} = \$8700 \times 0.025393 = \$220.92$$
$$\text{Total of payments} = 60 \times \$220.92 = \$13{,}255.20$$
$$\text{Finance charge} = \$13{,}255.20 - \$8700 = \$4555.20$$

16.4   Exercises

Find each of the following.

1. $\dfrac{1}{a_{\overline{15}|0.075}}$

2. $\dfrac{1}{a_{\overline{40}|0.075}}$

3. $\dfrac{1}{a_{\overline{36}|0.10}}$

4. $\dfrac{1}{a_{\overline{48}|0.12}}$

Find the payment necessary to amortize the following loans. Use column F of the interest table in Appendix D and the formula of this section.

	Amount of Loan	Interest Rate	Payments Made	Number of Years	Payment
5.	$3000	$7\frac{1}{2}\%$	annually	3	_____
6.	$3500	9%	annually	4	_____
7.	$4500	8%	semiannually	$7\frac{1}{2}$	_____
8.	$7200	14%	semiannually	$3\frac{1}{2}$	_____
9.	$96,000	8%	quarterly	$7\frac{3}{4}$	_____
10.	$210,000	12%	quarterly	8	_____
11.	$4876	12%	monthly	3	_____
12.	$6400	9%	monthly	$3\frac{1}{2}$	_____

Use Table 16.3 to find the monthly payment and then find the finance charge for each loan.

	Amount Financed	Number of Months	APR	Monthly Payment	Finance Charge
13.	$4800	36	9%	_____	_____
14.	$4800	24	12%	_____	_____
15.	$12,000	48	13%	_____	_____
16.	$8102	48	8%	_____	_____

Solve the following application problems. Use column F of the interest table in Appendix D.

17. **OPENING A RESTAURANT** Chuck and Judy Nielson agreed to buy a restaurant for $340,000. They paid $40,000 down and agreed to pay the remainder in quarterly payments over 7 years at 12% compounded quarterly. Find the quarterly payment and the total amount of interest paid over 7 years.

18. **NEW LIMOUSINE** Midtown Limousine Service bought a new Lincoln limousine for $57,000. The company agreed to pay 10% down and pay off the rest with monthly payments for 36 months at 9%. Find the amount of each monthly payment necessary to amortize the loan. Find the total amount of interest paid over 3 years.

19. **DIGITIZER** Grants Graphics buys a commercial digitizer and high-speed printer for $4000 and finances the entire amount. It amortizes the loan using 4 annual payments at 8% per year. Prepare an amortization schedule for this equipment.

Payment Number	Amount of Payment	Interest for Period	Portion to Principal	Principal at End of Period
0	—	—	—	$4000.00
1	_____	_____	_____	_____
2	_____	_____	_____	_____
3	_____	_____	_____	_____
4	_____	_____	_____	_____

20. TRUCK FINANCING   Long Haul Trucking purchases a used tractor for pulling large trailers on interstate highways at a cost of $72,000. It agrees to pay for it with a loan that will be amortized over 9 annual payments at 8% interest. Prepare an amortization schedule for the truck.

Payment Number	Amount of Payment	Interest for Period	Portion to Principal	Principal at End of Period
0	—	—	—	$72,000.00
1				
2				
3				
4				
5				
6				
7				
8				
9				

Solve the following application problems. Use Table 16.3.

21. ENGINEERING WORK STATIONS   An engineering firm purchases seven new work stations for $3500 each. It makes a down payment of $10,000 and amortizes the balance with monthly payments at 11% for 4 years. Prepare an amortization schedule showing the first 5 payments.

Payment Number	Amount of Payment	Interest for Period	Portion to Principal	Principal at End of Period
0	—	—	—	$14,500.00
1				
2				
3				
4				
5				

22. TAVERN REMODEL   Becky Johanson needed $25,000 to remodel the entrance to her small tavern. She had $5000 and borrowed the remaining $20,000. She agreed to amortize the balance with monthly payments for 5 years at 12% compounded monthly. Prepare an amortization schedule for the first 5 payments.

Payment Number	Amount of Payment	Interest for Period	Portion to Principal	Principal at End of Period
0	—	—	—	$20,000.00
1				
2				
3				
4				
5				

 23. Identify and explain three important items that you will see in an installment loan. (See Objectives 2 and 3.)

24. Explain how people can get in over their heads in terms of monthly payments. How can this be avoided?

Prepare an amortization schedule for the following loans. Use a spreadsheet package on a computer if you have one available. Do not forget to round interest to the nearest cent each month before finding the portion of each payment that goes to principal.

25. Tim Gates financed $8000 on a used car at 12% for 15 months.

Payment Number	Amount of Payment	Interest for Period	Portion to Principal	Principal at End of Period
0	—	—	—	$8000.00
1				
2				
3				
⋮	⋮	⋮	⋮	⋮
14				
15				

26. NETWORK LINK Caribbean Tours, Inc. financed $108,000 to set up a network link between its offices in Canada, the United States, and Mexico. It agrees to repay the 10% loan with 16 quarterly payments.

Payment Number	Amount of Payment	Interest for Period	Portion to Principal	Principal at End of Period
0	—	—	—	$108,000.00
1				
2				
3				
⋮	⋮	⋮	⋮	⋮
15				
16				

16.5 Real Estate Loans

OBJECTIVES

1 *Determine monthly payments on a home.*

2 *Prepare a repayment schedule.*

3 *Define escrow accounts.*

4 *Define fixed- and variable-rate loans.*

A home is *one of the most expensive purchases* made by the average person. The amount of the monthly payment is *a major concern* for prospective buyers. The size of this payment is found by the exact same methods and formulas used in **Section 16.4**, but because of the many different interest rates and repayment periods, special tables are often used.

Figure 16.8 shows that there have been two major trends in home mortgage rates during the past 40 years. Rates generally went up during the period 1965–1980, and rates generally fell during the period 1981–2004. The highest rate of over 15% in 1980 resulted in very high payments on homes. The lowest rates were in 1965 and again in 2009. Part of the reason for low rates in 2009 was federal government action to stabilize home prices by lowering the interest rates to offset falling home prices during the financial crisis that began in 2008. Use the World Wide Web to find current mortgage rates for your area.

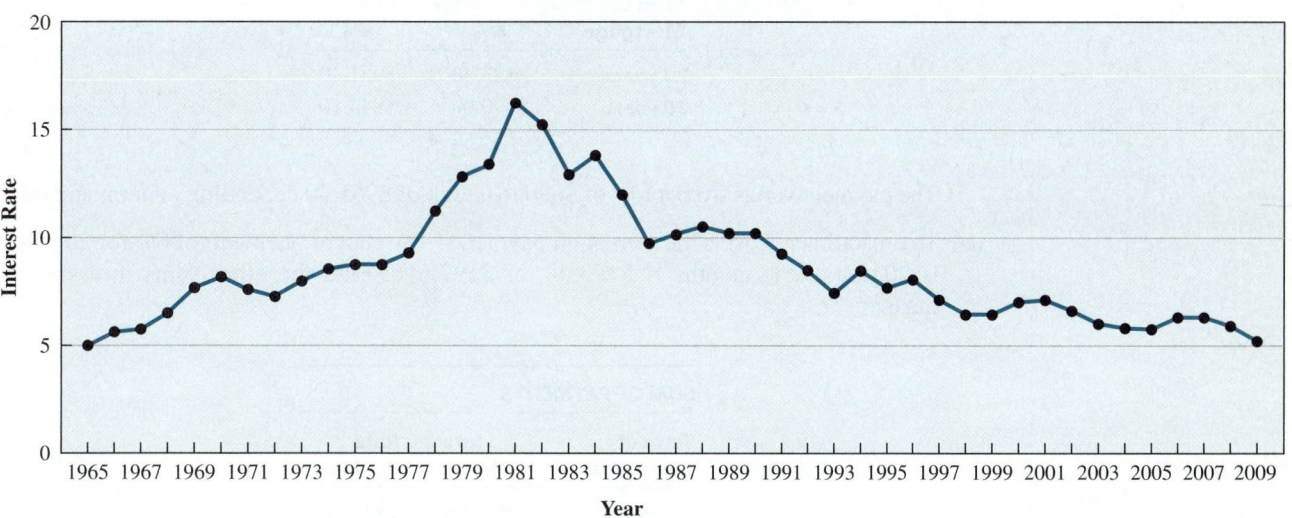

**Mortgage Interest Rates
30-Year Fixed-Rate Mortgages**

Source: Board of Governors of the Federal Reserve System, Federal Reserve Bulletin, 2008.

Figure 16.8

Objective

1   *Determine Monthly Payments on a Home.*   The real estate amortization table (Table 16.4) shows the monthly payment necessary to repay a $1000 loan for differing interest rates and lengths of repayment. This table is used to find the monthly payment by multiplying the loan amount, in thousands of dollars, by the correct factor from the table. Higher interest rates mean higher borrowing costs, as you can clearly see from the next example.

Table 16.4   AMORTIZATION (PRINCIPAL AND INTEREST PER THOUSAND DOLLARS)

Term in Years	5.00%	6.00%	7.00%	8.00%	9.00%	10.00%
10	$10.61	$11.10	$11.61	$12.13	$12.67	$13.22
15	$7.91	$8.44	$8.99	$9.56	$10.14	$10.75
20	$6.60	$7.16	$7.75	$8.36	$9.00	$9.65
25	$5.85	$6.44	$7.07	$7.72	$8.39	$9.09
30	$5.37	$6.00	$6.65	$7.34	$8.05	$8.78

EXAMPLE 1   Finding Payments to Amortize a Loan

After a 20% down payment, Bill and Judy Able need to borrow $115,000 to purchase a home and are debating whether they should use a 20-year or 30-year mortgage. They also want to know the effect of two different rates, 6% and 8%, on payments and costs. Find (a) the monthly payment for both rates at 20 years and at 30 years. Then find (b) the installment cost for each of the four combinations.

Solution

(a) The amount to be financed is $115,000 ÷ 1000 = $115 in thousands. The factor from Table 16.4 for 6% and 20 years is $7.16. The corresponding monthly payment is $115 × $7.16 = $823.40. Find the other payments in the same manner.

MONTHLY PAYMENTS

Term of Mortgage	Interest Rate	
	6%	8%
20 years	$823.40	$961.40
30 years	$690.00	$844.10

The payment varies from a low of $690 to a high of $961.40 depending on term and rate.

(b) The installment cost is the sum of all payments. The sum of payments at 6% for 20 years is 20 years $\times$ 12 months $\times$ $823.40, or $197,616. Find the other sums in a similar manner.

SUM OF PAYMENTS

Term of Mortgage	Interest Rate	
	6%	8%
20 years	$197,616	$230,736
30 years	$248,400	$303,876

To the nearest thousand, the installment costs range from a low of $198,000 to a high of $304,000, which is quite a difference for a mortgage of $115,000. The above tables show that keeping the interest rate constant, while shortening the term, results in a higher monthly payment but a lower installment cost.

However, short-term mortgages generally have slightly lower interest rates than a 30-year mortgage. It is to your advantage to use a shorter term if you wish to pay off your home loan more quickly and you can afford the monthly payments.

NOTE Be sure to divide the loan amount by $1000 before calculating the monthly payment.

For many years, mortgage payoffs of 25 or 30 years have been the most common. The last few years, however, have seen **accelerated mortgages**, with payoffs of 15 or 20 years. As you can see from the last example, an accelerated mortgage results in significantly less interest over the life of the loan.

EXAMPLE 2 **Finding Loan Amount**

The Mocks wish to purchase the largest, nicest home they can afford, but they are limited to a monthly payment of $900 not including insurance and taxes. If the current mortgage rate is 6% and they would like a 30-year mortgage, what is the most they can finance?

Solution The concept described in the first part of this section is

$$\text{Number of thousands of debt} \times \text{Factor from Table 16.4} = \text{Monthly payment}$$

Previously, the monthly payment was unknown. Now the payment ($900) and the factor from Table 16.4 (30 years, 6% interest yields a factor of 6.00) are known, but the debt is unknown. Using algebra, the equation above can be solved for debt.

$$\frac{\text{Number of thousands}}{\text{of debt}} = \frac{\text{Monthly payment}}{\text{Factor from Table 16.4}}$$

$$= \frac{\$900}{\$6.00}$$

$$= 150$$

Therefore, they can afford a mortgage of $150,000.

Objective

2 *Prepare a Repayment Schedule.* The interest on real estate loans is computed on *the decreasing balance* of the loan. Each monthly payment is first applied toward the interest for the previous month. The balance is then applied toward reduction of the amount owed. Payments in the *early years* of a real estate loan are mostly interest; only a small amount goes toward reducing the principal. The amount of interest gradually decreases each month, so that larger and larger amounts of the payment apply to the principal. During the last years of the loan, most of the monthly payment is applied toward the principal.

Many lenders supply an **amortization schedule**, also called a **repayment schedule** or **loan reduction schedule**, showing the amount of payments for interest, the amount for principal, and the principal balance for each month over the entire life of the loan. These calculations can be done by hand, as shown in the next example, but they are commonly done on computers.

EXAMPLE 3 Preparing a Repayment Schedule

Julie Kern borrows $120,000 at 7% interest for 30 years. Find the monthly payment and calculate a repayment schedule.

Solution Monthly payment = $120 × $6.65 = $798.00

Find the interest for the first month using the formula for simple interest, $I = PRT$.

1ST PAYMENT:

$$\text{Interest} = \$120,000 \times 0.07 \times \frac{1}{12} = \$700$$

$$\text{Amt. used to reduce debt} = \$798 - \$700 = \$98.00$$

$$\text{Debt after payment} = \$120,000 - \$98.00 = \$119,902$$

2ND PAYMENT:

$$\text{Interest} = \$119,902 \times 0.07 \times \frac{1}{12} = \$699.43$$

$$\text{Amt. used to reduce debt} = \$798 - \$699.43 = \$98.57$$

$$\text{Debt after payment} = \$119,902 - \$98.57 = \$119,803.43$$

The data is shown in the table.

REPAYMENT SCHEDULE

Payment Number	Monthly Payment	Interest Payment	Principal Payment	Loan Balance
0	—	—	—	$120,000.00
1	$798	$700.00	$98.00	$119,902.00
2	$798	$699.43	$98.57	$119,803.43

Table 16.5 shows payments 1–20, 256–263, and 352–360 for the loan in Example 3. During the first 20 years, the debt is large and most of each payment is used to pay interest. In fact, the 242nd payment, which occurs in year 20, is the first payment in which more than one-half of the monthly $798 payment is used to reduce principal. The debt is reduced to one-half of the original debt after the 262nd payment, or in the 21st year of payments. However, most of the last several years of payments are applied to reduce principal. The final payment is larger than $798 due to rounding, since it is the amount needed to reduce the balance to zero.

TABLE 16.5 LOAN REDUCTION SCHEDULE

Rate 7%, $120,000 loan amount, 30-year mortgage, $798 payment

Payment Number	Interest Payment	Principal Payment	Remaining Balance	Payment Number	Interest Payment	Principal Payment	Remaining Balance
1	$700.00	$98.00	$119,902.00	256	$366.12	$431.88	$62,331.73
2	$699.43	$98.57	$119,803.43	257	$363.60	$434.40	$61,897.33
3	$698.85	$99.15	$119,704.28	258	$361.07	$436.93	$61,460.40
4	$698.27	$99.73	$119,604.55	259	$358.52	$439.48	$61,020.92
5	$697.69	$100.31	$119,504.24	260	$355.96	$442.04	$60,578.88
6	$697.11	$100.89	$119,403.35	261	$353.38	$444.62	$60,134.26
7	$696.52	$101.48	$119,301.87	262	$350.78	$447.22	$59,687.04
8	$695.93	$102.07	$119,199.80	263	$348.17	$449.83	$59,237.21
9	$695.33	$102.67	$119,097.13	⋮	⋮	⋮	⋮
10	$694.73	$103.27	$118,993.86	352	$43.15	$754.85	$6,642.40
11	$694.13	$103.87	$118,889.99	353	$38.75	$759.25	$5,883.15
12	$693.52	$104.48	$118,785.51	354	$34.32	$763.68	$5,119.47
13	$692.92	$105.08	$118,680.43	355	$29.86	$768.14	$4,351.33
14	$692.30	$105.70	$118,574.73	356	$25.38	$772.62	$3,578.71
15	$691.69	$106.31	$118,468.42	357	$20.88	$777.12	$2,801.59
16	$691.07	$106.93	$118,361.49	358	$16.34	$781.66	$2,019.93
17	$690.44	$107.56	$118,253.93	359	$11.78	$786.22	$1,233.71
18	$689.81	$108.19	$118,145.74	360	$7.20	$1,233.71	$0.00
19	$689.18	$108.82	$118,036.92				
20	$688.55	$109.45	$117,927.47				
⋮							

Objective

3 *Define Escrow Accounts.* Many lenders require **escrow accounts** (also called **impound accounts**) for people taking out a mortgage. With an escrow account, buyers pay $\frac{1}{12}$ of the total estimated property tax and insurance each month. The lender holds these funds until the taxes and insurance fall due and then pays the bills for the borrower. Many consumer groups oppose this practice, since the lender earns interest on the money while waiting for payments to come due. In fact, a few states require that interest be paid to the homeowner on escrow accounts on any homes located in those states.

EXAMPLE 4   **Finding Total Monthly Payment**

Bob Jones used a $75,000 loan for 25 years at 8% to purchase a small summer cabin. Annual insurance and taxes on the property are $654 and $1329, respectively. Find the monthly payment.

Solution   Use Table 16.4 to find 7.72. Add monthly insurance and taxes to the loan amortization.

$$\text{Payment} = 75 \times 7.72 + \frac{\$654 + \$1329}{12}$$

$$= \$579 + \$165.25$$

$$= \$744.25$$

 Scientific Calculator Approach

The calculator solution to Example 4 is to first find the monthly payment on the principal by multiplying the number of thousands (75) by the number from the table. Add to this the monthly payment due to insurance and taxes.

$$75 \boxed{\times} 7.72 \boxed{+} \boxed{(} \; 654 \boxed{+} 1329 \boxed{)} \boxed{\div} 12 \boxed{=} 744.25$$

Objective

4   *Define Fixed- and Variable-Rate Loans.*   Home loans with fixed, stated interest rates are called **fixed-rate loans**. Fixed-rate loans keep payments from going up when interest rates go up, which helps consumers and hurts lenders. On the other hand, fixed-rate loans keep payments from going down when interest rates fall, which hurts consumers and helps lenders.

Variable-interest-rate loans, also called **adjustable-rate mortgages (ARM)**, have become popular and are offered by most mortgage lenders. These types of mortgages have interest rates that periodically move up or down as market rates move up or down. However, they usually have a **cap** so that rates do not go beyond some maximum number. Also, rates often have a cap on how much they can change at one time. In 2009, one lender offered the following mortgages.

30 year fixed	5.5% rate, payments are fixed for 30 years
15 year fixed	5.0% rate, payments are fixed for 15 years
1 year ARM	5.0% rate, it changes at the end of each year

NOTE   No one knows where interest rates will be in the future. Many families lock in their interest rates for 20 or 30 years because they do not want to take the risk of an increase in rate, and therefore monthly payments, going up too far on their homes.

Home ownership potentially offers benefits above and beyond a good place to live. For example, interest on home mortgages may be deductible on your income tax return and well-maintained homes in good areas have usually gone up in value with time. On the other hand, homeowners must pay for new roofs or other repairs to keep their homes in good condition.

> **NOTE**   In some countries, interest rates vary widely because inflation rates in those countries vary a lot. As a result, it is not possible to get 30-year fixed-rate mortgages in some countries.

16.5 | Exercises

Use Table 16.4 to find the monthly payment for the following loans.

	Amount of Loan	Interest Rate	Term of Loan	Monthly Payment
1.	$98,000	7%	30 years	_____
2.	$69,500	5%	25 years	_____
3.	$162,000	6%	15 years	_____
4.	$132,000	9%	25 years	_____
5.	$223,000	9%	20 years	_____
6.	$147,000	10%	30 years	_____

 7. Explain how different interest rates can make a large difference in interest charges over a 30-year loan. (See Objective 1.)

8. Explain how changing the term of a loan can result in significantly different interest charges over the life of the loan. (See Objective 2.)

Find the total monthly payment including taxes and insurance for the following loans. Round to the nearest cent.

	Amount of Loan	Interest Rate	Term of Loan	Annual Taxes	Annual Insurance	Monthly Payment
9.	$119,000	6%	30 years	$2050	$520	_____
10.	$154,000	5%	20 years	$3600	$840	_____
11.	$135,000	8%	20 years	$3200	$680	_____
12.	$68,400	9%	30 years	$1256	$350	_____
13.	$162,400	10%	25 years	$4350	$740	_____
14.	$210,000	7%	15 years	$4700	$980	_____

Solve the following application problems.

15. **HOME PURCHASE**   Peter and Betsy Mueller hope to buy a starter home costing $145,000 with annual insurance and taxes of $780 and $2950, respectively. They have $20,000 saved for a down payment and their real estate agent has told them that they can get a 7% rate for a 15-year mortgage. They are qualified for a home loan as long as the total monthly payment does not exceed $1500. Are they qualified for the loan?

16. **CONDOMINIUM PURCHASE**   The Appletons wish to buy a condo for $148,000 with annual insurance and taxes of $680 and $2270 respectively. They have $8000 to pay down, plan to amortize the balance at 9% for 30 years, and qualify for the loan if the total payment does not exceed $1200. Are they qualified?

17. REPAYMENT SCHEDULE Eric and Beth Eddy purchase a home and finance a debt of $212,000 for 20 years at 9%. Complete a repayment schedule for the first two monthly payments.

Payment Number	Total Payment	Interest Payment	Principal Payment	Balance of Principal
0	—	—	—	$212,000.00
1				
2				

18. REPAYMENT SCHEDULE Charlotte Cumings purchases a townhouse for her elderly mother that cost $164,000. Charlotte has $25,000 and her mother has $10,000 that they use for a down payment. They finance the balance at 7% for 10 years. Prepare a repayment schedule for the first two payments.

Payment Number	Total Payment	Interest Payment	Principal Payment	Remaining Balance
0	—	—	—	$129,000
1				
2				

19. DUPLEX Adam Vort purchases a duplex needing work for $108,000 and agrees to pay 20% down. Find (a) the monthly payment if the loan is financed at 10% for 25 years, and if insurance and taxes are $560 and $1432, respectively. Then find (b) the interest portion of the second monthly payment and (c) the remaining debt after that payment.

20. BORROWING PESOS Lety and Roberto Jaramillo borrowed 2,000,000 pesos to build a house on a mountain overlooking Guadalajara, Mexico. The loan was for 10 years and the rate was 10%. Find (a) the monthly payment. Then find (b) the interest portion of the second monthly payment and (c) the remaining debt after that payment.

21. AFFORDABLE MORTGAGE PAYMENT Paul Shingle can afford a mortgage payment of $980 per month not including insurance and taxes. Given a 30-year loan with a rate of 9%, find the maximum mortgage (to the nearest thousand) that he can afford.

22. AFFORDABLE MORTGAGE PAYMENT Jessie Baker can spend $1100 per month not including insurance and taxes. Given a 20-year loan with a rate of 9%, find the maximum mortgage (to the nearest thousand) that she can afford.

23. FOR RENTERS Take the amount either you or a friend currently pays for rent. Subtract $200 from that number as a rough estimate of insurance and taxes. Use this amount to estimate the home loan you or your friend can afford to buy, assuming a 7%, 30-year mortgage. Are there homes selling for this amount in your area? (See Example 2.)

24. FOR HOMEOWNERS Interest rates might have increased or decreased significantly since you financed your home. Find your loan balance and then use the World Wide Web to find mortgage rates in your area. Calculate the monthly payment on your existing debt for a 30-year fixed-rate mortgage at the new rate and compare to your current payment. In the event that the payment would be lower, it may be worth refinancing your mortgage, but you need to look carefully at the monthly savings, the length of time you expect to be in the home, and the cost of refinancing.

CHAPTER TERMS

Review the following terms to test your understanding of the chapter. For any terms you do not know, refer to the page number found next to that term.

accelerated mortgages [p. 578]
adjustable-rate mortgages (ARM) [p. 581]
amortization schedule [p. 572 or 579]
amortization table [p. 572]
amortized [p. 556 or 570]
amount financed [p. 558]
annual percentage rate (APR) [p. 552 or 556]
average daily balance [p. 550]
borrower [p. 546]
budget deficit [p. 546]
budget surplus [p. 546]
cap [p. 581]

Chapter 7 bankruptcy [p. 547]
Chapter 13 bankruptcy [p. 547]
credit accounts [p. 547]
consolidate loans [p. 553]
credit card [p. 548]
credit limit [p. 547]
creditor [p. 546]
debtor [p. 546]
deferred payment price [p. 558]
escrow accounts [p. 580]
Federal Truth-in-Lending Act [p. 556]
finance charges [p. 549 or 556 or 558]

fixed-rate loans [p. 581]
impound accounts [p. 580]
installment loan [p. 556]
itemized billing [p. 549]
late fees [p. 549]
lender [p. 546]
loan reduction schedule [p. 579]
loan repayment tables [p. 572]
nominal rate [p. 556]
open-end credit [p. 547]
over-the-limit fees [p. 549]
personal property [p. 570]
real estate [p. 570]
real property [p. 570]
Regulation Z [p. 556]

repayment schedule [p. 579]
repossessed [p. 570]
revolving charge account [p. 547]
Rule of 78 [p. 567]
Stafford loan [p. 559]
stated rate [p. 556]
sum-of-the-balances method [p. 567]
total installment cost [p. 558]
unearned interest [p. 567]
United States Rule [p. 564]
variable-interest-rate loans [p. 581]

CONCEPTS

EXAMPLES

16.1 Finding the finance charge on a revolving charge account using the average daily balance method

1. Find the unpaid balance on each day.
2. Add the daily unpaid balances and divide by the number of days in the billing period.
3. Calculate the finance charge by multiplying the average daily balance by the interest rate.

Previous balance, $115.45; November 1, Billing date; November 15, Payment of $35; November 22, Jacket $45. Find the finance charge if interest is 1% per month on the average daily balance.

1. 14 days at $115.45 = $1616.30
   7 days at ($115.45 − $35 = $80.45) = $563.15
   9 days at ($80.45 + $45 = $125.45) = $1129.05

2. 14 + 7 + 9 = 30 days
   $1616.30 + $563.15 + $1129.05 = $3308.50

   $$\text{Average daily balance} = \frac{\$3308.50}{30} = \$110.28$$

3. Finance charge = $110.28 × 0.01 = $1.10

16.2 Finding the total installment cost, finance charge, and amount financed

Total installment cost = Down payment + (Amount of each payment × Number of payments)

Finance charge = Total installment cost − Cash price

Amount financed = Cash price − Down payment

Joan Taylor bought a fur coat for $1580. She put $350 down and then made 12 payments of $115 each. Find the total installment cost, the finance charge, and the amount financed.

Total installment cost = $350 + (12 × $115) = $1730

Finance charge = $1730 − $1580 = $150

Amount financed = $1580 − $350 = $1230

16.2 Finding APR using a table

1. Determine the finance charge per $100.

$$\frac{\text{Finance charge}}{\text{Amount financed}} \times \$100$$

2. Find the number of payments in the leftmost column of Table 16.2; then go across to the number closest to the number found in Step 1 and read up to find APR.

Use the table to find the APR for the following example.

Finance charge = $992

Amount financed = $8200

$$\text{Finance charge per } \$100 = \frac{992}{8200} \times \$100 = \$12.10$$

Number of payments = 24; table value closest to $12.10 is $12.14; APR = 11.25%.

16.3 United States Rule for repayment of loans

1. Find interest from date of loan to date of partial payment.
2. Subtract interest from partial payment.
3. Reduce principal by any difference.
4. Find additional interest from date of partial payment to next partial payment or maturity date and add this interest to unpaid principal.

Sam Spade signed a 120-day note for $3000 at 11% on February 1. Spade made a partial payment of $1200 on March 18. What is the amount due at maturity?

1. There are 27 + 18 = 45 days from February 1 to March 18.

$$I = PRT$$

$$I = \$3000(0.11)\left(\frac{45}{360}\right) = \$41.25$$

2. $1200 − $41.25 = $1158.75 is applied to reduction of principal.
3. $3000 − $1158.75 = $1841.25 is balance owed.
4. There are 120 − 45 = 75 days until maturity, so additional interest is

$$I = \$1841.25(0.11)\left(\frac{75}{360}\right) = \$42.20$$

Then $1841.25 + $42.20 = $1883.45 is due at maturity.

16.3 Finding the unearned interest using the Rule of 78

Find the unearned interest:

$$U = F\left(\frac{N}{P}\right)\left(\frac{1 + N}{1 + P}\right)$$

where U = unearned interest,
F = finance charge,
N = number of payments remaining, and
P = total number of payments

Then find the amount left to pay and subtract the unearned interest to find balance remaining.

Tom Fish borrows $1500, which he is paying back in 36 monthly installments of $52.75 each. With 10 payments remaining, he decides to pay the loan in full. Find the amount of unearned interest and the amount necessary to pay the loan in full.

Installment cost = 36 × $52.75 = $1899

Finance charge = $1899 − $1500 = $399

$$\text{Unearned interest} = \$399 \times \frac{10}{36} \times \frac{(1 + 10)}{(1 + 36)} = \$32.95$$

The 10 payments of $52.75 that are left amount to $52.75 × 10 = $527.50.

$$\text{Balance} = \$527.50 − \$32.95 = \$494.55$$

16.4 Finding the periodic payment to amortize a loan

Use the number of periods for the loan n, interest rate per period i, and column F of the interest table to find $1 \div a_{\overline{n}|i}$. Then use the formula

$$R = A \cdot \left(\frac{1}{a_{\overline{n}|i}}\right)$$

to calculate the payment.

Bob agrees to pay $18,600 for a car. The amount will be repaid in monthly payments over 4 years at an interest rate of 9%. Find the amount of each payment.

$$n = 12 \times 4 = 48$$

$$i = \frac{9\%}{12} = \frac{3}{4}\%$$

$$\frac{1}{a_{\overline{48}|0.0075}} = 0.02488504$$

$$R = \$18,600 \times 0.02488504$$

$$= \$462.86$$

16.4 Setting up an amortization schedule

Find the periodic payment R; then find the interest for the first period using $I = PRT$ (R in this formula is rate). Subtract I from R and reduce the original debt by this amount, D. Find the balance by subtracting the debt reduction D from the original amount A. Repeat until the original debt is amortized.

Teri Meyer borrows $1800 for 2 years at 10%. She will repay this amount with semiannual payments. Set up an amortization schedule.

$$n = 4 \qquad i = \frac{10\%}{2} = 5\%$$

$$\frac{1}{a_{\overline{4}|0.05}} = 0.28201183$$

$$R = \$1800 \times 0.28201183$$

$$R = \$507.62$$

$$I = PRT$$

$$I = \$1800 \times 0.10 \times \frac{1}{2}$$

$$= \$90$$

$$\text{Applied to principal} = \$507.62 - \$90$$

$$= \$417.62$$

$$\text{Balance} = \$1800 - \$417.62$$

$$= \$1382.38$$

Continue to get table shown below.

Payment Number	Amount of Payment	Interest for Period	Portion Applied to Principal	Principal at End of Period
0	—	—	—	$1800.00
1	$507.62	$90.00	$417.62	1382.38
2	507.62	69.12	438.50	943.88
3	507.62	47.19	460.43	483.45
4	507.62	24.17	483.45	0

16.4 Finding monthly payments, total amount paid, and finance charge

Multiply the amount to be financed by the number from Table 16.3. This is the periodic payment. Find the total amount repaid by multiplying the periodic payment by the number of payments. Subtract the amount financed from the total amount repaid to obtain the finance charge.

Nick owes $9600 on a Ford Taurus. He wishes to pay the car off in 48 monthly payments. Find the amount of each payment and the finance charge if the APR on his loan is 12%.

$$\text{Amount financed} = \$9600$$

Table value (Table 16.3) for 48 payments and 12% is 0.026333.

$$\text{Payment} = \$9600 \times 0.026333 = \$252.80$$
$$\text{Total amount repaid} = \$252.80 \times 48 = \$12{,}134.40$$
$$\text{Finance charge} = \$12{,}134.40 - \$9600 = \$2534.40$$

16.5 Finding the amount of the monthly mortgage payments and total interest charges over the life of a mortgage

Use the number of years and the interest rate to find the amortization value per thousand dollars from Table 16.4. Then multiply the table value by the number of thousands in the principal to obtain the monthly payment. Find the total amount of payments and subtract the original amount owed from total payments to obtain interest paid.

Lou and Rose buy a house at the shore. After a large down payment, they owe $75,000. Find the monthly payment at 7% and the total charges over the life of a 25-year mortgage.

$$n = 25 \qquad i = 7\%$$

Table value (Table 16.4) = $7.07.

There are $\dfrac{\$75{,}000}{1000} = 75$ thousands in $75,000.

$$\text{Monthly payment} = 75 \times \$7.07$$
$$= \$530.25$$
$$\text{Total payments} = 25 \times 12 \times \$530.25$$
$$= \$159{,}075$$
$$\text{Interest paid} = \$159{,}075 - \$75{,}000$$
$$= \$84{,}075$$

CHAPTER 16 Review Exercises

The answer section includes answers to all Review Exercises.

Find the finance charge for each of the following revolving charge accounts. Assume interest is calculated on the average daily balance of the account. [16.1]

	Average Daily Balance	Monthly Interest Rate
1.	$243	$1\frac{1}{2}\%$
2.	$3240.60	$1\frac{1}{4}\%$
3.	$875.12	1.62%

Find the average daily balance for the following credit-card accounts. Assume the billing date is the same day of each month, and use the number of days in each month. Then find the finance charge if interest is $1\frac{1}{2}\%$ per month on the average daily balance. Finally, find the amount due at the end of the billing cycle. **[16.1]**

4. Previous balance $634.25

March 9	Billing date	
March 17	Payment	$125
March 30	Lunch	$34.26

5. Previous balance $236.26

July 10	Billing date	
July 15	Athletic shoes	$28.25
July 20	Payment	$75
July 31	Pillow cases	$35
August 5	Returns	$24.36

Find the cash price, total installment cost, and the finance charge for each of the following. **[16.2]**

	Amount Financed	Down Payment	Cash Price	Number of Payments	Amount of Payment	Total Installment Cost	Finance Charge
6.	$2300	$400	_____	18	$139.73	_____	_____
7.	$3800	$800	_____	20	$212	_____	_____
8.	$6500	$1500	_____	36	$225	_____	_____

Find the annual percentage rate using Table 16.2. **[16.2]**

	Amount Financed	Finance Charge	Number of Monthly Payments
9.	$4100	$435	18
10.	$5600	$698	20
11.	$8800	$766.48	15
12.	$10,270	$1065	20

Find the balance due on the maturity date and the total amount of interest on the following notes. Use the United States Rule. **[16.3]**

	Principal	Interest	Time in Days	Partial Payments
13.	$12,400	$8\frac{1}{2}\%$	180 days	$2000 on day 62
14.	$9000	12%	120 days	$2000 on day 40
15.	$6000	11%	120 days	$3200 on day 30
				$2000 on day 90
16.	$9000	9%	90 days	$3000 on day 30
				$1500 on day 45

Find the amount of each payment needed to amortize the following loans. Round to the nearest cent. [16.4]

17. $24,000 loan; repaid at 9% in 8 semiannual payments

18. $18,500 loan; repaid at 10% in 10 semiannual payments

19. $12,400 loan; repaid at 10% in 20 quarterly payments

20. $8600 loan; repaid at 9% in 24 monthly payments

Find the monthly payment and finance charge for the following loans using Table 16.3. Round to the nearest cent. [16.4]

21. $9400 financed for 24 months at 12%

22. $12,000 financed for 42 months at 10%

23. $9000 financed for 48 months at 14%

24. $15,000 financed for 30 months at 11%

Find the monthly payment for the following real estate loans using Table 16.4. [16.5]

25. $180,000 loan at 9% for 30 years

26. $112,800 loan at 7% for 20 years

27. $100,000 loan at 8% for 15 years

28. $235,400 loan at 8% for 25 years

Solve the following application problems.

29. Sandmeyer Concrete Company signed an 11% note for $5600 dated June 20 for 150 days. The firm made partial payments of $1330 on July 20 and $1655 on September 3. (a) What payment is required when the note is due? (b) What was the total interest paid on the note? **[16.3]**

30. Debbie Blaisdell has a revolving charge at a department store. Her monthly statement contained the following information. **[16.1]**

6-10	Billing date; previous balance	$157.35
6-20	Payment	$45 CR
6-25	Craft department	$52.20
7-2	Shoe department	$69

Find the average daily balance on the next billing date of July 10. Then, find the finance charge if the interest is 1.5% per month on the average daily balance.

31. Ben Franklin purchased a 1-year-old Honda Accord with a cash price of $15,780 with a down payment of $2780 and agreed to make 48 monthly payments of $332.84. Find the total installment cost and the annual percentage rate. **[16.2]**

32. ABC Plumbing borrows $28,100 to buy a new truck. The firm agrees to make quarterly payments for 3 years at 12% per year. Find the amount of the quarterly payment. **[16.4]**

33. Mr. and Mrs. Zagorin plan to buy a home costing $198,000, paying 20% down and financing the balance at 7% for 30 years. The taxes are $3400 per year and fire insurance costs $760 per year. Find the monthly payment (including taxes and insurance). **[16.5]**

34. Jerome Watson, owner of Watson Welding, purchases a building for his business and makes a $25,000 down payment. He finances the balance of $122,500 for 20 years at 8%. (a) Find the total monthly payment given taxes of $3200 per year and insurance of $1275 per year. (b) Assume that insurance and taxes do not increase and find the total cost of owning the building for 20 years (include the down payment). **[16.5]**

35. After his August 15 payment, Tony Garza's loan balance was $8432.18. He missed the September 15 monthly payment but made a payment of $500 on October 14. He did not make any charges during this time. No penalty was charged and the loan has a simple interest rate of 12%. Find (a) the number of days from August 15 to October 14 and (b) the loan balance after the October 14 payment. **[16.3]**

CHAPTER 16	Business Application Case #1
	Consolidating Loans

John and Kathy MacGruder have had credit problems in the past so they were able to get loans only by paying higher-than-market interest rates. They are struggling to make their current payments, but they have done so regularly for over a year. Now they are trying to reduce their monthly payments by refinancing at lower rates where possible and also by extending the terms on loans where possible.

(a) Find the monthly payments on each of the following purchases and the total monthly payment. Use column F in the interest tables in **Appendix D** and Table 16.4.

Purchase	Original Loan Amount	Interest Rate	Term of Loan	Monthly Payment
Honda Accord	$18,800	12%	4 years	_____
Ford truck	$14,300	18%	4 years	_____
Home	$96,500	9%	15 years	_____
2nd mortgage on home	$4500	12%	3 years	_____
Total				_____

(b) These monthly expenses do not include car insurance ($215 per month), health insurance ($120 per month), or taxes on their home ($3540 per year), among other expenses. Find their total monthly outlay for all of these expenses.

Expense	Monthly Outlay
Payments on debt from (a)	_____
Car insurance	_____
Health insurance	_____
Taxes on home	_____
Total	_____

(c) The MacGruders learn that they can (1) refinance the remaining $14,900 debt on the Honda Accord at 12% over 4 years, (2) refinance the remaining $8600 loan amount on the Ford truck at 12% over 3 years, (3) refinance the remaining $94,800 loan amount on their home at 8% over 30 years, and (4) reduce their car insurance payments by $28 per month. Complete the table below. Use column F in the interest tables in **Appendix D** and Table 16.4.

Item	New Loan Amount	New Interest Rate	New Term of Loan	New Monthly Payment
Honda Accord	$14,900	12%	4 years	_____
Ford truck	8600	12%	3 years	_____
Home	94,800	8%	30 years	_____
2nd mortgage on home	4500	12%	3 years	_____
Car insurance				_____
Health insurance				_____
Taxes on home				_____
Total				_____

(d) Find the reduction in their monthly payments.

NOTE   Part of the savings in the monthly payment came from reducing the interest rates. The remainder of the savings came from extending the loans further into the future.

CHAPTER 16	Business Application Case #2
	Starting out after College

Jessica Simms and Ben Waller met in the last year of college. Jessica received her degree in architecture at the same time that Ben received his in accounting. They married later that year and both found good jobs earning $78,640 per year between the two of them. However, they had accumulated a lot of student loans, credit-card debt, and car payments, as shown.

(a) Find the total of debt payments.

Debt	Loan Balance	Interest Rate	Minimum Monthly Payment
Her student loans	$12,380	8%	$251.02
His student loans	$28,600	9%	$419.00
Credit cards	$14,860	15%	$225.00
Her car	$18,230	9%	$453.65
His car	$6,350	12%	$298.92
		Total	

(b) Find the monthly FICA and Medicare taxes they must pay. **(c)** Then add the FICA and Medicare taxes to the other expenses shown below.

FICA and Medicare taxes (7.65% of monthly salary)	
Income tax withholding	$820.45
Rent	$985.00
Utilities, cable TV, cell phones	$358.00
Auto, medical, and life insurance	$236.00
Food and entertainment	$1100.00
Professional, clothing, miscellaneous	$380.00
Total	

(d) Find the sum of (a) and (c).

(e) Find the amount left over each month.

(f) Assume the Simms apply the extra left over at the end of each month from (e) and also their monthly rent to pay a mortgage. If interest rates are 8% on 30-year fixed-rate loans, estimate the largest debt they can finance to the nearest thousand.

(g) The mortgage broker has told the Simms that they must make a 10% down payment in order to borrow the full amount calculated in (f). Find the amount of the down payment needed if they borrow this full amount. Then estimate the number of months it will take to save the down payment needed if they save the cash left over each month from (e) and they earn 4% compounded monthly.

PART 4	Cumulative Review: Chapters 12–16

Round money amounts to the nearest cent, time to the nearest day, and rates to the nearest tenth of a percent.

Find the value of the unknown quantity using simple interest. Use banker's interest. [12.1–12.2]

	Interest	Principal	Rate	Time
1.	_____	$4500	8%	5 months
2.	_____	$6200	9.7%	250 days
3.	$46.67	_____	7%	100 days
4.	$302.60	_____	12.5%	70 days
5.	$50.93	$2100	_____	90 days
6.	$306	$6800	_____	120 days
7.	$202.22	$9100	10%	_____
8.	$915	$18,300	12%	_____

Find the discount and the proceeds. [13.2]

	Face Value	Discount Rate	Time (Days)
9.	$9000	12%	90
10.	$875	$6\frac{1}{2}$%	210

11. Convert a simple discount rate of 10% for 90 days to a simple interest rate and round to the nearest tenth of a percent. [13.3]

12. Convert a simple interest rate of 12% for 180 days to a simple discount rate and round to the nearest tenth of a percent. [13.3]

Find the compound amounts for the following deposits. [14.1]

13. $1000 at 4% compounded annually for 17 years

14. $3520 at 8% compounded annually for 10 years

Find the compound amounts and interest earned for the following deposits. Assume $3\frac{1}{2}$% interest compounded daily. [14.2]

	Amount	Date Deposited	Date Withdrawn
15.	$12,600	March 24	June 3
16.	$7500	November 20	February 14

Find the present value and the amount of interest earned for the following. Round to the nearest cent. [14.4]

	Amount Needed	Time (Years)	Interest	Compounded
17.	$1000	7	8%	Annually
18.	$19,000	9	5%	Semiannually

Find the amount of the following ordinary annuities. **[15.1]**

Amount of Each Deposit	Deposited	Rate	Time (Years)
19. $1000	Annually	4%	8
20. $3500	Semiannually	6%	4

Find the present value of the following annuities. **[15.2]**

Amount per Payment	Payment at End of Each	Time (Years)	Rate of Investment	Compounded
21. $925	6 months	11	8%	Semiannually
22. $27,235	Quarter	8	8%	Quarterly

Find the required payment into a sinking fund. **[15.3]**

Future Value	Interest Rate	Compounded	Time (Years)
23. $3600	8%	Annually	7
24. $4500	10%	Quarterly	7

Solve the following application problems. Use 360-day years where applicable.

25. Walter Bates sets aside $5000 today to help pay his son's college expenses, which will begin in 9 years. Given a rate of 8% compounded semiannually, find the future value of this investment. **[14.1]**

26. A divorce settlement calls for one spouse to pay the other a lump sum of $12,000 in 18 months. Assume funds earn 7% compounded semiannually. Find the lump sum that must be deposited today to satisfy this payment. **[14.4]**

27. Bill Jones borrowed $12,000 using a simple interest note at 8% for 40 days. Find (a) the maturity value and (b) the interest. **[13.1]**

28. Sherie Whatly borrowed $15,000 on a simple discount note at 10% for 100 days. Find (a) the interest and (b) the proceeds. **[13.2]**

29. Tom Davis owes $7850 to a relative. He has agreed to pay the money in 5 months, at a simple interest rate of 6%. One month before the loan is due, the relative discounts the loan at the bank. The bank charges a 7.92% discount rate. How much money does the relative receive? **[13.4]**

30. James Pool earned $23,500 last year. Find the gain in purchasing power for a year in which he receives a raise of 4.1% but inflation as measured by the CPI was 3.7%. **[12.4]**

31. Thomas Wood has an average daily balance of $6327.12 on a credit card that charges 1.5% per month. Find (a) the monthly finance charge, (b) the finance charge if he could change the loan to a credit card that charges 0.8% on the average daily balance, and (c) the savings. **[16.1]**

32. A used automobile costing $10,500 was purchased with $1000 down and payments of $315 per month for 36 months. Find (a) the total installment cost, (b) the finance charge, (c) the amount financed, and (d) the annual percentage rate. **[16.2]**

33. On July 7, Gene Harper borrows $3000 at 9% interest to pay for surgery to correct his nearsightedness. Find the balance owed immediately after a partial payment on September 30 of $720. Assume the United States Rule applies for partial payments. **[16.3]**

34. A public utility needs $60 million in 5 years for a major capital expansion. What annual payment must it place in a sinking fund earning 10% per year in order to accumulate the required funds? **[15.3]**

35. At 58, Thomas Jones knows that he must start saving for his retirement. He decides to invest $300 per quarter in an account paying 6% compounded quarterly. Find the accumulated amount (a) at age 65 and (b) at age 70. **[15.1]**

36. Ben Torres borrows $18,500 at 10% compounded monthly for 48 months to purchase a farm tractor. Find the monthly payment using Table 16.3. **[16.4]**

37. The owner of Jessica's Cookies has an extra $3200 that she puts into a savings account paying $3\frac{1}{2}\%$ per year compounded daily. Find the interest if the funds are left there for 65 days. **[14.2]**

38. Jonah Goldratt wants to borrow $189,000 at 7% for 30 years to purchase a home. Insurance and taxes combined are $3250 per year. Can he afford the home if he can only afford payments of $1300 per month at the maximum? **[16.5]**

CHAPTER

17

Depreciation

A business finds its net income (profit) by subtracting all expenses from the amount of money received by the business (revenues). Major expenses include the cost of goods sold, salaries, rent, and utilities. Other expenses include the cost of assets such as machines, buildings, and fixtures. These assets usually last several years, so it would not show the true income of the business if the entire cost of an asset were considered an expense in the year of purchase. Instead, a method called **depreciation** is used to spread the cost of the asset over the length of its useful life, which is measured in years.

Depreciation is used with assets having a useful life of more than one year. The asset to be depreciated must have a predictable life: a truck can be depreciated because its useful life can be estimated, but land cannot be depreciated because its life is indefinite. For example, Figure 17.1 shows the remaining value of a Kenworth truck as it is depreciated over its useful life. The truck in this example has a 5-year life.

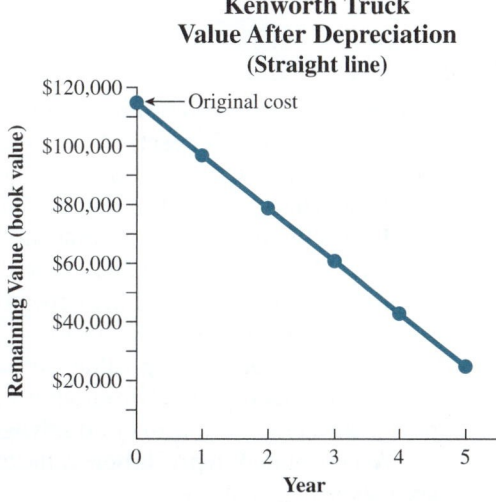

Kenworth Truck Value After Depreciation (Straight line)

Figure 17.1

STOP
and think

Employee salaries, rents, utilities, and other daily operating expenses are deducted on business income tax returns in the year paid, resulting in an immediate savings in taxes. However, only a small percent of the value of a long-term asset such as a building may be deducted in the year purchased. Why the difference? What would happen to current income taxes if managers could immediately deduct the cost of the building the same year it is purchased? If laws were changed to allow an immediate, full deduction of the cost of a building, would managers spend money differently? Explain.

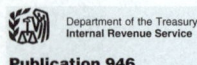

Department of the Treasury
Internal Revenue Service

Publication 946
Cat. No. 13081F

How To Depreciate Property

- Section 179 Deduction
- Special Depreciation Allowance
- MACRS
- Listed Property

Over the years, several methods of computing depreciation have been used, including *straight-line, declining-balance, sum-of-the-years'-digits,* and *units-of-production.* These methods are used in keeping company accounting records, and, in some states, for preparing state income tax returns. Assets purchased after 1981 are depreciated for federal tax returns with the accelerated cost recovery system or the modified accelerated cost recovery system discussed in **Section 17.5**. The use of depreciation for federal income tax purposes is detailed in an Internal Revenue Service Publication 946. The complete title of this publication is shown at the side.

A company need not use the same method of depreciation for all of its various assets. For example, the straight-line method of depreciation might be used on some assets and the declining-balance method on other assets. Furthermore, the depreciation method used in preparing a company's financial statements may be different from the method used in preparing income tax returns. Management goals for financial statements often differ from those for tax returns.

17.1	Straight-Line Method

OBJECTIVES

1 *Understand the terms used in depreciation.*

2 *Use the straight-line method to find the annual depreciation.*

3 *Use the straight-line method to find the book value of an asset.*

4 *Determine the book value of an asset after several years.*

5 *Calculate the accumulated depreciation.*

6 *Use the straight-line method to prepare a depreciation schedule.*

Objective

1   *Understand the Terms Used in Depreciation.*   Physical assets such as machinery, cars, or buildings are **tangible assets**. A tangible asset may be depreciated as long as its useful life can be estimated. The key terms used in depreciation are summarized below.

Cost is the basis for determining depreciation. It is the total amount paid for the asset.

Useful life is the period of time during which the asset will be used. The Internal Revenue Service (IRS) has guidelines as to the estimated life of assets used in a particular trade or business. However, useful life depends on the use of the asset, repair policy, replacement policy, obsolescence, and other factors.

Salvage value or **scrap value** (sometimes called **residual value**) is the estimated value of an asset when it is retired from service, traded in, disposed of, or exhausted. An asset may have a salvage value of zero or **no salvage value**.

Accumulated depreciation is the amount of depreciation taken so far, a running balance of depreciation to date.

Book value is the cost of an asset minus the total depreciation to date (cost minus accumulated depreciation). The book value at the end of an asset's life is equal to the salvage value. Book value can never be less than salvage value.

Objective

2   *Use the Straight-Line Method to Find the Annual Depreciation.*   The simplest method of depreciation, **straight-line depreciation**, assumes that assets lose an equal amount of value during each year of life. For example, suppose a heavy-equipment trailer is purchased by Village Nursery and Landscaping at a cost of $14,100. The trailer has an estimated useful life of 8 years and a salvage value of $2100. Find the amount to be depreciated (**depreciable amount**) using the following formula.

$$\text{Amount to be depreciated} = \text{Cost} - \text{Salvage value}$$

Here, the amount to be depreciated over the 8-year period is figured as follows.

$$
\begin{array}{rl}
\$14{,}100 & \text{Cost} \\
-\quad 2{,}100 & \text{Salvage value} \\
\hline
\$12{,}000 & \text{Amount to be depreciated}
\end{array}
$$

With the straight-line method, an equal amount of depreciation is taken each year of the 8-year life of the trailer.

$$\text{Annual depreciation} = \$12{,}000 \div 8 = \$1500$$

Or, use the following formula. The annual depreciation by the *straight-line method* for an item having a cost of c, a salvage value s, and a life of n years, is d, where

$$\text{Annual depreciation} = d = \frac{c - s}{n}$$

Use the formula for the example by substituting \$14,100 for c, \$2100 for s, and 8 for n.

$$d = \frac{\$14{,}100 - \$2100}{8} = \frac{\$12{,}000}{8} = \$1500$$

The annual straight-line depreciation is \$1500. Each year during the 8-year life of the trailer, \$1500 will be treated as an expense by the company owning the trailer. The annual depreciation of \$1500 is $\frac{1}{8}$ of the depreciable amount. The annual rate of depreciation is often given as a percent, in this case, $12\frac{1}{2}\%$ $\left(\frac{1}{8} = 12\frac{1}{2}\%\right)$.

Objective

3

Use the Straight-Line Method to Find the Book Value of an Asset. The **book value**, or remaining value of an asset at the end of a year, is the original cost minus the depreciation up to and including that year (the **accumulated depreciation**). In the example, the book value at the end of the first year is \$12,600.

$$
\begin{array}{rl}
\$14{,}100 & \text{Cost} \\
-\quad 1{,}500 & \text{First-year's depreciation} \\
\hline
\$12{,}600 & \text{Book value at the end of the first year}
\end{array}
$$

Book value is found with the following formula.

$$\text{Book value} = \text{Cost} - \text{Accumulated depreciation}$$

EXAMPLE 1 **Finding First-Year Depreciation and Book Value**

Commercial Fisheries purchased some navigation equipment at a cost of \$2650. The estimated life of the equipment is 5 years, with a salvage value of \$350. Find the (a) annual rate of depreciation, (b) annual amount of depreciation, and (c) book value at the end of the first year.

Solution

(a) The annual rate of depreciation is 20%, since a 5-year life means $\frac{1}{5}$ or 20% per year.

(b) First find the depreciable amount.

$$
\begin{array}{rl}
\$2650 & \text{Cost} \\
-\ 350 & \text{Salvage value} \\
\hline
\$2300 & \text{Depreciable amount}
\end{array}
$$

This $2300 will be depreciated evenly over the 5-year life for an annual depreciation of $460 ($2300 × 20% = $460, or $2300 ÷ 5 = $460). The annual depreciation can also be found by the following formula.

$$d = \frac{c - s}{n}$$

Substitute $2650 for *c*, $350 for *s*, and 5 for *n*.

$$d = \frac{\$2650 - \$350}{5} = \frac{\$2300}{5} = \$460$$

The annual depreciation by the straight-line method is $460.

(c) Since the annual depreciation is $460, the book value at the end of the first year will be found as follows.

$2650   Cost
− 460   First year's depreciation
$2190   Book value after 1 year

The book value of the navigation equipment after 1 year is $2190.

Scientific Calculator Approach

To solve Example 1 using a calculator, first use parentheses to find the depreciable amount. Next, divide to find depreciation. Finally, find the book value.

(2650 − 350) ÷ 5 = 460

2650 − 460 = 2190

If an asset has **no salvage value** at the end of the expected life, then the entire cost will be depreciated over the life of the asset. In Example 1, if the navigation equipment was expected to have no salvage value at the end of 5 years, the annual amount of depreciation would have been $530 (since $2650 ÷ 5 = $530).

NOTE   Find the book value at the end of any year by multiplying the annual amount of straight-line depreciation by the number of years and subtract this result, the accumulated depreciation to date, from the cost.

Objective

4   *Determine the Book Value of an Asset after Several Years.*

EXAMPLE 2   **Finding the Book Value at the End of Any Year**

A lighted display case at the Bead Works costs $3400 and has an estimated life of 10 years and a salvage value of $800. Find the book value at the end of 6 years.

Solution   The annual rate of depreciation is 10% (10-year life leads to $\frac{1}{10}$ or 10%).

$3400   Cost
− 800   Salvage value
$2600   Depreciable amount

Since $2600 is depreciated evenly over the 10-year life of the case, the annual depreciation is $260 ($2600 × 10% = $260, or $2600 ÷ 10 = $260).

Objective

5

Calculate the Accumulated Depreciation. The accumulated depreciation over the 6-year period follows.

$$\$260 \times 6 \text{ (years)} = \$1560 \quad \text{Accumulated depreciation (6 years)}$$

Find the book value at the end of 6 years by subtracting the accumulated depreciation from the cost.

$3400	Cost
− 1560	Accumulated depreciation (6 years)
$1840	Book value at the end of 6 years

After 6 years, this display case would be carried on the books with a value of $1840.

NOTE The book value helps the owner of a business estimate the value of the business, which is important when the owner is borrowing money or trying to sell the business.

Objective

6

Use the Straight-Line Method to Prepare a Depreciation Schedule. A **depreciation schedule** is often used to show the annual depreciation, accumulated depreciation, and book value over the useful life of an asset. As an aid in comparing the three methods of depreciation, the depreciation schedule of Example 3 and the schedules shown in the double-declining-balance method (see **Section 17.2**) and the sum-of-years'-digits method (see **Section 17.3**) use the same asset. The following example will be used in several places in this chapter so that you can better compare depreciation methods.

EXAMPLE 3 Preparing a Depreciation Schedule

Village Nursery and Landscaping bought a new pickup truck for $21,500. It is estimated that the truck will have a useful life of 5 years, at which time it will have a salvage value (trade-in value) of $3500. Prepare a depreciation schedule using the straight-line method of depreciation.

Solution The annual rate of depreciation is 20% (5-year life $= \frac{1}{5}$ per year $= 20\%$). Find the depreciable amount as follows.

$21,500	Cost
− 3,500	Salvage value
$18,000	Depreciable amount

This $18,000 will be depreciated evenly over the 5-year life, giving an annual depreciation of $3600 ($18,000 × 20% = $3600).

This depreciation schedule includes a year 0 to show the initial cost of the truck.

Year	Computation	Amount of Depreciation	Accumulated Depreciation	Book Value	
0	—	—	—	$21,500	
1	(20% × $18,000)	$3600	$3,600	$17,900	
2	(20% × $18,000)	$3600	$7,200	$14,300	
3	(20% × $18,000)	$3600	$10,800	$10,700	
4	(20% × $18,000)	$3600	$14,400	$7,100	
5	(20% × $18,000)	$3600	$18,000	$3,500	Salvage value

The depreciation is $3600 each year. The accumulated depreciation at the end of 5 years is equal to the depreciable amount, and the book value at the end of 5 years is equal to the salvage value.

■

NOTE   If the depreciation rate is a repeating decimal, use the fraction that is equivalent to the decimal. Instead of 33.3%, use the fraction $\frac{1}{3}$; instead of 16.7%, use the fraction $\frac{1}{6}$.

17.1	**Exercises**

Find the annual straight-line rate of depreciation, given each of the following estimated lives.

1. 5 years
2. 4 years
3. 8 years
4. 10 years
5. 20 years
6. 25 years
7. 15 years
8. 30 years
9. 80 years
10. 40 years
11. 50 years
12. 100 years

Find the annual amount of depreciation for each of the following, using the straight-line method.

13. Cost: $9000
    Estimated life: 20 years
    Estimated scrap value: None

14. Cost: $3400
    Estimated life: 4 years
    Estimated scrap value: $800

15. Cost: $2700
    Estimated life: 3 years
    Estimated scrap value: $300

16. Cost: $8100
    Estimated life: 6 years
    Estimated scrap value: $750

17. Cost: $4200
    Estimated life: 5 years
    Estimated scrap value: None

18. Cost: $12,200
    Estimated life: 10 years
    Estimated scrap value: $3200

Find the book value at the end of the first year for the following, using the straight-line method.

19. Cost: $3200
    Estimated life: 8 years
    Estimated scrap value: $400

20. Cost: $35,000
    Estimated life: 10 years
    Estimated scrap value: $2500

21. Cost: $5400
    Estimated life: 12 years
    Estimated scrap value: $600

22. Cost: $4500
    Estimated life: 5 years
    Estimated scrap value: None

Find the book value at the end of 5 years for the following, using the straight-line method.

23. Cost: $4800
    Estimated life: 10 years
    Estimated scrap value: $750

24. Cost: $16,000
    Estimated life: 20 years
    Estimated scrap value: $2000

25. Cost: $80,000
    Estimated life: 50 years
    Estimated scrap value: $10,000

26. Cost: $660
    Estimated life: 8 years
    Estimated scrap value: $100

27. Develop a single formula that will show how to find annual depreciation using the straight-line method of depreciation. (See Objective 2.)

28. Explain the procedure used to calculate depreciation when there is no salvage value. Why will the book value always be zero at the end of the asset's life?

Solve the following application problems.

29. **MACHINERY DEPRECIATION**   Dallas Tool and Diecasting Company selects the straight-line method of depreciation for a lathe costing $12,000 with a 3-year life and an expected scrap value of $3000. Prepare a depreciation schedule.

Year	Computation	Amount of Depreciation	Accumulated Depreciation	Book Value
0	—	—	—	$12,000
1				
2				
3				

30. **TRUCK DEPRECIATION**   Village Nursery and Landscaping paid $25,600 for a $1\frac{1}{2}$-ton dual-axle flatbed truck with an estimated life of 6 years and a salvage value of $7000. Prepare a depreciation schedule using the straight-line method of depreciation.

Year	Computation	Amount of Depreciation	Accumulated Depreciation	Book Value
0	—	—	—	$25,600
1				
2				
3				
4				
5				
6				

31. **OFFICE EQUIPMENT DEPRECIATION**   Shippers' Express paid $9400 for office equipment with an estimated life of 6 years and a salvage value of $2200. Prepare a depreciation schedule using the straight-line method of depreciation.

32. **BUSINESS FIXTURES**   Dorothy Sargent buys fixtures for her shop at a cost of $7800 and estimates the life of the fixtures as 10 years, after which they will have no salvage value. Prepare a depreciation schedule, calculating depreciation by the straight-line method.

33. **TUGBOAT**   A Dutch petroleum company purchased a tugboat for $1,300,000. The estimated life is 20 years, at which time it will have a salvage value of $200,000. (a) Use the straight-line method of depreciation to find the annual amount of depreciation. (b) Find the book value at the end of 5 years.

34. **DEPRECIATING COMPUTER EQUIPMENT**   The new computer equipment at Leisure Travel has a cost of $14,500, an estimated life of 8 years, and scrap value of $2100. Find (a) the annual depreciation and (b) the book value at the end of 4 years using the straight-line method of depreciation.

35. **BOAT RAMP** A freshwater boat ramp has an estimated life of 15 years and no scrap value. If the boat ramp cost $37,900 and the straight-line method is used, find (a) the annual depreciation and (b) the book value after 7 years. Round depreciation to the nearest dollar.

36. **PACKAGING EQUIPMENT** The packaging equipment at Rainbow Bakery has a cost of $132,400, an estimated life of 10 years, and a salvage value of $35,000. Find the book value of the packaging equipment after 8 years using the straight-line method of depreciation.

37. **FURNITURE DEPRECIATION** A bookcase costs $880, has an estimated life of 8 years, and has a scrap value of $160. Use the straight-line method of depreciation to find (a) the annual rate of depreciation, (b) the annual amount of depreciation, and (c) the book value at the end of the first year.

38. **WAREHOUSE SHELVING** Compu-Tech purchased new warehouse shelving for $37,500. The estimated life is 10 years, with a salvage value of $7500. Use the straight-line method of depreciation to find (a) the annual rate of depreciation, (b) the annual amount of depreciation, (c) the book value at the end of 5 years, and (d) the accumulated depreciation at the end of 8 years.

17.2	**Declining-Balance Method**

OBJECTIVES

1 *List the declining-balance methods.*

2 *Find the declining-balance rate.*

3 *Find depreciation and book value using the double-declining-balance method.*

4 *Use the formula to find depreciation by the double-declining-balance method.*

5 *Prepare a depreciation schedule using the double-declining-balance method.*

The straight-line method of depreciation assumes that the cost of an asset is spread equally and evenly over each year of its life. This is not realistic for many assets. For example, a new utility van loses much more value during its first year of life than during its fifth year. Using straight-line depreciation for such assets would give a book value higher than the actual value of the asset during the early years.

Methods of accelerated depreciation are used to more accurately reflect the rate at which most assets actually lose value. **Accelerated depreciation** produces larger amounts of depreciation in the earlier years of the life of an asset and smaller amounts in the later years. The total amount of depreciation taken over the life of an asset is the same as with the straight-line method (the difference of cost and salvage value), but the distribution of the annual amounts is different. The effect of accelerating depreciation on an income tax return is to reduce current income taxes now, at the expense of reducing taxes less in future years.

One of the more common accelerated methods of depreciation is the **declining-balance method**. This method requires that a *declining-balance rate* be first established. The rate is multiplied by last year's book value to get this year's depreciation. *Since the book value declines from year to year, the annual depreciation from year to year also declines.* This explains the method's name of declining balance.

Objective

1 *List the Declining-Balance Methods.*

Three Common Declining-Balance Methods

200%, or double-declining-balance, method. With this method, 200% of the straight-line rate, or twice the straight-line rate, is used.

150% declining-balance method. With this method, $1\frac{1}{2}$ times the straight-line rate is used.

125% declining-balance method. With this method, $1\frac{1}{4}$ times the straight-line rate is used.

When using the declining-balance method of depreciation, do not subtract salvage value before calculating the depreciation. Also, stop subtracting depreciation once the book value has reached the salvage value. The book value of the asset *never* goes below the salvage value.

Objective

2 *Find the Declining-Balance Rate.* Calculate depreciation using the declining-balance method by first finding the straight-line rate of depreciation. Then adjust the straight-line rate to the desired declining-balance rate (200%, 150%, or 125% as desired). The following examples of declining-balance depreciation show the **200% method**, or double-declining-balance method.

EXAMPLE 1 **Finding the 200% Declining-Balance Rate**

Find the straight-line rate and the double-declining-balance (200%) rate for each of the following years of life.

Solution

Years of Life	Straight-Line Rate	Double-Declining-Balance Rate
3	33.33% $\left(\frac{1}{3}\right)$	$\times 2 = 66.67\%$ $\left(\frac{2}{3}\right)$
4	25%	$\times 2 = 50\%$
5	20%	$\times 2 = 40\%$
8	12.5%	$\times 2 = 25\%$
10	10%	$\times 2 = 20\%$
20	5%	$\times 2 = 10\%$
25	4%	$\times 2 = 8\%$
50	2%	$\times 2 = 4\%$

NOTE Throughout the remainder of this chapter, money amounts will be rounded to the nearest dollar, a common practice when dealing with depreciation. The rounded value is then used in further calculations.

Objective

3   *Find Depreciation and Book Value Using the Double-Declining-Balance Method.*

> **EXAMPLE 2**   **Finding Depreciation and Book Value Using Double-Declining-Balance**
>
> Northridge Golf and Country Club purchased a portable storage building for $8100. It is expected to have a life of 10 years, at which time it will have a salvage value of $1000. Using the double-declining-balance method of depreciation, find the first and second years' depreciation and the book value at the end of the first and second year.
>
> **Solution**   Start by finding the double-declining-balance rate. Ignore the salvage value. Find the rate by doubling the straight-line rate. The straight-line rate for a life of 10 years is $\frac{1}{10}$, or 10%, and 10% doubled is 20%. The double-declining-balance rate (20%) is then multiplied by the book value, or in year 1, the *original cost.* The depreciation in year 1 is
>
> $$\text{Original cost} \times \text{Double-declining rate}$$
> $$\$8100 \times \quad 0.20 \quad = \$1620$$
>
> Depreciation in year 1 is $1620. Find the book value at the end of the first year as follows.
>
> $$\begin{array}{rl} \$8100 & \text{Cost} \\ -\ 1620 & \text{Depreciation to date} \\ \hline \$6480 & \text{Book value at the end of the first year} \end{array}$$
>
> The second year's depreciation is 20% of $6480 (last year's book value or declining balance).
>
> $$\$6480 \,(\text{declining balance}) \times 0.20 = \$1296 \quad \text{Depreciation in second year, rounded}$$
>
> The book value at the end of the second year is $8100 − $2916 (depreciation year 1 and year 2) = $5184.

Objective

4   *Use the Formula to Find Depreciation by the Double-Declining-Balance Method.*   Declining-balance depreciation can also be found with the following formula.

Finding Annual Depreciation Using Declining Balance

> The annual depreciation, d, by the declining-balance method, is given by
>
> $$d = r \times b$$
>
> where r is the declining-balance rate and b is the book value in the previous year. (In year 1, b is the original cost of the asset.)

> **EXAMPLE 3**   **Using a Formula to Find Depreciation and Book Value**
>
> Pioneer Beverage buys a small bottling machine for $59,400. The expected life of the bottling machine is 5 years, at which time it will have a salvage value of $3800. Using the double-declining-balance method of depreciation, find the first and second years' depreciation and the book value at the end of the first and second year.

Solution The straight-line depreciation rate for a 5-year life is 20%. The double-declining rate is 40% (20% times 2). The first year's depreciation is 40% of the declining balance or, in the first year, 40% of the cost. Use the formula, substituting 0.40 for r and \$59,400 for b.

$$d = r \times b$$
$$d = 0.40 \times \$59,400 = \$23,760$$

The depreciation in the first year is \$23,760. The book value at the end of the first year is as follows.

$59,400	Cost
− 23,760	Depreciation to date
$35,640	Book value at the end of the first year

The second year's depreciation is 40% of \$35,640 (last year's book value or declining balance).

$$d = r \times b$$
$$d = 0.40 \times \$35,640 = \$14,256$$

The depreciation in the second year is \$14,256. At the end of the second year the book value is figured as shown.

$59,400	Cost
− 38,016	Depreciation to date ($23,760 + $14,256)
$21,384	Book value at the end of the second year

NOTE The total amount of depreciation taken over the life of the asset is the same using either the straight-line or the double-declining-balance methods of depreciation, but the distribution of the annual amounts is different.

Objective

5 *Prepare a Depreciation Schedule Using the Double-Declining-Balance Method.* The next example shows a depreciation schedule for the same pickup truck used in Example 3 of **Section 17.1**. Here, the declining-balance method is used, where the same rate is used each year, and the rate is multiplied by the declining balance (last year's book value). This example shows that the amount of depreciation in a given year may have to be adjusted so that book value is never less than salvage value.

EXAMPLE 4 **Preparing a Depreciation Schedule**

Village Nursery and Landscaping bought a new pickup truck at a cost of \$21,500. It is estimated that the truck will have a useful life of 5 years, at which time it will have a salvage value (trade-in value) of \$3500. Prepare a depreciation schedule using the double-declining-balance method of depreciation.

Solution The annual rate of depreciation is 40% (20% straight-line × 2 = 40%). Do not subtract salvage value from cost before calculating depreciation. In year 1, the full cost is used to calculate depreciation.

Year	Computation	Amount of Depreciation	Accumulated Depreciation	Book Value
0	—	—	—	$21,500
1	(40% × $21,500)	$8600	$8,600	$12,900
2	(40% × $12,900)	$5160	$13,760	$7,740
3	(40% × $7740)	$3096	$16,856	$4,644
4		$1144*	$18,000	$3,500
5		$0	$18,000	$3,500 Salvage value

*In year 4, 40% of $4644 is $1858. If this amount were subtracted from $4644, the book value would drop below the salvage value of $3500. Since book value may **never be less than salvage value**, depreciation of $1144 ($4644 − $3500) is taken in year 4, so that book value equals salvage value. No further depreciation remains for year 5 or subsequent years. The total amount of depreciation taken over the life of the asset is the same using either the straight-line or the double-declining-balance method of depreciation.

17.2 Exercises

Find the annual double-declining-balance (200% method) rate of depreciation, given each of the following estimated lives.

1. 5 years   **2.** 20 years   **3.** 8 years

4. 25 years   **5.** 15 years   **6.** 4 years

7. 10 years   **8.** 30 years   **9.** 6 years

10. 40 years   **11.** 50 years   **12.** 100 years

Find the first year's depreciation for each of the following by using the double-declining-balance method of depreciation.

13. Cost: $18,000
    Estimated life: 10 years
    Estimated scrap value: $3000

14. Cost: $4950
    Estimated life: 20 years
    Estimated scrap value: None

15. Cost: $12,500
    Estimated life: 5 years
    Estimated scrap value: $500

16. Cost: $38,000
    Estimated life: 40 years
    Estimated scrap value: $5000

17. Cost: $3800
    Estimated life: 4 years
    Estimated scrap value: None

18. Cost: $1140
    Estimated life: 6 years
    Estimated scrap value $350

Find the book value at the end of the first year for each of the following by using the double-declining-balance method of depreciation. Round to the nearest dollar.

19. Cost: $4200
    Estimated life: 10 years
    Estimated scrap value: $1000

20. Cost: $2500
    Estimated life: 6 years
    Estimated scrap value: $400

21. Cost: $1620
    Estimated life: 8 years
    Estimated scrap value: None

22. Cost: $5640
    Estimated life: 5 years
    Estimated scrap value: $800

Find the book value at the end of 3 years for each of the following by using the double-declining-balance method of depreciation. Round to the nearest dollar.

23. Cost: $16,200
  Estimated life: 8 years
  Estimated scrap value: $1500

24. Cost: $8500
  Estimated life: 10 years
  Estimated scrap value: $1100

25. Cost: $6000
  Estimated life: 3 years
  Estimated scrap value: $750

26. Cost: $75,000
  Estimated life: 50 years
  Estimated scrap value: None

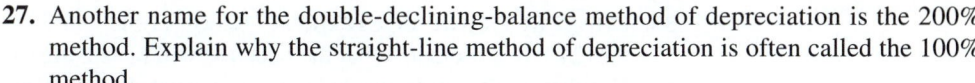

27. Another name for the double-declining-balance method of depreciation is the 200% method. Explain why the straight-line method of depreciation is often called the 100% method.

28. Explain why the amount of depreciation taken in the last year of an asset's life may be zero when using the double-declining-balance method of depreciation.

Solve the following application problems. Round to the nearest dollar.

29. WEIGHT-TRAINING EQUIPMENT Gold's Gym selects the double-declining-balance method of depreciation for some weight-training equipment costing $14,400. If the estimated life of the equipment is 4 years and the salvage value is zero, prepare a depreciation schedule.

Year	Computation	Amount of Depreciation	Accumulated Depreciation	Book Value
0	—	—	—	$14,400
1				
2				
3				
4				

30. STUDIO SOUND SYSTEM A studio sound system costing $11,760 has a 3-year life and a scrap value of $1400. Prepare a depreciation schedule using the double-declining-balance method of depreciation.

Year	Computation	Amount of Depreciation	Accumulated Depreciation	Book Value
0	—	—	—	$11,760
1				
2				
3				

31. ELECTRONIC ANALYZER Neilo Lincoln-Mercury decides to use the double-declining-balance method of depreciation on a Barnes Electronic Analyzer that was acquired at a cost of $25,500. If the estimated life of the analyzer is 8 years and the estimated scrap value is $3500, prepare a depreciation schedule.

32. CONVEYOR SYSTEM Prepare a depreciation schedule for the installation of a conveyor system using the double-declining-balance method of depreciation. Cost = $14,000; estimated life = 5 years; estimated scrap value = $2500.

33. **CARPET-CLEANING EQUIPMENT**   John Walker, owner of the Carpet Solution, purchased some truck-mounted carpet-cleaning equipment at a cost of $8200. The estimated life of the equipment is 8 years and the expected salvage value is $1250. Use the double-declining-balance method of depreciation to find the depreciation in the third year.

34. **CHOCOLATE YUMS**   Hiram Chocolates purchased two huge brass containers to hold a chocolate mix before pouring the candy. The total cost is $6800 and they have a useful life of 8 years with a salvage value of $1200. Find the depreciation in the second year using the double-declining-balance method of depreciation.

35. **CONSTRUCTION EQUIPMENT**   Cool Pools purchased a backhoe at a cost of $39,240. It is estimated that the backhoe will have a life of 5 years and no salvage value. Use the double-declining-balance method of depreciation to find the book value at the end of the third year.

36. **COMMUNICATION EQUIPMENT**   Caroline Fell purchased some communication equipment for her public relations firm at a cost of $19,700. She estimates the life of the equipment to be 8 years, at which time the salvage value will be $1000. Use the double-declining-balance method of depreciation to find the book value at the end of 5 years.

37. **POWER TOOLS**   West Construction purchased some power tools for the shop at a cost of $5800. They have a life of 8 years and a scrap value of $1000. Use the double-declining-balance method of depreciation to find (a) the annual rate of depreciation, (b) the amount of depreciation in the first year, (c) the accumulated depreciation at the end of the fifth year, and (d) the book value at the end of the fifth year.

38. **SCHOOL EQUIPMENT**   Gale Klein bought some white boards for her reading clinic at a cost of $3620. The estimated life of the white boards is 5 years, with a salvage value of $400. Use the double-declining-balance method of depreciation to find (a) the annual rate of depreciation, (b) the amount of depreciation in the first year, (c) the accumulated depreciation at the end of the third year, and (d) the book value at the end of the third year.

17.3   Sum-of-the-Years'-Digits Method

OBJECTIVES

1 *Understand the sum-of-the-years'-digits method.*

2 *Find the depreciation fractions for the sum-of-the-years'-digits method.*

3 *Use the formula to calculate the sum-of-the-years'-digits depreciation.*

4 *Prepare a depreciation schedule using the sum-of-the-years'-digits method.*

Objective

1   *Understand the Sum-of-the-Years'-Digits Method.*   The **sum-of-the-years'-digits method** of depreciation is another accelerated depreciation method. The double-declining-balance method of depreciation produces more depreciation than the straight-line method in the early years of an asset's life and less in the later years. The sum-of-the-years'-digits method, however, produces results in between the straight-line and the double-declining-balance method—more depreciation than straight-line at the beginning and more depreciation than double-declining at the end.

Objective

2   *Find the Depreciation Fractions for the Sum-of-the-Years'-Digits Method.*   The use of the sum-of-the-years'-digits method requires a **depreciation fraction** instead of the depreciation rate used earlier. The annual depreciation is this depreciation fraction multiplied by the depreciable amount (cost minus salvage value). The depreciation fraction decreases annually, as does the depreciation.

To find the depreciation fraction, first find the denominator, which remains constant for every year of the life of the asset. The denominator is the sum of all the years of the estimated life of the asset (sum of the years' digits). For example, if the life is 6 years, the denominator is 21 (since $1 + 2 + 3 + 4 + 5 + 6 = 21$). The numerator of the fraction decreases each year and represents the years of life remaining at the beginning of that year.

EXAMPLE **1** **Finding the Depreciation Fraction**

Find the depreciation fraction for each year if the sum-of-the-years'-digits method of depreciation is to be used for an asset with a useful life of 6 years.

Solution   First determine the denominator of the depreciation fraction. The denominator is 21 ($1 + 2 + 3 + 4 + 5 + 6 = 21$). Next determine the numerator for each year. The number of years of life remaining at the beginning of any year is the numerator.

Year	Depreciation Fraction
1	$\frac{6}{21}$
2	$\frac{5}{21}$
3	$\frac{4}{21}$
4	$\frac{3}{21}$
5	$\frac{2}{21}$
6	$\frac{1}{21}$
21 Sum of the year's digits	$\frac{21}{21}$ Sum of the fractions

Under the sum-of-the-years'-digits method, an asset having a life of 6 years is assumed to lose $\frac{6}{21}$ of its value the first year, $\frac{5}{21}$ the second year, $\frac{4}{21}$ the third year, and so on. The sum of the six fractions in the table is $\frac{21}{21}$, or 1, so that the entire depreciable amount is used over the 6-year life.

NOTE   It is common to not write these fractions in lowest terms so that the year in question can be seen.

A quick method of finding the sum of the years' digits is to use the formula

$$\text{Sum of the years' digits} = \frac{n(n + 1)}{2}$$

where n is the estimated life of the asset.

For example, if the life is 6 years, 6 is multiplied by 6 plus 1, resulting in 6×7, or 42. Then 42 is divided by 2, giving 21, the same denominator used in Example 1. This method eliminates adding digits and is especially useful when the life of an asset is long.

Objective

3   *Use the Formula to Calculate the Sum-of-the-Years'-Digits Depreciation.*   The depreciation fraction in any year is multiplied by the depreciable amount (as in the straight-line method) to calculate the amount of depreciation in any one year.

The formula for sum-of-the-years'-digits depreciation is

$$d = r \times (c - s)$$

where r is the depreciation fraction, c is the cost of the asset, and s is the salvage value.

EXAMPLE 2   Finding Depreciation Using the Sum-of-the-Years'-Digits Method

A Ditch Witch 1220 Trencher is purchased by Village Nursery and Landscaping at a cost of $8940. It has a useful life of 8 years and an estimated salvage value of $1200. Find the first and second years' depreciation using the sum-of-the-years'-digits method.

Solution   The depreciation fraction has a denominator of 36 (or $1 + 2 + 3 + 4 + 5 + 6 + 7 + 8$). The numerator for the first year of useful life is 8. The first-year fraction, $\frac{8}{36}$, is multiplied by the depreciable amount, $7740 ($8940 cost − $1200 salvage value). Substitute the proper numbers into the following formula.

$$d = r \times (c - s)$$

$$= \frac{8}{36} \times (\$8940 - \$1200)$$

$$= \frac{8}{36} \times \$7740 = \$1720$$

The first year's depreciation is $1720.

The book value at the end of the first year is $8940 (original cost) − $1720 (first year's depreciation) = $7220. For the second and succeeding years, always go back to the *original* depreciable amount and not to book value, as in the declining-balance method. The depreciation fraction for the second year, $\frac{7}{36}$, is multiplied by the original depreciable amount, $7740 ($8940 cost − $1200 salvage value). This gives

$$\frac{7}{36} \times \$7740 = \$1505$$

The second year's depreciation is $1505. In this example, the depreciation for any year is always found by multiplying the appropriate fraction by $7740.

Scientific Calculator Approach

The calculator solution to Example 2 finds $\frac{1}{36}$ of the depreciation amount and stores the result $\boxed{\text{STO}}$ in memory. This amount is then recalled $\boxed{\text{RCL}}$ to find future depreciation amounts.

8940 $\boxed{-}$ 1200 $\boxed{=}$ $\boxed{÷}$ 36 $\boxed{=}$ $\boxed{\text{STO}}$ $\boxed{\times}$ 8 $\boxed{=}$ 1720 $\boxed{\text{RCL}}$ $\boxed{\times}$ 7 $\boxed{=}$ 1505

EXAMPLE 3   Finding Depreciation When There Is No Salvage Value

City Saturn purchased an electronic smog analyzer for $9000. Using the sum-of-the-years'-digits method of depreciation, find the first and second years' depreciation if the analyzer has an estimated life of 4 years and no salvage value.

Solution The depreciation fraction has a denominator of 10 (or $1 + 2 + 3 + 4$). The numerator in the first-year is 4. The first-year depreciation fraction is $\frac{4}{10}$, which is multiplied by the amount to be depreciated, or $9000 ($9000 cost because there is no salvage value). Use the formula as follows.

$$d = r \times (c - s)$$

$$= \frac{4}{10} \times (\$9000 - \$0)$$

$$= \frac{4}{10} \times \$9000$$

$$= \$3600$$

The first year's depreciation is $3600.

The fraction for finding the depreciation in the second year is $\frac{3}{10}$, which is multiplied by the depreciable amount, or $9000.

$$\frac{3}{10} \times \$9000 = \$2700$$

The second year's depreciation is $2700.

Objective

4 *Prepare a Depreciation Schedule Using the Sum-of-the-Years'-Digits Method.* For comparison, the next example uses the same pickup truck discussed in **Sections 17.1** and **17.2**.

EXAMPLE 4 **Preparing a Depreciation Schedule**

Village Nursery and Landscaping bought a new pickup truck for $21,500. It is estimated that the truck will have a useful life of 5 years, at which time it will have a salvage value (trade-in value) of $3500. Prepare a depreciation schedule using the sum-of-the-years'-digits method of depreciation.

Solution Using the formula on page 609, the depreciation fraction has a denominator found as follows.

$$\frac{5 \times 6}{2} = 15$$

Year	Computation	Amount of Depreciation	Accumulated Depreciation	Book Value	
0	—	—	—	$21,500	
1	$\left(\frac{5}{15} \times \$18,000\right)$	$6000	$6,000	$15,500	
2	$\left(\frac{4}{15} \times \$18,000\right)$	$4800	$10,800	$10,700	
3	$\left(\frac{3}{15} \times \$18,000\right)$	$3600	$14,400	$7,100	
4	$\left(\frac{2}{15} \times \$18,000\right)$	$2400	$16,800	$4,700	
5	$\left(\frac{1}{15} \times \$18,000\right)$	$1200	$18,000	$3,500	Salvage value

NOTE The sum-of-the-years'-digits method of depreciation allows rapid depreciation in the early years of the asset's life and also provides some depreciation during the last years.

The three methods of depreciation can be compared visually by graphing the amounts of depreciation in each year and the book values at the end of each year. Figure 17.2 shows the depreciation using each of the three methods for the truck used by Village Nursery and Landscaping. Figure 17.3 shows the book value after depreciation for each of the three methods.

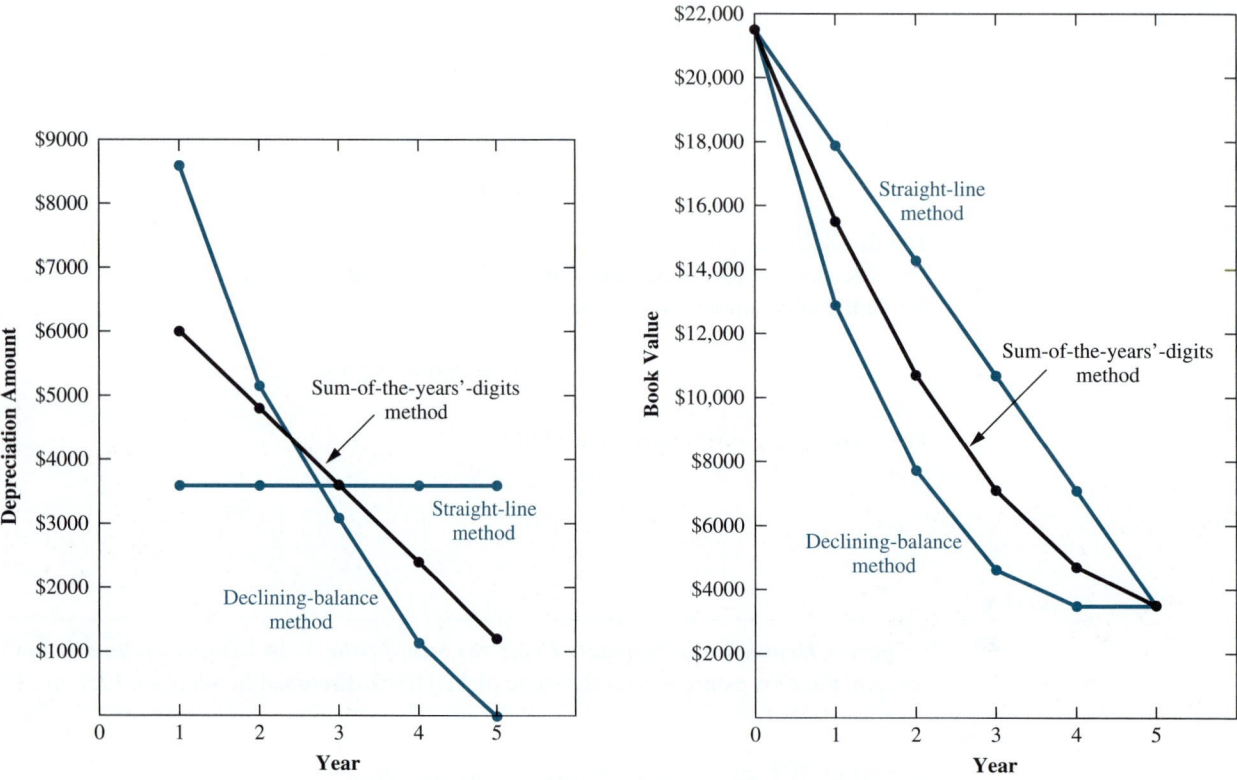

Figure 17.2 Comparing Methods of Depreciation

Figure 17.3 Comparison of Book Value Amounts

When used in preparing income tax returns, accelerated depreciation methods with higher, up-front depreciation result in lower income taxes in the early years compared to higher income taxes in later years. Remember to *never depreciate* the value of an asset below its salvage value.

Choosing a Method of Depreciation

Although there is no simple way to decide which method of depreciation is preferable in a given case, the following considerations may help to arrive at an answer.

- Will a larger deduction in the first year or years help pay for the asset with the tax dollars saved?
- Is it expected that earnings during the first years will be larger than in the following years? Larger depreciation deductions help to reduce taxes.
- Will a steady deduction over the life of the asset be advantageous?
- Accelerated deductions in early years mean little or no deductions in later years.
- Is profit expected to increase in the coming years during the life of the asset? If this is the case, a steady deduction over the life of the asset will allow depreciation in later years.
- Will repair bills be higher in later years? If so, these higher repair bills may offset the lower depreciation in later years that occurs with the declining-balance and the sum-of-the-years'-digits depreciation methods.

| **17.3** | **Exercises** |

Find the sum-of-the-years'-digits depreciation fraction for the first year given the following estimated lives.

1. 4 years   **2.** 3 years   **3.** 6 years   **4.** 5 years

5. 7 years   **6.** 8 years   **7.** 10 years   **8.** 20 years

Find the first year's depreciation for the following using the sum-of-the-years'-digits method of depreciation.

9. Cost: $4800
     Estimated life: 4 years
     Estimated scrap value: $700

10. Cost: $5600
     Estimated life: 5 years
     Estimated scrap value: $800

11. Cost: $60,000
     Estimated life: 10 years
     Estimated scrap value: $5000

12. Cost: $1440
     Estimated life: 8 years
     Estimated scrap value: None

13. Cost: $1350
     Estimated life: 3 years
     Estimated scrap value: $150

14. Cost: $9500
     Estimated life: 8 years
     Estimated scrap value: $1400

Find the book value at the end of the first year for the following using the sum-of-the-years'-digits method of depreciation. Round to the nearest dollar.

15. Cost: $9500
     Estimated life: 8 years
     Estimated scrap value: $1400

16. Cost: $25,000
     Estimated life: 10 years
     Estimated scrap value: None

17. Cost: $3800
     Estimated life: 5 years
     Estimated scrap value: $500

18. Cost: $15,650
     Estimated life: 6 years
     Estimated scrap value: $2000

Find the book value at the end of 3 years for the following using the sum-of-the-years'-digits method of depreciation.

19. Cost: $2240
     Estimated life: 6 years
     Estimated scrap value: $350

20. Cost: $27,500
     Estimated life: 10 years
     Estimated scrap value: None

21. Cost: $4500
     Estimated life: 8 years
     Estimated scrap value: $900

22. Cost: $6600
     Estimated life: 5 years
     Estimated scrap value: $1500

23. Write a description of how the depreciation fraction is determined in any year of an asset's life when using the sum-of-the-years'-digits method of depreciation. (See Objective 2.)

24. If you were starting your own business, what type of business would it be? Which of the three depreciation methods, straight line, double declining balance, or sum of the years' digits, would you decide to use? Why?

Solve the following application problems. Round to the nearest dollar.

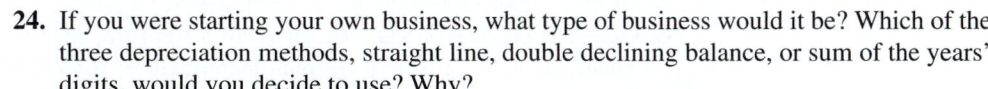

25. COMMERCIAL FREEZER   Big Town Market has purchased a new freezer at a cost of $10,800. The estimated life of the freezer is 6 years, at which time the salvage value is estimated to be $2400. Complete a depreciation schedule using the sum-of-the-years'-digits method of depreciation.

Year	Computation	Amount of Depreciation	Accumulated Depreciation	Book Value
0	—	—	—	$10,800
1				
2				
3				
4				
5				
6				

26. RESTAURANT EQUIPMENT Old South Restaurant has purchased a new steam table for $14,400. The expected life of the unit is 4 years, at which time the salvage value is estimated to be $2400. Complete a depreciation schedule using the sum-of-the-years'-digits method of depreciation.

Year	Computation	Amount of Depreciation	Accumulated Depreciation	Book Value
0	—	—	—	$14,400
1				
2				
3				
4				

27. OFFICE FURNITURE DEPRECIATION Sunset Real Estate Company has purchased office furniture at a cost of $2700. The estimated life of the furniture is 6 years, at which time the salvage value is estimated to be $600. Complete a depreciation schedule using the sum-of-the-years'-digits method of depreciation.

28. FORKLIFT DEPRECIATION Prepare a depreciation schedule for the following forklift using the sum-of-the-years'-digits method of depreciation. Cost is $15,000, estimated life is 10 years, and estimated scrap value is $4000.

29. WATER TAXI Find the depreciation in the third year for a water taxi using the sum-of-the years'-digits method of depreciation. Cost is $60,400, estimated life is 8 years, and estimated scrap value is $4600.

30. HOSPITAL EQUIPMENT Orangevale Rents uses the sum-of-the-years'-digits method of depreciation on all hospital rental equipment. If it purchases new hospital beds at a cost of $12,800 and estimates the life of the beds to be 10 years with no scrap value, find the book value at the end of the fourth year.

31. LIGHT-RAIL TOOLING Electro-car, a light-rail manufacturer, purchased a power-wheel and axle jig from a German manufacturer for $31,880. The jig has an expected life of 20 years and an estimated salvage value of $5000. Find the book value at the end of the third year.

32. SOLAR COLLECTOR Find the depreciation in the third year for a solar collector using the sum-of-the-years'-digits method of depreciation. The cost is $23,000, estimated life is 8 years, and the estimated scrap value is $5000.

33. COMMERCIAL CARPET Mercury Savings Bank has installed new floor covering at a cost of $25,200. It has a useful life of 6 years and no salvage value. Find (a) the first and (b) the second year's depreciation using the sum-of-the-years'-digits method.

34. ASSET DEPRECIATION Using the sum-of-the-years'-digits method of depreciation, find (a) the first and (b) the second year's depreciation for an asset that has a cost of $3375, an estimated life of 5 years and no salvage value.

35. FAST-FOOD RESTAURANTS In-N-Out Burgers purchased a new deep-fry unit at a cost of $12,420. The expected life of the unit is 8 years, with a scrap value of $1800. Use the sum-of-the-years'-digits method of depreciation to find (a) the first year's depreciation fraction, (b) the amount of depreciation in the first year, (c) the accumulated depreciation at the end of the eighth year, and (d) the book value at the end of the fourth year.

36. SEWER DEROOTER Armour Drain bought a new sewer derooter for $6725. The life of the machine is 10 years and the scrap value is $1500. Use the sum-of-the-years'-digits method of depreciation to find (a) the first year's depreciation fraction, (b) the amount of depreciation in the first year, (c) the accumulated depreciation at the end of the tenth year, and (d) the book value at the end of the sixth year.

17.4	**Units-of-Production Method and Partial-Year Depreciation**

OBJECTIVES

1 *Describe the units-of-production method of depreciation.*

2 *Use the units-of-production method to find the depreciation per unit.*

3 *Calculate annual depreciation by the units-of-production method.*

4 *Prepare a depreciation schedule using the units-of-production method.*

5 *Calculate partial-year depreciation by the straight-line method.*

6 *Calculate partial-year depreciation by the double-declining-balance method.*

7 *Calculate partial-year depreciation by the sum-of-the-years'-digits method.*

Objective

1 *Describe the Units-of-Production Method of Depreciation.* An asset often has a useful life given in terms of *units of production* or *units of output,* such as hours of use or miles of service. For example, an airliner or truck may have a useful life given as hours of air time or miles of travel. A steel press or stamping machine may have a life given as the total number of units that it can produce. With these assets, the **units-of-production method** of depreciation is used. Just as with the straight-line method of depreciation, a constant amount of depreciation is taken with the units-of-production method. With the straight-line method a constant amount of depreciation is taken each year. The units-of-production method depreciates a constant amount per unit of use or production.

Objective

2 *Use the Units-of-Production Method to Find the Depreciation per Unit.* Find the depreciation per unit with the following formula.

$$\text{Depreciation per unit} = \frac{\text{Depreciable amount}}{\text{Units of life}}$$

For example, suppose a stump chipper owned by Brent's Tree Service costs $15,000, has a salvage value of $3000, and is expected to operate 700 hours. Find the depreciation per hour of operation by dividing the depreciable amount by the number of hours of life.

The depreciable amount is $15,000 - $3000 = $12,000. Use the formula to find the depreciation per unit.

$$\frac{\$12{,}000 \text{ depreciable amount}}{700 \text{ hours of life}} = \$17.14 \quad \text{Depreciation per hour (rounded)}$$

Objective

3 ***Calculate Annual Depreciation by the Units-of-Production Method.*** Use the following formula and multiply the number of hours the machine was used during the year by the depreciation per unit to find the annual depreciation.

$$\text{Depreciation} = \text{Number of units (hours)} \times \text{Depreciation per unit (hour)}$$

EXAMPLE 1 **Using Units-of-Production Depreciation**

North American Trucking purchased a Kenworth truck for $115,000. The truck has a salvage value of $25,000 and an estimated life of 500,000 miles. Find the depreciation for a year in which the truck is driven 128,000 miles.

Solution   First find the depreciable amount.

$$
\begin{array}{ll}
\$115{,}000 & \text{Cost} \\
-\ 25{,}000 & \text{Scrap value} \\
\hline
\$90{,}000 & \text{Depreciable amount}
\end{array}
$$

Next find the depreciation per unit.

$$\frac{\$90{,}000 \text{ depreciable amount}}{500{,}000 \text{ miles of life}} = \$0.18 \text{ depreciation per mile}$$

Multiply to find the depreciation for the year.

$$128{,}000 \text{ miles} \times \$0.18 = \$23{,}040 \text{ depreciation for the year}$$

 Scientific Calculator Approach

The calculator solution to Example 2 uses parentheses to find the depreciable amount and then chain calculations to find the depreciation amount.

(115000 − 25000) ÷ 500000 = × 128000 = 23040

EXAMPLE 2 **Preparing a Depreciation Schedule**

Global Electronics purchased a shrink-wrapping machine that costs $52,300, has an estimated salvage value of $4000, and has an expected life of 690,000 units. Prepare a depreciation schedule using the units-of-production method of depreciation. Use the following packaging schedule.

Year 1	240,000 units
Year 2	150,000 units
Year 3	90,000 units
Year 4	120,000 units
Year 5	90,000 units

Solution   The depreciable amount is $48,300 ($52,300 − $4000). The depreciation per unit is found as follows.

$$\frac{\$48,300}{690,000 \text{ units}} = \$0.07 \text{ per unit}$$

The annual depreciation is found by multiplying the number of units packaged each year by the depreciation per unit.

Year 1 240,000 units × $0.07 = $16,800
Year 2 150,000 units × $0.07 = $10,500
Year 3 90,000 units × $0.07 = $6,300
Year 4 120,000 units × $0.07 = $8,400
Year 5 90,000 units × $0.07 = $6,300
Total: 690,000 units $48,300 *depreciable amount*

Objective

4   *Prepare a Depreciation Schedule Using the Units-of-Production Method.*   These results were used to help prepare the following depreciation schedule.

Year	Computation	Depreciation	Accumulated Depreciation	Book Value
0	—	—	—	$52,300
1	(240,000 × $0.07)	$16,800	$16,800	35,500
2	(150,000 × $0.07)	10,500	27,300	25,000
3	(90,000 × $0.07)	6,300	33,600	18,700
4	(120,000 × $0.07)	8,400	42,000	10,300
5	(90,000 × $0.07)	6,300	48,300	4,000

NOTE   In Example 2, the book value at the end of year 5 ($4000) is the amount of the salvage value. This is true because the total number of units of life (690,000) has been used up by the machine during the 5 years. The machine may continue in use producing more units; however, no additional depreciation may be taken.

Objective

5   *Calculate Partial-Year Depreciation by the Straight-Line Method.*   So far, each of the examples in depreciation assumed that the depreciable asset was purchased at the beginning of a year. If the asset is purchased during the year, only a fraction of the first year's depreciation may be taken. For example, if an asset is acquired on June 1, only $\frac{7}{12}$ (since 7 months remain) of the first year's depreciation may be taken. For an asset acquired on April 1, only $\frac{9}{12}$, or $\frac{3}{4}$, of the first year's depreciation may be taken. If the asset is purchased at a date other than the first of the month, then count that month for depreciation if purchased on or before the 15th of the month. This **partial-year depreciation** is explained in the following examples.

Each of the methods of depreciation studied so far (except the units-of-production method) is affected differently by a partial year. The units-of-production method is not affected by the partial first year since actual use determines depreciation.

EXAMPLE **3** **Finding Partial-Year Depreciation with Straight-Line**

A jewelry display rack purchased on October 1 at a cost of $6750 has an estimated salvage value of $750 and an expected life of 5 years. Using the straight-line method of depreciation, find the depreciation in the year of purchase.

Solution The depreciation for a full year is

$$\frac{\$6750 - \$750}{5 \text{ years}} = \frac{\$6000}{5} = \$1200$$

Since the purchase date is October 1, 3 months remain in the year. This means that only $\frac{3}{12}$, or $\frac{1}{4}$, of the $1200 may be taken in the year of purchase.

$$\$1200 \times \frac{1}{4} = \$300 \quad \text{Depreciation allowed in the year of purchase}$$

The next 4 years are depreciated at the full $1200 per year and the last 9 months $\left(\frac{3}{4}\right)$ of depreciation, figured as follows, are reported in the sixth calendar year.

$$\$1200 \times \frac{3}{4} = \$900 \quad \text{Partial-year depreciation}$$

As before, the total depreciation over all the years is the depreciable amount, or $6000.

Objective

6 *Calculate Partial-Year Depreciation by the Double-Declining-Balance Method.*

EXAMPLE **4** **Finding Partial-Year Depreciation with Double Declining Balance**

A boat dock with a life of 10 years is installed on April 12 at a cost of $72,000. If the double-declining-balance method is used, find the depreciation for the first partial year and the next full year.

Solution The double-declining-balance rate is 20% $\left(\frac{1}{10} \times 2 = \frac{2}{10} = \frac{1}{5} = 20\%\right)$. Calculate the first year's depreciation.

$$\$72,000 \times 0.2 = \$14,400 \quad \text{Depreciation first full year}$$

Now find the depreciation for 9 months, or $\frac{3}{4}$ year. (Since April 12 is on or before April 15, count all of April.)

$$\$14,400 \times \frac{3}{4} = \$10,800 \quad \text{Partial-year depreciation}$$

The book value (declining balance) is $61,200 ($72,000 − $10,800). Use this book value to find the first full-year depreciation.

$$\$61,200 \text{ declining balance} \times 0.2 = \$12,240$$

The depreciation for the first full year is $12,240. Depreciation for the following years would be calculated as usual. (Make sure that book value does not go below any scrap value.)

Objective

7 *Calculate Partial-Year Depreciation by the Sum-of-the-Years'-Digits Method.*

> **EXAMPLE 5** **Finding Partial-Year Depreciation with Sum of the Years' Digits**
>
> An industrial air-conditioning compressor is purchased on July 1 at a cost of $3800. It is estimated that the compressor will have a life of 4 years and a scrap value of $600. Use the sum-of-the-years'-digits method to find the depreciation for each year of the life of the asset.
>
> **Solution**

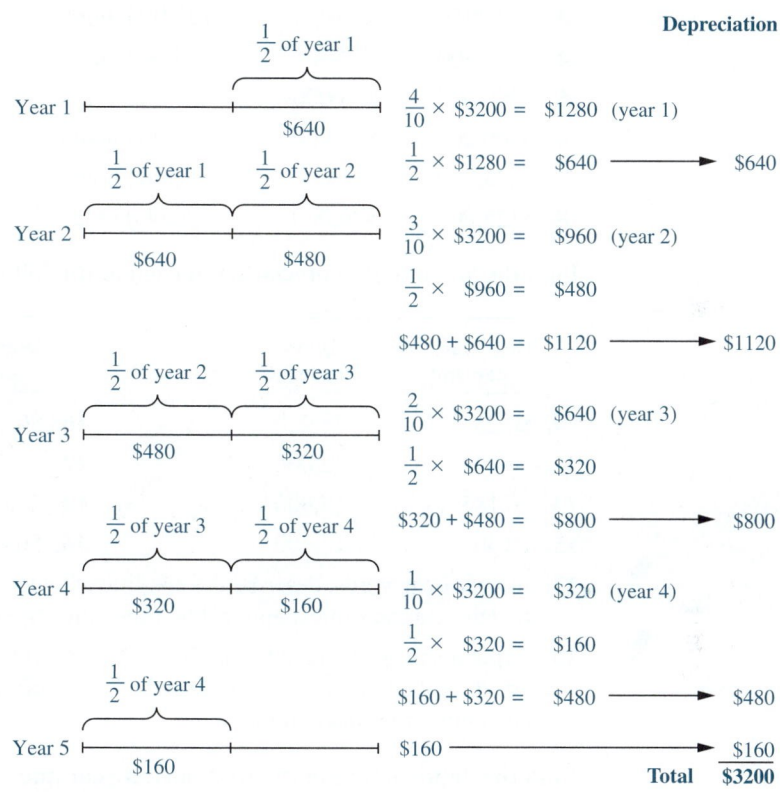

Figure 17.4

The partial year here is $\frac{1}{2}$ (6 months). The depreciation fraction in year 1 is $\frac{4}{10}$ and the depreciable amount is $3200 ($3800 − $600).

$$\frac{4}{10} \times \$3200 = \$1280 \quad \text{Depreciation year 1}$$

$$\$1280 \times \frac{1}{2} = \$640 \quad \text{Partial-year depreciation}$$

Partial-year depreciation in the sum-of-the-years'-digits method requires depreciation in the first full year (year 2) to be the sum of the second half of depreciation in year 1 and the first half of depreciation in year 2. Depreciation in year 3 will be the sum of the second half of year 2 and the first half of year 3 and so on for the remaining life. See Figure 17.4.

> **NOTE** If an asset is purchased on or before the 15th of the month, then count that month for depreciation. However, if an asset is purchased on the 16th of the month or after, begin depreciation with the following month.

| 17.4 | Exercises |

Find the depreciation per unit in each of the following. Round to the nearest thousandth of a dollar.

	Cost	Salvage Value	Estimated Life
1.	$22,500	$1500	60,000 units
2.	$5000	$400	10,000 units
3.	$3750	$250	120,000 units
4.	$7500	$500	15,000 units
5.	$300,000	$25,000	4000 hours
6.	$600,000	$50,000	2000 hours
7.	$175,000	$25,000	5000 hours
8.	$125,000	$20,000	500,000 miles

Find the amount of depreciation in each of the following.

	Depreciation per Unit	Units Produced			Depreciation per Unit	Units Produced
9.	$0.23	78,000		10.	$0.15	380,000
11.	$0.54	32,000		12.	$0.73	16,500
13.	$0.185	15,000		14.	$0.032	73,000
15.	$0.40	17,400		16.	$0.015	180,000

 17. In your own words, describe the conditions under which the units-of-production method of depreciation is most applicable. (See Objective 1.)

 18. Explain salvage value. Discuss how salvage value is used in all four depreciation methods described in this chapter: straight-line, declining-balance, sum-of-the-years'-digits, and units-of-production methods.

Find the depreciation in the first partial year and the next full year for each of the following. Round to the nearest dollar.

	Cost	Salvage Value	Life	Depreciation Method	Date Acquired
19.	$9700	$700	4 years	Straight line	June 1
20.	$5600	$1000	10 years	Straight line	Oct. 1
21.	$20,000	$1000	20 years	Double declining	Mar. 1
22.	$5250	$550	10 years	Double declining	May 1
23.	$3150	None	6 years	Sum of years' digits	July 12
24.	$9600	$600	5 years	Sum of years' digits	Sept. 10
25.	$6300	$900	8 years	Sum of years' digits	Mar. 28
26.	$14,375	$2000	10 years	Sum of years' digits	Apr. 19

Solve the following application problems. Round to the nearest dollar.

27. **GARBAGE COMPACTOR**   Cajun Catfish purchased a garbage compactor at a cost of $6800. The expected life is 5000 hours of production, at which time it will have a salvage value of $500. Prepare a depreciation schedule, using the units-of-production

method, given the following production: year 1: 1350 hours; year 2: 1820 hours; year 3: 730 hours; year 4: 1100 hours.

Year	Computation	Amount of Depreciation	Accumulated Depreciation	Book Value
0	—	—	—	$6800
1				
2				
3				
4				

28. **TRUCKING BUSINESS** Jack Armstrong purchased a small dump truck at a cost of $87,000. He estimates that it is good for 300,000 miles and will have a salvage value of $15,000. Use the units-of-production method to prepare a depreciation schedule given the following production: year 1: 108,000 miles; year 2: 75,000 miles; year 3: 117,000 miles.

Year	Computation	Amount of Depreciation	Accumulated Depreciation	Book Value
0	—	—	—	$87,000
1				
2				
3				

29. **SOFT-DRINK BOTTLING** A small soft-drink bottler purchased an automatic filling and capping machine for $185,000. The machine has a scrap value of $30,000 and an estimated life of 20,000 hours. Find the depreciation for a year in which the machine was in operation 3400 hours.

30. **CARDBOARD RECYCLING** A cardboard crusher costs $13,800, has an estimated salvage value of $2400, and has an expected life of 300,000 units. Find (a) the amount of depreciation each year and (b) the book value at the end of each year. Use the units-of-production method of depreciation given the following production schedule.

Year 1	36,000 units
Year 2	42,000 units
Year 3	39,000 units

31. **LOADER** Ajax Construction purchased a small loader for $156,000 and estimates the life of the machine to be 10 years with a salvage value of $10,000. If the straight-line method of depreciation is used and the system is purchased on October 1, find the first partial-year depreciation and the following full-year's depreciation.

32. **GRANITE COUNTERTOPS** The Copley Square Hotel had new granite countertops installed in the lobby at a cost of $64,400. The countertops have a useful life of 8 years and no salvage value. If the straight-line method of depreciation is used and the granite countertops were installed on March 11, find the first partial-year depreciation and the following full-year's depreciation.

33. **CELL PHONES** Tri-State Insurance Company purchased cellular phones for all outside salespeople at a cost of $4500. The phones were purchased on October 8, the estimated life of the phones is 5 years, and they are expected to have no salvage value. Use the double-declining-balance method of depreciation to find the first partial-year depreciation and the following full-year's depreciation.

34. **AUTOMATED TELEPHONES** Tele-Mation Services purchased a $14,200 auto-dial system on June 25. The estimated life of the system is 8 years and the salvage value is $3000. Use the double-declining-balance method of depreciation to find the first partial-year's depreciation and the following full-year's depreciation.

35. **COMMERCIAL REROOFING** A warehouse had a new roof installed on June 27 at a cost of $44,400. The estimated life is 15 years and there is no scrap value. Use the sum-of-the-years'-digits method to find the first partial-year's depreciation and the following full-year's depreciation.

36. **WAITING ROOM FURNITURE** On September 14, Dr. Umeda purchased new furniture for his office. The cost of the furniture was $7850, the salvage value is $500, and expected life is 6 years. Use the sum-of-the-years'-digits method to find the first partial-year's depreciation and the following full-year's depreciation.

| **17.5** | **Modified Accelerated Cost Recovery System** |

OBJECTIVES

1 *Understand the modified accelerated cost recovery system (MACRS).*

2 *Determine the recovery period of different types of property.*

3 *Find the depreciation rate given the recovery period and recovery year.*

4 *Use the MACRS method to find the amount of depreciation.*

5 *Prepare a depreciation schedule using the MACRS.*

Objective

1 *Understand the Modified Accelerated Cost Recovery System (MACRS).* A depreciation method known as the **accelerated cost recovery system (ACRS)** originated as part of the Economic Recovery Tax Act of 1981. It was later modified by the Tax Equity and Fiscal Responsibility Act of 1982 and again by the Tax Reform Act of 1984. The Tax Reform Act of 1986 brought the most recent and significant overhaul to the accelerated cost recovery system (ACRS) and applies to all property placed in service after 1986. This most recent method is known as the **modified accelerated cost recovery system (MACRS)**. The result is that there are now three systems for computing depreciation for *federal tax purposes.*

Federal Tax Depreciation Methods

1. The MACRS method of depreciation is used for all property placed in service after 1986.
2. The ACRS method of depreciation will continue to be used for all property placed in service from 1981 through 1986.
3. The straight-line, declining-balance, and sum-of-the-years'-digits methods continue to be used if the property was placed in service before 1981.

NOTE The units-of-production method of depreciation is still allowed under the MACRS.

Keep two things in mind about MACRS. First, the system is designed, really, for tax purposes (it is sometimes called the **income tax method**). Businesses often use some alternate method of depreciation (in addition to MACRS) for financial accounting purposes. Second, some states do not allow the modified accelerated cost recovery system of depreciation for finding state income tax liability. This means businesses must use the MACRS on the federal tax return and one of the previous methods on the state tax return.

Objective

2   *Determine the Recovery Period of Different Types of Property.*   Under the modified accelerated cost recovery system, assets are placed in one of nine recovery classes, depending on whether the law assumes a 3-, 5-, 7-, 10-, 15-, 20-, 27.5-, 31.5-, or 39-year life for the asset. These lives, or **recovery periods**, are determined as follows.

MACRS Recovery Classes

3-year property	Tractor units for over-the-road use, any racehorse that is over 2 years old, or any other horse that is over 12 years old
5-year property	Automobiles, taxis, trucks, buses, computers and peripheral equipment, office machinery, faxes, calculators, copiers, and research equipment
7-year property	Office furniture and fixtures (desks, files, safes), and any property not designated by law to be in any other class
10-year-property	Vessels, barges, tugs, and similar water transportation equipment
15-year property	Improvements made directly to land, such as shrubbery, fences, roads, and bridges, and any tree or vine bearing fruits or nuts
20-year property	Certain farm buildings
27.5-year property	Residential rental real estate such as rental houses, apartments, and mobile homes, not including land
31.5-year property	Nonresidential rental real estate such as office buildings, stores, and warehouses if placed in service before May 13, 1993, not including land
39-year property	Nonresidential property placed in service after May 12, 1993, not including land

NOTE   Land may not be depreciated. Only the cost of buildings and other improvements may be depreciated.

EXAMPLE 1   **Finding the Recovery Period for Property**

Rancher's Supply owns the following assets. Determine the recovery period for each of them.

(a) Computer equipment
(b) An industrial warehouse (after May 12, 1993)
(c) A pickup truck
(d) Office furniture
(e) A farm building (storage shed)

Solution   Use the list just given.

(a) 5 years
(b) 39 years
(c) 5 years
(d) 7 years
(e) 20 years

Objective

3   *Find the Depreciation Rate Given the Recovery Period and Recovery Year.*   With MACRS, salvage value is ignored so that *depreciation is based on the original cost of the asset.* The depreciation rates are determined by applying the double-declining-balance (200%) method

Table 17.1 **MACRS DEPRECIATION RATES**

Recovery Year	Applicable Percent for the Class of Property								
	3-year	5-year	7-year	10-year	15-year	20-year	27.5-year	31.5-year	39-year
1	33.33	20.00	14.29	10.00	5.00	3.750	1.818	1.587	2.568
2	44.45	32.00	24.49	18.00	9.50	7.219	3.636	3.175	2.564
3	14.81	19.20	17.49	14.40	8.55	6.677	3.636	3.175	2.564
4	7.41	11.52	12.49	11.52	7.70	6.177	3.636	3.175	2.564
5		11.52	8.93	9.22	6.93	5.713	3.636	3.175	2.564
6		5.76	8.92	7.37	6.23	5.285	3.636	3.175	2.564
7			8.93	6.55	5.90	4.888	3.636	3.175	2.564
8			4.46	6.55	5.90	4.522	3.636	3.175	2.564
9				6.56	5.91	4.462	3.637	3.175	2.564
10				6.55	5.90	4.461	3.636	3.174	2.564
11				3.28	5.91	4.462	3.637	3.175	2.564
12					5.90	4.461	3.636	3.174	2.564
13					5.91	4.462	3.637	3.175	2.564
14					5.90	4.461	3.636	3.174	2.564
15					5.91	4.462	3.637	3.175	2.564
16					2.95	4.461	3.636	3.174	2.564
17						4.462	3.637	3.175	2.564
18						4.461	3.636	3.174	2.564
19						4.462	3.637	3.175	2.564
20						4.461	3.636	3.174	2.564
21						2.231	3.637	3.175	2.564
22							3.636	3.174	2.564
23							3.637	3.175	2.564
24							3.636	3.174	2.564
25							3.637	3.175	2.564
26							3.636	3.174	2.564
27							3.637	3.175	2.564
28							3.636	3.174	2.564
29								3.175	2.564
30								3.174	2.564
31								3.175	2.564
32								3.174	2.564
33–39									2.564

Modified Accelerated Cost Recovery System (MACRS)

Useful Items
You may want to see:

Publication

☐ **225** Farmer's Tax Guide

☐ **463** Travel, Entertainment, and Gift Expenses

☐ **544** Sales and Other Dispositions of Assets

☐ **581** Basis of Assets

☐ **583** Taxpayers Starting a Business

☐ **587** Business Use of Your Home

☐ **917** Business Use of a Car

Source: IRS

to the 3-, 5-, 7-, and 10-year class properties, the 150% declining-balance method to the 15- and 20-year class properties, and the straight-line (100%) method to the 27.5-, 31.5-, and 39-year class properties. Since these calculations are repetitive and require additional knowledge, the Internal Revenue Service provides tables that show the depreciation rates expressed as percents. The rates are shown in Table 17.1. To determine the rate of depreciation for any year of life, find the recovery year in the left-hand column and then read across to the allowable recovery period.

Notice that the number of recovery years is one greater than the class life of the property. This is because only a half-year of depreciation is allowed for the first year the property is placed in service (for 31.5-year property or less), regardless of when the property is placed in service during the year. This is known as the **half-year convention** and is used by most taxpayers. Complete coverage of depreciation, including all depreciation tables, is provided in Internal Revenue Service **Publication 534**, *Depreciation*, and may be obtained by contacting the IRS Forms Distribution Center. Publication 534 lists several items that the taxpayer or tax preparer might find useful and is shown to the left.

NOTE MACRS is the income tax method of depreciation; several important points should be remembered.

1. No salvage value is used.
2. The life of the asset is determined by using the recovery periods assigned to different types of property.
3. A depreciation rate is usually found for each year by referring to a MACRS table of depreciation rates.

EXAMPLE 2 **Finding the Rate of Depreciation with MACRS**

Use Table 17.1 to find the rate of depreciation given the following recovery year and recovery period.

	(a)	(b)	(c)	(d)
Recovery year	4	2	3	9
Recovery period	5 years	3 years	10 years	27.5 years

Solution

(a) 11.52% (b) 44.45% (c) 14.40% (d) 3.637%

Objective

4 *Use the MACRS Method to Find the Amount of Depreciation.* No salvage value is subtracted from the cost of property. Under the MACRS method, the depreciation rate multiplied by the original cost determines the depreciation amount. Depreciation by the MACRS method is given by

$$d = r \times c$$

where d is the depreciation for a rate r (from Table 17.1) and an original cost c.

EXAMPLE 3 **Finding the Amount of Depreciation with MACRS**

Village Nursery and Landscaping purchased a pickup truck. Find the amount of depreciation in the third year if the truck had a cost of $21,500.

Solution A pickup truck has a recovery period of 5 years. From Table 17.1, the depreciation rate in the third year of recovery of 5-year property is 19.20%. Multiply this rate by the full cost of the property to determine the amount of depreciation.

$$19.20\% \times \$21,500 = \$4128$$

The amount of depreciation is $4128.

Objective

5 *Prepare a Depreciation Schedule Using the MACRS.*

EXAMPLE 4 **Preparing a Depreciation Schedule with MACRS**

Omaha Insurance Agency purchased desks and chairs at a cost of $24,160. Prepare a depreciation schedule using the modified accelerated cost recovery system.

Solution No salvage value is used with MACRS. Office desks and chairs have a 7-year recovery period. The annual depreciation rates for 7-year property from Table 17.1 are as follows.

Recovery Year	Recovery Percent (Rate)
1	14.29%
2	24.49%
3	17.49%
4	12.49%
5	8.93%
6	8.92%
7	8.93%
8	4.46%

Multiply the appropriate percents by $24,160 to get the results shown in the following depreciation schedule.

Year	Computation	Amount of Depreciation	Accumulated Depreciation	Book Value
0	—	—	—	$24,160
1	(14.29% × $24,160)	$3452	$3,452	20,708
2	(24.49% × $24,160)	5917	9,369	14,791
3	(17.49% × $24,160)	4226	13,595	10,565
4	(12.49% × $24,160)	3018	16,613	7,547
5	(8.93% × $24,160)	2157	18,770	5,390
6	(8.92% × $24,160)	2155	20,925	3,235
7	(8.93% × $24,160)	2157	23,082	1,078
8	(4.46% × $24,160)	1078	24,160	0

The MACRS method of depreciation allows a rapid rate of investment recovery and at the same time results in a less complicated computation. By eliminating the necessity of estimating the life of an asset and the need for using a salvage value, the tables provide a more direct method of calculating depreciation.

17.5 | Exercises

Use Table 17.1 to find the recovery percent (rate) given the following recovery year and recovery period.

	Recovery Year	Recovery Period			Recovery Year	Recovery Period
1.	3	5 years		**2.**	2	3 years
3.	4	10 years		**4.**	1	7 years
5.	1	5 years		**6.**	2	20 years
7.	14	27.5 years		**8.**	10	31.5 years
9.	6	5 years		**10.**	4	27.5 years
11.	14	39 years		**12.**	4	31.5 years

Find the first-year's depreciation for each of the following using the MACRS method of depreciation. Round to the nearest dollar.

| 13. | Cost: | $12,250 |
| | Recovery period: | 7 years |

| 14. | Cost: | $8790 |
| | Recovery period: | 5 years |

| 15. | Cost: | $9680 |
| | Recovery period: | 3 years |

| 16. | Cost: | $72,300 |
| | Recovery period: | 20 years |

| 17. | Cost: | $48,000 |
| | Recovery period: | 10 years |

| 18. | Cost: | $786,400 |
| | Recovery period: | 31.5 years |

Find the book value at the end of the first year for each of the following using the MACRS method of depreciation. Round to the nearest dollar.

| 19. | Cost: | $9380 |
| | Recovery period: | 3 years |

| 20. | Cost: | $32,750 |
| | Recovery period: | 10 years |

| 21. | Cost: | $18,800 |
| | Recovery period: | 10 years |

| 22. | Cost: | $137,000 |
| | Recovery period: | 27.5 years |

Find the book value at the end of 3 years for each of the following using the MACRS method of depreciation. Round to the nearest dollar.

| 23. | Cost: | $9570 |
| | Recovery period: | 5 years |

| 24. | Cost: | $6500 |
| | Recovery period: | 3 years |

| 25. | Cost: | $87,300 |
| | Recovery period: | 27.5 years |

| 26. | Cost: | $390,800 |
| | Recovery period: | 31.5 years |

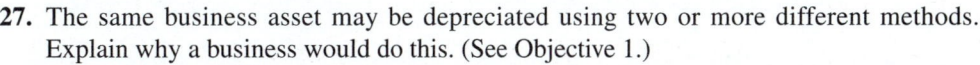

27. The same business asset may be depreciated using two or more different methods. Explain why a business would do this. (See Objective 1.)

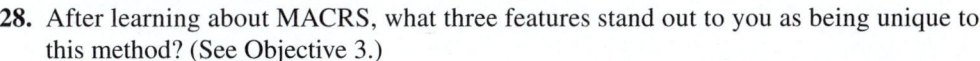

28. After learning about MACRS, what three features stand out to you as being unique to this method? (See Objective 3.)

Solve the following application problems. Use Table 17.1. Round to the nearest dollar.

29. RACE HORSE Rocking Horse Ranch purchased a race horse for $10,980. Prepare a depreciation schedule using the MACRS method of depreciation (3-year property).

Year	Computation	Amount of Depreciation	Accumulated Depreciation	Book Value
0	—	—	—	$10,980
1				
2				
3				
4				

30. COMPANY VEHICLES Village Nursery and Landscaping purchased a pickup truck at a cost of $21,500. Prepare a depreciation schedule using the MACRS method of depreciation (5-year property).

Year	Computation	Amount of Depreciation	Accumulated Depreciation	Book Value
0	—	—	—	$21,500
1				
2				
3				
4				
5				
6				

31. **OFFSHORE DRILLING** South Texas Drilling purchased a mud pump to circulate fluids when drilling wells for $122,700. Prepare a depreciation schedule using the MACRS method of depreciation.

32. **RESIDENTIAL RENTAL PROPERTY** Andy Kirkpatrick purchased some nonresidential rental real estate before May 12, 1993, for $415,000, not including land. Prepare a depreciation schedule for the first 10 years using the MACRS method of depreciation (31.5-year property).

33. **CORPORATE COMPUTERS** Beacon Engineering spent $285,000 for high-end workstations and associated network equipment. Find the book value at the end of the third year using the MACRS method of depreciation.

34. **DENTAL OFFICE FURNITURE** Harry Tepper, DDS, purchased new office furniture for the reception area of his dental office at a cost of $27,400. Find the book value at the end of the fifth year using the MACRS method of depreciation.

35. **OFFICE BUILDING** Brailey Bookkeeping purchased an office building. The value of the building was $480,000, not including the land. Find the amount of depreciation for each of the first 5 years using the MACRS method of depreciation (39-year property).

36. **INDEPENDENT BOOKSTORE** Maretha Roseborough, owner of the Barnstormer Bookstore, bought a building to use for her business. The cost of the building was $220,000, not including land. Find the amount of depreciation for each of the first 5 years using the MACRS method of depreciation (39-year property).

CHAPTER TERMS

Review the following terms to test your understanding of the chapter. For each term you do not know, refer to the page number found next to that term.

200% method [p. 603]
accelerated cost recovery
  system (ACRS) [p. 622]
accelerated depreciation
  [p. 602]
accumulated depreciation
  [p. 596 or 597]
book value [p. 596 or 597]
cost [p. 596]
declining-balance method
  [p. 602]

depreciable amount
  [p. 596]
depreciation [p. 595]
depreciation fraction
  [p. 608]
depreciation schedule
  [p. 599]
double-declining-balance
  method [p. 603]
half-year convention
  [p. 624]

income tax method [p. 622]
modified accelerated cost
  recovery system
  (MACRS) [p. 622]
no salvage value
  [p. 596 or 598]
partial-year depreciation
  [p. 617]
Publication 534 [p. 624]
recovery classes [p. 623]
recovery periods [p. 623]

residual value [p. 596]
salvage value [p. 596]
scrap value [p. 596]
straight-line method [p. 596]
sum-of-the-years'-digits
  method [p. 608]
tangible assets [p. 596]
units-of-production method
  [p. 615]
useful life [p. 596]

CONCEPTS

EXAMPLES

17.1 Straight-line method of depreciation

The depreciation is the same each year. Use the formula

$$d = \frac{c - s}{n}$$

with c = cost, s = salvage value, and n = life (in years).

Cost, $500; scrap value, $100; life of 8 years; find the annual amount of depreciation.

$$d = \frac{\$500 - \$100}{8} = \frac{\$400}{8} = \$50$$

17.1 Book value

Book value is the value remaining at the end of the year.

Book value = Cost − Accumulated depreciation

Cost, $400; scrap value, $100; life of 3 years; find the book value at the end of the first year.

$$d = \frac{\$400 - \$100}{3} = \frac{\$300}{3} = \$100$$

Book value = $400 − $100 = $300

17.2 Declining-balance rate

First, find the straight-line rate, then adjust it as follows.

  200%: Multiply by 2.
  150%: Multiply by $1\frac{1}{2}$.
  125%: Multiply by $1\frac{1}{4}$.

Life of an asset is 10 years. Find the double-declining-balance (200%) rate.

$$10 \text{ years} = 10\% \left(\frac{1}{10}\right) \text{ straight line}$$

$$2 \times 10\% = 20\%$$

17.2 Double-declining-balance depreciation method

First, find the double-declining-balance rate; then use the formula

$$d = r \times b$$

where b is total cost in the first year and the declining balance in the following years.

Cost, $1400; life of 5 years; find the depreciation in years 1 and 2 ($2 \times 20\%$ [straight-line rate] = 40%.)

Year 1:

$$\text{Depreciation} = 40\% \times \$1400 = \$560$$
$$\text{Book value} = \$1400 - \$560 = \$840$$

Year 2:

$$\text{Depreciation} = 40\% \times \$840 = \$336$$

17.3 Sum-of-years'-digits depreciation fraction

Add the years' digits together to get the denominator. The numerator is the number of years of life remaining at the beginning of the year. The denominator shortcut is as follows.

$$\text{Sum of the years' digits} = \frac{n(n + 1)}{2}$$

Useful life is 4 years; find the depreciation fraction for each year.

$$1 + 2 + 3 + 4 = 10$$

Year	Depreciation Fraction
1	$\frac{4}{10}$
2	$\frac{3}{10}$
3	$\frac{2}{10}$
4	$\frac{1}{10}$

17.3 Sum-of-years'-digits depreciation method

First find the depreciation fraction, and then use the formula.

$$d = r \times (c - s)$$

Cost, \$2500; salvage value, \$400; life of 6 years; find depreciation in year 1.

$$\text{Depreciation fraction} = \frac{6}{21}$$

$$d = \frac{6}{21} \times (\$2500 - \$400)$$

$$= \frac{6}{21} \times \$2100 = \$600$$

17.4 Units-of-production depreciation amount

Use the following formula.

$$\text{Depreciation per unit} = \frac{\text{Depreciable amount}}{\text{Units of life}}$$

Cost, \$10,000; salvage value, \$2500; useful life of 15,000 units; find depreciation per unit.

$$\frac{\text{Depreciation}}{\text{per unit}} = \frac{\$7500 \text{ depreciable amount}}{15{,}000 \text{ units of life}} = \$0.50$$

17.4 Units-of-production depreciation method

Multiply the number of units (hours) of production by the depreciation per unit (per hour).

Depreciation = Number of units (hours)
× Depreciation per unit (hour)

In the preceding example: the first year's production is 3800 units. Find depreciation in year 1.

$$3800 \times \$0.50 = \$1900$$

17.4 Partial-year depreciation

If an asset is purchased during the year, take only a fraction of the year's depreciation.

Depreciable amount, \$4500; life, 5 years; date purchased, June 7. Find first partial-year depreciation by the straight-line method.

$$7 \text{ months} = \frac{7}{12} \text{ year}$$

$$\frac{\$4500}{5} \times \frac{7}{12} = \$525$$

17.5 Modified accelerated cost recovery system (MACRS)

Established in 1986 for federal income tax. No salvage value. Recovery periods are:

3-year	5-year	7-year
10-year	15-year	20-year
27.5-year	31.5-year	39-year

Find the proper rate from the table and then multiply by the cost to find depreciation.

Use Table 17.1 to find the recovery period column at the top of the table and the recovery year in the left-hand column. Cost: $4850; recovery period 5 years; recovery year, 3; find the depreciation.

Find 5-year recovery period column at top of Table 17.1, and recovery year 3 in leftmost column; rate is 19.20%.

$$d = 19.20\% \times \$4850 = \$931.20$$

CHAPTER 17   Review Exercises

The answer section includes answers to all Review Exercises.

Find the annual straight-line and double-declining-balance rates (percents) of depreciation and the sum-of-the-years'-digits fractions in the first year for each of the following estimated lives. **[17.1–17.3]**

1. 5 years

2. 6 years

3. 4 years

4. 10 years

5. 20 years

6. 8 years

Use Table 17.1 to find the recovery percent (rate) given the following recovery year and recovery period. **[17.5]**

	Recovery Year	Recovery Period			Recovery Year	Recovery Period
7.	4	5-year		**8.**	1	3-year
9.	8	20-year		**10.**	3	7-year
11.	20	39-year		**12.**	20	31.5-year

Solve the following application problems. Round to the nearest dollar if necessary.

13. Cloverdale Creamery purchased an ice cream machine at a cost of $12,400. The machine has an estimated life of 10 years and a scrap value of $3000. Use the straight-line method of depreciation to find the annual depreciation. **[17.1]**

14. The water filtration system at Jackson Micro Brew costs $296,000, has an estimated life of 20 years, and an estimated scrap value of $48,000. Use the straight-line method of depreciation to find the book value of the machinery at the end of 10 years. **[17.1]**

15. Sunset Swimming Pools purchased a dump truck for $38,000. If the estimated life of the dump truck is 8 years, find the book value at the end of 2 years using the double-declining-balance method of depreciation. **[17.2]**

16. Star Bushing Company bought three drill presses from a Belgian firm at a total cost of $18,500. The estimated life of the drill presses is 5 years, and there is no scrap value. Find the depreciation in the first year using the double-declining-balance method of depreciation. **[17.2]**

17. The Feather River Youth Camp purchased a diesel generator for $8250. Use the sum-of-the-years'-digits method of depreciation to determine the amount of depreciation to be taken during *each of the 4 years* on the diesel generator that has a 4-year life and scrap value of $1500. **[17.3]**

18. Murray's Delicatessen purchased a new display case for $7375. It has an estimated life of 10 years and a salvage value of $500. Use the sum-of-the-years'-digits method of depreciation to find the book value at the end of the third year. **[17.3]**

19. A grape press costs $11,000, has a scrap value of $2500, and an estimated life of 5000 hours. Use the units-of-production method to find the depreciation for a year in which the machine was in operation 900 hours. **[17.4]**

20. Table Fresh Foods purchased a machine to package their presliced garden salads. The machine costs $20,100, has an estimated life of 30,000 hours, and a salvage value of $1500. Use the units-of-production method of depreciation to find (a) the annual amount of depreciation and (b) the book value at the end of each year, given the following use information: year 1: 7800 hours; year 2: 4300 hours; year 3: 4850 hours; year 4: 7600 hours. **[17.4]**

21. The Fashion Express purchased new clothing racks at a cost of $22,400. Using the straight-line method of depreciation, a 5-year life, and a scrap value of $3500, find the accumulated depreciation at the end of the fourth year. **[17.1]**

22. Using the sum-of-the-years'-digits method of depreciation, find the amount of depreciation to be charged off each year on a tour bus purchased by Bayside Tours. The bus has a cost of $85,000, an estimated life of 5 years, and a scrap value of $13,000. **[17.3]**

23. A recycled glass crusher costs $48,000, has an estimated life of 5 years, and a scrap value of $4500. If the straight-line method of depreciation is used and the system is purchased on September 10, find the first partial-year depreciation. **[17.4]**

24. A parking lot is resurfaced on June 1 at a cost of $9720. The estimated life is 8 years and there is no scrap value. Use the sum-of-the-years'-digits method to find the first partial-year depreciation and the following full-year's depreciation. **[17.4]**

25. Instant Copy Service purchased a new copy system at a cost of $28,400 on June 19. The estimated life of the system is 10 years and the salvage value is $6000. Use the double-declining-balance method of depreciation to find the first partial-year depreciation and the following full-year's depreciation. **[17.4]**

26. Karl Schmidt, owner of Toy Train Hobby, has added paging and intercom features to the communication systems of his four stores at a cost of $2800 per store. The estimated life of the systems is 10 years, with no expected salvage value. Using the sum-of-the-years'-digits method of depreciation, find the total book value of all the systems at the end of the third year. **[17.3]**

27. A book printer purchased an automatic composer at a cost of $15,000. If the estimated life of the composer is 8 years, find the book value at the end of 4 years, using the double-declining-balance method of depreciation. Assume no scrap value. **[17.2]**

28. Reef Fisheries purchased a commercial fishing boat for $222,375. The life of the boat is estimated to be 10 years and the scrap value is $45,000. Use the sum-of-the-years'-digits method of depreciation to find the book value of the fishing boat at the end of the fourth year. **[17.3]**

29. King's Table bought new dining room tables at a cost of $14,750. If the estimated life of the tables is 8 years, at which time they will be worthless, and the double-declining-balance method of depreciation is used, find the book value at the end of the third year. **[17.2]**

30. A private road costs $56,000 and has a 15-year recovery period. Find the depreciation in the third year using the MACRS method of depreciation. **[17.5]**

31. Kathy Woodward purchased a new refrigeration system (7-year property) for her flower shop at a cost of $8100. Find the amount of depreciation for each of the first 5 years using the MACRS method of depreciation. **[17.5]**

32. The Rice Growers Cooperative paid $2,800,000 to build a new rice-drying plant in 2007. The recovery period is 39 years. Use the MACRS method of depreciation to find the book value of the rice-drying plant at the end of the fifth year. **[17.5]**

33. The UPS Store purchased a new copy machine at a cost of $9480. Use the straight-line method of depreciation to find the amount of depreciation that should be charged off each year if the equipment has an estimated life of 4 years and a scrap value of $1500. **[17.1]**

34. The Music Circus has just installed new seating at a total cost of $228,000. The estimated life of the seating is 10 years, there is no salvage value, and the double-declining-balance method of depreciation is used. Find the depreciation in the first year. **[17.1]**

CHAPTER 17	Business Application Case #1
	Comparing Depreciation Methods

Trader Joe's purchased freezer cases at a cost of $285,000. The estimated life of the freezer cases is 5 years, at which time they will have no salvage value. The company would like to compare allowable depreciation methods and decides to prepare depreciation schedules for the fixtures using the straight-line, double-declining-balance, and the sum-of-the-years'-digits methods of depreciation. Using these depreciation schedules, find the answer to these questions for Trader Joe's.

(a) What is the book value at the end of 3 years using the straight-line depreciation method?

(b) Using the double-declining-balance method of depreciation, what is the book value at the end of the third year?

(c) With the sum-of-the-year's-digits method of depreciation, what is the accumulated depreciation at the end of 3 years?

(d) What amount of depreciation will be taken in year 4 with each of the methods?

CHAPTER 17	Business Application Case #2
	Effect of Depreciation on Corporate Taxes

The top accountant at Baja Oil Sands Operations wants to examine the effect of depreciation on income taxes for the next 10 years at the firm. The firm spends $28,400,000 for a variety of equipment for its oil-sands mining operation in Alberta, Canada. It has no salvage value at the end of its useful life. Based on research, the accountant determines that in this particular situation, it is possible for the equipment to fall either into the 5-year or the 7-year property MACRS definition, depending on several factors. The tax savings for one year is the amount of depreciation multiplied by the corporate tax rate of 40%, which includes federal and state taxes. Complete the following table.

Year	5-year MACRS	Depreciation	Tax Savings	7-year MACRS	Depreciation	Tax Savings
1						
2						
3						
4						
5						
6						
7						
8						
9						
10						

Since the total depreciation and the tax rate is the same either way, the total tax savings is the same. However, the 5-year MACRS results in quicker tax savings, but no tax savings at all after year 6. Management should make sure that the appropriate category of MACRS is used. If either can be used in this particular situation, then management can choose the option that is best for the firm.

Financial Statements and Ratios

The financial crisis that began in 2007 had a huge effect on most manufacturers and retailers around the world. For example, Figure 18.1 shows seasonally adjusted sales of new cars and light trucks in the United States in millions of cars. After many years of growth, U.S. sales peaked early in 2007. Sales continued to fall throughout 2008 and fell sharply at the end of the year, as stock markets fell and unemployment rapidly increased. By the beginning of 2009, U.S. automobile sales had plunged by over 40% from the peak. In this very chaotic environment, managers of global supply chains tried to quickly reduce the amount of inventory moving to final assembly and to automobile dealerships. To do so, they needed accurate forecasts of demand so that they could tell their suppliers what to produce and when to ship. However, forecasting had become extremely difficult, and managers struggled with many issues, including too much inventory on hand.

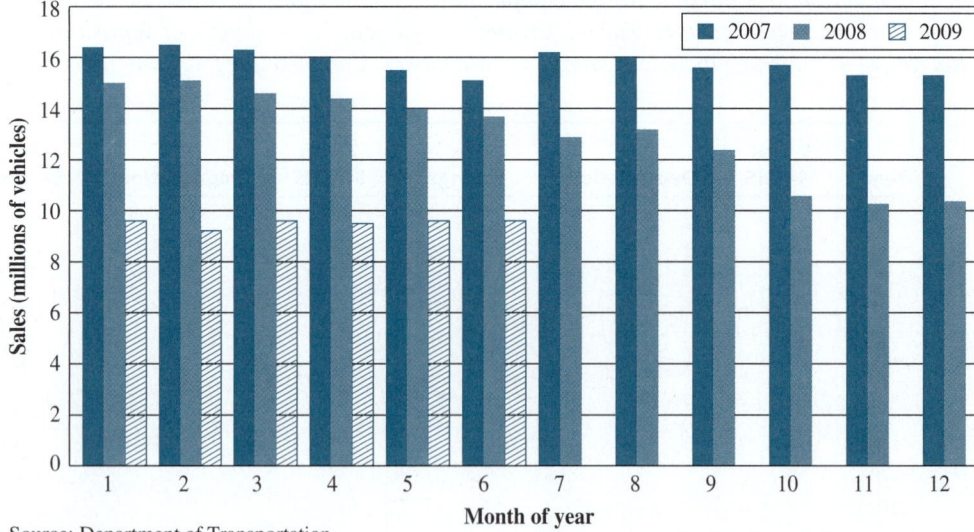

U.S. Sales of New Cars and Light Trucks (Seasonally Adjusted)

Source: Department of Transportation.

Figure 18.1

STOP
— and think

Even in normal times, it is very difficult to make an accurate forecast of future demand. What is the effect if managers in a global supply chain such as automobile manufacturing make a forecast of demand that is too high? Too low? Using only the data in Figure 18.1, what is your best guess for sales for the next three months? Would you predict sales to return to the levels of early 2008? Why or why not?

Business owners and managers must keep careful records of the expenses and income of their business. They need these records to help them manage the business, to inform other owners of current operations, to provide required information to lenders from whom they wish to borrow money, and for tax purposes.

Accountants are the employees who do the work of keeping track of income and expenses. They are concerned with issues such as meeting payroll, paying suppliers on time, and estimating and paying taxes, as well as estimating and handling revenues. This chapter covers some of the tools used by managers, accountants, lenders, and investors when looking at the financial health of a firm.

18.1 The Income Statement

OBJECTIVES

1 *Learn the terms used with income statements.*

2 *Understand the income statement of Wal-Mart.*

3 *Complete an income statement.*

In this chapter, we look at the financial statements of Wal-Mart Stores, Inc., the largest retailer in the world. Wal-Mart is a global company that buys goods produced around the world, especially products made in China. Products are shipped to one of the 6000+ Wal-Mart retail outlets located in over 15 countries. Wal-Mart is the largest private employer in the world, with over 2,000,000 associates according to its Web site, www.walmartstores.com. Shares of Wal-Mart trade on the New York Stock Exchange under the symbol WMT.

Objective

1 *Learn the Terms Used with Income Statements.* An **income statement** is used to summarize all income and expenses for a company for a given period of time such as a month, a quarter, or a year. Here are some important definitions related to financial statements.

> **Gross sales** or **total revenue** is the total amount of money received from customers.
> **Returns** are returns made by customers (usually used by smaller companies and not large ones).
> **Net sales** is the value of goods and services bought and kept by customers.
>
> $$\text{Net sales} = \text{Gross sales} - \text{Returns}$$
>
> **Cost of goods sold** is the amount paid by the firm for the items sold to customers.
> **Gross profit** or **Gross profit on** sales is the money left over after a firm pays for the cost of goods it sells.
>
> $$\text{Gross profit} = \text{Net sales} - \text{Cost of goods sold}$$
>
> **Operating expenses** or **overhead** is the firm's cost to run the business.
> **Net income before taxes** is the amount earned by the firm before income taxes are paid.
>
> $$\text{Net income before taxes} = \text{Gross profit} - \text{Operating expenses}$$
>
> **Net income** or **Net income after taxes** is the income remaining after income taxes have been paid.
>
> $$\text{Net income} = \text{Net income before taxes} - \text{Income taxes}$$

Banks do not wish to lend money to firms that may not be able to repay their loans. As a result, a bank will usually want to see all of the values identified in this section so far, in addition to other data, before making a loan to a firm. The values introduced here are typically included in an income statement, which we will now examine.

Objective

2 *Understand the Income Statement of Wal-Mart.* A portion of Wal-Mart's 2008 annual income statement is shown in Example 1. Rather than using a **calendar year** of January 1 to December 31 to report financial results as most individuals do, Wal-Mart uses a **fiscal year**. Its fiscal year for reporting purposes starts in February 1 of one year and ends January 31 of the following year. In this chapter, we will look at the financial statements for 2008, or for the fiscal year that ended January 31, 2008.

EXAMPLE 1 Finding Net Income

In fiscal year 2008, Wal-Mart had gross sales and other income of $378,799,000,000. (a) Write this number using words. Since the numbers are very large, we will round them to the nearest million dollars throughout the chapter. (b) Examine the income statement and identify the net income.

Solution

(a) 378,799,000,000 = Three hundred seventy-eight billion, seven hundred ninety-nine million

(b)

WAL-MART STORES, INC.
CONSOLIDATED STATEMENT OF INCOME
FISCAL YEAR ENDING JANUARY 31, 2008
(in millions of U.S. dollars)

Total revenue	$378,799
Cost of goods sold	−286,515
Gross profit	92,284
Operating expenses and other	− 72,645
Net income before taxes	19,639
Income taxes	− 6,908
Net income after taxes	$ 12,731

In 2008, Wal-Mart paid nearly $7 billion in income taxes and had an after-tax net income, or profit, of more than $12 billion. Check the numbers as follows:

Cost of goods sold	$286,515
Operating expenses and other	72,645
Income taxes	6,908
Net income after taxes	12,731
Total revenue	$378,799

Wal-Mart did much better during the financial crisis year of 2008 than many companies because its very low prices appealed to many cost-conscious shoppers.

■

The value of a company's stock is based on *financial results* and *perceived opportunities in the near future*. As a publicly held corporation, Wal-Mart must publish both quarterly and annual financial results and make them widely available. Generally, a firm's stock price rises when the company is doing well and the economy looks good. Similarly, stock prices tend to fall when the company is doing poorly and/or the economy is not healthy. You can obtain financial information about Wal-Mart from many financial Web sites or from the company's Web pages.

Objective

3 *Complete an Income Statement.* Example 1 gives the value for the cost of goods sold, whereas this amount would normally need to be calculated. The cost of goods sold can be found using the formula below. **Initial inventory** is the at-cost value of all goods on hand for sale at the beginning of the period, and **ending inventory** is the at-cost value of all goods on hand for sale at the end of the period.

$$\begin{array}{l} \text{Initial (or beginning) inventory} \\ + \text{ Cost of goods purchased during time period} \\ + \text{ Freight} \\ \underline{- \text{ Ending inventory}} \\ \text{Cost of goods sold} \end{array}$$

EXAMPLE **2** **Preparing an Income Statement**

One quarter, Lawn Equipment Co. had gross sales of $159,000 with returns of $9000. Inventory at the beginning of the quarter was $47,000. A total of $104,000 worth of goods was purchased during the quarter, with freight on the goods totaling $2000. Inventory at the end of the quarter was $56,000. Wages paid to employees totaled $18,000. Rent was $9000, advertising was $1000, utilities totaled $2000, and taxes on inventory and payroll totaled $4000. Miscellaneous expenses totaled $6000 and corporate income taxes were $500. Complete an income statement for the store.

Solution Go through the steps that follow, which refer to the income statement in Figure 18.2.

Working Through an Income Statement

STEP 1 Enter gross sales and sales returns. Subtract sales returns from gross sales to find net sales. Net sales in this example were $150,000.

STEP 2 Enter the cost of goods purchased and the freight. Add these two numbers.

STEP 3 Add the inventory at the beginning of the quarter and the total cost of goods purchased to find total of goods available for sale.

STEP 4 Subtract the inventory at the end of the quarter from the result of Step 3. This gives the cost of goods sold.

STEP 5 Subtract the cost of goods sold from net sales, which were found in Step 1. The result is the gross profit.

STEP 6 Enter all expenses and add them to get the total expenses.

STEP 7 Subtract the total expenses from the gross profit to find the net income before taxes.

STEP 8 Subtract income taxes from net income before taxes to find net income after taxes.

NOTE Be sure to check the results of your income statement by adding the cost of goods sold, expenses, and net income before taxes. This total should equal net sales.

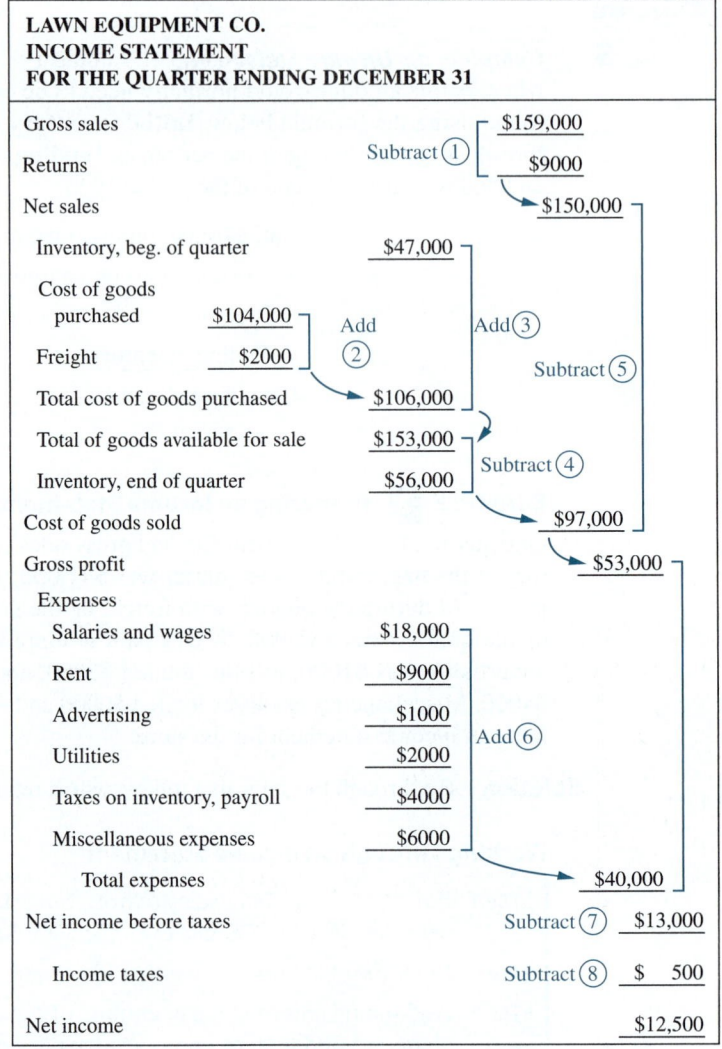

```
LAWN EQUIPMENT CO.
INCOME STATEMENT
FOR THE QUARTER ENDING DECEMBER 31
```

Gross sales		$159,000
Returns	Subtract ①	$9000
Net sales		$150,000
Inventory, beg. of quarter	$47,000	
Cost of goods purchased	$104,000	Add ③
Freight	$2000	Add ② Subtract ⑤
Total cost of goods purchased	$106,000	
Total of goods available for sale	$153,000	
Inventory, end of quarter	$56,000	Subtract ④
Cost of goods sold		$97,000
Gross profit		$53,000
Expenses		
Salaries and wages	$18,000	
Rent	$9000	
Advertising	$1000	
Utilities	$2000	Add ⑥
Taxes on inventory, payroll	$4000	
Miscellaneous expenses	$6000	
Total expenses		$40,000
Net income before taxes	Subtract ⑦	$13,000
Income taxes	Subtract ⑧	$ 500
Net income		$12,500

Figure 18.2

18.1 Exercises

Find (a) the gross profit, (b) the net income before taxes, and (c) the net income after taxes for each firm.

1. **BIKE STORE** Janis Jacobs opened a bike store in the mall 3 years ago. Last year, the cost of goods sold was $367,200, operating expenses were $228,300, income taxes were $22,700, gross sales were $685,900, and returns were $2350.

2. **CIGAR STORE** A cigar store in Ohio had net sales of $289,300, operating expenses of $68,200, cost of goods sold of $165,000, and paid $9900 in taxes.

Find the cost of goods sold in Exercises 3 and 4.

3. **VIDEO GAMES** The inventory at Yarborough Video Games, Inc. on January 1 was $263,400. Purchases during the year were $343,500, freight was $4800, and inventory at the end of the year was $287,500.

4. **SCUBA & BIKE** Jill Starkley enjoys both scuba diving and bike riding, so she opened a retail store selling equipment for both sports. Inventory was $385,200 on January 1 and $287,700 on December 31. She paid freight of $6250 during the year on purchases of $427,900.

5. **BURGLAR ALARMS** StopTheft Alarms had gross sales of $284,000 last quarter with returns of $6000. The inventory at the beginning of the quarter was $58,000. A total of $142,000 worth of goods was purchased during the quarter with freight charges of $3000. The inventory at the end of the quarter was $69,000. Wages and salaries were $19,400, rent was $6000, advertising was $2000, utilities paid by the company were $1800, taxes on inventory and payroll totaled $3000, miscellaneous expenses were $4000, and corporate income taxes were $14,650. Complete the income tax statement.

STOPTHEFT ALARMS
INCOME STATEMENT
QUARTER ENDING DECEMBER 31

Gross sales _____
Returns _____
Net sales _____
  Inventory, beg. of quarter _____
  Cost of goods
    purchased _____
  Freight _____
  Total cost of goods purchased _____
  Total of goods available for sale _____
  Inventory, end of quarter _____
Cost of goods sold _____
Gross profit _____
  Expenses
    Salaries and wages _____
    Rent _____
    Advertising _____
    Utilities _____
    Taxes on inventory, payroll _____
    Miscellaneous expenses _____
      Total expenses _____
Net income before taxes _____
  Income taxes _____
Net income _____

6. **DENTAL SUPPLY** New England Dental Supply is a regional wholesaler with gross sales last year of $2,215,000. Returns totaled $26,000. Inventory on January 1 was $215,000. Goods purchased during the year totaled $1,123,000. Freight was $4000. Inventory on December 31 was $265,000. Salaries and wages were $154,000, rent was $59,000, advertising was $11,000, utilities were $12,000, taxes on inventory and payroll totaled $10,000, and miscellaneous expenses were $9000. In addition, taxes for the year amounted to $287,400. Complete the following income statement for the firm.

NEW ENGLAND DENTAL SUPPLY
INCOME STATEMENT
YEAR ENDING DECEMBER 31

Gross sales		_____
Returns		_____
Net sales		_____
Inventory, January 1	_____	
Cost of goods purchased	_____	
Freight	_____	
Total cost of goods purchased	_____	
Total of goods available for sale	_____	
Inventory, December 31	_____	
Cost of goods sold		_____
Gross profit		_____
Expenses		
Salaries and wages	_____	
Rent	_____	
Advertising	_____	
Utilities	_____	
Taxes on inventory, payroll	_____	
Miscellaneous expenses	_____	
Total expenses		_____
Net income before taxes		_____
Income taxes		_____
Net income		======

7. INCOME STATEMENT FOR SELF-EMPLOYED Kathy Gilmore is self-employed as a computer consultant. She sells her services to customers and has no inventory, no returns, no freight, and no cost of goods sold. Gross sales were $170,500, salaries and wages were $63,000, rent was $28,000, advertising was $12,000, utilities were $4000, taxes on payroll were $3800, and miscellaneous office expenses were $9400. Complete the income statement for this firm given that income taxes were $6800.

KATHY GILMORE, CONSULTANT
INCOME STATEMENT
FOR THE YEAR ENDING DECEMBER 31

Gross sales		_____
Returns		_____
Net sales		_____
Inventory, January 1	_____	
Cost of goods purchased	_____	
Freight	_____	
Total cost of goods purchased	_____	
Total of goods available for sale	_____	
Inventory, December 31	_____	
Cost of goods sold		_____
Gross profit		_____
Expenses		
Salaries and wages	_____	
Rent	_____	
Advertising	_____	
Utilities	_____	
Taxes on inventory, payroll	_____	
Miscellaneous expenses	_____	
Total expenses		_____
Net income before taxes		_____
Income taxes		_____
Net income		======

8. What are the different factors that control gross profit? Is it important for management to continue to watch their gross profit? Why? (See Objective 1.)

 9. List the items on a family's income statement that a bank would need to look at when thinking of lending you money for a new automobile. (See Objective 2.)

10. Name several companies that compete with General Motors.

11. Explain why a lender might like to see an income statement before making a loan. (See Objective 1.)

 12. (a) Discuss the purpose of an income statement. (b) Outline the basic structure of an income statement. (See Objective 2.)

18.2 Analyzing the Income Statement

OBJECTIVES

> **1** *Compare income statements using vertical analysis.*
>
> **2** *Calculate percents of net sales.*
>
> **3** *Compare an income statement with published charts.*
>
> **4** *Prepare a horizontal analysis.*

By going through the steps presented in the previous section, a firm can find its net income for a given period of time. A question that might be asked is "What happened to each part of the sales dollar?" The first step toward answering this question is to *list each of the important items* on the income statement as a percent of net sales in a process called a **vertical analysis** of the income statement.

Objective

1 *Compare Income Statements Using Vertical Analysis.*   A vertical analysis of an income statement is another application of the fundamental formula for percent from **Chapter 3**, $P = RB$. Since a percent is needed, the formula must be solved for the rate R as follows. In a vertical analysis, each item is found as a percent of net sales.

$$\left(R = \frac{P}{B} \right) \quad \text{or} \quad \left(R = \frac{\text{Particular item}}{\text{Net sales}} \right)$$

For example, use data from the 2008 income statement for Wal-Mart on page 636 to find the following.

$$\text{Percent cost of goods sold} = \frac{\$286{,}515}{\$378{,}799} = 75.6\% \quad \text{Rounded}$$

In 2008, Wal-Mart spent 75.6% of total annual revenue to pay its thousands of suppliers for the cost of goods sold. Many of those funds were eventually paid to the employees of the suppliers. Although the cost of goods sold is very high at Wal-Mart, other companies may have little or no cost of goods sold. For example, Microsoft Corporation writes computer software and sells it to customers around the world. Microsoft has a very low cost of goods sold compared to Wal-Mart or any other firm that carries a lot of inventory.

EXAMPLE 1 **Doing a Vertical Analysis**

Do a vertical analysis of the 2007 and 2008 income statements shown next for Wal-Mart. Show your work in a **comparative income statement** table.

WAL-MART STORES, INC.
CONSOLIDATED STATEMENT OF INCOME
FISCAL YEAR ENDING JANUARY 31
(in millions of U.S. dollars)

	2007	2008
Total revenue	$348,650	$378,799
Cost of goods sold	− 264,152	− 286,515
Gross profit	84,498	92,284
Operating expenses and other	− 66,849	− 72,645
Net income before taxes	17,649	19,639
Income taxes	− 6365	− 6908
Net income after taxes	$ 11,284	$ 12,731

Solution Calculate each value in the column labeled 2007 as a percent of 2008 total revenue and round to the nearest tenth of a percent. Then do the same for 2008.

Comparative Income Statement

	2007	2008
Cost of goods sold	$\dfrac{\$264{,}152}{\$348{,}650} = 75.8\%$	$\dfrac{\$286{,}515}{\$378{,}799} = 75.6\%$
Gross profit	$\dfrac{\$84{,}498}{\$348{,}650} = 24.2\%$	$\dfrac{\$92{,}284}{\$378{,}799} = 24.4\%$
Operating expenses and other	$\dfrac{\$66{,}849}{\$348{,}650} = 19.2\%$	$\dfrac{\$72{,}645}{\$378{,}799} = 19.2\%$
Net income before taxes	$\dfrac{\$17{,}649}{\$348{,}650} = 5.1\%$	$\dfrac{\$19{,}639}{\$378{,}799} = 5.2\%$
Income taxes	$\dfrac{\$6365}{\$348{,}650} = 1.8\%$	$\dfrac{\$6908}{\$378{,}799} = 1.8\%$
Net income	$\dfrac{\$11{,}284}{\$348{,}650} = 3.2\%$	$\dfrac{\$12{,}731}{\$378{,}799} = 3.4\%$

Notice how consistent the percents are from 2007 to 2008. The sheer size of Wal-Mart and its global presence helps it maintain relatively consistent figures from year to year. The firm actually reduced its cost of goods sold slightly from 75.8% of revenue in 2007 to 75.6% of revenue in 2008. This may not seem like much, but even a tiny percent savings on nearly $400 billion in revenue amounts to a lot of money. Management at Wal-Mart is known to be very cost-conscious and to work at shaving pennies off of costs wherever it can. Notice that profits in 2008 were only 3.4% of total revenue. As an example, the net income expected on a sale of say $85 would be 3.4% of $85, or $2.89. This isn't much when you think about it, is it?

Objective

2 *Calculate Percents of Net Sales.* The formula given in the previous section for checking income statements is just as valid for percents as for dollar amounts.

Cost of goods sold + Operating expenses + Income taxes + Net income after taxes = Net sales

Use the information in Example 1 to verify this is true for the 2008 Wal-Mart data. Notice that net sales is the same as total revenue.

$$75.6\% + 19.2\% + 1.8\% + 3.4\% = 100\%$$

These figures may not always add to exactly 100% due to rounding. The next example shows how to find these percentages when there are returns.

EXAMPLE 2   Finding Percents of Net Sales

Write each of the following items as a percent of net sales. The salaries and wages for this firm are low because it is a small start-up business and the owner is currently not taking any income out of the business.

Gross sales	$209,000	Salaries and wages	$11,000
Returns	$9000	Rent	$6000
Cost of goods sold	$145,000	Advertising	$11,000

Solution   Use the formula for net sales, with gross sales = $209,000 and returns = $9000.

$$\text{Net sales} = \text{Gross sales} - \text{Returns}$$
$$= \$209,000 - \$9000 = \$200,000$$

Now find all the desired percents.

$$\text{Percent gross sales} = \frac{\$209,000}{\$200,000} = 104.5\%$$

NOTE   This percent is more than 100% because returns are included in it, but not in net sales.

$$\text{Percent returns} = \frac{\$9000}{\$200,000} = 4.5\%$$

$$\text{Percent cost of goods sold} = \frac{\$145,000}{\$200,000} = 72.5\%$$

$$\text{Percent salaries and wages} = \frac{\$11,000}{\$200,000} = 5.5\%$$

$$\text{Percent rent} = \frac{\$6000}{\$200,000} = 3\%$$

$$\text{Percent advertising} = \frac{\$11,000}{\$200,000} = 5.5\%$$

Objective

3   *Compare an Income Statement with Published Charts.*   Once the percent of net sales for each item on the income statement has been found, they can be compared to the percents for similar businesses. To do this, consult published charts that have the required data. One such chart is shown in Table 18.1. These charts are compiled by averaging statistics from many similar firms.

Table 18.1   TYPICAL PERCENTS

Type of Business	Cost of Goods	Gross Profit	Total Operating Expenses*	Net Income	Wages	Rent	Advertising
Supermarkets	82.7%	17.3%	13.9%	3.4%	6.5%	0.8%	1.0%
Men's and women's apparel	67.0%	33.0%	21.2%	11.8%	8.0%	2.5%	1.9%
Women's apparel	64.8%	35.2%	23.4%	11.7%	7.9%	4.9%	1.8%
Shoes	60.3%	39.7%	24.5%	15.2%	10.3%	4.7%	1.6%
Furniture	68.9%	31.2%	21.7%	9.6%	9.5%	1.8%	2.5%
Appliances	66.9%	33.1%	26.0%	7.2%	11.9%	2.4%	2.5%
Drugs	67.9%	32.1%	23.5%	8.6%	12.3%	2.4%	1.4%
Restaurants	48.4%	51.6%	43.7%	7.9%	26.4%	2.8%	1.4%
Service station	76.8%	23.2%	16.9%	6.3%	8.5%	2.3%	0.5%

*This column represents the total of all expenses involved in running the firm.
Total operating expenses include, but are not limited to, wages, rent, and advertising.

EXAMPLE 3   Compare Business Ratios

Gina Burton wishes to compare the business ratios of her shoe store to industry averages. Figures from her store and industry averages for shoe stores are shown below. Burton sees that her expenses are higher and her net income is lower than the industry averages. What might Ms. Burton do to decrease total expenses and increase net income?

	Cost of Goods	Gross Profit	Total Expenses	Net Income	Wages	Rent	Advertising
Burton's Shoes	58.2%	41.8%	28.3%	13.5%	11.7%	5.6%	2.8%
Shoes (from chart)	60.3%	39.7%	24.5%	15.2%	10.3%	4.7%	1.6%

Solution   Burton's wages, rent, and advertising all seem to be above the averages. If she can decrease any of these, or increase total sales without increasing any of these, then her net income will improve. Perhaps she can reschedule some employees to reduce overtime or shift more work to lower-wage employees. It may be that she can try to renegotiate her rent with her landlord or purchase her own building and move the store. Perhaps she can get the same advertising exposure by changing her advertising strategy to one that costs less.

On the other hand, her store may never compare favorably with national averages. That is fine as long as she makes an adequate profit.

Objective

4   *Prepare a Horizontal Analysis.* Another way to analyze an income statement is to prepare a **horizontal analysis**. A horizontal analysis finds percents of change (either increases or decreases) between the current time period and a previous time period. This comparison can expose *unusual changes*, such as a rapid increase in expenses or decline in net sales or profits.

Do a horizontal analysis by finding the amount of change from the previous year to the current year, both in dollars and as a percent. For example, the yearly income statement of Wal-Mart on page 642 shows that total revenue increased from $348,650 (in millions) in 2007 to $378,799 (in millions) in 2008. Find the percent increase in revenue as follows.

$$\text{Percent increase in revenue} = \frac{\$378,799 - \$348,650}{\$348,650} = 8.6\% \quad \text{Rounded}$$

So, Wal-Mart grew sales by 8.6% from 2007 to 2008. This is a very good, but not spectacular, growth rate for such a large company. In fact, at the time management was actively seeking additional growth by trying to penetrate more foreign markets, such as Japan and China. There were not that many locations left in the United States for its giant superstores. Figure 18.3 shows that Wal-Mart stock did very well from 1980 until 2000, but that it has been relatively flat since that time as the firm has struggled to grow and increase profits. Still, an investment in Wal-Mart made in 1980 would have done much better than the Dow Jones Industrial Average also shown in Figure 18.3.

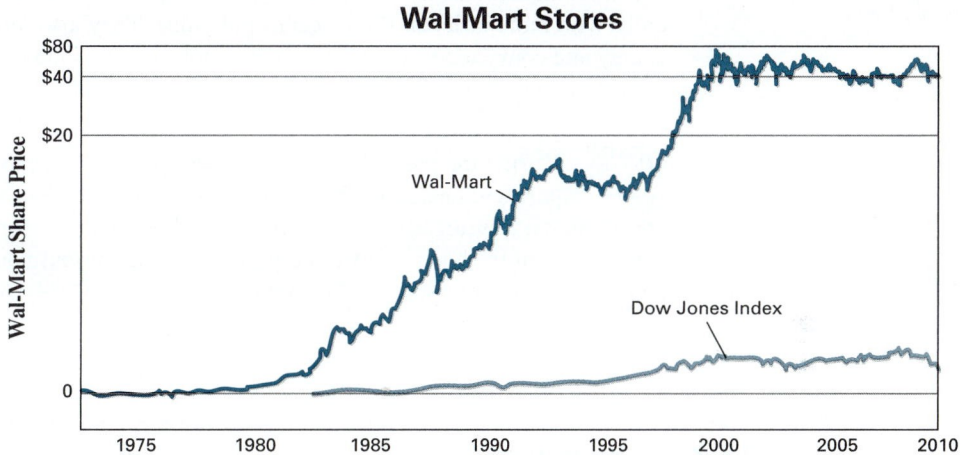

Figure 18.3

EXAMPLE 4   Doing a Horizontal Analysis

Do a horizontal analysis for the 2007 and 2008 Wal-Mart income statements using the data given in Example 1.

Solution   Find the increase by subtracting the 2007 figure from the 2008 figure. Then divide by the 2007 figure to find the percent increase (or decrease) to the nearest tenth.

WAL-MART STORES, INC.
CONSOLIDATED STATEMENT OF INCOME
(in millions of U.S. dollars)

	2007	2008	Increase	Percent
Total revenue	$348,650	$378,799	$30,149	8.6%
Gross profit	$ 84,498	$ 92,284	$ 7,786	9.2%
Net income before taxes	$ 17,649	$ 19,639	$ 1,990	11.3%
Net income	$ 11,284	$ 12,731	$ 1,447	12.8%

Although total revenue grew by only 8.6%, management did an excellent job controlling expenses so that net income before taxes increased by 11.3% and net income increased by 12.8%. These figures show that management is continuing to control expenses and trying to maximize profit.

Here are some of the things that management at Wal-Mart is doing to increase revenue and decrease costs.

1. Trying to increase sales throughout the world;
2. Working to understand what customers want;

3. Discontinuing products that do not sell well;
4. Reducing costs everywhere possible; and
5. Shifting purchasing to countries that offer lower costs.

A few years ago, Wal-Mart management was widely criticized for paying poor wages and offering an insurance plan that few employees could afford. In response, Wal-Mart made a number of changes in its labor relations policy. It now pays somewhat better wages and covers many more employees with insurance than it did a few years ago. Additionally, Wal-Mart has tried to be innovative by doing a few things to "go green" to support the environment. For example, management made a major effort to get people to replace their incandescent light bulbs with more efficient fluorescent light bulbs. They also modified some stores to use less energy and converted some stores to being powered by wind energy.

> **NOTE** During the past 40 years, many companies have moved manufacturing jobs to other countries to decrease labor costs. Now there is evidence that some technology and professional jobs are also being moved to other countries for the same reasons. Education is one of the basic ways to help protect yourself and your family from the job displacement brought about by this trend.

18.2 | Exercises

Prepare a vertical analysis for each of the following firms. Round percents to the nearest tenth of a percent.

1. **SCUBA SHOPPE** Reef Scuba, Inc. had net sales of $439,000, operating expenses of $143,180, and a cost of goods sold of $198,400.

2. **WOMEN'S FASHIONS** In the third year of business, Jarita's Fashion Shoppe had operating expenses of $198,400, a cost of goods sold of $287,104, and net sales of $589,250.

The following charts show some figures from the income statements of several companies. In each case, prepare a vertical analysis by expressing each item as a percent of net sales. Then write in the appropriate average percent from the table in the book. Round to the nearest tenth of a percent.

3. **CAPITAL DISTRICT APPLIANCES**

	Amount	Percent	Industry Percent from Table 18.1
Net sales	$900,000	100.0%	100.0%
Cost of goods sold	617,000	_____	_____
Gross profit	283,000	_____	_____
Wages	108,900	_____	_____
Rent	20,700	_____	_____
Advertising	27,000	_____	_____
Total expenses	216,000	_____	_____
Net income before taxes	67,000	_____	_____

4. ELLIS SEAFOOD

	Amount	Percent	Industry Percent from Table 18.1
Net sales	$600,000	100.0%	100.0%
Cost of goods sold	280,000	_____	_____
Gross profit	320,000	_____	_____
Wages	160,000	_____	_____
Rent	15,000	_____	_____
Advertising	8000	_____	_____
Total expenses	255,000	_____	_____
Net income before taxes	65,000	_____	_____

Complete the following comparative income statement. Round percents to the nearest tenth of a percent.

5. BEST TIRES, INC. COMPARATIVE INCOME STATEMENT

	This Year		Last Year	
	Amount	Percent	Amount	Percent
Gross sales	$1,856,000	_____	$1,692,000	_____
Returns	6000	_____	12,000	_____
Net sales	_____	100.0%	_____	100.0%
Cost of goods sold	1,202,000	_____	1,050,000	_____
Gross profit	648,000	_____	630,000	_____
Wages	152,000	_____	148,000	_____
Rent	82,000	_____	78,000	_____
Advertising	111,000	_____	122,000	_____
Utilities	32,000	_____	17,000	_____
Taxes on inventory, payroll	17,000	_____	18,000	_____
Miscellaneous expenses	62,000	_____	58,000	_____
Total expenses	456,000	_____	441,000	_____
Net income	_____	_____	_____	_____

Complete the following horizontal analysis for Best Tires, Inc. comparative income statement given above. Round percents to the nearest tenth of a percent. Use parentheses to show that a number is negative.

6. BEST TIRES, INC. COMPARATIVE INCOME STATEMENT

	This Year	Last Year	Increase (Decrease)	
			Amount	Percent
Gross sales	$1,856,000	$1,692,000	_____	_____
Returns	6000	12,000	_____	_____
Net sales	1,850,000	1,680,000	_____	_____
Cost of goods sold	1,202,000	1,050,000	_____	_____
Gross profit	648,000	630,000	_____	_____
Wages	152,000	148,000	_____	_____
Rent	82,000	78,000	_____	_____
Advertising	111,000	122,000	_____	_____
Utilities	32,000	17,000	_____	_____
Taxes on inventory, payroll	17,000	18,000	_____	_____
Miscellaneous expenses	62,000	58,000	_____	_____
Net income	192,000	189,000	_____	_____

The following tables give the percents for various items from the income statements of firms in various businesses. Complete these tables by including the appropriate percents from Table 18.1. Identify any areas that might require attention by management. Also list suggestions for improving any problem area.

Type of Store	Cost of Goods	Gross Profit	Total Operating Expenses	Net Income	Wages	Rent	Advertising
7. Supermarkets	84.5%	15.5%	14.4%	1.1%	6.4%	2.1%	0.9%
	___	___	___	___	___	___	___
8. Shoes	60.5%	39.5%	24.3%	15.2%	10.4%	4.8%	1.5%
	___	___	___	___	___	___	___
9. Drug store	71.2%	28.8%	26.5%	2.3%	12.9%	5.3%	2.0%
	___	___	___	___	___	___	___
10. Restaurant	57.8%	42.2%	38.6%	3.6%	28.1%	2.4%	1.0%
	___	___	___	___	___	___	___

 11. Compare a vertical analysis to a horizontal analysis. What are the strengths of each? (See Objectives 1 and 4.)

 12. Explain the purpose of comparing percent of net sales on an income statement to percents for similar businesses. (See Objective 2.)

 13. The average net income before taxes for supermarkets is 3.4%. Go to the supermarket where you normally shop and list 10 items that you normally buy and the price of each. Total these and find 3.4% of this total. Approximately what is the net income for the store for selling these 10 items?

 14. Why would a lender want to use both vertical and horizontal analyses before making a long-term loan to a firm? (See **Sections 18.1** and **18.2**.)

18.3   The Balance Sheet

OBJECTIVES

1 *Identify the terms used with balance sheets.*

2 *Prepare a balance sheet.*

An income statement summarizes the financial affairs of a business firm for a given period of time, such as a year. On the other hand, a **balance sheet** describes the financial condition of a firm *at one point in time*, such as the last day of a year. A balance sheet shows the worth of a business at a particular time by listing its **assets**, which are the things it owns, such as property, equipment, and money owed to the business, as well as its **liabilities**, which are amounts owed by the business to others. The difference between these two amounts gives the **owners' equity** in the business.

Objective

1 *Identify the Terms Used with Balance Sheets.* Both assets and liabilities are divided into two categories, **long-term** and **current (short-term)**. Long-term refers to assets or liabilities with a life in the firm of more than a year. Short-term applies to assets or liabilities that the company does not expect to have in one year.

Assets

Current assets: cash or items that can be converted into cash within a short period of time, such as a year

    Cash: cash in checking and savings accounts
    Marketable securities: stocks, bonds, and other securities that can quickly be converted to cash
    Accounts receivable: funds owed by customers of the firm
    Notes receivable: value of all notes owed to the firm
    Inventory: cost of merchandise that the firm has for sale

Plant and equipment: assets that are expected to be used for more than one year (also called **fixed assets** or **plant assets**)

    Land: book value of any land owned by the firm
    Buildings: book value of any building(s) owned by the firm
    Equipment: book value of equipment, store fixtures, furniture, and similar items owned by the firm

Liabilities

Current liabilities: items that must be paid by the firm within a short period of time, usually one year

    Accounts payable: amounts that must be paid to other firms
    Notes payable: value of all short-term notes owed by the firm

Long-term liabilities: items that will be paid after one year

    Mortgages payable: total due on all mortgages
    Long-term notes payable: total of all long-term notes

The difference between the total of all assets and the total of all liabilities is called the **owners' equity**, which is also referred to as **net worth** or, for a corporation, **stockholders' equity**. The relationship between owners' equity, assets, and liabilities is shown in the fundamental formula below.

$$\text{Owners' equity} = \text{Assets} - \text{Liabilities}$$
$$\text{or}$$
$$\text{Assets} = \text{Liabilities} + \text{Owners' equity}$$

Objective

2 ***Prepare a Balance Sheet.*** Now that all the terms have been defined, a balance sheet can be prepared.

EXAMPLE 1 **Preparing a Balance Sheet**

Farmers Market lists its current cash assets as $8000. Notes receivable total $11,000, accounts receivable total $15,000, and inventory is $51,000. Plant assets include land worth $48,000, buildings worth $110,000, and fixtures worth $18,000. Current liabilities include notes payable of $28,000 and accounts payable of $26,000. Mortgages total $62,800 and long-term notes payable total $24,000. Owners' equity is $120,200. Complete a balance sheet for the market, and use the fundamental formula for accounting to find owners' equity.

Solution To prepare a balance sheet, go through the following steps. Refer to the balance sheet in Figure 18.4.

> **STEP 1** Enter all current assets. On the balance sheet cash is $8000, notes receivable are $11,000, accounts receivable are $15,000, and inventory is $51,000.
>
> **STEP 2** Add the current assets. The total in the example is $85,000.
>
> **STEP 3** Enter all plant assets. In the example, land is $48,000, buildings are $110,000, and fixtures are $18,000.
>
> **STEP 4** Add the plant assets of Step 3. In the example, the total is $176,000.
>
> **STEP 5** Add the results from Steps 2 and 4. This gives the total value of all assets owned by the firm. Total assets in the example are $261,000.
>
> **STEP 6** Enter all current liabilities. In the example, notes payable are $28,000 and accounts payable are $26,000.
>
> **STEP 7** Add all current liabilities. The sum in the example is $54,000.
>
> **STEP 8** Enter long-term liabilities. In the example, mortgages total $62,800 and long-term notes payable total $24,000.
>
> **STEP 9** Add all long-term liabilities. The sum in the example is $86,800.
>
> **STEP 10** Add the results of Steps 7 and 9. This gives the total of all liabilities owed by the firm. The total of the liabilities in the example is $140,800.
>
> **STEP 11** Enter owners' equity. In the example, owners' equity is $120,200.
>
> **STEP 12** Add owners' equity to total liabilities to find $261,000.
>
> **STEP 13** Use the fundamental formula of accounting:
>
> $$\text{Total assets} = \text{Total liabilities} + \text{Owners' equity}$$

Total liabilities are $140,800, owners' equity is $120,200, and total assets are $261,000. Check to make sure no mistake has been made.

$$\$140,800 + \$120,200 = \$261,000$$

So, it is correct.

◼

NOTE Always make sure that the total assets equal *total liabilities plus owners' equity.*

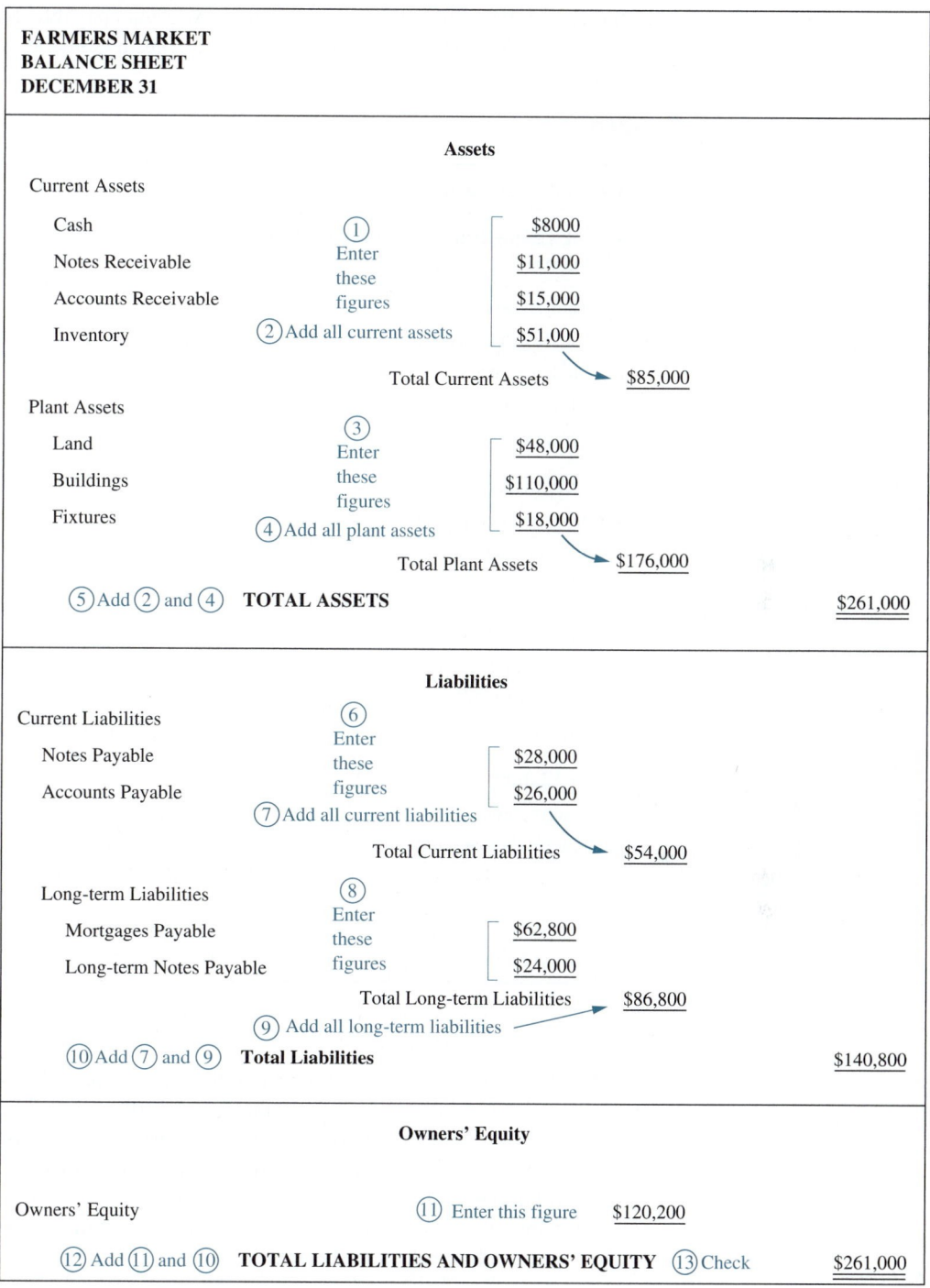

Figure 18.4

EXAMPLE 2 Preparing a Balance Sheet

Wal-Mart's assets in millions of dollars on January 31, 2008 were as follows: Cash and cash equivalents, $5569; Accounts receivables, $3654; Inventory and other, $38,362; Property and equipment, $97,017; Equity and other assets, $18,912. The firm's liabilities, in millions of dollars, on the same date follow: Accounts payable, $44,278; Other current liabilities, $14,176; Long-term debt, $33,402; Short-term debt and other, $7050. Complete the balance sheet.

Solution

WAL-MART STORES, INC.
CONSOLIDATED BALANCE SHEET
FISCAL YEAR ENDING JANUARY 31, 2008
(in millions of U.S. dollars)

Current Assets:		
Cash and cash equivalents	$5569	
Accounts receivable	$3654	
Inventory and other	$38,362	
Total current assets	$47,585	Sum of all current assets
Other Assets:		
Property and equipment	$97,017	
Equity and other assets	$18,912	
Total assets	$163,514	Sum of all current assets **and all other assets**
Current Liabilities:		
Accounts payable	$44,278	
Other current liabilities	$14,176	
Total current liabilities	$58,454	Sum of current liabilities
Other Liabilities:		
Long-term debt	$33,402	
Short-term debt and other	$7050	
Total liabilities	$98,906	Sum of current liabilities **and other liabilities**
Stockholders' Equity:	$64,608	Total assets minus total liabilities
Total liabilities and equity	$163,514	

A balance sheet shows assets and liabilities at one point in time. For example, the data in Example 2 was accurate only on January 31, 2008 and not on any other date. Wal-Mart has millions of transactions daily—the balance sheet was not even accurate two days later, on February 2, 2008. At the end of business on January 31, 2008, Wal-Mart had $5,569,000,000 in cash and cash equivalents and a nearly unbelievable $38,362,000,000 in inventory and other current assets. The firm had a lot of inventory on January 31, 2008! We will analyze a balance sheet in the next section.

18.3 | Exercises

Complete the balance sheets for the following business firms.

1. **GROCERY CHAIN** Brookshire's Grocery (all figures in millions): fixtures, $28; buildings, $290; land, $466; cash, $273; notes receivable, $312; accounts receivable, $264; inventory, $180; notes payable, $312; mortgages payable, $212; accounts payable, $63; long-term notes payable, $55.

BROOKSHIRE'S GROCERY
BALANCE SHEET FOR DECEMBER 31 (IN MILLIONS)

Assets		
Current assets		
Cash		
Notes receivable	_____	
Accounts receivable	_____	
Inventory	_____	
Total current assets		_____
Plant assets		
Land	_____	
Buildings	_____	
Fixtures	_____	
Total plant assets		_____
Total assets		_____

Liabilities		
Current liabilities		
Notes payable	_____	
Accounts payable	_____	
Total current liabilities		_____
Long-term liabilities		
Mortgages payable	_____	
Long-term notes payable	_____	
Total long-term liabilities		_____
Total liabilities		_____

Owners' equity		
Owners' equity	_____	
Total liabilities and owners' equity		_____

2. **MUFFLERS** Atlas Mufflers, Inc. has land valued at $87,500. Its accounts payable total $492,300; notes receivable are $26,000; accounts receivable are $378,200; cash is $148,000; buildings are $219,300; notes payable are $37,800; long-term notes payable total $187,400; mortgages total $263,300; inventory is $496,800; and fixtures are $168,200. Use the fundamental formula of accounting to find owners' equity.

ATLAS MUFFLERS, INC.
BALANCE SHEET FOR DECEMBER 31

Assets		
Current assets		
Cash	_____	
Notes receivable	_____	
Accounts receivable	_____	
Inventory	_____	
Total current assets		_____
Plant assets		
Land	_____	
Buildings	_____	
Fixtures	_____	
Total plant assets		_____
Total assets		_____

ATLAS MUFFLERS, INC.
BALANCE SHEET FOR DECEMBER 31

	Liabilities	
Current liabilities		
Notes payable	_____	
Accounts payable	_____	
Total current liabilities		_____
Long-term liabilities		
Mortgages payable	_____	
Long-term notes payable	_____	
Total long-term liabilities		_____
Total liabilities		═════════

	Owners' equity	
Owners' equity	_____	
Total liabilities and owners' equity		═════════

 3. Compare a balance sheet to an income statement. What are the similarities and the differences? How is each used? (See **Sections 18.1** and **18.3**.)

 4. Explain how the fundamental formula for accounting is used to check a balance sheet. (See Objective 1.)

 5. Prepare a balance sheet for your own family or for your parents.

6. List several reasons why a family needs to have some cash. List several reasons why a corporation needs to have some cash.

18.4	**Analyzing the Balance Sheet; Financial Ratios**

OBJECTIVES

1 *Compare balance sheets by vertical analysis.*

2 *Prepare a horizontal analysis.*

3 *Find the current ratio.*

4 *Find the acid-test ratio.*

5 *Find the ratio of net income after taxes to average owners' equity.*

6 *Find the accounts receivable turnover.*

7 *Find the average age of accounts receivable.*

8 *Find the debt-to-equity ratio.*

Objective

1   *Compare Balance Sheets by Vertical Analysis.*   A balance sheet can be analyzed in much the same way as an income statement. In a **vertical analysis**, each item on the balance sheet is expressed as a percent of total assets. A **comparative balance sheet** shows the vertical analysis for two different years. You may want to look at a firm's comparative balance sheet before buying their stock or before accepting a job offer.

> **EXAMPLE 1** **Comparing Balance Sheets**
>
> Do a vertical analysis for both the 2007 and 2008 balance sheets for Wal-Mart by calculating each value as a percent of the total assets for that year. Round to the nearest tenth of a percent. Then compare the percents to identify changes from 2007 to 2008.

Solution

WAL-MART STORES, INC.
CONSOLIDATED BALANCE SHEET
FISCAL YEAR ENDING JANUARY 31
(in millions of U.S. dollars)

	2007		2008	
ASSETS	**Amount**	**Percent**	**Amount**	**Percent**
Current Assets:				
Cash and cash equivalents	$7373	4.9%[1]	$5569	3.4%
Accounts receivable	$2840	1.9%	$3654	2.2%
Inventory and other	$36,375	24.1%	$38,362	23.5%
Total current assets	$46,588	30.8%[2]	$47,585	29.1%
Other Assets:				
Property and equipment	$88,440	58.5%	$97,017	59.3%
Equity and other assets	$16,165	10.7%	$18,912	11.6%
Total assets	$151,193	100.0%	$163,514	100.0%
LIABILITIES	**Amount**	**Percent**	**Amount**	**Percent**
Current Liabilities:				
Accounts payable	$43,471	28.8%	$44,278	27.1%
Other current liabilities	$8283	5.5%	$14,176	8.7%
Total current liabilities	$51,754	34.2%	$58,454	35.7%
Other Liabilities:				
Long-term debt	$30,735	20.3%	$33,402	20.4%
Short-term debt and other	$7131	4.7%	$7050	4.3%
Total liabilities	$89,620	59.3%	$98,906	60.5%
Stockholders' Equity:	$61,573	40.7%	$64,608	39.5%
Total liabilities and owners' equity	$151,193	100.0%	$163,514	100.0%

[1] The percent 4.9% for 2007 is found by dividing Cash and cash equivalents for 2007 of $7373 by Total assets of $151,193 for the same year, and rounding to the nearest tenth.
[2] Percents in column do not add to 30.8% due to rounding.

Current assets increased from $46,588 to $47,585 (both in millions). Investors, bankers, and managers want firms to maintain sufficient current assets for emergencies and also for operating funds. Current liabilities increased significantly from $51,754 to $58,454 (both in millions), which is not a trend that creditors like to see. However, it is somewhat comforting to see that total assets increased by more than total liabilities from 2007 to 2008.

NOTE Each value in the preceding table, including column subtotals, was divided by the respective value for total assets. Thus, the amounts add up to the appropriate subtotal, which cannot be said for all of the percent figures.

Objective

2 *Prepare a Horizontal Analysis.* Perform a **horizontal analysis** by finding the change, both in dollars and in percent, for each item on the balance sheet from one year to the next. As before, always use the *previous year* as a base when finding the percents.

EXAMPLE 2 **Doing a Horizontal Analysis**

Wal-Mart's cash and cash equivalents actually decreased from $7373 to $5569 (both in millions) from 2007 to 2008. The decrease is nearly $2 billion. Find the percent decrease or increase as follows.

$$\frac{\$5569 - \$7373}{\$7373} = -24.5\%$$

The large decrease in cash and cash equivalents in one year is significant. Complete a horizontal analysis of the current assets portion of Wal-Mart's balance sheet to see what else may have happened.

Solution

WAL-MART STORES, INC.
CONSOLIDATED BALANCE SHEET
FISCAL YEAR ENDING JANUARY 31
(in millions of U.S. dollars)

	2007	2008	Increase (Decrease) Amount	Percent
Current Assets:				
Cash and cash equivalents	$7373	$5569	−$1804	−24.5%
Accounts receivable	$2840	$3654	$814	28.7%
Inventory and other	$36,375	$38,362	$1987	5.5%
Total current assets	$46,588	$47,585	$997	2.1%

This shows that there was a fairly significant shift from cash and cash equivalents to accounts receivable and inventory and other. Investors and creditors might question why there was a shift away from cash and toward more debt and inventory. Sales may be slowing, causing inventory to back up in the global supply chain, or perhaps customers are paying off their bills more slowly. Astute bankers and investors would study this issue very carefully before lending money to, or buying stock in, Wal-Mart.

Objective

3 *Find the Current Ratio.* The **current ratio**, also known as **banker's ratio**, is found by dividing current assets by current liabilities.

$$\text{Current ratio} = \frac{\text{Current assets}}{\text{Current liabilities}}$$

EXAMPLE 3 **Finding the Current Ratio**

The 2008 balance sheet for Wal-Mart shows current assets of $47,585 and current liabilities of $58,454. Find the current ratio.

Solution

$$\text{Current ratio} = \$47,585 \div \$58,454 = 0.8 \quad \text{Rounded}$$

The ratio is often expressed as 0.8 to 1 or as 0.8:1.

Lending institutions look carefully at the current ratio before making a loan. A common rule of thumb, not necessarily applicable to all firms, is that the current ratio should be at least 1:1. A firm with a current ratio significantly lower may have an increased risk of financial problems. Wal-Mart has a current ratio that is slightly below this value, but its size and global operations probably allow it to operate with less cash than many other companies. In particular, Wal-Mart managers are very aggressive about keeping inventories extremely low in their supply chains although they want to keep their stores full of inventory. To really understand the significance of the current ratio for Wal-Mart, it is important to compare it to other similar firms, such as Target, which we do later in this section.

One disadvantage of the current ratio is that inventory is included in current assets. In a period of financial difficulty, a firm might have trouble disposing of the inventory at a reasonable price. Some accountants feel that the "acid test" for a firm's financial health is to consider only **liquid assets**: assets that are either cash or that can be converted to cash quickly, such as securities and accounts and notes receivable.

Objective

4   *Find the Acid-Test Ratio.*   The **acid-test ratio**, also called the **quick ratio**, is defined as follows.

$$\text{Acid-test ratio} = \frac{\text{Liquid assets}}{\text{Current liabilities}}$$

NOTE   As a general rule, the acid-test ratio should be at least 1 to 1, with the idea that liquid assets are at least enough to cover current liabilities.

EXAMPLE 4   **Finding the Acid-Test Ratio**

Find the acid-test ratio for Wal-Mart in 2008.

Solution   Liquid assets are cash and short-term investments plus accounts receivable. Inventory is not considered a liquid asset.

$$\text{Liquid assets} = \text{Current assets} - \text{Inventory}$$
$$= \$47{,}585 - \$38{,}362 = \$9223$$

$$\text{Acid-test ratio} = \text{Liquid assets} \div \text{Current liabilities}$$
$$= \$9223 \div \$58{,}454$$
$$= 0.2$$

This ratio is far below 1:1. So Wal-Mart is operating with very little liquid assets compared to current liabilities. It may be part of the Wal-Mart philosophy of minimizing costs, or it could be something related to the financial crisis that began in 2007. The financial statements may be showing some signs of financial stress within the company, but we would need to look at many other factors before drawing any conclusion.

Objective

5   *Find the Ratio of Net Income After Taxes to Average Owners' Equity.*   A company with a large amount of capital invested should have a higher net income than a company that has only a relatively small amount invested. To check on this, accountants often find the **ratio of net income after taxes to average owners' equity**. The average owners' equity is found by adding the owners' equity at the beginning and end of the year and dividing by 2.

$$\frac{\text{Average}}{\text{owners' equity}} = \frac{\dfrac{\text{Owners' equity}}{\text{at beginning}} + \dfrac{\text{Owners' equity}}{\text{at end}}}{2}$$

Then the ratio of net income after taxes to average owners' equity is found as follows.

$$\begin{array}{c}\text{Ratio of net income} \\ \text{after taxes to average} \\ \text{owners' equity}\end{array} = \frac{\text{Net income after taxes}}{\text{Average owners' equity}}$$

NOTE The ratio of net income after taxes to average owners' equity is also called "return on equity."

EXAMPLE 5 **Finding the Ratio of Net Income After Taxes**

Find the 2008 ratio of net income after taxes to average owners' equity for Wal-Mart.

Solution As seen in the balance sheet, stockholders' equity increased from $61,573 million at the end of 2007 to $64,608 million at the end of 2008.

$$\text{Average owners' equity} = \frac{\$61,573 + \$64,608}{2} = \$63,090.5 \text{ (in millions)}$$

Use the net income after taxes in 2008 from the income statement in **Section 18.1** on page 636 to find the following.

$$\begin{array}{c}\text{Ratio of net income after taxes} \\ \text{to average owners' equity}\end{array} = \frac{\$12,731}{\$63,090.5} = 0.20, \text{ or } 20\% \quad \text{Rounded}$$

The ratio of net income after taxes to average owners' equity should be higher than the interest rate paid on savings accounts or government bonds. Otherwise, the capital represented by those assets should be deposited in bank accounts or bonds, which have lower risk. The ratio for Wal-Mart of 20% is much better than yields from savings accounts or bonds, and is very satisfactory.

NOTE The ratio of net income after taxes to average owners' equity is the only ratio of the three we have looked at that requires you to look at both the income statement and the balance sheet.

Objective

6 *Find the Accounts Receivable Turnover.* The accounts receivable of a firm represent credit sales—goods sold on credit and later billed to the customer. The **accounts receivable turnover** is an indication of how fast the firm is collecting its bills. If this ratio *starts to decline*, then the firm may well need to be more aggressive in collecting its receivables from customers. By collecting receivables promptly, the firm will need to borrow less money, thus cutting its interest charges.

To find the accounts receivable turnover ratio, first find the average accounts receivable.

$$\begin{array}{c}\text{Average accounts} \\ \text{receivable}\end{array} = \frac{\begin{array}{c}\text{Accounts receivable} \\ \text{at beginning}\end{array} + \begin{array}{c}\text{Accounts receivable} \\ \text{at end}\end{array}}{2}$$

Then,

$$\frac{\text{Accounts receivable}}{\text{turnover}} = \frac{\text{Net sales}}{\text{Average accounts receivable}}$$

EXAMPLE 6   **Finding the Accounts Receivable Turnover**

Find the accounts receivable turnover for Wal-Mart for 2008.

Solution   The balance sheet shows that accounts receivable for Wal-Mart at the beginning and end of 2008 were, respectively, $2840 and $3654 in millions of dollars.

$$\text{Average accounts receivable} = \frac{\$2840 + \$3654}{2} = \$3247 \text{ (in millions)}$$

From the income statement on page 636, net sales or total revenue for 2008 was $378,799 in millions.

$$\text{Accounts receivable turnover} = \frac{\$378,799}{\$3247} = 116.7 \quad \text{Rounded}$$

This ratio indicates that Wal-Mart is turning over its accounts receivable by nearly 117 times per year, or more than twice a week on average. However, Wal-Mart customers are individuals and businesses that usually pay using cash, debit cards, or credit cards. So we would expect this ratio to be high, but we should watch it over time for trends.

Objective

7   *Find the Average Age of Accounts Receivable.*   As mentioned, a firm must collect its accounts receivable promptly to minimize its own need to borrow money. To tell how well accounts are being collected, the firm can find the **average age of accounts receivable**, or the average number of days needed to collect its receivables. This is found by this formula.

$$\frac{\text{Average age of}}{\text{accounts receivable}} = \frac{365}{\text{Accounts receivable turnover}}$$

EXAMPLE 7   **Finding the Average Age of Accounts Receivable**

Find the average age of accounts receivable for Wal-Mart during 2008.

Solution   Divide 365 by the accounts receivable turnover found in Example 6.

$$\frac{\text{Average age of}}{\text{accounts receivable}} = \frac{365}{116.7} = 3.1 \text{ days} \quad \text{Rounded}$$

Due to the nature of its business, Wal-Mart has very small accounts receivables and collects them rapidly. However, this is a ratio to watch over time for most companies. Again, you want to quickly discover any major trend or change that may be developing. The ratios may help identify important problem areas.

Objective

8   *Find the Debt-to-Equity Ratio.*   Companies borrow money to expand and take advantage of business opportunities. This is fine as long as total debt *does not* become excessive. One common measure used to see if debt is reasonable is the **debt-to-equity ratio**, which is the ratio of all liabilities to all owners' equity.

$$\text{Debt-to-equity ratio} = \frac{\text{Current liabilities} + \text{Long-term liabilities}}{\text{Owners' equity}}$$

EXAMPLE 8 **Finding the Debt-to-Equity Ratio**

Find the debt-to-equity ratio for Wal-Mart at the end of 2008.

Solution   From the balance sheet, owners' equity was $64,608 in millions.

$$\text{Current liabilities} + \text{Long-term debt} = \$58,454 + \$33,402$$
$$= \$91,856 \text{ (in millions)}$$

$$\text{Debt-to-equity ratio} = \frac{\$91,856}{\$64,608} = 1.4 \quad \text{Rounded}$$

Acceptable levels for the debt-to-equity ratio vary greatly by industry depending on how rapidly a firm can turn inventory into cash, among other things. A company that can quickly turn inventory into cash is said to be **liquid**. Generally, the smaller the debt-to-equity ratio, the safer the firm when/if financial problems or a recession occur. However, firms that manage debt well often generate larger profits. You can think of money as an asset that needs to be managed very well. In fact, managers at the best firms spend a good deal of time trying to efficiently manage the firm's financial resources.

Since companies in different industries, such as ExxonMobil in the oil and gas business and Wal-Mart Stores, Inc., are so different, the best way to evaluate a firm is to compare it to another, similar company. Figure 18.5 shows the various ratios for two very serious competitors: Wal-Mart and Target. Although competitors, Target is smaller than Wal-Mart, with total revenue of only about one-sixth that of Wal-Mart.

	Financial Ratios for 2008	
	Wal-Mart	**Target**
Current ratio	0.8	1.6
Acid-test ratio	0.2	1.0
Ratio of net income after taxes to average owners' equity	0.20	0.18
Accounts receivable turnover	116.7	8.2
Average age of accounts receivable	3.1 days	44.5 days
Debt-to-equity ratio	1.4	1.8

Figure 18.5

By looking at these two sets of ratios, a pattern begins to emerge. The current and acid-test ratios at Wal-Mart are much lower, indicating that Wal-Mart operates with less cash and inventory than does Target. Wal-Mart also has a slightly higher ratio of net income after taxes to average owners' equity (20% compared to 18%) and a much quicker turnover of receivables. So, Wal-Mart seems to be running a very lean organization, with managers trying to leverage its financial resources for maximum return as they fight to keep costs extremely low. Low costs and lean inventories are very much a part of the Wal-Mart business model.

Target seems to have a more conservative approach in terms of short-term debts and therefore perhaps has less risk in the event of a recession. However, the debt-to-equity ratios show that Wal-Mart uses less combined current and long-term debt compared to Target. These ratios give investors a place to begin when analyzing a company. More work would be needed before a serious investor or lender would invest in either Wal-Mart or Target.

18.4	Exercises

Complete the following.

1. **OFFICE SUPPLY**   Complete this balance sheet using vertical analysis. Round to the nearest tenth of a percent.

OTERO OFFICE SUPPLY
COMPARATIVE BALANCE SHEET (in thousands)

	This Year		Last Year	
	Amount	Percent	Amount	Percent
Assets				
Current assets				
Cash	$52,000	_____	$42,000	_____
Notes receivable	$8000	_____	$6000	_____
Accounts receivable	$148,000	_____	$120,000	_____
Inventory	$153,000	_____	$120,000	_____
Total current assets	_____	_____	_____	_____
Plant assets				
Land	$10,000	_____	$8000	_____
Buildings	$14,000	_____	$11,000	_____
Fixtures	$15,000	_____	$13,000	_____
Total plant assets	_____	_____	_____	_____
Total assets	_____	100.0%	_____	100.0%
Liabilities				
Current liabilities				
Accounts payable	$3000	_____	$4000	_____
Notes payable	$201,000	_____	$152,000	_____
Total current liabilities	_____	_____	_____	_____
Long-term liabilities				
Mortgages payable	$20,000	_____	$16,000	_____
Long-term notes payable	$58,000	_____	$42,000	_____
Total long-term liabilities	_____	_____	_____	_____
Total liabilities	_____	_____	_____	_____
Owners' equity	$118,000	_____	$106,000	_____
Total liabilities and owners' equity	_____	_____	_____	_____

2. **OFFICE SUPPLY**   Complete the horizontal analysis for a portion of the balance sheet for Otero Office Supply.

OTERO OFFICE SUPPLY
HORIZONTAL ANALYSIS (in thousands)

	This Year	Last Year	Increase (Decrease)	
			Amount	Percent
Assets				
Current assets				
Cash	$52,000	$42,000	_____	_____
Notes receivable	$8000	$6000	_____	_____
Accounts receivable	$148,000	$120,000	_____	_____
Inventory	$153,000	$120,000	_____	_____
Total current assets	$361,000	$288,000	_____	_____

OTERO OFFICE SUPPLY
HORIZONTAL ANALYSIS (in thousands)

	This Year	Last Year	Increase (Decrease) Amount	Percent
Plant assets				
Land	$10,000	$8000	_____	_____
Buildings	$14,000	$11,000	_____	_____
Fixtures	$15,000	$13,000	_____	_____
Total plant assets	$39,000	$32,000	_____	_____
Total assets	$400,000	$320,000	_____	_____

In Exercises 3–6, find (a) the current ratio and (b) the acid-test ratio. Round each ratio to the nearest hundredth. (c) Do the ratios suggest that the company is financially healthy using the guidelines given in the text?

3. **OTERO OFFICE SUPPLY** Use data from Exercises 1 and 2.

4. **MUSIC STORE** Virginia Music has current assets of $216,750, current liabilities of $213,000, cash of $25,400, notes and accounts receivable of $42,500, and an inventory of mostly electric pianos and various electronic equipment valued at $148,850.

5. **OXYGEN SUPPLY** BlueTex Oxygen Supply has current assets of $2,234,000, current liabilities of $840,000, total cash of $339,000, notes and accounts receivable of $1,215,000, and an inventory of $680,000.

6. **MOVIES** Aktron Movies has current liabilities of $356,000, cash of $32,800, notes and accounts receivable of $248,500, and an inventory valued at $82,400.

A portion of a comparative balance sheet is shown below. First complete the chart, then find the current ratio and the acid-test ratio for the indicated year. Round each ratio to the nearest hundredth.

7. This year

8. Last year

	This Year Amount	Percent	Last Year Amount	Percent
Current assets				
Cash	$12,000	_____	$15,000	_____
Notes receivable	4000	_____	6000	_____
Accounts receivable	22,000	_____	18,000	_____
Inventory	26,000	_____	24,000	_____
Total current assets	64,000	80.0%	63,000	84.0%
Total plant and equipment	16,000	_____	12,000	_____
Total assets	_____	_____	_____	_____
Total current liabilities	$30,000	_____	$25,000	_____

All amounts are in thousands

Find the debt-to-equity ratio for each of the following firms. Round to the nearest hundredth.

9. **OTERO OFFICE SUPPLY** Use data from Exercise 1 for this year.

10. **VIRGINIA MUSIC** Use data from Exercise 4; owners' equity of $265,000 and long-term liabilities of $174,300.

11. **BLUETEX OXYGEN** Use data from Exercise 5 along with owners' equity of $2,800,000 and long-term debt of $3,045,000.

12. **AKTRON MOVIES** Use data from Exercise 6 along with owners' equity of $380,000 and no long-term debt.

13. To the manager of a firm, explain the meaning of an increase in the age of accounts receivable. (See Objective 2.)

14. List three ratios that can be used to analyze a balance sheet and the purpose of each ratio.

Find the ratio of net income after taxes to average owners' equity for the following firms. Round to the nearest tenth of a percent.

15. **INTERNATIONAL AIRLINE** The stockholders' equity in TNA Airline, a small startup international airline that uses small airplanes to move freight to and from Mexico, is $845,000 at the beginning of the year and $928,500 at the end of the year. Net income after taxes for the year was $54,400.

16. **PIPELINE COMPANY** TransCanada Pipe is an international company that does business both in Canada and in the United States. In thousands of dollars, owners' equity at the beginning of the year was $48,340 and $62,842 at the end of the year. Net income after taxes for the year was $6838.

Find the accounts receivable turnover rate and the average age of the accounts receivable for the following firms. Round each rate to the nearest tenth.

17. **CAMEROONIAN TOBACCO** Accounts receivable at the beginning of the year of $139,000; accounts receivable at the end of the year of $284,500; and net sales of $1,805,000.

18. **PLATES AND PLANTS GALORE** Accounts receivable at the beginning of the year of $110,000; accounts receivable at the end of the year of $80,000; and net sales of $875,000.

19. Explain why the acid-test ratio is a better measure of the financial health of a firm than the current ratio. (See Objectives 3 and 4.)

20. Explain why increased risk requires a higher return on investment. (See Objective 8.)

CHAPTER TERMS

Review the following terms to test your understanding of the chapter. For any terms you do not know, refer to the page number found next to that term.

accountant [p. 635]

accounts receivable turnover [p. 658]

acid-test ratio [p. 657]

assets [p. 648]

average age of accounts receivable [p. 659]

balance sheet [p. 648]

banker's ratio [p. 656]

calendar year [p. 636]

comparative balance sheet [p. 654]

comparative income statement [p. 642]

consolidated [p. 636]

cost of goods sold [p. 635]

current assets [p. 649]

current liabilities [p. 649]

current ratio [p. 656]

debt-to-equity ratio [p. 659]

ending inventory [p. 637]

fiscal year [p. 636]

fixed assets [p. 649]

gross profit [p. 635]

gross profit on sales [p. 635]

horizontal analysis [p. 644 or 655]

income statement [p. 635]

initial inventory [p. 637]

liabilities [p. 648]

liquid assets [p. 657 or 660]

long-term assets [p. 649]

long-term liabilities [p. 649]

net income [p. 635]

net income after taxes [p. 635]

net income before taxes [p. 635]

net sales [p. 635]

net worth [p. 649]

operating expenses [p. 635]

overhead [p. 635]

owners' equity [p. 648 or 649]

plant and equipment [p. 649]

plant assets [p. 649]

quick ratio [p. 657]

ratio of net income after taxes to average owners' equity [p. 657]

returns [p. 635]

short-term assets/liabilities [p. 649]

stockholders' equity [p. 649]

total revenue [p. 635]

vertical analysis [p. 641 or 654]

CONCEPTS

EXAMPLES

18.1 Gross profit, net income before taxes, and net income after taxes

Gross profit = Net sales − Cost of goods sold

Net income before taxes = Gross profit − Operating expenses

Net income after taxes = Net income before taxes − Income taxes

September: cost of goods sold, $156,000; operating expenses, $35,000; net sales, $210,000; taxes, $4000. Find gross profit, net income both before and after taxes.

Gross profit = $210,000 − $156,000 = $54,000

Net income before taxes = $54,000 − $35,000

= $19,000

Net income after taxes = $19,000 − $4000 = $15,000

18.2 Finding the percent of net sales of individual items

Subtract returns from gross sales to determine net sales. Then divide the value of an item by net sales to obtain percent of net sales.

Express the following items for Capitol Appliance as percents of net sales: gross sales, $340,000; returns, $15,000; cost of goods sold, $210,000; wages, $19,000; gross profit. Round percents to the nearest tenth.

Net sales = $340,000 − $15,000 = $325,000

Gross profit = $325,000 − $210,000 = $115,000

$$\text{Percent gross sales} = \frac{\$340,000}{\$325,000} = 104.6\%$$

$$\text{Percent returns} = \frac{\$15,000}{\$325,000} = 4.6\%$$

$$\text{Percent cost of goods sold} = \frac{\$210,000}{\$325,000} = 64.6\%$$

$$\text{Percent wages} = \frac{\$19,000}{\$325,000} = 5.8\%$$

$$\text{Percent gross profit} = \frac{\$115,000}{\$325,000} = 35.4\%$$

18.2 Comparing income statements to published charts

In one chart, list the percents of net sales for each item from a published chart and a particular company.

Prepare a vertical analysis of Monica's Shoe Store.

Cost of Goods	Gross Profit	Wages	
65%	35%	6.4%	Monica's Shoe Store
60.3%	39.7%	10.3%	From chart

Her cost of goods is high, gross profit is low, and wages are low.

18.2 Preparing a horizontal analysis

List last year's and this year's values for each item. Then calculate the amount of the increase or decrease for each item and express it as a percent of the previous year.

The results of a horizontal analysis of the portion of a business is given. Calculate the percent of increase or decrease in each item.

	This Year	Last Year	Increase (Decrease) Amount	Percent
Gross sales	$735,000	$700,000	$35,000	5%
Returns	5000	10,000	(5000)	(50%)
Net sales	730,000	690,000	40,000	5.8%
Cost of goods sold	530,000	540,000	(10,000)	(1.9%)
Gross profit	200,000	150,000	50,000	33.3%

18.3 Fundamental formula for accounting

$$\text{Assets} = \text{Liabilities} + \text{Owners' equity}$$

or

$$\text{Assets} - \text{Liabilities} = \text{Owners' equity}$$

Stemco Tubing has assets of $842,300 and liabilities of $625,100. Find the owners' equity.

$$\$842,300 - \$625,100 = \$217,200$$

18.4 Current ratio; acid-test ratio; ratio of net income after taxes to the average owners' equity

$$\frac{\text{Current}}{\text{ratio}} = \frac{\text{Current assets}}{\text{Current liabilities}}$$

$$\frac{\text{Acid-test}}{\text{ratio}} = \frac{\text{Liquid assets}}{\text{Current liabilities}}$$

$$\text{Ratio} = \frac{\text{Net income after taxes}}{\text{Average owners' equity}}$$

The Circle Towne Agency has current assets of $250,000, current liabilities of $110,000, cash of $45,000, and accounts receivable of $80,000. The agency had owners' equity of $140,000 at the beginning of the year, and $180,000 at the end of the year. The net income after taxes was $25,000. Calculate the following ratios.

$$\frac{\text{Current}}{\text{ratio}} = \frac{\$250,000}{\$110,000} = 2.27$$

$$\frac{\text{Acid-test}}{\text{ratio}} = \frac{\$45,000 + \$80,000}{\$110,000} = 1.14 \quad \text{Rounded}$$

$$\begin{array}{l}\text{Average} \\ \text{owners'} \\ \text{equity}\end{array} = \frac{\$140,000 + \$180,000}{2}$$

$$= \$160,000$$

Ratio of net income after taxes to average owners' equity:

$$\frac{\$25,000}{\$160,000} = 0.156{:}1$$

18.4 Accounts receivable turnover

Accounts receivable turnover

$$= \frac{\text{Net sales}}{\text{Average accounts receivable}}$$

Average age of accounts receivable

Average age of accounts receivable

$$= \frac{365}{\text{Accounts receivable turnover}}$$

Debt-to-equity ratio

Debt-to-equity ratio

$$= \frac{\text{Current} \quad \text{Long-term}}{\text{liabilities} + \text{liabilities}}$$

A firm has net sales of $793,750; accounts receivable of $50,000 at the beginning of the year, $75,000 at the end of the year; current liabilities of $15,000; long-term liabilities of $10,000; and owners' equity of $80,000. Find the accounts receivable turnover, the average age of accounts receivable, and the debt-to-equity ratio.

Average accounts receivable

$$= \frac{\$50,000 + \$75,000}{2} = \$62,500$$

$$\text{Accounts receivable turnover} = \frac{\$793,750}{\$62,500} = 12.7$$

$$\text{Average age of accounts receivable} = \frac{365}{12.7} = 28.7 \text{ days}$$

$$\text{Debt-to-equity ratio} = \frac{\$15,000 + \$10,000}{\$80,000} = 0.31$$

CHAPTER 18   Review Exercises

The answer section includes answers to all Review Exercises.

Find the gross profit and net income before taxes for the following. [18.1]

	Cost of Goods	Operating Expenses	Net Sales
1.	$124,800	$89,200	$312,200
2.	$379,520	$124,800	$643,250
3.	$300,900	$98,400	$442,500
4.	$606,520	$212,300	$842,400

Find the cost of goods sold for each of the following. [18.1]

	Initial Inventory	Cost of Goods Purchased	Freight	Final Inventory
5.	$215,400	$422,000	$26,300	$247,100
6.	$125,400	$94,300	$8200	$101,400
7.	$84,000	$52,400	$4300	$98,000
8.	$184,200	$245,000	$18,300	$165,400

Find the net income after taxes for each. Then find the ratio of net income after taxes to average owners' equity. [18.1]

9. A surgeon has revenues of $660,500; no inventory and thus no cost of goods sold; total expenses of $412,900; average owners' equity of $340,000; and taxes of $58,800.

10. One quarter, Beck Floors had net sales of $894,200; cost of goods sold of $462,800; expenses of $304,100; average owners' equity of $389,700; and taxes of $36,700.

Complete the accompanying income statements for the following firms. [18.1]

11. Lori's Boutique had gross sales of $175,000 last year, with returns of $8000. The inventory on January 1 was $44,000. A total of $126,000 worth of goods was purchased with freight of $2000. The inventory on December 31 was $52,000. Salaries and wages were $9000, rent was $4000, advertising was $1500, utilities were $1000, taxes on inventory and payroll totaled $2000, and miscellaneous expenses totaled $3000.

LORI'S BOUTIQUE
INCOME STATEMENT FOR
THE YEAR ENDING DECEMBER 31

Gross sales		_____
Returns		_____
Net sales		_____
Inventory, January 1	_____	
Cost of goods		
purchased	_____	
Freight	_____	
Total cost of goods purchased	_____	
Total of goods available for sale	_____	
Inventory, December 31	_____	
Cost of goods sold		_____
Gross profit		_____
Expenses		
Salaries and wages	_____	
Rent	_____	
Advertising	_____	
Utilities	_____	
Taxes on inventory, payroll	_____	
Miscellaneous expenses	_____	
Total expenses		_____
Net income before taxes		========

12. The Guitar Warehouse had gross sales of $2,215,000 with returns of $26,000. The inventory on January 1 was $215,000. A total of $1,123,000 worth of goods was purchased with freight of $4000. The inventory on December 31 was $265,000. Salaries and wages were $154,000, rent was $59,000, advertising was $11,000, utilities were $12,000, taxes on inventory and payroll totaled $10,000, and miscellaneous expenses totaled $9000. Income taxes for the year were $242,300.

THE GUITAR WAREHOUSE
INCOME STATEMENT
FOR THE YEAR ENDING DECEMBER 31

Gross sales		_____
Returns		_____
Net sales		_____
Inventory, January 1	_____	
Cost of goods		
purchased	_____	
Freight	_____	
Total cost of goods purchased	_____	
Total of goods available for sale	_____	
Inventory, December 31	_____	
Cost of goods sold		_____

THE GUITAR WAREHOUSE
INCOME STATEMENT
FOR THE YEAR ENDING DECEMBER 31

Gross profit   _____

   Expenses

      Salaries and wages   _____

      Rent   _____

      Advertising   _____

      Utilities   _____

      Taxes on inventory, payroll   _____

      Miscellaneous expenses   _____

      Total expenses   _____

Net income before taxes   _____

   Income taxes   _____

Net income   _____

Prepare a vertical analysis for the following firms. Round to the nearest tenth of a percent. [18.2]

Cost of Goods Sold	Operating Expenses	Net Sales
13. $485,800	$104,300	$812,200
14. $813,200	$387,100	$1,329,400

Complete the following chart. Express each item as a percent of net sales and then write in the appropriate average percent from Table 18.1. Round each percent to the nearest tenth of a percent. [18.2]

15.

JALISCO MEXICAN FOODS (3RD QUARTER)

	Amount	Percent	Percent from Table 18.1
Net sales	$300,000	100%	100%
Cost of goods sold	$125,000	_____	_____
Gross profit	$175,000	_____	_____
Wages	$72,000	_____	_____
Rent	$12,000	_____	_____
Advertising	$5700	_____	_____
Total expenses	$123,000	_____	_____
Net income	$52,000	_____	_____

Complete the following balance sheet. [18.3]

16. Gaskets, Inc. manufactures gaskets for gasoline engines. It has been under intense financial pressure recently due to foreign competition. The firm has notes payable of $410,000; accounts receivable of $460,000; cash of $240,000; long-term notes payable of $194,000; buildings worth $260,000; inventory of $225,000; fixtures worth $48,000; notes receivable of $180,000; land worth $180,000; accounts payable of $882,000; and mortgages payable of $220,000. Use the fundamental formula of accounting to find owners' equity.

GASKETS, INC.
BALANCE SHEET FOR DECEMBER 31

Assets

Current assets

   Cash   _____

   Notes receivable   _____

   Accounts receivable   _____

   Inventory   _____

      Total current assets   _____

GASKETS, INC.
BALANCE SHEET FOR DECEMBER 31

Plant assets
  Land   _____
  Buildings   _____
  Fixtures   _____
    Total plant assets   _____
Total assets

Liabilities

Current liabilities
  Notes payable   _____
  Accounts payable   _____
    Total current liabilities   _____
Long-term liabilities
  Mortgages payable   _____
  Long-term notes payable   _____
    Total long-term liabilities   _____
Total liabilities

Owners' equity

Owners' equity   _____

Total liabilities and owners' equity

Calculate the current ratio, acid-test ratio, and debt-to-equity ratio for the following. Round to the nearest hundredth. [18.4]

	Current Assets	Current Liabilities	Long-Term Liabilities	Owners' Equity	Liquid Assets
17.	$342,000	$260,000	$140,000	$225,000	$120,000
18.	$95,000	$115,000	$85,000	$48,000	$5000
19.	$160,000	$205,000	$0	$185,000	$145,000

Find the accounts receivable turnover rate and the average age of the accounts receivable in the following firms. Round to the nearest tenth. [18.4]

20. Accounts receivable at beginning of year $875,400
    Accounts receivable at end of year $962,300
    Net sales $4,612,000

21. Accounts receivable at beginning of year $126,800
    Accounts receivable at end of year $92,400
    Net sales $942,500

22. Complete the following comparative balance sheet. Round to the nearest tenth of a percent. [18.4]

	This Year		Last Year	
	Amount	Percent	Amount	Percent
Current assets				
Cash	$28,000	_____	$22,000	_____
Notes receivable	$12,000	_____	$15,000	_____
Accounts receivable	$39,000	_____	$31,500	_____
Inventory	$22,000	_____	$20,000	_____
Total current assets	$101,000	_____	$88,500	_____
Total plant and equipment	$48,000	_____	$16,000	_____
Total assets	_____	_____	_____	_____
Total current liabilities	$38,000	_____	$36,000	_____

CHAPTER 18	Business Application Case #1
	Borrowing from a Bank

Tom Walker wants to expand his small bicycle shop and has gone to a bank for a loan. The commercial loan officer asks Walker for his most recent income statement and balance sheets based on the following data.

Gross sales	$212,000	Salaries and wages	$37,000
Returns	$12,500	Rent	$12,000
Inventory on January 1	$44,000	Advertising	$2000
Cost of goods purchased	$75,000	Utilities	$3000
Freight	$8000	Taxes on inventory, payroll	$7000
Inventory on December 31	$26,000	Miscellaneous expenses	$4500
		Income taxes	$4320

(a) Prepare an income statement.

WALKER BICYCLE SHOP
INCOME STATEMENT
YEAR ENDING DECEMBER 31

Gross sales	_____
Returns	_____
Net sales	_____
Inventory, January 1	_____
Cost of goods purchased _____	
Freight _____	
Total cost of goods purchased	_____
Total of goods available for sale	_____
Inventory, December 31	_____
Cost of goods sold	_____
Gross profit	_____
Expenses	
Salaries and wages _____	
Rent _____	
Advertising _____	
Utilities _____	
Taxes on inventory, payroll _____	
Miscellaneous expenses _____	
Total expenses	_____
Net income before taxes	_____
Income taxes	_____
Net income after taxes	_____

(b) Express the following items as a percent of net sales. Round to tenths of a percent.

Gross sales	_____	Salaries and wages	_____
Returns	_____	Rent	_____
Cost of goods sold	_____	Utilities	_____

(c) After the year is completed, Walker has $62,000 in cash, $2500 in notes receivable, $8200 in accounts receivable, and $26,000 in inventory. He has land valued at $7600, buildings valued at $28,000, and fixtures worth $13,500. He also has $4500 in notes payable and $27,000 in accounts payable, mortgages for $15,000, long-term notes payable of $8000, and owners' equity of $93,300. Prepare a balance sheet.

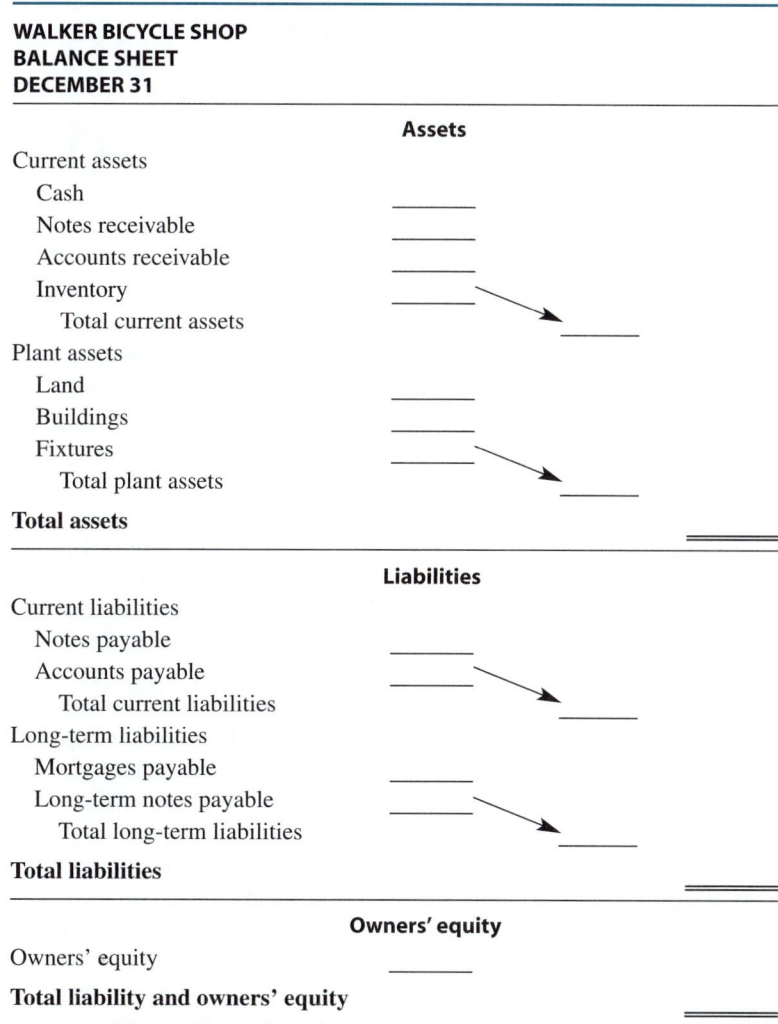

WALKER BICYCLE SHOP
BALANCE SHEET
DECEMBER 31

Assets

Current assets
   Cash   _____
   Notes receivable   _____
   Accounts receivable   _____
   Inventory   _____
     Total current assets   _____
Plant assets
   Land   _____
   Buildings   _____
   Fixtures   _____
     Total plant assets   _____
Total assets

Liabilities

Current liabilities
   Notes payable   _____
   Accounts payable   _____
     Total current liabilities   _____
Long-term liabilities
   Mortgages payable   _____
   Long-term notes payable   _____
     Total long-term liabilities   _____
Total liabilities

Owners' equity

Owners' equity   _____
Total liability and owners' equity

(d) Find the current ratio and the acid-test ratio for Walker's business. Round to nearest hundredth.

(e) If you were the commercial loan officer, would you approve Walker's requested loan? Why or why not?

CHAPTER 18 # Business Application Case #2
Analyzing Financial Statements

First, choose one large, publicly held company that you are familiar with, such as Apple, eBay, Nike, Microsoft, Toyota, Target, Best Buy, etc. Go to any of the financial Web sites (e.g., finance.yahoo.com) or to the company's home page on the Web and find the income statement and balance sheet for the two most recent years. Then find all of the following values: current ratio, acid-test ratio, ratio of net income after taxes to average owners' equity, accounts receivable turnover, average age of accounts receivable, and debt-to-equity ratio. Based on everything you know about the company, including personal experience, is the company doing well? If so, do you expect it to continue to do well in the future?

Securities and Distribution of Profit and Overhead

Businesses usually distribute some or all of their profits to the owners. The way in which profits are distributed depends on the type of company. For example, an individual who owns a small business, such as a hair salon, a small restaurant, or a small retail store, often operates the business as a **sole proprietorship**. In a sole proprietorship, there is no division between personal and company assets and the profits or losses pass directly through, to the owner. Both personal assets of the owner as well as business assets can be **attached** to pay debts in a sole proprietorship.

A **partnership** is a business formed by two or more people and is common for somewhat larger businesses such as a chain of two small retail stores or the ownership of a 50-unit apartment house. Unless they have a prior agreement, profits in a partnership are divided equally among the partners. Partners are jointly and severally liable for partnership debts. This means that the lender to the partnership can recover the entire indebtedness from any of the partners. So be very careful about going into a partnership with someone! You may end up having to pay off all of the debts. **Silent partners** invest money but are usually not directly involved in the day-to-day operations of the partnership. A **limited partnership** is one in which some partners invest money and then do not participate in the running of the business. Unlike in a regular partnership, a limited partner's loss is limited to the amount invested.

Because of the lack of protection for personal assets in regular partnerships, most larger businesses are set up as **corporations**. The people investing money in a corporation have **limited liability** and can lose no more than they have invested in the corporation. Another advantage of a corporation is that its structure and the laws make it relatively simple to have many different owners. Large companies sometimes incorporate in states or countries that have particularly favorable laws for them, such as the state of Delaware or the country of Antilles. However, most smaller firms incorporate in the state where they do most of their business and where their offices are located.

Figure 19.1 shows U.S. wages and corporate profits as a percent of **gross domestic product (GDP)**. GDP is one measure of the total economic activity in a country. Notice that wages have fallen from over 50% of GDP during 1950–1975 to less than 45% of GDP today. During the past 5 years in particular, corporate profits have risen to over 10% of GDP. Effectively, wages have not kept up with the increase in corporate profits during the last few years.

STOP
and think

Figure 19.1 really talks about the piece of the total income that goes for wages and also for corporate profits. Do you think corporations make too little or too much profit, or do you have enough information to make a decision? Explain. Are wages high enough? What would happen if corporate profits were somehow smaller and wages were higher? Remember, we live in a global world, so you have to consider the effects worldwide.

Employee Compensation and Corporate Profits as Share of GDP
Quarterly figures: shaded areas show recessions

Source: Dept. of Commerce; Economic Policy Institute.

Figure 19.1

| **19.1** | **Distribution of Profits in a Corporation** |

OBJECTIVES

1 *Compare preferred and common stocks.*

2 *Distribute profits to shareholders and calculate dividend per share.*

3 *Find earnings per share.*

A corporation is set up with money, or **capital**, raised by selling shares of **stock**. A share of stock represents partial ownership in a corporation. If 1 million shares of stock are sold to establish a new firm, the owner of one share is a **stockholder** who owns 1/1,000,000 of the corporation. A **publicly held corporation** is one whose stock is registered to trade in public stock markets such as the New York Stock Exchange. Stock ownership can be indicated by a **stock certificate**, as shown in Figure 19.2. Publicly held corporations must disclose their operating results to the public regularly. Managers must be careful that their employees do not participate in **insider trading**, or buying and selling stock on information that employees have but that has not yet been made available to the public. Managers also must be careful not to make significant misstatements in the information they release to the public since doing so can result in fines or imprisonment.

Corporations are required to hold an **annual meeting** that is open to all shareholders of the company. At this meeting, the management of the firm is open to questions from stockholders. The stockholders also elect a **board of directors**—a group of people who represent the stockholders. The board of directors hires the **executive officers** of the corporation, such as the president and vice presidents. The board of directors also typically authorizes the distribution of some of the profits in the form of dividends. Dividends are covered in more detail later in this section.

Objective

1 *Compare Preferred and Common Stocks.* Corporations of all sizes need money to operate and grow. Without growth, they will not hire additional employees and may even lay workers off. Corporations can raise money by selling ownership in the company by selling

Figure 19.2

stock, as discussed in **Section 19.2**. Or, they can borrow money from banks or other investors or sell bonds, as discussed in **Section 19.3**. Most stock issued by corporations is **common stock**, which has no guarantees. In the event of bankruptcy, common stockholders receive nothing until bankruptcy attorneys, debtors, and preferred shareholders are paid in full. However, common stockholders vote at the annual shareholder meeting, so they have some control over some of the issues faced by the corporation.

Some corporations also issue **preferred stock**, which has the following advantages over common stock:

Advantages of Preferred Stock

- Dividends on preferred stock are paid before any dividends are paid on common stock.
- In the event of bankruptcy, owners of preferred stocks are paid before common stockholders receive anything. Preferred shareholders receive nothing until all debts of the corporation have been paid.
- Each share has a **par value**—the amount that must be paid to its owner before common stockholders receive anything.
- Each share has a stated **dividend**, usually given as a percent of par value.

Holders of preferred stock are usually not allowed to vote at the annual meetings of the corporation. Also, most preferred stock is **nonparticipating**, meaning that the corporation will never pay dividends above the stated rate. However, holders of **participating** preferred stock could share in the successes of the corporation by an increase in the dividend.

Sometimes, preferred stock is given additional features to make it more attractive to potential buyers. For example, the stock may be **cumulative preferred stock**, which means that any dividends not paid in the past must be paid before common stockholders receive any money. The stock might also be **convertible preferred stock**, which means that one share is convertible into a stated number of shares of common stock at some future date.

Objective

2 *Distribute Profits to Shareholders and Calculate Dividend per Share.* The next examples show how the profits of a corporation might be distributed.

EXAMPLE 1 Calculating Dividend per Share

Thornton Electronics had a net income of $1,200,000 last year. The board of directors decides to reinvest $500,000 in the business and distribute the remaining $700,000 to stockholders as dividends. The company has 40,000 shares of $100 par value, 6% preferred stock, and 350,000 shares of common stock. Find (a) the amount per share paid to holders of preferred stock and (b) the amount per share given to holders of common stock.

Solution

(a) Each share of preferred stock has a par value of $100 and pays a dividend of 6%. The dividend per share is

Dividend rate
↓

Dividend per share = $100 × 6% = $100 × 0.06 = $6

A dividend of $6 must be paid for each share of preferred stock. Since there are 40,000 shares of preferred, a total of

$6 × 40,000 = $240,000

will be paid to owners of preferred shares.

(b) A total of $700,000 is available for stockholders, with $240,000 going to the owners of preferred shares, leaving

$700,000   Total
− 240,000   Preferred
$460,000

available for the common stockholders. There are 350,000 shares of common stock outstanding, with each share being paid a dividend of

$$\frac{\$460,000}{350,000} = \$1.31 \text{ per share} \quad \text{Rounded}$$

EXAMPLE 2 Finding Cumulative Dividends

Due to excessive debt, Alamo Energy paid no dividend last year. The company did much better this year and the board of directors has set aside $175,000 for the payment of dividends. The company has 12,500 outstanding shares of cumulative preferred stock having par value of $50, with an 8% dividend. The company also has 40,000 shares of common stock. What dividend will be paid to the owners of each type of stock?

Solution The dividend per share of preferred stock follows.

Dividend rate
↓

$50 par value × 8% = $4

Dividends have not been paid for 2 years (last year and this year), so each share of preferred stock must be paid

$4 per share × 2 years = $8

before any dividends can be paid to holders of common stock. Since there are 12,500 shares of cumulative preferred stock outstanding, a total of

$$\$8 \times 12{,}500 = \$100{,}000$$

must be paid to the owners of the preferred stock. This leaves

$$
\begin{array}{rl}
\$175{,}000 & \text{Total} \\
-\ \ 100{,}000 & \text{Preferred} \\
\hline
\$75{,}000 &
\end{array}
$$

to be divided among owners of common stock. Since there are 40,000 shares of common stock, each share will be paid a dividend of

$$\frac{\$75{,}000}{40{,}000} = \$1.88 \quad \text{Rounded}$$

> **NOTE**   In Example 2, the dividend for owners of preferred stock was paid for each of the last 2 years before any common stock dividends were paid.

Objective

3   *Find Earnings per Share.*   One way to measure the financial success of a corporation is by finding the **earnings per share** made by the corporation. Earnings per share is found with the following formula.

$$\text{Earnings per share} = \frac{\text{Net income} - \text{Dividends on preferred}}{\text{Number of shares of common outstanding}}$$

EXAMPLE 3   Finding Earnings per Share

Adam Nguyen started an import business as a sole proprietorship with an investment of $380,000. He then took on a partner who remains with the company as part owner. A few years later, they incorporated under the name of Asia Imports, Inc. The founding owners gave stock to three key employees so that they too will share in the success of the firm and therefore be motivated to stay and work harder.

(a) Asia Imports, Inc. had a net income of $420,000 last year after paying salaries and taxes. It had 500,000 shares of common stock outstanding and no preferred stock. Find the earnings per share.

$$\text{Earnings per share} = \frac{\$420{,}000 - \$0}{500{,}000 \text{ shares}} = \$0.84 \text{ per share}$$

(b) This year, the company issued preferred stock and paid $85,000 in dividends to preferred shareholders out of a net income of $544,000 after salaries and taxes. There are still 500,000 shares of common stock. Find the earnings per share for this year.

$$\text{Earnings per share} = \frac{\$544{,}000 - \$85{,}000}{500{,}000 \text{ shares}} = \$0.92 \text{ per share} \quad \text{Rounded}$$

(c) Find Mr. Nguyen's total dividend this year if he owns 300,000 shares of common stock and one-fourth of the preferred stock.

$$\text{Total dividend} = \text{Dividend from common stock} + \text{Dividend from preferred stock}$$

$$= 300{,}000 \times \$0.92 \qquad + \qquad \left(\frac{1}{4} \times \$85{,}000\right)$$

$$= \$297{,}250$$

(d) Find Mr. Nguyen's total dividends in a bad year with no profits, no dividends on common stock, and only a $10,000 dividend to preferred shareholders.

$$\text{Total dividend} = \frac{1}{4} \times \$10{,}000 = \$2500$$

19.1 | Exercises

Find the dividend that will be paid for each share of preferred stock and common stock.

	Common Stock (in shares)	Preferred Stock (in shares)	Total Dividends
1.	80,000	None	$0
2.	200,000	None	$16,000
3.	175,000	50,000, $10 par value, 3%	$40,000
4.	200,000	30,000, $5 par value, 5%	$80,000
5.	1,000,000	100,000, $1000 par value, 2%	$2,000,000
6.	500,000	40,000, $50 par value, 3%	$44,800

Solve the following application problems. Round percents to the nearest tenth and money to the nearest cent.

7. **ANIMAL HOSPITAL** Reeves Animal Hospital had a net income of $320,000 last year. If $280,000 was reinvested in an expansion of the business and the remainder was paid in dividends, what is the dividend per share on the 400,000 shares of common stock outstanding?

8. **TUGBOAT COMPANY** Fleet Operations, Inc. had a net income of $1,480,000 last year. The board of directors decided to purchase another tugboat for $850,000 and pay the remainder of the profits out as dividends. Find the dividend per share given 504,000 common shares of stock outstanding.

9. **FASHION GOODS** Junior Fashions operates three separate retail stores in the San Francisco Bay area. It has 250,000 shares of common stock and 15,000 shares of preferred stock with a $100 par value at $6\frac{1}{2}\%$. Find the dividend per share for both preferred and common stock if the total dividend is $280,000.

10. **MOVING COMPANY** A moving company affiliated with North American Van Lines has 200,000 shares of common stock and 8000 shares of preferred stock with a par value of $100 per share at 7%. Find the dividend per share for both preferred and common stock if the board of directors allocates $165,000 for dividends.

11. **PAPER PRODUCTS COMPANY** Northern Maine Paper Products has sold 25,000 shares of $40 par value, 4% preferred stock to help remodel its mill. It already had 300,000 shares of common stock. Find the dividend per share if the total profit is $850,000 and 35% was distributed to shareholders.

12. **DENTAL SUPPLIES** To help him start up a dental supply company, James Madison sold to investors 230,000 shares of common stock and 10,000 shares of preferred stock with a par value of $100 at 4%. Find the dividend per share for both types of shares if 60% of the $148,000 in profits is distributed to shareholders.

13. **COMPUTER COMPANY** Since the computer business is booming, a small new company has decided to pay no dividend for 3 years and, instead, reinvest the profits in expansion. During the fourth year, the board decides to pay a dividend of $2,675,000. Find the dividend per share if the company has outstanding 20,000 cumulative preferred shares of $100 par value at 5% and 450,000 common shares.

14. **RUBBER GOODS COMPANY** To pay for a new factory, Wilson Rubber Goods has paid no dividend for 2 years. Now, at the end of the third year, a dividend of $1,200,000 was declared. Find the dividend per share if the company has 10,000 cumulative preferred shares outstanding of $100 par value at 10% and 400,000 common shares.

15. **STETSON HATS** A manufacturer of Stetson hats reported an after-tax net income of $400,000. The firm had 120,000 common shares and no preferred shares. Find the earnings per share.

16. **WASHERS AND DRYERS** A large retailer of appliances had 750,000 common shares and no preferred shares. In a year with $2,350,000 in net income, find the earnings per share.

17. **FAR EAST IMPORTS** Eastern Manufacturing, Inc., operates two factories in Thailand that produce goods shipped to Asia, Australia, Europe, and the United States. The firm has 4,500,000 shares of common stock and 100,000 shares of preferred stock outstanding with a $100 par value at 6%. Last year, the company had a net income of $1,235,000 with $600,000 paid to preferred shareholders and the remainder paid to common stock shareholders. Find the earnings per share of common stock.

18. **FRUIT DISTRIBUTOR** Florida Fruit, Inc. has 50,000 shares of preferred stock outstanding with a $50 par value at 7%. It also had 4,000,000 shares of common stock outstanding. This year, the company has a net income of $138,000 with all of it going to shareholders. Find the earnings per share of common stock.

19. **EARNINGS PER SHARE** Arckat has 250,000 shares of common stock and 40,000 shares of preferred stock ($50 par, 4%) outstanding. Net income last year and this year were, respectively, $680,000 and $765,000. The board of directors disbursed 40% of net income as dividends in both years. Find the dividend per share of common stock (a) last year and (b) this year. (c) Find the percent increase in the *earnings per share* of this year over last year.

20. **RECORDING STUDIO** Rhythm Recording Studio has 60,000 shares of $1000 par value, 4% preferred stock. It also has 2,000,000 shares of common stock outstanding. This year the company increased its net income by 20% over last year's $4,300,000. In both years the board of directors authorized the payment of 60% of net income for payment of dividends. Find the dividend per share of common stock for (a) last year and (b) this year. (c) Find the percent increase in *earnings per share* of this year over last year.

21. **PAVING COMPANY** Bill Baker owns a paving company with 1,000,000 shares of common stock. He wishes to help provide for his six grandchildren, so he establishes 20,000 shares of preferred stock with a $100 par value, 8%, and donates the preferred stock to a trust for his grandchildren. Given a year with a net income of $620,000 and a payment of 30% of net income for dividends, find the dividend to be paid on behalf of *each* grandchild.

22. **PAVING COMPANY** In Exercise 21, find the dividend to be paid on behalf of *each* grandchild if net income is $85,000 and 30% of net income is used for dividends.

23. Explain the difference between common stock and preferred stock. (See Objective 1.)

24. List several reasons why a corporation would issue preferred stock in addition to common stock. (See Objective 1.)

19.2 Buying Stock

OBJECTIVES

1 *Know the basics of stock ownership.*

2 *Read stock tables.*

3 *Find the commission for buying or selling stocks.*

4 *Find the total to purchase or sell stock.*

5 *Find the current yield on a stock.*

6 *Find the PE ratio of a stock.*

7 *Define the common stock indices.*

8 *Define a mutual fund.*

Objective

1 *Know the Basics of Stock Ownership.* Buying stock in a corporation makes the stockholder a *part owner* of the corporation. In return for the money a person invests in stock, he or she shares in any profits the company makes. Hopefully, the company will do well and prosper. If this happens, many other people will want the company's stock, and they will be willing to pay a good price for its shares. If this happens, the stockholders may share in profits through dividends and then sell their stock at a profit.

On the other hand, if the company does not do well, then fewer people will want its stock and the price will fall. The price of the shares of most large, publicly held firms is set by supply and demand at institutions called **stock exchanges**. The largest stock exchange is the New York Stock Exchange, located on Wall Street in New York City. Many foreign countries, including Japan, Taiwan, England, China, Canada, and Mexico, have their own stock exchanges. Figure 19.3 was taken from *Barron's* online newspaper (online.barrons.com) published by Dow Jones & Co. This newspaper lists prices for many stocks and bonds as well as mutual funds.

There is almost unlimited advice about which stocks to buy. However, studies have shown that very few investors consistently make better-than-average returns on their investments. Many professionals suggest either that you purchase the stocks of companies that you know very well or that you purchase mutual funds that hold the stocks of many different companies. Mutual funds are discussed later in this section.

| 52 week | | | | | | | | Dividend | 52 week | | | | | | | | Dividend |
High	Low	Stock	Sym	Vol (100s)	Yld %	P/E	Close	Latest	High	Low	Stock	Sym	Vol (100s)	Yld %	P/E	Close	Latest
68.81	22.08	Aflac	AFL	632716	4.9	8	22.9	qp.28	19.95	5.1	B&G Foods	BGF	1133	15.2	...	10.13	qr.3845
71.19	17.74	AGCO Cp	AG	94762	...	5	19.96	...	11.8	2.54	B&G Foods A	BGS	2417	15.6	10	4.37	qr.17
39.13	24.02	AGL Res	ATG	13638	5.4	11	31	q.42	26.74	17.3	BB&T CapTrV		2833	2.4	...	24.4	.5905
10.35	1.21	AgriaCp ADS	GRO	z51724	...	...	1.36	...	45.31	17.56	BB&T Cp	BBT	628674	9.6	7	19.65	q.47
73.07	5.2	AK Steel	AKS	276755	2.2	2	8.93	q.05	18.85	4.7	BabcockBrwnAir	FLY	3659	16.6	4	4.81	q.20
38.38	13.5	Amcol	ACO	4330	4.0	10	17.92	q.18	62.74	17.58	BadgerMtr	BMI	5902	1.9	16	23.33	q.11
16.49	4	AMR	AMR	711178	...	dd	7.73	...	90.81	24.4	BakrHughs	BHI	153036	2.0	6	30.6	q.15
23	10.42	AMR Pines		z33375	15.2	...	12.95	q.4922	39.9	10.71	BaldorElec	BEZ	17058	4.6	7	14.83	q.17
92.6	31.03	ASA	ASA	1383	4.3	...	45.98	1.70	56.2	27.37	Ball Cp	BLL	42209	1.0	12	38.55	q.10
40.7	20.9	AT&T	T	990555	6.4	11	25.51	qp.41	101.61	73.37	Bard CR	BCR	31086	.7	24	88.41	q.16
30.22	13.27	AaronRent	RNT	27213	.3	17	26.31	qp.017	34.23	10.77	BarnesNoble	BKS	29082	5.6	11	17.83	q.25
25.92	13.25	AaronRent A	RNTA	19	.3	13	20.9	qp.017	32.33	8.51	BarnesGP	B	9742	5.0	6	12.72	q.16
60.78	45.75	AbbottLab	ABT	343384	2.7	17	53.01	q.36	54.74	17.27	BarckGld	ABX	569619	1.1	18	35.57	b.20
82.06	13.66	Abercrombie A	ANF	84497	3.5	4	20.29	q.175	32.97	7.32	BscEngySvs	BAS	9088	...	5	9.59	...
26.13	.24	AbitibiBowater	ABH	17218	...	dd	.59	Y	71.53	47.41	BaxterInt	BAX	178345	1.8	18	56.77	qp.26
25.72	8.68	AcadiaRlty	AKR	15103	7.2	10	11.66	q.21+.55	147,000	74,100	BerkHathwy A	BRKA	z3986	...	18	88,800	...
24.9	2.88	AdvMedOp	EYE	119340	...	59	21.73	...	49.65	16.42	Best Buy	BBY	352511	2.1	10	27.24	q.14
8.08	1.62	AdvMicro	AMD	451501	...	dd	2.02	...	35.33	12.9	BigLots	BIG	69756	...	7	14.11	...
37.4	12.52	Aeropostale	ARO	67910	...	10	20.59	...	66.96	14.93	BillBarrett	BBG	24693	...	9	19.74	...
54.9	14.21	Aetna	AET	165353	.1	9	29.07	a.04	29.5	5.88	BiomdTltyTr	BMR	58871	11.6	15	11.6	q.335

Source: From *Barron's*.

Figure 19.3

Objective

2 *Read Stock Tables.* Daily stock prices can easily be found on the World Wide Web, but some newspapers also print daily stock prices for at least some stocks. The format of the information given varies from one source of information to another, but we will be using the format used by *Barron's*, as shown in Figure 19.3.

> **NOTE** Historically, fractions were used for stock prices but that changed in 2001 and decimal numbers are now used.

EXAMPLE 1 Reading the Stock Table

Roman Rodriguez has been studying stocks. He particularly likes music and computers, so one of his favorite retail stores is Best Buy. Since he knows Best Buy from personal experience, he is interested in buying stock in the company. Analyze the following information on Best Buy taken from Figure 19.3.

| 52 week | | | | | | | | Dividend |
High	Low	Stock	Sym	Vol (100s)	Yld %	P/E	Close	Latest
49.65	16.42	Best Buy	BBY	352511	2.1	10	27.24	q.14

Solution

(a) The highest price the stock sold for during the past year was $49.65 per share.
(b) The lowest price the stock sold for during the past year was $16.42 per share.
(c) The company name is shown as Best Buy, but it refers to Best Buy Co., Inc.
(d) The stock trades under the symbol BBY on the New York Stock Exchange.
(e) The number of shares traded that day was $352511 \times 100 = 35{,}251{,}100$ shares.
(f) The dividend yield was 2.1% per year based on the close price of the stock.
(g) The ratio of the close price for the day to company earnings was 10.
(h) The close price for the stock that day was $27.24 per share.
(i) The latest quarterly dividend was $0.14 per share.

If the quarterly dividend continues at $0.14 per share, then the annual dividend will be 4 times that amount, or $0.56.

EXAMPLE 2 Finding the Cost to Buy Stock

Ignoring commissions, first find (a) Roman Rodriguez's combined cost to purchase 100 shares of Best Buy (BBY) at the close for the day and 200 shares of Barnes and Noble (BKS) at the close for the day. Then find (b) the combined dividend these shares would pay for a quarter. Finally, find (c) the annual dividend and the annual percent return on investment to the nearest tenth of a percent (annual dividend ÷ total cost). Does that rate compare favorably with interest paid on a certificate of deposit?

Solution

(a) Cost 100 shares BBY $= 100 \times \$27.24 = \$2724$
Cost 200 shares of BKS $= 200 \times \$17.83 = \underline{\$3566}$
Total cost $= \$6290$

(b) Add quarterly dividends from the two companies.
From 100 shares of BBY $= 100 \times \$0.14 = \$14.00$
From 200 shares of BKS $= 200 \times \$0.25 = \underline{\$50.00}$
Total quarterly dividend $= \$64.00$

(c) Annual dividend $= 4 \times \$64 = \$256$

$$\text{Return on investment} = \frac{\$256}{\$6290} = 4.1\% \quad \text{Rounded}$$

A rate of 4.1% compares favorably with CD rates.

Objective

3 *Find the Commission for Buying or Selling Stocks.* Individuals must use stockbrokers to trade publicly held stocks. Regular **stockbrokers** charge a higher **commission**, but they offer financial advice and expertise. Some people trade stocks using **discount brokers**, which offer less advice and a lower cost. Today, many people trade online, using **online brokers**, since the costs of trading are very low. Most online brokers charge one low flat fee for each purchase or sale of the shares of one company, although a few firms actually charge no commission for active traders with certain minimum balances. Firms charging no commission get their revenue from other sources, such as from ads on their Web sites or by holding cash. Some firms on the Internet will let you play a game of buying and selling stock to help you learn about trading.

Stocks are usually traded in multiples of 100 shares called **round lots**. An **odd lot** refers to the purchase of fewer than 100 shares at one time. For example, someone buying 300 shares of, say, Microsoft is buying in round lots, whereas someone who buys 50 shares of General Electric is buying an odd lot. In years past, a small extra fee called an **odd-lot differential** was added when odd lots were sold to discourage trades of odd lots. However, that rule has been changed.

Commissions vary widely but a typical commission charged by a regular stockbroker on a small trade is 1% of the total. A fee is also charged by the **Securities and Exchange Commission** (**SEC**) when shares are sold. The SEC fee is currently about 0.00093% of the sale price, but it changes frequently. The SEC is the branch of the U.S. government created in 1934 that has responsibility for regulating, monitoring, and enforcing the security laws. The SEC fee is small on any one transaction, but the fees quickly add up based on the many billions of dollars of transactions each year.

Cost of Buying Stock	Cost of Selling Stock
Broker's commission	Broker's commission + SEC fee of 0.00093% + Any transfer taxes (see below)

Some state and local governments charge a **transfer tax** when stock is sold. The amount of this tax is subtracted by the broker before turning over the balance to the seller. Since transfer taxes vary widely, none are included in the examples and exercises.

Objective

4 *Find the Total to Purchase or Sell Stock.* The next two examples show the total cost of purchasing stock and the total revenue from selling stock.

EXAMPLE **3** **Finding Total Cost of a Stock Purchase**

Jerita Baker bought 100 shares of Wal-Mart Stores, Inc. for $55.07 per share. Find the total cost if the broker who advised her charges a 1% commission.

Solution

Cost of shares	$5507.00	100 shares $\times$ $55.07
Commission	+ 55.07	1% of $5507
Total cost	$5562.07	

EXAMPLE 4 **Finding Total Cost of a Stock Sale**

Jerita Baker in Example 3 sold her 100 Wal-Mart shares 1 year later for $68.96 per share. (a) Find the amount received after paying a commission of 0.5% and the SEC fee. (b) Find her profit not including any dividends paid during the year she owned the stock.

Solution

(a)

Amount of sale	$6896.00	100 shares × $68.96
Commission	−34.48	0.5% of $6896
SEC fee	−0.06	0.00093% of $6896, rounded
Total received	$6861.46	

(b) Profit = Total received at sale − Total cost

$$= \$6861.46 - \$5562.07$$

$$= \$1299.39$$

Jerita Baker made a profit of $1299.39 from the 100 shares of Wal-Mart stock she owned for 1 year. This does not include any dividends paid by Wal-Mart during the period of time she owned the stock. It was a profitable investment for Baker. But, she knows that sometimes you make money in stocks and sometimes you lose money.

NOTE The broker's commission is calculated just on the value of the stock and not on any odd-lot fees or SEC fees.

Objective

5 *Find the Current Yield on a Stock.* There is no certain way of choosing stocks that will go up in price. However, two **stock ratios** that people commonly look at before buying shares of a company are the **current yield** and the **price-earnings ratio**.

Although current yield is shown in the stock tables as Yld %, we show how to find it here since you may not always have the tables available. It is used to compare the dividends paid by stocks selling at different prices. The result is commonly rounded to the nearest tenth of a percent.

$$\text{Current yield} = \frac{\text{Annual dividend per share}}{\text{Closing price per share}}$$

EXAMPLE 5 **Finding the Current Yield**

Use the latest dividend and close price in Figure 19.3 to find the current yield for (a) Best Buy (BBY) and (b) Abbott Labs (ABT). (*Hint:* You must first multiply a quarterly dividend by 4 to find the total annual dividend before finding the current yield.)

Solution

(a) Best Buy

$$\text{Annual dividend} = \$0.14 \times 4 = \$0.56$$

$$\text{Current yield} = \frac{\text{Annual dividend}}{\text{Close price}} = \frac{\$0.56}{\$27.24} = 2.1\% \quad \text{Rounded}$$

(b) Abbot Labs

$$\text{Annual dividend} = \$0.36 \times 4 = \$1.44$$

$$\text{Current yield} = \frac{\text{Annual dividend}}{\text{Close price}} = \frac{\$1.44}{\$53.01} = 2.7\% \quad \text{Rounded}$$

Note that both current yields correspond to the current yields shown for the respective companies in Figure 19.3.

NOTE   A company may not pay a dividend because of the following:
1. it is going through difficult financial times;
2. it needs the funds that would be paid out for research and development; or
3. it may be growing rapidly and needs the money to finance its growth.

Objective

6 *Find the PE Ratio of a Stock.*   Another number that some people use to help decide which stock to buy is the **price-earnings ratio**, also called the **PE ratio**. It is often rounded to the nearest whole number.

$$\text{PE ratio} = \frac{\text{Closing price per share}}{\text{Annual net income per share}}$$

EXAMPLE 6   Finding the PE Ratio

Find the price-earnings ratio for each of the following. Round to the nearest whole number.

(a) Wal-Mart with a close price of $51.35 and annual earnings of $3.46.
(b) ExxonMobil with a close price of $83.42 and annual earnings of $9.24.

Solution

(a) Wal-Mart PE ratio $= \dfrac{\$51.35}{\$3.46} = 15 \quad$ Rounded

(b) ExxonMobil PE ratio $= \dfrac{\$83.42}{\$9.24} = 9 \quad$ Rounded

A company that grows more rapidly should have significantly higher earnings in the future. As a result, investors are willing to pay more for rapidly growing firms, resulting in higher PE ratios. A low PE ratio may simply indicate that investors see a poor future for the company. It is best to compare the PE ratios of similar firms such as the giant retailers Wal-Mart Stores and Target Corporation. It does not make sense to compare the PE ratio of Target Corporation to ExxonMobil, since they are in very different industries.

Objective

7 *Define the Common Stock Indices.*   Several stock indices are used to identify trends in the market. The most common are the Dow Jones Industrial Average, the NASDAQ Composite Index, and Standard and Poor's 500.

Dow Jones Industrial Average—based on 30 of the largest and most widely owned companies in the United States and is no longer limited to "industrial" companies

NASDAQ Composite Index—computed from over 3000 international technology and growth companies

Standard and Poor's 500 or **S&P 500**—based on the price of 500 large companies that trade on stock exchanges in the United States

Figure 19.4 shows all three indices. Notice the sharp fall off in all three in late 2008 as the financial crisis became very serious. Even in early 2009, some feared that the serious recession would be rough, but no one knew exactly how things would turn out.

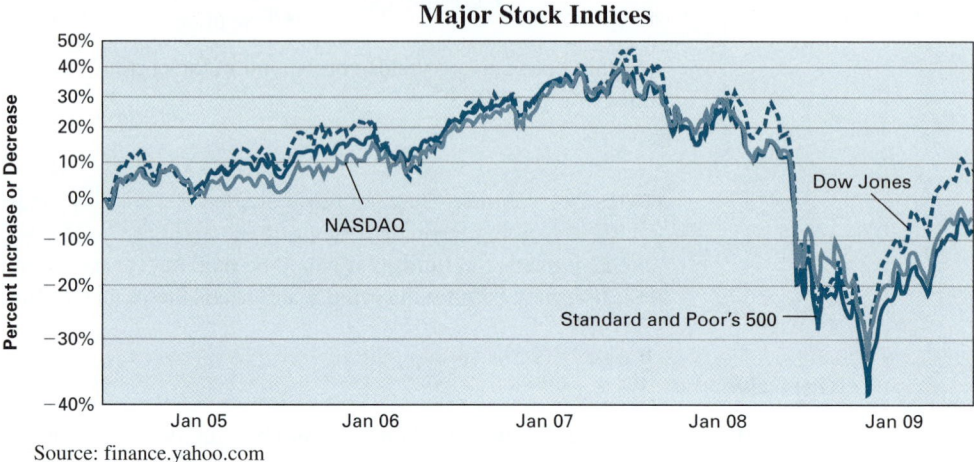

Source: finance.yahoo.com

Figure 19.4

The Dow Jones Industrial Average has been widely used for over 100 years, as shown in Figure 19.5. The Great Depression of 1929–1939 devastated many firms, investors, and

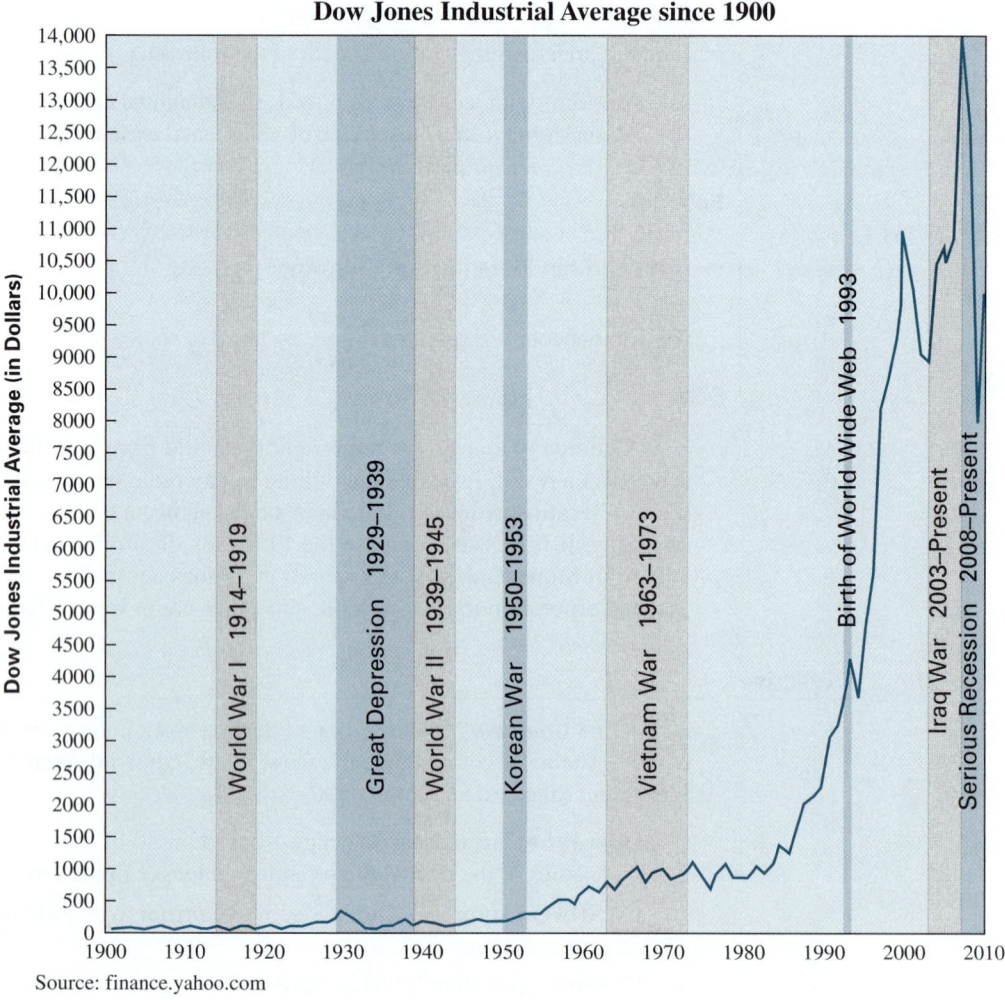

Source: finance.yahoo.com

Figure 19.5

families. Stock prices collapsed. It became difficult to borrow and many companies fired employees and declared bankruptcy. The entire world was mired in the depression until the war-related activities of World War II helped bring the world out of it. Stock prices did not recover until the 1950s. In spite of the Great Depression and the financial crisis beginning in 2008, it is important to note that the overall trend has clearly been up over the past 100 years.

Objective

8   *Define a Mutual Fund.*   Ownership of shares in a single company *can be risky*—the company may suffer poor financial results, causing the stock price to fall. This risk can be reduced by simultaneously investing in the stocks of several different companies. One way of doing this is to invest with a mutual fund that buys stocks. A **mutual fund** that invests in stocks receives investment funds from many different investors and uses the money to purchase stock in several different companies.

Another way to diversify and control the risk of losing money is to invest in **exchange traded funds** (**ETFs**). An ETF holds stocks, bonds, or futures contracts and trades throughout the day at the same price as the underlying assets. Most mutual funds are actively managed with managers constantly assessing what to own, when to buy, and when to sell. Originally, ETFs were not actively managed, but simply bought and held specific financial assets. However, some ETFs started in 2008 are also actively managed, such as those tracking futures contracts on commodities and a few others, too.

> **NOTE**   Historically, stocks have generally resulted in a better return on investment than savings accounts, certificates of deposit, or bonds. Most financial planners agree that stocks should be a part of any long-range investment plan.

Figure 19.6 shows that some mutual funds and exchange traded funds *specialize* by investing in the stocks *of different types* of publicly held companies. They may specialize in large-cap (large companies), small-cap (small companies), overseas (global), or specific industries (real estate, oil, banking, etc.). Many financial planners say that *the first fund* you should invest in is an **index fund** that tracks a broad index such as Standard and Poor's 500.

Investing Stocks in a Global World

Invest in a few of these funds and quickly create a diversified portfolio.

Fund	Invests in	Price	One-year Return
Mutual Funds			
Vanguard 500 Index (VFINX)	Large U.S. firms	$94.52	−3%
Fidelity Contrafund (FCNTX)	Intl. value stocks	$52.97	−2%
Dodge & Cox Diversified International (DODFX)	Large int. firms	$30.39	−1%
Amer. Funds Euro-Pacific Growth (AEPGX)	Europe & Asia	$36.56	−6%
Exchange Traded Funds			
Vanguard Total Stock Market (VTI)	Large U.S. firms	$51.86	−7%
iShares Russell 1000 Growth (IWF)	Large U.S. firms	$45.86	−1%
iShares S&P 500 (IVV)	Large U.S. firms	$102.85	−8%
MSCI EAFE Index (EFA)	Large int. firms	$52.66	−1%

Source: finance.yahoo.com

Figure 19.6

Funds that specialize in companies in one industry such as biotechnology or funds that specialize in international stock are usually more volatile or risky.

Notice that the 1-year returns on all of the mutual funds and exchange traded funds in Figure 19.6 were negative! Again, this was the result of the financial crisis that began in 2008 in the United States but spread quickly throughout the world. All of the funds have negative 1-year returns of about the same magnitude, although some obviously did worse than others. It is extremely rare when stocks across the world do so poorly in unison, since countries usually go into and out of recession at different times. However, this was a global recession, so stocks around the world fell sharply throughout 2008. However, look again at Figure 19.5 to remind yourself that stocks have generally increased throughout the past 100 years! Stocks can be poor investments over the short term, but they have usually done well over the past century or so.

> **NOTE** Many mutual-fund companies advertise on the World Wide Web, including Fidelity and Vanguard. Several of them will also let you track fund balances and make exchanges between funds using the World Wide Web.

EXAMPLE 7 **Comparing Investment Alternatives**

Cynthia Peck wants to know whether she should invest her retirement funds in certificates of deposit or in a mutual fund containing stock. Assume payments of $2000 per year for 30 years. Find the future value assuming (a) a certificate of deposit paying 4% compounded annually and (b) a mutual fund containing stocks that has returned 8% per year. (c) Then compare the two future values.

Solution

(a) Use 4% per year and 30 years in the Amount of Annuity column in **Appendix D** to find 56.08493775.

$$\text{Future value} = \$2000 \times 56.08493775 = \$112,169.88$$

(b) Use 8% per year and 30 years in the Amount of Annuity column in **Appendix D** to find 113.28321111.

$$\text{Future value} = \$2000 \times 113.28321111 = \$226,566.42$$

(c) Difference = $226,566.42 − $112,169.88 = $114,396.54

The mutual fund with stocks results in a much higher value in 30 years. However, neither the return on the CDs nor the mutual fund is guaranteed. Stocks may do better or worse than a bank CD in any year, but stocks have historically done much better over long periods of time than bank CDs.

> **NOTE** Some people feel they have lost money when stocks go down. Actually, for anyone making regular investments towards a long-term payoff, *it is good for stock prices to fall.* This allows them to buy more shares with the same amount of dollars. Studies have shown that regular investing is probably the best method for long-term investors.

| 19.2 | **Exercises** |

Find the following using the stock table in Figure 19.3.

1. Close price for the day for Aflac (AFL)

2. Close price for the day for Berkshire Hathaway (BRKA)

3. Low price for the year for AT&T (T)

4. Low price for the year for Ball Corporation (BLL)

5. Latest quarterly dividend for Bard CR (BCR)

6. Latest quarterly dividend for BabcockBrwnAir (FLY)

7. High price for the year for Baldor Electric (BEZ)

8. High price for the year for B&G Foods (BGF)

9. Annual dividend yield for BarckGld (ABX)

10. Annual dividend yield for Abercrombie A (ANF)

11. PE ratio for Acadia Realty (AKR)

12. PE ratio for AK Steel (AKS)

13. Daily volume for Baxter International (BAX)

14. Daily volume for BB&T Cp (BBT)

15. Annual dividend yield for Big Lots (BIG)

16. Annual dividend yield for Amcol (ACO)

17. Close price for the day for Aeropostale (ARO)

18. Close price for the day for Baker Hughes (BHI)

Find the total cost of the following stock purchases assuming a broker's commission of 1%.

19. 300 shares at $47.52

20. 100 shares at $20.45

21. 50 shares at $90.78

22. 200 shares at $17.40

23. 250 shares at $34.98

24. 700 shares at $40.69

Find the amount received by the sellers of the following stocks assuming a broker's commission of 1% and an SEC fee of 0.00093%.

25. 200 shares at $17.65

26. 100 shares at $48.32

27. 150 shares at $84.50

28. 300 shares at $19.42

29. 800 shares at $32.63

30. 400 shares at $112.27

Find the current yield for the following stocks. Round to the nearest tenth of a percent.

	Stock	Price per Share	Annual Dividend per Share
31.	Coca-Cola	$43.33	$1.52
32.	Chevron	$70.82	$2.60
33.	Wal-Mart	$48.35	$0.95
34.	Nike	$45.68	$1.00
35.	Microsoft	$17.20	$0.52
36.	Apple	$88.36	$0

Find the PE ratio for the following. Round to the nearest whole number.

	Stock	Price per Share	Net Income per Share
37.	Toyota	$62.58	$10.79
38.	Home Depot	$21.72	$1.78
39.	Intel	$13.12	$0.92
40.	Best Buy	$27.65	$2.76

Solve each of the following application problems. Exercises 47 and 48 require concepts from Chapter 15.

41. STOCK PURCHASES Triston Smith purchased 200 shares of Microsoft at $38.25 and 300 shares of General Electric at $44.58. Find the total cost if she was charged a commission of 1%.

42. STOCK PURCHASES Theresa Tabor purchased 200 shares of Coca-Cola at $50.25 and 100 shares of Wal-Mart for $48.90. Find the total cost if she was charged a commission of 0.75%.

43. STOCK TRADING Leslie Toombs purchased 250 shares of Intel at $22.02 with a 1% commission and later sold the shares for $36.80 and paid a 0.5% commission. Find her profit ignoring any dividends paid.

44. STOCK TRADING John O'Neill purchased 340 shares of Nike at $68.23 with a 1.5% commission and later sold the shares for $71.20 and paid a 1% commission. Find his profit ignoring any dividends paid.

 45. Explain current yield and the PE ratio. Why might investors be interested in these numbers? (See Objectives 5 and 6.)

46. List four advantages of mutual funds. Name any particular mutual fund(s) that you have read or heard about. (See Objective 8.)

47. TWO INVESTMENT ALTERNATIVES Toni Chavez is comparing two different investment alternatives for his $1200 semiannual contribution to a retirement plan. Plan A uses certificates of deposits currently yielding 5% compounded semiannually. Plan B uses a global stock mutual fund with Merrill Lynch that has historically yielded 8% compounded semiannually. Find the amount of an annuity after 25 years of (a) plan A and (b) plan B. (c) Find the difference between the two. (See **Section 15.1**.)

48. RETIREMENT ACCOUNT INVESTMENT Laurie Zimms is trying to decide whether she should place her quarterly $2000 retirement account investment in a certificate of deposit yielding 6% compounded quarterly or in a stock mutual fund that has historically yielded 10% compounded quarterly. Find the amount of an annuity after 12 years using (a) the CDs and (b) the mutual fund. (c) Find the difference between the two. (See **Section 15.1**.)

49. Use Figure 19.5 to estimate the length of the Great Depression.

50. Use Figure 19.5 to identify the year the Dow Jones Industrial Index was at 2000 and the year it reached its peak of about 14,000.

19.3   Bonds

OBJECTIVES

1 *Know the basics of bonds.*

2 *Read bond tables.*

3 *Find the cost of bonds, including commission.*

4 *Understand how mutual funds containing bonds can be used for monthly income.*

Businesses need money to invest and to pay operating expenses. They can obtain funds by selling stock, by borrowing short-term from banks, insurance companies, or investment firms, or by borrowing long-term using bonds. Stockholders are part owners of a corporation and share in profits and losses. Banks, investment firms, insurance companies, and individuals that lend money to firms are creditors of the corporation and not owners. Creditors expect to be paid back with interest, but they do not expect to own part of the future profits and do not receive dividends.

Objective

1   *Know the Basics of Bonds.*   For longer-term borrowing of, say, 5 years or more, corporations often borrow money by selling bonds to the public. A **bond** is a contractual *promise to repay the borrowed money at a specific date in the future*. The issuers of most bonds also agree to pay interest each year at a rate specified on the bond. For example, the owner of a bond that originally sold for a **face value** of $1000 with a 7.5% yield will receive interest of $75 each year and also receive a return of the $1000 at a specified date in the future. Most corporate bonds have a face value of $1000.

On the other hand, a corporation issuing a **zero-coupon bond** pays all interest at the maturity date (in the future) of the bond and does not pay interest each year. An example is a zero-coupon bond purchased for $600 in 2009 with no annual payment, and a payment of $1000 in 2016. This bond costs $600 but returns a future value of $1000 in 7 years, which results in a **yield-to-maturity** of 7.57% per year.

National governments, states and provinces, and some cities also issue bonds. Bonds issued by a state or local governmental authority are called **municipal bonds**. Bonds issued by a corporation are called **corporate bonds**. One advantage of municipal bonds is that the income from these bonds is usually *not* subject to federal income taxes, although it may be subject to a state income tax.

Treasury Inflation-Protected Securities (TIPS) are U.S. government bonds that are essentially a mixture of the two types of bonds discussed. TIPS pay a constant interest rate each year. In addition, the principal is adjusted up or down depending on the amount of inflation or deflation. TIPS protect a lender against rapid increases in inflation.

Objective

2   *Read Bond Tables.*   The **face value** or **par value** of a bond is *the original amount of money borrowed by a company*. Most corporations issue bonds with a par value of $1000. Suppose that a bond's owner needs money before the **maturity date** of the bond. In that event, the bond can be quickly sold through a bond dealer such as Merrill Lynch. However, the price of the bond is not determined by its initial price, but rather *by market conditions at the time of the sale*.

Market *interest rates fluctuate widely* from year to year, yet each bond pays exactly the same dollar amount of interest each year. If interest rates rise, investors will pay less for a bond because they want the new, higher interest yield. If interest rates fall, investors will pay more for a bond because they will still earn a favorable yield. As a result, the price of a bond fluctuates in the opposite direction of interest rates. A bond may have a face value of $1000, but it often trades at a different value than $1000, as shown in Example 1.

EXAMPLE 1   **Working with the Bond Table**

Brandy Barrett was in an automobile accident that put her in the hospital for 3 weeks and required months of rehabilitation. The other driver was at fault and his insurance company paid Barrett the liability limits on his policy of $50,000. Barrett needs monthly income and is thinking about investing the insurance proceeds in Wal-Mart Stores bonds that pay interest each year, but that are due in 2030. Data on this bond is taken from the information from *Barron's* in Figure 19.7.

Company	Coupon	Maturity	Rating	High	Low	Last	Change	Yield %
Wal-Mart Stores	7.550%	Feb 2030	Aa2/AA/AA	121.687	114.815	120.696	−1.461	5.830

Solution

(a) The coupon rate of 7.550% means that annual interest payments are 7.550% of the original face value of $1000, or $75.50.

(b) The bond matures in February 2030, at which time the principal of $1000 must be repaid.

(c) Rating gives an estimate of the quality of the bond by three different ratings agencies, in this order: Moody's, S&P, and Fitch. The highest possible ratings from the three agencies are Aaa, AAA, and AAA, respectively. So these bonds are rated slightly lower than highest quality but far above low-quality bonds.

(d) The high at which the bond traded during the day was 121.687, or 121.687% of $1000 = $1216.87.

(e) The low at which the bond traded during the day was 114.815, or 114.815% of $1000 = $1148.15.

(f) The last or close price of the bond for the day was 120.696, or 120.696% of $1000 = $1206.96.

(g) The change in the bond price compared to the previous day was −1.461, or a decrease of 1.461% of $1000 = $14.61.

(h) Yield % refers to the yield to maturity of the bond, which in this case is 5.830%. It is found using a formula that takes into consideration current price, annual interest, and length of time to maturity.

EXAMPLE 2 Using the Bond Table

Find the annual interest and closing price for each bond.

(a) General Electric Capital 2012
(b) First Data Corp
(c) International Business Machines Corp.

Solution The annual interest is the coupon rate times the face value of $1000.

Company	Annual Interest	Last Price
(a) General Electric Capital	$2.2\% \times \$1000 = \$22.00$	100.400% of $\$1000 = \$1004$
(b) First Data Corp	$9.875\% \times \$1000 = \$98.75$	54.375% of $\$1000 = \$543.75$
(c) International Business Machines Corp.	$8.000\% \times \$1000 = \$80.00$	127.347% of $\$1000 = \$1273.47$

Corporate Bonds

Issuer Name	Coupon	Maturity	Rating Moody's/S&P/ Fitch	High	Low	Last	Change	Yield %
VERIZON COMM	8.750%	Nov 2018	A3/A/A	119.039	115.276	116.813	−1.841	6.404
GENERAL ELECTRIC CAPITAL	2.200%	Jun 2012	Aaa/–/–	100.517	100.231	100.400	0.044	2.076
WAL-MART STORES	7.550%	Feb 2030	Aa2/AA/AA	121.687	114.815	120.696	−1.461	5.830
GENERAL ELECTRIC CAPITAL	6.875%	Jan 2039	Aaa/–/–	94.500	87.689	92.579	−2.569	7.500
INTL BUSINESS MACHINES CORP	8.000%	Oct 2038	A1/A+/A+	127.498	124.644	127.347	−0.035	6.013
FIRST DATA CORP	9.875%	Sep 2015	B3/B/B−	58.970	52.500	54.375	−3.125	23.873
SUNGARD DATA SYSTEMS	9.125%	Aug 2013	Caa1/B/B	84.500	83.250	83.500	−1.250	14.166
REALOGY CORP	10.500%	Apr 2014	Ca/C/–	25.250	24.500	25.250	1.000	55.184
GENERAL MOTORS	8.375%	Jul 2033	C/C/C	19.500	13.600	15.660	0.660	53.374
SUPERVALU	7.500%	May 2012	Ba3/B+/BB−	96.108	93.500	95.634	2.134	9.054
DYNEGY HLDG	7.750%	Jun 2019	B2/B/B+	78.000	76.750	76.750	−1.250	11.676
SPRINT NEXTEL CORP	6.000%	Dec 2016	Ba2/BB/BB+	67.500	66.000	66.000	−1.625	13.051

Source: Data from *Barron's*.

Figure 19.7

Objective

3 *Find the Cost of Bonds, Including Commission.*   Similar to stocks, bonds can be bought through stockbrokers or online brokers. The commission charged on bond sales varies significantly depending both on the broker and the size of the order. The commission on a smaller order is often about $5 per bond.

EXAMPLE 3 Finding the Cost to Buy Bonds and the Annual Interest

The sales charge on an order for 25 Dynegy Hldg bonds is $5 per bond. Find (a) the total purchase price at the close for the day, (b) annual interest paid by the corporation, and (c) the effective rate of interest earned the first year to the nearest tenth of a percent.

Solution   From Figure 19.7, the close price is 76.75% of $1000, or $767.50. The coupon rate used to find annual interest is 7.750%.

(a) Total cost $= 25$ bonds $\times$ ($767.50 + $5 commission per bond)

$\qquad\qquad = $19,312.50$

(b) Annual interest $= 25$ bonds $\times$ $1000 face value $\times$ 7.750%

$\qquad\qquad = 1937.50

(c) Effective rate for the year $=$ Annual interest $\div$ Total cost

$\qquad\qquad\qquad\qquad = \quad $1937.50 \quad \div $19,312.50$

$\qquad\qquad\qquad\qquad = 10.0\%$

The effective interest rate is far higher than the coupon rate since the bond sells at a discount to the $1000 face value.

NOTE   The effective interest rate is not the same as the last yield. The last yield takes into consideration the cost of the bond, the maturity value of the bond, the time to maturity, and all interest payments.

EXAMPLE 4 Find the Net Amount from the Sale of Bonds

Find the amount received from the sale of 30 Verizon Comm bonds sold at the close, if the commission is $5 per bond.

Solution

$$\text{Sale price} = 30 \times 116.813\% \text{ of } \$1000$$
$$= 30 \times 1.16813 \times \$1000$$
$$= \$35,043.90$$

$$\text{Net amount} = \text{Sale price} - \text{Commission of } \$5 \times 30 \text{ bonds}$$
$$= \$35,043.90 - \$150$$
$$= \$34,893.90$$

Bonds are a debt, since they indicate that a corporation owes money to its bondholders. As such, *bondholders have first claim,* after bankruptcy lawyers, taxing authorities, and wage earners, on the assets of the corporation if it goes into bankruptcy. Stockholders have the last claim. Even so, bonds may pay off only a few cents on the dollar in the event of bankruptcy. Bondholders have lost substantial sums in recent bankruptcies.

Some investors like to buy the bonds of bankrupt and troubled companies—such **junk bonds** or high-yield securities have been known to pay off handsomely when and if a company regains its financial health. Junk bonds are usually very risky and best left for professional investors.

Objective

4 *Understand How Mutual Funds Containing Bonds Can Be Used for Monthly Income.* A mutual fund can invest everything in stocks, everything in bonds, or part in stocks and part in bonds. Stock prices can be quite volatile, so financial planners recommend stock investments for people *who have a longer time horizon* over which to accumulate funds. Many planners recommend that *people invest in both stocks and bonds* during their lifetimes. Stocks may be a better investment *when investors are young* since stocks have tended to have a higher return. Bonds may be a better investment *for investors close to retirement* since there is less risk of losing principal in bonds and bonds pay regular interest.

EXAMPLE 5 Using a Bond Fund for Income

Brandy Barrett from Example 1 is undergoing rehabilitation and needs safety of principal. She also needs regular interest payments to help with medical expenses. She decides to place the $50,000 received from the insurance company in a mutual fund containing bonds. It is a no-load mutual fund, meaning that no commission is paid. (a) Find her annual income if the fund yields 6.5% per year. (b) How much would Barrett need to invest in the fund to earn $10,000 per year?

Solution

(a) Use the formula for simple interest: $I = PRT$.

$$\text{Interest} = \$50{,}000 \times 0.065 = \$3250$$

(b) Again use the formula for simple interest, but now the principal (P) is unknown. Divide both sides of $I = PRT$ by RT to find the following form of the equation.

$$\text{Principal} = P = \frac{I}{RT} = \frac{\$10{,}000}{0.065 \times 1} = \$153{,}846.15$$

19.3	**Exercises**

Use Figure 19.7 to find the following information for International Business Machine bonds. (See Examples 1–2.)

1. Close price per bond
2. Maturity date
3. Coupon rate
4. Annual interest
5. Yield to maturity (Yield %)
6. Price to buy 40 bonds at the last price if commission is $5 per bond

Use Figure 19.7 to find the cost for the following purchases at the last price if the commission is $4 per bond.

Bond	Maturity	Number Purchased
7. Sprint Nextel Corp	Dec 2016	30
8. General Electric Capital	Jan 2039	45
9. Supervalu	May 2012	20
10. Realogy Corp	Apr 2014	100
11. Intl Business Machines Corp	Oct 2038	80
12. Wal-Mart Stores	Feb 2030	500
13. Sungard Data Systems	Aug 2013	150
14. General Electric Capital	Jun 2012	200

15. Explain the purpose of bonds. (See Objective 1.)

16. Explain the differences between common stock, preferred stock, and bonds. (See **Sections 19.1** and **19.3.**)

Solve these application problems using bond prices from Figure 19.7. Unless stated otherwise, assume a commission of $5 per bond.

17. **BOND PURCHASE** Anita Fields purchased 50 International Business Machine bonds at the close. Find the total cost and annual interest.

18. **BOND PURCHASE** Mary Dunlap bought 25 Wal-Mart Stores bonds since she shops there and knows the store. She bought at the low for the day. Find the total cost and annual interest.

19. **BOND PURCHASE** A mutual-fund manager purchased 22,000 bonds of General Electric Capital maturing in January 2039 at the low for the day. Since the purchase is so large, the commission is $0.08 per bond. Find the total cost and annual interest.

20. **BOND PURCHASE** The manager of an exchange traded fund purchased 18,400 bonds of Supervalu at the high for the day. Since the purchase is large, the commission is $0.07 per bond. Find the total cost and annual interest.

21. **CARE OF MENTALLY ILL** On behalf of a mentally ill daughter who needs lifetime care, Kitty Wysong purchased 30 Verizon Comm bonds and 30 International Business Machines bonds, both at the close for the day. If the commission is $3 per bond, find (a) the total cost and (b) the annual interest. Then (c) find the effective interest rate for the first year to the nearest tenth of a percent.

22. **CARE OF DISABLED MOTHER** To help support his disabled mother, John Rankin purchased 50 General Electric bonds that mature in Jan 2039 and 30 Sungard Data Systems bonds, both at the low for the day. If the commission is $4 per bond, find (a) the total cost and (b) the annual interest. Then (c) find the effective interest rate for the first year to the nearest tenth of a percent.

23. **INTEREST** A wealthy couple places $100,000 in a municipal bond fund that allows them to reduce their taxes. Find their tax-free income from this investment if the fund earns $4\frac{1}{2}\%$ per year.

24. **ANNUAL INTEREST** Helmut Schmidt places all $150,000 of his retirement funds in a mutual fund containing only high-quality corporate bonds. Find his annual interest if the fund earns 8% per year.

25. INCOME FROM A DIVORCE Bill and Jane Fickland recently divorced. As a part of the divorce settlement, Mr. Fickland agrees to pay Ms. Fickland $7000 per year for several years. Find the amount that must be invested in a mutual fund containing bonds that is expected to yield 7.5% annually, to generate the needed income.

26. LAWSUIT AWARD Joan Klein lost a lawsuit to Milton Freeman. As a result, she must make annual payments of $28,500 to Freeman for several years. Find the amount that must be invested in a mutual fund containing bonds that is expected to yield 7.8% annually to generate the needed income.

19.4   Distribution of Profits and Losses in a Partnership

OBJECTIVES

1 *Divide profits by equal shares.*

2 *Divide profits by agreed ratio.*

3 *Divide profits by original investment.*

4 *Divide profits by salary and agreed ratio.*

5 *Divide profits by interest on investment and agreed ratio.*

In a partnership, a business is owned by two or more people. The partners may have invested equal amounts of money to start the business, or one may have invested money while another invested specialized knowledge. The partners must agree on the relative amounts of money and time that will be invested in the business. They must also agree on the method by which any profits will be distributed. This section considers the various methods by which partnership profits may be distributed.

Objective

1   *Divide Profits by Equal Shares.* The partners may simply agree to share all profits and losses equally. In fact, if there is no formal agreement stating the terms under which profits are to be divided, most states require that profits be divided equally.

> **EXAMPLE 1** **Dividing Profits by Equal Shares**
>
> Three partners open a menswear store. Each agrees to put up one-third of the investment funds needed and to work 40 hours per week in the business for no salary at first. They also agree to split profits equally. In a year with $96,000 in profits, each partner would get
>
> $$\tfrac{1}{3} \times \$96,000 = \$32,000$$

Objective

2   *Divide Profits by Agreed Ratio.* Partners may agree to divide the profits using some given rule. For example, two partners might agree that profits will be divided so that 60% goes to one partner and 40% to the other. Profit divisions are sometimes given as a ratio; this division could be written $60:40$, or in a reduced form, $3:2$, with profits said to be divided in an **agreed ratio**.

EXAMPLE 2 **Dividing Profits by Agreed Ratio**

Aaron Ortego and Gary Wayne purchase the Ter Marche Apartments in New Orleans, Louisiana, and agree to split profits in the ratio of $1:3$. How would profits of $18,000 be divided?

Solution The ratio $1:3$ says that profits will be divided into $1 + 3 = 4$ equal shares. Ortego gets 1 and Wayne gets 3 of the equal shares.

$$\$18,000 \div 4 = \$4500$$

Ortego's share:	$\$4500 \times 1 = \$\ 4,500$
Wayne's share:	$\$4500 \times 3 = \underline{\$13,500}$
Total:	$\$18,000$

Objective

3 *Divide Profits by Original Investment.* A common way of dividing the profits is on the basis of the **original investments** made by each partner. The fraction of the total original investment supplied by each partner is used to find the fraction of the profit that each partner receives.

EXAMPLE 3 **Dividing Profits by Original Investment**

Bob Huffman and Gary White form a partnership to drill a shallow well for oil. Huffman contributes $160,000 and White contributes $80,000. They sign an agreement that says that each partner will lose the money each invested if they drill a dry hole and that any profits will be distributed based on the original investment. If they discover an oil field and sell it for $600,000, find the share received by each.

Solution The total amount contributed to start the venture was

$$\$160,000 + \$80,000 = \$240,000$$

Of this total,

$$\text{Huffman contributed} = \frac{\$160,000}{\$240,000} = \frac{2}{3}$$

$$\text{White contributed} = \frac{\$80,000}{\$240,000} = \frac{1}{3}$$

So profits are distributed as follows.

$$\text{Profits to Huffman} = \frac{2}{3} \times \$600,000 = \$400,000$$

$$\text{Profits to White} = \frac{1}{3} \times \$600,000 = \$200,000$$

If the two men lost their investments by drilling dry holes, then Huffman would have lost $160,000 and White would have lost $80,000.

NOTE Each partner's fraction or percent of the total investment must be determined before the profit distribution is calculated.

EXAMPLE 4 **Dividing Losses by Original Investment**

Suppose the oil company in Example 3 had a loss of $40,000 the first year. Find the share of the loss that each partner must pay.

Solution Just as partners share profits, they may be called on to share losses. In this case, Huffman must pay $\frac{2}{3}$ of the loss, or

$$\frac{2}{3} \times \$40,000 = (\$26,666.67)$$

Losses are usually indicated with parentheses.

and White must pay $\frac{1}{3}$ of the loss.

$$\frac{1}{3} \times \$40,000 = (\$13,333.33)$$

Objective

4 *Divide Profits by Salary and Agreed Ratio.*   Sometimes one partner contributes money to get a business started, while a second partner contributes money and also operates the business on a daily basis. In such a case, the partner operating the business may be paid a salary out of profits, with any additional profits divided in some agreed-upon ratio, which is called dividing profits by **salary and agreed ratio**.

EXAMPLE 5 **Dividing Profits by Salary and Original Investment**

Ben Walker has managed a restaurant for 8 years and would like to open his own restaurant, but he does not have enough money. He finally decides to form a partnership with Herma Gonzalez to open a restaurant that will be managed by Walker at a guaranteed first-year salary of $18,000 in addition to his part of any profits. Walker invests $20,000 and Gonzalez invests $60,000. They agree to divide any profits based on the original investment. Find the amount each partner would receive from a first-year profit of $70,000.

Solution The first $18,000 is used for Walker's salary.

$$\begin{array}{rl} \$70,000 & \text{Profit} \\ -\ 18,000 & \text{Salary} \\ \hline \$52,000 & \text{Profit to be divided} \end{array}$$

Walker would also receive

$$\frac{1}{4} \times \$52,000 = \$13,000$$

and Gonzalez would receive

$$\frac{3}{4} \times \$52,000 = \$39,000$$

Thus, Walker receives $18,000 + $13,000 = $31,000 and Gonzalez receives $39,000.

Objective

5 *Divide Profits by Interest on Investment and Agreed Ratio.*   Sometimes one partner will put up a large share of the money necessary to start a firm, while other partners may actually operate the firm. In such a case, an agreement to divide profits by **interest on investment**

and agreed ratio may be reached by which the partner putting up the money gets interest on the investment before any further division of profits.

EXAMPLE 6 **Dividing Profits by Interest and Agreed Ratio**

Laura Cameron, Jay Davis, and Donna Friedman opened a tool rental business. Cameron contributed $250,000 to the opening of the business, which will be operated by Davis and Friedman. The partners agree that Cameron will first receive a 10% return on her investment before any further division of profits. Additional profits will be divided in the ratio $1:2:2$. Find the amount that each partner would receive from a profit of $75,000.

Solution   Cameron is first paid a 10% return on her investment of $250,000. This amounts to

$$\$250,000 \times 10\% = \$250,000 \times 0.10 = \$25,000$$

This leaves an additional

$75,000	Total profit
− 25,000	Amount to Cameron
$50,000	

to be divided. The additional profit of $50,000 is to be divided in the ratio $1:2:2$, respectively. First divide this amount into $1 + 2 + 2 = 5$ equal shares. Cameron gets 1 of these 5 shares, or

$$\frac{1}{5} \times \$50,000 = \$10,000$$

Davis and Friedman each get 2 of the 5 shares or

$$\frac{2}{5} \times \$50,000 = \$20,000$$

In summary, Cameron gets the following amount.

$25,000	Return on investment
+ 10,000	Share of profit
$35,000	Total

Davis and Friedman each receive $20,000.

NOTE   The return on investment is paid first and then the remaining profit is divided among the partners.

EXAMPLE 7 **Dividing Losses by Agreed Rates**

Suppose the tool rental business in Example 6 had a profit of only $15,000. What would be the distribution of this amount?

Solution   The partners agreed to give Cameron a 10% return, or $25,000. The profits were only $15,000, leaving a loss of $10,000.

$25,000
− 15,000
($10,000)

This loss of $10,000 will be shared in the ratio $1:2:2$, just as were the profits. Cameron's share of the loss is

$$\frac{1}{5} \times \$10,000 = (\$2000)$$

Losses are shown in parentheses.

while the share of both Davis and Friedman is

$$\frac{2}{5} \times \$10,000 = (\$4000)$$

Cameron gets $25,000, minus her share of the loss.

$$\begin{array}{ll} \$25,000 & \text{Due to Cameron} \\ -\quad 2,000 & \text{Her share of loss} \\ \hline \$23,000 & \text{Actually received by Cameron} \end{array}$$

Davis and Friedman must each *contribute* $4000 toward the loss. The $23,000 that Cameron actually receives is made up as follows.

$$\begin{array}{ll} \$15,000 & \text{Profit} \\ 4,000 & \text{From Davis} \\ +\quad 4,000 & \text{From Friedman} \\ \hline \$23,000 & \text{Total to Cameron} \end{array}$$

NOTE Cameron does absorb her share of the loss by accepting $23,000 instead of the $25,000 return on investment initially agreed upon.

19.4	**Exercises**

Divide the following profits. Round all answers to the nearest dollar.

	Partners	Investment	Method	Profits
1.	1	$40,000	Equal shares	$58,000
	2	$40,000		
2.	1	$20,000	Ratio $1:3:4$	$120,000
	2	$50,000		
	3	$50,000		
3.	1	$80,000	Ratio of investment	$92,000
	2	$20,000		
4.	1	$20,000	$22,000 salary to partner 3;	$72,000
	2	$20,000	balance divided $3:3:2$	
	3	$5,000		
5.	1	$40,000	12% return to partner 1;	$25,000
	2	$10,000	balance in ratio $3:2$	
6.	1	$40,000	10% return to partner 2;	$111,000
	2	$60,000	balance in ratio of	
	3	$50,000	investment	

	Partners	Investment	Method	Profits
7.	1	$20,000	$10,000 salary to partner 1;	$22,000
	2	$15,000	$12,000 salary to partner 2;	
	3	$40,000	balance in ratio of investment	
8.	1	$40,000	$20,000 salary to partner 3;	$133,000
	2	$40,000	10% return to partners 1	
	3	$5,000	and 2; balance divided	
	4	$35,000	$2:2:1:2$	

Solve the following application problems.

9. **CLOWN SCHOOL** Twin brothers became circus performers and finally decided to open a school to train clowns with the idea of sharing any profits or losses equally. Find the amount each receives given a profit of $78,300.

10. **SURGEONS** A firm with five surgeons has agreed to split the profits equally. Find the profit to each if the firm has a profit of $1,400,000 one year.

11. **MEXICAN RESTAURANT** Three brothers from Guadalajara invest $10,000, $20,000, and $20,000, respectively, to start up a Mexican restaurant. Find the share that each receives if profit the first year is $93,600 and profits are divided in the ratio of the original investments.

12. **BLOOD WORK** Two doctors established a lab in Mexico City to do blood work, such as testing for the HIV virus or tuberculosis. Dr. Rodriguez contributed 850,000 pesos and Dr. Pacas contributed 1,200,000 pesos to found the company. Find the division of 1,350,000 pesos of profit if profits are divided in the ratio of the original investments. Round to the nearest peso.

13. **INTERNATIONAL TRADE** Three international trade brokers combine their businesses into one company and agree to divide profits in the ratio $2:4:4$. Find the division of a profit of $220,000.

14. **INTERNATIONAL TRADE** Suppose the partners in Exercise 13 have a loss of $84,000. How much of the loss would be paid by each?

15. **TRAVEL AGENCY** Mary Finch and Pete Renz have started a new travel agency. Finch will run the agency. She gets a $15,000 salary, with any additional profits distributed in the ratio $1:4$. Find the distribution of a profit of $57,000.

16. **TOY STORE** June Thomas, Ben Walker, and his sister Sara Walker start a toy store to be managed by Thomas at a salary of $20,000 per year. They agree that any additional profits will be divided in the ratio of $1:3:2$. Find the division of a profit of $86,000.

17. **HARDWARE STORE** Bob Coker has invested $80,000 in a new hardware store. His partner, Will Toms, will actually run the store. The partners agree that Coker will get a 10% return on his investment, with any additional profits divided in the ratio $1:3$. Find the division of a profit of (a) $60,000 and (b) $6000.

18. **ELECTRONICS** Wilma Dickson has invested $350,000 in a small electronics plant, to be run by her partner, John Ardery. They agree that she will receive a 10% return on her investment and that any additional profits will be divided in the ratio $2:3$. Divide a profit of (a) $90,000 and (b) $30,000.

19. **PARTNERSHIP** Three partners invest $15,000, $25,000, and $30,000 in a business. The partners agree that partner 1 will receive a 10% return on investment, with partner 2

receiving a salary of $12,000. Any additional profits will be divided in the ratio of the original investments. Divide a profit of $110,000.

20. **WHOLESALE PLUMBING** A wholesale plumbing business has three partners. Partner 1 invested $50,000 in the business and is given a 10% return on investment. Partner 2 invested $75,000 and earns a 6% return on investment plus a salary of $21,000. Partner 3 invested $100,000 and earns a 12% return on investment. Any additional profits are divided in the ratio 2 : 1 : 2. Divide a profit of $180,000.

21. State the approach used to divide profits among three partners if partner 1 gets a fixed salary and the remaining profits are divided according to a ratio of 2 : 3 : 2. (See Objective 4.)

22. Explain the difference between the distribution of profits and losses in a partnership versus those in a corporation. (See **Sections 19.1** and **19.4**.)

19.5 Distribution of Overhead

OBJECTIVES

1 *Allocate overhead by floor space.*

2 *Allocate overhead by sales.*

3 *Allocate overhead by number of employees.*

Businesses have many expenses. For example, grocery stores tend to have profit margins of less than 3%, meaning that over 97% of the cost of items you buy at a grocery store is generally used to pay expenses. Firms must pay the following: salaries, rent, utilities, suppliers, insurance, taxes, and so on. **Overhead** refers to those expenses of a business that are *not directly attributable* to the production or sale of goods. For a grocery store, overhead would include rent, utilities, insurance premiums, taxes, and the salaries of corporate managers. It would *not include* funds paid to suppliers of grocery items.

Managers must continually determine if each line of business is profitable. In order to do so, overhead must be allocated (divided) among the various products or lines of business within a company. This is one area of **cost accounting**. Various methods are used to divide overhead and the choice often depends on industry practice. The **allocation of overhead** is usually done by forming a ratio of each product or department to the entire firm. There are several ways to form this ratio.

Objective

1 *Allocate Overhead by Floor Space.* Overhead can be allocated to departments according to the **floor space** used by each department of the company.

> **EXAMPLE** **1** **Allocating Overhead by Floor Space**
>
> Clover Printing has three departments, with floor space as shown.
>
> | Department | Floor Space |
> | --- | --- |
> | Magazine printing | 5,000 square feet |
> | Book printing | 3,000 square feet |
> | Catalog printing | 2,000 square feet |
> | **Total:** | 10,000 square feet |
>
> Allocate an overhead of $275,000.

Solution The magazine printing department has a floor space of 5000 square feet out of a total of 10,000 square feet. Therefore, this department is allocated

$$\frac{5000}{10,000} = \frac{1}{2}$$

of the overhead, or

$$\frac{1}{2} \times \$275,000 = \$137,500$$

When finding the expenses of this department, the company accountants would assign an overhead expense of $137,500 for the department.

The book printing department uses

$$\frac{3000}{10,000} = \frac{3}{10}$$

of the floor space and so would be allocated $\frac{3}{10}$ of the overhead, or

$$\frac{3}{10} \times \$275,000 = \$82,500$$

Finally, catalog printing would be allocated

$$\frac{2000}{10,000} = \frac{1}{5}$$

of the overhead, or

$$\frac{1}{5} \times \$275,000 = \$55,000$$

NOTE Check your answer by adding the individual departmental allocations. This sum should equal the total overhead.

Objective

2 *Allocate Overhead by Sales.* It is common to allocate overhead according to the **sales** of each department or product, as shown in the next example.

EXAMPLE 2 **Allocating Overhead by Sales Value**

A European firm owns a clothing manufacturing company in India that exports to the United States. It has these departments and sales figures.

Product Line	Production	Average Sale Price
Men's clothes	5,800 units	$42
Women's clothes	10,930 units	$54
Children's clothes	8,400 units	$38

Allocate an overhead of $186,000 by sales volume and round to the nearest dollar.

Solution   First complete the following table.

Product Line	Production		Average Sale Price		Sales Volume
Men's clothes	5,800	×	$42	=	$243,600
Women's clothes	10,930	×	$54	=	$590,220
Children's clothes	8,400	×	$38	=	$319,200
				Total:	$1,153,020

Now allocate overhead based on sales volume and round to the nearest dollar. Overhead to:

$$\text{Men's clothes} = \frac{\$243,600}{\$1,153,020} \times \$186,000 = \$39,296$$

$$\text{Women's clothes} = \frac{\$590,220}{\$1,153,020} \times \$186,000 = \$95,212$$

$$\text{Children's clothes} = \frac{\$319,200}{\$1,153,020} \times \$186,000 = \$51,492$$

Note that the three values total $186,000.

Objective

3   *Allocate Overhead by Number of Employees.*   Overhead can also be allocated by the **number of employees** associated with a department or product.

EXAMPLE 3   **Allocating Overhead by Number of Employees**

A local insurance agency has a building overhead-related charge of $80,000. Allocate this overhead expense based on the number of employees.

Solution   Allocate this expense based on a ratio of the number of employees in the department to the total number of employees.

Department	Number of Employees	Ratio of Employees	Overhead of Department
Commercial	5	$\frac{5}{8}$	$\frac{5}{8} \times \$80,000 = \$50,000$
Personal	2	$\frac{2}{8}$	$\frac{2}{8} \times \$80,000 = \$20,000$
Life	1	$\frac{1}{8}$	$\frac{1}{8} \times \$80,000 = \$10,000$
Total:	8		$80,000

19.5	Exercises

Allocate overhead as indicated. Round to the nearest dollar.

1.

Department	Floor Space
1	4000 square feet
2	8000 square feet
3	10,000 square feet

Overhead: $330,000

2.

Department	Floor Space
A	8000 square feet
B	14,000 square feet
C	10,000 square feet

Overhead: $288,000

3.

Department	Floor Space
1	2400 square feet
2	3600 square feet
3	4000 square feet
4	6000 square feet

Overhead: $120,000

4.

Department	Floor Space
1	4200 square feet
2	13,500 square feet
3	21,800 square feet
4	3600 square feet

Overhead: $420,000

5.

Product	Number Produced	Average Sale Price
M	15,000	$8.00
N	20,000	$3.50
P	35,000	$2.00

Overhead: $140,000

6.

Product	Number Produced	Average Sale Price
X	5000	$20
Y	8000	$25
Z	4000	$50

Overhead: $62,500

7.

Product	Number Produced	Average Sale Price
1	140	$100
2	2000	$15
3	150	$20
4	1000	$22

Overhead: $48,000

8.

Product	Number Produced	Average Sale Price
1	150	$6
2	200	$12
3	75	$3
4	125	$8

Overhead: $100,000

9.

Department	Number of Employees
X	110
Y	60
Z	80

Overhead: $1,300,000

10.

Department	Number of Employees
J	10
K	70
L	20

Overhead: $900,000

11.

Department	Number of Employees
1	25
2	30
3	35
4	15

Overhead: $800,000

12.

Department	Number of Employees
1	90
2	20
3	50
4	40

Overhead: $360,000

13. **AUTO PARTS STORE** Dayton Auto Parts allocates its $360,000 overhead based on the floor space used by each department. Allocate the overhead for the following departments.

Department	Floor Space
Hoses	2000 square feet
Radiators	8000 square feet
Water pumps	6000 square feet
Fuel pumps	9000 square feet
Gaskets	1000 square feet
Filters	4000 square feet

14. **OFFICE SUPPLIES** Savon Office and School Supplies wishes to allocate its $110,000 overhead among its various departments based on floor space. Allocate the overhead for the following departments.

Department	Floor Space
Pens, pencils	750 square feet
Copy machine paper	600 square feet
Copy machines	1000 square feet
Office furniture	1500 square feet
Filing cabinets	500 square feet
Calculators	650 square feet

15. **LUMBER PRODUCTION** Boght Lumber wishes to allocate 1 month's overhead of $68,000 according to sales based on bundles. Allocate overhead for the following products.

Product	Number of Bundles Produced	Average Sale Price
Construction 2 × 4s	150	$200
Plywood	200	$400
Veneers	100	$600
Wood chips	500	$75
Furniture wood	300	$150

16. **MEAT DISTRIBUTOR** The manager of Jason's Meats needs to allocate the $8732 in weekly overhead based on sales of packaged units. Allocate overhead for the following products.

Product	Number Produced	Average Sale Price
Beef	10	$800
Lamb	7	$300
Pork	5	$750
Chicken	14	$120
Sausage	12	$150
Luncheon meats	15	$300

17. TEA COMPANY Boston Teas has a weekly overhead of $6000 that it wishes to allocate based on the number of employees per department. Use the following chart.

Department	Number of Employees
Office	6
Marketing	8
Distribution	28
Accounting	8

18. HARDWARE STORE Allocate overhead of $247,100 among departments according to the number of employees.

Department	Number of Employees
Paint	4
Lumber	7
Appliances	4
Plumbing	6
All other	9

19. Define the term *overhead*. List at least three expenses that would be included in overhead. Explain why a manager needs to allocate overhead. (See Objective 1.)

20. Compare and contrast the three ways of allocating overhead that were discussed in this section. Give circumstances under which each of the three might be appropriate. (See Objectives 1–3.)

CHAPTER TERMS

Review the following terms to test your understanding of the chapter. For any terms you do not know, refer to the page number found next to that term.

CONCEPTS

19.1 Determining the amounts paid to holders of preferred and common stock

To find total paid to owners of preferred stock, multiply par value by dividend rate to obtain dividend per share, then multiply by number of shares.

To find the dividend paid to owners of common stock, subtract total paid to owners of preferred stock from total available to stockholders, then divide by number of shares of common stock.

19.1 Finding earnings per share

Subtract dividends on preferred stock from net income, then divide by the number of shares of common stock outstanding.

EXAMPLES

A company distributes $750,000 to stockholders. It has 15,000 shares of $100 par value 4% preferred stock and 150,000 shares of common stock. Find (a) amount paid to holders of preferred stock and (b) amount per share to holders of common stock.

(a) Dividend per share $= \$100 \times 0.04 = \$4$

Total to preferred stockholders $= \$4 \times 15,000$
$$= \$60,000$$

(b) Dividend to common

$$= \frac{\$750,000 - \$60,000}{150,000} = \$4.60$$

A company made $500,000 last year. The company has 750,000 shares of common stock outstanding and paid $75,000 to owners of preferred stock. Find the earnings per share.

$$EPS = \frac{\$500,000 - \$75,000}{750,000}$$

$$= \$0.57 \qquad \text{Rounded}$$

19.2 Reading the stock table

Locate the stock involved and determine the various quantities required.

Use Figure 19.3 to find the following information for Abercrombie A (ANF).

52 week		Stock	Sym	Vol (100s)	Yld %	P/E	Close	Dividend Latest
High	**Low**							
82.06	13.66	Abercrombie A	ANF	84497	3.5	4	20.29	q.175
↑	↑		↑	↑	↑	↑	↑	↑
High for the year	Low for the year		Symbol	Volume for day	Dividend yield	Price-to-earnings ratio	Close for day	Latest quarterly dividend

19.2 Selling shares of a stock

Find the basic price of the stock from Figure 19.3. Subtract the SEC fee and the broker's commission from the basic price of the stock.

Find the amount received by a person selling 300 shares of a stock at $45.82 if the commission is 1%.

$$\text{Sale price} = 300 \times \$45.82 = \$13,746$$

$$\text{Commission} = 0.01 \times \$13,746 = \$137.46$$

$$\text{SEC fee} = \$13,746 \times 0.0000093$$
$$= \$0.13$$

$13,746.00	Sale price
− 137.46	Broker's commission
− 0.13	SEC fee
$13,608.41	

19.2 Finding the current yield on a stock

$$\text{Current yield} = \frac{\text{Annual dividend}}{\text{Current price}}$$

Find the current yield of a stock if the purchase price is $65.42 per share and the annual dividend is $1.44.

$$\text{Current yield} = \frac{\$1.44}{\$65.42} = 2.2\%$$

19.2 Finding the price-to-earnings ratio (PE ratio)

To find the price-to-earnings ratio, use the formula

$$\text{PE ratio} = \frac{\text{Price per share}}{\text{Annual net income per share}}$$

Price per share, $42.50; annual net income per share, $2.75.

$$\text{PE ratio} = \frac{\$42.50}{\$2.75} = 15.45$$

19.2 Reading the Bond Table

Locate the bond table and determine the various quantities required.

Use Figure 19.7 to find the following information for a Sprint Nextel Corporation bond.

Company	Coupon	Maturity	Rating	High	Low	Last	Change	Yield %
Sprint Nextel Corp.	6.000%	Dec 2016	Ba2/BB/BB+	67.500	66.000	66.000	−1.625	13.051
↑	↑	↑	↑	↑	↑	↑	↑	↑
Company	Interest rate on $1000 face value	Maturity date	Rating of bond (quality)	High price for day	Low price for day	Last price for day	Change from previous day	Yield to maturity

19.3 Determining the cost of purchasing bonds

Locate the bond in Figure 19.7, then multiply the price of the bond by 1000 and the number of bonds purchased. Then, add the commission.

Find the cost, including sales charges of $5 per bond, of 30 Dynegy Holding bonds selling at the last price of the day.

$$\text{Price of 1 bond} = 76.750\% \text{ of } \$1000$$
$$= \$767.50$$
$$(30 \times \$767.50) + (30 \times \$5) = \$23,175$$

19.3 Determining the amount received from the sale of bonds

Locate the bond in the table, then multiply the price of the bond by 1000 and the number of bonds sold. Then subtract the commission.

Find the amount received from the sale of 20 Supervalu bonds at the high for the day if the commission is $5 per bond.

$$\text{Price of 1 bond} = 96.108\% \text{ of } \$1000$$
$$= \$961.08$$
$$(20 \times \$961.08) - (20 \times \$5) = \$19,121.60$$

19.3 Finding the annual income from a mutual fund containing bonds

Multiply the amount invested in the fund by the yield rate.

Find the annual income from $120,000 invested in a bond fund yielding $7\frac{1}{2}\%$.

$$\$120,000 \times 0.075 = \$9000$$

19.4 Dividing profits in a partnership

Use one of the following methods to determine each partner's ratio of the profits.

1. Equal shares
2. Agreed ratio
3. Original investment
4. Salary and agreed ratio
5. Interest on investment and agreed ratio
6. Multiply total profits by each partner's ratio.

Divide profits of $75,000 among three investors by the *original investment* if each partner invests the following amount.

Partner	Investment
1	$12,000
2	$15,000
3	$18,000

$$\text{Total initial investment} = \$12,000 + \$15,000$$
$$+ \$18,000 = \$45,000$$

Ratios for each partner:

$$1. \quad \frac{12,000}{45,000} = \frac{4}{15}$$
$$2. \quad \frac{15,000}{45,000} = \frac{1}{3}$$
$$3. \quad \frac{18,000}{45,000} = \frac{2}{5}$$

Profit for each partner:

$$1. \quad \frac{4}{15}(\$75,000) = \$20,000$$
$$2. \quad \frac{1}{3}(\$75,000) = \$25,000$$
$$3. \quad \frac{2}{5}(\$75,000) = \$30,000$$

19.5 Allocating overhead by floor space

First, find the total floor space. Then, determine the fraction of total floor space each department occupies. Multiply the fraction by the amount of overhead to be allocated.

Department	Floor Space
Printing	40,000 sq.ft
Cutting	25,000 sq.ft
Binding	55,000 sq.ft

Allocate $3,300,000 overhead.

$$\text{Printing: } \frac{40,000}{120,000} \times \$3,300,000 = \$1,100,000$$

$$\text{Cutting: } \frac{25,000}{120,000} \times \$3,300,000 = \$687,500$$

$$\text{Binding: } \frac{55,000}{120,000} \times \$3,300,000 = \$1,512,500$$

19.5 Allocating overhead by sales

Determine the fraction of total sales for each department. Multiply this fraction by the amount of overhead to be allocated.

Product	Number Produced	Average Sales Price
A	5000	$12
B	8000	$5
C	10,000	$10

Allocate $60,000 overhead.

$$\text{Total value} = (5000)(\$12) + (8000)(\$5) + (10,000)(\$10)$$

$$= \$200,000$$

$$\text{A: } \frac{(5000)(\$12)}{\$200,000} \times \$60,000 = \$18,000$$

$$\text{B: } \frac{(8000)(\$5)}{\$200,000} \times \$60,000 = \$12,000$$

$$\text{C: } \frac{(10,000)(\$10)}{\$200,000} \times \$60,000 = \$30,000$$

19.5 Allocating overhead by number of employees

Find the fraction of total employees in each department and multiply the fraction by the overhead to be allocated.

Dept.	Number of Employees
A	40
B	20

Allocate $180,000 overhead.

$$\text{A: } \frac{40}{40 + 20} \times \$180,000 = \$120,000$$

$$\text{B: } \frac{20}{40 + 20} \times \$180,000 = \$60,000$$

The answer section includes answers to all Review Exercises.

Find the amount per share paid to holders of (a) preferred stock and (b) common stock. **[19.1]**

	Net Income	Reinvested Funds	Par Value	Rate	Number of Shares of Preferred Stock	Number of Shares of Common Stock
1.	$460,000	$317,000	$50	$6\frac{1}{2}\%$	8000	180,000
2.	$2,375,000	$750,000	$150	4%	15,000	200,000
3.	$2,640,000	$425,000	$125	7%	22,750	750,000

Find the earnings per share. Round to the nearest cent. **[19.1]**

	Net Income	Dividends on Preferred Stock	Number of Shares of Common Stock
4.	$127,500	$0	82,000
5.	$1,425,000	$675,000	275,000
6.	$2,750,000	$900,000	500,000

Use Figure 19.3 to find each of the following. Round money answers to the nearest penny. **[19.2]**

7. 52-week low for Aetna (AET)

8. Volume for Ball Cp (BLL)

9. Close price for Aeropostale (ARO)

10. Quarterly dividend for BarnesGP (B)

11. 52-week low for BerkHathwy A (BRKA)

12. Annual yield for BigLots (BIG)

13. PE Ratio for BarckGld (ABX)

14. High for BB&T Cp (BBT)

15. Low for AK Steel (AKS)

Find the cost of the stock purchase. Ignore any broker's fees. **[19.2]**

Stock	Number of Shares	Transaction
16. BadgerMtr (BMI)	100	52-week low
17. Best Buy (BBY)	250	Close
18. AT&T (T)	400	Close

Find the cost of the stock purchase. Assume a broker's fee of 1%. **[19.2]**

19. 200 shares at $43.37

20. 450 shares at $52.12

Find the amount received from the sale of stock. Assume a broker's fee of 1% and an SEC fee of 0.00093%. **[19.2]**

21. 100 shares at $30.85

22. 180 shares at $47.25

Find the current yield for each stock. Round to the nearest tenth of a percent. [19.2]

23. Intel at $16.80 per share and a dividend of $0.56

24. Target at $41.80 per share and a dividend of $0.64

Find the PE ratio of the following. Round all answers to the nearest whole number. [19.2]

25. Apple at $98.42 per share with a net income of $6.01

26. British Petroleum at $53.79 per share with a net income of $9.73

Use Figure 19.7 to find the following for General Electric bonds due in Jan 2039. [19.3]

27. Last price

28. Low price for the day

29. Annual coupon rate

30. Yield to maturity

31. Change from day before

32. High price for the day

Find the total cost including the commission of $5 per bond, if purchased at the last price of the day. [19.3]

Bond	Number Purchased
33. Verizon Comm bonds	30
34. First Data Corp	25

In Exercises 35–37, divide the profits among the partners based on the indicated method. Round all answers to the nearest dollar. [19.4]

Partners	Investment	Method	Profits
35. 1	$8500	Equal shares	$72,000
2	$7000		
3	$10,500		
36. 1	$16,000	Ratio 2 : 3	$120,000
2	$25,000		
37. 1	$9000	Ratio of	$90,000
2	$12,000	investment	

In Exercises 38–40, allocate the overhead to each department of the company. Round to the nearest dollar. [19.5]

38. Department	Floor Space
A	3000 square feet
B	5000 square feet
C	4000 square feet

Overhead: $100,000

39. Product	Number Produced	Average Sale Price
1	8000	$12
2	40,000	$6
3	20000	$9

Overhead: $125,000

40.

Department	Number of Employees
A	70
B	55
C	45
D	60

Overhead: $850,000

Solve each of the following application problems. [19.3]

41. Ralph Toombs invested his retirement funds of $225,000 in a bond fund currently paying $8\frac{1}{4}\%$. Find his annual income.

42. George and Wanda Joyce invested their life's savings of $320,000 in a bond fund. If the fund charged them a 1% sales commission, find the annual income if the fund is currently paying 7.5%.

CHAPTER 19   # Business Application Case #1
Allocating Profits and Overhead

Dougherty Educational Services, Inc. was formed several years ago with an investment of $15,000 from Trish Shields, $10,000 from Katie Abbot, and $25,000 from Beth Dougherty. Every $1 of their initial contribution resulted in the purchase of 2 shares of common stock. They also sold 10,000 preferred shares of $50 par value at 8% to other investors. Last year the firm had a net income after taxes of $250,000, and the board of directors allocated 45% of net income to the shareholders.

(a) Find the number of common shares of stock owned by Shields, Abbot, and Dougherty.

(b) Find the dividend per share of preferred stock and common stock.

(c) Shields, Abbot, and Dougherty respectively earn salaries of $32,000, $40,000 and $48,000. Find the sum of salary plus dividend for each of the three.

(d) Twenty-five percent of the net income after dividends is paid to a profit-sharing plan that invests in a mutual fund containing both stocks and bonds. Recently the fund has yielded 9%. Find the contribution to the plan and 1 year's return on this investment, assuming the current yield continues.

(e) An overhead of $142,000 has to be allocated to three departments of the company based on the number of employees in the table to the right. Find the allocation to each department. Round to the nearest dollar.

Dept	No. of Employees
Math	7
English	5
Reading	4

(f) Would the profits represent a good return on their original investment if they formed the firm 5 years ago? If the company had been formed 30 years ago, would they be better off if they had placed their original investments in the stock market?

CHAPTER 19	Business Application Case #2
	Investing for Employees

Becky and Joe Rooter own their own small company. They have a retirement plan called a SEP IRA for all employees of the company. It is at Charles Schwab Corporation (www.schwab.com), where they can buy stocks or bonds within the SEP IRA. The Rooters have invested all previous funds in a very conservatively managed growth and income mutual fund containing both stocks and bonds. The $192,380 already in the fund before this quarterly contribution currently pays 4.2% per year, including dividends and interest.

The overall market is down sharply and a financial advisor has advised them to invest a portion of any new contributions in the stocks of a few of the best international companies. After careful consideration, the Rooters decided to buy 100 shares of each of the following international companies.

Company	Country	Close Price	Dividend	PE Ratio
Sony	Japan	$20.32	$0.37	9.9
Toyota	Japan	$62.58	$2.71	6.9
Siemens	Germany	$52.94	$1.47	7.3

(a) Find the total cost to buy the stock, including a commission of 1%.

(b) Find the annual dividend earned and effective rate of interest to the nearest tenth.

(c) The Rooters also purchased 10 International Business Machines Corporation bonds maturing in Oct 2038 at the close price for the day. Use Figure 19.7 to find the cost if the brokerage commission is $5 per bond.

(d) Find the annual interest paid on the bonds.

(e) Find the total annual interest and dividends from all sources.

| PART 5 | Cumulative Review: Chapters 17–19 |

Solve the following application problems.

1. Wild Oats Grocery purchased new store fixtures at a cost of $24,200. The estimated life of the fixtures is 4 years and the salvage value is estimated to be $3000. If straight-line depreciation, find (a) the annual rate of depreciation, (b) the annual amount of depreciation, and (c) the book value at the end of the *second* year. **[17.1]**

2. The owner of an Arco gas station purchased a new gasoline pump at a cost of $32,800. The pump is expected to have a useful life of 10 years but will then have no salvage value. Find (a) the first year's annual depreciation and (b) the second year's annual depreciation using the 200% declining-balance method. **[17.2]**

3. To control the rate at which the bananas ripen, Wholesale Bananas, Inc. bought a new walk-in cooler for $12,820. It is estimated to have a salvage value of $400 after 8 years. Find the first and second year's depreciation using the sum-of-the-years'-digits method. Then find the book value at the end of the second year. **[17.3]**

4. A robotic welding system costing $42,250 is expected to operate for 11,500 hours and to then have a salvage value of $2000. Use the units-of-production method to find the depreciation for the first year if the system is operated 12 hours per day for all 365 days of the year. Then find the book value at the end of the first year. **[17.4]**

5. An automobile manufacturing company bought a new stamping press for $115,800 to stamp out automobile fenders and placed it in service on April 1. The salvage value after an expected useful life of 5 years is $3800. Find the first year's partial depreciation using (a) the straight-line method, (b) the double-declining-balance method, and (c) the sum-of-the-years'-digits method. **[17.4]**

6. Find the recovery period under MACRS for (a) a tugboat, (b) a delivery van, (c) a 4-year-old race horse, (d) a 32-unit apartment house, and (e) a couch for the waiting room in a dentist's office. **[17.5]**

7. Atlas Moving and Storage purchased a tractor unit for moving people's household goods long distances. The cost of the truck was $96,000. Prepare a depreciation schedule using the MACRS method of depreciation. **[17.5]**

Year	Computation	Amount of Depreciation	Accumulated Depreciation	Book Value
0	—	—	—	$96,000
1				
2				
3				
4				

8. The Fashion Shoppe had gross sales of $240,800 with returns of $4300. Inventory at the beginning of the year was $48,300 and by the end of the year inventory was $41,500. A total of $102,000 worth of goods was purchased last year and freight charges were $2900. Wages were $32,400, rent was $15,000, advertising was $2200, utilities were $3100, and taxes on inventory and payroll totaled $6100. Miscellaneous expenses totaled $8900 and income taxes were $11,400. Complete an income statement for the company. **[18.1]**

THE FASHION SHOPPE	INCOME STATEMENT	YEAR ENDING DECEMBER 31		
Gross sales			_____	
Returns			_____	
Net sales				_____
Inventory, January 1		_____		
Cost of goods purchased	_____			
Freight	_____			
Total cost of goods purchased		_____		
Total of goods available for sale		_____		
Inventory, December 31		_____		
Cost of goods sold			_____	
Gross profit				_____
Expenses				
Salaries and wages		_____		
Rent		_____		
Advertising		_____		
Utilities		_____		
Taxes on inventory, payroll		_____		
Miscellaneous expenses		_____		
Total expenses			_____	
Net income before taxes			_____	
Income taxes			_____	
Net income			_____	

9. Analyze the income statement of Exercise 8 by finding cost of goods sold, gross profit, net income before taxes, and net income as a percent of net sales. Round to the nearest tenth of a percent. **[18.2]**

10. The Fashion Shoppe (see Exercise 8) has $28,400 cash, $8400 in notes receivable, $3800 in accounts receivable, and inventory of $41,500. It does not own the land or building that it uses, but fixtures have an estimated value of $12,200. The company has notes payable of $4800 and accounts payable of $32,500 but has neither mortgages nor long-term notes payable. Complete a balance sheet for this company. **[18.3]**

THE FASHION SHOPPE	BALANCE SHEET FOR DECEMBER 31	
	Assets	
Current assets		
Cash	_____	
Notes receivable	_____	
Accounts receivable	_____	
Inventory	_____	
Total current assets		_____
Plant assets		
Land	_____	
Buildings	_____	
Fixtures	_____	
Total plant assets		_____
Total Assets		_____

Liabilities

Current liabilities
  Notes payable   _____
  Accounts payable   _____
    Total current liabilities   _____
Long-term liabilities
  Mortgages payable   _____
  Long-term notes payable   _____
    Total long-term liabilities   _____
Total Liabilities   _____

Owners' Equity

Owner's equity   _____
Total Liabilities and Owners' Equity   _____

11. Find the current ratio, acid-test ratio, and ratio of net income after taxes to average owners' equity assuming owners' equity 1 year previous to the balance sheet of Exercise 10 was $42,800 and using the income statement from Exercise 8. **[18.4]**

12. Noel Saturn owns 50 shares of preferred stock with a par value of $80 and a dividend of 5%. Find his total dividend payment. **[19.1]**

13. Jackson Brewery paid no dividend last year but has set aside $80,750 for the payment of dividends this year. It has 10,000 shares of cumulative preferred stock outstanding with a par value of $60 and a 6% dividend. Find this year's dividend per share of common stock given 25,000 shares of common stock outstanding. **[19.1]**

14. ABC, Inc. was incorporated in 1990 and now has 200,000 shares of common stock outstanding. Given a net income of $85,000 and preferred dividends of $8000, find the earnings per share of common stock. **[19.1]**

15. Elizabeth Neault bought 200 shares of Intel at $23.22 per share and 100 shares of Toyota at $75.12 per share. Find the total cost if the broker charged 0.5% commission. **[19.2]**

16. A publicly held company that writes computer software had net income this year of $2.06 per share and paid a dividend this year of $0.40 per share. Given a stock price of $62\tfrac{1}{2}$, find (a) the current yield and (b) the PE ratio. **[19.2]**

17. Antonio Pondillo sold 200 shares of Wal-Mart stock at $47.70 per share and paid a commission of $12.95. Find the amount he received after expenses of the sale. (*Hint:* The SEC fee is included in the brokerage commission.) **[19.2]**

18. Use Figure 19.3 on page 679 to find the quarterly dividend yield and price-to-earnings ratio for Aetna (symbol AET). **[19.2]**

19. Use Figure 19.7 on page 690 to find the last price and yield to maturity for the day for Wal-Mart Stores. **[19.3]**

20. Use Figure 19.6 on page 685 to find the current price and two-year return for Fidelity Contrafund. **[19.2]**

21. Find the cost of purchasing 25 bonds selling at $97\tfrac{1}{4}$ assuming a commission of $5 per bond. **[19.3]**

22. Find the net proceeds after a $5 commission per bond from the sale of 40 bonds at a market price of $92\tfrac{3}{8}$. **[19.3]**

23. Two partners invested $40,000 and $60,000, respectively, in a business venture. If there was a profit of $48,000, find the distribution of profit to the two partners using (a) equal shares, (b) an agreed ratio of 3:1, and (c) the original investment. **[19.4]**

24. Alan Padgett and Gina Harden own a retail business that Harden manages at a salary of $28,000. Originally, Padgett invested $60,000 and Harden invested $20,000 to start the business. Find the amount each partner would receive from a profit of $85,000 if they agree to divide profits based on their original investment. **[19.4]**

25. Allocate an overhead of $340,000 by floor space. **[19.5]**

Department	Floor Space
Machining	30,000 square feet
Stamping	15,000 square feet
Assembly	35,000 square feet
	Total: 80,000 square feet

26. Allocate an overhead of $180,000 by number of employees. **[19.5]**

Department	Number of Employees
A	20
B	12
C	18
	Total: 50

27. Allocate an overhead of $140,000 by sales value. **[19.5]**

Product	Number Produced	Value of Each
1	12,800	$25
2	14,200	$15
3	180	$200

Calculator Basics

Calculators are among the more popular inventions of the last four decades. Each year better calculators are developed and costs drop. The first all-transistor desktop calculator was introduced to the market in 1966. It weighed 55 pounds, cost $2500, and was slow. Today, these same calculations are performed quite well on a calculator costing less than $10. And today's $100 pocket calculators have more ability to calculate than some of the early computers.

Many colleges allow students to use calculators in business mathematics courses. Some courses require calculator use. Although you can still purchase a basic four-function calculator, you're probably better off spending $10 to $20 on either a **scientific** or a **financial calculator**. These calculators allow you to do a lot more than the basic four-function calculators. A **graphing calculator** allows you to graph functions and visualize data; however, it is beyond the scope of this text.

In **Section A.1**, we discuss the common scientific calculator including percent key, reciprocal key, exponent keys, square root key, memory function, order of operations, and parentheses keys. In **Section A.2**, we discuss the financial calculator with its associated financial keys.

A.1	**Scientific Calculators**

OBJECTIVES

1 *Learn the basic calculator keys.*

2 *Understand the* $\boxed{C}$ *,* $\boxed{CE}$ *, and* $\boxed{ON/C}$ *keys.*

3 *Understand the floating decimal point.*

4 *Use the* $\boxed{\%}$ *and* $\boxed{1/x}$ *keys.*

5 *Use the* $\boxed{y^x}$ *,* $\boxed{e^x}$ *, and* $\boxed{\sqrt{x}}$ *keys.*

6 *Use the* $\boxed{a^b/_c}$ *key.*

7 *Solve problems with negative numbers.*

8 *Use the calculator memory function.*

9 *Solve chain calculations using order of operations.*

10 *Use the parentheses keys.*

11 *Use the calculator for problem solution.*

NOTE   The various calculator models differ significantly. *Use the instruction booklet that came with your calculator* for specifics about your calculator.

Objective

1   *Learn the Basic Calculator Keys.*   Most calculators use **algebraic logic**. Some problems can be solved by entering number and function keys in the same order as you would solve a problem by hand, but many others require a knowledge of the order of operations when entering the problem. Order of operations are discussed in Objective 9 of this Appendix.

EXAMPLE 1   Using the Basic Keys

(a) 12 + 25   **(b)** 456 ÷ 24

Solution

(a) The problem 12 + 25 would be entered as

$$12 \boxed{+} 25 \boxed{=}$$

and 37 would appear as the answer.

(b) Enter 456 ÷ 24 as

$$456 \boxed{\div} 24 \boxed{=}$$

and 19 appears as the answer.

Objective

2   *Understand the* $\boxed{C}$ *,* $\boxed{CE}$ *, and* $\boxed{ON/C}$ *Keys.*   All calculators have a $\boxed{C}$ key. Pressing this key erases everything in most calculators and prepares them for a new problem. Some calculators have a $\boxed{CE}$ key. Pressing this key erases only the number displayed, thus allowing for correction of a mistake without having to start the problem over. Many calculators combine the $\boxed{C}$ key and the $\boxed{CE}$ key and use an $\boxed{ON/C}$ key. This key is used both to turn the calculator on and to erase the calculator display. If ON/C is pressed after the

 = or after one of the operation keys + , − , × , or ÷ , everything in the calcu-

lator is erased. If the wrong operation key is pressed, simply press the correct key and the error

is corrected. For example, in 7 +   − 3 = 4 pressing the − key cancels out the previ-

ous + key entry.

> **NOTE**   Be sure to look at the directions that come with your calculator in terms of
> clearing the memory since keys and the operational sequence vary from calculator to
> calculator.

Objective

3   *Understand the Floating Decimal Point.*   Calculators have a **floating decimal**, which
locates the decimal point in the final result.

EXAMPLE 2   Calculating with Decimal Numbers

A contractor purchased 55.75 square yards of vinyl floor covering at a cost of $18.99 per
square yard. Find her total cost.

Solution   Proceed as follows.

$$55.75 \;\boxed{\times}\; 18.99 \;\boxed{=}\; 1058.6925$$

The decimal point is automatically placed in the answer. Since money answers are usually
rounded to the nearest cent, the answer is $1058.69.

EXAMPLE 3   Placing the Decimal Point in Money Answers

Add $21.38 and $1.22.

Solution

$$21.38 \;\boxed{+}\; 1.22 \;\boxed{=}\; 22.6$$

The final 0 is left off. Remember that the problem deals with dollars and cents, so write the
answer as $22.60.

Objective

4   *Use the* % *and* 1/x *Keys.*   The % key moves the decimal point two places to the left
when used following multiplication or division.

EXAMPLE 4   Using the % Key

Find 8% of $4205.

Solution

$$4205 \;\boxed{\times}\; 8 \;\boxed{\%}\; \boxed{=}\; 336.4 = \$336.40$$

The $1/x$ key replaces a number with the reciprocal of that number.

EXAMPLE 5 Using the $1/x$ Key

Find the multiplicative inverse, or reciprocal, of 40.

Solution

$$40 \boxed{1/x}\ 0.025$$

Objective

5 *Use the $\boxed{y^x}$, $\boxed{e^x}$, and $\boxed{\sqrt{x}}$ Keys.* The product of 3×3 can be written as follows.

$$3^2 \quad \text{exponent} \quad \text{base}$$

The **exponent** (2 in this case) shows how many times the **base** (3 in this case) is multiplied by itself. The $\boxed{y^x}$ key raises a base to a power. Be sure to enter the base first followed by the exponent.

EXAMPLE 6 Using the $\boxed{y^x}$ and $\boxed{e^x}$ keys

Note that e is a constant that is found on most calculators. It is approximately 2.71828, which is the same thing as e^1.

Solve the following: (a) 5^3 and (b) e^2.

Solution

(a)

$$\text{base} \qquad \text{exponent}$$
$$5 \boxed{y^x}\ 3 \boxed{=}\ 125$$

(b) In this case, the number e on your calculator is the base. Raise it to the second power by first entering the exponent 2 and then using the $\boxed{e^x}$ key.

$$2 \boxed{e^x}\ 7.389 \quad \text{Rounded}$$

Since $3^2 = 9$, the number 3 is called the **square root** of 9. The symbol $\sqrt{}$ is used to write the square root of a number.

$$\sqrt{9} = 3$$

EXAMPLE 7 Using the $\boxed{\sqrt{x}}$ Key

Find each square root.

(a) $\sqrt{144}$ **(b)** $\sqrt{20}$

Solution

(a) Using the calculator, enter

$$144 \boxed{\sqrt{x}}$$

and 12 appears in the display. The square root of 144 is 12.

(b) The square root of 20 is

$$20 \boxed{\sqrt{x}}\ 4.472136$$

which may be rounded to the desired position.

Objective

6 *Use the* $\boxed{a\%}$ *Key.* Many calculators have an $\boxed{a\%}$ key that can be used for problems containing fractions and mixed numbers. A mixed number is a number with both a whole number and a fraction, such as $7\frac{3}{4}$, which equals $7 + \frac{3}{4}$. The rules for adding, subtracting, multiplying, and dividing both fractions and mixed numbers are given in **Chapter 1**. Here, we simply show how these operations are done on a calculator.

EXAMPLE **8** **Using the** $\boxed{a\%}$ **Key with Fractions**

Solve the following.

(a) $\dfrac{6}{11} + \dfrac{3}{4}$ (b) $\dfrac{3}{8} \div \dfrac{5}{6}$

Solution

(a) 6 $\boxed{a\%}$ 11 $\boxed{+}$ 3 $\boxed{a\%}$ 4 $\boxed{=}$ $1\dfrac{13}{44}$

(b) 3 $\boxed{a\%}$ 8 $\boxed{\div}$ 5 $\boxed{a\%}$ 6 $\boxed{=}$ $\dfrac{9}{20}$

NOTE The calculator automatically reduces fractions for you.

EXAMPLE **9** **Using the** $\boxed{a\%}$ **Key**

Solve the following.

(a) $4\dfrac{7}{8} \div 3\dfrac{4}{7}$ (b) $\dfrac{5}{3} \div 27.5$ (c) $65.3 \times 6\dfrac{3}{4}$

Solution

(a) 4 $\boxed{a\%}$ 7 $\boxed{a\%}$ 8 $\boxed{\div}$ 3 $\boxed{a\%}$ 4 $\boxed{a\%}$ 7 $\boxed{=}$ $1\dfrac{73}{200}$

(b) 5 $\boxed{a\%}$ 3 $\boxed{\div}$ 27.5 $\boxed{=}$ 0.060606061

(c) 65.3 $\boxed{\times}$ 6 $\boxed{a\%}$ 3 $\boxed{a\%}$ 4 $\boxed{=}$ 440.775

Objective

7 ***Solve Problems with Negative Numbers.*** There are several calculations in business that result in a **negative number** or **deficit amount**.

EXAMPLE **10** **Working with Negative Numbers**

The amount in the advertising account last month was $4800, while $5200 was actually spent. Find the balance remaining in the advertising account.

Solution Enter the numbers in the calculator.

$$4800 \boxed{-} 5200 \boxed{=} -400$$

The minus sign in front of the 400 indicates that there is a deficit or negative amount. This value can be written as $-\$400$ or as ($400), which indicates a negative amount. Some calculators place the minus after the number, as $400-$.

Negative numbers may be entered into the calculator by using the $\boxed{-}$ before entering the number. For example, if $3000 is now added to the advertising account in Example 10, the new balance is calculated as follows.

$$\boxed{-}\ 400\ \boxed{+}\ 3000\ \boxed{=}\ 2600$$

The new account balance is $2600.

The $\boxed{+/-}$ key can be used to change the sign of a number that has already been entered. For example, 520 $\boxed{+/-}$ changes +520 to −520.

Objective

8   *Use the Calculator Memory Function.*   Many calculators feature **memory keys**, which are used to store intermediate steps in a calculation. On some calculators, a key labeled $\boxed{M}$ or $\boxed{STO}$ is used to store the numbers in the display, with $\boxed{MR}$ or $\boxed{RCL}$ used to recall the numbers from memory. Other calculators have $\boxed{M+}$ and $\boxed{M-}$ keys. The $\boxed{M+}$ key adds the number displayed to the number already in memory. For example, if the memory contains the number 0 at the beginning of a problem, and the calculator display contains the number 29.4, then pushing $\boxed{M+}$ will cause 29.4 to be stored in the memory (the result of adding 0 and 29.4). If 57.8 is then entered into the display, pushing $\boxed{M+}$ will cause

$$29.4 + 57.8 = 87.2$$

to be stored. If 11.9 is then entered into the display and $\boxed{M-}$ pushed, the memory will contain the difference of 75.3.

$$87.2 - 11.9 = 75.3$$

The $\boxed{MR}$ key is used to recall the number in memory as needed, with $\boxed{MC}$ used to clear the memory.

Scientific calculators typically have one or more storage registers in which to store numbers. These memory keys are usually labeled as $\boxed{STO}$ for store and $\boxed{RCL}$ for recall. For example, 32.5 can be stored in register 1 by

$$32.5\ \boxed{STO}\ 1$$

or it can be stored in memory register 2 by 32.5 $\boxed{STO}$ 2 and so forth. Values are retrieved from a particular memory register by using the $\boxed{RCL}$ key followed by the number of the register. For example, $\boxed{RCL}$ 2 recalls the contents of memory register 2.

With a scientific calculator, a number stays in memory until it is replaced by another number or until the memory is cleared. The contents of the memory are saved *even when the calculator is turned off.*

> **NOTE**   Always clear the memory before beginning work on a new problem. This is the only way to make sure there are no numbers remaining from the previous problem. Clear the memory by pressing 0 followed by $\boxed{STO}$ followed by the register number.

EXAMPLE 11 Using the Memory Registers

An elevator repairperson counted the number of people entering an elevator and also measured the weight of each group of people. Find the average weight per person.

Number of People	Total Weight
6	839 pounds
8	1184 pounds
4	640 pounds

Solution First, find the weight of all three groups and store in memory register 1.

$$839 \boxed{+} 1184 \boxed{+} 640 \boxed{=} 2663 \boxed{\text{STO}} 1$$

Then find the total number of people and store in register 2.

$$6 \boxed{+} 8 \boxed{+} 4 \boxed{=} 18 \boxed{\text{STO}} 2$$

Finally, divide the contents of memory register 1 by the 18 people.

$$\boxed{\text{RCL}} 1 \boxed{\div} \boxed{\text{RCL}} 2 \boxed{=} 147.94444 \text{ pounds}$$

This value can be rounded as needed.

Objective

9 *Solve Chain Calculations Using Order of Operations.* Long calculations involving several operations (adding, subtracting, multiplying, and dividing) must be done in a specific sequence called the **order of operations** and are called **chain calculations**. The logic of the following order of operations is built into most scientific calculators and can help us work problems without having to store a lot of intermediate values.

Solving Chain Calculations

STEP 1 Do all operations inside parentheses first.

STEP 2 Simplify any expressions with exponents (powers) and find any square roots.

STEP 3 Multiply and divide from left to right.

STEP 4 Add and subtract from left to right.

EXAMPLE 12 Using the Order of Operations

Solve the following.

(a) $3 + 7 \times 9\frac{3}{4}$ **(b)** $42.1 \times 5 - 90 \div 4$ **(c)** $6.75^2 \times 9 - 7$

Solution The calculator automatically keeps track of the order of operations for us.

(a) The order of operations tells us to multiply before doing the addition in the problem.

$$3 \boxed{+} 7 \boxed{\times} 9 \boxed{a\frac{b}{c}} 3 \boxed{a\frac{b}{c}} 4 \boxed{=} 71\frac{1}{4}$$

(b) The order of operations tells us to multiply, then divide, and only then subtract.

$$42.1 \boxed{\times} 5 \boxed{-} 90 \boxed{\div} 4 \boxed{=} 188$$

(c) The order of operations tells us to square 6.75 first, then multiply, and finally subtract.

$$6.75 \boxed{y^x} 2 \boxed{\times} 9 \boxed{-} 7 \boxed{=} 403.0625$$

NOTE Scientific calculators keep track of the order of operations for us. All we have to do is enter the problem correctly into the calculator and the calculator does the rest. However, the basic four-function calculator is not programmed to observe the order of operations and can be used only if you enter numbers in the proper order. If you do not get the answer above with your calculator, try using parentheses, as shown next.

Objective

10 *Use the Parentheses Keys.* The parentheses keys can be used to help establish the order of operations in a more complex chain calculation. For example, $\dfrac{4}{5+7}$ can be written as $\dfrac{4}{(5+7)}$, which can be solved as

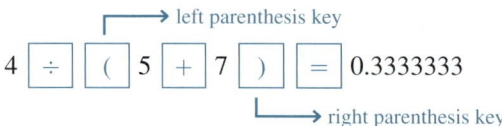

$$4 \;\boxed{\div}\; \boxed{(} \; 5 \; \boxed{+} \; 7 \; \boxed{)} \; \boxed{=} \; 0.3333333$$

left parenthesis key

right parenthesis key

EXAMPLE 13 Using Parentheses

Solve the following problem.

$$\frac{16 \div 2.5}{39.2 - 29.8 \times 0.6}$$

Solution Think of this problem as follows.

$$\frac{(16 \div 2.5)}{(39.2 - 29.8 \times 0.6)}$$

Using parentheses to set off the numerator and denominator will help you minimize errors.

$$\boxed{(}\; 16 \; \boxed{\div}\; 2.5 \; \boxed{)}\; \boxed{\div}\; \boxed{(}\; 39.2 \; \boxed{-}\; 29.8 \; \boxed{\times}\; 0.6 \; \boxed{)}\; \boxed{=}\; 0.3001876$$

Objective

11 *Use the Calculator for Problem Solution.*

EXAMPLE 14 Finding Sale Price

A gold necklace with an original price of $560 is on sale at 10% off. Find the sale price.

Solution If the discount from the original price is 10%, then the sale price is 100% − 10% of the original price.

$$560 \; \boxed{\times}\; \boxed{(}\; 100 \; \boxed{-}\; 10 \; \boxed{)}\; \boxed{\%}\; \boxed{=}\; 504$$

On some calculators the following keystrokes will also work.

$$560 \; \boxed{-}\; 10 \; \boxed{\%}\; \boxed{=}\; 504$$

> **EXAMPLE 15** **Applying Calculator Use to Problem Solving**
>
> After a good-sized down payment, a home buyer borrows $86,400 at 10% for 30 years. The monthly payment on the loan is $8.78 per $1000 borrowed. Annual taxes are $2780, and fire insurance is $670 a year. Find the total monthly payment including taxes and insurance.
>
> **Solution** The monthly payment is the *sum* of the monthly payment on the loan plus monthly taxes plus monthly fire insurance costs. The monthly payment on the loan is the number of thousands in the loan (86.4) times the monthly payment per $1000 borrowed ($8.78).

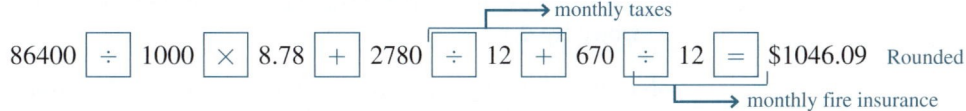

monthly taxes

$$86400 \boxed{\div} 1000 \boxed{\times} 8.78 \boxed{+} 2780 \boxed{\div} 12 \boxed{+} 670 \boxed{\div} 12 \boxed{=} \$1046.09 \quad \text{Rounded}$$

monthly fire insurance

> The monthly payment is $1046.09.

A.1	**Exercises**

Solve the following problems on a calculator. Round each answer to the nearest hundredth.

1.
$$\begin{array}{r} 384.92 \\ 407.61 \\ 351.14 \\ +\ \ 27.93 \\ \hline \end{array}$$

2.
$$\begin{array}{r} 85.76 \\ 21.94 \\ +\ 39.89 \\ \hline \end{array}$$

3.
$$\begin{array}{r} 6,850 \\ 321 \\ +\ 4,207 \\ \hline \end{array}$$

4.
$$\begin{array}{r} 781.42 \\ 304.59 \\ +\ 261.35 \\ \hline \end{array}$$

5.
$$\begin{array}{r} 4270.41 \\ -\ \ 365.09 \\ \hline \end{array}$$

6.
$$\begin{array}{r} 3000.07 \\ -\ \ \ 48.12 \\ \hline \end{array}$$

7.
$$\begin{array}{r} 384.96 \\ -\ 129.72 \\ \hline \end{array}$$

8. $36.84 - 12.17$

9.
$$\begin{array}{r} 365 \\ \times\ \ 43 \\ \hline \end{array}$$

10.
$$\begin{array}{r} 27.51 \\ \times\ \ 1.18 \\ \hline \end{array}$$

11. 3.7×8.4

12. 62.5×81

13. $\dfrac{375.4}{10.6}$

14. $\dfrac{9625}{400}$

15. $96.7 \div 3.5$

16. $103.7 \div 0.35$

Solve the following chain calculations. Round each answer to the nearest hundredth.

17. $\dfrac{9 \times 9}{2 \times 5}$

18. $\dfrac{15 \times 8 \times 3}{11 \times 7 \times 4}$

19. $\dfrac{87 \times 24 \times 47.2}{13.6 \times 12.8}$

20. $\dfrac{2 \times (3 + 4)}{6 + 10}$

21. $\dfrac{2 \times 3 + 4}{6 + 10}$

22. $\dfrac{4200 \times 0.12 \times 90}{365}$

23. $\dfrac{640 - 0.6 \times 12}{17.5 + 3.2}$

24. $\dfrac{16 \times 18 - 0.4 \div 2}{95.4 \times 3 - 0.8}$

25. $\dfrac{14^2 - 3.6 \times 6}{95.2 \div 0.5}$

26. $\dfrac{9^2 + 3.8 \div 2}{14 + 7.5}$

27. e^2

28. $9^2 \cdot e^{2.5}$

29. $175 \div e^1$

30. $15e^{1.2}$

Solve the following problems. Reduce any fractions to lowest terms or round to the nearest hundredth.

31. $7\frac{5}{8} \div \left(1 + \frac{3}{8}\right)$

32. $\left(5\frac{1}{4}\right)^2 \times 3.65$

33. $\left(\frac{3}{4} \div \frac{5}{8}\right)^3 \div 3\frac{1}{2}$

34. $\sqrt{6} \times \dfrac{3^2 + 2\frac{1}{2}}{7 \times \frac{5}{6}}$

35. Describe in your own words the order of operations to be used when solving chain calculations. (See Objective 9.)

36. Explain how the parentheses keys are used when solving chain calculations. (See Objective 9.)

Solve the following application problems on a calculator. Round each answer to the nearest cent.

37. A sporting goods store bought 15 pairs of skis at an average cost of $187 per pair, 30 parkas at an average cost of $128 each, and 10 mountain bikes at an average cost of $163 each. Find the total cost.

38. Ben Thompson fishes for halibut off the coast of Alaska. His daily catch over the past few days was 263.5 pounds, 122.7 pounds, 82.4 pounds, and 90.8 pounds. Find the average catch per day by adding the values and dividing the sum by 4.

39. Jessica Rodriguez owns a company that installs sprinkler systems. She has three crews made up of 3, 3, and 4 individuals, respectively. One of the workers in each crew is a crew chief who is paid $15.75 per hour. The others in each crew are paid $8.40 per hour. Find payroll for a week in which the first two crews worked 32 hours each and the third crew worked 40 hours.

40. Ben James is a college professor whose travel expenses to a conference are paid. His round-trip flight to Phoenix was $295, a shuttle to the conference in Sedona, Arizona was $65, the conference fee was $320, and he spent 2 nights at a hotel for $154.13 per night. Find the total cost.

41. In Virginia City, the sales tax is 6.5%. Find the tax on each of the following items: (a) a new car costing $17,908.43 and (b) an office word processor costing $1463.58.

42. Marja Strutz bought a used commercial fishing boat equipped for sardine fishing at a cost of $78,250. Additional safety equipment was needed at a cost of $4820, and sales tax of $7\frac{1}{4}$% was due on the boat and safety equipment. In addition she was charged a licensing fee of $1135 and a Coast Guard registration fee of $428. Strutz will pay $\frac{1}{3}$ of the total cost as a down payment and will borrow the balance. How much will she borrow?

43. Elizabeth Daigle purchased a home for $154,000. She paid $16,000 down and agreed to 30 years with payments of $1036.75 per month. Find the difference between the down payment plus all payments and the price of the home.

44. Linda Smelt purchased a 22-unit apartment house for $620,000. She made a down payment of $150,000, which she had inherited from her parents, and agreed to make monthly payments of $5050 for 15 years. By how much does the sum of her down payment and all monthly payments exceed the original purchase price?

45. Ben Hurd wishes to open a small repair shop but has only $32,400 in cash. He estimates that he will need $15,000 for equipment, $2800 for the first month's rent on a building, and about $28,000 operating expenses until the business is profitable. How much additional funding does he need?

46. Koplan Kitchens wishes to expand its retail store. In order to do so, it must first purchase the $26,000 vacant lot next door. The company then anticipates $120,000 in construction costs plus an additional $28,500 for additional inventory. It has $50,000 in cash and must borrow the balance from a bank. How much must the company borrow?

A.2   Financial Calculators

OBJECTIVES

1 *Learn the basic conventions used with cash flows.*

2 *Learn the basic financial calculator keys.*

3 *Understand which keys to use for a particular problem.*

4 *Use the financial calculator to solve financial problems.*

Financial calculators have added features that allow you to make certain compound interest calculations quickly and accurately. These calculators are commonly used by people in business. Financial calculators differ greatly from one another. *Be sure to use the booklet that came with your financial calculator* for specific information about your calculator.

Objective

1   *Learn the Basic Conventions Used with Cash Flows.*   Many financial calculators are based on logic that separates cash received by an individual or a company from cash paid out by the same individual or company using + and − signs. *Cash received is given a + sign, and cash paid out is given a − sign.*

Inflows of cash to a person or firm are **positive**. Outflows of cash from the same person or firm are **negative**. For example, suppose you put $100 per month into an investment for 10 years and then take out the balance of $23,000 at the end of 10 years. The $100 payment each month *is shown as a negative number*, since cash is leaving you. But the $23,000 received in 10 years *is shown as a positive number*, since cash flows to you at that time. We will use this convention throughout this text even though some financial calculators differ.

Objective

2   *Learn the Basic Financial Calculator Keys.*   Financial calculators have special functions that allow the user to solve financial problems involving time, interest rates, and money. Many of the compound interest problems presented in this text can be solved using a financial calculator rather than using tables as shown in the text. Most financial calculators have financial keys similar to those shown below.

These keys represent the following functions:

n	The number of compounding periods
i	The interest rate *per compounding period*
PV	**Present value:** the value in *today's* dollars
PMT	The amount of a **level payment** (e.g., $625 per month); this is used for annuity-type problems.
FV	**Future value:** the value at *some future date*

NOTE   Different financial calculators look and work somewhat differently from one another. *Look at the instruction booklet* that came with your calculator to determine how the keys are used with your particular calculator.

You will also find that different financial calculators will sometimes give slightly different answers to the same problems because of rounding.

Objective

3 *Understand Which Keys to Use for a Particular Problem.* Most simple financial problems require only four of the five financial keys described above. Both the number of compounding periods $\boxed{n}$ and the interest rate per compounding period $\boxed{i}$ are needed for each financial problem—these two keys will always be used. Which two of the remaining three financial keys ($\boxed{PV}$, $\boxed{PMT}$, and $\boxed{FV}$) are used depends on the particular problem. Using the convention described above, one of these monetary values will be negative and one will be positive. *The process of solving a financial problem is to enter values for the three variables that are known, then press the key for the unknown, fourth variable.*

For example, if you wish to know the future value of a series of known, equal payments, enter the specific values for $\boxed{n}$, $\boxed{i}$, and $\boxed{PMT}$. Then press $\boxed{FV}$ for the result. Or, if you wish to know how long it will take for an investment to grow to some specific value at a given interest rate, enter values for $\boxed{PV}$, $\boxed{i}$, and $\boxed{FV}$. Then press $\boxed{n}$ to find the required number of compounding periods.

> **NOTE** Be sure to enter a cash inflow as a positive number and a cash outflow as a negative number. Also be sure to clear all values from the memory of your calculator before working a problem.

Objective

4 *Use the Financial Calculator to Solve Financial Problems.*

EXAMPLE 1 **Given n, i, and PV, Find FV**

Mr. Willis invests $1000 in a fund containing bonds that pays 8% compounded quarterly. Find the future value in $1\frac{1}{2}$ years.

Solution The present value of $1000 (a cash outflow entered as a negative number) is compounded at 2% per quarter (8% ÷ 4 = 2%) for 6 quarters ($1\frac{1}{2} \times 4 = 6$).

Enter values for $\boxed{PV}$, $\boxed{i}$, and $\boxed{n}$.

$$-1000\ \boxed{PV}\ 2\ \boxed{i}\ 6\ \boxed{n}$$

Then press $\boxed{FV}$ to find the compound amount at the end of 6 quarters.

$$\boxed{FV}\ 1126.16$$

which is the future value.

EXAMPLE 2 **Given n, i, and PMT, Find FV**

Joan Jones plans to invest $100 at the end of each month in a mutual fund that she believes will grow at 9% per year compounded monthly. Find the future value in 20 years.

Solution She makes 240 payments ($12 \times 20 = 240$) of $100 each (cash outflows entered as a negative number) into an account earning 0.75% per month ($9\% \div 12 = 0.75\%$).

Enter values for $\boxed{n}$, $\boxed{\text{PMT}}$, and $\boxed{i}$.

$$240 \boxed{n} \ -100 \boxed{\text{PMT}} \ 0.75 \boxed{i}$$

Press $\boxed{\text{FV}}$ to find the future value.

$$\boxed{\text{FV}} \ 66{,}788.69$$

the future value is $66,788.69.

NOTE The order in which data are entered into the calculator does not matter. Just remember to *press the financial key for the unknown value last.*

Any one of the four values used to solve a particular financial problem can be unknown. Look at the next three examples in which the number of compounding periods $\boxed{n}$, the payment amount $\boxed{\text{PMT}}$, and the interest rate per compounding period $\boxed{i}$, respectively, are unknown.

EXAMPLE **3** **Given *i*, PMT, and FV, Find *n***

Mr. Trebor needs $140,000 for a new farm tractor. He can invest $8000 at the end of each month in an account paying 6% per year compounded monthly. How many monthly payments are needed?

Solution The $8000 monthly payment (cash outflow) will grow at 0.5% per compounding period ($6\% \div 12 = 0.5\%$) until a future value of $140,000 (cash inflow at a future date) is accumulated. Enter values for $\boxed{\text{PMT}}$, $\boxed{i}$, and $\boxed{\text{FV}}$.

$$-8000 \boxed{\text{PMT}} \ 0.5 \boxed{i} \ 140000 \boxed{\text{FV}}$$

Press $\boxed{n}$ to determine the number of payments.

$$\boxed{n} \ 17 \text{ monthly payments of } \$8000 \text{ each}$$

Actually, 17 payments of $8000 each in an account earning 0.5% per month will grow to slightly more than $140,000:

$$-8000 \boxed{\text{PMT}} \ 0.5 \boxed{i} \ 17 \boxed{n}$$

Press $\boxed{\text{FV}}$ to determine the future value.

$$\boxed{\text{FV}} \ 141578.41$$

which is the future value.

The 17th payment would need to be only

$$\$8000 - (\$141{,}578.41 - \$140{,}000) = \$6421.59$$

in order to accumulate exactly $140,000.

EXAMPLE 4 **Given *n*, *i*, and FV, Find PMT**

Jane Abel wishes to have $1,000,000 at her retirement in 40 years. Find the payment she must make at the end of each quarter into an account earning 8% compounded quarterly to attain her goal.

Solution   Abel makes 160 payments (40 × 4 = 160) into an account earning 2% per quarter (8% ÷ 4 = 2%) until a future value of $1,000,000 (cash inflow at a future date) is accumulated. Enter values for $\boxed{n}$, $\boxed{i}$, and $\boxed{\text{FV}}$.

$$160 \; \boxed{n} \; 2 \; \boxed{i} \; 1000000 \; \boxed{\text{FV}}$$

Press $\boxed{\text{PMT}}$ for the quarterly payment:

$$\boxed{\text{PMT}} \; -878.35$$

which is the required quarterly payment of cash. Hence, 160 payments of $878.35 at the end of each quarter in an account earning 8% compounded quarterly will grow to $1,000,000.

EXAMPLE 5 **Given *n*, PV, and FV, Find *i***

Tom Fernandez bought 200 shares of stock in an oil company at $33.50 per share. Exactly 3 years later he sold the stock at $41.25 per share. Find the annual interest rate, rounded to the nearest tenth of a percent, that Fernandez earned on this investment, assuming the company paid no dividends.

Solution   In 3 years, the per share price increased from a present value of $33.50 to a future value of $41.25. The purchase of the stock is a cash outflow and the eventual sale of the stock is a cash inflow. It is not necessary to multiply the stock price by the number of shares. The interest rate indicating the return on the investment is the same whether 1 share or 200 shares are used. Enter values for $\boxed{n}$, $\boxed{\text{PV}}$, and $\boxed{\text{FV}}$.

$$3 \; \boxed{n} \; -33.50 \; \boxed{\text{PV}} \; 41.25 \; \boxed{\text{FV}}$$

Press $\boxed{i}$ for the annual interest rate:

$$\boxed{i} \; 7.18\%$$

or about 7.2% per year. Fernandez's return on his original investment compounded at 7.2% per year.

Interest rates can have a great influence on both individuals and businesses. Individuals borrow for homes, cars, and other personal items, whereas firms borrow to buy real estate, expand operations, or cover operating expenses. A small difference in interest rates can make a large difference in costs over time, as shown in the next example.

EXAMPLE 6 **Compare Monthly House Payments**

Layne and Leticia Hare wish to refinance the remaining $62,000 debt on their home for 30 years. Find the monthly payment at interest rates of (a) 8% and (b) 9%. Show (c) the monthly savings at the lower rate and (d) the total savings in monthly payments over the 30 years.

Solution

(a) Enter a present value of $62,000 (cash inflow) with 360 compounding periods ($30 \times 12 = 360$) and a rate of 0.666667% per month ($8\% \div 12 = 0.666667$, rounded) and press PMT to find the monthly payment.

$$62000 \; \boxed{\text{PV}} \; 360 \; \boxed{n} \; 0.666667 \; \boxed{i}$$

 PMT -454.93 is the monthly payment at 8% per year, rounded to the nearest cent.

(b) Enter the values again using the new interest rate of 0.75% ($9\% \div 12 = 0.75\%$).

$$62000 \; \boxed{\text{PV}} \; 360 \; \boxed{n} \; 0.75 \; \boxed{i}$$

 PMT -498.87 is the monthly payment at 9% per year, again, rounded to the nearest cent.

(c) The difference in the monthly payments is

$$\$498.87 - \$454.93 = \$43.94$$

(d) The total difference saved over 30 years ($30 \times 12 = 360$ payments) is

$$\$43.94 \times 360 \text{ payments} = \$15,818.40$$

The lower interest rate will result in a savings of $15,818.40 over 30 years.

EXAMPLE 7 **Retirement Planning**

Courtney and Nathan Wright plan to retire in 25 years and feel that they will need $3500 per month beyond what Social Security will pay. They plan on needing the additional income for 20 years.

(a) Find the amount needed at retirement to fund the monthly retirement payments, assuming the annuity earns 9% compounded monthly while payments are being made.
(b) Find the amount of the quarterly payment they must make for the next 25 years to accumulate the necessary funds, assuming earnings of 6% compounded quarterly during the accumulation period.

Solution

(a) The accumulated funds at the end of 25 years is, at their retirement, a present value that must generate a cash inflow to the Wrights of $3500 per month for 240 months ($20 \times 12 = 240$), assuming earnings of 0.75% per month ($9\% \div 12 = 0.75\%$). Enter values for n , i , and PMT .

$$240 \; \boxed{n} \; 0.75 \; \boxed{i} \; 3500 \; \boxed{\text{PMT}}$$

Press PV to find the amount needed at the end of 25 years.

$$\boxed{\text{PV}} \; -389007.34$$

is the amount they must accumulate.

(b) The Wrights have 25 years of quarterly payments (100 payments that are cash outflows) in an account earning 1.5% per quarter ($6\% \div 4 = 1.5\%$) to accumulate a future value of $389,007.34. The question is one of what quarterly payment is required.

Enter values for $\boxed{n}$, $\boxed{i}$, and $\boxed{FV}$.

$$100 \boxed{n} \quad 1.5 \boxed{i} \quad 389007.34 \boxed{FV}$$

Press $\boxed{PMT}$ to find the quarterly payment needed:

$$\boxed{PMT} \quad -1700.18$$

is the required quarterly payment.

Thus, the Wrights must make 100 end-of-quarter deposits of $1700.18 each into an account earning 1.5% per quarter. They will then receive 20 years of payments of $3500 per month, assuming 9% per year during the time that payments are made.

A.2	**Exercises**

Solve the following problems for the missing quantity using a financial calculator. Round dollar answers to the nearest hundredth, interest rates to the nearest hundredth of a percent, and number of compounding periods to the nearest whole number. Assume that any payments are made at the end of the period.

	n	*i*	PV	PMT	FV
1.	10	8%	$3500	—	
2.	8	1.5%	$6400	—	
3.	10	3%		—	$12,000
4.	16	4%		—	$8200
5.	7	8%	—	$300	
6.	25	2%	—	$1000	
7.	30		—	$319.67	$12,000
8.	50		—	$4718.99	$285,000
9.	360	1%	$83,500		—
10.	180	0.5%	$125,000		—
11.		4%	$85,383	$5600	—
12.		2%	$3822	$100	—

Solve the following application problems. Round to the nearest cent.

13. Tremaine Walker received $2000 as a Christmas bonus. He placed the funds in a 4-year certificate of deposit earning 6% compounded quarterly. Find the future value.

14. Junella Ruiz decides to begin saving at a young age. She has $60 per month taken out of her paycheck and automatically deposited in an account containing technology stocks that she hopes will grow at 1% per month. Find the future value in 15, 30, and 45 years.

15. After making a down payment, Mr. and Mrs. Thrash borrowed $128,400 on a 30-year home loan at 8% per year. Find the monthly payment.

16. Terrance Walker wishes to have $20,000 in 10 years when his son begins college. What payment must he make at the end of each quarter in an investment earning 6% compounded quarterly?

17. The *Daily Gazette* needs $340,000 for new printing presses. It can invest $12,000 per month in bonds paying 0.8% per month. Find the number of payments that must be paid before reaching the goal. Round to the nearest whole number.

18. Mr. and Mrs. Peters wish to build their dream home and must borrow $248,500 on a 30-year mortgage to do so. Find the highest acceptable annual interest rate, to the nearest tenth of a percent, if they cannot afford a monthly payment above $1825.

19. A farmer purchases a farm costing $345,000, with 25% down and quarterly payments at 8% per year for 10 years. Find the payment.

20. A technical school purchases 25 classroom computers with projection systems at a cost of $2300 each. It pays 20% down and finances the balance at 0.8% per month for 3 years. Find the monthly payment.

APPENDIX TERMS

Review the following terms to test your understanding of the appendix. For any terms you do not know, refer to the page number found next to the term.

algebraic logic [p. 720]

base [p. 722]

calculator [p. 719]

chain calculations [p. 725]

deficit amount [p. 723]

exponent [p. 722]

financial calculator [p. 719]

floating decimal [p. 721]

future value [p. 729]

graphing calculator [p. 719]

level payment [p. 729]

memory keys [p. 724]

negative number [p. 723]

order of operations [p. 725]

present value [p. 729]

scientific calculator [p. 719]

square root [p. 722]

The Metric System

Today, the **metric system** is used just about everywhere in the world. In the United States, many industries are switching over to this improved system. The metric system is being taught in elementary schools, and it may eventually replace the current system.

A table on the English system is included here to refresh your memory. Notice that the time relationships are the same in the English and metric systems.

Length	Weight
1 foot (ft) = 12 inches (in.)	1 pound (lb) = 16 ounces (oz)
1 yard (yd) = 3 feet (ft)	1 ton (T) = 2000 pounds (lb)
1 mile (mi) = 5280 feet (ft)	

Capacity	Time
1 cup (c) = 8 fluid ounces	1 week (wk) = 7 days
1 pint (pt) = 2 cup (c)	1 day = 24 hours (hr)
1 quart (qt) = 2 pints (pt)	1 hour (hr) = 60 minutes (min)
1 gallon (gal) = 4 quarts (qt)	1 minute (min) = 60 seconds (sec)

OBJECTIVES

1 *Learn the metric system.*

2 *Learn how to convert from one system to the other.*

Objective

1 *Learn the Metric System.* The basic unit of length in the metric system is the **meter**. A meter is a little longer than a yard. For shorter lengths, the units **centimeter** and **millimeter** are used. The prefix "centi" means hundredth, so 1 centimeter is one-hundredth of a meter. Thus

$$100 \text{ centimeters} = 1 \text{ meter}$$

The prefix "milli" means thousandth, so 1 millimeter means one-thousandth of a meter. Thus

$$1000 \text{ millimeters} = 1 \text{ meter}$$

"Meter" is abbreviated m, "centimeter" is cm, and "millimeter" is mm.

Convert from centimeters to millimeters to meters by moving the decimal point, as shown in the following example.

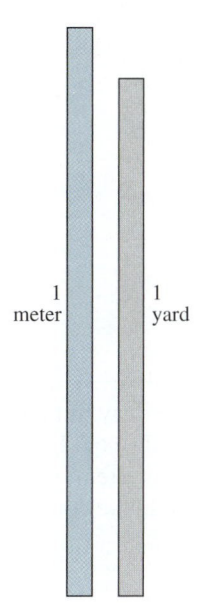

1
meter

1
yard

1 yard is 36 inches
1 meter is about 39.37
inches

Recall the basic metric
units for length, volume,
weight, and temperature

**Prefixes in the
Metric System**
deca = 10 times
kilo = 1000 times
deci = $\frac{1}{10}$ times
centi = $\frac{1}{100}$ times
milli = $\frac{1}{1000}$ times

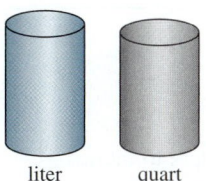

liter   quart

A liter equals about
1.06 quarts

kilogram   pound

A kilogram equals about
2.2 pounds.

EXAMPLE 1 **Converting Length Measurements**

(a) 6.4 m to cm   **(b)** 0.98 m to mm   **(c)** 34 cm to m

Solution

(a) A centimeter is a small unit of measure (a centimeter is about $\frac{1}{2}$ of the diameter of a penny) and a meter is a large unit (a little over 3 feet), so many centimeters make a meter. *Multiply* by 100 to convert meters to centimeters.

$$6.4 \text{ m} = 6.4 \times 100 = 640 \text{ cm}$$

(b) Multiply by 1000 to convert meters to millimeters.

$$0.98 \text{ m} = 0.98 \times 1000 = 980 \text{ mm}$$

(c) A meter is a large unit of measure, and a centimeter is a smaller unit, so 34 cm is less than a meter. Thus, *divide* by 100 to convert centimeters to meters.

$$34 \text{ cm} = \frac{34}{100} = 0.34 \text{ m}$$

Long distances are measured in **kilometer** (km) units. The prefix "kilo" means one thousand. Thus,

$$1 \text{ kilometer} = 1000 \text{ meters}$$

Since a meter is about a yard, 1000 meters is about 1000 yards, or 3000 feet. Therefore, 1 kilometer is about 3000 feet. One mile is 5280 feet, so 1 kilometer is about 3000/5280 of a mile. Divide 3000 by 5280 to find that 1 kilometer is about 0.6 miles.

The basic unit of volume in the metric system is the **liter** (L), which is a little more than a quart. You may have noticed that Coca-Cola is often sold in 2-liter plastic bottles. Again the prefixes "milli" and "centi" are used. Thus,

$$1 \text{ liter} = 100 \text{ centiliters}$$
$$1 \text{ liter} = 1000 \text{ milliliters}$$

Milliliter (mL) and **centiliter** (cL) are such small volumes that they find their main uses in science. In particular, drug dosages are often expressed in milliliters.

Weight is measured in **grams** (g). A nickel weighs about 5 grams. **Milligrams** (mg; one-thousandth of a gram) and **centigrams** (cg; one-hundredth of a gram) are so small that they are used mainly in science. A more common measure is the **kilogram** (kg), which is 1000 grams. A kilogram weighs about 2.2 pounds.

$$1000 \text{ grams} = 1 \text{ kilogram}$$

EXAMPLE 2 **Converting Weight and Volume Measurements**

(a) 650 g to kg   **(b)** 9.4 L to cL   **(c)** 4350 mg to g

Solution

(a) A gram is a small unit, and a kilogram is a large unit. Thus, *divide* by 1000 to convert grams to kilograms.

$$650 \text{ g} = \frac{650}{1000} = 0.65 \text{ kg}$$

(b) *Multiply* by 100 to convert liters to centiliters.

$$9.4\,\text{L} = 9.4 \times 100 = 940\,\text{cL}$$

(c) *Divide* by 1000 to convert milligrams to grams.

$$4350\,\text{mg} = \frac{4350}{1000} = 4.35\,\text{g}$$

Objective

2   *Learn How to Convert from One System to the Other.*   Eventually, everyone may think in the metric system as easily as in the **English system** of feet, quarts, pounds, and so on. However, during the period of changeover from the English system to the metric system, most people will find it necessary to convert from one system to the other. Approximate conversion can be made with the aid of Table B.1.

Table B.1   ENGLISH–METRIC CONVERSION TABLE (approximate)

From Metric	To English	Multiply By	From English	To Metric	Multiply By
Meters	Yards	1.09	Yards	Meters	0.914
Meters	Feet	3.28	Feet	Meters	0.305
Meters	Inches	39.37	Inches	Meters	0.0254
Kilometers	Miles	0.62	Miles	Kilometers	1.609
Grams	Pounds	0.00220	Pounds	Grams	454
Kilograms	Pounds	2.20	Pounds	Kilograms	0.454
Liters	Quarts	1.06	Quarts	Liters	0.946
Liters	Gallons	0.264	Gallons	Liters	3.785

EXAMPLE 3   Convert the Following Measurements

(a) 15 meters to yards   **(b)** 39 yards to meters   **(c)** 47 meters to inches
(d) 87 kilometers to miles **(e)** 598 miles to kilometers **(f)** 12 quarts to liters

Solution

(a) Look at Table B.1 for the meters-to-yards conversion, and find the number 1.09. Multiply 15 meters by 1.09.

$$15 \times 1.09 = 16.35\,\text{yards}$$

(b) Read the yards-to-meters row of Table B.1. The number 0.914 appears. Multiply 39 yards by 0.914.

$$39 \times 0.914 = 35.646\,\text{meters}$$

(c) 47 meters $= 47 \times 39.37 = 1850.39$ inches
(d) 87 kilometers $= 87 \times 0.62 = 53.94$ miles
(e) 598 miles $= 598 \times 1.609 = 962.182$ kilometers
(f) 12 quarts $= 12 \times 0.946 = 11.352$ liters

EXAMPLE 4   Solving a Proportion

At a depth of 16.5 feet under the water, a diver experiences additional pressure of 0.5 atmosphere. Estimate the additional pressure in atmospheres experienced by a submersible that is 400 feet under the water.

Solution   Set up a proportion with 16.5 feet to 0.5 atmosphere equal to 400 feet to an unknown number of atmospheres, which we represent with the variable x. Then solve the equation.

$$\frac{16.5 \text{ feet}}{0.5 \text{ atm.}} = \frac{400 \text{ feet}}{x}$$

$16.5 \times x = 400 \times 0.5$ Cross multiply.

$x = \dfrac{400 \times 0.5}{16.5}$ Divide both sides by 16.5.

$x = 12.1$ atmospheres of additional pressure   Rounded

°F   °C

Temperature in the metric system is measured in degrees **Celsius** (abbreviated C). Using the Fahrenheit system, water freezes at 32°F and boils at 212°F. In the Celsius scale, water freezes at 0°C and boils at 100°C. This is more sensible than degrees **Fahrenheit** (abbreviated F) in use now, in which a mixture of salt and water freezes at 0°F, and 100°F represents the temperature inside Gabriel Fahrenheit's mouth.

Converting from Fahrenheit to Celsius

STEP 1 Subtract 32 from the degrees Fahrenheit.

STEP 2 Multiply by 5.

STEP 3 Divide by 9.

These steps can be expressed by the following formula.

$$C = \frac{5(F - 32)}{9}$$

EXAMPLE 5   Convert 68° Fahrenheit to Celsius

Solution   Use the steps above.

STEP 1 Subtract 32. $68 - 32 = 36$

STEP 2 Multiply by 5. $36 \times 5 = 180$

STEP 3 Divide by 9. $\dfrac{180}{9} = 20$

Thus, 68°F = 20°C.

Converting from Celsius to Fahrenheit

STEP 1 Multiply degrees Celsius by 9.

STEP 2 Divide by 5.

STEP 3 Add 32.

These steps can be expressed by the following formula.

$$F = \frac{9 \times C}{5} + 32$$

EXAMPLE 6   **Convert 11° Celsius to Fahrenheit**

Solution   Use the steps above.

STEP 1 Multiply by 9. $9 \times 11 = 99$

STEP 2 Divide by 5. $99 \div 5 = 19.8$

STEP 3 Add 32. $19.8 + 32 = 51.8°F$

Thus, $11°C = 51.8°F$.

B.1	**Exercises**

Convert the following measurements.

1. 68 cm to m
2. 934 mm to m
3. 4.7 m to mm
4. 7.43 m to cm
5. 8.9 kg to g
6. 4.32 kg to g
7. 39 cL to L
8. 469 cL to L
9. 46,000 g to kg
10. 35,800 g to kg
11. 0.976 kg to g
12. 0.137 kg to g

Convert the following measurements. Round to the nearest hundredth.

13. 36 m to yards
14. 76.2 m to yards
15. 55 yards to m
16. 89.3 yards to m
17. 4.7 m to feet
18. 1.92 m to feet
19. 3.6 feet to m
20. 12.8 feet to m
21. 496 km to miles
22. 138 km to miles
23. 768 miles to km
24. 1042 miles to km
25. 683 g to pounds
26. 1792 g to pounds
27. 4.1 pounds to g
28. 12.9 pounds to g
29. 38.9 kg to pounds
30. 40.3 kg to pounds

Work the following application problems. Round to the nearest hundredth.

31. One nickel weighs 5 grams. How many nickels are in 1 kilogram of nickels?

32. Seawater contains about 3.5 grams of salt per 1000 milliliters of water. How many grams of salt would 5 liters of seawater contain?

33. Helium weighs about 0.0002 grams per milliliter. A balloon contains 3 liters of helium. How much would the helium weigh?

34. About 1500 grams of sugar can be dissolved in a liter of warm water. How much sugar could be dissolved in 1 milliliter of warm water?

35. Find your height in centimeters.

36. Find your height in meters.

Convert the following Fahrenheit temperatures to Celsius. Round to the nearest degree.

37. 104°F · · · · · · · · · · **38.** 86°F · · · · · · · · · · **39.** 536°F

40. 464°F · · · · · · · · · · **41.** 98°F · · · · · · · · · · **42.** 114°F

Convert the following Celsius temperatures to Fahrenheit. Round to the nearest degree.

43. 35°C · · · · · · · · · · **44.** 100°C · · · · · · · · · · **45.** 10°C

46. 25°C · · · · · · · · · · **47.** 135°C · · · · · · · · · · **48.** 215°C

In most cases today, medical measurements are given in the metric system. In the following problems, a doctor's prescription is given. Some of these are for reasonable amounts of medicine, and some are not. Decide which you think must not be correct.

49. 1940 grams of Kaopectate after each meal

50. 76.8 centiliters of cough syrup every 2 hours

51. 94.3 milliliters of antibiotic every 6 hours

52. 1.4 kilograms of vitamins every 3 hours

53. Apply a bandage 5 centimeters square as needed

54. Soak your feet in 3 milligrams of Epsom salts per 4 liters of water.

APPENDIX TERMS

Review the following terms to test your understanding of the appendix. For any terms you do not know, refer to the page number found next to the term.

Celsius (C) [p. 739] · · · · English system [p. 738] · · · · kilometer [p. 737] · · · · milligram [p. 737]
centiliter [p. 737] · · · · Fahrenheit (F) [p. 739] · · · · liter [p. 737] · · · · milliliter [p. 737]
centimeter [p. 736] · · · · gram [p. 737] · · · · meter [p. 736] · · · · millimeter [p. 736]
centigram [p. 737] · · · · kilogram [p. 737] · · · · metric system [p. 736]

Powers of *e*

x	e^x	x	e^x	x	e^x	x	e^x	x	e^x
0.00	1.00000000	0.35	1.41906755	0.70	2.01375271	1.05	2.85765112	1.40	4.05519997
0.01	1.01005017	0.36	1.43332941	0.71	2.03399126	1.06	2.88637099	1.41	4.09595540
0.02	1.02020134	0.37	1.44773461	0.72	2.05443321	1.07	2.91537950	1.42	4.13712044
0.03	1.03045453	0.38	1.46228459	0.73	2.07508061	1.08	2.94467955	1.43	4.17869919
0.04	1.04081077	0.39	1.47698079	0.74	2.09593551	1.09	2.97427407	1.44	4.22069582
0.05	1.05127110	0.40	1.49182470	0.75	2.11700002	1.10	3.00416602	1.45	4.26311452
0.06	1.06183655	0.41	1.50681779	0.76	2.13827622	1.11	3.03435839	1.46	4.30595953
0.07	1.07250818	0.42	1.52196156	0.77	2.15976625	1.12	3.06485420	1.47	4.34923514
0.08	1.08328707	0.43	1.53725752	0.78	2.18147227	1.13	3.09565650	1.48	4.39294568
0.09	1.09417428	0.44	1.55270722	0.79	2.20339643	1.14	3.12676837	1.49	4.43709552
0.10	1.10517092	0.45	1.56831219	0.80	2.22554093	1.15	3.15819291	1.50	4.48168907
0.11	1.11627807	0.46	1.58407398	0.81	2.24790799	1.16	3.18993328	1.51	4.52673079
0.12	1.12749685	0.47	1.59999419	0.82	2.27049984	1.17	3.22199264	1.52	4.57222520
0.13	1.13882838	0.48	1.61607440	0.83	2.29331874	1.18	3.25437420	1.53	4.61817682
0.14	1.15027380	0.49	1.63231622	0.84	2.31636698	1.19	3.28708121	1.54	4.66459027
0.15	1.16183424	0.50	1.64872127	0.85	2.33964685	1.20	3.32011692	1.55	4.71147018
0.16	1.17351087	0.51	1.66529119	0.86	2.36316069	1.21	3.35348465	1.56	4.75882125
0.17	1.18530485	0.52	1.68202765	0.87	2.38691085	1.22	3.38718773	1.57	4.80664819
0.18	1.19721736	0.53	1.69893231	0.88	2.41089971	1.23	3.42122954	1.58	4.85495581
0.19	1.20924960	0.54	1.71600686	0.89	2.43512965	1.24	3.45561346	1.59	4.90374893
0.20	1.22140276	0.55	1.73325302	0.90	2.45960311	1.25	3.49034296	1.60	4.95303242
0.21	1.23367806	0.56	1.75067250	0.91	2.48432253	1.26	3.52542149	1.61	5.00281123
0.22	1.24607673	0.57	1.76826705	0.92	2.50929039	1.27	3.56085256	1.62	5.05309032
0.23	1.25860001	0.58	1.78603843	0.93	2.53450918	1.28	3.59663973	1.63	5.10387472
0.24	1.27124915	0.59	1.80398842	0.94	2.55998142	1.29	3.63278656	1.64	5.15516951
0.25	1.28402542	0.60	1.82211880	0.95	2.58570966	1.30	3.66929667	1.65	5.20697983
0.26	1.29693009	0.61	1.84043140	0.96	2.61169647	1.31	3.70617371	1.66	5.25931084
0.27	1.30996445	0.62	1.85892804	0.97	2.63794446	1.32	3.74342138	1.67	5.31216780
0.28	1.32312981	0.63	1.87761058	0.98	2.66445624	1.33	3.78104339	1.68	5.36555597
0.29	1.33642749	0.64	1.89648088	0.99	2.69123447	1.34	3.81904351	1.69	5.41948071
0.30	1.34985881	0.65	1.91554083	1.00	2.71828183	1.35	3.85742553	1.70	5.47394739
0.31	1.36342511	0.66	1.93479233	1.01	2.74560102	1.36	3.89619330	1.71	5.52896148
0.32	1.37712776	0.67	1.95423732	1.02	2.77319476	1.37	3.93535070	1.72	5.58452846
0.33	1.39096813	0.68	1.97387773	1.03	2.80106583	1.38	3.97490163	1.73	5.64065391
0.34	1.40494759	0.69	1.99371553	1.04	2.82921701	1.39	4.01485005	1.74	5.69734342

x	e^x	x	e^x	x	e^x	x	e^x	x	e^x
1.75	5.75460268	1.95	7.02868758	2.15	8.58485840	2.35	10.48556972	2.55	12.80710378
1.76	5.81243739	1.96	7.09932707	2.16	8.67113766	2.36	10.59095145	2.56	12.93581732
1.77	5.87085336	1.97	7.17067649	2.17	8.75828404	2.37	10.69739228	2.57	13.06582444
1.78	5.92985642	1.98	7.24274299	2.18	8.84630626	2.38	10.80490286	2.58	13.19713816
1.79	5.98945247	1.99	7.31553376	2.19	8.93521311	2.39	10.91349394	2.59	13.32977160
1.80	6.04964746	2.00	7.38905610	2.20	9.02501350	2.40	11.02317638	2.60	13.46373804
1.81	6.11044743	2.01	7.46331735	2.21	9.11571639	2.41	11.13396115	2.61	13.59905085
1.82	6.17185845	2.02	7.53832493	2.22	9.20733087	2.42	11.24585931	2.62	13.73572359
1.83	6.23388666	2.03	7.61408636	2.23	9.29986608	2.43	11.35888208	2.63	13.87376990
1.84	6.29653826	2.04	7.69060920	2.24	9.39333129	2.44	11.47304074	2.64	14.01320361
1.85	6.35981952	2.05	7.76790111	2.25	9.48773584	2.45	11.58834672	2.65	14.15403865
1.86	6.42373677	2.06	7.84596981	2.26	9.58308917	2.46	11.70481154	2.66	14.29628910
1.87	6.48829640	2.07	7.92482312	2.27	9.67940081	2.47	11.82244685	2.67	14.43996919
1.88	6.55350486	2.08	8.00446891	2.28	9.77668041	2.48	11.94126442	2.68	14.58509330
1.89	6.61936868	2.09	8.08491516	2.29	9.87493768	2.49	12.06127612	2.69	14.73167592
1.90	6.68589444	2.10	8.16616991	2.30	9.97418245	2.50	12.18249396	2.70	14.87973172
1.91	6.75308880	2.11	8.24824128	2.31	10.07442466	2.51	12.30493006	2.71	15.02927551
1.92	6.82095847	2.12	8.33113749	2.32	10.17567431	2.52	12.42859666	2.72	15.18032224
1.93	6.88951024	2.13	8.41486681	2.33	10.27794153	2.53	12.55350614	2.73	15.33288702
1.94	6.95875097	2.14	8.49943763	2.34	10.38123656	2.54	12.67967097	2.74	15.48698510

Interest Tables

Rate $\frac{1}{3}$%	A Compound Interest	B Present Value	C Amount of Annuity	D Present Value of Annuity	E Sinking Fund	F Amortization
n	$(1 + i)^n$	$\dfrac{1}{(1 + i)^n}$	$s_{\overline{n}|i}$	$a_{\overline{n}|i}$	$\dfrac{1}{s_{\overline{n}|i}}$	$\dfrac{1}{a_{\overline{n}|i}}$
1	1.00333333	0.99667774	1.00000000	0.99667774	1.00000000	1.00333333
2	1.00667778	0.99336652	2.00333333	1.99004426	0.49916805	0.50250139
3	1.01003337	0.99006630	3.01001111	2.98011056	0.33222469	0.33555802
4	1.01340015	0.98677704	4.02004448	3.96688760	0.24875347	0.25208680
5	1.01677815	0.98349871	5.03344463	4.95038631	0.19867110	0.20200444
6	1.02016741	0.98023127	6.05022278	5.93061759	0.16528317	0.16861650
7	1.02356797	0.97697469	7.07039019	6.90759228	0.14143491	0.14476824
8	1.02697986	0.97372893	8.09395816	7.88132121	0.12354895	0.12688228
9	1.03040313	0.97049395	9.12093802	8.85181516	0.10963785	0.11297118
10	1.03383780	0.96726972	10.15134114	9.81908487	0.09850915	0.10184248
11	1.03728393	0.96405620	11.18517895	10.78314107	0.08940402	0.09273736
12	1.04074154	0.96085335	12.22246288	11.74399442	0.08181657	0.08514990
13	1.04421068	0.95766115	13.26320442	12.70165557	0.07539656	0.07872989
14	1.04769138	0.95447955	14.30741510	13.65613512	0.06989383	0.07322716
15	1.05118369	0.95130852	15.35510648	14.60744364	0.06512491	0.06845825
16	1.05468763	0.94814803	16.40629017	15.55559167	0.06095223	0.06428557
17	1.05820326	0.94499803	17.46097781	16.50058970	0.05727056	0.06060389
18	1.06173060	0.94185851	18.51918107	17.44244821	0.05399807	0.05733140
19	1.06526971	0.93872941	19.58091167	18.38117762	0.05107015	0.05440348
20	1.06882060	0.93561071	20.64618137	19.31678832	0.04843511	0.05176844
21	1.07238334	0.93250236	21.71500198	20.24929069	0.04605111	0.04938445
22	1.07595795	0.92940435	22.78738532	21.17869504	0.04388393	0.04721726
23	1.07954448	0.92631663	23.86334327	22.10501167	0.04190528	0.04523861
24	1.08314296	0.92323916	24.94288775	23.02825083	0.04009159	0.04342492
25	1.08675344	0.92017192	26.02603071	23.94842275	0.03842307	0.04175640
26	1.09037595	0.91711487	27.11278414	24.86553763	0.03688297	0.04021630
27	1.09401053	0.91406798	28.20316009	25.77960561	0.03545702	0.03879035
28	1.09765724	0.91103121	29.29717062	26.69063682	0.03413299	0.03746632
29	1.10131609	0.90800453	30.39482786	27.59864135	0.03290033	0.03623367
30	1.10498715	0.90498790	31.49614395	28.50362925	0.03174992	0.03508325
31	1.10867044	0.90198130	32.60113110	29.40561055	0.03067378	0.03400712
32	1.11236601	0.89898468	33.70980154	30.30459523	0.02966496	0.03299830
33	1.11607389	0.89599802	34.82216754	31.20059325	0.02871734	0.03205067
34	1.11979414	0.89302128	35.93824143	32.09361454	0.02782551	0.03115885
35	1.12352679	0.89005444	37.05803557	32.98366898	0.02698470	0.03031803
36	1.12727187	0.88709745	38.18156236	33.87076642	0.02619065	0.02952399
37	1.13102945	0.88415028	39.30883423	34.75491670	0.02543957	0.02877291
38	1.13479955	0.88121290	40.43986368	35.63612960	0.02472808	0.02806141
39	1.13858221	0.87828528	41.57466322	36.51441488	0.02405311	0.02738644
40	1.14237748	0.87536739	42.71324543	37.38978228	0.02341194	0.02674527
41	1.14618541	0.87245920	43.85562292	38.26224147	0.02280209	0.02613543
42	1.15000603	0.86956066	45.00180833	39.13180213	0.02222133	0.02555466
43	1.15383938	0.86667175	46.15181436	39.99847389	0.02166762	0.02500095
44	1.15768551	0.86379245	47.30565374	40.86226633	0.02113912	0.02447246
45	1.16154446	0.86092270	48.46333925	41.72318903	0.02063415	0.02396749
46	1.16541628	0.85806249	49.62488371	42.58125153	0.02015118	0.02348451
47	1.16930100	0.85521179	50.79029999	43.43646332	0.01968880	0.02302213
48	1.17319867	0.85237055	51.95960099	44.28883387	0.01924572	0.02257905
49	1.17710933	0.84953876	53.13279966	45.13837263	0.01882077	0.02215410
50	1.18103303	0.84671637	54.30990899	45.98508900	0.01841285	0.02174618

Rate $\frac{5}{12}$%	A Compound Interest	B Present Value	C Amount of Annuity	D Present Value of Annuity	E Sinking Fund	F Amortization
n	$(1 + i)^n$	$\dfrac{1}{(1 + i)^n}$	$s_{\overline{n}\rvert i}$	$a_{\overline{n}\rvert i}$	$\dfrac{1}{s_{\overline{n}\rvert i}}$	$\dfrac{1}{a_{\overline{n}\rvert i}}$
1	1.00416667	0.99585062	1.00000000	0.99585062	1.00000000	1.00416667
2	1.00835069	0.99171846	2.00416667	1.98756908	0.49896050	0.50312717
3	1.01255216	0.98760345	3.01251736	2.97517253	0.33194829	0.33611496
4	1.01677112	0.98350551	4.02506952	3.95867804	0.24844291	0.25260958
5	1.02100767	0.97942457	5.01484064	4.93810261	0.19834026	0.20250693
6	1.02526187	0.97536057	6.06284831	5.91346318	0.16493898	0.16910564
7	1.02953379	0.97131343	7.08811018	6.88477661	0.14108133	0.14524800
8	1.03382352	0.96728308	8.11764397	7.85205970	0.12318845	0.12735512
9	1.03813111	0.96326946	9.15146749	8.81532916	0.10927209	0.11343876
10	1.04245666	0.95927249	10.18959860	9.77460165	0.09813929	0.10230596
11	1.04680023	0.95529211	11.23205526	10.72989376	0.08903090	0.09319757
12	1.05116190	0.95132824	12.27885549	11.68122200	0.08144082	0.08560748
13	1.05554174	0.94738082	13.33001739	12.62860283	0.07501866	0.07918532
14	1.05993983	0.94344978	14.38555913	13.57205261	0.06951416	0.07368082
15	1.06435625	0.93953505	15.44549896	14.51158766	0.06474378	0.06891045
16	1.06879106	0.93563657	16.50985520	15.44722422	0.06056988	0.06473655
17	1.07324436	0.93175426	17.57864627	16.37897848	0.05688720	0.06105387
18	1.07771621	0.92788806	18.65189063	17.30686654	0.05361387	0.05778053
19	1.08220670	0.92403790	19.72960684	18.23090443	0.05068525	0.05485191
20	1.08671589	0.92020372	20.81181353	19.15110815	0.04804963	0.05221630
21	1.09124387	0.91638544	21.89852942	20.06749359	0.04566517	0.04983183
22	1.09579072	0.91258301	22.98977330	20.98007661	0.04349760	0.04766427
23	1.10035652	0.90879636	24.08556402	21.88887297	0.04151865	0.04568531
24	1.10494134	0.90502542	25.18592053	22.79389839	0.03970472	0.04387139
25	1.10954526	0.90127013	26.29086187	23.69516853	0.03803603	0.04220270
26	1.11416836	0.89753042	27.40040713	24.59269895	0.03649581	0.04066247
27	1.11881073	0.89380623	28.51457549	25.48650517	0.03506978	0.03923645
28	1.12347244	0.89009749	29.63338622	26.37660266	0.03374572	0.03791239
29	1.12815358	0.88640414	30.75685866	27.26300680	0.03251307	0.03667974
30	1.13285422	0.88272611	31.88501224	28.14573291	0.03136270	0.03552936
31	1.13757444	0.87906335	33.01786646	29.02479626	0.03028663	0.03445330
32	1.14231434	0.87541578	34.15544090	29.90021205	0.02927791	0.03344458
33	1.14707398	0.87178335	35.29775524	30.77199540	0.02833041	0.03249708
34	1.15185346	0.86816599	36.44482922	31.64016139	0.02743873	0.03160540
35	1.15665284	0.86456365	37.59668268	32.50472504	0.02659809	0.03076476
36	1.16147223	0.86097624	38.75333552	33.36570128	0.02580423	0.02997090
37	1.16631170	0.85740373	39.91480775	34.22310501	0.02505336	0.02922003
38	1.17117133	0.85384604	41.08111945	35.07695105	0.02434208	0.02850875
39	1.17605121	0.85030311	42.25229078	35.92725416	0.02366736	0.02783402
40	1.18095142	0.84677488	43.42834199	36.77402904	0.02302644	0.02719310
41	1.18587206	0.84326129	44.60929342	37.61729033	0.02241685	0.02658352
42	1.19081319	0.83976228	45.79516547	38.45705261	0.02183637	0.02600303
43	1.19577491	0.83627779	46.98597866	39.29333040	0.02128295	0.02544961
44	1.20075731	0.83280776	48.18175357	40.12613816	0.02075474	0.02492141
45	1.20576046	0.82935212	49.38251088	40.95549028	0.02025008	0.02441675
46	1.21078446	0.82591083	50.58827134	41.78140111	0.01976743	0.02393409
47	1.21582940	0.82248381	51.79905581	42.60388492	0.01930537	0.02347204
48	1.22089536	0.81907102	53.01488521	43.42295594	0.01886263	0.02302929
49	1.22598242	0.81567238	54.23578056	44.23862832	0.01843801	0.02260468
50	1.23109068	0.81228785	55.46176298	45.05091617	0.01803044	0.02219711

Rate $\frac{1}{2}$%	A Compound Interest	B Present Value	C Amount of Annuity	D Present Value of Annuity	E Sinking Fund	F Amortization
n	$(1 + i)^n$	$\dfrac{1}{(1 + i)^n}$	$s_{\overline{n}|i}$	$a_{\overline{n}|i}$	$\dfrac{1}{s_{\overline{n}|i}}$	$\dfrac{1}{a_{\overline{n}|i}}$
1	1.00500000	0.99502488	1.00000000	0.99502488	1.00000000	1.00500000
2	1.01002500	0.99007450	2.00500000	1.98509938	0.49875312	0.50375312
3	1.01507513	0.98514876	3.01502500	2.97024814	0.33167221	0.33667221
4	1.02015050	0.98024752	4.03010012	3.95049566	0.24813279	0.25313279
5	1.02525125	0.97537067	5.05025063	4.92586633	0.19800997	0.20300997
6	1.03037751	0.97051808	6.07550188	5.89638441	0.16459546	0.16959546
7	1.03552940	0.96568963	7.10587939	6.86207404	0.14072854	0.14572854
8	1.04070704	0.96088520	8.14140879	7.82295924	0.12282886	0.12782886
9	1.04591058	0.95610468	9.18211583	8.77906392	0.10890736	0.11390736
10	1.05114013	0.95134794	10.22802641	9.73041186	0.09777057	0.10277057
11	1.05639583	0.94661487	11.27916654	10.67702673	0.08865903	0.09365903
12	1.06167781	0.94190534	12.33556237	11.61893207	0.08106643	0.08606643
13	1.06698620	0.93721924	13.39724018	12.55615131	0.07464224	0.07964224
14	1.07232113	0.93255646	14.46422639	13.48870777	0.06913609	0.07413609
15	1.07768274	0.92791688	15.53654752	14.41662465	0.06436436	0.06936436
16	1.08307115	0.92330037	16.61423026	15.33992502	0.06018937	0.06518937
17	1.08848651	0.91870684	17.69730141	16.25863186	0.05650579	0.06150579
18	1.09392894	0.91413616	18.78578791	17.17276802	0.05323173	0.05823173
19	1.09939858	0.90958822	19.87971685	18.08235624	0.05030253	0.05530253
20	1.10489558	0.90506290	20.97911544	18.98741915	0.04766645	0.05266645
21	1.11042006	0.90056010	22.08401101	19.88797925	0.04528163	0.05028163
22	1.11597216	0.89607971	23.19443107	20.78405896	0.04311380	0.04811380
23	1.12155202	0.89162160	24.31040322	21.67568055	0.04113465	0.04613465
24	1.12715978	0.88718567	25.43195524	22.56286622	0.03932061	0.04432061
25	1.13279558	0.88277181	26.55911502	23.44563803	0.03765186	0.04265186
26	1.13845955	0.87837991	27.69191059	24.32401794	0.03611163	0.04111163
27	1.14415185	0.87400986	28.83037015	25.19802780	0.03468565	0.03968565
28	1.14987261	0.86966155	29.97452200	26.06768936	0.03336167	0.03836167
29	1.15562197	0.86533488	31.12439461	26.93302423	0.03212914	0.03712914
30	1.16140008	0.86102973	32.28001658	27.79405397	0.03097892	0.03597892
31	1.16720708	0.85674600	33.44141666	28.65079997	0.02990304	0.03490304
32	1.17304312	0.85248358	34.60862375	29.50328355	0.02889453	0.03389453
33	1.17890833	0.84824237	35.78166686	30.35152592	0.02794727	0.03294727
34	1.18480288	0.84402226	36.96057520	31.19554818	0.02705586	0.03205586
35	1.19072689	0.83982314	38.14537807	32.03537132	0.02621550	0.03121550
36	1.19668052	0.83564492	39.33610496	32.87101624	0.02542194	0.03042194
37	1.20266393	0.83148748	40.53278549	33.70250372	0.02467133	0.02967139
38	1.20867725	0.82735073	41.73544942	34.52985445	0.02396045	0.02896045
39	1.21472063	0.82323455	42.94412666	35.35308900	0.02328607	0.02828607
40	1.22079424	0.81913886	44.15884730	36.17222786	0.02264552	0.02764552
41	1.22689821	0.81506354	45.37964153	36.98729141	0.02203631	0.02703631
42	1.23303270	0.81100850	46.60653974	37.79829991	0.02145622	0.02645622
43	1.23919786	0.80697363	47.83957244	38.60527354	0.02090320	0.02590320
44	1.24539385	0.80295884	49.07877030	39.40823238	0.02037541	0.02537541
45	1.25162082	0.79896402	50.32416415	40.20719640	0.01987117	0.02487117
46	1.25787892	0.79498907	51.57578497	41.00218547	0.01938894	0.02438894
47	1.26416832	0.79103390	52.83366390	41.79321937	0.01892733	0.02392733
48	1.27048916	0.78709841	54.09783222	42.58031778	0.01848503	0.02348503
49	1.27684161	0.78318250	55.36832138	43.36350028	0.01806087	0.02306087
50	1.28322581	0.77928607	56.64516299	44.14278635	0.01765376	0.02265376

Rate $\frac{3}{4}$%	A Compound Interest	B Present Value	C Amount of Annuity	D Present Value of Annuity	E Sinking Fund	F Amortization
n	$(1 + i)^n$	$\dfrac{1}{(1 + i)^n}$	$s_{\overline{n}|i}$	$a_{\overline{n}|i}$	$\dfrac{1}{s_{\overline{n}|i}}$	$\dfrac{1}{a_{\overline{n}|i}}$
1	1.00750000	0.99255583	1.00000000	0.99255583	1.00000000	1.00750000
2	1.01505625	0.98516708	2.00750000	1.97772291	0.49813200	0.50563200
3	1.02266917	0.97783333	3.02255625	2.95555624	0.33084579	0.33834579
4	1.03033919	0.97055417	4.04522542	3.92611041	0.24720501	0.25470501
5	1.03806673	0.96332920	5.07556461	4.88943961	0.19702242	0.20452242
6	1.04585224	0.95615802	6.11363135	5.84559763	0.16356891	0.17106891
7	1.05369613	0.94904022	7.15948358	6.79463785	0.13967488	0.14717488
8	1.06159885	0.94197540	8.21317971	7.73661325	0.12175552	0.12925552
9	1.06956084	0.93496318	9.27477856	8.67157642	0.10781929	0.11531929
10	1.07758255	0.92800315	10.34433940	9.59957958	0.09667123	0.10417123
11	1.08566441	0.92109494	11.42192194	10.52067452	0.08755094	0.09505094
12	1.09380690	0.91423815	12.50758636	11.43491267	0.07995148	0.08745148
13	1.10201045	0.90743241	13.60139325	12.34234508	0.07352188	0.08102188
14	1.11027553	0.90067733	14.70340370	13.24302242	0.06801146	0.07551146
15	1.11860259	0.89397254	15.81367923	14.13699495	0.06323639	0.07073639
16	1.12699211	0.88731766	16.93228183	15.02431261	0.05905879	0.06655879
17	1.13544455	0.88071231	18.05927394	15.90502492	0.05537321	0.06287321
18	1.14396039	0.87415614	19.19471849	16.77918107	0.05209766	0.05959766
19	1.15254009	0.86764878	20.33867888	17.64682984	0.04916740	0.05666740
20	1.16118414	0.86118985	21.49121897	18.50801969	0.04653063	0.05403063
21	1.16989302	0.85477901	22.65240312	19.36279870	0.04414543	0.05164543
22	1.17866722	0.84841589	23.82229614	20.21121459	0.04197748	0.04947748
23	1.18750723	0.84210014	25.00096336	21.05331473	0.03999846	0.04749846
24	1.19641353	0.83583140	26.18847059	21.88914614	0.03818474	0.04568474
25	1.20538663	0.82960933	27.38488412	22.71875547	0.03651650	0.04401650
26	1.21442703	0.82343358	28.59027075	23.54218905	0.03497693	0.04247693
27	1.22353523	0.81730380	29.80469778	24.35949286	0.03355176	0.04105176
28	1.23271175	0.81121966	31.02823301	25.17071251	0.03222871	0.03972871
29	1.24195709	0.80518080	32.26094476	25.97589331	0.03099723	0.03849723
30	1.25127176	0.79918690	33.50290184	26.77508021	0.02984816	0.03734816
31	1.26065630	0.79323762	34.75417361	27.56831783	0.02877352	0.03627352
32	1.27011122	0.78733262	36.01482991	28.35565045	0.02776634	0.03526634
33	1.27963706	0.78147158	37.28494113	29.13712203	0.02682048	0.03432048
34	1.28923434	0.77565418	38.56457819	29.91277621	0.02593053	0.03343053
35	1.29890359	0.76988008	39.85381253	30.68265629	0.02509170	0.03259170
36	1.30864537	0.76414896	41.15271612	31.44680525	0.02429973	0.03179973
37	1.31846021	0.75846051	42.46136149	32.20526576	0.02355082	0.03105082
38	1.32834866	0.75281440	43.77982170	32.95808016	0.02284157	0.03034157
39	1.33831128	0.74721032	45.10817037	33.70529048	0.02216893	0.02966893
40	1.34834861	0.74164796	46.44648164	34.44693844	0.02153016	0.02903016
41	1.35846123	0.73612701	47.79483026	35.18306545	0.02092276	0.02842276
42	1.36864969	0.73064716	49.15329148	35.91371260	0.02034452	0.02784452
43	1.37891456	0.72520809	50.52194117	36.63892070	0.01979338	0.02729338
44	1.38925642	0.71980952	51.90085573	37.35873022	0.01926751	0.02676751
45	1.39967584	0.71445114	53.29011215	38.07318136	0.01876521	0.02626521
46	1.41017341	0.70913264	54.68978799	38.78231401	0.01828495	0.02578495
47	1.42074971	0.70385374	56.09996140	39.48616775	0.01782532	0.02532532
48	1.43140533	0.69861414	57.52071111	40.18478189	0.01738504	0.02488504
49	1.44214087	0.69341353	58.95211644	40.87819542	0.01696292	0.02446292
50	1.45295693	0.68825165	60.39425732	41.56644707	0.01655787	0.02405787

Rate $\frac{5}{6}$%	A Compound Interest	B Present Value	C Amount of Annuity	D Present Value of Annuity	E Sinking Fund	F Amortization
n	$(1+i)^n$	$\dfrac{1}{(1+i)^n}$	$s_{\overline{n}|i}$	$a_{\overline{n}|i}$	$\dfrac{1}{s_{\overline{n}|i}}$	$\dfrac{1}{a_{\overline{n}|i}}$
1	1.00833333	0.99173554	1.00000000	0.99173554	1.00000000	1.00833333
2	1.01673611	0.98353938	2.00833333	1.97527491	0.49792531	0.50625864
3	1.02520891	0.97541095	3.02506944	2.95068586	0.33057092	0.33890426
4	1.03375232	0.96734970	4.05027836	3.91803557	0.24689661	0.25522994
5	1.04236692	0.95935508	5.08403068	4.87739065	0.19669433	0.20502766
6	1.05105331	0.95142652	6.12639760	5.82881717	0.16322806	0.17156139
7	1.05981209	0.94356349	7.17745091	6.77238066	0.13932523	0.14765856
8	1.06864386	0.93576545	8.23726300	7.70814611	0.12139955	0.12973288
9	1.07754922	0.92803185	9.30590686	8.63617796	0.10745863	0.11579196
10	1.08652880	0.92036217	10.38345608	9.55654013	0.09630705	0.10464038
11	1.09558321	0.91275587	11.46998489	10.46929600	0.08718407	0.09551741
12	1.10471307	0.90521243	12.56556809	11.37450843	0.07958255	0.08791589
13	1.11391901	0.89773134	13.67028116	12.27223976	0.07315138	0.08148472
14	1.12320167	0.89031207	14.78420017	13.16255183	0.06763978	0.07597311
15	1.13256168	0.88295412	15.90740184	14.04550595	0.06286382	0.07119715
16	1.14199970	0.87565698	17.03996352	14.92116292	0.05868557	0.06701890
17	1.15151636	0.86842014	18.18196322	15.78958306	0.05499956	0.06333289
18	1.16111233	0.86124312	19.33347958	16.65082618	0.05172375	0.06005708
19	1.17078827	0.85412540	20.49459191	17.50495158	0.04879336	0.05712669
20	1.18054483	0.84706652	21.66538017	18.35201810	0.04615659	0.05448992
21	1.19038271	0.84006597	22.84592501	19.19208406	0.04377148	0.05210482
22	1.20030256	0.83312327	24.03630772	20.02520734	0.04160373	0.04993706
23	1.21030509	0.82623796	25.23661028	20.85144529	0.03962497	0.04795831
24	1.22039096	0.81940954	26.44691537	21.67085483	0.03781159	0.04614493
25	1.23056089	0.81263756	27.66730633	22.48349240	0.03614374	0.04447708
26	1.24081556	0.80592155	28.89786721	23.28941395	0.03460463	0.04293796
27	1.25115569	0.79926104	30.13868277	24.08867499	0.03317995	0.04151328
28	1.26158199	0.79265558	31.38983846	24.88133057	0.03185744	0.04019078
29	1.27209517	0.78610471	32.65142045	25.66743527	0.03062654	0.03895987
30	1.28269596	0.77960797	33.92351562	26.44704325	0.02947808	0.03781141
31	1.29338510	0.77316493	35.20621158	27.22020818	0.02840408	0.03673741
32	1.30416331	0.76677514	36.49959668	27.98698332	0.02739756	0.03573090
33	1.31503133	0.76043815	37.80375999	28.74742147	0.02645240	0.03478573
34	1.35298993	0.75415354	39.11879132	29.50157501	0.02556316	0.03389650
35	1.33703984	0.74792087	40.44478125	30.24949588	0.02472507	0.03305840
36	1.34818184	0.74173970	41.78182109	30.99123559	0.02393385	0.03226719
37	1.35941669	0.73560962	43.13000293	31.72684521	0.02318572	0.03151905
38	1.37074516	0.72953020	44.48941962	32.45637541	0.02247725	0.03081059
39	1.38216804	0.72350103	45.86016479	33.17987644	0.02180542	0.03013875
40	1.39368611	0.71752168	47.24233283	33.89739813	0.02116746	0.02950079
41	1.40530016	0.71159175	48.63601893	34.60898988	0.02056089	0.02889423
42	1.41701099	0.70571083	50.04131909	35.31470070	0.01998349	0.02831682
43	1.42881942	0.69987851	51.45833008	36.01457921	0.01943320	0.02776653
44	1.44072625	0.69409439	52.88714950	36.70867360	0.01890818	0.02724152
45	1.45273230	0.68835807	54.32787575	37.39703167	0.01840676	0.02674009
46	1.46483840	0.68266916	55.78060805	38.07970083	0.01792738	0.02626071
47	1.47704539	0.67702727	57.24544645	38.75672809	0.01746864	0.02580197
48	1.48935410	0.67143200	58.72249183	39.42816009	0.01702925	0.02536258
49	1.50176538	0.66588297	60.21184593	40.09404307	0.01660803	0.02494136
50	1.51428009	0.66037981	61.71361131	40.75442288	0.01620388	0.02453721

Rate 1%	A Compound Interest	B Present Value	C Amount of Annuity	D Present Value of Annuity	E Sinking Fund	F Amortization
n	$(1 + i)^n$	$\dfrac{1}{(1 + i)^n}$	$s_{\overline{n}\|i}$	$a_{\overline{n}\|i}$	$\dfrac{1}{s_{\overline{n}\|i}}$	$\dfrac{1}{a_{\overline{n}\|i}}$
1	1.01000000	0.99009901	1.00000000	0.99009901	1.00000000	1.01000000
2	1.02010000	0.98029605	2.01000000	1.97039506	0.49751244	0.50751244
3	1.03030100	0.97059015	3.03010000	2.94098521	0.33002211	0.34002211
4	1.04060401	0.96098034	4.06040100	3.90196555	0.24628109	0.25628109
5	1.05101005	0.95146569	5.10100501	4.85343124	0.19603980	0.20603980
6	1.06152015	0.94204524	6.15201506	5.79547647	0.16254837	0.17254837
7	1.07213535	0.93271805	7.21353521	6.72819453	0.13862828	0.14862828
8	1.08285671	0.92348322	8.28567056	7.65167775	0.12069029	0.13069029
9	1.09368527	0.91433982	9.36852727	8.56601758	0.10674036	0.11674036
10	1.10462213	0.90528695	10.46221254	9.47130453	0.09558208	0.10558208
11	1.11566835	0.89632372	11.56683467	10.36762825	0.08645408	0.09645408
12	1.12682503	0.88744923	12.68250301	11.25507747	0.07884879	0.08884879
13	1.13809328	0.87866260	13.80932804	12.13374007	0.07241482	0.08241482
14	1.14947421	0.86996297	14.94742132	13.00370304	0.06690117	0.07690117
15	1.16096896	0.86134947	16.09689554	13.86505252	0.06212378	0.07212378
16	1.17257864	0.85282126	17.25786449	14.71787378	0.05794460	0.06794460
17	1.18430443	0.84437749	18.43044314	15.56225127	0.05425806	0.06425806
18	1.19614748	0.83601731	19.61474757	16.39826858	0.05098205	0.06098205
19	1.20810895	0.82773992	20.81089504	17.22600850	0.04805175	0.05805175
20	1.22019004	0.81954447	22.01900399	18.04555297	0.04541531	0.05541531
21	1.23239194	0.81143017	23.23919403	18.85698313	0.04303075	0.05303075
22	1.24471586	0.80339621	24.47158598	19.66037934	0.04086372	0.05086372
23	1.25716302	0.79544179	25.71630183	20.45582113	0.03888584	0.04888584
24	1.26973465	0.78756613	26.97346485	21.24338726	0.03707347	0.04707347
25	1.28243200	0.77976844	28.24319950	22.02315570	0.03540675	0.04540675
26	1.29525631	0.77204796	29.52563150	22.79520366	0.03386888	0.04386888
27	1.30820888	0.76440392	30.82088781	23.55960759	0.03244553	0.04244553
28	1.32129097	0.75683557	32.12909669	24.31644316	0.03112444	0.04112444
29	1.33450388	0.74934215	33.45038766	25.06578530	0.02989502	0.03989502
30	1.34784892	0.74192292	34.78489153	25.80770822	0.02874811	0.03874811
31	1.36132740	0.73457715	36.13274045	26.54228537	0.02767573	0.03767573
32	1.37494068	0.72730411	37.49406785	27.26958947	0.02667089	0.03667089
33	1.38869009	0.72010307	38.86900853	27.98969255	0.02575744	0.03572744
34	1.40257699	0.71297334	40.25769862	28.70266589	0.02483997	0.03483997
35	1.41660276	0.70591420	41.66027560	29.40853009	0.02400368	0.03400368
36	1.43076878	0.69892495	43.07687836	30.10750504	0.02321431	0.03321431
37	1.44507647	0.69200490	44.05764714	30.79950994	0.02246805	0.03246805
38	1.45952724	0.68515337	45.95272361	31.48466330	0.02176150	0.03176150
39	1.47412251	0.67836967	47.41225085	32.16303298	0.02109160	0.03109160
40	1.48886373	0.67165314	48.88637336	32.83468611	0.02045560	0.03045560
41	1.50375237	0.66500311	50.37523709	33.49968922	0.01985102	0.02985102
42	1.51878989	0.65841892	51.87898946	34.15810814	0.01927563	0.02927563
43	1.53397779	0.65189992	53.39777936	34.81000806	0.01872737	0.02872737
44	1.54931757	0.64544546	54.93175715	35.45545352	0.01820441	0.02820441
45	1.56481075	0.63905492	56.48107472	36.09450844	0.01770505	0.02770505
46	1.58045885	0.63272764	58.04588547	36.72723608	0.01722775	0.02722775
47	1.59626344	0.62646301	59.62634432	37.35369909	0.01677111	0.02677111
48	1.61222608	0.62026041	61.22260777	37.97395949	0.01633384	0.02633384
49	1.62834834	0.61411921	62.83483385	38.58807871	0.01591474	0.02591474
50	1.64463182	0.60803882	64.46318218	39.19611753	0.01551273	0.02551273

Rate $1\frac{1}{4}$%	A Compound Interest	B Present Value	C Amount of Annuity	D Present Value of Annuity	E Sinking Fund	F Amortization
n	$(1 + i)^n$	$\dfrac{1}{(1 + i)^n}$	$s_{\overline{n}\mid i}$	$a_{\overline{n}\mid i}$	$\dfrac{1}{s_{\overline{n}\mid i}}$	$\dfrac{1}{a_{\overline{n}\mid i}}$
1	1.01250000	0.98765432	1.00000000	0.98765432	1.00000000	1.01250000
2	1.02515625	0.97546106	2.01250000	1.96311538	0.49689441	0.50939441
3	1.03797070	0.96341833	3.03765625	2.92653371	0.32920117	0.34170117
4	1.05094534	0.95152428	4.07562695	3.87805798	0.24536102	0.25786102
5	1.06408215	0.93977706	5.12657229	4.81783504	0.19506211	0.20756211
6	1.07738318	0.92817488	6.19065444	5.74600992	0.16153381	0.17403381
7	1.09085047	0.91671593	7.26803762	6.66272585	0.13758872	0.15008872
8	1.10448610	0.90539845	8.35888809	7.56812429	0.11963314	0.13213314
9	1.11829218	0.89422069	9.46337420	8.46234498	0.10567055	0.11817055
10	1.13227083	0.88318093	10.58166637	9.34552591	0.09450307	0.10700307
11	1.14642422	0.87227746	11.71393720	10.21780337	0.08536839	0.09786839
12	1.16075452	0.86150860	12.86036142	11.07931197	0.07775831	0.09025831
13	1.17526395	0.85087269	14.02111594	11.93018466	0.07132100	0.08382100
14	1.18995475	0.84036809	15.19637988	12.77055275	0.06580515	0.07830515
15	1.20482918	0.82999318	16.38633463	13.60054592	0.06102646	0.07352646
16	1.21988955	0.81974635	17.59116382	14.42029227	0.05684672	0.06934672
17	1.23513817	0.80962602	18.81105336	15.22991829	0.05316023	0.06566023
18	1.25057739	0.79963064	20.04619153	16.02954893	0.04988479	0.06238479
19	1.26620961	0.78975866	21.29676893	16.81930759	0.04695548	0.05945548
20	1.28203723	0.78000855	22.56297854	17.59931613	0.04432039	0.05682039
21	1.29806270	0.77037881	23.84501577	18.36969495	0.04193749	0.05443749
22	1.31428848	0.76086796	25.14307847	19.13056291	0.03977238	0.05227238
23	1.33071709	0.75147453	26.45736695	19.88203744	0.03779666	0.05029666
24	1.34735105	0.74219707	27.78808403	20.62423451	0.03598665	0.04848665
25	1.36419294	0.73303414	29.13543508	21.35726865	0.03432247	0.04682247
26	1.38124535	0.72398434	30.49962802	22.08125299	0.03278729	0.04528729
27	1.39851092	0.71504626	31.88087337	22.79629925	0.03136677	0.04386677
28	1.41599230	0.70621853	33.27938429	23.50251778	0.03004863	0.04254863
29	1.43369221	0.69749978	34.69537659	24.20001756	0.02882228	0.04132228
30	1.45161336	0.68888867	36.12906880	24.88890623	0.02767854	0.04017854
31	1.46975853	0.68038387	37.58068216	25.56929010	0.02660942	0.03910942
32	1.48813051	0.67198407	39.05044069	26.24127418	0.02560791	0.03810791
33	1.50673214	0.66368797	40.53857120	26.90496215	0.02466786	0.03716786
34	1.52556629	0.65549429	42.04530334	27.56045644	0.02378387	0.03628387
35	1.54463587	0.64740177	43.57086963	28.20785822	0.02295111	0.03545111
36	1.56394382	0.63940916	45.11550550	28.84726737	0.02216533	0.03466533
37	1.58349312	0.63151522	46.67944932	29.47878259	0.02142270	0.03392270
38	1.60328678	0.62371873	48.26294243	30.10250133	0.02071983	0.03321983
39	1.62332787	0.61601850	49.86622921	30.71851983	0.02005365	0.03255365
40	1.64361946	0.60841334	51.48955708	31.32693316	0.01942141	0.03192141
41	1.66416471	0.60090206	53.13317654	31.92783522	0.01882063	0.03132063
42	1.68496677	0.59348352	54.79734125	32.52131874	0.01824906	0.03074906
43	1.70602885	0.58615656	56.48230801	33.10747530	0.01770466	0.03020466
44	1.72735421	0.57892006	58.18833687	33.68639536	0.01718557	0.02968557
45	1.74894614	0.57177290	59.91569108	34.25816825	0.01669012	0.02919012
46	1.77080797	0.56471397	61.66463721	34.82288222	0.01621675	0.02871675
47	1.79294306	0.55774219	63.43544518	35.38064224	0.01576406	0.02826406
48	1.81535485	0.55085649	65.22838824	35.93148091	0.01533075	0.02783075
49	1.83804679	0.54405579	67.04374310	36.47553670	0.01491563	0.02741563
50	1.86102237	0.53733905	68.88178989	37.01287575	0.01451763	0.02701763

	A	B	C	D	E	F
Rate $1\frac{1}{2}$%	Compound Interest	Present Value	Amount of Annuity	Present Value of Annuity	Sinking Fund	Amortization
n	$(1 + i)^n$	$\dfrac{1}{(1 + i)^n}$	$s_{\overline{n}\vert i}$	$a_{\overline{n}\vert i}$	$\dfrac{1}{s_{\overline{n}\vert i}}$	$\dfrac{1}{a_{\overline{n}\vert i}}$
1	1.01500000	0.98522167	1.00000000	0.98522167	1.00000000	1.01500000
2	1.03022500	0.97066175	2.01500000	1.95588342	0.49627792	0.51127792
3	1.04567838	0.95631699	3.04522500	2.91220042	0.32838296	0.34338296
4	1.06136355	0.94218423	4.09090337	3.85438465	0.24444479	0.25944479
5	1.07728400	0.92826033	5.15226693	4.78264497	0.19408932	0.20908932
6	1.09344326	0.91454219	6.22955093	5.69718717	0.16052521	0.17552521
7	1.10984491	0.90102679	7.32299419	6.59821396	0.13655616	0.15155616
8	1.12649259	0.88771112	8.43283911	7.48592508	0.11858402	0.13358402
9	1.14338998	0.87459224	9.55933169	8.36051732	0.10460982	0.11960982
10	1.16054083	0.86166723	10.70272167	9.22218455	0.09343418	0.10843418
11	1.17794894	0.84893323	11.86326249	10.07111779	0.08429384	0.09929384
12	1.19561817	0.83638742	13.04121143	10.90750521	0.07667999	0.09167999
13	1.21355244	0.82402702	14.23682960	11.73153222	0.07024036	0.08524036
14	1.23175573	0.81184928	15.45038205	12.54338150	0.06472332	0.07972332
15	1.25023207	0.79985150	16.68213778	13.34323301	0.05994436	0.07494436
16	1.26898555	0.78803104	17.93236984	14.13126405	0.05576508	0.07076508
17	1.28802033	0.77638526	19.20135539	14.90764931	0.05207966	0.06707966
18	1.30734064	0.76491159	20.48937572	15.67256089	0.04880578	0.06380578
19	1.32695075	0.75360747	21.79671636	16.42616837	0.04587847	0.06087847
20	1.34685501	0.74247042	23.12366710	17.16863879	0.04324574	0.05824574
21	1.36705783	0.73149795	24.47052211	17.90013673	0.04086550	0.05586550
22	1.38756370	0.72068763	25.83757994	18.62082437	0.03870332	0.05370332
23	1.40837715	0.71003708	27.22514364	19.33086145	0.03673075	0.05173075
24	1.42950281	0.69954392	28.63352080	20.03040537	0.03492410	0.04992410
25	1.45094535	0.68920583	30.06302361	20.71961120	0.03326345	0.04826345
26	1.47270953	0.67902052	31.51396896	21.39863172	0.03173196	0.04673196
27	1.49480018	0.66898574	32.98667850	22.06761746	0.03031527	0.04531527
28	1.51722218	0.65909925	34.48147867	22.72671671	0.02900108	0.04400108
29	1.53998051	0.64935887	35.99870085	23.37607558	0.02777878	0.04277878
30	1.56308022	0.63976243	37.53868137	24.01583801	0.02663919	0.04163919
31	1.58652642	0.63030781	39.10176159	24.64614582	0.02557430	0.04057430
32	1.61032432	0.62099292	40.68828801	25.26713874	0.02457710	0.03957710
33	1.63447918	0.61181568	42.29861233	25.87895442	0.02364144	0.03864144
34	1.65899637	0.60277407	43.93309152	26.48172849	0.02276189	0.03776189
35	1.68388132	0.59386608	45.59208789	27.07559458	0.02193363	0.03693363
36	1.70913954	0.58508974	47.27596921	27.66068431	0.02115240	0.03615240
37	1.73477663	0.57644309	48.98510874	28.23712740	0.02041437	0.03541437
38	1.76079828	0.56792423	50.71988538	28.80505163	0.01971613	0.03471613
39	1.78721025	0.55953126	52.48068366	29.36458288	0.01905463	0.03405463
40	1.81401841	0.55126232	54.26789391	29.91584520	0.01842710	0.03342710
41	1.84122868	0.54311559	56.08191232	30.45896079	0.01783106	0.03283106
42	1.86884712	0.53508925	57.92314100	30.99405004	0.01726426	0.03226426
43	1.89687982	0.52718153	59.79198812	31.52123157	0.01672465	0.03172465
44	1.92533302	0.51939067	61.68886794	32.04062223	0.01621038	0.03121038
45	1.95421301	0.51171494	63.61420096	32.55233718	0.01571976	0.03071976
46	1.98352621	0.50415265	65.56841398	33.05648983	0.01525125	0.03025125
47	2.01327910	0.49670212	67.55194018	33.55319195	0.01480342	0.02980342
48	2.04347829	0.48936170	69.56521929	34.04255365	0.01437500	0.02937500
49	2.07413046	0.48212975	71.60869758	34.52468339	0.01396478	0.02896478
50	2.10524242	0.47500468	73.68282804	34.99968807	0.01357168	0.02857168

Rate $1\frac{3}{4}$%	A Compound Interest	B Present Value	C Amount of Annuity	D Present Value of Annuity	E Sinking Fund	F Amortization
n	$(1 + i)^n$	$\dfrac{1}{(1 + i)^n}$	$s_{\overline{n}\mid i}$	$a_{\overline{n}\mid i}$	$\dfrac{1}{s_{\overline{n}\mid i}}$	$\dfrac{1}{a_{\overline{n}\mid i}}$
1	1.01750000	0.98280098	1.00000000	0.98280098	1.00000000	1.01750000
2	1.03530625	0.96589777	2.01750000	1.94869875	0.49566295	0.51316295
3	1.05342411	0.94928528	3.05280625	2.89798403	0.32756746	0.34506746
4	1.07185903	0.93295851	4.10623036	3.83094254	0.24353237	0.26103237
5	1.09061656	0.91691254	5.17808939	4.74785508	0.19312142	0.21062142
6	1.10970235	0.90114254	6.26870596	5.64899762	0.15952256	0.17702256
7	1.12912215	0.88564378	7.37840831	6.53464139	0.13553059	0.15303059
8	1.14888178	0.87041157	8.50753045	7.40505297	0.11754292	0.13504292
9	1.16898721	0.85544135	9.65641224	8.26049432	0.10355813	0.12105813
10	1.18944449	0.84072860	10.82539945	9.10122291	0.09237534	0.10987534
11	1.21025977	0.82626889	12.01484394	9.92749181	0.08323038	0.10073038
12	1.23143931	0.81205788	13.22510371	10.73954969	0.07561377	0.09311377
13	1.25298950	0.79809128	14.45654303	11.53764097	0.06917283	0.08667283
14	1.27491682	0.78436490	15.70953253	12.32200587	0.06365562	0.08115562
15	1.29722786	0.77087459	16.98444935	13.09288046	0.05887739	0.07637739
16	1.31992935	0.75761631	18.28167721	13.85049677	0.05469958	0.07219958
17	1.34302811	0.74458605	19.60160656	14.59508282	0.05101623	0.06851623
18	1.36653111	0.73177990	20.94463468	15.32686272	0.04774492	0.06524492
19	1.39044540	0.71919401	22.31116578	16.04605673	0.04482061	0.06232061
20	1.41477820	0.70682458	23.70161119	16.75288130	0.04219122	0.05969122
21	1.43953681	0.69466789	25.11638938	17.44754919	0.03981464	0.05731464
22	1.46472871	0.68272028	26.55592620	18.13026948	0.03765638	0.05515638
23	1.49036146	0.67097817	28.02065490	18.80124764	0.03568796	0.05318796
24	1.51644279	0.65943800	29.51101637	19.46068565	0.03388565	0.05138565
25	1.54298054	0.64809632	31.02745915	20.10878196	0.03222952	0.04972952
26	1.56998269	0.63694970	32.57043969	20.74573166	0.03070269	0.04820269
27	1.59745739	0.62599479	34.14042238	21.37172644	0.02929079	0.04679079
28	1.62541290	0.61522829	35.73787977	21.98695474	0.02798151	0.04548151
29	1.65385762	0.60464697	37.36329267	22.59160171	0.02676424	0.04426424
30	1.68280013	0.59424764	39.01715029	23.18584934	0.02562975	0.04312975
31	1.71224913	0.58402716	40.69995042	23.76987650	0.02457005	0.04207005
32	1.74221349	0.57398247	42.41219955	24.34385897	0.02357812	0.04107812
33	1.77270223	0.56411053	44.15441305	24.90796951	0.02264779	0.04014779
34	1.80372452	0.55440839	45.92711527	25.46237789	0.02177363	0.03927363
35	1.83528970	0.54487311	47.73083979	26.00725100	0.02095082	0.03845082
36	1.86740727	0.53550183	49.56612949	26.54275283	0.02017507	0.03767507
37	1.90008689	0.52629172	51.43353675	27.06904455	0.01944257	0.03694257
38	1.93333841	0.51724002	53.33362365	27.58628457	0.01874990	0.03624990
39	1.96717184	0.50834400	55.26696206	28.09462857	0.01809399	0.03559399
40	2.00159734	0.49960098	57.23413390	28.59422955	0.01747209	0.03497209
41	2.03662530	0.49100834	59.23573124	29.08523789	0.01688170	0.03438170
42	2.07226624	0.48256348	61.27235654	29.56780136	0.01632057	0.03382057
43	2.10853090	0.47426386	63.34462278	30.04206522	0.01578666	0.03328666
44	2.14543019	0.46610699	65.45315367	30.50817221	0.01527810	0.03277810
45	2.18297522	0.45809040	67.59858386	30.96626261	0.01479321	0.03229321
46	2.22117728	0.45021170	69.78155908	31.41647431	0.01433043	0.03183043
47	2.26004789	0.44246850	72.00273637	31.85894281	0.01388836	0.03138836
48	2.29959872	0.43485848	74.26278425	32.29380129	0.01346569	0.03096569
49	2.33984170	0.42737934	76.56238298	32.72118063	0.01306124	0.03056124
50	2.38078893	0.42002883	78.90222468	33.14120946	0.01267391	0.03017391

	A	B	C	D	E	F
Rate 2%	Compound Interest	Present Value	Amount of Annuity	Present Value of Annuity	Sinking Fund	Amortization
n	$(1 + i)^n$	$\dfrac{1}{(1 + i)^n}$	$s_{\overline{n}|i}$	$a_{\overline{n}|i}$	$\dfrac{1}{s_{\overline{n}|i}}$	$\dfrac{1}{a_{\overline{n}|i}}$
1	1.02000000	0.98039216	1.00000000	0.98039216	1.00000000	1.02000000
2	1.04040000	0.96116878	2.02000000	1.94156094	0.49504950	0.51504950
3	1.06120800	0.94232233	3.06040000	2.88388327	0.32675467	0.34675467
4	1.08243216	0.92384543	4.12160800	3.80772870	0.24262375	0.26262375
5	1.10408080	0.90573081	5.20404016	4.71345951	0.19215839	0.21215839
6	1.12616242	0.88797138	6.30812096	5.60143089	0.15852581	0.17852581
7	1.14868567	0.87056018	7.43428338	6.47199107	0.13451196	0.15451196
8	1.17165938	0.85349037	8.58296905	7.32548144	0.11650980	0.13650980
9	1.19509257	0.83675527	9.75462843	8.16223671	0.10251544	0.12251544
10	1.21899442	0.82034830	10.94972100	8.98258501	0.09132653	0.11132653
11	1.24337431	0.80426304	12.16871542	9.78684805	0.08217794	0.10217794
12	1.26824179	0.78849318	13.41208973	10.57534122	0.07455960	0.09455960
13	1.29360663	0.77303253	14.68033152	11.34837375	0.06811835	0.08811835
14	1.31947876	0.75787502	15.97393815	12.10624877	0.06260197	0.08260197
15	1.34586834	0.74301473	17.29341692	12.84926350	0.05782547	0.07782547
16	1.37278571	0.72844581	18.63928525	13.57770931	0.05365013	0.07365013
17	1.40024142	0.71416256	20.01207096	14.29187188	0.04996984	0.06996984
18	1.42824625	0.70015937	21.41231238	14.99203125	0.04670210	0.06670210
19	1.45681117	0.68643076	22.84055863	15.67846201	0.04378177	0.06378177
20	1.48594740	0.67297133	24.29736980	16.35143334	0.04115672	0.06115672
21	1.51566634	0.65977582	25.78331719	17.01120916	0.03878477	0.05878477
22	1.54597967	0.64683904	27.29898354	17.65804820	0.03663140	0.05663140
23	1.57689926	0.63415592	28.84496321	18.29220412	0.03466810	0.05466810
24	1.60843725	0.62172149	30.42186247	18.91392560	0.03287110	0.05287110
25	1.64060599	0.60953087	32.03029972	19.52345647	0.03122044	0.05122044
26	1.67341811	0.59757928	33.67090572	20.12103576	0.02969923	0.04969923
27	1.70688648	0.58586204	35.34432383	20.70689780	0.02829309	0.04829309
28	1.74102421	0.57437455	37.05121031	21.28127236	0.02698967	0.04698967
29	1.77584469	0.56311231	38.79223451	21.84438466	0.02577836	0.04577836
30	1.81136158	0.55207089	40.56807921	22.39645555	0.02464992	0.04464992
31	1.84758882	0.54124597	42.37944079	22.93770152	0.02359635	0.04359635
32	1.88454059	0.53063330	44.22702961	23.46833482	0.02261061	0.04261061
33	1.92223140	0.52022873	46.11157020	23.98856355	0.02168653	0.04168653
34	1.96067603	0.51002817	48.03380160	24.49859172	0.02081867	0.04081867
35	1.99988955	0.50002761	49.99447763	24.99861933	0.02000221	0.04000221
36	2.03988734	0.49022315	51.99436719	25.48884248	0.01923285	0.03923285
37	2.08068509	0.48061093	54.03425453	25.96945341	0.01850678	0.03850678
38	2.12229879	0.47118719	56.11493962	26.44064060	0.01782057	0.03782057
39	2.16474477	0.46194822	58.23723841	26.90258883	0.01717114	0.03717114
40	2.20803966	0.45289042	60.40198318	27.35547924	0.01655575	0.03655575
41	2.25220046	0.44401021	62.61002284	27.79948945	0.01597188	0.03597188
42	2.29724447	0.43530413	64.86222330	28.23479358	0.01541729	0.03541729
43	2.34318936	0.42676875	67.15946777	28.66156233	0.01488993	0.03488993
44	2.39005314	0.41840074	69.50265712	29.07996307	0.01438794	0.03438794
45	2.43785421	0.41019680	71.89271027	29.49015987	0.01390962	0.03390962
46	2.48661129	0.40215373	74.33056447	29.89231360	0.01345342	0.03345342
47	2.53634352	0.39426836	76.81717576	30.28658196	0.01301792	0.03301792
48	2.58707039	0.38653761	79.35351927	30.67311957	0.01260184	0.03260184
49	2.63881179	0.37895844	81.94058966	31.05207801	0.01220396	0.03220396
50	2.69158803	0.37152788	84.57940145	31.42360589	0.01182321	0.03182321

Rate $2\frac{1}{2}$%	A Compound Interest	B Present Value	C Amount of Annuity	D Present Value of Annuity	E Sinking Fund	F Amortization
n	$(1 + i)^n$	$\dfrac{1}{(1 + i)^n}$	$s_{\overline{n}\rvert i}$	$a_{\overline{n}\rvert i}$	$\dfrac{1}{s_{\overline{n}\rvert i}}$	$\dfrac{1}{a_{\overline{n}\rvert i}}$
1	1.02500000	0.97560976	1.00000000	0.97560976	1.00000000	1.02500000
2	1.05062500	0.95181440	2.02500000	1.92742415	0.49382716	0.51882716
3	1.07689063	0.92859941	3.07562500	2.85602356	0.32513717	0.35013717
4	1.10381289	0.90595064	4.15251562	3.76197421	0.24081788	0.26581788
5	1.13140821	0.88385429	5.25632852	4.64582850	0.19024686	0.21524686
6	1.15969342	0.86229687	6.38773673	5.50812536	0.15654997	0.18154997
7	1.18868575	0.84126524	7.54753015	6.34939060	0.13249543	0.15749543
8	1.21840290	0.82074657	8.73611590	7.17013717	0.11446735	0.13946735
9	1.24886297	0.80072836	9.95451880	7.97086553	0.10045689	0.12545689
10	1.28008454	0.78119840	11.20338177	8.75206393	0.08925876	0.11425876
11	1.31208666	0.76214478	12.48346631	9.51420871	0.08010596	0.10510596
12	1.34488882	0.74355589	13.79555297	10.25776460	0.07248713	0.09748713
13	1.37851104	0.72542038	15.14044179	10.98318497	0.06604827	0.09104827
14	1.41297382	0.70772720	16.51895284	11.69091217	0.06053652	0.08553652
15	1.44829817	0.69046556	17.93192666	12.38137773	0.05576646	0.08076646
16	1.48450562	0.67362493	19.38022483	13.05500266	0.05159899	0.07659899
17	1.52161826	0.65719506	20.86473045	13.71219772	0.04792777	0.07292777
18	1.55965872	0.64116591	22.38634871	14.35336363	0.04467008	0.06967008
19	1.59865019	0.62552772	23.94600743	14.97889134	0.04176062	0.06676062
20	1.63861644	0.61027094	25.54465761	15.58916229	0.03914713	0.06414713
21	1.67958185	0.59538629	27.18327405	16.18454857	0.03678733	0.06178733
22	1.72157140	0.58086467	28.86285590	16.76541324	0.03464661	0.05964661
23	1.76461068	0.56669724	30.58442730	17.33211048	0.03269638	0.05769638
24	1.80872595	0.55287535	32.34903798	17.88498583	0.03091282	0.05591282
25	1.85394410	0.53939059	34.15776393	18.42437642	0.02927592	0.05427592
26	1.90029270	0.52623472	36.01170803	18.95061114	0.02776875	0.05276875
27	1.94780002	0.51339973	37.91200073	19.46401087	0.02637687	0.05137687
28	1.99649502	0.50087778	39.85980075	19.96488866	0.02508793	0.05008793
29	2.04640739	0.48866125	41.85629577	20.45354991	0.02389127	0.04889127
30	2.09756758	0.47674269	43.90270316	20.93029259	0.02277764	0.04777764
31	2.15000677	0.46511481	46.00027074	21.39540741	0.02173900	0.04673900
32	2.20375694	0.45377055	48.15027751	21.84917796	0.02076831	0.04576831
33	2.25885086	0.44270298	50.35403445	22.29188094	0.01985938	0.04485938
34	2.31532213	0.43190534	52.61288531	22.72378628	0.01900675	0.04400675
35	2.37320519	0.42137107	54.92820744	23.14515734	0.01820558	0.04320558
36	2.43253532	0.41109372	57.30141263	23.55625107	0.01745158	0.04245158
37	2.49334870	0.40106705	59.73394794	23.95731812	0.01674090	0.04174090
38	2.55568242	0.39128492	62.22729664	24.34860304	0.01607012	0.04107012
39	2.61957448	0.38174139	64.78297906	24.73034443	0.01543615	0.04043615
40	2.68506384	0.37243062	67.40255354	25.10277505	0.01483623	0.03983623
41	2.75219043	0.36334695	70.08761737	25.46612200	0.01426786	0.03926786
42	2.82099520	0.35448483	72.83980781	25.82060683	0.01372876	0.03872876
43	2.89152008	0.34583886	75.66080300	26.16644569	0.01321688	0.03821688
44	2.96380808	0.33740376	78.55232308	26.50384945	0.01273037	0.03773037
45	3.03790328	0.32917440	81.51613116	26.83302386	0.01226751	0.03726751
46	3.11385086	0.32114576	84.55403443	27.15416962	0.01182676	0.03682676
47	3.19169713	0.31331294	87.66788530	27.46748255	0.01140669	0.03640669
48	3.27148956	0.30567116	90.85958243	27.77315371	0.01100599	0.03600599
49	3.35327680	0.29821576	94.13107199	28.07136947	0.01062348	0.03562348
50	3.43710872	0.29094221	97.48434879	28.36231168	0.01025806	0.03525806

Rate 3%	A Compound Interest	B Present Value	C Amount of Annuity	D Present Value of Annuity	E Sinking Fund	F Amortization
n	$(1 + i)^n$	$\dfrac{1}{(1 + i)^n}$	$s_{\overline{n}\mid i}$	$a_{\overline{n}\mid i}$	$\dfrac{1}{s_{\overline{n}\mid i}}$	$\dfrac{1}{a_{\overline{n}\mid i}}$
1	1.03000000	0.97087379	1.00000000	0.97087379	1.00000000	1.03000000
2	1.06090000	0.94259591	2.03000000	1.91346970	0.49261084	0.52261084
3	1.09272700	0.91514166	3.09090000	2.82861135	0.32353036	0.35353036
4	1.12550881	0.88848705	4.18362700	3.71709840	0.23902705	0.26902705
5	1.15927407	0.86260878	5.30913581	4.57970719	0.18835457	0.21835457
6	1.19405230	0.83748426	6.46840988	5.41719144	0.15459750	0.18459750
7	1.22987387	0.81309151	7.66246218	6.23028296	0.13050635	0.16050635
8	1.26677008	0.78940923	8.89233605	7.01969219	0.11245639	0.14245639
9	1.30477318	0.76641673	10.15910613	7.78610892	0.09843386	0.12843386
10	1.34391638	0.74409391	11.46387931	8.53020284	0.08723051	0.11723051
11	1.38423387	0.72242128	12.80779569	9.25262411	0.07807745	0.10807745
12	1.42576089	0.70137988	14.19202956	9.95400399	0.07046209	0.10046209
13	1.46853371	0.68095134	15.61779045	10.63495533	0.06402954	0.09402954
14	1.51258972	0.66111781	17.08632416	11.29607314	0.05852634	0.08852634
15	1.55796742	0.64186195	18.59891389	11.93793509	0.05376658	0.08376658
16	1.60470644	0.62316694	20.15688130	12.56110203	0.04961085	0.07961085
17	1.65284763	0.60501645	21.76158774	13.16611847	0.04595253	0.07595253
18	1.70243306	0.58739461	23.41443537	13.75351308	0.04270870	0.07270870
19	1.75350605	0.57028603	25.11686844	14.32379911	0.03981388	0.06981388
20	1.80611123	0.55367575	26.87037449	14.87747486	0.03721571	0.06721571
21	1.86029457	0.53754928	28.67648572	15.41502414	0.03487178	0.06487178
22	1.91610341	0.52189250	30.53678030	15.93691664	0.03274739	0.06274739
23	1.97358651	0.50669175	32.45288370	16.44360839	0.03081390	0.06081390
24	2.03279411	0.49193374	34.42647022	16.93554212	0.02904742	0.05904742
25	2.09377793	0.47760557	36.45926432	17.41314769	0.02742787	0.05742787
26	2.15659127	0.46369473	38.55304225	17.87684242	0.02593829	0.05593829
27	2.22128901	0.45018906	40.70963352	18.32703147	0.02456421	0.05456421
28	2.28792768	0.43707675	42.93092252	18.76410823	0.02329323	0.05329323
29	2.35656551	0.42434636	45.21885020	19.18845459	0.02211467	0.05211467
30	2.42726247	0.41198676	47.57541571	19.60044135	0.02101926	0.05101926
31	2.50008035	0.39998715	50.00267818	20.00042849	0.01999893	0.04999893
32	2.57508276	0.38833703	52.50275852	20.38876553	0.01904662	0.04904662
33	2.65233524	0.37702625	55.07784128	20.76579178	0.01815612	0.04815612
34	2.73190530	0.36604490	57.73017652	21.13183668	0.01732196	0.04732196
35	2.81386245	0.35538340	60.46208181	21.48722007	0.01653929	0.04653929
36	2.89827833	0.34503243	63.27594427	21.83225250	0.01580379	0.04580379
37	2.98522668	0.33498294	66.17422259	22.16723544	0.01511162	0.04511162
38	3.07478348	0.32522615	69.15944927	22.49246159	0.01445934	0.04445934
39	3.16702698	0.31575355	72.23423275	22.80821513	0.01384385	0.04384385
40	3.26203779	0.30655684	75.40125973	23.11477197	0.01326238	0.04326238
41	3.35989893	0.29762800	78.66329753	23.41239997	0.01271241	0.04271241
42	3.46069589	0.28895922	82.02319645	23.70135920	0.01219167	0.04219167
43	3.56451677	0.28054294	85.48389234	23.98190213	0.01169811	0.04169811
44	3.67145227	0.27237178	89.04840911	24.25427392	0.01122985	0.04122985
45	3.78159584	0.26443862	92.71986139	24.51871254	0.01078518	0.04078518
46	3.89504372	0.25673653	96.50145723	24.77544907	0.01036254	0.04036254
47	4.01189503	0.24925876	100.39650095	25.02470783	0.00996051	0.03996051
48	4.13225188	0.24199880	104.40839598	25.26670664	0.00957777	0.03957777
49	4.25621944	0.23495029	108.54064785	25.50165693	0.00921314	0.03921314
50	4.38390602	0.22810708	112.79686729	25.72976401	0.00886549	0.03886549

Rate $3\frac{1}{2}$%	A Compound Interest	B Present Value	C Amount of Annuity	D Present Value of Annuity	E Sinking Fund	F Amortization
n	$(1 + i)^n$	$\dfrac{1}{(1 + i)^n}$	$s_{\overline{n}|i}$	$a_{\overline{n}|i}$	$\dfrac{1}{s_{\overline{n}|i}}$	$\dfrac{1}{a_{\overline{n}|i}}$
1	1.03500000	0.96618357	1.00000000	0.96618357	1.00000000	1.03500000
2	1.07122500	0.93351070	2.03500000	1.89969428	0.49140049	0.52640049
3	1.10871788	0.90194271	3.10622500	2.80163698	0.32193418	0.35693418
4	1.14752300	0.87144223	4.21494287	3.67307921	0.23725114	0.27225114
5	1.18768631	0.84197317	5.36246588	4.51505238	0.18648137	0.22148137
6	1.22925533	0.81350064	6.55015218	5.32855302	0.15266821	0.18766821
7	1.27227926	0.78599096	7.77940751	6.11454398	0.12854449	0.16354449
8	1.31680904	0.75941156	9.05168677	6.87395554	0.11047665	0.14547665
9	1.36289735	0.73373097	10.36849581	7.60768651	0.09644601	0.13144601
10	1.41059876	0.70891881	11.73139316	8.31660532	0.08524137	0.12024137
11	1.45996972	0.68494571	13.14199192	9.00155104	0.07609197	0.11109197
12	1.51106866	0.66178330	14.60196164	9.66333433	0.06848395	0.10348395
13	1.56395606	0.63940415	16.11303030	10.30273849	0.06206157	0.09706157
14	1.61869452	0.61778179	17.67698636	10.92052028	0.05657073	0.09157073
15	1.67534883	0.59689062	19.29568088	11.51741090	0.05182507	0.08682507
16	1.73398604	0.57670591	20.97102971	12.09411681	0.04768483	0.08268483
17	1.79467555	0.55720378	22.70501575	12.65132059	0.04404313	0.07904313
18	1.85748920	0.53836114	24.49969130	13.18968173	0.04081684	0.07581684
19	1.92250132	0.52015569	26.35718050	13.70983742	0.03794033	0.07294033
20	1.98978886	0.50256588	28.27968181	14.21240330	0.03536108	0.07036108
21	2.05943147	0.48557090	30.26947068	14.69797420	0.03303659	0.06803659
22	2.13151158	0.46915063	32.32890215	15.16712484	0.03093207	0.06593207
23	2.20611448	0.45328563	34.46041373	15.62041047	0.02901880	0.06401880
24	2.28332849	0.43795713	36.66652821	16.05836760	0.02727283	0.06227283
25	2.36324498	0.42314699	38.94985669	16.48151459	0.02567404	0.06067404
26	2.44595856	0.40883767	41.31310168	16.89035226	0.02420540	0.05920540
27	2.53156711	0.39501224	43.75906024	17.28536451	0.02285241	0.05785241
28	2.62017196	0.38165434	46.29062734	17.66701885	0.02160265	0.05660265
29	2.71187798	0.36874815	48.91079930	18.03576700	0.02044538	0.05544538
30	2.80679370	0.35627841	51.62267728	18.39204541	0.01937133	0.05437133
31	2.90503148	0.34423035	54.42947098	18.73627576	0.01837240	0.05337240
32	3.00670759	0.33258971	57.33450247	19.06886547	0.01744150	0.05244150
33	3.11194235	0.32134271	60.34121005	19.39020818	0.01657242	0.05157242
34	3.22086033	0.31047605	63.45315240	19.70068423	0.01575966	0.05075966
35	3.33359045	0.29997686	66.67401274	20.00066110	0.01499835	0.04999835
36	3.45026611	0.28983272	70.00760318	20.29049381	0.01428416	0.04928416
37	3.57102543	0.28003161	73.45786930	20.57052542	0.01361325	0.04861325
38	3.69601132	0.27056194	77.02889472	20.84108736	0.01298214	0.04798214
39	3.82537171	0.26141250	80.72490604	21.10249987	0.01238775	0.04738775
40	3.95925972	0.25257247	84.55027775	21.35507234	0.01182728	0.04682728
41	4.09783381	0.24403137	88.50953747	21.59910371	0.01129822	0.04629822
42	4.24125799	0.23577910	92.60737128	21.83488281	0.01079828	0.04579828
43	4.38970202	0.22780590	96.84862928	22.06268870	0.01032539	0.04532539
44	4.54334160	0.22010231	101.23833130	22.28279102	0.00987768	0.04487768
45	4.70235855	0.21265924	105.78167290	22.49545026	0.00945343	0.04445343
46	4.86694110	0.20546787	110.48403145	22.70091813	0.00905108	0.04405108
47	5.03728404	0.19851968	115.35097255	22.89943780	0.00866919	0.04366919
48	5.21358898	0.19180645	120.38825659	23.09124425	0.00830646	0.04330646
49	5.39606459	0.18532024	125.60184557	23.27656450	0.00796167	0.04296167
50	5.58492686	0.17905337	130.99791016	23.45561787	0.00763371	0.04263371

Rate $3\frac{3}{4}$%	A Compound Interest	B Present Value	C Amount of Annuity	D Present Value of Annuity	E Sinking Fund	F Amortization
n	$(1 + i)^n$	$\dfrac{1}{(1 + i)^n}$	$s_{\overline{n}|i}$	$a_{\overline{n}|i}$	$\dfrac{1}{s_{\overline{n}|i}}$	$\dfrac{1}{a_{\overline{n}|i}}$
1	1.03750000	0.96385542	1.00000000	0.96385542	1.00000000	1.03750000
2	1.07640625	0.92901727	2.03750000	1.89287270	0.49079755	0.52829755
3	1.11677148	0.89543834	3.11390625	2.78831103	0.32114005	0.35864005
4	1.15865042	0.86307310	4.23067773	3.65138413	0.23636875	0.27386875
5	1.20209981	0.83187768	5.38932815	4.48326181	0.18555189	0.22305189
6	1.24717855	0.80180981	6.59142796	5.28507162	0.15171219	0.18921219
7	1.29394774	0.77282874	7.83860650	6.05790036	0.12757370	0.16507370
8	1.34247078	0.74489517	9.13255425	6.80279553	0.10949839	0.14699839
9	1.39281344	0.71797125	10.47502503	7.52076677	0.09546517	0.13296517
10	1.44504394	0.69202048	11.86783847	8.21278725	0.08426134	0.12176134
11	1.49923309	0.66700769	13.31288241	8.87979494	0.07511521	0.11261521
12	1.55545433	0.64289898	14.81211550	9.52269392	0.06751230	0.10501230
13	1.61378387	0.61966167	16.36756983	10.14235558	0.06109642	0.09859642
14	1.67430076	0.59726426	17.98135370	10.73961984	0.05561317	0.09311317
15	1.73708704	0.57567639	19.65565447	11.31529623	0.05087595	0.08837595
16	1.80222781	0.55486881	21.39274151	11.87016504	0.04674483	0.08424483
17	1.86981135	0.53481331	23.19496932	12.40497835	0.04311280	0.08061280
18	1.93992927	0.51548271	25.06478067	12.92046106	0.03989662	0.07739662
19	2.01267662	0.49685080	27.00470994	13.41731187	0.03703058	0.07453058
20	2.08815200	0.47889234	29.01738656	13.89620421	0.03446210	0.07196210
21	2.16645770	0.46158298	31.10553856	14.35778719	0.03214862	0.06964862
22	2.24769986	0.44489926	33.27199626	14.80268645	0.03005531	0.06755531
23	2.33198860	0.42881856	35.51969612	15.23150501	0.02815339	0.06565339
24	2.41943818	0.41331910	37.85168472	15.64482411	0.02641890	0.06391890
25	2.51016711	0.39837985	40.27112290	16.04320396	0.02483169	0.06233169
26	2.60429838	0.38398058	42.78129001	16.42718454	0.02337470	0.06087470
27	2.70195956	0.37010176	45.38558838	16.79728630	0.02203343	0.05953343
28	2.80328305	0.35672459	48.08754794	17.15401089	0.02079540	0.05829540
29	2.90840616	0.34383093	50.89083099	17.49784183	0.01964991	0.05714991
30	3.01747139	0.33140331	53.79923715	17.82924513	0.01858762	0.05608762
31	3.13062657	0.31942487	56.81670855	18.14867001	0.01760046	0.05510046
32	3.24802507	0.30787940	59.94733512	18.45654941	0.01668131	0.05418131
33	3.36982601	0.29675123	63.19536019	18.75330063	0.01582395	0.05332395
34	3.49619448	0.28602528	66.56518619	19.03932591	0.01502287	0.05252287
35	3.62730178	0.27568702	70.06138067	19.31501293	0.01427320	0.05177320
36	3.76332559	0.26572242	73.68868245	19.58073535	0.01357060	0.05107060
37	3.90445030	0.25611800	77.45200804	19.83685335	0.01291122	0.05041122
38	4.05086719	0.24686072	81.35645834	20.08371407	0.01229159	0.04979159
39	4.20277471	0.23793805	85.40732553	20.32165212	0.01170860	0.04920860
40	4.36037876	0.22933788	89.61010024	20.55098999	0.01115946	0.04865946
41	4.52389296	0.22104855	93.97047900	20.77203855	0.01064164	0.04814164
42	4.69353895	0.21305885	98.49437196	20.98509739	0.01015286	0.04765286
43	4.86954666	0.20535793	103.18791091	21.19045532	0.00969106	0.04719106
44	5.05215466	0.19793535	108.05745757	21.38839067	0.00925434	0.04675434
45	5.24161046	0.19078106	113.10961223	21.57917173	0.00884098	0.04634098
46	5.43817085	0.18388536	118.35122269	21.76305709	0.00844943	0.04594943
47	5.64210226	0.17723890	123.78939354	21.94029599	0.00807824	0.04557824
48	5.85368109	0.17083268	129.43149579	22.11112866	0.00772609	0.04522609
49	6.07319413	0.16465800	135.28517689	22.27578666	0.00739179	0.04489179
50	6.30093891	0.15870651	141.35837102	22.43449317	0.00707422	0.04457422

Rate 4%	A Compound Interest	B Present Value	C Amount of Annuity	D Present Value of Annuity	E Sinking Fund	F Amortization
n	$(1 + i)^n$	$\dfrac{1}{(1 + i)^n}$	$s_{\overline{n}\mid i}$	$a_{\overline{n}\mid i}$	$\dfrac{1}{s_{\overline{n}\mid i}}$	$\dfrac{1}{a_{\overline{n}\mid i}}$
1	1.04000000	0.96153846	1.00000000	0.96153846	1.00000000	1.04000000
2	1.08160000	0.92455621	2.04000000	1.88609467	0.49019608	0.53019608
3	1.12486400	0.88899636	3.12160000	2.77509103	0.32034854	0.36034854
4	1.16985856	0.85480419	4.24646400	3.62989522	0.23549005	0.27549005
5	1.21665290	0.82192711	5.41632256	4.45182233	0.18462711	0.22462711
6	1.26531902	0.79031453	6.63297546	5.24213686	0.15076190	0.19076190
7	1.31593178	0.75991781	7.89829448	6.00205467	0.12660961	0.16660961
8	1.36856905	0.73069021	9.21422626	6.73274487	0.10852783	0.14852783
9	1.42331181	0.70258674	10.58279531	7.43533161	0.09449299	0.13449299
10	1.48024428	0.67556417	12.00610712	8.11089578	0.08329094	0.12329094
11	1.53945406	0.64958093	13.48635141	8.76047671	0.07414904	0.11414904
12	1.60103222	0.62459705	15.02580546	9.38507376	0.06655217	0.10655217
13	1.66507351	0.60057409	16.62683768	9.98564785	0.06014373	0.10014373
14	1.73167645	0.57747508	18.29191119	10.56312293	0.05466897	0.09466897
15	1.80094351	0.55526450	20.02358764	11.11838743	0.04994110	0.08994110
16	1.87298125	0.53390818	21.82453114	11.65229561	0.04582000	0.08582000
17	1.94790050	0.51337325	23.69751239	12.16566885	0.04219852	0.08219852
18	2.02581652	0.49362812	25.64541288	12.65929697	0.03899333	0.07899333
19	2.10684918	0.47464242	27.67122940	13.13393940	0.03613862	0.07613862
20	2.19112314	0.45638695	29.77807858	13.59032634	0.03358175	0.07358175
21	2.27876807	0.43883360	31.96920172	14.02915995	0.03128011	0.07128011
22	2.36991879	0.42195539	34.24796979	14.45111533	0.02919881	0.06919881
23	2.46471554	0.40572633	36.61788858	14.85684167	0.02730906	0.06730906
24	2.56330416	0.39012147	39.08260412	15.24696314	0.02558683	0.06558683
25	2.66583633	0.37511680	41.64590829	15.62207994	0.02401196	0.06401196
26	2.77246978	0.36068923	44.31174462	15.98276918	0.02256738	0.06256738
27	2.88336858	0.34681657	47.08421440	16.32958575	0.02123854	0.06123854
28	2.99870332	0.33347747	49.96758298	16.66306322	0.02001298	0.06001298
29	3.11865145	0.32065141	52.96628630	16.98371463	0.01887993	0.05887993
30	3.24339751	0.30831867	56.08493775	17.29203330	0.01783010	0.05783010
31	3.37313341	0.29646026	59.32833526	17.58849356	0.01685535	0.05685535
32	3.50805875	0.28505794	62.70146867	17.87355150	0.01594859	0.05594859
33	3.64838110	0.27409417	66.20952742	18.14764567	0.01510357	0.05510357
34	3.79431634	0.26355209	69.85790851	18.41119776	0.01431477	0.05431477
35	3.94608899	0.25341547	73.65222486	18.66461323	0.01357732	0.05357732
36	4.10393255	0.24366872	77.59831385	18.90828195	0.01288688	0.05288688
37	4.26808986	0.23429685	81.70224640	19.14257880	0.01223957	0.05223957
38	4.43881345	0.22528543	85.97033626	19.36786423	0.01163192	0.05163192
39	4.61636599	0.21662061	90.40914971	19.58448484	0.01106083	0.05106083
40	4.80102063	0.20828904	95.02551570	19.79277388	0.01052349	0.05052349
41	4.99306145	0.20027793	99.82653633	19.99305181	0.01001738	0.05001738
42	5.19278391	0.19257493	104.81959778	20.18562674	0.00954020	0.04954020
43	5.40049527	0.18516820	110.01238169	20.37079494	0.00908989	0.04908989
44	5.61651508	0.17804635	115.41287696	20.54884129	0.00866454	0.04866454
45	5.84117568	0.17119841	121.02939204	20.72003970	0.00826246	0.04826246
46	6.07482271	0.16461386	126.87056772	20.88465356	0.00788205	0.04788205
47	6.31781562	0.15828256	132.94539043	21.04293612	0.00752189	0.04752189
48	6.57052824	0.15219476	139.26320604	21.19513088	0.00718065	0.04718065
49	6.83334937	0.14634112	145.83373429	21.34147200	0.00685712	0.04685712
50	7.10668335	0.14071262	152.66708366	21.48218462	0.00655020	0.04655020

Rate $4\frac{1}{2}$%	A Compound Interest	B Present Value	C Amount of Annuity	D Present Value of Annuity	E Sinking Fund	F Amortization
n	$(1 + i)^n$	$\dfrac{1}{(1 + i)^n}$	$s_{\overline{n}|i}$	$a_{\overline{n}|i}$	$\dfrac{1}{s_{\overline{n}|i}}$	$\dfrac{1}{a_{\overline{n}|i}}$
1	1.04500000	0.95693780	1.00000000	0.95693780	1.00000000	1.04500000
2	1.09202500	0.91572995	2.04500000	1.87266775	0.48899756	0.53399756
3	1.14116613	0.87629660	3.13702500	2.74896435	0.31877336	0.36377336
4	1.19251860	0.83856134	4.27819112	3.58752570	0.23374365	0.27874365
5	1.24618194	0.80245105	5.47070973	4.38997674	0.18279164	0.22779164
6	1.30226012	0.76789574	6.71689166	5.15787248	0.14887839	0.19387839
7	1.36086183	0.73482846	8.01915179	5.89270094	0.12470147	0.16970147
8	1.42210061	0.70318513	9.38001362	6.59588607	0.10660965	0.15160965
9	1.48609514	0.67290443	10.80211423	7.26879050	0.09257447	0.13757447
10	1.55296942	0.64392768	12.28820937	7.91271818	0.08137882	0.12637882
11	1.62285305	0.61619874	13.84117879	8.52891692	0.07224818	0.11724818
12	1.69588143	0.58966386	15.46403184	9.11858078	0.06466619	0.10966619
13	1.77219610	0.56427164	17.15991327	9.68285242	0.05827535	0.10327535
14	1.85194492	0.53997286	18.93210937	10.22282528	0.05282032	0.09782032
15	1.93528244	0.51672044	20.78405429	10.73954573	0.04811381	0.09311381
16	2.02237015	0.49446932	22.71933673	11.23401505	0.04401537	0.08901537
17	2.11337681	0.47317639	24.74170689	11.70719143	0.04041758	0.08541758
18	2.20847877	0.45280037	26.85508370	12.15999180	0.03723690	0.08223690
19	2.30786031	0.43330179	29.06356246	12.59329359	0.03440734	0.07940734
20	2.41171402	0.41464286	31.37142277	13.00793645	0.03187614	0.07687614
21	2.52024116	0.39678743	33.78313680	13.40472388	0.02960057	0.07460057
22	2.63365201	0.37970089	36.30337795	13.78442476	0.02754565	0.07254565
23	2.75216635	0.36335013	38.93702996	14.14777489	0.02568249	0.07068249
24	2.87601383	0.34770347	41.68919631	14.49547837	0.02398703	0.06898703
25	3.00543446	0.33273060	44.56521015	14.82820896	0.02243903	0.06743903
26	3.14067901	0.31840248	47.57064460	15.14661145	0.02102137	0.06602137
27	3.28200956	0.30469137	50.71132361	15.45130282	0.01971946	0.06471946
28	3.42969999	0.29157069	53.99333317	15.74287351	0.01852081	0.06352081
29	3.58403649	0.27901502	57.42303316	16.02188853	0.01741461	0.06241461
30	3.74531813	0.26700002	61.00706966	16.28888854	0.01639154	0.06139154
31	3.91385745	0.25550241	64.75238779	16.54439095	0.01544345	0.06044345
32	4.08998104	0.24449991	68.66624524	16.78889086	0.01456320	0.05956320
33	4.27403018	0.23397121	72.75622628	17.02286207	0.01374453	0.05874453
34	4.46636154	0.22389589	77.03025646	17.24675796	0.01298191	0.05798191
35	4.66734781	0.21425444	81.49661800	17.46101240	0.01227045	0.05727045
36	4.87737846	0.20502817	86.16396581	17.66604058	0.01160578	0.05660578
37	5.09686049	0.19619921	91.04134427	17.86223979	0.01098402	0.05598402
38	5.32621921	0.18775044	96.13820476	18.04999023	0.01040169	0.05540169
39	5.56589908	0.17966549	101.46442398	18.22965572	0.00985567	0.05485567
40	5.81636454	0.17192870	107.03032306	18.40158442	0.00934315	0.05434315
41	6.07810094	0.16452507	112.84668760	18.56610949	0.00886158	0.05386158
42	6.35161548	0.15744026	118.92478854	18.72354975	0.00840868	0.05340868
43	6.63743818	0.15066054	125.27640402	18.87421029	0.00798235	0.05298235
44	6.93612290	0.14417276	131.91384220	19.01838305	0.00758071	0.05258071
45	7.24824843	0.13796437	138.84996510	19.15634742	0.00720202	0.05220202
46	7.57441961	0.13202332	146.09821353	19.28837074	0.00684471	0.05184471
47	7.91526849	0.12633810	153.67263314	19.41470884	0.00650734	0.05150734
48	8.27145557	0.12089771	161.58790163	19.53560654	0.00618858	0.05118858
49	8.64367107	0.11569158	169.85935720	19.65129813	0.00588722	0.05088722
50	9.03263627	0.11070965	178.50302828	19.76200778	0.00560215	0.05060215

Rate 5%	A Compound Interest	B Present Value	C Amount of Annuity	D Present Value of Annuity	E Sinking Fund	F Amortization
n	$(1+i)^n$	$\dfrac{1}{(1+i)^n}$	$s_{\overline{n}|i}$	$a_{\overline{n}|i}$	$\dfrac{1}{s_{\overline{n}|i}}$	$\dfrac{1}{a_{\overline{n}|i}}$
1	1.05000000	0.95238095	1.00000000	0.95238095	1.00000000	1.05000000
2	1.10250000	0.90702948	2.05000000	1.85941043	0.48780488	0.53780488
3	1.15762500	0.86383760	3.15250000	2.72324803	0.31720856	0.36720856
4	1.21550625	0.82270247	4.31012500	3.54595050	0.23201183	0.28201183
5	1.27628156	0.78352617	5.52563125	4.32947667	0.18097480	0.23097480
6	1.34009564	0.74621540	6.80191281	5.07569207	0.14701747	0.19701747
7	1.40710042	0.71068133	8.14200845	5.78637340	0.12281982	0.17281982
8	1.47745544	0.67683936	9.54910888	6.46321276	0.10472181	0.15472181
9	1.55132822	0.64460892	11.02656432	7.10782168	0.09069008	0.14069008
10	1.62889463	0.61391325	12.57789254	7.72173493	0.07950457	0.12950457
11	1.71033936	0.58467929	14.20678716	8.30641422	0.07038889	0.12038889
12	1.79585633	0.55683742	15.91712652	8.86325164	0.06282541	0.11282541
13	1.88564914	0.53032135	17.71298285	9.39357299	0.05645577	0.10645577
14	1.97993160	0.50506795	19.59863199	9.89864094	0.05102397	0.10102397
15	2.07892818	0.48101710	21.57856359	10.37965804	0.04634229	0.09634229
16	2.18287459	0.45811152	23.65749177	10.83776956	0.04226991	0.09226991
17	2.29201832	0.43629669	25.84036636	11.27406625	0.03869914	0.08869914
18	2.40661923	0.41552065	28.13238467	11.68958690	0.03554622	0.08554622
19	2.52695020	0.39573396	30.53900391	12.08532086	0.03274501	0.08274501
20	2.65329771	0.37688948	33.06595410	12.46221034	0.03024259	0.08024259
21	2.78596259	0.35894236	35.71925181	12.82115271	0.02799611	0.07799611
22	2.92526072	0.34184987	38.50521440	13.16300258	0.02597051	0.07597051
23	3.07152376	0.32557131	41.43047512	13.48857388	0.02413682	0.07413682
24	3.22509994	0.31006791	44.50199887	13.79864179	0.02247090	0.07247090
25	3.38635494	0.29530277	47.72709882	14.09394457	0.02095246	0.07095246
26	3.55567269	0.28124073	51.11345376	14.37518530	0.01956432	0.06956432
27	3.73345632	0.26784832	54.66912645	14.64303362	0.01829186	0.06829186
28	3.92012914	0.25509364	58.40258277	14.89812726	0.01712253	0.06712253
29	4.11613560	0.24294632	62.32271191	15.14107358	0.01604551	0.06604551
30	4.32194238	0.23137745	66.43884750	15.37245103	0.01505144	0.06505144
31	4.53803949	0.22035947	70.76078988	15.59281050	0.01413212	0.06413212
32	4.76494147	0.20986617	75.29882937	15.80267667	0.01328042	0.06328042
33	5.00318854	0.19978254	80.06377084	16.00254921	0.01249004	0.06249004
34	5.25334797	0.19035480	85.06695938	16.19290401	0.01175545	0.06175545
35	5.51601537	0.18129029	90.32030735	16.37419429	0.01107171	0.06107171
36	5.79181614	0.17265741	95.83632272	16.54685171	0.01043446	0.06043446
37	6.08140694	0.16443563	101.62813886	16.71128734	0.00983979	0.05983979
38	6.38547729	0.15660536	107.70954580	16.86789271	0.00928423	0.05928423
39	6.70475115	0.14914797	114.09502309	17.01704067	0.00876462	0.05876462
40	7.03998871	0.14204568	120.79977424	17.15908635	0.00827816	0.05827816
41	7.39198815	0.13528160	127.83976295	17.29436796	0.00782229	0.05782229
42	7.76158756	0.12883962	135.23175110	17.42320758	0.00739471	0.05739471
43	8.14966693	0.12270440	142.99333866	17.54591198	0.00699333	0.05699333
44	8.55715028	0.11686133	151.14300559	17.66277331	0.00661625	0.05661625
45	8.98500779	0.11129651	159.70015587	17.77406982	0.00626173	0.05626173
46	9.43425818	0.10599668	168.68516366	17.88006650	0.00592820	0.05592820
47	9.90597109	0.10094921	178.11942185	17.98101571	0.00561421	0.05561421
48	10.40126965	0.09614211	188.02539294	18.07715782	0.00531843	0.05531843
49	10.92133313	0.09156391	198.42666259	18.16872173	0.00503965	0.05503965
50	11.46739979	0.08720373	209.34799572	18.25592546	0.00477674	0.05477674

Rate $5\frac{1}{2}$%	A Compound Interest	B Present Value	C Amount of Annuity	D Present Value of Annuity	E Sinking Fund	F Amortization
n	$(1 + i)^n$	$\dfrac{1}{(1 + i)^n}$	$s_{\overline{n}\vert i}$	$a_{\overline{n}\vert i}$	$\dfrac{1}{s_{\overline{n}\vert i}}$	$\dfrac{1}{a_{\overline{n}\vert i}}$
1	1.05500000	0.94786730	1.00000000	0.94786730	1.00000000	1.05500000
2	1.11302500	0.89845242	2.05500000	1.84631971	0.48661800	0.54161800
3	1.17424138	0.85161366	3.16802500	2.69793338	0.31565407	0.37065407
4	1.23882465	0.80721674	4.34226637	3.50515012	0.23029449	0.28529449
5	1.30696001	0.76513435	5.58109103	4.27028448	0.17917644	0.23417644
6	1.37884281	0.72524583	6.88805103	4.99553031	0.14517895	0.20017895
7	1.45467916	0.68743681	8.26689384	5.68296712	0.12096442	0.17596442
8	1.53468651	0.65159887	9.72157300	6.33456599	0.10286401	0.15786401
9	1.61909427	0.61762926	11.25625951	6.95219525	0.08883946	0.14383946
10	1.70814446	0.58543058	12.87535379	7.53762583	0.07766777	0.13266777
11	1.80209240	0.55491050	14.58349825	8.09253633	0.06857065	0.12357065
12	1.90120749	0.52598152	16.38559065	8.61851785	0.06102923	0.11602923
13	2.00577390	0.49856068	18.28679814	9.11707853	0.05468426	0.10968426
14	2.11609146	0.47256937	20.29257203	9.58964790	0.04927912	0.10427912
15	2.23247649	0.44793305	22.40866350	10.03758094	0.04462560	0.09962560
16	2.35526270	0.42458109	24.64113999	10.46216203	0.04058254	0.09558254
17	2.48480215	0.40244653	26.99640269	10.86460856	0.03704197	0.09204197
18	2.62146627	0.38146590	29.48120483	11.24607447	0.03391992	0.08891992
19	2.76564691	0.36157906	32.10267110	11.60765352	0.03115006	0.08615006
20	2.91775749	0.34272896	34.86831801	11.95038248	0.02867933	0.08367933
21	3.07823415	0.32486158	37.78607550	12.27524406	0.02646478	0.08146478
22	3.24753703	0.30792567	40.86430965	12.58316973	0.02447123	0.07947123
23	3.42615157	0.29187267	44.11184669	12.87504239	0.02266965	0.07766965
24	3.61458990	0.27665656	47.53799825	13.15169895	0.02103580	0.07603580
25	3.81339235	0.26223370	51.15258816	13.41393266	0.01954935	0.07454935
26	4.02312893	0.24856275	54.96598051	13.66249541	0.01819307	0.07319307
27	4.24440102	0.23560450	58.98910943	13.89809991	0.01695228	0.07195228
28	4.47784307	0.22332181	63.23351045	14.12142172	0.01581440	0.07081440
29	4.72412444	0.21167944	67.71135353	14.33310116	0.01476857	0.06976857
30	4.98395129	0.20064402	72.43547797	14.53374517	0.01380539	0.06880539
31	5.25806861	0.19018390	77.41942926	14.72392907	0.01291665	0.06791665
32	5.54726238	0.18026910	82.67749787	14.90419817	0.01209519	0.06709519
33	5.85236181	0.17087119	88.22476025	15.07506936	0.01133469	0.06633469
34	6.17424171	0.16196321	94.07712207	15.23703257	0.01062958	0.06562958
35	6.51382501	0.15351963	100.25136378	15.39055220	0.00997493	0.06497493
36	6.87208538	0.14551624	106.76518879	15.53606843	0.00936635	0.06436635
37	7.25005008	0.13793008	113.63727417	15.67399851	0.00879993	0.06379993
38	7.64880283	0.13073941	120.88732425	15.80473793	0.00827217	0.06327217
39	8.06948699	0.12392362	128.53612708	15.92866154	0.00777991	0.06277991
40	8.51330877	0.11746314	136.60561407	16.04612469	0.00732034	0.06232034
41	8.98154076	0.11133947	145.11892285	16.15746416	0.00689090	0.06189090
42	9.47552550	0.10553504	154.10046360	16.26299920	0.00648927	0.06148927
43	9.99667940	0.10003322	163.57598910	16.36303242	0.00611337	0.06111337
44	10.54649677	0.09481822	173.57266850	16.45785063	0.00576128	0.06076128
45	11.12655409	0.08987509	184.11916527	16.54772572	0.00543127	0.06043127
46	11.73851456	0.08518965	195.24571936	16.63291537	0.00512175	0.06012175
47	12.38413287	0.08074849	206.98423392	16.71366386	0.00483129	0.05983129
48	13.06526017	0.07653885	219.36836679	16.79020271	0.00455854	0.05955854
49	13.78384948	0.07254867	232.43362696	16.86275139	0.00430230	0.05930230
50	14.54196120	0.06876652	246.21747645	16.93151790	0.00406145	0.05906145

Rate 6%	A Compound Interest	B Present Value	C Amount of Annuity	D Present Value of Annuity	E Sinking Fund	F Amortization
n	$(1 + i)^n$	$\dfrac{1}{(1 + i)^n}$	$s_{\overline{n}\rvert i}$	$a_{\overline{n}\rvert i}$	$\dfrac{1}{s_{\overline{n}\rvert i}}$	$\dfrac{1}{a_{\overline{n}\rvert i}}$
1	1.06000000	0.94339623	1.00000000	0.94339623	1.00000000	1.06000000
2	1.12360000	0.88999644	2.06000000	1.83339267	0.48543689	0.54543689
3	1.19101600	0.83961928	3.18360000	2.67301195	0.31410981	0.37410981
4	1.26247696	0.79209366	4.37461600	3.46510561	0.22859149	0.28859149
5	1.33822558	0.74725817	5.63709296	4.21236379	0.17739640	0.23739640
6	1.41851911	0.70496054	6.97531854	4.91732433	0.14336263	0.20336263
7	1.50363026	0.66505711	8.39383765	5.58238144	0.11913502	0.17913502
8	1.59384807	0.62741237	9.89746791	6.20979381	0.10103594	0.16103594
9	1.68947896	0.59189846	11.49131598	6.80169227	0.08702224	0.14702224
10	1.79084770	0.55839478	13.18079494	7.36008705	0.07586796	0.13586796
11	1.89829856	0.52678753	14.97164264	7.88687458	0.06679294	0.12679294
12	2.01219647	0.49696936	16.86994120	8.38384394	0.05927703	0.11927703
13	2.13292826	0.46883902	18.88213767	8.85268296	0.05296011	0.11296011
14	2.26090396	0.44230096	21.01506593	9.29498393	0.04758491	0.10758491
15	2.39655819	0.41726506	23.27596988	9.71224899	0.04296276	0.10296276
16	2.54035168	0.39364628	25.67252808	10.10589527	0.03895214	0.09895214
17	2.69277279	0.37136442	28.21287976	10.47725969	0.03544480	0.09544480
18	2.85433915	0.35034379	30.90565255	10.82760348	0.03235654	0.09235654
19	3.02559950	0.33051301	33.75999170	11.15811649	0.02962086	0.08962086
20	3.20713547	0.31180473	36.78559120	11.46992122	0.02718456	0.08718456
21	3.39956360	0.29415540	39.99272668	11.76407662	0.02500455	0.08500455
22	3.60353742	0.27750510	43.39229028	12.04158172	0.02304557	0.08304557
23	3.81974966	0.26179726	46.99582769	12.30337898	0.02127848	0.08127848
24	4.04893464	0.24697855	50.81557735	12.55035753	0.01967900	0.07967900
25	4.29187072	0.23299863	54.86451200	12.78335616	0.01822672	0.07822672
26	4.54938296	0.21981003	59.15638272	13.00316619	0.01690435	0.07690435
27	4.82234594	0.20736795	63.70576568	13.21053414	0.01569717	0.07569717
28	5.11168670	0.19563014	68.52811162	13.40616428	0.01459255	0.07459255
29	5.41838790	0.18455674	73.63979832	13.59072102	0.01357961	0.07357961
30	5.74349117	0.17411013	79.05818622	13.76483115	0.01264891	0.07264891
31	6.08810064	0.16425484	84.80167739	13.92908599	0.01179222	0.07179222
32	6.45338668	0.15495740	90.88977803	14.08404339	0.01100234	0.07100234
33	6.84058988	0.14618622	97.34316471	14.23022961	0.01027293	0.07027293
34	7.25102528	0.13791153	104.18375460	14.36814114	0.00959843	0.06959843
35	7.68608679	0.13010522	111.43477987	14.49824636	0.00897386	0.06897386
36	8.14725200	0.12274077	119.12086666	14.62098713	0.00839483	0.06839483
37	8.63608712	0.11579318	127.26811866	14.73678031	0.00785743	0.06785743
38	9.15425235	0.10923885	135.90420578	14.84601916	0.00735812	0.06735812
39	9.70350749	0.10305552	145.05845813	14.94907468	0.00689377	0.06689377
40	10.28571794	0.09722219	154.76196562	15.04629687	0.00646154	0.06646154
41	10.90286101	0.09171905	165.04768356	15.13801592	0.00605886	0.06605886
42	11.55703267	0.08652740	175.95054457	15.22454332	0.00568342	0.06568342
43	12.25045463	0.08162962	187.50757724	15.30617294	0.00533312	0.06533312
44	12.98548191	0.07700908	199.75803188	15.38318202	0.00500606	0.06500606
45	13.76461083	0.07265007	212.74351379	15.45583209	0.00470050	0.06470050
46	14.59048748	0.06853781	226.50812462	15.52436990	0.00441485	0.06441485
47	15.46591673	0.06465831	241.09861210	15.58902821	0.00414768	0.06414768
48	16.39387173	0.06099840	256.56452882	15.65002661	0.00389765	0.06389765
49	17.37750403	0.05754566	272.95840055	15.70757227	0.00366356	0.06366356
50	18.42015427	0.05428836	290.33590458	15.76186064	0.00344429	0.06344429

Rate $6\frac{1}{2}$%	A Compound Interest	B Present Value	C Amount of Annuity	D Present Value of Annuity	E Sinking Fund	F Amortization
n	$(1 + i)^n$	$\dfrac{1}{(1 + i)^n}$	$s_{\overline{n}|i}$	$a_{\overline{n}|i}$	$\dfrac{1}{s_{\overline{n}|i}}$	$\dfrac{1}{a_{\overline{n}|i}}$
1	1.06500000	0.93896714	1.00000000	0.93896714	1.00000000	1.06500000
2	1.13422500	0.88165928	2.06500000	1.82062642	0.48426150	0.54926150
3	1.20794963	0.82784909	3.19922500	2.64847551	0.31257570	0.37757570
4	1.28646635	0.77732309	4.40717462	3.42579860	0.22690274	0.29190274
5	1.37008666	0.72988084	5.69364098	4.15567944	0.17563454	0.24063454
6	1.45914230	0.68533412	7.06372764	4.84101356	0.14156831	0.20656831
7	1.55398655	0.64350621	8.52286994	5.48451977	0.11733137	0.18233137
8	1.65499567	0.60423119	10.07685648	6.08875096	0.09923730	0.16423730
9	1.76257039	0.56735323	11.73185215	6.65610419	0.08523803	0.15023803
10	1.87713747	0.53272604	13.49442254	7.18883022	0.07410469	0.13910469
11	1.99915140	0.50021224	15.37156001	7.68904246	0.06505521	0.13005521
12	2.12909624	0.46968285	17.37071141	8.15872532	0.05756817	0.12256817
13	2.26748750	0.44101676	19.49980765	8.59974208	0.05128256	0.11628256
14	2.41487418	0.41410025	21.76729515	9.01384233	0.04594048	0.11094048
15	2.57184101	0.38882652	24.18216933	9.40266885	0.04135278	0.10635278
16	2.73901067	0.36509533	26.75401034	9.76776418	0.03737757	0.10237757
17	2.91704637	0.34281251	29.49302101	10.11057670	0.03390633	0.09890633
18	3.10655438	0.32188969	32.41006738	10.43246638	0.03085461	0.09585461
19	3.30858691	0.30224384	35.51672176	10.73471022	0.02815575	0.09315575
20	3.52364506	0.28379703	38.82530867	11.01850725	0.02575640	0.09075640
21	3.75268199	0.26647608	42.34895373	11.28498333	0.02361333	0.08861333
22	3.99660632	0.25021228	46.10163573	11.53519562	0.02169120	0.08669120
23	4.25638573	0.23494111	50.09824205	11.77013673	0.01996078	0.08496078
24	4.53305081	0.22060198	54.35462778	11.99073871	0.01839770	0.08339770
25	4.82769911	0.20713801	58.88767859	12.19787673	0.01698148	0.08198148
26	5.14149955	0.19449579	63.71537769	12.39237251	0.01569480	0.08069480
27	5.47569702	0.18262515	68.85687725	12.57499766	0.01452288	0.07952288
28	5.83161733	0.17147902	74.33257427	12.74647668	0.01345305	0.07845305
29	6.21067245	0.16101316	80.16419159	12.90748984	0.01247440	0.07747440
30	6.61436616	0.15118607	86.37486405	13.05867591	0.01157744	0.07657744
31	7.04429996	0.14195875	92.98923021	13.20063465	0.01075393	0.07575393
32	7.50217946	0.13329460	100.03353017	13.33392925	0.00999665	0.07499665
33	7.98982113	0.12515925	107.53570963	13.45908850	0.00929924	0.07429924
34	8.50915950	0.11752042	115.52553076	13.57660892	0.00865610	0.07365610
35	9.06225487	0.11034781	124.03469026	13.68695673	0.00806226	0.07306226
36	9.65130143	0.10361297	133.09694513	13.79056970	0.00751332	0.07251332
37	10.27863603	0.09728917	142.74824656	13.88785887	0.00700534	0.07200534
38	10.94674737	0.09135134	153.02688259	13.97921021	0.00653480	0.07153480
39	11.65828595	0.08577590	163.97362996	14.06498611	0.00609854	0.07109854
40	12.41607453	0.08054075	175.63191590	14.14552687	0.00569373	0.07069373
41	13.22311938	0.07562512	188.04799044	14.22115199	0.00531779	0.07031779
42	14.08262214	0.07100950	201.27110981	14.29216149	0.00496842	0.06996842
43	14.99799258	0.06667559	215.35373195	14.35883708	0.00464352	0.06964352
44	15.97286209	0.06260619	230.35172453	14.42144327	0.00434119	0.06934119
45	17.01109813	0.05878515	246.32458662	14.48022842	0.00405968	0.06905968
46	18.11681951	0.05519733	263.33568475	14.53542575	0.00379743	0.06879743
47	19.29441278	0.05182848	281.45250426	14.58725422	0.00355300	0.06855300
48	20.54854961	0.04866524	300.74691704	14.63591946	0.00332505	0.06832505
49	21.88420533	0.04569506	321.29546665	14.68161451	0.00311240	0.06811240
50	23.30667868	0.04290616	343.17967198	14.72452067	0.00291393	0.06791393

Rate 7%	A Compound Interest	B Present Value	C Amount of Annuity	D Present Value of Annuity	E Sinking Fund	F Amortization
n	$(1 + i)^n$	$\dfrac{1}{(1 + i)^n}$	$s_{\overline{n}|i}$	$a_{\overline{n}|i}$	$\dfrac{1}{s_{\overline{n}|i}}$	$\dfrac{1}{a_{\overline{n}|i}}$
1	1.07000000	0.93457944	1.00000000	0.93457944	1.00000000	1.07000000
2	1.14490000	0.87343873	2.07000000	1.80801817	0.48309179	0.55309179
3	1.22504300	0.81629788	3.21490000	2.62431604	0.31105167	0.38105167
4	1.31079601	0.76289521	4.43994300	3.38721126	0.22522812	0.29522812
5	1.40255173	0.71298618	5.75073901	4.10019744	0.17389069	0.24389069
6	1.50073035	0.66634222	7.15329074	4.76653966	0.13979580	0.20979580
7	1.60578148	0.62274974	8.65402109	5.38928940	0.11555322	0.18555322
8	1.71818618	0.58200910	10.25980257	5.97129851	0.09746776	0.16746776
9	1.83845921	0.54393374	11.97798875	6.51523225	0.08348647	0.15348647
10	1.96715136	0.50834929	13.81644796	7.02358154	0.07237750	0.14237750
11	2.10485195	0.47509280	15.78359932	7.49867434	0.06335690	0.13335690
12	2.25219159	0.44401196	17.88845127	7.94268630	0.05590199	0.12590199
13	2.40984500	0.41496445	20.14064286	8.35765074	0.04965085	0.11965085
14	2.57853415	0.38781724	22.55048786	8.74546799	0.04434494	0.11434494
15	2.75903154	0.36244602	25.12902201	9.10791401	0.03979462	0.10979462
16	2.95216375	0.33873460	27.88805355	9.44664860	0.03585765	0.10585765
17	3.15881521	0.31657439	30.84021730	9.76322299	0.03242519	0.10242519
18	3.37993228	0.29586392	33.99903251	10.05908691	0.02941260	0.09941260
19	3.61652754	0.27650833	37.37896479	10.33559524	0.02675301	0.09675301
20	3.86968446	0.25841900	40.99549232	10.59401425	0.02439293	0.09439293
21	4.14056237	0.24151309	44.86517678	10.83552733	0.02228900	0.09228900
22	4.43040174	0.22571317	49.00573916	11.06124050	0.02040577	0.09040577
23	4.74052986	0.21094688	53.43614090	11.27218738	0.01871393	0.08871393
24	5.07236695	0.19714662	58.17667076	11.46933400	0.01718902	0.08718902
25	5.42743264	0.18424918	63.24903772	11.65358318	0.01581052	0.08581052
26	5.80735292	0.17219549	68.67647036	11.82577867	0.01456103	0.08456103
27	6.21386763	0.16093037	74.48382328	11.98670904	0.01342573	0.08342573
28	6.64883836	0.15040221	80.69769091	12.13711125	0.01239193	0.08239193
29	7.11425705	0.14056282	87.34652927	12.27767407	0.01144865	0.08144865
30	7.61225504	0.13136712	94.46078632	12.40904118	0.01058640	0.08058640
31	8.14511290	0.12277301	102.07304137	12.53181419	0.00979691	0.07979691
32	8.71527080	0.11474113	110.21815426	12.64655532	0.00907292	0.07907292
33	9.32533975	0.10723470	118.93342506	12.75379002	0.00840807	0.07840807
34	9.97811354	0.10021934	128.25876481	12.85400936	0.00779674	0.07779674
35	10.67658148	0.09366294	138.23687835	12.94767230	0.00723396	0.07723396
36	11.42394219	0.08753546	148.91345984	13.03520776	0.00671531	0.07671531
37	12.22361814	0.08180884	160.33740202	13.11701660	0.00623685	0.07623685
38	13.07927141	0.07645686	172.56102017	13.19347345	0.00579505	0.07579505
39	13.99482041	0.07145501	185.64029158	13.26492846	0.00538676	0.07538676
40	14.97445784	0.06678038	199.63511199	13.33170884	0.00500914	0.07500914
41	16.02266989	0.06241157	214.60956983	13.39412041	0.00465962	0.07465962
42	17.14425678	0.05832857	230.63223972	13.45244898	0.00433591	0.07433591
43	18.34435475	0.05451268	247.77649650	13.50696167	0.00403590	0.07403590
44	19.62845959	0.05094643	266.12085125	13.55790810	0.00375769	0.07375769
45	21.00245176	0.04761349	285.74931084	13.60552159	0.00349957	0.07349957
46	22.47262338	0.04449859	306.75176260	13.65002018	0.00325996	0.07325996
47	24.04570702	0.04158747	329.22438598	13.69160764	0.00303744	0.07303744
48	25.72890651	0.03886679	353.27009300	13.73047443	0.00283070	0.07283070
49	27.52992997	0.03632410	378.99899951	13.76679853	0.00263853	0.07263853
50	29.45702506	0.03394776	406.52892947	13.80074629	0.00245985	0.07245985

Rate $7\frac{1}{2}$%	A Compound Interest	B Present Value	C Amount of Annuity	D Present Value of Annuity	E Sinking Fund	F Amortization
n	$(1 + i)^n$	$\dfrac{1}{(1 + i)^n}$	$s_{\overline{n}|i}$	$a_{\overline{n}|i}$	$\dfrac{1}{s_{\overline{n}|i}}$	$\dfrac{1}{a_{\overline{n}|i}}$
1	1.07500000	0.93023256	1.00000000	0.93023256	1.00000000	1.07500000
2	1.15562500	0.86533261	2.07500000	1.79556517	0.48192771	0.55692771
3	1.24229688	0.80496057	3.23062500	2.60052574	0.30953763	0.38453763
4	1.33546914	0.74880053	4.47292187	3.34932627	0.22356751	0.29856751
5	1.43562933	0.69655863	5.80839102	4.04588490	0.17216472	0.24716472
6	1.54330153	0.64796152	7.24402034	4.69384642	0.13804489	0.21304489
7	1.65904914	0.60275490	8.78732187	5.29660132	0.11380032	0.18880032
8	1.78347783	0.56070223	10.44637101	5.85730355	0.09572702	0.17072702
9	1.91723866	0.52158347	12.22984883	6.37888703	0.08176716	0.15676716
10	2.06103156	0.48519393	14.14708750	6.86408096	0.07068593	0.14568593
11	2.21560893	0.45134319	16.20811906	7.31542415	0.06169747	0.13669747
12	2.38177960	0.41985413	18.42372799	7.73527827	0.05427783	0.12927783
13	2.56041307	0.39056198	20.80550759	8.12584026	0.04806420	0.12306420
14	2.75244405	0.36331347	23.36592066	8.48915373	0.04279737	0.11779737
15	2.95887735	0.33796602	26.11836470	8.82711975	0.03828724	0.11328724
16	3.18079315	0.31438699	29.07724206	9.14150674	0.03439116	0.10939116
17	3.41935264	0.29245302	32.25803521	9.43395976	0.03100003	0.10600003
18	3.67580409	0.27204932	35.67738785	9.70600908	0.02802896	0.10302896
19	3.95148940	0.25306913	39.35319194	9.95907821	0.02541090	0.10041090
20	4.24785110	0.23541315	43.30468134	10.19449136	0.02309219	0.09809219
21	4.56643993	0.21898897	47.55253244	10.41348033	0.02102937	0.09602937
22	4.90892293	0.20371067	52.11897237	10.61719101	0.01918687	0.09418687
23	5.27709215	0.18949830	57.02789530	10.80668931	0.01753528	0.09253528
24	5.67287406	0.17627749	62.30498744	10.98296680	0.01605008	0.09105008
25	6.09833961	0.16397906	67.97786150	11.14694586	0.01471067	0.08971067
26	6.55571508	0.15253866	74.07620112	11.29948452	0.01349961	0.08849961
27	7.04739371	0.14189643	80.63191620	11.44138095	0.01240204	0.08740204
28	7.57594824	0.13199668	87.67930991	11.57337763	0.01140520	0.08640520
29	8.14414436	0.12278761	95.25525816	11.69616524	0.01049811	0.08549811
30	8.75495519	0.11422103	103.39940252	11.81038627	0.00967124	0.08467124
31	9.41157683	0.10625212	112.15435771	11.91663839	0.00891628	0.08391628
32	10.11744509	0.09883918	121.56593454	12.01547757	0.00822599	0.08322599
33	10.87625347	0.09194343	131.68337963	12.10742099	0.00759397	0.08259397
34	11.69197248	0.08552877	142.55963310	12.19294976	0.00701461	0.08201461
35	12.56887042	0.07956164	154.25160558	12.27251141	0.00648291	0.08148291
36	13.51153570	0.07401083	166.82047600	12.34652224	0.00599447	0.08099447
37	14.52490088	0.06884729	180.33201170	12.41536952	0.00554533	0.08054533
38	15.61426844	0.06404399	194.85691258	12.47941351	0.00513197	0.08013197
39	16.78533858	0.05957580	210.47118102	12.53898931	0.00475124	0.07975124
40	18.04423897	0.05541935	227.25651960	12.59440866	0.00440031	0.07940031
41	19.39755689	0.05155288	245.30075857	12.64596155	0.00407663	0.07907663
42	20.85237366	0.04795617	264.69831546	12.69391772	0.00377789	0.07877789
43	22.41630168	0.04461039	285.55068912	12.73852811	0.00350201	0.07850201
44	24.09752431	0.04149804	307.96699080	12.78002615	0.00324710	0.07824710
45	25.90483863	0.03860283	332.06451511	12.81862898	0.00301146	0.07801146
46	27.84770153	0.03590961	357.96935375	12.85453858	0.00279354	0.07779354
47	29.93627915	0.03340428	385.81705528	12.88794287	0.00259190	0.07759190
48	32.18150008	0.03107375	415.75333442	12.91901662	0.00240527	0.07740527
49	34.59511259	0.02890582	447.93483451	12.94792244	0.00223247	0.07723247
50	37.18974603	0.02688913	482.52994709	12.97481157	0.00207241	0.07707241

Rate 8%	A Compound Interest	B Present Value	C Amount of Annuity	D Present Value of Annuity	E Sinking Fund	F Amortization
n	$(1 + i)^n$	$\dfrac{1}{(1 + i)^n}$	$s_{\overline{n}|i}$	$a_{\overline{n}|i}$	$\dfrac{1}{s_{\overline{n}|i}}$	$\dfrac{1}{a_{\overline{n}|i}}$
1	1.08000000	0.92592593	1.00000000	0.92592593	1.00000000	1.08000000
2	1.16640000	0.85733882	2.08000000	1.78326475	0.48076923	0.56076923
3	1.25971200	0.79383224	3.24640000	2.57709699	0.30803351	0.38803351
4	1.36048896	0.73502985	4.50611200	3.31212684	0.22192080	0.30192080
5	1.46932808	0.68058320	5.86660096	3.99271004	0.17045645	0.25045645
6	1.58687432	0.63016963	7.33592904	4.62287966	0.13631539	0.21631539
7	1.71382427	0.58349040	8.92280336	5.20637006	0.11207240	0.19207240
8	1.85093021	0.54026888	10.63662763	5.74663894	0.09401476	0.17401476
9	1.99900463	0.50024897	12.48755784	6.24688791	0.08007971	0.16007971
10	2.15892500	0.46319349	14.48656247	6.71008140	0.06902949	0.14902949
11	2.33163900	0.42888286	16.64548746	7.13896426	0.06007634	0.14007634
12	2.51817012	0.39711376	18.97712646	7.53607802	0.05269502	0.13269502
13	2.71962373	0.36769792	21.49529658	7.90377594	0.04652181	0.12652181
14	2.93719362	0.34046104	24.21492030	8.24423698	0.04129685	0.12129685
15	3.17216911	0.31524170	27.15211393	8.55947869	0.03682954	0.11682954
16	3.42594264	0.29189047	30.32428304	8.85136916	0.03297687	0.11297687
17	3.70001805	0.27026895	33.75022569	9.12163811	0.02962943	0.10962943
18	3.99601950	0.25024903	37.45024374	9.37188714	0.02670210	0.10670210
19	4.31570106	0.23171206	41.44626324	9.60359920	0.02412763	0.10412763
20	4.66095714	0.21454821	45.76196430	9.81814741	0.02185221	0.10185221
21	5.03383372	0.19865575	50.42292144	10.01680316	0.01983225	0.09983225
22	5.43654041	0.18394051	55.45675516	10.20074366	0.01803207	0.09803207
23	5.87146365	0.17031528	60.89329557	10.37105895	0.01642217	0.09642217
24	6.34118074	0.15769934	66.76475922	10.52875828	0.01497796	0.09497796
25	6.84847520	0.14601790	73.10593995	10.67477619	0.01367878	0.09367878
26	7.39635321	0.13520176	79.95441515	10.80997795	0.01250713	0.09250713
27	7.98806147	0.12518682	87.35076836	10.93516477	0.01144810	0.09144810
28	8.62710639	0.11591372	95.33882983	11.05107849	0.01048891	0.09048891
29	9.31727490	0.10732752	103.96593622	11.15840601	0.00961854	0.08961854
30	10.06265689	0.09937733	113.28321111	11.25778334	0.00882743	0.08882743
31	10.86766944	0.09201605	123.34586800	11.34979939	0.00810728	0.08810728
32	11.73708300	0.08520005	134.21353744	11.43499944	0.00745081	0.08745081
33	12.67604964	0.07888893	145.95062044	11.51388837	0.00685163	0.08685163
34	13.69013361	0.07304531	158.62667007	11.58693367	0.00630411	0.08630411
35	14.78534429	0.06763454	172.31680368	11.65456822	0.00580326	0.08580326
36	15.96817184	0.06262458	187.10214797	11.71719279	0.00534467	0.08534467
37	17.24562558	0.05798572	203.07031981	11.77517851	0.00492440	0.08492440
38	18.62527563	0.05369048	220.31594540	11.82886899	0.00453894	0.08453894
39	20.11529768	0.04971341	238.94122103	11.87858240	0.00418513	0.08418513
40	21.72452150	0.04603093	259.05651871	11.92461333	0.00386016	0.08386016
41	23.46248322	0.04262123	280.78104021	11.96723457	0.00356149	0.08356149
42	25.33948187	0.03946411	304.24352342	12.00669867	0.00328684	0.08328684
43	27.36664042	0.03654084	329.58300530	12.04323951	0.00303414	0.08303414
44	29.55597166	0.03383411	356.94964572	12.07707362	0.00280152	0.08280152
45	31.92044939	0.03132788	386.50561738	12.10840150	0.00258728	0.08258728
46	34.47408534	0.02900730	418.42606677	12.13740880	0.00238991	0.08238991
47	37.23201217	0.02685861	452.90015211	12.16426741	0.00220799	0.08220799
48	40.21057314	0.02486908	490.13216428	12.18913649	0.00204027	0.08204027
49	43.42741899	0.02302693	530.34273742	12.21216341	0.00188557	0.08188557
50	46.90161251	0.02132123	573.77015642	12.23348464	0.00174286	0.08174286

Rate 9%	A Compound Interest	B Present Value	C Amount of Annuity	D Present Value of Annuity	E Sinking Fund	F Amortization
n	$(1 + i)^n$	$\dfrac{1}{(1 + i)^n}$	$s_{\overline{n}\,i}$	$a_{\overline{n}\,i}$	$\dfrac{1}{s_{\overline{n}\,i}}$	$\dfrac{1}{a_{\overline{n}\,i}}$
1	1.09000000	0.91743119	1.00000000	0.91743119	1.00000000	1.09000000
2	1.18810000	0.84167999	2.09000000	1.75911119	0.47846890	0.56846890
3	1.29502900	0.77218348	3.27810000	2.53129467	0.30505476	0.39505476
4	1.41158161	0.70842521	4.57312900	3.23971988	0.21866866	0.30866866
5	1.53862395	0.64993139	5.98471061	3.88965126	0.16709246	0.25709246
6	1.67710011	0.59626733	7.52333456	4.48591859	0.13291978	0.22291978
7	1.82803912	0.54703424	9.20043468	5.03295284	0.10869052	0.19869052
8	1.99256264	0.50186628	11.02847380	5.53481911	0.09067438	0.18067438
9	2.17189328	0.46042778	13.02103644	5.99524689	0.07679880	0.16679880
10	2.36736367	0.42241081	15.19292972	6.41765770	0.06582009	0.15582009
11	2.58042641	0.38753285	17.56029339	6.80519055	0.05694666	0.14694666
12	2.81266478	0.35553473	20.14071980	7.16072528	0.04965066	0.13965066
13	3.06580461	0.32617865	22.95338458	7.48690392	0.04356656	0.13356656
14	3.34172703	0.29924647	26.01918919	7.78615039	0.03843317	0.12843317
15	3.64248246	0.27453804	29.36091622	8.06068843	0.03405888	0.12405888
16	3.97030588	0.25186976	33.00339868	8.31255819	0.03029991	0.12029991
17	4.32763341	0.23107318	36.97370456	8.54363137	0.02704625	0.11704625
18	4.71712042	0.21199374	41.30133797	8.75562511	0.02421229	0.11421229
19	5.14166125	0.19448967	46.01845839	8.95011478	0.02173041	0.11173041
20	5.60441077	0.17843089	51.16011964	9.12854567	0.01954648	0.10954648
21	6.10880774	0.16369806	56.76453041	9.29224373	0.01761663	0.10761663
22	6.65860043	0.15018171	62.87333815	9.44242544	0.01590499	0.10590499
23	7.25787447	0.13778139	69.53193858	9.58020683	0.01438188	0.10438188
24	7.91108317	0.12640494	76.78981305	9.70661177	0.01302256	0.10302256
25	8.62308066	0.11596784	84.70089623	9.82257960	0.01180625	0.10180625
26	9.39915792	0.10639251	93.32397689	9.92897211	0.01071536	0.10071536
27	10.24508213	0.09760781	102.72313481	10.02657992	0.00973491	0.09973491
28	11.16713952	0.08954845	112.96821694	10.11612837	0.00885205	0.09885205
29	12.17218208	0.08215454	124.13535646	10.19828291	0.00805572	0.09805572
30	13.26767847	0.07537114	136.30753855	10.27365404	0.00733635	0.09733635
31	14.46176953	0.06914783	149.57521702	10.34280187	0.00668560	0.09668560
32	15.76332879	0.06343838	164.03698655	10.40624025	0.00609619	0.09609619
33	17.18202838	0.05820035	179.80031534	10.46444060	0.00556173	0.09556173
34	18.72841093	0.05339481	196.98234372	10.51783541	0.00507660	0.09507660
35	20.41396792	0.04898607	215.71075465	10.56682148	0.00463584	0.09463584
36	22.25122503	0.04494135	236.12472257	10.61176282	0.00423505	0.09423505
37	24.25383528	0.04123059	258.37594760	10.65299342	0.00387033	0.09387033
38	26.43668046	0.03782623	282.62978288	10.69081965	0.00353820	0.09353820
39	28.81598170	0.03470296	309.06646334	10.72552261	0.00323555	0.09323555
40	31.40942005	0.03183758	337.88244504	10.75736020	0.00295961	0.09295961
41	34.23626789	0.02920879	369.29186510	10.78656899	0.00270789	0.09270789
42	37.31753197	0.02679706	403.52813296	10.81336604	0.00247814	0.09247814
43	40.67610984	0.02458446	440.84566492	10.83795050	0.00226837	0.09226837
44	44.33695973	0.02255455	481.52177477	10.86050504	0.00207675	0.09207675
45	48.32728610	0.02069224	525.85873450	10.88119729	0.00190165	0.09190165
46	52.67674185	0.01898371	574.18602060	10.90018100	0.00174160	0.09174160
47	57.41764862	0.01741625	626.86276245	10.91759725	0.00159525	0.09159525
48	62.58523700	0.01597821	684.28041107	10.93357546	0.00146139	0.09146139
49	68.21790833	0.01465891	746.86564807	10.94823436	0.00133893	0.09133893
50	74.35752008	0.01344854	815.08355640	10.96168290	0.00122687	0.09122687

	A Compound Interest	B Present Value	C Amount of Annuity	D Present Value of Annuity	E Sinking Fund	F Amortization
Rate 10%						
n	$(1 + i)^n$	$\dfrac{1}{(1 + i)^n}$	$s_{\overline{n}\rvert i}$	$a_{\overline{n}\rvert i}$	$\dfrac{1}{s_{\overline{n}\rvert i}}$	$\dfrac{1}{a_{\overline{n}\rvert i}}$
1	1.10000000	0.90909091	1.00000000	0.90909091	1.00000000	1.10000000
2	1.21000000	0.82644628	2.10000000	1.73553719	0.47619048	0.57619048
3	1.33100000	0.75131480	3.31000000	2.48685199	0.30211480	0.40211480
4	1.46410000	0.68301346	4.64100000	3.16986545	0.21547080	0.31547080
5	1.61051000	0.62092132	6.10510000	3.79078677	0.16379748	0.26379748
6	1.77156100	0.56447393	7.71561000	4.35526070	0.12960738	0.22960738
7	1.94871710	0.51315812	9.48717100	4.86841882	0.10540550	0.20540550
8	2.14358881	0.46650738	11.43588810	5.33492620	0.08744402	0.18744402
9	2.35794769	0.42409762	13.57947691	5.75902382	0.07364054	0.17364054
10	2.59374246	0.38554329	15.93742460	6.14456711	0.06274539	0.16274539
11	2.85311671	0.35049390	18.53116706	6.49506101	0.05396314	0.15396314
12	3.13842838	0.31863082	21.38428377	6.81369182	0.04676332	0.14676332
13	3.45227121	0.28966438	24.52271214	7.10335620	0.04077852	0.14077852
14	3.79749834	0.26333125	27.97498336	7.36668746	0.03574622	0.13574622
15	4.17724817	0.23939205	31.77248169	7.60607951	0.03147378	0.13147378
16	4.59497299	0.21762914	35.94972986	7.82370864	0.02781662	0.12781662
17	5.05447028	0.19784467	40.54470285	8.02155331	0.02466413	0.12466413
18	5.55991731	0.17985879	45.59917313	8.20141210	0.02193022	0.12193022
19	6.11590904	0.16350799	51.15909045	8.36492009	0.01954687	0.11954687
20	6.72749995	0.14864363	57.27499949	8.51356372	0.01745962	0.11745962
21	7.40024994	0.13513057	64.00249944	8.64869429	0.01562439	0.11562439
22	8.14027494	0.12284597	71.40274939	8.77154026	0.04100506	0.11400506
23	8.95430243	0.11167816	79.54302433	8.88321842	0.01257181	0.11257181
24	9.84973268	0.10152560	88.49732676	8.98474402	0.01129978	0.11129978
25	10.83470594	0.09229600	98.34705943	9.07704002	0.01016807	0.11016807
26	11.91817654	0.08390545	109.18176538	9.16094547	0.00915904	0.10915904
27	13.10999419	0.07627768	121.09994191	9.23722316	0.00825764	0.10825764
28	14.42099361	0.06934335	134.20993611	9.30656651	0.00745101	0.10745101
29	15.86309297	0.06303941	148.63092972	9.36960591	0.00672807	0.10672807
30	17.44940227	0.05730855	164.49402269	9.42691447	0.00607925	0.10607925
31	19.19434250	0.05209868	181.94342496	9.47901315	0.00549621	0.10549621
32	21.11377675	0.04736244	201.13776745	9.52637559	0.00497172	0.10497172
33	23.22515442	0.04305676	222.25154420	9.56943236	0.00449941	0.10449941
34	25.54766986	0.03914251	245.47669862	9.60857487	0.00407371	0.10407371
35	28.10243685	0.03558410	271.02436848	9.64415897	0.00368971	0.10368971
36	30.91268053	0.03234918	299.12680533	9.67650816	0.00334306	0.10334306
37	34.00394859	0.02940835	330.03948586	9.70591651	0.00302994	0.10302994
38	37.40434344	0.02673486	364.04343445	9.73265137	0.00274692	0.10274692
39	41.14477779	0.02430442	401.44777789	9.75695579	0.00249098	0.10249098
40	45.25925557	0.02209493	442.59255568	9.77905072	0.00225941	0.10225941
41	49.78518112	0.02008630	487.85181125	9.79913702	0.00204980	0.10204980
42	54.76369924	0.01826027	537.63699237	9.81739729	0.00185999	0.10185999
43	60.24006916	0.01660025	592.40069161	9.83399753	0.00168805	0.10168805
44	66.26407608	0.01509113	652.64076077	9.84908867	0.00153224	0.10153224
45	72.89048369	0.01371921	718.90483685	9.86280788	0.00139100	0.10139100
46	80.17953205	0.01247201	791.79532054	9.87527989	0.00126295	0.10126295
47	88.19748526	0.01133819	871.97485259	9.88661808	0.00114682	0.10114682
48	97.01723378	0.01030745	960.17233785	9.89692553	0.00104148	0.10104148
49	106.71895716	0.00937041	1057.18957163	9.90629594	0.00094590	0.10094590
50	117.39085288	0.00851855	1163.90852880	9.91481449	0.00085917	0.10085917

Rate 11%	A Compound Interest	B Present Value	C Amount of Annuity	D Present Value of Annuity	E Sinking Fund	F Amortization
n	$(1 + i)^n$	$\dfrac{1}{(1 + i)^n}$	$s_{\overline{n}\rvert i}$	$a_{\overline{n}\rvert i}$	$\dfrac{1}{s_{\overline{n}\rvert i}}$	$\dfrac{1}{a_{\overline{n}\rvert i}}$
1	1.11000000	0.90090090	1.00000000	0.90090090	1.00000000	1.11000000
2	1.23210000	0.81162243	2.11000000	1.71252333	0.47393365	0.58393365
3	1.36763100	0.73119138	3.34210000	2.44371472	0.29921307	0.40921307
4	1.51807041	0.65873097	4.70973100	3.10244569	0.21232635	0.32232635
5	1.68505816	0.59345133	6.22780141	3.69589702	0.16057031	0.27057031
6	1.87041455	0.53464084	7.91285957	4.23053785	0.12637656	0.23637656
7	2.07616015	0.48165841	9.78327412	4.71219626	0.10221527	0.21221527
8	2.30453777	0.43392650	11.85943427	5.14612276	0.08432105	0.19432105
9	2.55803692	0.39092477	14.16397204	5.53704753	0.07060166	0.18060166
10	2.83942099	0.35218448	16.72200896	5.88923201	0.05980143	0.16980143
11	3.15175729	0.31728331	19.56142995	6.20651533	0.05112101	0.16112101
12	3.49845060	0.28584082	22.71318724	6.49235615	0.04402729	0.15402729
13	3.88328016	0.25751426	26.21163784	6.74987040	0.03815099	0.14815099
14	4.31044098	0.23199482	30.09491800	6.98186523	0.03322820	0.14322820
15	4.78458949	0.20900435	34.40535898	7.19086958	0.02906524	0.13906524
16	5.31089433	0.18829220	39.18994847	7.37916178	0.02551675	0.13551675
17	5.89509271	0.16963262	44.50084281	7.54879440	0.02247148	0.13247148
18	6.54355291	0.15282218	50.39593551	7.70161657	0.01984287	0.12984287
19	7.26334373	0.13767764	56.93948842	7.83929421	0.01756250	0.12756250
20	8.06231154	0.12403391	64.20283215	7.96332812	0.01557564	0.12557564
21	8.94916581	0.11174226	72.26514368	8.07507038	0.01383793	0.12383793
22	9.93357404	0.10066870	81.21430949	8.17573908	0.01231310	0.12231310
23	11.02626719	0.09069252	91.14788353	8.26643160	0.01097118	0.12097118
24	12.23915658	0.08170498	102.17415072	8.34813658	0.00978721	0.11978721
25	13.58546380	0.07360809	114.41330730	8.42174466	0.00874024	0.11874024
26	15.07986482	0.06631359	127.99877110	8.48805826	0.00781258	0.11781258
27	16.73864995	0.05974197	143.07863592	8.54780023	0.00698916	0.11698916
28	18.57990145	0.05382160	159.81728587	8.60162183	0.00625715	0.11625715
29	20.62369061	0.04848793	178.39718732	8.65010976	0.00560547	0.11560547
30	22.89229657	0.04368282	199.02087793	8.69379257	0.00502460	0.11502460
31	25.41044919	0.03935389	221.91317450	8.73314646	0.00450627	0.11450627
32	28.20559861	0.03545395	247.32362369	8.76860042	0.00404329	0.11404329
33	31.30821445	0.03194050	275.52922230	8.80054092	0.00362938	0.11362938
34	34.75211804	0.02877522	306.83743675	8.82931614	0.00325905	0.11325905
35	38.57485103	0.02592363	341.58955480	8.85523977	0.00292749	0.11292749
36	42.81808464	0.02335462	380.16440582	8.87859438	0.00263044	0.11263044
37	47.52807395	0.02104020	422.98249046	8.89963458	0.00236416	0.11236416
38	52.75616209	0.01895513	470.51056441	8.91858971	0.00212535	0.11212535
39	58.55933991	0.01707670	523.26672650	8.93566641	0.00191107	0.11191107
40	65.00086731	0.01538441	581.82606641	8.95105082	0.00171873	0.11171873
41	72.15096271	0.01385983	646.82693372	8.96491065	0.00154601	0.11154601
42	80.08756861	0.01248633	718.97789643	8.97739698	0.00139086	0.11139086
43	88.89720115	0.01124895	799.06546504	8.98864593	0.00125146	0.11125146
44	98.67589328	0.01013419	887.96266619	8.99878011	0.00112617	0.11112617
45	109.53024154	0.00912990	986.63855947	9.00791001	0.00101354	0.11101354
46	121.57856811	0.00822513	1096.16880101	9.01613515	0.00091227	0.11091227
47	134.95221060	0.00741003	1217.74736912	9.02354518	0.00082119	0.11082119
48	149.79695377	0.00667570	1352.69957973	9.03022088	0.00073926	0.11073926
49	166.27461868	0.00601415	1502.49653350	9.03623503	0.00066556	0.11066556
50	184.56482674	0.00541815	1668.77115218	9.04165318	0.00059924	0.11059924

Rate 12% n	A Compound Interest $(1 + i)^n$	B Present Value $\dfrac{1}{(1 + i)^n}$	C Amount of Annuity $s_{\overline{n}\rvert i}$	D Present Value of Annuity $a_{\overline{n}\rvert i}$	E Sinking Fund $\dfrac{1}{s_{\overline{n}\rvert i}}$	F Amortization $\dfrac{1}{a_{\overline{n}\rvert i}}$
1	1.12000000	0.89285714	1.00000000	0.89285714	1.00000000	1.12000000
2	1.25440000	0.79719388	2.12000000	1.69005102	0.47169811	0.59169811
3	1.40492800	0.71178025	3.37440000	2.40183127	0.29634898	0.41634898
4	1.57351936	0.63551808	4.77932800	3.03734935	0.20923444	0.32923444
5	1.76234168	0.56742686	6.35284736	3.60477620	0.15740973	0.27740973
6	1.97382269	0.50663112	8.11518904	4.11140732	0.12322572	0.24322572
7	2.21068141	0.45234922	10.08901173	4.56375654	0.09911774	0.21911774
8	2.47596318	0.40388323	12.29969314	4.96763977	0.08130284	0.20130284
9	2.77307876	0.36061002	14.77565631	5.32824979	0.06767889	0.18767889
10	3.10584821	0.32197324	17.54873507	5.65022303	0.05698416	0.17698416
11	3.47854999	0.28747610	20.65458328	5.93769913	0.04841540	0.16841540
12	3.89597599	0.25667509	24.13313327	6.19437423	0.04143681	0.16143681
13	4.36349311	0.22917419	28.02910926	6.42354842	0.03567720	0.15567720
14	4.88711229	0.20461981	32.39260238	6.62816823	0.03087125	0.15087125
15	5.47356576	0.18269626	37.27971466	6.81086449	0.02682424	0.14682424
16	6.13039365	0.16312166	42.75328042	6.97398615	0.02339002	0.14339002
17	6.86604098	0.14564434	48.88367407	7.11963049	0.02045673	0.14045673
18	7.68996580	0.13003959	55.74971496	7.24967008	0.01793731	0.13793731
19	8.61276169	0.11610678	63.43968075	7.36577686	0.01576300	0.13576300
20	9.64629309	0.10366677	72.05244244	7.46944362	0.01387878	0.13387878
21	10.80384826	0.09255961	81.69873554	7.56200324	0.01224009	0.13224009
22	12.10031006	0.08264251	92.50258380	7.64464575	0.01081051	0.13081051
23	13.55234726	0.07378796	104.60289386	7.71843370	0.00955996	0.12955996
24	15.17862893	0.06588210	118.15524112	7.78431581	0.00846344	0.12846344
25	17.00006441	0.05882331	133.33387006	7.84313911	0.00749997	0.12749997
26	19.04007214	0.05252081	150.33393446	7.89565992	0.00665186	0.12665186
27	21.32488079	0.04689358	169.37400660	7.94255350	0.00590409	0.12590409
28	23.88386649	0.04186927	190.69888739	7.98442277	0.00524387	0.12524387
29	26.74993047	0.03738327	214.58275388	8.02180604	0.00466021	0.12466021
30	29.95992212	0.03337792	241.33268434	8.05518397	0.00414366	0.12414366
31	33.55511278	0.02980172	271.29260646	8.08498569	0.00368606	0.12368606
32	37.58172631	0.02660868	304.84771924	8.11159436	0.00328033	0.12328033
33	42.09153347	0.02375775	342.42944555	8.13535211	0.00292031	0.12292031
34	47.14251748	0.02121227	384.52097901	8.15656438	0.00260064	0.12260064
35	52.79961958	0.01893953	431.66349649	8.17550391	0.00231662	0.12231662
36	59.13557393	0.01691029	484.46311607	8.19241421	0.00206414	0.12206414
37	66.23184280	0.01509848	543.59869000	8.20751269	0.00183959	0.12183959
38	74.17966394	0.01348078	609.83053280	8.22099347	0.00163980	0.12163980
39	83.08122361	0.01203641	684.01019674	8.23302988	0.00146197	0.12146197
40	93.05097044	0.01074680	767.09142034	8.24377668	0.00130363	0.12130363
41	104.21708689	0.00959536	860.14239079	8.25337204	0.00116260	0.12116260
42	116.72313732	0.00856728	964.35947768	8.26193932	0.00103696	0.12103696
43	130.72991380	0.00764936	1081.08261500	8.26958868	0.00092500	0.12092500
44	146.41750346	0.00682978	1211.81252880	8.27641846	0.00082521	0.12082521
45	163.98760387	0.00609802	1358.23003226	8.28251648	0.00073625	0.12073625
46	183.66611634	0.00544466	1522.21763613	8.28796115	0.00065694	0.12065694
47	205.70605030	0.00486131	1705.88375247	8.29282245	0.00058621	0.12058621
48	230.39077633	0.00434045	1911.58980276	8.29716290	0.00052312	0.12052312
49	258.03766949	0.00387540	2142.98057909	8.30103831	0.00046686	0.12046686
50	289.00218983	0.00346018	2400.01824858	8.30449849	0.00041666	0.12041666

Rate 13%	A Compound Interest	B Present Value	C Amount of Annuity	D Present Value of Annuity	E Sinking Fund	F Amortization
n	$(1 + i)^n$	$\dfrac{1}{(1 + i)^n}$	$s_{\overline{n}\|i}$	$a_{\overline{n}\|i}$	$\dfrac{1}{s_{\overline{n}\|i}}$	$\dfrac{1}{a_{\overline{n}\|i}}$
1	1.13000000	0.88495575	1.00000000	0.88495575	1.00000000	1.13000000
2	1.27690000	0.78314668	2.13000000	1.66810244	0.46948357	0.59948357
3	1.44289700	0.69305016	3.40690000	2.36115260	0.29352197	0.42352197
4	1.63047361	0.61331873	4.84979700	2.97447133	0.20619420	0.33619420
5	1.84243518	0.54275994	6.48027061	3.51723126	0.15431454	0.28431454
6	2.08195175	0.48031853	8.32270579	3.99754979	0.12015323	0.25015323
7	2.35260548	0.42506064	10.40465754	4.42261043	0.09611080	0.22611080
8	2.65844419	0.37615986	12.75726302	4.79877029	0.07838672	0.20838672
9	3.00404194	0.33288483	15.41570722	5.13165513	0.06486890	0.19486890
10	3.39456739	0.29458835	18.41974915	5.42624348	0.05428956	0.18428956
11	3.83586115	0.26069765	21.81431654	5.68694113	0.04584145	0.17584145
12	4.33452310	0.23070589	25.65017769	5.91764702	0.03898608	0.16898608
13	4.89801110	0.20416450	29.98470079	6.12181152	0.03335034	0.16335034
14	5.53475255	0.18067655	34.88271190	6.30248807	0.02866750	0.15866750
15	6.25427038	0.15989075	40.41746444	6.46237882	0.02474178	0.15474178
16	7.06732553	0.14149624	46.67173482	6.60387506	0.02142624	0.15142624
17	7.98607785	0.12521791	53.73906035	6.72909298	0.01860844	0.14860844
18	9.02426797	0.11081231	61.72513819	6.83990529	0.01620085	0.14620085
19	10.19742280	0.09806399	70.74940616	6.93796928	0.01413439	0.14413439
20	11.52308776	0.08678229	80.94682896	7.02475158	0.01235379	0.14235379
21	13.02108917	0.07679849	92.46991672	7.10155007	0.01081433	0.14081433
22	14.71383077	0.06796327	105.49100590	7.16951334	0.00947948	0.13947948
23	16.62662877	0.06014448	120.20483667	7.22965782	0.00831913	0.13831913
24	18.78809051	0.05322521	136.83146543	7.28288303	0.00730826	0.13730826
25	21.23054227	0.04710195	155.61955594	7.32998498	0.00642593	0.13642593
26	23.99051277	0.04168314	176.85009821	7.37166812	0.00565451	0.13565451
27	27.10927943	0.03688774	200.84061098	7.40855586	0.00497907	0.13497907
28	30.63348575	0.03264402	227.94989040	7.44119988	0.00438693	0.13438693
29	34.61583890	0.02888851	258.58337616	7.47008839	0.00386722	0.13386722
30	39.11589796	0.02556505	293.19921506	7.49565344	0.00341065	0.13341065
31	44.20096469	0.02262394	332.31511301	7.51827738	0.00300919	0.13300919
32	49.94709010	0.02002119	376.51607771	7.53829857	0.00265593	0.13265593
33	56.44021181	0.01771786	426.46316781	7.55601643	0.00234487	0.13234487
34	63.77743935	0.01567953	482.90337962	7.57169596	0.00207081	0.13207081
35	72.06850647	0.01387569	546.68081897	7.58557164	0.00182922	0.13182922
36	81.43741231	0.01227937	618.74932544	7.59785101	0.00161616	0.13161616
37	92.02427591	0.01086670	700.18673775	7.60871771	0.00142819	0.13142819
38	103.98743178	0.00961655	792.21101365	7.61833426	0.00126229	0.13126229
39	117.50579791	0.00851022	896.19844543	7.62684447	0.00111582	0.13111582
40	132.78155163	0.00753117	1013.70424333	7.63437564	0.00098648	0.13098648
41	150.04315335	0.00666475	1146.48579497	7.64104039	0.00087223	0.13087223
42	169.54876328	0.00589801	1296.52894831	7.64693840	0.00077129	0.13077129
43	191.59010251	0.00521948	1466.07771159	7.65215787	0.00068209	0.13068209
44	216.49681583	0.00461901	1657.66781410	7.65677688	0.00060326	0.13060326
45	244.64140189	0.00408762	1874.16462994	7.66086450	0.00053357	0.13053357
46	276.44478414	0.00361736	2118.80603183	7.66448185	0.00047196	0.13047196
47	312.38260608	0.00320120	2395.25081596	7.66768306	0.00041749	0.13041749
48	352.99234487	0.00283292	2707.63342204	7.67051598	0.00036933	0.13036933
49	398.88134970	0.00250701	3060.62576691	7.67302299	0.00032673	0.13032673
50	450.73592516	0.00221859	3459.50711660	7.67524158	0.00028906	0.13028906

Answers to Selected Exercises

Chapter 1

Section 1.1 (page 5)

1. 382 miles   **3.** 467 passengers   **5.** 1.7 billion tons   **7.** 2477 pounds   **9.** 23,993,000 small and midsize businesses   **11.** 328,500 veterans   **13.** $750   **15.** $20,961   **17.** 20 seats   **19.** 35.2 hours   **21.** 65.5 million shares   **23.** 26 coins   **25. (a)** 0.43 inch **(b)** 4.3 inches   **27. (a)** 180.6 hours **(b)** $18.00   **29.** $14,790

Section 1.2 (page 16)

1. $\frac{11}{8}$ **3.** $\frac{17}{4}$ **5.** $\frac{183}{8}$ **7.** $\frac{101}{8}$ **9.** $\frac{1}{2}$ **11.** $\frac{8}{15}$ **13.** $\frac{5}{8}$ **15.** $\frac{4}{5}$ **17.** $\frac{11}{12}$ **19.** $\frac{8}{15}$ **21.** $3\frac{1}{2}$ **23.** $3\frac{4}{5}$ **25.** $1\frac{3}{11}$ **27.** $1\frac{2}{5}$ **29.** $1\frac{15}{16}$ **31.** $2\frac{17}{32}$ **35.** $\frac{3}{5}$
37. $\frac{17}{20}$ **39.** $1\frac{7}{60}$ **41.** $\frac{19}{22}$ **43.** $1\frac{23}{36}$ **45.** $2\frac{5}{24}$ **47.** $97\frac{4}{5}$ **49.** $80\frac{3}{4}$ **51.** $53\frac{17}{24}$ **53.** 187   **55.** $\frac{1}{2}$ **57.** $\frac{1}{2}$ **59.** $\frac{17}{48}$ **61.** $\frac{1}{3}$ **63.** $4\frac{3}{8}$ **65.** $3\frac{11}{24}$
67. $9\frac{1}{24}$ **69.** $6\frac{1}{4}$ **75.** $\frac{31}{40}$ inch   **77.** $4\frac{3}{8}$ miles   **79.** $\frac{3}{16}$ inch   **81.** $22\frac{1}{2}$ hours   **83.** $1\frac{5}{8}$ cubic yards   **85.** $19\frac{5}{6}$ cases   **87.** $9\frac{1}{6}$ hours
89. $104\frac{5}{8}$ feet

Section 1.3 (page 27)

1. $\frac{5}{12}$ **3.** $\frac{99}{160}$ **5.** $4\frac{1}{2}$ **7.** 69   **9.** $4\frac{7}{12}$ **11.** 90   **13.** $\frac{1}{2}$ **15.** $\frac{3}{4}$ **17.** $1\frac{1}{2}$ **19.** $\frac{2}{3}$ **21.** $3\frac{1}{3}$ **23.** $4\frac{4}{5}$ **27.** $12   **29.** $25.50   **31.** $15.75
33. $\frac{4}{5}$ **35.** $\frac{6}{25}$ **37.** $\frac{73}{100}$ **39.** $\frac{7}{8}$ **41.** $\frac{3}{80}$ **43.** $\frac{3}{16}$ **45.** 3.5; 3.52   **47.** 0.1; 0.08   **49.** 8.6; 8.64   **51.** 59.0; 58.96   **53.** 23.0; 23.05
55. 39.5; 39.50   **57.** 0.75   **59.** 0.375   **61.** 0.167   **63.** 0.813   **65.** 0.32   **67.** 0.010   **69.** 0.625   **71.** 0.833   **77.** 36 yards
79. 88 dispensers   **81.** 12 homes   **83.** $21\frac{7}{8}$ ounces   **85.** 471 gallons   **87.** 60 trips   **89.** $2632\frac{1}{2}$ inches

Chapter 1 Review Exercises (page 33)

1. $\frac{3}{5}$ **2.** $\frac{1}{2}$ **3.** $\frac{1}{3}$ **4.** $\frac{1}{2}$ **5.** $\frac{9}{10}$ **6.** $\frac{7}{11}$ **7.** $\frac{1}{50}$ **8.** $\frac{3}{8}$ **9.** $8\frac{1}{8}$ **10.** $4\frac{2}{3}$ **11.** $1\frac{7}{12}$ **12.** $7\frac{6}{7}$ **13.** $2\frac{2}{3}$ **14.** $8\frac{1}{6}$ **15.** $8\frac{1}{16}$ **16.** $3\frac{1}{32}$ **17.** $1\frac{5}{24}$
18. $\frac{7}{8}$ **19.** $\frac{8}{21}$ **20.** $\frac{1}{12}$ **21.** $71\frac{5}{6}$ **22.** $91\frac{5}{6}$ **23.** $4\frac{1}{4}$ **24.** $81\frac{1}{16}$ **25.** $3799   **26.** 14,454 gallons saved   **27.** $22\frac{1}{2}$ hours   **28.** $35\frac{7}{8}$ gallons
29. $319\frac{1}{2}$ ft.   **30.** $54\frac{11}{24}$ lb.   **31.** $\frac{5}{12}$ **32.** $\frac{7}{40}$ **33.** $\frac{1}{2}$ **34.** 16   **35.** $\frac{2}{3}$ **36.** $2\frac{2}{9}$ **37.** $20\frac{5}{6}$ **38.** $6\frac{1}{6}$ **39.** $3.93   **40.** 3.6 million shares
41. $42\frac{1}{2}$ acres   **42.** 2480 anchors   **43.** 36 pull cords   **44.** $140,550   **45.** $\frac{1}{4}$ **46.** $\frac{5}{8}$ **47.** $\frac{93}{100}$ **48.** $\frac{1}{200}$ **49.** 68.4; 68.43
50. 975.5; 975.54   **51.** 0.4; 0.35   **52.** 8.0; 8.03   **53.** 7.0; 6.97   **54.** 0.4; 0.43   **55.** 1.0; 0.96   **56.** 71.2; 71.25   **57.** 0.625   **58.** 0.75
59. 0.833   **60.** 0.438

Chapter 1 Business Application Case #1 (page 34)

(a) $432,000   **(b)** $\frac{5}{12}, \frac{1}{4}, \frac{1}{12}, \frac{1}{16}, \frac{1}{16}, \frac{1}{8}$ **(c)**

Miscellaneous $\frac{1}{8}$; Insurance $\frac{1}{16}$; Advertising $\frac{1}{16}$; Utilities $\frac{1}{12}$; Rent $\frac{1}{4}$; Salaries $\frac{5}{12}$

Chapter 1 Business Application Case #2 (page 35)

1. 1 foot $3\frac{5}{8}$ inches   **2.** 387 shares
3. Answers will vary.
4. Answers will vary.

Chapter 2

Section 2.1 (page 42)

1. 42   **3.** 305   **5.** 13   **7.** 4.2   **9.** 12   **11.** 2
13. 3   **15.** 2.2   **17.** 0.8   **19.** 400   **21.** 294
23. 7   **25.** 12   **27.** 25   **29.** $\frac{5}{6}$ **31.** $\frac{5}{36}$ **33.** 4
35. $11\frac{4}{7}$ **37.** 4.65   **39.** $1\frac{5}{24}$ **41.** $\frac{2}{3}$ **43.** 1   **45.** 3.5   **47.** 13   **49.** 2   **51.** 5   **53.** 7   **55.** 10   **57.** $\frac{16}{19}$ **59.** $\frac{2}{3}$ **61.** $1\frac{1}{6}$ **63.** 2.1   **65.** 0.8

Section 2.2 (page 48)

1. $27 + x$ **3.** $22 + x$ **5.** $x - 4$ **7.** $x - 3\frac{1}{2}$ **9.** $3x$ **11.** $\frac{3}{5}x$ **13.** $\frac{9}{x}$ **15.** $\frac{16}{x}$ **17.** $2.1(4 + x)$ **19.** $7(x - 3)$ **21.** $12y$
23. $472 - x$ **25.** $73 - x$ **27.** $\frac{22,210}{x}$ **29.** $21 - x$ **31.** 13   **33.** 1.5   **35.** 1   **37.** $1\frac{3}{7}$ **39.** 59 stereos   **41.** 207   **43.** $20,500
45. 42 deluxe; 63 economy   **47.** $7875 announcers; $13,125 all other employees   **49.** office space $30,000; retail stores $105,000
51. 3 new; 19 experienced   **53.** 81 Altimas; 39 Sentras

Section 2.3 (page 54)

1. $586.50 **3.** $10,080 **5.** $16.50 **7.** 14 **9.** 2250 **11.** 151.2 **13.** $749.86 **15.** 7.5 **17.** 7 **19.** 24,000 **21.** $\frac{A}{W}$ **23.** $\frac{nRT}{P}$
25. $\frac{M}{(1 + i)^n}$ **27.** $\frac{(A - P)}{P}$ **29.** $\frac{(M - P)}{MT}$ **31.** $\frac{2A}{(b + B)}$ **33.** $2.40 **35.** $93.80 **37 (a)** $427 **(b)** $502.50
39. $236 million **41.** $2.29 **43.** $644,400 **45.** $390 **47.** 0.13, or 13% **49.** 4 years **51.** $4000 **53.** $4500

Section 2.4 (page 61)

1. $\frac{9}{32}$ **3.** $\frac{27}{1}$ **5.** $\frac{4}{3}$ **7.** $\frac{3750}{1}$ **9.** $\frac{225}{1}$ **11.** $\frac{8}{5}$ **13.** $\frac{1}{6}$ **15.** $\frac{4}{15}$ **17.** $\frac{9}{2}$ **19.** T **21.** F **23.** F **25.** F **27.** F **29.** F **31.** T
33. T **35.** F **37.** T **39.** 7 **41.** 72 **43.** 105 **45.** $3\frac{1}{2}$ **47.** 24 **49.** 8 **53.** 1575 tickets **55.** $516,000 **57.** $360
59. Further increase of 2.6° Fahrenheit **61.** 1020 miles **63.** $713,211.20 **65.** $128,000 **67.** 350 miles
69. 3,500,000 cubic meters **71.** U.S. $214.26

Chapter 2 Review Exercises (page 66)

1. 51 **2.** 50.7 **3.** 16.3 **4.** $5\frac{1}{4}$ **5.** 252 **6.** 136 **7.** 56 **8.** $13\frac{1}{2}$ **9.** 7 **10.** $1\frac{2}{3}$ **11.** 21 **12.** 3.6 **13.** $94x$ **14.** $\frac{1}{2}x$ **15.** $6x + x$
16. $5x - 11$ **17.** $3x + 7$ **18.** $92.35 **19.** $3000 **20.** $108 water; $432 phone **21.** 76 **22.** 70 child; 30 adult **23.** $P = $4000
24. $P = $3250 **25.** $P = $8200 (rounded) **26.** $\frac{I}{PT}$ **27.** $\frac{M - P}{PR}$ **28.** $\frac{B}{R}$ **29.** $\frac{34}{1}$ **30.** $\frac{18}{1}$ **31.** $\frac{20}{1}$ **32.** $\frac{12}{5}$ **33.** $\frac{8}{3}$ **34.** 3 **35.** $6\frac{3}{4}$
36. $4\frac{1}{2}$ **37.** 165 **38.** 24 **39.** 4293 bass **40.** 4734 pounds per square inch (rounded) **41.** 6624 pounds **42.** 105
43. $112,008 **44.** $139.50 **45.** 5 DVDs

Chapter 2 Business Application Case #1 (page 67)

(a) $12,570 **(b)** $\frac{3}{10}$ **(c)** $\left(\frac{3}{10} \cdot \$24.80 \cdot N\right) - \$12,570$ or $7.44N - \$12,570$ **(d)** 1690 books **(e)** The owner would probably receive a lower salary **(f)** 2496 books

Chapter 2 Business Application Case #2 (page 68)

(a) $961,538 **(b)** $961,538 \cdot (26,000 + N)$ **(c)** $30 billion **(d)** Answers will vary.

Chapter 3

Section 3.1 (page 74)

1. 20% **3.** 72% **5.** 140% **7.** 37.5% **9.** 462.5% **11.** 0.25% **13.** 0.15% **15.** 345% **17.** 25% **19.** 10% **21.** 2% **23.** 37.5%
25. 12.5% **27.** 0.5% **29.** 87.5% **31.** 6% **33.** 0.65 **35.** 0.75 **37.** 0.006 **39.** 0.0025 **41.** 3.15 **43.** 2.006 **45.** 5.406
47. 0.0007 **53.** 0.5; 50% **55.** $\frac{3}{20}$; 0.15 **57.** $\frac{1}{4}$; 25% **59.** 6.125; 612.5% **61.** $7\frac{1}{4}$; 725% **63.** $\frac{1}{400}$; 0.25% **65.** $0.33\overline{3}$; $33\frac{1}{3}\%$
67. $\frac{3}{400}$; 0.0075 **69.** $\frac{1}{8}$; 0.125 **71.** $2\frac{1}{2}$; 250% **73.** $10\frac{767}{2000}$; 10.3835 **75.** 4.375; 437.5% **77.** $\frac{27}{400}$; 0.0675 **79.** $8\frac{4}{5}$; 880%
81. $\frac{1}{400}$; 0.0025

Section 3.2 (page 80)

1. 16 bicycles **3.** $244.35 **5.** 4.8 feet **7.** 10,185 miles **9.** 182 homes **11.** 148.444 yds **13.** $5366.65 **15.** $6.50
19. 264 adults **21.** $275.84 **23.** 2024 shoppers **25.** 206 scientists **27.** (a) 37.5% (b) 16.5 million female workers
29. 3.78 million office workers **31.** 2156 products **33.** $135 million **35.** $51,844.20 **37.** $2098.80 **39.** $199.89
41. $116.93

Section 3.3 (page 85)

1. 1060 **3.** 187.5 **5.** 1000 **7.** 4800 **9.** 22,000 **11.** 20,000 **13.** $90,320 **15.** 1750 **17.** 312,500 **19.** 65,400 **21.** 40,000
25. 5022 juniors and seniors **27.** 7761 students **29.** $3800 **31.** 1055 people (rounded) **33.** $104.2 billion **35.** $185,500

Section 3.3 Supplementary Exercises (page 87)

1. 16 ounces (rounded) **3.** $288.150 **5.** 478,175 Mustangs **7.** $93.9 million **9.** $39,000 **11.** 836 drivers **13.** $61.4 million

Section 3.4 (page 92)

1. 10 **3.** 125 **5.** 28.3 **7.** 9.3 **9.** 4.1 **11.** 5.9 **13.** 102.5 **15.** 17.6 **17.** 27.8 **21.** 5.6% **23.** 2% **25.** 8.7% **27.** 9.1% **29.** 20%

Section 3.4 Supplementary Exercises (page 94)

1. 300 doctors **3.** 40% **5.** 16,910 hotels **7.** 2,900,844 injuries **9.** $396.05 **11.** (a) 30% (b) 70% **13.** $134 sale price
15. 2.98% **17.** 12.5% **19.** 5.5% **21.** 960 candy bars **23.** $4473 **25.** 23.6% **27.** 391 million **29.** 36%

Section 3.5 (page 101)

1. $375 **3.** $27.91 **5.** $25 **7.** $854.50 **11.** $173,534 **13.** (a) $1900 (b) $152 **15.** $2.3 billion **17.** $15,161.90
19. $118,080 **21.** $78,854 **23.** $3864 **25.** 145.24 million (rounded) **27.** 51.2 million **29.** 34,741 students **31.** 695 deaths
33. 361,461 phones

Chapter 3 Review Exercises (page 106)

1. 150 members   **2.** 24 vans   **3.** 1100 shippers   **4.** 2.5%   **5.** $3.75   **6.** $\frac{6}{25}$ **7.** 960 loads   **8.** $\frac{7}{8}$ **9.** 8.5%   **10.** $\frac{1}{200}$
11. $5185; $25,315   **12.** 224,000 units   **13.** 6.22 million   **14.** 21.43 million people   **15. (a)** 35% **(b)** $28,560
16. 68%   **17.** $350   **18.** 1200 backpacks   **19.** 2.8%   **20.** 21.4 million   **21.** 75%   **22.** 12.5 ounces   **23.** 97,757 copies
24. $39,840   **25.** 48.7%   **26.** 0.7%   **27.** 314,395,000 people   **28.** $1.365 billion   **29.** 1673%   **30.** 6.0%   **31.** 1.1%
32. 1,800,000 tourists   **33.** $140.8 million   **34.** 148,507 units   **35.** $11.90 per hour   **36.** 97 units

Chapter 3 Business Application Case #1 (page 108)

172.7%; 39.45; 3.14; 18.5%; 52.1%; 55.30; 23.27; 42.11; 52.68; 159.9%

Chapter 3 Business Application Case #2 (page 109)

(a) $271,095   **(b)** $504,000   **(c)** 7.1%   **(d)** Answers will vary.   **(e)** Answers will vary.

Chapter 4

Section 4.1 (page 117) (page 109)

1. 17.7%   **3.** 3.91 times as much in investments as in banks   **5.** It has increased.   **7.** 4   **9.** 6   **11.** 5
13.

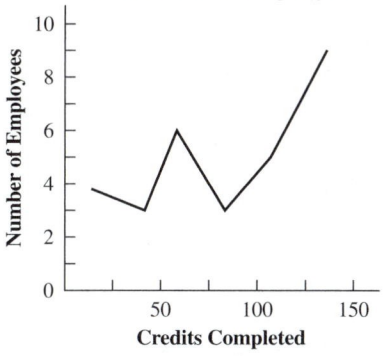

15. 23   **17.** 7   **21. (a)** almost 1 acre **(b)** almost $3\frac{7}{8}$ acres **(c)** 2 mph **(d)** 99 inches
23.   **Computer Skills Evaluation**

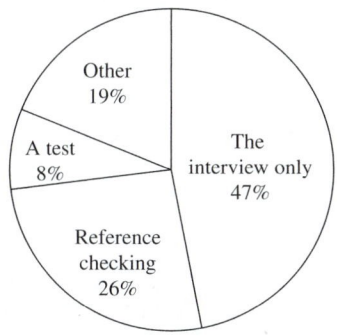

25. (a) 2% **(b)** 8% to 13% **(c)** 2% to $6\frac{1}{2}$% **(d)** up; down
27.

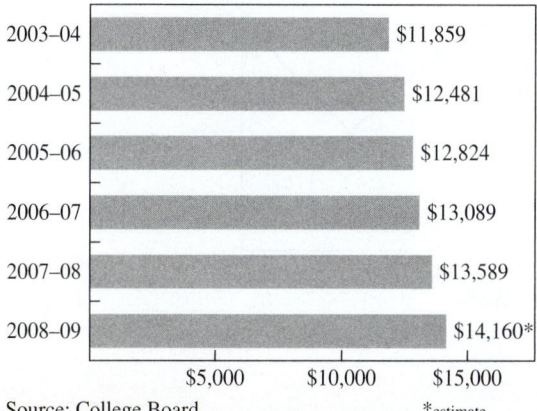

Section 4.2 (page 126)

1. 228 **3.** 3689.6 **5.** 73 pounds **7.** $1300 **9.** 10.3 inches **11.** 39.4 **13.** 167.2 **17.** $31,000 **19.** 1.62 **21.** 76.3 **23.** 105.8 **25.** 68% **27.** 55 inches

Section 4.3 (page 132)

1. 32 **3.** 88 **5.** 0.83 **7.** 60 **9.** none **11.** 4 and 6 **15.** 81.2 feet; 82 feet **19.** 115.1; 114.5; 114.5 **21.** Mean $1.7275; Median $1.715 **23.** 3.01 pounds; probably so

Section 4.4 (page 139)

1. 18; 1.9 **3.** 21; 1.6 **5.** 55.9; 3.1 **7.** 43 **9.** 388 **13.** 100 **15.** 136 **17.** 27 **19.** 190 **21.** 50% **23.** 95% **25.** 50% **27.** 16% **29.** 95% **31.** $\frac{1}{2}$% **33.** 84% **35.** 97.5% **37.** 84% **39.** 97.5% **41.** 68% **43.** 3 swimmers

Section 4.5 (page 143)

1. 244.4 **3.** 60 **5.** 560 **7.** $213.40 **9.** $168.50 **11.** $371.90 **13.** $127,000 **15.** $679.52 **17.** Medical costs

Chapter 4 Review Exercises (page 149)

1. 1; 3; 10; 3; 2; 1 **2.** 6

3.

Weekly Gasoline Sales

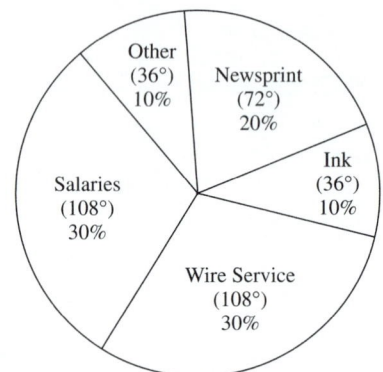

4. 72°; 10%; 108°; 108°; 36°

5.

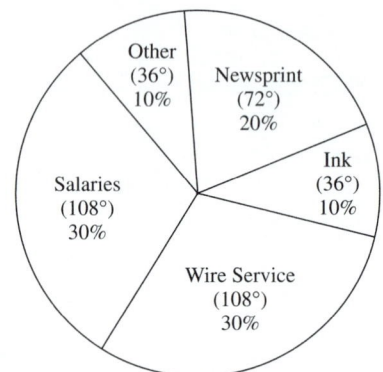

6. 60% **7.** 23.4; 20; no mode **8.** 85.6; 85; 82 **9.** 20.3; 20.5; 21 **10.** 43.3; 44; 44 **11.** 6.9; 7; 7 **12.** 2.4; 2.4; 2.4 **13.** 26.1 **14.** 34.8 **15.** 8; 3 **16.** 74.5; 74.5 **17.** 67; 22.77 **18.** 13; 4.05 **19.** 21; 7.21 **20.** 42; 14.88 **21.** 143.6 **22.** 164.0 **23.** 52.8 **24.** 162.2 **25.** $41,427 **26.** 84%

27. Sales are relatively flat.

Weekly Sales for Current's Restaurant

28. 2.54; 2.31   **29.** 237.4

30.

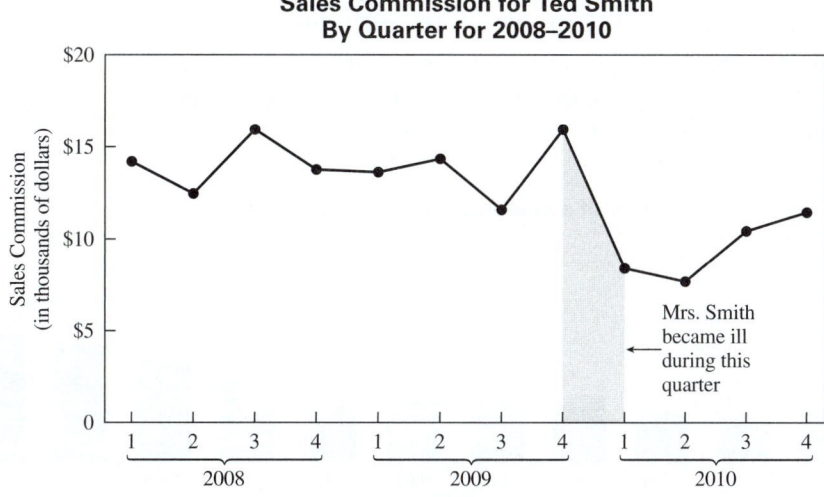

Sales Commission for Ted Smith By Quarter for 2008–2010

Mrs. Smith's illness affected Mr. Smith's work.

Chapter 4 Business Application Case #1 (page 153)

(a) Midland: 18.8, 18.5, no mode
Lockhart: 8.5, 9.4, 10.2

(b)

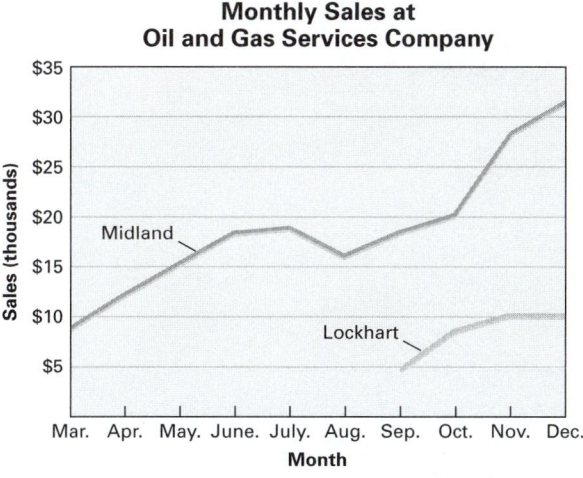

Monthly Sales at Oil and Gas Services Company

(c) Sales grew rapidly in Midland, and are also growing in Lockhart.

(d) Sales have grown more rapidly in Midland. Pat Farmer has worked in Midland for several years and knows a lot of people. She does not know as many people in Lockhart.

Chapter 4 Business Application Case #2 (page 154)

(a) Income taxes paid: mean = \$5.8 billion; median = \$6.0 billion
Profit: mean = \$10.9 billion; median = \$11.2 billion

(b) Average before-tax profit = \$16.7 billion; 34.7% tax rate

(c) Sales have a clear upward trend, indicating that Wal-Mart Stores continues to grow even though the company is the largest retailer in the world.

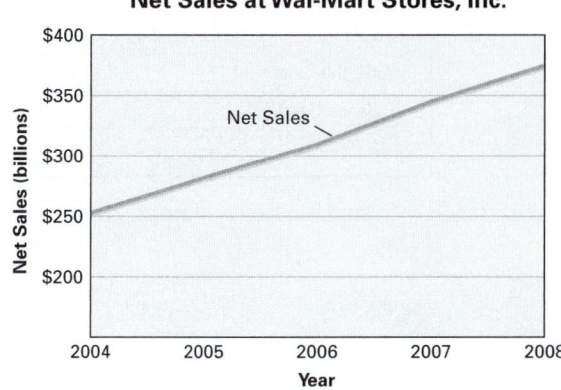

Net Sales at Wal-Mart Stores, Inc.

Part 1 Cumulative Review Chapters 1–4 (page 155)

1. $60 per month   **2.** $20,961   **3.** $31,658.27   **4.** 24 payments   **5.** $\frac{8}{9}$ **6.** $\frac{65}{8}$ **7.** $7\frac{2}{15}$ **8.** $4\frac{5}{12}$ **9.** $13\frac{13}{24}$ **10.** $1\frac{3}{4}$ **11.** 3   **12.** $2\frac{2}{9}$

13. $42\frac{1}{2}$ acres   **14.** $22\frac{1}{2}$ hours   **15.** 130 feet   **16.** $\frac{1}{12}$ of the total   **17.** $\frac{7}{20}$ **18.** 0.667   **19.** 78.57   **20.** 4732.49   **21.** 62.7

22. 215.675   **23.** 26   **24.** 85.4   **25.** 112   **26.** 12   **27.** $\frac{3}{4}x$ **28.** $5x + x$ **29.** $8x - 8$ **30.** $6x + 5$ **31.** $T = 3$ **32.** $P = \$1850$

33. $\frac{5}{1}$ **34.** $\frac{7}{5}$ **35.** 9   **36.** $35\frac{1}{5}$ **37.** 525 students   **38.** $154,000   **39.** 62.5%   **40.** 0.0025   **41.** 450 prospects   **42.** $107.20

43. 25%   **44.** 150%   **45.** 9.3%   **46.** 21,888 people   **47.** 58,484 students   **48.** $16,760   **49.** 90,000%

50. 16.7% (rounded)   **51. (a)** $3.80, $7.25, 91%; **(b)** $2.29, $7.25, 217%; **(c)** Trend is down.

52.

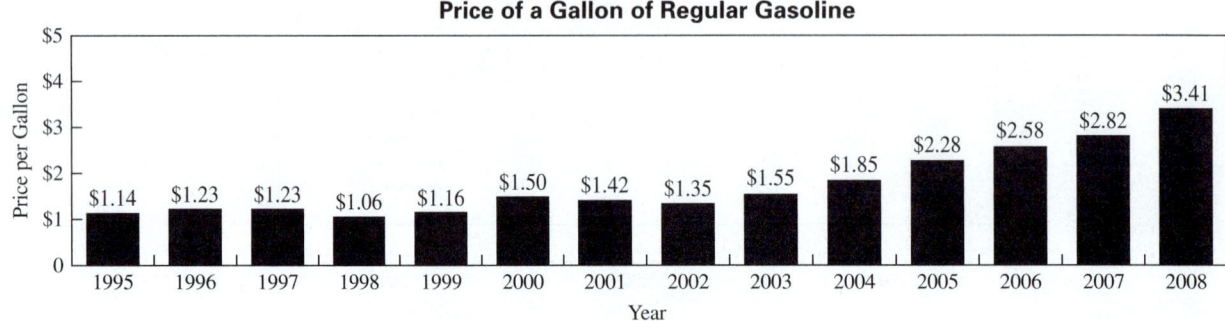

Price of a Gallon of Regular Gasoline

53.

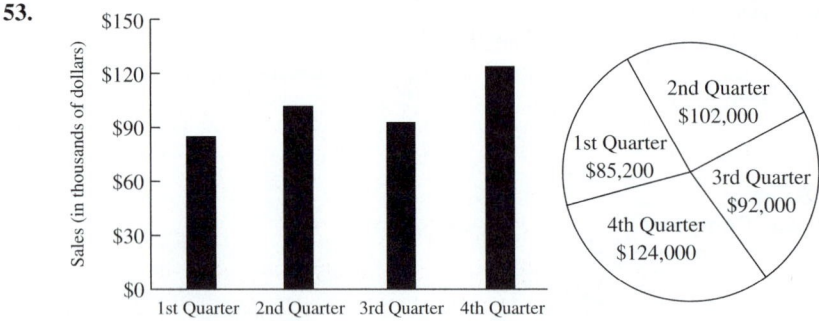

54. 2.69   **55.** 75; 13; 5.2   **56.** 47.5%   **57.** 57   **58.** $642

Chapter 5

Section 5.1 (page 168)

1. $14.20   **3.** $0   **5.** $17.10   **7.** $13.10

9.

857		
Mar. 8 20 ____		
Amount $380.71		
To Patty Demko		
For Tutoring		
Bal. Bro't. For'd.	3971	28
Am't. Deposited	79	26
Total	4050	54
Am't. this Check	380	71
Balance For'd.	3669	83

11.

735		
Dec. 4 20 ____		
Amount $37.52		
To Paul's Pools		
For Chemicals		
Bal. Bro't. For'd.	1126	73
Am't. Deposited		
Total	1126	73
Am't. this Check	37	52
Balance For'd.	1089	21

17.

5312		
Oct. 10 20 ___		
Amount $39.12		
To *County Clerk*		
For *License*		
Bal. Bro't. For'd.	5972	89
Am't. Deposited	752	18
	23	32
Total	6748	39
Am't. this Check	39	12
Balance For'd.	6709	27

19. 1379.41; 1230.41; 1348.14; 1278.34; 1608.20; 2026.50; 1916.74; 1302.62; 1270.44; 1791.39   **21.** 3709.32; 3590.92; 3877.24; 3797.24; 2811.02; 2435.52; 3637.34; 2901.66; 2677.72; 3175.73; 3097.49

Section 5.2 (page 174)

1. (a) $2419.76 **(b)** $203.86 **(c)** $2215.90 **(d)** $66.48 **(e)** $2149.42   **3. (a)** $1591.44 **(b)** $189.39 **(c)** $1402.05 **(d)** $56.08 **(e)** $1345.97   **5. (a)** $1064.72 **(b)** $72.83 **(c)** $991.89 **(d)** $29.76 **(e)** $962.13

Section 5.3 (page 182)

1. $5095.47   **3.** $7690.62   **5.** $18,314.72   **7.** $6967.88   **9.** $7498.20   **11.** $4496.01 **17.** $6728.20

Chapter 5 Review Exercises (page 186)

1. $15.90   **2.** $19   **3.** $10.20   **4.** 9517.70   **5.** 9831.34   **6.** 19,415.20   **7.** $1064.72   **8.** $72.83   **9.** $991.89   **10.** $19.84 **11.** $972.05   **12.** $6043.16   **13.** $8992.02   **14.** $1267.21

Chapter 5 Business Application Case #1 (page 188)

(a) $8178.46 gross profit   **(b)** $7974 credit   **(c)** $9810.36 total of checks outstanding   **(d)** $4882.58 deposits not recorded **(e)** $7274.56 balance

Chapter 5 Business Application Case #2 (page 189)

1. $7.40   **2. (a)** $2570 **(b)** $2531.45   **3.** Answers will vary.   **4.** Answers will vary.

Chapter 6

Section 6.1 (page 198)

1. 40; 0; $12.15   **3.** 38.75; 0; $11.70   **5.** 40; 5.25; $17.22   **7.** $324; $0; $324   **9.** $302.25; $0; $302.25   **11.** $459.20; $90.41; $549.61   **13.** $13.20; $347.60; $0; $347.60   **15.** $21.60; $576; $97.20; $673.20   **17.** $13.77; $367.20; $58.52; $425.72   **19.** 51; 11; $3.70; $377.40; $40.70; $418.10   **21.** 50.25; 10.25; $4.30; $432.15; $44.08; $476.23   **23.** 50.25; 10.25; $5.10; $512.55; $52.28; $564.83   **25.** 35; 6; $14.25; $332.50; $85.50; $418.00   **27.** 39.5; 3.75; $17.10; $450.30; $64.13; $514.43   **29.** 39.75; 3.5; $15.30; $405.45; $53.55; $459.00   **33.** $496; $537.33; $1074.67; $12,896   **35.** $426; $923; $1846; $22,152   **37.** $501.92; $1003.85; $2175; $26,100   **39.** $618.46; $1236.92; $1340; $32,160   **41.** $830; $1660; $1798.33; $3596.67   **43.** $832 **45.** $487.70   **47.** $703.08   **49.** $436.80   **51.** $678.90   **53.** $1127   **55.** $925.16   57. **(a)** $1260 biweekly **(b)** $1365 semimonthly **(c)** $2730 monthly **(d)** $32,760 annually

Section 6.2 (page 206)

1. $208.16   **3.** $421.65   **5.** $1941.75   **7.** $433.37   **9.** $1405   **11.** $688.40   **13.** $748   **15.** $2136   **19.** $5030; $201.20; $491.20 **21.** $4085; $245.10; $745.10   **23.** $19,530; $585.90; $585.90   **25.** $2897; $144.85; $354.85   **27.** $916.20   **29.** $5646 **31. (a)** $2495 **(b)** $1695   **33.** $874.27

Section 6.3 (page 211)

1. 652; $378.16   **3.** 451; $338.25   **5.** 665; $452.20   **7.** 588; $270.48   **9.** 670; $522.60   **11.** $190.00   **13.** $230.24   **15.** $421.75 **17.** $260.19   **19.** $284.65   **21.** $297   **23.** $274.80   **25.** $439.52   **27.** $503.80   **29.** $322.57   **31.** $340.73   **35.** $844   **37.** $777.75 **39.** $648.40

Section 6.4 (page 218)

1. $20.13; $4.71   **3.** $28.72; $6.72   **5.** $52.99; $12.39   **7.** $67.35; $15.75   **9.** $261.55   **11.** $39.66   **13.** $28.46   **15.** $368.80; $76.07; $444.87; $27.58; $6.45; $4.45   **17.** $412; $61.80; $473.80; $29.38; $6.87; $4.74   **19.** $327.20; $61.35; $388.55; $24.09; $5.63; $3.89   **21.** $700; $177.19; $877.19; $54.39; $12.72; $8.77   **23. (a)** $24.07 **(b)** $5.63   **25. (a)** $95.67 **(b)** $22.38 **(c)** $15.43 **27.** $7221.60; $1688.92   **29.** $4317.33; $1009.70   **31.** $3328.61; $778.46

Section 6.5 (page 229)

1. $175   **3.** $38   **5.** $46   **7.** $40   **9.** $23   **11.** $77   **13.** $8.30   **15.** $8.89   **17.** $88.58   **19.** $35.73; $8.36; $15.30; $516.89 **21.** $155.78; $36.43; $268.13; $2052.19   **23.** $141.16; $33.01; $193.55; $1909.11   **25.** $122.21; $28.58; $82.06; $1738.21 **27.** $168.02; $39.30; $415.94; $2086.74   **29.** $110.76; $25.90; $355.07; $1294.71   **31.** $114.84; $26.86; $129.86; $1580.64 **35.** $749.20   **37.** $570.23   **39.** $3765.89

Section 6.6 (page 234)

1. $2392.04 **3.** $2671.70 **5.** $2162.14 **7.** $9558.80 **9.** $1570.26 **11.** $13,129.72 **13.** $12,831.18 **15.** $17,914.01 **19.** $3355 **21.** $2791.98 **23. (a)** $1120 **(b)** $69.44 **25. (a)** $1600 **(b)** $99.20

Chapter 6 Review Exercises (page 239)

1. 40; 8.5; $482.14 **2.** 40; 8; $442 **3.** 38.25; 0; $415.01 **4.** 40; 17.25; $803.68 **5.** $821.60; $890.07; $1780.13; $21,361.60 **6.** $530; $1148.33; $2296.67; $27,560 **7.** $346.15; $692.31; $750; $1500 **8.** $403.85; $807.69; $1750; $21,000 **9.** $760 **10.** $427.50 **11.** $3641.12 **12.** $3374.55 **13.** $532.10 **14.** $134 **15.** $3525 **16.** $465 **17.** $600 **18.** $265.02 **19. (a)** $576.60 **(b)** $134.85 **20. (a)** $477.40 **(b)** $134.85 **21.** $42 **22.** $48 **23.** $187 **24.** $47 **25.** $44 **26.** $13 **27.** $1485.53 **28.** $563.58 **29.** $804.87 **30.** $1946.18 **31.** $9386.32 **32. (a)** $31.90 **(b)** $7.46 **(c)** $5.14 **33. (a)** $110.98 **(b)** $38.43 **34.** $5451.25 **35. (a)** $4810.61 **(b)** $1125.06 **36. (a)** $3424.70 **(b)** $800.94 **37. (a)** $913 **(b)** $56.61 **38. (a)** $2140 **(b)** $132.68

Chapter 6 Business Application Case #1 (page 241)

(a) $740 **(b)** $333 **(c)** $1073 **(d)** $66.53 **(e)** $15.56 **(f)** $154.30 **(g)** $10.73 **(h)** $37.56 **(i)** $220 **(j)** $568.32

Chapter 6 Business Application Case #2 (page 242)

(a) 25.5 million; 51 million; 100% **(b)** FICA, $1029.20; Medicare, $240.70

Chapter 7

Section 7.1 (page 248)

1. $2.29; $8.38; $86.87 **3.** $2.15; $1.43; $51.28 **5.** $7.43; $30.36; $186.29 **7.** $57.55; $98.66; $978.39 **9.** $1837.50; $504; $31,741.50 **11.** $160; $169.60 **13.** $157.50; $163.80 **15.** $330; $351.45 **17.** $1276.80; $1340.64 **19.** $102.20; $5.11 **21.** $520.30; $31.22 **23.** $19.76; $0.84 **25.** $315; $18.90 **27.** $2753.05; $192.71 **31. (a)** $7.19 **(b)** $13.18 **(c)** $140.17 **33.** $258.53 **35.** $1250 **37.** $58,544.64 **39. (a)** $149.48 **(b)** $12.70 too high **41.** $2192 **43.** $16,500

Section 7.2 (page 254)

1. $136,480 **3.** $60,830 **5.** $325,125 **7.** 5.6% **9.** 3.7% **11.** 3% **13. (a)** 2.8% **(b)** $2.80 **(c)** $28 **15. (a)** $2.41 **(b)** $24.10 **(c)** 24.1 **17. (a)** 7.08% **(b)** $70.80 **(c)** 70.8 **21.** $5861.60 **23.** $47,498.22 **25.** $4464 **27.** 5.8% **29.** $6273 **31.** $5.25 **33.** $236,800 **35.** 3.4% **37.** $13,817.55 **39.** $200,925 **41. (a)** The second county **(b)** $300.96 **43.** 2.5% **45.** $2500

Section 7.3 (page 269)

1. $23,131 **3.** $21,710 **5.** $39,031 **7.** $23,650; $3156 **9.** $17,851; $1895 **11.** $42,600; $5608 **13.** $22,310; $2955 **15.** $34,750; $5111 **17.** $47,323; $7006 **19.** $1301.75 tax refund **21.** $611.81 tax refund **23.** $3832.50 tax due **27.** $80,346; $12,934 **29.** $70,550; $14,061 **31.** $70,880; $12,895 **33.** $102,828; $18,555

Chapter 7 Review Exercises (page 273)

1. $51.13; $85.22; $988.50 **2.** $6.89; $9.48; $102.52 **3.** $825; $1342; $18,667 **4.** $24.22; $52.16; $422.34 **5.** $1134 **6.** $284 **7.** $280 **8.** $327.15 **9.** $422 **10.** $125 **11.** $279 **12.** $159.68 **13.** 4.06%; $40.60; 40.6 **14.** 2.7%; $2.70; $27 **15.** $1.27; $12.70; 12.7 **16.** 1.95%; $1.95; 19.5 **17.** $13,632 **18.** $18.50 **19.** $46,500 **20.** 2.8% **21.** $96,200 **22.** $2797.20 **23.** $29,665; $4059 **24.** $60,928; $8357 **25.** $46,870; $6248 **26.** $101,260; $20,490 **27.** 2.2% **28.** $194.88 **29.** $39,124.50 **30.** $73,420; $11,203 **31.** $19,740; $2401 **32.** $46,732; $6227 **33.** $1451.80 tax refund **34.** $97.10 tax refund **35.** $1699.36 tax due **36.** $972.40 tax refund

Chapter 7 Business Application Case #1 (page 275)

(a) Anderson: $3,143,664; Bentonville: $3,488,706 **(b)** Anderson: $785,916; Bentonville: $697,741.20 **(c)** Anderson: $25,149.31; Bentonville: $52,330.59 **(d)** Anderson: $3,395,157.10; Bentonville: $4,012,011.90 **(e)** Anderson

Chapter 7 Business Application Case #2 (page 276)

(a) $1718.25 **(b)** $3757.56 **(c)** $4016.25 **(d)** $33,440 **(e)** $4233.50 **(f)** $800.03 **(g)** $14,525.59 **(h)** 25.8% rounded

Chapter 8

Section 8.1 (page 285)

1. $4707 **3.** $3158 **5.** $9299 **7.** $8648 **9.** $432.40 **11.** $3985.20 **13.** $828.85 **15.** $243 **17. (a)** $2010 **(b)** $670 **19. (a)** $2552.08 **(b)** $1822.92 **21. (a)** $2654 **(b)** $2654 **23.** $19,850 **25.** $92,201.90 **27.** $36,500 **29.** $12,554.95 **31.** A: $60,000; B: $20,000 **33.** 1: $292,500; 2: $260,000; 3: $97,500 **35. (a)** $300,000 **(b)** A: $175,000, B: $125,000 **(c)** $60,000 **37. (a)** $12,500 **(b)** 1: $7500; 2: $5000 **(c)** $7500 **39.** $18,804 **41.** $1084 **43.** $1057.50 **45.** $930 **47. (a)** $1112.50 **(b)** $1557.50 **49. (a)** $1134 **(b)** $810 **53. (a)** $19,936.71 **(b)** $2563.29 **55. (a)** $30,681.82 **(b)** $14,318.18

59. A: $274,000 B: $182,667 C: $91,333   **61. (a)** $375,000 **(b)** A: $281,250; B: $93,750   **63. (a)** $75,000 **(b)** 1: $41,667; 2: $20,833; 3: $12,500

Section 8.2 (page 295)

1. $770   **3.** $932   **5.** $609   **7.** $814   **9.** $748   **11.** $810   **15.** $1223.25   **17.** $655   **19. (a)** $25,000 **(b)** $11,500   **21. (a)** $1628 **(b)** $6936 **(c)** $100,000 **(d)** $15,250   **23. (a)** $60,000 **(b)** $20,250

Section 8.3 (page 306)

1. $952.50; $485.78; $247.65; $86.49   **3.** $849.10; $433.04; $220.77; $77.10   **5.** $516.80; $263.57; $134.37; $46.93
7. $297; $151.47; $77.22; $26.97   **9.** $531; $270.81; $138.06; $48.21   **11.** $1836.10; $936.41; $477.39; $166.72
13. $3175; $1619.25; $825.50; $288.29   **17.** $15,500   **19.** $30,000   **21.** $196,800   **23.** 23 yr. 315 days   **25.** $289   **27.** 18 years
29. $160.20   **31. (a)** $384 **(b)** $50,000   **33.** $592.62   **35.** $110.41   **37. (a)** $444.72 **(b)** $226.72 **(c)** $79.18 **(d)** $889.44; $906.88;
$950.16   **39. (a)** $5660 **(b)** $11,580 **(c)** 23 yr. 315 days   **41.** $149,500   **43. (a)** $211.50 **(b)** approx. 20 years **(c)** $115.75
(d) $109.50   **45. (a)** $345.50 **(b)** 18 yr. **(c)** $297 **(d)** $286.50

Chapter 8 Review Exercises (page 311)

1. $4630   **2.** $3510   **3.** $434   **4.** $1028   **5.** $1152.45   **6.** $323.40   **7.** $222.90   **8.** $1007.30   **9. (a)** $1312.50 **(b)** $1837.50
10. (a) $1481.25 **(b)** $493.75   **11. (a)** $1230 **(b)** $246   **12. (a)** $464 **(b)** $2320   **13.** $39,473.68   **14.** $72,689.19
15. $2731.66   **16.** $35,707.69   **17.** $796   **18.** $1086.55   **19.** $1157.80   **20.** $746   **21.** $2281.30   **22.** $246   **23.** $133.50
24. $192   **25.** A: $36,000; B: $21,600; C: $14,400   **26. (a)** $125,762 **(b)** 1: $80,030; 2: $45,732   **27. (a)** $25,000 **(b)** $13,400
28. (a) $15,000 **(b)** $0   **29. (a)** $40,000 **(b)** $36,800   **30. (a)** $494.70 **(b)** $252.20 **(c)** $88.08 **(d)** $989.40; $1008.80; $1056.96
31. $67,500   **32. (a)** $11,320 **(b)** $23,160 **(c)** 23 yr. 315 days   **33. (a)** $552.80 **(b)** about 12 yr. **(c)** $475.20 **(d)** $392.80
34. (a) $231.20 **(b)** about 18 yr. **(c)** $185.20 **(d)** $179.60

Chapter 8 Business Application Case #1 (page 314)

(a) $39,940.40   **(b)** $370.39   **(c)** $40,310.79   **(d)** $1389.21

Chapter 8 Business Application Case #2 (page 314)

(a) $2796.96   **(b)** P. Russo: $129, $1457, $240,75, $1926.75; E. Martin: $492, $2777.60, $649.60, $3919.20; T. Hicks: $984, $3596,
$841, $5421   **(c)** $140,363.91

Part 2 Cumulative Review Chapters 5–8 (page 315–316)

1. $1014.40   **2.** $208.15   **3.** $806.25   **4.** $18.14   **5.** $788.11   **6.** $17,984.04   **7.** $595.20   **8. (a)** $2710 **(b)** $1510   **9.** $679.43
10. (a) $102.58 **(b)** $23.99 **(c)** $16.54   **11.** $863.84   **12.** $4359.38   **13.** $272   **14. (a)** $2.68% **(b)** $26.80 **(c)** $26.8
15. (a) $4.62 **(b)** $46.20 **(c)** 46.2   **16.** $37,389.93   **17.** $1330.56   **18. (a)** $150,000 **(b)** A: $83,333; B: $41,667; C: $25,000
19. $861   **20. (a)** $6090 **(b)** $25,000 **(c)** $50,000 **(d)** $125,050   **21. (a)** $1662.09 **(b)** $847.34 **(c)** $295.92 **(d)** $3324.18; $3389.36;
$3551.04

Chapter 9

Section 9.1 (page 324)

1. foot   **3.** sack   **5.** great gross   **7.** case   **9.** drum   **11.** cost per thousand   **13.** gallon   **15.** cash on delivery   **17.** $226.80;
$37.80; $126.36; $848.96: $3610.36; $4850.28; $4887.73   **21.** 0.72   **23.** 0.512   **25.** 0.54   **27.** 0.4025   **29.** 0.532   **31.** 0.342
33. $267.52   **35.** $7.01   **37.** $7.14   **39.** $4919.67   **41.** $11.81   **43.** $640   **49.** $242.99   **51. (a)** 20/15 **(b)** $4.08   **53.** $16,416
55. $2.14 for each music player   **57.** $189   **59. (a)** $274.02 **(b)** $18.27

Section 9.2 (page 330)

1. 0.72; 28%   **3.** 0.5525; 44.75%   **5.** 0.64; 36%   **7.** 0.576; 42.4%   **9.** 0.675; 32.5%   **11.** 0.75; 25%   **13.** 0.648; 35.2%
15. 0.243; 75.7%   **17.** 0.45; 55%   **19.** 0.7; 30%   **21.** 0.5184; 48.16%   **23.** 0.5054; 49.46%   **27.** $720   **29.** $700   **31.** $1920
33. (a) $25.89 **(b)** $28.76 **(c)** $2.87   **35.** $740   **37. (a)** $544.32 **(b)** $604.80 **(c)** $60.48   **39.** 25.0%   **41.** $3857.14
43. 5.0%

Section 9.3 (page 337)

1. Oct. 18; Nov. 7   **3.** Mar. 25; Mar. 30   **5.** Sept. 21; Nov. 10   **7.** Jan. 24; Mar. 15   **9.** Jan. 20; Mar. 6   **11.** $3.03; $160.90
13. $0; $101.28   **15.** $14.48; $747.66   **17.** $0; $659.50   **19.** $29.15; $607.03   **23.** $1990.59   **25.** $674.42   **27.** $1571.62
29. $2511.13   **31.** $2021.32   **33. (a)** April 24; May 4; May 14 **(b)** June 3   **35. (a)** April 25 **(b)** May 5   **37.** $3547.50
39. $3106.60

Section 9.4 (page 343)

1. Mar. 10; Mar. 30   **3.** Dec. 22; Jan. 11   **5.** June 16; July 6   **7.** Aug. 10; Aug. 30   **9.** Aug. 24; Sep. 13   **11.** $20.47; $661.81
13. $0; $194.04   **15.** $59.20; $2900.80   **17.** $168.80; $4051.20   **19.** $0.25; $12.13   **21.** $97.52; $3153.08   **23.** $68.33; $1639.85

27. $1900; $1250 **29.** $720; $1030 **31.** $100; $60 **35. (a)** Sept. 15 **(b)** Oct. 5 **37. (a)** Dec. 23 **(b)** Jan. 12
39. $280,645.20 **41. (a)** Dec. 13 **(b)** $2334.93 **43.** $742.84 **45. (a)** $1000 **(b)** $920 **47.** $1495.58 **49.** $93.02
51. (a) $306.12 **(b)** $220.68 **53. (a)** $597.94 **(b)** $522.21 **55. (a)** $489.13 **(b)** $183.17

Chapter 9 Review Exercises (page 350)

1. $345.60 **2.** $195.62 **3.** $1828.18 **4.** $826.20 **5. (a)** 0.6375 **(b)** 36.25% **6. (a)** 0.576 **(b)** 42.4% **7. (a)** 0.54 **(b)** 46%
8. (a) 0.4536 **(b)** 54.64% **9.** $502.08 **10.** $1545.21 **11.** $537.09 **12.** $2262.11 **13.** Mar. 15; April 4 **14.** May 30; June 19
15. Jan. 10; Jan. 30 **16.** Dec. 19; Jan. 8 **17.** $38.41; $1318.17 **18.** $28.37; $917.23 **19.** $35.02; $907.66 **20.** $44.21; $2166.39
21. $306.12; $353.88 **22.** $2597.94; $2712.06 **23.** $505.05; $354.95 **24.** $2113.40; $1736.60 **25. (a)** $394.40 **(b)** $386.51
(c) $398.06 **26. (a)** Builders Supply **(b)** $1.91 **27.** $48,450 **28.** 10% **29.** $1779.95 **30.** $218.73 **31. (a)** April 15 **(b)** $821.24
32. (a) $1875 **(b)** $3405 **(c)** $75

Chapter 9 Business Application Case #1 (page 352)

(a) $17,750.66 **(b)** October 15 **(c)** November 4 **(d)** $17,966.52 **(e)** $10,309.28; $8189.76

Chapter 9 Business Application Case #2 (page 352)

(a) Trident, Inc., $135,193; Shanghai Industries, $148,024 **(b)** Trident, Inc.; Savings = $12,831 **(c)** Answers will vary.

Chapter 10

Section 10.1 (page 359)

1. $4.96; $17.36 **3.** 50%; $35.25 **5.** $39.80; 25.1% **7.** $67.50; 20% **9.** $118; 56.2% **11.** $133.65; $628.65 **15.** $102.22
17. $13.73 **19.** $3609.60 **21.** 29.8% **23. (a)** $95.96 **(b)** 25% **(c)** 125% **25. (a)** 132% **(b)** $97.02 **(c)** $23.52 **27. (a)** $70
(b) 27.2% **(c)** $19.04 **29.** $5172.40 **31.** $6.63

Section 10.2 (page 366)

1. $7; $28 **3.** $131.48; $243.48 **5.** $37.20; $55.80 **7.** $46.36; $24.96 **9.** $77.82; 35.2% **11.** $230; $287.50 **13.** $8.46; $22.26;
61.3% **15.** $750; $1050; 28.6% **17.** $357.52; 22% **19.** 25% **21.** 35.1% **23.** 33.3% **25.** 66.7% **29.** $48.98 **31.** $386.75
33. $119 **35. (a)** $4.50 **(b)** $2.88 **(c)** 64% **37.** 26.5% **39. (a)** 72% **(b)** $259.99 **(c)** $72.80 **41. (a)** $0.72 **(b)** 100%
43. (a) $13,680 **(b)** $6080 **(c)** 44.4% **(d)** 80% **45. (a)** $472 **(b)** 150% **47. (a)** 43.8% **(b)** 30.4% **49. (a)** $64.80 **(b)** 25.9%
51. (a) $24.90 **(b)** 12.5% **(c)** 14.2%

Section 10.3 (page 372)

1. $1.11 **3.** $3.13 **5.** $9 **7.** $1.65 **9.** 24; $8.94 **11.** 18; $22 **13.** 76; $3.75 **15.** 1900; $16.58 **17.** 160; 40; $3.36
19. 34; 6; $78.53 **21.** 108; 36; $4.17 **23.** 700; 300; $4.71 **27.** $4.22 **29.** $78.75 **31.** $30 **33.** $308.75 **35.** $177.78
37. $24.13

Supplementary Exercises: Markup (page 374)

1. $22.35 **3.** 19.1% **5.** $6.98 **7.** $125.50 **9. (a)** 76% **(b)** $179.99 **(c)** $43.20 **11.** $0.65

Chapter 10 Review Exercises (page 377)

1. $6.40; $38.40 **2.** $24.60; $30.75 **3.** $147; 50% **4.** $45.90; 42.5% **5.** $18.08; $90.40 **6.** $105; 25% **7.** $34.70; $52.05
8. 38.5%; $460.20 **9.** $1920; $2400; 25% **10.** $64.50; 100%; 50% **11.** $8; 46%; 31.5% **12.** $474.28; $948.56; 50%
13. $22.08; 50%; $33\frac{1}{3}$% **14.** $150.16; $525.56; 28.6% **15.** 25% **16.** 50% **17.** 18.1% **18.** $16\frac{2}{3}$% **19.** $1.25 **20.** $32.50
21. $13.59 **22.** $17.04 **23.** 135; 15; $6.67 **24.** 72; 18; $2.38 **25.** 216; 72; $8.27 **26.** 700; 300; $4.71 **27.** $34.31
28. $632 **29.** 40% **30. (a)** $37.99 **(b)** 19.0% **(c)** 23.5% **31. (a)** $19,050.25 **(b)** 47% **32.** $6 **33. (a)** 20% **(b)** 25%
34. $12.35

Chapter 10 Business Application Case #1 (page 378)

(a) $16,116.41 **(b)** $20,127 **(c)** $4010.59 **(d)** 20% **(e)** 25%

Chapter 10 Business Application Case #2 (page 379)

(a) 5.2% **(b)** $373,375.60 **(c)** 63.4% **(d)** 38.8%

Chapter 11

Section 11.1 (page 386)

1. 25%; $645 **3.** 45%; $13.86 **5.** $6.50; $1.30 **7.** $2.70; $1.62 **9.** $21.75; $21.75 **11.** $857; 20% **13.** $60; $10; none
15. $16; $22; $6 **17.** $385; $250; $60 **19.** $29; $10; $39 **23.** $239 **25.** 18% **27.** $298 operating loss **29. (a)** $63.62
(b) $40.75 **(c)** 27% **31. (a)** $256.50 **(b)** 11%

Section 11.2 (page 391)

1. $11,680 **3.** $22,673 **5.** $24,500 **7.** 2.81; 2.83 **9.** 7.94; 7.98 **11.** 10.25; 10.25 **13.** 4.66; 4.69 **17.** $49,717.15 **19.** 5.43 **21.** 6.32 **23.** 11.09 **25.** 4.17

Section 11.3 (page 399)

1. $827 **3.** $560 **5. (a)** $182 **(b)** $195 **(c)** $170 **7. (a)** $2352 **(b)** $2385 **(c)** $2313 **9.** $1770 **11. (a)** $48 **(b)** $50 **(c)** $51 **13. (a)** $1251 **(b)** $1430 **(c)** $1040 **15. (a)** $6144 **(b)** $6784 **(c)** $5500 **17.** $130,600 **19.** $30,641

Chapter 11 Review Exercises (page 404)

1. $28.80; $67.20 **2.** $15; $5 **3.** $5.40; $2.70 **4.** 25%; $585 **5.** $48; $66 **6.** $100; $7; none **7.** $100; $70; $8 **8.** $6.25; $0.75; none **9.** $41,051 **10.** $348,468 **11.** $76,411.80 **12.** $32,859.80 **13.** 5.73; 5.76 **14.** 7.94; 7.98 **15.** 4.66; 4.69 **16.** 4.56; 4.63 **17.** $556 **18.** $1242 **19.** $3640 **20.** $6017 **21.** 28% **22. (a)** $78.40 **(b)** 7% **23.** $32,568 **24.** 10.77 **25.** 12.64 **26. (a)** $6489 **(b)** $5887.50 **(c)** $6675 **27.** $115,000 **28.** $75,600

Chapter 11 Business Application Case #1 (page 406)

(a) $187.50 **(b)** $3093.75 **(c)** $562.50 **(d)** $0

Chapter 11 Business Application Case #2 (page 406)

(a) Small boats, 27.2%; Mid-sized boats, 34.8%; Parts, 60%; Misc, 50.9% **(b)** Total Cost, $271,890; Original Selling Price, $370,820; 36.4% **(c)** $283,677.30 **(d)** 4.3%

Part 3 Cumulative Review Chapters 9–11 (page 407)

1. $201.60 **2.** $240.47 **3.** 0.72; 28% **4.** 0.64; 36% **5.** 0.532; 46.8% **6.** 0.27; 73% **7.** $14.81; $762.57 **8.** $34.97; $839.25 **9.** $113.65; $3745.73 **10.** $93.85; $4598.65 **11.** $288.14; 100%; 50% **12.** $114.66; $152.88; 25% **13.** 700 pr.; 300 pr.; $2.36 **14.** 135; 15; $20 **15.** $48; $66; $18 **16.** $50; $35; $4 **17.** $64,877 **18.** $211,981 **19.** 5.73 at retail; 5.76 at cost **20.** 4.66 at retail; 4.69 at cost **21. (a)** $1533.44 **(b)** $1916.80 **(c)** $383.36 **22.** $3506.44 **23.** $730 **24.** 20% **25. (a)** $124.99 **(b)** 25% **(c)** $33\frac{1}{3}$% **26.** 28% **27. (a)** $131.10 operating loss **(b)** $45.60 absolute loss **28.** $65,139 average inventory **29.** $12,978 weighted-average method **30. (a)** $11,775 FIFO **(b)** $13,350 LIFO

Chapter 12

Section 12.1 (page 414)

1. $850 **3.** $785.33 **5.** $1340.63 **7.** $644.90 **9.** $3821.17 **11.** $500 **13.** $4062.50 **15.** 7% **17.** 14 **19.** 1.5 years **21.** $4200 **23.** 11 months **25.** 8% **27.** $146.25 **29.** $1,525,000 **31.** 8 months **33.** 2.5% **37.** $170.67 **39.** 11.1% **41.** $13.48 **43.** $1660

Section 12.2 (page 421)

1. 209 days **3.** 36 days **5.** 196 days **7.** October 12 **9.** March 10 **11.** April 11 **13.** $450 **15.** $162.50 **17.** $336.46 **19.** $67.13 **21.** $104.11 **23.** $115.56 **25.** $114.68 **27.** $157.04 **31.** $118.36 **33.** $2092.54 **35.** $3234 **37.** $18,229.17 **39. (a)** $532.60 **(b)** $540 **(c)** $7.40 **41. (a)** $9057.53 **(b)** $9183.33 **(c)** $125.80 **43.** $249.05 **45.** First Bank; $9.34

Section 12.3 (page 428)

1. $637.50; $9137.50 **3.** $191.72; $5991.72 **5.** $1080; $9720 **7.** $133.33; $4933.33 **9.** 70; $8733.78 **11.** $10\frac{1}{2}$%; $14,490 **13.** $16,400; $717.50 **15.** $14,800; 180 **17.** $126; 180 **19.** $42,459.44; 15% **21.** $490; $12,490 **23.** 140 days; $512.36 **25.** $1200; 12% **27.** $59,315.59; $5684.41

Section 12.4 (page 436)

1. $4932 **3.** $11,462.50 **5.** $4529.22 **7.** $2400 **9.** $8400 **11.** $8700 **15.** $6,755,576.39 **17.** $58,437.50 **19.** $78,333.34 **21.** $7104.85 **23.** $3377.33 **25.** $397.50 loss **27.** $17,400 in 150 days

Chapter 12 Review Exercises (page 441)

1. $840 **2.** $840 **3.** $8710 **4.** $2400 **5.** 9% **6.** 7.5% **7.** 9 months **8.** 30 months **9.** 114 days **10.** 115 days **11.** $258.90 **12.** $336.58 **13.** $222.51 **14.** $867.95 **15.** $43.17 **16.** $3241.33 **17.** $12,199.80 **18.** $6181.82 **19.** 7% **20.** $8\frac{1}{4}$% **21.** 40 days **22.** 90 days **23.** $6270 **24.** $7272.60 **25.** $12,000 **26.** $6500 **27.** 9% **28.** 12% **29.** $6418.15 **30.** $11,612.90 **31.** $8093.75 **32.** $19,550.56 **33.** $809.69 **34.** $15,598.34 **35.** $84.38 **36.** $19,297.50 **37.** 250 days **38.** $3600 **39.** 9.5% **40.** 17.3%; no **41.** 322 days **42.** $9127.31 **43.** $19,528.16 **44.** $11,948.33 **45.** $852 gain **46.** $2811 loss

Chapter 12 Business Application Case #1 (page 444)

September 3, $600, $12,600; July 16, $186, $6386; January 25 of the following year, $971.11, $19,371.11; Totals: $1757.11, $38,357.11

Chapter 12 Business Application Case #2 (page 444)

(a)

	Interest	Maturity Value
Shanghai Bank	$558,080	$13,358,080
Bacon Funds	$1,228,800	$14,028,800
Jidlaka Investments	$707,093.33	$13,507,093.33

(b) The loan from Jidlaka Investments is only for 1 more month than the one from Shanghai Bank but the interest rate is quite a bit higher. So that does not appear to be a good choice. The loan from Shanghai Bank looks best unless Navistar Shipping needs the longer term of 12 months from Bacon Funds.

Chapter 13

Section 13.1 (page 450)

1. Helen Spence   **3.** Leta Clendenen   **5.** 90 days   **7.** January 25   **9.** September 20   **11.** June 30   **13.** March 17   **15.** April 23
17. November 9; $6225   **19.** June 10; $5354.17   **21.** $8400   **23.** 120 days   **25.** 11%   **27.** $12,954   **31. (a)** April 25 **(b)** $19,396.67
33. (a) November 15 **(b)** $90,206.25   **35.** $12,500   **37. (a)** April 7 **(b)** $28,400   **39.** 90 days   **41.** 8%   **43.** $2004

Section 13.2 (page 460)

1. $103.50; $4496.50   **3.** $779.17; $7720.83   **5.** $66.50; $8333.50   **7.** April 13; $8143.33   **9.** February 17; $11,430
11. 8/3; $1140; $22,860   **13.** 11%; $13,740   **15.** $7200; 6%; 2/10   **17.** $220; $5780   **19.** 120 days   **21.** 6.5%   **23.** $3329.48
25. $7358; 9.0%   **27.** $415,891.80; 4.3%   **29. (a)** $24,625,000 **(b)** $25,000,000 **(c)** $375,000 **(d)** 6.09%

Section 13.3 (page 465)

1. 9.28%   **3.** 11.15%   **5.** 8.22%   **7.** 8.27%   **9.** 11.18%   **11.** 9.73%   **15.** 13% simple interest   **17.** $22.98   **19.** First Financial; $193.33

Section 13.4 (page 470)

1. 83 days   **3.** 59 days   **5.** $7981.33   **7.** $14,100   **9.** 61 days; $73.30; $3531.70   **11.** 68 days; $159.98; $6897.85   **13.** 81 days; $286.50; $10,324.61   **15. (a)** 93 days **(b)** $274.48 **(c)** $8579.69   **17. (a)** $719.77 **(b)** $18,473.98   **19. (a)** $22,950 **(b)** $23,340 **(c)** $390   **21. (a)** $33,093.33 **(b)** $35,202.22 **(c)** $2108.89   **23. (a)** $95,200 **(b)** $1923.08 **(c)** $98,076.92 **(d)** 4.91%

Chapter 13 Review Exercises (page 475)

1. $462.78; $10,262.78   **2.** $10\frac{1}{2}$%; $3078.75   **3.** 240 days; $8640   **4.** $14,500; $15,170.63   **5.** May 8; $12,360   **6.** January 5; $6416.67   **7.** $480; $17,520   **8.** $1365; $24,635   **9. (a)** 99 days **(b)** $410.85 **(c)** $12,039.15   **10. (a)** 50 days **(b)** $146.92 **(c)** $8668.29   **11.** 11.53%   **12.** 9.40%   **13.** 11.32%   **14.** $24,642.36   **15.** $547.61   **16.** 9%   **17.** 180 days   **18.** 200 days
19. 10.75%   **20.** 11%; 10.71%   **21.** 13.04%   **22.** $13,874.39   **23.** 150 days   **24.** $2216.67   **25.** 15.9%   **26.** $18,400
27. $8318.53   **28.** 170 days   **29.** $1900; $23,100   **30.** $36,000   **31.** $24,366.67   **32.** $15,750.67   **33.** $85,420.83   **34.** $38,000
35. $11,279.51   **36.** 12.66%; 8.98%

Chapter 13 Business Application Case #1 (page 477)

(a) $1,037,500; Interest to be paid to the Chinese investment house:
$I = \$80,000,000 \times 0.05 \times \frac{180}{360} = \$2,000,000$
Interest from the Canadian firm:
$I = \$38,000,000 \times 0.07 \times \frac{180}{360} = \$1,330,000$
Interest from the British contractor:
$B = \$27,500,000 \times 0.082 \times \frac{180}{360} = \$1,127,500$
Interest from the Louisiana company:
$B = \$14,500,000 \times 0.08 \times \frac{180}{360} = \$580,000$

Interest received by Bank of America:	$1,330,000
	1,125,500
	+ 580,000
	$3,037,500

Interest received by Bank of America:	$3,037,500
Interest paid by Bank of America:	−$2,000,000
Difference:	$1,037,500

(b) $78,292,500

Loan		Amount loaned out
First		$38,000,000
Second	$27,500,000 − $1,127,500 =	$26,372,500
Third	$14,500,000 − $580,000 =	$13,920,000
	Total loaned out	$78,292,500

Chapter 13 Business Application Case #2 (page 478)

(a) Bank U.S., $19,419,889.50, $204,419,889.50; Japan FundCo, $18,130,000.00, $203,130,000.00; Niacin Strong, $21,473,214.29, $206,473,214.29. The best loan is the one with the lowest total interest for the one-year loan, or the loan offered by Japan FundCo.
(b) The most expensive loan is the one offered by Niacin Strong. Difference in interest = $3,343,214.29

Chapter 14

Section 14.1 (page 487)

1. $15,116.54; $3116.54   **3.** $6626.92; $626.92   **5.** $21,724.52   **7.** $17,024.33   **9.** $6032.76   **11.** $5755.82   **13.** $300; $338.23; $38.23   **15.** $3163.37; $3775.92; $612.55   **17.** 8.24%   **19.** 9.38%   **21. (a)** $5978.09 **(b)** $5983.40   **23. (a)** $2624.77 **(b)** $2667.70 **(c)** $2689.86 **(d)** $2704.89 **(e)** $2400   **25.** $12,043.41   **27. (a)** $11,248.64; $11,268.25 **(b)** $19.61   **29.** $577,152.52   **31.** 6.09%; 5.12%; the first option   **33.** $18,119.24   **35.** $12,250.08   **39.** $587.92   **41.** $85,280.20

Section 14.2 (page 497)

1. $38.16   **3.** $35.62   **5.** $7267.81   **7.** $2992.00   **9.** $5637.43   **11.** $17,271.15   **13.** $4673.06   **15.** $867.50   **19.** $5845.41   **21. (a)** $118.49 **(b)** $11,638.49   **23.** $0   **25.** $175.61   **27.** $9019.97; $1019.97   **29.** $14,656.83; $2656.83   **31.** $4333.15   **33.** $18,758.03   **35. (a)** $901,988.58 **(b)** $101,988.58   **37.** 7% compounded semiannually; $5726.58

Section 14.3 (page 502)

1. 3   **3.** 3   **5.** 6%   **7.** 8%   **11.** about $2\frac{1}{2}$ years   **13. (a)** $14,347.42 **(b)** $16,162.26   **15.** 10%   **17.** 3 years   **19.** 28 years   **21.** 20 years   **23.** 35 years   **25.** $40,224.31   **27.** $8219.12   **29.** $21,247.04

Section 14.4 (page 507)

1. $3810.39; $989.61   **3.** $9077.95; $3122.05   **5.** $7543.32; $956.68   **9.** $3564.93; $1435.07   **11.** $8401.69   **13.** $7096.44   **15.** $3800 in 5 years   **17.** $38,288.45; $31,409.86   **19.** $23,520; $18,534.49   **21. (a)** $26,620 **(b)** $20,989.69

Chapter 14 Review Exercises (page 513)

1. $18,093.36; $5693.36   **2.** $8867.39; $1867.39   **3.** $27,454.28; $4954.28   **4.** $23,758.73; $5758.73   **5.** $11,261.45; $2261.45   **6.** $14,576.65; $2576.65   **7.** 7.19%   **8.** 8.24%   **9.** 4.04%   **10.** 9.38%   **11.** $24.29   **12.** $24.21   **13.** $22.68   **14.** $3523.23   **15.** $7248.84   **16.** $9648.39   **17.** $4647.29   **18.** $7328.66   **19.** $12,213.89   **20.** $22,058.47; $9458.47   **21.** $5809.17; $809.17   **22.** 6%   **23.** 10%   **24.** 8%   **25.** 3   **26.** $3\frac{1}{2}$ **27.** $12,178.08; $2121.92   **28.** $3551.89; $448.11   **29.** $3661.63; $2338.37   **30.** $2361.30; $638.70   **31.** $4120.01   **32.** $5238.54   **33.** $2983.58; $983.58   **34.** $5399.30; $1399.30   **35.** $49,699.68   **36. (a)** $15,173.40 **(b)** $13,481.37   **37.** 4 years   **38.** approximately 12 years

Chapter 14 Business Application Case #1 (page 515)

(a) $4,053,386; $3,016,100 **(b)** $2,539,386; $1,889,542 **(c)** $2,798,302; $2,082,199 **(d)** $2,539,386; $1,889,542; $2,798,302; $2,082,199; $4,053,386; $3,016,100

Chapter 14 Business Application Case #2 (page 515)

(a) $47,504,179.84 **(b)** $2,495,820.16 **(c)** $1,949,730.72

Chapter 15

Section 15.1 (page 526)

1. 18.59891389   **3.** 15.19292972   **5.** $58,248.89; $34,448.89   **7.** $73,105.94; $48,105.94   **9.** $67,410.39; $22,610.39   **11.** $46,016.57; $7616.57   **13.** $13,475.82; $3875.82   **15.** $138,997.66; $33,733.66   **17.** $11,320.10   **19.** $13,673.64   **21.** $16,577.77   **23.** $36,895.94   **25.** $57,782.55   **27.** $59,794.96   **29.** $122,676.78   **31.** $263,879.29   **35.** $24,687.62; $4687.62   **37.** $5303.43; $1703.43   **39.** $1413.72   **41.** $952.33   **43.** 28 quarterly payments; $15,516.67   **45.** 37 monthly payments; $35,030.62   **47.** $7188.27   **49. (a)** $17,256.21 **(b)** $2856.21   **51.** $34,186.78; $14,706.78   **53.** 31 months; $4075.14   **55. (a)** $15,100.50 **(b)** $13,566.97

Section 15.2 (page 533)

1. 8.82711975 **3.** 6.81086449 **5.** $16,004.78 **7.** $11,901.98 **9.** $6540.57 **13.** $839,255.24 **15.** $239,326.76
17. $12,675.75; $4124.25 **19. (a)** $252,691.00 **(b)** $209,764.50 **21. (a)** $48,879.75 **(b)** No **23.** $93,636.35 **25.** $51,000 down
and $8000 per year **27.** $335,000 today **29.** $28,847.04 **31.** $27,050.13

Section 15.3 (page 538)

1. 0.05427783 **3.** 0.00295961 **5.** $1957.50 **7.** $576.19 **11. (a)** $106,747.76 **(b)** $699.22 **13. (a)** $305,866.11 **(b)** $2003.48
15. (a) $274,802.78 **(b)** $151,183.32 **17.** $9572.45 **19.** $404,143.76; $766,849.92 **21.** $17,047.28; $443,229.18; $443,229.18;
$213,090.95; $35,458.33; $691,778.46; $691,778.46; $213,090.98; $55,342.28; $960,211.72 **23. (a)** $604,910.16 **(b)** $437,596.64

Chapter 15 Review Exercises (page 543)

1. $69,152.45 **2.** $34,426.47 **3.** $113,736.00 **4.** $49,153.29 **5.** $163,383.42 **6.** $97,457.37 **7.** $20,114.46; $2514.46
8. $134,489.45; $21,989.45 **9.** $38,253.24 **10.** $5948.27 **11.** $8055.06 **12.** $5094.30 **13.** $11,298.18 **14.** $1332.74
15. $22,217.87 **16.** $623.89 **17.** $80,627.53 **18.** 31 years **19.** $6427.17 **20.** $20,891.12 **21.** $25,723.79 **22.** $2676.72
23. $32,625.58 **24.** $98,713.33 **25. (a)** $886,898.80 **(b)** $713,918.56 **26.** $21,866.87; $21,886.87; $1968.02; $45,701.76;
$45,701.76; $21,866.87; $4113.16; $71,681.79; $71,681.79; $21,866.85; $6451.36; $100,000.00

Chapter 15 Business Application Case #1 (page 545)

(a) $517,204.85 **(b)** $53,046.70 **(c)** $520,820.32 **(d)** Almost, but not quite.

Chapter 15 Business Application Case #2 (page 545)

(a) $6,165,389.97 **(b)** $15,134,610.03 **(c)** $2,658,160.27

Chapter 16

Section 16.1 (page 554)

1. $10.03 **3.** $4.87 **5.** $132.64; $1.99; $133.80 **7.** $2764.63; $41.47; $2881.75 **9.** $938.73; $14.08; $857.83 **11.** $681.52;
$10.22; $769.01 **13. (a)** $42.01 **(b)** $28 **(c)** $14.01 **15. (a)** $72.76 **(b)** $38.80 **(c)** $33.96 **21.** $276

Section 16.2 (page 562)

1. $20,896.40; $3496.40 **3.** $180; $30 **5.** $1200; $120 **7.** 12.50% **9.** 10.25% **11.** 11.25% **15.** 12.00% **17.** 11.00%
19. (a) 732,212.32 pesos **(b)** 13.75% **21. (a)** $209,239.80 **(b)** 12.00%

Section 16.3 (page 568)

1. $5130.57; $130.57 **3.** $3754.46; $254.46 **5.** $4333.78; $333.78 **7.** $385.52 **9.** $21.90 **11.** $139.81 **17. (a)** $6569.44
(b) $131,569.44 **19.** $148.50 **21. (a)** $51.82 **(b)** $490.58 **23.** $41,176.11; $1876.11 **25. (a)** 66 days **(b)** $11,564.31

Section 16.4 (page 573)

1. 0.11328724 **3.** 0.10334306 **5.** $1153.61 **7.** $404.73 **9.** $4185.25 **11.** $161.95 **13.** $152.64; $695.04 **15.** $321.92;
$3452.16 **17.** $15,987.97; $147,663.16

19.

Payment Number	Amount of Payment	Interest for Period	Portion to Principal	Principal at End of Period
0	—	—	—	$4000.00
1	$1207.68	$320.00	$887.68	3112.32
2	1207.68	248.99	958.69	2153.63
3	1207.68	172.29	1035.39	1118.24
4	1207.70	89.46	1118.24	0

21.

Payment Number	Amount of Payment	Interest for Period	Portion to Principal	Principal at End of Period
0	—	—	—	$14,500.00
1	$374.77	$132.92	$241.85	14,258.15
2	374.77	130.70	244.07	14,014.08
3	374.77	128.46	246.31	13,767.77
4	374.77	126.20	248.57	13,519.20
5	374.77	123.93	250.84	13,268.36

25.

Payment Number	Amount of Payment	Interest for Period	Portion to Principal	Principal at End of Period
0	—	—	—	$8000.00
1	$576.99	$80.00	$496.99	7503.01
2	576.99	75.03	501.96	7001.05
3	576.99	70.01	506.98	6494.07
⋮	⋮	⋮	⋮	⋮
14	576.99	11.37	565.62	571.28
15	576.99	5.71	571.28	0

Section 16.5 (page 582)

1. $651.70   **3.** $1367.28   **5.** $2007.00   **9.** $928.17   **11.** $1451.93   **13.** $1900.39   **15.** Yes, they are qualified. The payment would be $1434.58.

17.

Payment Number	Total Payment	Interest Payment	Principal Payment	Balance of Principal
0	—	—	—	$212,000.00
1	$1908	$1590.00	$318.00	$211,682.00
2	$1908	$1587.62	$320.38	$211,361.62

19. (a) $951.38 **(b)** $718.07 **(c)** $85,935.31   **21.** $121,000

Chapter 16 Review Exercises (page 587)

1. $3.65   **2.** $40.51   **3.** $14.18   **4.** $552.56; $8.29; $551.80   **5.** $216.51; $3.25; $203.40   **6.** $2700; $2915.14; $215.14
7. $4600; $5040; $440   **8.** $8000; $9600; $1600   **9.** 13%   **10.** 13.75%   **11.** 12.75%   **12.** 11.5%   **13.** $10,876.33; $476.33
14. $7309.87; $309.87   **15.** $915.66; $115.66   **16.** $4641.89; $141.89   **17.** $3638.63   **18.** $2395.83   **19.** $795.42   **20.** $392.89
21. $442.51; $1220.24   **22.** $339.80; $2271.60   **23.** $245.94; $2805.12   **24.** $574.16; $2224.80   **25.** $1449   **26.** $874.20
27. $956   **28.** $1817.29   **29. (a)** $2788.22 **(b)** $173.22   **30.** $171.85; $2.58   **31.** $18,756.32; 10.50%   **32.** $2822.98
33. $1400.03   **34. (a)** $1397.02 **(b)** $360,284.80   **35. (a)** 60 days **(b)** $8100.82

Chapter 16 Business Application Case #1 (page 590)

(a) $495.08; $420.06; $978.51; $149.46; $2043.11 **(b)** $2043.11; $215.00; $120.00; $295; $2673.11 **(c)** $392.37; $285.64; $695.83; $149.46; $187.00; $120.00, $210.83, $2041.13 **(d)** $631.98

Chapter 16 Business Application Case #2 (page 591)

(a) $1647.59 **(b)** $501.33 **(c)** $4380.78 **(d)** $6028.37 **(e)** $524.96 **(f)** $206,000 **(g)** $22,888.89; 41 months

Part 4 Cumulative Review Chapters 12–16 (page 592)

1. $150   **2.** $417.64   **3.** $2400.17   **4.** $12,449.83   **5.** 9.7%   **6.** 13.5%   **7.** 80 days   **8.** 150 days   **9.** $270; $8730
10. $33.18; $841.82   **11.** 10.3%   **12.** 11.3%   **13.** $1947.90   **14.** $7599.42   **15.** $12,686.07; $86.07   **16.** $7562.10; $62.10
17. $583.49; $416.51   **18.** $12,182.15; $6817.85   **19.** $9214.23   **20.** $31,123.18   **21.** $13,367.28   **22.** $639,160.10
23. $403.46   **24.** $112.90   **25.** $10,129.08   **26.** $10,823.31   **27. (a)** $12,106.67 **(b)** $106.67   **28. (a)** $416.67 **(b)** $14,583.33
29. $7993.14   **30.** $94   **31. (a)** $94.91 **(b)** $50.62 **(c)** $44.29   **32. (a)** $12,340 **(b)** $1840 **(c)** $9500 **(d)** 12%   **33.** $2343.75
34. $9.828 million (rounded)   **35. (a)** $10,344.44 **(b)** $20,869.57   **36.** $469.22   **37.** $20.01   **38.** No, the monthly payment would be $1527.68

Chapter 17

Section 17.1 (page 600)

1. 20%   **3.** 12.5%   **5.** 5%   **7.** $6\frac{2}{3}$%   **9.** 1.25%   **11.** 2%   **13.** $450   **15.** $800   **17.** $840   **19.** $2850   **21.** $5000   **23.** $2775
25. $73,000

29.

Year	Computation	Amount of Depreciation	Accumulated Depreciation	Book Value
0	—	—	—	$12,000
1	$\left(33\frac{1}{3}\% \times \$9000\right)$	$3000	$3000	$9000
2	$\left(33\frac{1}{3}\% \times \$9000\right)$	$3000	$6000	$6000
3	$\left(33\frac{1}{3}\% \times \$9000\right)$	$3000	$9000	$3000

31. Book values: $8200; $7000; $5800; $4600; $3400; $2200   **33. (a)** $55,000 depreciation **(b)** $1,025,000 book value
35. (a) $2527 depreciation **(b)** $20,211 book value   **37. (a)** $12\frac{1}{2}$% **(b)** $90 **(c)** $790

Section 17.2 (page 606)

1. 40%   **3.** 25%   **5.** $13\frac{1}{3}$%   **7.** 20%   **9.** $33\frac{1}{3}$%   **11.** 4%   **13.** $3600   **15.** $5000   **17.** $1900   **19.** $3360   **21.** $1215
23. $6834   **25.** $750
29.

Year	Computation	Amount of Depreciation	Accumulated Depreciation	Book Value
0	—	—	—	$14,400
1	(50% × $14,400)	$7200	$7200	$7200
2	(50% × $7200)	$3600	$10,800	$3600
3	(50% × $3600)	$1800	$12,600	$1800
4	—	$1800*	$14,400	$0

*To depreciate to $0 scrap value

31. Book values: $19,125; $14,344; $10,758; $8068; $6051; $4538; $3500; $3500   **33.** $1153   **35.** $8476   **37. (a)** 25% **(b)** $1450
(c) $4425 **(d)** $1375

Section 17.3 (page 613)

1. $\frac{4}{10}$ **3.** $\frac{6}{21}$ **5.** $\frac{7}{28}$ **7.** $\frac{10}{55}$ **9.** $1640   **11.** $10,000   **13.** $600   **15.** $7700   **17.** $2700   **19.** $890   **21.** $2400
25.

Year	Computation	Amount of Depreciation	Accumulated Depreciation	Book Value
0	—	—	—	$10,800
1	$\left(\frac{6}{21} \times \$8400\right)$	$2400	$2400	$8400
2	$\left(\frac{5}{21} \times \$8400\right)$	$2000	$4400	$6400
3	$\left(\frac{4}{21} \times \$8400\right)$	$1600	$6000	$4800
4	$\left(\frac{3}{21} \times \$8400\right)$	$1200	$7200	$3600
5	$\left(\frac{2}{21} \times \$8400\right)$	$800	$8000	$2800
6	$\left(\frac{1}{21} \times \$8400\right)$	$400	$8400	$2400

27. Book values: $2100; $1600; $1200; $900; $700; $600   **29.** $9300   **31.** $24,584   **33. (a)** $7200 **(b)** $6000   **35. (a)** $\frac{8}{36}$
(b) $2360 **(c)** $10,620 **(d)** $4750

Section 17.4 (page 620)

1. $0.35   **3.** $0.029   **5.** $68.75   **7.** $30   **9.** $17,940   **11.** $17,280   **13.** $2775   **15.** $6960   **19.** $1313; $2250   **21.** $1667;
$1833   **23.** $450; $825   **25.** $900; $1088
27.

Year	Computation	Amount of Depreciation	Accumulated Depreciation	Book Value
0	—	—	—	$6800
1	(1350 × $1.26)	$1701	$1701	$5099
2	(1820 × $1.26)	$2293	$3994	$2806
3	(730 × $1.26)	$920	$4914	$1886
4	(1100 × $1.26)	$1386	$6300	$500

29. $26,350   **31.** $3650; $14,600   **33.** $450; $1620   **35.** $2775; $5365

Section 17.5 (page 626)

1. 19.2%   **3.** 11.52%   **5.** 20%   **7.** 3.636%   **9.** 5.76%   **11.** 2.564%   **13.** $1751   **15.** $3226   **17.** $4800   **19.** $6254
21. $16,920   **23.** $2756   **25.** $79,364

29.

Year	Computation	Amount of Depreciation	Accumulated Depreciation	Book Value
0	—	—	—	$10,980
1	(33.33% × $10,980)	$3660	$3660	$7320
2	(44.45% × $10,980)	$4881	$8541	$2439
3	(14.81% × $10,980)	$1626	$10,167	$813
4	(7.41% × $10,980)	$813*	$10,980	$0

*Due to rounding in prior years

31. Book values: $110,430; $88,344; $70,675; $56,540; $45,227; $36,184; $28,147; $20,110; $12,061; $4024; $0   **33.** $82,080
35. year 1: $12,326; years 2–5: $12,307

Chapter 17 Review Exercises (page 631)

1. 20%; 40%; $\frac{5}{15}$ **2.** $16\frac{2}{3}$%; $33\frac{1}{3}$%; $\frac{6}{21}$ **3.** 25%; 50%; $\frac{4}{10}$ **4.** 10%; 20%; $\frac{10}{55}$ **5.** 5%; 10%; $\frac{20}{210}$ **6.** $12\frac{1}{2}$%; 25%; $\frac{8}{36}$ **7.** 11.52%
8. 33.33%   **9.** 4.522%   **10.** 17.49%   **11.** 2.564%   **12.** 3.174%   **13.** $940   **14.** $172,000   **15.** $21,375   **16.** $7400   **17.** year 1:
$2700; year 2: $2025; year 3: $1350; year 4: $675   **18.** $4000   **19.** $1530   **20. (a)** $4836; $2666; $3007; $4712 **(b)** $15,264;
$12,598; $9591; $4879   **21.** $15,120   **22.** $24,000; $19,200; $14,400; $9600; $4800   **23.** $2900   **24.** $1260; $2003   **25.** $2840;
$5112   **26.** $5702   **27.** $4746   **28.** $112,725   **29.** $6222   **30.** $4788   **31.** $1157; $1984; $1417; $1012; $723   **32.** $2,440,928
33. $1995   **34.** $45,600

Chapter 17 Business Application Case #1 (page 633)

(a) $114,000 **(b)** $61,560 **(c)** $228,000 **(d)** $57,000 straight-line; $24,624 double-declining balance; $38,000 sum-of-the-years'-digits

Chapter 17 Business Application Case #2 (page 633)

Year	5-year MACRS	Depreciation	Tax Savings	7-year MACRS	Depreciation	Tax Savings
1	20.00	$5,680,000	$2,272,000	14.29	$4,058,360	$1,623,344
2	32.00	$9,088,000	$3,635,200	24.49	$6,955,160	$2,782,064
3	19.20	$5,452,800	$2,181,120	17.49	$4,967,160	$1,986,864
4	11.52	$3,271,680	$1,308,672	12.49	$3,547,160	$1,418,864
5	11.52	$3,271,680	$1,308,672	8.93	$2,536,120	$1,014,448
6	5.76	$1,635,840	$654,336	8.92	$2,533,280	$1,013,312
7	0	$0	$0	8.93	$2,536,120	$1,014,448
8	0	$0	$0	4.46	$1,266,640	$506,656
9	0	$0	$0	0	$0	$0
10	0	$0	$0	0	$0	$0

Chapter 18

Section 18.1 (page 638)

1. (a) $316,350 **(b)** $88,050 **(c)** $65,350   **3.** $324,200

5.

THEFTPROOF ALARMS
INCOME STATEMENT
QUARTER ENDING DECEMBER 31

Gross sales		$284,000
Returns		$6000
Net sales		$278,000
Inventory, beg. of quarter	$58,000	
Cost of goods purchased	$142,000	
Freight	$3000	
Total cost of goods purchased	$145,000	
Total of goods available for sale	$203,000	
Inventory, end of quarter	$69,000	

THEFTPROOF ALARMS
INCOME STATEMENT
QUARTER ENDING DECEMBER 31

Cost of goods sold		$134,000
Gross profit		$144,000
Expenses		
Salaries and wages	$19,400	
Rent	$6000	
Advertising	$2000	
Utilities	$1800	
Taxes on inventory, payroll	$3000	
Miscellaneous expenses	$4000	
Total expenses		$36,200
Net income before taxes		$107,800
Income taxes		$14,650
Net income		$93,150

7.

KATHY GILMORE, CONSULTANT
INCOME STATEMENT
FOR THE YEAR ENDING DECEMBER 31

Gross sales		$170,500
Returns		0
Net sales		$170,500
Inventory, January 1	0	
Cost of goods purchased	0	
Freight	0	
Total cost of goods purchased	0	
Total of goods available for sale	0	
Inventory, December 31	0	
Cost of goods sold		0
Gross profit		$170,500
Expenses		
Salaries and wages	$63,000	
Rent	$28,000	
Advertising	$12,000	
Utilities	$4000	
Taxes on inventory, payroll	$3800	
Miscellaneous expenses	$9400	
Total expenses		$120,200
Net income before taxes		$50,300
Income taxes		$6800
Net income		$43,500

Section 18.2 (page 646)

1. 32.6%; 45.2%

3.

CAPITAL DISTRICT APPLIANCES

	Amount	Percent	Percent from Table 18.1
Net sales	$900,000	100.0%	100.0%
Cost of goods sold	617,000	68.6%	66.9%
Gross profit	283,000	31.4%	33.1%
Wages	108,900	12.1%	11.9%
Rent	20,700	2.3%	2.4%
Advertising	27,000	3%	2.5%
Total expenses	216,000	24%	26%
Net income before taxes	67,000	7.4%	7.2%

5.

BEST TIRES, INC.
COMPARATIVE INCOME STATEMENT

	This Year		Last Year	
	Amount	Percent	Amount	Percent
Gross sales	$1,856,000	100.3%	$1,692,000	100.7%
Returns	6000	0.3%	12,000	0.7%
Net sales	1,850,000	100.0%	1,680,000	100.0%
Cost of goods sold	1,202,000	65.0%	1,050,000	62.5%
Gross profit	648,000	35.0%	630,000	37.5%
Wages	152,000	8.2%	148,000	8.8%
Rent	82,000	4.4%	78,000	4.6%
Advertising	111,000	6.0%	122,000	7.3%
Utilities	32,000	1.7%	17,000	1.0%
Taxes on inventory, payroll	17,000	0.9%	18,000	1.1%
Miscellaneous expenses	62,000	3.4%	58,000	3.5%
Total expenses	456,000	24.6%	441,000	26.3%
Net income	192,000	10.4%	189,000	11.3%

7. 82.7%; 17.3%; 13.9%; 3.4%; 6.5%; 0.8%; 1.0%; No major problems   **9.** 67.9%; 32.1%; 23.5%; 8.6%; 12.3%; 2.4%; 1.4%; Cost of goods and operating expenses are both high, resulting in a small net income.

Section 18.3 (page 652)

1.

BROOKSHIRE'S GROCERY
BALANCE SHEET FOR DECEMBER 31 (IN MILLIONS)

Assets		
Current assets		
Cash	$273	
Notes receivable	$312	
Accounts receivable	$264	
Inventory	$180	
Total current assets		$1029
Plant assets		
Land	$466	
Buildings	$290	
Fixtures	$28	
Total plant assets		$784
Total assets		$1813

Liabilities		
Current liabilities		
Notes payable	$312	
Accounts payable	$63	
Total current liabilities		$375
Long-term liabilities		
Mortgages payable	$212	
Long-term notes payable	$55	
Total long-term liabilities		$267
Total liabilities		$642

Owners' equity		
Owners' equity	$1171	
Total liabilities and owners' equity		$1813

Section 18.4 (page 661)

1.

OTERO OFFICE SUPPLY
COMPARATIVE BALANCE SHEET

	This Year		Last Year	
	Amount	Percent	Amount	Percent
Assets				
Current assets				
Cash	$52,000	13%	$42,000	13.1%
Notes receivable	$8000	2%	$6000	1.9%
Accounts receivable	$148,000	37%	$120,000	37.5%
Inventory	$153,000	38.3%	$120,000	37.5%
Total current assets	$361,000	90.3%	$288,000	90%
Plant assets				
Land	$10,000	2.5%	$8000	2.5%
Buildings	$14,000	3.5%	$11,000	3.4%
Fixtures	$15,000	3.8%	$13,000	4.1%
Total plant assets	$39,000	9.8%	$32,000	10%
Total Assets	$400,000	100.0%	$320,000	100.0%
Liabilities				
Current liabilities				
Accounts payable	$3000	0.8%	$4000	1.3%
Notes payable	$201,000	50.3%	$152,000	47.5%
Total current liabilities	$204,000	51%	$156,000	48.8%
Long-term liabilities				
Mortgages payable	$20,000	5%	$16,000	5%
Long-term notes payable	$58,000	14.5%	$42,000	13.1%
Total long-term liabilities	$78,000	19.5%	$58,000	18.1%
Total Liabilities	$282,000	70.5%	$214,000	66.9%
Owners' Equity	$118,000	29.5%	$106,000	33.1%
Total Liabilities and Owners' Equity	$400,000	100.0%	$320,000	100.0%

3. (a) 1.77 **(b)** 1.02 **(c)** No, current ratio is low.   **5. (a)** 2.66 **(b)** 1.85 **(c)** Yes, ratios are okay.   **7.** 2.13; 1.27   **9.** 2.39   **11.** 1.39
15. 6.1%   **17.** 8.5 times; 42.9 days

Chapter 18 Review Exercises (page 666)

1. $187,400; $98,200   **2.** $263,730; $138,930   **3.** $141,600; $43,200   **4.** $235,880; $23,580   **5.** $416,600   **6.** $126,500
7. $42,700   **8.** $282,100   **9.** $188,800; 0.56   **10.** $90,600; 0.23

11.

LORI'S BOUTIQUE
INCOME STATEMENT FOR
THE YEAR ENDING DECEMBER 31

Gross sales		$175,000
Returns		$8000
Net sales		$167,000
Inventory, January 1	$44,000	
Cost of goods purchased	$126,000	
Freight	$2000	
Total cost of goods purchased	$128,000	
Total of goods available for sale	$172,000	
Inventory, December 31	$52,000	

LORI'S BOUTIQUE
INCOME STATEMENT FOR
THE YEAR ENDING DECEMBER 31

Cost of goods sold		$120,000
Gross profit		$47,000
Expenses		
Salaries and wages	$9000	
Rent	$4000	
Advertising	$1500	
Utilities	$1000	
Taxes on inventory, payroll	$2000	
Miscellaneous expenses	$3000	
Total expenses		$20,500
Net income before taxes		$26,500

12.

THE GUITAR WAREHOUSE
INCOME STATEMENT
FOR THE YEAR ENDING DECEMBER 31

Gross sales			$2,215,000
Returns			$26,000
Net sales			$2,189,000
Inventory, January 1		$215,000	
Cost of goods			
purchased	$1,123,000		
Freight	$4000		
Total cost of goods purchased		$1,127,000	
Total of goods available for sale		$1,342,000	
Inventory, December 31		$265,000	
Cost of goods sold			$1,077,000
Gross profit			$1,112,000
Expenses			
Salaries and wages		$154,000	
Rent		$59,000	
Advertising		$11,000	
Utilities		$12,000	
Taxes on inventory, payroll		$10,000	
Miscellaneous expenses		$9000	
Total expenses			$255,000
Net income before taxes			$857,000
Income taxes			$242,300
Net income			$614,700

13. 59.8%; 12.8%   **14.** 61.2%; 29.1%

15.

JALISCO MEXICAN FOODS (3RD QUARTER)

	Amount	Percent	Percent from Table 18.1
Net sales	$300,000	100%	100%
Cost of goods sold	$125,000	41.7%	48.4%
Gross profit	$175,000	58.3%	51.6%
Wages	$72,000	24.0%	26.4%
Rent	$12,000	4.0%	2.8%
Advertising	$5700	1.9%	1.4%
Total expenses	$123,000	41.0%	43.7%
Net income	$52,000	17.3%	7.9%

16.

GASKETS, INC.
BALANCE SHEET FOR DECEMBER 31

Assets

Current assets		
Cash	$240,000	
Notes receivable	$180,000	
Accounts receivable	$460,000	
Inventory	$225,000	
Total current assets		$1,105,000
Plant assets		
Land	$180,000	
Buildings	$260,000	
Fixtures	$48,000	
Total plant assets		$488,000
Total assets		$1,593,000

Liabilities

Current liabilities		
Notes payable	$410,000	
Accounts payable	$882,000	
Total current liabilities		$1,292,000
Long-term liabilities		
Mortgages payable	$220,000	
Long-term notes payable	$194,000	
Total long-term liabilities		$414,000
Total liabilities		$1,706,000

Owners' equity

Owners' equity	($113,000)	
Total liabilities and owners' equity		$1,593,000

17. 1.32; 0.46; 1.78   **18.** 0.83; 0.04; 4.17   **19.** 0.78; 0.71; 1.11   **20.** 5.0; 73 days   **21.** 8.6; 42.4 days

22.

	This Year		Last Year	
	Amount	**Percent**	**Amount**	**Percent**
Current assets				
Cash	$28,000	18.8%	$22,000	21.1%
Notes receivable	$12,000	8.1%	$15,000	14.4%
Accounts receivable	$39,000	26.2%	$31,500	30.1%
Inventory	$22,000	14.8%	$20,000	19.1%
Total current assets	$101,000	67.8%	$88,500	84.7%
Total plant and equipment	$48,000	32.2%	$16,000	15.3%
Total assets	$149,000	100.0%	$104,500	100.0%
Total current liabilities	$38,000	25.5%	$36,000	34.4%

Chapter 18 Business Application Case #1 (page 670)

(a)

WALKER BICYCLE SHOP
INCOME STATEMENT
YEAR ENDING DECEMBER 31

Gross sales			$212,000
Returns			$12,500
Net sales			$199,500
Inventory, January 1		$44,000	
Cost of goods purchased	$75,000		
Freight	$8000		
Total cost of goods purchased		$83,000	
Total of goods available for sale		$127,000	
Inventory, December 31		$26,000	
Cost of goods sold			$101,000
Gross profit			$98,500
Expenses			
Salaries and wages		$37,000	
Rent		$12,000	
Advertising		$2000	
Utilities		$3000	
Taxes on inventory, payroll		$7000	
Miscellaneous expenses		$4500	
Total expenses			$65,500
Net income before taxes			$33,000
Income taxes			$4320
Net income after taxes			$28,680

(b) 106.3%; 18.5%; 6.3%; 6%; 50.6%; 1.5%

(c)

WALKER BICYCLE SHOP
BALANCE SHEET
DECEMBER 31

	Assets		
Current assets			
Cash	$62,000		
Notes receivable	$2500		
Accounts receivable	$8200		
Inventory	$26,000		
Total current assets		$98,700	
Plant assets			
Land	$7600		
Buildings	$28,000		
Fixtures	$13,500		
Total plant assets		$49,100	
Total assets			$147,800

WALKER BICYCLE SHOP
BALANCE SHEET
DECEMBER 31

Liabilities			
Current liabilities			
Notes payable	$4500		
Accounts payable	$27,000		
Total current liabilities		$31,500	
Long-term liabilities			
Mortgages payable	$15,000		
Long-term notes payable	$8000		
Total long-term liabilities		$23,000	
Total liabilities			$54,500

Owners' equity			
Owners' equity	$93,300		
Total liability and owners' equity			$147,800

(d) 3.13; 2.31 **(e)** Probably not, profits are too small. Any small problem could result in an inability to repay the loan.

Chapter 18 Business Application Case #2 (page 671)

Answers will vary.

Chapter 19

Section 19.1 (page 677)

1. $0; $0   **3.** $0.30; $0.14   **5.** $20; $0   **7.** $0.10   **9.** $6.50; $0.73   **11.** $1.60; $0.86   **13.** $20; $5.06   **15.** $3.33   **17.** $0.14
19. (a) $0.77 **(b)** $0.90 **(c)** 14.2%   **21.** $26,666.67 each since there are sufficient dividends

Section 19.2 (page 686)

1. $22.90   **3.** $20.90   **5.** $0.16   **7.** $39.90   **9.** 1.1%   **11.** 10   **13.** 17,834,500 shares   **15.** 0%   **17.** $20.59   **19.** $14,398.56
21. $4584.39   **23.** $8832.45   **25.** $3494.67   **27.** $12,548.13   **29.** $25,842.72   **31.** 3.5%   **33.** 2.0%   **35.** 3.0%   **37.** 6   **39.** 14
41. $21,234.24   **43.** $3593.86   **47. (a)** $116,981.22 **(b)** $183,200.50 **(c)** $66,219.28   **49.** 10 years

Section 19.3 (page 692)

1. $1273.47   **3.** 8.000%   **5.** 6.013%   **7.** $19,920   **9.** $19,206.80   **11.** $102,197.60   **13.** $125,850   **17.** $63,923.50; $4000
19. $19,293,340; $1,512,500   **21. (a)** $73,428 **(b)** $5025 **(c)** 6.8%   **23.** $4500   **25.** $93,333.33

Section 19.4 (page 698)

1. $29,000 each   **3.** $73,600 for 1; $18,400 for 2   **5.** $16,920 for 1; $8080 for 2   **7.** $10,000 for 1; $12,000 for 2; $0 for 3
9. $39,150   **11.** $18,720; $37,440; $37,440   **13.** $44,000; $88,000; $88,000   **15.** $23,400 for Finch; $33,600 for Renz
17. (a) $21,000 for Coker; $39,000 for Toms **(b)** $7500 for Coker; $1500 by Toms to Coker   **19.** $22,179 to 1; $46,464 to 2;
$41,357 to 3

Section 19.5 (page 703)

1. $60,000; $120,000; $150,000   **3.** $18,000; $27,000; $30,000; $45,000   **5.** $64,615; $37,692; $37,692   **7.** $9739; $20,870;
$2087; $15,304   **9.** $572,000; $312,000; $416,000   **11.** $190,476; $228,571; $266,667; $114,286   **13.** $24,000; $96,000; $72,000;
$108,000; $12,000; $48,000   **15.** $8079; $21,545; $16,158; $10,099; $12,119   **17.** $720; $960; $3360; $960

Chapter 19 Review Exercises (page 711)

1. (a) $3.25 **(b)** $0.65   **2. (a)** $6 **(b)** $7.68   **3. (a)** $8.75 **(b)** $2.69   **4.** $1.55   **5.** $2.73   **6.** $3.70   **7.** $14.21   **8.** 4,220,900
9. $20.59   **10.** $0.16   **11.** $74,100   **12.** 0%   **13.** 18   **14.** $45.31   **15.** $5.20   **16.** $1758   **17.** $6810   **18.** $10,204
19. $8760.74   **20.** $23,688.54   **21.** $3054.12   **22.** $8419.87   **23.** 3.3%   **24.** 1.5%   **25.** 16   **26.** 6   **27.** $925.79
28. $876.89   **29.** 6.875%   **30.** 7.500%   **31.** −$25.69   **32.** $945.00   **33.** $35,193.90   **34.** $13,718.75   **35.** $24,000 to each
36. $48,000 to 1; $72,000 to 2   **37.** $38,571 to 1; $51,429 to 2   **38.** $25,000; $41,667; $33,333   **39.** $23,256; $58,140; $43,605
40. $258,696; $203,261; $166,304; $221,739   **41.** $18,562.50   **42.** $23,760

Chapter 19 Business Application Case #1 (page 713)

(a) 30,000; 20,000; 50,000 **(b)** $4 preferred; $0.73 common **(c)** $53,900; $54,600; $84,500 **(d)** $34,375; $3093.75 **(e)** Math—$62,125; English—$44,375; Reading—$35,500 **(f)** Yes; difficult to know without more information

Chapter 19 Business Application Case #2 (page 714)

(a) $13,719.84 **(b)** $455; 3.3% **(c)** $12,784.70 **(d)** $800 **(e)** $9334.96

Part 5 Cumulative Review Chapters 17–19 (page 715)

1. (a) 25% **(b)** $5300 **(c)** $13,600 **2. (a)** $6560 **(b)** $5248 **3.** $2760; $2415; $7645 **4.** $15,330; $26,920 **5. (a)** $16,800 **(b)** $34,740 **(c)** $28,000 **6. (a)** 10 years **(b)** 5 years **(c)** 3 years **(d)** 27.5 years **(e)** 7 years

7.

Year	Computation	Amount of Depreciation	Accumulated Depreciation	Book Value
0	—	—	—	$96,000
1	(33.33% × $96,000)	$32,000	$32,000	$64,000
2	(44.45% × $96,000)	$42,672	$74,672	$21,328
3	(14.81% × $96,000)	$14,218	$88,890	$7110
4	(7.41% × $96,000)	$7110*	$96,000	$0

*To depreciate to $0.

8.

THE FASHION SHOPPE	INCOME STATEMENT	YEAR ENDING DECEMBER 31	
Gross sales		$240,800	
Returns		$4300	
Net sales			$236,500
Inventory, January 1		$48,300	
Cost of goods purchased	$102,000		
Freight	$2900		
Total cost of goods purchased		$104,900	
Total of goods available for sale		$153,200	
Inventory, December 31		$41,500	
Cost of goods sold			$111,700
Gross profit			$124,800
Expenses			
Salaries and wages		$32,400	
Rent		$15,000	
Advertising		$2200	
Utilities		$3100	
Taxes on inventory, payroll		$6100	
Miscellaneous expenses		$8900	
Total expenses			$67,700
Net income before taxes			$57,100
Income taxes			$11,400
Net income			$45,700

9. 47.2%, 52.8%, 24.1%, 19.3%

10.

THE FASHION SHOPPE	BALANCE SHEET FOR DECEMBER 31	

Assets

Current assets		
Cash	$28,400	
Notes receivable	$8400	
Accounts receivable	$3800	
Inventory	$41,500	
Total current assets		$82,100
Plant assets		
Land	$0	
Buildings	$0	
Fixtures	$12,200	
Total plant assets		$12,200
Total Assets		**$94,300**

Liabilities

Current liabilities		
Notes payable	$4800	
Accounts payable	$32,500	
Total current liabilities		$37,300
Long-term liabilities		
Mortgages payable	$0	
Long-term notes payable	$0	
Total long-term liabilities		$0
Total Liabilities		**$37,300**

Owners' Equity

Owner's equity		$57,000
Total Liabilities and Owners' Equity		**$94,300**

11. 2.20; 1.09; 0.92   **12.** $200   **13.** $0.35   **14.** $0.385 per share   **15.** $12,216.78   **16. (a)** 0.6% (rounded) **(b)** 30 (rounded)
17. $9527.05   **18.** 0.1%; 9   **19.** $1206.96 per bond; 5.83%   **20.** $42.24; −38%   **21.** $24,437.50   **22.** $36,750   **23. (a)** $24,000
to each **(b)** $36,000 to partner 1; $12,000 to partner 2 **(c)** $19,200 to partner 1; $28,800 to partner 2   **24.** Padgett—$42,750;
Harden—$42,250   **25.** $127,500; $63,750; $148,750   **26.** $72,000; $43,200; $64,800   **27.** $78,734.62; $52,407.73; $8857.64

Appendix A

Section A.1 (page 727)
1. 1771.60   **3.** 11,378   **5.** 3905.32   **7.** 255.24   **9.** 15,695   **11.** 31.08   **13.** 35.42   **15.** 27.63   **17.** 8.1   **19.** 566.14   **21.** 0.63
23. 30.57   **25.** 0.92   **27.** 7.39   **29.** 64.38   **31.** $5\frac{6}{11}$ **33.** 0.49   **37.** $8275   **39.** $3721.20   **41. (a)** $1164.05 (b) $95.13
43. $235,230   **45.** $13,400

Section A.2 (page 734)
1. $7556.24   **3.** $8929.13   **5.** $2676.84   **7.** 1.5%   **9.** $858.89   **11.** 24   **13.** $2537.97   **15.** $942.15   **17.** 26   **19.** $9458.80

Appendix B

Section B.1 (page 740)
1. 0.68 m   **3.** 4700 mm   **5.** 8900 g   **7.** 0.39 L   **9.** 46 g   **11.** 976 g   **13.** 39.24 yards   **15.** 50.27 m   **17.** 15.42 feet   **19.** 1.10 m
21. 307.52 miles   **23.** 1235.71 km   **25.** 1.50 pounds   **27.** 1861.4 g   **29.** 85.58 pounds   **31.** 200   **33.** 0.6 g   **35.** Answers will vary.
37. 40°C   **39.** 280°C   **41.** 37°C   **43.** 95°F   **45.** 50°F   **47.** 275°F   **49.** Unreasonable   **51.** Reasonable   **53.** Reasonable

Glossary

For further information on any of these terms, see the index.

1040EZ This form is used by some single individuals when filing their income tax returns.

1099 forms These forms show miscellaneous income received such as stock dividends or interest income.

absolute or **gross loss** The loss resulting when the selling price is less than the cost.

accelerated cost recovery system (ACRS) The method of depreciation required on all federal income tax returns for property acquired after January 1, 1981 and before 1986.

accelerated depreciation Depreciation which has a rate greater than a straight-line rate of depreciation. For example, declining balance, sum-of-the-years'-digits, or ACRS.

accelerated mortgages Home mortgages that are paid off faster than the typical 30 years for most home mortgages.

accidental death benefit Coverage which pays an additional death benefit if the insured dies as the result of an accident.

accountant A professional who keeps track of costs, depreciation, revenues, etc. both to help managers make decisions and also to report to various agencies such as the Internal Revenue Service.

accounts payable Funds owed by a firm that must be paid within a short period of time such as a year or less.

accounts receivable Funds owed to a firm, by customers, that must be paid within a short period of time such as a year or less.

accounts receivable turnover Net sales divided by average accounts receivable.

accumulated depreciation A running balance or total of the depreciation to date on an asset.

acid-test ratio The ratio of current assets and current liabilities. Also called quick ratio.

actual selling price *See* reduced price.

actuary A person who determines insurance premiums.

addition rule The same value can be added to both sides of an equation.

adjustable-rate mortgage (ARM) A mortgage on a house in which the interest rate is adjusted periodically.

adjusted bank balance This number represents the current checking account balance.

adjusted gross income (AGI) The sum total of all income received from wages, salaries, interest, and dividends less any adjustments to income such as sick pay and moving expenses.

adult operator A driver of a motor vehicle over a certain age, usually 25 years of age or older.

agreed ratio Partners of a business divide the profits using some rule. These profit divisions are sometimes given as a ratio.

algebraic logic The logic used by most electronic calculators.

allocation of overhead Dividing the overhead among the various products or lines of business of a company.

allowances *See* withholding allowances.

amortization schedule A table showing the equal payment necessary to pay off a loan for a specific amount of money including interest, for a specific amount of time. Also called a repayment schedule.

amortization table *See* amortization schedule.

amortized When principal and interest are paid by a sequence of equal payments (on a loan).

amount financed The amount borrowed or financed.

amount of an annuity The sum of the compound amounts of all the periodic payments into an annuity, compounded to the end of the term.

annual meeting A meeting open to all owners of stock where the management of the firm is open to questions from stockholders and where the board of directors is elected.

annual percentage rate A rate of interest that must be stated for each loan, by federal regulation. This annual percentage rate is designed to help consumers compare interest rates. This is the true or effective rate of interest.

annuity Periodic payments of a given, fixed amount of money.

annuity certain An annuity with a fixed beginning date and a fixed ending date.

annuity due An annuity with payments made at the beginning of a time period.

anticipation The seller's offer of interest for early payment of an invoice, in addition to a cash discount.

APR *See* annual percentage rate.

AS OF An invoice which is postdated "AS OF" a future date.

assessed The procedure whereby a local official, called the assessor, makes an estimate of the fair market value of property.

assessed valuation The value for property tax purposes set by the tax assessor on a piece of property.

assessment rate A certain percent used in an area to determine assessed valuation.

assets Items of value owned by a firm.

ATM cards Many people now carry automatic teller machine cards, which results in a debit to their account when they obtain cash from an ATM machine or when they make a purchase.

attached A seizure of property by court order.

automated teller machine (ATM) A machine allowing 24-hour banking.

average *See* mean.

average age of accounts receivable One year (365 days) divided by accounts receivable turnover rate.

average daily balance A method of calculating the balance owed on a revolving charge account. With this method, the balance on the account is found at the end of each day in the month and the total is divided by the number of days in the month.

average inventory Determined by dividing the sum of all inventories taken by the number of times inventory was taken.

bad check A check that is not honored because there are insufficient funds in the checking account.

balance brought forward The amount left in a checking account after previous checks written have been subtracted; the current balance.

balance forward *See* balance brought forward.

balance sheet A summary of the financial condition of a firm at one point in time.

balanced Agreement reached between the bank statement amount and the depositor's checkbook balance.

bank discount *See* discount.

bank statement A list of all charges and deposits made against and to a checking account, usually sent out monthly by the bank.

bank statement balance This is the checking account balance appearing on the front of the bank statement.

banker's interest *See* ordinary interest.

banker's ratio *See* current ratio.

bar graph A graph that uses bars to show data.

base In the number 3^2, the number 3 is the base. *See* exponent. The starting point or reference point or that to which something is being compared.

base year A previous year against which something is being compared.

basic percent equation Rate $\times$ Base $=$ Part, or $R \times B = P$.

bell-shaped curve This refers to the normal probability distribution function which is a symmetric curve often used to describe data.

beneficiary The person receiving insurance benefits upon the occurrence of a certain event.

bimodal A set of data in which two numbers occur equally often.

blank endorsement The endorsement of a check with a signature alone.

board of directors A group of people who represent the stockholders.

bodily injury insurance Another name for liability insurance.

bond A promise by a corporation or government to pay a certain fixed amount of money at a certain time in the future.

book value The cost of an asset minus any depreciation to date.

borrow Taking a number from one column of numbers in a problem in order to make a larger number in the column to which the borrowed number is added.

bouncing a check A check is said to be bounced when there are insufficient funds in the account on which the check was written.

break-even point The cost of an item plus the operating expenses associated with the item. Above this amount a profit is made; below it, a loss is incurred.

breaking even This occurs when the reduced price at which at item is sold just covers cost plus operating expenses.

brick-to-click banks Refers to the trend from banking in a building (brick) to banking over the Internet (clicking the mouse).

budget deficit A budget deficit occurs when a governmental entity spends more than they take in through taxes and other revenues.

budget surplus A budget surplus occurs when a governmental entity takes in more money than they spend.

business checking account The type of checking account used by businesses.

business owner's package policy A business insurance policy insuring many additional perils beyond fire.

calendar year A calendar year is a year starting on January 1 and ending on December 31. Although most individuals file income taxes based on calendar year information, many firms do not, using a fiscal year instead.

canceled check A check is canceled after credit has been received for the amount of the check by the depositor's bank.

cancellation A process used to simplify multiplication and division of fractions using a modification of the method of writing fractions in lowest terms.

cancellation rate Another name for short-term rate.

cap The maximum interest rate on an ARM loan.

capital The amount of money originally invested in a firm.

carrier The insurance company. Also known as the insurer.

cash discount A discount offered by the seller allowing the buyer to take a discount if payment is made within a specified period of time.

cash settlement option Life insurance benefits that are paid in cash.

cash value The value in cash remaining after a policy holder has canceled or borrowed against a life insurance policy.

cashier's check A check written by the financial institution itself and having the full faith and backing of the institution.

certificate of deposit Money placed in a time deposit account.

chain calculation A long sequence of calculations.

chain discount Involves two or more individual discounts.

Chapter 7 bankruptcy Results in the liquidation of the borrower's assets with funds used to pay creditors.

Chapter 11 bankruptcy Requires borrowers to enter into a repayment plan and make payments until debt has been repaid.

charge account An account that allows an individual to charge purchases at a specific store.

chargeback A fee charged to a production employee for a rejected item of production.

Check 21 A federal law known as the 21st Century Act. It allows financial institutions to take electronic photos of all canceled checks and then destroy the originals.

check register A single-page record of checks written and deposits made to a checking account.

checks outstanding Checks written that have not reached and cleared the bank as of the statement date.

check stub A stub attached to the check and retained for keeping a record of checks written.

circle graph A circle broken up into various parts, based on percentages of 360°.

class frequency The frequency of values for each class.

class mark The midpoint of an interval.

classes The intervals of a frequency distribution.

COD A shipping term meaning *cash on delivery.*

coefficient A number multiplied by a variable.

coinsurance clause A fire insurance clause that places part of the risk of fire loss upon the insured.

collateral Goods pledged as security for a loan—in the event that a loan is not paid off, the collateral can be seized by the lender and sold to pay the debt.

collision insurance A form of automobile insurance that pays for repairs to the insured's car in case of an accident.

commission A fee paid to an employee for transacting a piece of business or performing a service. A charge for buying or selling stock.

common denominator A number that all the denominators of a fraction problem divide into evenly.

common stock Ordinary stock not sharing the privileges of preferred stock and showing ownership in corporation.

companion or **spouse insurance** This lets the insured add a companion or spouse to a policy, resulting in both being insured.

comparative balance sheet A balance sheet used to compare the assets and liabilities of a firm at two different periods.

comparative income statement Preparation of a vertical analysis for two or more years in order to compare income or expense items for each year analyzed.

comparative line graph One graph that shows how several different things relate.

compensatory time (comp time) Time off given an employee to compensate for overtime previously worked.

complement The number that must be added to a given discount to get 1 or 100%.

compound amount The final amount, both principal and interest, after money is deposited at compound interest.

compound interest Interest computed on both principal and interest.

compounded daily Interest is paid for every day that money is on deposit in a savings account.

comprehensive insurance A form of automobile insurance that pays for damage to the insured's car caused by fire, theft, vandalism, and so on.

consolidate loans Several smaller loans can sometimes be consolidated, or brought together into one larger loan, in order to reduce payments or gain more favorable terms.

consolidated A consolidated statement is one that includes the financial results of all subsidiaries of a company.

consumer The ultimate user of a product or service, the public.

Consumer Price Index (CPI) A monthly publication by the federal government showing the change in the cost of living.

contingent annuity An annuity with a variable beginning or ending date.

continuous compounding An account offering continuous compounding features interest compounded every instant.

conversion formulas These formulas allow one to convert from percent markup on cost to percent markup on selling price or from percent markup on selling price to percent markup on cost.

convertible preferred stock One share is convertible into a stated number of shares of common stock at some date.

corporate bond A bond issued by a corporation.

corporation A form of business organization offering limited liability to shareholders—no more money may be lost than has been invested.

cost The price paid to a supplier after trade and cash discounts have been taken. This price includes transportation and insurance charges. The amount paid for a depreciable asset. This is the amount used to determine depreciation.

cost accounting A detailed look at the costs of material, labor, and overhead underlying a product or a production process.

cost of goods sold The amount paid by a firm for the goods it sold during the time period covered by an income statement.

country club billing A type of billing received on revolving charge plans in which actual carbon copies of charges are returned.

credit cards Cards that allow an individual to make charges at several different businesses such as retail stores and restaurants.

credit limit The limit on the amount an individual can charge.

creditor *See* lender.

credit union share draft account A credit union account that may be used as a checking account.

cross products In the proportion $\frac{a}{b} = \frac{c}{d}$, the cross products are ad and bc.

cumulative preferred stock Stock requiring that any dividends not paid in the past must be paid before common stockholders receive any dividends.

current assets Cash or items that can be converted into cash within a given period of time, such as a year.

current balance *See* adjusted bank balance.

current (short-term) liabilities Those items that must be paid by a firm within a given period of time, such as a year.

current ratio The quotient of current assets and current liabilities. Also called banker's ratio.

current yield The annual dividend per share of stock divided by the current price per share.

daily overtime Some companies pay overtime on all hours over 8 that are worked in one day.

debit card A bank card used at a point of sale terminal. The amount of the purchase is instantly subtracted from the customer's account and credit is given to the seller's account.

debtor The person or firm borrowing money.

debt-to-equity ratio All liabilities divided by owner's equity.

decimal A number written with a decimal point, such as 4.3 or 7.22.

decimal equivalent of a fraction The decimal fraction that is equal to a proper fraction. For example, $\frac{1}{2} = 0.5, \frac{3}{8} = 0.375$.

decimal number A fraction with a denominator that is a power of 10, which is written with a decimal point, such as 4.3 or 7.22.

decimal point The starting point in the decimal system (.).

declining-balance depreciation An accelerated depreciation method.

declining-balance method A method of depreciation using a declining balance rate.

(200%) declining-balance method An accelerated method of depreciation using twice, or 200%, of the straight-line rate. Also called double-declining-balance method.

(150%) declining-balance method An accelerated method of depreciation using one and one-half, or 150%, of the straight-line rate.

(125%) declining-balance method An accelerated method of depreciation using one and one-fourth, or 125%, of the straight-line rate.

decrease problem Often called a difference problem; the part equals the base minus some portion of the base. Usually the base must be found.

decreasing term insurance A form of life insurance in which the insured pays a fixed premium until age 60 or 65 with the amount of life insurance decreasing periodically.

deductible The amount of the deductible is paid by the insured with the balance of the loss being paid by the insurance company.

deductions Amounts that are subtracted from the gross earnings of an employee to arrive at the amount of money the employee actually receives as net pay.

deferred payment price The cash price of an item, plus any finance charge.

deficit number *See* negative number.

denominator The number below the line in a fraction. For example, in the fraction $\frac{7}{9}$, 9 is the denominator.

deposit slip (deposit ticket) The form used for making a bank savings or checking account deposit.

depreciable amount The amount to be depreciated over the life of the asset.

depreciation A method used to spread the value of an asset over the several years of its life.

depreciation fraction The fraction used with sum-of-the-years'-digits depreciation. The numerator is the year and the denominator is the sum of the years of life of the asset.

depreciation schedule A schedule or table showing the depreciation rate, amount of depreciation, book value, and accumulated depreciation for each year of an asset's life.

destination The city or town where goods or merchandise are being shipped.

developed world The developed world refers to the more economically developed countries such as Germany, France, the United Kingdom, and the U.S., among others.

differential-piece plan A pay rate designed to pay a greater amount for each unit of production as the number of units produced is increased.

diability insurance This type of insurance covers individuals who become disabled.

discount An amount subtracted from the price of a product or service that helps the buyer purchase at a lower cost and increase profits. The amount of interest charged on a note. Also called a bank discount.

discount broker A stockbroker who charges less than full price for buying and selling stocks.

discount fee A bank collects a discount fee on credit-card deposits from the merchant.

discount note A note where interest is deducted in advance.

discount period The period of time in the discounting process.

discounting a note The holder of a note sometimes sells the note to a bank before its maturity date. This gives cash to the holder earlier than otherwise.

dispersion Spread of data.

distributive property A property of algebra that says a number on the outside of the parentheses should be multiplied times each term inside the parentheses.

distributors Firms that buy in bulk and then distribute goods to various retail outlets.

dividends Money paid by a company to the holders of a stock.

divisibility rules These rules allow us to quickly determine if a number is evenly divisible by 2, 3, 4, 5, 6, 8, 9, and/or 10.

docking Same meaning as chargeback.

dollars per $100 Property tax rates are sometimes stated in dollars per $100 of appraised value.

dollars per $1000 Property tax rates are sometimes stated in dollars per $1000 of appraised value.

double-declining-balance method *See* (200%) declining-balance method.

double time Twice the regular hourly rate. A premium often paid for working holidays and Sunday.

Dow Jones Industrial Average A commonly quoted average of the stock prices of 30 large industrial, publicly held corporations.

down payment An amount paid when an item is bought.

draw An amount paid by an employer to salespeople at regular intervals. This is often paid against future income.

drawing account An account from which a salesperson can receive payment against future commissions.

duplicate statement A duplicate of a checking account statement issued by the bank.

early withdrawal penalty A fine or amount of money charged by the lending institution for withdrawal of money earlier than the time agreed upon by the depositor and the institution. These penalties apply only to interest, not to principal.

earnings per share The difference of the net income of a corporation and any dividends on preferred shares, divided by the number of common shares outstanding.

e-commerce The buying and selling of products over the Internet or other network system.

effective annual yield *See* effective rate of interest.

effective rate of interest The simple interest rate corresponding to a given discount rate. Also called true rate of interest. The actual percent of interest earned during a year.

electronic banking The use of electronic technology in banking. Such services as direct deposits, ATM cards, debit cards, and home and business banking are all a part of electronic banking.

electronic commerce People and companies can now purchase products and pay bills electronically using the Internet.

Electronic Federal Tax Payment System (EFTPS) This system allows taxpayers to make tax payments electronically.

electronic funds transfer Many companies choose to move money electronically using computer networks, rather than using checks that are mailed.

Employer's Quarterly Federal Tax Return The form (Form 941) is sent to the IRS along with quarterly payments of FICA and withholding tax.

ending inventory The value at cost of inventory at the end of a period.

end-of-month dating (EOM) In cash discounts, the time period beginning at the end of the month the invoice is dated. Proximo and prox. have the same meaning.

endowment policy A form of life insurance guaranteeing the payment of a fixed amount of money to a given individual whether or not the insured person lives.

equal shares Partners in a business share all profits equally.

equation A statement that says two expressions are equal.

equivalent cash price A single amount today equal to the present value of an annuity.

escrow account An account maintained by real estate lenders and used to pay taxes and insurance. Also called an impound account.

exact interest Simple interest calculated using 365 days in a year.

Exchange Traded Fund (ETF) An ETF holds stocks and bonds and trades at about the same price as the underlying assets throughout the day. These have become very popular investment vehicles.

excise tax A tax charged on specific items that are purchased. Tobacco, alcoholic beverages, and gasoline have an excise tax.

executive officers President, vice president, and so on, of a corporation.

exponent In the number 3^2 the small number 2 is the exponent. It says to multiply 3 by itself. A number that tells how many times a number is used in a product. For example, $3^2 = 3 \times 3 = 9$.

expression Here are three examples of expressions: 7, 8.5x, 6y − 9.

extended term insurance The nonforfeiture option that gives the insured term insurance for a fixed number of years and days.

extension total On an invoice, the product of the number of items times the unit price.

extra dating (extra, ex., or x) Extra time allowed in determining the net payment date of a cash discount.

Exchange Traded Fund (ETF) An ETF holds stocks and bonds and trades at about the same price as the underlying assets throughout the day. These have become very popular investment vehicles.

face value The amount shown on the face of a note. *See* par value.

face value of the policy The amount of an insurance policy.

factor A person who buys accounts receivable of a firm (accounts receivable represent money owed to the firm).

factoring The term for when a business sells part of its accounts receivable to a financial institution.

Fair Labor Standards Act A federal law setting work conditions and standards of employee treatment.

fair market value The price for which a piece of property could reasonably be expected to be sold in the market.

FAS (free alongside ship) Free alongside the ship on the loading dock with all freight charges to that point paid by the shipper.

Federal Deposit Insurance Corporation (FDIC) This branch of the government insures funds at members' banks. It protects small investors from losses when a member bank goes out of business.

Federal Insurance Contributions Act (FICA) A federal act requiring that a specified amount of money be collected from the paycheck of almost all nongovernmental employees, which is used by the federal government to pay pensions, survivors benefits, and disability.

Federal Savings and Loan Insurance Corporation (FSLIC) This branch of the government insures funds at member savings and loan associations. It protects small investors from losses.

Federal Tax Deposit Coupon (Form 8109) Employers use this form when depositing taxes due to the IRS.

Federal Truth in Lending Act (Regulation Z) An act passed in 1969 that requires that all interest rates be given as comparable percents.

Federal Unemployment Tax Act (FUTA) A federal act covering unemployment insurance.

finance charges Charges paid to obtain credit.

financial calculator A calculator that includes common business applications such as present value, future value, payments, and interest rates.

first-in, first-out method (FIFO) Inventory valuation method following the flow of goods, first-in, first-out.

fiscal year Many firms use a fiscal year which starts and ends on dates other than January 1 and December 31. They file their income taxes and report financial results based on their fiscal year.

fixed-amount annuity A settlement option that pays a fixed amount per month to life insurance beneficiaries.

fixed assets *See* plant and equipment assets.

fixed-period annuity A settlement option for life insurance beneficiaries paying a sum of money for a fixed period of time.

fixed-rate loan A home loan made at a fixed rate of interest for a fixed period of time.

flat-fee checking account Some banks offer checking accounts that charge a flat fee each month for a checking account and perhaps an ATM card, debit card, and credit card.

float In finance, float refers to the time between the actual deposit of a sum of money and the time at which those funds are credited to an account.

floating decimal point A feature on electronic calculators that locates the decimal point in the answer.

floor space Overhead is sometimes allocated among lines of business based on the amount of floor space used by each line.

FOB (free on board) Free on board shipping point means that the buyer pays for shipping. Free on board destination means that the seller pays for shipping.

Form 1040A Many people use this form when filling out their income tax returns.

formula A rule showing how quantities are related.

formula for base In a percent problem, the base is the part divided by the rate.

formula for rate In a percent problem, the rate is the part divided by the base.

fraction Used to indicate a part of a whole. For example, $\frac{3}{4}$ means that the whole is divided into 4 parts and we are considering 3 of them.

frequency distribution table A table showing the number of times one or more events occur.

fringe benefits Companies often provide benefits other than a paycheck, including child care or medical insurance.

future amount The future amount, also called future value, is the amount of money an investment grows to at a future date.

future value The amount an investment grows to at some future date.

graph A visual presentation of numeric data.

graphing calculator A calculator that allows functions to be graphed.

gross domestic product (GDP) GDP is one measure of the total of income and output for a country. Economists and journalists constantly refer to GDP.

gross earnings The total amount of money earned by an employee before any deductions are taken.

gross loss *See* absolute loss.

gross profit The difference between the amount received from customers for goods and what the firm paid for the goods.

gross-profit method A method used to estimate inventory value at cost that utilizes cost amounts.

gross sales The total amount of money received from customers for the goods or services sold by the firm.

group insurance plan An insurance plan that includes a group of people employed by the same company or belonging to the same organization.

grouped data Items combined into groups (taken from a table) to simplify information for more immediate comprehension.

guaranteed conversion privilege This provision allows the insured to convert term insurance to ordinary or variable life insurance without physical examination.

half-year convention Under MACRS, property placed in service or disposed of is allowed one-half year of depreciation.

head of household A filing status on an income tax return for an unmarried person who provides a home for others, such as a dependent child or children or parent(s) of the taxpayer.

home banking A system that allows the customer to do banking from the home or business using the telephone and computer.

homeowner's policy A policy for homeowners providing fire, theft, and vandalism protection.

horizontal analysis Prepared by finding the amount of any change from last year to current year, both in dollars and as a percent.

hourly wage A rate of pay expressed as so much per hour. *See* time rate.

hundredths Refers to the number of parts out of one hundred.

I Bond A bond issued by the federal government that pays a low fixed interest rate plus a rate based on inflation.

IMMA *See* insured money market accounts.

impound account *See* escrow account.

improper fraction A fraction with a numerator larger than or equal to the denominator. For example, $\frac{7}{5}$ is an improper fraction; $\frac{1}{9}$ is not.

incentive rate A payment system based on the amount of work completed.

income statement A summary of all the income and expenses involved in running a business for a given period of time.

income tax withholding Federal income tax withheld from gross earnings by the employer.

increase problem Often called an amount problem; the part equals the base plus some portion of the base, resulting in a new value. Usually the base must be found.

indicator words These words help indicate to us whether addition, subtraction, multiplication, or division is used in solving the problem.

individual retirement account (IRA) An account that permits an individual to establish a retirement plan and to deduct any contributions to the account.

inflation The increase over time in the price levels of goods and services.

initial inventory The value at cost of inventory at the beginning of a period.

insider trading An illegal practice in which someone trades the stocks and/or bonds of publicly held corporations using information that has not been released to the public.

inspection Sometimes we can quickly find a common denominator by inspecting the denominators of two or three fractions.

installment loan A loan paid off in a series of equal payments made at equal periods of time. Car loans are examples of installment loans.

insufficient funds (NSF) Not enough funds in a checking account for the bank to honor the check.

insured A person or business that has purchased insurance. Also known as the policyholder.

insured money market accounts (IMMAs) Accounts that are insured up to a certain maximum by the federal government and that offer a higher rate than passbook accounts.

insurer The insurance company.

intangible assets These are assets of a company that are not physical and include something like the good name and reputation of a company.

interest A charge paid for borrowing money or a fee received for lending money.

interest-in-advance note *See* simple discount note.

interest on investment and agreed ratio Sometimes one partner will put up a large share of money to start a firm, while other partners operate it. The partner putting up the larger share of money gets interest on the investment before any further division of profits.

interest paying accounts Some checking accounts receive interest based on the amount in the account.

interest rate spread The difference between the interest rate charged on loans and interest rate paid on deposits.

Internal Revenue Service (IRS) The IRS is the branch of the United States Government that is responsible for collecting the taxes due to the government.

inventory The value of all goods on hand for sale.

inventory turnover The number of times each year that the average inventory is sold; also called stock turnover.

inventory turns *See* turns.

inventory valuation Determining the value of merchandise in stock. Four common methods are specific identification, weighted average cost, FIFO, and LIFO.

invoice A document that helps businesses keep track of sales and purchases.

invoice total The total amount owed on an invoice.

IRA *See* individual retirement account.

irregulars Items that are blemished or have flaws and must be sold at a reduced price.

itemized billing A method of credit-card billing in which purchases are listed, along with payments, with no actual receipts returned to the user.

itemized deductions A taxpayer can itemize certain expenses, such as interest and taxes on a home and cash donations, among others, and deduct from income before calculating taxes.

junk bonds Bonds of bankrupt or troubled companies.

last-in, first-out method (LIFO) Inventory valuation method following the flow of goods, last-in, first-out.

late fees Fees charged by lenders for late payments.

least common denominator The smallest whole number that all the denominators of two or more fractions evenly divide into.

left side In the equation $4x = 28$, the left side is $4x$.

lender The person or firm making the loan.

liabilities Expenses that must be paid by a firm.

liability or **bodily injury insurance** Coverage that provides protection from suit by an injured party.

like fractions Two fractions that have the same denominator.

like terms Algebraic terms that have the same variables raised to the same power.

limited liability No more money can be lost than has been invested.

limited partnership A partnership with partners who have limited liability and no management authority.

limited-payment life insurance A form of life insurance in which premiums are paid for only a certain fixed number of years.

line graph A graph that uses a line to show data.

liquid assets Cash or items that can be converted to cash quickly.

liquidity A firm is liquid if it has the ability to pay its bills as they come due.

list price The suggested retail price or final consumer price given by the manufacturer or supplier.

loan repayment table A table used to decide on the payment that will amortize a loan.

long-term liabilities Those items that will be paid after one year.

lowest terms A fraction is written in lowest terms when no number except the number 1 divides evenly into both the numerator and denominator of the fraction.

lump sum Benefits from a retirement plan can be paid all at once in a lump sum.

luxury tax A name sometimes given to excise tax.

maintenance charge per month A flat charge for maintaining a checking account.

maker The person borrowing the money on a note.

manufacturer The assembler of component parts or finished products.

margin *See* gross profit.

marital status A married individual pays less income tax than does a single person with the same income.

markdown A reduction from the original selling price. It may be expressed as a dollar amount or as a percent of the original selling price.

marketable securities Stocks, bonds, and other securities that can be converted quickly to cash.

marketing channels The path or steps that goods take from manufacturer to consumer.

markup (margin or **gross profit)** The difference between the cost and the selling price.

markup conversion formula A formula used to convert markup from one base to the other base.

markup equivalents A markup of 20% on selling price is equivalent to a markup of 25% on cost.

markup formula The formula used when working with markup. Cost + Markup = Selling price.

markup on cost Markup that is calculated as a percent of cost.

markup on selling price Markup that is calculated as a percent of selling price.

markup with spoilage The calculation of markup including deduction for spoiled or unsaleable merchandise.

MasterCard A credit-card plan.

mathematics of buying The mathematics involving trade and cash discounts.

maturity date The date a loan is due.

maturity value The total amount, principal and interest, that must be repaid when a loan is paid off. It equals face value plus interest.

mean The sum of numbers divided by the number of numbers.

measure of central tendency A number that tries to estimate the middle of a set of data. Measures of central tendency include the mean, median, and mode.

median The middle number in an ordered array.

medical and dental expenses Medical and dental expenses in excess of a certain percent of an individual's adjusted gross income may be deducted.

medical insurance Insurance providing medical protection in the event of accident or injury.

Medicare tax Part of the Social Security tax (FICA) until 1991. Since 1991 Medicare tax has been collected separately.

memory keys A feature on electronic calculators that allows answers to be stored for future use and recalled.

merchant batch header ticket A form used to deposit credit-card sales in a business checking account.

method of prime numbers The least common denominator of two or more fractions can be found using this method.

metric system A system of measurement established by a group of scientists after the French Revolution of 1789.

middlemen Those along the marketing channels, such as wholesalers, brokers, and retailers.

mill A mill is one-tenth of a cent or one-thousandth of a dollar.

minimum wage The federal government and some states define a minimum wage to be paid. It does not apply to managers or salaried employees, but to hourly employees.

miscellaneous deductions In some cases, deductions such as union dues, qualified education expenses, income tax preparation fees, etc. may be deducted from income before calculating income taxes.

mixed number The sum of a fraction and a whole number. For example, $1\frac{1}{5}$ or $2\frac{5}{9}$ are mixed numbers.

mode The most common number in a list of numbers.

modified accelerated cost recovery system (MACRS) The Tax Reform Act of 1986 replaces the ACRS with the MACRS.

money market A money market is a short-term investment account that pays a small amount of interest but allows money to be quickly withdrawn without penalty.

money order An instrument that is purchased and used in place of cash. It is usually preferred over a personal or business check.

mortality table A table showing statistics on life expectancy, survival, and death rates.

multiple carriers More than one insurance company sharing an insurable risk.

multiplication rule Both sides of an equation can be multiplied by the same number.

municipal bond A bond issued by a municipality such as a city or school district.

mutual company An insurance company owned by the policyholders, who receive a dividend.

mutual fund Typically receives money from many different small investors and reinvests the funds in stocks and/or bonds.

negative number (deficit number) A number that is less than zero; a negative balance or deficit. For example, −$800 or ($800).

net cost The cost or price after allowable discounts have been taken.

net cost equivalent or **percent paid** The decimal number derived from the product of the complements of the trade discounts. This number may be multiplied by the list price to find the net cost (price).

net income Net income before taxes minus taxes.

net income after taxes *See* net income.

net income before taxes Gross sales minus Returns minus Cost of goods sold minus Operating expenses.

net pay The amount of money actually received by an employee after deductions are taken from gross pay.

net price The net price is the list price minus the trade discount minus the cash discount.

net profit (or **net earnings**) The difference between gross margin and expenses. After the cost of goods and operating expenses are subtracted from total sales, the remainder is net profit.

net sales The value of goods bought by customers after subtracting goods returned.

net worth Same as owners' equity.

no-fault insurance Motor vehicle insurance that pays directly to the insured no matter who causes the accident.

nominal rate *See* stated rate.

noncustomer check cashing A service that allows an individual who is not a bank customer to cash a check upon payment of a fee.

nonforfeiture options Options available to the insured when canceling the insurance policy.

nonparticipating A form of stock that will never pay dividends above the stated rate.

nonparticipating policy This is an insurance policy sold by a stock company. If the company prospers, the stockholders, not the policyholders, receive a dividend.

nonsmokers discount A discount given to nonsmokers because they are better insurance risks.

nonsufficient funds (NSF) Not enough funds in a checking account for the bank to honor the check.

normal curve The bell-shaped curve commonly used in statistics.

notary service A service that provides notarization, which is required on certain business documents and transfers.

NOW account This account uses a "Negotiable Order of Withdrawal," which works and looks like a check.

numerator The number above the line in a fraction. For example, in the fraction $\frac{5}{8}$, 5 is the numerator.

odd lot Fewer than 100 shares of stock.

odd-lot differential An additional charge for buying or selling stocks when the number of shares is not a multiple of 100.

offshoring Offshoring refers to moving work out of the country. The main advantage of offshoring would be the substantially lower wages paid in many countries such as Mexico or China.

online brokers Online brokers allow you to buy or sell stock through them using the Internet.

open-end credit An account that is not paid off in a fixed period of time; MasterCard and Visa accounts are examples of open-end credit.

operating expenses (or **overhead**) Expenses of operating a business. Wages, salaries, rent, utilities, and advertising are examples of operating expenses.

operating loss The loss resulting when the selling price is less than the break-even point.

order of operations The rules determining which calculations must be done first in chain calculations.

ordered array An arrangement of a list of numbers from smallest to largest.

ordinary annuity An annuity with payments made at the end of a given period of time.

ordinary dating method A method for calculating the discount date and the net payment date. Days are counted from the date of the invoice.

ordinary interest Simple interest calculated assuming 360 days in a year. Also called banker's interest.

ordinary life insurance (whole-life insurance, straight life insurance) A form of life insurance in which the insured pays a constant premium until death or retirement, whichever occurs sooner. Upon retirement, monthly payments are made by the company to the insured until the death of the insured.

original investment Partners divide profits of a business on the basis of original investments by each partner.

overdraft This occurs when a customer writes a check for which there are insufficient funds in the account.

overdraft protection The bank service of honoring checks written on an account that has insufficient funds.

overhead *See* operating expenses.

override A commission received by a sales supervisor or department head based on total sales of the sales group or department.

over the limit fees Many lenders charge a fee in the event the debt exceeds the amount authorized by the issuer of the card.

overtime The number of hours worked by an employee in excess of 40 hours per week, or 8 hours per day.

overtime premium method Payment of overtime as a premium. All hours worked are paid at regular rate. Overtime hours are paid at $\frac{1}{2}$ rate. Gross earnings are the sum of these.

owners' equity The difference between assets and liabilities. Also called proprietorship or net worth.

paid-up insurance A nonforfeiture option that provides paid-up insurance of a certain amount.

par value The amount printed on a stock certificate; usually the price at which a share of stock is first offered to the public.

part The result of multiplying the base times the rate.

partial payment A payment that is less than the total owed on an invoice; a cash discount may be earned.

partial-year depreciation The amount of depreciation that is determined for the asset during a period of less than one year.

participating A type of stock that could be affected by an increase in the dividend.

participating policy The type of life insurance policy issued by a mutual insurance company.

partnership A business formed by two or more people.

passbook account A bank account used for day-in and day-out deposits of money. These accounts usually have the lowest interest rates of any accounts but have no penalties when money is withdrawn.

pay period The time period for which an employee is paid.

payee The person who loans the money and will receive payment on a note.

payer *See* maker.

payment period The time between the payments of an annuity.

payments for life A life insurance settlement option that pays an annuity for life.

payments for life with a guaranteed number of years A life insurance settlement option that pays a certain amount per month for the life of the insured but guarantees a certain length of time in the event that the insured dies before this guaranteed time period.

payroll ledger A chart showing all payroll information.

PE ratio *See* price-earnings ratio.

peak oil Refers to the idea that world oil production may peak and then decline.

per debit charge A charge per check. Usually continues regardless of the number of checks written.

percent A percent is one hundredth. For example, 2 percent means 2 parts of a hundred.

percent formula The basic percent formula is $P = B \times R$, or Part = Base $\times$ Rate.

percent key The electronic calculator key $\boxed{\%}$ that moves the decimal point two places to the left when used following multiplication or division.

percent or **rate of markdown** The markdown expressed as a percent of original price.

percent or **rate of markup** The markup expressed as a percent of original price.

percentage method of withholding Used to determine federal withholding tax. This method does not require the several pages of tables needed with the wage bracket method.

peril insurance Insurance that pays upon a loss by the insured.

period of compounding Amount of time between the addition of interest to a deposit or loan.

periodic inventory A physical inventory taken at regular intervals.

periodic payments A series of payments made at regular intervals in time.

perpetual inventory A continuous inventory system normally utilizing a computer.

personal checking account The type of checking account used by individuals.

personal exemption Each taxpayer currently gets a deduction for each dependent, including the taxpayer.

personal identification number (PIN) A special code that must be entered when using an ATM card or a debit card.

personal income tax A type of tax charged by states and the federal government to individuals. The tax is based on income.

personal property Property other than real estate, such as furnishings, appliances, cars, trucks, clothing, boats, and money.

physical inventory An actual physical count of each item in stock at a given time.

pie chart A chart in the shape of a pie that is used to show data.

piecework rate A method of pay by which an employee receives so much money per item completed.

PIN A personal identification number is needed in addition to an ATM card in order to make a cash withdrawal.

plant assets *See* plant and equipment assets.

plant and equipment assets Items owned by a firm that will not be converted to cash within a year. Also called fixed assets or plant assets.

point-of-sale terminal This refers to the point in a store where the sale is actually made—commonly at a cash register where scanners are used to record the items purchased.

policy A contract between an insured and an insurance company.

policy fee An annual fee charged by insurance companies to cover the cost of processing the policy.

policyholder A person or business that has purchased insurance. Also known as the insured.

population The entire group being studied.

postdating Dating in the future; on an invoice, **"AS OF"** dating.

preferred stock Stock that pays dividends before common stockholders receive any dividends.

premium The amount of money charged for an insurance policy.

premium factor A factor used to convert annual premiums to either semiannual, quarterly, or monthly premiums of an insurance policy.

premium payment An additional payment for extra service.

premium rate A higher amount of pay given for additional hours worked or additional units produced.

present value An amount that can be invested today to produce a given amount in the future.

present value of an annuity (1) The lump sum that can be deposited today that will amount to the same final total as would the periodic payment of an annuity. (2) A lump sum that could be deposited today so that equal periodic withdrawals could be made.

price-earnings ratio (PE ratio) The price per share of stock divided by the firm's annual earnings per share of the stock.

price relative The quotient of the current price and the price in some past year with the quotient multiplied by 100.

prime number A number divisible without remainder only by itself or 1 (such as 7 or 13).

prime rate The interest rate at which large, financially secure corporations borrow money.

principal An amount of money either borrowed, loaned, or deposited. The initial amount of money deposited.

proceeds The amount of money the borrower receives after subtracting the discount from the face value of a note.

processing (check) A check given to a merchant is processed by being deposited with the merchant's bank, where it is then routed to a Federal Reserve bank and then to the payer's bank.

profit margin The profit margin refers to the (usually) small portion of the total revenues earned by a firm that actually goes to profit. For example, many grocery stores have profit margins of about 3%, meaning that only 3% of their total sales end up as profit.

promissory note A document in which one person agrees to pay money to another person, a certain amount of time in the future, and at a certain rate of interest.

proper fraction A fraction in which the numerator is smaller than the denominator. For example, $\frac{2}{3}$ is a proper fraction; $\frac{9}{5}$ is not.

property damage insurance A type of automobile insurance that pays for damages caused to the property of others.

property tax rate The tax rate applied to the assessed value of property.

proportion A proportion says that two ratios are equal.

proprietorship *See* owners' equity.

prox. *See* proximo dating.

proximo dating In cash discounts, the time period beginning at the end of the month the invoice is dated. End-of-month dating (EOM) and "prox." have the same meaning.

Publication 534 The Internal Revenue Service publication that gives a complete coverage of depreciation.

publicly held corporation A company owned by the public, rather than by one or a very few individuals.

purchase invoice The invoice or document received by the purchaser of goods or services from the seller.

quick ratio *See* acid-test ratio.

quota bonus system A plan that pays a bonus to an employee after reaching a quota.

range The difference between the largest value and the smallest value in a set of numbers.

rate A number followed by "%" or "percent."

rate of commission Many people in sales are paid based on a commission or percent of sales.

rate of interest The percent of interest charged for one year.

ratio A quotient of two quantities.

ratio of net income after taxes to average owners' equity Net income divided by average owners' equity.

raw data A set of data before analysis.

raw materials suppliers These firms supply raw materials such as steel, copper, etc.

real estate Real property such as land and buildings.

real property All land, buildings, and other improvements attached to the land.

receipt-of-goods dating (ROG) In cash discounts, time is counted from the date that goods are received.

reciprocal The result of interchanging the numerator and denominator of a fraction.

reconciliation The process of checking a bank statement against the depositor's own personal records.

recourse Merchants sometimes sell debts that are owed them. If the person owing the money is unavailable and the bank buying the debt has recourse to the merchant—the merchant is liable for the debt.

recovery class The class into which property is placed under MACRS (3-, 5-, 7- 10-, 15-, 20-, 27.5-, 31.5-, or 39-year class).

recovery period The number of years over which the cost of an asset is recovered using the MACRS.

rediscounting The process in which one financial institution discounts a note at a second institution.

reduced net profit This occurs when a markdown decreases the selling price to a point that is still above the break-even point.

reduced price The selling price after subtracting the markdown; also called sale price and actual selling price.

Regulation DD A federal law requiring that interest paid on funds in savings accounts be paid based on the exact number of days.

Regulation Z *See* Federal Truth in Lending Act.

repayment schedule *See* amortization schedule.

repeating decimal A decimal that repeats one or more digits without ending. A bar is often placed over the repeating digit(s). For example, $.333\overline{3}$ and $.16\overline{16}$ are both repeating decimals.

repossess The act by a lender of taking back ownership of an item when payments have not been made.

Request for Earnings and Benefit Estimate Statement This form is used by individuals when checking with the Social Security Administration to see if they have the correct information on the individuals' previous Social Security contributions.

residual value *See* salvage value.

restricted endorsement Endorsement of a check so that only the person or company given the check may cash it.

retail method A method used to estimate inventory value at cost that utilizes both cost and retail amounts.

retail price The price at which merchandise is offered for sale to the public.

retailer A firm that sells directly to the consumer.

returned check A check that has been deposited but returned to the bank due to nonsufficient funds (NSF) is said to be returned.

returned-deposit item The return to the bank of an item that has been deposited, due to any number of irregularities.

returned goods Merchandise returned due to incorrect shipment or damage.

returns The total value of all goods returned by customers.

revolving charge account *See* open-end credit.

right side In the equation $4x = 28$, the right side is 28.

ROG *See* receipt-of-goods dating.

Roth IRA Contributions to this type of IRA are not deductible when made, but funds in the IRA grow tax-free and eventual withdrawals are also tax-free.

round lot Multiple of 100 shares of stock.

rounded decimals Decimals reduced to a number with fewer decimals.

Rule of 78 A method of calculating interest charges that need not be paid because the loan was paid off earlier than planned.

rules for divisibility Rules that help determine whether a number is evenly divisible by another number.

salary A fixed amount of money per pay period.

salary and agreed ratio Same as agreed ratio, except that a salary may be allowed to one partner or the other in addition to the profit division.

salary plus commission A commission is paid as a premium in addition to salary.

sale price *See* reduced price.

sales invoice The invoice or document retained by the seller of goods or services, a copy of which is sent to the purchaser.

sales quota An expected level of production. A premium may be paid for surpassing quota.

sales tax A tax placed on sales to the final consumer. The tax is collected by the state, county, or local government.

sales value Value of sales for each department of a company.

salvage value or **scrap value** The value of an asset at the end of its useful life. For depreciation purposes, this is often an estimate.

sample A portion of the entire population being studied.

savings account *See* passbook account.

Schedule 1 (Form 1040) This is the basic form used for reporting interest dividend income.

scientific calculator A calculator that includes common math operations used in science, including the grouping of operations using parentheses.

SDI (State Disability Insurance) deduction The deduction for a state disability insurance program.

Securities and Exchange Commission (SEC) The SEC is an organization within the U.S. government that is responsible for enforcing laws related to securities and regulating that industry.

self-employed individuals Individuals who work for themselves instead of for the government or a company owned by someone else.

selling price The price at which merchandise is offered for sale to the public. The cost of an item plus its markup.

series discount *See* chain discount.

settlement options Methods of receiving life insurance benefits in addition to a cash payment.

shift differential A premium paid for working a less desirable shift, such as swing shift or graveyard shift.

shipping point The location from which merchandise is shipped by the seller to the buyer.

short-term or cancellation rate A rate used when charging for short-term policies and the refunds given when policies are canceled by the policyholder.

silent partner A partner who invests in a partnership but takes no part in running it.

similar terms *See* like terms.

simple annuity An annuity with payment dates matching the compounding period.

simple discount note A note whose interest is deducted in advance from the face value, with only the difference given to the borrower.

simple interest Interest computed only on the principal.

simple interest notes Notes on which interest is found by formulas for simple interest.

single discount A discount expressed as a single percent and not as a series or chain discount.

single discount equivalent to a series discount A series or chain discount that is expressed as a single discount.

sinking fund A fund set up to receive equal periodic payments in order to pay off an obligation at some fixed time in the future.

sliding-scale commission A graduated commission plan giving a higher rate to top-producing salespeople.

SMP The abbreviation for a special multiperils policy. This policy gives additional insurance coverage to businesses. *See* business owner's package policy.

Social Security *See* Federal Insurance Contributions Act (FICA).

sole proprietorship A business owned by one person.

solution A number that can replace a variable in an equation and result in a true statement.

special endorsement An endorsement to a specific payee.

specific-identification method Inventory valuation method that identifies the cost of each individual item.

split-shift premium A premium paid for working a split shift. For example, an employee who is on 4 hours, off 4 hours, and then on 4 hours.

spoilage Merchandise that becomes unsaleable. Usually considered when calculating markup.

square root The square root ($\sqrt{\ }$) of a number is a number that when multiplied by itself equals that number. The square root of 9, $\sqrt{9}$, is 3, since $3 \times 3 = 9$.

square root key The electronic calculator key $\boxed{\sqrt{\ }}$ that calculates the square root of the number on the calculator.

Stafford loan Government loans that can be subsidized—they are frequently used by students.

Standard and Poor's 500 (S&P 500) This is an index that reflects the combined prices of the stocks of 500 of the largest and best companies in the U.S. It is often used as one measure of how well the stock market is doing.

standard deduction A deduction used to reduce taxable income for taxpayers who do not itemize their deductions.

standard deviation A measurement of the dispersion of a set of data.

state income tax Some states levy a state income tax on income.

state unemployment insurance (SUTA) Many states have unemployment insurance to help those who have become unemployed.

state withholding State income tax withheld from gross earnings by the employer.

stated rate The rate of interest quoted by a bank; also called the nominal rate.

statistics Data and/or the analysis of data.

stock A share of stock represents partial ownership of a corporation.

stock certificates Documentation of stock ownership.

stock company An insurance company owned by stockholders. No dividend is paid to policyholders.

stock exchange A place or mechanism at or through which stocks can be bought and sold.

stock fund There are many mutual funds that own stocks.

stock ratio Numbers used to compare stocks—typically the current yield and the PE ratio.

stock turnover *See* inventory turnover.

stockbroker A person who buys and sells stock for the public.

stockholders The owners of a corporation.

stockholders' equity The difference between a corporation's assets and liabilities.

stop-payment order A request that the bank not pay on a check previously written.

straight commission A fixed amount or percent for each unit of work. Earnings are based on performance alone.

straight life insurance Another name for ordinary or whole-life insurance.

straight-line depreciation A depreciation method whereby depreciation is spread evenly over the life of the asset.

subsidiary A company controlled by another company or corporation.

substitution Replacing the variable in an equation by the solution; substitution is used to check a solution.

suicide clause A clause that excludes suicide as an insurable cause of death (usually for the first two years of the policy).

sum-of-the-balances method *See* Rule of 78.

sum-of-the-years'-digits method An accelerated depreciation method using a depreciation fraction.

supply chain Retailers and manufacturers depend on their supply chain to keep goods coming to them.

T-account form This is a method for reconciling a bank statement in which the bank statement balance is on the left and the checkbook balance is on the right side.

T-bills *See* U.S. Treasury bills.

tangible assets These are physical assets such as machinery, trucks, and buildings.

tax deduction Any expense that the IRS will allow a taxpayer to subtract from adjusted gross income.

tax rate schedule A schedule that shows the individual tax rates for tax filing status.

taxable income Adjusted gross income, minus exemptions, minus deductions.

taxes Individuals and companies pay many types of taxes, including sales tax, income tax, and property tax, among others.

telephone transfer The transfer of funds with a verbal request over the telephone.

term A single letter, a single number, or the product of a number and a letter.

term insurance A form of insurance providing protection for a fixed length of time.

term of an annuity The time from the beginning of the first payment into an annuity until the end of the last payment.

term of the note The length of time until a note is due.

territorial ratings Insurance companies use territorial ratings to adjust for the fact that automobile accidents occur more often in certain territories than in others.

third world country Third world refers to countries that are underdeveloped and include countries such as Ethiopia and Mexico.

time The number of years or fraction of a year for which the loan is made.

time-and-a-half rate Many employees are paid $1\frac{1}{2}$ times the normal rate of pay for any hours worked in excess of 40 hours per week or 8 hours per day.

time card A card that is helpful in preparing the payroll. The time card includes such information as the dates of the pay period, the employee's name, and the number of hours worked.

time deposit account A savings account in which the depositor agrees to leave money for a certain period of time.

time rates Earnings based on hours worked, not work accomplished.

time value of money, or **value of money** The average interest rate for which money is loaned at a given time.

total installment cost Find the total installment cost by multiplying the amount of each payment on a loan and the number of payments; then add any down payment.

total invoice amount The sum of all the extension totals on an invoice.

total revenue Total revenue from all sources.

trade discount The discount offered to businesses. This discount is expressed either as a single discount (such as 25%) or

a series discount (such as 20/10) and is subtracted from the list price.

transaction costs Transaction costs refer to the costs of making a transaction. For example, it costs banks to handle each check (a transaction).

transaction register A single-page record of checks written, deposits made, and other transactions made to a checking account.

transfer tax A tax charged by some cities and states on the purchase or sale of stock.

Treasury bills *See* U.S. Treasury bills.

Treasury-bill fund Some funds invest most of their assets in Treasury bills.

Treasury Inflation-Protected Securities (TIPS) TIPS refer to government bonds that pay a stated interest in addition to additional interest to offset inflation. Many believe that they are a good way to save during a time when inflation is increasing.

true rate of interest *See* effective rate of interest.

turnover at cost Found by the following formula.

$$\frac{\text{Cost of goods sold}}{\text{Amount of inventory at cost}}$$

turnover at retail Found by the following formula.

$$\frac{\text{Retail sales}}{\text{Average inventory at retail}}$$

turns Inventory turns refer to how many times a year a company turns over its inventory and is one of the measures of the efficiency with which the firm manages its inventory.

underinsured motorist insurance Insurance coverage that covers the insured when involved in an accident with a driver who is underinsured. Coverage for bodily injury above the amounts of insurance carried by the underinsured driver.

underwriter An insurance company employee who determines the risk factors involved in the occurrence of various insurable losses. This helps determine the insurance premium.

unearned interest The amount of interest not owed when a loan is paid off early.

unemployment insurance tax A tax paid by employers. The money is used to pay unemployment benefits to qualified unemployed workers.

uniform product codes (UPC) Bar codes found on each product in most stores; used for efficient inventory control by stores. It also provides greater accuracy and perhaps faster service to the customer.

uninsured motorist insurance Insurance coverage that covers the insured when involved in an accident with a driver who is not insured.

unit price The cost of each unit on an invoice.

units-of-production method A depreciation method using the units produced to determine depreciation allowance.

units shipped The number of units shipped.

United States Rule A method of handling partial loan payoffs; any payment is first applied to the interest owed on the loan, with any balance then used to reduce the principal amount of the loan.

universal life insurance Allows the insured to vary the amount of premium and type of protection depending on changing insurance needs.

unlike fractions Fractions having different denominators.

unpaid balance The balance outstanding on a revolving charge account at the end of a billing period.

unpaid balance method A method of calculating the finance charge on a revolving charge account by using the balance at the end of the previous month.

unsaleable items Merchandise that cannot be sold. Usually considered when calculating markup.

useful life The estimated life of an asset. The IRS gives guidelines of useful life for depreciation purposes.

U.S. Treasury bills A loan of money to the United States government. Treasury bills (or T-bills) are a very safe way to invest money.

variability The spread in the values in a set of data. For example, the height of students in a sixth grade class has variability (or variation) since not all students are the same height.

variable A letter that represents a number.

variable commission A rate of commission that depends on the total amount of the sales, with the rate increasing as sales increase.

variable life insurance Provides life insurance protection and allows the insured to select investment funds to invest the balance of the premium.

variable interest rate loan A home loan made at an interest rate that varies with market conditions.

variance The square of the standard deviation.

vertical analysis The process of listing each of the important items on an income statement as a percent of total net sales or each item on a balance sheet as a percent of total assets.

virtual bank A virtual bank is one that can be accessed over the Internet but may not have a lobby that a customer can walk into to make a transaction.

Visa A credit-card plan.

W–2 form The wage and tax statement given to the employee each year by the employer.

wage bracket method of withholding Used to determine federal withholding tax. This method requires several pages of tables.

waiver of premium clause Allows insurance to continue without payment of premium when the insured becomes disabled.

weighted-average method Inventory valuation method where the cost of all purchases during a time period is divided by the number of units purchased.

weighted mean A mean calculated by using weights so that each number is multiplied by its frequency.

whole-life insurance (ordinary or **straight life insurance)** A form of life insurance in which the insured pays a constant premium until death or retirement, whichever occurs sooner. Upon retirement, monthly payments are made by the company to the insured until the death of the insured.

wholesaler The middleman; purchases from manufacturers or other wholesalers and sells to retailers.

wire transfer The instant electronic transfer of funds from one account to another.

withholding allowances These allowances, for employees, their spouses, and dependents, determine the amount of withholding tax taken from gross earnings.

worker's compensation insurance Insurance that provides payments to an employee who is unable to work due to a job-related injury or illness.

youthful operator A driver of a motor vehicle under a certain age, usually 25 years of age or younger.

zero-coupon bond A bond that does not pay annual interest, rather it only pays the face value of the bond at maturity.

Index

The Number of Each of the Days of the Year*

Number of Days	Jan.	Feb.	Mar.	Apr.	May	June	July	Aug.	Sept.	Oct.	Nov.	Dec.	Number of days
1	1	32	60	91	121	152	182	213	244	274	305	335	1
2	2	33	61	92	122	153	183	214	245	275	306	336	2
3	3	34	62	93	123	154	184	215	246	276	307	337	3
4	4	35	63	94	124	155	185	216	247	277	308	338	4
5	5	36	64	95	125	156	186	217	248	278	309	339	5
6	6	37	65	96	126	157	187	218	249	279	310	340	6
7	7	38	66	97	127	158	188	219	250	280	311	341	7
8	8	39	67	98	128	159	189	220	251	281	312	342	8
9	9	40	68	99	129	160	190	221	252	282	313	343	9
10	10	41	69	100	130	161	191	222	253	283	314	344	10
11	11	42	70	101	131	162	192	223	254	284	315	345	11
12	12	43	71	102	132	163	193	224	255	285	316	346	12
13	13	44	72	103	133	164	194	225	256	286	317	347	13
14	14	45	73	104	134	165	195	226	257	287	318	348	14
15	15	46	74	105	135	166	196	227	258	288	319	349	15
16	16	47	75	106	136	167	197	228	259	289	320	350	16
17	17	48	76	107	137	168	198	229	260	290	321	351	17
18	18	49	77	108	138	169	199	230	261	291	322	352	18
19	19	50	78	109	139	170	200	231	262	292	323	353	19
20	20	51	79	110	140	171	201	232	263	293	324	354	20
21	21	52	80	111	141	172	202	233	264	294	325	355	21
22	22	53	81	112	142	173	203	234	265	295	326	356	22
23	23	54	82	113	143	174	204	235	266	296	327	357	23
24	24	55	83	114	144	175	205	236	267	297	328	358	24
25	25	56	84	115	145	176	206	237	268	298	329	359	25
26	26	57	85	116	146	177	207	238	269	299	330	360	26
27	27	58	86	117	147	178	208	239	270	300	331	361	27
28	28	59	87	118	148	179	209	240	271	301	332	362	28
29	29		88	119	149	180	210	241	272	302	333	363	29
30	30		89	120	150	181	211	242	273	303	334	364	30
31	31		90		151		212	243		304		365	31

*Add 1 to each date after February 29 for a leap year

Comparing Simple Interest and Simple Discount Rates	The simple interest rate R and the simple discount rate D are calculated by the formulas $$R = \frac{D}{1 - DT} \quad \text{and} \quad D = \frac{R}{1 + RT}$$ where T is time in years.
Compound Interest	If P dollars are deposited at a rate of interest i per period for n periods, then the *compound amount M*, or the final amount on deposit, is $$M = P(1 + i)^n$$ The interest earned I is $$I = M - P$$ (Use column A of the interest table.)
Present Value at Compound Interest	The *present value P* of the future amount M at an interest rate of i per period for n periods is $$P = \frac{M}{(1 + i)^n} \qquad \text{(Use column B of the interest table.)}$$
Unearned Interest	The *unearned interest* is given by $U = F\left(\dfrac{N}{P}\right)\left(\dfrac{1 + N}{1 + P}\right)$ where: U = Unearned interest $\qquad N$ = Number of payments remaining F = Finance charge $\qquad\quad\ P$ = Total number of payments
Annuities, Sinking Funds, and Amortization	**Lump Sums.** A lump sum is deposited today; to find the *compound amount* in the future, use the formula $M = P(1 + i)^n$ and column A of the interest table in Appendix D. To find the lump sum that is the *present value* today of a known amount in the future, use $P = \dfrac{M}{(1 + i)^n}$ and column B. **Making Periodic Payments.** To find the *amount of an annuity* when periodic payments are made for a fixed period of time, use $S = R \cdot s_{\overline{n}|i}$ and column C. To find the amount that could be deposited today that would be equivalent to a series of periodic payments, find the *present value of an annuity* by using the formula $A = R \cdot a_{\overline{n}|i}$ and column D. **Find Periodic Payments.** To find the periodic payment that must be made to produce some fixed total in the future, use the formula for a *sinking fund*, $$R = S\left(\frac{1}{s_{\overline{n}|i}}\right),$$ and column E. The periodic payment that will pay off, or amortize, a loan is given by $$R = A\left(\frac{1}{a_{\overline{n}|i}}\right)$$ and column F.